Handbook of
Children
and the Media

SECOND EDITION

We dedicate this book with love to
Jon, Bruce and Mary, Jefferson and Anne

Handbook of
Children
and the Media

SECOND EDITION

Dorothy G. Singer • Jerome L. Singer

Yale University

Los Angeles | London | New Delhi
Singapore | Washington DC

Los Angeles | London | New Delhi
Singapore | Washington DC

FOR INFORMATION:

SAGE Publications, Inc.
2455 Teller Road
Thousand Oaks, California 91320
E-mail: order@sagepub.com

SAGE Publications Ltd.
1 Oliver's Yard
55 City Road
London EC1Y 1SP
United Kingdom

SAGE Publications India Pvt. Ltd.
B 1/I 1 Mohan Cooperative Industrial Area
Mathura Road, New Delhi 110 044
India

SAGE Publications Asia-Pacific Pte. Ltd.
33 Pekin Street #02-01
Far East Square
Singapore 048763

Acquisitions Editor: Chris Cardone
Editorial Assistant: Sarita Sarak
Production Editor: Brittany Bauhaus
Copy Editors: Jeni Dill, Kim Husband
Typesetter: C&M Digitals (P) Ltd.
Proofreader: Dennis W. Webb
Indexer: Rick Hurd
Cover Designer: Gail Buschman
Marketing Manager: Liz Thornton
Permissions Editor: Karen Ehrmann

Copyright © 2012 by SAGE Publications, Inc.

Printed in the United States of America

Library of Congress Cataloging-in-Publication Data

Handbook of children and the media / Dorothy G.
Singer, Jerome L. Singer, editors. — 2nd ed.

p. cm.
Includes bibliographical references and index.

ISBN 978-1-4129-8242-9 (pbk.)

1. Television and children—United States. 2. Mass
media and children—United States. 3. Video games—
Psychological aspects. I. Singer, Dorothy G. II. Singer,
Jerome L.

HQ784.T4H29 2011
302.23'1083—dc23   2011019174

This book is printed on acid-free paper.

11 12 13 14 15 10 9 8 7 6 5 4 3 2 1

Contents

About the Editors and Contributors

Dorothy G. Singer is retired senior research scientist, Department of Psychology, Yale University. Dr. Singer is also co-director, with Jerome L. Singer, of the Yale University Family Television Research and Consultation Center affiliated with the Zigler Center for Child Development and Public Policy. She is a fellow of the American Psychological Association. Her research and publications are in the areas of early childhood imaginative play and development, television's effects on youth, and parent training. She received the Distinguished Alumni Award from Teachers College, Columbia University in 2006; and in 2009, she received the Award for Distinguished Lifetime Contributions to Media Psychology from the American Psychological Association.

Jerome L. Singer is professor emeritus of psychology and child study at Yale University and a fellow of the American Psychological Association. His specialty is research on the psychology of imagination and daydreaming. Dr. Singer has authored articles on thought processes, imagery, personality, psychotherapy, children's play, and the effects of television. Recent books include *Imagination and Play in the Electronic Age* and *Imagery in Psychotherapy*. He has been president of the Division of Aesthetics, Creativity, and the Arts in the American Psychological Association. In 2008, he was awarded the Rudolf Arnheim Award for Distinguished Contributions to the Psychology of Aesthetics, Creativity, and the Arts from the American Psychological Association; and in 2009, he was awarded the Paul Farnsworth Award for Lifetime Contribution and Service, Division 10, American Psychological Association.

Alison Alexander, PhD, Ohio State University, is professor and senior associate dean for Academic Affairs of the Grady College at the University of Georgia. Her work focuses on media audiences, particularly children and youth, and on the economics of media organizations.

J. Cory Allen is the director of audience measurement at WGBH-Boston, the leading producer of primetime and children's series for PBS. Before joining WGBH, he was the associate director of research at PBS. He has a master's degree from the Annenberg School for Communication at the University of Pennsylvania.

Craig A. Anderson, PhD, Stanford University, is distinguished professor of psychology and director of the Center for the Study of Violence at Iowa State University. He has published over 150 works, most in top scientific outlets. Oxford University Press recently published his book *Violent Video Game Effects on Children and Adolescents* (2007).

Joy Keiko Asamen, PhD, is professor of psychology at Pepperdine University, Graduate School of Education and Psychology. She has co-edited four books with Dr. Gordon Berry, the most recent volume titled *The SAGE Handbook of Child Development, Multiculturalism, and Media.*

Smita C. Banerjee, PhD, Rutgers University, is assistant attending behavioral scientist in the Department of Psychiatry & Behavioral Sciences at Memorial Sloan-Kettering Cancer Center, New York. Her research focuses on persuasive message design, media literacy, and adolescent risk taking behaviors.

Gordon L. Berry, EdD, is professor emeritus in the Graduate School of Education & Information Studies at UCLA. He also holds the same title in the Department of Communication Studies. He has been a consultant for numerous children's television programs, such as *Fat Albert and The Cosby Kids, Ghostwriter, Happily Ever After, Fairy Tales for Every Child, Barney and Friends, Liberty's Kids, Hip Hop Harry, Zoom,* and Disney's series, *Spot.*

David S. Bickham, PhD, University of Texas, is a research scientist at the Center on Media and Child Health at Children's Hospital Boston and an instructor of pediatrics at Harvard Medical School. His research examines the impact of media on children's health and includes assessing the effectiveness of media literacy education and examining the consequences of online food advertising to children.

Kelly D. Brownell, PhD, is professor of Psychology, Epidemiology, and Public Health at Yale University, where he also serves as director of the Rudd Center for Food Policy and Obesity. His work focuses on the intersection of science and public policy, particularly in the areas of nutrition and obesity prevention.

J. Alison Bryant, PhD, University of Southern California, is president and founder of PlayScience, a research, innovation, and consulting firm specializing in children, families, and media. She is the former head of digital research for Nickelodeon and has published several books, including *Television and the American Family* (2nd ed., with Jennings Bryant). She is also the associate editor for the *Journal of Children & Media.*

Jennings Bryant, PhD, Indiana University, is associate dean for graduate studies and research, CIS Distinguished Research Professor, and Reagan Chair of Broadcasting at The University of Alabama. He was founding editor of the journal *Media Psychology*. His research interests are in entertainment theory, media effects, and media, children, and family.

Brad J. Bushman is professor of communication and psychology at The Ohio State University. He is also a professor of Communication Science at the VU University, Amsterdam, the Netherlands. His research focuses on the causes and consequences of human aggression. It has challenged several societal myths, such as violent media have a trivial effect on aggression, venting anger reduces aggression, violent people suffer from low self-esteem, violence and sex in the media sell products, and warning labels on TV programs and video games repel potential audiences.

Sandra L. Calvert, PhD, is professor of psychology at Georgetown University and director of the Children's Digital Media Center, a multisite interdisciplinary research center funded by the National Science Foundation and the Robert Wood Johnson Foundation. Her current research focuses on the effects of media on very early development and on the effects of interactive food marketing and exergames on children's diets and health. Dr. Calvert, a fellow of the American Psychological Association, has authored more than 60 journal articles and book chapters as well as several books about children and media.

Joanne Cantor is professor emerita and outreach director of the Center for Communication Research at the University of Wisconsin-Madison. Her research interests center on the impact of media on emotional responses, productivity, and creativity. Her most recent book is *Conquer CyberOverload: Get More Done, Boost Your Creativity, and Reduce Stress.*

Jessica Castonguay is a doctoral student in the Department of Communication at the University of Arizona. Her research focuses on the advertising of health-related products, with particular emphasis on children's and parents' interpretations of persuasive messages.

Peter G. Christenson, professor of rhetoric and media studies at Lewis & Clark College, studies children , adolescents, and media, with particular emphasis on children's and adolescent's uses of and responses to popular music. Recent publications include *It's Not Only Rock and Roll: Popular Music in the Lives of Adolescents* and *Substance Use in Popular Movies and Music.*

Michael Cohen, PhD, Graduate Center City University of New York, is a research psychologist and president of the Michael Cohen Group LLC. Dr. Cohen conducts inquiry and evaluation globally, with children, youth, and families focusing on education, media, health, and entertainment. He currently serves as principal investigator for the U.S. Department of Education Ready To Learn Grant exploring media and early childhood learning.

George Comstock, PhD, Stanford University is the SI Newhouse Professor emeritus at the SI Newhouse School of Public Communications at Syracuse University. He was science adviser to the Surgeon General's Scientific Advisory Committee on Television and Social Behavior, which issued the 1972 federal report, *Television and Growing Up: The Impact of Televised Violence.* Recent publications (with Erica Scharrer as co-author) include *Media and the American Child* (2007), *The Psychology of Media and Politics* (2005), and *Television: What's On, Who's Watching, and What It Means.* (1999).

Roger Desmond, PhD, University of Iowa, is a professor in the School of Communication at the University of Hartford, in West Hartford, Connecticut. His research interests are in media and children, media literacy, and the knowledge gap in adult newsreaders.

Karen E. Dill, PhD, University of Missouri-Columbia, is the director of the Media Psychology Doctoral Program at Fielding Graduate University in Santa Barbara, California. Karen is a social psychologist whose focus is on the relation between media portrayals and narratives (especially as related to gender and race and to aggression and stereotyping) and their consequences, both positive and negative. She is the author of *How Fantasy Becomes Reality: Seeing Through Media Influence* (2009).

Barna William Donovan is an associate professor of communication at Saint Peter's–The Jesuit College of New Jersey. His research interests include film and media history and studies of audiences and fan communities. He is the author of the books *The Asian Influence on Hollywood Action Films* and *Blood, Guns, and Testosterone: Action Films, Audiences, and A Thirst for Violence.*

Ed Donnerstein, PhD, Florida State University, is professor of communication at the University of Arizona. His major research interests are in mass-media violence and mass-media policy, and he has published over 225 scientific articles in these general areas. He is a past-president of the International Society for Research on Aggression, and in 2008 he received the American Psychological Association Div 46 Award for Distinguished Scientific Contributions to Media Psychology.

Wes Fondren, PhD, University of Alabama, is the assistant professor of methods, research, and theory at Coastal Carolina University. His research focuses on cognition and media effects, developmental aspects of children's media consumption, and attention. Before earning his PhD, he was the director of technology for a group of 35 newspapers, so he also has a strong interest in communication technology.

Douglas A. Gentile, PhD, University of Minnesota, is associate professor of developmental psychology at Iowa State University. His research focuses on multiple domains of media's effects, including studies on both the positive and negative effects of video games on children in several countries, the validity of the American media rating systems, and video game "addiction." He is the editor of the book *Media Violence and Children* (2003) and co-author of the book *Violent Video Game Effects on Children and Adolescents: Theory, Research, and Public Policy* (2007).

Alice Ann Howard Gola received her PhD in developmental psychology from the University of Connecticut. Until recently, she worked as a postdoctoral research fellow in the Children's Digital Media Center at Georgetown University investigating how the language and features of screen media influence very young children's social and cognitive development. She is currently a Research Specialist at MANILA Consulting Group, Inc.

Bradley S. Greenberg is university distinguished professor emeritus of communication, telecommunication, information studies, and media at Michigan State University, where he continues to sit and think. When not sitting and thinking, he makes an effort to get others to think.

Patricia Greenfield, PhD, Harvard University, is distinguished professor of psychology at the University of California, Los Angeles and director of Children's Digital Media Center @ Los Angeles. She is the co-editor of *Children, Adolescents, and the Internet: A New Field of Inquiry in Developmental Psychology* (2006) and co-editor of *Social Networking on the Internet: Developmental Implications* (2008). In January 2009, her article, "Technology and Informal Education: What is Taught, What is Learned," appeared in a special issue of *Science* on technology and education.

Jennifer L. Harris, PhD, MBA, is director of marketing initiatives at the Rudd Center for Food Policy and Obesity. She received her MBA in marketing at The Wharton School, University of Pennsylvania. She worked for 11 years as a marketing executive and consultant and then received her doctoral degree in social psychology at Yale University. Her work examines the effects of marketing on health-related beliefs and behaviors and documents young people's exposure to food marketing of all forms.

Karen Hill-Scott, EdD, UCLA Learning and Development, is president of the Karen Hill Scott Company, a children's media and public policy consulting firm. She is an adjunct associate professor at UCLA, teaching in both the Urban Planning Program and in the UCLA Graduate School of Management. Her consulting practice includes extensive work on series television with NBC, Disney, Nickelodeon, Discovery Communications, and PBS. Including specials and development projects, Hill-Scott has consulted on close to 2,000 episodes of children's and teen programming, including programs that have won the Emmy, Humanitas, and Prism Awards.

Marjorie J. Hogan, MD, is a practicing pediatrician at Hennepin County Medical Center in Minneapolis and is an associate professor of pediatrics at the University of Minnesota. Areas of expertise include adolescent medicine, the effects of media on children and teens, and child maltreatment.

Katherine Battle Horgen, PhD, received her degree in clinical psychology at Yale University. Her research and clinical interests focus on eating disorders and obesity. She is especially interested in the application of policy to psychological problems. Her published works are on policy approaches to the obesity epidemic, targeting the toxic environment as a major component in the increasing prevalence of obesity.

L. Rowell Huesmann is Amos N. Tversky Collegiate Professor of Psychology and Communication Studies at the University of Michigan and director of the Research Center for Group Dynamics at Michigan's Institute for Social Research. Huesmann's research focuses on the psychological foundations of aggressive behavior and, in particular, on how violence in the mass media and video games influences the development of aggressive and violent behavior. Huesmann has authored over 100 widely cited scientific articles and books, including *Aggressive Behavior* (1994). He is editor of the international journal *Aggressive Behavior* and was the 2005 recipient of the American Psychological Association's award for Distinguished Lifetime Contributions to Media Psychology.

Nina Huntemann, PhD, is an associate professor of media at Suffolk University in the Department of Communication and Journalism. Her research focuses on new media technologies, particularly video and computer games, and incorporates feminist, critical cultural studies, and political economy perspectives. She is co-editor with Matthew Thomas Payne of the anthology *Joystick Soldiers: The Politics of Play in Military Video Games* (2010), and producer and director of the educational video, *Game Over: Gender, Race and Violence in Video Games* (2000), distributed by the Media Education Foundation.

Aletha C. Huston is the Priscilla Pond Flawn Regents Professor of Child Development at the University of Texas at Austin. Her research on media focused on the potential of television to promote learning and prosocial behavior. She is first author of *Big World, Small Screen: The Role of Television in American Society.*

Nancy A. Jennings, PhD, is an associate professor at the University of Cincinnati, Department of Communication. Her research focuses on children's cognitive and social development and their use of media through experimental study and evaluation of television content and media literacy promotion programs. Dr. Jennings has served on local and national task forces for screen-time reduction, and she provides parent education programs on children's media use.

Amy B. Jordan is director of the Media and the Developing Child Sector at the Annenberg Public Policy Center of the University of Pennsylvania. Dr. Jordan's research focuses on children's media policy. Her studies have examined the implementation and public reception of the educational television mandate known as the Three-Hour Rule, the V-chip legislation, the American Academy of Pediatrics' media use recommendations, and the industry's effort to self-regulate food marketing to children. She received her PhD in 1990 from the Annenberg School for Communication at the University of Pennsylvania.

Mami Komaya, PhD, Ochanomizu University, is an associate professor in the Department of Elementary Education at Showa Women's University, Tokyo. Her research focuses on media literacy education from early childhood through later childhood, with particular emphasis on creating educational programs and materials.

Robert Kubey is director of the Center for Media Studies and professor of Journalism & Media Studies at Rutgers University in New Brunswick, New Jersey. Professor Kubey has co-authored "Television and the Quality of Life" with Mihaly Csikszentmihalyi and, more recently, "Creating Television." He has authored more than 50 articles and chapters.

Dale Kunkel is professor of communication at the University of Arizona. His research emphasizes children and media policy concerns, addressing such topics as exposure to media violence and advertising to children.

Neil M. Malamuth is professor of psychology, communication studies, and women's studies at UCLA, where he is also a faculty associate of the Center for Society and Genetics. He was previously on the faculties of the University of Manitoba, Canada and the University of Michigan, Ann Arbor. He has published more than 100 scholarly publications and is a fellow of the American Psychological Association and of the American Psychological Society.

Marie-Louise Mares is an associate professor in the Department of Communication Arts at the University of Wisconsin-Madison. Her research focuses on life-span developmental changes in media uses and effects, with particular emphasis on children's interpretations of prosocial media content.

Lara Mayeux received her PhD from the University of Connecticut, and she is currently an associate professor in the Department of Psychology at the University of Oklahoma. Her expertise is in social and emotional development, particularly peer relationships in childhood and adolescence. Her research focuses on the interplay of aggression (physical, verbal, relational) and peer status (acceptance, rejection, popularity).

Kathryn C. Montgomery is a professor in the School of Communication at American University. During the 1990s, as president of the nonprofit Center for Media Education, she spearheaded the successful campaign that led to passage of the Children's Online Privacy Protection Act (COPPA). Montgomery holds a PhD from the University of California, Los Angeles, and is the author of *Generation Digital: Politics, Commerce, and Childhood in the Age of the Internet* (2007).

Michael Morgan is a professor in the Department of Communication at the University of Massachusetts Amherst. He has conducted many national and international studies on the effects of television on audience conceptions of violence, sex-roles, aging, health, science, the family, political orientations, and other issues.

Letitia R. Naigles, PhD, is a professor of psychology at the University of Connecticut. She studies the processes and products of language acquisition in typically developing children and those with autism. She also studies children who are acquiring a variety of languages, including English, Turkish, Mandarin, Japanese, Spanish, and French.

Wei Qiu is a doctoral candidate in the Program of Educational Psychology and Educational Technology at Michigan State University. Her dissertation focuses on social networking and cross-cultural adjustment. She is also interested in e-learning and game design.

Lynn Rampoldi-Hnilo is currently driving the strategic direction of user research and design for the next generation mobile applications at Oracle. Lynn completed her PhD at Michigan State University with an emphasis on technology and cognition. She has taught communication theories and social science methodologies at Stanford, Michigan State University, and St. Mary's College.

Donald F. Roberts is the Thomas More Storke Professor in Communication emeritus at Stanford University. His research focuses on how young people use and respond to mass media, a topic on which he has published extensively. He also consults with producers of children's TV and children's interactive media to develop content that is simultaneously educational and entertaining.

Erica Scharrer, PhD, Syracuse University, is associate professor in the Department of Communication at University of Massachusetts

Amherst. She studies media content, opinions of media, media effects, and media literacy, especially pertaining to violence and gender. Her work has appeared in journals including *Communication Research, Human Communication Research*, and *Media Psychology.*

Marie Evans Schmidt, PhD, University of Massachusetts at Amherst, is a research associate at the Center on Media and Child Health at Children's Hospital Boston and an instructor of pediatrics at Harvard Medical School. Her research focuses on the effects of media on infants' and very young children's development and has been published in such journals as *Child Development, Media Psychology,* and *Pediatrics.*

Nancy Signorielli, PhD, University of Pennsylvania, is professor of communication at the University of Delaware. Her research focuses on media content relating to gender, age- and minority-roles, and cultivation analysis. She has published several books, including *Violence in the Media* (2005).

Victor C. Strasburger, MD, is professor of pediatrics, professor of Family & Community Medicine, and chief of the Division of Adolescent Medicine at the University of New Mexico School of Medicine in Albuquerque, New Mexico. He is the co-author with Barbara Wilson, PhD, and Amy Jordan, PhD, of *Children, Adolescents, and the Media* (2nd ed., 2009). He has also published 11 other books and more than 150 journal articles and book chapters on the topics of adolescent medicine and children and media.

Kaveri Subrahmanyam, PhD, University of California, Los Angeles, is professor of psychology at California State University, Los Angeles and associate director of the Children's Digital Media Center @ Los Angeles. She has published several research articles on youth and digital media and has co-edited a special issue on social networking for the *Journal of Applied Developmental Psychology* (2008). She is the co-author (with David Smahel) of *Digital Youth: The Role of Media in Development* (2010).

Todd Tarpley is a media strategist specializing in digital and emerging media. He served on the launch team of The History Channel and has overseen online divisions of media companies including A&E, Bravo, AMC, and Nielsen. He is the author of two children's books.

Laurie A. Trotta has produced and directed projects on media and society for more than 15 years. A professional journalist, she has published and lectured widely on media-related topics, and she is currently a doctoral candidate in educational technology at Arizona State University.

Patti M. Valkenburg, PhD, University of Leiden, the Netherlands, is professor of Youth and Media at the Amsterdam School of Communication Research at the University of Amsterdam and director of CCAM, the Center for Research on Children, Adolescents, and the Media. Her research focuses on the cognitive, affective, and behavioral effects of old and new media on children and adolescents. She has published over 140 scientific articles, books, and book chapters on this topic. Professor Valkenburg is a recipient of the prestigious Netherlands Organization for Scientific Research Spinoza prize in recognition of her ground-breaking research about youth and media.

Cecilia von Feilitzen is professor in Media and Communication Studies, Södertörn University, Sweden, and scientific coordinator of The International Clearinghouse on Children, Youth and Media, at Nordicom, University of Gothenburg, Sweden. As a media researcher since 1964, she has published 250 research reports, articles, and books in the field, most of them on children and media.

Ellen A. Wartella is Al-Thani professor of communication, professor of psychology, human development and social policy and director of the Center on Media and Human Development at Northwestern University.

She has published widely in the area of media's role in children's development. She currently is co-principal investigator on a National Science Foundation grant on Children's Digital Media Centers.

Brian L. Wilcox, PhD, University of Texas, is professor of psychology and director of the Center on Children, Families, and the Law at the University of Nebraska-Lincoln. His research focuses on linkages between child and adolescent development and social policy, including media policy. He is also a senior program associate with the William T. Grant Foundation.

Emory H. Woodard, PhD, University of Pennsylvania, is associate professor and director of Graduate Studies in Communication at Villanova University. His research focuses on niche media audiences across the life span, with a focus on African-American media experiences.

Paul J. Wright is a member of the telecommunications faculty at Indiana University (Bloomington). His disciplinary interests are health and mass communication; his specialty interests within these domains are sexual socialization and sexual health.

Naiyi Xie is a doctoral candidate in educational psychology and educational technology at College of Education, Michigan State University. Her research interests are technology-enhanced second language learning and literacy development, computer-mediated communication, and the development of digital and intercultural competence through technology-mediated language learning.

Yong Zhao is a distinguished professor of education at Michigan State University. His research interests include diffusion of innovation, gaming and education, and the impact of technology on children. He has published extensively, including the book *Catching Up or Leading the Way*.

Acknowledgments

We wish to thank Olivia Grossman for her valuable assistance in preparing this revision. We commend her patience, careful editing, and her good spirit. We also want to thank Jenifer Dill and Kim Husband for their copyediting of each chapter. We give a special thank you to our Sage editors Brittany Bauhaus, Christine Cardone, and Sarita Sarak who guided and encouraged us throughout this process.

—DOROTHY G. SINGER
—JEROME L. SINGER
Yale University

Introduction

Why a Handbook on Children and the Media?

Dorothy G. Singer

Jerome L. Singer

The Emergence of Mediated Learning in Children's Lives

In the decade since this handbook first appeared, there has been an amazing proliferation of new forms of electronic media, such as video-and-Internet-enabled mobile phones, iPods, iPads, and Kindle, that are accessible to even some of the youngest children. We have seen the introduction of blogs, Twitter, Facebook, YouTube, MySpace, Skype, and texting as forms of communication among young people and adults. Until less than 200 years ago, the vast majority of the world's children and adults depended on the immediate experiences of their senses in a setting limited to the people of tribe and family, and the livestock, wild animals, and physical characteristics of a narrow milieu. How could they learn, for example, that there were other tribes or nations, people of different colors or customs, perhaps just over the hills or up the river or across the vast forbidding sea? They heard stories from the family elders or clan wise men. For many human cultures, priests of various religions who had access to ancient, sacred writings could tell tales as part of worship rituals of how the world began, of deities and demons, or of a unique but often invisible God. Temple statuary and, for some religions, painted representations that could be viewed in sacred places on occasional visits during feasts or holy days may have strongly impressed children in ancient Greece or Rome, in India and China, or in medieval and Renaissance Europe.

News of important changes was long delayed. Often, people depended on passing traders, marauding bands, or the very occasional traveling theatrical performers who might appear at an annual festival. This poor communication affected the financial world. Less than 200 years ago, for example, in the London stock market, prices plummeted in the absence of news about the outcome of the battle of Waterloo being fought by England and Prussia against France just a few hundred miles away across the English Channel. Those few bankers who had a faster signaling and courier boat system learned of the defeat of Napoleon before most of England did. They were vastly enriched because they bought up shares at the lowest prices. What a contrast with the instantaneous news we receive electronically today! Not only adults are affected nowadays by the rapidity of news dissemination. Children all over the United States, while watching television, directly witnessed the murder of President Kennedy's assassin, Lee Harvey Oswald, in Texas; the explosion of the Challenger space shuttle in Florida; and the destruction of the World Trade Center in 2001. The television broadcasts of the fireworks displays and other celebrations of each incoming year moving hour by hour around the world create an exciting experience of a "global village" for at least one day.

One might argue that, with the emergence perhaps 6,000 years ago of written language, adults and children might then have had access to learning about the world through reading. The profound impact of reading on modern civilization, especially after the technology of printing was developed 500 years ago at Mainz in Western Europe, is well documented. Until the 19th century, however, the vast majority of children even in America and Western Europe were not educated to read (Murray, 1998). Only the sons (and some daughters) of the aristocracy or upper middle classes had the opportunity to learn about history, philosophy, geography, legends, science, and the cultures of other nations or continents, and thus to create for themselves a far-ranging world of the imagination beyond immediate experience.

Consider how world literature and poetry have been enriched because an upwardly mobile glove maker from Stratford, England, sent his son Will to grammar school to learn to read in English and also to acquire "small Latin and less Greek." Such an education outside the aristocracy was so rare that even today there are those who still regard Shakespeare's name as really a cover for the actual poetic creations of "well-born" nobility like Lord Bacon or the Earl of Oxford.

This handbook is not, however, a treatise on the tremendous impact of reading on human imagination. Even before the vast world increase in literacy that emerged in the 20th century in Japan, Russia, and, most recently, China, new sources of information became available to hundreds of millions of children with the scientific development of radio and cinema in the first decades of that same century. Motion pictures spread so rapidly after 1910 that, by the mid-1920s, the silent-film comic character of Charlie Chaplin was known to children on all continents. Phonograph records so proliferated during this same period that children (and adults) began to envision new worlds and cultures from the Italian opera arias sung by Enrico Caruso and the Scottish humor and tunes of Sir Harry Lauder. By the late 1920s, with the further distribution of these sound reproduction processes via radio, a whole new musical form entered human consciousness: the jazz music of African Americans such as Louis Armstrong and its offshoots into "popular" music and "big band swing," promoted by Paul Whiteman, Benny Goodman, and the primarily New York City–based "Tin Pan Alley" lyricists and composers such as Irving Berlin, Jerome Kern, George and Ira Gershwin, Larry Hart, Oscar Hammerstein, Richard Rodgers, and Cole Porter.

Radio in the early 1930s also brought directly into millions of homes the voices of political leaders. During the Great Depression, families from all walks of life gathered together in American homes to listen to the firm and mellifluent voice of President Franklin D. Roosevelt. Millions in Germany during the same period listened and, alas, were inspired by the strident, hate-filled shouting of Chancellor Adolf Hitler.

For children and many adults, radio also brought story telling into the home on a daily basis, which opened new vistas for the imagination. Children in the United States listened to serial episodes of Tarzan in a largely imaginary Africa, the Lone Ranger in a nearly mythical U.S. West, Chandu the Magician with world-ranging episodes, and "Buck Rogers in the 25th Century!" By this time, low-cost talking movies in theaters outside the home were tremendously popular, and these two media became rich sources of incidental education, along with so-called pulp books, magazines, and comic strips in newspapers and book forms.

Books, magazines, and comics required at least moderate literacy and intellectual effort. Radio storytelling demanded some imaginative stretching by the listener. The movies, however, portrayed for children in an almost directly experiential manner a vast outside world ranging from American cowboy adventures in Western mountain ranges to dramatic confrontations between British colonial troops and Hindu or Afghan "native rebels."

Sometimes these conflicts were even resolved without bloodshed by the delightful intervention of the dimpled child actress Shirley Temple. Even the more "realistic," contemporary-setting films of the depression era often displayed wealthy urban apartments or salons in which actors such as Norma Shearer, Myrna Loy, William Powell, Melvyn Douglas, or Katharine Hepburn, appareled in tuxedos or high-fashion dresses, engaged in witty exchanges. And, of course, there were the ultra-sophisticated music and dance films of beautifully groomed Fred Astaire and Ginger Rogers. In effect, films created for child and adolescent viewers an immediate experience of a virtual reality that became at once central to the fantasy lives of the young. The fantasies were so powerful, indeed, that the stars of these films have become celebrated almost beyond the glory of the ancient Greco-Roman gods.

The Impact of Television and the Computer

Consider then the next electronic advance—the television set that entered the homes of millions by the mid-1950s. For millennia before, young children from their earliest ages learned directly from observing or modeling parents, relatives, older siblings, or peers, but there was now a new member of the family that portrayed actions and far-flung settings to them every day for hours at a time. Can there be any real doubt that just in the past half century the television medium has radically altered human experience? It has ushered in an electronic age incorporating all the features stemming from 20th-century electricity, moving pictures, music reproduction, radio news, music, sports, and storytelling. What impact does the near omnipresence of this medium of entertainment and information have on the cognitive, emotional, social, and behavioral responses of children? These are questions that have stimulated extensive ongoing research. The findings of such studies must take us beyond the accumulation of personal anecdotes to a body of more systematic evidence.

The reader may also ask, however, about the great acceleration of information and electronic media in just the past two decades.

We have video games in arcades and in millions of homes. Personal computers have introduced the Internet and World Wide Web into homes and schools. Vast new commercial, entertainment, and informational opportunities beckon from these newest electronic sources of input for children and adolescents. Once we moved into the 21st century, almost imponderable new forms of delivery of entertainment, information, and education to children and youth began to emerge.

The *Handbook of Children and the Media* therefore represents an effort to review, through the contributions of research experts, the past and potential future impact of the electronic media on growing children in America and to some extent all over the world. This volume places its greatest emphasis on the television medium as it has developed over the past 60 years. The most recent research evidence still makes it clear that children between the ages of 2 and 5 spend, on average, almost 32 hours weekly watching television. Children aged 6 to 11 watch about 28 hours a week (McDonough, 2009). The number of television-viewing hours increases between ages 8 and 18. This age group spends an average of 7 hours and 38 minutes using entertainment media across a typical day (Kaiser Family Foundation, 2010[1]). In a study involving 16 nations ranging from China, India, and Indonesia to England, France, the United States, and other countries around the world, mothers reported that 72% of the children aged 2 to 12 years watched television as their favorite pastime when not in school (Singer, Singer, D'Agostino, & Delong, 2009). Clearly, television still dominates the attention of our youth, and we must understand its impact, the hazards, and also the constructive educational potential of such heavy viewing of this medium.

There has been a great deal of popular attention on the cognitive, social, and even physiological dangers of television viewing from early childhood to adolescence. Much of this concern has been based on speculation rather than on carefully assembled scientific research data. We, ourselves, as confirmed book lovers, have wondered about the risks of growing up in this picture-centered media world. Our guesses, however, are just useful as suggestions for systematic research. There are no true experts who can pontificate on the hazards or values of television without recourse to the great body of accumulated research evidence. No single research in a given area is usually definitive, of course. What we try to provide in this volume are the issues raised by the electronic media and what methods have been used to gather data that can address these issues. The contributors are themselves experienced investigators who point out the limitations and advantages of particular research methods. Our hope is that a critical reading of these chapters can dispel media myths, dubious generalizations about television hazards, or unsupported and hasty judgments. Readers may not find ultimate truths in these chapters, but we believe they will be guided into a more careful and deliberate examination of how our growing children and grandchildren use, enjoy, learn from, and are advantaged or disadvantaged from regular exposure to television and other electronic media.

Developmental Processes in Children and Adolescents

Our expectation is that this handbook will appeal to a wide-ranging audience: child development researchers, educators, parents or other child-caregivers, journalists, state or federal government policy makers or legislators, child advocates, graduate and undergraduate students, and even those younger students who often write or e-mail us with questions for their school reports. We can hardly expect that anyone will read this book through at one sitting like a Judy Blume or John Grisham novel. We have tried, therefore, to attain some unity and focus for all the chapters by asking our authors to keep in mind basic principles of child development and socialization. Even our more policy-oriented or industry-related chapters examine such issues as they bear on the *age-specific cognitive, emotional, motivational*, or *social processes* of childhood and adolescence.

In our own 40 years of research on children's television viewing, we have been dismayed to find that this area of investigation has not been integrated into the basic field of child study. Authors of developmental psychology textbooks often completely ignored the fact that children were spending more

hours watching TV programs than talking to their parents, playing, exploring their physical environment, or mastering reading. On the other hand, many researchers of television sought to answer specific questions about the physical or social hazards of regular viewing without putting their findings into the context of the basic cognitive or emotional capacities of children at different age levels. Unfortunately, producers and writers of children's TV shows often seemed oblivious to the great differences between children ages 3 to 5, 7 to 11, and 13 to 15 in attending to, comprehending, and imitating or emotionally responding to not only the content of programming, but also to the formal features or conventions of the medium.

The goal in this handbook, therefore, is to integrate the usage and effects of electronic media exposure on children and adolescents with the basic behavioral research on child development. When do particular skills of attention and concentration develop? How do children learn to understand language and to imitate the words they hear, not only from parents but also from television characters? Our own research over many years—and, of course, the earlier studies and theories of Jean Piaget (1962), Kurt Lewin (1935), Sigmund Freud (1908/1962), and L. S. Vygotsky (1978)—has emphasized how children, usually through symbolic, pretend, or make-believe play, gradually develop a capacity for imaginative thought. Such symbolic play can have enormous adaptive potential (Singer & Singer, 2005). To what extent can television programming, either through its content or its format, influence children's developing imagination? We sought some answers to such questions in the 1970s (Singer & Singer, 1981), but much more study is needed.

A continuing preoccupation of child development research has been the origins and modification of aggressive behavior in children. For the first 60 years of the 20th century, conceptions such as Freud's (1923/1962) theory of a fundamental aggressive drive or instinct predominated. The critical analyses and careful research on social learning of Albert Bandura (1971a, 1971b) and literally scores of psychophysiological and behavioral empirical studies beginning in the 1960s have pointed much more to aggression as a learned response (Singer, 1971). To the extent that a great deal of aggressive behavior in childhood and adolescence reflects observation, modeling, and imitation of the aggression of parents, siblings, and peers, can we ignore the impact on children of their exposure through television and films or, more recently, to computer games, home console, and arcade video games that involve vast amounts of violent actions? What are the contingencies of age, cognitive capacity, type of program content, or reality or fantasy depiction that might moderate possible influences on children of the high frequency of vicarious violence that makes up so much of the content of television or of video and computer games?

These few examples should make clear that the great accumulation of research on children and the media can contribute to our understanding of child development more generally and also that principles of developmental psychology can help us interpret the social impact of these media. We urge our readers to keep these issues in mind in examining each chapter.

The Organization of This Volume

Let us next turn to how we have organized the sections and chapters of this book as a guide to the interests of specific readers. Part I is structured to examine the fundamental research knowledge about the possible ways in which the popular media serve (for better or worse) as incidental or planned educators and socializers of children. In the early 1980s, we both participated in the preparation of a large National Institute of Mental Health report on television and behavior (Pearl, Bouthilet, & Lazar, 1982). Perhaps the single major conclusion that emerged from that massive review was that children learn from television even though they watch predominantly for their own entertainment. What they learn, however, is a key question that Part I addresses, drawing on more than 40 years of research.

Part I begins with five chapters that discuss, in up-to-date fashion, an area that was one of the earliest studied in media research: How do children use these new technologies, what needs seem gratified by their availability, and

how are the media used for social networking? These chapters set forth the historical background for electronic media use. Although reading itself is not featured in this handbook, we do include a chapter dealing with popular literature and comic books as a context against which most television viewing or use of videos can be set. These five chapters are critical foundations of basic information on how, when, where, how often, and at what ages children or adolescents watch television or engage themselves with the Internet, videos, or computers. Researchers or journalists who wish to begin a study or write an article with reference to the preceding questions will find the most current, carefully researched data in this section.

We turn next to the most frequently asked questions about the impact of media usage: their influence on cognitive functions such as attention, comprehension, imagination, and language. We also include chapters on social behaviors such as alertness or vigilance, fearfulness, aggression, and sexuality. We next address health, including drug usage and eating patterns. The chapters in this section also explore the constructive potential of television viewing in promoting school readiness for very young children or prosocial behaviors such as civility, sharing, and cooperation. Next we consider the fact that most of the television industry in the United States (and, increasingly, around the world) relies on commercials for income. What is the impact of the deluge of such messages on children? We also look more broadly on identity formation, stereotyping, multicultural awareness or tolerance, family life, and ethics or morality.

Parts II and III of this volume turn to the broader social impact of the media environment: the media industry and formal educational and policy considerations. In these sections, we provide the latest available information and the accumulated research on commercial and public broadcasting approaches to children. These chapters are concerned with issues of advocacy for quality programming, parental control, applications of research for producers of programming, and specific school uses of television. They also address the government's role of oversight and regulation of the airwaves, which truly belong to all of us and are only leased to private groups.

The economic structure of the television industry is also examined. Finally, the chapters address questions of what needs to be done to ensure privacy, parental control, and quality programming, and how we can foster media literacy and intelligent and discriminating viewing in children and youth.

We believe that educators, child advocates, policy makers, parents, and journalists will find the second and third parts of this volume especially helpful. Even though innovations in technology occur rapidly, the basic questions on child–media interactions are features of this book, along with an emphasis on how we can investigate the issues in a systematic, reasonably scientific fashion. Our authors are largely science trained, and we have asked them to draw as much as possible on formal research. At the same time, we have asked them to avoid the use of technical jargon and statistical or mathematical content. The extensive bibliographies of each chapter are a valuable resource for researchers who wish to pursue the full technical details of particular investigations summarized here. We believe that the broad readership we expect for a book on children and the popular media will find the subject matter and presentations of this volume engaging, challenging, and deeply informative.

Note

1. This report, sponsored by the Kaiser Family Foundation (2010), is described in detail in various chapters of the handbook.

References

Bandura, A. (Ed.). (1971a). *Psychological modeling*. New York: Alaine-Atherton.

Bandura, A. (1971b). *Social learning theory*. New York: General Learning Press.

Freud, S. (1908/1962). Creative writers and daydreaming. In J. Strachey (Ed.), *The standard edition of the complete psychological works of Sigmund Freud* (Vol. 9, pp. 141–154). London: Hogarth Press. (Original work published 1908)

Freud, S. (1923/1962). The ego and the id. In J. Strachey (Ed.), *The standard edition of the complete psychological works of Sigmund Freud* (Vol. 19, pp. 3–66). London: Hogarth Press. (Original work published 1923)

Kaiser Family Foundation. (2010). *Generation M2: Media in the lives of 8- to 18-year-olds*. Menlo Park, CA: The Henry J. Kaiser Family Foundation. Retrieved April 21, 2010, from www.kff.org

Lewin, K. (1935). *A dynamic theory of personality*. New York: McGraw-Hill.

McDonough P. (2009). TV viewing among kids at an eight-year high. Nielsenwire. October 26, 2009. Retrieved April 2, 2011, from http://blog.nielsen.com/nielsenwire/media_entertainment/tv-viewing-among-kids-at-an-eight-year-high/

Murray, G. S. (1998). *American children's literature and the construction of childhood*. New York: Twayne/Macmillan.

Pearl, D., Bouthilet, L., & Lazar, J. (Eds.). (1982). *Television and behavior: Ten years of scientific progress and implications for the eighties* (Vols. 1–2). Washington, DC: National Institute of Mental Health.

Piaget, J. (1962). *Play, dreams, and imitation in childhood*. New York: Norton.

Singer, D.G., Singer, J. L., D'Agostino, H., & Delong, R. (2009, Winter). Children's pastimes and play in sixteen nations: Is free play declining? *American Journal of Play, 1*(3), 283–312.

Singer, D.G., & Singer, J. L. (2005). *Imagination and play in the electronic age*. Cambridge, MA: Harvard University Press.

Singer, J. L. (Ed.). (1971). *The control of aggression and violence: Cognitive and physiological factors*. New York: Academic Press.

Singer, J. L., & Singer, D. G. (1981). *Television, imagination, and aggression: A study of preschoolers*. Hillsdale, NJ: Lawrence Erlbaum.

Vygotsky, L. S. (1978). *Mind in society*. Cambridge, MA: Harvard University Press.

PART I

The Popular Media as Educators and Socializers of Growing Children

Preliminary Comments From the Editors

Our handbook opens with the most extensively researched areas in the study of children and the media. What does it mean for children's development to be growing up in a milieu in which popular reading literature and especially electronic sources of input compete daily with what children can learn from parents, family, or teachers—the "live" people around them? In the sections that follow, we examine efforts to answer many of the questions that scholars, educators, parents, and policy makers have asked about the influences of the media on children's enjoyment, time distribution, attention and understanding, development of imagination, and language. Can watching television lead to constructive influences such as improved school readiness or universally agreed upon values of cooperation, sharing, and common civility? Are there special features of television and related media that may yield socially undesirable influences on children such as fostering excessive fears, unwarranted aggression, problems of identity, problems in family interaction, sexual doubts, or confusions? What impact does television

viewing have on health habits such as substance abuse or eating patterns, on social attitudes and prejudices, on excessive materialism and even fundamental morality?

Children's Uses and Gratifications

We begin by examining, in the first five chapters, one of the classic areas for studying the new media. How do children use and enjoy extrafamilial sources of input? Chapter 1, by George Comstock and Erica Scharrer, provides a scholarly overview of the historical emergence of film, television, and the Internet as developments of the 20th century that have become pervasive sources of input for children and youth. It draws us deeply into the ways in which our youth actually watch and devote time to the electronic media, particularly television. This chapter lays out in systematic detail the research issues and studies that have examined the principal variables of concern, the modes of the viewing experience, the time spent viewing, and the contingent circumstances such as family settings, children's ages, household attributes, and situational factors. Although each individual reader may have anecdotal experiences about how, when, and where one viewed TV, this chapter provides the clear research evidence on the normative national uses of the medium. Chapter 2, by Roger Desmond, sets these electronic media against a background of the reading of popular literature, a phenomenon that influenced mainly more educated middle-class children in the late 19th century but spread widely to all children in the past century. To what extent does reading comics or "pop" magazines and books intersect and interact with attending movies and watching television? There is evidence that encouraging children to read books at home (given by publishers) over a three year period leads to an increase in student's later test scores (Brooks, 2010).

Chapter 3, by Todd Tarpley, looks ahead to the newest technologies, from digital television and high-definition television to personal video recorders and the Internet. He examines the relevant research on the uses of these approaches, their health and safety hazards, and their constructive possibilities. Skype is a response to the concern that electronic media isolate children from experiencing the direct reactions of other persons. With Skype, children can now see others at play. In contrast with most of the electronic communication possibilities that depend heavily on words, children can interact with others, aware of facial expressions and gestures.

Chapter 4, by Kaveri Subrahmanyam and Patricia Greenfield, carries us beyond popular reading, movies, and television into the burst of new electronic media that marked the last decade of the 20th century and that reflects the forms of entertainment of the 21st century: video games, the new computer uses, and many new communication devices. What are the special psychological and sociological features of video games and of the increasingly varied uses of the Internet? Schools are offering opportunities for children to engage in creating virtual worlds as a possible alternative to formal lectures and textbooks. Older students report that the use of simulated selves (avatars) and made up environments in classes ranging from hygiene to social studies

attract otherwise inhibited students. There are indications that such exposures stimulate the applications of problem solving skills and rational thinking to considerations of everyday difficult situations (Hu, 2010). Chapter 4 provides what we now know from research, but it also points to the many new questions that we shall have to ask and for which we shall try to find the answers in the coming decades.

Chapter 5, by Yong Zhao, Wei Qiu, and Naiyi Xie, seeks to understand the similarities and differences of teenagers around the world in terms of their social media consumption, the motivations behind their acceptance of social media, and the potential effects facing them. Social media are defined by these authors as a group of Internet-based applications that allow the creation and exchange of user-generated content. Some examples of social media are blogs, social network sites (SNS), virtual worlds, games, Wikipedia, and YouTube, among others.

In the next section we present the rich research literature on the possible significance for the growing child of the extensive exposure to electronic media, especially television. Proving a direct influence of television viewing on children's information-processing capacities, overt behavior, and personality or societal attitudes is no easy task. The chapters in this section detail how difficult it is to show cause-and-effect relationships, but they also exemplify a host of imaginative research methods that have been employed to close in cumulatively on answers to these questions.

Cognitive Function and School-Readiness Skills

Chapter 6, by David Bickham, Marie Evans Schmidt, and Aletha Huston, addresses one of the most frequent and often controversial concerns about television viewing in preschool children. To what extent does the format of American television—characterized as it is by rapid pacing, frequent interruptions either for commercial messages or for changes of subject matter, and shifts in loudness or interpolations of music—have a significant impact on children's attention spans and their ability to comprehend and later to retrieve program information? This is a matter of special concern when we consider whether programs designed especially for children can have an educational value. In the 1970s, as commercial networks and local stations largely abandoned children's programming, leaving that field to the Public Broadcasting System, two models of formatting emerged. These were exemplified by *Sesame Street,* which adopted a variation of the faster-paced, lively, short episode and fast-talking pattern of commercial programming, and *Mister Rogers' Neighborhood,* which emphasized a slow-talking adult host and relatively longer episodes with a pacing more like that of a parent directly addressing a preschool child. These two programs had somewhat different goals (cognitive teaching vs. social and personal development) and therefore could not be directly compared. Still, some critics felt that the faster-paced *Sesame Street* style was (a) ineffective in yielding school-readiness learning and "in-depth" processing and (b) potentially training children to anticipate a jazzy, short-sequenced mode of presentation from their first-grade teachers.

Over the last quarter of a century, these issues have been addressed in research described in Chapter 6. We have also witnessed changes in *Sesame Street* and related programming toward somewhat longer sequences and toward the use of more adult-mediated teaching. The implications for learning from *Sesame Street* are documented in this chapter. The emergence of the *Barney & Friends* series for preschoolers, which seeks to strike a balance between mediation of new information and longer episodes and a livelier, music-rich format, reflects an important new step toward integrating the possible presentation modes. Our own research (in a series of 10 studies) has shown that each half-hour episode of the *Barney* series contains almost 100 mediated teaching instances (as rated by panels of developmentally trained judges), that preschoolers and toddlers actually seem to grasp these same examples, and that (especially if there is adult follow-up) children do improve in vocabulary, general information, and civility after viewing 10 episodes in day care settings (Singer & Singer, 1998). Chapter 6 lays out the critical issues in this area and reviews how one can even investigate longer-term constructive effects on school-readiness skills for preschoolers under various viewing conditions.

In Chapter 7, Alice Ann Howard Gola, Lara Mayeux, and Letitia Naigles, language development specialists, consider whether television viewing can foster or impede the regularly viewing child's vocabulary and grammatical usage. We know from our earlier chapters that very young children are watching, on average, 3 hours of television daily and are exposed to a great range of words and usages far beyond what they might encounter in contacts with parents, siblings, or peers. What are the potential constructive or even negative consequences of viewing on word learning and effective communication?

Chapter 8, by Patti Valkenburg and Sandra Calvert, presents an up-to-date review of how television viewing may be playing a role in the development of young children's creativity and imagination. One might at first surmise that, just as reading exposed children to far-flung lands and myths, legends, or scientific knowledge and clearly fostered imagery and fantasy, the vividness and daily easy availability of television might also stir up creative thought processes. The authors examine what research tells us about the contingent circumstances that may foster or inhibit the emergence of the inner dimension of experience in the television viewing of youngsters.

We continue this section of the potential good news about television as a constructive learning tool with Chapter 9, by Jennings Bryant, Wes Fondren, and Alison Bryant. These authors address very critical questions about the extent to which emotional arousal, liveliness, humor, and excitement can spur effective learning from television or can simply lead to enjoyment of what was watched at the moment with little subsequent recall of the content. Our older readers may remember that there was once a popular TV show called *Laugh-In* in which sight gags and word play filled the screen at such a rapid pace that we would be laughing throughout the program. Despite the pleasurable experience (which made us want to see the show the following week), only rarely could we reconstruct more than a minute portion of the actual jokes in a given episode. Clearly, if television for children is to serve some educational function, some balance must be found between sheer liveliness and effective information processing. Chapter 9 examines this issue in a theoretical and research-data-derived practical fashion. Throughout the chapter, the authors reflect on possibilities for producers to enhance the attention-getting power of educational programs.

This section on the constructive teaching potential of television viewing concludes with Chapter 10, by Marie-Louise Mares and Emory Woodard, in which the so-called prosocial contributions of television are considered. What parents or educators would deny that we would hope to see children encouraged to be more helpful to others and to show cooperation, courtesy, civility, and a reduction in unwarranted aggression? The authors also touch briefly on issues of morality on television. Chapter 10 reviews the results of the cumulative research from television viewing and other media use in this vital area of child development—what has been done, and what more can be done.

Some Hazards of Television Viewing: Fears, Aggression, and Sexual Attitudes

We turn in this next group of chapters to the bad news about television-viewing for children. The stark reality, well-documented by many years of content analyses conducted by the Annenberg School for Communication at the University of Pennsylvania under the leadership of its former dean, George Gerbner (Gerbner, Gross, Morgan, & Signorielli, 1994), is that commercial television programming in news content and entertainment shows is replete with instances of violence. The epidemiological studies of Brandon Centerwall (1989, 1994) strongly suggest that, as television was introduced in the United States and Canada, there was within a few years a sharp increase in the rate of homicides among adults. In South Africa, which resisted the influx of television, the homicide rates for White adults, which were closely comparable to those of the North American countries before the spread of television there, remained level. When, however, television was introduced into South Africa, the same increases in homicide rates emerged a few years later. These suggestive results must be taken seriously for their implications regarding the exposure of millions of young children and adults to incidents of televised violence.

Chapter 11, by Joanne Cantor, addresses the impact of the heavy exposure of violence that child viewers experience at home on their fears and their experiences of possible dangers in their daily lives. The author discusses how the news on television also can contribute to a child's fears because of the constant replaying of major catastrophes. Chapter 12, by Brad Bushman and L. Rowell Huesmann, takes us beyond emotions and attitudes to the realm of overt behaviors. To what extent can we formulate psychological theories to explain how television viewing can influence children to engage in overt aggressive behavior or other antisocial acts? And by what methods can we test these theories either in the laboratory or in field studies of children based on their home viewing of violent program content? This seminal chapter addresses not only American research findings but also those from several European countries and Israel. Bushman and Huesmann also consider factors that might mitigate these negative influences of viewing violent media. The issue of free speech is addressed in terms of a law in California that would prevent the sale of violent video games to minors. An entire issue of the *Review of General Psychology* edited by Ferguson (2010) raises questions about whether the concerns of harmful effects of fear arousing or violent video games may be exaggerated. This journal issue also includes papers that point out useful functions of video game play that are discussed in other chapters in this handbook and especially in Chapter 13, by Anderson, Gentile, and Dill. In this chapter, the authors focus on the effects of playing recreational video games, that is, games *not* specifically designed for use in educational or therapeutic contexts. They begin by describing the main theoretical perspectives needed to understand video game effects. Next, they review the known effects of recreational video games, focusing on prosocial effects (e.g., helping others), antisocial effects (e.g., hurting others, stereotyping others), and other effects on the individual (e.g., addiction, cognitive skills, exercise, attention control).

Another area of concern for parents and educators, as well as for those officials confronting public health and social policy issues, is children's sexual attitudes. What are the implications of the very considerable exposure of child viewers to relatively explicit sexual material in film and even more pervasively on television? Chapter 14, by Paul Wright, Neil Malamuth, and Ed Donnerstein, examines what we know about this issue from actual research study. The theoretical and data-based concerns that children may be prematurely aroused and that they may adopt potentially self-defeating or socially risky attitudes are considered here. Although certain religious groups may be offended by almost any sexual exposure or sexual references, the emphasis in this chapter is on identifying evidence of potential harm to children and the creation of public health problems. This approach is extended further by examining the impact of sexual portrayals on television and the Internet. Currently, there is an increase of explicit sexual scenes on television. If a young person is exploring the Internet, he or she can easily find a chat room that may be titillating but inappropriate for young viewers. As the authors indicate, there is a need for further careful research concerning the effects of sexual material on the Internet on young people.

Personality, Social Attitudes, and Health

We move in these next chapters to a consideration of how moderate to heavy viewing of television may be influencing children in their personal development and gender role awareness and in their orientation toward family, the social groups around them, and their substance use or eating behavior. Chapter 15, by Nina Huntemann and Michael Morgan, examines the subtle features of a sense of identity, the experience of "who am I?" and "what are my personal qualities?" What features of television content can be shown to influence how young viewers may form a sense of self? Chapter 16, by Nancy Signorielli, moves into the role of gender stereotyping and how television content represents boys and girls and men and women for the child viewer. Her review points out important effects as well as "content" research approaches. It also contains constructive suggestions for further research as well as for more educationally sound representations of the sexes.

Chapter 17, by Robert Kubey, Smita Banerjee, and Barna William Donovan, carries the theme of self a step further, to self in family. The authors consider the research

evidence on how television is watched in the family context (using the important experience sampling method) and then examine what the content of family programming presents to the viewer. One concern of researchers is the dependence on technology and its detraction from family and friends in the real world. Because the brain is still developing, the constant digital stimulation may also lead to attention problems in some children (Richtel, 2010). As with most of our chapters, suggestions for amelioration of the more negative effects of viewing are discussed. Chapter 18, by Joy Keiko Asamen and Gordon Berry, further points out the risks for children of narrowly focused cultural stereotyping based on the available current television programming. The authors review how cultural stereotype research is carried out and summarize available effect data. They also point toward ways in which television and the emerging computer-based media can lead children toward a richer awareness of the range of human cultural, physical, and social variations. *Sesame Street*, for example, has created 25 international co-productions wherein each country's show has its own identity (Shapiro, 2009). Cecilia von Feilitzen continues the discussion of multicultural awareness and the media in Chapter 19. She presents glimpses of a few topics on children, youth, and media and limits her discussion primarily to some different aspects of young people's media access and media use. The chapter also comments on the deceptive concept of media globalization. Findings on media reception and influences of the media on children and youth can often not be generalized across borders, which is why there is a great need for research in most countries. How do families from diverse backgrounds use television to structure their everyday lives? An entire issue of *Televizion* (2010) is devoted to the topic of the lack of diversity in children's TV, indicating that this medium does not reflect the numerous ethnic audiences.

A feature of most television in the United States, and increasingly worldwide, that is so pervasive that its message may actually be overlooked, is the commercial basis of the medium. Chapter 20, by Dale Kunkel and Jessica Castonguay, musters a huge panoply of evidence to demonstrate that one of the most powerful of television's socializing influences is that it exposes viewers to thousands of commercials and to a continuous stream of temptations that may create excessive materialism and also the conflicts of aspirations for possessions beyond their own or their families' capacities for achievement. The vulnerability of the young lies in the fact that they (a) may not be capable of clearly separating externally generated commercial messages from their own desires and (b) may not yet be capable, as most adults are, of building up some defense structures or cynicism about advertising appeals. What responsibilities do the industry, parents, or policy makers have in the face of the data reported?

Our next two chapters review the available literature on how television viewing may be directly influencing children's health habits. A very powerful and disquieting Chapter 21, by Victor Strasburger, reviews in detail the methods of study and the findings bearing linkages between television viewing and substance abuse, drinking, or smoking in children and youth. Chapter 22, by Katherine Battle Horgen, Jennifer Harris, and Kelly Brownell, carries this thrust further into an examination of how television commercials create trends toward unhealthy eating habits.

Still another area of television's and other media's appeal lies in children's attraction to popular music. What messages are conveyed in music, on audiotapes and compact discs, and on television in the powerful images of MTV and its variants? The authors of Chapter 23, Donald Roberts and Peter Christenson, examine the scientific literature in this field. For example, they raise the question "Is there a heavy metal syndrome?" and review the available research literature correlating preferences for such music with reckless driving or drug abuse. That watching MTV can be influential at least in changing recreational preferences has recently been demonstrated with the report on the CBS *60 Minutes* program about the tiny Shangri-La monarchy of Bhutan in the Himalayan Mountains. This country allowed television use only in the last year of the 20th century. A government leader somewhat ruefully reports that children and youth, hitherto seemingly happily conforming to Buddhist ritual and recreation, have now taken to dancing and imitating American MTV!

In summary, Part I provides a pervasive and careful review of the positive and negative influences of television on children and youth. The reader will see that most children watch a great deal of television and that research demonstrates a variety of ways in which their cognitive, social, and health habits reflect that pervasive, intrusive new "member of the family."

References

Brooks, D. (2010, July 9). The medium is the medium. *The New York Times*, p. A23.

Centerwall, B. S. (1989). Exposure to television as a cause of violence. *Public Communication and Behavior, 2,* 1–57.

Centerwall, B. S. (1994). Television and the development of the superego: Pathway to violence. In C. Chiland, J. G. Young, & D. Kaplan (Eds.), *Children and violence: The child in the family* (Monograph series of the International Association for Child and Adolescent Psychiatry and Allied Professions, pp. 178–197). Northvale, NJ: Jason Aronson, XIII.

Ferguson, C. J. (Ed.). (2010). Video games: Old fears and new directions [Special issue]. *Review of General Psychology*, *14*(2), pp. 65–187.

Gerbner, G., Gross, L., Morgan, M., & Signorielli, N. (1994). Growing up with television: The cultivation perspective. In J. Bryant & D. Zillmann (Eds.), *Media effects: Advances in theory and research* (pp. 17–42). Hillsdale, NJ: Lawrence Erlbaum.

Hu, W. (2010, May 7). Avatars go to school, letting students get a feel for the work world. *The New York Times*, p. A23.

Richtel, M. (2010, June). Hooked on gadgets, and paying a mental price. *The New York Times,* pp. A1, A12, A13.

Shapiro, S. M. (2009, October 4). Can the Muppets make friends on the West Bank? *The New York Times Magazine*, pp. 39–44.

Televizion. (2010). *Diversity in children's TV*. Internationales Zentralinstitut für das Jugend- und Bildungsfernsehen (IZI).

Singer, J. L., & Singer, D. G. (1998). *Barney & friends* as entertainment and education: Evaluating the quality and effectiveness of a television series for preschool children. In J. K. Asamen & G. Berry (Eds.), *Research paradigms in the study of television and social behavior* (pp. 305–367). Thousand Oaks, CA: Sage.

CHAPTER 1

The Use of Television and Other Screen Media

GEORGE COMSTOCK
Syracuse University

ERICA SCHARRER
University of Massachusetts Amherst

Television and other screen media account for a substantial portion of the time expenditures of children and adolescents. Recent estimates (Rideout, Foehr, & Roberts, 2010) place viewing at almost 5 hours a day for those 8 to 18, with 7 hours and 38 minutes devoted to all entertainment media (Kaiser Family Foundation, 2010). Screen media account for almost half of their media exposure, with television preeminent (with about 95% of screen media use). This implies, for most young people, an extensive consumption of undemanding entertainment, including many portrayals of conflict and violence, with potential consequences for affect, cognition, and behavior. There may be a loss as well of the benefits of foregone opportunities. Our present task is to examine the behavior of the young in their use of television and other screen media, by which we mean whatever appears on the television screen from whatever source, television content on other platforms (such as a computer or iPod), and movies seen in theaters.

There are very good reasons to give attention to young people's use of screen media. These media certainly provide many moments of piqued interest and enjoyment for children and adolescents, as they do for adults. In this respect, they are merely one of the pleasures afforded by modern life. However, it would be a mistake to think of them as limited to such outcomes. There is ample evidence that, for some young people, either the amount viewed or what is viewed may have adverse consequences (Comstock & Scharrer, 1999).

Television and other screen media have been implicated in the displacement of time that might be spent acquiring the basic scholastic skills of reading, mathematics, and writing (Comstock & Scharrer, 1999; Neuman, 1991; Van Evra, 1998; Williams, 1986); in the encouragement of attitudes and practices that diminish concentration while reading and promote a preference for undemanding pictures and texts, such as comic books (Koolstra & van der Voort, 1996); in affecting mood and behavior by contributing to fearfulness, physiologically measured excitation, hyperactivity, and reduced impulse control and attention span (Cantor, 1994a, 1994b; Singer, Singer, Desmond, Hirsch, & Nicol, 1988); in shaping daydreaming, play, and imaginative processes (Valkenburg & van der Voort, 1994; Valkenburg, Voojis, van der Voort, & Wiegman, 1992); in encouraging food choices that promote obesity and poor nutrition (Adler et al., 1980; Comstock & Scharrer, 2007); and in the facilitation of aggressive and antisocial behavior (Anderson et al., 2003; Comstock & Scharrer, 1999, 2007; Kirsh, 2006; National Television Violence Study, 1996, 1997, 1998; Singer & Singer, 1981; U.S. Department of Health & Human Services, 2001).

Screen media also have been associated with prosocial outcomes. They can contribute importantly, through educational programming, to children's scholastic achievement, as exemplified by gains in knowledge of letters and numbers attributable to the viewing of *Sesame Street* (Cook et al., 1975). They can be a part of child-rearing practices that lead to slightly enhanced performance years later in high school (Comstock & Scharrer, 1999; Wright & Huston, 1995; Zill, Davies, & Daly, 1994). By the examples they may give of positive forms of behavior, they can facilitate generosity, tolerance, cooperation, and other modes of behavior that promote constructive social interaction. There is also the mundane but hardly insignificant relief of stress from entertainment (Comstock & Scharrer, 1999, 2007).

The exposure of children to a specific program or movie, as Hamilton (1998) pointed out in his economic analysis of the marketplace for television violence, is to a substantial degree the product of what economists call *externalities,* or unintended consequences, and the balancing of costs and benefits by television executives and parents. Executives may attract children to unsuitable programs as a by-product of scheduling them to maximize an older audience sought by advertisers. They may also schedule educational programs at times when the available audience of children is not at its peak because other programs are more profitable in those time slots. Parents may not supervise viewing to an optimum degree because of the inconvenience, or costs, of determining which programs might be harmful or beneficial and of exerting

authority. Thus, both media executives and parents often act in their narrow, short-term interests rather than acting in terms of longer-range benefits to children and society.

We conceive of the study of media audiences as very broad (Comstock & Scharrer, 1999), including orientation toward a medium; motivations for its use; content selection; various household and situational variables that affect use; the regularities that mark audience flow throughout the day, week, and season; and the demographic variables that describe media consumption. We attempt to describe young people's use of television and other screen media in the same terms.

We draw often on the Kaiser Foundation surveys of media use by the young (Rideout et al., 2010; Rideout & Hamel, 2006; Roberts & Foehr, 2004). They supply tabulations of media use that cover all media and are also nationally representative. They are remarkably up-to-date, with the most recent survey in 2009. They also employ a taxonomy that meticulously describes electronic media use and the new platforms that figure in access to television content.

We use the term *television and other screen media* to encompass all access to television content and time spent at theaters watching movies. *Television content* covers what might be received on a TV screen by whatever means it might be accessed (for example, time-shifted programs, DVDs and videos, the Internet, iPods and MP-3 players, and cell phones). We sometimes reassemble categories, such as combining movie going and use of videos and DVDs as an overall estimate of exposure to movies.

We recognize the distinction employed by the Kaiser surveys between media exposure and media use when describing aggregate consumption. *Exposure* is defined as the time spent with media, however achieved. *Use* is defined as the amount of time spent with media, however crowded with multiple use. One hour of attending to television while using the Internet would sum to two hours of media exposure produced by one hour of media use. Exposure by definition is always greater than (if two or more media are used at the same time) or equal to use (if there is no multiple consumption). This device captures media exposure that might be ignored while not exaggerating the allocation of time to media.

Otherwise, we employ the two terms *use* and *exposure* interchangeably to represent the time spent with the named source or type of content regardless of other media consumption that may be taking place at the same time.

Children and Electronic Media

Television

Every new electronic communication medium has faced questions about effects on children and adolescents. (See Chapter 1 in Singer and Singer, 2001, for a full discussion of history of the media.)Television in particular has understandably aroused concerns. There was extensive research in the 1950s (Schramm, Lyle, & Parker, 1961); a report by the President's Commission on the Causes and Prevention of Violence, a media task force, in the late 1960s (Baker & Ball, 1969); and federal inquiries in the 1970s (Surgeon General's Scientific Advisory Committee, 1972) and 1980s (Pearl, Bouthilet, & Lazar, 1982). In fact, television was so popular it took away much of the audience for comic books (Comstock, 1991; Comstock & Scharrer, 2007). More recently, video games (Anderson, Gentile, & Buckley, 2007) and the Internet have received extensive attention.

When television was first developed in the 1920s and 1930s, the film and radio industries looked on it as more of a novelty than a threat. About three years after radio broadcasting became a reality in 1920, a very primitive version of a television system was available. In 1928, telecasting began on an experimental basis, without commercials or an audience. This was followed by television's first major public demonstration at the 1939 World's Fair and the first commercial telecast in 1941. Even after television became a major mass medium, the amount of time that children and adolescents spent with radio remained substantial. Confirming radio's consistent listenership, Lyle and Hoffman (1972a) reported in the early 1970s that, even when television was the most favored medium, half of the first graders and 80% of the sixth graders among their respondents reported listening to radio on the preceding day, and 24% of 10th graders reported listening five hours or more a day.

Television probably would have been developed as a commercial mass medium sooner except for three barriers: the depression, which severely constrained the consumer market; the popularity of movies, which seemed to satisfy needs for mass entertainment; and World War II, which dramatically monopolized human and technological resources. At the end of the war, however, the situation changed. There was what one analyst called a "supervening necessity" (Winston, 1986) on behalf of the new medium—the economy was resurgent, the growth of the suburbs favored in-home entertainment, and the industrial and technological capacities of war invited peacetime application. The need to invest in the economy translated into a market for a new mass medium. It became evident that television would constitute a serious threat to movies and radio (Barnouw, 1990).

The structure of early television closely resembled that of radio. There were three television networks—the National Broadcasting Company (NBC), the Columbia Broadcasting System (CBS), and the American Broadcasting Company (ABC)—and a programming spectrum that covered comedies, quiz shows, soap operas, suspense programs, variety shows, and westerns. The similarity resulted from the migration of personnel from radio (e.g., technicians, writers, directors, actors, musicians, and singers), pursuit of the same audience (Whetmore, 1981), and the aggressive advantage of radio broadcasters in obtaining television licenses from the Federal Communications Commission (FCC) (Boddy, 1990).

Schramm et al. (1961), in their benchmark study of the effects of the introduction of television, recorded that sixth-grade children were spending four fifths of their viewing time on programs intended for adult viewers. Even in first grade, nearly two fifths of viewing time was devoted to adult programs. This pattern of early use and extensive exposure to adult programs persists to the present day.

Whether children watch television alone or with parents, siblings, or peers is a significant component of the viewing experience. In the late 1940s and early 1950s, television typically was a major purchase and was placed in the living room. Viewing with parents was common; television physically brought families together (Lawrence & Wozniak, 1989; McDonagh, 1950), but such family viewing, whatever the case when television was a novelty and whatever the minor pleasures of togetherness, eventually was categorized by many viewers as comparatively unrewarding (Kubey & Csikszentmihalyi, 1990). The young, with the help of affluence and technology, would increasingly view alone or with others their own age.

Today, almost 90% of households have more than one set, and many are in children's bedrooms. In addition, television is now available on a number of different platforms, such as the Internet via computers, iPods, cell phones, and similar devices (Rideout et al., 2010). The result has been a clear trend toward greater viewing alone. This increased independence has reduced the parental role in how much is viewed, what is viewed, and what young people learn from or think about what they view (Comstock, 1991a).

Cable, freed many years ago from regulatory restraints, and direct satellite services delivering a similar diversity of channels now reach about 85% of households. These carry adult programming that often is graphic in regard to sex and violence. They also make available children's channels (e.g., Nickelodeon, the Disney Channel, and Cartoon Network), family-oriented networks that carry some children's programming (e.g., Turner Broadcasting System [TBS], USA Network, the Discovery Channel, Turner Network Television [TNT], the Arts and Entertainment Channel [A&E]), and music channels primarily attended to by the young (such as MTV).

Ironically, this diversity may not improve the educational value of the viewing of some young people. The ease of viewing without parental involvement often means less viewing of educationally beneficial programs. For example, Huston and Wright (1996) found that cable access increased cartoon viewing by children because it made more cartoons available.

Computer-Based Media

Television introduced a new experience in mass media into American households: the screen media. Today, a second novel household transition is well underway: the introduction of computer-based technologies.

Educational Software

The personal computer software market has been producing "edutainment" (education + entertainment) programs for children since its earliest days. Typical programs for 6- to 9-month-old infants involve shapes, colors, animal sounds, and nursery rhymes. For toddlers, programs teach numbers and vocabulary while developing computer mouse skills. Some of these programs were spin-offs of television programs for children 12 to 18 months (e.g., *Play with the Teletubbies* from PBS and the British Broadcasting Company [BBC] and *Blue's Clues* from Nickelodeon). The software industry was soon able to extend the market to older children and adolescents.

Video Games

The first interactive video games originated in 1962. However, in the 1970s, computers were mostly mainframe computers and thus inaccessible to most people. During that time, video games were played in video arcades. Then, in 1972, microcomputer games were introduced alongside arcade systems, and by the 1980s, even home computers were thought of as game computers. In the mid-1980s, video game popularity surged, until market saturation with similar games led to a decline in sales. Then in the late 1980s, the Nintendo system was introduced—a computer solely for games—and the video game industry regained its popularity. In the 1990s, with the growth of CD technology, CD-ROM games led the market with much-improved graphics and realism. These trends were the foundation for the past decade—continuing high-popularity, stand-alone devices and ever-increasing realism and graphic impact.

The Internet

The idea of the Internet dates back to the 1950s, but the current design can be traced to 1969, when the Defense Department computer network allowed military contractors and universities doing military research to exchange information with each other electronically. However, the birth of the Internet as a public domain had to await the development of the personal computer by International Business Machines (IBM) in 1975 and the price reductions necessary for mass affordability in the early 1980s.

Finally, in 1987, the basic structure of the current Internet was formed when the National Science Foundation created a network giving researchers access to five supercomputing centers that were connected to hundreds of other networks operated by educational institutions, government agencies, and research organizations (Cozic, 1997; Hudson, 1997). Today, supercomputers play no role in driving the Internet. It is based on the many, many thousands of smaller computers.

Growth has been encouraged by the interest of ordinary computer users in the World Wide Web (WWW) and other Internet features (Dizard, 2000). On average, children and adolescents today spend about an hour and a half a day using computers for recreational purposes (Rideout et al., 2010), about an hour more than a decade ago. Only about a quarter of an hour is devoted to video games, leaving an enormous one hour and 12 minutes for Internet use—communication (email, instant messaging), social networking (MySpace, Facebook), video sites (YouTube), and other applications.

The Internet is in its infancy. So far, Internet use by the young has only slightly affected use of other media while at the same time enjoying popularity and growth because so much use now involves multitasking (use of two or more media at the same time). This is the phenomenon that Robinson and Godbey (1997) labeled "time deepening."

Principal Variables

The principal variables that play a role in young people's use of television and other screen media can be divided into four categories: societal and structural factors, household characteristics, personal attributes, and situational influences.

Societal and Structural Factors

Societal and structural factors determine the number of channels available, their content, the costs of obtaining access to them, and, thus, the options open to the young viewer. These factors include governmental and regulatory policies that shape the way the media operate, the economics of program production and distribution that influence what will be offered, and the state of technology that determines what can be received or viewed in the home. In recent years, technology has been the center of attention for the dramatic increases in sources of programming and means of reception it has made possible.

Household Characteristics

Household characteristics play an enormous role in children's use of television and other media. These characteristics include socioeconomic status; the norms specifying the degree to which television is central to household life and leisure, including the ubiquity of television use; and the available resources, including the number of television sets, other media such as computers, media in children's bedrooms, and alternative leisure opportunities.

Personal Attributes

Personal attributes affect how much is viewed, what is viewed, and, importantly, the how—the attentional manner—of consuming television and other screen media. The principal variables are age, mental ability, and an outcome affected by both—comprehension—which figures in the shift from a child to an adult mode of viewing.

Situational Influences

Situational influences include transient but sometimes repetitive factors that are not inextricably part of the practices or make-up of the household. These include the presence of others (e.g., parents, peers, and siblings) while the child is viewing; clock- and calendar-based influences such as hour of the day, day of the week, and season; and states of mind such as anger and loneliness.

The Viewing Experience

The viewing of television and other screen media is such an everyday activity that it is easy to overlook its uniqueness among mass media consumption. Every mode of how people attend to media is encompassed—"browse, momentarily ignore, assemble into a mosaic of contrasting bits, passingly follow, attentively consume" (Comstock & Scharrer, 1999, p.61)—with the most striking feature being the large amounts of time in which viewers are indifferent. The combining of varying degrees of cognitive involvement with waxing and waning physical attentiveness in a context of social conventions and competing activities requires, in our view, an examination of the viewing process as prerequisite to looking at data on time spent viewing and its correlates. This is because hours and minutes spent with television and other screen media only take on meaning and can only be meaningfully interpreted with knowledge of what constitutes viewing. We cover four topics: the purposes and motives of viewing; the role in viewing of three typical modes of response; the adoption of these adult-like viewing patterns as children learn to use television; and our explication and operationalization of the concept of viewing.

Purposes and Motives

The two orientations that describe both viewing behavior at a given moment and an individual's typical disposition toward the medium so well among teenagers and adults (Comstock & Scharrer, 1999) at first seem embarrassingly obtuse when applied to children. *Instrumental viewing* surely connotes too much in the way of use of the medium for information to describe the behavior of children; *ritualistic viewing* seems to belie the enthusiasm that children bring to favorite programs and their characters. However, the data convince us that these distinctions can be usefully applied to children, although it is only through changes that occur during childhood that children, as a group, come to parallel the viewing behavior of teenagers and adults.

The distinguishing element is the degree to which the specific content of a program is responsible for viewing (Comstock & Scharrer, 1999, 2007; Rubin, 1983, 1984). The first priority in ritualistic viewing is exposure to television. Gratifications are then maximized by choosing the most pleasing of the available options. Correlates of regular ritualistic viewing are greater overall viewing and a preference for undemanding, entertaining content. Instrumental viewing, in contrast, is motivated by interest in a specific program or specific content. Correlates of regular instrumental viewing are lesser overall viewing and a preference for programs that satisfy a particular interest. Instrumental viewing, then, represents greater selectivity. Programs universally are of importance but at a subordinate level in ritualistic viewing. Most viewing is ritualistic; the proportion, however, may be declining because of the greater selectivity made possible by new technology—especially among the young because they are more likely to use such technology.

Ritualistic viewing accounts for the large amount of time that has been recorded as devoted to television viewing among all age groups. The devoted concentration called forth by highly interesting fare could only support a few hours of viewing a week. Ritualistic viewing is particularly likely to be characterized by monitoring, in which audience members attend only enough to follow the narrative and use cues in the audio track to determine when to direct attention to the screen (Comstock & Scharrer, 1999, 2007). It is this behavior that underlies the financial foundation of much of the medium—the assembling of the huge audiences that advertisers seek to reach.

The three major motives that operate within these two orientations for viewing at all ages are (a) diversion and an escape from comparatively less attractive options; (b) surveillance on behalf of social comparison, by which an individual evaluates the merits of his or her personal attributes; and (c) awareness. We define the latter as embracing not only what is transpiring in the world but also what is occurring on television (programs, personalities) and the way the medium covers those events (film, tape, controversy).

In our view, escape in its various guises is primary. Our rationale is the frequency with which stress in a variety of forms predicts greater viewing among both children and older people (Anderson, Collins, Schmitt, & Jacobvitz, 1996; Canary & Spitzberg, 1993; Kubey & Csikszentmihalyi, 1990; Maccoby, 1954; Potts & Sanchez, 1994), as well as the dominance of pleasure and relaxation when adults cite reasons for viewing (Albarran & Umphrey, 1993; Bower, 1985). The other two are nevertheless important. This is evident in the case of surveillance from the frequency with which viewers have been found to pay more attention to personages on the screen who are like themselves, whether the link is race (Comstock, 1991), age (Harwood, 1997), or gender (Maccoby & Wilson, 1957; Maccoby, Wilson, & Burton, 1958; Sprafkin & Liebert, 1978). In the case of awareness, it is evident from the frequency with which learning is cited as a motive by adults for attending to television (Albarran & Umphrey, 1993; Bower, 1985) and the frequency with which presentational elements—visual imagery, a compelling construction of the spoken and the seen—figure in the quality ascribed to the viewing experience by audience members (Levy, 1978; Neuman, 1982).

Three Modes of Response

The predominance of ritualistic viewing is exemplified by three modes of response to the medium that come to typify viewing as children mature, are characteristic of the viewing of teenagers and adults, and are surprisingly frequent throughout childhood. We emphasize that these modes of response are not universal. There are frequent exceptions to each, typically in the form of the time spent at all ages with favorite programs, major sports events, or particularly attractive movies. Nevertheless, they are the dominant motifs that characterize the bulk of attending to screen media and particularly television. They are the *primacy* given to the media, *low involvement,* and *monitoring.*

Primacy

The primacy of the medium—a collection now of a bundle of media platforms that deliver television content—is one of the most consistently and clearly documented phenomena of mass audience behavior. Although the popularity of specific programs is crucial to the success of the channels on which the programs appear, the audience at a given time, for the most part, is not assembled because of a particular offering but rather to enjoy what the medium in general has to offer. The primacy, in particular, is represented by the well-known *two-step decision* process by which programs to be viewed are chosen and by the governing role of *time available* in whether or not television will be viewed.

The initial step is typically whether or not to view television (Barwise, Ehrenberg, & Goodhardt, 1982; Comstock, Chaffee, Katzman, McCombs, & Roberts, 1978). The second step is to select the most satisfying among the possible options for the person or persons making the decision. The role of specific programs in determining who will view at a given time is comparatively minor.

Viewing is largely (but not wholly) governed by time available. Viewing by those older and younger, by females and males, and by children varies across the time of day, the day of the week, and the season, depending on the availability of the members of the demographic category to become part of the television audience (Comstock & Scharrer, 1999; Webster & Phalen, 1997). People almost always choose the same option again and again if options remain the same when viewing at a particular time, but substantially more than half the time they fail to see the forthcoming episode of something they have previously chosen to view—news, talk, situation comedy, action adventure—because some obligation or preferred activity takes them out of the vicinity of the operating television set (Barwise et al., 1982). When the United Nations Educational, Scientific, and Cultural Organization (UNESCO) surveyed time use in cities around the globe, including cities in the United States, Eastern and Western Europe, and South America, in the mid-1960s, an extraordinary pattern emerged in regard to television use. Despite the enormous differences that existed in the quality, type, amount, and variety of programming available, the set owners worldwide were very much alike in the amount of time spent with television (Comstock, 1991: Robinson & Converse, 1972; Robinson & Godbey, 1997). Recent data (Klepp et al., 2007) confirm the pattern among children across Europe: Children in Austria, Belgium, Denmark, Iceland, the Netherlands, Norway, Portugal, Spain, and Sweden, in data collected via the Pro Children Project and comprising well over 13,000 children from age 8 to 14, watched an average of 2.1 to 2.7 hours of television per day. These figures imply a relative consistency in exposure times for those in developed countries with ready access to the medium.

These varied data make it clear that the enjoyment of television and not the specific programs scheduled is primary most of the time in assembling an audience. One exception is the rare program that seemingly has no equivalent—that is not one of a largely fungible genre. A second exception is major events, such as the Super Bowl and other sports spectaculars (Barwise & Ehrenberg, 1988). Annual events like awards programs are also major draws. The size of the Academy Awards audience, for example, has ranged from 32 to 43 million in the past eight years, with the 2010 Oscar broadcast pulling in 41.3 million viewers (O'Neil, 2010).

Thus, it is programming that conforms to the availability of demographic segments to become part of the audience, with the popularity of specific programs primarily governing the division of the available audience. An example is the role of children on Saturday mornings and, to a lesser extent, weekday afternoons. Children tend to be otherwise unoccupied and therefore available for viewing at these times, inspiring media executives to tailor programs offered during these parts of the day to child audiences. Similar "targeting" of audience segments occurs in other parts of the day, such as the scheduling of soap operas on weekday afternoons to appeal to nonworking women.

Low Involvement

Viewers much of the time are only passively involved in what they view. When large, representative national samples were asked what they viewed the night before, few mentioned a specific program. A majority cited the rewards of viewing television (a further reason to think of the medium as having primacy over individual programs in the assembly of an audience), and not many thought what they had seen was particularly rewarding, pleasurable, memorable, or exciting (Bower, 1985; LoSciuto, 1972). More than one third did not actively choose what they had viewed but watched whatever came on next or a program chosen—there were fewer multi-set households then—by someone else (LoSciuto, 1972). In a detailed study of the viewing behavior of two dozen families, between about one half and two thirds of adults said they did not give full attention to programs they considered as having viewed (Hopkins & Mullis, 1985); the higher figure was recorded for women because of their more frequent involvement in household tasks (Robinson & Godbey, 1997). Time-lapse photography (Allen, 1965) and video recording of viewers (Anderson, Lorch, Field, Collins, & Nathan, 1986; Bechtel, Achelpohl, & Akers, 1972) confirm that attention is typically erratic, with viewers giving no attention to the screen about 40% of the time. People treasure the medium, and many viewers have favorite programs they particularly enjoy, but as these data attest, much of the time they are not deeply engaged in attending to what is on the screen (Barwise & Ehrenberg, 1988). The selectivity made possible by today's much greater diversity has undoubtedly somewhat enhanced viewer interest in particular, but a diluted disposition toward the screen persists because the circumstances of much viewing remain the same. The data attest that viewers of all ages most of the time broadly seek entertainment and specific content is secondary.

Low levels of involvement should not be surprising for an activity that for the past several decades has consumed two dozen hours a week or more for the average person (Comstock & Scharrer, 1999) and that clocks in at an enormous 141 hours per month (that's an average of 4.7 hours per day in a 30-day month) according to 2009 Nielsen figures (Nielsen Wire, 2010). Such a large allocation of time does not, in most households, permit an investment of intense concentration. Thus, the huge audiences that constitute the economic foundation of those sectors of the medium deriving much of their income from advertising are in equilibrium with the modest cognitive demands of most programming. It is no accident that those channels that somewhat more often venture into more demanding programming are those least dependent on advertising—cable, particularly premium cable, and public television. Low involvement makes a mass audience possible as well as leaves viewers in a state of vague pleasure within which advertisers may effectively court them.

Monitoring

Although, in deference to common usage, we use the term *viewing* to refer to attending to screen media, the more apt term is *monitoring* (which we use when we want to emphasize the nature of the activity). The various indexes that point to low levels of involvement in the typical viewing of most programs lead to the conclusion that most of the time viewers pay only sufficient attention to comprehend the unfolding narrative and take in depictions, portrayals, events, and exchanges of particular interest. This phenomenon has been examined primarily among young children, whose attention to the screen varies as a function of the audio and visual cues offered by the medium and the degree to which others in the vicinity are attending to the screen

(Anderson, & Lorch, 1983; Bryant, Zillmann, & Brown, 1983; Collins, 1981; Huston & Wright, 1989; Krull, 1983; Lorch, Anderson, & Levin, 1979). Drama, sound, and the behavior of fellow viewers—those are the cues that govern attention to the screen.

In effect, the viewer, disinclined to invest viewing with much in the way of concentration, seeks signs that will attest to an enhanced likelihood that one or another gratification will be satisfied or that an immediately forthcoming element will be important to understanding what is taking place. The same phenomenon characterizes adult viewing. On average, attention to the screen is at its lowest for content that is either episodic or redundant, or stereotypic and conventionalized. Episodic or redundant content, such as news, sports, and commercials, does not require prior attention to one item for future comprehension of another. Stereotypic and conventionalized content, such as soap operas, contain elements that, even if unattended to, can be readily inferred. Attention is at its highest for extended narratives that may present the unexpected, such as movies and crime dramas (Bechtel et al., 1972), because such attention is necessary for comprehension.

Television viewing, unlike attending to the screen at a movie theater, conforms to the principle of minimal expended effort because of the greater presence of distracting stimuli. Viewers most of the time adopt a strategy of attending closely only when reward or necessity dictates such an expenditure of effort, and the process involved makes the term *monitoring* more accurate than *viewing* in describing what takes place.

Learning to Use Television

Children literally grow into these patterns of behavior. They learn to use the medium, and by about the age of 12, when amount of viewing will peak, their behavior in response to television will approximate that of adults— although there will be many specific programs they will not yet find of much interest.

Viewing on a regular basis in a household with television usually begins between the ages of two-and-a-half and three, with an average estimated in one study of about 1.5 hours per day (Huston et al., 1983). Giving regular attention to the screen, however, has been recorded as early as six months of age (Hollenbeck & Slaby, 1979). The recent Kaiser Foundation survey (Rideout & Hamel, 2006) of the very young estimates an average of 49 minutes a day in total screen use for those zero to one and 1 hour 51 minutes for those two to three. Screen media use, then, begins very early, and this has been a long-standing pattern in child rearing.

Viewing then quickly increases, with later estimates by the same group of investigators (Huston, Wright, Rice, Kerkman, & St. Peters, 1990) rising to 2.75 hours for those between the ages of three and six, then declining about a half-hour between the ages of five-and-a-half and seven, when activities associated with beginning school temporarily limit available time. As most data indicate, viewing increases again until about ages 12 to 14. Thus, a peak in viewing begins in late childhood and continues into early adolescence. In the latest Kaiser data, 11- to 14-year-olds viewed an average of just over five hours of television per day, compared to 3 hours 41 minutes for 8- to 10-year-olds and 4 hours 22 minutes for 15- to 18-year-olds (Rideout et al., 2010). Our Figure 1.1 is valid in the shape of the curves, but amount of viewing would be somewhat higher were it based on contemporary data.

Obviously, at the earliest of these ages, the following of a narrative would not be one of the satisfactions of viewing. However, if what is seen performed on the screen is within their physical capability, children as young as 12 and 24 months of age are able to internalize what they see, imitate it on request, and retain this capability for as long as 24 hours after the initial exposure (Meltzoff, 1988). Thus, comprehension of what is represented physically on the screen begins quite early.

Preferences develop very early (see Table 1.1, page 23). About four fifths of the three-year-olds in the Los Angeles area sample of 160 children ages three, four, and five named a favorite program when asked to do so by Lyle and Hoffman (1972b); by age five, almost everyone did. Gender and age are major predictors. Both preschool boys and girls are attracted to appealing animal characters, as exemplified by *Sesame Street*. Girls will watch superhero programming in which they have only token representation, as attested to by the

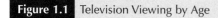

Figure 1.1 Television Viewing by Age

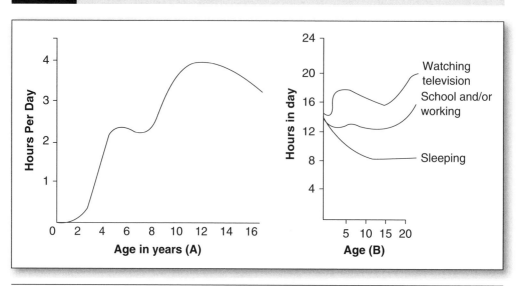

Source: Comstock, Chaffee, Katzman, McCombs, and Roberts (1978).

child audience for Saturday morning programming (Comstock, 1991). Gender exerts an influence even among very young children, with twice as many girls as boys (39% vs. 19%) among those ages three, four, and five naming a family cartoon (*The Flintstones*) as a favorite and three times as many boys as girls (17% vs. 5%) naming a violent cartoon as a favorite. More recently, very young children, in first and second grade, were asked to list up to three favorite television programs (Aubrey & Harrison, 2004). Animated fare expressly created for children dominated the list (with *Rugrats, Doug, Arthur*, and *Pokémon* among the top choices), thus pointing to the enduring appeal of the cartoon format for the young child. Additional recent data from 183 children from 5 to 12 years of age found characters need not be realistic to become a child's favorite (Rosaen & Dibble, 2008). Indeed, 73% of the children in the sample chose a favorite character who neither appeared nor acted real (such as an animated character and/or one with super powers).

Age differences are pronounced. In the data Lyle and Hoffman (1972a) obtained from about 1,600 Los Angeles area 1st-, 6th-, and 10th-grade students, about half of those in the first grade named a situation comedy and about a fourth named a cartoon as favorite. By the sixth grade, only one in 20 named a cartoon;

situation comedies remained the most popular but to a somewhat reduced degree; and all varieties of adult formats were increasing in favoritism. By the 10th grade, the most popular formats were action adventures, dramas, and music, variety, and talk shows (music and variety now partly replaced by MTV and other music channels). Further, as children grew older, they were more likely to have favorite television characters who looked and behaved in ways similar to what is encountered in the "real world" (Rosaen & Dibble, 2008).

The viewing of *Sesame Street* and other educational programs designed specifically to appeal to the very young increases between the ages of three and four and then begins to decline precipitously (Huston et al., 1990). The early gender and age shifts observed by Lyle and Hoffman (1972a, 1972b) represent enduring phenomena because children have not changed in their cognitive and affective makeup and, consequently, television essentially has not changed in what it makes available to them. Thus, about 20 years later, Huston and colleagues (1990) observed the same trends in their Topeka sample of more than 300 children three to five and five to seven years old. And more than 30 years later, Aubrey and Harrison (2004) and Rosaen and Dibble (2008) confirmed the special appeal of animation and cartoons for children.

Table 1.1	Child and Teenage Viewing Preferences, by Type of Program					
	Percentage Named as Favorites					
	Preschool Age			Grade		
	3	*4*	*5*	*1st*	*2nd*	*3rd*
Sitcom	—	4	12	22	17	9
Family sitcom	5	2	6	25	23	9
Flintstones	11	29	36	—	—	—
Mickey Mouse	3	4	12	—	—	—
General cartoon	8	16	6	24	5	1
Violent cartoon	3	15	12	—	—	—
Bozo, etc.	8	2	—	—	—	—
Sesame Street	30	13	12	—	—	—
Mister Rogers	3	2	6	—	—	—
Don't understand the question	19	4	3	—	—	—

Source: Lyle and Hoffman (1972a, 1972b).

Note: Percentages are rounded to the nearest whole number.

Two concepts proposed by von Feilitzen and Linne (1975) help explain these patterns: *similarity* and *wishful identification.* Similarity refers to the preference for characters like oneself and is very evident among children in the greater attention and greater favoritism they give to portrayals of those of the same gender, age, or race (Comstock, 1991; Harwood, 1997; Lyle & Hoffman, 1972a; Maccoby & Wilson, 1957; Maccoby et al., 1958; Sprafkin & Liebert, 1978). Wishful identification refers to a preference for characters the young viewer would like to resemble, and it increases with viewer age. Thus, children increasingly come to view programs portraying those who are older, more powerful, and higher in status, while when very young they will prefer programs portraying those who are somewhat dependent on others, as they are, such as cute animals (Comstock, 1991).

What increasingly becomes the case is the adoption of patterns that characterize teenage and adult viewing, but what is surprising is the occurrence of some of these patterns in the earliest years of viewing. The motive of surveillance, or using television as a source for evaluating oneself, apparently begins very early, as evidenced by very young viewers' preference for those on screen who have something in common with them. The gratification derived from awareness about the medium similarly would seem to be satisfied by the decided shifts in favorite programs, which also begins among the very young. Escape is omnipresent, and the central role of simple pleasure in attending to the images on a television screen is manifest in an oddity of the behavioral science laboratory. Television imagery or its withdrawal can be used to shape the behavior of young children (as could any pleasurable or noxious stimulus) and thus is inherently rewarding (Baer, 1962).

Children are reputed to be tremendous fans of favored programs and their characters, and we have no reason to doubt the accuracy of parental anecdotes, newspaper articles, or the testimony of the shelves and stacks in stores of toys and paraphernalia representing television programs. This devotion is reflected in the greater attention preschool children give to the screen when watching a cartoon compared with a situation comedy (Argenta, Stoneman, & Brody, 1986) and the visual attention that young children give to children's programming in general (Bechtel et al., 1972). In these instances, they are undeniably instrumental viewers.

However, their viewing of other content and at other times, which will constitute a majority of the viewing of all children, is clearly more ritualistic in nature, and their increasing adoption of a less involved stance toward viewing is quite apparent when the frequency of viewing favorite programs is examined (see Figure 1.2). It increases up to about the age of nine; children are exercising their preferences (which by then would place situation comedies in the forefront, with cartoons dwindling in favor and general audience formats other than situation comedies showing small gains). Then the viewing of favorites declines; children begin to

Figure 1.2 Change in Frequency of Television Viewing From Grades 1 to 5: Favorite Programs

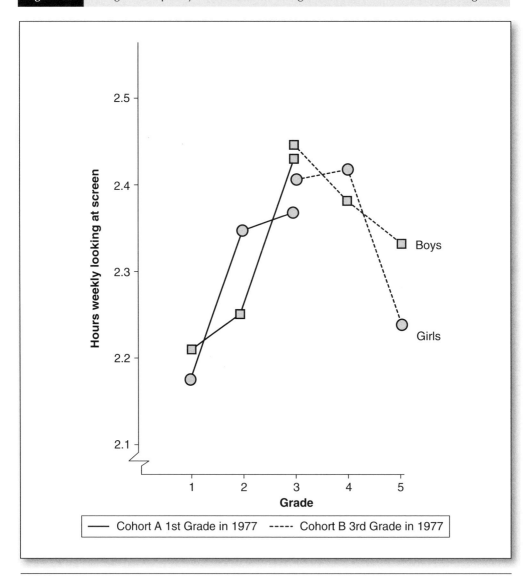

Source: Eron, Huesmann, Brice, and Mermelstein (1983).

conform to the constraints of the time available to view favorites, as their overall viewing at this point in the life span, on average, is actually increasing (see Figure 1.1). Children are beginning to resemble adults, who often miss favorites in their truncated exercise of preferences, an exercise that for both adults and children is only slightly enhanced by the DVR and other home recording devices because only modest amounts of regular recording and replay occur in most households (Comstock & Scharrer, 1999, 2007; Lin, 1990, 1993).

Attention to the screen in general typically also will have been rising during these earlier years (see Figure 1.3) because the shifts toward general audience programming on the part of children increasingly requires their greater attention if they are to understand what is taking place and derive some gratification from following the narrative (Anderson et al., 1986). Then, at about the same age that time constraints begin

Figure 1.3 Weekly Attention to the Screen as a Function of Age

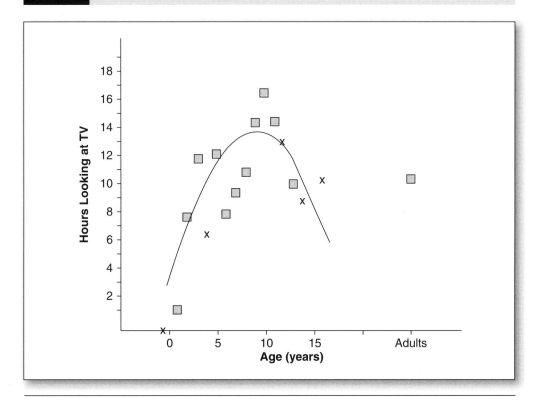

Source: Anderson, Lorch, Field, Collins, and Nathan (1986).

to delimit the viewing of favorite programs, attention to the screen begins to decline (compare Figures 1.2 and 1.3). Children now have had sufficient experience with television and have sufficient cognitive capacity to make inferences about what is being portrayed. They are well into the "concrete operational" stage, in the vocabulary of Piaget (Piaget & Inhelder, 1969), so they are able to comprehend much of what is on television about as well as most adults do

(Comstock, 1991), and consequently, less attention to the screen is required to follow a narrative. They are now monitoring the medium much of the time. Nevertheless, as a careful examination of the data (Figure 1.3) makes clear, young teenagers give more attention to the screen than young children do to satisfy their motive to monitor the general audience programming to which they are now more often attending with comprehension.

By the time young persons are at the midpoint of their teenage years, they will have adopted the adult pattern of viewing in which much of television use is ritualistic. The medium will have primacy over specific content, involvement will be comparatively low, and monitoring will better describe the sporadic attention that is typically given to the screen than viewing. However, some programs some of the time will command enough attention and some viewers will be selective of content in which they are highly interested enough of the time that, for those times and those viewers, television use is instrumental.

The Concept of Viewing

We believe that the definition and operationalization of the concept of viewing must acknowledge the irregular activity represented by monitoring. Clancey (1994), in this very vein, proposed that presence in the room when a set is operating should be sufficient to be counted as a viewer.

We offer the definition formulated by the first author and his colleagues (Comstock et al., 1978): "a discontinuous, often interrupted, and frequently nonexclusive activity for which a measure in hours and minutes serves only as the outer boundary of possible attention" (Comstock et al., 1978, pp. 146–147). We operationalize—that is, would measure— these hours and minutes in terms of the time individuals record themselves as using the medium, with use divided into three levels: *primary*, *secondary*, and *tertiary* (Comstock & Scharrer, 1999; Robinson & Godbey, 1997). The first consists of television recorded as a sole activity or foremost activity; it has accounted in the average household for slightly more than two thirds of use. The second covers television when it is recorded as specifically secondary to some other activity; this has accounted for about one fifth of use. The third includes television that is subordinate to other activities (usually two or more) but is nevertheless operating in the vicinity (and thus subject to monitoring); this has accounted for the remaining approximately 10% of use. The data (Robinson & Godbey, 1997) establish television as an activity that ranks high overall in the priorities of time allocation despite the irregularities and inconsistencies of attention. They also make it

clear that the majority of use from the perspective of the viewer constitutes the most important activity underway at the time.

Viewing Behavior

We begin our examination of the amount of use of television and other screen media with a critique of the measurement of viewing. We then turn to the context of other activities within which viewing occurs; the role of our principal variables; developmental processes as they relate to children's television use; cross-cultural patterns; and changes that have taken place since the introduction of the medium more than six decades ago. The focus will be on television, including content received from a variety of platforms, because motion picture theater attendance accounts for a comparatively small proportion of the time allocated by children and adolescents to screen media.

Measurement

There are wide variations in the quality of the data available on television viewing by children and adolescents. Two major issues are the validity of the measurement techniques and the representativeness of the sample. However, rapid technological change makes recency and sensitivity to changing behavior also very important. Often, measurement, the samples, or recency are less than ideal.

We prefer *diary data* that can be recorded post hoc (usually by parents) to data produced by Nielsen Media Research's "people meter," which requires real-time entry on a remote-control-like device. The meter risks underestimating the viewing of children (Comstock & Scharrer, 1999), whose behavior at the moment may be ignored by adults and who are likely themselves to skip the task of entry as the result of fatigue, indifference, or distraction. We obviously also prefer representative national samples because these produce estimates (within small and known margins of error) for the nation as a whole.

In our judgment, the best sources of national data are the Kaiser Foundation surveys, which collected data from nationally representative samples of 8- to 18-year-olds in 1999, 2004, and 2009 (Rideout et al., 2010;

Roberts & Foehr, 2004; Roberts, Foehr & Rideout, 2005). In addition, Kaiser has sponsored national surveys of media use by the very young—those six months to six years in age (Rideout & Hamel, 2006; Rideout, Vandewater & Wartella, 2003). These are pioneering efforts in their scope (range of ages), comprehensiveness (all media), and representativeness (the nation), and they cannot be faulted on recency.

The recent national survey, which is typical, had a sample of 2,002 young people 8 to 18 years in age (3rd through 12th grade) who completed questionnaires in classrooms. The sample was chosen in two stages, with schools randomly selected first and then classrooms within schools, and the survey was conducted from late October 2008 to early May 2009.

The most recent preschool survey obtained data by telephone interview from 1,051 parents of children six months to six years in age. The sample was chosen by random-digit dialing, and the survey was conducted from early September to late November 2003.

We have drawn on the time-budget data of Robinson and Godbey (1997) in identifying the three levels of television use—primary, secondary, and tertiary. Large though the numbers are, the Kaiser measurement techniques probably somewhat underestimate screen media exposure. This is because the survey questions are attention-centric, asking for time spent viewing from the user's perspective. This procedure risks ignoring some background use of media such as television (and radio) that do not require strict attention. For example, it is hard to imagine using an iPod to view television without consciously giving attention to the screen, just as using a computer as background to another activity would be difficult to ignore, but passive exposure to television content when a set is operating without any motive or interest in viewing is quite conceivable. Thus, the Kaiser estimates for television and radio are actually conservative.

At many points, data from recent or representative national samples are not available. In these cases, we emphasize that while the relationships among variables to which we call attention in our view are valid (or we would not present the data), the exact figures or proportions cannot be extrapolated to children and adolescents in general.

Other Activities

Our summary of the data on activities that might compete with or be diminished by the use of screen media covers two topics. The first is the ranking of television and other screen media when compared with other activities. The second is the relationship between greater amounts of screen media use and engaging in voluntary activities such as social interaction, play, lessons, hobbies, and excursions.

Ranking

Among the population in general across the life span in the many different societies where UNESCO examined time use, television invariably has ranked third behind sleep, which typically has been first, and work or school (Condry, 1989; Robinson & Godbey, 1997). The pattern is similar for children and adolescents.

The diary data meticulously collected from about 400 children and teenagers between the ages of 3 and 17 in the early 1980s (see Table 1.2) by Timmer, Eccles, and O'Brien (1985) indicate that, at the earliest ages (three to five), television took up only about half of the time of free play, which ranked second only to sleep at this age, and began to rival play only among those slightly older (six to eight). After this point, television was consistently third on weekdays (behind sleep and school), and on weekends, when there is no school, it ranked second.

These estimates are remarkably similar to those obtained almost three decades later using a large nationally representative sample (Rideout & Hamel, 2006). These more current estimates of screen use are 1 hour 51 minutes for those two to four and 1 hour 50 minutes for those four to six (see Table 1.3). These data testify to great stability in children's time use when the functions of activities—in this case, entertainment—remain the same; screens, and to some extent their content, have changed, but their role has not and, thus, neither has the amount of time allocated to them.

The broader context of media use, in contrast, displays significant increases in exposure to television content and music (see Table 1.4), as well as use of computers and video games (Rideout et al., 2010). Total *media use* for those 8 to 18 was 7 hours 38 minutes, an increase of more than an hour in

Table 1.2 Time Spent by Children and Teenagers in Primary Activities (Mean Hours:Minutes)

Activities	Week Days					Weekend Days					Significant Effects
	3-5[a]	6-8	9-11	12-14	15-17	3-5	6-8	9-11	12-14	15-17	
Market work[b]	—	0:14	0:08	0:14	0:28	—	0:04	0:10	0:29	0:48	
Personal care	0:41	0:49	0:40	0:56	1:00	0:47	0:45	0:44	1:00	0:51	A, S, A x S (F>M)
Household work	0:14	0:15	0:18	0:27	0:34	0:17	0:27	0:51	1:12	1:00	A, S, A x S (F>M)
Eating	1:22	1:21	1:13	1:09	1:07	1:21	1:20	1:18	1:08	1:05	A
Sleeping	10:30	9:55	9:08	7:53	8:19	10:34	10:41	9:56	10:04	9:22	A
School	2:17	4:52	5:15	5:44	5:14	—	—	—	—	—	
Studying	0:02	0:08	0:29	0:33	0:33	0:01	0:02	0:12	0:15	0:30	A
Church	0:04	0:09	0:09	0:09	0:03	0:55	0:56	0:53	0:32	0:37	A
Visiting	0:14	0:15	0:10	0:21	0:20	0:10	0:08	0:13	0:22	0:56	A (Weekend only)
Sports	0:05	0:24	0:21	0:40	0:46	0:03	0:30	0:42	0:51	0:37	A, S (M>F)
Outdoor activities	0:04	0:09	0:06	0:07	0:11	0:06	0:23	0:39	0:25	0:26	
Hobbies	0:00	0:02	0:02	0:04	0:06	0:01	0:05	0:03	0:06	0:03	
Art activities	0:05	0:04	0:03	0:03	0:12	0:04	0:04	0:04	0:07	0:10	
Other passive leisure	0:09	0:01	0:02	0:06	0:04	0:06	0:01	0:07	0:10	0:18	A
Playing	3:38	1:51	1:05	0:31	0:14	4:27	3:00	1:32	0:35	0:21	A, S (M>F)
TV	1:51	1:39	2:26	2:22	1:48	2:02	2:16	3:05	2:49	2:37	A, S, A x S (M>F)
Reading	0:05	0:05	0:09	0:10	0:12	0:04	0:09	0:10	0:10	0:18	A
Being read to	0:02	0:02	0:00	0:00	0:00	0:03	0:02	0:00	0:00	0:00	A

Source: Timmer, Eccles, and O'Brien (1985).

Note: A = age effect, significant at $p < .05$ for both weekday and weekend activities unless otherwise specified; S = sex effect, significant at $p < .05$; F>M = females spend more time than males; M>F = males spend more time than females; A × S = age by sex interaction, significant at $p < .05$ a. Age in years. b. Market work = obligations outside the home.

Table 1.3	Media and the Very Young

	(Hours: minutes; [ ] % using each day)			
		Age		
Time Use	*0–1*	*2–3*	*4–6*	*Overall*
Reading (or Being Read To)	:33 [77]	:42[+] [87]	:42[+] [87]	:40 [83]
Music	:57[+++] [88]	:50[+++] [84]	:41 [78]	:48 [82]
Television	: 34 [56]	1:11[+] [81]	1:02[+] [79]	:59 [75]
Playing Outside	:56 [55]	1:26[+] [80]	1:34[+] [81]	1:22 [74]
Watching Video or DVD	:13 [24]	:32[+] [41]	:25[+] [32]	:24 [32]
Reading Electronic Book	:05 [11]	:06 [18]	:04 [13]	:05 [14]
Computer	:01 [02]	:05[+] [12]	:12[++] [26]	:07 [16]
Videogames	:00 [01]	:03[+] [08]	:10[++] [18]	:06 [11]
Total Screen Media*	:49 [61]	1:51[+] [88]	1:50[+] [90]	1:36 [83]

[+] Statistically significant ($p < .05$) vs. 0–1; [++] vs. 0–1 and 2–3; [+++] vs. 4–6.

N= 1,051 parents of children six months to six years in age.

*Television, video/DVR, videogame, computer.

Source: Rideout & Hamel, 2006. Menlo Park, CA: Kaiser Foundation.

Table 1.4	Media Use Over Time

(8–18 year olds) (hours:minutes)			
	YEAR		
Medium	*2009*	*2004*	*1999*
TV Content	4:29[a]	3:51[b]	3:47[b]
Music/audio	2:31[a]	1:44[b]	1:48[b]
Computer	1:29[a]	1:02[b]	:27[c]

(Continued)

Table 1.4 (Continued)

(8–18 year olds) (hours:minutes)			
	YEAR		
Medium	*2009*	*2004*	*1999*
Video games	1:13[a]	:49[b]	:26[c]
Print	:38[a]	:43[ab]	:43[a]
Movies	:25[a]	:25[ab]	:18[b]
TOTAL MEDIA EXPOSURE	10:45[a]	8:33[b]	7:29[c]
Multitasking Proportion	29%[a]	26%[a]	16%[b]
TOTAL MEDIA USE	7:38[a]	6:21[b]	6:19[b]

Statistical significance ($p < .05$) across rows indicated by nonmatching subscripts. Total media exposure = sum of hours and minutes spent with media. Total media use = amount of hours and minutes allocated to media in a day. Media activity covers watching television and movies, playing video games, listening to music, using computers, and reading newspapers, magazines, and books. Data confined to nonschool related recreational use of media. Class projects, homework, in-school computing excluded.

Source: Rideout, Foehr, and Roberts (2010).

the 10 years since 1999; *media exposure*, which reflects the sum of time with individual media, was an extraordinary 10 hours and 45 minutes, about 3 hours and 15 minutes more than was registered in 1999. This discrepancy of exposure and use represented almost a doubling of media multitasking, from 16% to 29% of media use. Print saw a small decline (although the estimates included text read on computer screens); theater movie-going saw a small increase.

Screen Media as Competition

Options for the allocation of discretionary time changed with the introduction of television in the late 1940s. There was a substantial rearrangement of time for many, with greater amounts of time spent with mass media overall, principally accounted for by television. There was a decline in the time spent on a wide variety of other activities, including the use of other mass media (Comstock & Scharrer, 1999; Himmelweit, Oppenheim, & Vince, 1958; Murray & Kippax, 1978; Robinson, 1972; Robinson & Converse, 1972; Schramm, et al., 1961). Similarly, longitudinal data drawn from nearly 2,000 South African 7th to 12th graders before and after the introduction of television there in the mid-1970s showed radio

listening and movie attendance most often displaced—though only modestly—and particularly when the medium of television was novel (Mutz, Roberts, & van Vuuren, 1993).

With one possible exception, there is very little evidence that greater amounts of screen media use—specifically television set use in the data available—currently have a detrimental effect on children engaging in other activities. Whether the activity in question is socializing with peers or parents, play, lessons, hobbies, or excursions, the relationship with viewing repeatedly has been found to be null or only very modestly inverse, with the latter usually attributable to those who view very little or a very great deal (Lyle & Hoffman, 1972a; Medrich, Roizen, Rubin, & Buckley, 1982; Neuman, 1991; Roberts & Foehr, 2004; Robinson, 1990). In one instance (Roberts & Foehr, 2004), engaging in activities with parents was more likely among those higher in media use. Our interpretation is that children and adolescents do not typically abandon activities that are enjoyable and interesting for television and that much of their viewing is the reciprocal of the availability of such options. The modest inverse relationships principally represent either particularly strong preferences for alternatives among a few (who view very little) or the unavailability (from the perspective of the young viewers) of much in the way of alternatives among another few (who view a great deal). In sum, a few hours one way or another of television per week doesn't make much difference for most young people in how they spend their time. The possible exception is reading, for which television can serve as a less demanding, more accessible sedentary substitute (Comstock & Scharrer, 1999; Huston, Wright, Marquis, & Green, 1999; Mutz et al., 1993; Williams, 1986).

Viewing Patterns

The best estimate available of television screen use is the average of 4 hours and 39 minutes a day for children and adolescents 8 to 18 years in age (Rideout et al., 2010), which represents access to television content from a variety of sources (see Table 1.5). The average of 25 minutes per day spent at the movies brings the total of screen exposure to an average of 4 hours 54 minutes a day.

These Kaiser Foundation figures represent significant change in three respects. First, total screen exposure has increased impressively over the past decade. Second, viewing television content at the time it is broadcast (called *live TV* by the investigators) declined noticeably. Third, viewing on platforms that in earlier years were not considered worth measuring—the Internet, iPods and MP-3 players, and cell phones—accounted for 56 minutes of viewing in 2009, about one fifth of all exposure to television content.

There is a moderate degree of stability as young people grow up in the amount of screen media that they view. Tangney and Feshbach (1988), in a sample of 400 elementary school children, found correlations of .67 and .65 between adjacent years and .54 between the first and third year in hours spent with television. Some stability would be expected because, for many young people, the principal variables that influence screen use would not much change. What the variability in the data

| **Table 1.5** | Screen Media Use Over Time |

(8–18 year olds) Hours:Minutes per day			
	YEAR		
TV Content	*2009*	*2004*	*1999*
Live TV	2:39[a]	3:04[b]	3:05[b]
Time-shifted TV (total)	:22[a]	:14[b]	:14[b]
On Demand	:12	~	~
Self-recorded TV (TiVo/DVR/VCR)	:09[a]	:14[b]	:14[b]
DVDs/videos (total)	:32[a]	:32[ab]	:28[b]
On a TV	:26	~	~
On a computer	:06	~	~
TV on other platforms (total)	:56	~	~
Internet	:24	~	~
iPod/MP3 player	:16	~	~
Cell phone	:15	~	~
TOTAL TV CONTENT	4:29[a]	3:51[b]	3:47[b]
Movies	:25	:25	:18
TOTAL SCREEN USE	4:54[a]	4:16[b]	4:22[b]
Statistical significance (*p* < .05) across rows indicated by non-matching subscripts.			

Source: Rideout, Foehr, and Roberts (2010).

attest to (and particularly the lower coefficient for first and third years), then, is that, in fact, as young people grow up there is considerable change in the obligations, alternatives, and preferences for other activities that govern the time available on which screen use depends.

Societal and Structural Factors

How much young people view is not much influenced by programming schedules; it is influenced by the hours and minutes that they are able to view. However, the programming available importantly affects what is viewed at a given time and the allocation of time between educational and cultural fare and entertainment. Time allocated to television by everyone has been very similar across societies and sites despite considerable variation in the number of available channels, hours of operation, and the diversity and emphases of programming (Comstock et al., 1978; Robinson & Godbey, 1997). For example, when a single government-sponsored channel was introduced to a remote British Columbia community, viewing patterns in terms of amount quickly came to resemble those of a similar community that had long had access to five channels—two Canadian and three American networks (Williams, 1986). And when the school day was cut in California for fiscal reasons, children's viewing sharply increased with no change in television schedules (Robinson & Godbey, 1997).

However, the degree to which a national television system resembles that of the United States, with its comparative lack of a prescriptive paternalism in regard to how the public should be served and its reliance on advertising for support, is an important determinant of the emphasis of the medium on entertainment and the availability of educational and cultural programming that young people might view. While readiness to adopt new technology has increased access to television and other screen media, diversity is somewhat suppressed by the competition that makes entertainment the most effective means to attract audiences of interest to advertisers. The result is that there may not be much in the way of educational and cultural fare for children to view as they grow older (Hamilton, 1998; Huston et al., 1990). Thus, societies that impose more demanding standards of public service are likely to offer more options to young people for viewing television that might have some constructive influence.

Governmental and regulatory practices also influence what is available. Thus, in the 1990s, the demands in the United States made by Congress and the FCC for more educational and cultural programming as a condition of retaining a broadcast license led to the production of much new programming that would meet these requirements.

Finally, as exemplified by the past decade in the United States, technological developments constitute a major influence. New technology in dissemination (satellites and cable) has been important in the longer term, but in the past few years viewing of television content has been driven by new media that are particularly adaptable to multitasking by individuals.

We originally divided the history of television in the United States into three periods (Comstock & Scharrer, 1999). The *introductory* period between the late 1940s and the end of the 1950s saw the widespread diffusion of the medium and essentially the emergence of the television we know today; *equilibrium,* from the early 1960s through the 1970s, was the era of dominance by the three networks (ABC, CBS, and NBC), with limited diversity of channels and programming in communities and homes; what we called *transition,* beginning with the 1990s, saw the breakup of the established pattern with greater diversity of choice by new broadcast outlets, cable, new channels, and in-home recording and playback. We would now divide this third stage into *emergent diversity*, beginning with the 1990s and extending through about 2005, and *technological elaboration*, beginning in about 2005. The shift is documented across the three Kaiser surveys, where personal devices and alternative screens by 2009 (compared to 1999 and 2004) importantly amplify access to television content and significantly increase viewing. Our intent is to recognize the current wave of new technology in making content more available across places and times as a new era.

Household Attributes

The four principal household variables that influence the amount of exposure to television content by young people are norms for media use, socioeconomic status, race, and resources available. However, family research also indicates that the general attitudinal and communicatory atmosphere established by parents makes some difference.

Norms favoring heavy use of television (e.g., the absence of rules specifying when viewing is appropriate and a television set constantly operating) are associated with greater viewing by young people in households that otherwise are apparently comparable (Comstock & Scharrer, 1999; Medrich et al., 1982; Rideout et al., 2010). Fewer than half of parents say they often impose rules about how much, when, and what programs may be viewed (Bower, 1985; Rideout et al., 2010), although this figure is somewhat higher for younger children and declines with age. Viewing is inversely associated with socioeconomic status, with education a more powerful predictor than income, and is greater in

Figure 1.4   Centrality of Television in the Home

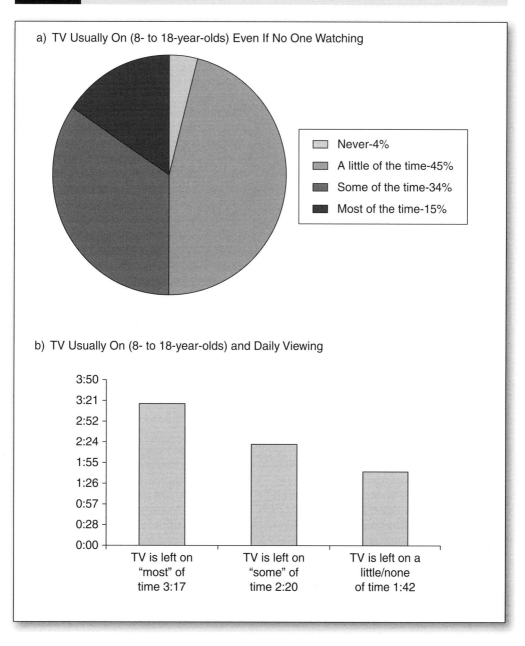

a) TV Usually On (8- to 18-year-olds) Even If No One Watching

Never-4%
A little of the time-45%
Some of the time-34%
Most of the time-15%

b) TV Usually On (8- to 18-year-olds) and Daily Viewing

TV is left on "most" of time 3:17

TV is left on "some" of time 2:20

TV is left on a little/none of time 1:42

Black and to a lesser degree in Hispanic households than in White households (Anderson, Mead, & Sullivan, 1986; Blosser, 1988; Comstock, 1991; Comstock et al., 1978; Comstock & Scharrer, 1999; Medrich et al., 1982; Rideout et al., 2010). Norms favoring screen media use and Black or Hispanic ethnicity are inversely associated with socioeconomic status, but each (socioeconomic status, Black and Hispanic ethnicity) independently predicts greater or lesser viewing.

The governing role of time availability obviously imposes a ceiling on the effects of this greater centrality of television, but they are nonetheless substantial in both the short and long run. Our estimate about three decades ago from the sample of 750 sixth-grade children examined by Medrich and colleagues (1982) is that a pervasive, unrestricted use of television in the household led to about 20% more television use by children (Comstock, 1991). This factor is even more important today, for the most recent Kaiser Foundation survey (Rideout et al., 2010) records viewing among those 8 to 18 as about an hour greater when "TV is left on 'most' of the time" (see Figure 1.4, p. 33). Similarly, Rosengren and Windahl (1989) found in Scandinavia that the amount of viewing of a sample of 11- and 13-year-olds was directly correlated with the amount of parental use. This parental endorsement has long-range implications because the amount of viewing by teenagers was predicted by much earlier amounts of parental viewing (Rosengren & Windahl, 1989), and the amount of viewing by young adults was predicted by the amount of parental viewing when they were growing up (Kenny, 1985).

Resources in the household make a major contribution. Multi-sets, available in almost 90% of households, mean that young people more often will view alone or with other young people and more often will choose their own programming. Almost three fourths (71%) of those 8 to 18 were recorded as having a television set in their bedrooms in the most recent Kaiser survey (Rideout et al., 2010), as well as an array of other platforms (see Table 1.6). Media of all types in the household promote their use by the young (Roberts & Foehr, 2004). Media availability in the bedrooms of the young is associated with much greater viewing of television content.

Table 1.6 TV Usually On (8- to 18-year-olds) and Daily Viewing

(% 8- to 18-year-olds)			
	YEAR		
Medium	*2009*	*2004*	*1999*
Radio	75%[a]	84%[b]	86%[b]
TV	1%[a]	68%[ab]	65%[b]
CD player	68%[a]	86%[b]	88%[b]
DVD or VCR player	57%[a]	54%[a]	36%[b]
Cable/satellite TV	49%[a]	37%[b]	29%[c]
Computer	36%[a]	31%[b]	21%[c]
Internet access	33%[a]	20%[b]	10%[c]
Video game console	50%	49%	45%
Premium channels	24%[a]	20%[b]	15%[c]
TiVo/other DVR	13%[a]	10%[b]	~
Statistical significance ($p < .05$) across rows indicated by non-matching subscripts.			

Source: Rideout, Foehr, and Roberts (2010).

DVRs or VCRs, available in about 85% of households, mean that the young will view more movies and have easier access to those carrying restricted labels. In-home recording for later playback sees very little use among the young—fewer than 10 minutes a day (see Table 1.4) out of the almost four and a half hours of consuming television content and greater viewing alone. How much and what is viewed shift with personal preference.

Parental communication practices also affect a young person's media use. Lack of interaction with parents in the home as a result of the out-of-home employment of mothers or the absence of fathers is associated with more time spent viewing among adolescents (Brown, Childers, Bauman, & Koch, 1990). Left alone, the young turn to media. An emphasis on communication and discussion rather than prescription and the exercise of power in the disciplinary practices of parents demonstrably has been associated with an impressive list of positive outcomes—greater viewing of programs portraying constructive behavior (Abelman, 1985); the providing by parents of supplementary information and evaluation in connection with programs (e.g., geographical, historical, or scientific facts; moral implications; the make-believe aspects of stories; see Messaris & Kerr, 1983); and improved comprehension on the part of the child (Singer et al., 1988).

Encouraging the expression of opinions and the exchange of ideas in the household increases as a child grows older (Meadowcroft, 1986), presumably because many parents believe this is a province for the more mature. Such encouragement has been associated with less total television viewing, greater print use, greater instrumental use of the medium, and higher levels of news consumption among young people (Chaffee & McLeod, 1972; Chaffee, McLeod, & Atkin, 1971). When the emphasis was on maintaining social harmony without an accompanying emphasis on expression and opinion, total viewing was greater, entertainment viewing was higher, and news consumption was lower. When expression and opinion were also emphasized, the heightened viewing of both television in general and entertainment specifically vanished, and news consumption was enhanced. In our view, these data overall identify the communication atmosphere established by parents as an important factor in the development of constructive, instrumental use of media in which entertainment is somewhat diminished (but of course—for most young viewers—remains predominant).

Personal Attributes

Four major child or person variables affect viewing, with almost all of the data representing television. They are age, mental ability, comprehension, and innate affinity for viewing.

The amount of viewing increases during the elementary school years, reaching a peak between 11 and 14 (see Figure 1.1). Then it declines as the greater obligations, opportunities, and time outside the household during the teenage years suppress the amount of time spent with screen media (Comstock & Scharrer, 2007; Roberts & Foehr, 2004).

Mental ability among children has been consistently inversely associated with television use (Gortmaker, Salter, Walker, & Dietz, 1990; Schramm et al., 1961), but only very modestly so (Lyle & Hoffman, 1972a)—and this negative association has been growing smaller with the passage of time (Comstock & Scharrer, 2007). The decline has been the result of changing norms, which have made television use more acceptable among almost all young people and in most households. The modest size reflects a somewhat paradoxical pattern. Very bright children, when young, are often enthusiastic users of television as well as other media. In the past, they turned toward print at an earlier age and to a more pronounced degree than their peers (Comstock & Scharrer, 2007; Schramm, et al., 1961). Today, this shift toward media that are more informational, sometimes more demanding of intellect and emotion, and often more exploratory of events and people presumably would embrace, in addition to print, the Internet and various television channels and video sources that rest on technological developments. Thus, the modest size of the relationship masks a more complex process in which young people are pursuing somewhat different paths in media use as a consequence of mental ability—some toward greater involvement and information and others toward greater entertainment.

Comprehension plays little role in the amount of television use in total, as is clear from the many hours spent viewing by those too young to fully understand all that is taking place. However, as we have observed, it plays a large role in the degree of attention actually given to the screen and therefore in the amount of viewing as a primary activity. Attention rises as children need to pay closer attention to understand the narrative (see Figure 1.3), then declines as greater knowledge about subject matter and the conventions of the medium make close attention less necessary for understanding.

Children (and presumably those older) also differ in the degree to which television use (and possibly use of other screen media) is innately gratifying. Plomin, Corely, DeFries, and Fulker (1990), using the widely recognized methodology for separating genetic from environmental influences among a sample of 220 children ages three, four, and five (and their siblings and adoptive and natural parents) in the well-known Colorado Adoption Project (Plomin & DeFries, 1985), found that amount of television viewing was a product of both heredity and environment. Our tentative interpretation is that television is inherently pleasurable, which would help explain why set use is so similar across societies, and that the degree of innate gratification has a basis in the degree of pleasure derived from alpha waves, or holistic, nonverbal, affective right-brain processing (Comstock & Scharrer, 1999; Krugman, 1971; Rothschild, Thorson, Reeves, Hirsch, & Goldstein, 1986), and this would vary genetically among individuals.

Situational Influences

We divide situational influences into three categories: the presence of others, temporal factors, and mental states. The first covers the role of parents and other young persons; the second, the hour of the day, day of the week, and the season; and the third, stress, psychological discomfort, and the desire to relax or be entertained.

A young person's attention to the screen will vary with the attention given by others in the room (Anderson, Lorch, Smith, Bradford, & Levin, 1981). This social cue joins audio and visual cues in governing responses to the screen. Parents and other children also will increase viewing by a particular child in the

short run by turning on a set and thereby placing the child in the role of a viewer.

Temporal influences are quite marked (Comstock & Scharrer, 1999; Robinson & Godbey, 1997; Webster & Phalen, 1997). There is a day cycle in which children's viewing rises in the afternoon and continues through prime time, with a peak at about 8:30 p.m. for those younger (two to five) and at shortly before 9 p.m. for those older (6 to 11). The younger children view at a higher rate in the early morning and early afternoon. There is a week cycle, with children's viewing at its highest on Fridays and Saturdays when there is no school the next day; this is in contrast to young adults (and older teenagers), whose viewing is at a minimum on these two days because of competing social and entertainment options. There is also seasonal variation, with children's viewing higher during the summer when school is out.

Children cite television as a favored activity to relax, to be entertained, and to fend off loneliness (Comstock & Scharrer, 2007; Lyle & Hoffman, 1972a). Young people more generally have consistently been found to use screen media more when in states of stress, conflict, or psychological discomfort (Comstock & Scharrer, 1999, 2007). There is also evidence that young women in particular use comedy and drama to alleviate feelings of anger, while young men may bolster hostile responses and aggravation by turning to violent entertainment (Zillmann, 1988; Zillmann & Bryant, 1985). Thus, mood affects how much and what is watched.

Developmental Processes

If we take the initial hours of viewing before the age of three and peak levels reached between the ages of 11 and 14, the process from attending to imagery with very limited meaning to viewing in an adult mode—if not with the tastes of an adult— covers about nine years. How much young people view is primarily a function of the time they have available without obligations or preferred alternatives. What they view with comprehension and interest changes as they grow up. Cartoons and cartoon-like storytelling swiftly give way to situation comedies. Attention rises as more information is needed for comprehension; the medium becomes more central, as does ritualistic viewing, as the opportunity to view favorite programs decreases.

Household characteristics and child attributes affect changes in the amount of viewing and in the division between ritualistic and instrumental use as young people mature. Households lower in socioeconomic status and households higher in television centrality will have greater viewing by children and less instrumental use as specific content takes a decidedly subsidiary place to the pleasures of monitoring the most satisfactory of available options. Early instrumental use as exemplified by viewing children's educational programs (of which the best known has been *Sesame Street*), which often will have been the product of thoughtful parental guidance, will lead to less total viewing and greater instrumental viewing when the child becomes a teenager (Rosengren & Windahl, 1989); this is another example of the important role of household characteristics in the media behavior of young people and why the environment established by parents has long-range consequences for their children. Foremost among child attributes is mental ability, with those more cognitively capable in the past making comparatively greater use of print and at the present time using print and Internet information sources more as they grow older.

Comprehension is also an important factor. Up to about six years of age, greater attention to the screen—which, in our view, represents involvement—is largely confined to cartoons and other children's programs (Bechtel et al., 1972). Then attention increases for television in general up to about age 10 as the narratives of adult programs requiring greater attention for understanding become of interest; attention to the screen then begins to decline as children have begun to achieve an adult relationship with the medium (Anderson et al., 1986). This peak essentially coincides with ages seven to nine, when children move from Piaget's preoperational to his concrete operational stage and become more able to understand subtleties of plot and character and place comparatively greater emphasis on meaning and verbal elements than appearances and action. Prior to this time, visual elements play a larger role, although one that is decreasing with age; children are more perceptually bound and guided by what can be seen rather than inferred (Comstock & Scharrer, 2007). However, much of television—in terms of interpreting its narratives—becomes understandable with a little effort before this transition period (Wolf, 1987), which explains why the curve representing attention to the screen presented by D. R. Anderson and colleagues (1986) rises stoutly beginning at age five. Similarly, children's viewing of favorite programs will peak and decline as there is reduced opportunity, as with teenagers and adults, to view their favorites; at the same time, the amount of viewing in a less attentive way—what we have called monitoring—will continue to increase up until about the age of 12 (Comstock, 1991).

The national television system influences how much of this experience is likely to be entertainment or to have some cultural or educational value. Programming of the latter sort is more prevalent when reliance on advertiser support is less and the triumvirate of nonpaternalism, competition, and entertainment that characterizes American television is restrained (Comstock, 1989).

Movies played a very minor role in the lives of children with television in the 1960s and 1970s. Then modern marketing, with its multiplexes and the VCR, returned some popularity to movies. For example, Lyle and Hoffman (1972a), in their survey of 1,600 1st, 6th, and 10th graders found that, even by the 6th grade, the average amount of time allocated per week to watching movies (other than those shown on broadcast television) was less than 20 minutes, and only 15% had seen a movie at a theater during the past week. This is in sharp contrast to the heyday of American movie-going. We estimate that focused marketing and the VCR have increased this figure significantly (Comstock, 1991). Currently, those 8 to 18 spend about 25 minutes per day on average at the movies, or about three-and-a-quarter hours a week (Rideout et al., 2010). DVDs account for about another half hour, or three-and-a-half hours per week, for total movie exposure of approximately 6 hours 45 minutes a week. The developmental significance is that the VCR, and now the DVD, gives young people access to movies, which are more emotionally and psychologically involving than much of television and may, for older children and teenagers, include titles with restricted labels.

Cross-Cultural Comparison

Von Feilitzen (1999) collated A. C. Nielsen people meter data on television viewing by children and teenagers in 10 countries.[1] Groebel (1999) summarized a survey of use of major media among more than 5,000 children who were 12 years of age in 23 countries.[2] Livingstone, Holden, and Bovill (1999) surveyed media use by more than 15,000 children and teenagers in 11 European countries[3] and Israel.

The most indelible impression is the degree to which television use by young people is much the same in all countries. In developed countries, access (households with television) approaches 100%, and the amount of viewing (which excluded most secondary and tertiary use) was about two hours or more per day. Even in less developed regions, access registered at more than 80% of households. Television can be fairly described as the universal medium.

The second most noticeable pattern is the frequency of differences in use of media other than broadcast and cable television. For example, in the 12-country data collected by Livingstone and colleagues (1999), the amount of time spent reading books differed from a low of 14 minutes per day in Flanders to a high of 35 minutes per day in Finland. As Livingstone and colleagues pointed out, some differences reflect marketing and technological developments (e.g., a great variety of cable offerings that would suppress rental video viewing), while others reflect cultural differences in norms, tastes, and preferences.

Changes

There have been significant, documented changes in the past decade in the consumption by the young of television and other screen media. These reflect important technological developments that have affected what is available to view, how much is viewed, which media platforms are used to access screen media, and how these platforms are used.

The basic contours of growing up have been highly stable. Children mature as they always have, and in the case of television and other screen media, they acquire the cognitive skills to use these media as they grow up. They enjoy (as well as benefit from) free play, and so it continues to occupy a major place in the allocation of time among young children. Teenagers pursue a social life outside the home, and so movie-going remains a modest but persisting factor in time use. Young children are perpetually drawn to the color and action of animated cartoons; teenagers desert them almost entirely in favor of comedy and drama that rest to a greater degree on the understanding of motive and character. Screen media use goes up and down with available time. These are all essentially permanent pillars of childhood and adolescence around which media become arrayed.

A pervasive change in television and other screen media is the growth in the variety of programming available. Earlier, this greater diversity could be traced to large increases in available channels: new stations, new networks, cable systems, premium cable channels, pay-per-view, and in-home recording with VCRs. In recent years, this trend has continued, with the DVR somewhat replacing the VCR. Video remains a staple, now replayed on DVDs. The major recent change, however, is that these sources are now available on numerous new platforms.

Screen media use is up dramatically. The present 4 hours 45 minutes per day (for those 8 to 18) is an extraordinary figure when compared with the 3 hours 7 minutes estimated by these authors in the first edition of the present volume.* A major and probably surprising change is not only the diversity of platforms employed to view television content (see Table 1.5), but the use of platforms beyond imagination a decade ago—the cell phone, iPod or MP-3 player, and the Internet—that now account for almost an hour of daily exposure to television content and fairly could be said to be responsible for much of the increase in screen media use. The result is that the viewing of live television—the term employed in one survey (Rideout et al., 2010) to refer to programs on the screen of a TV set—is down by 25 minutes compared to 2004, while total exposure to television content has increased.

---

*Note: Our 1999 estimate was for those 2 to 11 years of age. However, this results in an underestimate of the changes since then because teenagers (12–17) at that time viewed markedly less than those younger.

The stunning amounts (and we think this term connotes the proper respect) of media use and exposure (see Table 1.4) have been made possible by the use of more than one medium at a time. Between 1999 and 2009, this practice of media multitasking increased from 16% to 29% of all media exposure. The same practice has allowed computer use and video game playing to increase (see Table 1.4) without a decrease in exposure to television content.

Technology and multitasking have increased exposure to screen media, but time available remains the major factor in amount of viewing. Viewing is governed largely by the time available (but not wholly; specialized content not fungible with most programs may draw a few viewers who otherwise would not be viewing television at that time). These two factors should probably be thought of as expanding time available by convenience (technology) and by more efficient deepening of use (multitasking).

One consequence of these changes is that young people more easily may view adult content or confine viewing to one type of content. Nevertheless, at present in the United States, the amount of programming in which young people can take an honest interest as well as derive some pleasure and an enriching experience is vast compared with past decades, as is the amount of time they spend with such programming.

Notes

1. Argentina, Australia, Chile, the Czech Republic, Lebanon, the Philippines, South Africa, South Korea, Spain, and the United States.

2. Angola, Argentina, Armenia, Brazil, Canada, Costa Rica, Croatia, Egypt, Fiji, Germany, India, Japan, Mauritius, the Netherlands, Peru, the Philippines, Qatar, South Africa, Spain, Tadjikistan, Togo, Trinidad and Tobago, and Ukraine.

3. Denmark, Finland, Flanders/Belgium, France, Germany, Italy, the Netherlands, Spain, Sweden, Switzerland, and the United Kingdom.

References

Abelman, R. (1985). Styles of parental disciplinary practices as a mediator of children's learning from prosocial television portrayals. *Child Study Journal, 17*, 46–57.

Adler, R. P., Lesser, G. S., Meringoff, L. K., Robertson, T. S., Rossiter, J. R., & Ward, S. (1980). *The effects of television advertising on children: Review and recommendations.* Lexington, MA: Lexington Books.

Albarran, A. B., & Umphrey, D. (1993). An examination of television motivations and program preferences by Hispanics, blacks, and whites. *Journal of Broadcasting and Electronic Media, 37*(1), 95–103.

Allen, C. L. (1965). Photographing the TV audience. *Journal of Advertising Research, 5*, 208.

Anderson, B., Mead, N., & Sullivan, S. (1986). *Television: What do national assessment tests tell us?* Princeton, NJ: Educational Testing Service.

Anderson, C. A., Gentile, D. A., & Buckley, K. E. (2007). *Violent video game effects on children and adolescents: Theory, research and public policy.* New York: Oxford University Press.

Anderson, C., Berkowitz, L., Donnerstein, E., Huesmann, L. R., Johnson, J. D., Linz, D., Malamuth, N. M., & Wartella, E. (2003). The influence of media on youth. *Psychological Science in the Public Interest, 4,* 81–110.

Anderson, D. R., Collins, P. A., Schmitt, K. L., & Jacobvitz, R. S. (1996). Stressful life events and television viewing. *Communication Research, 23*(3), 243–260.

Anderson, D. R., & Lorch, E. P. (1983). Looking at television: Action or reaction? In J. Bryant & D. R. Anderson (Eds.), *Children's understanding of television: Research on attention and comprehension* (pp. 1–34). New York: Academic Press.

Anderson, D. R., Lorch, E. P., Field, D. E., Collins, P. A., & Nathan, J. G. (1986). Television viewing at home: Age trends in visual attention and time with TV. *Child Development, 57*, 1024–1033.

Anderson, D. R., Lorch, E. P., Smith, R., Bradford, R., & Levin, S. R. (1981). Effects of peer presence on preschool children's television-viewing behavior. *Developmental Psychology, 17*(4), 446–453.

Argenta, D. M., Stoneman, Z., & Brody, G. H. (1986). The effects of three different television programs on young children's peer interactions and toy play. *Journal of Applied Developmental Psychology, 7*(4), 355–371.

Aubrey, J. S., & Harrison, K. (2004). The gender-role content of children's favorite television programs and its links to their gender-related perceptions. *Media Psychology, 6*(2), 111–146.

Baer, D. M. (1962). Laboratory control of thumb-sucking by withdrawal and representation of enforcement. *Journal of the Experimental Analysis of Behavior, 5*, 525–528.

Baker, R. K., & Ball, S. J. (1969). *Mass media and violence: Staff report to the National Commission on the Causes and Prevention of Violence* (Vol. 9). Washington, DC: U.S. Government Printing Office.

Barnouw, E. (1990). *Tube of plenty.* New York: Oxford University Press.

Barwise, T. P., & Ehrenberg, A. S. C. (1988). *Television and its audience.* Newbury Park, CA: Sage.

Barwise, T. P., Ehrenberg, A. S. C., & Goodhardt, G. J. (1982). Glued to the box? Patterns of TV repeat viewing. *Journal of Communication, 32*(4), 22–29.

Bechtel, R. B., Achelpohl, C., & Akers, R. (1972). Correlates between observed behavior and questionnaire responses on television viewing. In E. A. Rubenstein, G. A. Comstock, & J. P. Murray (Eds.), *Television and social behavior: Vol. 4. Television in day-to-day life: Patterns of use.* Washington, DC: U.S. Government Printing Office.

Blosser, B. J. (1988). Ethnic differences in children's media use. *Journal of Broadcasting and Electronic Media, 32*(4), 453–470.

Boddy, W. (1990). *Fifties television: The industry and its critics.* Urbana: University of Illinois Press.

Bower, R. (1985). *The changing television audience in America.* New York: Columbia University Press.

Brown, J. D., Childers, K. W., Bauman, K. E., & Koch, G. G. (1990). The influence of new media and family structure on young adolescents' television and radio use. *Communication Research, 17*(1), 65–82.

Bryant, J., Zillmann, D., & Brown, D. (1983). Entertainment features in children's educational television: Effects on attention and information acquisition. In J. Bryant & D. R. Anderson (Eds.), *Children's understanding of television: Research on attention and comprehension* (pp. 221–240). New York: Academic Press.

Canary, D. J., & Spitzberg, B. H. (1993). Loneliness and media gratification. *Communication Research, 20*(6), 800–821.

Cantor, J. (1994a). Confronting children's fright responses to mass media. In D. Zillmann, J. Bryant, & A. C. Huston (Eds.), *Media, children, and the family: Social scientific, psychodynamic, and clinical perspectives* (pp. 139–150). Hillsdale, NJ: Lawrence Erlbaum.

Cantor, J. (1994b). Fright reactions to mass media. In J. Bryant & D. Zillmann (Eds.), *Media effects: Advances in theory and research* (pp. 213–246). Hillsdale, NJ: Lawrence Erlbaum.

Chaffee, S. H., & McLeod, J. M. (1972). Adolescent television use in the family context. In G. A. Comstock & E. A. Rubinstein (Eds.), *Television and social behavior: Vol. 3. Television and adolescent aggressiveness* (pp. 149–172). Washington, DC: U.S. Government Printing Office.

Chaffee, S. H., McLeod, J. M., & Atkin, C. K. (1971). Parental influences on adolescent media use. *American Behavioral Scientist, 14*, 323–340.

Clancey, M. (1994). The television audience examined. *Journal of Advertising Research, 34*(4), 1–10.

Collins, W. A. (1981). Recent advances in research on cognitive processing of television viewing. *Journal of Broadcasting, 25*(4), 327–334.

Comstock, G. (1991). *Television and the American child.* San Diego, CA: Academic Press.

Comstock, G. (1989). *The evolution of American television.* Thousand Oaks, CA: Sage.

Comstock, G., Chaffee, S., Katzman, N., McCombs, M., & Roberts, D. (1978). *Television and human behavior.* New York: Columbia University Press.

Comstock, G., & Scharrer, E. (1999). *Television: What's on, who's watching, and what it means.* San Diego, CA: Academic Press.

Comstock, G., & Scharrer, E. (2007). *Media and the American child.* San Diego, CA: Elsevier/ Academic Press.

Condry, J. (1989). *The psychology of television.* Hillsdale, NJ: Lawrence Erlbaum.

Cook, T. D., Appleton, H., Conner, R. F., Schaffer, A., Tamkin, G., & Weber, S. J. (1975). *Sesame Street revisited.* New York: Russell Sage.

Cozic, C. (1997). *The future of the Internet.* San Diego, CA: Greenhaven Press.

Dizard, W. P. (2000). *Old media, new media: Mass communications in the information age* (3rd ed.). Reading, MA: Addison-Wesley.

Gortmaker, S. L., Salter, C. A., Walker, D. K., & Dietz, W. H. (1990). The impact of television viewing on mental aptitude and achievement: A longitudinal study. *Public Opinion Quarterly, 54*(4), 594–604.

Groebel, J. (1999). Media access and media use among 12-year-olds in the world. In C. von Feilitzen & U. Carlsson (Eds.), *Children and media: Image, education, participation* (pp. 61–67). Göteborg, Sweden: Göteborg University, UNESCO International Clearinghouse on Children and Violence on the Screen.

Hamilton, J. T. (1998). *Channeling violence.* Princeton, NJ: Princeton University Press.

Harwood, J. (1997). Viewing age: Lifespan identity and television viewing choices. *Journal of Broadcasting and Electronic Media, 41*(2), 203–213.

Himmelweit, H. T., Oppenheim, A. N., & Vince, P. (1958). *Television and the child.* London: Oxford University Press.

Hollenbeck, A., & Slaby, R. (1979). Infant visual and vocal responses to television. *Child Development, 50,* 41–45.

Hopkins, N. M., & Mullis, A. K. (1985). Family perceptions of television viewing habits. *Family Relations, 34,* 171–181.

Hudson, D. (1997). *Rewired: A brief (and opinionated) Net history.* Indianapolis, IN: Macmillan Technical.

Huston, A. C., & Wright, J. C. (1996). Television and socialization of young children. In T. M. MacBeth (Ed.), *Tuning in to young viewers: Social science perspectives on television* (pp. 37–60). Thousand Oaks, CA: Sage.

Huston, A. C., & Wright, J. C. (1989). The forms of television and the child viewer. In G. Comstock (Ed.), *Public communication and behavior* (Vol. 2, pp. 103–159). New York: Academic Press.

Huston, A. C., Wright, J. C., Marquis, J., & Green, S. B. (1999). How young children spend their time: Television and other activities. *Developmental Psychology, 35,* 912–925.

Huston, A. C., Wright, J. C., Rice, M. L., Kerkman, D., Siegle, J., & Bremer, M. (1983, April). *Family environment and television use by preschool children.* Paper presented at the biennial meeting of the Society for Research in Child Development, Detroit, MI.

Huston, A. C., Wright, J. C., Rice, M. L., Kerkman, D., & St. Peters, M. (1990). Development of television viewing patterns in early childhood: A longitudinal investigation. *Developmental Psychology, 26*(3), 409–420.

Kaiser Family Foundation. (2010). *Generation M²: Media in the lives of 8- to 18-year olds.* Menlo Park, CA: The Henry J. Kaiser Family Foundation. Retrieved April 21, 2010, from www.kff.org.

Kenny, J. F. (1985). *The family as a mediator of television use and the cultivation phenomenon among college students.* Unpublished doctoral dissertation, Syracuse University, Syracuse, NY.

Kirsh, S. J. (2006). *Children, adolescents, and media violence.* Thousand Oaks, CA: Sage.

Klepp, K. I., Wind, M., de Bourdeauhuij, I., Rodrigo, C. P., Due, P., Bjelland, M., & Brug, J. (2007). Television viewing and exposure to food-related commercials among European school children, associations with fruit and vegetable intake: A cross sectional study. *International Journal of Behavioral Nutrition and Physical Activity, 4,* 46–64.

Koolstra, C. M., & van der Voort, T. H. A. (1996). Longitudinal effects of television on children's leisure time reading: A test of three explanatory models. *Human Communication Research, 23*(1), 4–335.

Krugman, H. E. (1971). Brain wave measures of media involvement. *Journal of Advertising Research, 11*(1), 3–9.

Krull, R. (1983). Children learning to watch television. In J. Bryant & D. R. Anderson (Eds.), *Children's understanding of television: Research on attention and comprehension* (pp. 103–123). New York: Academic Press.

Kubey, R. W., & Csikszentmihalyi, M. (1990). *Television and the quality of life: How viewing shapes everyday experience.* Hillsdale, NJ: Lawrence Erlbaum.

Lawrence, F. C., & Wozniak, P. H. (1989). Children's television viewing with family members. *Psychological Reports, 65,* 396–400.

Levy, M. R. (1978). The audience experience with television news. *Journalism Monographs, 55,* 1–29.

Lin, C. A. (1990). Audience activity and VCR use. In J. R. Dobrow (Ed.), *Social and cultural aspects of VCR use* (pp. 75–92). Hillsdale, NJ: Lawrence Erlbaum.

Lin, C. A. (1993). Exploring the role of VCR use in the emerging home entertainment culture. *Journalism Quarterly, 70*(4), 833–842.

Livingstone, S., Holden, K. J., & Bovill, M. (1999). Children's changing media environment: Overview of a European comparative study. In C. von Feilitzen & U. Carlsson (Eds.), *Children and media: Image, education, participation* (pp. 61–67). Göteborg, Sweden: Göteborg University, UNESCO International Clearinghouse on Children and Violence on the Screen.

Lorch, E. P., Anderson, D. R., & Levin, S. R. (1979). The relationship of visual attention to children's comprehension of television. *Child Development, 50,* 722–727.

LoSciuto, L. A. (1972). A national inventory of television viewing behavior. In E. A. Rubinstein, G. A. Comstock, & J. P. Murray (Eds.), *Television and social behavior: Vol. 4. Television in day-to-day life: Patterns of use* (pp. 33–86). Washington, DC: U.S. Government Printing Office.

Lyle, J., & Hoffman, H. R. (1972a). Children's use of television and other media. In E. A. Rubinstein, G. A. Comstock, & J. P. Murray (Eds.), *Television and social behavior: Vol. 4,*

Television in day-to-day life: Patterns of use (pp. 129–256). Washington, DC: U.S. Government Printing Office.

Lyle, J., & Hoffman, H. R. (1972b). Explorations in patterns of television viewing by preschool-age children. In E. A. Rubinstein, G. A. Comstock, & J. P. Murray (Eds.), *Television and social behavior: Vol. 4, Television in day-to-day life: Patterns of use* (pp. 257–273). Washington, DC: U.S. Government Printing Office.

Maccoby, E. E. (1954). Why do children watch television? *Public Opinion Quarterly, 18*(3), 239–244.

Maccoby, E. E., & Wilson, W. C. (1957). Identification and observational learning from films. *Journal of Abnormal and Social Psychology, 55,* 76–87.

Maccoby, E. E., Wilson, W. C., & Burton, R. V. (1958). Differential movie-viewing behavior of male and female viewers. *Journal of Personality, 26,* 259–267.

McDonagh, E. C. (1950). Television and the family. *Sociology and Social Research, 35*(2), 113–122.

Meadowcroft, J. M. (1986). Family communication patterns and political development: The child's role. *Communication Research, 13*(4), 603–624.

Medrich, E. A., Roizen, J., Rubin, V., & Buckley, S. (1982). *The serious business of growing up: A study of children's lives outside of school.* Los Angeles: University of California Press.

Meltzoff, A. N. (1988). Imitation of televised models by infants. *Child Development, 59,* 1221–1229.

Messaris, P., & Kerr, D. (1983). Mothers' comments about TV: Relation to family communication patterns. *Communication Research, 10,* 175–194.

Murray, J. P., & Kippax, S. (1978). Children's social behavior in three towns with differing television experience. *Journal of Communication, 28*(4), 19–29.

Mutz, D. C., Roberts, D. F., & van Vuuren, D. P. (1993). Reconsidering the displacement hypothesis: Television's influence on children's time use. *Communications Research, 20*(1), 51–75.

National Television Violence Study. (1996). *National television violence study: Scientific papers, 1994–95.* Studio City, CA: Mediascope.

National Television Violence Study. (1997). *National television violence study* (Vol. 2). Santa Barbara: University of California, Center for Communication and Social Policy.

National Television Violence Study. (1998). *National television violence study* (Vol. 3). Santa Barbara: University of California, Center for Communication and Social Policy.

Neuman, S. B. (1991). *Literacy in the television age.* Norwood, NJ: Ablex.

Neuman, W. R. (1982). Television and American culture: The mass medium and the pluralistic audience. *Public Opinion Quarterly, 46*(4), 471-487.

Nielsen Wire. (2010). Three screen report: Media consumption and multi-tasking continue to increase across TV, Internet, and mobile. Available at: http://blog.nielsen.com/nielsen wire/media_entertainment/three-screen -report-media-consumption-and-multi-tasking -continue-to-increase

O'Neil, T. (March 8, 2010). Oscars ratings highest in five years. *Los Angeles Times.* Retrieved April 12, 2011, from http://goldderby.latimes. com/awards_goldderby/2010/03/oscars-rat ings-highest-in-five-years-html

Pearl, D., Bouthilet, L., & Lazar, J. (Eds.). (1982). *Television and behavior: Ten years of scientific progress and implications for the eighties: Vol. 1. Summary report.* Washington, DC: U.S. Government Printing Office.

Piaget, J., & Inhelder, B. (1969). *The psychology of the child.* New York: Basic Books.

Plomin, R., Corely, R., Defries, J. C., & Fulker, D. W. (1990). Individual differences in television viewing in early childhood: Nature as well as nurture. *Psychological Science, 6*(1), 371–377.

Plomin, R., & DeFries, J. C. (1985). *Origins of individual differences in infancy: The Colorado Adoption Project.* New York: Academic Press.

Potts, R., & Sanchez, D. (1994). Television viewing and depression: No news is good news. *Journal of Broadcasting and Electronic Media, 38*(1), 79–90.

Rideout, V. J., Foehr, U. G., & Roberts, D. F. (2010). *Generation M²: Media in the lives of 8-18 year-olds.* Kaiser Family Foundation.

Rideout, V., & Hamel, E. (2006). *The media family: Electronic media in the lives of infants, toddlers, preschoolers and their parents.* Menlo Park, CA: Kaiser Family Foundation.

Rideout, V. J., Vandewater, E. A., & Wartella, E. A. (2003). *Zero to six: Electronic media in the lives of infants, toddlers and preschoolers* (Report): Menlo Park, CA: The Henry J. Kaiser Family Foundation; Children's Digital Media Centers.

Roberts, D., & Foehr, U. (2004). *Kids and media in America.* Cambridge, UK: Cambridge University Press.

Roberts, D. F., Foehr, U. G., & Rideout, V. (2005). *Generation M: Media in the lives of 8–18 year-olds.* A Kaiser Family Foundation Study. Accessed April 12, 2011, from http://www.kff .org/entmedia/upload/Generation-M-Media -in-the-Lives-of-8-18-Year-olds-Report.pdf

Robinson, J. P. (1972). Television's impact on everyday life: Some cross-national evidence. In G. A. Comstock & J. P. Murray (Eds.), *Television and social behavior: Vol. 4, Television in everyday life: Patterns of use* (pp. 410–431), Washington, DC: U.S. Government Printing Office.

Robinson, J. P. (1990). Television's effects on families' use of time. In J. Bryant (Ed.), *Television and the American family* (pp. 195–210). Hillsdale, NJ: Lawrence Erlbaum.

Robinson, J. P., & Converse, P. E. (1972). The impact of television on mass media usages: A cross national comparison. In A. Szalai (Ed.), *The use of time: Daily activities of urban and suburban populations in twelve countries* (pp. 197–212). The Hague, Netherlands: Mouton.

Robinson, J. P., & Godbey, G. (1997). *Time for life: The surprising ways Americans use their time.* University Park: Pennsylvania State University Press.

Rosaen, S. F., & Dibble, J. L. (2008). Investigating the relationships among child's age, parasocial interactions, and the social realism of favorite television characters. *Communication Research Reports, 25*(2), 145–154.

Rosengren, K. E., & Windahl, S. (1989). *Media matter: TV use in childhood and adolescence.* Norwood, NJ: Ablex.

Rothschild, N., Thorson, E., Reeves, B., Hirsch, J. E., & Goldstein, R. (1986). EEG activity and the processing of television commercials. *Communication Research, 13*(2), 182–220.

Rubin, A. M. (1983). Television uses and gratifications: The interaction of viewing patterns and motivations. *Journal of Broadcasting, 27*(1), 37–51.

Rubin, A. M. (1984). Ritualized and instrumental television viewing. *Journal of Communication, 34*(3), 67–77.

Schramm, W., Lyle, J., & Parker, E. B. (1961). *Television in the lives of our children.* Stanford, CA: Stanford University Press.

Singer, J. L., & Singer, D. G. (1981). *Television, imagination, and aggression: A study of preschoolers.* Hillsdale, NJ: Lawrence Erlbaum.

Singer, J. L., & Singer, D. G. (2001). *Handbook of children and the media.* Thousand Oaks, CA: Sage.

Singer, J. L., Singer, D. G., Desmond, R., Hirsch, R., & Nicol, A. (1988). Family mediation and children's cognition, aggression, and comprehension of television: A longitudinal study. *Journal of Applied Developmental Psychology, 9*(3), 329–347.

Sprafkin, J. N., & Liebert, R. M. (1978). Sex-typing and children's preferences. In G. Tuchman, A. K. Daniels, & J. Benet (Eds.), *Hearth and home: Images of women in the mass media* (pp. 288–339). New York: Oxford University Press.

Surgeon General's Scientific Advisory Committee on Television and Social Behavior. (1972). *Television and growing up: The impact of televised violence* [Report to the surgeon general, U.S. Public Health Service]. Washington, DC: U.S. Government Printing Office.

Tangney, J. P., & Feshbach, S. (1988). Children's television-viewing frequency: Individual differences and demographic correlates. *Personality and Social Psychology Bulletin, 14*(1), 145–158.

Timmer, S. G., Eccles, J., & O'Brien, K. (1985). How children use time. In F. T. Juster & F. P. Stafford (Eds.), *Time, goods, and well-being* (pp. 353–382). Ann Arbor: University of Michigan, Institute for Social Research.

U. S. Department of Health and Human Services. (2001). *Youth violence: A report of the surgeon general.* Rockville, MD: U.S. Department of Health and Human Services. Centers for Disease Control and Prevention, National Center for Injury Prevention and Control; Substance Abuse and Mental Health Services Administration, Center for Mental Health Services; and National Institutes of Health, National Institute of Mental Health.

Valkenburg, P. M., & van der Voort, T. H. A. (1994). Influence of TV on daydreaming and creative imagination: A review of research. *Psychological Bulletin, 116*(2), 316–339.

Valkenburg, P. M., Voojis, M. W., van der Voort, T. H. A., & Wiegman, O. (1992). The influence of television on children's fantasy styles: A secondary analysis. *Imagination, Cognition, and Personality, 12,* 55–67.

Van Evra, J. (1998). *Television and child development* (2nd ed.). Mahwah, NJ: Lawrence Erlbaum.

von Feilitzen, C. (1999). Children's amount of TV viewing: Statistics from 10 countries. In C. von Feilitzen & U. Carlsson (Eds.), *Children and media: Image, education, participation* (pp. 61–67). Göteborg, Sweden: Göteborg University, UNESCO International Clearinghouse on Children and Violence on the Screen.

von Feilitzen, C., & Linne, O. (1975). Identifying with television characters. *Journal of Communication, 25*(4), 51–55.

Webster, J. G., & Phalen, P. F. (1997). *The mass audience: Rediscovering the dominant model.* Mahwah, NJ: Lawrence Erlbaum.

Whetmore, E. J. (1981). *The magic medium: An introduction to radio in America.* Belmont, CA: Wadsworth.

Williams, T. M. (Ed.). (1986). *The impact of television: A natural experiment in three communities.* New York: Praeger.

Winston, B. (1986). *Misunderstanding media.* Cambridge, MA: Harvard University Press.

Wolf, M. A. (1987). How children negotiate television. In T. R. Lindlof (Ed.), *Natural audiences: Qualitative research of media uses and effects* (pp. 58–94). Norwood, NJ: Ablex.

Wright, J. C., & Huston, A. C. (1995). *Effects of educational TV viewing of lower income preschoolers on academic skills, school readiness, and school adjustment one to three years later* [Technical report]. Lawrence: University of Kansas.

Zill, N., Davies, E., & Daly, M. (1994). *Viewing of Sesame Street by preschool children in the United States and its relationship to school readiness* [Report prepared for Children's Television Workshop]. Rockville, MD: Westat.

Zillmann, D. (1988). Mood management: Using entertainment to full advantage. In L. Donohew, H. E. Sypher, & E. T. Higgins (Eds.), *Communication, social cognition, and affect* (pp. 147–171). Hillsdale, NJ: Lawrence Erlbaum.

Zillmann, D., & Bryant, J. (1985). Affect, mood, and emotion as determinants of selective media exposure. In D. Zillmann & J. Bryant (Eds.), *Selective exposure to communication* (pp. 157–190). Hillsdale, NJ: Lawrence Erlbaum.

CHAPTER 2

The Role of Reading for Children and Adolescents in a Digital Age

Roger Desmond
University of Hartford

Introduction

When the first edition of this book was published over a decade ago my emphasis was on the role of "free reading," or reading for pleasure, in the lives of children and adolescents. While that topic is still relevant, the vast changes in the media landscape add enormous complexity to the issue. Certainly, children are still reading, but much of their reading is done from a screen. With each passing month, those screens have become ubiquitous and more portable than ever. The distinction between reading for school and reading for pleasure begins to blur as stories are used in electronic games in schools and lessons from history classes are incorporated into games that children and teens play at home or at any location of their choice. Product placements are used to advertise products in books that children read for pleasure. A recent book series, *Mackenzie Blue,* aimed at preteen girls, contains embedded references to brands of candy, drinks, clothing, and other commodities, and the products are used by characters; other marketers are regularly riddling books with products (Nagy, 2009). The frozen-in-mind image of a child reading a book beside a river on a summer day no longer describes how, what, and why children read.

This time, the chapter will explore free, out-of-school reading as well as the implications of the digital platform for reading in the lives of children and adolescents. Still important are questions regarding the onset of reading, the amount that children read, and what that reading contributes to their social and intellectual lives—but there are new questions. When "screen time" competes with book and magazine reading, how attractive are traditional print and illustrations? Does digitalization alter the process of reading in terms of rate, retention, or comprehension?

Will portable digital reading devices spell the end of bound books or stapled magazines? Are multimedia editions of books for children and adolescents more or less satisfying for a young audience? These and other questions will be used to explore the implications of reading in the digital age. While many of these questions lack solid research evidence for answers, the process has begun.

How Much Do Children Read?

Since the first edition of this volume, the amount of time children spend reading is the only use of a medium that has decreased. In 1999, an analysis of Kaiser Foundation survey data from over 3,000 children and adolescents revealed that respondents aged 2 to 14 reported an overall average of 43 minutes of reading per day, with 21 minutes devoted to books, 15 minutes to magazines, and 7 minutes to newspapers (Roberts, Ulla, Rideout, & Brodie, 1999). In 2010, a report from the same foundation found a decrease of about 5 minutes in overall reading, to 38 minutes per day (Rideout, Foehr, & Roberts, 2010). While the proportion of 8 to 18 year olds who read books has remained stable (46%), the proportion of respondents who read newspapers has decreased (from 42% to 23%), as has magazine reading (from 55% to 35%).

Not all of this reading was done from print sources: Computers bring large amounts of text. About 10% of this age cohort reported reading newspapers and magazines online, at an average of 21 minutes per day. Thus, about two minutes of journal reading has been made up for by reading from a screen. Regardless of the time differences across two decades, reading from print sources occupies the least time in the media diet, dwarfed as it is by over four and one half hours of television content.

Many children choose to not read often or in great quantities. Scholars from a variety of disciplines have studied the amount of time young people read and its effect on cognitive functions. A group of studies involving hundreds of students found that very few preschool and primary grade children chose to look at books during free-choice time at school (Morrow & Weinstein, 1986). Greaney (1980) found that fifth-grade students spent

only 5.4% of their out-of-school free time engaged in reading, and 23% of them chose not to read at all. Anderson, Fielding, and Wilson (1988) found that students spend less than 2% of their free time reading. Furthermore, as students get older, the decline in reading becomes more pronounced. The decline in reading for pleasure is most pronounced among adolescents. The percentage of young people who read for "at least 5 minutes" the previous day in 2004 was 63% for 8 year olds, but only 34% of 15 to 18 year olds read the previous day (National Endowment for the Arts, 2007).

What Are They Reading?

Perennial classics such as *The Pokey Little Puppy* by Janet S. Lowrey, S. E. Hinton's *Outsiders,* and E. B. White's *Charlotte's Web* continue to be in the "Top 10" on Publications International's list of best-selling children's books of all time since. (Publications International, 2011). At that time, the Harry Potter craze was in full blossom, with librarians breathlessly celebrating the return of reading as a major factor in children's leisure time. With over 400 million copies sold, the series clearly ranks as the most popular in history. In 2005 and 2006, news reports mentioned a British survey that claimed that 59% of a sample of children said that they had never read a book before Harry Potter and that a larger percentage said that reading them helped them in school. Attempts to verify this and other investigations result in a diagnosis of a kind of media virus; while the press reported research results, sources merely quoted each other. Primary data were nowhere in evidence. All of this attention was accompanied by severe criticism from religious groups who feared that the primary outcome of reading the books was a preoccupation with witchcraft and magic.

Whatever the ultimate legacy of J. K. Rowling's Harry Potter books, the impact has faded. No new "superstars" of children's literature have emerged. Rowling has declared that the series has ended; only the last book in the series remains to be filmed. Critic A. S. Byatt (2003) said of the world of Harry Potter, "It is written for people whose imaginative lives are confined to TV cartoons, and the exaggerated (more exciting, not threatening) mirror-worlds of soaps, reality TV and celebrity gossip" (p. B1).Other critics have leveled similar critiques, saying that the books are popular because they are so television-like. Things happen to Harry, his family, and his friends that have no implication for others in the world. Regardless of critics' attacks, several generations of young readers are likely to continue their enjoyment of the world of Hogwarts.

For the preteen reader (aged 9–12), Creative Juices (2009) still lists several classics as best sellers. Among them are C. S. Lewis' *Narnia* series, Laura Ingalls Wilder's *Little House in the Big Woods* and its sequels, and Caroline Keene's *Nancy Drew* and sequels. Thirteen to 15 year olds are reading Katherine Paterson's *Bridge to Terabithia* and *The Great Gilly Hopkins*. Both teens and preteens are reading Stephenie Meyer's Twilight series, as well as viewing the popular films based on the books. Vampires have a long shelf life for teens and young adults. According to culture critic Karen Valby (2008),

> There are young girls and grown women alike wearing homemade T-shirts with slogans like "I Love Hot Guys With Superpowers (and Fangs)" and "I Love Vegan Vampires." There are gleeful members from the online community Twilight Moms, who Meyer had breakfast with that morning despite being at a signing until 1 a.m. the previous night, and grandmothers who say if they knew how to use a computer they'd start their own fansite too. There are women who've quit their day jobs and now make a living online selling *Twilight*-inspired T-shirts and jewelry, and a teenage girl clutching a letter for Meyer that says the books persuaded her not to take her own life. (p. 12)

Benefits of Reading

Children whose parents read to them tend to become better readers and to perform better in school than those who are not read to (Snow, Burns, & Griffin 1998). Other family activities such as telling stories and singing songs also encourage children's acquisition of literacy skills (Moss & Fawcett, 1995). A large

body of research revealing the effectiveness of reading aloud in helping children to become effective readers was emerging during the first edition of this volume. Children who are frequently read to before first grade will then "read" their favorite books by themselves by engaging in oral language-like and written language-like routines (Teale, 1995). For most children at this age, emergent reading routines include attending to pictures and occasionally to salient print, such as that found in illustrations or labels. A few begin to attend to the print in the main body of the text, and a few make the transition into conventional reading with their favorite books. Another investigation in this tradition found that first graders who were read to from children's trade books outperformed controls on a number of measures of reading comprehension (Feitelson, Kita, & Goldstein, 1986). In a review of research on play, the authors cite a number of renowned scholars and authors, including Goethe, E. B. Browning, G. B. Shaw, and many others, who report vivid memories of their parents' reading to them and the impact of these read-aloud experiences on their literary accomplishments (Singer & Singer, 1990).

Trelease's (1995) review of reading research revealed that in a number of investigations, competent early readers were read to as young children. The U.S. Department of Education (1985) study "Becoming a Nation of Readers," a review of over 10,000 research findings, stated that "the single most important activity for building the knowledge required for eventual success is reading aloud to children" (p. 247).

Not every investigation has found positive results of reading aloud, especially if the reader was a teacher. Meyer, Stahl, Wardrop, and Linn (1994) completed a longitudinal investigation of two large cohorts of K through second-grade students and found that among kindergarten students, there was a *negative* relationship between reading aloud by kindergarten teachers and students' reading achievement, and there was no relationship for first graders. This was explained in terms of a displacement effect, where teachers who read the most spent the least amount of time teaching activities positively correlated with reading. For parents, no relationship between reading aloud and reading achievement in their children was found, but there was a positive association between time spent with print and reading achievement.

Parents' reading to children has been found to have benefits that transfer into reading achievement as measured by in-school assessments. A longitudinal study of a large sample of children from preschool to Grade 3 found that children's early exposure to books was related to their development of vocabulary and listening comprehension skills and that these language skills were directly related to their reading in Grade 3 (Sénéchal & LeFevre, 2002). A secondary result was that parents teaching children about reading and writing words was related to the development of early literacy skills, and these skills predicted reading ability in Grade 1. A meta-analysis of 20 published studies of parental involvement in reading found significant effect sizes suggesting that parents of children in kindergarten through Grade 3 can help their children learn to read (Sénéchal & Young, 2008). Parents are most helpful when they are trained to teach specific skills to their children.

Stanovich and Cunningham (1993) studied 268 college students and found that exposure to print predicted differences in knowledge in a variety of subject domains, after controlling for individual differences on four indicators of general ability. Although correlational, the results provide strong evidence that exposure to print sources of information is an independent contribution to the acquisition of content knowledge.

As Cullinan (2006) pointed out in an extensive review of the outcomes of reading, reading to children does not by itself automatically lead to literacy. The causal factor seems to lie in the talking between adults and children that occurs during story reading. Asking questions, pointing out relationships, and providing the names of things are examples of interactions that lead to literacy. Successful outcomes of reading involve interactions in which readers and listeners actively construct meaning based on texts.

The bulk of research on the outcomes of reading aloud to children suggest that it leads to free reading by children and begins a life-long process of reading for pleasure. The benefits of adult literacy have their seeds in young children and parents or caregivers engaging in reading and talking.

Mythic Dimensions of Reading

Reading has traditionally introduced children to the realm of myth. Every culture has myths that serve to entertain and to instruct; the heroic stories of any culture convey the norms and values of a people by illustrating their highest and lowest aspirations through the activities of heroes and villains. Just as characters like Hestia, in the Greek myths, embodied the characteristics of home and hearth, classical children's characters also celebrate key values and goals. Certainly, the 20th-century hero Tom Swift represented innovation and intelligence, along with the courage to employ his inventions to positive goals. Frontier stories of Davy Crockett and Daniel Boone reflect the strong individualism of the pioneer.

It is because of the power of myths that feminists have sought to discover female heroes who represent strong, intelligent responses to human problems. The Nancy Drew stories that served as summer reading for many baby boomers featured an intelligent female hero, but one who still lived and worked in a man's world. Judy Blume's books, including *Hello, God, It's Me, Margaret*, were a departure radical enough to get them excluded from many school and public libraries. Blume's books, while still maintaining the innocence of pre-adolescents, also portrayed girls as sexual beings. In this manner, myths show a young reader who and what is valued in a society, and when conflicting subcultures emerge, myths may be a source of deep concern to those who hold power.

Can other children's media such as comics and TV programs serve mythic functions? Joseph Campbell (1949) observed that there are some key fixed elements of mythic stories. Mythic heroes must respond to a *call to adventure* and *cross thresholds*, often overcoming a *guardian*. With the help of *assistants*, they overcome a series of *tests* leading to the *supreme ordeal* to achieve a reward. They then make a return journey where there is a *reemergence* in their now peaceful everyday world.

In a comic series like *Superman* there are signs of this mythic pattern. Most of the stories begin with a call to action; Superman reads a newspaper headline announcing the theft of uranium, for example. Superman is often tested—"that's kryptonite, not uranium!" Helpers may come, in the form of his colleagues Lois Lane and Jimmy at the *Daily Planet* newspaper—"Lois, see what you can find out about these thugs!" Guardians (Lex Luthor's henchmen) are confronted. The supreme ordeal is confronted: "I will put on a lead suit, which will let me get past the kryptonite and into their lair!" The mythic pattern may break down here, at the reemergence stage. As comic book author Joel Grineau (1997) pointed out, in comics "there is rarely that last return home, the final loss of powers, and restoration of the world to its former, better condition. Why? The first axiom in comics is that characters rarely stay dead or retired" (p. 2). Unlike the Japanese manga comics, it is bad form to terminate the ongoing adventures of an American hero.

The *Superman* story has biblical elements as well. Like Moses, the young Superboy was discovered and raised by parents who were not biologically his after traveling a great distance (in Superboy's case, in a starship from his home planet). The hero was discovered to have super powers that must be used for leading people to a safe and good place.

While the reader often sees Superman as drab reporter Clark Kent in his restored everyday world, the comic cannot make a story out of such a humdrum life. But within any one comic, a critical mass of mythic elements seems to be present. A typical story concludes with the elements of reemergence and restoration, at least until the next issue. Children's books can certainly also qualify as mythic, especially those that, like the Harry Potter books, offer a story of triumph over adversity. Many popular children's books are simply good narratives, with no mythical dimension at all.

Animated television characters, even those based on books, operate in only a partial realm of myth. While there are obstacles to overcome, the most typical mythic elements present are *tests* or action-packed events, few of which lead up to the conquest of a dark force and a return to the everyday world.

The functions of reading mythic stories include the vicarious experience of adventures that, in real life, might prove dangerous. Children meet and experience the thoughts of complex characters who embody many dimensions of people they will meet in life. Mythic stories tell children how we should act toward one another. Good stories help children to discover what and who their culture loves and hates, and they are a non-negotiable, irreplaceable part of growing up.

Who Is Reading Aloud?

According to U.S. Department of Education (2006) statistics, there is reason for optimism regarding the amount of reading in the family: The practice is on the increase. The percentage of prekindergarten children ages three to five read to by a family member (three or more times in the week preceding the survey) increased from 78% in 1993 to 86% in 2005. The percentage of children whose family members frequently told them a story rose from 43% to 54%.

Also according to the U.S. Department of Education (2006), all children were more likely to have an adult read to them frequently in 2005 than in 1993; however, the increase among poor children (from 68% to 78%) was greater than the increase among middle income children (from 87% to 90%). Despite the greater increase for poor children, middle class children were still more likely than poor children to have a family member read to them frequently in 2005 (as was also the case in 1993). For example, in 2005, a greater percentage of middle or upper income children were read to than poor children (90% vs. 78%). However, in 2005, there were no measurable differences found between middle income and poor children for the other literacy-related activities (e.g., teaching them numbers, letters, or songs). The percentage of children who engaged in literacy activities in 2005 varied by parents' education and race/ethnicity. Children whose parents had at least a high school diploma or equivalent were more likely to be read to and taught letters, words, or numbers than those children whose parents had less than a high school diploma. White children were more likely than Black or Hispanic children to have a family member read to them.

What Kind of Families Read Aloud?

Since the average child spends eight times the number of hours outside of school as she spends in school, it is important to stress that the home as teacher is likely to be a stronger predictor of admiration for reading than is the school. A longitudinal investigation by Weigel, Martin, and Bennett (2010) on the role of family assets and lifestyles found that among a number of family descriptors studied (presence of technology, family stress, etc.), the most important predictor of preschool children's emerging literacy skills was that the more regular the routines in the household, the more likely parents were to engage their children in literacy enhancing activities and, in turn, the higher the children's print knowledge and reading interest. This was the case both initially and a year later. Similarly, a study of over 400 K through first grader's home environments found that household order (but not a household free of noise) was associated with early reading skills among children whose mothers were of above-average reading ability (Johnson, Martin, Brooks-Gunn, & Petrill, 2008). *Order,* as defined in this research, is simply a measure of physical clutter in the home.

Social class is, not unexpectedly, a strong factor in the home environment of young readers. A longitudinal U.S. Departmental of Education study of the relationships among reading aloud and oral communication between parents of children (birth to 4 years) found that when the daily number of words for each group of children was projected across four years, the four-year-old child from the professional family would have heard 45 million words, the working-class child 26 million, and the welfare child only 13 million (Trelease, 2006). According to a reviewer, "If No Child Left Behind expects the teacher (of the welfare child) to get this child caught up, she'll have to speak 10 words *a second* for nine hundred hours to reach the 32-million mark by year's end" (Trelease, 2006, p. 15).

An investigation of children's interest in books analyzed children and parents from 29 kindergarten classrooms in terms of their interest in books and aspects of their home environments (Morrow, 1983). Children with a relatively high interest in books came from homes with significantly more books than those of children lower in book interest, and they were more likely to have visited libraries, owned library cards, and been read to by parents.

Parents' education level has been found to strongly influence the amount and quality of children's reading, but the relationship is strongly mediated by other factors (Myrberg & Rosen, 2009). Using structural equation modeling to estimate the effects of parent education on 10,000 third graders' reading ability in Sweden, Myrberg and Rosen (2009) found substantial effects of parents' education, but nearly half of these effects were mediated by other variables. These included the number of books in the home, but also the child's reading ability entering school, which was in turn strongly predicted by the amount of reading aloud in the home. Educated parents had many books in the home and read them to their children early in life, with positive results among preschool children.

Intervention Facilitates Reading at Home

Despite research suggesting differences in ethnicity and social class in reading in the home, there is clear evidence that intervention programs can improve the reading-aloud patterns of any family. Mendez (2010) reported the results of an intervention developed to promote parent involvement with children attending Head Start preschool programs and with their teachers. In a small southern city, 288 predominantly African American families received an intervention designed to promote reading aloud, among other activities. Results showed an increase in the frequency of reading aloud as compared to parents who did not receive the program. Parent–teacher relationship quality was significantly correlated with parents' participation in the intervention. Program participation and the parent–teacher relationship were correlated with higher levels of children's school readiness abilities. Children in the intervention condition showed stronger end-of-year receptive vocabulary and parent-rated social competence as compared with children who did not receive the treatment.

An investigation of intervention with an older sample (fourth grade) of primarily low income Hispanic families concluded that a summer reading intervention program increased the amount of summer reading by children, particularly if parents accompanied their children to several literary events (Kim & Guryan, 2010). There was no significant increase in reading comprehension from June to September, however.

Since the first edition of this volume, a number of factors have facilitated new directions in research on reading outcomes. President Bush signed the No Child Left Behind act into law in 2001, which contained mandates regarding teacher and school effectiveness. The resultant preoccupation with evaluation resulted in press releases stating that an enormous number of elementary and secondary students in American schools did not perform to the standards dictated by the law. One of the trends that emerged from this downturn was that schools and, later, researchers began investigating methods to improve reading scores. Free, or outside of school, reading was one target for investigators. Some research in the past decade focused on the relationships among free reading and performance in school.

New technologies were also a factor in shifting research questions. As computers in the home (and in public libraries and other shared environments) became more available, stories to be read or printed from computers became more common. In-school reading and reading for pleasure began to blur, at least from the perspective of reading research. Scholars from a variety of nations have collaborated on research on the relationships among demographic and family variables, realizing that many of their problems were shared.

An example of this kind of approach is an investigation that provided computerized storybooks for 5-year-old immigrants from low income households in the Netherlands who were at risk for reading difficulties in the language of instruction in their schools (Verhallen & Bus, 2010). Books with both still and video images were effective in increasing vocabularies, but video books were more effective in the acquisition of expressive vocabulary. Computerized "talking books" have also been used to target at-risk populations of 5 and 6 year olds (Wood, Pillinger, & Jackson, 2010) Lower-achieving children who used computer-generated talking books in conjunction with adult interaction while reading gained phonological awareness more than did children who used the electronic books alone.

Reading as Children Mature

A survey by Nipold, Duthie, and Larson (2005) of two groups of students, in Grade 6 and Grade 9, investigated the role of reading among all leisure activities preferred by students of these ages. For both age groups, reading was only moderately popular; as an activity, it ranked below watching TV, running, swimming, shopping at the mall, and talking on the phone. Reading became less popular by ninth grade; only 30% of boys and 44% of girls listed reading as a part of their leisure activities. In terms of time spent reading, average estimates were approximately 20 to 30 minutes per day, with girls of both age groups reporting more time. In terms of what they like to read, for all students combined, the most popular reading materials were magazines, novels, and comics; least popular were plays, technical books, and newspapers. Older students showed a stronger preference than younger ones for magazines, and girls showed a stronger preference than did boys for poems.

Self-reports from a sample of junior high school students reflected a decline in reading for pleasure as children matured (Zender-Merrell, 2002). Only 12% of eighth-grade students reported reading seven or more books in the past three months, as compared to 22% of sixth graders. Almost a third (30%) of eighth graders reported having read no books in that period, as compared to only 15% of sixth graders. In a survey of seventh- and eighth-grade students, respondents reported frequent free reading before seventh grade but virtually no reading not required by teachers after that. In another investigation, recreational reading ranked lowest in leisure activities after Grade 7 (McCoy, 1991).

Cummings and Vandewater's (2007) analysis of survey data from a large sample of 10 to 19 year olds revealed differences between adolescent players and non-players of video games in time spent reading. On average, gamers (36% of the sample) played for an hour on the weekdays and an hour and a half on the weekends. Compared with non-gamers, adolescent gamers spent 30% less time reading and 34% less time doing homework. Among gamers (both genders), time spent playing video games without parents or friends was negatively related to time spent with parents and friends in other activities. This effect is more pronounced for males, since only 20% of players were female. Only reading for pleasure and homework were displaced by game-playing; time spent with friends and family was not affected by playing.

In 2007, National Endowment for the Arts issued a report linking flat or declining national reading test scores among teenagers with the slump in the proportion of adolescents who said they read for fun (Rich, 2008). According to Department of Education data cited in Rich's (2008) report, just over a fifth of 17-year-olds said they read almost every day for fun in 2004, down from nearly a third in 1984. Nineteen percent of 17 year olds said they never or hardly ever read for fun in 2004, up from 9% in 1984. (It was unclear whether they thought of what they did on the Internet as reading.)

There are gender differences in what adolescents read, similar to those evident in childhood (Parkhurst, 2008). Boys read much more nonfiction than do girls, who prefer fiction. Comprehension of nonfiction is important for teens, but the books that they choose tend not to provide the experience with sustained text that will promote growth in ability to handle more complex text structures and text types (Sullivan, 2004). Parkhurst (2008) noted that nonfiction books checked out by boys include books that are largely photographs and drawings—of World War II fighter planes, for example—and that many of these books are full of pictures, with little

sustained text. He also cited a large body of research that suggests that humorous fiction is read by boys, but that there isn't much age-appropriate humorous fiction available for them. That category is occupied by movies.

As every parent knows, adolescence is characterized by social interaction with friends. Whether in person, on cell phones, or on computers, adolescents spend most of their leisure time communicating with peers and boyfriends or girlfriends. In a typical week, high school students will spend twice as much time with their peers as with adults (Csikszentmihalyi, Larson, & Prescott, 1977). Data from several longitudinal studies confirm that initial membership in a peer group that is academically and reading-oriented is correlated with higher grades, more time spent on homework, and more involvement in extracurricular activities (Steinberg, 1996). Just as peers influence adolescent musical and clothing tastes, whether young people read for pleasure and, if so, what they read, are certainly woven into the fabric of peer culture.

Reading From Electronic Media

No matter how much time children and adolescents spend with computers, they are doing some kind of reading. Whether they use (or misuse) a search engine to locate information for a term paper, modify their profiles on Facebook or other social media, or text message friends, they are decoding texts and encoding sentences. According to the 2010 Kaiser Foundation report, they spend, on average, nearly two hours using computers every day (Rideout et al., 2010). No responsible educator would argue that Internet reading is the same experience as reading a story or a novel. Internet texts are skimmed, hypertext links carry the reader to new texts, and rarely is information conveyed in serial fashion.

A study of 700 children in 6th through 10th grade in Detroit found a large amount of Internet reading among a variety of other reading media within the sample (Rich, 2008). The only kind of reading, however, that related to higher academic performance was frequent novel reading, which predicted better grades in English and higher overall grade point averages. But critics of Internet reading who point to the superiority of fiction in terms of concentration and reflection ignore the realities of child and adolescent reading choices. They don't always choose stories or novels; they read magazines, comics, and many literary forms less complex than novels.

Donald J. Leu (2007a), director of the New Literacies Research Team at the University of Connecticut, argued that Internet reading is a fundamentally different, not inferior, form of information processing than reading from print texts. Because Internet reading is not what is tested in NCLB standardized reading assessments, skillful web readers do not necessarily perform well on those tests. Leu argued that skillful Internet reading always begins with a question framed by the reader, as opposed to with "Once upon a time." A growing body of research suggests that this process of beginning with a question to be answered facilitates any type of reading for information by children in the elementary grades (Taboada & Guthrie, 2006).

In one investigation, Leu (2007a) and colleagues mounted a web page that contained incorrect information about a fictitious creature (Pacific Northwest Tree Octopus). A seventh grade class was asked to evaluate the information and, if they deemed it valid, to recommend it to another class doing research on endangered species. All but one student recommended the website as valid information. Unsophisticated Internet readers lack critical skills to evaluate information, and they are inefficient searchers; they typically take many more "clicks" to locate information than capable readers, and they do not understand which information to ignore. Leu (2007b) believes that because of NCLB, schools have stressed phonemic awareness, phonics, vocabulary, and comprehension as isolated skills and ignored more general strategic skills necessary for Internet comprehension.

Reading from computers, while demanding particular search skills, relies on the basic reading skills traditionally taught in schools. But the digital world clearly represents new opportunities for reading. The Disney Corporation recently offered 500 age-appropriate digital books (eBooks) for downloading. Scholastic will soon add eBooks to a line of short films based on books from their collection. Digital versions of print books, eBooks offer several features not found in print books. Pages can be located instantly, without the reader having to turn individual pages. They often come with games, instant pronunciation guides, and dictionaries. Many feature animation, sounds, and other media. They can be CD-ROM storybooks or books downloaded from the Internet onto computers or portable reading devices.

Portable reading devices have become popular in the past five years among children and adolescents. They offer portability, and the digital versions are much less expensive than are paper books. Many are available for downloading free from virtual libraries. While the reading devices now available are somewhat fragile for young children, downloading onto more durable laptop computers may present a practical solution. Since 2007, Amazon's Kindle has been the most popular eBook reader, with bundled software that allows users to purchase, download (wirelessly), and read books from Amazon.com. Later models allowed the software to be loaded onto cell phones and music devices like Apple's iPod. With a current price just under 300 dollars, it has dominated the emerging market with virtually no competition. A new tablet computer, the Apple iPad, was released in the spring of 2010 and presents serious competition for Kindle. It runs iPad-specific applications as well as those written for the iPhone and iPod touch pad, including an eBook reader application. The iPad allows users to play games, surf the Internet, and create content using a touch screen keypad. The iPad retails for more than twice as much as the Kindle, but it has more applications. It also offers a larger reading surface than other readers on the market.

Children enjoy reading eBooks. A small sample of six to nine year olds was given eBooks loaded with traditional stories in children's centers and asked to rate them on several dimensions of use (Bellaver, 2006). The majority of children found them easy to use and adapted to them without difficulty, but they did not use the dictionary software that came with the machines. One major goal of the research was to determine whether eBooks could help to alleviate the "backpack syndrome" where children have endured back injuries from carrying textbooks and readers. In a second investigation, 20 fourth graders used eBooks in a classroom setting, and the majority reported that the books were more fun to use than traditional books and that, given the opportunity, they would read more frequently using the new medium (Bellaver, 2007). When given comparable paper and electronic opportunities, kindergarten and first-grade students preferred to wait for a chance to use the electronic version, even if a print version was available immediately (Mitchell & Fox, 2001).

In terms of basic reading processes, one investigation found that eBooks with animated cues (dictionaries, highlighted words, etc.) significantly improved vocabulary acquisition in a sample of third graders (Higgins & Cocks, 1999). Korat and Shamir (2008) found that children ages five to six reading eBooks (as compared to adults reading equivalent books aloud) significantly improved phonological awareness and word recognition regardless of the students' low socio-economic status. Weber and Cavanaugh (2006) found similar gains in these skills for gifted children who read eBooks.

Parents and preschool children reading eBooks together have been observed to have productive conversations, with high levels of abstraction, of the type seen in print co-reading, particularly when the child determined which story path to take when the digital book offered a choice (Fish, Shulman, Ackerman, & Levin, 2002).

Nearly every investigation of children reading from eBooks mentions an inherent problem with them: distraction. Because many of them offer games and other extras, children interrupt reading and become distracted by features not directly related to understanding the content. Since most of the preliminary studies were done in a school or laboratory setting, there is little data about how these devices are employed for free reading—but there may be less motivation for readers to continue through a book in a focused manner. In some studies, children in experimental groups were given eBooks with automatic "pop-up" dictionaries, while control groups were given print dictionaries. Children with print dictionaries were rarely observed using them. Each medium, then, features inherent trade-offs in terms of how readers come to use them.

Consequences of Not Reading

The National Endowment for the Arts (NEA) (2007) report on reading cited survey data that suggest that declines in reading have civic, social, and economic implications. According to the report, "advanced readers accrue personal, professional, and social advantages. Deficient readers run higher risks of failure in all three areas" (p. 6). Nearly two thirds of employers ranked reading comprehension as "very important" for high school graduates. Yet 38% consider most high school graduates deficient in this basic skill.

Poor readers also suffer in the health care system. Marwick (1997) documented longer hospital stays and higher incidences of illness for poor readers than for minimally literate patients, primarily because they were unable to follow directions for therapy and medication. Beyond these specific areas, Edwards (1979) presented evidence that the cultural disadvantages that accrue from the lack of stimulation offered by reading can result in adults who are generally less socially connected and satisfied at the end of their lives than are capable readers.

It is not surprising that children who have difficulties in reading in the early grades perform poorly in subsequent secondary and college environments (Kamil, 2003). Adults who read poorly also suffer in the search for employment. A large organization reported that only 16% of applicants for an entry-level position could pass a basic reading comprehension test; the majority who failed were denied employment (Perry, 1988).

The majority of prison inmates are functionally illiterate, as are 85% of adolescent offenders in the United States, according to actual proficiency tests (National Assessment of Adult Literacy, 2003). While there is no evidence of a causal relationship between functional illiteracy and crime, inmates have a 16% chance of returning to prison if they receive literacy help, as opposed to 70% if they do not. One reason for this difference is that poor readers are less likely to enroll in vocational programs while incarcerated than are readers. Increasingly, due to changes in workplace technology, many rehabilitation programs are centered on information technologies, which are near impossible for less capable readers to participate in.

Newspaper readership is in decline, and it has been for at least two decades. Although statistics differ across agencies reporting readership, all converge in a drop of from 1% to 2% for each year since 1980 (Step, 2003). The decline is most pronounced among young adults (18–34), as well as among Asian, Black, and Hispanic readers. Television network news viewing follows a similar pattern. The share of the total viewing audience has declined by 51% since 1980, characterized as an ever-graying audience with a median age of nearly 60 (Project for Excellence in Journalism, 2006). News reading and viewing by adolescents has always been the gateway to adult news consumption, but there is no cohort preparing for a lifetime awareness of current events. These trends are alarming, and they are more or less pronounced in Europe and South America. A three-country survey of 3,500 teens and young adults concluded that regular newspaper readers are more informed, engaged, and connected to community than non-readers (World Association of Newspapers, 2008).

Since 2005, the amount of time young people (8–18) spend reading magazines or newspapers in print in a typical day has declined by seven minutes, from 19 to 12 minutes per day (Rideout et al., 2010). Some adolescents now spend time reading magazines and newspapers online. In a typical day, 10% of young people report reading magazines or newspapers online, and those who report online reading spend an average of 21 minutes per day doing so.

If young people are gleaning information from the Internet, blogs, and other electronic sources, what do we know from the perspectives of psychology, media research, computer science, and other disciplines that may help us to predict the possible outcomes of digital consumption of news and information? What will generation M know? Will digitally delivered information result in a general lack of world knowledge? Many investigations have found that adult news readers learn and retain more information from print than from broadcast news (Findahl & Hoijer, 1985; Stauffer, Frost, & Rybolt, 1981), but the intensity of this difference may be mediated by differences in how the information is retrieved (Leshner & Coyle, 2000). Print has been found to be superior to online information in terms of comprehension of stories and retention of facts (Eyetrack III, 2006). Television and Internet use are not highly correlated with current events knowledge; newspaper reading is (Amadeo, Torney-Purta, & Barber, 2004). Early research on websites attractive to young web surfers, designed to increase levels of political knowledge, reveals no gain in knowledge (Sherr, 2005).

Multitasking

Multitasking means doing several things at once. A recent survey revealed that 61% of a large sample of 8 to 18 year olds is surfing the web or watching television "most" or "some" of the time they are doing homework (Kaiser Family Foundation, 2005). Media multitasking has increased so much since 2000, for example, that media exposure (time spent with one or more media) must now be separated from media use (time spent with one medium) to predict cognitive and behavioral outcomes of these activities.

There is evidence that young adults in the workplace are also multitasking. Continuous partial attention (CPA) scanning is a designation that means simultaneously monitoring incoming information from two or more channels for an important or interesting opportunity. First mentioned in an address at the 2006 ETech conference by former Microsoft executive Linda Stone, the process is in evidence when users open two or more laptops, writing on one, for example, while monitoring e-mail or the Internet for interesting content (Torkington, 2006). Her contention was that CPA is rapidly increasing and that it leads to distraction and loss of focus, or in her words "Constantly being accessible makes you *in*accessible" (Levy, 2006). Research on the outcomes of these and other patterns of knowledge is emerging in several disciplines. The emphasis of this section is on how patterns of information seeking in the print and digital universes affect the information that people possess.

An investigation of multitasking by college students offered strong evidence that the practice impairs learning new information (Foerde, Poldrack, & Knowlton, 2007). Performing a classification task with auditory distraction reduced knowledge of how to perform the task a short time later in college students. Two kinds of memories appear to dwell in two different areas of the brain. The two systems that are often defined in opposition to each other are a declarative memory system, thought to depend on the hippocampus, and a procedural learning system, thought to depend on the striatum. Declarative memory represents memory of facts and events, whereas procedural learning encompasses a variety of motor and perceptual skills. Using magnetic resonance imaging to examine subject's brain activity revealed that, for the task learned without distraction, the hippocampus was involved. For the task learned with the distraction, the hippocampus was not involved—but the striatum was, which means that while subjects could learn the task, they could not recall details of procedures, or how they did it.

A research team at Stanford University found that college students who are frequent multitaskers are more susceptible to interference from competing stimuli than are users of one medium at a time (Ophir, Nass, & Wagner, 2009). Using a trait index of multitasking and a series of simple experimental tasks, they were surprised to find heavy media multitaskers performed worse on a test of task-switching ability than did non-multitaskers. They reasoned that these differences were likely due to a reduced ability to filter out interference from irrelevant tasks. According to one of the authors, Eyal Ophir, in a Stanford press release "Multitaskers couldn't help thinking about the task they weren't doing. The high multitaskers are always drawing from all the information in front of them. They can't keep things separate in their minds" (Gorlick, 2009). In light of the difficulty in information processing in evidence in this research, the conclusion is that reading while gaming, instant messaging, or using cell phones will detract from the ability to process and recall information from computer screens for people younger than college students. Yet that is the very landscape where adolescents dwell.

What Children and Adolescents Say About Reading

In 2008, representatives from the publishing and public opinion research industries studied 501 young people aged 5 to 17 regarding the place occupied by reading, computers, and other activities in their leisure time (Scholastic & Yankelovich, 2008). In their answers to interviewers' questions, these children and adolescents reported that reading is fully integrated into, not an alternative to, the digital world. Among the findings was that over 75% of young people aged 5 to 17 agreed with the statement, "No matter what I can do online, I'll always want to read books printed on paper," and 62% of them said they preferred to read books printed on paper rather than on a computer or a handheld device. The majority of the sample had read all or part of a book on a digital platform, but only 12% had read on a handheld device. Despite their preference for print books, across all age groups, over two thirds of the sample believed that within the next 10 years, most books that are read for fun will be read digitally—either on a computer or on another kind of electronic device.

About 9 in 10 children in the Scholastic and Yankelovich (2008) survey agree that they need to be strong readers to "get into a good college and to get a good job," but as in most investigations, daily reading declines after age eight—and this is most pronounced in boys. By age 15, only 21% of boys report that reading is "extremely important." Of 9–17 year olds, the predominant reason for not reading more is that "It's hard to find good books for boys and girls my age" (p. 18). The blogosphere is a place where it is possible to listen to children talk about reading in their words. For the past several years, CNN has invited readers as young as 5 and as old as 9 to provide video reviews of popular children's books (CNN.com, 2008). While younger children may react to a book by saying that it is "weird and happy!" the reviews also reveal that children are still reading in depth and reacting emotionally to what they read. In one review, an eight year old named Andrew reacts to Nikki Giovanni's *Rosa,* about the life of Rosa Parks, by saying "Parts of it are kind of boring, and the pictures are dark and gloomy, but I think that parents should read it to their children who are too young to read alone." The message—that Black people won their rights by fighting for them—is very important. Blogs by children, particularly if they are well monitored and secure from predators, are just one more example of the symbiosis of the print and digital domains.

Conclusion

Early in this second decade of the 21st century, it is clear that children are still reading. Reading for pleasure occupies a place in the leisure diets of children and adolescents, although in terms of sheer time, the last place. There is no compelling evidence for media displacement of reading by cell phones, the plethora of games, or the Internet; reading time has been on the decline for decades. What is evident is that multitasking with other media while reading is on the rise, and this may have implications for how stories are enjoyed and understood, and perhaps for the way they will be written by authors in the future. While parents and educators have valid reasons for concern about the rise of screen time, there is also clear evidence that many children are led into new domains of reading that weren't possible by browsing bookstores and libraries. Children talk about books and stories with each other without much interference, and they can be severe critics of what they read.

The digital world brings children new possibilities for seeing and vicariously being in places they could only go in their imaginations a few decades ago. Because of the visual richness of the cyberworld, they have come to expect multimedia and animation where they previously had only their inner voices to enliven their reading experience. It is therefore not surprising that a good deal of their reading has become more film- and television-like, since that is what they expect from storytelling. But the classics of children's literature still survive. The majority of them were written before the invention of cyberspace, but they have a way of engaging the imagination that isn't possible with Saturday morning cartoons—a medium that surely has declined. There is something about the long ago, far away, mythic interplay of heroes and adventures that fills a child's needs for good stories.

The child who reads on her own in junior high was read to early in her life, beginning long before age two, in an orderly home with regular routines. This pattern served her well in the early elementary grades, where she had the benefit of increased vocabulary, letter and word recognition, and phonic knowledge. The early attachment to reading resulted in reading achievement scores that far surpassed her classmates who weren't read to on a regular basis.

But it is important to stress that this child was no "bookworm." She spent many hours watching television, playing computer games, and communicating with peers on a variety of electronic media. What set her apart from her friends who didn't spend a lot of time reading was that some of the content of the conversations with her friends was about books and short stories, some age-appropriate and some material that would make parents balk. For her, a life-long fabric of reading for pleasure was woven from the threads of her early experiences with reading.

Because of a lack of longitudinal research, what happens next is less clear. We know that the trends in all kinds of reading begin to slide downward after Grade 8, most severely among boys—especially if they are Black or Hispanic. Although adolescents read, their reading begins to divide along gender lines; girls read more fiction and narratives, boys read more action-adventure stories and "how things work" books and articles. Do these content differences have implications for the contribution of free reading to adult social- or work-related skills? Research on how the fruit of reading is incorporated into social and work networks would be helpful in providing insights into the benefits of reading for adults. And we also have very little data on adult free reading, including whether life changes such as divorce or the birth of a child or the death of a spouse play a role in the amount and kind of reading done by mature people.

There is discomforting certainty regarding the decline of news reading (and viewing) by boys and girls before and during adolescence. Although many report that they get news from the Internet, evaluations of their knowledge of current events reveals that they don't know very much about the institutions and developments that determine their world. For several decades, the Pew Research Center for People and the Press regularly surveyed adults and adolescents about their sources of news and their knowledge of current events (Pew Research Center for People and the Press, 2010). Of all age groups in the most recent surveys, young people knew the least: Only 15% of 18 to 29 year olds were among the most informed third of the public, compared with 43% of those ages 65 and older.

In the age of information, people know less than they did 30 years ago. This is because of a number of the factors outlined earlier in this chapter, including a sharp decline in news consumption and, in light of the ever-increasing tendency of young people to multitask, the way that information is processed. Pew data and a mountain of earlier research conclude that people who know about their world are more likely to participate in it than are the less informed. How will democracy work if voters are uninformed about issues and positions if they do vote? How will they prevent developing diseases and participate in a complex economy? A number of news organizations are trying to lure young people back to the news, but future research is needed to determine the success of their efforts.

Reading texts from computers and handheld portable devices offers some options not available in a print text. Animated characters, online dictionaries, and sound clips may enhance the reading experience. These electronic books are inexpensive, even compared to paperbacks. Many are free. The number of titles is limitless, and it is growing each week. Yet children have not embraced them. They prefer, so far, reading from books. This may simply represent the novelty of these media. But there is some concern about the experience of reading from screens. The tendency to multitask and the ease of skipping

through text with eBooks offer opportunities for young readers that may alter the way stories are understood and incorporated into the lives of children. In light of the potential for textbooks to be disseminated electronically, research into this domain is sure to come.

Media critic Ken Auletta (2010) argued that a unique competitive environment among Google, Amazon, and Apple will breathe new life into the book business and simultaneously lower the price and increase the availability of every book ever published. While Amazon and Apple dominate the reading device market, Google surpasses both in its vast ownership of content. As competition increases and the price of best-sellers hovers below 10 dollars, consumers expect to pay less for digital copies than for paper and cloth versions. While publishers and bookstores will likely be the casualties of this battle, the ultimate outcome for the consumer will be less expensive books.

We have enough knowledge now to realize that reading must be kept alive—and that takes some effort. Parents should read to their children early and often. Both schools and parents need to find new ways of inviting children to read, especially during long summer vacations. With the vastness of the Internet, parents have unprecedented resources to help children and adolescents discover new books to read "just for fun." With adult supervision, children should be encouraged to visit blogs where other children talk about reading. The bulk of research summarized in this chapter suggests that keeping reading alive is worth all of our time and energy.

References

Amadeo, J-A., Torney-Purta, J., & Barber, C. (2004). *Attention to media and trust in media sources: Analysis of data from the IEA civic education study* [Electronic version]. College Park, MD: Center for Information and Research on Civic Learning and Engagement, University of Maryland, College Park.

Anderson, R., Fielding, C., & Wilson, P. (1988). Growth in reading and how children spend their time outside of school. *Reading Research Quarterly, 23*, 285–304.

Auletta, K. (2010, April 26). Publish or perish: Can the iPad top the Kindle and save the book business? *The New Yorker*, pp. 24–31.

Bellaver, R. (2006). *Children's eBook usability.* Muncie, IN: Center for Information and Communication Sciences, Ball State University. Retrieved March 4, 2010, from http://www.bsu .edu/web/rbellave/childrens_usability.htm

Bellaver, R. (2007). *The fight continues: A synopsis of continuing use of eBooks by elementary school children.* Muncie, IN: Center for Information and Communication Sciences, Ball State University. Retrieved April 3, 2010, from http://www.teleread.org/blog/?p=6787# comment-451526

Byatt, A. S. (2003, July 7). Harry Potter and the childish adult. *The New York Times*, pp. B1, B2

Campbell, J. (1949). *Hero with a thousand faces.* Princeton, NJ: Princeton University Press.

CNN.com. (2008). *Review: What children say about children's books*. Retrieved March 30, 2010, from http://www.cnn.com/2008/SHOWBIZ/ books/07/01/childrens.books/#cnnSTCText

Creative Juices. (2009). *Guide to best books for teens & most popular teen books*. Retrieved February 17, 2010, from http://www.creative juicesbooks.com

Csikszentmihalyi, M., Larson, R., & Prescott, S. (1977). The ecology of adolescent activity and experience. *Journal of Youth and Adolescence*, 6, 281–294.

Cullinan, B. (2006). Independent reading and school achievement. *School Library Media Research, 3*. Retrieved March 11, 2010, from http://www .ala.org/ala/mgrps/divs/aasl/aaslpubsandjour nals/slmrb/slmrcontents/volume32000/indepen dent.cfm

Cummings, H., & Vandewater, E. (2007). Relation of adolescent video game play to time spent in other activities. *Archives of Pediatrics and Adolescent Medicine, 161*(7), 684–689.

Edwards, J. R. (1979). *Language and disadvantage.* New York: Elsevier.

Eyetrack III. (2006). *Recall of information presented in text vs. multimedia format.* Retrieved April 7, 2010, from http://poynterextra.org/ eyetrack2004/multimediarecall.htm

Feitelson, D., Kita, B., & Goldstein, C. (1986). Effects of listening to series stories of first graders comprehension and use of language. *Research in the Teaching of English, 20*, 339–356.

Findahl, O., & Hoijer, B. (1985). Some characteristics of news memory and comprehension. *Journal of Broadcasting & Electronic Media, 29*(4), 379–396.

Fish, S., Shulman, J., Ackerman, A., & Levin, G. (2002). Reading between the pixels; Parent-child interaction while reading online story books. *Early Education & Development, 13*(4), 435–451.

Foerde, K., Poldrack, R., & Knowlton, B. (2007). Secondary-task effects on classification learning. *Memory & Cognition, 35*(5), 864–874.

Gorlick, A. (2009, August 24). Media multitaskers pay heavy price. *Stanford University News*, p. 4.

Greaney, V. (1980). Factors related to amount and type of leisure reading. *Reading Research Quarterly, 15*, 337–357.

Grineau, J. (1997). Comic books and the mythic pattern. In *Comic book conundrum* (issue 3). Retrieved April 11, 2010, from http://www .sideroad.com/comics/column3.html

Higgins, N. C., & Cocks, P. (1999). The effects of animation cues on vocabulary development. *Reading Psychology, 20*(1), 1–10

Johnson, A., Martin, A., Brooks-Gunn, J., & Petrill, S. (2008). Order in the house! Associations among household chaos, the home literacy environment, maternal reading ability, and children's early reading. *Merrill-Palmer Quarterly, 54*(4), 445–472.

Kaiser Family Foundation. (2005). *Generation M: Media in the lives of 8-18 year olds*. Retrieved March 21, 2010, from http://www.kff.org/ entmedia

Kamil, M. L. (2003). Reading for the 21st century: Adolescent literature teaching and learning strategies. *Alliance for Excellent Education*. Retrieved March 7, 2010, from http://www .all4ed.org/files/Reading_21stCentury.pdf

Kim, J., & Guryan, J. (2010). The efficacy of a voluntary summer book reading intervention for low-income Latino children from language minority families. *Journal of Educational Psychology, 102*(1), 20–31.

Korat, O., & Shamir, A. (2008). The educational electronic book as a tool for supporting children's emergent literacy in low versus middle SES groups. *Computers & Education, 50*(1), 110–124.

Leshner, G., & Coyle, J. R. (2000). Memory for television news: Match and mismatch between processing and testing. *Journal of Broadcasting & Electronic Media, 44*(4), 599–612.

Leu, D. J. (2007a, May). *What happened when we weren't looking? How reading comprehension has changed and what we need to do about it.* Paper presented to the International Reading Association's Research Conference, Toronto, Ontario, Canada.

Leu, D. J. (2007b, April). *The new literacies of online reading comprehension: Preparing all students for their reading.* Presentation to Pearson Education's Instructional Leadership Council, San Diego, CA. Retrieved April 2, 2010, from http://www.newliteracies.uconn .edu/events.html

Levy, S. (2006, March). (Some) attention must be paid. *Newsweek*, p. 22.

Marwick, C. (1997). Rising care costs due to patients' lack of literacy. *Journal of the American Medical Association, 278*(12), 971–973.

McCoy, D. (1991, May). *Surveys of independent reading: Pinpointing the problems, seeking the solutions.* Paper presented at the annual meeting of the College Reading Association, Crystal City, VA. (ERIC Document Reproduction Service No. ED238692)

Mendez, J. (2010). How can parents get involved in preschool? Barriers and engagement in education by ethnic minority parents of children attending Head Start. *Cultural Diversity and Ethnic Minority Psychology, 16*(1), 26–36.

Meyer, L., Stahl, S. A., Wardrop, J., & Linn, R. (1994). Effects of reading storybooks aloud to children. *Journal of Educational Research, 88,* 69–85.

Mitchell, M. J., & Fox, B. J. (2001). The effects of computer software for developing phonological awareness in low-progress readers. *Reading Research and Instruction, 40*(4), 315–332.

Morrow, L. M. (1983). Home and school correlates of early interest in literature. *Journal of Educational Research, 76,* 221–230.

Morrow, L. M., & Weinstein, C. (1986). Encouraging voluntary reading: The impact of a literature program on children's use of library centers. *Reading Research Quarterly, 21*(3), 330–346.

Moss, B., & Fawcett, G. (1995). Bringing the curricula of the world of the home to the school. *Reading and Writing Quarterly, 11,* 247–256.

Myrberg, E., & Rosen, M (2009). Direct and indirect effects of parents' education on reading achievement among third graders in Sweden. *British Journal of Educational Psychology, 79*(4), 695–711.

Nagy, E. (2009, April 6). Multi-platform Mackenzie Blue arrives. *Publishers Weekly,* 14.

National Assessment of Adult Literacy. (2003). *Literacy behind bars: Results from the national assessment of adult literacy.* Washington, DC: U.S. Department of Education. Retrieved March 10, 2010, from http://nces.ed.gov/naal/ fct_prison.asp

National Endowment for the Arts. (2007). *To read or not to read: A question of national consequence.* Washington, DC: NEA.

Nipold, M., Duthie, J., & Larson, J. (2005). Literacy as a leisure activity: Free-time preferences of older children and young adolescents. *Language, Speech, and Hearing Services in Schools, 36*(2), 93–102.

Ophir, E., Nass, C., & Wagner, A. D. (2009). Cognitive control in media multitaskers. *Proceedings of the National Academy of Sciences, 106*(37), 15583–15587.

Parkhurst, H. (2008). Engaging male adolescents in reading: Humor in young adult fiction. *The Charter Schools Resource Journal, 5,* 11–16.

Perry, N. J. (1988, November 7). Saving the schools: How business can help. *Fortune,* 42–47

Pew Research Center for People and the Press. (2010). *What Americans know: 1989–2007.* Retrieved April 29, 2010, from http://people-press.org/report/319/public-knowledge-of-current-affairs-little-changed-by-news-and-information-revolutions

Project for Excellence in Journalism. (2006). The state of the news media 2006. Retrieved February 20, 2010, from http://www.stateofthe newsmedia.org/2006

Publications International (2011). Twenty best-selling children's books of all time. Retrieved April 7, 2011, from http://www.howstuff works.com/arts/literature/20-best-selling-childrens-books-of-all-time.htm

Rich, M. (2008, July 27). Literacy debate: Online, r u really reading? *New York Times,* pp. A1.

Rideout, V. J., Foehr, U. G., & Roberts, D. F. (2010). *Generation M2: Media in the lives of 8 to 18 year olds.* Palo Alto: The Kaiser Foundation.

Roberts, D. F., Ulla, G. F., Rideout, V. J., & Brodie, M. (1999). *Kids and media at the new millennium.* Palo Alto: The Kaiser Foundation.

Scholastic & Yankelovich (2008). *The 2008 kids and family reading report.* Retrieved March 11, 2010, from http://www.scholastic.com/about scholastic/news/readingreport.htm

Sénéchal, M., & LeFevre, J. (2002). Parental involvement in the development of children's reading skill: A 5-year longitudinal study. *Child Development, 73,* 445–460.

Sénéchal, M., & Young, L. (2008).The effect of family literacy interventions on children's acquisition of reading from kindergarten to grade 3: A meta-analytic review. *Review of Educational Research, 78*(8), 880–907.

Sherr, S. (2005). News for a new generation. Retrieved July 9, 2010, from www.civicyouth .org/PopUps/WorkingPapers/WP29Sherr.pdf

Singer, D. G., & Singer, J. L. (1990). *The house of make-believe: Children's play and the developing imagination.* Cambridge, MA: Harvard University Press.

Snow, C., Burns, M., & Griffin, P. (1998). *Preventing reading difficulties in young children*. Washington, DC: National Academy Press.

Stanovich, K. E., & Cunningham, A. E. (1993). Where does knowledge come from? Specific associations between print exposure and information acquisition. *Journal of Educational Psychology, 85*(2), 211–229.

Stauffer, J., Frost, R., & Rybolt, W. (1981). Recall and learning from broadcast News: Is print better? *Journal of Broadcasting, 25,* 251–262,

Steinberg, L. (1996). *Beyond the classroom: Why school reform has failed and what parents need to do*. New York: Touchstone.

Step, C. S. (2003). What they like. *American Journalism Review, 25*(8), 18–24.

Sullivan, M. (2004). Why Johnny won't read. *School Library Journal, 50*(8), 36–39.

Taboada, A., & Guthrie, J. T. (2006). Contributions of student questioning and prior knowledge to construction of knowledge from reading information text. *Journal of Literacy Research, 38,* 1–35.

Teale, W. H. (1995). Young children and reading: Trends across the twentieth century. *Journal of Education, 177*(9), 5–128.

Torkington, N. (2006). E-tech: Linda Stone. O'Reilly Radar. Retrieved April 8, 2011, from http://radar.oreilly.com/archives/2006/03/etech-linda-stone-1.html

Trelease, J. (1995). *The read-aloud handbook*. New York: Penguin Books.

Trelease, J. (2006). *The read-aloud handbook*. (5th ed.). New York: Penguin Books.

U.S. Department of Education. (1985). *Becoming a nation of readers: A compendium of research on reading and academic achievement*. Washington, DC: U.S. Department of Education.

U.S. Department of Education. (2006). *The condition of education 2006*. Washington, DC: U.S. Department of Education, National Center for Education Statistics.

Valby, K. (2008, July 31). Stephenie Meyer: Inside the "Twilight" saga. *Entertainment Weekly,* 12–15.

Verhallen, M., & Bus, A. (2010). Low-income immigrant pupils learning vocabulary through digital picture storybooks. *Journal of Educational Psychology, 102*(1), 54–61

Weber, C., & Cavanaugh, T. (2006). Promoting reading: Using eBooks with gifted and advanced readers. *Gifted Child Today, 29*(4), 56–63

Weigel, D., Martin, S., & Bennett, K. (2010). Pathways to literacy: Connections between family assets and preschool children's emergent literacy skills. *Journal of Early Childhood Research, 8*(1), 5–22.

Wood, C., Pillinger, C., & Jackson, E. (2010). Understanding the nature and impact of young readers' literacy interactions with talking books and during adult reading support. *Computers & Education, 54*(1), 190–198.

World Association of Newspapers. (2008). *Annual report 2007–2008*. Göteborg Sweden: Author.

Zender-Merrell, J. (2002). *Kids count in Michigan: Data book 2002. County profiles of child and family well-being*. Report to the Annie E. Casey Foundation. Retrieved April 29, 2010, from http://www.aecf.org/KnowledgeCenter/Publications.aspx?pubguid={EA2CBD17-BE56-4FDF-93A8-50A2421A1A55}

CHAPTER 3

Children and New Technologies

TODD TARPLEY

An Explosion of New Technologies

3:45 P.M. Johnnie arrives home from grade school. On the bus ride home he sent 15 text messages; he sent four more between the bus stop and his front door. Once at home, he parks himself in front of the TV—and in front of his laptop computer with Internet access—in the family room. His mobile phone remains in his hand, receiving more text messages. Johnnie's own voice informs him that he has email. (Last week, he chose the voice of his favorite pro wrestler, "Violent Vinnie," and the week before that the female star of the top-rated TV show *Nude Beach*.) Fifteen new email messages today: nine invitations to visit porn websites, five offers for medical prescriptions from Canada, and—at last!—a personal reply from the convicted serial killer Johnnie met last month in an online chat room.

Turning his attention momentarily to the TV, Johnnie notes that the DVR automatically recorded three TV shows it thinks Johnnie might like based on his past preferences: *Co-Ed Ultimate Fighting* from the Pro Wrestling Channel, an R-rated movie (*Fraternity Bloodbath*) from HBO 12, and the latest episode of *Nude Beach* in high-def. After previewing each, Johnnie opts to watch them all—while continuing to multitask, of course; if he runs out of time, he'll watch the highlights of *Nude Beach* online. Before he can settle in for another long evening of interactive entertainment, he receives another text message from his classmate: "Hmwrk done: got book rprts frm TermPapers.com & sent to yr email :)"

Mass media continue to evolve at breakneck speed. Over the past decade, new devices and formats have entered the fray, from time-shifted television to video-and-Internet-enabled mobile phones to iPods and iPads. Rather than replacing TV, these new devices are adding to children's overall media consumption. Over the past five years, young people aged 8 to 18 have increased the amount of time they spend consuming media by over an hour a day: from 6 hours, 21 minutes to 7 hours, 38 minutes. Because they multitask, they consume a total of 10 hours and 45 minutes worth of media content into those daily 7½ hours—an increase of almost 2¼ hours of media exposure per day. This does not include time spent texting on mobile phones, which would add considerably to the total (Rideout, Foehr, & Roberts, 2010). Younger people tend to be particularly adept at multitasking: A recent study showed that younger generations multitask more than older generations, and they find multitasking to be easier (Carrier, Cheever, Rosen, Benitez, & Change, 2009).

What New Technologies Mean for Children

Will our children's futures be made better or worse by new technology? Technological advancements have both positive and negative repercussions. Greater accessibility to information means that children have the world at their fingertips. Books and documents from distant libraries are available instantaneously. Classrooms in different states—or countries—can communicate with each other in real time. Educators can share knowledge with peers or parents easily and instantly. Materials for homeschooling parents are easily accessible and often free. And websites created specifically for educators and special-interest groups facilitate the transfer of information in new ways. The online phone program, Skype, allows users to talk while seeing each other on the computer screen. Skype requires a computer with a camera and an Internet connection in order to receive and send moving pictures.

This chapter offers a brief overview of various new media technologies and discusses the available evidence or needed research addressing the role of new media in influencing the cognitive, social, behavioral, emotional, and physical development of the growing child.

Television

Not so long ago, if someone said, "I'm watching a show," it meant they were in their living room watching television. Now it could just as well mean any of the following:

- "I'm watching a TV show in the backseat of a minivan on the way to the mall."
- "I'm watching a compilation of clips from various TV shows on my iPod at the beach."
- "I'm watching an original Web series on YouTube on my iPad on an airplane."

- "I'm watching a video on my Xbox created by someone I've never met, in response to a video I created yesterday, while texting about it with a friend."

Despite this plethora of new options, traditional television viewing continues to dominate video consumption. Children 2 to 11 spend just over 25 hours a week watching traditional TV, 1 hour and 30 minutes watching time-shifted TV (recorded and played back at a later time), 24 minutes using the Internet, and 4 minutes watching video on the Internet. Younger children (ages 2–5) now spend more than 32 hours a week on average in front of a TV screen. Slightly older children (ages 6–11) spend about 28 hours per week watching TV ("TV Viewing," 2009). Teens spend less time than younger children watching traditional TV and more time on the Internet. However, their TV usage still far out-paces their Internet usage: over 100 hours a month of television versus only 11 hours 30 minutes of Internet. And they are watching more TV than ever (Nielsen, 2009c).

The increase in TV viewing may be driven in part by increased convenience (Digital Video Recorders), improved quality of the experience (high-definition and flat-screen TVs), and more channels.

Digital Television and High-Definition Television

Standard broadcast television is transmitted "over the air" via a spectrum of radio frequencies. Digital television (DTV) is a transmission standard that uses the existing broadcast spectrum more efficiently. This enables broadcasters to offer television with better picture and sound quality and additional programming choices, called multicasting. Since June 13, 2009, all full-power U.S. television stations have broadcast over-the-air signals in digital only.

High-definition television (HDTV) is a form of DTV that offers improved picture and sound quality. It uses a wide-screen format and requires an HDTV-enabled television set. Digital technology affects cable and satellite television in much the same way as broadcast television. By digitally compressing the video signal, even more channels are made available to subscribers. One third of U.S. homes now have at least one HD television set. When households add an HD television set, they often retain their old, non-HD set for other uses (e.g., video gaming, DVD viewing). This adds to the availability of media in the household (Nielsen, 2009a). More programming options and better technical quality may be a factor in the recent increase in television viewing across all age groups; if so, the impact may be greater as penetration of HDTV increases.

Digital Video Recorders

Digital Video Recorders (DVRs) allow television viewers to pause, rewind, and replay programs in real time, as well as to record programs for future playback (time-shifting). In addition, DVRs are capable of "learning" their owner's viewing preferences. For example, a DVR in a household that watches a lot of children's programming will automatically record children's programming,

then "suggest" it to the viewer when the television is turned on. DVRs can be either stand-alone set-top devices, like TiVo, or built into the cable TV box.

DVRs are now in over a third of U.S. homes, with usage up 25% in the past year (Nielsen, 2009c). Children 2 to 11 now spend 1 hour and 30 minutes each week watching time-shifted TV. That comprises about 5% of their total TV time, which has increased since the inception of DVRs ("TV Viewing," 2009). Children comprise 14% of the broadcast TV viewing audience, but 25% of the DVR audience, indicating their relatively heavy usage of DVRs (Nielsen VideoCensus, 2009).

The primary impacts of the DVR are more viewer control of the television viewing experience, less reliance on network scheduling, and less viewing of television commercials. This can raise the quality of TV time while avoiding conflicts with family activities. The ability to bypass commercials potentially reduces the amount of commercial messages seen by children. However, the convenience of DVRs may lead to even more television viewing.

| Figure 3.1 | Percentage of Media Viewing Audiences by Age |

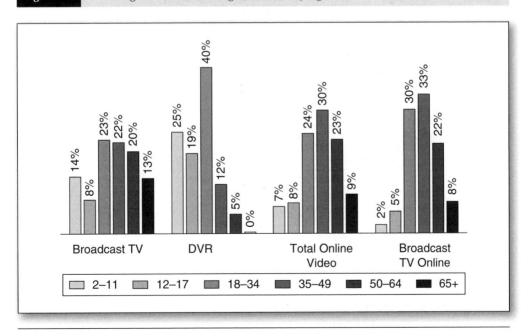

Source: Nielsen VideoCensus, Combined Home and Work. Npower Live + 7 12/1-12/31/09.

Mobile

Twenty percent of media consumption among young people ages 8 to 18 (over 2 hours a day) occurs on mobile devices—cell phones, iPods, or handheld video game players. Over the past five years, the proportion of 8- to 18-year-olds who own their own mobile phone has grown from 39% to 66%. The proportion with iPods or other MP3 players increased even more dramatically, jumping from 18% to 76% (Rideout et al., 2010). The age at which children and teens receive their first mobile phone has consistently grown younger. In 2004, 18% of 12-year-olds and 64% of 17-year-olds owned a mobile phone. In 2009, 58% of 12-year-olds and 83% of 17-year-olds owned a mobile phone (Lenhart, 2009).

Texting

Texting, also known as *text messaging,* refers to sending a short text message via mobile phone to another mobile phone user. Texting is also used to enter contests or promotions, to vote in online or TV polls, and by advertisers to send promotional messages to mobile phone owners. Photos or short videos can also be embedded in text messages.

In technical jargon, texting is sometimes referred to as SMS (for Short Messaging Service). Texting that includes embedded photos or videos is sometimes referred to as MMS (for Multimedia Messaging Service). Texting is by far the most popular feature of mobile phones among teens. Eighty-three percent of U.S. mobile teens use text messaging, and 56% use picture messaging (Nielsen, 2009b).

| Figure 3.2 | Most Popular Mobile Features Used by Teens |

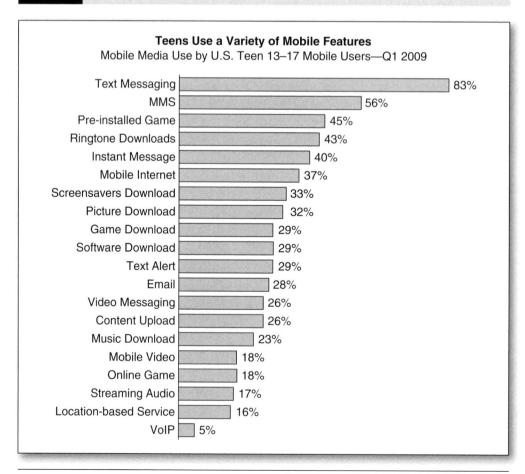

Teens Use a Variety of Mobile Features
Mobile Media Use by U.S. Teen 13–17 Mobile Users—Q1 2009

Feature	Percent
Text Messaging	83%
MMS	56%
Pre-installed Game	45%
Ringtone Downloads	43%
Instant Message	40%
Mobile Internet	37%
Screensavers Download	33%
Picture Download	32%
Game Download	29%
Software Download	29%
Text Alert	29%
Email	28%
Video Messaging	26%
Content Upload	26%
Music Download	23%
Mobile Video	18%
Online Game	18%
Streaming Audio	17%
Location-based Service	16%
VoIP	5%

Source: The Nielsen Company.

The average U.S. mobile teen sent or received an average of 2,899 text messages per month in 2009, compared to 191 calls. The average number of texts has increased 566% in just two years, while calls have declined slightly (Nielsen, 2009b).

Subsequent research indicates that texting among teens has continued to increase, to more than 3,500 text messages a month by the end of 2009 ("Big Screen, Small Screen," 2009).

To illustrate the phenomenon, a 17-year-old boy, caught sending text messages in class, was sent to the vice principal's office. The vice principal told the boy he needed to focus on the teacher, not on his cell phone. The boy listened politely and nodded; then the vice principal noticed the student's fingers moving on his lap. He was texting while being reprimanded for texting (Zaslow, 2009).

Sexting

Sexting is the sending of nude or seminude photos via a mobile phone. Photos are taken using the built-in camera feature of the phone and then embedded as a text message.

According to the Pew Research Center's Internet & American Life Project, 15% of U.S. teens ages 12 to 17 with mobile phones report having received nude or nearly nude photos by text message. Four percent say they have sent sexually suggestive nude or seminude photos of themselves to someone else via text messaging (Lenhart, 2009).

Sexting generally takes place between people who are in a relationship, or when at least one person hopes to be. Sometimes exchanges of images are then shared with others, either with or without the consent of the original sender. Girls and boys are equally likely to have sent a suggestive picture to another person. Older teens are much more likely to send and receive these images: 8% of 17-year-olds have sent a sexually provocative image via cell phone, compared to 4% of 12-year-olds (Lenhart, 2009).

Child pornography laws vary from state to state, but most are directed at preventing adults from exploiting children. These laws are often not aimed at preventing youth from sharing images among themselves. This has created a new area of concern for parents and legal officials. Among recent incidents, a Maryland middle school student allegedly rented his iPod to classmates, who clicked through images of female classmates and other girls in various states of undress. In Virginia, a 12-year-old and 14-year-old were arrested for sending each other naked images and video (Johnson, 2010).

Figure 3.3 Average Number of Monthly Texts and Phone Calls by U.S. Mobile Teens 13–17

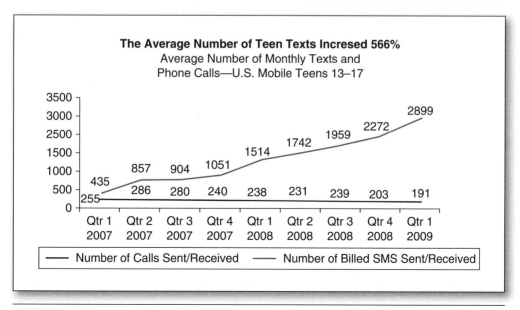

Mobile Video

Mobile video use is increasing rapidly: from 11 million users in 2008 to almost 18 million in 2009 (Nielsen, 2009c). One in five U.S. teens (13–17) with mobile phones has watched some form of video content on the phone. Teens who watch mobile video watch an average of 6 hours 30 minutes a month, compared to about 3 hours 30 minutes by all other age groups (Nielsen, 2009b).

Almost a third of mobile video content is user generated. As such, the barriers between content creators and consumers are steadily eroding.

Little data are available on mobile video use by preteens, as fewer have mobile phones of their own. Potential effects include increased overall media consumption. If the trend toward younger ownership of mobile devices continues, this concern will become more pronounced.

Other Electronic Devices and New Technologies

Other new devices and technologies have recently entered the market that may impact children's media consumption. These include e-book digital readers (e.g., Kindle); computer tablets (e.g., iPad), which in addition to providing e-books in full-color, provide gaming and access to the Internet; Internet-enabled TVs, which allow for streaming of online content directly to the TV; and low-power radio chips that can pick up signals from any source—broadcast TV, radio, mobile phones.

The common denominator of these new technologies is ever greater accessibility to media. Just as the advent of the transistor led to the portability of radio (followed in subsequent decades by portable TVs and portable

---

Figure 3.4 Top Categories of Online Video

Top Categories Q3 2009			
Rank	Categories	Unique Audience (000s)	Share of Mobile Video Viewers
.	All Categories	15,744	1
1	Comedy	6,557	41.7%
2	Music	5,287	33.6%
3	Weather	5,208	33.1%
4	Sports	4,927	31.3%
5	User-Generated Video Content	4,579	29.1%
6	Movie Trailers	4,517	28.7%
7	News and Finance	4,132	26.2%
8	Entertainment News	3,994	25.4%
9	Animated	3,533	22.4%
10	Reality TV	3,307	21.0%

Source: The Nielsen Company. Q3 2009 Mobile Video Report.

phones), new devices may lead to further intrusion of media into daily lives.

The Internet

Contrary to common perception, children and teens spend less time on the Internet than any other age group. This is largely a function of availability: Adults have greater access during work hours, and older adults have more available leisure hours.

About 20% of younger children (ages 2–5) and almost half of slightly older children (ages 6–11) spend time on the Internet each month ("TV Viewing," 2009). On average, 8- to 18-year-olds spend 1 hour and 30 minutes a day using the computer outside of school work, an increase of almost 30 minutes over the past five years. In the same time period, home Internet access has expanded from 74% to 84% among young people. The quality of Internet access has also improved, with high-speed access increasing from 31% to 59% (Rideout et al., 2010).

Several facets of the Internet are of particular interest to parents and educators: online video, online communities/virtual worlds (also known as social networks), and multiplayer gaming.

Online Video

Children aged 2 to 11 view an average of almost 2 hours of online video each month, while teens (12–17) view slightly more ("Nielsen Data," 2008). However, online viewing does not typically replace TV viewing. Instead, it is generally used to catch up on programs missed, or when the TV is unavailable (Nielsen, 2009c). Online videos include TV shows and clips, independent and short films, and videos created specifically for Internet viewing, either by professional producers or directly by users. YouTube remains the most popular online video site, generating almost 100 million viewers each month.

Implications for children include easy access to a wide range of video content, both appropriate and inappropriate, and increased overall media usage.

| **Figure 3.5** | Average Monthly Time Spent Using Internet in U.S. |

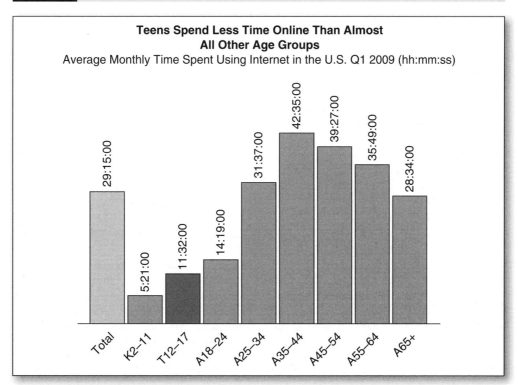

Figure 3.6 Top Online Video Brands

Top 10 U.S. Online Video Brands, Home & Work March 2010			
Rank	Brand	Total Streams (000)	Unique Viewers (000)
1	YouTube	4,672,376	96,075
2	Hulu	707,547	12,196
3	Yahoo!	244,422	30,469
4	MSN/WindowsLive/Bing	170,034	14,828
5	Nickelodeon Kids and Family Network	149,950	5,938
6	CBS Entertainment Network	144,085	6,665
7	Turner Sports and Entertainment Digital Network	141,917	5,588
8	CNN Digital Network	129,721	10,992
9	Blinkx	107,190	419
10	Facebook	104,097	23,339

Source: Nielsen VideoCensus (2010).

Online Communities and Virtual Worlds

Online communities, sometimes referred to as *social networks,* facilitate chat, messaging, and sometimes sharing of personal or professional information among members of a particular demographic or interest group. Seventy-three percent of online teens (12–17) visit social network sites (Lenhart, Purcell, Smith, & Zickuhr, 2010), with MySpace and Facebook being the most popular, each visited by almost half of online teens each month (Zaslow, 2009). Social network participation jumps from 46% at age 12 to 63% at 13, the age at which membership is officially allowed on MySpace and Facebook (Lenhart et al., 2010); a growing number of younger children are flouting minimum age requirements (Gross, 2009).

Virtual worlds are online communities that take the form of a simulated world in which users can interact with each other, often using animated characters called avatars to represent themselves. Online communities for children often adopt this format, which allows for easier interaction than less visual or purely text-based online communities.

Examples of popular virtual worlds for children include Club Penguin (owned by Disney), Webkinz World (associated with Ganz stuffed animals of the same name), and Nicktropolis (owned by Nickelodeon). Other toy brands such as Barbie, Build-a-Bear Workshop, and American Girls also maintain online communities.

Massively multiplayer online games (also called MMOGs) are virtual worlds that encompass a video game aspect. They can support hundreds or thousands of players simultaneously and are played on the Internet. They can also be played on newer game consoles with Internet access, including PlayStation, Xbox, Nintendo DS, and Wii. Fantasy and Sci-fi titles predominate, including current market leader *World of Warcraft,* with more than 11 million monthly subscribers.

Current Research on Effects on Cognitive Development

The American Academy of Pediatrics (AAP) recommends that children's screen time (defined as watching TV and videotapes, playing video and computer games, and surfing the Internet) be limited to no more than 1 to 2 hours a day for older children. Children under the age of 2 should have no screen time (American Academy of Pediatrics, 1999).

Higher amounts of screen time have been associated with lower physical activity rates. Both higher screen time and lower physical activity rates are linked with higher odds of psychological distress, including emotional symptoms, conduct problems, and peer relationship problems (Hamer, Stamatakis, & Mishra, 2009). Too much screen time has also been linked to obesity, irregular sleep, behavioral problems, depression, anxiety, and impaired academic performance ("Children and TV," 2009). A recent study by the Kaiser Family Foundation found a correlation between heavy media exposure and lower academic performance, lower personal contentment, and more frequent boredom (Rideout et al., 2010).

Current Research on Effects on Social, Behavioral, and Emotional Development

Internet use has been linked with a positive influence on self-concept and self-esteem (Jackson et al., 2009). Feedback on social network profiles has been associated with both positive and negative changes in self-esteem; positive feedback from other users had a positive impact, whereas negative feedback had the opposite effect (Valkenburg, Peter, & Schouten, 2006). An example of such feedback is a Facebook page called "Bathroom Stall," which encourages users to post anonymous gossip about others. Like the walls of a real bathroom stall, the comments can be inappropriate, particularly for adolescents.

At the extreme, online harassment—also referred to as *cyber-bullying*—can lead to self-inflicted harm. Recently, nine teens were charged in the bullying of a 14-year-old girl who subsequently committed suicide. In 2006, a 13-year-old girl killed herself after being harassed on MySpace by a neighbor's mother who was posing as a 16-year-old teenage boy. Several other well-publicized instances have followed ("9 Teens Charged," 2010).

Researchers at the University of Maryland reported that college students who voluntarily gave up social media showed signs of withdrawal similar to those of drug addicts going cold turkey ("24 Hours: Unplugged," 2010). A New York City middle school conducted a similar experiment in which students voluntarily gave up instant messaging, chat, texts, and Facebook for two days. The results were more encouraging: The students described their free time as unusually relaxing and expressed surprise at how quickly they finished their homework when undistracted by the hundreds of text messages they normally received (Dominus, 2010).

Current Research on Effects of Physical Health and Safety

The Children's Online Privacy Protection Act requires commercial websites aimed at children to obtain parental permission before collecting personal information from children under 13. However, chat rooms on children's sites are generally accessible to anyone; the anonymity of the Internet means that anyone can claim to be any age or sex.

Pedophiles go online with regularity, not only to visit chat rooms, but to seek tips for getting near children at camps, through foster care, at community gatherings, and at countless other events (Eichenwald, 2006).

Texting is as an increasingly dangerous distraction. The Department of Transportation noted an increase in the use of handheld devices among drivers of all ages, but especially in the youngest drivers—those under 20—carrying a dangerous potential for accidents (U.S. Department of Transportation, 2009). Forty-six percent of teens say they have been distracted behind the wheel due to texting ("Teen Risky Driving Habits, 2007).

The Internet can play a positive role in fostering children's health and safety. Thirty-one percent of online teens get health, dieting, or physical fitness information from the Internet. Seventeen percent of online teens report they use the Internet to gather information about health topics that are hard to discuss with others, such as drug use and sexual health topics (Lenhart et al., 2010). Virtual worlds have been utilized to provide hospitalized or autistic children with a comfortable and safe environment to which they can escape and in which they can interact with others and relieve stress ("Avatars Help Asperger," 2007).

Conclusions and Directions for Future Research

New technologies, like old ones, are simply tools. The extent to which they improve or hinder the cognitive, behavioral, social, and physical aspects of children's lives is ultimately a factor of the way in which they are used. Research on the effects of new technologies is limited by the relative infancy of the technologies themselves. Long-term tracking studies have not yet been possible, and the most relevant questions for study are likely just now being formulated.

The speed at which new media technologies have developed is both encouraging and alarming, and it underscores the need for educators, parents, and researchers to stay abreast of their rapid changes. Although new technologies raise concerns about the cognitive, emotional, social, and physical welfare of children, they also open up the world to positive new ideas and possibilities. Unlocking this vast potential is ultimately the responsibility of educators, parents, and researchers alike.

References

24 hours: Unplugged. (2010). International Center for Media & the Public Agenda, University of Maryland. Retrieved April 16, 2011, from http://withoutmedia.wordpress.com

9 teens charged for unrelenting bullying. (2010, March 29). *CBSNews.com*. Retrieved April 16, 2011, from http://www.cbsnews.com/stories/2010/03/29/national/main6343798.shtml?tag=stack

American Academy of Pediatrics. (1999). *Understanding the impact of media on children and teens* [Brochure]. Elk Grove Village, IL: Author.

Avatars help Asperger Syndrome patients learn to play the game of life. (2007, November 18). *University of Texas at Dallas News Center* [Press Release]. Retrieved April 16, 2011, from http://www.utdallas.edu/news/2007/11/18-003.html

Big screen, small screen, smart screen. (2009, December 15). *NielsenWire*. Retrieved April 16, 2011, from http://blog.nielsen.com/nielsenwire/online_mobile/big-screen-smart-screen-small-screen

Carrier, L., Cheever, N., Rosen, L., Benitez, S., & Change, J. (2009). Multitasking across generations: Multitasking choices and difficulty ratings in three generations of Americans. *Computers in Human Behavior, 25*(2), 483-489.

Children and TV: Limiting your child's screen time. (2009, April 3). *MayoClinic.com*. Mayo Foundation for Medical Education and Research. Retrieved April 16, 2011, from http://www.mayoclinic.com/health/children-and-tv/MY00522

Dominus, S. (2010, April 26). Encouraging the text generation to rediscover its voice. *The New York Times*. Retrieved April 16, 2011, from http://www.nytimes.com/2010/04/27/nyregion/27bigcity.html

Eichenwald, K. (2006, August 21). On the web, pedophiles extend their reach. *The New York Times*. Retrieved April 16, 2011, from http://www.nytimes.com/2006/08/21/technology/21pedo.html

Gross, D. (2009, November 3). Social networks and kids: How young is too young? *CNN.com*. Retrieved April 16, 2011, from http://www.cnn.com/2009/TECH/11/02/kids.social.networks/index.html

Hamer, M., Stamatakis, E., & Mishra, G. (2009). Psychological distress, TV viewing and physical activity in children aged 4-12 yrs. *Pediatrics, 123*(5), 1263–1268.

Jackson, L., Zhao, Y., Witt, E., Fitzgerald, H., von Eye, A., & Harold, R. (2009). Self-concept, self-esteem, gender, race, and technology use. *CyberPsychology & Behavior, 12*(4), 437–440.

Johnson, J. (2010, April 17). Montgomery police are investigating how middle school sexting photos were obtained. *The Washington Post*. Retrieved April 16, 2011, from http://www.washingtonpost.com/wp-dyn/content/article/2010/04/16/AR2010041603657.html

Lenhart, A. (2009). *Teens and sexting*. Washington, DC: Pew Research Center.

Lenhart, A., Purcell, K., Smith, A., & Zickuhr, K. (2010). *Social media & young adults*. Washington, DC: Pew Research Center.

Nielsen. (2009a). *HDTV: The picture is getting clearer* [Analyst report]. New York: Author.

Nielsen. (2009b). *How teens use media* [Analyst report]. New York: Author.

Nielsen. (2009c). *Television, internet, and mobile usage in the U.S.: Three screen report, 4th Quarter, 2009* [Analyst report]. New York: Author.

Nielsen data illuminates habits of the online video generation. (2008, June 13). *NielsenWire*. Retrieved April 16, 2011, from http://blog.niel sen.com/nielsenwire/online_mobile/nielsen-data-illuminates-habits-of-the-%e2%80%9c online-video-generation%e2%80%9d/

Nielsen VideoCensus. (2010). *More than Nine Billion Video Streams Viewed in the U.S. in March.* Retrieved from http://blog.nielsen .com/nielsenwire/online_mobile/more-than-nine-billion-video-streams-viewed-in-the-u-s-in-march/

Rideout, V., Foehr, U., & Roberts, D. (2010). *Generation M²; media in the lives of 8-18-year-olds*. Menlo Park, CA: Kaiser Family Foundation.

Teen risky driving habits include text messaging behind the wheel. (2007, July 10). *AAA NewsRoom*. Retrieved November 1, 2010, from http://www.aaanewsroom.net/main/ Default.asp?CategoryID=7&ArticleID=554

TV viewing among kids at eight-year high. (2009, October 26). *NielsenWire*. Retrieved April 16, 2011 from http://blog.nielsen.com/nielsen-wire/media_entertainment/tv-viewing-among-kids-at-an-eight-year-high

U.S. Department of Transportation. (2009, September 30). *Transportation secretary Ray LaHood kicks off historic summit to tackle dangers of distracted driving* [Press release]. Washington, DC: Author. Retrieved April 16, 2011, from http://www.dot.gov/affairs/2009/ dot15509.htm

Valkenburg, P., Peter, J., & Schouten, A. (2006). Friend networking sites and their relationship to adolescents' well-being and social self-esteem. *CyberPsychology & Behavior, 9*(5), 584–590.

Zaslow, J. (2009, November 5). The greatest generation (of networkers). *The Wall Street Journal*. Retrieved April 16, 2011, from http:// online.wsj.com/article/SB100014240527487 04746304574505643153518708.html

CHAPTER 4

Digital Media and Youth

Games, Internet, and Development

KAVERI SUBRAHMANYAM AND PATRICIA GREENFIELD
California State University, Los Angeles &
Children's Digital Media Center @ Los Angeles

Acknowledgement

We thank Bob Kraut for his comments on an earlier draft of this chapter.

Digital Media and Youth: Games, Internet, and Development

Digital media such as computers, interactive games, the Internet, cell phones, and other handheld devices have become an integral part of the media landscape surrounding young people. According to some estimates, 93% of U.S. children between 12 and 17 years of age are online (Jones & Fox, 2009); 87% of 8- to 18-year-olds in the United States live in a home with at least one video game console (Rideout, Foehr, & Roberts, 2010); and 79% of 13- to 19-years old have a mobile device (Harris Interactive, 2008). This was not always the case. In 1994, 39% of American households with children had personal computers; by 1999, this had jumped to over 60% for married couples with children (Roberts, Foehr, Rideout, & Brodie, 1999; Turow & Nir, 2000). In 2004, 86% of 8- to 18-year-olds in the United States lived in a home with at least one computer. Time with these different entertainment media has similarly been increasing over the years. According to the 2010 Kaiser report, youth in the United States spend approximately 7 hours and 38 minutes daily using a variety of entertainment media. Because of the multi-tasking nature of their media use, in actuality, they consume 10 hours and 45 minutes of media content during this time (Rideout et al., 2010). Apart from television and music/audio content, which are not the focus in this chapter, computers and video games are the two major media forms that young people access and interact with. In the results of the Kaiser report, respondents reported that outside of school work, they used the computer for 1 hour and 29 minutes per day to go online and access various applications and games; in addition, they reported spending an average of 1 hour and 13 minutes playing games on a variety of platforms (e.g., consoles, handheld systems, etc.). Online communication applications, such as email and instant messaging, and social networking sites, such as MySpace and Facebook, are popular among youth (Subrahmanyam & Greenfield, 2008a).

It is important to point out at the start that even more now than at previous times, distinctions between hardware and software are getting blurred as youth are able to use a range of hardware tools to access a variety of functions such as searching for information and entertainment, playing games, and importantly, interacting and communicating with each other. For instance, interactive games can be played on a variety of platforms, including consoles (such as the Nintendo Wii or the Xbox), stand-alone computers, handheld devices such as the PS2 or cell phones, and the Internet. Similarly, online applications such as email and instant messaging can be accessed on a desktop, laptop, or smart phone. As the lines between hardware and content are getting blurred, it is more meaningful to focus on the various digital applications rather than the particular hardware that supports them (Subrahmanyam & Smahel, 2010). Our goal here is to examine young people's informal, out of school use of these technologies and their implications for development. Accordingly, we focus here broadly on interactive games and the Internet, regardless of the particular platforms that may be used to access them.

Demographics and the Digital Divide

Although it has narrowed, there continues to be a digital divide based on parental education, family income, and race/ethnicity with regard to the presence of a home computer

and access to the Internet. By the end of 1998, 88% of American adults with family incomes greater than $75,000 reported owning a personal computer, compared to 47% with incomes between $30,000 and $50,000, and only 19% with family incomes less than $20,000. In homes with children from 2 to 18, 78% of European American respondents reported a family computer, whereas only 55% of African American and 48% of Hispanic respondents did so (Roberts et al., 1999). In 2010, according to the Pew Report, only 70% of youth in households with annual household incomes less than $30,000 had a home computer, compared to 92% in households with higher incomes (Lenhart, Ling, Campbell, & Purcell, 2010). According to the 2010 Kaiser report, computer ownership ranged from 87% among youth whose parents had a high school education to 97% among those whose parents were college graduates (Rideout et al., 2010). Similarly, online access and time on computers tends to be strongly correlated with income and education (Roberts et al., 1999; Stanger, 1998); for instance, previously, 12% of families with annual incomes under $30,000 subscribed to the Internet, compared to 61.1% of families with annual incomes over $75,000 (Stanger, 1998). Although Internet access among youth has become relatively high across all ethnic groups, the 2010 Kaiser report reveals a range of 74% among Latinos, 78% among Blacks, and 88% among European Americans; furthermore it is 74% among those whose parents have a high school education and 91% among those with college educated parents (Rideout et al., 2010).

There are also other demographic differences in young people's use of technologies and consumption of media content that are deserving of attention. Previously, stand-alone video game platforms did not vary systematically with income and race (Roberts et al., 1999), leading us to speculate that they may be the most democratic means for spreading computer literacy (Greenfield, 1994; Subrahmanyam, Kraut, Greenfield, & Gross, 2001). Our speculation turned out to have some truth because in the 2010 Kaiser report, Latino (1 hour 35 minutes) and African American (1 hour 25 minutes) youth reported spending more time playing video games across all platforms compared to European

American youth (56 minutes). Equally important, African American and Latino youth consume almost 4 hours and 30 minutes more media per day than do European American youth, and the difference is greatest for television content.

Finally, there are interesting differences in how youth access the Internet and what sites they may access while online. Forty-one percent of teens from households with annual incomes less than $30,000 report using their cell phones to access the Internet. Among teens from low-income households, 44% of African American, 35% of Latino, and 21% of European American youth use cell phones to access the Internet (Lenhart et al., 2010). Similarly, in the Kaiser report, African American (1 hour 28 minutes) and Latino (1 hour 4 minutes) youth report using cell phones to access media content (music, games, and television) at much higher rates than European American (26 minutes) youth. With regard to the kinds of sites accessed online, there are indications that, compared to European Americans, Latinos are more likely to use MySpace (Hargittai, 2007; Subrahmanyam, Reich, Waechter, & Espinoza, 2008).

Gender is another important demographic variable that is relevant to understanding young people's use of interactive media. In the early years, there was a big gender gap in video game playing—boys played video games more often and spent more time playing (Dominick, 1984; Linn & Lepper, 1987). Indeed, video arcades, which were the primary means of accessing this technology at the time, were well known to be male preserves (Kiesler, Sproull, & Eccles, 1985). With the advent of newer technologies, including handheld games, the Internet, and games for mobile phones, the gender gap has remained in some aspects of technology use, but it has been erased, and, at times, even reversed in other areas. One aspect that has remained the same is gaming: In the Kaiser report, boys were exposed to an hour more of media each day (11 hours 12 minutes vs. 10 hours 17 minutes), partly because they spend more time on computers, primarily playing games (25 minutes vs. 8 minutes) and watching videos on sites such as YouTube (17 minutes vs. 12 minutes). With regard to online use, there are no gender differences in time spent on email, instant messaging, visiting websites, graphics/photos, and reading newspapers/magazines. However, girls spend more time on social networking sites (25 minutes vs. 19 minutes). Although both genders were equally likely (40%) to visit the sites, girls reported spending more time (1 hour 1 minute vs. 47 minutes); girls also spend more time—both texting and calling—with cell phones (Rideout et al., 2010). In our chapter in the first edition of this volume, we speculated that girls may be getting socialized with the Internet at an earlier age, and that the social nature of online applications might appeal more to preteen girls than to preteen boys (Subrahmanyam et al., 2001). While these data do not speak to whether girls are getting socialized with the Internet at earlier ages compared to boys, they certainly do indicate that the social applications of the Internet appeal to girls and have helped to erase the gender gap in at least one form of technology use.

Understanding the Influence of Digital Media on Development

To understand the influence of games on development, we start with Vygotsky's (1978) sociocultural theory, which posits that the context and, in particular, tools provided by the culture play a mediating role in development. Some cultural tools that Vygotsky considered to be important for the development of higher mental functions included the abacus, language, and mathematics. Drawing on Tikhomirov (1974) and Salomon (1979), we have extended this idea in prior work and posited that different cultural tools elicit and develop different sets of cognitive skills. Computers, digital games, and the Internet are the newest cultural tools in technological societies, and they will likely influence the development of thinking and learning (Greenfield, 1994; Maynard, Subrahmanyam, & Greenfield, 2005). Within this theoretical framework, there are at least three potential pathways through which digital media might influence development (Subrahmanyam, 2009).

The first pathway is based on the idea that time with digital media not only involves time spent on that particular activity, but presumably time away from other potentially more valuable activities—a proposal called the time displacement hypothesis (Nie & Hillygus, 2002). For children, time with computer games and the Internet could take away from book reading, engaging in physical activities, and interacting face-to-face with friends and family members. The second and third pathways stem from the nature of interactive media themselves. In prior work, we proposed that in order to understand the influence of a particular media form on thinking and learning, we had to distinguish among the *physical platform or hardware* (i.e., television, computer, or video game system), *formal features* (i.e., audio visual production features that characterize a medium), and the *content* (i.e., the topic or focus of a game or online site) within it (Subrahmanyam & Greenfield, 2008b).

The second pathway of digital media influence is via its *formal features*, which are the symbolic and representational systems that it uses—for instance, enactive (action-based representations), iconic (image-based representations), or symbolic (symbol-based representations) (Bruner, Olver, & Greenfield, 1966)—and that the user has to decode to grasp the message. Consequently, repeated use of a media form will likely lead to internalization of the skills utilized by it and influence the development of those particular representational skills (Salomon, 1979).

The third pathway of influence involves *media content*, which consists of the message conveyed by the formal features. With regard to games, content could involve the particular topic area (math, history, science, or fantasy) or themes such as aggression. In online contexts, content could similarly include aggressive, prosocial, or academic themes. Just as we expect particular formal features of media to mediate development, message content in digital media may also influence development.

In addition to the preceding three pathways, a fourth pathway of influence involves the *communication environment* within online contexts such as social networking sites, games, and virtual worlds. Features of online contexts that may be relevant for development include the potential for anonymity; disembodied users; ease of interaction; lack of face-to-face cues, including eye contact and gestures; as well as the potential for contact with strangers (Subrahmanyam & Greenfield, 2008a). For instance, the potential for anonymity and the lack of readily available information about the body (e.g., age, gender, etc.) in contexts such as games and virtual worlds may have implications for identity development and social interaction. In the next sections, we will take into account each of these pathways as we examine the implications of interactive games and the Internet for development.

Interactive Games

As we have already noted, interactive games can be played on a variety of platforms, including video game systems (e.g., Nintendo Wii, X Box), computers, the Internet, and handheld devices such as portable game systems (Nintendo DS, PS2) and mobile phones. Following Roberts et al. (1999), we will refer to games played on game systems as video games, games on the computer as computer games, and games played via the Internet as online games; the term *interactive games* will be used to refer to all three types of games. Video games were among the earliest forms of interactive media that were widely used by youth (Subrahmanyam & Greenfield, 1994). Interactive gaming has increased in popularity in the last five years; however, much of this increase has been because of the increased popularity of gaming via cell phones and handheld devices. On average, youth spend about 1 hour and 13 minutes playing interactive games; on a given day, 60% report playing games—47% on a handheld device and 39% on a console player. Those who do play on a given day report spending approximately 2 hours per day on interactive game playing across all platforms (Rideout et al., 2010). As with other digital media forms, interactive gaming varies as a function of age (11- to 14-year-olds spend the most amount of time), race/ethnicity (Latino and African American youth spend more time than European American youth), and gender (boys spend more time than girls, and among players, boys spend more time at the controller than girls).

Does Time Spent With Interactive Games Replace Other Activities?

Because of the difficulties involved in obtaining accurate estimates of young people's media use, we can not say whether computer game playing replaces other activities such as television watching, reading, and physical activities. In recent years, concerns have been raised that sedentary activities such as game playing may be associated with well-documented increases in youth obesity. This is of particular concern among young children, whose first exposure to technology is via computer and video games (Rideout, Vandewater, & Wartella, 2003). A study of 922 Swiss elementary school children found a twofold increase in the risk of obesity for every hour spent playing electronic games (Stettler, Singer, & Sutter, 2004). However, another study, based on a national sample of 2,831 U.S. children younger than 12 years, did not find a linear relation between television viewing and obesity. Instead, they found a U-shaped relationship between obesity and time spent playing electronic games: Children with higher weights reported spending moderate amounts of time playing games, whereas children with lower weights played either a lot or very little (Vandewater, Shim, & Caplovitz, 2004). Thus, the relation between computer games and obesity is not entirely straightforward.

Another activity that may get replaced by interactive gaming is sleep, and there is evidence that children with a gaming computer in their room go to bed later on weekdays; those who spend more time playing computer games go to sleep later on weekdays and weekends and get up later on weekends (Van den Bulck, 2004). Van den Bulck (2004) suggests that the problem might stem from the fact that game playing is an unstructured activity with no firm start and end times and that setting time limits might help counteract the associated sleep loss. Especially as youth get older, and as they enter adolescence, reduced sleep may be associated with a variety of other problems, such as depression, school and academic problems, and even driving accidents (Subrahmanyam & Smahel, 2010).

Regardless of whether time spent playing interactive games replaces other activities, media use may be associated with school grades and psychological adjustment. The 1999 Kaiser report found a significant negative correlation between video game playing and feelings of contentment and adjustment:

The lowest average adjustment scores were received by children and adolescents who reported spending the most time on video games (Roberts et al., 1999). The 2010 Kaiser report found a negative relation between media use and grades and between media use and personal contentment (Rideout et al., 2010). Because media use was collapsed across all media forms, we do not know the particular role of video games in this relationship. More generally, because of the correlational nature of the data, we do not know to what extent game playing or media use in general is a constructive outlet for relatively maladjusted young people versus to what extent it was a causal factor in the maladjustment.

Excessive time spent playing computer and online games is also a concern. For a small minority of youth, such extreme game playing may even be considered a form of addiction. In one large survey of online gamers, the game playing of approximately 12% of respondents met the diagnostic criteria of an addiction (Grüsser, Thalemann, & Griffiths, 2006). We know that adolescents with addictive behavior on the Internet also have problems in other aspects of their lives, including academics (a drop in grades, avoiding school), family relations (conflicts and having to hide their excessive Internet use from parents), physical health (sleep deprivation), mental health (depression), financial (Internet expenses), substance abuse, and cyberbullying (Chou, Condron, & Belland, 2005; Griffiths, 2000; Ko et al., 2006; Kraut et al., 1998; Kubey, Lavin, & Barrows, 2001; Subrahmanyam & Smahel, 2010; Tsai & Lin, 2003; Young, 1998); we would expect similar consequences for excessive game playing.

Interactive Games and the Development of Cognitive Skills

The second pathway of media influence, described earlier, suggests that the formal features of media can influence thinking and learning (Subrahmanyam & Greenfield, 2008b). Video games are spatial, iconic, and dynamic, and they have things going on simultaneously in different locations on the screen; these features utilize and have been shown to develop a variety of attentional, spatial, and iconic skills. Because the features are common to computer applications of all kinds, the suite of skills that the games develop constitutes a foundational computer literacy. Next, we summarize the experimental evidence for the role of interactive games in developing the particular attentional, spatial, and iconic representational skills that they utilize.

Practice on a computer game (*Marble Madness*) reliably improved 10-year-olds' spatial performance (e.g., anticipating targets, extrapolating spatial paths) compared to practice on a computerized word game (Subrahmanyam & Greenfield, 1994). Similarly, practice on the computer game *Tetris* (a game which requires the rapid rotation and placement of 7 different-shaped blocks) significantly improved undergraduate students' mental rotation time and spatial visualization time on computerized spatial performance tests (Okagaki & Frensch, 1994). Playing *Tetris* improved mental rotation skills even among 3rd graders, and the effects were especially pronounced for girls (De Lisi & Wolford, 2002). The research to date suggests that video game playing enhances visual spatial skills and that the benefits may be greater for those who initially have weaker visual spatial skills. It is important to keep in mind that transfer effects from such use are most likely to accrue in the same or similar medium and on tasks that utilize the same suite of skills as the game.

Another skill embodied in interactive games is that of iconic or analog representation—in other words, games privilege image over word. In a cross-cultural study carried out in Rome and Los Angeles, participants who played *Concentration* on the computer became more iconic and less symbolic in their communication about the animated computer simulation in software called *Rocky's Boot* compared to those who played the same game on a board (Greenfield, Camaioni, et al., 1994). The study results also indicated that exposure to video games is related to both the comprehension and production of iconic representation.

Another study explored the role of interactive games in developing strategies for keeping track of events at multiple locations on a screen. In a task where an icon could appear at either of two locations (but with unequal probabilities), the researchers found that expert video game players had faster response times than novices at both high and low probability positions of the icon. Furthermore they found that 5 hours of playing an action arcade video game, *Robotron*, improved strategies for keeping track of events at multiple locations, but only for the low probability target position (Greenfield, DeWinstanley, Kilpatrick, & Kaye, 1994).

Recent research has provided further evidence that video game playing improves attentional skill, an effect that was found to transfer to very different attentional tasks (Green & Bavelier, 2003). In a correlational study, video game players (those who reported that they had consistently played in the 6 months prior to the study) had better attentional capacity compared to non-players (participants who had little video game usage in the 6 months prior to the study). These correlations were substantiated in a cross-sectional developmental study in which positive effects of video game play increased as players progressed in age from 7 to 17 years of age (Dye & Bavelier, 2010). In a training study comparing the action game *Medal of Honor* and the puzzle game *Tetris*, the action game led to greater improvements on all the attentional tests compared to *Tetris*. *Medal of Honor* is a battle game in which multiple entities are simultaneously engaged in various actions, whereas *Tetris* is a dynamic puzzle game in which only one event takes place at a time. These studies suggest that individuals who play interactive games may be better at monitoring two or more locations on a game screen and that repeated playing over time might improve strategies for monitoring low-probability targets. They show that video game training in the lab can have immediate short-term effects on the development of divided attention strategies and that expert game players have better-developed attention skills than novices.

Divided attention is the cognitive basis for screen-based multitasking, which that involves more than one window or application on a computer screen. We hypothesize that the divided attention required by most action games is the reason video game expertise has a positive effect on screen-based multitasking in a virtual real-world task. Kearney (2005) found that playing two hours of a shooting game, *Counterstrike*, improved performance in a simulated multitask work environment (called *SynWork*); it comprised four simultaneous tasks that are useful in the military job of standing guard.

Most of the research on the impact of interactive games on cognitive processing has assessed short-term transfer effects; although some of the evidence presented earlier suggested relations between game playing expertise and cognitive or occupational skills, we know very little about the cumulative impact of electronic games. Greenfield (1998) suggested that the proliferation of computer games and the corresponding development of iconic representational skills may have a causal role in the recent dramatic increases in nonverbal or performance IQ scores that have occurred in the period of years when modern computer technology was developing and becoming widespread (Flynn, 1999).

The best study of the long-term effects of video game play is a study of the effect of video game expertise on skill in laparoscopic surgery (Rosser et al., 2007). Laparoscopic surgery provides an example in which visual skills developed by video games have implications for training.

> Surgeons recognize that laparoscopy has changed the required skill profile of surgeons and their training needs. In laparoscopic surgery, a small incision is made, and a viewing tube with a small camera on the eyepiece is inserted through it. The surgeon examines internal organs on a video monitor connected to the tube and can also use the viewing tube to guide actual surgical procedures. Navigating through and operating in a three-dimensional space represented on a two-dimensional screen with minimal tactile feedback constitute basic parallels between laparoscopy and action video games. A study of the relation between video game skill and success in training for laparoscopic surgery yielded positive results: Action video game skill (as demonstrated in the laboratory) and past video game experience (assessed through self-report) predicted laparoscopic skills; in contrast, neither laparoscopic experience in the operating room nor years of training significantly predicted laparoscopic skill. The best game players (the top third) made

> 47% fewer errors and performed 39% faster in the laparoscopy tasks than the worst players (the bottom third). These results indicate the value of video game play as informal educational background for specific training in laparoscopic surgery, a finding that is applicable to other lines of work (such as piloting a plane) whose skill profiles overlap with those required by action video games. (Greenfield, 2009, p. 70)

Much of the research on the cognitive impact of game playing has been done with the older generation of arcade games and game systems. Despite advances in interactive technology and the capabilities of current computer games, we believe that the fundamental nature of computer games has remained unchanged. The need for divided attention, spatial imagery, and iconic representation continue to be features of the current generation of games. Based on previous research we would predict no changes in the nature of the effects of computer game playing that stem from structural features of the medium, although the strength of visual effects could change with increasing sophistication of the graphics. For example, the newer generations of games such as EA Sports' Football and basketball games have very realistic images that appear to be almost three-dimensional. How will these games influence representational skill development? In fact, Green and Bavelier (2003) found more consistent effects of video game play on divided attention than had Greenfield, Camaioni, et al. (1994) almost a decade earlier. One possible reason for this difference is that young people are starting earlier and/or playing more than they were a decade before. Another possible reason is that the more sophisticated visual graphics are having a greater effect.

The Wii sports games and music video games such as the *Dance Dance Revolution* series utilize a whole new set of skills. For instance, in *Dance Dance Revolution*, a player uses his or her feet to press on a dance pad with four arrow panels (left, right, up, and down) that are connected to the computer. The player has to press the panels in response to visual information consisting of rapidly changing arrows (corresponding to those on the pad) on a screen that are synchronized to the beat of a song that is being played simultaneously. Success on the game requires intermodal integration—the player has to see the arrows that have to be pressed and then press the correct ones with his or her feet. Additional research is needed to understand how these newer games, as well as multiparty games on the Internet, influence the cognitive skills of youth.

Content of Interactive Games and Development

The third pathway of influence occurs via the thematic content of digital media. Interactive games contain a wide array of themes such as fantasy, prosociality, and aggression, as well as topic domains such as history or math. The effects of prosocial and aggressive content on development are discussed in Chapter 12 and Chapter 13 of this volume. Here we focus on educational games; these have variously been called instructional games, entertainment games, edutainment, or serious games. They range from those that provide drill and practice (e.g., for spelling, multiplication) to those that present subject content (e.g., social studies, geography; e.g., *The Oregon Trail*). The premise behind these serious games is that students will be more engaged and presumably learn more when the information is presented in a game-like context. The effects of computers and video games on learning outcomes are in fact mixed.

A survey of the educational publications of 20 years revealed very little hardcore academic benefits of playing educational games (Kafai, 2006). Another recent review of 20 studies on this topic concluded that students can learn from computer games and that most appreciate the use of games in the classroom (Egenfeldt-Nielsen, 2009). However, Egenfeldt-Nielson (2009) also pointed out that "we can certainly say that you learn from computer games but the support for saying something more valuable is weak" (p. 268); for instance, we do not know how educational software compares to other teaching methods, and more important, we do not know the particular game feature or sets of features that best promote learning. In addition, a recent well-designed longitudinal study commissioned by the U.S. Department of Education compared a national sample of 1st-, 4th-, and 6th-grade classrooms that used reading and mathematics software with classrooms that did not. No statistically significant differences were found between the test scores of students in the classrooms that used the software products and those in classrooms that did not (Dynarski et al., 2007). More research is needed to understand the motivating role of interactive games, particularly for drill-based activities that children may consider boring. It is very likely that for digital youth, the benefit of software/computer games to education may lie more in their motivational and social advantages.

In all of the research mentioned previously, the goal was to examine whether playing interactive games would lead to learning. However, Kafai has shown that allowing students to make games might help them develop new understandings of content knowledge. In one case study, students were asked to create their own games with their own worlds, characters, and storylines to teach fractions to a group of younger students in their school. The students enjoyed making games for learning, and they were able to develop their programming skills; after analyzing the games that the students designed, the authors hypothesized that the context of designing games helped them to develop more sophisticated and complex representations of fractions (Kafai, Franke, Ching, & Shih, 1998).

Games on the Internet: Role of the Communication Environment

The fourth pathway of influence—the communication environment—comes into play with multiplayer games on the Internet (Steen, Greenfield, Davies, & Tynes, 2006). A study of an online multiplayer game, *Sims Online*, revealed impacts of the structure of the game on social interaction (Steen et al., 2006). Each player has an avatar representing the self in the game. Avatars can interact with other avatars for online social interaction. However, several factors impeded social interaction in this game. First of all, the avatars were controlled robotically (through instructions concerning direction of movement) rather than directly (by moving a cursor). This made interaction slow and artificial and was one barrier to social interaction. Second, the motivational structure of the game was economic, with economic gains made by leaving an avatar unattended in a money-making situation. In such a case, there was no one to interact with, making social interaction impossible.

These characteristics also weakened identification between avatar and player. If you can leave your avatar's body behind, there is clearly a psychological separation of player from avatar. The lack of realism of robotic control undoubtedly weakens identification with an avatar. We also found that players experimented with avatars, using them to express various identities, from fantastical to realistic, to ideal, to "off-the-wall." As we will see, real and ideal selves are also constructed on social networking sites; however, fantastical and off-the-wall are probably specific to the more imaginative settings of a game world and may have been enhanced by the structural characteristics of *Sims Online* that caused the dissociation between player and avatar. In the development of a less game-like simulation, Second Life, there seems to be a much greater incidence of player–avatar identification. At its height, *Sims Online* had subscribers in the thousands, way below initial expectations and estimates. *World of Warcraft*, another massive multiplayer game with 6.5 million subscribers as of 2006, is at the other end of the spectrum, and is one of the best-selling online game in the United States. Its structure enhances various sorts of collaboration with offline friends and strangers as well as leads to scaffolded learning concerning the rules and opportunities in the game, not only from other players but from resources such as websites and forums (Nardi & Harris, 2006).

Gender Issues in Interactive Games

As we noted earlier, there remains a gender imbalance in the playing of electronic games, with boys continuing to spend more time playing them than girls (Rideout et al., 2010). It was initially believed that girls were turned off by electronic games by the lack of female protagonists and the violent nature of the games (Malone, 1981). The early efforts of the software industry to create nonviolent games with female protagonists were largely a failure (Subrahmanyam & Greenfield, 1998). Although one "girl software," *Barbie Fashion Designer*, was very successful, other girl games, such as *Lets Talk About Me*, *Rockett*, and *Barbie Print and Play*, were not. The Barbie character certainly has importance in itself: A number of Barbie games have become best sellers among girls. It has been suggested that the success of *Barbie Fashion Designer* did not stem from the mere presence of Barbie and the lack of aggression, but instead stemmed from the fact that it contained features that fit in with girls' play and their tastes in reading and literature in general (Subrahmanyam & Greenfield, 1998; Tizard, Philips, & Plewis, 2006). We proposed that by helping girls create outfits for Barbie, the computer became a creative tool for girls' pretend play, which tends to be based more on reality and real-life models compared to boys' pretend play. Unlike most games where the electronic fantasy is primary, the electronic medium became a tool to design a product that could then be used in play with Barbie dolls. Our analysis suggests that girls like nonaggressive software that allows them to enhance popular play themes with realistic-familiar characters. Not much has changed since we proposed this. Based on their ethnographic work, Ito and Bittani (2009) suggest that although more girls are playing games, boys still play more games, and more boys are engaged in what they call recreational gaming; this involves more sophisticated, "geeked-out" gaming. Ito and Bittani suggest that there is more of a gender balance when it comes to playing games simply to hang out or to kill time. The gender imbalance in more sophisticated kinds of gaming is important because such informal activities might provide access to networks of technology expertise and learning.

Children, Adolescents, and The Internet

Since the previous edition of the *Handbook of Children and the Media* was published, there have been rapid and dramatic changes in the Internet—not just in how it is accessed, but also in the various applications and activities that it affords. Dial-up access has given way to broadband and wireless networks, and the Internet can now be accessed via high-speed wired computers, wireless networks on laptops, as well as a variety of handheld devices, such as the iPhone, BlackBerry, and Sidekick. In addition, there are a variety of online applications with very diverse functions that are available—email, chat rooms, instant messaging, social networking sites (e.g., MySpace and Facebook), web blogs, microblogs (e.g., Twitter, mylifeisaverage.com), Formspring, and virtual worlds (e.g., Whyville, Teen Second Life); text messaging, while not strictly an online application, is nonetheless very popular among youth and so must be considered as part of the digital landscape.

Together with changes in the nature of the Internet itself, there has been its rapid diffusion, and as we noted earlier, more than 90% of U.S. youth are online. With most of their peers online, it is not surprising that the communication uses of the Internet remain popular among youth (Subrahmanyam & Greenfield, 2008a; Subrahmanyam & Smahel, 2010). Recent research has confirmed that most young people in the United States interact and communicate online with people from their offline worlds (Reich, Subrahmanyam, & Espinoza, 2009; Subrahmanyam & Smahel, 2010); this is in contrast to the earlier years of the Internet, when youth were more likely to interact with strangers (Subrahmanyam et al., 2001). Although there has been a decline in youth reports of unwanted sexual solicitation and harassment by predatory adults, probably because of better education and law enforcement (Mitchell, Wolak, & Finkelhor, 2007), there is an increased incidence of cyberbullying at the hands of peers (Hinduja & Patchin, 2008; Juvonen & Gross, 2008; Chapters 5 and 33 in this volume). At the same time, youth have come to depend on the Internet for information (e.g., for school work, for health information) as well as for entertainment (e.g., for downloading music, videos, and television shows). In the next sections, we utilize the pathways of influence framework that we described earlier as we consider the implications of the Internet for child and adolescent development.

Implications of Online Time on Development

Consistent with the displacement hypothesis, an important question is whether time spent online displaces activities important for adolescent social development, such as face-to-face interactions with peers (Nie & Hillygus, 2002). On this line of reasoning, Internet use displaces adolescents' "real interactions" with peers and family, and so greater Internet use may be associated with weaker social ties as well as lowered well-being (e.g., greater depression). Early research revealed that greater use of the Internet was associated with declines in adolescents' well-being as well as weaker social ties (Kraut et al., 1998). Mesch (2003) also found that adolescents' perceptions about the quality of their family relationships were negatively related to their frequency of Internet use. Other studies have not found a reliable connection between adolescents' online time use and psychological well-being as measured by dispositional or daily well-being (Gross, Juvonen, & Gable, 2002; Subrahmanyam & Lin, 2007). Similarly, no relation was found between time online and aspects of social networks, such as size of local and distant social circles and amount of face-to-face communication (Kraut et al., 2002).

Furthermore, the research suggests that the developmental implications of online time use may be moderated by a variety of factors. When different types of online activity are considered, more time spent in chatrooms, online browsing, and games was related to higher levels of social anxiety among older adolescent and young adult males, but not females (Mazalin & Moore, 2004). Because the study was correlational, we do not know whether participants became more depressed because of their chat room use, whether they were drawn to chat rooms in the first place because they were depressed and were looking for support that they were not getting from their offline relationships, or both. Longitudinal research has shown that Internet use has differential effects based on user characteristics (e.g., Bessière, Kiesler,

Kraut, & Boneva, 2008; Kraut et al., 2002; Steinfield, Ellison, & Lampe, 2008). Bessière and colleagues (2008) found that using the Internet to meet new people and using it for entertainment lead to reduced depressive affect, but only for people with better social resources. For people with poor social resources, using the Internet to meet people was actually associated with reduced depressive affect. Steinfield et al. (2008) found that participants with lower self-esteem reported more gains in their social capital from their Facebook use. Neither of these studies focused exclusively on children and adolescents, but they are relevant to our discussion since 15% of the participants in Bessière et al.'s (2008) study were younger than 19 years and Steinfield and colleagues' (2008) sample consisted of college students. Other variables that may mediate the relation between time use and well-being include young people's perceptions about their online relationships (Subrahmanyam & Lin, 2007) as well as the quality their online interactions (Valkenburg, Peter, & Schouten, 2006).

Formal Feature of the Internet— Effects on Cognition and Learning

We have previously suggested that the Internet's formal or symbolic features are a combination of those found in all other previous media forms—"like books, the Internet contains text; like the radio, the Internet contains audio; like television, the Internet contains audiovisual representations; and like computer and video games, the Internet contains interactive audio and video" (Subrahmanyam & Greenfield, 2008b, p. 178). There is sparse literature with regard to whether formal features of the Internet have effects on cognitive skills. In previous work, we have speculated that because the information and communication uses of the Internet center around the production and comprehension of text, Internet use will likely have an impact on verbal, spatial, and other representational skills.

One important issue is that text-based online communication has features of both oral and written representation, and therefore, online text frequently consists of novel abbreviations (lol, brb) and short forms for words (e.g., srsly for seriously), as well as incomplete and grammatically simple or even incorrect sentences (Greenfield & Subrahmanyam, 2003; Herring, 1996). Such text message abbreviations are called *textisms* (Plester, Wood, & Joshi, 2009; Rosen, Chang, Erwin, Carrier, & Cheever, 2010). Rosen and colleagues (2010) found that among young adults, the greater use of such textisms and more simultaneous instant messaging conversations was related to worse formal writing (e.g., a letter about a defective product); interestingly, there was a positive relationship between textisms and informal writing (Rosen et al., 2010). Among children 10- to 12-years of age, word reading, vocabulary, and phonological awareness measures were positively related to the ratio of textisms to total words used in a text message composing task (Plester et al., 2009). Textism use also predicted word reading ability over and above age, short-term memory, vocabulary, phonological awareness, and length of mobile phone ownership; furthermore, use of textisms was positively associated with word reading ability. Although preliminary, these results point to the need for more research to understand the relation between informal online writing and the more formal and informal reading and writing that occurs in offline contexts.

Spatial representation skills, particularly with regard to two-dimensional representations of three-dimensional space, may also be impacted by online activities. Unlike traditional books, which arrange pages in a linear fashion, the Internet utilizes a more complex set of links, linking content within a page and pages within and across sites. An example of this includes the personal home pages of adolescent cancer patients, which contained hyperlinks to a variety of other sites (Suzuki & Beale, 2006). Just as video games require players to create mental maps of game worlds, constructing and navigating websites might require users to create mental maps of the site organization and help them develop spatial visualization skills. Avatars, which serve as users' three-dimensional motion-enabled online identities, are also a part of the formal representational language of some contexts, such as online games and virtual worlds; for instance, within some virtual worlds, an avatar with few accessories indicates a "newbie," and children inhabiting these worlds must learn this "language" in order to successfully navigate within them. Research is needed to evaluate avatars as symbol systems and to understand how use of these three-dimensional symbols might relate to young children's online and offline self-presentation and perception of others.

A final aspect of online symbol systems that we consider is multitasking. One type of multitasking involves utilizing multiple windows or multiple tabs within a window, each one representing a different activity. This type of multitasking is the phenomenon of using multiple computer applications (e.g., Internet and word processing applications) or multiple windows of the same application (e.g., multiple instant message windows) at the same time. A second type of multitasking is media-multitasking, "which is the practice of using different media at the same time such as the telephone, computer, and television" (Subrahmanyam & Greenfield, 2008b, p. 180). A third type of multitasking involves both a medium and a real-life interaction (e.g., texting while having a family dinner). Online multitasking (e.g., several concurrent conversations via instant messaging, or checking social networking profiles while also having an instant messaging conversation) has come to characterize young people's use of digital media (Carrier, Cheever, Rosen, Benitez, & Chang, 2009; Rideout et al., 2010). However, we do not have a very good understanding of the cognitive costs or benefits of engaging in online multitasking, especially while studying or doing homework.

Foerde, Knowlton, and Poldrack (2006) have examined the cognitive and neural effects of media multitasking in which one task was presented aurally and the other visually, on a computer screen. While this is not the Internet per se, there is no reason to believe that results would differ if someone were accessing a visual task on the Internet. Although dual task conditions (i.e., multitasking) did not affect performance on a weather-prediction task (the visual task) wherein participants had to learn the cues associated with weather outcomes (being able to use cues to predict the weather), it did decrease the acquisition of metaknowledge about the task. In the dual task condition, participants could use the cues to predict the weather, but they could not say how they had done it. Neural processing also was affected by multitasking, and the neural processing of the task was shifted from the medial temporal lobe, which supports flexibly accessible knowledge and metaknowledge, to the striatum, which supports habit learning. In a study of the cognitive cost of the first kind of multitasking (multiple computer applications used simultaneously), college students who were heavy multitaskers took twice as long to write a critique (Calvert & Wells, 2007). There was no difference between heavy and light multitaskers with regard to the quality of the critiques.

A study of the third type of multitasking—between a medium and human interaction—revealed that text interruptions during a class lecture had significant, though moderate, decrements on a test based on the lecture (Lim & Rosen, 2010). A similar study was done by Hembrooke and Gay (2003). Students in a communication studies class were encouraged to use laptops during class in order to explore lecture topics in greater detail on the Internet and through library research. All the students had laptops, but half were randomly selected to keep their laptops closed during class. A surprise quiz at the end of class revealed that the students with open laptops learned significantly less of the lecture material. These studies suggest, in several different ways, that multitasking causes a decrement in higher-level cognitive skills; the study by Foerde et al. (2006) suggests a neural basis for this decrement.

Effects of Online Content on Youth

The Internet is a repository of content and provides access to vast amounts of freely available information. Search engines such as Google, encyclopedic websites such as Wikipedia, and online bulletin boards are some of the tools that youth can use to access these resources. The Internet provides access to useful information, such as for school as well as for health-related needs, but it also exposes youth to hateful, violent, and other undesirable content. There are simply too many different content kinds to enumerate here; instead, we focus on the developmental implication of young people's access to health-related material and exposure to online hate.

Survey studies suggest that youth use the Internet to access health information, and such use has been increasing since these trends have been tracked (Rideout, 2001; Roberts, Foehr, & Rideout, 2005). Suzuki and Calzo (2004) conducted a content analysis of a health-related online bulletin board for adolescents and found that the most frequent health-related concerns and questions dealt with the following topics: sexual health, pregnancy/birth control, body image, and grooming of genital areas. The Kaiser report similarly found that sexual health issues such as pregnancy, AIDS, and other sexually transmitted diseases (STDs) were the second most frequently searched topic after diseases like cancer and diabetes (Rideout, 2001). These results suggest that youth access online resources to find out more about specific adolescent concerns, especially sensitive ones, which they may not be comfortable discussing with parents, teachers, or physicians. Although the information they obtain from the Internet may result in their talking to their peers or adults, it does not consistently lead to long lasting behavior changes, and only a very small minority report going to the doctor because of information they saw online (Rideout, 2001). Online health resources have other benefits, such as their 24/7 availability and passive access to information (e.g., questions and the responses on bulletin boards and other sites remain long after they are initially posted). Moreover, they also expand support networks as youths can go online and get information, advice, and support from a wider network of people than would be possible from offline contacts alone (Suzuki & Calzo, 2004). These advantages could be especially valuable for youths who may be too shy to post questions themselves, or who might not have adequate offline support because of their location (e.g., rural areas, areas steeped in poverty), social isolation, or illness (e.g., teens with cancer). Research has documented online access of health information by rural teens living in Accra, Ghana (Borzekowski, Fobil, & Asante, 2006), teens with cancer (Kyngas et al. 2001; Suzuki & Beale, 2006), as well as youth with self-injurious behaviors (Whitlock, Powers, & Eckenrode, 2006) and eating disorders (Winzelberg, 1997).

Despite these advantages, online health content also presents some challenges—for instance, youth are not very good at searching and retrieving high quality health information (Skinner, Biscope, Poland, & Goldberg, 2003) or at evaluating the credibility of sources (e.g., a government website versus one hosted by a commercial entity; Eysenbach, 2008). There is also the concern that the Internet provides easy access to dangerous and potentially harmful content, such as those that portray and sell prescription drugs that adolescents tend to abuse (e.g., stimulants; Schepis, Marlowe, & Forman, 2008) or those that endorse eating disorders (Wilson, Peebles, Hardy, & Litt, 2006). In experimental work with college students who were exposed to different kinds of websites (a pro-anorexic website, a website of female fashion showing average-sized models, or a home décor site), those who viewed the pro-anorexic website showed a decrease in self-esteem, appearance, self-efficacy, and perceived attractiveness, and an increase in negative affect and perceptions of being overweight (Bardone-Cone & Cass, 2006). In addition, because self-injurious behaviors seem to follow epidemic-like patterns in hospitals and other institutions, Whitlock and colleagues (2006) cautioned that problem behaviors such as cutting might become socially contagious through the Internet.

Two aspects of online content that we briefly examine are violence on websites and interactive online games with violent content. Websites that youth may access include those with violent and aggressive themes that advocate violence and aggression and websites that sometimes provide detailed directions for committing violent actions: examples include those that provide bomb making information, contain violent gore content such as pictures of torture and mutilation, online music (particularly rap and hip hop music), and hate sites (Subrahmanyam & Smahel, 2010). Given the dynamic and vast nature of the World Wide Web, it is hard to know what percentage of content includes such violent and disturbing themes. Although estimates vary, many teens report exposure to online violence (Fleming, Greentree, Cocotti-Muller, Elias, & Morrison, 2006), much of it inadvertent or unintentional (Aisbett, Authority, & Insights, 2001; Livingstone, Bober, & Helsper, 2005). Based on a review of extant survey research (Slater, 2003; Slater, Henry, Swaim, & Anderson, 2003), Subrahmanyam and Smahel (2010) concluded that violence-oriented websites may not be harmful for a majority of adolescents, but may pose threats for a subset of youth, particularly those who are alienated from their immediate contexts, are sensation-seekers, and are generally at risk for problem behaviors.

Online hate sites generally contain violent and aggressive messages against individuals and groups (Tynes, 2005), and researchers have begun to document both the nature of their content and the strategies they use to target and recruit young people to their cause (Gerstenfeld, Grant, & Chiang, 2003; Tynes, 2005). Relevant is an experimental study that investigated the persuasiveness of hate messages such as those found on White supremacist web pages. The results revealed that even brief exposure to negative messages such as those found on online hate sites can lead to persistent changes in young adolescent Internet users' attitudes. Furthermore, youth who were already susceptible to such messages were most at risk for such changes (Lee & Leets, 2002).

Finally, we consider the role that online content can play with regard to learning. Because of their immersive nature, virtual worlds have been touted for their potential to engage young people in learning activities. It is argued that, compared to traditional modes of classroom instruction, they are more appealing for even disinterested learners and can help them develop critical thinking and problem solving skills that can be applied to real-world settings (Wu, 2010). A participatory simulation study integrated a virtual experience with a science curriculum at school (Neulight, Kafai, Kao, Foley, & Galas, 2007). The virtual world was Whyville, which targeted 8- to 16-year-olds and provided opportunities to engage in science and social activities (Fields & Kafai, 2007). Participants were two sixth grade classrooms who experienced a virtual epidemic of Whypox, an infectious disease within Whyville. Concurrently, as part of their science curriculum, they learned about natural infectious diseases. From the answers on a pre- and posttest, it was clear that although the students' had made significant advances in their understanding of natural disease, their explanations still emphasized prebiological mechanisms (e.g., mechanical transfer of disease through contact) versus truly biological ones (e.g., biology of germs or white blood cells). As in the case of interactive games, this finding is disappointing and more research is necessary to determine the true potential of online contexts for learning and to see whether such learning transfers to more traditional academic contexts.

A new approach to the issue of learning online has been pioneered by Ito and Bittani (2009). Utilizing the example of Japanese anime fans who create subtitles on Japanese animation, they point to interest-driven online communities (called *networked publics*), within which learning activities are primary. These communities promote and develop sophisticated technical skills, which are motivated by publicity and fame. There is also a step-by-step learning progression built into each genre and scaffolded by peers in the network. In the case of anime, fans progress from consumption to production. This progression eventually leads to what might be called precocious professionalism. As the authors point out, there is a need for formal institutions such as schools to recognize the cognitive and technical skills being developed in these informal online learning communities and to interface with them in classroom-based teaching and testing.

Online Communication Contexts and Development

As we noted earlier, online communication tools such as email, instant messaging, and social networking are popular among youth. The communication environment within them has important developmental implications, and in this section we consider this fourth pathway of influence. Most mediated environments are disembodied, and information about the body, face, and other face-to-face cues such as gestures and eye contact are not readily available. Even though true anonymity on the Internet is something of an illusion, users do have control as to how anonymous they wish to be. Research to date suggests that, at least among adolescents, online interactions center around core offline developmental concerns such as sexuality, intimacy, and identity (Smahel & Subrahmanyam, 2007; Subrahmanyam, Greenfield, & Tynes, 2004; Subrahmanyam, Smahel, & Greenfield, 2006). To understand how the disembodied and potentially anonymous nature of online contexts might mediate development, we provide examples that relate to the development of intimacy and identity.

In an earlier section, we examined the issue of time online and well-being. Here we reconsider this question, taking into account the particular affordances of online communication environments. First, many Internet forums enable communication with strangers, and such interactions may be more superficial and poorer in quality. Second, most mediated contexts (e.g., email, text messaging, and instant messaging) do not contain facial cues, voice, gestures, or other elements of body language. Consequently, online communication might not be of the same quality as face-to-face communication, and online interactions may lead to superficial and weak ties (Krackhardt, 1994; Kraut et al., 1998). Therefore, an important question is whether online interactions and relationships provide the same kinds of intimacy and support as their offline counterparts.

Research on this topic has presented a complex picture. To start with, at the time of writing this chapter in 2010, relationships that were exclusively online were not the norm among youth, at least in the United States and other Western countries. When purely online relationships do occur, they are qualitatively different from offline ones. For instance, Mesch and Talmud (2006) found that among Israeli adolescents, online friendships were shorter in duration and not as close when one considered the topics discussed (e.g., less personal topics) and the frequency of shared activities. Furthermore, adolescents' online relationships rarely move from online to offline contexts (Wolak, Mitchell, & Finkelhor, 2002).

Young people's online interactions (via text messaging and social networking sites) seem to mostly involve peers their offline worlds, including schools, after-school settings (e.g., sports and clubs), and neighborhoods. (See Subrahmanyam & Smahel, 2010, for an in-depth discussion of this issue.) Interestingly, their online communication with their offline friends may actually have positive effects on these offline friendships. In Valkenburg and Peter's (2007) survey of adolescents, 80% reported that they used the Internet to maintain existing friendship networks. Those who communicated more often on the Internet felt closer to existing friends, but only if they interacted online with friends rather than strangers. Participants who felt that online communication was more effective for self-disclosure also reported feeling closer to their offline friends compared to adolescents who did not view online communication as allowing for more intimate self-disclosure compared to offline communication. At the same time, online communication may present some costs. For instance, youth participants in one study found instant messaging to be less enjoyable than phone and face-to-face conversations, and they also reported that they felt psychologically less close to their instant messaging partners than in phone or face-to-face communication (Boneva, Quinn, Kraut, Kiesler, & Shklovski, 2006).

Regardless of the quality of intimacy and support accrued from online communication, tools such as instant messaging, text messaging, and social networking sites have made it possible for young people to access their offline friends and peer groups at any time, anywhere, and in any manner, public or private (e.g., Kaare, Brandtzaeg, Heim, & Endestad, 2007; Subrahmanyam & Smahel, 2010). Interestingly, this increased online peer contact does not seem to be at the expense of face-to-face interactions (Subrahmanyam & Smahel, 2010). In addition, digital tools have helped to widen or broaden young people's peer networks. For instance, in one study of high school students' social networking use, the number of social networking "friends" ranged from 0 to 793, with a mean of 176, a standard deviation of 166, and a median of 130 (Reich et al., 2009). Clearly, the notion of friendship is undergoing a transformation, and for youth, the word *friends* now seems to include both close, intimate others as well as acquaintances, with whom they might not otherwise interact with face-to-face. Subrahmanyam and Smahel (2010) noted that such a "wider circle of friends" could be valuable for adolescents and help them learn more about themselves and their social world. Future research should also examine the developmental implications of online peer interactions that occur, at times in very public ways, such as on social networking sites.

Another domain that may be impacted by the unique affordances of online contexts is that of identity and self-development. Given the disembodied and potentially anonymous nature of many online forums, scholars initially speculated that online users could leave their bodies behind and create new and different selves or personas online (Kendall, 2003; Stallabrass, 1995; Turkle, 1997). Turkle (1997) famously wrote about a youth who assumed four different selves in three different MUDs (Multi User Dungeons): a seductive woman, a "macho cowboy" type, a rabbit of unspecified gender, and a furry animal; in his words, "'rl' [real life] is just one more window, and it's not usually my best one" (p. 13). Formulating a coherent sense of self is an important task for adolescents, and we examine some of the ways that young people might use technology to negotiate and present aspects of their developing selves.

Contrary to early speculation, the evidence indicates that "identity experiments" are not very common among youth. For instance, among U.S. adolescents in 7th (12- and 13-year-olds) and 10th grade (15- and 16-year-olds), Gross (2004) found that assuming a different identity was rare; it occurred when youths pretended to be someone older or when they wanted to make fun of friends and not as part of an alternative or preferred identity.

Although youths do not actively assume different identities while online, nonetheless, they adopt a variety of strategies for identity expression and self-presentation. For instance, they use digital tools (e.g., nicknames, avatars, profiles, photos, and videos) and digital contexts (e.g., blogs and social networking sites) to test aspects of their self in front of a

peer audience and to create narratives about themselves (Subrahmanyam & Smahel, 2010). Here we briefly describe their use of nicknames, avatars, and blogs in the context of their online self-presentation. In our own research with online teen chat rooms, we have found that users adopt nicknames that present aspects of their selves such as their gender (e.g., *prettygurl245*) and sexualized identities (e.g., *straitangel*) as well as interests (e.g., *soccerchick*). Within the anonymous and disembodied chat space, such nicknames could serve as a proxy for a person's body and intentions. Thus, sexualized nicknames may be adopted by chat users to portray a sexual persona or an interest in sexual activities (Subrahmanyam et al., 2006).

As mentioned in the section on video games, identity expression and development are relevant to avatars, which are three-dimensional versions of nicknames and are adjustable, motion-enabled graphical representations assumed by users within online contexts such as computer games (e.g., Massively Multi Player Online Role Playing Games, or MMORPGs) and complex virtual worlds (e.g., Second Life). Depending on the particular online space, avatars can assume a variety of forms, ranging from human-like to fantastical creatures. A qualitative study of Whyville, a virtual world, found that youth users adopted a variety of avatars: Some were like them in offline life, others were different, and still others were either for or against a popular trend (Kafai, Fields, & Cook, 2007). Other research has found that children's avatars in a MUD mostly mirrored offline properties such as their gender and interests (Calvert, Mahler, Zehnder, Jenkins, & Lee, 2003). Again, contrary to speculation, gender-bending (where users assume the gender opposite to their offline one) was infrequent; when it did occur, children were generally interacting with familiar peers. Similarly, content analysis of teen web blogs, or *blogs*, revealed that blog entries were narrative and reflective in style, and they generally described the authors' peers and everyday activities (e.g., school, after-school activities) and often carried a strong emotional tone (Subrahmanyam, Garcia, Harsono, Li, & Lipana, 2009). Based on McAdams's (1997) suggestion that such life stories help individuals to construct a coherent sense of their self, Subrahmanyam et al. (2009) speculated that these online narratives might help youths with formulating their sense of self. Although it is clear that youths are taking advantage of digital tools for self-presentation and to construct self-narratives, we do not fully understand how these online negotiations mediate their identity development.

While identity exploration is developmentally appropriate for adolescents, social networking sites have now become very popular with children. Club Penguin, with 22 million accounts, is now owned by Disney (Marsh, 2010). Marsh's (2010) study in the United Kingdom of children between the ages of 5 and 11 who used Club Penguin found that their play on Club Penguin and a second online children's game, Barbie Girls, mirrored offline activities for this age group. However, age-appropriate gaming is prominently featured in social networking sites for this age group. In contrast, the social networking aspect is totally downplayed by participating children. Comparing this pattern to that of adolescents, we see that each is different but equally age appropriate. Caring for virtual pets is another popular activity in Club Penguin and other children's social networking sites. Again, this activity is distinct from what is going on in the social networking of emerging adults, but equally developmentally appropriate. It confirms a theme we have struck for a number of years: that old developmental issues are projected onto new media (Subrahmanyam et al., 2006; Subrahmanyam & Smahel, 2010).

Conclusions

In conclusion, the proliferation of digital media such as computers, interactive games, the Internet, cell phones, and other handheld devices has raised questions about the extent of their use by youth and the impact of such use on their activities and development. Survey studies suggest that youth are spending an increasing number of hours consuming media content through a variety of platforms. Despite the diffusion of digital technologies, there remain differences based on parental education, family income, and racial and ethnic differences in the presence of a home computer and access

to the Internet, playing of video games, overall media consumption, and mobile access to the Internet. Although gender differences in the use of the Internet are mostly narrowed, there remain gaps in computer game playing that could impact access to technology networks.

To understand the role of interactive games and the Internet on development, we considered four potential pathways. The first pathway examined whether time with media displaces other activities such as physical play, sleep, and face-to-face social interaction. Because of the multitasking nature of much media use, it is not possible to know the extent to which such displacement actually occurs. However, research to date suggests that time spent gaming might be related to obesity, sleep difficulties, and adjustment challenges. Of particular concern are those youths who spend excessive amounts of time gaming, to the detriment of their school and family activities. Research regarding the effects of time spent online is similarly complex, and it suggests that other factors play a role, such as user characteristics and the particular activities that youth engage in while spending time online.

The second pathway of influence considers the effects that may stem from the particular symbolic and representational systems utilized by a media form. Research suggests that interactive games may help to change the balance of cognitive skills from the verbal to the visual. From a cognitive perspective, they prepare children and adolescents for the increasingly visual domains of science and technology. Although there is little research on the verbal, spatial, and other representational skills utilized by the Internet, the multitasking that it affords has been shown to have cognitive costs.

The third pathway of influence takes into account the particular thematic content in a media form and its potential effect on development. The content effects of interactive games and online virtual worlds with regard to learning in academic contexts have generally been disappointing, and we need more research to understand whether and how the learning that occurs in informal interactive contexts can transfer to more formal settings. Some online content can be useful, and youth report using online content for school, health information, and entertainment purposes; but the Internet can also provide easy access to inappropriate and potentially dangerous content, and some youth might be more at risk than others.

The fourth pathway of influence considers the features of online communication environments, such as disembodied and potentially anonymous users. There is no question that youth are taking advantage of the opportunities afforded by digital tools to connect with their peers and to express their identities. They are also forming interest-based communities online. Children have also begun to use social network sites in large numbers; their interests are quite different from those of teens and emerging adults. They confirm the principle that the same developmental issues that manifest offline are projected into young people's online worlds. Nevertheless, we need to know more about whether and how new digital technologies are transforming fundamental developmental processes and what effect they will ultimately have on young people's development.

References

Aisbett, K., Authority, A. B., & Insights, E. (2001). *The Internet at home: A report on Internet use in the home*. Retrieved January 16, 2009, from http://www.acma.gov.au/webwr/aba/newspubs/documents/internetathome.pdf

Bardone-Cone, A. M., & Cass, K. M. (2006). Investigating the impact of pro-anorexia websites: A pilot study. *European Eating Disorders Review, 14*, 256.

Bessière, K., Kiesler, S., Kraut, R. E., & Boneva, B. (2008). Effects of Internet use and social resources on changes in depression. *Information Community and Society, 11*, 47–70.

Boneva, B. S., Quinn, A., Kraut, R. E., Kiesler, S., & Shklovski, I. (2006). Teenage communication in the instant messaging era. In R. E. Kraut, M. Brynin, & S. Kiesler (Eds.), *Computers, phones, and the internet: Domesticating information technology* (pp. 201–218). New York: Oxford University Press.

Borzekowski, D. L. G., Fobil, J. N., & Asante, K. O. (2006). Online access by adolescents in Accra: Ghanaian teens' use of the Internet for health information. *Developmental Psychology, 42*, 450.

Bruner, J. S., Olver, R. R., & Greenfield, P. M. (1966). *Studies in cognitive growth*. New York: McGraw-Hill.

Calvert, S. L., Mahler, B. A., Zehnder, S. M., Jenkins, A., & Lee, M. S. (2003). Gender differences in preadolescent children's online interactions: Symbolic modes of self-presentation and self-expression. *Journal of Applied Developmental Psychology, 24*, 627–644.

Calvert, S. L., & Wells, J. (2007). *Age and gender effects of multitasking on academic performance*. Paper presented at the Hawaii International Conference on Education, Honolulu, Hawaii.

Carrier, L. M., Cheever, N. A., Rosen, L. D., Benitez, S., & Chang, J. (2009). Multitasking across generations: Multitasking choices and difficulty ratings in three generations of Americans. *Computers in Human Behavior, 25*, 483–489.

Chou, C., Condron, L., & Belland, J. C. (2005). A review of the research on Internet addiction. *Educational Psychology Review, 17*, 363–368.

De Lisi, R., & Wolford, J. (2002). Improving children's mental rotation accuracy with computer game playing. *Journal of Genetic Psychology, 163*, 272–282.

Dominick, J. R. (1984). Videogames, television violence, and aggression in teenagers. *Journal of Communication, 34*, 136–147.

Dye, M. W., & Bavelier, D. (2010). Differential development of visual attention skills in school-age children. *Vision Research, 50*, 452–459.

Dynarski, M., Agodini, R., Heaviside, S., Novak, T., Carey, N., Campuzano, L., et al. (2007). Effectiveness of reading and mathematics software products: Findings from the first student cohort. Retrieved March 5, 2009, from http://hal.archives-ouvertes.fr/hal-00190019/

Egenfeldt-Nielsen, S. (2009). Third generation educational use of computer games. *Learning and Teaching with Electronic Games*, 263–281.

Eysenbach, G. (2008). Credibility of health information and digital media: New perspectives and implications for youth. In M. J. Metzger & A. J. Flanagin (Eds.), *Digital media, youth, and credibility* (pp. 123–154). Cambridge, MA: MIT Press.

Fields, D. A., & Kafai, Y. B. (2007). *Stealing from grandma or generating cultural knowledge? Contestations and effects of cheats in a tween virtual world*. Paper presented at the Situated Play, Proceedings of DiGRA 2007 Conference. Retrieved March 4, 2009, from http://www.gseis.ucla.edu/faculty/kafai/paper/whyville_pdfs/DIGRA07_cheat.pdf

Fleming, M. J., Greentree, S., Cocotti-Muller, D., Elias, K. A., & Morrison, S. (2006). Safety in cyberspace: Adolescents' safety and exposure online. *Youth & Society, 38*, 135–154.

Flynn, J. R. (1999). Searching for justice: The discovery of IQ gains over time. *American Psychologist, 54*, 5–20.

Foerde, K., Knowlton, B. J., & Poldrack, R. A. (2006). Modulation of competing memory systems by distraction. *Proceedings of the National Academy of Sciences, 103*, 11778–11783.

Gerstenfeld, P. B., Grant, D. R., & Chiang, C. P. (2003). Hate online: A content analysis of extremist Internet sites. *Analyses of Social Issues and Public Policy, 3*, 29–44.

Green, C. S., & Bavelier, D. (2003). Action video game modifies visual selective attention. *Nature, 423*, 534–537.

Greenfield, P. M. (1994). Video games as cultural artifacts. *Journal of Applied Developmental Psychology, 15*, 3–12.

Greenfield, P. M. (1998). The cultural evolution of IQ. In U. Neisser (Ed.), *The rising curve. Long-term gains in IQ and related measures* (pp. 81–123). Washington, DC: American Psychological Association.

Greenfield, P. M. (2009). Technology and informal education: What is taught, what is learned. *Science, 323*, 69–71.

Greenfield, P. M., Camaioni, L., Ercolani, P., Weiss, L., Lauber, B. A., & Perucchini, P. (1994). Cognitive socialization by computer games in two cultures: Inductive discovery or mastery of an iconic code? *Journal of Applied Developmental Psychology, 15*, 59–85.

Greenfield, P. M., DeWinstanley, P., Kilpatrick, H., & Kaye, D. (1994). Action video games and informal education: Effects on strategies for dividing visual attention. *Journal of Applied Developmental Psychology, 15*, 105–123.

Greenfield, P. M., & Subrahmanyam, K. (2003). Online discourse in a teen chatroom: New codes and new modes of coherence in a visual medium. *Journal of Applied Developmental Psychology, 24*, 713–738.

Griffiths, M. (2000). Does Internet and computer "addiction" exist? Some case study evidence. *Cyberpsychology & Behavior, 3*, 211–218.

Gross, E. F. (2004). Adolescent Internet use: What we expect, what teens report. *Journal of Applied Developmental Psychology, 25*, 633–649.

Gross, E. F., Juvonen, J., & Gable, S. L. (2002). Internet use and well-being in adolescence. *Journal of Social Issues, 58*, 75–90.

Grüsser, S. M., Thalemann, R., & Griffiths, M. D. (2006). Excessive computer game playing: Evidence for addiction and aggression? *CyberPsychology & Behavior, 10*, 290–292.

Hargittai, E. (2007). Whose space? Differences among users and non-users of social network sites [Electronic version]. *Journal of Computer-Mediated Communication, 13, Article 14.* Retrieved November 27, 2009, from http://jcmc.indiana.edu/vol13/issue1/hargittai.html

Harris Interactive. (2008). Teenagers: A generation unplugged. Retrieved March 1, 2010, from http://files.ctia.org/pdf/HI_TeenMobileStudy_ResearchReport.pdf

Hembrooke, H., & Gay, G. (2003). The laptop and the lecture: The effects of multitasking in learning environments. *Journal of Computing in Higher Education, 15*, 46–64.

Herring, S. C. (1996). Introduction. In S. C. Herring (Ed.), *Computer-mediated communication: Linguistic, social, and cross-cultural perspectives* (pp. 1–12). Philadelphia, PA: John Benjamins.

Hinduja, S., & Patchin, J. W. (2008). Cyberbullying: An exploratory analysis of factors related to offending and victimization. *Deviant Behavior, 29*, 129–156.

Ito, M., & Bittani, M. (2009). Gaming. In M. Ito, S. Baumer, & M. Bittani (Eds.), *Hanging out, messing around, geeking out: Living and learning with new media.* Cambridge, MA: MIT Press.

Jones, S., & Fox, S. (2009). *Generations online in 2009.* Retrieved February 9, 2009, from http://pewresearch.org/pubs/1093/generations-online

Juvonen, J., & Gross, E. F. (2008). Extending the school grounds? Bullying experiences in cyberspace. *The Journal of School Health, 78*, 496–505.

Kaare, B. H., Brandtzaeg, P. B., Heim, J., & Endestad, T. (2007). In the borderland between family orientation and peer culture: The use of communication technologies among Norwegian tweens. *New Media & Society, 9*, 603–624.

Kafai, Y. B. (2006). Playing and making games for learning: Instructionist and constructionist perspectives for game studies. *Games and Culture, 1*, 36–40.

Kafai, Y. B., Fields, D. A., & Cook, M. S. (2007). *Your second selves: Resources, agency, and constraints in avatar designs and identity play in a tween virtual world.* Paper presented at the Situated Play, Proceedings of Digital Games Research Association 2007 conference, Tokyo, Japan.

Kafai, Y. B., Franke, M. L., Ching, C. C., & Shih, J. C. (1998). Game design as an interactive learning environment for fostering students' and teachers' mathematical inquiry. *International Journal of Computers for Mathematical Learning, 3*, 149–184.

Kearney, P. (2005). *Cognitive calisthenics: Do fps computer games enhance the player's cognitive abilities.* Paper presented at the DIGRA 2005 Conference: Worlds in Play, Vancouver, Canada.

Kendall, L. (2003). Cyberspace. In S. Jones (Ed.), *Encyclopedia of new media* (pp. 112–114). Thousand Oaks, CA: Sage.

Kiesler, S., Sproull, L., & Eccles, J. S. (1985). Pool halls, chips, and war games: Women in the culture of computing. *Psychology of Women Quarterly, 9*, 451–462.

Ko, C.-H., Yen, J.-Y., Chen, C.-C., Chen, S.-H., Wu, K., & Yen, C.-F. (2006). Tridimensional personality of adolescents with Internet addiction and substance use experience. *The Canadian Journal of Psychiatry/La Revue Canadienne de Psychiatrie, 51*, 887–894.

Krackhardt, D. (1994). The strength of strong ties: The importance of philos in organizations. In N. Nohria & R. Eccles (Eds.), *Networks and organizations: Structure, form, and action,* (pp. 216–239). Boston, MA: Harvard Business School Press.

Kraut, R. E., Kiesler, S., Boneva, B. S., Cummings, J., Helgeson, V., & Crawford, A. (2002). Internet paradox revisited. *Journal of Social Issues, 58*, 49–74.

Kraut, R. E., Patterson, M., Lundmark, V., Kiesler, S., Mukopadhyay, T., & Scherlis, W. (1998). Internet paradox: A social technology that reduces social involvement and psychological well-being? *American Psychologist, 53*, 1017–1031.

Kubey, R. W., Lavin, M. J., & Barrows, J. R. (2001). Internet use and collegiate academic performance decrements: Early findings. *Journal of Communication, 51*, 366–382.

Kyngas, H., Mikkonen, R., Nousiainen, E. M., Rytilahti, M., Seppanen, P., Vaattovaara, R., et al. (2001). Coping with the onset of cancer: Coping strategies and resources of young people with cancer. *European Journal of Cancer Care, 10*, 6–11.

Lee, E., & Leets, L. (2002). Persuasive storytelling by hate groups online: Examining its effects on adolescents. *American Behavioral Scientist, 45*, 927.

Lenhart, A., Ling, R., Campbell, S., & Purcell, K. (2010). *Teens and mobile phones*: Pew Internet. Retrieved June 4, 2010, from http://pewinternet.org/Reports/2010/Teens-and-Mobile-Phones.aspx?r=1

Lim, A. F., & Rosen, L. D. (2010, April 23). *The impact of text message interruptions on memory during classroom lectures*. Paper presented at the Western Psychological Association, Cancun, Mexico.

Linn, S., & Lepper, M. (1987). Correlates of children's usage of video games and computers. *Journal of Applied Social Psychology, 17*, 72–93.

Livingstone, S., Bober, M., & Helsper, E. (2005). Internet literacy among children and young people: Findings from the UK children go online project. Retrieved January 16, 2009, from http://eprints.lse.ac.uk/397/1/UKCGO onlineLiteracy.pdf

Malone, T. W. (1981). Toward a theory of intrinsically motivating instruction. *Cognitive Science: A Multidisciplinary Journal, 5*, 333–369.

Marsh, J. (2010). Young children's play in online virtual worlds. *Journal of Early Childhood Research, 8*, 23–39.

Maynard, A. E., Subrahmanyam, K., & Greenfield, P. M. (2005). Technology and the development of intelligence: From the loom to the computer. In R. J. Sternberg & D. D. Preiss (Eds.), *Intelligence and technology: The impact of tools on the nature and development of human abilities* (pp. 29–53). Mahwah, NJ: Lawrence Erlbaum.

Mazalin, D., & Moore, S. (2004). Internet use, identity development and social anxiety among young adults. *Behavior Change, 21*, 90–102.

McAdams, D. P. (1997). The case for unity in the (post)modern self: A modest proposal. In R. D. Ashmore & L. J. Jussim (Eds.), *Self and identity: Fundamental issues* (pp. 46–78). New York: Oxford University Press.

Mesch, G. S. (2003). The family and the Internet: The Israeli case. *Social Science Quarterly, 84*, 1039–1050.

Mesch, G., & Talmud, I. (2006). The quality of online and offline relationships: The role of multiplexity and duration of social relationships. *The Information Society, 22*, 137–148.

Mitchell, K. J., Wolak, J., & Finkelhor, D. (2007). Trends in youth reports of sexual solicitations, harassment and unwanted exposure to pornography on the internet. *Journal of Adolescent Health, 40*, 116–126.

Nardi, B., & Harris, J. (2006). *Strangers and friends: Collaborative play in World of Warcraft*. Paper presented at the proceedings of the 2006 20th anniversary conference on Computer Supported Cooperative Work, Alberta, Canada.

Neulight, N., Kafai, Y. B., Kao, L., Foley, B., & Galas, C. (2007). Children's participation in a virtual epidemic in the science classroom: Making connections to natural infectious diseases. *Journal of Science Education and Technology, 16*, 47–58.

Nie, N. H., & Hillygus, D. S. (2002). Where does Internet time come from? A reconnaissance. *IT & Society, 1*, 1–20.

Okagaki, L., & Frensch, P. A. (1994). Effects of video game playing on measures of spatial performance: Gender effects in late adolescence. *Journal of Applied Developmental Psychology, 15*, 33–58.

Plester, B., Wood, C., & Joshi, P. (2009). Exploring the relationship between children's knowledge of text message abbreviations and school literacy outcomes. *British Journal of Developmental Psychology, 27*, 145–161.

Reich, S. M., Subrahmanyam, K., & Espinoza, G. E. (2009, April 3). *Adolescents' use of social networking sites—Should we be concerned?* Paper presented at the biennial meeting of the Society for Research on Child Development, Denver, CO.

Rideout, V. (2001). Generation rx.Com: How young people use the Internet for health information [Electronic version]. Retrieved December 18, 2008, from http://www.kff.org/entmedia/upload/Toplines.pdf

Rideout, V. J., Foehr U, G., & Roberts, D. F. (2010). *Generation M²: Media in the lives of 8- to 18-year-olds*: Menlo Park, CA: A Kaiser Family Foundation Study. Retrieved June 5, 2010, from http://www.kff.org/entmedia/mh012010pkg.cfm

Rideout, V. J., Vandewater, E. A., & Wartella, E. A. (2003). Zero to six: Electronic media in the lives of infants, toddlers and preschoolers. Retrieved November 10, 2009, from http://www.kff.org/entmedia/3378.cfm

Roberts, D. F., Foehr, U. G., & Rideout, V. (2005). Generation M: Media in the lives of 8- to 18-year-olds [Electronic version]. Retrieved December 16, 2008, from http://www.kff.org/entmedia/7251.cfm

Roberts, D. F., Foehr, U. G., Rideout, V. J., & Brodie, M. (1999). *Kids and media@ the new millennium: A comprehensive national analysis of children's media use*. Menlo Park, CA: Kaiser Family Foundation.

Rosen, L. D., Chang, J., Erwin, L., Carrier, L. M., & Cheever, N. A. (2010). The relationship between "textisms" and formal and informal writing among young adults. *Communication Research, 37*, 420–440.

Rosser, J. C., Jr., Lynch, P. J., Cuddihy, L., Gentile, D. A., Klonsky, J., & Merrell, R. (2007). The impact of video games on training surgeons in the 21st century. *Archives of Surgery, 142*, 181.

Salomon, G. (1979). Interaction of media, cognition, and learning. San Francisco, CA: Jossey-Bass.

Schepis, T. S., Marlowe, D. B., & Forman, R. F. (2008). The availability and portrayal of stimulants over the Internet. *The Journal of Adolescent Health, 42*, 458–465.

Skinner, H., Biscope, S., Poland, B., & Goldberg, E. (2003). How adolescents use technology for health information: Implications for health professionals from focus group studies. *Journal of Medical Internet Research, 5*:e32. doi: 10.2196/jmir.5.4.e32

Slater, M. D. (2003). Alienation, aggression, and sensation seeking as predictors of adolescent use of violent film, computer, and website content. *The Journal of Communication, 53*, 105–121.

Slater, M. D., Henry, K. L., Swaim, R. C., & Anderson, L. L. (2003). Violent media content and aggressiveness in adolescents: A downward spiral model. *Communication Research, 30*, 713–736.

Smahel, D., & Subrahmanyam, K. (2007). "Any girls want to chat press 911": Partner selection in monitored and unmonitored teen chat rooms. *CyberPsychology & Behavior, 10*, 346–353.

Stallabrass, J. (1995). Empowering technology: The exploration of cyberspace. *New Left Review, I*(211), 3–32.

Stanger, J. D. (1998). *Television in the home 1998: The third annual national survey of parents and children*. Philadelphia: University of Pennsylvania.

Steen, F. F., Greenfield, P. M., Davies, M. S., & Tynes, B. (2006). What went wrong with *The Sims Online*? Cultural learning and barriers to identification in a massively multiplayer online role-playing game. In P. Vorderer & J. Bryant (Eds.), *Playing computer games—Motives, responses, and consequences* (pp. 307–323). Mahwah, NJ: Erlbaum.

Steinfield, C., Ellison, N. B., & Lampe, C. A. C. (2008). Social capital, self-esteem, and use of online social network sites: A longitudinal analysis. *Journal of Applied Developmental Psychology, 29*, 434–445.

Stettler, N., Singer, T., & Sutter, P. (2004). Electronic games and environmental factors associated with childhood obesity in Switzerland. *Obesity Research, 12*, 896–903.

Subrahmanyam, K. (2009). Developmental implications of children's virtual worlds. *Washington and Lee Law Review, 66*, 1065–1084.

Subrahmanyam, K., Garcia, E. C., Harsono, S. L., Li, J., & Lipana, L. (2009). In their words: Connecting online weblogs to developmental processes. *British Journal of Developmental Psychology, 27*, 219–245.

Subrahmanyam, K., & Greenfield, P. M. (1994). Effect of video game practice on spatial skills in girls and boys. *Journal of Applied Developmental Psychology, 15*, 13–32.

Subrahmanyam, K., & Greenfield, P. M. (1998). Computer games for girls: What makes them play? In J. Cassell & H. Jenkins (Eds.), *From Barbie to Mortal Kombat: Gender and computer games* (pp. 46–71). Cambridge, MA: MIT Press.

Subrahmanyam, K., & Greenfield, P. M. (2008a). Communicating online: Adolescent relationships and the media. *The Future of Children, 18*, 119–146.

Subrahmanyam, K., & Greenfield, P. M. (2008b). Media symbol systems and cognitive processes. In S. Calvert & B. Wilson (Eds.), *The Blackwell handbook of children, media, and development.* (pp. 166–187). England, UK: Blackwell Publishing.

Subrahmanyam, K., Greenfield, P. M., & Tynes, B. M. (2004). Constructing sexuality and identity in an online teen chat room. *Journal of Applied Developmental Psychology: An International Lifespan Journal, 25,* 651–666.

Subrahmanyam, K., Kraut, R., Greenfield, P., & Gross, E. (2001). New forms of electronic media: The impact of interactive games and the Internet on cognition, socialization, and behavior. In D. Singer & J. Singer (Eds.), *Handbook of children and the media* (pp. 73–99). Thousand Oaks, CA: Sage.

Subrahmanyam, K., & Lin, G. (2007). Adolescents on the net: Internet use and well-being. *Adolescence, 42,* 659–677.

Subrahmanyam, K., Reich, S. M., Waechter, N., & Espinoza, G. (2008). Online and offline social networks: Use of social networking sites by emerging adults. *Journal of Applied Developmental Psychology, 29,* 420–433.

Subrahmanyam, K., & Smahel, D. (2010). *Digital youth: The role of media in development.* New York: Springer.

Subrahmanyam, K., Smahel, D., & Greenfield, P. M. (2006). Connecting developmental constructions to the Internet: Identity presentation and sexual exploration in online teen chat rooms. *Developmental Psychology, 42,* 395–406.

Suzuki, L. K., & Beale, I. L. (2006). Personal web home pages of adolescents with cancer: Self-presentation, information dissemination, and interpersonal connection. *Journal of Pediatric Oncology Nursing, 23,* 152–161.

Suzuki, L. K., & Calzo, J. P. (2004). The search for peer advice in cyberspace: An examination of online teen bulletin boards about health and sexuality. *Journal of Applied Developmental Psychology, 25,* 685–698.

Tikhomirov, O.K. (1974). Man and computer: The impact of psychological processes on the development of psychological processes. In D. E. Olson (Ed.), *Media and symbols: The forms of expression, communication, and education* (pp. 357–382). Chicago: University of Chicago Press.

Tizard, B., Philips, J., & Plewis, I. (2006). Play in pre-school centres: Play measures and their relation to age, sex, and IQ. *Journal of Child Psychology and Psychiatry, 17,* 251–264.

Tsai, C.-C., & Lin, S. S. J. (2003). Internet addiction of adolescents in Taiwan: An interview study. *Cyberpsychology & Behavior, 6,* 649–652.

Turkle, S. (1997). *Life on the screen: Identity in the age of the Internet.* New York: Simon & Schuster.

Turow, J., & Nir, L. (2000). *The Internet and the family 2000: The view from parents, the view from kids.* Annenberg Public Policy Center of the University of Pennsylvania. ERIC Document Reproduction Service No. ED448874.

Tynes, B. M. (2005). Children, adolescents and the culture of online hate. In N. E. Dowd, D. E. Singer, & R. F. Wilson (Eds.), *Handbook of children, culture, and violence* (pp. 267–289). Thousand Oaks, CA: Sage.

Valkenburg, P. M., & Peter, J. (2007). Preadolescents' and adolescents' online communication and their closeness to friends. *Developmental Psychology, 43,* 267–277.

Valkenburg, P. M., Peter, J., & Schouten, A. P. (2006). Friend networking sites and their relationship to adolescents' well-being and social self-esteem. *CyberPsychology & Behavior, 9,* 584–590.

Van den Bulck, J. (2004). Television viewing, computer game playing, and Internet use and self-reported time to bed and time out of bed in secondary-school children. *Sleep, 27,* 101–104.

Vandewater, E. A., Shim, M., & Caplovitz, A. G. (2004). Linking obesity and activity level with children's television and video game use. *Journal of Adolescence, 27,* 71–85.

Vygotsky, L. S. (1978). *Mind in society: The development of higher psychological processes.* Cambridge, MA: Harvard University Press.

Whitlock, J. L., Powers, J. L., & Eckenrode, J. (2006). The virtual cutting edge: The Internet and adolescent-self-injury. *Developmental Psychology, 42,* 407.

Wilson, J. L., Peebles, R., Hardy, K. K., & Litt, I. F. (2006). Surfing for thinness: A pilot study of pro-eating disorder web site usage in adolescents with eating disorders. *Pediatrics, 118,* e1635.

Winzelberg, A. (1997). The analysis of an electronic support group for individuals with eating disorders. *Computers in Human Behavior, 13,* 393–407.

Wolak, J., Mitchell, K. J., & Finkelhor, D. (2002). Close online relationships in a national sample of adolescents. *Adolescence, 37,* 441–456.

Wu, W. (2010, May 6). Avatars go to school, letting students get a feel for the work world. *The New York Times.* Retrieved May 6, 2010, from http://www.nytimes.com/2010/05/07/nyregion/07avatar.html

Young, K. S. (1998). *Caught in the net.* New York: John Wiley & Sons.

CHAPTER 5

Social Networking, Social Gaming, Texting

YONG ZHAO, WEI QIU, AND NAIYI XIE
Michigan State University

Social media are dominating forces in the lives of teenagers nowadays. They spend an average of more than 7.5 hours a day and seven days a week on social media—more time than in any other activity besides (maybe) sleeping, according to the 2010 survey study by the Kaiser Family Foundation on the media consumption of American teenagers from 8- to 18-years-old (Rideout, Foehr, & Roberts, 2010). While not all media consumption is related to social media, it is not exaggeration that social media occupy a sizable portion of teenagers' media consumption. In fact, the same study showed that 7th to 12th graders spend an average of 1 hour and 30 minutes per day on just one media activity: text messaging (Rideout et al., 2010, p.3).

Against the backdrop of teenagers' avid social media consumption, parents, educators, and the general public have been trying to understand and debate about the phenomenon of social media mania among teenagers. By putting this phenomenon into a global perspective, this chapter seeks to understand the similarities and differences of teenagers around the world, in terms of their social media consumption, the motivations behind their embracement of social media, and the potential effects facing them. A global view of teenagers' social media activities might facilitate parents, educators, and policy makers to make reasonable judgment about and constructive responses to teenagers' engagement with social media. More important, it will help us as a society to consider how to integrate digital media into current curricula and to transform learning experiences, so that the young generation will be better prepared for a world that is ever-changing.

What Are Social Media?

As the case with all new phenomena, it is almost impossible to define social media because they are evolving constantly and rapidly. Scholars, the social media industry, and social media enthusiasts provide various definitions of social media. An example of scholarly interpretation of social media comes from a study that defined social media as a group of Internet-based applications that allow the creation and exchange of user-generated content (Kaplan & Haenlein, 2010). Based on this definition, typical examples of social media are blogs, social network sites (SNS), virtual worlds, games, Wikipedia, and YouTube.

As an example of the social media industry's effort to capture the essence of social media, Mayfield (2008) interpreted social media as a group of emerging online media with a number of characteristics: participation, openness, conversation, community, and connectedness. Mayfield included blogs, wikis, podcasts, forums, content communities, and micro-blogging (e.g., Twitter) as six types of social media.

One independent consultant and blogger depicts on his blog that social media reflect a landscape encompassing an extensive trove of social media services and tools (Cavazza, 2009). Cavazza's (2009) concept of social media landscape is just one of those popular visualized definitions of social media online that are tweeted, tagged, and shared by millions of individuals inhabiting the social media landscape. According to Cavazza (2009), the social media landscape consists of four main chunks (expressing, sharing, networking, and gaming) that are structured around social platforms.

The diversity of social media definitions reveals an interesting quality of social media. It depicts social media as a term and a space that encourages grassroots-based, individualized, and democratic voices, rather than one that sets an authoritative, universal, and static tone. Further, while social media are interpreted differently, a common theme runs through all these definitions: That, above all, social media remain an extension of our physical existence (McLuhan & Gordon, 2003). If McLuhan and Gordon's (2003) argument—*the medium is the message*—still stands today, then social media send out a clear and strong message: social media are designed to connect and to influence, anytime and anywhere. Teenagers interact with and influence their friends through expressing, sharing, networking, and gaming, as Table 5.1, a summary of major social media that are presently popular among the young generation and which is based on Cavazza's (2009) social media landscape.

According to this table, social media are not necessarily confined to the Internet. Mobile phone, for example, has become a globally popular social media as it provides various Web services. In fact, according to a study conducted by the Pew Research Center, texting is the only media activity that outgrew other activities among teenagers (Lenhart, Madden, Macgill, & Smith, 2007). The same study also pointed out

Table 5.1 Social Media, Tools, and Examples

Function	Tools	Examples
Expressing	Publication tools	blogs (blogger), wikis (Wikipedia), microblogs (Twitter), citizen news (digg), livecast (blogtv), texting
	Discussion tools	forums (Tianya), IM (MSN), 3D chats (IMVU), texting
	Aggregation tools	FriendFeed, etc.
Sharing	Content sharing	video (YouTube), pictures (Flickr), music (Last.fm), links (Delicious), document (Slideshare)
	Product sharing	recommendation platforms (Crowdstorm, douban), collaborative feedback (FeedBack2.0), swapping platforms (LibraryThing)
	Place sharing	local address (Whrrl), events (Upcoming), trips (TripWolf)

Function	Tools	Examples
Networking	Ex-classmates	Classmates
	Niche networks	Boompa
	BtoB networks	LinkedIn
	Mobile networks	Groovr
	Network Building	Ning
Gaming	Casual games	Pogo, BigFish
	Social games	Zynga, PlayFish, MMORPG (World of Warcraft), MMO (Drift City), Casual MMO (Club Penguin)
Platforms		Facebook, MySpace, Bebo, Orkut, Mixi, Cyworld, Xiaonei

that SNS and social games have remained as popular social media among teenagers since 2006, whereas Instant Messages and landline phones have become less popular. In this chapter, we focus on three social media: texting, SNS, and social games. Meanwhile, we use the following terms interchangeably—*teenagers, young generation, adolescents, children,* and *youth*—to represent Generation M (M stands for media), who grew up during the birth and rise of the Internet (Rideout et al., 2010).

How Do Teenagers Consume Social Media Globally?

During the early days of social media, researchers noticed that teenagers' social media consumption varied from region to region. For example, American teenagers seemed more active on computer-based social applications, such as email, chat rooms, and video games, whereas teenagers from Japan and Scandinavia were more avid adopters of mobile phone and other mobile services (Lyman, Billings, Ellinger, Finn, & Perkel, 2005).

This section synthesizes the literature that compares teenagers' social media consumption in the West, such as in the United States and the United Kingdom, with that from the East, such as in China, Japan, and South Korea. These countries are selected because, individually, they are very different from each other in terms of the spread and

consumption of social media, and collectively, these countries more or less reflect the current "pulse" and future trends of social media around the globe.

Texting

Texting, short for *text messaging,* is an exchange of information between people through mobile devices or the Internet. Ever since its inception, texting has been rapidly adopted by teenagers worldwide. It becomes more and more popular around the world as cell phone ownership among the young generation increases dramatically and the cost of texting becomes more affordable. In the United States, almost two out of three young people (66%) own a cell phone in 2010, as compared to 39% in 2005 (Rideout et al., 2010). According to a 2009 Nielsen study, American teenagers sent an average of 3,146 text messages a month in the fall of 2009, or 10 messages every waking hour in their after-school life (Entner, 2010). Demographically, girls tend to spend more time on texting than boys, and Black and Hispanic children tend to spend more time on it than their White peers. In the United Kingdom, half of 5- to 9-year-old children own a cell phone (Naish, 2009). While no specific data are available on how many text messages British children send on a daily basis, it is not hard to imagine the magnitude of British children's texting activity, based on the fact that British people sent 11 million text messages an hour in 2009 (MDA, 2010).

In Asia, the cell phone penetration rate reached a record high in 2009: 48.9% in China, 77.3% in Japan, and 80.6% in South Korea according to a study co-sponsored by the GSM Association and NTT Docomo (GSMA & NTT Docomo, 2009). New data showed that 20% of Japanese high school girls own two phones, and some own even more (Mundy, 2010). It was also found that teenagers use mobile phones more for short message service (SMS) and mobile email than for voice calling (GSMA & NTT Docomo, 2009). Its low cost might be the main reason for the popularity of texting among Asian teenagers. According to the MIIT (Ministry of Industry and Information Technology), the price for sending a message in China, for example, is 0.1 RMB (Renminbi, equivalent of U.S. $0.012), which is much cheaper than a local call (0.3 RMB/minute, equivalent of U.S. $0.03) or a long-distance call (0.7 RMB/minute, equivalent of U.S. $0.10). Meanwhile, there is no fee charged on a text message, but it takes 0.05 RMB per minute to receive a call on a cell phone. Because a majority (70.4%) of teenagers in China have a monthly allowance of a mere 20 RMB (iResearch, 2009), it is not unusual for text messages to be so popular among Chinese teenagers.

Teenagers use texting for a variety of purposes. In a thematic analysis research that studied the theme of text messages among young people, the researchers found that a majority (61%) of messages were related to relationship maintenance, such as social arrangement, salutary, friendship maintenance, romantic and sexual; another large chunk (31%) of messages involved informational exchange and practical arrangement (Thurlow & Brown, 2002). This study suggested that texting was an indispensable communication channel for young people to keep in touch with their friends and parents. Meanwhile, texting is a way for young people to participate in political campaigns and civic services, such as voting (Lenhart et al., 2008). However, this texting mania also causes serious concerns among parents and educators about things such as text addiction, text bullying, sexting (text messaging with sexual content), and literacy development

(Ambrogi, 2009; Wood, Jackson, Plester, & Wilde, 2009).

Social Networking

Online social networking is another dominant force behind teenagers' social media consumption. Rideout et al.'s (2010) study showed that American teenagers on average spend 22 minutes a day on SNS, which is 25% of their computer time. Forty percent of young people visit SNS regularly, and they spend almost an hour (54 minutes) on SNSs a day. More than half (55%) of online teenagers have profiles on SNSs (Lenhart et al., 2007). Lenhart et al.'s (2007) study also showed that most teenagers restrict access to their profiles in some way: 66% set their profile as invisible to the public, nearly half (46%) of teenagers reveal that they give at least some false information, and most teenagers rarely post information on public profiles that would help strangers actually locate them, such as their full name, home phone number, or cell phone number. The study also noted that parents, usually (49%), know if their children have an online SNS profile.

Internationally, teenagers are similarly avid about online social networking. But there are regional differences in terms of how and where children conduct online social networking (Cosenza, 2009). Cosenza (2009) also summarized the top three SNSs in major countries (Table 5.2).

There is extensive reportage on the popularity of Facebook and MySpace in the Western world; however, relatively little is known about the development of SNSs in other regions. For instance, 91.5% of Chinese teenagers consider QQ, Kaixin, or Xiaonei as their major SNS (iResearch, 2009). Nearly every Chinese adolescent has an account in QQ, the largest social networking platform in China, where one can simultaneously chat in text, audio, and video; play *QQ games*; find friends on *QQ campus*; and manage profiles in *Qzone*. In South Korea, nearly every young person has a virtual home on Cyworld, and there is even a new word in South Korea for people who spend too much time in Cyworld: *Cyholic* (Business Week, 2005). The Infinita Market Research Report (2007) shows that Mixi, from

Table 5.2	Top Three SNSs		
Countries	*SNS #1*	*SNS #2*	*SNS #3*
Australia	FaceBook	MySpace	Twitter
Canada	FaceBook	MySpace	Flickr
China	QQ	Xiaonei	51
France	FaceBook	Skyrock	MySpace
Germany	FaceBook	StudiVZ	MySpace
Italy	FaceBook	Netlog	Badoo
Russia	V Kontakte	Odnoklassniki	LiveJournal
Spain	FaceBook	Tuenti	Fotolog
U.K.	FaceBook	Bebo	MySpace
U.S.	FaceBook	MySpace	Twitter

Japan, occupies 80% of the Japanese social networking market. Orkut, another popular SNS, is the most popular among Indians and Brazilians (Orkut, 2010).

While a majority of teenagers participate in SNS, there are still a sizable number of teenagers who are nonparticipants. In her study, boyd (2007) identified two types of nonparticipants in her study: *disenfranchised teens* and *conscientious objectors*. According to boyd's definition, disenfranchised teens are those without Internet access, those whose parents succeed in banning them from participation, and the online teens that primarily access the Internet through school and other public venues where social network sites are banned. Conscientious objectors include politically minded teens who wish to protest against Murdoch's News Corp (the corporate owner of MySpace), obedient teens who have respected or agree with their parents' moral or safety concerns, marginalized teens who feel that social network sites are for the "cool kids," and other teens who feel as though they are too cool for these sites.

Social Games

Another popular social media activity among young people is social games (Heim, Brandtzæg, Kaare, Endestad, & Torgersen, 2007). Social games are the video games driven by turn-taking actions between two or more players (O'Neill, 2008). Social games can be played on stand-alone game consoles, mobile devices, or SNSs, such as Facebook. The most popular social games currently in the United States are Facebook games such as *FarmVille* and *PetVille* (Morrison, 2010), iPhone games such as *Lux Touch* and *Galcon* (Kohler, 2009), and MMOs (massively multiplayer online games such as *World of Warcraft* (WoW) and *Second Life*. In China, the top social games in 2009 included *Happy Farm, House Buying, Parking Wars, and Renren Restaurant* (Lukoff, 2009).

Teens spend a significant amount of time playing social games. According to the 2008 PEW Study (Lenhart et al., 2008) on teens and video games, nearly all American teens (i.e., 97% of 12–17-years-olds) play games on computers, the Internet, consoles, or cell phones. Girls (94%) are as likely to play games as boys (99%), but with less frequency and for shorter periods of time. Nearly one third (31%) of teens are daily gamers (meaning they play games every day). Popular games among teens are racing, puzzle, sports, rhythm, simulation, and MMOs. In China, adolescent game players amounted to 35 million people in 2009, which is 46.1% of the entire social game player population in China, and the game population is increasing at an annual rate of more than 20% (CNNIC, 2009).

MMOs are especially popular among teens. Every one out of five (21%) teens claims to have played MMOs, and nearly one third (30%) of boys report that they have had MMO experiences (Lenhart et al., 2008). This is the latest step in a progression of social games from paper-and-pencil fantasy games (e.g., *Dungeons and Dragons*) to text-based multi-user dungeons (MUDs) on computer and later to the virtual digital worlds online (Steinkuehler & Williams, 2006). In MMOs, players build virtual economies and social worlds by trading and engaging in community involvement activities. MMOs also provide a virtual reality for young people to actively study scientific reasoning (Steinkuehler & Duncan, 2009), social sciences (Squire, 2002), literacies (Gee, 2007), foreign languages (Zhao & Lai, 2008) and digital literacies (Steinkuehler, 2008).

Why Do Teenagers Love Social Media?

Teenagers love social games, live on SNSs, and text each other constantly. A single question on the mind of parents and educators is "Why are social media so attractive and important to them?" In fact, social media fulfill a number of psychological, social, and emotional needs of teenagers, which makes them not only extremely popular, but also an essential part of teenagers' lives.

Escape

To begin with, social media offer a place for teenagers to escape. Today's social media provide virtually boundless possibilities for escaping from real life—parental supervision, boredom, depression, and so on. Escapism seems to be a main source of gratification for young Internet users (Leung, 2003). The escapism of social media has both positive and negative consequences. On one hand, it serves as a coping strategy for adolescents to deal with disturbing family environments, boredom, isolation, discrimination, and depression (Cabiria, 2008; Hwang, Cheong, & Feeley, 2009). Hwang, Cheong, and Feeley (2009) found that, among adolescents in Taiwan, the higher their depression was, the more they reported engaging in online communication,

entertainment, and information searches. Cabiria (2008) argued that virtual worlds provided marginalized gay and lesbian adolescents a place to maintain a sense of personal integrity, community, and well-being.

On the other hand, escapism that occurs at pathological levels may lead to harmful social relationships, obesity and other negative health consequences from a lack of activity, and further depression (Bessière, Pressman, Kiesler, & Kraut, 2010). More important, escaping from challenges in the real world may further the phenomenon of moratorium: a delay in the development of independence and cognitive maturity to handle challenges (Pickhardt, 2009).

Entertainment

Social media provide a place for entertainment. For teenagers, social media function as a "third space" to build their social lives (Oldenburg, 1999; Soukup, 2006). Oldenburg (1999) noted that it is essential to the well-being of adults to have a third space beyond home and workplace that allows people to socialize, such as cafés or bookstores. Likewise, for adolescents, a third place beyond home and school, such as a playground, is important for their social development. However, it becomes increasingly difficult for children to find a third space to hang out because the adults' hold on space is more thorough, and the rules on young people's gatherings and behaviors at shopping centers, on sidewalk, and at city parks become tighter (Childress, 2004). Not only spatially restricted, children nowadays are deprived of time to socialize with their friends because they participate far more often in professionally supervised activities (Gaster, 1991).

Under such circumstances, children adopt the virtual third space carved out by SNSs, texting, and social games for socialization. Social media possess a number of qualities to function as a third place (Soukup, 2006). In social media, children are able to claim the ownership of the space without having to negotiate with adults. Meanwhile, social media provide a place where children can be temporarily free of their social status and background in real life, which oftentimes are a barrier to their efforts to make friends. Also, social media such as SNSs and texting are easy to access, searchable, persistent, and playful, which provides a lasting sense of belonging (boyd, 2007). Taken together, social media make it possible for adolescents to build a social life that is hard to establish in their offline space.

Connections

Social media help teenagers connect with their peers, friends, parents, and strangers. As mentioned earlier, a majority of teenagers play social games to cement their offline friendships and to meet new people online (Hundley & Shyles, 2010). In a study on children's perception of social media, Hundley and Shyles (2010) found that children can have more than 200 friends on the "friend list" of their MySpace, and they spend time on SNSs mainly for the purpose of socialization and entertainment, such as talking with friends, updating profiles, checking other profiles, checking messages, meeting friends, and getting in touch with old friends.

Cell phones and text messaging offer the potential of always-on companionship and connectedness. As a mobile and private tool, texting fulfills children's constant curiosity about the lives of their peers and lowers their anxiety about being out of the loop. As a mother confessed in a *New York Times* blog (Parker-Pope, 2009),

> Texting is how kids stay connected with their peers. It is as ubiquitous as the notes we used to pass in school. For many kids, it's a major part of their social world, and not having it makes them feel like an outcast. At least, that's what my daughter says . . . I feel her pain.

Indeed, texting helps children stay in touch with those friends with whom they have a hard time getting together physically after school because of the living condition predefined by suburban life style, or because their friends have moved to another school district or region for various reasons.

In addition, social media have become an important tool for children to communicate with their parents. A single text message of "hello" helps to make the unvoiced care visible and to cement the bond between parents and children. In a more practical sense, texting and SNSs make it possible for parents and children to know each other's whereabouts, to change plans, and to say things that are hard to say when talking on the cell phone or in person. In addition, texting offers an easier way for parents to reach their children when they are in different time zones because of travel, relocation, or family changes (Chen, 2009).

Exploration

Social media also serve as an "identity laboratory" for children to explore their possible selves (Turkle, 1995) and inhabit roles that are inaccessible to them (Gee, 2007). In *Life on the Screen*, Sherry Turkle (1995) observed that "MUDs provide worlds for anonymous social interactions in which one can play a role as close to or as far away from one's 'real self' as one chooses" (p.183). This is the same case with MMOs, where young players construct their identities or personas by taking on distinctive avatar names, profiles, and actions and by assuming the corresponding social responsibilities and consequences in the virtual world. Similarly, young people adopt social networking tools for self-expression (boyd, 2007). Meanwhile, cell phones gradually become an extension of young people's body and mind (Turkle, 2007) because of all the personal information, numbers, photos, and previous messages stored in cell phones.

What Are the Social Media Effects on Teenagers?

With the ever increasing consumption of social media among children and teenagers, researchers across disciplines have started to attend to the effects of social media on their development. So far, a considerable amount of literature has addressed the content and experience of children's social media use and the projected influence of such experiences. Empirical studies investigating longitudinally the actual psychological and social effects of social media consumption are still in their initial stages (Livingstone, 2003). Overall, there are three major areas of concern about how social networking, social gaming, and texting can affect the development of children: (1) their social-emotional development, (2) the risks presented by social media settings and the assumed resultant harms, and (3) education, learning, and cognitive development. Within these three areas, researchers have found both positive and negative scenarios of how social media may affect children.

Effects on Social-Emotional Development

Childhood and adolescence are considered crucial for one's development, in that during these periods of time children will form their self-concept, come to realize their identity in society, develop essential social skills, and start to learn to participate in public life. Today's children are born with a computer mouse in their hands, and many of them have access to social networking sites at a very early age (Bauman & Tatum, 2009). Engagement in a variety of social media has been found to correlate with children's formation of self-concept and self-esteem and to play an important role in children's presentation, negotiation, and formation of identity (Jackson et al., 2008). Evidence collected to date from qualitative studies has found that the nature and affordances of social media can both enhance and hinder children's social and emotional development.

For the positive and promising scenario, social media can effectively facilitate the process of identity formation and socialization in at least three aspects. First, social media provide more opportunities and spaces for young children to experience different identities. Since the stakes are "perceived to be low, online spaces can be treated as 'safe' places to explore identities, work through personal issues, or even 'act out' unresolved conflicts with others" (James et al., 2009, p. 15). Studies have found that through various activities, from creating and updating their profiles (boyd, 2008; boyd & Heer, 2006), blogging (Huffaker, 2006), and sharing and creating textual, audio, and video artifacts in different social media settings (Livingstone, 2003; Stern, 2008), children are given opportunities to express and present themselves. Given the invisibility of the physical body and the lack of non-verbal cues in social interaction, children

need to "write themselves into being" (boyd, 2008) and present their lives so as to let others know about them. These activities of constructing narratives and sharing stories about their daily life are considered to be powerful channels for their identity formation and socialization (James et al., 2009; Valentine & Holloway, 2002).

Second, engaging in social media encourages more self-reflection and self-evaluation in children. It is found that in diverse social settings afforded by social media, children are learning to present themselves according to their imagined community of audience and to navigate through various social situations (boyd, 2008; boyd & Heer, 2006). During this process, they are found to be constantly reflecting and evaluating in order to better express who they are, which in turn can help them refine their social skills and enhance their engagement in public life (Green & Hannon, 2007; Jackson et al., 2008).

Finally, social media also provide children the opportunity to gain the feedback they need to form their self concept and for social development (James et al., 2009). It is argued that feedback can help children come to understand the reception they get from different communities concerning the different selves they try to present and the opinions they want to express, all of which help them make possible changes to improve their presence (boyd, 2008). For instance, Huffaker (2006) suggested that blog characteristics such as opportunities for reader feedback or links to other bloggers foster the formation and maintenance of children's identities, social ties, social interaction, and online communities. However, positive and negative feedback may work differently in terms of affecting children's self-perception. For example, Valkenburg, Peter, and Schouten (2006) found that positive feedback on the profiles enhanced adolescents' social self-esteem and well-being, whereas negative feedback decreased their self-esteem and well-being.

There is also evidence, however, that the affordances of social media that could be promoting children's identity formation may also do them harm if misused or overused. First, while experimenting with multiple identities may enhance the children's social emotional development, exploring incoherent, deceptive, or harmful identities could cause a negative effect on oneself and others (James et al., 2009). In their study, Harman, Hansen, Cochran, and Lindsey (2005) found that children who reported the most faking behaviors on the Internet (e.g., pretending to be someone quite different) had poorer social skills, lower levels of self-esteem, higher levels of social anxiety, and higher levels of aggression. Moreover, some social media settings, such as virtual spaces and massively multiplayer online role-play games (MMORPGs), due to their unique characteristics, make it possible for children to explore harmful identities, which could result in negative consequences in their offline lives (James et al., 2009).

Second, since social interaction mediated by social media sites is in and of itself different from traditional face-to-face interaction, with less experience in social communication, children may find it more difficult to interpret messages they have received online because of the lack of social cues such as nonverbal gestures and facial expression. Misinterpretation of social cues in online spaces can also lead to harmful consequences for children (Bauman & Tatum, 2009; Dwyer, 2008).

Last, but not least, while the feedback children receive from others may be facilitative in their identity formation, being overly dependent on the feedback can also lead to an unstable identity and an insufficient ability in problem-solving and decision-making (James et al., 2009). As boyd (2008) found, as far as "being cool" is the primary goal of presenting oneself in MySpace, children all tend to manage their presence according to external factors such as their peers' views on what is cool and their feedback, even though some of the acts are against the expectation of themselves or their teachers and parents.

Effects on Psychological Well-Being

When considering the effects children may gain from participating in social media, perhaps the biggest concern for parents, teachers, and schools is safety. Indeed, numerous cases have been reported to warn parents, educators, and children how dangerous it can be when children are exposed to those social media settings without careful scrutiny (Lenhart & Madden, 2007). In the news, the safety of popular social networking sites often comes to the spotlight (e.g., Rawe et al., 2006). National and international surveys about the safety of online social networks have revealed that there are two major areas of concern related to this issue, namely contact and content (e.g., Byron, 2008; Lenhart & Madden, 2007). It is found that by far the most serious public concern about children using social networking sites are the dangerous contacts encountered by children, including sexual predators, cyber-stalkers, and cyberbullies. Data show that a considerable amount of children and teenagers have reported being contacted by strangers with sex-related requests and messages (e.g., Livingstone, 2003). Reported cases of cyber-stalking and cyberbullying are also of high frequency (Palfrey, Sacco, boyd, DeBonis, & Tatlock, 2008). In terms of the inappropriate content, it includes the content children are exposed to during their use of social media, such as pornography and commercials, or that created and shared by themselves that may be abused by others, such as their private information, all of which can result in negative psychological and behavioral effects (Palfrey et al., 2008; Sharples, Graber, Harrison, & Logan, 2009).

However, evidence collected to date about how children interpret and deal with this content seems to imply that the reality is less peculiar and definite than people have thought. For instance, it is found that children do have the awareness of and skills for issues like how to deal with unwanted messages and requests they have received and how to manage their presence, privacy, and profiles to avoid undesirable consequences, such as making decisions of what not to say to audiences of different types (Livingstone, 2008). It has also been found that the danger and risk are not equal across all demographics (Palfrey et al., 2008).

In fact, the evidence so far indicates that "the risk of children being duped by online predators is small and the public image of online predators who trick naive children into becoming victims of abuse is largely inaccurate" (Crook & Harrison, 2008, p. 29); for another thing, the intense and frequent use of social media does not, of itself, indicate that children are naïve or significantly vulnerable to dangerous behavior (Livingstone, 2008).

There are a few studies done recently that may help us better understand this situation. For example, Ybarra, Mitchell, Wolak, and Finkelhor (2006) investigated the impact of Internet harassment on children and young people, who reported varied level of distress and depression due to the harassment they had received. In a later study, Ybarra and Mitchell (2008) looked into the risks children and young people may have according to different social networking sites, and they found that different sites hold different types of risks. The same research team (Wolak, Finkelhor, Mitchell, & Ybarra, 2008) also presented an in-depth analysis of the characteristics of those children who are particularly vulnerable to Internet sex crimes and the characteristics of certain social networking sites that may increase the likelihood of such crimes occurring.

Effects on Cognitive Development and Learning

Besides the concerns of how different social media settings may affect children's development socially and psychologically, there has been growing interest in how different social media technologies may affect children cognitively. Questions have been raised, such as if they have effects on how children learn and know about the world we are living in and how we can promote learning through social media. Researchers have already proposed that information processing in virtual worlds indeed requires some cognitive skills different from those we need in the physical world, both mechanically and pragmatically (Green & Hannon, 2007; Greenfield, 2004; Montero & Stokols, 2003). This is considered particularly significant for children because childhood is a critical period for the development of the brain and learning abilities; therefore, their experience with social media could have long-term impact on their cognitive development (Byron, 2008; Wang, Kinzie, McGuire, & Pan, 2009). However, at this moment, empirical investigation into how engaging in different social media settings may actually affect children cognitively is scarce.

Nonetheless, available evidence already indicates that social media hold substantial promises in facilitating and enhancing learning.

Around the world, some pioneering projects have already been carried out to integrate social networking applications in school settings to promote creative and collaborative learning and research, critical thinking, and problem-solving ability (Sharples et al., 2009). For example, the Becta Project investigated how Web 2.0 technologies had been adopted in U.K. schools (Crook & Harrison, 2008). Various applications of social media that were used in teaching and learning were examined, including blogs, podcasts, wikis, forums, social bookmarking, and so forth. Although the significance of the findings varied, the research team proposed that, when used effectively, Web 2.0 technologies can have a positive impact on motivation and engagement. Four potential educational benefits of Web 2.0 technologies have also been identified, namely "stimulating new modes of enquiry, engaging in collaborative learning activities, engaging with new literacies, and online publication of content" (Crook & Harrison, 2008, pp. 4-5). These findings are consistent with some other studies on the impact of social media technology on learning (Green & Hannon, 2007; Redecker, Ala-Mutka, & Punie, 2010; Sun, 2009; Vie, 2008; Wang et al., 2009; Wellings & Levine, 2009).

Along the same line, researchers have also been exploring the potential of social gaming for learning and teaching (Gee, 2005; Prensky, 2001). Earlier findings indicated that video game playing improves visual-spatial skills, which are considered important to performance in mathematics, science, and technology (Jackson et al., 2008). Moreover, recent research has implied that across various age groups, the affordances of social gaming, particularly MMORPGs, can support learning in many ways, including literacy development (Steinkuehler, 2007), acquiring subject area knowledge (Young, Schrader, & Zheng, 2006), developing life and social skills (Ducheneaut & Moore, 2005), and enhancing creativity (Kirriemuir & McFarlane, 2004). Intellectually challenging game playing, in particular, provides opportunities for children to develop a wide range of skills, especially some metacognitive abilities (Crook & Harrison, 2008; Green & Hannon, 2007). For example, the Quest Atlantis project, a learning project that employed a multiuser, virtual environment to immerse children, ages 9 through 12, in educational tasks, was designed based on commercial gaming environments, with lessons from educational research on learning and motivation. It exemplifies the affordances of social gaming in supporting and promoting children's learning in various subjects, intercultural learning, and the development of higher level cognitive ability (Barab, Thomas, Dodge, Carteaux, & Tuzun, 2005).

Last, but not least, the various mobile platform-based social media tools, with their easy and convenient access, have gained increasing popularity as being powerful tools to enhance learning. Emerging evidence from research has already indicated that texting and other mobile technologies can enhance children's literacy and communication skills (eNotAlone.com, 2009) and foster situated, participatory, and collaborative learning (Shuler, 2009).

On the other hand, some researchers also have concerns that engaging in social media at a too early age might gradually stifle children's creativity and imagination (Bauman & Tatum, 2009). Their opportunities for exploring a wider range of perspectives and knowledge could be limited or narrowed because of the personalized information consumption, customized preferences, and commitment to certain communities (James et al., 2009).Yet again, there is no empirical study so far to explore if such effects do exist.

Overall, various social media, especially social networking sites, are considered to be important places for children's development and socialization. With the variety of themes and focuses, children can experience diverse social settings where they connect and interact with different people, both known or unknown. More significantly, it is widely recognized by researchers that the line between online and offline social lives does not necessarily exist; rather, they are two parts of life that are mutually constructed and incorporated into each other (e.g., Livingstone, 2003, 2008; Valentine & Holloway, 2002).

Implications

The previous sections have highlighted the trends of Generation M's social media consumption:

- Today's children are deeply immersed in a variety of social media, and they are simultaneously using different social media tools for different purposes and to meet different needs in their lives.
- Such extensive and in-depth participation has nurtured them into being "multiliterate" in a variety of technologies and has developed a wide range of skills that have not been covered adequately in schools (Green & Hannon, 2007).
- Through Web 2.0 oriented activities such as creating, sharing, and gaming, they have engaged themselves in and enjoyed the kind of informal learning that is considered largely different from what they experience in schools.

Moreover, not only the developmental course, lifestyle, and learning experience are changing for today's children, the entire world is under profound transformation driven by globalization and technology (Zhao, 2009). A number of pioneering researchers and organizations have defined a set of skills and knowledge that students need to acquire in order to be successful in the new global economy (e.g., "Framework for 21st Century Learning," 2009). Among the set of crucial knowledge and abilities, information literacy, media literacy, and ICT (Information and Communication Technology) literacy are listed as critical skills for success in the 21st century. It is argued that students are supposed to not just master the skills of using the new technologies and new media, but also to be able to utilize these technologies, media, as well as other essential cognitive and social abilities to communicate with others, create, evaluate and analyze information, and solve real-life problems in the age of globalization. As researchers and educators this means that to prepare our children for the 21st century, we are facing a series of challenges.

For Researchers

More empirical studies are definitely needed to provide solid evidence on the actual effects of social media participation on children's social, emotional, psychological, and cognitive development. In each of the areas concerning the possible effects of social media consumption, in-depth exploration is necessary in order to test our assumptions about social media and to find out how the affordances and constraints of social media can affect children's development. Considering the evidence we have at hand, we are now in need of an in-depth understanding of questions like how children interact with different social media for various purposes; what effects, both positive and negative, such interaction may have on children's development; and how we can evaluate students' knowledge and skills in using social media, and so forth.

For Educators

It is our belief that social networking sites, social gaming, and texting do bear educational benefits through providing ample opportunities for children to develop the skills and acquire the knowledge they need in the 21st century through authentic activities (James et al., 2009; Redecker et al., 2010; Sharples et al., 2009). However, it has been widely recognized that schools today are not keeping pace with the change in children's life and learning in terms of the technologies they are familiar with and the activities they are truly passionate for (Green & Hannon, 2007; Palfrey & Gasser, 2008; Redecker et al., 2010; Sharples et al., 2009; Wellings & Levine, 2009). Rather, what a lot of schools have been doing is to block and strictly limit student's access to new technologies, including various social media tools, which in turn has deepened the gap. However, schools and educators need to realize that while such action may make the safety issue invisible in the school right now, it may result in deepening the gap between the digital generation and their school education in the long term, or even result in simply storing up the problem for the society in the future (Crook & Harrison, 2008).

Therefore, the challenges for today's schools and educators are (1) to effectively make use of the educational benefits of social media for formal learning and teaching; (2) to help students transfer, reinforce, and further develop the knowledge and skills they have acquired through the new technologies within school—under effective guidance and facilitation; and (3) to create and maintain a safe and supportive learning environment for the students. Teachers, too, are confronted with the challenge that, given the richness of social media, they are no longer the only source where students can obtain information, that their students may be more proficient than they are in using the new Web 2.0 technologies, and that the kind of learning their students find interesting and engaging tends to be quite at odds with the kind that they have had in the classroom. Meanwhile, teachers also need to be aware of the opportunities and risks to their students when they are using social media and of the strategies to balance the good and the bad aspects of it.

Suggestions

Transforming the Learning Environment

Schools and educators need to reconsider their roles and work out ways to release the learning potential of social media in school. First of all, it is necessary for school leaders to not only have the vision of integrating various Web 2.0 technologies into curriculum, but to also create a learning culture that supports and nurtures risk-taking innovations across the school. For one thing, school leaders and teachers need to recognize, understand, and value the wide range of skills and interests children have today and then provide them the space and opportunity to refine and reinforce those skills in a formal educational setting. While it is true that children today are born into a world rich in technologies that enable access to numerous possibilities in life, it does not necessarily mean that they are inherently able to use these technologies in a sophisticated, responsible, and productive way ("Framework for 21st Century Learning," 2009). Therefore, it is the school's responsibility to provide students with resources, assistance, and guidance in effectively using social media for their learning and development.

In addition, teachers need to be encouraged and empowered to adopt Web 2.0 technologies and to make use of social media settings for instruction. This implies changes on at least two levels. First, in order to understand and make effective use of various social media technologies, teachers themselves have to be fluent in information, digital, and media literacy (Green & Hannon, 2007). Second, the role of teachers needs to be transformed from a centered and authoritative role of information giving to someone that offers guidance and mentoring to enable and facilitate learner-centered learning (Redecker et al., 2010).

Managing the Risk of Social Media

Schools need to distinguish the current fears of society from the actual risks to children. As Livingstone (2003) pointed out, "the link between risks, incidents and actual harm is genuinely tenuous: Not all risks taken result in worrying incidents, not all worrying incidents result in actual or lasting harm" (p. 157). What schools could do is to educate children about the risks, helping them to be aware of them, to learn to recognize and deal with them, and to practice how to take responsibility in using social media.

Furthermore, schools can proactively use social media and Web 2.0 technologies to present positive messages to teenagers. Studies show that parents and schools, joined by advocacy groups, foundations, and community organizations, are now using Facebook, Twitter, and other social media platforms to promote adolescent well-being (Donahue, Haskins, & Nightingale, 2008). In Donahue, Haskins, and Nightingale's (2008) report, there are a number of exemplary reach-out efforts of using social media to convey positive messages to the young generation regarding a number of critical issues, such as childhood obesity, unplanned pregnancy, tobacco, HIV, global awareness, and civic engagement. The key is to engage the digital generation by "harnessing its passion for media and technology and incorporating it into rigorous, more participatory learning experiences" (Wellings & Levine, 2009, p. 5).

To achieve this, schools needs to fight fire with fire by creatively using media to provide youth with positive messages that counteract the negative and potentially damaging messages to which they are so frequently exposed (Donahue et al., 2008). More important, schools have the responsibility to prepare the young generation to be both discerning consumers and brave creators in the expanding landscape of social media.

References

Ambrogi, S. (2009). "Sexting" craze on the rise among British children [Electronic version]. Reuters. Retrieved March 31, 2010, from http://www.reuters.com/article/idUSTRE5733SG20090804

Barab, S., Thomas, M., Dodge, T., Carteaux, R., & Tuzun, H. (2005). Making learning fun: Quest Atlantis, a game without guns. *ETR&D, 53*(1), 86–107.

Bauman, S., & Tatum, T. (2009). Web sites for young children: Gateway to online social networking? *ASCA, 13*(1), 1–7.

Bessière, K., Pressman, S., Kiesler, S., & Kraut, R. (2010). Effects of Internet use on health and depression: A longitudinal study. *Journal of Medical Internet Research, 12*(1), e6.

boyd, d. (2007). Why youth (heart) social network sites: The role of networked publics in teenage social life. In D. Buckingham (Ed.), *MacArthur Foundation series on digital learning—Youth, identity, and digital media* (pp. 119–142). Cambridge, MA: MIT Press.

boyd, d. (2008). Why youth (heart) social network sites: The role of networked publics in teenage social life. In D. Buckingham (Ed.), *Youth, identity, and digital media* (pp. 119–142). Cambridge, MA: MIT Press.

boyd, d., & Heer, J. (2006). *Profiles as conversation: Networked identity performance on Friendster.* Paper presented at the Hawai'i International Conference on System Sciences, Kauai, HI.

Business Week. (2005, September 26). E-society: My world is Cyworld. *Business Week.* Retrieved April 9, 2009, from http://www.businessweek.com/magazine/content/05_39/b3952405.htm

Byron, T. (2008). Safer children in a digital world: The report of the Byron Review [Electronic version]. Retrieved April 9, 2009, from http://www.dcsf.gov.uk/byronreview/

Cabiria, J. (2008). Virtual world and real world permeability: Transference of positive benefits for marginalized gay and lesbian populations. *Journal of Virtual Worlds Research, 1*(1), 1–13.

Cavazza, F. (2009). Social media landscape redux [Electronic version]. Retrieved April 16, 2010, from http://www.fredcavazza.net/2009/04/10/social-media-landscape-redux/

Chen, P. (2009, November 5). Texting as a health tool for teenagers. *New York Times*. Retrieved April 16, 2010, from http://www.nytimes.com/2009/11/05/health/05chen.html

Childress, H. (2004). Teenagers, territory and the appropriation of space. *Childhood, 11*(2), 195–205.

CNNIC. (2009). 2009 Chinese online game market research report [Electronic version]. Retrieved April 2, 2010, from www.cnnic.net.cn/upload files/pdf/2009/11/24/110832.pdf

Cosenza, V. (2009). World map of social networks [Electronic version]. Retrieved May 12, 2010, from http://www.vincos.it/world-map-of-social-networks/

Crook, C., & Harrison, C. (2008). Web 2.0 technologies for learning at key stages 3 and 4: Summary report [Electronic version]. Retrieved April 9, 2010, from http://research.becta.org.uk/upload-dir/downloads/page_documents/research/web2_ks34_summary.pdf

Donahue, E. H., Haskins, R., & Nightingale, M. (2008). Using the media to promote adolescent well-being. *The Future of Children: Policy Brief, 18*(1), 7.

Ducheneaut, N., & Moore, R. J. (2005). More than just 'XP': Learning social skills in massively multiplayer online games. *Interactive Technology and Smart Education, 2*(2), 89–100.

Dwyer, C. (2008). *Digital relationships in the "MySpace" generation: Results from a qualitative study.* Paper presented at the 40th annual Hawaii International Conference on System Sciences, Waikoloa, HI.

eNotAlone.com. (2009). Benefits of text messaging for children [Electronic version] Retrieved from http://www.enotalone.com/article/19396.html

Entner, R. (2010). Under-aged texting: Usage and actual cost [Electronic version]. Retrieved May 12, 2010, from http://blog.nielsen.com/nielsenwire/online_mobile/under-aged-texting-usage-and-actual-cost/

Framework for 21st Century Learning. (2009, April 13). Retrieved April 16, 2010, from http://www.p21.org/documents/framework_

Gaster, S. (1991). Urban children's access to their neighborhood: Changes over three generations. *Environment and Behavior, 23*(1), 70–85.

Gee, J. P. (2005). Learning by design: Good video games as learning machines. *E–Learning, 2,* 5–16.

Gee, J. P. (2007). *What video games have to teach us about learning and literacy.* New York: Macmillan.

Green, H., & Hannon, C. (2007). Their space: Education for a digital generation [Electronic version]. Retrieved April 16, 2010, from http://www.demos.co.uk/publications/theirspace

Greenfield, P. (2004). Developmental considerations for determining appropriate Internet use guidelines for children and adolescents. *Applied Developmental Psychology, 25,* 751–762.

GSMA & NTT Docomo. (2009). *Children's use of mobile phones: An international comparison* [Electronic version]. Retrieved April 16, 2010, from http://www.gsmworld.com/documents/Final_report.pdf

Harman, J., Hansen, C., Cochran, M., & Lindsey, C. (2005). Liar, liar: Internet faking but not frequency of use affects social skills, self-esteem, social anxiety, and aggression. *CyperPsychology & Behavior, 8*(1), 1–6.

Heim, J., Brandtzæg, P. B., Kaare, B. H., Endestad, T., & Torgersen, L. (2007). Children's usage of media technologies and psychosocial factors. *New Media Society, 9*(3), 425–454.

Huffaker, D. (2006). *Teen blogs exposed: The private lives of teens made public,* Paper presented at the American Association for the Advancement of Science (AAAS), in St. Louis, MO.

Hundley, H. L., & Shyles, L. (2010). US teenagers' perceptions and awareness of digital technology: A focus group approach. *New Media Society, 12,* 417–433. doi:10.1177/1461444809342558

Hwang, J. M., Cheong, P. H., & Feeley, T. H. (2009). Being young and feeling blue in Taiwan: Examining adolescent depressive mood and online and offline activities. *New Media Society, 11*(7), 1101–1121.

Infinita Market Research Report. (2007). *Mixi: A case study of Japan's most successful social networking service.* Tokyo Japan: Infinita.

iResearch. (2009). 2009 iResearch report on Chinese teenagers' behavior on the Internet [Electronic version]. Retrieved April 16, 2010, from http://report.iresearch.cn/1270.html

Jackson, L. A., Zhao, Y., Witt, E. A., Fitzgerald, H. E., Eye, A. v., & Harold, R. (2008). Self-concept, self-esteem, gender, race, and information technology use. *CyberPsychology & Behavior, 12*(4), 437–440.

James, C., Davis, K., Flores, A., Francis, J. M., Pettingill, L., Rundle, M., et al. (2009). *Young people, ethics, and the new digital media: A synthesis from the Good Play Project* [Electronic version]. Retrieved from http://pzweb.harvard.edu/ebookstore/pdfs/goodwork54.pdf

Kaplan, A., & Haenlein, M. (2010). Users of the world, unite! The challenges and opportunities of social media. *Business Horizons, 53*(1), 59–68.

Kirriemuir, J., & McFarlane, A. (2004). *Literature review in games and learning* [Electronic version]. Retrieved April 9, 2010, from http://halshs.archives-ouvertes.fr/docs/00/19/04/53/PDF/kirriemuir-j-2004-r8.pdf

Kohler, C. (2009). Top 10 iPhone games, as voted by Wired.com readers. *Wired*. Retrieved May 10, 2010, from http://www.wired.com/gamelife/2009/02/readers-picks-o/

Lenhart, A., Kahne, J., Middaugh, E., Macgill, A., Evans, C., & Vitak, J. (2008). *Teens, video games and civics*. Washington, DC: Pew Internet & American Life Project.

Lenhart, A., & Madden, M. (2007). *Teens, privacy and online social networks* [Electronic version]. Retrieved February 26, 2010, from http://www.pewinternet.org/Reports/2007/Teens-Privacy-and-Online-Social-Networks.aspx

Lenhart, A., Madden, M., Macgill, A., & Smith, A. (2007). *Teens and social media. PEW Internet & American life project*. Washington, DC: Pew Charitable Trusts.

Leung, L. (2003). Impacts of Net-generation attributes, seductive properties of the Internet, and gratifications-obtained on Internet use. *Telematics and Informatics, 20*(2), 107–129.

Livingstone, S. (2003). Children's use of the Internet: Reflections on the emerging research agenda. *New Media Society, 5*, 147–166.

Livingstone, S. (2008). Taking risky opportunities in youthful content creation: Teenagers' use of social networking sites for intimacy, privacy and self-expression. *New Media & Society, 10*(3), 393–411.

Lukoff, K. (2009). Top 10 social games in China [Electronic version]. *The Next Web.com*. Retrieved April 17, 2010, from http://thenextweb.com/asia/2009/12/15/top-10-social-games-china/

Lyman, P., Billings, A., Ellinger, S., Finn, M., & Perkel, D. (2005). Literature review kids' informal learning and digital-mediated experiences. White paper for MacArthur Foundation.

Mayfield, A. (2008). *What is social media? (V.1.4)*. Retrieved April 16, 2010, from www.icrossing.co.uk/ . . . /What_is_Social_Media_iCrossing_ebook.pdf

McLuhan, M., & Gordon, W. T. (2003). *Understanding media: The extensions of man*. Corte Madera, CA: Gingko Press.

MDA. (2010). *UK sends 11 million text messages an hour* [Electronic version]. Retrieved April 16, 2010, from http://www.themda.org/mda-press-releases/the-q4-2009-uk-mobile-trends-report.php

Montero, M., & Stokols, D. (2003). Psychology and the Internet: A social ecological analysis. *CyberPsychology & Behavior, 6*(1), 59–72.

Morrison, C. (2010). *Zynga takes the top three on this week's list of top FaceBook gainers by DAU*. Retrieved April 1, 2010, from http://www.insidesocialgames.com/2010/03/31/zynga-takes-the-top-three-on-this-weeks-list-of-top-facebook-gainers-by-dau/

Mundy, L. (2010, March 28). In Japan, teenage cell phone culture makes real connections. *Washington Post*. Retrieved May 10, 2010, from http://www.washingtonpost.com/wp-dyn/content/article/2010/03/26/AR2010032602218.html

Naish, J. (2009). Mobile phones for children: A boon or a peril? [Electronic version]. *Timesonline*. Retrieved April 16, 2010, from http://women.timesonline.co.uk/tol/life_and_style/women/families/article6556283.ece

O'Neill, N. (2008). What exactly are social games? [Electronic version]. *Social Times*. Retrieved April 17, 2010, from http://www.socialtimes.com/2008/07/social-games/

Oldenburg, R. (1999). *The great good place: Cafés, coffee shops, bookstores, bars, hair salons, and other hangouts at the heart of a community*. New York: Marlowe & Company.

Orkut. (2010). *Orkut demographics* [Electronic version]. Retrieved March 31, 2010, from http://www.orkut.co.in/MembersAll.aspx

Palfrey, J., & Gasser, U. (2008). *Born digital: Understanding the first generation of digital natives*. New York: Basic Books.

Palfrey, J., Sacco, D. T., boyd, d., DeBonis, L., & Tatlock, J. (2008). *Enhancing child safety and online technologies* [Electronic version]. Retrieved April 6, 2009, from http://cyber.law.harvard.edu/pubrelease/isttf/

Parker-Pope, T. (2009). When dad banned text messaging. *New York Times*. Retrieved May 12, 2010, from http://well.blogs.nytimes.com/2009/03/30/when-dad-banned-text-messaging/

Pickhardt, C. (2009). Adolescence in the age of electronic entertainment [Electronic version]. *Psychology Today*. Retrieved April 17, 2010, from http://www.psychologytoday.com/print/35304

Prensky, M. (2001). *Digital game-based learning*. New York: McGraw-Hill.

Rawe, J., August, M., Bennett, B., Schmidt, T., Hylton, H., & Ressner, J. (2006). How safe is MySpace? *TIME, 168*, 34–36.

Redecker, C., Ala-Mutka, K., & Punie, Y. (2010). *Learning 2.0—The impact of social media on learning in Europe* [Electronic version]. Retrieved from http://ftp.jrc.es/EURdoc/JRC56958.pdf

Rideout, C. J., Foehr, U. G., & Roberts, D. F. (2010). *Generation M²: Media in the lives of 8- to 18-year-olds (A Kaiser Family Foundation study)*. Menlo Park, CA: Henry J. Kaiser Family Foundation.

Sharples, M., Graber, R., Harrison, C., & Logan, K. (2009). E-Safety and Web2.0 for children aged 11–16. *Journal of Computer-Assisted Learning, 25*(1), 70–84.

Shuler, C. (2009). *Pockets of potential: Using mobile technologies to promote children's learning* [Electronic version] Retrieved from http://www.joanganzcooneycenter.org/pdf/pockets_of_potential.pdf

Soukup, C. (2006). Computer-mediated communication as a virtual third place: Building Oldenburg's great good places on the World Wide Web. *New Media Society, 8*(3), 421–440.

Squire, K. D. (2002). Rethinking the role of games in education. *Game Studies, 2*(1), 29.

Steinkuehler, C. A. (2007). Massively multiplayer online gaming as a constellation of literacy practices. *E–Learning, 4*(3), 297–318.

Steinkuehler, C. (2008). Cognition and literacy in massively multiplayer online games. In J. Coiro, M. Knobel, C. Lankshear, & D. Leu (Eds.), *Handbook of research on new Literacies* (pp. 611–634). Mahwah, NJ: Erlbaum.

Steinkuehler, C., & Duncan, S. (2009). Informal scientific reasoning in online virtual worlds. *Journal of Science Education & Technology, 17*(6), 530–543.

Steinkuehler, C., & Williams, D. (2006). Where everybody knows your (screen) name: Online games as "third places." *Journal of Computer-Mediated Communication, 11*(4), 885–909.

Stern, S. (2008). Producing sites, exploring identities: Youth online authorship. In D. Buckingham (Ed.), *Youth, identity, and digital media* (pp. 95–118): Cambridge, MA: MIT Press.

Sun, Y.-C. (2009). Voice blog: An exploratory study of language learning. *Language Learning & Technology, 13*(2), 88–103.

Thurlow, C., & Brown, A. (2002). Generation txt? The sociolinguistics of young people's text-messaging. *Discourse Analysis Online, 1*(1).

Turkle, S. (1995). *Life on the screen.* New York: Simon & Schuster.

Turkle, S. (2007). *Evocative objects: Things we think with.* Cambridge, MA: MIT Press.

Valentine, G., & Holloway, S. L. (2002). Cyberkids? Exploring children's identities and social networks in on-line and off-line worlds. *Annals of the Association of American Geographers, 92*(2), 302–319.

Valkenburg, P., Peter, J., & Schouten, A. (2006). Friend networking sites and their relationship to adolescents' well-being and social self-esteem. *CyberPsychology & Behavior, 9*(5), 584–590.

Vie, S. (2008). Digital divide 2.0: "Generation M" and online social networking sites in the composition classroom. *Computers and Composition 25*(1), 9–23.

Wang, F., Kinzie, M. B., McGuire, P., & Pan, E. (2009). Applying technology to inquiry-based learning in early childhood education. *Early Childhood Education Journal, 37*(5), 381–389.

Wellings, J., & Levine, M. H. (2009). *The digital promise: Transforming learning with innovative uses of technology* [Electronic version]. Retrieved April 2, 2010, from http://www.digitalpromise.org/Files/Apple.pdf

Wolak, J., Finkelhor, D., Mitchell, K. J., & Ybarra, M. L. (2008). Online "predators" and their victims: Myths, realities, and implications for prevention and treatment. *American Psychologist, 63*(2), 111–128.

Wood, C., Jackson, E., Plester, B., & Wilde, L. (2009). *Children's use of mobile phone text messaging and its impact on literacy development in primary school* [Electronic version]. Retrieved March 31, 2010, from http://partners.becta.org.uk/upload-dir/downloads/page_documents/research/reports/childrens_use_of_mobile_phone_text_messaging.pdf

Ybarra, M. L., & Mitchell, K. J. (2008). How risky are social networking sites? A comparison of places online where youth sexual solicitation and harassment occurs [Electronic version]. *Pediatrics.* Retrieved April 16, 2010, from http://pediatrics.aappublications.org/cgi/content/abstract/peds.2007-0693v1

Ybarra, M. L., Mitchell, K. J., Wolak, J., & Finkelhor, D. (2006). Examining characteristics and associated distress related to Internet harassment: Findings from the second youth Internet safety survey. *Pediatrics, 118*, 1169–1177.

Young, M., Schrader, P. G., & Zheng, D. (2006). MMOGs as learning environments: An ecological journey into Quest Atlantis and The Sims Online. *Innovate, 2*(4).

Zhao, Y. (2009). *Catching up or leading the way: American education in the age of globalization.* Alexandria, VA: ASCD.

Zhao, Y., & Lai, C. (2008). Massively multi-player online role playing games (MMORPGS) and foreign language education. In R. Ferdig (Ed.), *Handbook of research on effective electronic gaming in education.* New York: IDEA Group.

CHAPTER 6

Attention, Comprehension, and the Educational Influences of Television and Other Electronic Media[1]

DAVID S. BICKHAM AND MARIE EVANS SCHMIDT
Center on Media and Child Health
Children's Hospital Boston

ALETHA C. HUSTON
University of Texas at Austin

I magine, for a moment, that we enter a room where a young child is watching television. The child's eyes are fixed on the screen. Her face is almost expressionless, and the flashing of the screen is reflected in her unblinking eyes. We judge that she is entranced, engulfed, possibly even addicted. Is this an accurate observation of what is happening (or not happening) in the mind of the child? Questionable.

Is it one that many parents and teachers believe is typical? Definitely.

It is a prevalent assumption in the United States that the physical inactivity common in television watching implies mental and cognitive inactivity. This belief has become so ingrained in our perceptions of the television experience that it has infiltrated our everyday language: Children are said to have become

[1]The authors would like to acknowledge the considerable intellectual contribution made by the late John Wright to the concepts and conclusions put forth in this chapter.

"couch potatoes" and to "veg-out" in front of television. Inherent in this assumption of passivity is an attribution concerning television's power over the young viewer. The bright lights, loud sounds, and quick movements of the television's images are thought to seize and hold captive the child's attention. The viewer is said to be a passive recipient of television and its messages. She is unable to look away, and the viewing act itself interferes with and inhibits any critical thought processes.

Stemming from these assumptions are policies of educators and beliefs of parents about television's alleged inability to teach. Many assume that television, *as a medium*, interferes with active processing, and they therefore believe that it is not conducive to learning, school achievement, or school-readiness. Teachers rarely incorporate television into their curriculum or encourage targeted viewing as an at-home activity.

If we imagine slight changes in the scene described previously, our preconceived notions can shift. For example, what if the viewer is an infant, say 6 or 8 months old? How would that fact alter our understanding and assumptions about the viewing event? What if, instead of television, she is using an interactive medium such as a video game or a computer? How might this change our belief that she's a passive receiver of images and messages?

It is the purpose of this chapter to examine the ideas behind these popular conceptions of how children attend to and learn from electronic media. Considering that television continues to be the medium that occupies more of the American child's waking hours than any other mass media device (Rideout, Foehr, & Roberts, 2010), much time will be spent discussing the processes that guide attention to this device. The questions that we address, however, will also be applied to other electronic audiovisual media. Are images from audio-visual media overpowering to the child, or does she play an active role in her own attention? How do the types of content and styles of production influence the child's attention to the screen and development of general attention skills? How do the child's goals, experiences, and stage of cognitive development shape the

media use experience and help determine its long-term effects?

We will also review the potential for educational material delivered via electronic media to have positive effects on users. Is it possible to have attractive and well-made educational television that uses the enticing qualities of the medium to teach children and prepare them for school and a life of learning? Or do the essential properties of the medium itself make this impossible? What if the viewer is under the age of two? Does the learning potential from audio-visual media change? Is the very young viewer capable of drawing connections between two-dimensional content and the dynamic and social world in which she lives? What about computers and video games; does the interactivity of these media ensure that they deliver educational content effectively? Are the skills that video games teach consistent with educational success?

It is the goal of this chapter to highlight the ways that young media users are active in the allocation of their attention to and cognitive processing of screen media. We hope to invoke a new image: a picture of a child capable of using media to make her own attentional decisions; a child who actively decides what is worth watching and how to get the most out of it; and a child who gradually learns how to attend to a screen to better understand and master her world and to choose among the various life goals and options it offers her. Such a picture will do more than dispel hasty and superficial judgments about media per se. It will focus the attention of those who raise and educate children on the media's ability, when well designed and produced, to have positive, lasting effects on its young viewers.

In the first part of this chapter, we focus on the active–passive dimension with regard to children's attention to and processing of television and other media, examining how features of the media as well as goals of the user can guide attention. We also discuss the potential impact of media use on attention skills and how very young children watch television. In the second part of the chapter, we turn to the related issue of children's learning from media. We present research evidence to support our view that children at certain ages can learn important facts and critical skills from well-designed educational television. We also review evidence showing that very young children lack the cognitive abilities necessary to learn from television. Overall, we hope to demonstrate that producers of educational media are, and will continue to be, most successful when they implement strategies derived from well-researched concepts of children's attentional and cognitive processes related to media use.

Children's Attention to and Comprehension of Screen Media

Visual and Auditory Attention to Television and Video Games

A number of physical features of visual and auditory stimuli are known to elicit attention to them and, together, to constitute the properties that make stimuli perceptually salient. These "automatic" attention-eliciting characteristics were listed by Berlyne (1960). They include intensity, contrast, change, movement, novelty, and incongruity. To this list we must add stimuli whose content has important learned meanings, such as sirens, the sensation of momentary weightlessness, and symbols like the dollar sign or the swastika.

Auditory attention is surely an important factor because the audio portion of a television program often provides the viewer with information that contextualizes and elaborates the visual content (Anderson & Field, 1983; Lorch, Anderson, & Levin, 1979). Perhaps not surprisingly, auditory attention predicts auditory comprehension (recall of verbal sound track), while visual attention predicts visual comprehension (recall of actions and images) (Rolandelli, Wright, Huston, & Eakins, 1991). Children can attend to the auditory stream of a program and direct their visual attention when a salient sound indicates the need to look at the screen. In this manner, the young viewer uses listening to guide looking.

A similar strategy is not possible with video games because they require constant visual attention to play and attention to games is more task relevant and goal driven than it is for viewing television (Jie & Clark, 2008). In order to track the multiple, co-occurring images and events in video games, players must divide their visual attention. Researchers comparing game players and non-players documented that players responded more quickly to events that could occur at one of two locations on a computer screen (Greenfield, deWinstanley, Kilpatrick, & Kaye, 1994). An intervention that included practice on a video game that required this skill increased participants' ability to divide their attention. Video game play, it seems, requires and in turn fosters the ability to simultaneously visually monitor multiple areas on a screen.

For a final point on visual attention to media, it is important to note that our understanding of these strategies is built on studies that examined children with normally developed attentional processes. How do children with attention problems view television? Do they differ in their allocation of visual attention to the screen? For some time there has been anecdotal evidence that children diagnosed with attention problems can give their undivided attention to television. Research has found that children with and without attention deficit hyperactivity disorder (ADHD) do not differ from other children in the amount of time they spend looking at a screen during viewing (Pugzles Lorch et al., 2004). However, there is evidence that children with ADHD have fewer sustained looking events, are more easily distracted when toys are present during viewing, and have more difficulty recalling aspects of the story than similarly aged comparison children (Acevedo-Polakovich, Pugzles Lorch, Milich, & Ashby, 2006; Lorch, Milich, Flake, Ohlendorf, & Little, 2010). While the amount of time spent looking may be the same regardless of attentional problems, the quality of those looks and their ability to lead to comprehension appear different.

Interestingly, television viewing may also impact the development of attentional skills differently for children with and without ADHD. Problematic outcomes of television viewing over time, including worse cognitive processing and visual attention skills, have been found to be evident in comparison children but not in children with ADHD (Acevedo-Polakovich et al., 2006). The authors who found these results point to the possibility that the biological contributors of the disorder are so strong that environmental attributes that might impact other children have far less effect on children with ADHD. The findings examining how children with attention problems use, process, and are impacted by television add additional complexity to our understanding of children's attention to television and remind us that attributes of the viewers shape their experience with and effects of the medium.

Processing Television Content

Because television has existed for much longer than interactive media, we know considerably more about how children watch, understand, and process this medium. In this section, we will review how attention to and comprehension of television are linked and describe the active and passive models that seek to explain this linkage. Finally, we will discuss similar processes with interactive media.

If attention is a prerequisite for comprehension, then producers of educational programs need to concentrate as much on capturing ears and eyeballs as on teaching the content. This assumption has guided much of the research on attention and comprehension, and many researchers have found results supporting a relationship between attention to television and later recall of its messages (Field & Anderson, 1985; Zillman, Williams, Bryant, Boynton, & Wolf, 1980; Zuckerman, Ziegler, & Stevenson, 1978). The assumed causal relationship from attention to comprehension, however, has also been repeatedly challenged. Lorch et al., (1979), for example, reduced children's attention to *Sesame Street* by introducing toys into the environment. However, children with or without toys present did not differ on their level of comprehension. Visual attention and comprehension were related, but not in a way that implied more attention simply led to greater comprehension. Comprehensibility of a segment appeared to

drive attention because the segments that children comprehended the best were the ones they attended to the most. The authors concluded that cues from the auditory track informed the children of the presence of comprehensible content, which in turn led to the participant's full visual attention.

Formal Features and the "Syntax of Television." The content of messages on television is conveyed by the use of various production techniques and conventions that have their own syntactic structure. For example the use of a "lap dissolve" between scenes almost always indicates a change in time or place within the story. Other formal features have been used so often in specific contexts that they have come to communicate semantic information. Scary music, for example, helps the viewer anticipate a scary scene. Because the two are regularly juxtaposed in movies and TV programs, they come to be associated by the child.

Still other features encode program genre, context, and characters (e.g., detective/police story, reality show, situation comedy, news, sports, children's cartoon, etc.). With viewing experience, children come to know the signs that can be used to identify such attributes as well as the likely intended audience, both of which contribute to the decision to attend or not. The age of intended audience tells how comprehensible the program story will be (or how much mental effort will be required to process and understand it), while the genre can tell a child who does not know the particulars of the series whether or not it is the kind of show she usually likes to watch.

The Passive Viewer Model. This model posits that control of attention and processing lie mostly in the television program's form and content, and it is more applicable to young children than to older ones. Building upon the known reactivity of everyone to stimuli of higher physical salience as described previously, this model predicts that children's attention and processing will be governed primarily by the glitz of the production—that is, the rapidity of movement and change and the intensity and salience of both auditory and visual stimuli. Some researchers have proposed that the use of fast paced production techniques does not elicit or permit the desired thorough processing of the content (Singer, 1980). In the passive model, therefore, most children's television is seen as inhibiting the careful processing necessary to glean from each scene its most critical content in order to consider its meaning reflectively.

Regardless of the level of active cognition behind the attending, there are certain features of television that embody Berlyne's (1960) attention-getting attributes. These include, in addition to perceptually salient features, program switch points like commercials and station breaks (Anderson & Levin, 1976; Duck, Gregson, Jones, Noble, & Noy, 1988; Huston & Wright, 1997; Huston et al., 1981).The alleged effects of perceptual salience on attention are well known among producers, as evidenced by the high levels of rapid action, rapid tempo, variability, animation, music, and noise in Saturday morning commercial programs (Huston et al., 1981). Assuming a relationship between attention and comprehension, perceptual salience could also affect what children understand about a television message. Children allegedly can more easily learn material that is linked with perceptually salient and attention-enticing features because that is what passive viewers are preprogrammed to attend to.

The Active Viewer Model. The active model does not reject all of the assumptions on which the passive model is based. Its adherents accept the idea that certain forms and content are prepotent in eliciting attention in infancy and that such features thereby offer some basic supports for active processing that should be taken advantage of in designing positive and constructive children's programs.

The role of the child viewer in the active theory, however, is one where the child is cognitively involved in the television experience (Anderson & Field, 1983). The child's attending is not determined by the images on the screen, but by her own agendas and goals (Huston & Wright, 1989). Instead of capturing her attention, formal features are utilized by the viewer to make her own attentional decisions and viewing choices. In this model, formal features influence comprehension by guiding attention selectively to content that is interesting to and comprehensible by the viewer (Calvert, Huston, Watkins, & Wright, 1982). In short, the active model views children as working deliberately to solve problems of decoding, interpreting, and thus understanding the content. It credits them with using knowledge about the medium and its formal features to do so. The distinction between early passive reactivity and later active control of inputs corresponds to what Wright and Vliestra (1975) called *the distinction between exploration and search.*

The feature-marker or stimulus-sampling model of formal features, a theory assuming the active role of the viewer, posits that features supply experienced viewers with information essential to the processing of the content (Hawkins, Yong-Ho, & Pingree, 1991; Huston & Wright, 1983; Lorch et al., 1979). As a child spends more and more of his life viewing television, he begins to learn the common production uses of formal features. Through this experience, he acquires the ability to recognize and predict content based upon the viewing of specific production techniques.

This theory allows for an effective, goal-driven division of attention where the child uses program features to determine where to direct her attention in order to fulfill her needs and not waste her energy on uninteresting or incomprehensible content (Campbell, Wright, & Huston, 1987). By taking periodic samples of the features and content of television, a child can direct the bulk of his attention elsewhere when the television's offering is of little interest. Children can monitor the soundtrack and attend to the screen only when types of voices, sounds, or music imply the presence of child-oriented material. If the content is not sufficiently enticing to the potential viewer, the sampling does not stop all together: Other program features and contextual features of the viewing environment will lead to further monitoring of program content. Exceptionally salient auditory events such as screams, sirens, and explosions can elicit further samples of content. Much like the other theories assuming an active role for the viewer, the stimulus-sampling model illustrates how a child comes to utilize formal features as an aid in making informed decisions concerning the allocation of attentional energy and effort.

Anderson, Lorch, Field, and Sanders (1981) pioneered the theory that a child's perceptions of the comprehensibility of a message determine her attention to it. To further measure and understand children's attention, Anderson and his colleagues edited segments of *Sesame Street* to create bits with varying levels of apparent comprehensibility. Three types of program manipulation were tested. Some segments were edited so the characters were speaking Greek instead of English. Others were changed to backward speech; in still others the bits of content were sequentially rearranged into a random order. In all situations, subjects paid attention to the bits for a higher percentage of the time when they were unaltered. Greek and backward speech were instantly known to be entirely incomprehensible, and they held attention the least. The random segments were not so manifestly incomprehensible, and the subjects paid correspondingly more attention to them. These results suggest that Cognitive Functions and School-Readiness Skills a child's perceptions of the probable comprehensibility of the bit dictated the amount of attention it received.

Research has yielded support for the active viewer model. The early studies found that changes in scene, character, and bit—all formal features that highlight the need to attend to the screen to evaluate the new status of the program—led to recruitment of attention in those not watching at the moment of change. Conversely, those viewing at the moment of change promptly looked away (Anderson, Alwitt, Lorch, & Levin, 1979; Calvert et al., 1982; Huston & Wright, 1989; Wright et al., 1984).

Brain Activity and the Active Viewer. Central to the active viewer model of television viewing is the idea that viewers activate neurological resources in order to make decisions about how to allocate their attention. Until fairly recently, the specific neurological processes that occur while children watch television were unknowable. With the advancement of work using EEG and fMRI to observe brain activity at the moment of television viewing, researchers have been able to investigate the neurological activities activated to understand televised images (Anderson, Bryant et al., 2006).

In general, studies examining brain activity during television viewing have found that the areas of the brain activated by television content correspond to those areas that would be activated with similar, real-world stimuli. For example, nonverbal material on television appears to be processed in the right hemisphere while material requiring linguistic understanding activates the left hemisphere (Rothschild & Hyun, 1990; Rothschild, Hyun, Reeves, Thorson, & Goldstein, 1988). Violent content activated parts of the brain similar to those involved with traumatic and long-term memory storage (Murray et al., 2006). To investigate the parts of the brain that contribute to the understanding of edited video material, Anderson, Bryant, and colleagues (2006) used fMRI to measure brain activity of eight adults (five men and three women) who were watching normal video segments from movies and random and scrambled video clips. Results indicated that a network of multiple areas of the brain, coordinated by high-level cognitive processes, is activated to comprehend edited video material. Areas handling tasks such as visual identification, inferences about the motivations of other people, and sequence construction, comprised the network. This network was not activated when participants viewed the incoherent video sequences. By demonstrating the activation of this network, the researchers provided concrete evidence that viewers are cognitively active during the viewing of edited video. Their neurological circuitry is hard at work employing the appropriate parts of the brain to comprehend the complex images present in narrative video content.

Video Games and Active-Passive Models of Attention

It is much easier to consider a child who is playing a video game an active participant in their media use experience; they are clearly visually and physically engaged in the game. Aspects of video games that drive players' attention to specific screen content are less easily recognized. Researchers have identified two processes of visual attention that apply to video game play and parallel the active and passive roles of television viewing: the bottom-up (where features attract attention) and top-down (where the goals of the player drive attention) approaches (El-Nasr & Yan, 2006).

Research has shown that there are salient features of video games that attract and shape visual attention. Using eye-tracking technology, researchers examined features of games that impact two types of attention in video games—eye fixation and eye pursuit (Jie & Clark, 2008). Eye fixation is the allocation of visual attention to a specific point; duration of fixation is a key aspect of this behavior. Eye pursuit is the tracking of a moving object. By comparing the complexity of images that were the target of eye fixation, the study found that the more complex an image is the longer and less distractible fixated looks at the image are. Results of this work also showed that when players perform eye pursuit, their visual attention is focused in front of the moving object. Researchers in this study implemented their findings in the design of a video game in order to further substantiate their results. They were able to increase the difficulty of the game by having targets corresponding to the goals of the game appear when the player was looking at a complex image elsewhere on the screen or behind a moving object. Overall, this study showed that the formal features of image complexity and image movement both play a role in how video game players allocate their attention to the screen.

Another study that utilized eye-tracking procedures during participant video game play found examples of both feature-driven and goal-driven attention strategies. Examining the looking patterns of six college-aged students, researchers found that color and motion were both successful at attracting visual attention (El-Nasr & Yan, 2006). However, their overall findings led them to conclude that player goals are stronger drivers of attention than salient visual features. They provided an example where a game required the player to find an exit. The player's attention went first to dark colored doors rather than the brightly colored wall that actually provided an exit. It seems that while bright colors and movements can attract attention, a game player will first visually seek out game features that are in line with his or her goals before turning to features that seem unrelated but salient.

Resolution of the Active and Passive Models

At first glance the active and reactive models appear diametrically opposed. Children are either controlled by a medium or they use it deliberately to allocate their attention. In the preceding video game examples, however, it is possible that these two processes are occurring simultaneously: players direct their attention toward goal-consistent objects but shift attention when another object is sufficiently salient or if their attention strategy is not leading to game advancement. For television, theories like the feature-sampling model illustrate how the active and passive models can be smoothly integrated so as to complement each other. At different points in the viewing process, formal features serve different purposes in attention and cognition. Similarly, at different points in a viewer's development, features may play different roles. It takes time and experience, for example, for children to learn the connections between form and content. For example, children under six do not recognize instant replay as a repetition of the same event, but instead believe the event actually occurred twice (Rice, Huston, & Wright, 1986).

Implied in the previous results and theory is the notion that the feature-sampling model deals not only with the viewer's attention but also with her cognitive processing and motivational judgments. Salient features and segment transitions may attract attention through their audiovisual properties, but in the active models, they merely set the occasion for a viewer to decide to continue to invest attention if the program matches her current abilities and needs, but otherwise not. As sampling occurs, the viewer gains information from the features observed and can consider specific cognitive and motivational questions: "Is this a program I recognize? Is it a program for people like me? Can I understand it? Does it meet my current viewing goals? Will it be fun to watch?" Positive answers to these questions lead to further attention. This attention, however, is constantly reevaluated: "Am I understanding this? How much mental energy is required to continue to understand? Is this memorable enough to merit my investment of energy?" Transitions in the program elicit a re-questioning of the current attentional state based on the cognitive and motivational goals of the child viewer (Huston & Wright, 1989).

Children use different methods of seeking information as they develop. In any particular initially novel setting, they progress from exploring their environment where interesting stimuli can capture their attention, to searching systematically for the specific knowledge they need at any given moment. In the realm of television, formal features guide this transformation. Infants, knowing little about the connection between form and content, explore their television environment, attending automatically whenever perceptually salient events occur. Toddlers between one and two years of age attend when features mark information interesting to them or relevant to their current goals. In other words, this theory predicts that infants are more reactive, while preschool and older children are familiar with most television contexts and are therefore more cognitively active. This does not mean that older children completely stop attending to salient stimuli; in fact, age differences in attention to certain salient features have been found to be small and to occur mostly in specific situations (Calvert et al., 1982; Wartella & Ettema, 1974).

The developmental processes hypothesized by the exploration-search model have met with moderate support. In one study, younger children attended slightly more to high pace rather than low pace programs; no difference was found in the older children, who responded most to continuity of plot (Wright et al., 1984). Another study found that the limitations younger children have in discriminating central from incidental information is reduced when relevant content is deliberately marked by salient features (Calvert et al., 1982; Campbell et al., 1987). This finding adds credence to the argument that a developmental shift occurs between a very early dependence of attention on stimulus salience (passive exploration) on the one hand, and the quest for markers to help decode content messages (active search) on the other.

In combining the active and reactive models of attention, this developmental theory also indicates a shift in the relationship between comprehension and attention. The attention of a very young, inexperienced viewer is organized around salient formal features. This process leads to the comprehension of the material highlighted by such features: Attention leads to comprehension. Slightly older, slightly more experienced viewers, on the other hand, control their attention and allocate it to the television screen when something interesting and comprehensible is happening. Here, anticipated comprehension and relevance, the products of active analysis, control attention. Studies examining attention to videos altered to change comprehensibility have provided evidence for this developmental process in how attention and comprehension are linked (Hawkins et al., 1991; Pingree, 1986).

This developmental model could be applied to help build our understanding of how children attend to and make sense of computer-based content. While television and computers use a similar audio-visual system to convey most information (Lee & Huston, 2003) and almost identical techniques when the computers show videos through the Internet, iTunes, or DVD players, there are numerous and important differences in the way information is presented by these two types of media. For example, when using a browser to access information online, the user must actively seek content; there is no stream of information to sample for features or other indicators of relevance and comprehensibility. The formal features of websites differ depending on their audience and the type of content they are providing (consider the differences between sites such as Lego.com and etrade.com), but research has yet to be conducted that examines how children may use these differences to guide their attention.

Video games, conveyed through computer, handheld, or television-based systems, are another case deserving more consideration in the research. As already described, features of a game can attract attention to content that is relevant to problem solving within a game (El-Nasr & Yan, 2006). Solving puzzles and mastering the physical challenges of a video game, therefore, may be parallel constructs to comprehending content in television. Revealing the relationships among features of video games, players' attention to these features, and players' abilities to solve the puzzles could lead to a better understanding of the processing that occurs during children's video game play.

Multitasking and Splitting Attention: Impacts on Development

The feature-sampling model seeks to explain how the features of a single medium attract attention and influence cognition. But what if multiple auditory or visual informational sources are simultaneously competing for a child's attention? The modern media environment can pose considerably more complex material than a single video image, requiring that a young media user sample from multiple sources (both electronic and not) in order to allocate attention. As media platforms have become more portable and ever present, media multitasking (using multiple types of media at once) has become a commonplace activity. Children aged 8 to 18 spend over 3 hours a day using more than one type of media at a time (Rideout et al., 2010).

Studies examining efforts to use media and simultaneously perform a cognitively demanding task (e.g., a reading comprehension task) have found support for a limited capacity model; when the media and the task compete for similar cognitive resources, the completion of the task is more difficult (Armstrong & Chung, 2000; Lang, Bolls, Potter, & Kawahara, 1999; Pool, Koolstra, & van der Voort, 2003). Given that children are now developing in a multitasking rich environment, it is possible that frequent multitaskers develop information processing styles that allow them to more efficiently allocate cognitive resources. Early research in this area has not found evidence to support this hypothesis. In a series of studies with undergraduate participants, Ophir, Nass, and Wagner (2009) compared heavy and light

media multitaskers in several tests of cognitive control. Heavy multitaskers were found to be easily disrupted by irrelevant, interfering stimuli and were slower in a task switching procedure. Additional work in this area is necessary to better understand if young people who grow up in a multimedia environment develop new exploration-search strategies.

Video Games as Split Attention. As discussed earlier, video games require the user to divide visual attention among multiple stimuli. Much like multitasking, extensive experience with this activity may shape young people's attention skills. There is some evidence that playing video games can increase visual processing and visual attention skills. In a series of lab-based studies examining young adults, Green and Bavelier (2003, 2007) compared video game players' and non-video game players' abilities in a variety of visual skills tasks. Overall, they found that frequent action game players are better than non-gamers at identifying and locating target symbols in the presence of distracters. In addition, these studies found that when non-gamers play an action-based video game for 30 hours (no more than 2 hours a day) in a lab, their visual processing abilities improved more than non-gamers who played a puzzle game.

Children have also been examined in studies that explore how video game play may impact processing skills related to visual attention. Using a larger sample of 114 and a broader age range (7 to 22), researchers had action video game players and non-game players complete three tasks that tested the speed at which they could locate a target image among distracters, the rate their attention recovered, and the extent that they could allocate attention to numerous images at one time (Dye & Bavelier, 2010). Action video game players outperformed non-players on each of these tasks regardless of whether the task was one that was stable or improved across the different age groups. The authors concluded that video game players exhibit attentional skills that are more similar to older non-gamers.

Together, these studies provide some strong evidence that playing action video games contributes to visual processing and attention skills. While there are certainly positive attributes related to developing these skills, some researchers and theorists caution that the visual intelligences fostered in video games and other electronic media may come at a cost of limited development of deeper processing skills that are promoted by traditional media such as print (Greenfield, 2009). Further studies in this area should use longitudinal methods in order to track the development of these skills alongside real-world video game play. With appropriate measures, this work could also examine if the skills fostered by action video game play can transfer into important attentional abilities that are linked to academic success and other life skills.

Television and Attention Problems

The evidence from the multitasking and video game research sets forth the possibility that attention allocation strategies developed to understand media may impact young people's attentional skills and strategies in other venues. This has been a long-standing concern among educators and parents—that using electronic media fosters shorter attention spans and results in children without the skills necessary to be successful in traditional educational environments. TV viewing in infancy may be associated with attention problems in childhood (Christakis, Zimmerman, DiGiuseppe, & McCarty, 2004), but the evidence is mixed (Mistry, Minkovitz, Strobino, & Borzekowski, 2007; Obel et al., 2004; Stevens & Mulsow, 2006). In 2004, Christakis and his colleagues analyzed data from a large, longitudinal study (conducted in the 1980s) of approximately 1,300 children and found that the more TV children watched as infants (age 1) and toddlers (age 3), the more likely they were to have attention problems at age 7.

Other researchers have disputed these results (Mistry et al., 2007; Obel et al., 2004; Stevens & Mulsow, 2006), in particular the notion that TV plays a causal role in the onset of ADHD. In Christakis et al. (2004), the reported association between TV viewing and attention problems was small (OR = 1.09), and the outcome of interest was attention problems as reported retrospectively by parents, not medical diagnoses of ADHD. Further, Foster and Watkins (2010) reanalyzed the data used by Christakis and his colleagues and found that only a small subset (10%) of the sample, who watched over 7 hours of TV a day, had any negative effects from TV viewing. When maternal characteristics and poverty status were added to the analysis as covariates, even this relationship disappeared.

Program content may also influence how and whether TV influences attention. Zimmerman and Christakis (2007) found that viewing violent programs or non-violent, non-educational programs in infancy was associated with later attention problems, but educational program viewing was not.

Associations reported between TV viewing and attention problems, when derived from correlational studies (which do not allow causal inferences), may, more likely, reflect the influence of attention problems on TV viewing (Acevedo-Polakovich, Lorch, & Milich, 2007). Studies suggest that children with attention problems watch more TV, and parents of children with attention problems are more likely to use TV to manage their children's behavior (Acevedo-Polakovich, Lorch, & Milich, 2005; Milich & Lorch, 1994).

Several studies, in fact, have not found associations between early TV viewing and ADHD. In a Danish study, Obel et al. (2004) did not find a significant association between TV viewing in infancy and behavior problems in preschool. In addition, Stevens and Muslow (2006) failed to find a relationship between TV viewing by kindergarteners and symptoms of attention disorders at entry to first grade.

Overall, research has yet to conclude how television viewing impacts attention problems. Clearly, there is a dedicated group of researchers examining this area, and hopefully their continued efforts will help clarify the current inconsistent findings.

Background Television and Infants. When children are very young, the development of their attentional skills may be impacted by background television. The television is on for 8 hours per day (on average) in most American homes (Gertner, 2005), and studies suggest that most infants are exposed to about 2 hours of background television per day (Mendelsohn et al., 2008; Pierroutsakos, Hanna, Self, Lewis, & Brewer, 2004).

In a study by Evans Schmidt et al. (2008), television in the background disrupted very young children's toy play and attention during play. In this study, 1-, 2-, and 3-year-old children were individually invited to play with a variety of age-appropriate toys in the laboratory for one hour. For one half hour the TV was on, and for one half hour the TV was off. The TV played an episode of Jeopardy, with commercials, and parents were instructed not to play or interact with their children unless the children demanded it or became fussy.

When the TV was on in the background, there was less play overall and children's episodes of play and focused attention were shorter. Children also switched among toys more frequently during play when TV was on in the background. Evans Schmidt and her colleagues (2008) speculated that television disrupted play by diverting children's attention toward the TV and away from their ongoing play episodes, thus forcing the children to refocus in order to return to play. TV may also disrupt play as a kind of background noise or general interference. Although the long-term consequences of play episode disruption are unknown, short play episodes and less focused attention during play are considered a marker for developmental delays or poor developmental outcomes (e.g., Faden & Graubard, 2000; Handen, McAuliffe, Janosky, Feldman, & Breaux, 1998; Malone, 1997).

According to the feature-sampling process model, infants primarily react to the features of television. The repeated process of focusing and refocusing attention in response to salient television features may disrupt the development of important attentional facilities. As the research in this area continues, we will hopefully gain a full understanding of how the background media environment impacts the cognitive development of young people.

The Traveling Lens Model

Let us return now to examining models that explain children's television viewing in terms of their attention and comprehension. The traveling lens model is a more comprehensive model that incorporates the attention and comprehension findings along with the well-explored phenomena of attentional habituation and attentional inertia (Rice, Huston, & Wright, 1982). While built from research examining television viewing, it is applicable to other types of screen media as well. The model's key features are shown in Figure 6.1.

An inverted U function, the lens from which the model gets its name, serves as a graphical explanation of the theory. The x-axis can denote any variable that indicates changing levels of ease of comprehension of the stimulus. Examples include familiarity versus novelty, simplicity versus complexity, redundancy versus unpredictability, orderliness versus randomness, and consistency versus incongruity. The y-axis is the level of arousal of interest and the level of attention of the child. The peak of the curve therefore denotes where the stimuli are that receive maximum time and attention from the child. The stimuli are, in this example, television moments, bits, segments, episodes, or series. Moderate levels of comprehensibility characterize a peak in interest, while information falling to the left of the peak is overly familiar or boring. The further to the right of the peak, the more nearly incomprehensible the material. Thus, the two tails fail to arouse interest or receive attention for opposite reasons: one (the left) is too well known already to be interesting, and the other (right) is two complex and difficult to be readily understood. Between the middle and the right tail of the curve, attention and interest to rather difficult, but not totally incomprehensible, events begins to occur, but it requires greater mental effort than the most preferred intermediate level stimuli, as found by Hawkins et al. (1991).

While the lens predicts attention to content at any given moment in time, its movement over time from left to right in the stimulus array is its dynamic aspect. As a child watches more television, his familiarity with the stimuli increases. On the left side (increasing boredom), the same repetition that is initially responsible for familiarity eventually inhibits interest through the process of habituation of attention over repeated exposures. Habituation

Figure 6.1 The Traveling Lens Model

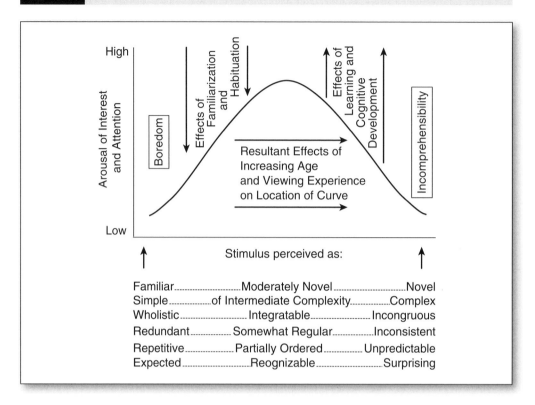

is therefore a reduction in attention as a part of the "been there, done that" reaction. The same process of familiarization, however, has the opposite effect on attention and interest on the right side, or the leading edge of the lens. Here, although exposure is limited at first, as familiarity slowly grows, perceived comprehensibility is enhanced and truly difficult materials become challenging and then interesting. As the elevation of interest is suppressed on the left and raised on the right, the whole lens moves to the right with respect to the ordered array of stimuli. As a result of both cognitive development and experience with the medium over time, a child's allocation of attention shifts toward increasingly complex material. The child's ability to comprehend drives her attention. The lens moves, not because the stimuli themselves are changing, but only because items on one side are rising to a peak, while those on the other side are continuously declining in interest value. The result is a wave-like migration of interest

and attention toward the yet-to-be-mastered stimuli found at the relatively more complex and difficult end of the gradient.

Attentional Inertia. While attention on the leading edge of the lens is at first sporadic, accidental, and ineffective, over time looking there increases, not only because content on the left is boring, but also because occasional or even unintended looking at the mostly incomprehensible gets a boost from another phenomenon of attention: attentional inertia (Anderson et al., 1979). Attentional inertia is the well-documented phenomenon where looks are most vulnerable to ending in their earliest moments (Anderson & Lorch, 1983). Conversely, the longer they continue, the lower the probability of their ending in the next moment. The more time a look has lasted and the more attention one has invested in it, the stronger the forces that sustain its continuance, and the weaker the impulse to look away—making these longer looks less susceptible to distraction (Anderson, Choi, & Lorch, 1987). Inertial properties can, therefore, carry looks into material that would otherwise lose attention because of other qualities of the content. The sustained and focused looking of attentional inertia can then lead to the processing of television content as indicated by high levels of cognitive engagement, resulting in greater memory of the program's material (Burns & Anderson, 1993).

Differences in characteristics of attentional inertia across individuals and television content type indicate that other looking patterns are also employed during viewing. In a study of undergraduate men and women, researchers observed participants as they viewed different types of televised content in an environment with available alternate nonelectronic activities (Hawkins et al., 2005). The viewing was recorded, and the researchers coded for four different types of looks according to their duration (monitoring, orienting, engaged, and stares). Proportion of these different types of looks varied both across and within individuals, indicating that individuals did not employ consistent, characteristic looking patterns. The viewing strategies reported in this study employed short looks (under 15 seconds) much more than stares (more than 15 seconds). In fact, short looks are much more common in general than longer looks (Hawkins, Pingree, Bruce, & Tapper, 1997). This does not mean that deep processing of material is not occurring. While long looks may indicate that a higher degree of cognition is underway, many short monitoring looks is also a valid viewing strategy that is associated with better comprehension of material (Hawkins et al., 1997).

While individuals may not have consistent attention strategies, television genres do produce fairly consistent viewing styles. In the study examining adult viewing behaviors, there was a higher percentage of monitoring looks in drama and news programs than in situational comedies, a finding that the authors attribute to the more demanding narrative structures of these types of programs (Hawkins et al., 2005). Higher monitoring also has been observed when adults view

television commercials (Hawkins et al., 1997), but attention among all but very young children drops when these advertisements are on screen (Schmitt, Woolf, & Anderson, 2003). The style of attention employed by a viewer at any given time, therefore, appears to be driven in part by specific characteristics of what they are viewing.

Even though individual differences and television content may influence the extent to which attentional inertia occurs, it does not impact the ability of the traveling lens model to explain children's attention to television. Other factors of the event can also encourage viewers to expend the necessary cognitive resources to attend to content at the right cusp of the curve. If, for example, the topic of the program or a character being shown is of special interest to the viewer, she could attend to otherwise overly challenging information. Overall, the traveling lens model synthesizes our understanding of the relationship between attention and comprehension into a single framework that can cross program type, content, and even medium.

Educational Media Design and Impact

Let us return for a moment to the viewing experience described at the beginning of this chapter. Our perspective of what the child is experiencing and what she will take away from the experience will be very different when we begin to focus on what she is watching. Suddenly we realize that she is attending to a well-produced program designed to teach children her age developmentally significant material. In other words, she is watching an educational program. Concerns about the power of the medium over the child have been addressed, and now with the introduction of educational content, the viewing experience can be seen to have a potentially positive impact on the viewer's readiness for school and her academic achievement when she gets there. Let us next consider the evidence on such deliberate manipulations of the traveling lens and the endeavor to create quality media content, both on television and on other platforms, that exists at the forward cusp of the curve.

Techniques of Educational Media

One production technique utilized by many television program designers, including Sesame Workshop, is the incorporation of attention-holding, salient features into programs such as *Sesame Street*. While this technique was once criticized as creating a television environment that is too fast paced to allow for deep processing (Singer, 1980), it can be done so as to aid in teaching messages to children. A program designed in this manner can contain humor, puppets, children's and women's voices, or any of the previously described salient features that draw attention. Capturing and holding attention is necessary, but not sufficient, to teach a message, especially when the audience of younger children is unable to separate the central messages from the incidental ones. By utilizing salient features selectively to highlight central content, producers can guide children toward a fuller understanding and better recall of the message (Calvert et al., 1982).

In a technique know as layering, producers insert into a well-designed, attention-holding program, bits of information slightly more complicated than the majority of the program's content. Viewers are exposed to content that they may have otherwise ignored, allowing for novel and complex material to become familiar. Layering is based on Vygotsky's (1978) notion that there is for every concept and for every child a "zone of proximal development" (ZPD), that is, a level of difficulty between the hardest already mastered and the best a child can do with supporting, prompting help. In a layered program, children are offered content that is not immediately familiar and accessible, but that is moderately novel and challenging. To be effective, layering must offer one level of content that falls on the edge of each child's ability to understand. When multiple levels of complexity of the same material are deliberately provided, not only does the program hold interest for a wider range of ages and abilities, but repeated viewing of familiar segments can advance the child's comprehension

to successively deeper layers of the same presentation without losing attention.

Repetition, another simple technique designed to deepen processing, is a common practice of today's producers. While repetition is usually repeating the same central content within an episode or scene, the Nickelodeon program *Blue's Clues* rebroadcasted the same episode every day for a five-day period. Research indicated that the audience for that episode grew each day (Crawley, Anderson, Wilder, Williams, & Santomero, 1999). *Blue's Clues* also provided layered content: three similar puzzles of increasing difficulty for each activity. Investigations into the effectiveness of this repetition approach found that comprehension of the material was expectedly higher, as was use of the demonstrated problem-solving strategies, for a group of young children who saw the program five times than for a group that only saw it once (Crawley et al., 1999). The combination of these techniques helped ensure that children were exposed to previously incomprehensible material, allowing the attentional lens to travel into new domains of difficulty without producing failure or discouragement for the child.

An educational strategy in children's television that is showing considerable success at shaping attention and increasing comprehension is encouraging the audience to overtly participate in the program. Characters speak directly to the viewing audience and ask for their opinion, advice, assistance, or other type of response, and then they pause to allow time for a reaction directed at the screen. *Blue's Clues* was the first program to focus on this educational strategy, and its success has lead to programs such as *Dora the Explorer* and the Elmo's World segment of *Sesame Street* following suit. With repeated viewing of a *Blue's Clues* episode, children's interaction with the show increased and their visual attention did not diminish (Crawley et al., 1999). In two studies that examined the differences in audience participation between experienced and inexperienced viewers of *Blue's Clues*, Crawley and her colleagues (2002) found that experienced viewers actually looked less at the program (especially at program specific, rather than episode specific, information). These experienced viewers interacted more with a new program that used similar audience participation strategies as *Blue's Clues,* indicating that children can learn specific television viewing patterns. The authors concluded that familiarity with format allows for higher levels of content mastery, thereby increasing audience participation. These findings support the notion that the skills required to decode and comprehend televised material are learned and develop with experience.

Apart from specific characteristics within a show, the overall structure of the program (defined as the program's *metastructure*) can also have the potential to support learning. When material is presented in a narrative format—telling a story rather than using magazine style or other formats—educational programs have been shown to lead to increases in the acquisition of language and literacy skills among both very young children (Linebarger & Walker, 2005) and school-aged children (Linebarger & Piotrowski, 2010). This structure also enhances the cognitive processing of the program's content as indicated by higher levels of comprehension and more successful identification of story events in viewers (Linebarger & Piotrowski, 2010). The authors of this research conclude that the narrative structure requires fewer cognitive demands from young viewers as this format follows a well known and easily recognized organization of information, thereby making more resources available for processing the educational material. Overall, the metastructure of program content acts alongside other, specific program characteristics to determine the extent to which young people follow the story and learn educational content.

The Capacity Model. With his Capacity Model, Fisch (2000, 2004) proposed a cognitive process through which children comprehend educational television content. Based on the information processing approach, the Capacity Model suggests that there is a limited amount of cognitive resources available for the comprehension of educational material, and television designed to teach children will not be effective if it has demands that

exceed these limits. The capacity of working memory is central to defining these limits. As children view educational television, they must process both the narrative of the show and the educational content. Fisch proposed that cognitive resources compete to accomplish both of these tasks. As such, these resources are strained the most when there is a large difference between the narrative and educational content. The most successful educational program, therefore, is one that reduces this difference by making the educational lesson central and critical to the plot of the show. When used effectively, this strategy allows for parallel processing of the two types of content, rather than having them compete for limited cognitive resources. This model is the first to propose a mechanism that explains how children extract and understand information from educational content. It applies the notion of cognitively active viewers to the comprehension of educational material in a way that informs the theoretical understanding in this area as well as the application of these concepts to the creation of effective programming.

Educational Computer Games and Software. Educational computer games and software are structurally different from television programs with similar goals. The effective strategies of these media, therefore, will also differ. Unlike television, computers have an interactive interface that has been generally seen as helping advance the cognitive development of its users. However, interactivity has yet to be systematically defined, and its impact on learning has yet to be rigorously tested (Lee & Huston, 2003). Applying aspects of Fisch's (2002, 2004) Capacity Model, interactivity will likely enhance educational content most effectively when it is used to reinforce educational content rather than to detract from it. Research on interactive storybooks supports this concept. When content secondary to the educational goals of the book are interactive (e.g., character or scenery images that animate when the user clicks on them), they can interfere with the educational effectiveness of the book (Labbo & Kuhn, 2000). Similarly, if the interactivity supports, reinforces, and otherwise assists in the processing of the educational content, this approach could be especially effective. These findings and this theoretical perspective would expect that an educational computer program that integrates a rich, relevant storyline with interactivity used as a tool for reinforcing educational content will be more successful in its teaching goals than a program that has a highly interactive game but presents educational content separately from both the narrative and the interactive components of the game.

Children's computer use is no longer limited to programs that are installed on their home machine or that contain finite and relatively static information and content. Instead, children have access to information, games, and communication through the Internet that are constantly in flux and require very different types of cognition and skills to process. This structure combines multiple features that may influence its potential as an educational medium. Consider the comparison of a CD-based encyclopedia to Wikipedia. The first is much more similar to a printed encyclopedia, with its content determined by a set number of authors and finalized on the CD. Wikipedia, on the other hand, presents content that is written by various (unnamed) authors, is of varying levels of accuracy, can be different on a daily basis, is linked to other resources on the same topic, can be discussed and debated, and can be altered by the user. The basic cognitive processing required to extract information from these sources would be very similar as they both involve visual and linguistic information conveyed using a computer interface and they likely use similar wordings that need to be interpreted. There are, however, some considerable differences in the processing required to fully and correctly interpret the data from these two sources. In Johnson's (2006) theoretical framework for cognition and Internet use, she proposed the differences in these cognitive requirements. Websites such as Wikipedia require users to employ metacognitive abilities, including planning and searching strategies as well as evaluation of online material. In addition, the interactive component of Wikipedia, or other sites, necessitates sophisticated written language skills as well as the ability to decode intent and meaning in asynchronous communication exchanges (i.e., not occurring in real time). Exercising these areas may very well improve and promote important cognitive processes such as language, communication skills, and the development of a more expansive knowledge base (Johnson, 2006).

Characteristics inherent in educational computer and video games allow for them to constantly present material at the forward cusp of the curve presented in the traveling lens model previously described, thereby giving them a high potential for success. Television and other static, non-interactive media have to rely on layering and other strategies to ensure that members of their broad audience all have their cognitive needs met. Computer games and other similar software or web applications, on the other hand, can present activities and tasks that vary according to slight increases in difficulty, allowing the user to constantly face material that is optimally challenging. More ambitious software can respond to the individual user's abilities with tailored material that is designed to specifically engage and test them. Each of the stimuli listed in Figure 6.1 can be independently altered at any point in interactive software, guaranteeing that a user experiences an optimum learning environment. Of course, this strategy of engaging and educating users by employing concepts of the traveling lens model takes intentional effort on the end of the programmers and content creators.

Luckily, entertainment games already utilize some of the concepts described previously to engage their users. Materials ranging from complex problem-based puzzles to rhythm-based hand-eye coordination tasks are designed to increase in difficulty throughout a game. Theorists such as Gee (2003) and Lieberman (2006) have made intriguing claims that these video games present material in a manner that is optimal for learning. By utilizing interactivity within a rich virtual world that allows users to explore, fail, and succeed at their own rate, games have an unprecedented opportunity to teach young people everything from specific skills to attitudes and values to thinking and problem solving. In a review of these theories, Amy Thai and others at The Joan Ganz Cooney Center at Sesame Workshop propose a research funding and development agenda that capitalizes on the potential of electronic games and, if implemented, that would potentially change the landscape of education, increase the availability of well-designed teaching games, and change public perspective of this platform (Thai, Lowenstein, Ching, & Rejeski, 2009).

As illustrated in the Sesame Workshop report (Thai et al., 2009), the discussions on this topic continue to address the teaching potential of video games because there is a relatively small pool of existing research that examines the teaching success of these games. In a review of research investigating the educational outcomes of video games among adults, the authors found no systematic evidence indicating that games teach on their own, most likely because many of the instruction-based games and simulators do not employ the intentional structural support for learning that Gee (2003) and others have identified in well-designed games (O'Neil, Wainess, & Baker, 2005). Apparently, there is nothing magical about interactivity or simulation that will guarantee educational success; strategies that follow sound learning principals must be employed in these platforms to help ensure positive outcomes.

The Use of Educational Video Games in Schools. In research examining children, there is some evidence that video game play can enhance problem-solving skills and teach factual information better than less interactive computer-based learning (Tsung-Yen & Wei-Fan, 2009). Much of the research that examines the effectiveness of educational video games does so in the context of school-based game use. For example, in a study conducted in Chile, young school-aged children played handheld educational video games that provided material supporting their lessons on reading comprehension, spelling, and math (Rosas et al., 2003). Those who were given the games performed better on posttests in all these areas than children in other schools who were not given games but otherwise had similar school experiences. The findings that a control group at the same school as the game players did not differ in abilities from the experimental group do, to

some extent, call into question the impact of the games. In a similarly designed study, kindergarten students were assigned to either a group that played educational games during school or one that did not (Din & Calao, 2001). The game-playing group showed increases in their spelling and reading skills. These studies have demonstrated that educational video games can be successfully integrated into school environments to supplement traditional teaching methods, but additional research is needed that examines the long-term impact of these games.

Positive and Long-Term Effects of Educational Television

Our perception of the television experience described at the beginning of the chapter has changed dramatically. We now understand that the viewer not only actively participates in the viewing process, but she may attend to a program designed to hold her attention and elicit her highest potential of cognitive processing. Will she take with her information that will educate and prepare her for school, or will the effects of her attention to an educational program quickly dissipate? To find an answer we turn to long-term studies of the cumulative effects of viewing different kinds of programming on subsequent achievement in school.

Consider one exemplary program as representative of the best research-based use of the techniques described previously for producing optimal attention and processing of educational content. Since its inception, the designers of *Sesame Street* have utilized child development experts as consultants in the creation of their programs. A curriculum carefully designed to prepare children for school was adopted, and production techniques designed to maximize visual attention were employed. Early in its now 40-plus year-old life, researchers began to assess *Sesame Street*'s ability to educate. The first studies found that children encouraged to watch *Sesame Street* scored higher than a control group on tests of skills that the program was designed to teach (Ball & Bogatz, 1970; Bogatz & Ball, 1971). The methods of these studies, however, were seen by some as flawed. Researchers reanalyzing the data argued that the involvement of the parents in the child's viewing choices accounted for at least part of the observed effects of *Sesame Street* (Cook et al., 1975).

The Early Window Project. In a study called "The Early Window Project," the Center for Research on the Influences of Television on Children (CRITC) undertook a three-year longitudinal investigation of the effects of educational television viewing from age two to five and from four to seven in relatively low-income families (Huston, Wright, Marquis, & Green, 1999; Wright & Huston, 1995; Wright, Huston, Murphy et al., 2001; Wright, Huston, Scantlin, & Kotler, 2001). From 1990 to 1994, four waves of data collection occurred. A battery of measures was collected, including academic and language skills, measures of the home learning environment, and time-use diaries that included the titles of television programs the children watched. In order to account for the effects of the home environment and other family differences, relevant measures were included as controls in the overall model.

Viewing *Sesame Street* and similar programs at ages 2 and 3 predicted higher scores at age 5 on measures of language, math, and school readiness. Viewing at age 4 and beyond, however, did not significantly affect later scores. Apparently, there is a window of opportunity where educational television can have its longest, most powerful effects. During this time, however, viewing general audience (adult) entertainment programs and, to a lesser extent, commercial cartoons was found to be detrimental to children's academic future. Viewing such entertainment programming at early ages predicted lower levels of school readiness at age 5 (Huston et al., 1999; Wright & Huston, 1995).

Long-Term Effects: The Recontact Project. The findings that early viewing of educational programs like *Sesame Street* enhances the scholastic potentials of a 5-year-olds may be easily accepted, but what is learned from early television that could still influence them in their adolescence? *Sesame Street* does not teach information that is taught and tested in

high school courses, so how could watching it at a young age help academic performance in high school? Is it not more likely that early educational viewing effects simply fade away by the time children enter third or fourth grade?

To answer that question, a follow-up study was undertaken in the early 1990s to re-contact 15- to 19-year-old young people who had participated in one of two projects, by two different research teams, 10 to 13 years earlier (Anderson, Huston, Schmitt, Linebarger, & Wright, 2001). Because both studies had used many of the same measures on their separate preschool samples, the authors pooled their samples. The located youths completed an hour-long phone interview that included a variety of measures related to their family, schooling, and television viewing. Their creativity was also assessed with a fluency of recategorization procedure, sometimes called the *unusual uses test*. High school transcripts were also obtained.

The results showed both positive relations of preschool educational program viewing and negative relations of general audience entertainment viewing to transcript grades in English, science, and math. These associations were in the same direction for boys and girls, but much stronger for boys than for girls. A boy who watched five hours per week of educational programming at age five had a grade point average of approximately .35 higher than if he had never watched the program. A girl, having watched the same amount of such programs, could only expect about a .10 increase in her high school GPA associated with that early viewing. For girls, conversely, the negative relation of commercial entertainment viewing to achievement was stronger than it was for boys.

Preschool educational viewing was also found to be associated positively with creativity for both sexes (Anderson et al., 2001). Children who watched more educational television, and especially *Mister Rogers' Neighborhood*, scored higher on the test for creativity.

The long-term effects obtained demand a latent mediating variable to complete the explanation. The authors proposed that a positive attitude toward school, enjoyment of learning, the experience of early academic success, and related latent variables would account for the continuity between early viewing and high school achievement. Research to confirm or correct that interpretation is needed.

Just as the bottom line in the first part of this chapter was that viewing is an active process involving perceiving, learning, thinking about, and encoding the content, so it is the conclusion of the second part that it is not the medium that has effects, but the processing of its content. Television in the United States today is not a homogeneous and monolithic entity, and one may well doubt that it ever was such. When educational or violent messages are presented in children's favorite medium at an early age, they have long lasting effects. Analogous findings may be seen in the work of Huesmann and his colleagues (Huesmann & Miller, 1994; Huesmann, Moise-Titus, Podolski, & Eron, 2003), who have shown that violence viewing at age eight is a better predictor of aggressive behavior at age 28, and even 38, than is adult violence viewing. A case for the primacy of early experience with media can clearly be made.

Infant Cognition

The Early Window Project showed the positive impact of educational television viewing by 2- and 3-year-old children. The Recontact Study found that viewing educational content around the age of 5 predicted long-term academic achievement. But, as previously discussed, very young children are also watching television. Are children as young as six months old able to make sense of televised images and messages? How does this viewing impact the development of abilities that are crucial for cognitive development? Research that seeks to answer these questions is, in part, in response to the wide market of baby videos and the numerous educational claims made by their advertisers (Goodrich, Pempek, & Calvert, 2009).

Effects of TV on Cognition

Although few studies have been conducted, most find that the number of hours a child views TV in infancy has no effect or modest effects on cognitive test scores in childhood. Zimmerman and Christakis (2005) reported that each one hour increase in TV viewing before age 3 was associated with small decreases in reading recognition (−0.31 points) and comprehension (−0.58) scores, and digit span memory (−0.10), at age 6. Evans Schmidt et al. (2009) found that each one hour increase in TV viewing before age 2 was not associated with vocabulary (PPVT) or visual motor test scores (WRAVMA) at age 3, when controlling for relevant socioeconomic variables, such as maternal age, income, education, parity, and maternal PPVT scores.

As it is with older children, content may be an important determinant of the effects of TV viewing on infants. In a study by Barr, Lauricella, Zack, and Calvert (2010), children who were heavily exposed to adult-directed TV programs as infants scored lower on tests of cognitive function, school readiness, and executive function at age 4; exposure to child-directed content was not associated with age 4 cognitive skills.

Television Viewing and Language

While some studies have found negative relationships between TV viewing in infancy and language development, particularly among heavy viewers (Chonchaiya & Pruksananonda, 2008; Tanimura, Okuma, & Kyoshima, 2007; Zimmerman, Christakis, & Meltzoff, 2007), other studies have found no effects, particularly when parental variables are taken into account. Evans Schmidt et al. (2009), in an analysis of prospective longitudinal data, found that TV viewing in infancy had no influence on PPVT scores at age 3 when relevant family variables where controlled.

Other studies, however, found that the content of TV programs (which Evans Schmidt et al. [2009] did not study) determines the effects of TV on the development of language. In a study by Zimmerman et al. (2007), each hour of viewing of baby videos (by infants, between 8 and 16 months of age) was associated with a 17-point drop in MacArthur Bates Communicative Development Inventory (CDI) scores. However, overall viewing and viewing at older ages did not influence CDI scores. Linebarger and Walker (2005) similarly found that viewing some programs between 6 and 30 months of age (*Dora the Explorer, Arthur*) was associated with improved language skills at 30 months, whereas viewing other programs (*Teletubbies*) was associated with reduced 30-month-old language skills.

Research by Zimmerman et al. (2009) suggested that TV may negatively influence language development by inhibiting conversation between adults and children. In their study, young children (ages 2 months to 4 years) wore recording devices for 12 hours per day for 6 months. Initial analyses found a relationship between TV viewing and language scores. However, the number of conversational turns engaged in by the child was also associated with language scores. When these conversational turns were included in the analyses, the relationship between TV and language scores disappeared, suggesting that any negative effects of TV on language may be due, at least in part, to reduced opportunities for parent–child conversation in the home. In fact, studies suggest that parents rarely interact with their children during TV exposure (Mendelsohn et al., 2008; Schmitt et al., 2003).

Other research examining background television also indicates that its presence may disrupt parent–child interactions. In a study by Kirkorian, Pempek, Murphy, Schmidt, and Anderson (2009), 1-, 2-, and 3-year-old children were individually invited to play with a variety of age-appropriate toys in the laboratory for one hour. For one half hour the TV was on, and it played one of a variety of prime-time programs prerecorded and selected by the parent. For the other half hour, the TV was off. Throughout the study, parents were instructed to act with their child as they normally would at home. When the TV was on, there was less verbal interaction, less interaction overall, and parents were less responsive to their children. Parents were more likely to engage in passive type interactions with their children (e.g., verbally communicating with the child without looking at him or her), and less likely to engage in active type interactions, such as helping a child build a block tower.

Several studies suggest infants do not learn words from TV as easily as they do from live speakers. In one study, by Krcmar, Grela, and Lin (2007), children under 22 months had difficulty learning verbal labels from TV. Babies between 15 and 24 months were exposed to words in four separate conditions: by a live speaker looking at the named object (joint reference), a live speaker looking at something other than the named object, a speaker on television, or an infant TV program with a voice-over. Children were most likely to learn the object labels presented in the joint reference condition with the live speaker, and they were least likely to learn the labels from the infant television program.

In research by Richert, Robb, Fender, and Wartella (2010), infants did not learn words from commercially produced baby videos intended to teach language. Infants between 12 and 25 months of age watched an episode of *Baby Wordsworth* repeatedly in their homes. The children did not appear to learn any of the words specifically taught in the program. Further, exposure to the DVD program (and to other *Baby Einstein* DVDs) did not correlate with any measures of general language learning.

Research by Kuhl, Tsao, and Liu (2003) indicated that, for language learning, TV is a poor substitute for exposure to live language speakers. Children are born with the ability to distinguish contrasts in all language, but they lose this ability between 6 and 12 months of age. In Kuhl et al.'s study, 9- to 10-month-old American infants were repeatedly exposed to live, televised, or audio recordings of speakers of Mandarin. Only the children exposed to live speakers of Mandarin maintained their ability to distinguish non-native Mandarin sounds.

Well-designed educational television targeting children over the age of 2 has been shown to result in positive and long-lasting academic outcomes. However, current evidence suggests that when children are very young, programs designed specifically to teach them language skills have no impact. These infants, who are, as proposed by the feature-sampling method, primarily reactive to the features of television, may not get much more from a screen than stimuli to react to. The goal-driven, active attention allocation of older children may be a prerequisite for learning from television or an indicator that the child has developed the cognitive tools necessary to make meaning from educational television.

Conclusion

Television through its form and content is capable of drawing children into its programming, teaching them age-specific messages, and affecting their lives long after its screen has gone black. Emerging evidence shows that other audiovisual media have these same abilities, but the processes that guide them and their long-term impact are still being revealed. What is clear is that throughout any media use experience, older children are actively processing information and utilizing salient cues, their own goals, and their level of understanding to guide their attention to content that meets their needs and matches their interests. While not yet completely determined, it seems that the experience of attending to some types of media and to multiple media sources at the same time may play a role in shaping critical attention-based skills of young people. Research must continue to explore this area so that we can equip teachers, parents, and media producers with an understanding of how future generations will seek out information and in what type of educational environment they will thrive.

According to Marshall McLuhan's famous dictum (McLuhan, 1964), the medium is the message. For very young children, this may be the case. Infants appear extremely limited in their ability to process the message of screen media, and the very presence of television can potentially disrupt developmentally important opportunities. It seems that the medium and its features dictate their experience. For older children, the content of the program, video game, or computer application is of paramount importance in determining its lasting impact. The medium, therefore, is the conveyance that must be decoded, but the message is the message.

The research reviewed in this chapter brings good news for parents, in that opportunity can be maximized and risk factors minimized

by choosing for their children only the very best of media content made to serve the informational and educational needs of children. We owe them no less.

References

Acevedo-Polakovich, I. D., Lorch, E. P., & Milich, R. (2007). Comparing television use and reading in children with ADHD and non-referred children across two age groups. *Media Psychology, 9*(2), 447–472.

Acevedo-Polakovich, I. D., Pugzles Lorch, E., Milich, R., & Ashby, R. D. (2006). Disentangling the relation between television viewing and cognitive processes in children with Attention-Deficit/Hyperactivity Disorder and comparison children. *Archives of Pediatrics & Adolescent Medicine, 160*, 354–360.

Acevedo–Polakovich, I. D., Lorch, E. P., & Milich, R. (2005). TV or not TV: Questions and answers regarding television and ADHD. *ADHD Report, 13*(6), 6–11.

Anderson, D. R., Alwitt, L. F., Lorch, E. P., & Levin, S. R. (1979). Watching children watch television. In G. Hale & M. Lewis (Eds.), *Attention and cognitive development* (pp. 331–362). New York: Plenum.

Anderson, D. R., Bryant, J., Murray, J. P., Rich, M., Rivkin, M. J., & Zillmann, D. (2006). Brain imaging: An introduction to a new approach to studying media processes and effects. *Media Psychology, 8*(1), 1–6.

Anderson, D. R., Choi, H. P., & Lorch, E. P. (1987). Attentional inertia reduces distractibility during young children's TV viewing. *Child Development, 58*(3), 798–806.

Anderson, D. R., & Field, D. E. (1983). Children and the formal features of television. In M. Meyer (Ed.), *Children's attention to television: Implications for production* (pp. 56–96). Munich, Germany: Saur.

Anderson, D. R., Fite, K. V., Petrovich, N., & Hirsch, J. (2006). Cortical activation while watching video montage: An fMRI study. *Media Psychology, 8*(1), 7–24.

Anderson, D. R., Huston, A. C., Schmitt, K. L., Linebarger, D. L., & Wright, J. C. (2001). Adolescent outcomes associated with early childhood television viewing: The recontact study. *Monographs of the Society for Research in Child Development, 66*(1).

Anderson, D. R., & Levin, S. R. (1976). Young children's attention to "Sesame Street." *Child Development, 47*, 806–811.

Anderson, D. R., & Lorch, E. P. (1983). Looking at television action or reaction? In J. Bryant & D. R. Anderson (Eds.), *Children's understanding of television: Research on attention and comprehension* (pp. 1–33): New York: Academic Press.

Anderson, D. R., Lorch, E. P., Field, D. E., & Sanders, J. (1981). The effects of TV program comprehensibility on preschool children's visual attention to television. *Child Development, 52*(1), 151–157.

Armstrong, G. B., & Chung, L. (2000). Background television and reading memory in context. *Communication Research, 27*(3), 327.

Ball, S., & Bogatz, G. A. (1970). *The first year of Sesame Street: An evaluation.* Princeton, NJ: Educational Testing Service.

Barr, R., Lauricella, A., Zack, E., & Calvert, S. L. (2010). Infant and early childhood exposure to adult-directed and child-directed television programming. *Merrill-Palmer Quarterly 56*(1), 21–48.

Berlyne, D. E. (1960). *Conflict, arousal, and curiosity.* New York: McGraw-Hill.

Bogatz, G. A., & Ball, S. (1971). *The second year of Sesame Street: A continuing evaluation.* Princeton, NJ: Educational Testing Service.

Burns, J. J., & Anderson, D. R. (1993). Attentional inertia and recognition memory in adult television viewing. *Communication Research, 20*(6), 777–799.

Calvert, S. L., Huston, A. C., Watkins, B. A., & Wright, J. C. (1982). The relation between selective attention to television forms and children's comprehension of content. *Child Development, 53*(3), 601–610.

Campbell, T. A., Wright, J. C., & Huston, A. C. (1987). Form cues and content difficulty as determinants of children's cognitive processing of televised educational messages. *Journal of Experimental Child Psychology, 43*(3), 311–327.

Chonchaiya, W., & Pruksananonda, C. (2008). Television viewing associates with delayed language development. *Acta Paediatrica, 97*(7), 977–982.

Christakis, D. A., Zimmerman, F. J., DiGiuseppe, D. L., & McCarty, C. A. (2004). Early television exposure and subsequent attentional problems in children. *Pediatrics, 113*(4), 708–713.

Cook, T. D., Appleton, H., Conner, R. F., Shaffer, A., Tamkin, G., & Weber, S. J. (1975). "Sesame Street" revisited. New York: Russell Sage.

Crawley, A. M., Anderson, D. R., Santomero, A., Wilder, A., Williams, M., Evans, M. K., et al. (2002). Do children learn how to watch television? The impact of extensive experience with *Blue's Clues* on preschool children's television viewing behavior. *Journal of Communication, 52*(2), 264.

Crawley, A. M., Anderson, D. R., Wilder, A., Williams, M., & Santomero, A. (1999). Effects of repeated exposures to a single episode of the television program *Blue's Clues* on the viewing behaviors and comprehension of preschool children. *Journal of Educational Psychology, 91*(4), 630–637.

Din, F. S., & Calao, J. (2001). The effects of playing educational video games on kindergarten achievement. *Child Study Journal, 31*(2), 95–102.

Duck, J. M., Gregson, R. A., Jones, E. B., Noble, G., & Noy, M. (1988). Children's visual attention to "Playschool": A time series analysis. *Australian Journal of Psychology, 40*(4), 413–420.

Dye, M. W. G., & Bavelier, D. (2010). Differential development of visual attention skills in school-age children. *Vision Research, 50*(4), 452–459.

El-Nasr, M. S., & Yan, S. (2006). *Visual attention in 3D video games.* Paper presented at the proceedings of the 2006 ACM SIGCHI international conference on advances in computer entertainment technology, Hollywood, CA.

Evans Schmidt, M., Pempek, T. A., Kirkorian, H. L., Lund, A. F., & Anderson, D. R. (2008). The effects of background television on the toy play behavior of very young children. *Child Development, 79*(4), 1137–1151.

Evans Schmidt, M., Rich, M., Rifas-Shiman, S. L., Oken, E., & Taveras, E. M. (2009). Television viewing in infancy and child cognition at 3 years of age in a US cohort. *Pediatrics, 123*(3), 370–375.

Faden, V. B., & Graubard, B. I. (2000). Maternal substance use during pregnancy and developmental outcome at age three. *Journal of Substance Abuse, 12*(4), 329–340.

Field, D. E., & Anderson, D. R. (1985). Instruction and modality effects on children's television attention and comprehension. *Journal of Educational Psychology, 77*(1), 91–100.

Fisch, S. M. (2000). A capacity model of children's comprehension of educational content on television. *Media Psychology, 2*(1), 63–91.

Fisch, S. M. (2004). *Children's learning from educational television: Sesame Street and beyond.* Mahwah, NJ: Lawrence Erlbaum.

Foster, E. M., & Watkins, S. (2010). The value of reanalysis: TV viewing and attention problems. *Child Development, 81*(1), 368–375.

Gee, J. P. (2003). *What video games have to teach us about learning and literacy.* New York: Palgrave/Macmillan.

Gertner, J. (2005, April 10). Our ratings, ourselves. *New York Times Magazines,* 34–41.

Goodrich, S. A., Pempek, T. A., & Calvert, S. L. (2009). Formal production features of infant and toddler DVDs. *Archives of Pediatric and Adolescent Medicine, 163*(12), 1151–1156.

Green, C. S., & Bavelier, D. (2003). Action video game modifies visual selective attention. *Nature, 423*(6939), 534–537.

Green, C. S., & Bavelier, D. (2007). Action-video-game experience alters the spatial resolution of vision. *Psychological Science, 18*(1), 88–94.

Greenfield, P. M. (2009). Technology and informal education: What is taught, what is learned. *Science, 323*(5910), 69–71.

Greenfield, P. M., deWinstanley, P., Kilpatrick, H., & Kaye, D. (1994). Action video games and information education: Effects of strategies for dividing visual attention. *Journal of Applied Developmental Psychology, 15,* 105–123.

Handen, B. L., McAuliffe, S., Janosky, J., Feldman, H., & Breaux, A. M. (1998). A playroom observation procedure to assess children with mental retardation and ADHD. *Journal of Abnormal Child Psychology, 26*(4), 269–277.

Hawkins, R. P., Pingree, S., Bruce, L., & Tapper, J. (1997). Strategy and style in attention to television. *Journal of Broadcasting & Electronic Media, 41*(2), 245.

Hawkins, R. P., Pingree, S., Hitchon, J., Radler, B., Gorham, B. W., Kahlor, L., et al. (2005). What produces television attention and attention style?: Genre, situation, and individual differences as predictors. *Human Communication Research, 31*(1), 162–187.

Hawkins, R. P., Yong-Ho, K., & Pingree, S. (1991). The ups and downs of attention to television. *Communication Research, 18*(1), 53–76.

Huesmann, L. R., & Miller, L. S. (1994). Long-term effects of repeated exposure to media violence in childhood. In L. R. Huesmann (Ed.), *Aggressive behavior: Current perspectives* (pp. 153–186). New York: Plenum Press.

Huesmann, L. R., Moise-Titus, J., Podolski, C.-L., & Eron, L. D. (2003). Longitudinal relations between children's exposure to TV violence and their aggressive and violent behavior in young adulthood: 1977–1992. *Developmental Psychology, 39*(2), 201–221.

Huston, A. C., & Wright, J. C. (1983). Children's processing of television: The informative functions of formal features. In J. Bryant & D. R. Anderson (Eds.), *Children's understanding of television: Research on comprehension and attention* (pp. 35–68): New York: Academic Press.

Huston, A. C., & Wright, J. C. (1989). The forms of television and the child viewer. In G. Comstock (Ed.), *Public communication and behavior* (Vol. 2, pp. 103–158). San Diego, CA: Academic Press.

Huston, A. C., & Wright, J. C. (1997). Mass media and children's development. In W. Damon, I. E. Sigel, & K. A. Renninger (Eds.), *Handbook of child psychology: Vol. 4. Child psychology in practice* (4th ed., pp. 999–1058): New York: Wiley.

Huston, A. C., Wright, J. C., Marquis, J., & Green, S. B. (1999). How young children spend their time: Television and other activities. *Developmental Psychology, 35*(4), 912–925.

Huston, A. C., Wright, J. C., Wartella, E., Rice, M. L., Watkins, B. A., Campbell, T., et al. (1981). Communicating more than content: Formal features of children's television programs. *Journal of Communication, 31*(3), 32–48.

Jie, L., & Clark, J. J. (2008). Video game design using an eye-movement-dependent model of visual attention. *ACM Transactions on Multimedia Computing, Communications, and Applications, 4*(3), 1–16.

Johnson, G. (2006). Internet use and cognition development: A theoretical framework. *E-Learning, 3*(4), 565–573.

Kirkorian, H. L., Pempek, T. A., Murphy, L. A., Schmidt, M. E., & Anderson, D. R. (2009). The impact of background television on parent–child interaction. *Child Development, 80*(5), 1350–1359.

Krcmar, M., Grela, B., & Lin, K. (2007). Can toddlers learn vocabulary from television? An experimental approach. *Media Psychology, 10*(1), 41–63.

Kuhl, P. K., Tsao, F.-M., & Liu, H.-M. (2003). Foreign-language experience in infancy: Effects of short-term exposure and social interaction on phonetic learning. *Proceedings of the National Academy of Sciences of the United States of America, 100*(15), 9096–9101.

Labbo, L. D., & Kuhn, M. R. (2000). Weaving chains of affect and cognition: A young child's understanding of CD-ROM talking books. *Journal of Literacy Research, 32*(2), 187–210.

Lang, A., Bolls, P., Potter, R. F., & Kawahara, K. (1999). The effects of production pacing and arousing content on the information processing of television messages. *Journal of Broadcasting & Electronic Media, 43*(4), 451–475.

Lee, J. H., & Huston, A. C. (2003). Educational televisual media effects. In E. L. Palmer & B. M. Young (Eds.), *The faces of televisual media: Teaching, violence, selling to children* (pp. 83–106). Mahwah, NJ: Lawrence Erlbaum.

Lieberman, D. A. (2006). What can we learn from playing interactive games? In J. Bryant & P. Vorderer (Eds.), *Playing video games: Motives, responses, and consequences.* Mahwah, NJ: Lawrence Erlbaum.

Linebarger, D. L., & Piotrowski, J. T. (2010). Structure and strategies in children's educational television: The roles of program type and learning strategies in children's learning. *Child Development, 81*(5), 1582–1597.

Linebarger, D. L., & Walker, D. (2005). Infants' and toddlers' television viewing and language outcomes. *American Behavioral Scientist, 48*(5), 624–645.

Lorch, E. P., Anderson, D. R., & Levin, S. R. (1979). The relationship of visual attention to children's comprehension of television. *Child Development, 50*(3), 722-727.

Lorch, E. P., Milich, R., Flake, R., Ohlendorf, J., & Little, S. (2010). A developmental examination of story recall and coherence among children with ADHD. *Journal of Abnormal Child Psychology, 38*(3), 291–301.

Malone, D. M. (1997). Preschoolers' categorical and sequential toy play: Change over time. *Journal of Early Intervention, 21*(1), 45–61.

McLuhan, M. (1964). *Understanding media: The extensions of man.* New York: McGraw-Hill.

Mendelsohn, A. L., Berkule, S. B., Tomopoulos, S., Tamis-LeMonda, C. S., Huberman, H. S., Alvir, J., et al. (2008). Infant television and video exposure associated with limited parent–child verbal interactions in low socioeconomic status households. *Archives of Pediatric and Adolescent Medicine, 162*(5), 411–417.

Milich, R., & Lorch, E. P. (1994). Television viewing methodology to understand cognitive processing of ADHD children. In R. J. T. H. Ollendick & R. J. Prinz (Ed.), *Advances in clinical child psychology* (pp. 107–201). New York: Plenum.

Mistry, K. B., Minkovitz, C. S., Strobino, D. M., & Borzekowski, D. L. G. (2007). Children's television exposure and behavioral and social outcomes at 5.5 years: Does timing of exposure matter? *Pediatrics, 120*(4), 762–769.

Murray, J. P., Liotti, M., Ingmundson, P. T., Mayberg, H. S., Pu, Y., Zamarripa, F., et al. (2006). Children's brain activations while viewing televised violence revealed by fMRI. *Media Psychology, 8*(1), 25–37.

O'Neil, H. F., Wainess, R., & Baker, E. L. (2005). Classification of learning outcomes: Evidence from the computer games literature. *Curriculum Journal, 16*(4), 455–474.

Obel, C., Henriksen, T. B., Dalsgaard, S., Linnet, K. M., Skajaa, E., Thomsen, P. H., et al. (2004). Does children's watching of television cause attention problems? Retesting the hypothesis in a Danish cohort. *Pediatrics, 114*(5), 1372–1373.

Ophir, E., Nass, C., & Wagner, A. D. (2009). Cognitive control in media multitaskers. *Proceedings of the National Academy of Sciences, 106*(37), 15583-15587.

Pierroutsakos, S. L., Hanna, M. M., Self, J. A., Lewis, E. N., & Brewer, C. (2004). *Baby Einsteins everywhere: The amount and nature of television and video viewing of infants birth to 2 years.* Paper presented at the International Conference for Infant Studies, Chicago, IL.

Pingree, S. (1986). Children's activity and television comprehensibility. *Communication Research: An International Quarterly, 13*(2), 239–256.

Pool, M. M., Koolstra, C. M., & van der Voort, T. H. A. (2003). The impact of background radio and television on high school students' homework performance. *Journal of Communication, 53*(1), 74–87.

Pugzles Lorch, E., Eastham, D., Milich, R., Lemberger, C. C., Polley Sanchez, R., Welsh, R., et al. (2004). Difficulties in comprehending causal relations among children with ADHD: The role of cognitive engagement. *Journal of Abnormal Psychology, 113*(1), 56–63.

Rice, M. L., Huston, A. C., & Wright, J. C. (1982). The forms and codes of television: Effects of children's attention, comprehension and social behavior. In D. Pearl (Ed.), *Television and behavior: Ten years of scientific progress and implications for the eighties.* Washington, DC: Government Printing Press.

Rice, M. L., Huston, A. C., & Wright, J. C. (1986). Replays as repetitions: Young children's interpretation of television forms. *Journal of Applied Developmental Psychology, 7*(1), 61–76.

Richert, R. A., Robb, M. B., Fender, J. G., & Wartella, E. (2010). Word learning from baby videos. *Archives of Pediatric and Adolescent Medicine, 164*(5), 432–437.

Rideout, V. J., Foehr, U. G., & Roberts, D. F. (2010). *Generation M²: Media in the lives of 8- to 18-year-olds.* Menlo Park, CA: Kaiser Family Foundation.

Rolandelli, D. R., Wright, J. C., Huston, A. C., & Eakins, D. (1991). Children's auditory and visual processing of narrated and nonnarrated television programming. *Journal of Experimental Child Psychology, 51*(1), 90–122.

Rosas, R., Nussbaum, M., Cumsille, P., Marianov, V., Correa, M., Flores, P., et al. (2003). Beyond Nintendo: Design and assessment of educational video games for first and second grade students. *Computers & Education, 40*(1), 71.

Rothschild, M. L., & Hyun, Y. J. (1990). Predicting memory for components of TV commercials from EEG. *Journal of Consumer Research, 16*(4), 472.

Rothschild, M. L., Hyun, Y. J., Reeves, B., Thorson, E., & Goldstein, R. (1988). Hemispherically lateralized EEG as a response to television commercials. *Journal of Consumer Research, 15*(2), 185.

Schmitt, K. L., Woolf, K. D., & Anderson, D. R. (2003). Viewing the viewers: Viewing behaviors by children and adults during television programs and commercials. *Journal of Communication, 53*(2), 265–281.

Singer, J. L. (1980). The power and limits of television: A cognitive-affective analysis. In P. Tannenbaum (Ed.), *The entertainment function of television* (pp. 31–65). Hillsdale, NJ: Erlbaum.

Stevens, T., & Mulsow, M. (2006). There is no meaningful relationship between television exposure and symptoms of Attention-Deficit/Hyperactivity Disorder. *Pediatrics, 117*(3), 665–672.

Tanimura, M., Okuma, K., & Kyoshima, K. (2007). Television viewing, reduced parental utterance, and delayed speech development in infants and young children. *Archives of Pediatric and Adolescent Medicine, 161*(6), 618–619.

Thai, A., Lowenstein, D., Ching, D., & Rejeski, D. (2009). *Game changer: Investing in digital play to advance children's learning and health.* New York: The Joan Ganz Cooney Center at Sesame Workshop.

Tsung-Yen, C., & Wei-Fan, C. (2009). Effect of computer-based video games on children: An experimental study. *Journal of Educational Technology & Society, 12*(2), 1–10.

Vygotsky, L. (1978). *Mind in society.* Cambridge, MA: Harvard University Press.

Wartella, E., & Ettema, J. S. (1974). A cognitive developmental study of children's attention to television commercials. *Communication Research, 1*(1), 69–88.

Wright, J. C., & Huston, A. C. (1995). *Effects of educational TV viewing of lower income preschoolers on academic skills, school readiness, and school adjustment on to three years later.* New York: Children's Television Workshop.

Wright, J. C., Huston, A. C., Murphy, K. C., St. Peters, M. F., Piñon, M. F., Scantlin, R. M., et al. (2001). The relations of early television viewing to school readiness and vocabulary of children from low-income families: The early window project. *Child Development, 72*(5), 1347–1366.

Wright, J. C., Huston, A. C., Ross, R. P., Calvert, S. L., Rolandelli, D., Weeks, L. A., et al. (1984). Pace and continuity of television programs: Effects on children's attention and comprehension. *Developmental Psychology, 20*(4), 653–666.

Wright, J. C., Huston, A. C., Scantlin, R. M., & Kotler, J. A. (2001). The early window project: *Sesame Street* prepares children for school. In S. Fisch & R. Truglio (Eds.), *"G" is for growing: Thirty years of research on Sesame Street.* (pp. 97–114). Mahwah, NJ: Lawrence Erlbaum.

Wright, J. C., & Vlietstra, A. G. (1975). The development of selective attention: From perceptual exploration to logical search. In H. W. Reese (Ed.), *Advances in child development and behavior* (Vol. 10, pp. 195–239).

Zillman, D., Williams, B. R., Bryant, J., Boynton, K. R., & Wolf, M. A. (1980). Acquisition of information from educational television programs as a function of differently paced humorous inserts. *Journal of Educational Psychology, 72*(2), 170–180.

Zimmerman, F. J., & Christakis, D. A. (2005). Children's television viewing and cognitive outcomes: A longitudinal analysis of national data. *Archives of Pediatric and Adolescent Medicine, 159*(7), 619–625.

Zimmerman, F. J., & Christakis, D. A. (2007). Associations between content types of early media exposure and subsequent attentional problems. *Pediatrics, 120*(5), 986–992.

Zimmerman, F. J., Christakis, D. A., & Meltzoff, A. N. (2007). Associations between media viewing and language development in children under age 2 years. *Journal of Pediatrics, 151*(4), 364–368.

Zimmerman, F. J., Gilkerson, J., Richards, J. A., Christakis, D. A., Xu, D., Gray, S., et al. (2009). Teaching by listening: The importance of adult-child conversations to language development. *Pediatrics, 124*(1), 342–349.

Zuckerman, P., Ziegler, M., & Stevenson, H. W. (1978). Children's viewing of television and recognition memory of commercials. *Child Development, 49*(1), 96–104.

CHAPTER 7

Electronic Media as Incidental Language Teachers

ALICE ANN HOWARD GOLA
Georgetown University

LARA MAYEUX
University of Oklahoma

LETITIA R. NAIGLES
University of Connecticut

Movies often portray language learning as a fast and simple process—so easy, in fact, it can be learned by watching television. Consider Cassandra from *Wayne's World,* who claimed she learned English from watching the *Police Academy* movies, or Madison in *Splash*, who learned English after a day of watching television at Bloomingdale's. Perhaps it is no surprise that the covers of infant and toddler DVDs currently on the market advertise that babies can learn sign language or even learn to read through watching television. In real life, though, learning a language is not so straightforward. As anyone who has ever tried to learn a second language can attest, becoming fluent in Spanish, for example, involves much more than watching a DVD in Spanish. Language researchers have known for years that language is best learned through conversations between interacting people, one of which is the language learner herself (Clark & Clark, 1977). However, the question we investigate in this chapter is this: *Can* children learn any aspects of language from electronic media? We use the term *electronic media* here to refer to television and video content that is viewed on a screen.

Nearly 90% of toddlers and preschoolers watch television or video programs each day, with over 40% viewing two or more hours a day (Rideout & Hamel, 2006). Therefore,

Address correspondence to Alice Ann Howard Gola, Georgetown University, 37th and O Streets, NW, 309 White Gravenor Building, Washington, DC 20057. alice.h.gola@gmail.com.

what children can learn from this prevalent pastime is a very important question. Contrary to popular belief, young children are frequently active participants as they watch television. Children call attention to, or label objects on the screen (Lemish & Rice, 1986), laugh at the appropriate points, and repeat parts of the ongoing dialogue (Singer & Singer, 1998). Children also rarely watch TV alone, which provides them with an opportunity to ask questions of their co-viewer about what is on the screen (Lemish & Rice, 1986; Zimmerman, Christakis, & Meltzoff, 2007). Thus, the possibility remains that children can acquire at least some aspects of language through watching television and videos; the purpose of our chapter is to survey the available evidence to see what aspects of language children actually *do* learn. We will first examine the influences of electronic media on children's grammatical development before addressing the effects on lexical development.

Do Electronic Media Influence Phonological or Grammatical Development?

Before evaluating the effects of electronic media on phonological or grammatical development, it is necessary to understand the child's task in acquiring the phonology and grammar of her native language, along with how natural language input (i.e., the language used during social interactions with the child) facilitates this acquisition. We will briefly discuss these topics before addressing (a) whether television and video input includes language-facilitatory properties and (b) the evidence relating electronic media exposure to phonological and grammatical development.

Phonological and Grammatical Acquisition

Learning a language involves discovering the relations between various *forms*—sounds, words, phrases, sentences, discourse—and various *meanings*—objects, categories, events, propositions, and social interactions (Gleitman & Wanner, 1984). Moreover, the forms and

meanings, themselves, must be discovered. None of these discoveries can be thought of as easy or straightforward.

The phonology of a language captures the patterns by which individual sounds are combined to form meaningful units (i.e., content words such as *bed* and *run* and grammatical words such as *the* and *-ing*). Languages differ in the sound contrasts they use, such as the [r/l] contrast that English uses but Japanese does not, or the [ts/s] contrast that Mandarin uses but English does not. Moreover, languages differ in the combinations of sounds that are permitted; for example, /tr/ is fine in English but not in Mandarin, while /bn/ is fine in Hebrew but not in English. Babies acquire these contrasts and patterns without deliberate or explicit attention. However, especially in cultures with an alphabetic writing system, older children must be able to bring the sound patterns into conscious awareness—called phonological awareness—to master the mapping of sound and letter.

Natural human speech does not produce every sound in isolation, with spaces between words, commas between phrases, or periods at the ends of sentences. A more accurate visual depiction of running speech (say, ordering at a restaurant) might be *illhavethebowloftomato- soupwithacupofcoffeeandshellhavethehotdog- butwithoutmustardandsomechocolatemilk*. To extract phrases and sentences, infants must *segment* the continuous stream of sound they hear. Children must also determine their language's canonical *word order:* For example, sentences typically proceed in Subject(S)- Verb(V)-Object(O) order in English:

(1) Gregory gave a book to Beverly

but in SOV order in Japanese (from Clancy, 1985, p. 374):

(2) Taroo ga Hanako ni hon o age - ta

Taroo SUBJ[1] Hanako IO book DO give - PAST

The functions and arrangements of the *grammatical* words must also be discovered. For example, children must learn that *a* and *the* both precede nouns, but *a* indicates non-specific nouns (*a cat*) whereas *the* indicates specific ones (*the cat*), and that the modals, or "helping verbs," *can, will, may, have, do,* and *be* typically follow the subjects in statements but precede them in questions (e.g., *She can walk now* versus *Can she walk now?*)

As if that weren't enough, children must also arrive at an adult-like understanding of the relevant objects, events, and relations to which these forms refer. That is, children must conceive of the referring event of "She can walk now" as [*young female reveals ability to walk*] and not [*young female only stumbles occasionally*] or [*young female makes mom and dad happy*] to learn the appropriate meaning for that sentence.[2]

How Natural Language Input Facilitates Phonological and Grammatical Development

Newborns discriminate the sound contrasts of many languages; by 10 months of age they typically only discriminate the contrasts of their ambient language (Werker & Tees, 1984). Therefore, listening to the speech used around them helps infants narrow in on their to-be-native language contrasts. Phonological awareness does not emerge until much later, around 4 to 6 years of age, and it usually involves some explicit instruction concerning the similarities of sounds across words (e.g., *see, say, saw;* Fowler, 1991).

More pertinent to grammatical acquisition is the fact that, especially in developed cultures, adults (and older children) typically speak differently to young children than they do to other adults. This *child-directed speech* (CDS) has several properties that are considered helpful for children's grammatical development. For example, CDS has a distinctive *prosody,* which is relatively slow and melodic, with dramatic but regular pitch changes throughout utterances, lengthening of the final syllable of the utterance, and longer pauses between clauses and sentences (Fernald et al., 1989; Gleitman, Gleitman, Landau, & Wanner, 1988):

(1) Loook at the BIRD, baaaaaby. [pause] Seee the biiiird?

These properties might help the child segment the sound stream by highlighting the beginnings and ends of clauses and sentences

within longer utterances (Morgan & Demuth, 1996). CDS is also heavily weighted toward questions (Both Yes-No: "Do you want some milk?" and Wh-: "Where did you put that ball?") and repetitions that minimally change their own or the child's speech:

(2) Child: I want milk

Adult: Do you want more chocolate milk or white milk?

In one of the most robust findings in the language acquisition literature, mothers' frequent use of Yes-No questions consistently predicts their children's subsequent frequent use of modal verbs (Hoff-Ginsberg, 1985, 1986; Newport, Gleitman, & Gleitman, 1977). It's easy to see why: In Yes–No questions, modals occupy the first position in the sentence, which is usually highly stressed (e.g., pronounced loudly) and so more salient to the child. The frequency of adult repetitions also seems to positively predict the speed with which children's utterances grow in length and complexity (Hoff-Ginsberg, 1986).

Other properties of CDS help highlight the meanings of utterances. For example, children and parents frequently *jointly construct* their social interactions so that each more easily understands the others' intentions, and so are more likely to understand the others' language. Thus, hearing "Do you want some water" while climbing the stairs for a nap might be considered to be confusing to a child. If the child routinely asks for water at just this point in the nap-taking routine, then the utterance may accurately reflect the child's current thinking (for more discussion, see Clark, 1996; Clark & Grossman, 1998; Tomasello, 1990, 2001).

Does the Content of TV and Video Include Such Facilitative Properties?

Mabel Rice and her colleagues (Rice, 1984; Rice & Haight, 1986) performed detailed analyses of the language used in educational TV programs, such as *Mister Rogers' Neighborhood, Sesame Street*, and *Electric Company*. Overall, these programs contained several of the relevant properties of CDS. That is, characters' utterances included frequent repetitions of key terms and Yes-No questions, and they were predominantly *event casts,* or descriptions, of ongoing events visible on the screen. Although the melody and prosodic stress of the utterances were not assessed, the overall rate of speech (averaging 111.5 words per minute) did compare favorably with the rate of speech found in naturalistic mother-child storytelling situations (see Broen, 1972).

Given these properties, the biggest drawback to television input for language development is that it is *not* jointly constructed with the child viewer. Consider a hypothetical situation where Mr. Rogers is describing what he is doing as he is building a wooden chair. If the child is not focusing on the building aspect of the scene, but is instead wondering why Mr. Rogers isn't wearing his sweater, then the child would not be able to make the form-meaning pairings that are critical for learning language. The question becomes, How frequently might this be the case? Can we find any evidence that children exposed to TV and videos have learned something about grammar or phonology, or that children who watch more TV content progress more rapidly in their phonological or grammatical development?

Do Electronic Media Influence Phonological or Grammatical Development?

Because it is unethical to purposely deprive children of language interactions, there is only one study that has examined the language of a child whose only language input was from television. Sachs, Bard, and Johnson (1981) carried out a detailed analysis of the speech of a 3-year-old hearing boy of deaf parents. Until he began preschool at age 3.8, his only exposure to English came from the family's TV. About the time he began preschool, a sample of his spontaneous speech was recorded and analyzed. With regard to phonology, this boy's articulation was initially quite poor, with some utterances being unintelligible. While he did produce English words in multiword utterances, his word order did not conform to English SVO order (e.g., "I want that make," "my

mommy in house apple," and "off my mittens"). Also, some grammatical morphemes were entirely missing (the copula, conjunctions), while others (modals, plural [-s], past [-ed], articles *a* and *the*) appeared only about 30% of the time in their obligatory contexts (compared with 71% of the time from typically developing children producing utterances of the same length). Overall, he produced idiosyncratic combinations of English words, uninformed by conventional English sentence structure. Clearly, this boy had *not* acquired the conventions of English phonology or grammar from his television viewing, although we do not know what programs he watched and the extent to which they included relevant properties of CDS.

Experimental studies investigating whether children can learn phonology or grammar from television have been rare. Recently, though, Kuhl, Feng-Ming, and Huei-Mei, (2003) investigated infants' ability to retain phoneme contrasts of non-native languages through exposure to video, audio, or live adult interaction. Recall that exposure to a particular language helps infants to focus on the contrasts of that language but also reduces their sensitivity to the sounds of other languages. Kuhl et al. (2003) exposed 9-month-olds raised in English-only households to five hours of a live adult speaking Mandarin across a four-week period. Compared to infants who were only exposed to an English-speaking adult, those who heard the Mandarin maintained their sensitivity to Mandarin contrasts. However, infants exposed to five hours of Mandarin by an adult on a DVD did not maintain this sensitivity, suggesting that increased or decreased sensitivity to phonetics cannot be acquired from video exposure alone.

Correlational studies have investigated whether children who watch more TV display more sophisticated grammar or faster grammatical development. The data, however, are mixed. Selnow and Bettinghaus (1982) collected spontaneous language samples from 3- to 5-year-olds and asked their parents to keep a week-long diary of the television programs the children watched. The language samples were scored for their syntactic complexity (e.g., longer utterances and correct uses of grammatical morphemes yielded higher scores), and the diaries were coded for number of hours of TV watched, both overall and by program type (i.e., educational, family drama, sports). Few correlations were obtained, and the only one that approached significance was *negative*: The more television viewed, the *lower* the child's language score. However, Singer and Singer (1981) found modest *positive* correlations between the amount of educational television preschool-aged children watched over a 2-week period and their uses of imperative sentences (commands) and exclamations in spontaneous speech.

Summary

Research examining the relationship between phonological or grammatical development and television input is scarce. Of the studies available, there is little indication that children are learning much phonology or grammar from television viewing. The infants exposed to Mandarin by an adult on a DVD were no more able to distinguish the phonemes of the language than children who were never exposed to Mandarin (Kuhl et al., 2003). Moreover, the child studied by Sachs et al. (1981) displayed fairly aberrant phonological and grammatical development during the period when he was only exposed to television input. (Subsequently, after entering preschool and speech therapy, his language developed to near-normal conditions.) The correlational studies do not suggest there is a strong relationship between television viewing and grammatical development (Selnow & Bettinghaus, 1982; Singer & Singer, 1981). Thus, it seems unlikely that children learn much about phonology or grammar specifically from television input. Although the language of children's television is similar to that of CDS (Rice, 1984; Rice & Haight, 1986), our conclusion supports the notion that phonological and grammatical development also require linguistic interactions that are socially based and carried out jointly by children and their caregivers (Clark & Clark, 1977; Tomasello, 2001).

In spite of our conclusion, it may not be possible for a moderate amount of television viewing to influence overall grammatical development. In a comparison of families of different SES levels, Hoff-Ginsberg (1998) demonstrated that differences in the sheer amount of speech children hear do not seem to influence their early grammatical development. Instead, there appears to be a threshold of input that children must receive in order to acquire their grammar; variation above that threshold has little effect (e.g., Pinker, 1994). Likewise, moderate variations in television input might be expected to have little effect because the children's natural linguistic input is already above threshold.

It is also important to note that definitive studies have not been conducted showing that children *cannot* learn phonology or grammar from television. The studies conducted to date have either targeted only one aspect of *grammatical/phonological* outcomes (e.g., phoneme recognition) or have looked at television input too generally. As we will see in the next section, what children can learn from television and videos depends greatly on the content of the program. For example, a recent study by Uchikoshi (2007) found that Spanish-English bilingual kindergarteners who were shown a television show focusing on phonics three times a week for seven months increased significantly more on one measure of phonological awareness than children who viewed another type of show or no show at all. More studies with an experimental design such as Uchikoshi's are needed to assess how *specific* content might influence multiple aspects of children's phonological or grammatical development (e.g., mean length of utterance, correct uses of grammatical morphemes). Given that a plethora of programs have been made for young children in the last 10 years, it is possible that there are other shows currently available that *do* influence children's grammatical or phonological development. However, until such studies are conducted, our conclusion is that watching television has little impact on children's phonological and grammatical development.

Do Electronic Media Influence Lexical Development?

The child's task of learning the meanings of words bears considerable—although not complete—resemblance to her task of learning grammar. For example, the challenge of segmenting the sound stream is similar, except that the child must distinguish individual *words* in addition to phrases and sentences. The restaurant order mentioned above (*illhavethebowloftomatosoupwithacupofcoffeeandshellhavethehotdogbutwithoutmustardandsomechocolatemilk*) must be segmented so that *the, bowl, of, tomato*, and *soup* are recognized as distinct lexical items. Meanings must also be mapped onto these words, and here the child faces Quine's (1960) problem of translation and induction. Namely, the child's visual-spatial world is so rich in *possible* meanings that any given word's meaning is vastly under-determined. Notice first that the visual-spatial context of the restaurant order does not include any of the referents of the words! Moreover, even if a parent says "here comes my bowl of soup" when the order comes, there are a plethora of possible referents for *bowl*: *bowl, soup, red* (the color of the soup), *plastic* (the substance of the bowl), *round* (the shape of the bowl), *hot* (the temperature of the soup), *spoon, tray* (other salient objects), *place-in-front* (a salient action), and so on. Somehow, the child must determine which meaning is the correct one.

A third issue for lexical development involves establishing the relations *between* word meanings. (We present here just a sketch; for more in-depth discussions, see Gleitman & Gleitman, 1997; Woodward & Markman, 1998.) It is not enough to know that *soup* refers to soup; children must also come to know, for example, that soup is a kind of food and that chicken noodle is a kind of soup. Noun meanings often stand in taxonomic or hierarchical relations to each other, going from the most general relation (*food, animal, vehicle*) to the most specific (*chicken noodle, cocker spaniel, cable car*) (see Keil, 1979; Rosch, Mervis, Gray, Johnson, & Boyes-Braem, 1976; Waxman & Kosowski, 1990). Verb meanings relate to each other on other dimensions, such as *causality* (distinguishing *come* and *go* from *bring* and *take*), *directionality* (*enter* vs. *exit*), *manner* (*run* vs. *walk*), and *certainty* (*think* vs. *know*) (see Levin, 1993; Talmy, 1985; Urmson, 1963). It is not enough to know what walking or thinking *is*; children must also learn how each action or process fits in the organization of other actions and processes.

How Natural Language Input Facilitates Lexical Development

Certainly, the child does not face the task of learning words with only a continuous stream of speech on the one hand and an incredibly rich visual-spatial world on the other. The prosodic qualities of CDS, especially the dramatic pitch excursions and regular patterns of emphasis, serve to highlight some syllables in an utterance over others. In languages like English, those highlighted (or stressed) syllables most often correspond to the content words of the utterance (e.g., "LOOK, the DOG is RUNning!"; see Fernald & Mazzie, 1991). Thus, the task of segmenting the sound stream into words with meanings is made easier by the melody and emphasis naturally used in the speech of adults to children.

The task of determining the meanings of words can be facilitated by specific types of adult–child interaction and input. For example, adults label objects for young children typically after having established *joint attention* to a given object with the child. That is, the adult makes sure that the child is looking at the same place that the adult is looking. In a clever series of studies, Dare Baldwin (1991, 1993) showed that children 18-months-old and older can exploit this joint attention (and can establish it themselves) to figure out which of several novel objects a single novel word refers to (see also Hollich, Hirsh-Pasek, & Golinkoff, 1998). However, joint attention may not be deterministic enough to learn verb meanings because a given action can be viewed from any number of perspectives (e.g., *throwing* a ball can also be seen as *catching* and *flying through the air;* see Gleitman, 1990). Luckily, adults provide more clues by placing the verbs in sentences: "She is X-ing the ball" could refer to *throw* or *catch*, but not *fly*, whereas "the ball is X-ing" can refer to *fly* but not to *throw* or *catch*. Naigles and Hoff-Ginsberg (1998) analyzed the speech of mothers to their toddlers, and the speech of the toddlers 10 weeks later, and found that those verbs that mothers used in more diverse sentences were the same verbs that the toddlers subsequently used more frequently (see also Gillette, Gleitman, Gleitman, & Lederer, 1999; Landau & Gleitman, 1985). Thus, the task of learning the meanings of words is made easier through social interactions and exposure to diverse sentence frames.

Does TV and Video Content Include Such Facilitative Properties?

We refer again to the analyses Mabel Rice and her colleagues performed on the language used in educational television programs (Rice, 1984; Rice & Haight, 1986). The prosody of single words spoken on children's educational television appears to be similar to those of CDS. For example, Rice (1984) reported that many new or novel words in programs such as *Electric Company* were spoken more loudly than the rest of the words in the sentence. Therefore, children might easily distinguish these words from the rest of the speech stream.

Two additional aspects of educational television that might facilitate children's determination of word meanings emerge from Rice's work. First, Rice and Haight (1986) found that approximately 60% of the utterances on *Mister Rogers* and *Sesame Street* referred to objects or events that were immediately present on the screen (see also Anderson, 2004). Thus, for a majority of the time, children need not look far to find possible referents for unfamiliar words. In fact, Anderson (2004) found that 3- and 5-year-olds looked longer at the screen when the referents were immediately available, suggesting preschoolers pay more attention to characters' utterances that provide immediate reference. Second, although sentence frame information was not analyzed explicitly, Rice and Haight (1986) reported that both *Sesame Street* and *Mister Rogers* included numerous utterance repetitions. To the extent that these included full sentences and were not always exact repetitions, they might be considered to provide diverse information about verbs and their meanings. Therefore, it appears that the

language and visuals of children's educational television provide at least some of the characteristics of CDS that have been shown to facilitate "natural" lexical development.

Do Electronic Media Influence Lexical Development?

This subsection is divided into three parts. The first part presents evidence from experimental studies revealing that children can learn novel words from custom-produced videos. The second part presents naturalistic studies suggesting that children's vocabulary development is supported by the content of the programs viewed. The third part presents studies assessing whether children learn the specific words highlighted in commercial videos.

In an experimental study examining whether children can learn words from video, Rice and Woodsmall (1988) demonstrated that preschoolers were indeed able to learn (and retain) low-frequency words (e.g., *gramophone*) from television when paired with voice-over narration. Importantly, the researchers found that children learned objects and attribute words (e.g., *sick*) more easily than action or affective-state (e.g., *happy*) words. Recall, there are many things to consider when learning a new verb: causality, directionality, manner, and certainty, making verb learning from television potentially more difficult than noun learning. Thus, we separate research examining children's verb learning from electronic media from studies that focus on children's noun learning.

Naigles and her colleagues (Naigles, 1990; Naigles, 1998; Naigles & Kako, 1993) used a video paradigm to investigate whether toddlers could learn the meanings of novel verbs by exploiting the sentence frames in which the verbs were presented. On a typical "program," two novel actions were presented simultaneously, one of which was causative (e.g., a duck pushing a rabbit over) and one of which was noncausative (e.g., the duck and rabbit bending their arms in unison). The audio introduced a novel verb in either a transitive sentence ("the duck is blicking the bunny") or an intransitive sentence ("the duck and the bunny are blicking"). After several presentations, the two actions were separated and children were asked to "find blicking." Throughout, their eye movements were tracked, and the findings were that the children who heard the verb in the transitive frame preferred to watch the causative action when asked to find blicking, whereas the children who had heard the verb in the intransitive frame preferred to watch the noncausative action. Studies like these demonstrate that very young children can link actions and verbs when the actions are presented as dynamic videos and the verbs are presented in simultaneous voice-overs.

A recent study by Roseberry, Hirsh-Pasek, Parish-Morris, and Golinkoff (2009) created videos using clips from *Sesame Beginnings* to teach 30- to 40-month-olds novel verbs. During training, the clips (e.g., Cookie Monster wiggling) were presented on the screen and children heard *both* a live adult and the video label the novel verb (e.g., "Look at Cookie Monster wezzling! He's wezzling!). The clips then disappeared and two novel test clips appeared: a new actor performing the same action (e.g., baby wezzling), and the same new actor performing a different action (e.g., baby playing on parent's leg). The audio then asked children to find the novel verb presented during training; thus, these trials tested whether the child could *extend* the verb to the same action performed by a new actor. Children as young as 30 months old looked longer at the action corresponding to the novel verb. A follow-up study removed the live experimenter from the study design so that children heard only the video label the novel actions (Roseberry et al., 2009). Only the older children (36- to 40-month-olds) looked longer at the action corresponding to the novel verb heard during training. These results suggest that video alone is not sufficient for 30- to 36-month-olds to extend novel verbs; social interaction must also be involved.

Both of the previous studies suggest children can learn verbs from video if they are given additional cues: either through social interaction or through the presence of informative sentence frames. We now turn to research investigating whether children can learn nouns from custom-made video.

Using an experimental design, Scofield and Williams (2009) examined whether 2-year-olds could learn novel nouns from custom videos. A novel object (e.g., a t-joint) was presented on screen and labeled three times via an audio track (e.g., This is a *koba*.). The novel object then disappeared and reappeared alongside another novel distracter object. The children were asked by an audio track to find the *koba*. The 2-year-olds looked to the target object significantly more often than they did to the distracter object. Moreover, they were able to extend the novel verb to an exemplar of the novel object differing in color and size when it appeared alongside a novel distracter object (see also Tek, Jaffery, Swensen, Fein, & Naigles, 2008). These results suggest that children as young as two years old can learn nouns from television *and* extend these novel nouns to another, taxonomically related object. However, they were not able to disambiguate by matching a new novel word (different from the word learned in training) to the novel distracter (e.g., "This is a zav. Can you help me find the lug?").

Krcmar, Grela, and Lin (2007) compared different types of live and televised presentations to examine which type best helped 15- to 24-month-olds learn nouns. Using a repeated-measures design, children's noun learning was assessed in five conditions: (1) adult video—a video of an adult displaying and labeling the target object; (2) children's television program—a clip from *Teletubbies* in which a periscope (the novel target object) emerged from the ground with a corresponding audio track label; (3) adult live-joint reference—a live adult labeled the target object only when child was looking at the object; (4) adult live-discrepant reference—a live adult labeled the target object only when the child was *not* looking at the object; (5) no language control. After viewing the presentations, an experimenter handed the children five objects and asked them to find the target object. Two interesting findings emerged. First, children's performance in the adult video condition was similar to their performance in the live adult-joint reference condition, indicating they learned the novel words as well from the adult on television as they did from the live adult (joint reference condition). Interestingly, children chose the target object significantly more often in the adult video condition than they did in the children's programming condition, demonstrating that children learned the novel word better from an onscreen adult than they did from a typical children's program.

The results from these experimental studies suggest that children as young as 15 months of age can learn novel nouns from video if the objects are presented in conjunction with the novel label (Krcmar et al., 2007; Scofield & Williams, 2009). However, research also suggests that the type of presentation greatly affects if, and how well, children learn the words. That is, 15- to 24-month-olds did not learn nouns presented in a clip from a children's television show as well as they did when the words were presented by an adult on the video (Krcmar et al., 2007). Moreover, children as young as two years old can learn novel verbs from video if the verbs are presented in an informative sentence frame (e.g., "The duck is blicking the bunny") (Naigles, 1990). However, 3-year-olds had a difficult time *extending* verbs to novel actors in custom versions of commercial video clips when a live adult did not also label the verb (Roseberry et al., 2009). In all of these studies, the videos from which children successfully learned words were experimentally controlled. The next question is, Can children learn words while watching commercial television or videos at home or in day care?

Past research assessing children's vocabulary growth over a 2.5 year span via the Peabody Picture Vocabulary Test (PPVT) found that children who watched more hours of *Sesame Street* showed greater gains in vocabulary between the ages of 3 and 5 years than children who watched fewer hours (Rice, Huston, Truglio, & Wright, 1990). This positive correlation remained after controlling for vocabulary-influencing variables such as parental education, number of siblings, and initial PPVT scores. The direction of causality seems clear—greater amounts of *Sesame Street* watching lead to higher subsequent vocabulary scores, but higher vocabulary scores do not lead to greater *Sesame Street* viewing.

More recent studies have produced similar findings. Using a longitudinal design, Wright and colleagues (2001) examined how the content and amount of television exposure affected 236 low-income children's language

comprehension and IQ. The children were either 2- or 4-years-old at the start of the study and were seen annually for four years. Through periodic phone interviews with parents, the number and type of television programs the children viewed was collected. Experimenters classified all television viewed into three types of programs: child-audience educational (e.g., *Sesame Street*), child-audience animated (i.e., fully animated with no educational purpose), and general audience (i.e., made for a general adult audience). At each annual visit, children's receptive vocabulary, school readiness, reading skills, number skills, and family variables were assessed. After controlling for family variables, the most compelling finding was that frequent viewers of child-audience educational television at 2 and 3 years of age performed better on all academic measures at age 3 compared to the infrequent viewers. In contrast, frequent viewers of child-audience animated shows at 2 and 3 years of age had lower scores on measures of letter-words skills at age 3 and receptive language at age 5. Similarly, children in both cohorts who watched a lot of general audience programming performed more poorly on these four measures than children who were infrequent viewers. These results suggest that the *type* of programming viewed, not just the amount, plays a significant role in the development of children's early lexical learning and other academic skills.

A similar study by Linebarger and Walker (2005) investigated the naturalistic television viewing of 51 infants in relation to their patterns of language development. All children began the study at 6 months of age. Parents were asked to report the amount and type of television viewed every 3 months until their children were 30 months old. Experimenters classified the programs by the intended audience (child or adult) and the type (informative, entertainment, sports, news). Children's vocabulary production was measured using the MacArthur Communicative Developmental Inventory (MCDI; Fenson et al., 1993), while their general expressive communication (which included gestures, vocalizations, single- and multiple-word utterances) was measured using the Early Communication Indicator (Luze et al., 2001). After controlling for children's cognitive development and family characteristics, children's combined viewing of the shows *Arthur* and *Clifford the Big Red Dog* and combined viewing of the shows *Blue's Clues* and *Dora the Explorer* were each independently related to their production of more words and utterances at 30 months and to an increase in word growth rate, compared to nonviewers. In contrast, viewers of *Barney and Friends* or *Teletubbies* produced 11.68 fewer words at 30 months compared to nonviewers, as measured by the MCDI. Similar to the study by Wright et al. (2001), these results demonstrate that the type of programming children watch affects their language development in different ways.

These three studies provide very convincing evidence that watching television can positively influence children's language development *if* the programs are educational and made for a child audience. Linebarger and Walker (2005) hypothesized that children may learn novel words better from shows like *Dora the Explorer* and *Blue's Clues* because they use strategies known to support language-learning in everyday life (e.g., speaking directly to the child, actively eliciting participation, labeling objects, providing opportunities to respond). Children's language development may also have been helped by exposure to shows like *Arthur* and *Clifford* because of their storybook-like nature (strong narrative, visually appealing, contains opportunities to hear vocabulary words). Overall, the *content* of the program, not the *amount* of exposure, seems to be the driving force behind whether children's language is positively affected.

One concern with the previous studies is that the link between television viewing and the word learned is not direct. That is, a direct link between specific words used during the television programs and the words acquired by the children has not been substantiated. Past studies by Singer and Singer (1998) and Naigles (2000) tried to make this link more explicit. Both studies pretested preschoolers on their vocabulary before exposing them to two to three weeks of the television show *Barney and Friends*. The vocabulary measures consisted only of words involved in the central themes of the shows the children watched. At the end of the intervention, children were then tested again on their vocabulary. Although the

dependent language measures differed across the studies, both studies revealed that children who watched the *Barney* episodes made significant gains in their vocabulary development compared to children who did not watch *Barney*.

Two recent studies have yielded mixed results on the direct link between children's language development and one particular DVD: *Baby Einstein's Baby Wordsworth*. Vandewater (2010) assessed 8- to 15-month-olds' word learning from this video across a 16-week time period. The video features 30 words for objects and rooms found inside a house. A picture of each object is displayed on the screen and is labeled with its corresponding word. Children's understanding and production of 21 words found in the DVD were measured at three time points: at baseline, after 1 month of viewing, and 3 months after the viewing period ended. Children were randomly assigned to an experimental group or the control group. The parents in the experimental group were instructed to show their child the video twice a week for four weeks and were given no instructions for the following 12 weeks. Parents in the control group were asked to keep their children from watching the video during the first 12 weeks and were given no instructions during the remaining 4 weeks. Analyses controlled for variables pertinent to children's language development (e.g., maternal education, the number of hours per week the children were talked to or read to, children's social, self-help, fine-motor, and gross-motor maturity—as measured by the Infant Developmental Inventory; Ireton, 1994). Results indicated that at Time 3, children in the video-viewing group understood significantly more words specific to the DVD compared to children in the control group.

Robb, Richert, and Wartella (2009) used a similar procedure with 12- to 15-month-olds, but they had different results. Half of the parents in this study were asked to show their children *Baby Wordsworth* five times every two weeks for six weeks, while the other half were given no specific instructions. Children's language was assessed using a parental vocabulary checklist at four time points: once at baseline and then every two weeks for six weeks. The vocabulary questionnaire consisted of the 30 words featured in the video; parents were asked to indicate the words their children understood and produced. After controlling for children's age, Robb et al. found that time spent viewing the video was not a significant predictor either of children's receptive or expressive vocabulary acquisition. Moreover, there were no differences between those who watched the video and those who did not on expressive or receptive language at any time point. These results suggest that infant DVD-viewing is not directly related to children's learning of vocabulary words.

The mixed findings from these two recent studies might have emerged due to a procedural difference. In Vandewater's (2010) study, children's language was measured four months after baseline (three months after the four-week viewing period), whereas the children in the study by Robb et al. (2009) were assessed six weeks after baseline (immediately after the viewing period). Vandewater hypothesized that the earlier DVD viewing in her study might have laid the foundation for later word learning.

It is also important to note that compared to the experimental studies that used novel objects and labels, these two studies investigated growth in familiar labels as indicators of objects to measure children's word-learning (e.g., *kitchen*). Vandewater, Park, Lee, and Barr (2010) hypothesized that the use of the familiar words and objects during a period of rapid language acquisition may have masked differences in word learning between the control and experimental groups. A recent study evaluated the effect of a commercial video on children's learning of a novel word-shape mapping (Vandewater, Barr, Park, & Lee, 2010). This study assessed whether infants could map a novel word onto a novel object already embedded and labeled in a commercially available video, Brainy Baby's® *Baby Shapes & Colors*. Toddlers ranging from 18 to 33 months were randomly assigned to the experimental or control group. Parents in the experimental group were asked to show their child the video featuring lessons on shapes at least once a day for 15 days. The toddlers were brought into the lab at the end of the viewing period and were given a series of forced-choice measures to assess their understanding of the shapes (i.e., after hearing a label, they were asked to point to one of two

pictures). Children who watched the video were 22 times more likely to correctly identify a novel crescent shape than children not exposed to this video. Moreover, at testing, parents in the experimental group were significantly more likely than parents in the control group to report that their children produced the word *crescent*. There were no significant differences between the groups on correctly identifying any of the other, more familiar shapes (square, circle, triangle, and rectangle). These results indicate that children learned a novel word, but not familiar words, from a commercial video better than children who did not view the video.

It is important to point out that a study by Zimmerman et al. (2007) found a negative relationship between the language development of 8- to 16-month-olds and their viewing of baby DVDs (e.g., *Baby Einstein, Brainy Baby*). In particular, viewing baby DVDs was associated with 16.99 fewer words on the MCDI score for this age group; however, this relationship did not hold for children 17 to 24 months of age. The negative findings of this study might have emerged in the youngest age group because too much viewing at this age could interfere with parent–child interactions known to promote language learning. However, two other studies found simply no relationship between children's lexical learning and television. DeLoache et al. (under review) measured the vocabulary of 12- to 18-month-olds using a forced-choice measure. Compared to children who heard the words from their parents, those who heard them in a baby DVD did not improve in their vocabulary. Similarly, Schmidt, Rich, Rifas-Shiman, Oken, and Taveras (2009) found no relationship between 6-, 12-, and 24-month-olds' language and number of hours of television exposure. (See Patterson, 2002, for research on bilingual toddlers.)

Overall, the majority of recent studies provide strong evidence that children's language acquisition from television seems highly dependent on the type of content viewed. If the video mimics live adult interaction, as it did in the experimental studies (e.g., only an adult on screen with one object), children learned nouns and verbs from television. As Krcmar et al. (2007) demonstrated, children's shows such as *Teletubbies* might provide an overload of information, making it difficult for children to focus on and extract the novel word. Similarly, Wright et al. (2001) found that children's language is positively affected if children view the appropriate programs—those made for educating children (also see Linebarger & Walker, 2005). Shows such as *Dora the Explorer* and *Blue's Clues* (those that were positively related to language development) often mimic live interaction by turning to face the audience, asking questions, and pausing for a reply.

The findings are mixed on whether children can acquire vocabulary words from programs that are not specifically designed for them. Linebarger and Walker (2005) found a small positive relationship between children's expressive communication and the frequency with which they viewed adult programming. However, Wright et al. (2001) found that children who watched more general audience programs (i.e., programs not made for children) performed more poorly on cognitive and vocabulary measures than the children who did not frequently watch this type of programming. Research has shown that adult programming, even if on in the background, disrupts the quantity and quality of parent–child interaction and child-play (Christakis et al., 2009; Kirkorian, Pempek, Murphy, Schmidt, & Anderson, 2009). For example, parents provide fewer words and utterances per minute during interactions with their children when the TV is on compared to when it is off (Pempek, Kirkorian, & Anderson, 2010). Relatedly, in a direct correlation, Zimmerman et al. (2009) found that children's TV viewing is negatively related to their concurrent vocabulary scores; however, when adult conversational turns are included as a factor, this negative effect disappears. In other words, conversational turns are the strongest predictors of vocabulary scores; to the extent that these may decrease during TV viewing, TV may seem to have a negative effect. It is only natural that adult programming might serve as a bigger distraction for parents than child-audience programming, whereas programs made for children might encourage adult–child interaction that subsequently aids in children's language development. Thus, the next question is this: How does

adult mediation influence children's language development during television shows that are made for children?

How Does Adult Mediation Influence Language Development via Electronic Media?

Young children may watch television entirely by themselves (St. Peters, Fitch, Huston, Wright, & Eakins, 1988), or with an adult or older child present who is available for consultation and conversation (Barr, Zack, Garcia, & Muentener, 2008; Lemish & Rice, 1986). Recent research by Zimmerman et al. (2007) found that of the 1,009 families they interviewed, approximately 82% of the parents watched television with their children at least half of the time, with approximately 32% *always* watching with their children. Moreover, what parents say to their infants while watching videos with them predicts the infants' responsiveness to the video, as measured by their verbal responses, questions, pointing, and play (Barr et al., 2008). To what extent does the language input during co-viewing account for the observed findings that children learn the meanings of words from television programs? Recall that Roseberry et al. (2009) found that 30- to 36-month-olds only learned a novel verb from a video when a live adult labeled the novel action too. Because research suggests arousal is important in children's ability to encode and remember information (Kuhl, 2007), the authors hypothesized that arousal was the key to why children typically learn language better from live adults than from video. However, it is also possible that children glean additional information about the television program from their parents—information that aids in their language development.

Imagine a 3-year-old and her mother who are watching *Sesame Street*. While Bert and Ernie are talking about a game of soccer they played, flashbacks of the game are also shown; at one point, Ernie kicked the ball and missed the goal. The screen likely shows the ball bounding past the goal and Ernie voicing his dismay. *Miss* is a difficult concept to abstract from the relevant event. The child picks up on the word *miss* and repeats it: "Missed the goal?" The mother elaborates, "'Miss the goal' means that Ernie wanted to kick the ball into the goal, and although he tried, he did not succeed—the ball did not go into the goal, so he *missed* the goal." How much of the child's acquisition of the meaning of *miss* can be attributed to her viewing of the television program, and how much to her mother's elaboration? If the mother had gone on to give her own example of *missing*, which manifestation would be most important in the child's subsequent representation? These are questions for which we have no definitive answers now.

Two studies have tried to address the adult mediation issue by assessing vocabulary growth under varying viewing conditions. The strongest findings of adult mediation come from Singer and Singer's (1998) study of noun learning via the *Barney and Friends* episodes. In addition to the *Barney*-watchers and non-watchers, a third group was included: These children both watched the 10 *Barney* episodes and participated in 30-minute lessons about the episodes. Each lesson, led by the children's preschool teacher, was held immediately after the episode was shown. The unfamiliar words in each episode, a subset of which formed the basis for the vocabulary test, were included in each lesson plan provided for the teachers. During the testing phase, Singer and Singer found that the children in this third *Barney* and Teaching group outperformed both of the other groups on the vocabulary test. That is, while the *Barney* Only group significantly improved from pre- to posttest, and the non-watching group did not, the *Barney* and Teaching group improved considerably more than the *Barney* Only group did.[3] In sum, when adult mediation is presented in a formal teaching mode, it clearly enhances the lessons available from television. It is important to remember, though, that the findings for those children who did not receive any lessons after viewing the *Barney* episodes were also positive, indicating that they had acquired some aspects of word meaning simply from watching the program.

Another study of adult mediation is more closely concerned with adult co-viewing—that is, of the possible effects of adult input during the actual viewing of the television programs. This is closer to the natural situation for most young children. These data come from the aforementioned longitudinal study of vocabulary development performed by Rice et al. (1990). Their viewing diaries included information concerning which television-watching sessions were co-viewed with an adult and which were experienced by the child alone. When Rice et al. considered these two types of sessions separately, they found that viewing *without* an adult at age 3 to 3.5 years positively predicted vocabulary at age 5, but viewing *with* an adult at the same ages yielded no significant relations to later vocabulary (Rice et al., 1990, p. 426). At the very least, then, the child's growth in vocabulary that was related to television viewing cannot be attributed to the adult commentary during the viewing.

Taken together, these findings suggest that children's vocabulary development can be partly explained by the linguistic and social influences of adult co-viewers. However, as Singer and Singer's (1998) study revealed, an adult presence is not necessary for children to learn words from television. Studies assessing adult–child interactions during television programs that include many unfamiliar words and concepts are needed. This might be the type of situation in which adult co-viewing *is* facilitative of vocabulary growth because the adult can provide explicit definitions, explain potential confusions, and include additional exemplars. More in-depth analyses of the type of linguistic interaction provided by the parent during co-viewing are needed. In particular, it would be interesting to examine what type of program provides the right format for parents to interact with their children to promote their language development.

Do Electronic Media Influence Narrative Development?

Recent research has begun to investigate the effects of television on children's development of language use; that is, the way(s) language is used in conversation, storytelling, disputing, and other kinds of discourse.

A child with good narrative skills is able to tell a story that has a beginning, a middle, and an end; he or she can link the events in a causal structure and can include relevant information about the characters and setting. Narrative development begins around 3 years of age and continues into the grade school years (Berman & Slobin, 1994). Parents may provide scaffolding for the components of storytelling as they read books and reminisce about past events with their children; teachers, too, frequently provide explicit instruction (Andersen, 1990).

Because narrative skills are strong predictors of children's language and literacy development, the extent to which children learn these skills from television is important to consider, but the investigations are few at the moment. Linebarger and Piotrowski (2009) pretested preschoolers from economically disadvantaged homes on their story knowledge and their comprehension of wordless picture books. The children were then shown one television show once a day while in daycare for 40 days. The children were randomly assigned at the classroom level to one of four conditions: (1) expository stimuli—program that explained, described, and provided information about a particular topic (*Zoboomafoo*); (2) embedded narrative—program that contained a narrative within a narrative (*Pinky Dinky Doo*); (3) traditional narrative—program in a traditional storybook format (*Clifford the Big Red Dog*); or (4) a non-viewing condition. Children's age, gender, pretest scores, and the classroom literacy environment were included as covariates. For all of the narrative measures (e.g., telling a relevant story, making connections between pictures), children in one of the narrative conditions, either traditional or embedded, outperformed the children in the non-viewing or expository condition.

A similar study by Uchikoshi (2005) examined the narrative skills of bilingual kindergarteners as a result of their exposure to one of two types of television shows. The children were from primarily Spanish-speaking homes. Half of the children were assigned to watch *Arthur*, a show that focuses on narrative structure, while half were assigned to watch *Between the Lions*, a show that focuses on phonics and story mechanics.

Children watched the shows in their Spanish-English classrooms three times a week throughout the school year (October through May). The children's narrative skills were measured three times: once before the intervention, once midway through the intervention, and once at the end of the intervention. The most compelling finding was that children who watched *Arthur* improved in their narrative skills at a faster rate than children who viewed *Between the Lions*. These results suggest that children's language benefitted from television, even when English was their second language.

Two important points can be taken away from the research described previously. First, children developed better narrative skills by watching a television program with a strong narrative than by viewing a different type of television program or no television at all. Second, when the content of the television show is appropriately aligned with the dependent variable of the study, a positive relationship between children's language development and television is more likely to emerge. In other words, if specific aspects of language are examined in relation to specific types of television content, we might begin to understand precisely what children can learn from television and why.

Conclusions

Can children learn language from watching television and videos? Our conclusion remains "Yes and no." Where vocabulary acquisition is concerned, the answer is "Yes." Research documents that children can learn both nouns and verbs from television, and they can even extend the new words to other, taxonomically related objects. However, word-learning most often occurred when the programs were educational and made for a child audience. If the content was purely entertainment or made for adults, children's vocabulary was rarely positively affected. Studies on narrative development are quite new, but this area of language also seems positively influenced by television viewing. However, if the language domains in question are phonology or grammar, then the answer seems to be "No." Far fewer studies have been performed, but the overall gist is clear: Television input does not provide any facilitation of phonological or grammatical development. Perhaps development in these domains is so robust that a few extra hours of television input per week does little to change its course (e.g., Hoff-Ginsberg, 1998; Pinker, 1994). Indeed, when learning a language after puberty, people rarely achieve native language levels, particularly in their grammatical development (Johnson & Newport, 1989). Johnson and Newport's (1989) finding certainly, and to some extent the discrepancy in findings between video input and grammatical/phonological development versus lexical/narrative development, suggests there is something unique about the former domains compared to the latter ones.

The findings over the past decade point strongly to the fact that the content of the television programs plays a large role in how children's language acquisition is affected. The research we have reviewed reveals a strong link between custom-made videos and language-learning, while the link between commercial videos and language-learning is not as strong. Could it be that the formal features (e.g., zooms, cuts, music, pacing) commonly used in commercial videos are too distracting for children to process the content? Many DVDs and television shows made for children include a lot of cuts (Goodrich, Pempek, & Calvert, 2009; Rice, 1984). Recent eye-tracking research by Kirkorian, Whitcomb, and Anderson (2010) found that 4-year-olds do not anticipate that a ball moving from right to left across a TV screen will again appear on the left side of the screen after a cut. This suggests that unlike adult viewers, 4-year-olds may not be processing or understanding the content surrounding the commonly occurring cuts. Future research should focus on how television content can be better produced so that it is more comprehensible for children.

Future research should also examine how the environment in which the child is watching the television or videos interacts with the screen content to create a better learning atmosphere. In particular, what type of language do parents and children use while watching television, and how might their conversations differ by the program they view? Relatedly,

updated research on the type of language used in the DVDs and television shows, themselves, and how this might be related to what children learn from the show is needed. We are not suggesting television and videos could ever replace natural language input for child language learners. In fact, electronic media can be counterproductive if it replaces the natural parent–child interactions that are known to enhance language development. As reported in the case study by Sachs et al. (1981), if a child's entire linguistic database consists only of television input, she may succeed in picking up a few words; however, her vocabulary will be limited and her combinations and articulations of words are unlikely to resemble those of the target language. However, we can work to ensure that the content our children are already viewing on television and videos is as facilitatory as possible.

Notes

1. SUBJ indicates the *subject* marker, IO the *indirect object* marker, and DO the *direct object* marker.

2. This is only a brief sketch of the child's task in learning a language. For more complete descriptions, please see Hoff (2009) and Pinker (1994).

3. The control group, Teaching Only, exposed to the *Barney* lessons without viewing the television, showed minimal impact of teacher attention plus lessons. The statistical significance was limited by the smaller number of subjects.

References

Andersen, E. (Ed.). (1990). *Speaking with style: The sociolinguistic skills of children.* New York: Routledge.

Anderson, D. (2004). Watching children watch television and the creation of *Blue's Clues*. In H. Hendershot (Ed.). *Nickelodeon nation* (pp. 241–268). New York: New York University Press.

Baldwin, D. (1991). Infants' contribution to the achievement of joint reference. *Child Development, 62,* 875–890.

Baldwin, D. (1993). Early referential understanding: Infants' ability to recognize referential acts for what they are. *Developmental Psychology, 29,* 832–843.

Barr, R., Zack, E., Garcia, A., & Muentener, P. (2008). Infants' attention and responsiveness to television increases with prior exposure and parental interaction. *Infancy, 13*, 30–56.

Berman, R., & Slobin, D. (1994). *Relating events in narrative: A crosslinguistic developmental study*. Hillsdale, NJ: Lawrence Erlbaum.

Broen, P. A. (1972). The verbal environment of the language learning child. *American Speech and Hearing Association Monograph, 17*.

Christakis, D., Gilkerson, J., Richards, M., Zimmerman, F., Garrison, M., Xu, D., et al. (2009). Audible television and decreased adult words, infant vocalizations, and conversational turns. *Archives of Pediatrics and Adolescent Medicine, 163*, 554–558.

Clancy, P. (1985). The acquisition of Japanese. In B. MacWhinney (Ed.), *Mechanisms of language acquisition: Vol. 1. The data* (pp. 373–524). Hillsdale, NJ: Lawrence Erlbaum.

Clark, E., & Grossman, J. (1998). Pragmatic directions and children's word learning. *Journal of Child Language, 25*, 1–18.

Clark, H. (1996). *Using language*. Cambridge: Cambridge University Press.

Clark, H., & Clark, E. (1977). *Psychology and language*. New York: Harcourt Brace Jovanovich.

DeLoache, J., Chiong, C., Vanderborght, M., Sherman, K., Islam, N., Troseth, G., et al. (under review). Do babies learn from baby media? *Psychological Science*.

Fenson, L., Dale, P. S., Reznick, J. S., Thal, D., Bates, E., Hartung, J. P., et al. (1993). *MacArthur communicative development inventories: User's guide and technical manual*. Baltimore, MD: Paul H. Brookes Publishing.

Fernald, A., & Mazzie, C. (1991). Prosody and focus in speech to infants and adults. *Developmental Psychology, 27*, 209–221.

Fernald, A., Taeschner, T., Dunn, J., Papousek, M., deBoysoon-Bardies, P., & Fukui, I. (1989). A cross-linguistic study of prosodic modification in mothers' and fathers' speech to preverbal infants. *Journal of Child Language, 16*, 477–501.

Fowler, A. (1991). How early phonological development might set the stage for phoneme awareness. In S. Brady & D. Shankweiler (Eds.), *Phonological processes in literacy.* (pp. 97–117). Hillsdale, NJ: Lawrence Erlbaum.

Gillette, J., Gleitman, H., Gleitman, L., & Lederer, A. (1999). Human simulation of vocabulary learning. *Cognition, 73*, 135–176.

Gleitman, L. (1990). The structural sources of verb meanings. *Language Acquisition 1*, 3–55.

Gleitman, L., & Gleitman, H. (1997). What is a language made of? *Lingua, 100*, 29–67.

Gleitman, L.R., Gleitman, H., Landau, B., & E. Wanner (1988). Where learning begins: Initial representations for language learning. In F. Newmeyer (Ed.), *The Cambridge linguistic survey* (Vol. 3, pp. 150–193). Cambridge: Cambridge University Press.

Gleitman, L., & Wanner, E. (1984). Current issues in language learning. In M. Bornstein & M. Lamb (Eds.), *Developmental psychology: An advanced textbook: Vol. 2. Perceptual, cognitive, and linguistic development* (pp. 181–240). Hillsdale, NJ: Lawrence Erlbaum.

Goodrich, S., Pempek, T., & Calvert, S. (2009). Formal production features of infant and toddler DVDs. *Archives of Pediatric and Adolescent Medicine, 163*, 1151–1156.

Hoff, E. (2009). *Language development* (4th ed.). Belmont, CA: Wadsworth/Cengage Learning.

Hoff-Ginsberg, E. (1985). Some contributions of mothers' speech to their children's syntactic growth. *Journal of Child Language 13*, 367–385.

Hoff-Ginsberg, E. (1986). Function and structure in maternal speech: Their relation to the child's development of syntax. *Developmental Psychology, 22*, 155–163.

Hoff-Ginsberg, E. (1998). The relation of birth order and socioeconomic status to children's language experience and language development. *Applied Psycholinguistics, 19*, 603–629.

Hollich, G., Hirsh-Pasek, K., & Golinkoff, R. (1998). Introducing the 3-D intermodal preferential looking paradigm: A new method to answer an age-old question. In C. Rovee-Collier, L. Lipsitt, & H. Hayne (Eds.), *Advances in infancy research* (Vol. 12, pp. 355–374). Stamford, CT: Ablex.

Ireton, H. (1994). *Infant development inventory*. Minneapolis, MN: Behavior Science Systems.

Johnson, J. S., & Newport, E. L. (1989). Critical period effects in second language learning: The influence of maturational state on the acquisition of English as a second language. *Cognitive Psychology, 21*, 60–99.

Keil, F. (1979). *Semantic and conceptual development*. Cambridge, MA: Harvard University Press.

Kirkorian, H., Pempek, T., Murphy, L., Schmidt, M., & Anderson, D. (2009). The impact of background television on parent–child interaction. *Child Development, 80*, 1350–1359.

Kirkorian, H., Whitcomb, A., & Anderson, D. (2010). *Integrating information across shots during video viewing: Eye movement research*. Paper presented at the biennial International Conference on Infant Studies, Baltimore, MD.

Krcmar, M., Grela, B., & Lin, K. (2007). Can toddlers learn vocabulary from television? An experimental approach. *Media Psychology, 10,* 41–63.

Kuhl, P. K. (2007). Is speech learning "gated" by the social brain? *Developmental Science,* 10, 110–120.

Kuhl, P. K., Feng-Ming, T., & Huei-Mei, L. (2003). Foreign-language experience in infancy: Effects of short-term exposure and social interaction on phonetic learning. *Proceedings of the National Academy of Sciences, 100,* 9096–9101.

Landau, B., & Gleitman, L. (1985). *Language and experience: Evidence from the blind child.* Cambridge, MA: Harvard University Press.

Lemish, D., & Rice, M. (1986). Television as a talking picture book: A prop for language acquisition. *Journal of Child Language, 13,* 251–274.

Levin, B. (1993). *English verb classes and alternations.* Chicago: University of Chicago Press.

Linebarger, D., & Piotrowski, J. (2009). TV as storyteller: How exposure to television narratives impacts at-risk preschoolers' story knowledge and narrative skills. *British Journal of Developmental Psychology,* 27, 47–69.

Linebarger, D., & Walker, J. (2005). Infants' and toddlers' television viewing and language outcomes. *American Behavioral Scientist, 48,* 624–645.

Luze, G. J., Linebarger, D. L., Greenwood, C. R., Carta, J. J., Walker, D., Leitschuh, C., et al. (2001). Developing a general outcome measure of growth in expressive communication of infants and toddlers. *School Psychology Review, 30,* 383–406.

Morgan, J., & Demuth, K. (1996). *Signal to syntax: Bootstrapping from speech to grammar in early acquisition.* Mahwah, NJ: Lawrence Erlbaum.

Naigles, L. (1990). Children use syntax to learn verb meanings. *Journal of Child Language, 17,* 357–374.

Naigles, L. (1998). Developmental changes in the use of structure in verb learning: Evidence from preferential looking. In C. Rovee-Collier, L. Lipsitt, & H. Hayne (Eds.), *Advances in infancy research* (Vol. 12, pp. 298–318). Stamford, CT: Ablex.

Naigles, L. (2000). Manipulating the input: Studies in mental verb acquisition. In B. Landau, J. Sabini, J. Jonides, & E. Newport (Eds.), *Perception, cognition and language* (pp. 245–274). Cambridge, MA: MIT Press.

Naigles, L., & Hoff-Ginsberg, E. (1998). Why are some verbs learned before other verbs? Effects of input frequency and structure on children's early verb use. *Journal of Child Language, 25,* 95–120.

Naigles, L., & Kako, E. (1993). First contact: Biases in verb learning with and without syntactic information. *Child Development, 64,* 1665–1687.

Newport, E., Gleitman, H., & Gleitman, L. (1977). Mother, I'd rather do it myself: Some effects and non-effects of maternal speech style. In C. Snow & C. Ferguson (Eds.), *Talking to children: Language input and acquisition* (pp. 109–150). Cambridge, MA: Cambridge University Press.

Patterson, J. (2002). Relationships of expressive vocabulary to frequency of reading and television experience among bilingual toddlers. *Applied Psycholinguistics, 23,* 493–508.

Pempek, T., Kirkorian, H., & Anderson, D. (2010). The impact of background TV on the quantity and quality of parents' verbal input. Paper presented at the biennial International Conference on Infant Studies, Baltimore, MD.

Pinker, S. (1994). *The language instinct.* New York: William Morrow and Co.

Quine, W. V. O. (1960). *Word and object.* Cambridge, MA: Harvard University Press.

Rice, M. (1984). The words of television. *Journal of Broadcasting, 28,* 445–461.

Rice, M., & Haight, P. (1986). The "motherese" of Mr. Rogers: The dialogue of educational television programs. *Journal of Speech and Hearing Disorders, 51,* 272–281.

Rice, M., Huston, A., Truglio, R., & Wright, J. (1990). Words from "Sesame Street": Learning vocabulary while viewing. *Developmental Psychology, 2,* 421–428.

Rice, M., & Woodsmall, L. (1988). Lessons from television: Children's word learning when viewing. *Child Development, 59,* 420–429.

Rideout, V., & Hamel, R. (2006). *The media family: Electronic media in the lives of infants, toddlers, preschoolers, and their parents.* Menlo Park, CA: Henry J. Kaiser Family Foundation.

Robb, M., Richert, R., & Wartella, E. (2009). Just a talking book? Word learning from watching baby videos. *British Journal of Developmental Psychology, 27,* 27–45.

Rosch, E., Mervis, C., Gray, W., Johnson, D., & Boyes-Braem, P. (1976). Basic objects in natural categories. *Cognitive Psychology, 8,* 382–439.

Roseberry, S., Hirsh-Pasek, K., Parish-Morris, J., & Golinkoff, R. (2009). Live action: Can children learn verbs from video? *Child Development, 80,* 1360–1375.

Sachs, J., Bard, B., & Johnson, M. (1981). Language learning with restricted input: Case studies of two hearing children of deaf parents. *Applied Psycholinguistics, 2,* 33–54.

Schmidt, M. E., Rich, M., Rifas-Shiman, S., Oken, E., & Taveras, E. (2009). Television viewing in infancy and child cognition at 3 years of age in a US cohort. *Pediatrics, 123,* 370–375.

Scofield, J., & Williams, A. (2009). Do 2-year-olds disambiguate and extend words learned from video? *First Language, 29,* 228–240.

Selnow, G. W., & Bettinghaus, E. (1982). Television exposure and language development. *Journal of Broadcasting, 26,* 469–479.

Singer, J., & Singer, D. (1981). Television, imagination, and aggression: A study of preschoolers. Hillsdale, NJ: Lawrence Erlbaum.

Singer, J., & Singer, D. (1998). Barney & Friends as entertainment and education: Evaluating the quality and effectiveness of a television series for preschool children. In W. K. Asamen & G. Berry (Eds.), *Research paradigms in the study of television and social behavior.* (pp. 305–367). Thousand Oaks, CA: Sage.

St. Peters, M., Fitch, M., Huston, A., Wright, J., & Eakins, D. (1988). *Television and families: What do young children watch with their families?* New Orleans, LA: Southwestern Society for Research in Human Development.

Talmy, L. (1985). Lexicalization patterns: Semantic structure in lexical forms. In T. Shopen (Ed.), *Language typology and syntactic description* (Vol. 3). (pp. 57–160). New York: Cambridge University Press.

Tek, S., Jaffery, G., Swensen, L., Fein, D., & Naigles, L. (2008). Do children with autism spectrum disorders show a shape bias in word learning? *Autism Research, 1,* 208–222.

Tomasello, M. (1990). The social bases of language acquisition. *Social Development, 1,* 67–87.

Tomasello, M. (2001). Perceiving intentions and learning words in the second year of life. In M. Bowerman & S. Levinson (Eds.), *Language acquisition and conceptual development.* (pp. 132–158). Cambridge, UK: Cambridge University Press.

Uchikoshi, Y. (2005). Narrative development in bilingual kindergarteners: Can Arthur help? *Developmental Psychology, 41,* 464–478.

Uchikoshi, Y. (2007). Early reading in bilingual kindergarteners: Can educational television help? *Scientific Studies of Reading, 10,* 89–120.

Urmson, J. (1963). Parenthetical verbs. In C. Caton (Ed.), *Philosophy and ordinary language* (pp. 220–246). Urbana: University of Illinois Press.

Vandewater, E. A. (2010, April). *Infant word learning from commercially available video.* Paper presented at the Conference on Human Development, New York, NY.

Vandewater, E., Park, S. E., Lee, S. J., & Barr, R. (2010). Transfer of learning from video to books during toddlerhood in the US: Matching words across context change. *Journal of Children and Media, 4,* 451–466.

Vandewater, Barr, Park, & Lee. (2010).

Waxman, S., & Kosowski, T. (1990). Nouns mark category relations: Toddlers' and preschoolers' word-learning biases. *Child Development, 61,* 1461–1490.

Werker, J., & Tees, R. (1984). Cross-language speech perception: Evidence for perceptual reorganization during the first year of life. *Infant Behavior and Development, 7,* 49–63.

Woodward, A., & Markman, E. (1998). Early word learning. In W. Damon (Ed.), *Handbook of child psychology: Volume 2: Cognition, perception, and language* (pp. 371–420). Hoboken, NJ: John Wiley & Sons.

Wright, J., Huston, A., Murphy, K., St. Peters, M., Piñon, M., Scantlin, R., & Kotler, J. (2001). The relations of early television viewing to school readiness and vocabulary of children from low-income families: The early window project. *Child Development, 72,* 1347–1366.

Zimmerman, F., Christakis, D., & Meltzoff, A. (2007). Television and DVD/video viewing in children younger than 2 years. *Archives of Pediatrics and Adolescent Medicine, 161,* 473–479.

Zimmerman, F., Gilkerson, J., Richards, J., Christakis, D., Xu, D., Sharmistha, G., & Yapanel, U. (2009). Teaching by listening: The importance of adult-child conversations to language development. *Pediatrics, 124,* 342–349.

CHAPTER 8

Media and the Child's Developing Imagination

Patti M. Valkenburg
University of Amsterdam

Sandra L. Calvert
Georgetown University

Media and the Child's Developing Imagination

Over the past four decades, a variety of studies have investigated environmental and developmental influences on creative achievement. One of the most clear-cut findings obtained in these studies is that individuals who make creative contributions as an adult tend to come from families in which a favorable background for the development of intellectual abilities is provided (see Mumford & Gustafson, 1988). If environmental forces in childhood can affect later creative achievement, one might also expect that cumulative exposure to media, beginning in infancy, is a socializing factor with a great potential to influence children's developing imagination.

The question of whether and how the media impact children's imagination has been debated since the medium became part of everyday life, and there is still little consensus on the issue. On the one hand, media such as television and films are believed to produce a passive intellect and reduce imaginative capacities. On the other hand, there has been enthusiasm about educational programming fostering children's creative thinking skills (see Anderson, Huston, Schmitt, Linebarger & Wright, 2001; Valkenburg, 1999a; Valkenburg & van der Voort, 1994; van der Voort & Valkenburg, 1994). However, if media do have a positive or negative impact on children's imagination, it is especially important to understand the nature of their impact.

Media-related research on imagination has focused largely on television. Therefore, we first review the available research evidence on television's effects on children's imagination. We present the different stimulation and reduction hypotheses that have been proposed in the literature and discuss the validity of each of these hypotheses. Then we discuss the emerging evidence for the opportunities and risks of computer games and the Internet for children's imagination. We end with our conclusions about what is currently known about the influence of television, computer games, and the Internet on children's imagination.

Defining Two Manifestations of Imagination

Before reviewing the effects literature, it is necessary to define two developmental manifestations of imagination that have been identified in the media-related literature: (a) imaginative play and (b) creative imagination. Imaginative play (fantasy play, pretend play) can be defined as play in which children transcend the constraints of reality by acting "as if" (van der Voort & Valkenburg, 1994). In imaginative play, children pretend that they are someone else, that an object represents something else, or that the participants are in a different place and time (James & McCain, 1982). Imaginative play is usually investigated by observing children while engaging in imaginative play.

Creative imagination is defined as the capacity to generate many different novel or unusual ideas. It is a central facet of narrative thinking, which entails story-like, imaginistic thinking, whose object is not truth but "verisimilitude" or "lifelikeness" (Bruner, 1986, p. 11; Valkenburg & Peter, 2006). According to Singer and Singer (2005), the creative process involves the potential for imaginative novelty, in which there is a free flow of ideas, images, and mini stories, all facets of divergent processing, followed by an evaluation of the quality of these ideas within a domain of expertise. Creative imagination is typically measured in television studies by divergent thinking tests (tests that require creative thinking in response to open-ended problems) and by creative tasks like drawing, problem solving, and making up stories (Valkenburg & van der Voort, 1994). Participation in extracurricular activities such as the visual arts, music, drama, and journalism has also been defined as an index of creative imagination (Anderson et al., 2001).

Both imaginative play and creative imagination can make an important contribution to the cognitive and social development of the child (Piaget, 1972; Singer & Singer, 1990). Children who exhibit a great deal of imagination in their play are better able to concentrate, develop greater empathic ability, and are better able to consider a subject from different angles (Singer & Singer, 1990). They are happier, more self-assured, and more flexible in unfamiliar situations (Singer & Singer, 1990). Moreover, there are indications that a high level of imaginative play in childhood is positively related to creative imagination in adulthood (Dansky, 1980; Fisher, 1992). It has been suggested that the as-if nature of imaginative play helps the child in breaking free of established associations or meanings and, thereby, encourages children's creative imagination in the long term (Sutton-Smith, 1966).

The emergence of imaginative play and creative imagination follows a developmental path. The first manifestations of imaginative play appear at about 12 or 13 months of age (see Fein, 1981). A child closes his or her eyes, pretending to sleep without actually doing so, or pretends to drink out of an empty cup. Between 20 and 26 months, children's imaginative play becomes increasingly independent of the immediate reality. An inanimate object, such as a teddy bear, might be treated as if it were an animate, living being, and a great many objects might be used to stand in for another object, such as a stick being used as a magic wand (Fein, 1981).

By age 3, children's imaginative play becomes more social. Children increasingly begin to play with other children. In addition, their imaginative play develops from loose fragments into play based on elaborated plots. The development of imaginative play peaks between ages 5 and 7 (Fein, 1981). In this period, children start to distinguish between fantasy and reality and recognize that other children can have different perspectives (thoughts, feelings, and motives) than they have themselves (Selman, 1980). This is the period in which children seem to delight in the most elaborated forms of social imaginative play.

Overt imaginative play, however, progressively declines after age 7. By this time, school achievement starts to gain prominence in the child's life, and overt utterances of imaginative play are often discouraged by parents and teachers. It has been suggested that this emphasis on conventional behavior is the reason why children's internal processes, in the form of fantasizing and imaginative capacities, start to blossom (Singer & Singer, 1990).

Creative imagination seems to begin around 5 or 6 years of age (see Mumford & Gustafson, 1988). Some researchers believe that younger children cannot be creative because they are unable to differentiate outer stimuli from the internal experience of the stimuli (Smith & Carlsson, 1985). This could explain why divergent thinking tests, which are used to tap into creative imaginative processes, have been shown to be useless instruments with kindergarten children (Runco, 1992).

The Impact of Television on Children's Imaginative Play and Creative Imagination

Researchers have advanced contradictory opinions about the influence of television on imaginative play and creative imagination. Some scholars believe that television encourages imaginative play and creative imagination. We refer to this view as the stimulation hypothesis. Many others, however, argue that television hinders imaginative play and creative imagination, a position we call the reduction hypothesis.

Stimulation Hypothesis: The Potential of Educational Programs

According to the stimulation hypothesis, well-designed television programs can enrich the store of ideas from which children can draw when engaged in imaginative play or creative tasks. Adherents of the stimulation hypothesis argue that television characters and events are picked up, transformed, and incorporated into children's play and

products of creative imagination and that, as a result, the quality or quantity of their play and creative products is improved.

There is indeed evidence to suggest that children often use television content in their imaginative play (e.g., James & McCain, 1982) and creative products (e.g., Vibbert & Meringhoff, 1981). However, the fact that children incorporate television content into their play and creative products does not necessarily mean that their television-related play or creative products are more imaginative. There is as yet no empirical evidence that the quality or quantity of imaginative play and creative products is improved through television viewing in general. None of the studies that have been conducted demonstrate that overall television viewing is positively related to imaginative play (Shmukler, 1981; J. Singer & Singer, 1976; Singer & Singer, 1981; Singer, Singer, & Rapaczynski, 1984a) or creative imagination (Childs, 1979; Furu, 1971; Peterson, Peterson, & Caroll, 1987; Singer et al., 1984a; Wade, 1971; Zuckerman, Singer, & Singer, 1980). Overall, then, there is little indication that overall television viewing stimulates children's imaginative play or creative imagination.

While a stimulating effect does not appear to be true of TV viewing in general, it has been suggested that educational viewing that is designed to cultivate imagination stimulates children's imagination (Anderson et al., 2001; Calvert, Strong, Jacobs, & Conger, 2007; Schmitt et al., 1997). Observational-experimental evidence finds that children's television programs, such as *Mister Rogers' Neighborhood* and *Dora the Explorer*, can promote imaginative play (Calvert et al., 2007; Friedrich-Cofer, Huston-Stein, McBride Kipnis, Susman, & Clewett, 1979; Singer & Singer, 1976; Tower, Singer, Singer, & Biggs, 1979).

The positive effects of educational viewing have also been demonstrated in two longitudinal studies (Anderson et al., 2001; Schmitt et al., 1997), which showed that viewing educational programs over time leads to an increase in children's creative imagination. Although the stimulation effects have been found in both experimental and longitudinal research, the elements of educational programming that lead to these beneficial effects are unclear. At least three elements of such programs may account for these effects: (a) the pace of the program, (b) an imaginary lead character, and (c) interactivity.

The Pace of the Program. To create, children need to be able to reflect (Singer & Singer, 2005). Television programs that allow time for reflection, for instance those that are slowly paced such as *Mister Rogers' Neighborhood*, may improve imaginative activities. Current production practices in children's educational television programs include the use of pauses built into the story at key program points (Anderson et al., 2001). These pauses allow children time to think and to reflect on the content, a characteristic that could promote imaginative activity.

An Imaginary Lead Character. Many times educational programs have a lead character who acts as a social model. These models display imaginative activities and provide children with prototypes about how to generate creative responses to situations. Children who observe these models may be likely to learn that behavior and to use it when it is appropriate for a situation (Bandura, 1986). In addition, children who develop parasocial relationships, in which they treat certain media characters as friends (Hoffner, 2008), might also have their imaginative activities stimulated. After all, behavior will be acted out more readily when it is adopted from a well-liked friend (Calvert et al., 2007).

Interactivity. In children's educational television programs, the lead character sometimes asks the viewing child a question, the child presumably replies, and the character then acts as if they hear or see the child's response. This allows children time to respond to characters. This interactivity in children's programs may at least in part account for the positive effects of educational programming on imagination. This interactivity assumption may be promising for computer games and

the Internet, in which children can create, interact with, and even become the characters that act onscreen (see end of chapter; Calvert, 2002).

Reduction Hypotheses: Does Television Stifle Children's Creative Capacities?

The majority of studies suggest that television in general and television violence in particular have a reductive effect on imaginative play and creative imagination (Valkenburg & van der Voort, 1994; van der Voort & Valkenburg, 1994). In the case of imaginative play, each of the different types of research that have been conducted report a negative relation between television viewing and imaginative play. First, most quasi-experimental studies carried out in the early years of television found that the introduction of television resulted in a loss of playtime (Maccoby, 1951; Schramm, Lyle, & Parker, 1961). Second, the correlational studies showed that children who watch a great deal of violence engage less frequently in imaginative play (Shmukler, 1981; J. Singer & Singer, 1976; Singer et al., 1984a). And finally, a series of experimental studies indicates that programs with a high level of violence hinder imaginative play (Huston-Stein, Fox, Greer, Watkins, & Whitaker, 1981; Noble, 1970, 1973).

In the case of creative imagination, the overall results are in the same negative direction. First, a quasi-experimental study carried out in the introductory stage of television found that the arrival of television into a community was linked to a decrease in creative imagination over time (Harrison & Williams, 1986). Second, the majority of the correlational studies demonstrated that overall television viewing is negatively related to creative imagination (Childs, 1979; Furu, 1971; Peterson et al., 1987; Singer et al., 1984a; Wade, 1971; Zuckerman et al., 1980). Finally, most experiments that established the short-term effects of exposure to films suggested that viewing television programs leads to less creative imagination than does listening to radio broadcasts or reading written texts (Greenfield & Beagles-Roos, 1988; Greenfield, Farrar, & Beagles-Roos, 1986; Kerns, 1981;

Meline, 1976; Valkenburg, & Beentjes, 1997; Vibbert & Meringoff, 1981).

To date, six types of reduction hypotheses have been proposed to explain the negative effects of television on imagination: the displacement hypothesis, passivity hypothesis, rapid pacing hypothesis, visualization hypothesis, arousal hypothesis, and fear hypothesis. Four hypotheses pertain to the impact of television on both imaginative play and creative imagination, whereas two hypotheses have only been proposed for imaginative play (the fear hypothesis) or for creative imagination (the visualization hypothesis). In each of the hypotheses, the reductive effect of television is attributed to a special property of television. The first four reduction hypotheses attribute the reductive effect of television on imagination to some structural characteristic of television, such as its visual nature or its rapid pace. The other two hypotheses attribute television's negative influence on imaginative play and creative imagination to a specific type of program, namely action-oriented and violent programs.

Displacement Hypothesis. In this hypothesis, the reductive effect of television on imaginative play and creative imagination is a result of the popularity of the medium. It is argued that children spend a considerable portion of their free time watching television, at the expense of other leisure activities. In case of imaginative play, the displacement hypothesis assumes that television viewing takes up time that could otherwise be spent on imaginative play (e.g., Singer & Singer, 1990). In the case of creative imagination, it is argued that television viewing occurs at the expense of activities like reading or listening to the radio that are thought to stimulate creative imagination more than does television viewing.

The displacement hypothesis was tested in studies conducted during the introductory stage of television, when households with and without television could still be compared (Maccoby, 1951; Murray & Kippax, 1978; Schramm et al., 1961). Although none of the studies investigated the effect of the arrival of television on the time devoted to imaginative play, they did investigate the consequences for playtime in general. Two of the three studies found that television watching occurred at the expense of playtime in general (Maccoby, 1951; Schramm et al., 1961). Since approximately one third of general play is spent on imaginative play during early childhood (Fein, 1981), it is likely that television has a reductive effect on imaginative play as well.

In the case of creative imagination, the displacement hypothesis argues that television viewing takes time from other activities that are thought to be more beneficial for creative imagination than television viewing. The result is that creative imagination is hindered. Evidence does suggest that the arrival of television displaces other media, such as comic books and radio (see Anderson & Collins, 1988). It is still unknown, however, whether this displacement of verbal media (i.e., books and radio) leads to a reduction in creative imagination. A study that was conducted during the introductory stage of television in Canada demonstrated that the arrival of television resulted in a decrease in children's imagination (Harrison & Williams, 1986), but this study did not assess whether this reductive effect was caused by a diminished use of books and radio by children.

Passivity Hypothesis. Adherents of the passivity hypothesis see television as an "easy" medium, requiring little mental effort (Salomon, 1984). When there is a minimum of mental effort, the child-viewer is content to consume the fantasies produced by others. According to the passivity hypothesis, this leads to a passive, "let you entertain me" attitude that undermines children's willingness to use their own imagination in play and creative products (Harrison & Williams, 1986; Singer et al., 1984a).

The passivity hypothesis has never been tested, neither for imaginative play nor for creative imagination. The first assumption of the passivity hypothesis is that processing television requires little mental effort. Despite popular stereotypes of children just sitting and staring at the screen, there is evidence that the child-viewer is far from cognitively passive. Even very young children actively view television offerings for attractiveness and understandability and make an effort to interpret television images in their own terms (Collins, 1982). Although viewers do actively process television content (Anderson & Burns, 1991; Richards & Anderson, 2004), reading a book does require more mental effort than watching a television program does (Beentjes, 1989; Salomon, 1984).

The second assumption of the passivity hypothesis is that the low levels of effort that are purportedly commonplace during television viewing generalize to other situations. This assumption has not been tested. Nor do we know if this process is expected to occur for all screen media or is unique to viewing lean-back media such as television or films. It also assumes that children's willingness to put effort into play and creative thinking is undermined because they consume fantasies produced by others.

In summary, while there is some evidence that television viewing requires relatively little mental effort, empirical investigations have not examined whether this leads to a general tendency to expend little mental effort, including a diminished tendency to invest mental effort in imaginative play or creative activities. Of course child-viewers consume fantasies produced by others, but one cannot then logically assume that this leads to reductions in fantasy play or creative imagination. Children who read a story, listen to a radio story, or watch a play also consume fantasies produced by others—but no one has ever argued that print stories or theater hinder children's imaginative play or creative imagination. Therefore, there is little reason to assume that television's reductive effect on imaginative play and creative imagination is caused by a television-induced, passive let-you-entertain-me attitude.

Rapid Pacing Hypothesis. The rapid pacing hypothesis attributes television's reductive effect on imaginative play and creative imagination to the rapid pace of television programs. According to this hypothesis, the viewer is confronted with images that must be instantaneously processed because scenes are presented in rapid succession. Viewers are thus allowed little time to process the information

at their own rate or to reflect upon program content. The hypothesis argues that rapidly paced television programs encourage cognitive overload, impulsive thinking, hyperactivity, and a non-reflective style of thinking (Anderson, Levin, & Lorch, 1977). Because both imaginative play and creative tasks require children to fix their attention for a sustained period of time, the quality or quantity of imaginative play and creative products could be impaired.

Of course, rapidly paced programs leave children less room for reflection on program content than slowly paced programs do. Until now, however, there have been no indications that a rapidly paced television program *per se* leads to cognitive overload, impulsive thinking, and shortened attention spans. Anderson et al. (1977) found no immediate effect of rapidly paced television programs on perseverance in puzzle solving and impulsive thinking. Zillmann (1982) suggested that fast-paced programs may even foster the child's attention. In particular, Zillmann observed that the fast-paced interspersion of attention-catching stimuli in educational programs, compared with the slow-paced interspersion of the same materials, resulted in superior information acquisition.

Because there is no evidence of the ill effects of fast-paced programs on children's attention spans and cognitive style, it is not likely that children's imaginative play and creative imagination will be hindered by program pace. It is no surprise, therefore, that several experimental studies reported that program pace did not affect children's imaginative play (Anderson et al., 1977; Greer, Potts, Wright, & Huston, 1982; Tower et al., 1979). It should be noted, however, that these experiments used only benign, nonviolent programs. It is possible that the combination of rapid pace and violence, which is common in many action-adventure children's programs, does lead to hyperactivity, impulsive thinking, and reduced attention spans. The rapid pacing hypothesis has never been tested with these types of programs, neither for imaginative play nor for creative imagination.

Visualization Hypothesis. The visualization hypothesis has only been proposed and tested with respect to creative imagination—not with respect to imaginative play. This hypothesis attributes the reductive effect of television on creative imagination to the medium's visual nature. Television, unlike radio and print, presents viewers with ready-made visual images and leaves them little room to form their own images. When engaged in creative thinking, viewers find it hard to dissociate themselves from the images supplied by television, so that they have difficulty generating novel ideas (Greenfield & Beagles-Roos, 1988; Meline, 1976; Valkenburg & Beentjes, 1997).

Seven experimental studies have been designed to test the visualization hypothesis. In all of these *media-comparison experiments*, children were presented with either a story or a problem. The stories or problems were presented in either television (audiovisual), radio (audio), or print (written text) format. The text of the story or problem was usually kept the same, whereas the presentation modality was varied. After the presentation of the stories and problems, children were given a creative task. They were asked, for instance, to find a solution for a problem, make a drawing, or complete a story that was stopped just prior to the end.

Six of the experiments were carried out in the United States (Greenfield & Beagles-Roos, 1988; Greenfield et al., 1986; Kerns, 1981; Meline, 1976; Runco & Pezdek, 1984; Vibbert & Meringoff, 1981), and one was conducted in the Netherlands (Valkenburg & Beentjes, 1997) to test the visualization hypothesis. With the exception of one study (Runco & Pezdek, 1984), all of the media comparison studies showed that verbally presented information evoked more novel ideas than did televised information. According to the authors, the television presentations led to fewer novel ideas than did the radio and print presentations because children in the video condition had difficulty dissociating themselves from television images during creative thinking.

However, the results of the media experiments can also be explained in a different way. According to a rival hypothesis, verbal presentations, such as radio and print, might elicit more novel responses than television presentations, not because verbal presentations are more stimulating for creative imagination, but

because they are *remembered less well*. The faulty-memory hypothesis disputes the premise that the superior production of novel ideas after a verbal presentation should be attributed to creative imagination. According to this hypothesis, the novel ideas produced by children after radio listening are not creative responses but merely inventions to fill in holes in a faulty memory.

A part of the faulty-memory hypothesis is that radio information is remembered less well than television information. This assumption is supported by experimental evidence. Several studies have shown that children remember information presented on radio less well than information presented on television (e.g., Beagles-Roos & Gat, 1983). However, none of those media-comparison experiments investigated whether the relatively poor recall of radio information was responsible for the incorporation of more novel ideas in children's creative products.

A Dutch experiment was specifically designed to test the faulty-memory hypothesis (Valkenburg & Beentjes, 1997). Children in two age groups were asked to think up an ending for an incomplete television or radio story. An extra radio condition was included in which children were exposed twice to the same radio story. Because there is ample evidence that repetitive stimulus presentation improves recall, it was expected that double presentation of a radio story would improve children's recall. Therefore, the faulty-memory hypothesis was tested by examining whether a double presentation of a radio story would result in fewer novel ideas than a single presentation. As expected, double presentation of the radio story improved children's story recall. However, the faulty memory hypothesis did not receive support: In comparison with a single radio presentation, double presentation of a radio story did not lead to fewer novel ideas.

Because the faulty-memory hypothesis was not supported, the visualization hypothesis is as yet still the only plausible explanation for differences in novel ideas following radio presentations. The majority of the media-comparison experiments suggest that verbal information is more stimulating to creative imagination than is television information, although it should be recognized that the effect sizes of the differences in favor of radio have usually been small.

The Effects of Television Violence on Imagination

The Arousal Hypothesis. Like the rapid pacing hypothesis, the arousal hypothesis assumes that television promotes hyperactive and impulsive behavior. However, the hyperactivity is not seen as a result of the rapid pace of television programs, but is attributed to the arousing quality of action-oriented and violent programs. This arousing quality is assumed to foster a physically active and impulsive behavior orientation in children, which in turn disturbs the sequential thought and planning necessary for organizing plots of make-believe games and creative tasks (Singer et al., 1984a).

Although television viewing generally appears to be associated with relaxation, violent programs can produce intense arousal in children (e.g., Zillmann, 1991). In addition, there is evidence that the frequency with which children watch violent or action-oriented programs is positively related to restlessness in a waiting room (Singer et al., 1984b) and impulsivity at school (Anderson & McGuire, 1978). Finally, watching violent programs diminishes children's tolerance of delay and persistence in free play (Friedrich & Stein, 1973).

Because research does indicate that violent programs can induce an impulsive behavior orientation, it is no surprise that many television–imagination effect studies have demonstrated that watching violent programs can adversely affect children's imaginative play (Anderson et al., 2001; Huston-Stein et al., 1981; Noble, 1970, 1973; Shmukler, 1981; J. Singer & Singer, 1976; Singer & Singer, 1981; Singer et al., 1984a) and creative imagination (Singer et al., 1984a; Zuckerman et al., 1980). However, although these studies established that violent programs can hinder children's imaginative play and creative imagination, they failed to investigate whether it was the arousal provoked by television violence that was responsible for the reductions in imaginative play and creative imagination. In other words, although there is convincing evidence that violent programs can foster a physically and cognitively impulsive behavior orientation, it has not been directly investigated whether a heightened level of arousal was responsible for the observed reductions in imaginative play and creative imagination.

Fear Hypothesis. The fear hypothesis provides a plausible rival explanation for the reductive effect of television violence on children's imagination. This hypothesis also argues that violent programs hinder children's imaginative play, but the reduction effect is not attributed to the arousal that violent programs produce, but to the fright reactions they generate. The fear hypothesis assumes that the television-induced fright leads to regression in behavior, which is expressed in a reduction in the quantity or quality of imaginative play (Noble, 1970, 1973).

Although the fear hypothesis has only been advanced with respect to television's influence on imaginative play, in our view it also provides a plausible explanation for the reductive effects of violent programs on creative imagination. First, there is ample evidence that violent programs can induce intense fright reactions in children (Cantor, 1998). Second, there are indications that high levels of fear can disrupt fantasy play (see Fein, 1981) and creative imagination (e.g., Smith & Carlson, 1985). What remains to be proven, however, is whether television-induced fright is responsible for the reductive effects on imaginative play and creative imagination.

In summary, there is evidence that television violence has a negative effect on children's imaginative play and creative imagination and that the causal mechanisms proposed by the arousal and fear hypothesis actually operate. However, what remains to be proven is whether it is arousal or fear which is responsible for television-induced decreases in imaginative play and creative imagination. In fact, it is possible that both the arousal and the fear hypotheses are valid reduction hypotheses. It is widely recognized that different types of media violence evoke different reactions in different viewers (Paik & Comstock, 1994). It could be that an arousing children's program affects imaginative play and creative imagination through arousal, whereas frightening movies that have been shown to disturb many young viewers (Cantor, 1998) reduce children's imaginativeness through fear.

The Effects of Computer Games and the Internet: Some Preliminary Results

Although television is still the preferred pastime of children, with 72% of children from 16 countries reporting that television viewing is their favorite out-of-school activity (Singer, Singer, D'Agostino & Delong, 2009), computer and Internet use are weaving their way into the fabric of daily life (Rideout, Foehr, & Roberts, 2010). An important question is whether the effects of these newer media are different from those found in the television literature. Computer games and the Internet have a number of characteristics that have been used to explain television's reductive effects on imagination, such as their potential to displace other leisure activities and to increase arousal and fright in children. However, there are also some obvious differences between television and computer games that disqualify some reduction hypotheses advanced about television's impact on imagination. For example, unlike lean-back media such as television and films, newer media often require a high level of cognitive involvement. Using these media is certainly not a passive activity (Denot-Ledunois, Vardon, Perruchet, & Gallego, 1998). As a result, few people would argue that computer games impair children's creative imagination because they lead to a passive let-you-entertain-me attitude.

Unfortunately, there is little empirical evidence for the positive or negative effects of newer media on imaginative play and creative imagination. However, we can give some preliminary results and thoughts about their potential effects on children's imagination, which may inspire future researchers interested in this research question. We will discuss which mechanisms that were proposed in existing hypotheses on television's influence on imagination and creative imagination may also hold for newer interactive media.

Stimulation Hypothesis. As discussed earlier, educational television programs designed to cultivate imagination have the potential to do so. Many educational computer games and online tools are also designed to foster imagination. These media are often interactive, and children can determine their own pace while playing or consuming these media. These very characteristics are the presumed explanations for the positive effects of educational television programs on imagination, and therefore, they definitely need our research attention when investigating effects of games and the Internet on imagination.

It is quite possible that educational computer games and online tools designed to foster imagination can encourage children's creative capacities. Games and online tools designed for children typically include ways in which children can individualize the character and media environment: One way is to name the character; another way involves the roles played through that character (Calvert, 2002). In a study by Calvert, Mahler, Zehnder, Jenkins, and Lee (2003) on a virtual community created for children, children were free to choose and name their own character. Several children selected creative character names, derived from fantasy and mythology, concepts or objects, and nonsense words. They sometimes pretended to be basketball players shooting imaginary balls in the virtual city scene, or they pretended like they were drowning at the virtual beach scene (Calvert et al., 2003; Calvert, Strouse, Strong, Huffaker, & Lai, 2009).

Online interactions in virtual communities may be associated with children's role play because these kinds of sites have minimal structure. Preschool-aged children, for instance, demonstrate more novel responses in low-structure than in high-structure activities (Carpenter & Huston-Stein, 1980). Therefore, it may be that certain kinds of online activities lend themselves to imaginative responses more than others.

Interactive media activities also allow children the opportunity to make content, some of which can be creative. Kafai (1995, 1996), for instance, had children create video games to learn fractions. One of the first steps in game creation was to write a script. Girls created diverse stories, such as games where the player had to avoid a spider or ski down a hill without falling (Kafai, 1996). Although boys' stories often clustered around action-oriented themes, they sometimes made very clever stories en route to solving fractions (Kafai, 1995). These studies showed that any time a child is making content, creative output is likely to occur.

Displacement Hypothesis. Games and the Internet are rapidly gaining prominence as a preferred leisure activity, and thus, they have the potential to displace other activities, such as imaginative play and reading, as does television viewing. A study by Creasey and Myers (1986), in which computer game users were compared with nonusers, demonstrated that a newly introduced video game computer in the home mainly displaced television viewing and movie attendance. The introduction of the video game computer had no significant reductive effect on reading for pleasure, radio listening, peer interactions, and homework. The study also found that the displacement effects were short-lasting. Early decreases in television viewing, for example, started to disappear after several weeks. Although newer media could presumably displace older media use, this pattern has not emerged. Instead, all media use among children has increased dramatically, with multitasking, in which more than one medium is used at a time, emerging as a normative behavior (Rideout et al., 2010).

A variant of the displacement hypothesis proposes that computer games impair children's imagination because they are played according to preset rules. It is argued that children, who predominantly play rule-based games, do not get sufficient practice in "divergent" and as if experiences and that, as a result, their development of imaginal skills is impaired. However, not all video and computer games have preset rules (Valkenburg, 1999b). In some adventures and fantasy role-play games, children are provided with ample opportunity to give free reign to their fantasies and ideas. They can draw, compose music, and create stories, and although nobody would recommend that parents replace all real-life drawings and stories with computer-generated ones, there is little reason to assume that these computer games hinder children's creative imagination through lack of practice in divergent thinking tasks.

Rapid Pacing Hypothesis. Like television, some action-oriented computer games use a high tempo, which qualifies them for the rapid pacing hypothesis. As discussed earlier, there is little data to support the argument that children's imagination is hindered through the rapid pace of television because there is no evidence that a rapid pace *per se* leads to impulsivity and a nonreflective style of thinking. Therefore, there is also little reason to assume that the rapid pace of computer games will impair children's imagination.

Arousal and Fear Hypotheses. Finally, many computer games are at least as violent in nature as certain television programs (e.g., Provenzo, 1991), and therefore, they have a similar potential to induce arousal and fright in children. In order to tease out which causal mechanisms are responsible for a potential negative effect on children's imaginative play and creative imagination, research into the effects of violent computer games should include measures of arousal and fright and compare arousing-frightening with arousing-nonfrightening computer games.

Concluding Comments and Suggestions for Further Research

Research into the impact of television on children's imagination originated in the 1950s (Maccoby, 1951; Himmelweit, Oppenheim, & Vince, 1958), developed in the 1970s, flourished in the 1980s, and waned in the early 1990s. With the exception of the works of Dorothy and Jerome Singer, the study of the relationship between television and imagination is characterized by an ephemeral research interest. Researchers contributed with at most one or two studies, after which they disappeared again. The overall lack of continuity in the scholars in this area disrupts the ability of scholars to build on their prior research line to disentangle the underlying theoretical reasons for their findings.

Most studies have examined the relation between television viewing and imagination as an input-output measure, without attempting to explore the mechanisms that might be responsible for television's reductive or stimulating effect. Therefore, the existing research does not allow us to single out which of the hypotheses discussed in this chapter is the most plausible. Future research should derive from more sophisticated theoretical models, and it should pay closer attention to the question of *how* television, computer games, and the Internet may affect imaginative play and creative imagination.

Further research should also determine whether the content or structure of media moderates the relationship with imagination. As argued earlier, most previous research in this field has treated television viewing as a one-dimensional construct. However, including total viewing time as an independent variable only makes sense if the displacement hypothesis is tested. Tests of all other hypotheses demand a differentiation in types of content, types of media, or technology, at least in terms of violent and educational content, but also in terms of structural characteristics such as pace, character use, and interactivity.

Finally, new research should pay more attention to child characteristics. A basic assumption in modern theories of media effects is that children are active and motivated explorers of what they see on television (Valkenburg & Cantor, 1999). Another assumption is that any effect of television on children is enhanced, channeled, or mitigated by what the child viewer makes of it. In order to understand media effects on children, it is crucial to gain insight into the different antecedents of children's selective exposure to media (e.g., Valkenburg & Janssen, 1999).

In summary, the literature to date makes too few attempts to explore the dynamic elements of child variables in the media–imagination relationship. There is a strong need for more elaborated theoretical models, in which media factors (e.g., pace, content, characters, interactivity), child factors (e.g., developmental level, intelligence), and different environmental agents (e.g., media exposure, family influences) all operate as interacting determinants of children's developing imagination.

References

Anderson, D. R., & Burns, J. (1991). Paying attention to television. In D. Zillmann & J. Bryant (Eds.), *Responding to the screen: Perception and reaction processes* (pp. 3–26). Hillsdale, NJ: Lawrence Erlbaum.

Anderson, D. R., & Collins, P. A. (1988). *The impact on children's education: Television's influence on cognitive development* (Working Paper No. 2). Washington, DC: Office of Educational Research and Improvement. (ERIC Document Reproduction Service No. ED 295 271)

Anderson, D. R., Huston, A. C., Schmitt, K., Linebarger, D., & Wright, J. C. (2001). Early childhood television viewing and adolescent behavior. *Monographs of the Society for Research in Child Development*, 68(1, Serial No. 264), 1–143.

Anderson, D. R., Levin, S. R., & Lorch, E. P. (1977). The effects of TV program pacing on the behavior of preschool children. *AV Communication Review*, 25, 159–166.

Anderson, C., & McGuire, T. (1978). The effect of TV viewing on the educational performance of elementary school children. *The Alberta Journal of Educational Research*, 24, 156–163.

Bandura, A. (1986). *Social foundations of thought and action: A social cognitive theory*. Englewood Cliffs, NJ: Prentice Hall.

Beagles-Roos, J., & Gat, I. (1983). Specific impact of radio and television on children's story comprehension. *Journal of Educational Psychology*, 75, 128–137.

Beentjes, J. W. J. (1989). Salomon's model for learning from television and books: A Dutch replication study. *Educational Technology: Research and Development*, 37(2), 47–58.

Bruner, J. S. (1986). *Actual minds, possible worlds*. Cambridge, MA: Harvard University Press.

Calvert, S. L. (2002). Identity construction on the Internet. In S. L. Calvert, A. B. Jordan, & R. R. Cocking (Eds.), *Children in the digital age: Influences of electronic media on development* (pp. 57–70). Westport, CT: Praeger.

Calvert, S. L., Mahler, B. A., Zehnder, S. M., Jenkins, A., & Lee, M. (2003). Gender differences in preadolescent children's online interactions: Symbolic modes of self-presentation and self-expression. *Journal of Applied Developmental Psychology*, 24, 627–644.

Calvert, S. L., Strong, B. L., Jacobs, E. L., & Conger, E. E. (2007). Interaction and participation for young Hispanic and Caucasian children's learning of media content. *Media Psychology*, 9(2), 431–445.

Calvert, S. L., Strouse, G. A., Strong, B., Huffaker, D. A., & Lai, S. (2009). Preadolescent boys' and girls' virtual MUD play. *Journal of Applied Developmental Psychology*, 30, 250–264.

Cantor, J. (1998). *Mommy I'm scared: How TV and movies frighten children and what we can do to protect them.* San Diego: Harcourt Brace.

Carpenter, C. J., & Huston-Stein, A. C. (1980). Activity structure and sex-typed behavior in preschool children. *Child Development, 51,* 862–872.

Childs, J. H. (1979). Television viewing, achievement, IQ and creative imagination. *Dissertation Abstracts International, 39,* 6531A.

Collins, W. A. (1982). Cognitive processing in television viewing. In D. Pearl, L. Bouthilet, & J. Lazar (Eds.), *Television and behavior: Ten years of scientific progress and implications for the eighties* (pp. 9–23). (DHHS Publication No. ADM 82-1196). Washington, DC: U.S. Government Printing Office.

Creasey, G. L., & Myers, B. J. (1986). Video games and children: Effects on leisure activities, schoolwork, and peer involvement. *Merrill-Palmer Quarterly, 32,* 251–262.

Dansky, J. L. (1980). Make-believe: A mediator of the relationship between play and associative fluency. *Child Development, 51,* 576–579.

Denot-Ledunois, S., Vardon, G., Perruchet, P., & Gallego, J. (1998). The effect of attentional load on the breathing pattern in children. *International Journal of Psychophysiology, 29(1),* 13–21.

Fein, G. G. (1981). Pretend play in childhood: An integrative review. *Child Development, 52,* 1095–1118.

Fisher, E. P. (1992). The impact of play on development: A meta analysis. *Play and Culture, 5,* 159–181.

Friedrich, L. K., & Stein, A. H. (1973). Aggressive and prosocial television programs and the natural behavior of preschool children. *Monographs of the Society for Research in Child Development, 38*(4, Serial No. 151, pp. 1–64).

Friedrich-Cofer, L. K., Huston-Stein, A., McBride Kipnis, D., Susman, E. J., & Clewett, A. S. (1979). Environmental enhancement of prosocial television content: Effects on interpersonal behavior, imaginative play, and self-regulation in a natural setting. *Developmental Psychology, 15,* 637–646.

Furu, T. (1971). *The function of television for children and adolescents.* Tokyo: Monumenta Nipponica, Sophia University.

Greenfield, P. M., & Beagles-Roos, J. (1988). Radio vs. television: Their cognitive impact on children of different socioeconomic and ethnic groups. *Journal of Communication, 38*(2), 71–92.

Greenfield, P. M., Farrar, D., & Beagles-Roos, J. (1986). Is the medium the message? An experimental comparison of the effects of radio and television on imagination. *Journal of Applied Developmental Psychology, 7,* 201–218.

Greer, D., Potts, R., Wright, J. C., & Huston, A. C. (1982). The effects of television commercial form and commercial placement on children's social behavior and attention. *Child Development, 53,* 611–619.

Harrison, L. F., & Williams, T. M. (1986). Television and cognitive development. In T. M. Williams (Ed.), *The impact of television: A natural experiment in three communities* (pp. 87–142). New York: Academic Press.

Himmelweit, H., Oppenheim, A. N., & Vince, P. (1958). *Television and the child: An empirical study of the effects of television on the young.* London: Oxford University Press.

Hoffner, C. (2008). Parasocial and online social relationships. In S. L. Calvert & B. J. Wilson (Eds.), *The handbook of children, media, and development* (pp. 309–333). Malden, MA: Blackwell.

Huston-Stein, A., Fox, S., Greer, D., Watkins, B. A., & Whitaker, J. (1981). The effects of action and violence on children's social behavior. *Journal of Genetic Psychology, 138,* 183–191.

James, N. C., & McCain, T. A. (1982). Television games preschool children play: Patterns, themes and uses. *Journal of Broadcasting, 26,* 783–800.

Kafai, Y. (1995). *Minds in play: Computer game design as a context for children's learning.* Mahwah, NJ: Lawrence Erlbaum.

Kafai, Y. (1996). Gender differences in children's constructions of video games. In P. M. Greenfield & R. R. Cocking (Eds.), *Interacting with video.* Norwood, NJ: Ablex.

Kerns, T. Y. (1981). Television: A bisensory bombardment that stifles children's creative imagination. *Phi Delta Kappan, 62,* 456–457.

Maccoby, E. E. (1951). Television: Its impact on school children. *Public Opinion Quarterly, 15,* 421–444.

Meline, C. W. (1976). Does the medium matter? *Journal of Communication, 26*(3), 81–89.

Mumford, M. D., & Gustafson, S. (1988). Creative imagination syndrome: Integration, application, and innovation. *Psychological Bulletin, 103,* 27–43.

Murray, J. P., & Kippax, S. (1978). Children's social behavior in three towns with differing television experience. *Journal of Communication, 28*(1), 19–29.

Noble, G. (1970). Film-mediated aggressive and creative play. *British Journal of Social & Clinical Psychology, 9,* 1–7.

Noble, G. (1973). Effects of different forms of filmed aggression on children's constructive and destructive play. *Journal of Personality and Social Psychology, 26*, 54–59.

Paik, H., & Comstock, G. (1994). The effects of television violence on antisocial behavior: A meta analysis. *Communication Research, 21*, 516–546.

Peterson, C. C., Peterson, J. L., & Caroll, J. (1987). Television viewing and imaginative problem solving during preadolescence. *Journal of Genetic Psychology, 147*, 61–67.

Piaget, J. (1972). *Play, dreams and imitation in childhood.* London: Routledge & Kegan Paul.

Provenzo, E.F. (1991). *Video kids: Making sense of Nintendo.* Cambridge, MA: Harvard University Press.

Richards, J., & Anderson, D. R. (2004). Attentional inertia in children's extended looking to television. *Advances in Child Development and Behavior, 32*, 163–212.

Rideout, V., Foehr, U., & Roberts, D. (2010, January). *Generation M^2: Media in the lives of 8- to 18-year-olds.* Menlo Park, CA: The Kaiser Family Foundation.

Runco, M. A. (1992). Review: Children's divergent thinking and creative ideation. *Developmental Review, 12*, 233–264.

Runco, M. A., & Pezdek, K. (1984). The effect of television and radio on children's creative imagination. *Human Communication Research, 11*, 109–120.

Salomon, G. (1984). Television is "easy" and print is "tough": The differential investment of mental effort as a function of perceptions and attributions. *Journal of Educational Psychology, 76*, 647–658.

Schmitt, K. L., Linebarger, D., Collins, P. A., Wright, J. C., Anderson, D. R., Huston, A. C., & McElroy, E. (1997, April). *Effects of preschool television viewing on adolescent creative thinking and behavior.* Poster presented at the biennial meeting of the Society for Research in Child Development, Washington, DC.

Selman, R. L. (1980). *The growth of interpersonal understanding.* New York: Academic Press.

Schramm, W., Lyle, J., & Parker, E. (1961). *Television in the lives of our children.* Stanford, CA: Stanford University Press.

Shmukler, D. (1981). A descriptive analysis of television viewing in South African preschoolers and its relationship to their spontaneous play. *South-African Journal of Psychology, 11*, 106–109.

Singer, D. G., & Singer, J. L. (1976). Family television viewing habits and the spontaneous play of preschool children. *American Journal of Orthopsychiatry, 46*, 496–502.

Singer, D. G., & Singer, J. L. (1990). *The house of make-believe.* Cambridge, MA: Harvard University Press.

Singer, D. G., & Singer, J. L. (2005). *Imagination and play in the electronic age.* Cambridge, MA: Harvard University Press.

Singer, D. G., Singer, J. L., D'Agostino, H., & Delong, R. (2009, Winter). Children's pastimes and play in sixteen nations: Is free play declining? *American Journal of Play, Vol. 1*(3), 283–312.

Singer, J. L. (1975). *The inner world of daydreaming.* New York: Harper & Row.

Singer, J. L., & Singer, D. G. (1976). Can TV stimulate imaginative play? *Journal of Communication, 26(3)*, 74–80.

Singer, J. L., & Singer, D. G. (1981). *Television, imagination and aggression: A study of preschoolers.* Hillsdale, NJ: Lawrence Erlbaum.

Singer, J. L., Singer, D. G., & Rapaczynski, W. S. (1984a). Children's imagination as predicted by family patterns and television viewing: A longitudinal study. *Genetic Psychology Monographs, 110*, 43–69.

Singer, J. L., Singer, D. G., & Rapaczynski, W. S. (1984b). Family patterns and television viewing as predictors of children's beliefs and aggression. *Journal of Communication, 34*(2), 73–89.

Smith, G., & Carlsson, I. (1985). Creative imagination in middle and late school years. *International Journal of Behavioral Development, 8*, 329–343.

Sutton-Smith, B. (1966). Piaget on play: A critique. *Psychological Review, 73*, 104–110.

Tower, R. B., Singer, D. G., Singer, J. L., & Biggs, A. (1979). Differential effects of television programming on preschoolers' cognition, imagination, and social play. *American Journal of Orthopsychiatry, 49*, 265–281.

Valkenburg, P. M. (1999a). Television and creative imagination. In M. Runco & S. Pritzker (Eds.), *Encyclopedia of creative imagination* (Vol. I., pp. 651–658). New York: Academic Press.

Valkenburg, P. M. (1999b). *Vierkante ogen: Opgroeien met TV en PC* [Square eyes: Growing up with TV and PC]. Amsterdam: Rainbow Pocket Books.

Valkenburg, P. M., & Beentjes, J. W. J. (1997). Children's creative imagination in response to radio and television stories. *Journal of Communication, 47*(2), 21–38.

Valkenburg, P. M., & Cantor, J. (1999). Children's likes and dislikes in entertainment.

In D. Zillmann & P. Vorderer (Eds.), *Entertainment: The psychology of its appeal*. Hillsdale, NJ: Lawrence Erlbaum.

Valkenburg, P. M., & Janssen, S. J. (1999). What do children value in entertainment programs? A cross-cultural investigation. *Journal of Communication, 49*, 3–21.

Valkenburg, P. M., & Peter, J. (2006). Fantasy and imagination. In J. Bryant & P. Vorderer (Eds.), *The psychology of entertainment* (pp. 105–117). Mahwah, NJ: Lawrence Erlbaum.

Valkenburg, P. M., & van der Voort, T. (1994). Influence of TV on daydreaming and creative imagination: A review of research. *Psychological Bulletin, 116*, 316–339.

van der Voort, T. H. A., & Valkenburg, P. M. (1994). Television's impact on fantasy play: A review of research. *Developmental Review*, 27–51.

Vibbert, M. M., & Meringoff, L. K. (1981). *Children's production and application of story imagery: A cross-medium investigation* (Technical Report No. 23). Cambridge, MA: Project Zero, Harvard University. (ERIC Document Reproduction Service No. ED 210 682)

Wade, S. E. (1971). Adolescents, creative imagination, and media: An exploratory study. *American Behavioral Scientist, 14*, 341–351.

Zillmann, D. (1982). Television viewing and arousal. In D. Pearl, L. Bouthilet, & J. Lazar (Eds.), *Television and behavior: Ten years of scientific progress and implications for the eighties*. Vol. 2 Technical reviews (pp. 53–67). (DHHS Publication No. ADM 82-1196). Washington, DC: U.S. Government Printing Office.

Zillmann, D. (1991). Television viewing and psychological arousal. In J. Bryant & D. Zillmann (Eds.), *Responding to the screen: Reception and reaction processes* (pp. 103–133). Hillsdale, NJ: Lawrence Erlbaum.

Zuckerman, D. M., Singer, D. G., & Singer, J. L. (1980). Television viewing, children's reading, and related classroom behavior. *Journal of Communication, 30*(1), 166–174.

CHAPTER 9

Creating Vigilance for Better Learning From Television

JENNINGS BRYANT
University of Alabama

WES FONDREN
Coastal Carolina University

J. ALISON BRYANT
PlayScience, LLC

This chapter examines the relationships between attention, especially vigilance, and children's learning from television programming. The first two sections discuss concepts. The third section presents theories of attentional processes that address learning from television. Section four elaborates on factors that affect learning from television. Throughout the chapter, we reflect on possibilities for producers to enhance the attention-getting power of educational programs.

Vigilance and Learning

Cognitive psychologists seem to agree that learning is the process by which relatively permanent changes occur in behavioral potential (or probability) as a result of experience. In this chapter, we examine learning that occurs from watching television. Bandura's social learning (1977) and social cognitive (1994) theories, which address vicarious learning, posit that four processes—attention, retention, motor reproduction, and motivation—mediate learning. Our discussion will focus on the role of attention in learning from television.

Whereas learning typically refers to the process of adapting behavior, memory is considered the product of the change—the relatively permanent record of the experience that underlies learning (Anderson, 1995; Mowrer & Klein, 1989). In this chapter, retention will be the typical measure of learning. When we speak of attention as a factor in learning, we usually refer to vigilance: that is, sustained attention, defined as a steady state of alertness and wakefulness (Weinberg & Harper, 1993). This includes the ability of observers to maintain the focus of their attention and to remain alert to stimuli for prolonged periods of time (Davies & Parasuraman, 1982; Parasuraman, Warm, & Dember, 1987; Warm, 1984, 1993; Warm, Dember, & Hancock, 1996; Weinberg & Emslie, 1991).

Vigilance and Attention

The way an organism responds to various stimuli depends on which areas of the brain are activated by the respective stimuli and to what level. One role of attention is to modulate this process of selective activation. Neuroscientists distinguish three major attention functions: orienting or stimulus foveation, focusing or signal/target detection, and vigilance or maintenance of a state of alertness (Posner & Petersen, 1990). Vigilance in the most restricted sense is maintenance of a state of alertness associated with expectation of a target (Deese, 1955). In television, program designers, through strategic sequential presentation of stimuli, can create such expectations. Viewers experience vigilance as alertness to the stimuli they expect. The role of vigilance in a strict sense is to allow fast selection of a response based on a lower quality of information, which results in a higher rate of response errors. Vigilance thus defined does not affect the build-up of information in the sensory or memory systems, but it does affect the rate of response (Posner & Petersen, 1990).

Vigilance and Information Processing

Researchers have looked at the effects of television on information processing from two broad perspectives: arousal systems and cognitive processes. We will discuss theories proposed from each perspective.

Arousal Systems

Traditionally, arousal is discussed in connection with vigilance as a way to account for attentional decrement resulting from excessively low levels of stimulation. Causes of understimulation may be stimulus simplicity or repetition, and the effect is a decrease in responsiveness to external stimulation, leading to a decline in the efficiency of signal detection (Warm et al., 1996). Mackworth (1970a, 1970b) proposed a habituation theory to account for a decrement in short-term vigilance.

Routtenberg (1968, 1971) distinguished two arousal systems with distinct anatomical structures and functions. The cortical system, or reticular activating system, was found to produce cortical arousal and to serve attention, perception, and response preparation. The limbic system was found to be responsible for basic vegetative processes, including affective and emotional reactions (independent of hedonic valence). From the perspective of educational television, the problem is how to choose stimuli to trigger the appropriate kind of arousal and attentional processes to optimize the learning of different kinds of information. The choice is not simple because, although the two types of arousal are distinct, they are closely related in a functional way. Both the orienting response and the defensive response produce cortical arousal, which serves attention, but they also tend to produce limbic/autonomic arousal, which serves to maintain the cortical arousal.

Research on diminished cortical and limbic arousal as an effect of exposure to television focused on the "zombie viewer" type (Lesser, 1972, 1974, 1977). This label was used to describe children's alleged passive-mindless-hypnotic-addictive viewing of television. In an attempt to provide a definitive answer to the question of whether television has a hypnotizing effect on viewers or makes them more passive, Miller (1985) conducted six experiments on a total of 56 research participants, mostly college students. He concluded that, "with respect to our brainwave patterns, television viewing appears to be nothing special" (p. 514). According to Miller's data, television viewing is predominantly a beta brainwave pattern that indicates a more active than inactive viewer; beta activity tends to increase rather than decrease over half-hour and hour viewing times (and, conversely, alpha tends to decrease), indicating that television tends to activate viewers rather than make them passive. Furthermore, television viewing is not primarily a right-brain activity (involving pattern rather than sequential processing of visual rather than verbal information), and neither hemisphere tends to dominate during television viewing. In conclusion, the zombie viewer line of research initiated in the 1970s was theoretically closed by Miller's findings in the mid-1980s. Nevertheless, residual smoke from the hot flames persists in the form of speculation that television "may be subtly yet profoundly changing the structure of consciousness" (Miller, 1985, p. 508) or be linked to attention deficit-type behavior (Levine & Waite, 2000).

Another theoretical issue of pragmatic relevance for educational television is the optimal level of arousal. Researchers tend to agree that, because arousal underlies and energizes attention, its relationship with learning has the same inverted-U pattern as the relationship between attention and learning or attention and performance (Yerkes & Dodson, 1908). Very low and very high levels of arousal are accordingly expected to result in poor learning, and moderate levels are believed to enhance attention and learning. Low levels of arousal likely produce automation, which reduces the cognitive workload and produces "understimulation" (Warm et al., 1996, p. 185). High arousal narrows attention, reduces fine discriminations (Kahneman, 1973), reduces cue utilization (Easterbrook, 1959), and, in case of divided attention, increases the attentional bias in favor of the primary task (Eysenck, 1982).

Two major lessons can be derived from these considerations for educational television strategies. The general lesson is that excessive reliance on arousing stimuli to enhance attention may sometimes result in comparatively high levels of arousal in the short run and/or unexpectedly low arousal in the long run. Both phenomena diminish attention and jeopardize learning. An additional lesson concerns the tendency to make children's programs too simple, with a lowest-denominator audience standard in mind. The implication of this observation for educational television is that an effort to make information too easy to process may have the undesirable effects of under-stimulation, low arousal, and, consequently, poor vigilance and retention. That is why the appropriate, moderate level of difficulty should

be a crucial concern for producers of educational programs for children.

Cognitive Strategies

The cognitive processes associated with sustained attention are also important. Huston and Wright (1983) proposed a sampling model of attention, according to which viewers make sequential decisions to continue or discontinue (or resume) watching based on programming cues and learned associations with cognitive and affective expectations of television content. A sequence of decisions involves progress in terms of depth and detail of cue analysis, and a continued and increasingly elaborate processing is conducive to deeper involvement with the content. The model predicts that incomprehensible content will cease to be attended.

Attentional Inertia

Paradoxically, this strategic sampling approach is facilitated by an opposite non-strategic phenomenon called *attentional inertia* (Anderson, Alwitt, Lorch, & Levin, 1979; Anderson, Choi, & Lorch, 1987; Anderson & Lorch, 1983), which is a lag in reacting to changes in television content: The more attention viewers have been paying to the program, the more likely they are to continue to do so. Automatic short-term vigilance persistence helps the viewer extend processing to apparently incomprehensible elements of television content, trying to make sense of them, and thus promotes learning. Distractibility lowers significantly (i.e., inertia becomes manifest) after a child has maintained attention to television for 15 seconds or longer (Anderson et al., 1987).

Thorson, Reeves, and Schleuder (1985) proposed a more elaborate model of attention decisions that includes two types of judgments: one based on the continuous assessment of immediately incoming stimuli—in Omanson's (1982) terms, *on-line processing*—and another based on judgments about "chunks" (i.e., meaningful clusters of information items)—in Omanson's terms, *off-line processing*. According to Hawkins, Kim, and Pingree (1991), the first type would involve mostly heuristic decisions based on formal features, whereas the second type would involve schematic decisions that take more time and more television content. If we consider attentional inertia within the framework of Thorson et al.'s (1985) model, we may expect the automatic short-term processing lag to expand with age and knowledge by incorporating discrete incomprehensible content elements into meaningful chunks and by deriving expectations about subsequent content based on chunks rather than isolated elements. Research results seem to support this hypothesis, showing that older children are capable of more sustained attention and tend to extend effort longer to understand incomprehensible content (Hawkins et al., 1991). Even the expectations associated with the program genre appear to modify attentional inertia (Hawkins et al., 2002). The discussion of the importance of schema knowledge for children's attention will be resumed in the next section in connection with programming features that elicit attention.

Does Comprehension Drive Attention?

Thorson et al.'s (1985) two-tiered model of attention and Omanson's (1982) distinction between on-line (data-driven) and off-line (schema-driven) processing are conciliating products of a dispute that pushes for a trend reversal in television processing theory. The initiator of the dispute was Daniel R. Anderson, who, in the early 1980s, proposed a cognitive involvement model, arguing that attention to television is attracted and maintained by "cognitive involvement and active comprehension of content" rather than by "salient noncontent features" (Anderson, Lorch, Field, Collins, & Nathan, 1986, p. 1025). Anderson emphasized the progressive nature of cognitive processing and the contingency of the attention/involvement level on understanding.

Supporters of data-driven processing challenged Anderson's "understanding and looking hypothesis" (Verbeke, 1988, p. 67), arguing that there is no understanding without looking. They claimed that visual attention is a prerequisite for understanding and perceived Anderson's model as a claim that understanding is an antecedent of attention.

This chicken-and-egg dispute needs to be put into context. If we think of the role of arousal as an energizer of cognitive processes (Zillmann, 1982) and admit the need for adjusting the level of arousal to meet current cognitive needs, then Anderson's level of "understanding" provides this feedback. On the other hand, as proposed by Chaiken (1980), heuristic, schema-based processing tends to be preferred to systematic processing because it saves mental effort. The use of schemata facilitates understanding, which decreases the need for arousal as energizer of the understanding (sense-making) process and thus reduces attention to material that is easy to understand. This framework is not incompatible with Verbeke's (1988) thesis that viewers, while paying attention to television, work their way through the material, trying to make sense of it by "locating a sequence of causally or purposefully connected events or states" (p. 73); this locating process involves the use of both TV content knowledge and world knowledge. What Anderson's theory did was to transcend the bit-by-bit processing view that posited attention as a condition for understanding in order to account for sustained attention. His higher-level, process-in-progress approach simply added the feedback loop from understanding to attention. Efforts to disprove Anderson's cognitive involvement model failed, and a "concession" was made that "how much a child is watching is . . . a reflection of an attention managing style" (Verbeke, 1988, p. 89). But this, again, is not incompatible with the situated version of Anderson's (1983) model, in which schema-based understanding of TV content is only one component of motivation to watch (i.e., the feedback for sustained attention), in competition with alternative attractions.

Viewing Styles

So far, we have examined roles of attention captured by models proposed to explain television processing. We will now refer to viewing styles as patterns of behavior involving choices that in some way or another affect attention to and learning from television. The viewing style topic bloomed in television literature in the early 1980s when Bryant, Zillmann, and Brown (1983) revisited Lesser's (1972, 1974) classification of children's styles as zombie (passive), dual-attention (sharing attention with other activities, monitoring the television flow for personally relevant content), and modeling (actively relating and responding to TV content). At the same time, Anderson and Lorch (1983) discussed different perceptions that theorists (and the public at large) entertained about television viewing, reflected in two types of theories that concern the processing of television. One type assumed reactive viewers whose attention was automatically captured by salient features of the television material, whose processing and comprehension of the material was limited (under a limited-capacity assumption) by frequent reorienting to new stimuli, and whose learning was imperfect or incomplete—leading to "considerable recognition . . . without efficient retrieval" (Singer, 1980, p. 38). The other type of theories assumed active viewers who distributed their attention between television and other events in their environment and among various elements of the program. Under the active viewing model, children would be able to gauge their mental effort depending on how much they wanted to understand and retain from the program.

An interesting angle on active viewing was introduced by Salomon's (1981, 1983a, 1983b, 1984) theory of differential investment of mental effort. According to Salomon, learners' perceptions about media messages included perceived self-efficacy in handling them. The perceived difficulty of a message could be associated with the medium (print generally being considered harder than television), the format of the message, or the specific information conveyed by the message. The viewers' perceptions of self-efficacy determined the amount of invested mental effort (AIME), which affected learning. Salomon (1984) found that self-efficacy correlated positively with AIME in print and negatively in television. The theory implies an inherent disadvantage of television in eliciting mental effort (which can include attention). The perception of realism, found by Salomon (1984) to contribute to the impression of easiness, is enhanced in television by film footage and live performances. On the other hand, animation, largely used in children's television, involves message simplification. And the easier a TV message is to perceive, the less focused attention it will get.

This is potentially problematic given the current trend in children's educational programming toward the use of animation instead of live action. If that continues, it will become particularly important to understand how different levels of realism in animation style (flat 2-D animation vs. rich 3-D animation) affect the level of mental effort.

It is hoped that the discussion of attention in relation to processing strategies has sensitized designers of educational programs to a couple of issues that have practical relevance. First, relying on attentional inertia to help children process and understand new or difficult items of information is risky—especially with young children, whose attention span is smaller because of lower schematization of knowledge, which results in poorer anticipation. Extensive schematization of content intended to expand the attention span and facilitate understanding triggers more schematic processing and reduces the depth of understanding. On the other hand, the build-up of cognitive involvement cannot be controlled through program qualities because of the situatedness of TV viewing that involves competition for children's attention. The use of form-related stimuli to create and maintain arousal as a component of or condition for attention may focus young children's attention away from what is intended to be central content. Last but not least, given the intermittent nature of focused attention and the fragmentariness of viewing because of children's high distractibility, educational content needs to be sequentially organized in small fragments with a high level of independence, in which new items are nested in a framework repeated in each fragment to ensure comprehension even without watching preceding fragments. The framework repetition requires formal variation to avoid being perceived as a known schema and being disregarded (possibly, together with embedded new items).

Factors Involved in Vigilance

An attempt will be made in this section to cover major factors of attention to and learning from television. We will discuss variables related to viewers, programming features, and situation factors.

Viewer-Related Factors

The amount of attention a child pays to television at any particular moment depends on factors that vary in their stability over time. The viewer's gender, for instance, influences attentional patterns and is a fixed characteristic of the person. At the other extreme, age is inexorably changing. The attentional factors situated between these extremes can be assessed in terms of degree of stability, degree of controllability, and relevance to producers of educational programming.

Gender

Great consistency across a large number of studies indicates that boys' visual attention to television is greater than girls' (Alvarez, Huston, Wright, & Kerkman, 1988; Anderson et al., 1987; Field & Anderson, 1985; Greer, Potts, Wright, & Huston, 1982; Potts, Huston, & Wright, 1986; Rolandelli, Wright, & Huston, 1985; Wright, Calvert, Huston-Stein, & Watkins, 1980; Wright et al., 1984). The finding holds when appealing distractors are provided (Anderson et al., 1987; Wright et al., 1984). But gender differences in visual attention are not typically associated with differences in comprehension, and males' greater visual attention does not typically lead to greater recall of content (Alvarez et al., 1988).

Rather inconsistent findings about the differential impact of programming containing action and violence on children's attention maintained controversies in media effects literature. Feminist critics of television blamed television for its male bias, the arguments being that the majority of main characters are male, and male characters engage in most of the interesting activities (Sternglantz & Serbin, 1974; Williams, Baron, Phillips, Travis, & Jackson, 1986). Moreover, many programs (e.g., cartoons, action-adventure series) have plots, content themes, and behaviors that are masculine sex-typed (Signorielli, Gross, & Morgan, 1982). A popular hypothesis among researchers and theorists is that the formal features of television—such as animation, rapid action, sound effects, and frequent cuts—might appeal to boys more than to girls because those features are associated with masculine sex-typed content (Welch, Huston-Stein, Wright, & Plehal, 1979) and carry masculine connotations

even when used with neutral content (Huston, Greer, Wright, Welch, & Ross, 1984).

Although violence is a frequent ingredient of action programming that increases arousal and attention, some authors claim that action and the formal features associated with it are actually more critical than violent content per se for maintaining young children's attention (Huston-Stein, Fox, Greer, Watkins, & Whitaker, 1981; Potts et al, 1986). The fact that differences in attention to high and low action were found to be greater for live than for animated shows (Potts et al., 1986) suggests as a general explanation the orienting reactions elicited by action programming, which may be stronger with males under a hypothesis of gender specialization for environmental surveillance and danger detection (because of either the genetic development of the species or different gender socialization). Such a hypothesis has some support in findings that girls' attention is higher under low-action than under high-action conditions (Alvarez et al., 1988). But this finding might also be explained through Anderson's (Anderson & Lorch, 1983; Anderson, Lorch, Field, & Sanders, 1981) involvement model of attention because slower action allows for deeper processing and thus facilitates involvement and sustained attention. Further research is needed to clarify (a) whether boys are more susceptible than girls to formal high-action cues and therefore more likely to be distracted from central processing, and (b) whether boys' and girls' attention is differently affected by programming rich in orienting cues (eliciting stronger cortical arousal) and by emotional programming (eliciting stronger limbic arousal).

Another gender-related peculiarity is the fact that boys' attention to the audio and video tracks of television is less dissociated than is girls' attention (Rolandelli, Wright, & Huston, 1982). Girls appear to use single modality cues more readily than boys (Rolandelli et al., 1982), but they tend to orient more to the audio track (Halpern, 1986) and have better memory for auditory information than boys (Rolandelli, 1985). Girls tend to listen without looking more often, but they still retain the same amount of information from the program. An explanation that may account for these observations is that, during preschool and early school years, girls' verbal development is, on the average, slightly more advanced than boys' (Halpern, 1986).

These findings relative to gender as a factor of attention to and learning from television indicate that boys and girls might profit differentially from information presented in the two modalities (Alvarez et al., 1988). To the extent that producers of educational programs produce programs designed more for one gender than the other, this information may be useful for choosing the predominant modality for conveying the most important information.

Intelligence

A legitimate question raised by Swanson and Cooney (1989) is whether individual differences in sustained attention relate to primary mental abilities. Research findings are inconsistent: Some studies found evidence that intelligence does affect vigilance, whereas others found no significant correlations.

The limited-resource model posits relatively stable interpersonal differences in attentional resources across task situations, directly correlated with IQ levels. The arousal model of attention assumes that increased time on tasks leads to a decrement in arousal levels as a function of IQ. Empirical findings show low positive correlations between attentional capacity and IQ. Carter and Swanson (1995) claimed that the findings do not provide enough support either for a direct relationship between intelligence and attention or for a relationship mediated by arousal. Swanson (1989) proposed an alternative model in which the correlation between IQ and vigilance is mediated by central processing capacity, which involves the use of attention strategies.

Temperament and Personality

An individual's temperament includes behavioral features that are relatively stable over time. Such features discussed in the literature as relevant to attentional processes are attention span, persistence, and inhibitory control.

The attention span refers to how long an activity is being pursued. Persistence refers to the continuation of an activity in the face of obstacles (Silverman & Gaines, 1996; Thomas, Chess, & Birch, 1968) and the ability to work on dull, tiring, or boring tasks (Buss & Plomin, 1975). Inhibitory control is the capacity to delay responding to an attractive stimulus. Performance on all three measures improves with age (Ruff, 1990; Vaughn, Kopp, & Krakow, 1984), but the three features appear to be relatively independent (e.g., Silverman & Gaines, 1996).

Interpersonal differences in inhibitory control emerge as early as 24 months of age and develop throughout childhood and adolescence (Golden, Montare, & Bridger, 1977; Ippolito, 1993; Levy, 1980; Luria, 1959; Silverman & Ippolito, 1995; Silverman & Ragusa, 1990). Persistence is a costs-rewards trade-off and develops as a component of strategic attention through exercise that may be emphasized by educators both at home and at school. Given the limited opportunity for children to interact with television on specific tasks, the role of the medium in educating or promoting persistence and inhibitory control is small.

As far as the attention span is concerned, fears were repeatedly expressed that the fragmentariness and fast pace of children's programming are undermining the development of their attention span, triggering item-by-item processing with emphasis on formal features rather than processing of meaningful chunks. What critics would like to see is programming with more structure and continuity that presents information at a slower pace, leaving children time for more elaborate cognitive processing. Such programming would facilitate the exercise of sequential-task vigilance that focuses more on content cues. This correction is suggested as a means of counterbalancing the almost exclusive exercise of alertness to simultaneous stimuli imposed by programming loaded with formal attention getters, which may increase arousal and elicit orienting response but take processing resources away from central content.

Depending on their typical alertness, people can be classified as more or less vigilant (Type A vs. Type B). Type A personalities involve hypervigilance (Price, 1982), superior inhibitory control, and persistence. Type A persons focus on tasks (Jennings, 1983) and tend to ignore external peripheral stimuli and to suppress internal cues that might interfere with their performance (Carver, Coleman, & Glass, 1976; Strube, Turner, Patrick, &

Perrillo, 1983; Weidner & Matthews, 1978). Although most studies addressed Type A personality as an antecedent of coronary heart disease and were conducted on middle-aged males, research by Matthews (1978, 1980) showed that children as young as kindergarten age can be successfully classified as Type A or Type B. According to Price (1982), Type A behavior is to a large extent "learned very early in life" (p. 48) from models provided by family, school, and mass media. Educators push children to "hurry up," "try harder," "be number one," and to be competitive. On the other hand, the media emphasize suspense (anticipatory reactions) as well as success through fast, opportunistic, and aggressive action.

Using Bandura's (1971) theory that consistent models enhance social learning, we can assume that each generation will exhibit stronger Type A behavior than the preceding one. As observed by Price (1982), extreme Type A behavior may hinder rather than facilitate children's success because "hypervigilance can lead to a chronic inability to concentrate, due in large part to racing thoughts and intrusive worries" (p. 123). In addition, Type A responses to situations are faster at the cost of being more schematic—that is, nonspecific and therefore less adequate. Another problem seems to be gender stereotyping, particularly through exemplification in the media, with males being pushed harder than females toward Type A behavior. Added to boys' higher rate of Type A behavior resulting from their higher level of androgens (male hormones), stereotyped modeling enhances boys' arousability and risks of schematic and aggressive reactions to stimuli. Television producers should be aware that the overuse of suspense to heighten arousal and maintain attention tends to create chronic hypervigilance in the audience that jeopardizes learning from television.

A personality distinction that involves vigilance ability is between extroverts and introverts, who differ in their excitation-inhibition balance. Introverts were hypothesized to have a higher level of basal/tonic/habitual cortical arousal (Eysenck, 1983; Parasuraman, 1985) or higher arousability (Eysenck, 1982, 1988, 1989). Higher arousal helps introverts to better sustain their attention, which makes them more efficient learners. In a study by Checcino (1997) on seventh graders, introversion did not appear to affect grade point averages (GPAs) directly, but it correlated negatively with self-concept. These two variables, together with gender, accounted for 15% of the GPA variance. Girls were found to have lower self-concept and higher GPAs. Since gender and extroversion or introversion appear to affect learning in general, research is warranted on the impact of these factors on children's learning from television.

Age

The Piagetian operational theory of intelligence (Piaget, 1947/1973) outlined four stages of cognitive development. Sensorimotor intelligence (ages 0 to approximately 2 years) was described as nonreflective intelligence in action. During the preoperational stage (2 to 6 or 7 years), children develop representational skills and intuitive regulation closely modeled on perceptual data. Concrete logical operations develop during the early school years (ages 6 or 7 through 11 or 12), and formal operations with abstractions begin at the age of 11 or 12. In Piagetian terms, cognitive activity consists of assimilation of new information to existing knowledge and accommodation (restructuring/change) of existing knowledge to coherently include new information.

Gibson and Rader's (1979) theory of attention development similarly posited a progress with age from focusing on perceptual features for the purpose of object differentiation to focusing on conceptual features for the purpose of identifying utility, which derives from functionality, which in turn involves causal relationships.

If we consider television viewing within this theoretical framework, preschool children can be expected to pay the most attention to salient formal features of programming and to process sensory material primarily in terms of differentiations, with more assimilation (additions to previous knowledge) than accommodation (changes in stored knowledge). The video track is likely to elicit attention through such elements as colors, shapes, contrasts, and change, and the audio track through music, noises, or different voices. Even in the late preschool years, children attend to and comprehend visual information more than verbal information (e.g., Bellack, 1984; Ward & Wackman, 1973).

Vigilance improves with age. The ability to develop an expectation for an event and to attend to the place of occurrence in its absence was observed in 5-month-old infants (Ruff, Capozzoli, Dubiner, & Parrinello, 1990), and a dramatic rise in visual attention to television was found between ages 12 and 23 months (Carew, 1980). Ruff, Capozzoli, and Weissberg (1998) argued that attention during television viewing changes most in the period from 30 to 42 months. According to Anderson et al. (1986), visual attention increases sharply in the years from 1 to 5 and then slowly throughout later childhood. After age 3, they say, individual differences become more prominent than age differences.

If we were to single out the most important benefit of growing up in terms of attention, it would be the development of attentional strategies, which is driven by two factors. On the one hand, television is a dual-modality medium that requires parallel processing. The efficiency of learning from television depends on the development of skills and strategies for distributing attentional resources between the two channels that convey information simultaneously. For example, even though children younger than 2 years old may be attending to the visual track, they often lack the foundational knowledge (e.g., vocabulary, phonetics, etc.) to comprehend the audio track (Krcmar, 2010). Supporting this hypothesis is research showing that 12- to 24-month-old children who watch vocabulary training videos show no measurable benefit in regard to word learning (Krcmar, Grela, & Lin, 2007; Richert, Robb, Fender, & Wartella, 2009). Preschool children older than 2, however, do show marked improvement in vocabulary and number recognition from watching educational videos (Rice, Huston, Truglio, & Wright, 1990). These results indicate that both attention and adequate knowledge to comprehend audio tracks are necessary for learning to occur—not simply exposure (See Chapters 7 and 10 in this volume for a further discussion of learning from television).

Monitoring skills and strategies develop with age (Baer, 1997) and are made possible by neurological changes (Thatcher, 1994) that make the right-hemisphere vigilance system more available (Posner & Petersen, 1990; Ruff & Rothbart, 1996). According to Pingree (1986), children as young as 3 monitor the television audio track even when they are looking elsewhere and can shift their attention back to the screen when an auditory cue suggests that something significant is occurring. Researchers (Baer, 1997; Baer & Lorch, 1990) found that children ages 7 to 10 tended to look at television when it was most necessary to do so to build a coherent story representation, and they recalled auditory information most when it was story relevant. Field and Anderson (1985) found that the correlation between learning from the auditory channel and learning from the visual channel diminished with age (between 5 and 9 years), which indicated increasingly independent processing in the two channels.

Moreover, there appears to be an interaction effect between maturation and exposure with children. In an examination of preschool children who had not viewed the educational television show *Blue's Clues,* compared with experienced viewers of a similar age, researchers found that although experienced viewers looked less frequently at the screen, they were more likely to respond to onscreen cues (Crawley et al., 2002). The findings indicated that children had learned from previous viewing how to manage attention to the program.

Schema Development

Under Chaiken's (1980) heuristic-systematic processing model, by default, individuals use heuristics to minimize cognitive effort. In the case of television viewing, especially under heavy cognitive load (due to program complexity at the formal or semantic levels), the use of schemata facilitates the selection and processing of information. When children are engaged in parallel activities, one of which is television watching, schemata are crucial filters for monitoring (minimally processing) the information related to secondary activities. Such monitoring makes possible a flexible allocation of attention among activities depending on comparative levels of salience at each particular moment.

The most useful schemata for processing television content are generally believed to be the story schemata, defined as "memory structures which consist of clusters of knowledge about stories and how they are typically structured and the ability to use this knowledge in processing stories" (Meadowcroft, 1985, p. 7). Children with a good grasp of story schemata exhibit reduced processing effort, increased memory of central story content, increased efficiency in the deployment of cognitive resources, and greater flexibility of capacity allocation to program content (Meadowcroft, 1985).

Variance in knowledge of story grammar was found mostly among very young children, from about 2 to 5 years of age (e.g., Applebee, 1977). Story schemata appear to be well mastered after age 7 (at the Piagetian [1947/1973] stage of concrete operations). Preschoolers at the preoperational stage of development (ages 2 to 6–7 years) are able to use story schemata only when the content is simply structured and causal linkages are clearly stated (Mandler & Johnson, 1977). This means that the use of schemata stored in long-term memory depends on the schematization level of the material to be processed. This interaction will be discussed in connection with programming features relevant to vigilance.

Another type of schemata useful for processing television content is those related to television practices, formats, and techniques. As persistently suggested and demonstrated by Dorothy and Jerome Singer (e.g., Singer, Singer, & Zuckerman, 1981; Singer, Zuckerman, & Singer, 1980), educating children about television-related schemata benefits comprehension of programming. In addition, once children habituate to television techniques, their attention to visual and sound effects may diminish, leaving more processing capacity available for content.

Both story schemata and television-related schemata function as frameworks for encoding, storage, and retrieval processes. Their relevance to our discussion of vigilance comes from the fact that they influence both what television material is attended to and the amount of effort allocated for that material. An immature selection style is characterized by the allocation of attention to stimuli with highly salient features, such as movement, and it shows little evidence of habituation (e.g., Fishbein, 1976; Gibson & Rader, 1979). Mature attention styles are more flexible and are guided by the individual's knowledge and goals. Development is assumed to be in the direction of increased control, flexibility, and efficiency of attention deployment (i.e., less attentional effort for comprehending and learning). Skills associated with the execution of mature selection styles develop throughout childhood, with dramatic progress between 6 and 8 years of age (e.g., Brown & French, 1976; Collins, Wellman, Keniston, & Westby, 1978; Dent & Thorndyke, 1979).

As far as children's strategic behavior is concerned, educators may help by promoting metacognition: that is, "awareness of what skills, strategies, and resources are needed to perform a task effectively and the ability to use self-regulatory mechanisms to ensure successful completion of the task" (Schindler, 1986, p. 132). According to Flavell (1979; Flavell & Wellman, 1977), three categories of metacognitive knowledge may help children become better learners: knowledge about their own enduring characteristics, especially their potential to engage in certain tasks; knowledge about the purposes, scopes, and requirements of the task; and knowledge of strategies relevant to the task. If we consider vigilance during television watching from a metacognitive perspective, a child's attentional self-regulation would involve awareness of his or her ability to sustain attention to television, assessment of how much attention is needed to understand a program (and eventually to learn from it), and the use of skills and strategies for maintaining attention.

A metacognitive-training question is how to enhance these three categories of knowledge in early childhood. Within the Piagetian (1947/1973) framework, operations with abstractions such as "attention" are unlikely before school age. Instructions such as "Pay attention" must be made more specific (e.g., "Look there") in order to get young children to act on them. Most frequently in early childhood, attention to television is simply elicited and automatically sustained by the flow of stimuli in conjunction with children's comprehension of content and format. Young viewers pay attention to television until they get distracted by other stimuli. Deliberate, conscious self-monitoring of attention is unlikely because self-perception in parallel with stimulus perception would be too complex for young children's cognitive capacity. On the other hand, children's television typically is a recreational medium. Its content is neither hard nor compelling enough to require self-monitoring and strategic resource deployment. Consequently, attention allocation is spontaneously made.

The main trigger of preschoolers' attention to television is stimulus salience (due to formal features and personal relevance). Stimuli guide and sustain attention. But two more factors are also involved: broad assessments of medium difficulty and program difficulty. According to Salomon (1983b, 1984), cumulative watching of television results in an overall perception of how hard or easy television is when compared with other media, as well as particular perceptions about how difficult the programs they watch are. These perceptions gauge the allocation of attentional and processing resources. Hard versus easy assessments are also a component of program preferences. A *hard* label is bad to the extent that it reduces chances that a child will attend to a program. But if expected gains exceed expected processing costs and the child chooses to attend, the same label becomes good because it causes more cognitive resources to be allocated during watching, which results in better understanding and learning.

Once perception of difficulty was acknowledged as a significant factor of attention to television, educators were called on to enhance children's metacognition by teaching them story schemata and television conventions and techniques. That required more participation and effort from parents and teachers. The task involved directing children's attention to story patterns and television practices and tricks and providing explanations. The goal was to initially increase vigilance to schemata, gradually habituate children to conventions, and ultimately enable them to use those schemata for more efficient processing of the television fare. This kind of metacognitive support is easy for educators, who can provide online commentary and eventually recapitulate or rehearse the new information at the end of the viewing session and link new information items from session to session.

What has not been addressed so far as an educational objective is children's metacognition in terms of awareness of personal ability to follow and understand television programming. The reason may be that facilitating this kind of metacognition is more difficult. It would involve more structuring of children's experience with television by manipulating the level of program difficulty as well as the type and level of distraction. The participative role of educators from this perspective would be to coach children to assess what they have understood and what they have missed and why. Repeated exposure with increased attention (mandated/directed vigilance or decreased distraction) would help children become aware of the benefits of sustained attention and the attentional strategies that are available. This kind of metacognitive support requires much more effort from educators, who are supposed to choose videos or record television programs and organize viewing sessions around teaching objectives (e.g., understanding how much external distractors obstruct comprehension and memory or how much focusing attention and repeating the exposure help comprehension).

In light of these metacognitive considerations, future research may address questions such as the following: Do children start to benefit from the two types of metacognitive support (i.e., enrichment of story and television schemata and assessment of their own processing ability) at different ages? Do the two types of support affect children's attention to and learning from educational programs differently?

Programming-Related Factors

Many concerns have been expressed about the limitations imposed by television as a medium on the processing of its content. For example, McLuhan (1964, 1978) claimed that the low resolution of the TV picture required a constant reflexive perceptual closure response on the part of the viewer, which accounted for the paradoxical passive involvement of TV viewers. Salomon (1983a, 1983b, 1984) proposed that television is perceived as easier to process than other media and consequently is processed more superficially, with the effect of poorer learning.

As technology advances toward higher fidelity of image and sound, thus reducing the sensory gap between real life and television content, concerns shift away from the peculiarities of television as a carrier technology and focus on the real(istic)-unreal(istic) distinction at the level of programming. This has become a critical issue because the blurring line between reality and fantasy on television may cause children to develop a distorted image of reality. On the other hand, the interest in medium effects migrated from television (one-way) communication to computer-mediated communication, which is interactive (e.g., e-mail, video conferencing). So current television-effects research is mostly devoted to programming effects, and research on the effects of programming features is proliferating.

From a vigilance perspective, both formal features and content features of television programming can be discussed as facilitators or inhibitors of attention. Traditionally, emphasis on form and exploitation of attention-getting production techniques was criticized for diverting children's attention away from content and jeopardizing the educational potential of television.

Formal Features of Programming

The potential of formal features to affect vigilance is related to humans' orienting response to changes and unusualness in the environment. According to Berlyne (1960), such properties as intensity, contrast, change, movement, novelty, and incongruity make stimuli perceptually salient—that is, alerting.

An essential element of change is pace, or scene change, which automatically triggers the orienting response. Research confirms that pace tends to enhance attention, but only for younger children, who are more perceptually oriented and therefore more attentive to salient formal features than to reflective features of content (Campbell, Wright, & Huston, 1987; Greer et al., 1982; Huston & Wright, 1983; Huston et al., 1981; Huston-Stein & Wright, 1979; Wright & Huston, 1981). Moreover, pace improves younger children's vigilance only to less schematically organized magazine programs (Wright et al., 1984). Some studies failed to find a consistent influence of pace on attention (e.g., Anderson & Levin, 1976), probably because scene change is often associated with other salient formal features such as fades, dissolves, zooms, or pans, or by auditory features such as music, sound effects, or speech (Wright et al., 1984), all of which have confounding effects.

When high pace is coupled with high density of salient formal features, young children's attentional capacity is overburdened and semantic processing of content is reduced, particularly under conditions of poor schematization of content. J. L. Singer (1980) suggested that sensory bombardment may leave young viewers with no time to think about what they are being presented and thus undermines rehearsal and storage of information. Research conducted by Singer and Singer (1998) on children's learning from *Barney & Friends* accounted for the educational effectiveness of the program in terms of clear explanation of procedures and attitudes being taught "at a pace children can grasp" (pp. 363–364). The researchers suggested that "we need a new type of aesthetic in video cinematography . . . geared to the cognitive level of the viewing audience" (p. 364).

As children get older, they attend increasingly to reflective features (Calvert, Huston, Watkins, & Wright, 1982; Wartella & Ettema, 1974). Also, habituation to formal manipulations in television makes children orient less to visual and auditory effects, and knowledge schematization helps them to use their processing capacity more efficiently and strategically. Consequently, older children's attention to and learning from television are less likely to be impaired by manipulation of formal-feature salience.

The notion that fast-paced programming is detrimental to vigilance was challenged by Zillmann (1982; Zillmann, Williams, Bryant, Boynton, & Wolf, 1980), who argued that the "rapid fire" presentation in educational television tends to produce cortical arousal and therefore should be expected to create alertness at least for short periods of time, especially in children with little motivation to pay close attention and learn from exposition.

The two positions may be reconciled by considering the likelihood of beneficial effects (through arousal) of moderately fast-paced programming and the pernicious effects (due to limited processing capacity) of exceedingly fast-paced programming. Consequently, producers may consider testing programs in order to reach the optimal pace. For entertainment, arousal benefits of rapid-fire presentation may prevail, but for educational purposes, information load should be the primary concern.

Content Features of Programming

The effects of content-related factors on attention to and learning from television are much more complicated and are often compounded by formal-feature variability, either spontaneous or manipulated. From a content perspective, vigilance can be regarded as alertness, primarily to stimuli that carry threat information and secondarily to those carrying opportunity information. Cues of enjoyment may be considered opportunity indicators. A third possibility is vigilance driven by the individual's long-term, transitory, or momentary interests. Stimuli belonging to the three categories may simultaneously come from television and children's viewing environments. They compete for children's attention with other stimuli that have no meaning but still elicit orienting responses as mere change phenomena. In addition, alternatively or simultaneously, children's attention may be inwardly directed to physiological information or their own thoughts. Cases of exclusive attention to television content are rare.

We limit our discussion in this section to three major issues. One is the role of emotionally negative and positive information in the orienting response. Another issue is arousal as a factor of vigilance to content cues and of learning. The third aspect is content difficulty as a factor of attention and learning.

Emotionally Negative and Positive Content

Attention to television content is most likely to be automatically engaged by threatening content. Children's programming that contains threatening material belongs to the dangerous-action and fear-appeal categories. Occasionally, news, history, and science programs also include threatening stimuli and cause automatic deployment of attention.

According to the Pollyanna principle (Matlin & Stang, 1978), people tend to view desirable events as common, frequent, and typical and undesirable events as uncommon, infrequent, and atypical. Consequently, the information value of undesirable traits is higher (Pratto & John, 1991). Shoemaker (1996) interpreted this statistical bias as an outcome of natural selection for survival. She argued that humans are hardwired for bad news, that they scan the environment for danger more than for opportunities, and that they allocate cognitive resources preferentially to negative information. The outcome of this asymmetry in information processing is a higher accessibility of negative information stored in long-term memory, regardless of stimulus base rate (Pratto & John, 1991). This phenomenon indicates a close association between attention, judgment, and memory during automatic, non-goal-directed information-processing purposes. From this theoretical perspective, the claims that television watching tends to be a mindless activity (e.g., Mander, 1978; Winn, 1977) appear to be misguided.

The potential of children's programming to attract automatic attention increases with the amount of negative information related to threats and dangers. The strength of negative stimuli as vigilance triggers depends directly on the intensity of their perceptual features and inversely on their base rate. The problems with the intensity of negative stimuli frequently presented on television are viewer habituation and desensitization, which reduce children's capacity to react to real-life dangers. Producers of educational programming may exploit the natural advantage of threat- or fear-based messages in eliciting vigilance and use them to stimulate deployment of cognitive resources to subsequently presented methods for dealing with critical or dangerous situations, thus facilitating learning. But producers must keep in mind that the more threat and danger are shown on television in general, the less effective each instance will be in eliciting arousal and attention. This is one more example of the classical tragedy of the commons, in which individual users of a common good (in this case, the arousing potential of fear stimuli) make excessive use of that good and deplete the resource.

In the psychology literature devoted to coping behavior, vigilance is often used to designate an "intensified intake and processing of threatening information" (Khrone, Hock, & Kohlmann, 1992, p. 73). In this sense, it is opposed to cognitive avoidance, which means turning away from threat-related cues. According to Khrone's (1978) model of attention allocation in threatening situations, the first phase involves attention for the purpose of identifying threat-related cues, and in the second phase, attention is directed toward or away from such stimuli. The direction is dictated, respectively, by either intolerance of uncertainty and the need to learn more about the danger or intolerance of emotional (somatic) arousal and the need to block processing of threatening information. These theoretical possibilities indicate that vigilance to programming, including negative stimuli, depends on the producers' ability to enhance uncertainty and the need for information without exceeding a bearable level of arousal. Their target needs to be curiosity rather than extreme emotionality.

The role of emotionally positive stimuli as attention getters is also important. According to the feature/signal hypothesis (Huston & Wright, 1983), children learn the regular and consistent associations between formal features and content quite early. That knowledge makes their choices more dependent on formal features than educators would like. We must admit that learning is work and that what children are after is enjoyment, not effort. Stimulating curiosity, the spontaneous need to know, is probably the best way to promote learning from television. But cues of newness and direct relevance to children may not suffice to elicit attention when competing with enjoyment cues. Therefore, producers of educational programs understandably favor enjoyment cues over curiosity enticers. But an exaggeration in this direction, especially in the absence of curiosity-eliciting stimuli, conveys the wrong message that the program is pure entertainment, and according to Salomon's (1981, 1983a, 1983b, 1984) theory of mental effort, children will pay superficial attention to it and will learn less than from nonentertaining material.

Research until the 1980s examined a large diversity of program features that convey the promise of enjoyment. Experiments were not concerned with the systematicity of the stimuli being tested as much as with their common function and strength as attention getters and cues for children. This explains why formal and content features were often thrown in together (e.g., animation, second-person address, character-voice narration, and sprightly music; Campbell et al., 1987). But research became increasingly sophisticated in terms of stimuli comparison and classification and goals. The pragmatic interest in effects began to be replaced by a theoretical interest in explaining the development of cues as stable associations between formal features and content. A study by Ruff and colleagues (1990) found that infants as young as 5 months repeatedly exposed to puppet events came to have expectations in connection with salient formal features such as variety of puppets, volume and animation of sound, light brightness, and degree of movement, and they began to attend to the place of occurrence at times of nonoccurrence. This phenomenon indicates that the development of interest, presumably based on increased arousal and enjoyment associated with the puppet events, motivated the infants to be vigilant.

In addition to formal features promising enjoyment (e.g., lively music, cheerful voices), the content itself may enhance vigilance through semantically entertaining features such as humor. Research by Zillmann et al. (1980) with preschoolers and first graders showed that, although initial attention to nonhumorous and humorous programs did not differ, humor prevented vigilance decrement associated with nonhumorous material and produced superior information acquisition. Zillmann and Bryant (1983) found that nonvivid humor facilitated attention and learning only minimally with younger children but considerably with older children. On the other hand, vivid humor had strong facilitatory effects with all children. Extremely funny humor, however, may engage and preoccupy children to a degree that nullifies the positive effect of increased vigilance (Schramm, 1972; Zillmann & Bryant, 1983). More sophisticated forms of humor such as irony, which contains distortions and contradictions that are not readily recognizable, tend to be counterproductive for learning (Cantor & Reilly, 1979; McGhee, 1979) because they produce confusion. Comprehension and enjoyment of distorting humor become possible only at the formal operational level of cognitive development—that is, in early adolescence (Helmers, 1965; McGhee, 1979). Producers of educational programming need to consider not only age appropriateness of various forms of humor but also complexity and intensity that may challenge viewers' processing capacity and jeopardize learning.

Arousing Content

The arousal model of vigilance (Davies & Parasuraman, 1982; Dember & Warm, 1979; Frankmann & Adams, 1962; Loeb & Alluisi, 1984; Parasuraman, 1984) predicts attention decrement through habituation (Mackworth, 1968, 1969) caused by repetitive, monotonous stimuli presented at a slow pace. According to Posner (1978), stimulus repetition creates pathway inhibition: that is, it decreases responsiveness to that stimulus and reduces the ability of the stimulus to elicit central processing. This implies that low vigilance is associated with peripheral, nonsystematic processing, which is consistently claimed to be a major problem for children's learning from television.

To be able to sustain central processing, television programming needs to be semantically salient or interesting. As already mentioned, this can be achieved through information that is novel and relevant to child viewers and is delivered at a conformably fast pace. Also as mentioned earlier, neural responsiveness can be maintained through quantitative and qualitative changes in the pattern of stimulation (Sharpless & Jasper, 1956). In semantic terms, this involves a wide range of themes and frequent thematic changes. Diversity and sustained pace enhance arousal but at the same time increase program complexity. This raises the question of how much material can be retained and how well.

In his review of the relationship between arousal and retention, J. R. Anderson (1995) mentioned Levonian's (1972) findings that arousal diminished encoding but enhanced memory of information encoded in a high arousal state. A comprehensive body of research in the 1960s and early 1970s (Kleinsmith & Kaplan, 1963, 1964; Levonian, 1967, 1968, 1972) indicated that a low level of arousal—like that observed during much of children's television watching—is conducive

to poor short-term memory but good long-term memory, whereas high arousal serves short-term memory better (Crane, Dieker, & Brown, 1970). One implication of these findings is that little arousing educational television helps children acquire a larger amount of information that they hold in their memory for a longer time. Another implication is that information retained from highly arousing programming may be less complete but is more accessible in short-term memory. So producers who consider using arousing contexts are faced with a trade-off between the quantity and the quality of the information that can be retained. They also need to take into account a serious risk associated with the use of fear and violence as means of enhancing arousal and attention: Children are likely to forget the contingent circumstances and to recall and rehearse only the fear or aggression. Over time, television that arouses through violence may build up an inventory of negative feelings and aggressive behavior schemata, which may vitiate the psychological and social climate of a whole generation of viewers. Such harmful overall side effects may outweigh any positive main effects in terms of curriculum learning.

Perceived Difficulty of Content

The most intricate aspect of vigilance is its relationship to content difficulty. Research findings support the hypothesis of a curvilinear relationship between content difficulty and attention, with attention being greatest at intermediate levels of difficulty (Anderson & Lorch, 1983; Campbell et al., 1987; Rice, Huston, & Wright, 1982). Very easy and familiar content tends to receive low attention because it has become redundant and predictable, therefore useless and unexciting. Vigilance decrement in this case results in low arousal. Very difficult content also tends to depress attention because the child is poorly equipped with the schemata or other cognitive structures needed for processing the material. Vigilance decrement in this case can be accounted for through low comprehension. At moderate levels of difficulty, attention and learning (comprehension and recall) are highest (Campbell et al., 1987) because novelty arouses interest and prior knowledge provides the framework for assimilating the new information.

Programming difficulty has been operationalized in terms of objective features of the television material (e.g., information quantity/density, pace, order/structure/schematization) or viewers' subjective evaluations of the material (e.g., predictability, discriminability/salience, comprehensibility). We focus our discussion on the latter category, with incidental references to the objective factors.

Vigilance described as expectation of certain stimuli involves the notion of predictability. Higher levels of uncertainty about the occurrence and schedule of critical signals result in lower vigilance (Lanzetta, 1986) and a more conservative response performance (Baddley & Colquhoun, 1969; Colquhoun, 1961). The expectancy theory predicates expectations about the temporal distribution of critical signals on their previous occurrence (Baker, 1963; Deese, 1955). In programming terms, a relatively stable pattern of occurrence of the stimuli to be attended can be expected to improve alertness to them.

Vigilance can also be regarded as a discrimination exercise in which critical signals occur against and have to be distinguished from a background of regularly occurring neutral events. The distinction is made along certain specified dimensions (Lanzetta, 1986). Vigilance can be enhanced by increasing the discriminability of critical signals (Adams, 1956; Thurmond, Binford, & Loeb, 1970; Warm, Loeb, & Alluisi, 1970; Wiener, 1964). In the case of television programming, that can be achieved by increasing contrasts between the stimuli of interest and the neutral material. Another possibility would be to educate viewers about distinctive features that are not salient enough, which may happen more often at the level of meaning than at the level of form. The formal features that pose problems for children's attentional response, comprehension, and learning are probably the make-believe artifacts used in television. The more educated the children are about such features, the more adequately they deploy their attention.

According to Lanzetta (1986), vigilance may involve comparative judgment—that is, simultaneous discrimination among co-occurring stimuli (e.g., identifying the needed tool among other tools in a tool box)—or absolute judgment—that is, successive discrimination between currently perceived stimuli and information present in memory (e.g., thinking about what tool would be appropriate for a specific task and who might have it and be willing to lend it). Most viewing situations involve vigilance to several stimuli and simultaneous use of both types of judgments. This may raise demands on cognitive resources to critical levels and may thus entail a vigilance decrement (Davies & Parasuraman, 1982; Parasuraman, 1979). Producers should be aware of this danger and keep the density of simultaneous stimuli low, especially when the learning task requires absolute judgment.

One challenge to discrimination is high similarity between target and background stimuli. According to Posner (1978), such situations involve processing of both types of stimuli in more or less the same pathways, and that jeopardizes the ability to react to the target. For example, it is harder to distinguish a turquoise pencil from blue or green pencils than from red or yellow ones. Conversely, research has shown that a high degree of dissimilarity between the primary object of a video and secondary objects often creates *inattentional blindness* to the secondary object, suggesting a lower attentional impact by the secondary objects (Most, Scholl, Clifford, & Simons, 2005; Simons & Chabris, 1999).

Another threat to discriminability is the repetition of background neutral events, which habituates the nonspecific alpha block and thus increases neural noise (Mackworth, 1968, 1969). Vigilance capacity is unnecessarily dispersed between target and background stimuli, and the response to the target becomes less effective. For instance, if the purpose of a program is to teach turquoise, and the color samples presented to children to choose from repeat purple more often than turquoise, the viewers tend to forget about turquoise and develop vigilance for purple. This phenomenon can be aggravated by the high rate (fast pace) of background events (Metzger, Warm, & Senter, 1974) that some authors believe to be a prepotent psychophysical factor in sustained attention (Bowers, 1983; Dember & Warm, 1979; Mackworth, 1968, 1969; Warm & Berch, 1984; Warm & Jerison, 1984). In our example, the faster the succession of color samples that include purple more often than turquoise, the faster the extinction of vigilance for turquoise and the emergence of vigilance for purple.

As a general conclusion to discriminability, attentional capacity can be concentrated on central elements of programming by reducing the density and pace of noncentral stimuli, as well as reducing their similarity to central stimuli. If we want to teach turquoise, we must show it together with few and sharply contrasting colors, in a slow to moderately paced succession of color samples in which turquoise is consistently repeated and the other colors are never or rarely repeated.

A third subjective factor of content difficulty is comprehensibility. According to the cognitive involvement model (Anderson et al., 1981; Lorch, Anderson, & Levin, 1979), perceived comprehensibility of the content facilitates attention. Wright et al. (1984) found that comprehensibility predicts attention more than attention predicts comprehensibility. This means that content comprehension is more critical to attention than vigilance is to comprehension and learning.

Comprehensibility as a function of knowledge, which develops with age, poses different vigilance problems for different age groups. Older children have more knowledge that they can use as a framework for processing new information, so they understand novel things faster and better. Younger children are more dependent on formal features of content, and their vigilance depends to a large extent on sensory feature recognizability.

Comprehensibility as a function of content may involve a wide range of variables. First, if we try to convey a large amount of information at the same time, alertness to myriad targets will result in missing many of them or attending little to any one of them. Reduced processing of each information item will diminish comprehension. So if better learning is the ultimate goal, simultaneously presenting fewer things should be more effective. Second, redundancy between the video and the audio tracks, order, coherence, and schematization of content make a program look more comprehensible, reduce cognitive costs, and eliminate the waste of cognitive resources. Structure injected into programs guides attention and facilitates processing. For example, stories were found to receive more attention than magazine programs (which have less structured information), and attention and comprehension were found to covary with one another more in animated (structured) than in live (less

structured) shows (Wright et al., 1984). But on the other hand, too complex structures may require too much effort for grasping components and their links, which will diminish resources available for schema instantiation (i.e., matching the incoming information to known schemata). For example, if we see three children running after a soccer ball, we immediately assume they are playing soccer. But if we see 6 children swimming toward a floating ball in a pool while 10 others are standing on the pool border, we are not sure whether the swimmers are trying to rescue the ball for the 10 children who are waiting or the 6 are playing polo while the 10 are watching. We need to keep monitoring the scene, collecting more information, and analyzing details such as children's clothing and attitudes before we can decide.

The effectiveness of content schematization in enhancing comprehensibility depends on the viewers' level of schema development. Wright et al. (1984) noticed that the covariance between attention and comprehension was highest with older children (who have stronger schema skills) exposed to animated (structured) programming.

An experiment conducted by Meadowcroft (1985) on children aged 5 to 8 examined the independent and combined effects of these two factors on attention and learning. She found that, in general, children with more developed schemata allocated less attention (had higher efficiency) than children with poor schema development. All children allocated more capacity to central content than to incidental content. Children with more developed schemata paid more attention to central content when the material presented to them was structured as a story (the attention to incidental content was not different between story and nonstory). Children with poor schema development allocated more attention to nonstructured material and were less efficient in processing the story (structured material). In the case of children with poor schema development, the levels of attention to central and incidental content were not affected by the presence or absence of a story schema.

Meadowcroft's (1985) results indicate that the patterns of relations among variables are complex and often paradoxical (e.g., comprehensibility may engage viewers and sustain their attention, but it may also decrease the need for attending to the material). And the more variables are examined in combination, the worse the theoretical confusion. For example, the influence of pace on vigilance can be expected under an arousal hypothesis to benefit attention deployment and under a comprehensibility hypothesis to burden children's processing and reduce attention (Wright et al., 1984). Opposite predictions and inconsistent empirical data that support both hypotheses threaten to void the theories of explanatory power. More systematic research is needed to overcome the dilemmas and explicate nonlinear relationships. As we have already suggested, in the case of pace, the arousal hypothesis may be more applicable up to a certain event rate, beyond which the limited-capacity model governs the process. It is possible that, within a certain pace range, both arousal and limited-capacity effects occur and cancel each other out. That may explain complaints in literature that findings about pace effects are inconclusive (e.g., Anderson, & Levin, 1976; Wright et al., 1984).

The pace issue is not trivial for producers in the context of findings that private television has fast-paced shorter events (Hooper & Chang, 1998). Visual overload caused by high event rates alters the way visual information is processed. Visual search tasks become slow and serial (Posner & Petersen, 1990), and comprehension relies more on schematic/automatic processing. If the educational goal of a program is to get children to think about, understand, and connect new things to previous knowledge, then information overload is bad. If the goal is to rehearse information and promote automation in the use of existing information, then a higher informational load paired with content schematization will serve the purpose. On the other hand, if we consider a televised message as incorporating educational information and form information, then children with developed/schematized knowledge of television and story conventions will make less effort to understand form and will have more cognitive resources available for processing educational content.

Although very serious, the problem of pace is not insoluble. A study by Tamborini and Zillmann (1985) addressed Singer and Singer's (1979) concern that pace reduces thinking and tested three methods suggested by the critics for improving format to counteract negative pace effects: curiosity-arousing questions, personalized communication style (direct address and eye contact), and pauses for thinking. The first two methods involve the use of schemata that have an engaging effect. The third method is expected to eliminate the pace-related time crunch responsible for diminished thinking. Experimental results showed significant main effects of personalized communication style on attention, total learning, and verbal learning; a significant main effect of thinking time on visual learning; and a tendency of personalized style to interact with thinking time as predictors of total and visual learning. Questions without a personalized style were not found effective in eliciting attention. A surprising finding was that questions delivered using a personalized style increased eyes-off-screen. This phenomenon was interpreted as a sign of deeper thinking manifested as an attention shift from perception (vigilance) inward to thinking.

Tamborini and Zillmann's (1985) experiment once again emphasized the complex nature of the relationship between pacing and schematization as factors of vigilance. We may conclude the discussion of program-related factors of attention to and learning from television with Wright et al.'s (1984) observation:

> Neither comprehensibility nor salience alone determine the nature and extent of processing. Rather, it appears that they are determined instead by a combination of schematic knowledge and strategic decision making at key points in the response to the level of processing demanded or supported by the program's format and structure. (p. 665)

Situational Factors

The least apparent and frequently ignored situational variable that affects vigilance is the time of day. The circadian rhythm has been found to influence the level of arousal. As arousal increases from morning toward evening, cognitive efficiency should be expected to increase too. Nevertheless, research findings seem to converge on a decrease of vigilance (response speed and accuracy) in the second part of the day. In general, vigilance performance was found to be best in the morning (Coyle, 1992; Dunne, Roche, & Hartley, 1990; Mathur, 1991; Rana, Rishi, & Sinha, 1996) and worst in the afternoon (Rana et al., 1996). But circadian variability of vigilance is high. One reason is that humans may be "morning types" (more vigilant in the first part of the day) or "evening types" (Akerstedt & Froberg, 1976; Home & Ostberg, 1977). Also, an interaction between sex and time of day as vigilance factors was documented on certain types of tasks (Baker, 1987; Christie & McBreauty, 1979; Rana et al., 1996). Girls were found to be more accurate (to make fewer omission errors) than boys in the morning and early afternoon but not in the evening (Rana et al., 1996).

Variation in vigilance during the day affects memory and learning not only quantitatively but also qualitatively. Findings by Folkard, Monk, Bradbury, and Rosenthal (1977) showed that retention of information depended on the variation of arousal levels related to time of day, as follows: Short-term memory (immediate recall) was better for information acquired in the morning (9:00 A.M.), at a time of relatively low arousal, whereas long-term memory (recall 1 week later) was better for information acquired in the afternoon (3:00 P.M.), at a time of relatively higher arousal.

These findings indicate to programmers and producers that, in general, educational material is bound to receive more attention in the morning. Matinal viewing may benefit children more in terms of instrumental knowledge for short-term use, whereas evening viewing may serve long-term memory objectives better.

If we consider stimulus type as a situational factor of vigilance, then real life, where all senses can be engaged, is a stronger attention getter than television, which uses only the visual and the auditory modalities. This, together with the opportunity for action in real life, makes the environment more engaging than the world of television. The attractiveness of television can be expected to depend on its complementarity to real life. TV presentations of realities beyond children's reach, fiction, and high levels of excitement and enjoyment can capture children's attention and retain it for a while. But young children are hyperactive, and the very limited opportunity for action and interaction that television provides dooms it to intermittent attendance and it is often relegated to being a secondary activity.

The educators' question is how to integrate the pockets of TV watching in a child's life and use the medium more effectively as an educational tool. The traditional approach is to have children coview with peers or adults for the purpose of discussion, which makes possible the rehearsal of knowledge and its expansion by pooling and sharing coviewers' knowledge. This method helps children learn that knowledge develops through additions and changes of perspective.

Another possible approach is to create activity and interactivity situations based on the program. For example, "how to" or "let's do" tasks can be proposed to children, prompting them to use the knowledge provided by the program. The immediate applicability of knowledge made available on television is likely to enhance children's attention to and retention from the program.

If we transfer the notion of difficulty from television content to the viewing situation, the TV flow of information meanders between center and periphery in the children's attentional field. When the child is more alert to television than to other elements in the environment, nontelevision stimuli function as distractors and introduce noise that diminishes and can eventually reorient or divert attention to more compelling sources. Making television competitive through a high density of salient and arousing stimuli increases the risk of cognitive overload and poor attendance to educational content. A more effective strategy may be a sparing, intermittent use of salient cues to hook in viewers who have defected.

For children who watch in solitude, the situation may be understimulating, and monotonous programming may depress arousal and vigilance to levels that are insufficient to ensure systematic processing of central information. Actions in the program to counteract vigilance decrement, such as, for instance, taking a pen to draw something, or having a drink, or looking up a rare and intriguing word in a dictionary, may suggest frequent simple actions in the immediate environment. For young children, lively songs to sing along with and dance to may be arousing.

An additional set of variables to be understood comes with the proliferation of television programs available on multiple media. The same episode of *Dora the Explorer* may be viewed by a child on their big screen living room television set, their parents' laptop, and their portable media device. Some aspects of that programming, such as the formal features of the program and the type and valence of content, remain constant; but other variables, such as screen size (Bellman, Schweda, & Varan, 2009; Reeves, Lang, Kim, & Tatar, 1999), availability (and movement) of surrounding interactive content, and context of viewing (such as in the car), may have significant effects on how educational content is viewed and on children's vigilance with that program in the moment.

Some of the effects of those more constant features may also be less consistent. For example, user's reception to the program's pacing may vary depending on whether they are viewing it on a large screen at home or on a small screen in a moving vehicle. Moreover, what is the impact of motivation for viewing programming using a particular device on attention given to the program? If a mom passes back her iPod in the car to keep her child quiet, does the child pay as much attention to it as to a program he or she has chosen to watch at home? These questions are critical in the context of vigilance in television because the same videos being produced with the television screen in mind are increasingly being viewed by children on a wide variety of other screens. From a production standpoint, understanding how the same content will be viewed and understood across platforms, and how that can affect vigilance, is a critical part of moving educational television forward.

That said, from a vigilance perspective, children's learning from television seems to be, ultimately, a function of producers' abilities to go beyond program design and construct viewing-acting-learning situations. Such an integrative approach will require more complex research to beat the barrier between children's real world and the virtual world of television. The emphasis in educational television research will probably shift from stimuli processing toward interaction and motivation.

References

Adams, J. A. (1956). Vigilance in the detection of low-intensity visual stimuli. *Journal of Experimental Psychology, 52,* 204–208.

Akerstedt, T., & Froberg, J. E. (1976). Interindividual differences in circadian patterns of catecholamine excretion, body temperature, performance, and subjective arousal. *Biological Psychology, 4,* 277–292.

Alvarez, M. M., Huston, A. C., Wright, J. C., & Kerkman, D. D. (1988). Gender differences in visual attention to television form and content. *Journal of Applied Developmental Psychology, 9,* 459–475.

Anderson, D. R. (1983). *Young children's television viewing: The problem of cognitive continuity* (Working Paper). University of Massachusetts, Department of Psychology.

Anderson, D. R., Alwitt, L., Lorch, E., & Levin, S. (1979). Watching children watch television. In G. Hale & M. Lewis (Eds.), *Attention and cognitive development* (pp. 331–361). New York: Plenum.

Anderson, D. R., Choi, H. P., & Lorch, E. P. (1987). Attentional inertia reduces distractibility during young children's TV viewing. *Child Development, 58,* 798–806.

Anderson, D. R., & Levin, S. R. (1976). Young children's attention to "Sesame Street." *Child Development, 47,* 806–811.

Anderson, D. R., & Lorch, E. P. (1983). Looking at television: Action or reaction? In J. Bryant & D. R. Anderson (Eds.), *Children's understanding of television: Research on attention and comprehension* (pp. 1–34). New York: Academic Press.

Anderson, D. R., Lorch, E. P., Field, D. E., Collins, P. A., & Nathan, J. G. (1986). Television viewing at home: Age trends in visual attention and time with TV. *Child Development, 57,* 1024–1033.

Anderson, D. R., Lorch, E. P., Field, D. E., & Sanders, J. (1981). The effects of TV program comprehensibility on preschool children's visual attention to television. *Child Development, 52,* 151–157.

Anderson, J. R. (1995). *Learning and memory: An integrated approach.* New York: John Wiley.

Applebee, A. N. (1977). A sense of story. *Theory Into Practice, 16,* 342–347.

Baddley, A. D., & Colquhoun, W. P. (1969). Signal probability and vigilance: A reappraisal of the "signal-rate" effect. *British Journal of Psychology, 60,* 169–178.

Baer, S. A. (1997). Strategies of children's attention to and comprehension of television (Doctoral dissertation, University of Kentucky, 1996). *Dissertation Abstracts International, 57*(11-B), 7243.

Baer, S. A., & Lorch, E. P. (1990). *Effects of importance on children's visual attention to television.* Paper presented at the biennial meeting of the Southeastern Conference on Human Development, Richmond, VA.

Baker, C. H. (1963). Signal duration as a factor in vigilance tasks. *Science, 141,* 1196–1197.

Baker, M. A. (1987). *Sex differences in human performance.* New York: John Wiley.

Bandura, A. (Ed.). (1971). *Psychological modeling: Conflicting theories.* Chicago: Aldine-Atherton.

Bandura, A. (1977). *Social learning theory.* Englewood Cliffs, NJ: Prentice Hall.

Bandura, A. (1994). Social cognitive theory of mass communication. In J. Bryant & D. Zillmann (Eds.), *Media effects: Advances in theory and research* (pp. 61–90). Hillsdale, NJ: Lawrence Erlbaum.

Bellack, D. R. (1984). An investigation of developmental differences in attention and comprehension of television (Doctoral dissertation, University of Kentucky, 1983). *Dissertation Abstracts International, 44*(7-B)*,* 2263.

Bellman, S., Schweda, A., & Varan, D. (2009). Viewing angles matter: Screen size does not. *Journal of Communication, 59*, 609–634.

Berlyne, D. E. (1960). *Conflict, arousal, and curiosity.* New York: McGraw-Hill.

Bowers, J. C. (1983). *Stimulus homogeneity and the event rate effect in sustained attention.* Unpublished doctoral dissertation, University of Cincinnati, OH.

Brown, A. L., & French, L. A. (1976). Construction and regeneration of logical sequences using causes or consequences as the point of departure. *Child Development, 47,* 930–940.

Bryant, J., Zillmann, D., & Brown, D. (1983). Entertainment features in children's educational television: Effects on attention and information acquisition. In J. Bryant & D. R. Anderson (Eds.), *Children's understanding of television: Research on attention and comprehension* (pp. 221–240). New York: Academic Press.

Buss, A. H., & Plomin, R. (1975). *A temperament theory of personality development.* New York: John Wiley.

Calvert, S. L., Huston, A. C., Watkins, B. A., & Wright, J. C. (1982). The effects of selective attention to television forms on children's comprehension of content. *Child Development, 53*, 601–610.

Campbell, T. A., Wright, J. C., & Huston, A. C. (1987). Form cues and content difficulty as determinants of children's cognitive processing of televised educational messages. *Journal of Experimental Child Psychology, 43,* 311–327.

Cantor, J., & Reilly, S. (1979, August). *Jocular language style and relevant humor in educational messages.* Paper presented at the second International Conference on Humor, Los Angeles, CA.

Carew, J. (1980). Experience and the development of intelligence in young children at home and in day care. *Monographs of the Society for Research in Child Development, 45*(6–7, Serial No. 187).

Carter, J. D., & Swanson, H. L. (1995). The relationship between intelligence and vigilance in children at risk. *Journal of Abnormal Child Psychology, 23,* 201–220.

Carver, C. S., Coleman, A. E., & Glass, D. C. (1976). The coronary-prone behavior pattern and the suppression of fatigue on a treadmill test. *Journal of Personality and Social Psychology, 33,* 460–466.

Chaiken, S. (1980). Heuristic versus systematic processing and the use of source versus message cues in persuasion. *Journal of Personality and Social Psychology, 39,* 752–766.

Checcino, D. J. (1997). Relationships among personality type, self-concept, grade point average, and gender of seventh graders (Doctoral dissertation, George Mason University, 1996). *Dissertation Abstracts International, 57*(8-A), 3401.

Christie, M. J., & McBreauty, E. M. T. (1979). Psychophysiological investigations of post lunch style in male and female subjects. *Ergonomics, 22,* 307-323.

Collins, W. A., Wellman, H., Keniston, A. H., & Westby, S. D. (1978). Age-related aspects of comprehension and inference from a televised dramatic narrative. *Child Development, 49,* 389–399.

Colquhoun, W. P. (1961). The effect of "unwanted" signals on performance in a vigilance task. *Ergonomics, 4,* 42–51.

Coyle, K. (1992). Circadian variation in cognitive functioning (Doctoral dissertation, University of Wales College of Cardiff, 1989). *Dissertation Abstracts International, 51,* 1914.

Crane, L. D., Dieker, R. J., & Brown, C. T. (1970). The psychological response to the communication modes: Reading, listening, speaking, and evaluating. *Journal of Communication, 20,* 231–240.

Crawley, A. M., Anderson, D. R., Santomenro, A., Wilder, A., Williams, M., Evans, M. K., & Bryant, J. (2002). Do children learn how to watch television? The impact of extensive experience with *Blue's Clues* on preschool children's television viewing behavior. *Journal of Communication, 52,* 264–280.

Davies, D. R., & Parasuraman, R. (1982). *The psychology of vigilance.* London: Academic Press.

Deese, J. (1955). Some problems in the theory of vigilance. *Psychological Review, 62,* 359–368.

Dember, W. N., & Warm, J. S. (1979). *Psychology of perception* (2nd ed.). New York: Holt, Rinehart & Winston.

Dent, C., & Thorndyke, P. W. (1979). *The use of schemata in children's comprehension and recall of narrative texts.* Santa Monica, CA: RAND.

Dunne, M. P., Roche, F., & Hartley, L. R. (1990). Effects of time of day on immediate recall and sustained retrieval from semantic memory. *Journal of General Psychology, 117,* 403–410.

Easterbrook, J. A. (1959). The effect of emotion on cue utilization and the organization of behavior. *Psychological Review, 66,* 183–201.

Eysenck, H. J. (1983). Is there a paradigm in personality research? *Journal of Research in Personality, 17,* 369–397.

Eysenck, M. W. (1982). *Attention and arousal.* Berlin: Springer.

Eysenck, M. W. (1988). Individual differences, arousal, and monotonous work. In J. P. Leonard (Ed.), *Vigilance: Methods, models, and regulation* (pp. 111–118). Frankfurt, Germany: Peter Lang.

Eysenck, M. W. (1989). Individual differences in vigilance performance. In A. Coblentz (Ed.), *Vigilance and performance in automatized systems* (pp. 31–40). Dordrecht, The Netherlands: Kluwer.

Field, D. E., & Anderson, D. R. (1985). Instruction and modality effects on children's television attention and comprehension. *Journal of Educational Psychology, 77,* 91–100.

Fishbein, H. D. (1976). *Evolution, development, and children's learning.* Pacific Palisades, CA; Goodyear.

Flavell, J. H. (1979). Metacognition and cognitive monitoring: A new era of cognitive-developmental inquiry. *American Psychologist, 34,* 906–911.

Flavell, J. H., & Wellman, H. M. (1977). Metamemory. In R. V. Kailand & J. W. Hagan (Eds.), *Perspectives on the development of memory and cognition* (pp. 3–33). Hillsdale, NJ: Lawrence Erlbaum.

Folkard, S., Monk, T. H., Bradbury, R., & Rosenthal, J. (1977). Time of day effects in school children's immediate and delayed recall of meaningful material. *British Journal of Psychology, 68,* 45–50.

Frankmann, J. P., & Adams, J. A. (1962). Theories of vigilance. *Psychological Bulletin, 59,* 257–272.

Gibson, E. J., & Rader, N. (1979). The perceiver as performer. In G. A. Hale & M. Lewis (Eds.), *Attention and cognitive development* (pp. 1–21). New York: Plenum.

Golden, M., Montare, A., & Bridger, W. (1977). Verbal control of delay behavior in two-year-old boys as a function of social class. *Child Development, 48,* 1107–1111.

Greer, D., Potts, R., Wright, J. C., & Huston, A. C. (1982). The effects of television commercial form and commercial placement on children's social behavior and attention. *Child Development, 53,* 611–619.

Halpern, D. F. (1986). *Sex differences in cognitive abilities.* Hillsdale, NJ: Lawrence Erlbaum.

Hawkins, R. P., Kim, J. H., & Pingree, S. (1991). The ups and downs of attention to television. *Communication Research, 18,* 53–76.

Hawkins, R. P., Pingree, S., Hitchon, J. B., Gilligan, E., Kahlor, L., Gorham, B. W., et al. (2002). What holds attention to television? Strategic inertia of looks at content boundaries. *Communication Research, 29,* 3–30.

Helmers, H. (1965). *Sprache und Humor des Kindes* [Children's speech and humor]. Stuttgart, Germany: Ernst Klett.

Home, J. A., & Ostberg, O. (1977). Individual differences in human circadian rhythms. *Biological Psychology, 5,* 179–190.

Hooper, M.-L., & Chang, P. (1998). Comparison of demands of sustained attentional events between public and private children's television programs. *Perceptual and Motor Skills, 86,* 431–434.

Huston, A. C., Greer, D., Wright, J. C., Welch, R., & Ross, R. (1984). Children's comprehension of televised formal features with masculine and feminine connotations. *Developmental Psychology, 20,* 707–716.

Huston, A. C., & Wright, J. C. (1983). Children's processing of television: The informative function of formal features. In J. Bryant & D. R. Anderson (Eds.), *Children's understanding of television: Research on attention and comprehension* (pp. 35–68). New York: Academic Press.

Huston, A. C., Wright, J. C., Wartella, E., Rice, M. L., Watkins, B. A., Campbell, T., et al. (1981). Communicating more than content: Formal features in children's television programs. *Journal of Communication, 31*(3), 32–48.

Huston-Stein, A., Fox, S., Greer, D., Watkins, B. A., & Whitaker, J. (1981). The effects of TV action and violence on children's social behavior, *Journal of Genetic Psychology, 138,* 183–191,

Huston-Stein, A., & Wright, J. C. (1979). Children and television: Effects of the medium, its content, and its form. *Journal of Research and Development in Education, 13,* 20–31.

Ippolito, M. F. (1993). *Standards as a correlate of delay of gratification in 24-month-old children.* Unpublished master's thesis, Bowling Green State University, Bowling Green, OH.

Jennings, J. R. (1983). Attention and coronary heart disease. In D. S. Krantz, A. Baum, & J. E. Singer (Eds.), *Handbook of psychology and health* (Vol. 3, pp. 85–124). Hillsdale, NJ: Lawrence Erlbaum.

Kahneman, D. (1973). *Attention and effort.* Englewood Cliffs, NJ: Prentice Hall.

Khrone, H. W. (1978). Individual differences in coping with stress and anxiety. In C. D. Spielberger

& I. G. Sarason (Eds.), *Stress and anxiety* (Vol. 5, pp. 233–260). Washington, DC: Hemisphere.

Khrone, H. W., Hock, M., & Kohlmann, C.-W. (1992). Coping dispositions, uncertainty, and emotional arousal. In K. T. Strongman (Ed.), *International review of studies on emotion* (Vol. 2, pp. 73–95). Chichester, UK: Wiley.

Kleinsmith, L. J., & Kaplan, S. (1963). Paired-associate learning as a function of arousal and interpolated activity. *Journal of Experimental Psychology, 65,* 190–193.

Kleinsmith, L. J., & Kaplan, S. (1964). Interaction of arousal and recall interval in nonsense syllable paired-associate learning. *Journal of Experimental Psychology, 67*(2), 124–126.

Krcmar, M. (2010). Assessing the research on media, cognitive development, and infants. *Journal of Children & Media, 4,* 119–143.

Krcmar, M., Grela, B., & Lin, K. (2007). Can toddlers learn vocabulary from television? An experimental approach. *Media Psychology, 10,* 41–63.

Lanzetta, T. M. (1986). Effects of stimulus heterogeneity and information processing load on the event rate function in sustained attention (Doctoral dissertation, University of Cincinnati, 1985), *Dissertation Abstracts International, 46*(10-B)*,* 3623.

Lesser, G. S. (1972). Learning, teaching, and television production for children: The experience of *Sesame Street. Harvard Educational Review, 42,* 231–272.

Lesser, G. S. (1974). *Children and television: Lessons from* Sesame Street. New York: Random House.

Lesser, G. S. (1977). *Television and the preschool child.* New York: Academic Press.

Levine, L. E., & Waite, B. M. (2000). Television viewing and attentional abilities in fourth and fifth grade children. *Journal of Applied Developmental Psychology, 21,* 667–679.

Levonian, E. (1967). Retention of information in relation to arousal during continuously presented material. *American Educational Research Journal, 4*(2)*,* 103–116.

Levonian, E. (1968). Short-term retention in relation to arousal. *Psychophysiology, 4,* 284–293.

Levonian, E. (1972). Retention overtime in relation to arousal during learning: An explanation of discrepant results. *Acta Psychologica, 36,* 290–321.

Levy, F. (1980). The development of sustained attention (vigilance) and inhibition in children: Some normative data. *Journal of Child Psychology and Psychiatry, 21,* 77–84.

Loeb, M., & Alluisi, E. A. (1984). Theories of vigilance. In J. S. Warm (Ed.), *Sustained attention in human performance* (pp. 179–200). Chichester, UK: Wiley.

Lorch, E. P., Anderson, D. R., & Levin, S. R. (1979). The relationship of visual attention to children's comprehension of television. *Child Development, 50,* 722–727.

Luria, A. R. (1959). Experimental study of the higher nervous activity of the abnormal child. *Journal of Mental Deficiency Research, 3,* 1–22.

Mackworth, J. F. (1968). Vigilance, arousal, and habituation. *Psychological Review, 75,* 308–322.

Mackworth, J. F. (1969). *Vigilance and habituation.* Baltimore, MD: Penguin.

Mackworth, J. F, (1970a). *Vigilance and attention: A signal detection approach.* New York: Penguin.

Mackworth, J. F. (1970b). *Vigilance and habituation: A neuropsychological approach.* Baltimore, MD: Penguin.

Mander, J. (1978). *Four arguments for the elimination of television.* New York: Quill.

Mandler, J., & Johnson, N. (1977). Remembrance of things parsed: Story structure and recall. *Cognitive Psychology, 9,* 111–151.

Mathur, K. (1991). TOD dependent performance efficiency in student nurses. *Journal of Human Ergology, 20,* 67–75.

Matlin, M., & Stang, D. (1978). *The Pollyanna principle.* Cambridge, MA: Schenkman.

Matthews, K. A. (1978). Assessment and developmental antecedents of Pattern A behavior in children. In T. M. Dembrowski, S. M. Weiss, J. L. Shields, S. G. Haynes, & M. Feinleib (Eds.), *Coronary-prone behavior* (pp. 207–217). New York: Springer.

Matthews, K. A. (1980). Measurement of Type A behavior pattern in children: Assessment of children's competitiveness, impatience-anger, and aggression. *Child Development, 51,* 466–475.

McGhee, P. E. (1979). *Humor: Its origin and development.* San Francisco: Freeman.

McLuhan, M. (1964). *Understanding media: The extensions of man.* New York: McGraw-Hill.

McLuhan, M. (1978, April 3). A last look at the tube. *New York Times Magazine,* p. 45.

Meadowcroft, J. M. (1985). *Children's attention to television: The influence of story schema development on allocation of cognitive capacity and memory.* Unpublished doctoral dissertation, University of Wisconsin, Madison.

Metzger, K. R., Warm, J. S., & Senter, R. J. (1974). Effects of background event rate and artificial signals on vigilance performance. *Perceptual and Motor Skills, 38,* 1175–1181.

Miller, W. (1985). A view from the inside: Brainwaves and television viewing. *Journalism Quarterly, 62,* 508–514.

Most, S. B., Scholl, B. J., Clifford, E. R., & Simons, D. J. (2005). What you see is what you set: Sustained inattentional blindness and the capture of awareness. *Psychological Review, 112*, 217–242.

Mowrer, R. R., & Klein, S. B. (1989). Traditional learning theory and the transition to contemporary learning theory. In S. B. Klein & R. R. Mowrer (Eds.), *Contemporary learning theories: Pavlovian conditioning and the status of traditional learning theory* (pp. 3–17). Hillsdale, NJ: Lawrence Erlbaum.

Omanson, R. (1982). An analysis of narratives. *Discourse Processes, 2*, 195–224.

Parasuraman, R. (1979). Memory load and event rate control sensitivity decrements in sustained attention. *Science, 205*, 924–927.

Parasuraman, R. (1984). The psychology of sustained attention. In J. S. Warm (Ed.), *Sustained attention in human performance* (pp. 61–101). Chichester, UK: Wiley.

Parasuraman, R. (1985). Sustained attention: A multifactorial approach. In M. I. Posner & O. S. M. Marin (Eds.), *Attention and human performance* (Vol. 11, pp. 493–511). Hillsdale, NJ: Lawrence Erlbaum.

Parasuraman, R., Warm, J. S., & Dember, W. N. (1987). Vigilance: Taxonomy and utility. In L. S. Mark, J. S. Warm, & R. L. Huston (Eds.), *Ergonomics and human factors: Recent research* (pp. 11–32). New York: Springer.

Piaget, J. (1947/1973). *The psychology of intelligence.* Totowa, NJ: Littlefield & Adams.

Pingree, S. (1986). Children's activity and television comprehensibility. *Communication Research, 13*, 239–256.

Posner, M. I. (1978). *Chronometric explorations of the mind.* Hillsdale, NJ: Lawrence Erlbaum.

Posner, M. I., & Petersen, S. E. (1990). The attention system of the human brain. *Annual Review of Neuroscience, 13*, 25–42.

Potts, R., Huston. A. C, & Wright, J. C. (1986). The effects of television form and violent content on boys' attention and social behavior. *Journal of Experimental Child Psychology, 41*, 1–17.

Pratto, F., & John, O. P. (1991). Automatic vigilance: The attention-grabbing power of negative social information. *Journal of Personality and Social Psychology, 61*, 380–391.

Price, V. A. (1982). *Type A behavior pattern: A model for research and practice.* New York: Academic Press.

Rana, N., Rishi, P., & Sinha, S. P. (1996). Vigilance performance in children in relation to time of the day. *Psychological Studies, 47*(1–2), 10–15.

Reeves, B., Lang, A., Kim, E., & Tatar, D. (1999). The effects of screen size and message content on attention and arousal. *Media Psychology, 1*, 49–68.

Rice, M. L., Huston, A. C., Truglio, R., & Wright, J. C. (1990). Words from *Sesame Street:* Learning vocabulary while viewing. *Developmental Psychology, 26*, 421–428.

Rice, M. L., Huston, A. C., & Wright, J. C. (1982). The forms of television: Effects on children's attention, comprehension, and social behavior. In D. Pearl, L. Bouthilet, & J. Lazar (Eds.), *Television and behavior: Ten years of scientific progress and implications for the eighties* (pp. 24–38). Washington, DC: U.S. Government Printing Office.

Richert, R., Robb, M., Fender, J. G., & Wartella, E. (2009). Word learning from baby videos. *Archives of Pediatric & Adolescent Medicine, 164*(5). doi:10.1001/archpediatrics.2010.24

Rolandelli, D. R. (1985). *Young children's auditory and visual processing of narrated and nonnarrated television programming.* Unpublished doctoral dissertation, University of Kansas, Lawrence.

Rolandelli, D. R., Wright, J. C., & Huston, A. C. (1982, April). *Auditory attention to television: A new methodology.* Paper presented at the biennial meeting of the Southwestern Society for Research in Human Development, Galveston, TX.

Rolandelli, D. R., Wright, J. C., & Huston, A. C. (1985, May). *Children's auditory and visual processing of narrated and nonnarrated television programming.* Paper presented at the annual meeting of the International Communication Association, Honolulu, HI.

Routtenberg, A. (1968). The two-arousal hypothesis: Reticular formation and limbic system. *Psychological Review, 75*, 51–80.

Routtenberg, A. (1971). Stimulus processing and response execution: A neurobehavioral theory. *Psychology and Behavior, 6*, 589–596.

Ruff, H. A. (1990). Individual differences in sustained attention during infancy. In J. Colombo & J. Fagen (Eds.), *Individual differences in infancy: Reliability, stability, and prediction* (pp. 247–270). Hillsdale, NJ: Lawrence Erlbaum.

Ruff, H. A., Capozzoli, M., Dubiner, K., & Parrinello, R. (1990). A measure of vigilance in infancy. *Infant Behavior and Development, 13*, 1–20.

Ruff, H. A., Capozzoli, M., & Weissberg, R. (1998). Age, individuality, and context as factors in sustained visual attention during preschool years. *Developmental Psychology, 34*, 454–464.

Ruff, H. A., & Rothbart, M. K. (1996). *Attention in early development: Themes and variations.* New York: Oxford University Press.

Salomon, G. (1981). Introducing AIME: The assessment of children's mental involvement with television. In H. Kelly & H. Gardner (Eds.), *Viewing children through television* (pp. 89–102). San Francisco: Jossey-Bass.

Salomon, G. (1983a). The differential investment of mental effort in learning from different sources. *Educational Psychologist, 18*(1), 42–50.

Salomon, G. (1983b). Television watching and mental effort: A social psychological view. In J. Bryant & D. Anderson (Eds.), *Children's understanding of television: Research on attention and comprehension* (pp. 181–198). New York: Academic Press.

Salomon, G. (1984). Television is "easy" and print is "tough": The differential investment of mental effort in learning as a function of perceptions and attributions. *Journal of Educational Psychology, 76,* 647–658.

Schindler, R. A. (1986). Hyperactive and non-hyperactive children's knowledge and use of factors affecting attention (Doctoral dissertation, Texas A&M University, 1985). *Dissertation Abstracts International, 47*(1-A), 132.

Schramm, W. (1972). What the research says. In W. Schramm (Ed.), *Quality in instructional television.* Honolulu: University Press of Hawaii.

Sharpless, S., & Jasper, H. H. (1956). Habituation of the arousal reaction. *Brain, 79,* 655–680.

Shoemaker, P. J. (1996). Hardwired for news: Using biological and cultural evolution to explain the surveillance function. *Journal of Communication, 46*(3), 32–48.

Signorielli, N., Gross, L., & Morgan, M. (1982). Violence in television programs: Ten years later. In D. Pearl, L. Bouthilet, & J. Lazar (Eds.), *Television and behavior: Ten years of scientific progress and implications for the eighties* (Vol. 2, pp. 158–173). Washington, DC: U.S. Government Printing Office.

Silverman, I. W., & Gaines, M. (1996). Using standard situations to measure attention span and persistence in toddler-aged children: Some cautions. *Journal of Genetic Psychology, 157,* 397–410.

Silverman, I. W., & Ippolito, M. F. (1995). Maternal antecedents of delay ability in young children. *Journal of Applied Developmental Psychology, 16,* 569–591.

Silverman, I. W., & Ragusa, D. M. (1990). Child and maternal correlates of impulse control in 24-month-old children. *Genetic, Social, and General Psychology Monographs, 116,* 435–473.

Simons, D. J., & Chabris, C. F. (1999). Gorillas in our midst: Sustained inattentional blindness for dynamic events. *Perception, 28,* 1059–1074.

Singer, D. G., Singer, J. L., & Zuckerman, D. M. (1981). *Teaching television: How to use TV to your child's advantage.* New York: Dial Press.

Singer, D. G., Zuckerman, D. M., & Singer, J. L. (1980). Helping elementary children learn about TV. *Journal of Communication, 30*(3), 84–93.

Singer, J. L. (1980). The power and limitations of television: A cognitive-affective analysis. In P. Tannenbaum (Ed.), *The entertainment functions of television* (pp. 31–65). Hillsdale, NJ: Lawrence Erlbaum.

Singer, J. L., & Singer, D. G. (1979, March). Come back, Mister Rogers, come back. *Psychology Today,* pp. 56, 59–60.

Singer, J. L., & Singer, D. G. (1998). *Barney & Friends* as entertainment and education: Evaluating the quality and effectiveness of a television series for preschool children. In J. K. Asamen & G. L. Berry (Eds.), *Research paradigms, television, and social behavior* (pp. 305–367). Thousand Oaks, CA: Sage.

Sternglantz, S. H., & Serbin, L. A. (1974). Sex role stereotyping in children's television programs. *Developmental Psychology, 10,* 710–715.

Strube, M., Turner, C., Patrick, S., & Perrillo, R. (1983). Type A and Type B attentional responses to aesthetic stimuli: Effects on mood and performance. *Journal of Personality and Social Psychology, 45,* 1369–1379.

Swanson, H. L. (1989). The effects of central processing strategies on learning disabled, mildly retarded, average, and gifted children's elaborative encoding abilities. *Journal of Experimental Child Psychology, 47,* 370–397.

Swanson, H. L., & Cooney, J. B. (1989). Relationship between intelligence and vigilance in children. *Journal of School Psychology, 27,* 141–153.

Tamborini, R., & Zillmann, D. (1985). Effects of questions, personalized communication style, and pauses for reflection in children's educational programs. *Journal of Educational Research, 79*(1), 19–26.

Thatcher, R. W. (1994). Cyclic cortical reorganization: Origins of human cognitive development. In G. Dawson & K. W. Fischer (Eds.), *Human behavior and the developing brain* (pp. 232–266). New York: Guilford.

Thomas, A., Chess, S. S., & Birch, H. G. (1968). *Temperament and behavior disorders in children,* New York: New York University Press.

Thorson, E., Reeves, B., & Schleuder, J. (1985). Message complexity and attention to television. *Communication Research, 12,* 427–454.

Thurmond, J. B., Binford, J. R., & Loeb, M. (1970). Effects of signal-to-noise variability over repeated sessions in an auditory vigilance task. *Perception and Psychophysics, 7,* 100–102.

Vaughn, B. E., Kopp, C. B., & Krakow, J. B. (1984). The emergence and consolidation of self-control from eighteen to thirty months of age: Normative trends and individual differences. *Child Development, 55,* 990–1004.

Verbeke, W. (1988). Preschool children's visual attention and understanding behavior towards a visual narrative. *Communication & Cognition, 21,* 67–94.

Ward, S., & Wackman, D. B. (1973). Children's information processing of television advertising. In P. Clark (Ed.), *New models for mass communication research* (Vol. 2, pp. 119–146). Beverly Hills, CA: Sage.

Warm, J. S. (1984). An introduction to vigilance. In J. S. Warm (Ed.), *Sustained attention in human performance* (pp. 1–14), Chichester, UK: Wiley.

Warm, J. S. (1993). Vigilance and target detection. In B. M. Huey & C. D. Wickens (Eds.), *Workload transition: Implications for individual and team performance* (pp. 139–170). Washington, DC: National Research Council, National Academy Press.

Warm, J. S., & Berch, D. B. (1984). Sustained attention in the mentally retarded: The vigilance paradigm. In N. R. Ellis & N. W. Bray (Eds.), *International review of research in mental retardation* (Vol. 13, pp. 1–41). New York: Academic Press,

Warm, J. S., Dember, W. N., & Hancock, P. A. (1996). Vigilance and workload in automatic systems. In R. Parasuraman & M. Mouloua (Eds.), *Automation and human performance: Theory and applications* (pp. 183–200). Mahwah, NJ: Lawrence Erlbaum.

Warm, J. S., & Jerison, H. J. (1984). The psychophysics of vigilance. In J. S. Warm (Ed.), *Sustained attention in human performance* (pp. 15–60). New York: John Wiley.

Warm, J. S., Loeb, M., & Alluisi, E. A. (1970). Variations in watchkeeping performance as a function of the rate and duration of visual signals. *Perception and Psychophysics, 7,* 97–99.

Wartella, E., & Ettema, J. S. (1974). A cognitive developmental study of children's attention to television commercials. *Communication Research, 1,* 69–88.

Weidner, G., & Matthews, K. A. (1978). Reported physical symptoms elicited by unpredictable events and the Type A coronary prone behavior pattern. *Journal of Personality and Social Psychology, 36,* 1213–1220.

Weinberg, W. A., & Emslie, G. J. (1991). Attention deficit hyperactivity disorder: The differential diagnosis. *Journal of Child Neurology, 6* (Suppl.), S23–S36.

Weinberg, W. A., &. Harper, C. R. (1993). Vigilance and its disorders. *Neurologic Clinics, 11,* 59–78.

Welch, R. L., Huston-Stein, A., Wright, J. C., & Plehal, R. (1979). Subtle sex-role cues in children's commercials. *Journal of Communication, 29*(3), 202–209.

Wiener, E. L. (1964). Transfer of training in monitoring: Signal amplitude. *Perceptual and Motor Skills, 18,* 104.

Williams, T. M., Baron, D., Phillips, S., Travis, L., & Jackson, D. (1986, August). *The portrayal of sex roles on Canadian and U.S. television.* Paper presented to the working group on sex roles at the conference of the International Association for Mass Communication Research, New Delhi, India.

Winn, M. (1977). *The plug-in drug.* New York: Viking.

Wright, J. C., Calvert, S. L., Huston-Stein, A., & Watkins, B. A. (1980, May). *Children's selective attention to television forms: Effects of salient and informative production features as functions of age and viewing experience.* Paper presented at the meeting of the International Communication Association, Acapulco, Mexico.

Wright, J. C., & Huston, A. C. (1981). The forms of television: Nature and development of television literacy in children. In H. Gardner & H. Kelly (Eds.), *Viewing children through television* (pp. 73–88). San Francisco: Jossey-Bass.

Wright, J. C., Huston, A. C, Ross, R. P., Calvert, S. L., Rolandelli, D., Weeks, L. A., et al. (1984). Pace and continuity of television programs: Effects on children's attention and comprehension. *Developmental Psychology, 20,* 653–666.

Yerkes, R. M., & Dodson, J. D. (1908). The relation of strength of stimulus to rapidity of habit formation. *Journal of Comparative and Neurological Psychology, 18,* 459–482.

Zillmann, D. (1982). Television viewing and arousal. In D. Pearl, L. Bouthilet, & J. Lazar (Eds.), *Television and behavior: Ten years of scientific progress and implications for the eighties* (Vol. 2, pp. 53–67). Washington, DC: U.S. Government Printing Office.

Zillmann, D., & Bryant, J. (1983). Uses and effects of humor in educational ventures. In P. E. McGhee & J. H. Goldstein (Eds.), *Handbook of humor research: Vol. 2. Applied studies* (pp. 173–193). New York: Springer-Verlag.

Zillmann, D., Williams, B. R., Bryant, J., Boynton, K. R., & Wolf, M. A. (1980). Acquisition of information from educational television programs as a function of differently paced humorous inserts. *Journal of Educational Psychology, 72,* 170–180.

CHAPTER 10

Effects of Prosocial Media Content on Children's Social Interactions

MARIE-LOUISE MARES
University of Wisconsin-Madison

EMORY H. WOODARD
Villanova University

Over the years, public and scholarly attention has focused on the accumulation of evidence that television contributes to violence and hostility. (See Sparks, Sparks, & Sparks, 2009, for a review.) The possibility that television viewing may also foster friendly, prosocial interactions has received less attention (Mares & Woodard, 2005). The aim of this chapter is to discuss the weight of evidence that television viewing and other forms of media use can have positive effects on children's social encounters and to review the conditions under which such effects are strongest.

There is no inherent reason why exposure to television content should have only negative effects, and in fact, the same mechanisms used to explain antisocial outcomes of media experiences are also used to explain prosocial ones. Observational learning of behaviors and social scripts has been used to explain both aggression (Bandura, Ross, & Ross, 1963) and helping behavior (Friedrich & Stein, 1975). Berkowitz (1984) suggested that cognitive priming could predict both prosocial and antisocial responses to media portrayals, depending upon the nature of the portrayal.

In an effort to create a more parsimonious model that combines the overlapping features of these theories, Anderson and his colleagues (e.g., Buckley & Anderson, 2006) developed the General Learning Model (GLM), which describes the various pathways by which both prosocial and antisocial learning from the media can occur. The model proposes that a person's behavior is the result of personal variables such as attitudes, beliefs, goals, behavioral tendencies, previous experiences, and emotions, as well as situational variables such as media, objects, settings, and other people. These personal and situational variables can affect behavior by altering the individual's thoughts (cognitions), emotions, and level of arousal.

Another promising model for explaining prosocial effects of entertainment programming is found in Moyer-Gusé's (2008) explication of the processes involved in effective entertainment-education campaigns. In entertainment-education, social issue messages (e.g., encouraging condom use) are embedded into popular media content. Using social cognitive theory and the extended elaboration likelihood model, Moyer-Gusé (2008) suggested that entertainment programming fosters narrative and character involvement through parasocial interaction, identification, and increased liking. Narrative and character involvement (including a sense of transportation) reduces viewer resistance to embedded prosocial messages, increasing the likelihood of message-consistent attitudes and behaviors. Though, just as GLM could be used to explain prosocial and antisocial effects, the entertainment-education model forecasts not only reduced resistance to shows with a positive message, but also content that is more violent in nature.

But What *Is* Prosocial?

Most of the broad theoretical definitions of prosocial behavior include the idea of voluntary, intentional actions that result in benefits for another person (Eisenberg & Miller, 1987; Radke-Yarrow & Zahn-Waxler, 1986) or society at large (Rushton, 1979). Most recently, Smith et al. (2009) slightly narrowed these boundaries by arguing that prosocial behavior had to be legal and had to involve actions beyond simple sociability or duties associated with the person's role.

Our focus here (as elsewhere in our research, e.g., Mares & Woodard, 2005) is on the use of media to encourage or enable children to interact with each other in friendly, inclusive ways. Thus, the outcome variables of interest are all related to the idea of positive interactions (e.g., friendly play, inclusiveness, aggression reduction, altruism, and stereotype reduction). This approach is consistent with recent reconceptualizations of prosocial behavior (Ostrov, Gentile, & Crick, 2006) and, indeed, with middle-school children's own conceptualizations of what it means to be a nice person (Greener & Crick, 1999). Nonetheless, Greener (2000) made a compelling point that in extremely hostile environments, being kind and inclusive may, at times, be inconsistent with the ability to function within that environment. Therefore, we acknowledge that the benefits and costs of particular acts vary by the context in which they are performed, and ideally, theorizing and research should begin to consider the effects of context.

Policy Issues Around the Definition of Prosocial Programming

Producers and regulators face the same questions about what to consider prosocial or educational. Kunkel (1991, 1998) outlined the history of struggles between producers, advocacy groups such as Action for Children's Television, and regulators over what should constitute prosocial and educational programming and how many hours per week should be required. We do not attempt to duplicate Kunkel's expert recounting of these epic battles. However, it is worth noting that, prior to the 1990 Children's Television Act, there were no real attempts on the part of regulators to define such content, let alone to regulate how much of it there should be on television or what time it should be shown.

In the 1990 Children's Television Act, policy makers stated that programs would meet requirements for children's educational or informational content if they "further[ed] the positive development of the child in any respect, including the child's cognitive/ intellectual or emotional/social needs" (Federal Communications Commission [FCC], 1991, p. 2114). It was left to the broadcaster to determine what this would mean and when the programming should be aired. To clarify apparent confusion in the industry and to increase compliance with the law, the FCC enacted a processing guideline known as the *3-hour rule* that went into effect in 1997. Under the 3-hour rule, broadcasters who wish to have their license renewals expedited are required to air a minimum of 3 hours a week of educational and informational (E/I) television that meets the cognitive/intellectual or social/emotional needs of children. The E/I programs must be specifically designed for children ages 16 and under and must air between the hours of 7:00 a.m. and 10:00 p.m. Broadcasters are required to place an on-air symbol at the beginning of E/I programs to indicate to the public that they are educational, and they must provide this information to listing services such as the local newspaper and *TV Guide.*

Content analyses (e.g., Schmitt, 1999) suggest that a substantial proportion of E/I programming has continued to focus on socio-emotional messages rather than on traditional academic content related to reading, science, or math. This emphasis on life lessons makes sense for producers because general themes such as honesty or friendship can be targeted toward fairly broad audiences (rather than the narrow age-ranges needed for meaningful teaching of academic content) and can be embedded within entertaining narratives rather than taught as an obvious piece of education. The challenge, of course, is in figuring out how to make sure that such programs are effective. In early 2007, the Federal Communications Commission decided to fine Univision $24 million because it claimed in its submissions for license renewals to have met the E/I requirement by showing a telenovela about twins separated at birth (Labaton, 2007). Thus, the struggle to define and evaluate prosocial content is an ongoing and serious issue.

How Much Prosocial Content Is There on Television?

Early content analyses conducted in the United States during the 1970s found considerable variability in the frequency with which various types of prosocial behaviors were presented. Liebert and Poulos (1975) analyzed broadcasting programming for 1974 and reported that, although there were an average of 11 altruistic acts and 6 sympathetic behaviors per hour of programming, resistance to temptation and control of aggressive impulses occurred less than once per hour (see also Poulos, Harvey, & Liebert, 1976). Liebert and Sprafkin (1988) concluded that children watching during the 1970s (when a number of the studies discussed in this chapter were

conducted) were exposed to a fair number of prosocial interpersonal behaviors but few instances of self-control behaviors. Moreover, early content analyses also indicated that prosocial acts often appeared in the context of aggression (Greenberg, Edison, Korzenny, Fernandez-Collado, & Atkin, 1980).

In the 1990s, in the wake of the Children's Television Act, the Annenberg Public Policy Center conducted a series of content analyses of all children's programs aired over the course of a composite week in Philadelphia, a large urban media market. Woodard (1999) reported that 50% of all children's shows contained at least one social lesson. These were mostly concentrated in programming for preschool children: 77% of preschool children's programming contained a social lesson. PBS programming for children contained the most social lessons (72% of programs), followed by premium cable channels such as the Disney Channel and HBO (59% of children's programs).

Smith et al. (2006) examined the frequency and context of altruistic acts on U.S. television in 2005. They noted that there were approximately four instances of helping or sharing per hour in children's cable programming and close to three per hour in public broadcasting programming (a high proportion of which is children's content). Roughly half of all altruistic acts in children's cable or public broadcast programs were initiated and received by human characters; the rest were performed or received by animals or other anthropomorphic characters. Half or slightly less than half were in realistic contexts, and a number involved humor (21% in public broadcasting, 43% in children's cable).

How Do Children Interpret Prosocial Lessons in Books and on TV?

The research in this section suggests that prosocial narratives are not always interpreted in the ways that authors and producers intend. This may be in large part because of developmental changes in cognitive processing. In addition, research by Narvaez and her colleagues suggests that understanding the intended moral lesson of a story is particularly challenging for children because of developmental changes in children's moral schemas (see Narvaez, 2002). Judgments about *what* is bad and *why* it is bad are not the same for a 4-year-old and a 10-year-old or an adult. Thus, what seems like an obvious moral lesson to an adult may be much less clear to a youthful audience. For example, in one study, Narvaez, Gleason, Mitchell, and Bentley (1999) had 3rd and 5th graders and undergraduates read stories in which the main character faced a moral dilemma (e.g., whether to return extra change) and then choose which of four short messages and four short vignettes best captured the moral theme of the story. The 3rd graders chose the correct vignette only 11% of the time (well below the chance level of 25%). The 5th graders made the correct choice 45% of the time, compared to 91% for the undergraduates.

What about stories that children really *want* to read? Whitney, Vozzola, and Hofmann (2005) studied reactions to the Harry Potter series among 4th to 6th graders, 7th to 12th graders, undergraduates, and graduate students. How readers evaluated the characters (particularly the unpleasant but ultimately good character, Snape) varied considerably with age, amount of education, and amount of expertise. Those children who had read the books multiple times had more nuanced moral interpretations than those who had read them less often. Thus, texts with moral themes are often open to interpretation, and those interpretations are shaped to a large degree by cognitive and moral development. Not surprisingly, young children find it easier to identify moral themes and relate them to their own life if a story is realistic rather than a fable or folktale (Goldman, Reyes, & Varnhagen, 1984; Lehr, 1988).

Similar age patterns are found in research on children's understanding of televised narratives. For example, Rosenkoetter (1999) had 81 first, third, and fifth graders watch an episode of *The Cosby Show*, an American live-action situation comedy featuring the comedian Bill Cosby and his television family. Rosenkoetter identified six different moral issues in the episode he showed students (e.g., it is wrong to steal, wrong to lie, good to forgive). Virtually all students in each grade correctly identified at least one lesson, but it took rather more probing (up to five questions per lesson) to elicit the others. In another study reported in the same paper, only 32% of first graders and 46% of third graders correctly articulated the lesson of a different situation comedy, *Full House,* in which the main character had to decide whether to throw easy pitches to her boyfriend on an opposing baseball team and thereby make her team lose, or risk him not liking her any more. Thus, the more complex, unfamiliar lesson about weighing loyalties was more challenging.

Several studies have suggested that children are particularly likely to be confused by stories in which there is an initial moral error (e.g., a character refuses to play with a socially stigmatized individual) that is then overcome (ultimately the character learns better and plays happily with the former outcast). For example, Fisch, Brown, and Cohen (2001) showed 3- to 5-year-olds short vignettes from *Sesame Street* in which the characters faced an initial struggle that was then resolved. The children could remember that the characters' solution to competing over a toy was to share it, but they had difficulty remembering that the solution to the temptation to lie was to tell the truth. The authors suggested that being honest was difficult to represent concretely and that children were confused by a visual sequence in which the character contemplated lying.

Mares and Acosta (2008) examined kindergarteners' comprehension of an episode of the animated series, *Clifford the Big Red Dog,* which seemed to intend to teach positive attitudes toward people with disabilities. The story was about Clifford and his fellow dog friends who learned to overcome their initial reactions to a dog who only had three legs. One of the friends was afraid of the three-legged dog and remained so for the substantial majority of the episode—until the brief happy ending. Despite the fact that kindergarteners were at the upper end of the target range for the program, children in both conditions found it difficult to identify the moral lesson. In many instances, they took the story at face value, regarding it only as a story about being kind to three-legged dogs. Among those who saw the original version, some of the open-ended characterizations of the lesson were the opposite of that intended, suggesting that watching the episode increased anxiety about germs rather than fostering greater tolerance toward people with disabilities. In a follow-up study (discussed in more detail later in this chapter), Mares and Acosta (2010) found similar miscomprehension of episodes from other programs where the story had the same narrative structure (initial hostility followed by brief friendliness).

Finally, there is also considerable evidence that children who are acquiring social schemas (or frameworks) about how the world operates often have difficulty noticing and remembering events that do not fit within those schemas. That is, nontraditional portrayals designed to alter stereotypes have to fight against the cognitive processes at play in early childhood. For example, Bigler and Liben (1993) had children listen to stories in which African American and European American characters interacted. In one condition, the African American character was lazy (or mean, or dirty); in the counter-stereotypical condition, the African American character was presented positively and the European American character held the negative attributes. Children who were more cognitively mature and could classify stimuli along multiple dimensions were better able to remember the counter-stereotypical story. Less advanced children and those who initially held the most negative racial stereotypes often misremembered the counter-stereotypical stories. In their version, the attributes were reversed to conform to their initial perceptions that the African American character would have the negative attributes. Other studies have demonstrated the same memory reversals for depictions of counter-stereotypical gender roles (e.g., Cordua, McGraw, & Drabman, 1979; Liben & Signorella, 1993).

All of these are studies of children's interpretations of content rather than studies of the effects of such content on children's behavior or attitudes. Obviously, one need not always understand the producer's intent or the details of the plot in order for positive effects of exposure to occur. However, in instances where children focus on depictions of conflict rather than happy endings or when they misremember story elements to conform to their preexisting schemas, then prosocial effects seem relatively unlikely.

What, then, do studies of exposure to prosocial content find? We focus first on the effects of televised content because that is where the majority of research has been done, but we then consider effects of other media in later sections.

Investigating Prosocial Effects

Correlational Studies

Most correlational studies report only small effects of home viewing of prosocial content, particularly if the researchers control for background demographic variables. For example, in an early study, Sprafkin and Rubinstein (1979) asked 500 middle-class 7- to 9-year-olds in the United States how often they watched each of 55 television series (later coded for frequency of prosocial and antisocial acts). Two weeks later, the children and teachers completed a roster rating measure indicating which children in their classroom engaged in specific behaviors such as helping, sharing, or trying to make others feel good. Prosocial television viewing was only weakly related to nominations after controlling for background variables (partial r = .12). Total television viewing was negatively related to prosocial nominations.

The implication that children's regular television diets tend not to promote prosocial outcomes for young viewers is supported by two additional studies. Rosenkoetter, Huston, and Wright (1990) found that for a sample of 72 kindergartners (but not second or fourth graders), heavy television viewing (as measured by mothers' reports) was moderately associated with less advanced moral reasoning on a variety of measures. More recently, Linder and Gentile (2009) asked 5th-grade girls to list their three favorite programs and asked the girls' teachers to rate the girls' behavior in school. The authors noted that children's programs had roughly the same amount of verbal aggression as and even more physical aggression than general audience programs. Having favorite programs with more physical aggression was associated with lower teacher ratings of prosocial behavior (r = −.29).

Rosenkoetter (1999) studied first- and third-grade children's exposure to prosocial adult situation comedies (i.e., judged to be high in prosocial content by a panel of undergraduates and mothers' reports about the frequency with which their child shared, helped others, and so on. He found a significant positive relationship (.57) between prosocial situation comedy viewing and prosocial behavior, but only among 1st graders (not 3rd graders) and without any controls except for gender. In a second study reported in the same paper, Rosenkoetter found a small, marginally significant correlation between viewing prosocial adult situation comedies and mothers' ratings of their child's behavior, but only among children who were able to identify the moral lesson in a sample episode of *Full House* (a family situation comedy). There was no relationship between prosocial viewing and behavior among the children who did not perform well on this task. This finding fits with our suggestion that young viewers may often have difficulty understanding the intended lesson, which may, in turn, limit the positive outcomes of viewing.

Mares and Acosta (2010) studied a U.S. sample of 128 four- to six-year-olds and found no significant relationships between children's self-reported frequency of viewing 20 programs that purportedly taught inclusiveness and positive interactions and children's interest in having classmates of a different race, ethnicity, or gender. There were also no significant effects on students' level of moral reasoning about short scenarios in which children excluded someone of a different gender.

It is worth noting that Abelman (1985) found that the strength of the relationship between watching prosocial TV programs and children's reports about how they would react in hypothetical social dilemmas (e.g., coping with bullies) depended on family style. He surveyed mothers of fourth- and fifth-grade children about their disciplinary styles (inductive techniques such as reasoning, explanation, and appeals to the child's pride vs. sensitizing techniques such as physical punishment and deprivation of privileges or objects). Children whose parents used inductive disciplinary techniques showed a stronger relationship (r = .48) between prosocial TV viewing and prosocial solutions than children whose parents used sensitizing techniques (r = .14). Thus, prosocial media messages viewed at home may have stronger effects when they resonate with messages from other sources, such as parents.

Longitudinal Studies

As we noted earlier, longitudinal studies allow researchers to examine how prosocial viewing and outcomes unfold, but they are rare, given the labor involved. To our knowledge, there are only a few longitudinal studies of self-selected prosocial television viewing and prosocial outcomes.

Wiegman, Kuttschreuter, and Baarda, (1992) studied 466 second- and third-grade children in the Netherlands for a period of 3 years. Every year, children's prosocial and antisocial exposure was measured by the frequency of viewing specific programs, and prosocial behavior was assessed by peer nominations. Wiegman and his colleagues found no sign of positive relationships between prosocial viewing and prosocial behavior. If anything, the relationships tended to be very weakly negative rather than positive. The researchers noted that watching prosocial content was very highly correlated (i.e., r = .90) with watching antisocial content; children who saw the most prosocial content were simply heavy television viewers and thus were exposed to numerous antisocial models as well.

In a more recent longitudinal study of self-selected exposure, Ostrov et al. (2006) investigated the effects of favorite TV programs and movies on the aggressive and prosocial behaviors of 76 preschoolers (average age was 47 months at the start of the investigation) over a 2-year period separated into four phases with approximately 4 months between phases. At each of the four phases, the researchers coded the children's preschool interactions in term of physical and verbal aggression, relational aggression (i.e., gossiping, spreading malicious rumors, lies, ignoring, and exclusion) and prosocial behavior (e.g., sharing, helping, including others in activities). They also collected teacher reports of behavior. Media exposure was assessed in Phase 2 by having parents list the child's three favorite TV shows and three favorite movies or videos and rate how violent and educational they considered each to be.

Watching more educational content at home in Phase 2 was associated with less physical aggression four months later, even after controlling for the child's earlier levels of physical aggression (partial r = −.32). However, the researchers reported that among girls, watching more educational content in Phase 2 was also associated with more (rather than less) relational aggression at Phase 4 (r = .61), though they did not report the analyses controlling for initial relational aggression. The authors noted that relational aggression appeared relatively frequently in many programs that parents considered educational (such as *Arthur* and ABC's *One Saturday Morning*) and suggested that these storylines may be particularly salient for girls. The authors did not report any significant effects of Phase 2 educational viewing on subsequent prosocial behaviors.

Although much of their work remains proprietary and unpublished, researchers at Sesame Workshop have repeatedly used international co-productions of *Sesame Street* to try to promote inclusive, positive attitudes in areas where there is long-standing, deep-seated political tension. Clearly, these are interventions under challenging circumstances. Cole et al. (2003) examined what happened when two related co-productions of *Sesame Street* aired in Israel and Palestine. The producers' initial goal was that the versions would be parallel: The Israeli version would feature positive images of Arabs as well as scenes of friendly interactions between Israeli and Palestinian characters; the Palestinian version would similarly feature positive images of Israeli Jews and friendly interactions. The researchers measured children's initial attitudes before the program was broadcast and then reassessed the attitudes 4 months after the programs began airing. The children's levels of exposure to the programs and the context of their viewing (home or school, with adults or without) were not recorded but there was no intervention to make them watch the program.

Among the 113 Jewish Israeli children, there were positive changes in attitudes over the time period of the study. That is, when asked, "What is an Arab?" the percent of negative responses such as "dirty" or "makes war against us" decreased from 19% to 6%, and the number of relatively positive responses, such as "from a different country" or "is nice" increased from 35% to 82%. In addition, significantly more children said that both Arab and Jewish children engaged in various activities, indicating increased recognition of similarity between the two groups. Among the 63 Arab Israeli children (who were exposed to the same version because they lived in Israel), there was a significant increase (from 29% to 53%) in positive responses to the question, "What is a Jew?" though other outcomes did not change significantly.

The 99 Palestinian children saw a different version of the program that ultimately was not parallel to the Israeli version. There were fewer episodes and less emphasis on cross-group interactions and positive depictions of the out-group. Rather, the focus was on positive depictions of Palestinian culture, which was seldom represented on television at the time. In contrast to the other two groups, Palestinian children's negative responses to "What is a Jew?" increased over the 4 months, from 61% to 75%.

Caution is needed in making causal attributions about any of these changes, given the complexity of the real-world context over the 4-month period and the lack of measurement of children's exposure. On the other hand, the results suggest that when particular issues are extremely salient (such as land and religion in the Israeli–Palestinian context), media representations can operate in conjunction with the social environment to have important positive or negative effects, rather than the weak effects that often seem to prevail when the issues are less vivid.

Experimental Studies

Effects of One-Time Exposure to Different Depictions

Most experiments on the effects of prosocial depictions of children's generosity or helping behavior were conducted during the 1970s. They typically involved showing children a short film in which a child model behaved in a positive or negative way. Afterward, children were placed in a similar situation and their behaviors were observed.

For example, Elliott and Vasta (1970) showed 5- to 7-year-old children a film about "Johnny the birthday boy" who got candy for his birthday from his parents and chose to mail some of it to another little boy whose parents were too poor to buy candy. Some of the children saw Johnny perform the action without being rewarded, some saw Johnny get rewarded with a teddy bear, and some saw Johnny get the teddy bear and be praised as "a good boy." (There was no true control group.) Afterward, the children were asked to pretend that it was their birthday and were given a large bag of candies and were given the opportunity to put some in an envelope for a little boy "who has no candy and no money" (Elliot & Vasta, 1970, p. 10). To observe whether the learning generalized to a similar but not identical behavior, they were then given a pile of pennies and allowed to decide whether to put some in a box for the unfortunate child. Elliott and Vasta found no significant difference between the no-reward and the teddy-bear-reward conditions in terms of number of candies or pennies donated, but the combination of reward and praise led to more items being donated. They also noted that older children donated more than younger children did.

In another well-known early study of helping behavior, Poulos, Rubinstein, and Liebert (1975) randomly assigned 30 first-grade children to one of three viewing conditions: a prosocial episode of *Lassie* in which Jeff risked his life to save a puppy; a neutral episode of *Lassie*; or a neutral episode of *The Brady Bunch*. Afterward, the children were shown how to play a game in which they could accumulate points by pressing a button. The more points they earned, the larger the prize they would win. At the same time, they were asked to listen to puppies in a distant kennel and to push a help button if the puppies seemed distressed. As children played the game, the recorded puppy sounds grew increasingly loud and intense. The researchers measured the average number of seconds children spent pushing the help button (thereby sacrificing points in the game). Children who saw the prosocial episode pushed the help button nearly twice as long as did children in the other two conditions.

What about friendly, inclusive play? Gorn, Goldberg, and Kanungo (1976) assigned 205 White, English Canadian children 3- to 5-years old to watch 12 minutes of *Sesame Street* programming with multicultural inserts or without the inserts. The children were then shown two sets of four photos taken from the inserts. One set contained White children and the other showed Asian and Indian children. The child then chose which of the photographed children should be brought to the nursery school the next day. The control group that did not see the inserts showed a marked preference for playing with the White children rather than the Asian and Indian children (67% vs. 33%). This was reversed among children who saw the multiracial inserts; 71% preferred the Asian and Indian children and 29% preferred Whites. However, in a second study, when children were tested a day after exposure, those who saw the multicultural inserts were no longer significantly more interested in nonwhite playmates than those who had not seen the inserts (Goldberg & Gorn, 1979).

Other experiments in which the researchers attempted to alter children's social role judgments or beliefs by showing characters in nontraditional roles also found mixed or limited effects. For example, Pingree (1978) showed 227 children in third and eighth grade commercials featuring women in either traditional or nontraditional roles. One third of the children were told that those they would see were real people who actually did the things portrayed, one third were told that they would see actors who did not do such things in real life, and the final third were given no instructions. The third graders and the eighth-grade girls showed reduced stereotyping in the nontraditional condition, particularly when they were told that these were real people. However, among eighth-grade boys, there appeared to be something of a contrary reaction; stereotyping was significantly higher in the nontraditional condition than in the traditional condition.

Experiments With Longer, Repeated Exposure

Given that children often watch the same material repeatedly (Mares, 1998), one possibility is that with repetition, they would come to understand the material better, including the intended prosocial lessons. The evidence for the benefits of repetition is mixed. Presumably, the effects depend on how much repetition there is and how consistent the prosocial message.

Persson and Musher-Eizenman (2003) compared the effects of showing European American preschoolers 10 minutes of pro-diversity television programming that either featured animated humans, puppets that resembled humans, or live humans. None of the conditions reduced children's preferences for photographs of Caucasians rather than photographs of Blacks and Asians or their preferences for White Fisher-Price Little People dolls rather than Black and Asian Little People dolls. In a second study reported in the same paper, children watched the same episode four times over 12 days. Although children who saw the episode repeatedly understood some of the basic elements of the plot slightly better, their preferences did not change.

In a study of stereotype reduction, O'Bryant and Corder-Bolz (1978) showed 67 children who were 5 to 10 years old nine half-hour cartoons over a month. Embedded in each cartoon were commercials for a fruit juice drink. In the traditional condition, the commercials featured a female telephone operator, fashion model, file clerk, and manicurist. In the nontraditional condition, the commercials featured a female pharmacist, welder, butcher, and laborer. Over the course of the month, children saw many repetitions of the commercials. Comparisons between pre- and posttest scores on tests of occupational stereotyping found that children exposed to the nontraditional commercials were significantly more likely to say that a traditionally male job was also appropriate for a woman. Moreover, girls in the nontraditional condition gave higher ratings to traditionally male jobs when asked how much they would like to have that job in the future. Boys' ratings of future interest in traditionally male jobs were lower in the experimental condition—apparently, seeing a woman in those roles was a deterrent. This effect is consistent with Pingree's (1978) findings of a backlash among boys and underlines the point that seemingly prosocial content can have unintended effects on subgroups.

Elias (1983) examined whether videos could be used as one component of treatment for boys with serious emotional and educational disturbances. The 10 videos, shown twice a week for 5 weeks, portrayed realistic scenarios of common problematic situations such as teasing and bullying, dealing with peer pressure, learning how to express feelings, and coping with new social situations. After watching each video, the boys were encouraged to discuss what they had seen and how they felt about it. The boys were measured on a variety of behavioral and emotional outcomes related to interactions, both for 3 months before and 2 months after the video series. Compared with control children who did not see the videos, experimental participants were rated by their counselors as less emotionally detached, less isolated, having improved in their ability to delay gratification, and having decreased in overall personality problems. These effects were still evident 2 months after the intervention.

Positive, though small, effects were also observed in D. R. Anderson et al.'s (2000) 2-year long longitudinal study of 120 children, aged 2 to 5 years old, and their exposure to *Blue's Clues*. Initially none of the children in the study had access to the program; subsequently, children who had access and watched regularly were compared with those who did not have access. By the end of the second year, caregiver ratings of prosocial behaviors (e.g., helping others) were 9% higher for regular viewers of *Blue's Clues* than for nonviewers.

Experiments Combining Prosocial TV Content With Related Curriculum

Friedrich and Stein conducted a series of studies on prosocial effects using *Mister Rogers' Neighborhood*. In the first study (Friedrich & Stein, 1973), 93 preschool children watched television or films 12 times over a 4-week period. The prosocial group watched *Mister Rogers' Neighborhood;* the aggressive group watched *Batman* and *Superman;* and the control group watched neutral films (e.g., about farms and animals). Observers rated the children's aggressive and prosocial behavior during free play for 3 weeks before the experimental period, during the 4-week experimental period, and then for 2 weeks afterward. Children who watched *Mister Rogers' Neighborhood* showed several positive changes. They persisted longer on tasks, were more likely to obey rules, and were more likely to delay gratification without protest. In addition, children from families with lower socioeconomic status also showed an increase in prosocial playground interactions (e.g., more cooperation and friendliness). These effects continued, though they tapered off somewhat, over the 2-week post-viewing period. Children from higher socioeconomic backgrounds had initially been more prosocial, and they did not change significantly after seeing *Mister Rogers' Neighborhood.* Despite the positive effects of watching *Mister Rogers* as part of the preschool day, there was no correlation between the frequency of watching *Mister Rogers' Neighborhood* at home and children's baseline measures of prosocial behavior.

In a second study, Friedrich and Stein (1975) assigned 73 kindergarten children to watch four episodes of *Mister Rogers' Neighborhood* and receive differing types of training: verbal labeling (children were taught to describe how characters had felt and behaved) and role playing (children used hand puppets to reenact scenes from the episodes). Over the next few days, the children were tested for their memory of the content and their willingness to help. Helping related to the program was assessed by observing whether the child helped a puppet from the program during a reenactment of one of the scenes. More generalized helping was measured by observing how children responded when shown a torn collage that had been made and accidentally damaged by another child. Friedrich and Stein found slightly higher helping behaviors among the children who had watched *Mister Rogers' Neighborhood* than among those in the control group. For boys, the role-playing training appeared to strengthen the effects of the program, and verbal labeling was actually associated with some decreases in helping.

In their third project, Friedrich-Cofer, Huston-Stein, Kipnis, Susman, and Clewett (1979) focused on the effects *of Mister Rogers' Neighborhood* on "urban poor children" (p. 637). They had 141 children in urban Head Start programs watch 20 episodes over a period of 8 weeks. Comparisons

were made between children who watched *Mister Rogers* at the Head Start Center without any additional prosocial materials; those who watched it and also had access to prosocial books, games, and so on; and those who watched it, had access to the prosocial materials, and also had follow-up activities such as verbal labeling and role playing. A control group simply saw neutral films. Friedrich-Cofer et al. (1979) found that *Mister Rogers' Neighborhood* alone produced relatively few behavioral changes. Those who watched the program and had access to the prosocial materials became more active overall; they had more positive interactions but more aggressive interactions as well. Children who watched the program and also received training in role playing and verbal label showed significant increases in positive social interactions without any increases in aggression.

In all three of these studies, then, *Mister Rogers' Neighborhood* did have some positive effects, but the effects were much stronger when viewing was accompanied by activities designed to explicitly teach the types of behaviors modeled in the program. Similarly, Singer and Singer (1983) reported that children who saw short television segments in the context of lessons emphasizing prosocial themes and activities were more likely to show increases in prosocial behaviors than were those who saw the segments without the additional training.

Singer and Singer (1998) conducted a series of studies evaluating the effectiveness of *Barney & Friends.* In the first study, 121 preschool children, largely from White, middle-class families, were assigned to one of four groups. The first group watched 10 episodes of *Barney* over 2 weeks, with each episode followed by a lesson designed to expand on the message of the episode. The second group watched the 10 episodes without the follow-up lessons. The third group received the lessons without watching the program, and the fourth group simply followed the usual day care routine. Children were pre- and posttested on their knowledge of the material presented in the programs, including lessons from *Barney* about good manners. The pattern of results was very consistent. Children showed the strongest gains when viewing was combined with follow-up lessons, moderate gains from viewing without the lessons, and negligible gains just from the lessons. In a second study reported in the same paper, the Singers investigated whether the same strong positive effects would be observed with children of lower socioeconomic status and greater ethnic and racial diversity. Within each day care, children were assigned to one of three groups: *Barney & Friends* with follow-up lessons, *Barney & Friends* without the lessons, or a control group that received no special treatment. In this study, the pattern of results was somewhat different. The viewing-plus-lessons group performed significantly better on most measures of learning from the program, but there were no consistent significant effects of watching the program without the lessons. Moreover, there were no effects of either viewing condition on measures related to good manners and civility.

In one of the largest and most impressive studies of stereotype reduction, Johnston and Ettema (1982) examined the effectiveness of *Freestyle*. Their field experiment involved more than 7,000 fourth- through sixth-grade children in seven sites across the United States. Classrooms were randomly assigned to watch 26 episodes of *Freestyle*, a public television program designed to reduce stereotypes about gender roles. Children were assigned to watch the program in school and to engage in teacher-led discussions about the material, watch it at school without any such discussions, or watch it at home. The students completed extensive questionnaires before seeing any episodes and then after the exposure period. Compared with a control group, there were significant positive changes in perceptions of personal ability and interest in various types of jobs and reductions in stereotypes about gender roles in employment. These effects were strongest when the program was viewed in the classroom and accompanied by teacher-led discussions. Much smaller effects were observed among students who simply watched the program in school or at home.

Connolly, Fitzpatrick, Gallagher, and Harris (2006) examined the effects of a pro-tolerance ad campaign aired on commercial television in Northern Ireland. The goals of the short, animated skits depicting children playing in a park were to teach preschool viewers to recognize social exclusion and to encourage them to play with children from various socially stigmatized out-groups, such as Chinese children and those with eye-patches (a common correction for astigmatism at the time). Of particular interest, given the historical context of long-standing conflict between Catholics and Protestants in the area, was a skit that depicted interactions between children from both religious/cultural groups. Each 2-minute ad featured a character who initially expressed fear or distaste about another child (e.g., "I never go and play with her 'cause her skin's not like mine."). That discomfort was then quickly resolved by the need to cooperate (e.g., getting a kite down from a tree).

Connolly and his associates (2006) compared the pre-post scores of 193 children, aged 3 and 4, who watched the ads in preschool and spent half an hour a day for three weeks on related curriculum, with the pre-post scores of 88 children in the control condition. Seeing the ads in school accompanied by teacher-led explanations and activities was associated with increased awareness of the emotional consequences of being excluded and increased willingness to play with hypothetical Chinese girls (but not boys) and hypothetical girls with eye patches (but not boys with eye patches). There was no effect on children's willingness to play with the religious out-group (Protestants/Catholics). The authors noted that children were relatively positive about the religious out-groups to begin with (hence there were ceiling effects). However, they also noted that teachers tended not to discuss this topic out of concern about parents' reactions.

Overall, the results of experimental interventions in which viewing is accompanied by related activities and curriculum are generally encouraging, particularly in comparison to the weaker or nonexistent effects observed without such additional materials.

Meta-Analyses of Prosocial Effects

Meta-analyses involve averaging statistical information across studies on a particular topic in order to estimate the overall strength of an effect. In an early meta-analysis, Hearold

(1986) analyzed 230 studies on television and social behavior published prior to 1978 and compared positive and negative outcomes of viewing. Her estimate of the average strength of antisocial effects combined a variety of outcomes such as aggression, criminal behavior, and stereotyping. Her estimate of the average prosocial effect size included a wide range of positive outcomes, including friendly interactions, imagination, buying books, library use, safety activism, and "conversation activism." Hearold concluded that positive effects of viewing were twice as strong and more enduring than antisocial effects, both in the laboratory and in more natural conditions.

Two more recent meta-analyses suggest that positive and negative effects may be roughly equivalent in strength, at least if they are more narrowly defined. Paik and Comstock (1994) provided a partial update of Hearold's (1986) estimates of antisocial effects, limiting their analysis to studies of the effects of television violence on viewer aggression or criminal activity. They reported an overall negative effect of violent television content that was approximately double the antisocial effect found by Hearold. Whereas she had reported very weak antisocial effects (equivalent to a Pearson correlation of .15), they reported a correlation of .32.

Inspired by Paik and Comstock (1994), we updated Hearold's (1986) estimates of prosocial outcomes, including a number of studies published after Hearold's cut-off date of 1978 (Mares & Woodard, 2005). Our final estimate of the effect of prosocial content was virtually the same as Hearold's: Prosocial content had a weak to moderate effect (roughly equivalent to a Pearson correlation of .27). Not surprisingly, effects were stronger when the content depicted specific behaviors that were identical to the outcomes measured after viewing (e.g., donating candy) than when the researchers were studying whether children could generalize to other behaviors or were examining the effects of broad prosocial themes.

Negative Effects of Combining Antisocial and Prosocial Content

Based on a small handful of studies available at the time, the results of our meta-analysis suggested that combining initial antisocial content with a short prosocial outcome might be particularly problematic (Mares & Woodard, 2005). Across several studies, children who watched aggressive-prosocial content compared to those who watched purely prosocial content (i.e., with no initial aggression or hostility) had more negative outcomes (r = .39). For example, Silverman and Sprafkin (1980) had children aged 3 to 7 watch 16 minutes of *Sesame Street* featuring either initial conflict followed by peaceful resolution or prosocial-only interactions. Control groups saw material with no social lessons. Pairs of children then played a marble game designed to measure cooperation: They could maximize the number of marbles they both got by taking turns, or they could ruin each other's chances by pulling simultaneously. Silverman and Sprafkin found that the prosocial-only conditions had virtually no effect on cooperation measured by the marble game; scores were equivalent to those in the control group. The conflict-resolution strategy seemed to backfire: Children who saw the conflict tended to cooperate *less* than those in the control group.

Similarly, Liss, Reinhardt, and Fredriksen (1983) showed children either a nonaggressive excerpt of a *Superfriends* cartoon, or one in which the superheroes used aggression to teach someone not to steal. Those who saw the aggressive (though ultimately prosocial) content were subsequently less cooperative than those who saw the nonaggressive content, and in a subsequent interview, they showed less comprehension of the plot and moral lesson of the episode.

Most recently, Mares and Acosta (2010) assigned 4- to 6-year-olds to watch one of two TV episodes that appeared designed to teach inclusiveness, but which did so by depicting initial hostility (either between boys and girls or between cats and mice) followed by friendliness. Half the children in each condition saw the episodes with short audiovisual inserts at the beginning and middle that explained the intended lesson and criticized the initial hostility; half saw them as originally aired. A control group watched a *Berenstain Bears* episode about helping out with chores. Afterward, children were asked to indicate which of a variety of hypothetical classmates they would like to have in class and to evaluate an exclusion scenario in which children of one gender were reluctant to play with a child of the opposite gender.

Those who saw the boy–girl episode as originally aired (without inserts) showed significantly less prosocial reasoning about the gender exclusion scenario than the control group and were significantly less likely to show gender balance in their choice of hypothetical classmates; those who saw it with the inserts did not differ significantly from the control group. Children who saw the cat–mouse episode as originally aired (without inserts) did not differ from the control group; those who saw it with inserts showed significantly more prosocial reasoning about gender-based exclusion than the control group. Children's evaluations of the initial hostility in the episode and their understanding of the intended moral lesson provided partial mediation of the effects of viewing condition. Thus, the use of an initial moral error (such as prejudice) to teach an ultimate moral lesson (such as inclusiveness) may be effective for young viewers, but only if their interpretations of the content fall in line with the producers' intent. Sometimes they appear to need help with those interpretations.

To be fair, there are instances where this storyline seems to work. Truglio, Kotler, Cohen, and Housley-Juster (2005) reported on the effects of a *Sesame Street* episode in which Big Bird's pen pal, Gulliver, was briefly unwilling to play with anyone who was not a bird. After being confronted by Big Bird ("If you don't want to play with my friend, then I don't want to play with you!"), he learned better. Children gave significantly more positive responses to a hypothetical exclusion scenario a week after watching the episode than they had before they saw it. On the other hand, in another study reported in the same paper, Truglio et al. (2005) described the effects of an episode in which Telly Monster fantasized about beating up another character who kept taking his triangles. Although the story ended positively, children who saw the episode gave more negative responses when asked what a child should do in a parallel situation than they had before they saw the episode. Presumably, the differences in outcomes of the two studies

had to do with the visual salience of the initial negative behavior and the speediness of the prosocial resolution.

Prosocial Effects of Other Media

Teaching With Storybooks

What evidence is there that reading or listening to stories can alter children's attitudes or behaviors in social interactions? In one study, Cameron and Rutland (2006) assigned 67 children aged 5 to 10 years old in the United Kingdom to listen to six stories over six weeks, featuring children interacting happily with peers who had learning or physical disabilities. The stories were based on real, age-appropriate books but were modified to feature different levels of emphasis on the fictional characters' disabilities. In the neutral condition, the stories featured nondisabled and disabled children in friendship and adventure situations where the fact of differences in ability was mentioned only once, at the beginning of each story. In the "decategorization" condition, the idea was to help the listeners perceive children with disabilities as individuals with unique qualities. Thus, the fact of the character's disability was mentioned only once, and in addition to depicting the friendship, the stories and subsequent discussion emphasized the individual characteristics of each of the characters, such as their kindness, or their fondness for chocolate, or their enjoyment of computer games. The "intergroup" condition was intended to help listeners perceive the connections between the positive qualities of the characters in the stories and real-world exemplars of children with disabilities. Thus, the stories and discussion placed more emphasis on the distinction between characters with and without disabilities and specifically mentioned that the characters in each group were typical of others in their category and that there were many others who were similar.

Children in the intergroup condition (i.e., emphasizing real-world typicality of disabled characters) showed significant improvement in their attitudes toward others with disabilities. Children in the other two conditions did not show significant changes, though all children were fairly positive in their attitudes. Finally, when asked how they would react if they met a hypothetical disabled acquaintance from school, children in the intergroup and decategorization (all characters are individuals) conditions showed significantly more positive responses after the intervention than before. Those in the neutral condition showed no significant changes.

In a similar study, Cameron, Rutland, Brown, and Douch (2006) examined the effects of listening to stories about refugee children living in the United Kingdom. Once again, the stories featured friendships between two groups (in this case, English children and refugee children) and were based on preexisting, age-appropriate books. As before, in the decategorization condition, the stories and subsequent discussions only mentioned refugee status briefly and went on to emphasize the individual qualities of the story characters. In the "common ingroup identity" condition, the characters in the stories (both refugee and English) went to the same school as the listeners and had the same teacher and principal. The discussion focused on the school connection between the listener and characters and the exploration of additional similarities. In the "dual identity" condition, the stories featured the common identity of the same school but the narrative and subsequent discussion also emphasized refugee status (English or refugee) and the typicality of characters as exemplars of their group. As in the study of attitudes toward children with disabilities, participants' attitudes and intended behaviors were measured 1 to 2 weeks after the 6-week intervention.

Children in all three story conditions had significantly more positive attitudes toward refugees compared to children who did not hear any stories. However, the effects were significantly stronger for those who heard the dual identity stories that emphasized the typicality of the characters compared to those who heard the stories that emphasized individualism or common identity without typicality. With regard to intended behavior, there were no effects of condition among older children, but among younger children, those who heard the common identity and the dual identity/typicality stories thought they would behave more positively than those who heard the stories that emphasized individual characteristics.

Taken together, the two studies suggest that stories can significantly alter attitudes and intended behavior and that encouraging children to see story characters as typical of real-world group members but also sharing similarities with themselves (as in the dual identity group condition) is particularly helpful.

Prosocial Effects of Video Games

In an early study of the effects of video game play, Chambers and Ascione (1987) assigned 160 students in 3rd, 4th, 7th, and 8th grade to play either a prosocial or aggressive video game, either singly or cooperatively, or not to play any game. The prosocial game (*Smurfs*) involved rescuing a character after avoiding a series of hazards. The aggressive game involved boxing. After playing the game, children were given $1.00 in nickels and were left alone to donate as many nickels as they wished in a donation box "For Logan's Poor." They were also given the option of helping the experimenter by sharpening pencils for another project or reading quietly. Those who played the prosocial game, whether alone or cooperatively, did not differ from the control group on either measure of prosocial behavior. More recently, an experiment with college undergraduates provided (somewhat mixed) evidence that playing a violent, shooting video game (*Halo*) cooperatively rather than alone or competitively was associated with less aggressive cognitions but not less aggressive affect (Schmierbach, 2010).

Gentile et al. (2009) conducted a series of studies on the effects of prosocial video game play. In the first, the authors surveyed 727 Singaporean middle-school students, asking them to list their three favorite games, to estimate the time per week spent playing them, and to rate how often the characters in the game helped versus hurt or killed others. (The authors noted that the students' estimates of prosocial and antisocial character behavior were highly correlated with expert content analyses for a subset of the games.) Students' prosocial orientations were assessed with self-reports of helping, cooperation, sharing, empathy, and emotional awareness. Although prosocial and violent game exposure were highly related, prosocial game exposure was significantly positively related to all of the prosocial outcomes (particularly helping and sharing) after statistically controlling for total amount of gaming, violent game exposure, gender, and age.

To assess the direction of causality, the authors then conducted longitudinal surveys with 5th-, 8th-, and 11th-grade students in Japan, assessing both their game playing and prosocial behaviors twice, with four months between the two assessments. At both times of measurement, students rated how often in the previous month they had played video games in which characters helped one another or there were scenes of friendships or parent–child affection. Students were also asked how often in the previous month they had engaged in four prosocial behaviors. The authors found both that those children who were initially most prosocial played more prosocial games four months later *and* that children who played more prosocial games initially reported more prosocial behaviors four months later. The strength of these two relationships was very similar. The authors interpreted this as indication of an upward spiral of prosocial gaming and behavior. Their conclusions about the causal effects of prosocial video game play were further strengthened by an experiment with college students in the United States, in which those who were assigned to play prosocial games (*Super Mario Sunshine* or *Chibi Robo*) were subsequently more helpful and less hurtful to a partner in a tangram task, relative to those who played neutral or violent games. (See Chapter 13 in this volume for a fuller discussion of prosocial effects of video games.)

Prosocial Effects of Music

To our knowledge, very little research has been done on the effects of listening to music on children's prosocial behaviors. Rickson and Watkins (2003) reported on a pilot intervention in which 15 youths with substantial aggressive behavior and other emotional or learning difficulties were assigned to music therapy or a control group. The music therapy consisted of 8 weeks of listening to self-selected music, playing rhythms, and discussing each other's choices. The authors reported no effects of the intervention, though this is hardly surprising given the gravity of the youths' psychological condition and the small

sample size. A study examining the effects of background music during math class on the behavior of 10 similarly troubled children found some effects on reducing disruptive classroom behavior as well as the children's math performance (Hallam & Price, 1998).

Two studies with adults suggested that soothing music elicited more helping behavior than aversive or no music (Fried & Berkowitz, 1979) and that upbeat music was associated with more helping behavior (distributing leaflets to help charity) than "annoying" music (North, Tarrant, & Hargreaves, 2004). More recently, Greitemeyer (2009a) conducted a series of three experiments with college students in Germany. In the first, students were assigned to listen either to two songs with prosocial lyrics or to songs by the same artists with neutral lyrics. Those who heard the prosocial lyrics showed greater accessibility of prosocial cognitions (as assessed by the choice of letters to complete word fragments, e.g., *help* vs. *here*). In the second experiment, those who heard prosocial songs reported feeling more empathy for the authors of two essays describing personal hardship. In the third experiment, participants who listened to a song with prosocial lyrics were more likely to donate their study participation incentive (2 €) than participants who listened to a song with neutral lyrics. In a subsequent study, Greitemeyer (2009b) demonstrated that empathy functioned as a mediator in the relationship between exposure to prosocial song lyrics and helping behavior. This work has yet to be conducted with child audiences.

Conclusion

When we wrote the earlier version of this chapter 10 years ago, we bewailed the fact that there was far more research on negative effects of media than on positive outcomes. This is still undoubtedly the case—but the field has changed considerably nonetheless. Theorizing has expanded to acknowledge that the same processes that can cause antisocial outcomes are also at work for prosocial effects. There are more studies (including more longitudinal work) of the effects of exposure to prosocial content, across a broader range of media, with more socially important outcome variables. These are all extremely hopeful signs. Not surprisingly, the basic lesson remains the same: Television and other media are not a magic bullet for instant social improvement, but they can be used for positive ends in conjunction with other prosocial influences.

References

Abelman, R. (1985). Styles of parental disciplinary practices as a mediator of children's learning from prosocial television portrayals. *Child Study Journal, 15,* 131–145.

Anderson, D., Bryant, J., Wilder, A., Santomero, A., Williams, M., & Crawley, A. (2000). Researching *Blue's Clues*: Viewing behavior and impact. *Media Psychology, 2,* 179–194.

Bandura, A., Ross, D., & Ross, S. A. (1963). Imitation of film-mediated aggressive models. *Journal of Abnormal and Social Psychology, 66,* 3–11.

Berkowitz, L. (1984). Some effects of thoughts on anti- and prosocial influences of media events: A cognitive-neoassociation analysis. *Psychological Bulletin, 95*(3), 410–427.

Bigler, R. S., & Liben, L. S. (1993). A cognitive-developmental approach to racial stereotyping and reconstructive memory in Euro-American children. *Child Development, 64*(5), 1507–1518.

Buckley, K. E., & Anderson, C. A. (2006). A theoretical model of the effects and consequences of playing video games. In P. Vorderer & J. Bryant (Eds.), *Playing video games—Motives, responses, and consequences* (pp. 363–378). Mahwah, NJ: Lawrence Erlbaum.

Cameron, L., & Rutland, A. (2006). Extended contact through story reading in school: Reducing children's prejudice toward the disabled. *Journal of Social Issues, 62,* 469–488.

Cameron, L., Rutland, A., Brown, R., & Douch, R. (2006). Changing children's intergroup attitudes toward refugees: Testing different models of extent contact. *Child Development, 77,* 1208–1219.

Chambers, J. H., & Ascione, F. R. (1987). The effects of prosocial and aggressive videogames on children's donating and helping. *The Journal of Genetic Psychology, 148*(4), 499–505.

Cole, C. F., Arafat, C., Tidhar, C., Tafesh, W. Z., Fox, N. A., Killen, M., et al. (2003). The educational impact of *Rechov Sumsum/Shara'a Sim sim: A Sesame Street* television series to promote respect and understanding among children living in Israel, the West Bank and Gaza. *International Journal of Behavioral Development, 27,* 409–422.

Connolly, P., Fitzpatrick, S., Gallagher, T., & Harris, P. (2006). Addressing diversity and inclusion in the early years in conflict-affected societies: A case study of the Media Initiative for Children in Northern Ireland. *International Journal of Early Years Education, 14,* 263–278.

Cordua, G. D., McGraw, K. O., & Drabman, R. S. (1979). Doctor or nurse: Children's perception of sex typed occupations. *Child Development, 50*(2), 590–593.

Eisenberg, N., & Miller, P. (1987). The relation of empathy to prosocial and related behaviors. *Psychological Bulletin, 101,* 91–119.

Elias, M. J. (1983). Improving coping skills of emotionally disturbed boys through television-based social problem solving. *American Journal of Orthopsychiatry, 53,* 61–72.

Elliott, R., & Vasta, R. (1970). The modeling of sharing: Effects associated with vicarious reinforcement, symbolization, age, and generalization. *Journal of Experimental Child Psychology, 10,* 8–15.

Federal Communications Commission. (1991). Policies and rules concerning children's television programming: Memorandum opinion and order. *Federal Communications Commission Record, 6,* 2111–2127.

Fisch, S. M., Brown, S. K. M., & Cohen, D. I. (2001). Young children's comprehension of educational television: The role of visual information and intonation. *Media Psychology, 3,* 365–378.

Fried, R., & Berkowitz, L. (1979). Music hath charms . . . and can influence helpfulness. *Journal of Applied Social Psychology, 9,* 199–208.

Friedrich, L., & Stein, A. H. (1973). Aggressive and prosocial television programs and the natural behavior of preschool children. *Monographs of the Society for Research in Child Development, 38*(4, Serial No. 151).

Friedrich, L., & Stein, A. H. (1975). Prosocial television and young children: The effects of verbal labeling and role playing on learning and behavior. *Child Development, 46,* 27–38.

Friedrich-Cofer, L. K., Huston-Stein, A., Kipnis, D. M., Susman, E. J., & Clewett, A. S. (1979). Environmental enhancement of prosocial television content: Effect on interpersonal behavior, imaginative play, and self-regulation in a natural setting. *Developmental Psychology, 15,* 637–646.

Gentile, D. A., Anderson, C. A., Yukawa, S., Ihori, N., Saleem, M., Ming, L. K., et al. (2009). The effects of prosocial video games on prosocial behaviors: International evidence from correlational, longitudinal, and experimental studies. *Personality and Social Psychology Bulletin, 35,* 752–763.

Goldberg, M. E., & Gorn, G. J. (1979). Television's impact on preferences of non-white playmates: Canadian "Sesame Street" inserts. *Journal of Broadcasting, 23,* 27–32.

Goldman, S. R., Reyes, M., & Varnhagen, D. (1984). Understanding fables in first and second languages. *NABE Journal, 8,* 35–66.

Gorn, G. J., Goldberg, M. E., & Kanungo, R. N. (1976). The role of educational television in changing the intergroup attitudes of children. *Child Development, 42,* 277–280.

Greenberg, B. S., Edison, N., Korzenny, F., Fernandez-Collado, C., & Atkin, C. K. (1980). Antisocial and prosocial behaviors on television. In B. S. Greenberg (Ed.), *Life on television: Content analyses of U.S. TV drama* (pp. 99–128). Norwood, NJ: Ablex.

Greener, S. (2000). Peer assessment of children's prosocial behaviour. *Journal of Moral Education, 29,* 47–60.

Greener, S., & Crick, R. C. (1999). Normative beliefs about prosocial behavior in middle childhood: What does it mean to be nice? *Social Development, 8,* 349–363.

Greitemeyer, T. (2009a). Effects of songs with prosocial lyrics on prosocial thoughts, affect, and behavior. *Journal of Experimental Social Psychology, 45*(1), 186–190.

Greitemeyer, T. (2009b). Effects of songs with prosocial lyrics on prosocial behavior: Further evidence and a mediating mechanism. *Personality and Social Psychology Bulletin, 35*(11), 1500–1511.

Hallam, S., & Price, J. (1998). Can the use of background music improve the behavior and academic performance of children with emotional and behavioural difficulties? *British Journal of Special Education, 25,* 88–91.

Hearold, S. (1986). A synthesis of 1,043 effects of television on social behavior. In G. Comstock (Ed.), *Public communication and behavior* (Vol. 1, pp. 65–133). New York: Academic Press.

Johnston, J., & Ettema, J. S. (1982). *Positive images: Breaking stereotypes with children's television.* Beverly Hills, CA: Sage.

Kunkel, D. (1991). Crafting media policy: The genesis and implications of the Children's Television Act of 1990. *American Behavioral Scientist, 35,* 181–202.

Kunkel, D. (1998). Policy battles over defining children's educational television. *Annals of the American Academy of Political and Social Science, 557,* 39–53.

Labaton, S. (2007, February 24). Record fine expected for Univision. *New York Times.* Retrieved May 24, 2010, from http://www.nytimes.com/2007/02/24/business/24fcc.html

Lehr, S. (1988). The child's developing sense of theme as a response to literature. *Reading Research Quarterly, 23,* 337–357.

Liben, L., & Signorella, M. (1993). Gender-schematic processing in children: The role of initial interpretations of stimuli. *Developmental Psychology, 29,* 141–149.

Liebert, R. M., & Poulos, R. W. (1975). Television and personality development: The socializing effects of an entertainment medium. In A. Davids (Ed.), *Child personality and psychopathology: Vol. 2. Current topics* (pp. 61–97). New York: John Wiley.

Liebert, R. M., & Sprafkin, J. (1988). *The early window: Effects of television on children and youth.* New York: Pergamon.

Linder, J. R., & Gentile, D. A. (2009). Is the television rating system valid? Indirect, verbal, and physical aggression in programs viewed by fifth grade girls and associations with behavior. *Journal of Applied Developmental Psychology, 30,* 286–297.

Liss, M. B., Reinhardt, L. C., & Fredriksen, S. (1983). TV heroes: The impact of rhetoric and deeds. *Journal of Applied Developmental Psychology, 4*(2), 175–187.

Mares, M. L. (1998). Children's use of VCRs. *Annals of the American Academy of Political and Social Science, 557,* 120–132.

Mares, M. L., & Acosta, E. E. (2008). Be kind to three-legged dogs: Children's literal interpretations of TV's moral lessons. *Media Psychology, 11,* 377–399.

Mares, M. L., & Acosta, E. E. (2010). Teaching tolerance via TV narratives in the US: Young viewers need help with the message. *Journal of Children and Media, 4,* 231–247.

Mares, M. L., & Woodard, E. (2005). Positive effects of television on children's social interactions: A meta-analysis. *Media Psychology, 7*(3), 301–322.

Moyer-Gusé, E. (2008). Toward a theory of entertainment persuasion: Explaining the persuasive effects of entertainment-education messages. *Communication Theory, 18*(3), 407–425.

Narvaez, D. (2002). Does reading moral stories build character? *Educational Psychology Review, 14,* 155–171.

Narvaez, D., Gleason, T., Mitchell, C., & Bentley, J. (1999). Moral theme comprehension in children. *Journal of Educational Psychology, 91,* 477–487.

North, A. C., Tarrant, M., & Hargreaves, D. J. (2004). The effects of music on helping behavior: A field study. *Environment and Behavior, 36*(2), 266–275.

O'Bryant, S. L., & Corder-Bolz, C. R. (1978). The effects of television on children's stereotyping of women's work roles. *Journal of Vocational Behavior, 12,* 233–244.

Ostrov, J. M., Gentile, D., & Crick, N. (2006). Media exposure, aggression and prosocial behavior during early childhood: A longitudinal study. *Social Development, 15(4),* 612–627.

Paik, H., & Comstock, G. (1994). The effects of television violence on antisocial behavior: A meta-analysis. *Communication Research, 21,* 516–546.

Persson, A., & Musher-Eizenman, D. R. (2003). The impact of a prejudice-prevention television program on young children's ideas about race. *Early Childhood Research Quarterly, 18,* 530–546.

Pingree, S. (1978). The effects of nonsexist television commercials and perceptions of reality on children's attitudes about women. *Psychology of Women Quarterly, 2,* 262–277.

Poulos, R. W., Harvey, S. E., & Liebert, R. M. (1976). Saturday morning television: A profile of the 1975–76 children's season. *Psychological Reports, 39,* 1047–1057.

Poulos, R. W., Rubinstein, E. A., & Liebert, R. M. (1975). Positive social learning. *Journal of Communication, 25,* 90–97.

Radke-Yarrow, M., & Zahn-Waxler, C. (1986). The role of familial factors in the development of prosocial behavior: Research findings and questions. In D. Olweus, J. Block, & M. Radke-Yarrow (Eds.), *Development of antisocial and prosocial behavior: Research, theories, and issues* (pp. 207–233). New York: Academic Press.

Rickson, D. J., & Watkins, W. G. (2003). Music therapy to promote prosocial behaviors in aggressive adolescent boys—A pilot study. *Journal of Music Therapy, 40,* 283–301.

Rosenkoetter, L. I. (1999). The television situation comedy and children's prosocial behavior. *Journal of Applied Social Psychology, 29,* 979–993.

Rosenkoetter, L., Huston, A., & Wright, J. (1990). Television and the moral judgment of the young child. *Journal of Applied Developmental Psychology, 11,* 123–137.

Rushton, J. P. (1979). Effects of prosocial television and film material on the behavior of viewers. In L. Berkowitz (Ed.), *Advances in experimental social psychology* (pp. 321–351). New York: Academic Press.

Schmierbach, M. (2010). "Killing spree": Exploring the connection between competitive game play and aggressive cognition. *Communication Research, 37,* 256–274.

Schmitt, K. L. (1999). *The three hour rule: Is it living up to expectations?* (Report No. 30).

Philadelphia: University of Pennsylvania, Annenberg Public Policy Center.

Silverman, L. T., & Sprafkin, J. N. (1980). The effects of *Sesame Street's* prosocial spots on cooperative play between young children. *Journal of Broadcasting, 24,* 135–147.

Singer, J. L., & Singer, D. G. (1983). Implications of childhood television viewing for cognition, imagination, and emotion. In J. Bryant & D. R. Anderson (Eds.), *Children's understanding of television* (pp. 265–295). New York: Academic Press.

Singer, J. L., & Singer, D. G. (1998). *Barney & Friends* as entertainment and education. In J. K. Asamen & G. Berry (Eds.), *Research paradigms, television, and social behavior* (pp. 305–367). Thousand Oaks, CA: Sage.

Smith, S. L., Smith, S. W., Pieper, K. M., Downs, E., Yoo, J. H., Bowden, B., et al. (2009). Measuring prosocial behavior, altruism, and compassionate love on US television. In B. Fehr, S. Sprecher, & L. G. Underwood (Eds.), *The science of compassionate love: Theory, research, and applications* (pp. 53–77). Hoboken: NJ: Wiley-Blackwell.

Smith, S. W., Smith, S. L., Pieper, K. M., Yoo, J. H., Ferris, A. L., Downs, E., et al. (2006). Altruism on American television: Examining the amount of, and context surrounding, acts of helping and sharing. *Journal of Communication, 56(4),* 707–727.doi:10.1111/j.1460-2466.2006.00316.x

Sparks, G. G., Sparks, C. W., & Sparks, E. A. (2009). Media violence. In J. Bryant & M. B. Oliver (Eds.), *Media effects: Advances in theory and research* (3rd ed., pp. 269–324). New York: Routledge.

Sprafkin, J. N., & Rubinstein, E. A. (1979). Children's television viewing habits and prosocial behavior: A field correlational study. *Journal of Broadcasting, 23,* 265–276.

Truglio, R. T., Kotler, J. A., Cohen, D. I., & Housley-Juster, A. (2005). Modeling life skills on *Sesame Street. Televizion, 18,* 15–19.

Whitney, M. P., Vozzola, E. C., & Hofmann, J. (2005). Children's moral reading of *Harry Potter*: Are children and adults reading the same books? *Journal of Research in Character Education, 3,* 1–24.

Wiegman, O., Kuttschreuter, M., & Baarda, B. (1992). A longitudinal study of the effects of television viewing on aggressive and prosocial behaviors. *British Journal of Social Psychology, 31,* 147–164.

Woodard, E. H. (1999). *The 1999 state of children's television report: Programming for children over broadcast and cable television* (Report No. 28). Philadelphia: University of Pennsylvania, Annenberg Public Policy Center.

CHAPTER 11

The Media and Children's Fears, Anxieties, and Perceptions of Danger

JOANNE CANTOR
University of Wisconsin-Madison

Television, movies, and other media provide a multitude of images that have the capacity to worry, frighten, or even traumatize children. Moreover, the intensity and variety of these images have grown over the last generation. This may be a function of the huge expansion in the number of cable channels, which makes available a wide variety of sensational, violent, and disturbing content any time of day. Furthermore, the popularity of round-the-clock news channels, which compete with each other to attract the largest audience, has led to an increasing display of video footage of catastrophic and sensational events (Klite, Bardwell, & Salzman, 1997). The fact that nearly everyone seems to have a gadget that can capture video images means that more and more disturbing images wind up on television (Cantor, 2009a).

New developments in media technology have also made children's emotional disturbances more likely. As televisions have become cheaper, more and more homes have multiple TVs. Recent data indicate that more than two thirds of 8- to 18-year-olds have a television in their bedroom (e.g., Rideout, Foehr, & Roberts, 2010). Moreover, the wide adoption of computers has given youth ready access to pornography, sadistic violence, and YouTube fare that goes well beyond what commercial media present. And young people's enthusiasm for portable electronic devices such as cell phones, smart phones, and video game consoles means that they have access to all sorts of disturbing content practically all the time. A 2010 report by the Kaiser Family Foundation showed a dramatic increase in the amount of time youth spend with media. The media are so essential to young people's daily lives that a *New York Times* story on the release of the Kaiser report was headlined, "If Your Kids are Awake, They're Probably Online" (Lewin, 2010).

Although the impact of media violence on children's aggressive behavior has been at the center of research debates and public attention for decades, the impact of images of violence, danger, death, and destruction on children's perceptions, worries, and fears has received much less attention.

The Impact of Habitual Viewing Practices on Perceptions, Fears, and Anxieties

One way in which the impact of media on children's perceptions and worries has been studied is by the "cultivation" paradigm, in which a child's amount of television viewing is related to his or her perceptions of how dangerous the world is (e.g., Gerbner, Gross, Morgan, & Signorielli, 1994). One of the assumptions underlying this body of work is that the most important features of the television landscape pervade all forms of programming. Accordingly, predictions about a child's view of the world are made on the basis of how much television a child watches—independent of his or her choice of particular shows. The research of Gerbner and his associates (1994) has shown, for example, that heavy television viewers perceive the chances of being involved in violence as greater than light viewers do. They are also more prone to believe that others cannot be trusted (e.g., Gerbner, Gross, Morgan, & Signorielli, 1980).

Although cultivation analysis has been criticized for the assumption that television content is rather homogeneous (Hawkins & Pingree, 1981), research has documented the association between heavy television viewing, independent of program choice, and negative emotional consequences. A survey of more than 2,000 third through eighth graders in Ohio public schools revealed that, as the number of hours of television viewing per day increased, so did the prevalence of symptoms of psychological trauma such as anxiety, depression, and posttraumatic stress (Singer, Slovak, Frierson, & York, 1998). Similarly, a survey of the parents of almost 500 public school children in kindergarten through fourth grade in Rhode Island revealed that the amount of children's television viewing (especially television viewing at bedtime) and having a television in their own bedroom were significantly related to sleep disturbances (Owens et al., 1999). Although these survey data cannot rule out the alternative explanation that children experiencing trauma or sleep difficulties are more likely to turn to television for distraction, they are consistent with the conclusion that exposure to frightening and disturbing images on television contributes to a child's level of stress and anxiety. Indeed, 9% of the parents in the study by Owens et al. (1999) reported that their child experienced TV-induced nightmares at least once a week. More recent research further documented that media exposure can cause sleep disturbances in children (Johnson, Cohen, Kasen, First, & Brook, 2004; Paavonen, Pennonen, Roine, Valkonen, & Lahikainen, 2006; Van den Bulck, 2004).

Effects of Exposure to Individual Programs and Movies

The fright-producing impact of media depictions has most often been studied in terms of the immediate emotional impact of specific programs and movies, and the study of children's fright reactions to media fare goes back long before the introduction of television. For example, as early as the 1930s, Blumer (1933) reported that 93% of the children he questioned said they had been frightened or horrified by a motion picture. More recently, about 75% of the respondents in two separate samples of preschool and elementary school children said that they had been scared by something they had seen on television or in a movie (Wilson, Hoffner, & Cantor, 1987). Cantor and Nathanson (1996) indicated that 43% of a random sample of parents of elementary school children in Madison, Wisconsin, said that their child had experienced enduring fright as a function of exposure to television. In the first random national survey of its kind in the United States, Gentile and Walsh (1999) stated that 62% of parents with children between the ages of 2 and 17 said that their child had become scared that something they saw in a TV program or movie might happen to them. Finally, in a random national survey of 7- to 12-year-old children in the Netherlands, 31% of the respondents reported having been frightened by television during the preceding year (Valkenburg, Cantor, & Peeters, 2000).

An experimental study explored the impact of witnessing scary media events on the subsequent behavioral choices of children in kindergarten through fifth grade (Cantor & Omdahl, 1991). In this experiment, exposure to dramatized depictions of a deadly house fire or a drowning increased children's self-reports of worry about similar events in their own lives. More important, these fictional depictions affected the children's preferences for normal, everyday activities that were related to the tragedies they had just witnessed. Children who had seen a movie depicting a drowning expressed less willingness to go canoeing than did other children; those who had seen the program about a house fire were less eager to build a fire in a fireplace. Although the duration of such effects was not measured, the effects were undoubtedly short-lived because debriefings were employed and safety guidelines were taught so that no child would experience long-term distress (Cantor & Omdahl, 1999).

There is growing evidence, in fact, that the fear induced by mass media exposure is often intense and long-lasting, with sometimes debilitating effects (Cantor, 1998). In a study designed to assess the severity of enduring fright reactions to media, Johnson (1980) asked a random sample of adults whether they had ever seen a motion picture that had disturbed them "a great deal." Forty percent replied in the affirmative, and the median length of the reported disturbance was 3 days. Respondents also reported on the type, intensity, and duration of symptoms such as nervousness, depression, fear of specific things, and recurring thoughts and images. On the basis of these reports, Johnson judged that 48% of these respondents (19% of the total sample) had experienced, for at least 2 days, a "significant stress reaction" as the result of watching a movie. Johnson argued the following:

> It is one thing to walk away from a frightening or disturbing event with mild residue of the images and quite another thing to ruminate about it, feel anxious or depressed for days, and/or to avoid anything that might create the same unpleasant experience. (p. 786)

On the basis of his data, Johnson concluded that such reactions were more prevalent and more severe than had previously been assumed.

Retrospective studies of adults' detailed memories of having been frightened by a television show or movie provide more evidence of the severity and duration of media-induced fear (Harrison & Cantor, 1999; Hoekstra, Harris, & Helmick, 1999). In these studies, involving samples of undergraduates from three universities, the presence of vivid memories of enduring media-induced fear was nearly universal. All of the participants in the Hoekstra, Harris, and Helmick (1999) research reported such an incident. In the Harrison and Cantor (1999) study, 90% reported an intense fear reaction to something in the media, despite the fact that the respondents could receive full extra credit for participating in the study, and thereby would avoid writing a paper and filling out a three-page questionnaire, if they simply said "no" (meaning "I never had such an experience").

As for the effects reported, both studies revealed a variety of intense reactions. In Hoekstra et al.'s (1999) study, 61% reported a generalized fear or free-floating anxiety after viewing; 46% reported what they called "wild imagination" (e.g., monsters under the bed or someone sneaking up on you); 29% reported a specific fear (e.g., sharks, power tools, spiders); and more than 20% reported a variety of sleep disturbances, including fear of sleeping alone, nightmares, insomnia, or needing to sleep with the lights on. Of the students reporting fright reactions in Harrison and Cantor's (1999) study, 52% reported disturbances in eating or sleeping, 22% reported mental preoccupation with the disturbing material, and 35% reported subsequently avoiding or dreading the situation depicted in the program or movie. Moreover, one third of those who reported having been frightened said that the fear effects had lasted more than a year. Indeed, more than one fourth of the respondents said that the emotional impact of the program or movie (viewed an average of 6 years earlier) was still with them at the time of reporting.

A recent study solicited children's retrospective reports of having been scared by particular media offerings (Cantor, Byrne, Moyer-Gusé, & Riddle, 2010). Of the sample of elementary school children interviewed, 76% reported having been frightened by something on TV or in a movie. When these children were asked to indicate which side-effects they experienced, 71% said that they couldn't stop thinking about the program or movie, 59% reported sleep problems, 51% said they worried about it, and 44% said that they didn't want to do something that reminded them of what they had seen. When asked to describe the side-effects in their own words, they typically mentioned being afraid of the dark, fearing their own bedroom or bathroom, fearing media exposure, and being afraid to be alone. Of those children who said they had been afraid to do something after exposure to the scary media, 23% said the fear was still ongoing at the time of the interview.

The news is often a source of long-term fears in children. Although younger children are less often exposed to and affected by the news than older children and adults, a catastrophic news story such as those around the terrorist attacks of September 11, 2001, can have intense effects on all ages. For example, a study of children in New York City schools (Applied Research and Consulting et al., 2002) reported a broad range of mental health problems 6 months after the 9/11 attacks, including agoraphobia (15%), separation anxiety (12%), and posttraumatic stress disorder (11%). Children who reported heavy exposure to the news coverage had higher rates of posttraumatic stress disorder (PTSD) than children with less television exposure. This was true for children living near Ground Zero as well as for those inhabiting the rest of New York City. Reports of intense reactions to the terrorist attacks were documented in children in other parts of the country as well (e.g., Saylor, Cowart, Lipovsky, Jackson, & Finch, 2003; Smith, Moyer, Boyson, & Pieper, 2002).

The most extreme stress reactions to media reported in the literature come from psychiatric case studies in which acute and disabling anxiety states enduring several days to several weeks or more (some necessitating hospitalization) are said to have been precipitated by the viewing of horror movies such as *The Exorcist, Invasion of the Body Snatchers,* and *Ghostwatch* (Buzzuto, 1975; Mathai, 1983; Simons & Silveira, 1994). Most of the patients in the cases reported had not had previously diagnosed psychiatric problems, but the viewing of the film was seen as occurring in conjunction with other stressors in the patients' lives.

Limited Evidence for Catharsis or Anxiety Reduction

Given the prevalence of intense anxiety reactions to scary media images, the question naturally arises as to why horror films, violent fare, and other frightening images are so popular. A variety of theories have been advanced to account for the enduring popularity of frightening media. (See Goldstein, 1998, for a variety of viewpoints on the attractions of violence.) Prominent among the theories is the notion of sensation seeking (Zuckerman, 1979), which contends that risk taking helps individuals seek their optimal level of arousal. Apter (1992) argued that individuals can experience excitement rather than anxiety when confronting danger when the event is experienced through a *protective frame.* He further argued that our modern society, which has reduced most day-to-day threats to an individual's safety, makes it more necessary than ever to seek safe ways to experience excitement.

There have been some arguments, particularly in the psychoanalytic literature, that scary images in the media reduce rather than increase anxieties by allowing children to confront their real fears in a safe context. Bettelheim (1975) is most frequently associated with this argument, although his claims were related to violent fairy tales that are presented orally rather than to mass media presentations that involve moving images. In any event, no systematic evidence for this therapeutic effect of fairy tales has been presented (Cantor, 1998).

There are some limited circumstances, however, when a frightening media depiction might be effective in alleviating anxiety. This anxiety-reducing effect appears to occur only when the story induces no more than a mild level of fear and when the outcome of the story reveals that the danger can be effectively counteracted (Bryant, Carveth, & Brown, 1981; see also Cantor & Nathanson, 1997).

Instances in which frightening media depictions reduce anxiety seem to be the exception rather than the rule, especially when children are concerned. As detailed previously, many studies demonstrate that enduring emotional disturbances occur in a large proportion of children and that these responses are often intense and disruptive of a child's well-being.

Developmental Differences and Media-Induced Fear

A large body of research has examined two major developmental issues in fright reactions to media: (a) the types of mass media stimuli and events that frighten children at different ages, and (b) the strategies for preventing or reducing unwanted fear reactions that are most effective for different-aged children (Cantor, 2009b). Experiments and surveys have been conducted to test expectations based on theories and findings in cognitive development research. The experiments have had the advantage of testing rigorously controlled variations in program content and viewing conditions, using a combination of self-reports, physiological responses, the coding of facial expressions of emotion, and behavioral measures. For ethical reasons, only small excerpts from relatively mild stimuli are used in experiments. In contrast, the surveys have investigated the responses of children who were exposed to a particular mass media offering in their natural environment, without any researcher intervention. Although less tightly controlled, the surveys permit the study of responses to much more intensely frightening media fare.

Developmental Differences in the Media Stimuli That Produce Fright

One might expect that, as children get older, they become less and less susceptible to all media-produced emotional disturbances. However, this is not the case. As children mature cognitively, some things become less likely to disturb them, whereas other things become potentially more upsetting. This generalization is consistent with developmental differences in children's fears in general.

According to a variety of studies using diverse methodologies, children from approximately 3 to 8 years of age are frightened primarily by animals; the dark; supernatural beings such as ghosts, monsters, and witches; and anything that looks strange or moves suddenly. The fears of 9- to 12-year-olds are more often related to personal injury and physical destruction and the injury and death of family members. Adolescents continue to fear personal injury and physical destruction; in addition, school fears and social fears arise at this age, as do fears regarding political, economic, and global issues. (See Cantor, Wilson, & Hoffner, 1986, for a review; see also Laing, Fernyhough, Turner, & Freeston, 2009.)

Perceptual Dependence

The findings regarding the media stimuli that frighten children at different ages are consistent with observed changes in children's fears in general. This section summarizes broad generalizations and supportive findings. The first generalization about fright-provoking stimuli is that the relative importance of the immediately perceptible components of a fear-inducing media stimulus decreases as a child's age increases. Research on cognitive development indicates that, in general, very young children react to stimuli predominantly in terms of their perceptible characteristics and that, with increasing maturity, they respond more and more to the conceptual aspects of stimuli (see Flavell, 1963; Melkman, Tversky, & Baratz, 1981). Research findings support the generalization that preschool children (approximately 3–5 years old) are more likely to be frightened by something that *looks* scary but is actually harmless than by something that looks attractive but is actually harmful; for older elementary school children (approximately 9–11), appearance carries much less weight relative to the behavior or destructive potential of a character, animal, or object.

One set of data that supports this generalization comes from a survey conducted in 1981 (Cantor & Sparks, 1984) that asked parents to name the programs and films that had frightened their children the most. In this survey, parents of preschool children most often mentioned offerings with grotesque-looking, unreal characters, such as the television series

The Incredible Hulk and the feature film *The Wizard of Oz;* parents of older elementary school children more often mentioned programs or movies (e.g., *The Amityville Horror*) that involved threats without a strong visual component and that required a good deal of imagination to comprehend. Sparks (1986) replicated this study using children's self-reports rather than parents' observations and obtained similar findings. Both surveys included controls for possible differences in exposure patterns in the different age groups.

A second investigation that supported this generalization was a laboratory study involving an episode of *The Incredible Hulk* (Sparks & Cantor, 1986). In the 1981 survey of parents, this program had spontaneously been mentioned by 40% of the parents of preschoolers as a show that had scared their child (Cantor & Sparks, 1984). The laboratory study concluded that preschool children's unexpectedly intense reactions to this program were partially due to their overresponse to the visual image of the Hulk character. When participants were shown a shortened episode of the program and were asked how they had felt during different scenes, preschool children reported the most fear after the attractive, mild-mannered hero was transformed into the monstrous-looking Hulk. Older elementary school children, in contrast, reported the least fear at this time because they understood that the Hulk was really the benevolent hero in another physical form and that he was using his superhuman powers to rescue a character who was in danger.

Another study (Hoffner & Cantor, 1985) tested the effect of appearance more directly by creating four versions of a story in which a major character was either attractive and grandmotherly looking or ugly and grotesque. The character's appearance was factorially varied with her behavior; she was depicted as behaving either kindly or cruelly. In judging how nice or mean the character was and in predicting what she would do in the subsequent scene, preschool children were more influenced than older children (6–7 vs. 9–10 years) by the character's looks and less influenced than older children by her kind or cruel behavior. As the age of the child increased, the character's looks became less important and her behavior carried increasing weight.

A follow-up experiment revealed that all age groups engaged in physical-appearance stereotyping in the absence of information about the character's behavior.

Harrison and Cantor's (1999) retrospective study of fright responses also provided evidence in support of the diminishing influence of appearance. When descriptions of the program or movie that had frightened respondents were categorized as involving immediately perceptible stimuli (e.g., monstrous-looking characters, eerie noises) or not, the percentage of respondents whose described scene fell into the former category declined as the respondent's age at exposure increased.

Fantasy Versus Reality as Fear Inducers

A second generalization that emerges from research is that, as children mature, they become more responsive to realistic dangers and less responsive to fantastic dangers depicted in the media. The data on trends in children's fears suggest that very young children are more likely than older children and adolescents to fear things that are not real (i.e., their occurrence in the real world is impossible; e.g., monsters). The development of more mature fears seems to presuppose the acquisition of knowledge regarding the objective dangers posed by different situations. One important component of this knowledge includes an understanding of the distinction between reality and fantasy, a competence that develops only gradually throughout childhood (see Flavell, 1963; Kelly, 1981; Morison & Gardner, 1978; Rapaczynski, Singer, & Singer, 1982).

This generalization is supported by Cantor and Sparks's (1984) survey of parents. In general, the tendency to mention fantasy offerings (depicting events that could not possibly occur in the real world) as sources of fear decreased as the child's age increased, and the tendency to mention fictional offerings (depicting events that could possibly occur) increased. Again, Sparks (1986) replicated these findings using children's self-reports. Further support for this generalization comes from a study of children's fright responses to television news (Cantor & Nathanson, 1996). A random survey of parents of children in kindergarten and second, fourth, and sixth grade showed that fear produced by fantasy programs decreased as the child's grade increased, whereas fear induced by news stories increased with age. Valkenburg et al. (2000), in their random survey of Dutch children, also found a decrease in fright responses to fantasy content between the ages of 7 and 12.

Responses to Abstract Threats

The third generalization from research is that, as children mature, they become frightened by media depictions involving increasingly abstract concepts. This generalization is clearly consistent with the general sources of children's fears cited earlier. It is also consistent with theories of cognitive development (e.g., Flavell, 1963), which indicate that the ability to think abstractly emerges relatively late in cognitive development.

Data supporting this generalization come from a survey of children's responses to the television movie *The Day After* (Cantor et al., 1986). Although many people were concerned about young children's reactions to this movie, which depicts the devastation of a Kansas community by a nuclear attack (Schofield & Pavelchak, 1985), developmental considerations led to the prediction that the youngest children would be the least affected by it. In a random telephone survey of parents conducted the night after the broadcast of this movie, children under 12 were reportedly much less disturbed by the film than were teenagers, and parents were the most disturbed. The very youngest children seem to have been the least frightened. The findings seem to be due to the fact that the emotional impact of the film comes from the contemplation of the potential annihilation of the earth as we know it—a concept that is beyond the grasp of the young child. The visual depictions of injury in the movie were quite mild compared with what most children had become used to seeing on television.

A study of children's reactions to television coverage of the war in the Persian Gulf also supports the generalization that, as they mature, children are increasingly responsive to abstract as opposed to concrete aspects of frightening media (Cantor, Mares, & Oliver, 1993). In a random survey of the parents of children in public school in Madison, Wisconsin, that was conducted shortly after the Gulf War, there were no significant differences between 1st, 4th, 7th, and 11th graders regarding the prevalence or intensity of negative emotional reactions to television coverage of the war. However, children in different grades were upset by different aspects of the coverage. In their descriptions of the elements that had disturbed their child the most, parents of younger children, but not of adolescents, stressed the visual aspects of the coverage and the direct, concrete consequences of combat (e.g., the missiles exploding). As the child's age increased, the more abstract, conceptual aspects of the coverage (e.g., the possibility of the conflict spreading) were cited by parents as the most disturbing. More recently, Smith and Moyer-Gusé (2006) reported very similar developmental differences in 5- to 17-year-olds' fear responses to television coverage of the war in Iraq.

In summary, research on the relationship between cognitive development and emotional responses to television can be very helpful in predicting the types of television programs and movies that are more or less likely to frighten children of different ages. In addition to providing empirical tests of the relationship between cognitive development and affective responses, these developmental findings can help parents and other caregivers make more sensible viewing choices for children (Cantor, 1998).

Developmental Differences in the Effectiveness of Coping Strategies

No matter how well intentioned or careful or sensitive parents are to the emotional vulnerabilities of their children, children are likely to be frightened at one time or another by what they see on television. Research in cognitive development has also been used to determine the best ways to help children cope with fear-producing stimuli or to reduce children's fear reactions once they occur (Cantor, 1998).

Developmental differences in children's information-processing abilities yield differences in the effectiveness of strategies to prevent or reduce their media-induced fears

(Cantor & Wilson, 1988). The findings of research on coping strategies can be summed up in the following generalization: Preschool children benefit more from *noncognitive* than from *cognitive* strategies; both cognitive and noncognitive strategies can be effective for older elementary school children, although this age group tends to prefer cognitive strategies.

Noncognitive Strategies

Noncognitive strategies are those that do not involve the processing of verbal information and that appear to be relatively automatic. The process of visual desensitization, or gradual exposure to threatening images in a nonthreatening context, is one such strategy that has been shown to be effective for both preschool and older elementary school children. In one experiment, gradual visual exposure to filmed footage of snakes tended to reduce fear reactions to the "snake pit" scene from the action-adventure film *Raiders of the Lost Ark* (Wilson & Cantor, 1987). In a second experiment (Wilson, 1987), exposure to a realistic rubber replica of a tarantula reduced the emotional impact of a scene involving tarantulas in *Kingdom of the Spiders.* In a third experiment (Wilson, 1989a), exposure to a live lizard reduced children's expression of fear while watching a scene involving deadly lizards in *Frogs.* In a fourth experiment (Weiss, Imrich, & Wilson, 1993), exposure to graphic photographs of worms taken from the horror film *Squirm* reduced children's self-reports of fear during a scene from that movie. Finally, fear reactions to the Hulk character in *The Incredible Hulk* were reduced by exposure to footage of Lou Ferrigno, the actor who played the character, having his makeup applied so that he gradually took on the menacing appearance of the character (Cantor, Sparks, & Hoffner, 1988). None of these experiments revealed developmental differences in the technique's effectiveness.

Other noncognitive strategies involve physical activities such as clinging to an attachment object or having something to eat or drink. Although these techniques are available to viewers of all ages, there is reason to believe that they are more effective for younger than for older children. First, it has

been argued that the effectiveness of such techniques is likely to diminish as the infant's tendency to grasp and suck objects for comfort and exploration decreases (Bowlby, 1973). Second, it seems likely that the effectiveness of such techniques is partially attributable to distraction, and distraction techniques should be more effective in younger children, who have greater difficulty allocating cognitive resources to two simultaneous activities (e.g., Manis, Keating, & Morison, 1980).

Children seem to be aware that physical techniques work better for younger than for older children. In a study of children's *perceptions* of the effectiveness of strategies for coping with media-induced fright, preschool children's evaluations of holding onto a blanket or a toy and getting something to eat or drink were significantly more positive than were those of older elementary school children (Wilson et al., 1987). Harrison and Cantor's (1999) retrospective study also showed that the percentage of respondents who reported having used a behavioral (noncognitive) coping strategy to deal with media-induced fear declined as age at exposure to the frightening content increased.

Another noncognitive strategy that has been shown to have more appeal and more effectiveness for younger than for older children is covering one's eyes during frightening portions of a presentation. In an experiment by Wilson (1989b), when covering the eyes was suggested as an option, younger children used this strategy more often than older children. Moreover, the suggestion of this option reduced the fear of younger children but actually increased the fear of older children. Wilson noted that the older children recognized the limited effectiveness of covering their eyes (while still being exposed to the audio features of the program) and may have reacted by feeling *less* in control, and therefore more vulnerable, when this strategy was offered to them.

Cognitive Strategies

In contrast to noncognitive strategies, cognitive strategies involve the provision of information that is used to cast the threat in a different light. These strategies involve relatively complex cognitive operations, and research consistently finds such strategies to be more effective for older than for younger children.

When dealing with fantasy depictions, the most typical cognitive strategy seems to be to provide an explanation focusing on the unreality of the situation. This strategy should be especially difficult for preschool children, who do not have a full grasp of the implications of the fantasy–reality distinction. In an experiment by Cantor and Wilson (1984), older elementary school children who were told to remember that what they were seeing in *The Wizard of Oz* was not real showed less fear than their classmates who received no instructions. The same instructions did not help preschoolers, however. A later study (Wilson & Weiss, 1991) again showed developmental differences in the effectiveness of reality-related strategies.

Children's beliefs about the effectiveness of focusing on the unreality of the stimulus have been shown to be consistent with these experimental findings. In the study of perceptions of fear-reducing techniques, preschool children's ranking of the effectiveness of "tell yourself it's not real" was significantly lower than that of older elementary school children (Wilson et al., 1987). In contrast to both preschool and elementary school children, who apparently view this strategy accurately, parents do not seem to appreciate the inadequacy of this technique for young children. Of the parents of both the preschool and elementary school children who participated in another study (Wilson & Cantor, 1987), 80% reported that they employed a "tell them it's not real" coping strategy to reduce their child's media-induced fear.

For media depictions involving realistic threats, the most prevalent cognitive strategy seems to be to provide an explanation that minimizes the perceived severity of the depicted danger. Not only is this type of strategy more effective with older children than with younger children, in certain situations it has been shown to have a fear-enhancing rather than anxiety-reducing effect with younger children. In the experiment involving the snake-pit scene from *Raiders of the Lost Ark* mentioned earlier (Wilson & Cantor, 1987), a second experimental variation involved the presence or absence of reassuring information

about snakes (e.g., the statement that most snakes are not poisonous). Although this information tended to reduce the fear of older elementary school children, kindergarten and first-grade children seemed to have only partially understood the information, responding to the word *poisonous* more intensely than to the word *not*. For them, negative emotional reactions were more prevalent if they had heard the supposedly reassuring information than if they had not heard it.

Data also indicate that older children use cognitive coping strategies more frequently than preschool children do. In the survey of reactions to *The Day After* (Cantor et al., 1986), parents' reports that their child had discussed the movie with them after viewing it increased with the age of the child. In a laboratory experiment involving exposure to a scary scene (Hoffner & Cantor, 1990), significantly more 9- to 11-year-olds than 5- to 7-year-olds reported spontaneously employing cognitive coping strategies (thinking about the expected happy outcome or thinking about the fact that what was happening was not real). Finally, Harrison and Cantor's (1999) retrospective study showed that the tendency to report employing a cognitive strategy to cope with media-induced fear increased with the respondent's age at the time of the incident.

Studies have also shown that the effectiveness of cognitive strategies for young children can be improved by providing visual demonstrations of verbal explanations (Cantor et al., 1988) and by encouraging repeated rehearsal of simplified, reassuring information (Wilson, 1987). In addition, research has explored some of the specific reasons for young children's inability to profit from verbal explanations such as those involving relative quantifiers (e.g., "some are dangerous, but most are not"; Badzinski, Cantor, & Hoffner, 1989) and probabilistic terms (e.g., "this probably will not happen to you"; Hoffner, Cantor, & Badzinski, 1990). It is clear from these studies that it is an extremely challenging task to explain away threats that have induced fear in a child, particularly when there is a strong perceptual component to the threatening stimulus and when the reassurance can only be partial or probabilistic rather than absolute (see Cantor & Hoffner, 1990).

The fact that younger children do not benefit from cognitive strategies should not be interpreted as meaning that children do not like to talk to their parents or caregivers when they are scared. Recent research suggests that young children enjoy talking with their caregivers, not so much to hear explanations of what they have seen, but to let them know how they are feeling and to solicit their comfort and support (Cantor, Byrne, Moyer-Gusé, & Riddle, 2007). Children's picture books designed for fear-reduction, such as *Teddy's TV Troubles* (Cantor, 2004), can facilitate such conversations.

Gender Differences in Media-Induced Fear

Gender Differences in Fright Reactions

There is a common stereotype that girls are more easily frightened than boys (Birnbaum & Croll, 1984; Cantor, Stutman, & Duran, 1996) and, indeed, that females in general are more emotional than males (e.g., Fabes & Martin, 1991; Grossman & Wood, 1993). There is quite a bit of research that seems to support this contention, although the gender differences may be weaker than they appear at first glance.

Peck (1999) conducted a meta-analysis of the studies of media-induced fear that were produced between 1987 and 1996. Her analysis, which included 59 studies that permitted a comparison between males and females, reported a moderate gender-difference effect size (.41), with females exhibiting more fear than males. Females' responses were more intense than those of males for all dependent measures. However, the effect sizes were largest for self-report and behavioral measures (those that are under the most conscious control) and smallest for heart rate and facial expressions. In addition, the effect size for gender differences increased with age. A recent study by Walma van der Molen and Bushman (2008) also found that among 8- to 12-year-old children, girls reported more fright and worry than boys in response to television programming.

Peck (1999) also conducted an experiment in which male and female college students were exposed to two scenes from the *Nightmare on Elm Street* series of movies, one featuring a male victim and the other featuring a female victim. She found that women's self-reports of fear were more intense than those of males, especially when the victim was female. However, when the victim was male, certain responses (pulse amplitude and hemispheric asymmetry) suggested that men were experiencing more intense physiological reactions than women.

Although more research is needed to explore the extent of gender differences in media-induced fear and the factors that contribute to them, these findings suggest that the size of the gender difference may be partially a function of social pressures to conform to gender-appropriate behavior.

Gender Differences in Coping Strategies

There is some evidence of gender differences in the coping strategies used to counteract media-induced fear, and these gender differences may also reflect gender-role socialization pressures. Hoffner (1995) found that adolescent girls reported using more noncognitive coping strategies than boys did but that there were no gender differences in the use of cognitive strategies. Similarly, Valkenburg et al. (2000) found that, among 7- to 12-year-old Dutch children, girls reported resorting to social support, physical intervention, and escape more often than boys, but there was no gender difference in the use of cognitive reassurance as a coping strategy.

Both of these findings are consistent with Hoffner's (1995) explanation that, because boys are less willing to show their emotions than girls are, they avoid noncognitive strategies, which are usually apparent to others. In contrast, the two genders employ cognitive strategies with equal frequency because these strategies are less readily observable.

Implications for Parents and Educators

Parental Knowledge and Children's Exposure

It has been noted that parents often are not aware of the frequency or severity of their children's fright reactions. For example, Cantor and Reilly (1982) found that parents' estimates of the frequency of their children's media-induced fright reactions were significantly lower than their children's self-reports. This finding may be due in part to children's reluctance to admit to their parents that they have been scared in an attempt to appear mature or to avert parental restrictions over their future viewing. Parents also underestimate their children's exposure to scary media. Research suggests that children often experience fright reactions to programs that many parents would not expect to be scary. For example, a recent study that interviewed children (Cantor et al., 2010) reported that more than one third of the children scared by movies named a movie rated G or PG as causing their fear. Nevertheless, there is evidence that children are widely exposed to televised stimuli that were originally intended for adults and that are considered frightening by a large proportion of adult moviegoers. Sparks (1986), for example, reported that almost 50% of the 4- to 10-year-olds he interviewed had seen *Poltergeist* and *Jaws,* and substantial proportions of his sample had seen *Halloween* and *Friday the 13th* (see, also, Cantor et al., 2010). Most of this viewing was done in the home, on cable television. Parents may be unaware of what their children are viewing if they are not present when the viewing occurs. Cantor et al. (2010) found that having a TV in one's bedroom was the best predictor of the severity of a child's fright reaction to media.

Coviewing and Emotional Responses

Research has focused on the role that coviewing can play in reducing fright reactions to media. Hoffner and Haefner (1997) asked first- through sixth-grade children to recall a time when they watched a television show with someone who became scared and to describe how (if at all) they had attempted to comfort the frightened coviewer. Almost 40% said that they recalled watching a program with a frightened sibling. (Indeed, 5% said they remembered watching a program during which their mother had become frightened!) Approximately half of the girls and 30% of the boys said that they had tried to comfort the frightened coviewer. Comforting behaviors ranged from simple distraction attempts to a discussion and explanation of the coviewer's fear. Even the youngest children adjusted the sensitivity of their comforting strategy based on the intensity of the coviewer's fright response.

How effective are siblings at providing comfort for one another? Wilson and Weiss (1993) studied preschoolers' reactions to a scary television program when viewed with or without an older sibling. More than half of the sibling pairs talked about how scary the program was while watching the movie, and more than a third of the older siblings actively tried to provide comfort by offering reassurance, a hug, or a hand to hold. The older siblings' comforting attempts seem to have worked: Compared with children who watched the scary program alone, preschoolers who viewed with an older sibling were less emotionally aroused and liked the program more.

Advice for Parents

The research presented here suggests that media content can have substantial negative effects on children's emotional well-being and that these effects can sometimes endure for long periods of time. Moreover, unhealthy effects on a child can be physical as well as emotional, such as when children are suddenly reluctant to sleep alone (or to sleep at all) or to engage in everyday activities that remind them of the fear-provoking television show or movie. These findings highlight the importance of taking the child's media exposure seriously and of trying to prevent severe emotional disturbances to the extent possible.

The research leads to a variety of recommendations for parents:

1. The amount of time children spend watching television should be limited.

2. Parents should be especially concerned about children's viewing before bedtime and should not allow children to have a television or computer in their bedroom.

3. Parents should become aware of the content of the television programs and movies their children see, by watching programs and movies beforehand, by acquiring whatever information is available from

television and movie ratings, by reading reviews and program descriptions, and by watching programs with their children.

4. Parents should monitor their own television viewing and realize that children may be affected by programming that their parents watch—even if they do not seem to be paying attention.

5. Parents should consider various available blocking technologies, such as the V-chip, which is available in virtually all televisions, and other devices available for purchase.

6. An awareness of the developmental trends in the stimuli that frighten children can help parents make wiser choices about the programming that their children may safely view.

7. An understanding of the types of coping strategies for dealing with media-induced fears at different ages can allow parents to help their children reduce their fears once they have been aroused.

Conclusions and Future Directions

The issue of media and children's fears provides a vivid illustration of how powerfully the media can disrupt children's lives. In addition to the spread of computers and other portable devices, the technology by which media content is transmitted is rapidly evolving to permit the display of bigger, more realistic, and more vivid high-definition images. Virtual reality systems take this process even further, resulting in experiences that seem astonishingly similar to undergoing a real event. It seems only logical that these advances will make scary images all the more frightening to children.

References

Applied Research and Consulting, LLC, Columbia University Mailman School of Public Health, & New York State Psychiatric Institute. (2002). *Effects of the World Trade Center attack on NYC public school students.* New York, NY: New York City Board of Education.

Apter, M. (1992). *The dangerous edge: The psychology of excitement.* New York: Free Press.

Badzinski, D. M., Cantor, J., & Hoffner, C. (1989). Children's understanding of quantifiers. *Child Study Journal, 19,* 241–258.

Bettelheim, B. (1975). *The uses of enchantment: The meaning and importance of fairy tales.* New York: Vintage Books.

Birnbaum, D. W., & Croll, W. L. (1984). The etiology of children's stereotypes about sex differences in emotionality. *Sex Roles, 10,* 677–691.

Blumer, H. (1933). *Movies and conduct.* New York: Macmillan.

Bowlby, J. (1973). *Separation: Anxiety and anger.* New York: Basic Books.

Bryant, J., Carveth, R. A., & Brown, D. (1981). Television viewing and anxiety: An experimental examination. *Journal of Communication, 31*(1), 106–119.

Buzzuto, J. C. (1975). Cinematic neurosis following *The Exorcist. Journal of Nervous and Mental Disease, 161,* 43–48.

Cantor, J. (1998). *"Mommy, I'm scared": How TV and movies frighten children and what we can do to protect them.* San Diego, CA: Harcourt.

Cantor, J. (2004). *Teddy's TV troubles.* Madison, WI: Goblin Fern Press.

Cantor, J. (2009a). *Conquer CyberOverload: Get more done, boost your creativity, and reduce stress.* Madison, WI: CyberOutlook Press.

Cantor, J. (2009b). Fright reactions to mass media. In J. Bryant & M. B. Oliver (Eds.), *Media effects: Advances in theory and research* (3rd ed., pp. 287–303). New York: Routledge.

Cantor, J., Byrne, S., Moyer-Gusé, E., & Riddle, K. (2007, May). Young children's descriptions of their media-induced fright reactions. Paper presented at the Convention of the International Communication Association, San Francisco, CA.

Cantor, J., Byrne, S., Moyer-Gusé, E., & Riddle, K. (2010). Descriptions of media-induced fright reactions in a sample of U.S. elementary school children. *Journal of Children and Media, 4*(1), 1–17.

Cantor, J., & Hoffner, C. (1990). Children's fear reactions to a televised film as a function of perceived immediacy of depicted threat. *Journal of Broadcasting & Electronic Media, 34,* 421–442.

Cantor, J., Mares, M. L., & Oliver, M. B. (1993). Parents' and children's emotional reactions to televised coverage of the Gulf War. In B. Greenberg & W. Gantz (Eds.), *Desert Storm and the mass media* (pp. 325–340). Cresskill, NJ: Hampton Press.

Cantor, J., & Nathanson, A. (1996). Children's fright reactions to television news. *Journal of Communication, 46*(4), 139–152.

Cantor, J., & Nathanson, A. (1997). Predictors of children's interest in violent television programming. *Journal of Broadcasting & Electronic Media, 41*, 155–167.

Cantor, J., & Omdahl, B. (1991). Effects of fictional media depictions of realistic threats on children's emotional responses, expectations, worries, and liking for related activities. *Communication Monographs, 58*, 384–401.

Cantor, J., & Omdahl, B. (1999). Children's acceptance of safety guidelines after exposure to televised dramas depicting accidents. *Western Journal of Communication, 63*(1), 1–15.

Cantor, J., & Reilly, S. (1982). Adolescents' fright reactions to television and films. *Journal of Communication, 32*(1), 87–99.

Cantor, J., & Sparks, G. G. (1984). Children's fear responses to mass media: Testing some Piagetian predictions. *Journal of Communication, 34*(2), 90–103.

Cantor, J., Sparks, G. G., & Hoffner, C. (1988). Calming children's television fears: Mr. Rogers vs. the Incredible Hulk. *Journal of Broadcasting & Electronic Media, 32*, 271–288.

Cantor, J., Stutman, S., & Duran, V. (1996). *What parents want in a television rating system: Results of a national survey.* Chicago: National PTA. Available from http://yourmindonmedia .com/wp-content/uploads/parent_survey.pdf

Cantor, J., & Wilson, B. J. (1984). Modifying fear responses to mass media in preschool and elementary school children. *Journal of Broadcasting, 28*, 431–443.

Cantor, J., & Wilson, B. J. (1988). Helping children cope with frightening media presentations. *Current Psychology: Research & Reviews, 7*, 58–75.

Cantor, J., Wilson, B. J., & Hoffner, C. (1986). Emotional responses to a televised nuclear holocaust film. *Communication Research, 13*, 257–277.

Fabes, R. A., & Martin, C. L. (1991). Gender and age stereotypes of emotionality. *Personality and Social Psychology Bulletin, 17*, 532–540.

Flavell, J. (1963). *The developmental psychology of Jean Piaget.* New York: Van Nostrand.

Gentile, D. A., & Walsh, D. A. (1999). *Media-Quotient™: National survey of family media habits, knowledge, and attitudes.* Minneapolis, MN: National Institute on Media and the Family.

Gerbner, G., Gross, L., Morgan, M., & Signorielli, N. (1980). The "mainstreaming" of America: Violence profile no. 11. *Journal of Communication, 30*(3), 10–29.

Gerbner, G., Gross, L., Morgan, M., & Signorielli, N. (1994). Growing up with television: The cultivation perspective. In J. Bryant & D. Zillmann (Eds.), *Media effects: Advances in theory and research* (pp. 17–40). Hillsdale, NJ: Lawrence Erlbaum.

Goldstein, J. (Ed.). (1998). *Why we watch: The attractions of violent entertainment.* New York: Oxford University Press.

Grossman, M., & Wood, W. (1993). Sex differences in the intensity of emotional experience: A social role interpretation. *Journal of Personality and Social Psychology, 65*, 1010–1022.

Harrison, K., & Cantor, J. (1999). Tales from the screen: Enduring fright reactions to scary media. *Media Psychology, 1*(2), 97–116.

Hawkins, R. P., & Pingree, S. (1981). Uniform messages and habitual viewing: Unnecessary assumptions in social reality effects. *Human Communication Research, 7*, 291–301.

Hoekstra, S. J., Harris, R. J., & Helmick, A. L. (1999). Autobiographical memories about the experience of seeing frightening movies in childhood. *Media Psychology, 1*(2), 117–140.

Hoffner, C. (1995). Adolescents' coping with frightening mass media. *Communication Research, 22*, 325–346.

Hoffner, C., & Cantor, J. (1985). Developmental differences in responses to a television character's appearance and behavior. *Developmental Psychology, 21*, 1065–1074.

Hoffner, C., & Cantor, J. (1990). Forewarning of a threat and prior knowledge of outcome: Effects on children's emotional responses to a film sequence. *Human Communication Research, 16*, 323–354.

Hoffner, C., Cantor, J., & Badzinski, D. M. (1990). Children's understanding of adverbs denoting degree of likelihood. *Journal of Child Language, 17*, 217–231.

Hoffner, C., & Haefner, M. J. (1997). Children's comforting of frightened coviewers: Real and hypothetical television-viewing situations. *Communication Research, 24*, 136–152.

Johnson, B. R. (1980). General occurrence of stressful reactions to commercial motion pictures and elements in films subjectively identified as stressors. *Psychological Reports, 47*, 775–786.

Johnson, J. G., Cohen, P., Kasen, S., First, M. B., & Brook, J. S. (2004). Association between television viewing and sleep problems during adolescence and early adulthood. *Archives of Pediatrics and Adolescent Medicine, 158*, 562–568.

Kelly, H. (1981). Reasoning about realities: Children's evaluations of television and books.

In H. Kelly & H. Gardner (Eds.), *Viewing children through television* (pp. 59–71). San Francisco: Jossey-Bass.

Klite, P., Bardwell, R. A., & Salzman, J. (1997). Local TV news: Getting away with murder. *Press/Politics, 2*(2), 102–112.

Laing, S. V., Fernyhough, C., Turner, M., & Freeston, M. H. (2009). Fear, worry, and ritualistic behaviour in childhood: Developmental trends and interrelations. *Infant and Child Development, 18,* 351–366.

Lewin, T. (2010, January). If your kids are awake, they're probably online. *The New York Times.* Retrieved April 26, 2011, from http://www.nytimes.com/2010/01/20/education/20wired.html?scp=1&sq=if%20your%20kids%20are%20awake,%20they're%20probably&st=cse

Manis, F. R., Keating, D. P., & Morison, F. J. (1980). Developmental differences in the allocation of processing capacity. *Journal of Experimental Child Psychology, 29,* 156–169.

Mathai, J. (1983). An acute anxiety state in an adolescent precipitated by viewing a horror movie. *Journal of Adolescence, 6,* 197–200.

Melkman, R., Tversky, B., & Baratz, D. (1981). Developmental trends in the use of perceptual and conceptual attributes in grouping, clustering, and retrieval. *Journal of Experimental Child Psychology, 31,* 470–486.

Morison, P., & Gardner, H. (1978). Dragons and dinosaurs: The child's capacity to differentiate fantasy from reality. *Child Development, 49,* 642–648.

Owens, J., Maxim, R., McGuinn, M., Nobile, C., Msall, M., & Alario, A. (1999). Television-viewing habits and sleep disturbance in school children [Abstract]. *Pediatrics, 104*(3), 552. Retrieved April 26, 2011, from http://pediatrics.aappublications.org/cgi/content/full/104/3/e27

Paavonen, E. J., Pennonen, M., Roine, M., Valkonen, S., & Lahikainen, A. R. (2006). TV exposure associated with sleep disturbances in 5- to 6-year-olds. *Journal of Sleep Research, 15,* 154–161.

Peck, E. Y. (1999). *Gender differences in film-induced fear as a function of type of emotion measure and stimulus content: A meta-analysis and a laboratory study.* Unpublished doctoral dissertation, University of Wisconsin-Madison.

Rapaczynski, W., Singer, D. G., & Singer, J. L. (1982). Teaching television: A curriculum for young children. *Journal of Communication, 32*(2), 46–55.

Rideout, V., Foehr, U., & Roberts, D. G. (2010). *Generation M²: Media in the lives of 8- to 18-year-olds.* Menlo Park, CA: Kaiser Family Foundation. Retrieved April 26, 2011, from http://www.kff.org/entmedia/mh012010pkg.cfm

Saylor, C. F., Cowart, B. L., Lipovsky, J. A., Jackson, C., & Finch, A. J., Jr. (2003). Media exposure to September 11: Elementary school students' experiences and posttraumatic symptoms. *American Behavioral Scientist, 46,* 1622–1642.

Schofield, J., & Pavelchak, M. (1985). "The Day After": The impact of a media event. *American Psychologist, 40,* 542–548.

Simons, D., & Silveira, W. R. (1994). Post-traumatic stress disorder in children after television programmes. *British Medical Journal, 308,* 389–390.

Singer, M. I., Slovak, K., Frierson, T., & York, P. (1998). Viewing preferences, symptoms of psychological trauma, and violent behaviors among children who watch television. *Journal of the American Academy of Child and Adolescent Psychiatry, 37*(10), 1041–1048.

Smith, S. L., & Moyer-Gusé, E. (2006). Children and the war on Iraq: Developmental differences in fear responses to television news coverage. *Media Psychology, 8,* 213–237.

Smith, S. L., Moyer, E. J., Boyson, A. R., & Pieper, K. M. (2002). Parents' perceptions of their child's fear reactions to TV news coverage of the terrorists' attacks. In B. S. Greenberg (Ed.), *Communication and terrorism: Public and media responses to 9/11* (pp. 193–209). Cresskill, NJ: Hampton Press.

Sparks, G. G. (1986). Developmental differences in children's reports of fear induced by the mass media. *Child Study Journal, 16,* 55–66.

Sparks, G. G., & Cantor, J. (1986). Developmental differences in fright responses to a television program depicting a character transformation. *Journal of Broadcasting & Electronic Media, 30,* 309–323.

Valkenburg, P. M., Cantor, J., & Peeters, A. L. (2000). Fright reactions to television: A child survey. *Communication Research, 27,* 82–99.

Van den Bulck, J. (2004). Media use and dreaming: The relationship among television viewing, computer game play, and nightmares or pleasant dreams. *Dreaming, 14,* 43–49.

Walma van der Molen, J. H., & Bushman, B. J. (2008). Children's direct fright and worry reactions to violence in fiction and news television programs. *The Journal of Pediatrics, 153,* 420–424.

Weiss, A. J., Imrich, D. J., & Wilson, B. J. (1993). Prior exposure to creatures from a horror film:

Live versus photographic representations. *Human Communication Research, 20,* 41–66.

Wilson, B. J. (1987). Reducing children's emotional reactions to mass media through rehearsed explanation and exposure to a replica of a fear object. *Human Communication Research, 14,* 3–26.

Wilson, B. J. (1989a). Desensitizing children's emotional reactions to the mass media. *Communication Research, 16,* 723–745.

Wilson, B. J. (1989b). The effects of two control strategies on children's emotional reactions to a frightening movie scene. *Journal of Broadcasting & Electronic Media, 33,* 397–418.

Wilson, B. J., & Cantor, J. (1987). Reducing children's fear reactions to mass media: Effects of visual exposure and verbal explanation. In M. McLaughlin (Ed.), *Communication yearbook 10* (pp. 553–573). Beverly Hills, CA: Sage.

Wilson, B. J., Hoffner, C., & Cantor, J. (1987). Children's perceptions of the effectiveness of techniques to reduce fear from mass media. *Journal of Applied Developmental Psychology, 8,* 39–52.

Wilson, B. J., & Weiss, A. J. (1991). The effects of two reality explanations on children's reactions to a frightening movie scene. *Communication Monographs, 58,* 307–326.

Wilson, B. J., & Weiss, A. J. (1993). The effects of sibling coviewing on preschoolers' reactions to a suspenseful movie scene. *Communication Research, 20,* 214–248.

Zuckerman, M. (1979). *Sensation seeking: Beyond the optimal level of arousal.* New York: John Wiley.

CHAPTER 12

Effects of Violent Media on Aggression

BRAD J. BUSHMAN
The Ohio State University
VU University Amsterdam

L. ROWELL HUESMANN
University of Michigan

Effects of Violent Media on Aggression

"We played the game by day and lived the game by night."

(Anonymous, incarcerated gang member who says he and his friends used the Grand Theft Auto *games as a kind of virtual reality training. His gang has been linked to several car thefts and at least seven murders.)*

"I have been to something like 50 gang funerals where the guy in the coffin was no more than 20. The game companies don't see the family crying and the people

in the coffin. They don't see the impact this has on our culture. They make or play their games in the studio, but for kids on the street it's a real life." (Terrance Stone, former gang member)

Violent video games, TV programs, films, Internet websites, and music are often blamed for causing young people to commit acts of violence. Although it is not possible to know whether a particular violent video game caused a particular young person to commit a particular violent crime, one can test whether there is a relationship between exposure to violent media and violent crime rates. One can also test whether violent media cause people to commit aggressive acts that are not serious enough to be classified as violent crimes. The theme of this chapter is *not* that media violence is *the* cause of aggression and violence in our society, or even that it is the *most* important cause. The theme is that accumulating research evidence has revealed that media violence is *one* significant factor that contributes to aggression and violence in our society. We also discuss other possible effects of violent media, such as making people more afraid of becoming a victim of violence themselves and making people numb to the pain and suffering of others.

Definitions

In sports and in business, the term *aggressive* is frequently used when the terms *assertive, enthusiastic,* or *confident* would be more accurate. For example, an aggressive salesperson is one who tries really hard to sell you something. Among researchers, the term aggression means something different. *Aggression* is generally defined as any behavior that is intended to harm another person who wants to avoid the harm (Baron & Richardson, 1994). This definition includes three important features. First, aggression is an external behavior that you can see. For example, you can see a person shoot, stab, hit, slap, or verbally abuse someone. Aggression is not an emotion that occurs inside a person, such as an angry feeling. Aggression is not a thought that occurs inside someone's brain, such as mentally rehearsing a murder. Aggression is a behavior that can be seen by others. Note also that aggression is a social behavior because it always involves at least two people. Second, aggression is intentional. Aggression is not accidental, such as when a drunk driver accidentally runs over a child on a tricycle. In addition, not all intentional behaviors that hurt others are aggressive behaviors. For example, a dentist might intentionally give a patient a shot of Novocain (and the shot hurts!), but the goal is to help rather than hurt the patient. Third, the victim wants to avoid the harm. Thus, again, the dental patient is excluded because she or he is not seeking to avoid the harm (in fact, the patient probably scheduled the appointment weeks in advance and paid to

have the dental work done). Suicide would also be excluded because the person who commits suicide does not want to avoid the harm. Sadomasochism would likewise be excluded because the masochist enjoys being harmed by the sadist.

Researchers and laypeople also differ in their use of the term violence. A meteorologist may call a storm *violent* if it has intense winds, rain, thunder, and lightning. Among researchers, *violence* is aggression that has extreme physical harm such as injury or death as its goal. For example, one child intentionally pushing another child down is an act of aggression but is not an act of violence. One person intentionally hitting, kicking, shooting, or stabbing another person is an act of violence. Violence is a subset of aggression. All violent acts are aggressive, but not all aggressive acts are violent. Only extreme physical acts of aggression are considered violent. The U.S. Federal Bureau of Investigation (FBI) classifies four crimes as violent: murder, assault, rape, and robbery. Researchers would also classify other physically aggressive acts as violent even if they do not meet the FBI definition of a violent crime, such as slapping someone really hard across the face. Thus, violent media are those that depict extreme acts of physical aggression.

Violent Media Consumption

Children today spend over 7 and a half hours per day consuming entertainment media (over 53 hours per week; Kaiser Family Foundation, 2010). Because children spend much of that time "media multitasking" (using more than one form of media at the same time), they actually manage to squeeze 10 and three quarter hours worth of media content into those 7 and a half hours. There is plenty of violence in the entertainment media, including TV, film, music, and video games (e.g., Dill, Gentile, Richter, & Dill, 2005; Hetsroni, 2007; Hunnicutt & Andrews, 2009; Kubrin, 2005; Lachlan et al., 2009; Monk-Turner et al., 2004). Parents, policy makers, and other members of society might wonder what impact exposure to violent media has on those who consume it. The purpose of this chapter is to review scientific research on the effects of violent media. In this chapter we divide media effects into three categories: (1) the *aggressor* effect—the more violent media you consume, the more aggressive you become, (2) the *fear-of-victimization* effect—the more violent media you consume, the more afraid you are of becoming a victim of violence, and (3) the *conscience-numbing* effect—the more violent media you consume, the less you care about others being victimized. Similar psychological processes underlie all three of these effects, and we will discuss those processes as well.

Violent Media Effects

The Aggressor Effect

Over five decades of scientific data lead to the irrefutable conclusion that exposure to violent media increases aggression. Findings are similar across studies that use very different methodologies (Anderson & Bushman, 2002a; Anderson et al., 2010). Each research method has its unique strengths and weaknesses, yet across the different methods there is a convergence of evidence. Scientists call this convergence *triangulation.* Regardless of the method used, the conclusion is the same: Exposure to violent media increases aggression and violence.

Experimental studies have shown that exposure to media violence *causes* people to behave more aggressively immediately afterwards. Experimental studies typically expose participants to violent media for relatively short amounts of time (usually about 15–30 minutes) before measuring aggressive thoughts, feelings, and, most important, behaviors. For example, research has shown that exposure to violent media immediately makes people more willing to give others painful electric shocks (Geen & O'Neal, 1969) and loud noise blasts (Bushman, 1995) and makes young children and adolescents more likely to attack each other physically (Bjorkqvist, 1985; Josephson, 1987). One recent experiment showed that playing violent video games causes men to behave more aggressively 24 hours later, but only if they ruminate about the violent content in the game (Bushman & Gibson, 2010).

Experimental studies have been criticized for their somewhat artificial nature (for reviews and rebuttals of these criticisms, see Anderson, Lindsay, & Bushman, 1999), but field experiments have produced similar results in more realistic settings. For example, delinquent boys who were shown violent films every night for five nights were more likely than those shown nonviolent films to get into fights with other boys (Leyens, Parke, Camino, & Berkowitz, 1975) or to display higher levels of verbal aggression (Sebastian, Parke, Berkowitz, & West, 1978). Similar effects have been found with nondelinquent children who saw a single episode of a violent children's television program (Boyatzis, Matillo & Nesbitt, 1995).

However, it is not so much the immediate effects of media violence that are of concern, but rather the aggregated long-term effects. Longitudinal studies offer evidence of a relationship between exposure to violent television as a child and aggressive and violent behavior many years later as an adult. Children who have a heavy diet of violent television are more likely to behave aggressively later in life. For example, one longitudinal study showed that a boy's exposure to TV violence at age 8 predicted his "change" in aggression over the next 10 years until he was 19 (Eron, Huesmann, Lefkowitz, & Walder, 1972). The more a boy watched television violence at age 8, the more aggressive he was at age 19—regardless of how aggressive he had been at age 8. Furthermore, his aggressiveness at age 8 did not predict how much TV violence he watched later on, which rules out the possibility that aggressive boys are attracted to TV violence. The surgeon general cited these results in justifying his 1972 national warning that "television violence, indeed, does have an adverse effect on certain members of our society" (Steinfeld, 1972, p. 26). A follow-up analysis showed that violent criminal behavior at age 30 in these same participants was predicted by their age 8 violence viewing (Huesmann, 1986). A cross-national longitudinal study found that exposure to TV violence at ages 6 or 8 predicted aggression 2 years later among many boys and girls in the United States, Finland, Poland, and Israel (Huesmann & Eron, 1986).

However, perhaps the most important longitudinal data on TV violence are from a 15-year study that followed a large sample of first- and third-grade children into their middle 20s (Huesmann, Moise-Titus, Podolski, & Eron, 2003). The results showed that boys and girls who had watched more TV violence in early childhood were significantly more aggressive young adults, independent of how aggressive they had been in childhood. Moreover, these effects remained significant when parenting differences, early intellectual functioning, social class, and other variables were statistically controlled. Importantly, adult aggression was assessed through other reports as well as self-reports and included some very serious acts of aggression. For example, the males who had watched large amounts of violent television during childhood were nearly twice as likely to have assaulted their spouses 15 years later, 18% more likely to have threatened or used a knife or a gun on someone in the last year, and significantly more likely to have been arrested for a crime. Even more recently, a study of delinquents and high-risk high school students found that very serious delinquent and violent acts were predicted from prior exposure to violent media (Boxer, Huesmann, Bushman, O'Brien, & Moceri, 2009).

Although the majority of longitudinal studies to date have focused on violent television and movies, the same general pattern of effects appears to be present after exposure to different forms of media, including violent music (Anderson, Carnagey, & Eubanks, 2003; Johnson, Jackson, & Gatto, 1995) and violent video games (Anderson et al., 2010).

Of course, violent media is not the only risk factor for violent and aggressive behavior, or even the most important risk factor, yet it is an important risk factor that cannot be dismissed as trivial or inconsequential. Although the typical effect size for exposure to violent media is relatively small by conventional standards (Cohen, 1977), and is therefore dismissed by some critics, this "small effect" translates into significant consequences for society as a whole, which may

be a better standard by which to measure the magnitude of the effect (Abelson, 1985; Yeaton & Sechrest, 1981). For example, the U.S. Surgeon General Report on youth violence found that violent media is as large a risk factor for youth violence as other well-known factors such as poverty, substance abuse, and bad parenting (Anderson, Berkowitz, et al., 2003; U.S. Department of Health and Human Services, 2001).

In summary, the scientific data lead to the same inescapable conclusion: Media violence increases aggression. Laboratory experiments have shown conclusively that exposing people to violent media causes them to behave more aggressively immediately afterwards, and even up to 24 hours later if they ruminate about the violent content. Field experiments have shown conclusively that the people who are playing more violent games or watching more media violence are the same people who are behaving more aggressively. Longitudinal studies have shown that children who grow up exposed to a lot of violence are likely to behave more aggressively later in childhood, in adolescence, and in young adulthood. This finding holds up even if one controls for differences in initial aggressiveness, intellectual functioning, and social class. The bottom line is that media violence is making kids behave more aggressively in childhood, and the aggressive habits they learn from the media in childhood carry over into adolescence and even young adulthood.

The Fear-of-Victimization Effect

Research has shown that heavy TV viewers (defined as those viewing at least 4 hours per day) are more fearful about becoming victims of violence, are more distrustful of others, and are more likely to perceive the world as a dangerous, mean, and hostile place than are light TV viewers (e.g., Gerbner & Gross, 1976, 1981). In one study, television exposure was predictive of fear of crime, whereas actual exposure to crime was not (Van den Bulck, 2004). A similar but stronger relationship has been reported between watching television news and fear of crime (Romer, Jamieson, & Aday, 2003). Like the *aggressor* effect, this *fear-of-victimization* effect seems to begin early in childhood, with even 7- to 11-year-olds displaying this effect (Peterson & Zill, 1981).

In general, the *fear-of-victimization* effect only seems to apply when people are evaluating unfamiliar environments. Although violent media makes people more afraid of crime in their city and increases their estimates of the prevalence of crime in general, it has relatively little impact on people's feelings of fear in their own neighborhoods (Heath & Petraitis, 1987; Hughes, 1980; Sparks & Ogles, 1990). This suggests that the *fear-of-victimization effect* may be related to the availability heuristic (Tversky & Kahneman, 1973). The *availability heuristic* is the tendency to judge the frequency or likelihood of an event by the ease with which relevant instances come to mind. People make evaluations based on salient or noticeable information, and when people have relatively little firsthand experience with an environment, they may draw upon television as an additional source of information. People usually don't need to draw on television for information about crime in their own neighborhood because they already know how dangerous it is.

The Conscience-Numbing Effect

People who consume a lot of violent media become less sympathetic to victims of violence. They become numb to the pain and suffering of others. In one study, people who played violent video games assigned less harsh penalties to criminals than those who played nonviolent games (Deselms & Altman, 2003). People exposed to violent media also perceive victims as less injured (Linz, Donnerstein, & Adams, 1989) and display less empathy toward them (Linz, Donnerstein, & Penrod, 1988). The *conscience-numbing effect* appears to be an enduring one. Even several days after watching violent, sexually explicit scenes, men still displayed an increased tolerance to aggression directed toward women (Malamuth & Check, 1981; Mullin & Linz, 1995).

The reduced empathy for victims of violence causes people to become less willing to help a victim of violence in the real world (Drabman & Thomas, 1974, 1976; Molitor & Hirsh, 1994). Children in these studies who had been exposed to violent programs were less willing to intervene when they saw two younger children fighting. Similar effects were found for adults who played a violent video game or watched a violent movie (Bushman & Anderson, 2009). After exposure to violence in the virtual world, people become numb to the pain and suffering of others in the real world. One reason why people may become more tolerant of violence and less sympathetic toward violence victims is because they become desensitized to it over time. Consistent with this interpretation, research has shown that after consuming violent media, people are less physiologically aroused by real depictions of violence (Carnagey, Anderson, & Bushman, 2007; Cline, Croft, & Courrier, 1973; Thomas, 1982).

The effects of violent video games on children's empathy toward victims are of particular concern. Feeling empathy requires taking the perspective of the victim, and violent video games encourage players to take the perspective of the aggressor. While in at least some television and video depictions of violence the viewer has the choice of taking the perspective of the aggressor or victim, in most violent video games the player is forced into taking the perspective of the aggressor. Thus, playing violent video games may have a particularly strong effect on diminishing the empathy the player feels for the victim (Funk, Baldacci, Pasold, & Baumgardner, 2004). This conscience-numbing effect of media violence is a process that contributes to the aggressor effect described previously.

Why Do People Deny Media Effects?

Although scientific evidence shows that violent media effects are undeniable, many people still deny these effects. There are at least four reasons why. First, people may think "I (or my teenage son, or other people I know) watch a lot of violent shows and we've never killed anyone. Furthermore, I never heard of anyone watching a lot of violence and then killing someone. Therefore, media violence has no effect."

This fallacious reasoning is a good example of how the availability heuristic coupled with the *base rate problem* distorts logical reasoning (Tversky & Kahneman, 1973). People have great difficulty judging influences on events when the base rate probability of the event is very low. It is not surprising that people who consume violent media have not killed anyone because very few people kill anyone. For example, fewer than 6 people per 100,000 are murdered each year in the United States (U.S. Federal Bureau of Investigation, 2010). It is very difficult to predict rare events, such as murder, using exposure to violent media or any other factor. However, murder is the most salient violent event to most people. When people don't have available in memory any cases of people viewing media violence and then murdering, they ignore the base rate of murder and conclude that media violence has no effect. They do this despite the fact that one *can* predict more common violent behaviors from media violence viewing. For example, in one 15-year longitudinal study (Huesmann et al., 2003), heavy viewers of violent TV shows in first and third grade were three times more likely to be convicted of criminal behavior by the time they were in their 20s. They were also more likely to have abused their spouses and assaulted other people at least once in the past year.

Second, people believe the media have a much stronger effect on others than on themselves. This effect is very robust and is called the *third person effect* (Davison, 1983; Innes & Zeitz, 1988; Perloff, 1999). The consequence of this psychological effect is that people may often agree that media violence harms some people, but not themselves, their own children, or other children who they feel were "brought up" like their own.

Third, the entertainment industry frequently claims that violent media do not increase aggression (Bushman & Anderson, 2001). Even though the public may recognize that making such claims is in the economic self-interest of the entertainment industry, the repetition of the claims still has an influence. In 1972, the U.S. surgeon general issued a warning about the harmful effects of TV violence. Since then, the scientific evidence has grown even stronger (Anderson & Bushman, 2002b, see Figure 12.1). But an analysis of over 600 news reports shows that over time, news stories have become more likely to deny the harmful effects of media violence (see Figure 12.1). Most Americans aren't even aware that the U.S. surgeon general issued a warning about TV violence in 1972. Perhaps this is because most Americans get their information from the mass media, and media officials are reluctant to admit that they are marketing a harmful product, much like the tobacco officials were reluctant to admit that they were marketing a harmful product.

Fourth, people do not understand psychological processes as well as they understand biological processes. If you see a violent video game player assault another person, it is difficult to know the direct cause of the assault. Was it playing violent video games for hours on end, or was it something else? The psychological process by which playing violent video games produces this result is not as intuitive to most people as are biological processes. People are probably more accepting of the idea that smoking causes lung cancer, for example, because it is much easier to grasp the idea that smoke going into the lungs damages cells and starts tumor growth. These psychological processes combine to create an atmosphere in which not only nonexpert journalists but also scholars who have not done research in the area write articles and books arguing that there are no effects (see Huesmann & Taylor, 2003). However, the vast majority of social scientists working in the area now accept that media violence poses a danger to society (Murray, 1998).

Why Do Violent Media Increase Aggression?

The psychological processes that help explain media-related aggression can be divided into those that produce more immediate, but transient, short-term effects on behavior and those that produce more delayed, but enduring, long-term effects on behavior (e.g., Bushman & Huesmann, 2006; Huesmann, 1988, 1997; Huesmann & Kirwil, 2007).

Figure 12.1	Conservative Scientific (Lower Boundary of 99.9% Confidence Interval) Versus News Reports of the Effect of Media Violence on Aggression (Anderson & Bushman, 2002b)

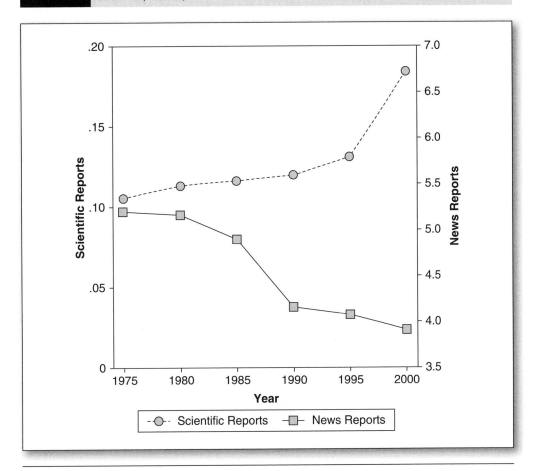

Source: Adapted from "Media Violence and the American Public: Scientific Facts versus Media Misinformation" (Figure 7), by B. J. Bushman and C. A. Anderson, 2001, *American Psychologist, 56,* p. 486. Reproduced with permission from the American Psychological Association.

Explaining Short-Term Violent Media Effects

Research shows that short-term increases in children's aggressive behavior following the observation of violence are mainly due to three psychological processes: (1) the priming of already existing aggressive behavioral scripts, aggressive cognitions, or angry emotional reactions; (2) simple mimicking of aggressive scripts; and (3) changes in emotional arousal stimulated by the observation of violence. In films and plays, scripts tell actors what to say and do. In memory, scripts

define situations and guide behavior. The person first selects a script from memory to represent the situation, and then he or she assumes a role in the script. Scripts can be learned by direct experience or by observing others, including media characters.

Priming

Neuroscientists and cognitive psychologists posit that the human mind can be represented as an associative network that consists of nodes and links. The nodes represent concepts in memory, and the links represent associations or relations among concepts. Thoughts, feelings, and behavioral tendencies are linked together in memory. Exposure to a stimulus can activate or prime concepts in memory (Fiske & Taylor, 1984). The activation produced by an observed stimulus spreads along network links to associated concepts as well. Thus, exposure to a stimulus can prime related concepts, ideas, and emotions in a person's memory, even without the person being aware of it (e.g., Bargh & Pietromonaco, 1982). For example, exposure to a weapon can increase aggressive thoughts and behaviors (Berkowitz & LePage, 1967).

Mimicry

Human and primate young have an innate tendency to mimic whomever they observe (e.g., Hurley & Chatter, 2004; Meltzoff & Moore, 2000). Neuroscientists have discovered *mirror neurons* in primates that seem to promote such mimicry and longer-term imitation (Rizzolati, Fadiga, Gallese, & Fogassi, 1996). The immediate mimicry of aggressive behaviors does not require a complex cognitive representation of the observed act, but only a simple mirror representation of it. Consequently, children who observe (in the media or in the environment around them) others doing a specific aggressive behavior are more likely to do the same aggressive behavior immediately after observing it (Bandura, 1977). Theoretically, the more similar children think they and the observed model are, the more readily mimicry will take place—but the mimicry mechanism is so powerful that even fantasy characters will be imitated by young children.

Arousal and Excitation Transfer

Media violence often consists of exciting, action-packed scenes that increase physiological arousal (e.g., heart rate, blood pressure). There are three possible reasons why arousal may increase aggression in the short run. First, high levels of arousal may be experienced as aversive (e.g., Mendelson, Thurston, & Kubzansky, 2008), and they may therefore stimulate aggression in the same way as other aversive stimuli (Berkowitz, 1983). Second, high arousal generated by exposure to violence

makes any dominant response tendency more likely to be carried out in the short run. Consequently, the child with aggressive tendencies behaves even more aggressively (e.g., Geen & O'Neal, 1969). Third, when a child is highly aroused by viewing violence, a mild specific emotion (e.g., mild anger) experienced sometime later may be "felt" as more severe (e.g., intense anger) than otherwise because some of the emotional arousal stimulated by the violent media presentation is misattributed as due to the provocation. This process is called *excitation transfer* (Bryant & Zillmann, 1979; Zillmann, Bryant, & Comisky, 1981).

Explaining Long-Term Violent Media Effects

Research shows that long-term increases in children's aggressive behavior are mainly due to two psychological processes: (1) observational learning, and (2) activation and desensitization of emotional processes.

Observational Learning

By *observational learning* we mean the process through which behavioral scripts, world schemas, and normative beliefs become encoded in a child's mind simply as a consequence of the child observing others (Huesmann, 1988, 1997). Observational learning is a powerful extension of imitation in which logical induction and abstraction are used to encode complex representations in memory. For example, extensive observation of violence biases children's world schemas toward hostility; they then attribute more hostility to others' actions, which in turn increases the likelihood of aggression (e.g., Dodge, Pettit, & Bates, 1995). Similarly, through repeated observation of aggressive role models in the media and in the real world, children develop normative beliefs that aggression is appropriate, and they acquire social scripts for how to behave aggressively. Whereas short-term mimicry requires only one exposure to an observed behavior, long-term observational learning usually requires repeated exposures. The more the child's attention is riveted on the observed behavior, the fewer the number of repetitions are needed. However, numerous other factors besides attention affect the extent of observational learning. For example, the more the child identifies with the observed models, and the more the observed scripts for behavior are rewarded and portrayed as appropriate, the more firmly the scripts will be encoded in memory. Similarly, if the world schemas and normative beliefs that a child acquires through observing others (again, in real life and in the media) lead to valuable outcomes for the child, they will become more firmly encoded and more resistant to change (Huesmann & Guerra, 1997).

Activation and Desensitization of Emotional Processes

The long-term effects on children of exposure to violence also involve the vicarious conditioning of emotional reactions. Through classical conditioning, fear or anger can become linked with specific stimuli after only a few exposures (e.g., Cantor, 1998). These emotions influence behavior in social settings away from the media source through stimulus generalization. A child may then react with inappropriate fear or anger in a novel situation similar to one that the child has observed in the media. Repeated exposure to emotionally arousing media or video games can also lead to habituation of certain natural emotional reactions. This process is often called *desensitization*, and it has been used to explain a reduction in distress-related physiological reactivity to media portrayals of violence.

The same process can make people more likely to act aggressively. For example, most people seem to have an innate negative emotional response to observing blood and violence, as evidenced by increased physiological arousal and self-reports of discomfort that often accompany such exposure. However, with repeated exposure, this negative emotional response habituates, and even children become "desensitized." People can then think about behaving aggressively without experiencing negative affect.

Moderators of Violent Media Effects

Although research has shown that violent media stimulate aggressive behavior in the short run and in the long run, there are a number of important moderators of these effects (Anderson, Carnagey, et al., 2003). The effects seem to depend both on how the violence is presented and on who is watching the violence.

What Kinds of Violent Media Have the Biggest Effects?

Media that glamorize, justify, and reward violence may have a particularly strong influence on aggressive behavior and attitudes. Content analyses have shown that about 75% of violent acts on TV go unpunished and about 40% are committed by attractive and heroic characters (National Television Violence Study, 1998). Observational learning theory proposes that these are the "best" kinds of violence to show if we want children to imitate the violent scripts they see and adopt attitudes and beliefs condoning violence (Bandura, 1986). Violent acts that are perceived as morally justified and that are rewarded produce the strongest learning effects (Berkowitz, 1993). Thus, the violent behavior of heroes is more likely to influence young viewers than the violent behavior of villains. Other characteristics of the format of almost any violent presentation increases learning effects compared to many nonviolent presentations. For example, learning does not occur without viewer attention, and the rapid movements, changes in audio levels, and changes in emotions produced by violent scenes are very good at attracting children's attention (Comstock & Paik, 1991).

There are at least three reasons to believe that violent video games might have a stronger effect on aggression than do violent TV programs. First, video game play is active, whereas watching TV is passive. People learn better when they are actively involved. Suppose you wanted to teach a person how to fly an airplane. What would be the best method to use: read a book, watch a TV program, or use a video game flight simulator? The obvious answer is the flight simulator. Indeed, research has shown that playing a violent video game leads to more aggression than watching a violent game (Polman, Orobio de Castro, & van Aken, 2008). Second, players of violent video games are more likely to identify with a violent character. If the game is a first person shooter, players have the same visual perspective as the killer. If the game is third person, the player controls the actions of the violent character from a more distant visual perspective. In both first and third person violent games, the player is linked to a violent character. In a violent TV program, viewers might or might not identify with a violent character. Third, violent games directly reward violent behavior by awarding points or allowing players to advance to the next game level. In some games, players are rewarded through verbal praise, such as hearing the words "Nice shot!" or "Impressive!" after killing an enemy. It is well known that rewarding behavior increases its frequency. In TV programs, reward is not directly tied to the viewer's behavior.

At the same time, different interpretations of violent content have been shown to be important in determining how much influence TV violence has on a viewer. Longitudinal data from several different countries have shown that children who perceive TV violence as more realistic and who identify more with the aggressive characters in the violent programs are influenced more by the violence (Huesmann & Eron, 1986). The children most at risk for behaving violently when they become young adults are those who not only watched a steady diet of TV violence but those who also perceived it as realistic and who identified with the aggressive characters (Huesmann et al., 2003).

Who Is Most Affected by Television Violence?

A number of individual differences put some people at greater risk than others for harmful violent media effects. One key individual difference is trait aggressiveness. People who score high in trait aggressiveness behave more aggressively after being exposed to violent media than those low in trait aggressiveness

(Bushman, 1995; Josephson, 1987). However, this does not mean that people low in trait aggressiveness are not stimulated to be more aggressive than they otherwise would be; they are (Eron et al., 1972; Huesmann et al., 2003). Nobody is immune to the harmful effects of violent media.

The relationship between media violence and aggressiveness may be reciprocal. Exposure to media violence increases trait aggressiveness, which in turn increases the likelihood of aggressive behavior (Anderson, Carnagey, et al. 2003). In addition, there is some evidence that, in the long run, more aggressive individuals expose themselves to violent media for social comparison motivations (Huesmann et al., 2003) This leads to a downward spiral into greater levels of aggression (Slater, Henry, Swaim, & Anderson, 2003).

Younger children appear to be particularly vulnerable to the effects of violent media (Bushman & Huesmann, 2006; Eron et al., 1972; Huesmann et al., 2003; Paik & Comstock, 1994). Some studies have found that boys are more influenced by media violence than girls are (Eron et al., 1972), but these effects are inconsistent; other researchers find little difference between boys and girls (Huesmann et al., 2003). This inconsistency may be a result of using different measures of aggression (Anderson, Carnagey, & Flanagan, 2004), different gender norms in the sample populations, or changes in gender norms over time. Longitudinal studies have shown that gender differences in aggression have decreased over time, probably because aggressive female models are becoming more common in the media and because it has become more socially acceptable for females to behave aggressively. One clear difference is that the combination of exposure to sex *plus* violence appears to be particularly potent in males. In one experiment, for example, college students watched movies portraying violence, sex and violence, or neither sex nor violence (Donnerstein & Berkowitz, 1981). Men exposed to both sex and violence were more aggressive toward a female who provoked them than were men exposed to only violence or men exposed to no sex or violence.

Reducing Violent Media Effects

Government Policy

The U.S. government has been involved in the TV violence debate since the 1950s. In 1972, the surgeon general concluded that TV violence was harmful to children and issued his famous warning about it (Steinfeld, 1972). However, it took almost 25 years for Congress to actually do something about the problem. In 1996, the Telecommunications Act was passed and signed into law. This Act mandated that new television sets be manufactured with a V-chip that allows parents to block out TV programs with objectionable content. This Act also mandated that TV programs be rated or labeled to provide information that can be read by the V-chip. When the V-chip is activated by a special code inserted by broadcasters into the TV signal, it scrambles the reception of the incoming picture. One problem with the V-chip is that some parents have difficulty with modern technology and cannot program the V-chip. Parents also do not understand the various labels, such as TV-MA for mature audiences (Bushman & Cantor, 2003). All of the different letters can seem like alphabet soup to parents. A bigger problem, however, concerns the effects of the rating system on children. Within a year of passage of the 1996 Telecommunications Act, the TV industry announced an age-based rating system that is similar to the movie-rating system used by the Motion Picture Association of America (e.g., "TV-14, Parents Strongly Cautioned . . . many parents would find this program unsuitable for children under 14"). Some violent programs also contain a warning label (e.g., "Due to some violent content, viewer discretion is advised"). Research has shown that such labels just make violent media forbidden fruits that attract young audiences (Bushman & Cantor, 2003). It is somewhat ironic that although labels can increase the attractiveness of violent TV programs, the TV industry can claim that it is attempting to be more responsible and proactive about the potentially harmful effects of TV violence. Similar findings have been reported for video games: Age-based ratings and violent content

labels are like magnets that attract players to violent video games, including very young children and girls (Nije Bijvank, Konijn, Bushman, & Roelofsma, 2009).

In June, 2011, the U.S. Supreme Court struck down California's law forbidding the sale of violent video games to children (Egelko, 2011; Liptak, 2010). California's law imposes fines of up to $1,000.00 on retailers who sell violent video games to anyone under the age of 18. When states have tried to pass such laws in the past, they have been judged unconstitutional because they supposedly violated the First Amendment, which protects freedom of speech: Video games are considered a form of free speech.

The Role of Parents and Schools

Sitting a child in front of a TV set or computer or having them play a video game can buy the parent time—a precious commodity to any parent, especially those who are single or have to work at more than one job. However, these electronic devices are shoddy babysitters because they do not monitor the child. The electronic mass media—TV, video games, movies, Internet—are powerful teachers, but what they teach depends on the substantive content of the media. Caretakers must control both the amount and the content of the electronic media that children use. Parents are in the best position to do this. The primary mass media exposure a young child experiences occurs in the home. Mass media habits are established early in life and are quite persistent over time. The harmful effects of violent media are also greatest for young children (e.g., Bushman & Huesmann, 2006; Paik & Comstock, 1994). Thus, the parent should take an active role rather than a passive role in counteracting the potentially harmful effects of media violence. If the parent establishes strong self-regulating standards and habits for media use in children at a young age, children will regulate themselves in adolescence and young adulthood, even in the face of peer pressure.

The schools could be a primary source for training for parents about the dangers of media violence and what to do in response. Training programs should inform them of the negative effects violent media can have on their child, teach them how to control their child's media use, and teach them how to counteract the negative effects of media violence. Research shows that coviewing violent programs or coplaying violent games with children is not enough (Nathanson, 2002). By itself, it can exacerbate the effects of the violence because children think their parents approve of the violence (because they watch it with them and do not saying anything about it). Parents need to coview, but also to discuss the unreality of the violence they see (Tangney & Feshbach, 1988). Restricting time and content of media exposure can also have some unintended consequences, including less positive attitudes toward parents, more positive attitudes toward the content, and more viewing of the content with friends (Nathanson, 2002).

Although the existing empirical evidence suggests that so-called media literacy programs in the school do not help reduce the effects of violence on children, school interventions directed at changing children's attitudes and beliefs about media violence have been shown to have some value (Huesmann, Eron, Klein, Brice, & Fischer, 1983).

The Role of the Media Industry

Some in the TV, film, and electronic game industries claim that viewing violence or playing violent games is therapeutic because it allows individuals to drain their angry and aggressive impulses into harmless channels, producing a cathartic effect. Consider the following quotes from movie directors:

> One of television's greatest contributions is that it brought murder back into the home where it belongs. Seeing a murder on television can be good therapy. It can help work off one's antagonism.
>
> — Alfred Hitchcock,
> director of *Psycho*

> Maybe we need the catharsis of bloodletting and decapitation like the ancient Romans needed it, as ritual but not real like the Roman circus.
>
> — Martin Scorsese,
> director of *GoodFellas*

> I come out of "Alien" or "The Texas Chainsaw Massacre" refreshed. Movies can provide catharsis.
>
> — Jonathan Demme, director
> of *Silence of the Lambs*

> I think it's a kind of purifying experience to see violence.
>
> — Paul Verhoeven, director of
> *Robocop, Total Recall,* and
> *Basic Instinct*

Despite what these movie directors say, viewing violence or playing violent games is not cathartic. In her review of the relevant literature, Tavris (1988) concluded, "it is time to put a bullet, once and for all, through the heart of the catharsis hypothesis. The belief that observing violence (or "ventilating it") gets rid of hostilities has virtually never been supported by research" (p. 194). The results from hundreds of studies converge on the finding that viewing violence increases aggressive thoughts, feelings, and behaviors (e.g., Anderson, Carnagey, et al., 2003).

Media executives also claim that violent media have a trivial effect on aggressive behavior. Consider the following quotes:

> If you cut the wires of all TV sets today, there would still be no less violence on the streets in two years.
>
> — Jack Valenti, Former President of
> Motion Picture Association of America

> No TV set ever killed a kid.
>
> — Lucie Salhany, Chairperson of Fox
> Broadcasting

> I don't think there is any correlation between violence on TV and violence in society.
>
> — Jim Burke of Rysher Entertainment

These kinds of opinions seem foolish in light of the evidence summarized in this chapter. But media executives have never seemed to care much about appearing foolish if it generates a profit. On the one hand, the TV industry charges hundreds of thousands of dollars for a few minutes of commercial airtime (or millions of dollars for high profile events like the Oscars or the Super Bowl), claiming that TV advertisements can sell virtually anything. On the other hand, the TV industry asserts that the hours of programming surrounding the few minutes of advertisements have no effect on viewers. This is an absurd contradiction. FCC Chairman Reed Hundt said: "If a sitcom can sell soap, salsa and cereal, then who could argue that TV violence cannot affect to some degree some viewers, particularly impressionable children?" (Eggerton, 1994, p. 10).

Historically, violent TV programs have attracted *smaller* audiences than nonviolent programs (Hamilton, 1998). However, advertisers value violent programs because they attract younger viewers (e.g., 18–49 year olds) and because they are slightly less expensive for the networks to purchase (Hamilton, 1998). Violent programming is also more likely to be exported to foreign broadcast markets than other types of programming, perhaps because violence loses less in translation than, for example, situation comedies that rely on some knowledge of popular culture (Hamilton, 1998). But if someone shoots a gun at you, you duck—regardless of where you live. According to Gerbner, "Violence travels well in foreign markets. It is a low-cost high-circulation commodity" (cited in Jenish, 1992, p. 40;). In time, violent media might become America's most exportable commodity, making the United States the "bread-casket for the world" (Hammerman, 1990, p. 79).

It is unlikely that moral appeals from parents and other concerned citizens will influence the TV industry to reduce the amount of violent programming. The bottom line really determines what programs are shown on television. If advertisers refused to sponsor them, violent TV programs would become extinct. Several years ago, a spokesperson for the J. Walter Thompson Company stated, "The more we probe the issue, the more we are convinced that sponsorship of television violence is potentially bad business, as well as a social risk" ("Lousy Frames," 1977, p. 56). The available research evidence is consistent with this conclusion in ways that TV executives might not realize. Commercial messages actually seem to be less effective if they are embedded in violent programs (e.g., Bushman, 2005), and product placements may be less effective if they are embedded in violent games than if they are embedded in nonviolent games (Gibson, Bushman, Melzer, & Zielaskowski, 2010).

Conclusion

In this chapter, we have reviewed the evidence showing that violent media increase aggression, increase fear of victimization, and decrease feelings of compassion and concern for others. We have concluded that these effects are not limited to only aggressive children, only poor children, or only less intelligent children.

Researchers have made substantial progress in understanding the psychological processes involved in how media violence affects children. Children who watch violent movies and TV or who play violent video games imitate the aggressive scripts they see; become more condoning of violence, start to believe the world is a more hostile place, become emotionally desensitized to violence, and lose empathy for victims. The violence they see justifies to them their own violent acts; the violence they see arouses them; and the violence they see cues aggressive ideas for them.

Unfortunately, understanding the process by which media violence may engender aggression in children does not immediately suggest a solution. Still, several points provide us with guidelines. First, we need to be more concerned about the effects of media violence on children than about the effects of media violence on adults. Media violence may have short-term effects on adults, but the real long-term effects seem to occur only with children. This makes some societal controls more palatable in a free society. Second, the violent video games, films, and programs that may have the most deleterious effects on children are not always the ones that adults and critics believe are the most violent. It is the violent scene in which a charismatic, heroic perpetrator of violence is rewarded that will have the most influence. Parents need to be educated about these facts. Third, we need to be aware that media violence can affect any child from any family. It is not, as some have suggested, only the already violence prone child who is likely to be affected. True, media violence is not likely to turn an otherwise fine child into a violent criminal. But just as every cigarette one smokes increases a little bit the likelihood of a lung tumor some day, every violent game one plays increases a little bit the likelihood of behaving more aggressively in some situation. Fourth, broadcasters, film producers, and electronic game makers need to be put on notice that they cannot avoid all responsibility and expect parents, governments, and others to control viewing violence. The argument that "people watch or play it, so we give it to them," is not valid in a modern, socially conscious society. It is unrealistic to expect parents to completely control what children watch or play in a society with video games everywhere, multiple TVs in each household, DVDs and handheld devices everywhere, and both parents working.

What is the solution? Perhaps we need better parental control, more government control, education and training for children to not be affected by media violence, computers and TVs put in shared places in the home rather than in the child's bedroom, electronic chips that cut out violence, and to boycott sponsors of violence. Society needs to make decisions based on an appropriate balance between freedom of expression and protection of our children. It is time for society to take this problem seriously and respond accordingly. The future of our children and society is too precious for us not to act.

References

Abelson, R. P. (1985). A variance explanation paradox: When a little is a lot. *Psychological Bulletin, 97,* 128–132.

Anderson, C. A., Berkowitz, L., Donnerstein, E., Huesmann, R. L., Johnson, J. D., Linz, D., Malamuth, N. M., & Wartella, E. (2003). The influence of media violence on youth. *Psychological Science in the Public Interest, 4,* 81–110.

Anderson, C. A., & Bushman, B. J. (2002a). Media violence and societal violence. *Science, 295,* 2377–2378.

Anderson, C. A., & Bushman, B. J. (2002b). Media violence and the American public revisited. *American Psychologist, 57,* 448–450.

Anderson, C. A., Carnagey, N. L., & Eubanks, J. (2003). Exposure to violent media: The effects of songs with violent lyrics on aggressive thoughts and feelings. *Journal of Personality & Social Psychology, 84,* 960–971.

Anderson, C. A., Carnagey, N. L., & Flanagan, M. (2004). Violent video games: Specific effects of violent content on aggressive thoughts and behavior. *Advances in Experimental Social Psychology, 36,* 199–249.

Anderson, C. A., Lindsay, J. J., & Bushman, B. J. (1999). Research in the psychological laboratory: Truth or triviality? *Current Directions in Psychological Science, 8,* 3–9.

Anderson, C. A., Shibuya, A., Ihori, N., Swing, E. L., Bushman, B. J., Sakamoto, A., et al., (2010). Violent video game effects on aggression, empathy, and prosocial behavior in Eastern and Western countries: A meta-analytic review. *Psychological Bulletin, 136*(2), 151–173.

Bandura, A. (1977). *Social learning theory.* New York: Prentice Hall.

Bandura, A. (1986). *Social foundations of thought and action: A social cognitive theory.* Englewood Cliffs, NJ: Prentice Hall.

Bargh, J. A., & Pietromonaco, P. (1982). Automatic information processing and social perception: The influence of trait information presented outside of conscious awareness on impression formation. *Journal of Personality and Social Psychology, 43,* 437–449.

Baron, R. A., & Richardson, D. R. (1994). *Human aggression* (2nd ed.). New York: Plenum.

Berkowitz, L. (1983). Aversively stimulated aggression: Some parallels and differences in research with animals and humans. *American Psychologist, 38,* 1135–1144.

Berkowitz, L. (1993). *Aggression: Its causes, consequences, and control.* New York: McGraw-Hill.

Berkowitz, L., & LePage, A. (1967). Weapons as aggression-eliciting stimuli. *Journal of Personality and Social Psychology, 7,* 202–207.

Bjorkqvist, K. (1985). *Violent films, anxiety and aggression.* Helsinki, Finland: Finnish Society of Sciences and Letters.

Boxer, P., Huesmann, L. R., Bushman, B. J., O'Brien, M., & Moceri, D. (2009). The role of violent media preference in cumulative developmental risk for violence and general aggression. *Journal of Youth and Adolescence, 38*(3), 417–428.

Boyatzis, C. J., Matillo, G. M., & Nesbitt, K. M. (1995). Effects of the 'Mighty Morphin

Power Rangers' on children's aggression with peers. *Child Study Journal, 25*, 45–55.

Bryant, J., & Zillmann, D. (1979). Effect of intensification of annoyance through unrelated residual excitation on substantially delayed hostile behavior. *Journal of Experimental Social Psychology, 15,* 470–480.

Bushman, B. J. (1995). Moderating role of trait aggressiveness in the effects of violent media on aggression. *Journal of Personality and Social Psychology, 69,* 950–960.

Bushman, B. J. (2005). Violence and sex in television programs do not sell products in advertisements. *Psychological Science, 16,* 702–708.

Bushman, B. J., & Anderson, C. A. (2001). Media violence and the American public: Scientific facts versus media misinformation. *American Psychologist, 56,* 477–489.

Bushman, B. J., & Anderson, C. A. (2009). Comfortably numb: Desensitizing effects of violent media on helping others. *Psychological Science, 21*(3), 273–277.

Bushman, B. J., & Cantor, J. (2003). Media ratings for violence and sex: Implications for policy makers and parents. *American Psychologist, 58*, 130–141.

Bushman, B. J., & Gibson, B. (2011). Violent video games cause an increase in aggression long after the game has been turned off. *Social Psychological and Personality Science, 2,* 29–32.

Bushman, B. J., & Huesmann, L. R. (2006). Short-term and long-term effects of violent media on aggression in children and adults. *Archives of Pediatrics & Adolescent Medicine, 160*, 348–352.

Cantor, J. (1998). *"Mommy, I'm scared":* How TV and movies frighten children and what we can do to protect them. San Diego, CA: Harvest/Harcourt.

Carnagey, N. L., Anderson, C. A., & Bushman, B. J. (2007). The effect of video game violence on physiological desensitization to real life violence. *Journal of Experimental Social Psychology*, *43*, 489–496.

Cline, V. B., Croft, R. G., & Courrier, S. (1973). Desensitization of children to television violence. *Journal of Personality and Social Psychology, 27,* 360–365.

Cohen, J. (1977). *Statistical power analysis for the behavioral sciences* (Revised ed.). Hillsdale, NJ: Lawrence Erlbaum.

Comstock, G. A., & Paik, H. (1991). The effects of television violence on aggressive behavior: A meta-analysis. In *A preliminary report to the National Research Council on the understanding and control of violent behavior.* Washington, DC: National Research Council.

Davison, W. P. (1983). The third-person effect in communication. *Public Opinion Quarterly, 47*, 1–15.

Deselms, J. L., & Altman, J. D. (2003). Immediate and prolonged effects of videogame violence. *Journal of Applied Social Psychology, 33,* 1553–1563.

Dill, K. E., Gentile, D. A., Richter, W. A., & Dill, J. C. (2005). Violence, sex, race, and age in popular video games: A content analysis. In E. Cole & J. H. Ellen (Eds.), *Featuring females: Feminist analyses of media* (pp. 115–130). Washington, DC: American Psychological Association.

Dodge, K. A., Pettit, G. S., & Bates, J. E. (1995). Social information-processing patterns partially mediate the effect of early physical abuse on later conduct problems. *Journal of Abnormal Psychology, 104,* 632–643.

Donnerstein, E., & Berkowitz, L. (1981). Victim reactions in aggressive erotic films as a factor in violence against women. *Journal of Personality and Social Psychology, 41,* 710–724.

Drabman, R. S., & Thomas, M. H. (1974). Does media violence increase children's tolerance of real-life aggression? *Developmental Psychology, 10,* 418–421.

Drabman, R. S., & Thomas, M. H. (1976). Does watching violence on television cause apathy? *Pediatrics, 57,* 329–331.

Egelko, B. (2011, June 27). Court strikes down California video games. *San Francisco Chronicle* App for iPad. http://www.sfgate.com/cgi-bin/article.cgi?f=/c/a/2011/06/27/BA9Q1K37ED.DTL. Retrieved June 27, 2011.

Eggerton, J. (1994, January 31). Hundt hits television violence. *Broadcasting and Cable, 124*(5), 10.

Eron, L. D., Huesmann, L. R., Lefkowitz, M. M., & Walder, L. O. (1972). Does television violence cause aggression? *American Psychologist, 27,* 253–263.

Fiske, S. T., & Taylor, S. E. (1984). *Social cognition.* Reading, MA: Addison-Wesley.

Funk, J. B., Baldacci, H. B., Pasold, T., & Baumgardner, J. (2004). Violence exposure in real-life, video games, television, movies, and the Internet: Is there desensitization? *Journal of Adolescence, 27,* 23–39.

Geen, R. G., & O'Neal, E. C. (1969). Activation of cue-elicited aggression by general arousal. *Journal of Personality and Social Psychology, 11,* 289–292.

Gerbner, G., & Gross, L. (1976). Living with television: The violence profile. *Journal of Communication, 26,* 172–199.

Gerbner, G., & Gross, L. (1981). The violent face of television and its lessons. In E. I. Palmer &

A. Dorr (Eds.), *Children and the faces of television: Teaching, violence, selling* (pp. 149–162). New York: Academic Press.

Gibson, B., Bushman, B. J., Melzer, A., & Zielaskowski, K. (2010). Killing avatars in video games kills the effectiveness of in-game ads. Manuscript under review.

Hamilton, J. T. (1998). *Channeling violence: The economic market for violent television programming.* Princeton, NJ: Princeton University Press.

Hammerman, J. K. (1990, October). Dead men don't smirk. *Esquire, 114*(4), 79.

Heath, L., & Petraitis, J. (1987). Television viewing and fear of crime: Where is the mean world? *Basic and Applied Social Psychology, 8,* 97–123.

Hetsroni, A. (2007). Four decades of violent content on prime-time network programming: A longitudinal meta-analytic review. *Journal of Communication, 57*(4), 759–784.

Huesmann, L. R. (1986). Psychological processes promoting the relation between exposure to media violence and aggressive behavior by the viewer. *Journal of Social Issues, 42*(3), 125–139.

Huesmann, L. R. (1988). An information processing model for the development of aggression. *Aggressive Behavior, 14,* 13–24.

Huesmann, L. R. (1997). Observational learning of violent behavior: Social and biosocial processes. In A. Raine, P. A. Brennen, D. P. Farrington, & S. A. Mednick (Eds.), *Biosocial bases of violence* (pp. 69–88). London: Plenum.

Huesmann, L. R., & Eron, L. (1986). *Television and the aggressive child: A cross-national comparison.* Hillsdale, NJ: Lawrence Erlbaum.

Huesmann, L. R. Eron, L.D., Klein, R., Brice, P., & Fischer, P. (1983). Mitigating the imitation of aggressive behaviors by changing children's attitudes about media violence. *Journal of Personality and Social Psychology, 44*(5), 899–910.

Huesmann, L. R., & Guerra, N. (1997). Children's normative beliefs about aggression and aggressive behavior. *Journal of Personality and Social Psychology, 72(2),* 408–419.

Huesmann, L. R., & Kirwil, L. (2007). Why observing violence increases the risk of violent behavior in the observer. In D. J. Flannery, A. T. Vazsonyi, & I. D. Waldman (Eds.), *The Cambridge handbook of violent behavior and aggression* (pp. 545–570). Cambridge, UK: Cambridge University Press.

Huesmann, L. R., Moise-Titus, J., Podolski, C. L., & Eron, L. D. (2003). Longitudinal relations between children's exposure to TV violence and their aggressive and violent behavior in young adulthood: 1977–1992. *Developmental Psychology, 39,* 201–221.

Huesmann, L. R., & Taylor, L. D. (2003). The case against the case against media violence. In D. Gentile (Ed.), *Media violence and children* (pp. 107–130). Westport, CT: Greenwood Press.

Hughes, M. (1980). The fruits of cultivation analysis: A reexamination of some effects of television watching. *Public Opinion Quarterly, 44,* 287–302.

Hunnicutt, G., & Andrews, K. H. (2009). Tragic narratives in popular culture: Depictions of homicide in rap music. *Sociological Forum, 24*(3), 611–630.

Hurley, S., & Chatter, N. (2004). *Perspectives on imitation: From cognitive neuroscience to social science.* Cambridge, MA: MIT Press.

Innes, J. M., & Zeitz, H. (1988). The public's view of the impact of the mass media: A test of the "third person" effect. *European Journal of Social Psychology, 18,* 457–463.

Jenish, D. (1992, December 7). Prime-time violence: Despite high ratings for violent shows, revulsion is growing over bloodshed on TV. *Macleans, 105,* 40.

Johnson, J. D., Jackson, L. A., & Gatto, L. (1995). Violent attitudes and deferred academic aspirations: Deleterious effects of exposure to rap music. *Basic and Applied Social Psychology, 16,* 27–41.

Josephson, W. L. (1987). Television violence and children's aggression: Testing the priming, social script, and disinhibition predictions. *Journal of Personality and Social Psychology, 53,* 882–890.

Kaiser Family Foundation. (2010). Generation M[2]: Media in the lives of 8- to 18-year-olds. Retrieved April, 20, 2010, from http://www.kff.org/entmedia/entmedia012010nr.cfmi

Kubrin, C. R. (2005). 'I see death around the corner': Nihilism in rap music. *Sociological Perspectives, 48*(4), 433–459.

Lachlan, K. A., Tamborini, R., Weber, R., Westerman, D., Skalski, P., & Davis, J. (2009). The spiral of violence: Equity of violent reprisal in professional wrestling and its dispositional and motivational features. *Journal of Broadcasting & Electronic Media, 53*(1), 56–75.

Leyens, J. P., Parke, R. D., Camino, L., & Berkowitz, L. (1975). Effects of movie violence on aggression in a field setting as a function of group dominance and cohesion. *Journal of Personality & Social Psychology, 32,* 346–360.

Linz, D. G., Donnerstein, E., & Adams, S. M. (1989). Physiological desensitization and judgments about female victims of violence. *Human Communication Research, 15,* 509–522.

Linz, D. G., Donnerstein, E., & Penrod, S. (1988). Effects of long-term exposure to violent and sexually degrading depictions of women. *Journal of Personality and Social Psychology,* 55, 758–768.

Liptak, A. (2010, April 26). Justices to consider law limiting the sale of violent video games. *New York Times,* p. A14

Lousy frames for beautiful pictures: Are they changing? (1977, May 23). *Advertising Age, 48,* 56.

Malamuth, N. M., & Check, J. V. P. (1981). The effects of mass media exposure on acceptance of violence against women. *Journal of Research in Personality, 15,* 436–446.

Meltzoff, A. N., & Moore, M. K. (2000). Imitation of facial and manual gestures by human neonates: Resolving the debate about early imitation. In D. Muir & A. Slater (Eds.), *Infant development: The essential readings* (pp. 167–181). Malden, MA: Blackwell.

Mendelson, T., Thurston, R. C., & Kubzansky, L. D. (2008). Arousal and stress: Affective and cardiovascular effects of experimentally-induced social status. *Health Psychology, 27*(4), 482–489.

Molitor, F., & Hirsch, K. W. (1994). Children's toleration of real-life aggression after exposure to media violence: A replication of the Drabman and Thomas studies. *Child Study Journal, 24,* 191–207.

Monk-Turner, E., Ciba, P., Cunningham, M., McIntire, P. G., Pollard, M., & Turner, R. (2004). A content analysis of violence in American war movies. *Analyses of Social Issues and Public Policy (ASAP), 4*(1), 1–11.

Mullin, C. R., & Linz, D. (1995). Desensitization and resensitization to violence against women: Effects of exposure to sexually violent films on judgments of domestic violence victims. *Journal of Personality and Social Psychology, 69,* 449–459.

Murray, J. P. (1998). Studying television violence: A research agenda for the 21st century. In J. K. Asamen & G. L. Berry (Eds.), *Research paradigms, television, and social behavior* (pp. 369–410). Thousand Oaks, CA: Sage.

Nathanson, A. I. (2002). The unintended effects of parental mediation of television on adolescents. *Media Psychology, 4*(3), 207–230.

National Television Violence Study. (1998). *National television violence study* (Vol. 3). Santa Barbara, CA: The Center for Communication and Social Policy, University of California, Santa Barbara.

Nije Bijvank, M., Konijn, E. A., Bushman, B. J., & Roelofsma, P. H. M. P. (2009). Age and content labels make video games forbidden fruit for youth. *Pediatrics, 123,* 870–876.

Paik, H., & Comstock, G. (1994). The effects of television violence on antisocial behavior: A meta-analysis. *Communication Research, 21,* 516–546.

Perloff, R. M. (1999). The third-person effect: A critical review and synthesis. *Media Psychology, 1,* 353–378.

Peterson, J. L., & Zill, N. (1981). Television viewing in the United States and children's intellectual, social, and emotional development. *Television and Children, 2,* 21–28.

Polman, H., Orobio de Castro, B., & van Aken, M. (2008). Experimental study of the differential effects of playing versus watching violent video games on children's aggressive behavior. *Aggressive Behavior, 34*(3), 256–264.

Rizzolati, G., Fadiga, L., Gallese, V., & Fogassi, L. (1996). Premotor cortex and the recognition of motor actions. *Cognitive Brain Research, 3,* 131–141.

Romer, D., Jamieson, K. H., & Aday, S. (2003). Television news and the cultivation of fear of crime. *Journal of Communication, 53,* 88–104.

Sebastian, R. J., Parke, R. D., Berkowitz, L., & West, S. G. (1978). Film violence and verbal aggression: A naturalistic study. *The Journal of Communication, 28,* 164–171.

Slater, M. D., Henry, K. L., Swaim, R. C., & Anderson, L. L. (2003). Violent media content and aggressiveness in adolescents: A downward spiral model. *Communication Research, 30,* 713–736.

Sparks, G. G., & Ogles, R. M. (1990). The difference between fear-of-victimization and the probability of being victimized: Implications for cultivation. *Journal of Broadcast Electronic Media, 34,* 351–358.

Steinfeld, J. (1972). *Statement in hearings before Subcommittee on Communications of Committee on Commerce* (United States Senate, Serial #92-52, pp. 25–27). Washington, DC: United States Government.

Tangney, J. P., & Feshbach, S. (1988). Children's television viewing frequency: Individual differences and demographic correlates. *Personality and Social Psychology Bulletin, 14,* 145–158.

Tavris, C. (1988). Beyond cartoon killings: Comments on two overlooked effects of television. In S. Oskamp (Ed.), *Television as a social issue* (pp. 189–197). Newbury Park, CA: Sage.

Thomas, M. H. (1982). Physiological arousal, exposure to a relatively lengthy aggressive film, and aggressive behavior, *Journal of Research in Personality, 16,* 72–81.

Tversky, A., & Kahneman, D. (1973). Availability: A heuristic for judging frequency and probability. *Cognitive Psychology, 5,* 207–232.

U.S. Department of Health and Human Services. (2001). *Youth violence: A report of the surgeon general.* Rockville, MD: U.S. Government Printing Office.

U.S. Federal Bureau of Investigation. (2010). *Uniform crime reports.* Washington, DC: U. S. Government Printing Office.

Van den Bulck, J. (2004). Research note: The relationship between television fiction and fear of crime: An empirical comparison of three causal explanations. *European Journal of Communication, 19,* 239–248.

Yeaton, W., & Sechrest, L. (1981). Meaningful measures of effect. *Journal of Consulting and Clinical Psychology, 49,* 766–767.

Zillmann, D., Bryant, J., & Comisky, P. W. (1981). Excitation and hedonic valence in the effect of erotica on motivated inter-male aggression. *European Journal of Social Psychology, 11,* 233–252.

CHAPTER 13

Prosocial, Antisocial, and Other Effects of Recreational Video Games

CRAIG A. ANDERSON AND DOUGLAS A. GENTILE
Iowa State University

KAREN E. DILL
Fielding Graduate University

Prosocial, Antisocial, and Other Effects of Recreational Video Games

Video games are immensely popular around the world. They are played on computers, handheld devices, cell phones, and game consoles. They are played at home, at arcades, at school, in automobiles, and virtually anywhere that an electronic device can be operated. The video game industry's revenues surpassed the movie industry's several years ago and surpassed the music industry's in 2008. A recent, nationally representative sample of U.S. teens found that 99% of boys and 94% of girls played video games (Lenhart et al., 2008). The amount of time spent playing games has increased over time (Escobar-Chaves & Anderson, 2008; Gentile & Anderson, 2003). Many children and adolescents play more than 20 hours each week; 40 hours of gaming per week is not uncommon among males (e.g., Bailey, West, & Anderson, 2010).

Much research has examined potential positive and negative effects of playing various types of video games. Most has focused on the deleterious effects of violent games (e.g., Anderson et al., 2010). Other research has focused on educational games (e.g., Murphy et al., 2002). Still other work has found that total time playing video games

Author's Note: Correspondence concerning this chapter should be addressed to Craig A. Anderson, Iowa State University, Department of Psychology, W112 Lagomarcino Hall, Ames, IA 50011-3180. Phone: 515–294–3118; Fax: 515–294–6424; E-mail: caa@iastate.edu

is negatively associated with school performance (e.g., Anderson & Dill, 2000; Anderson, Gentile, & Buckley, 2007), that prosocial video games can increase prosocial behavior (Gentile et al., 2009; Taylor, 2006), that exercise games are an attractive form of physical activity (Rhodes, Warburton, & Bredin, 2009; Sell, Lillie, & Taylor, 2008), and that some types of games can improve game-related visual attention skills (e.g., Green & Bavelier, 2003; Okagaki & Frensch, 1994). Some of the latest research has studied the implications of avatar use on outcomes as diverse as self-concept, social behavior, and even exercise. Thus, the simple good–bad dichotomy frequently posed by the general public and the press ("Are video games bad for children?") is inappropriate.

In this chapter, we focus on the effects of playing recreational video games—that is, games *not* specifically designed for use in educational or therapeutic contexts. (For a brief review of all types of video games, see Barlett, Anderson, & Swing, 2009.) We begin by describing the main theoretical perspectives needed to understand video game effects. Next, we review the known effects of recreational video games, focusing on prosocial effects (e.g., helping others), antisocial effects (e.g., hurting others; stereotyping others), and other effects on the individual (e.g., addiction, cognitive skills, exercise, attention control).

Theoretical Overview

Three complementary theoretical perspectives are particularly useful when contemplating the effects of playing video games. The *General Aggression Model* and its offshoot, the *General Learning Model*, describe the basic learning processes and effects involved in both short-term and long-term effects of playing various types of games. The *Five Dimensions of Video Game Effects* perspective describes different aspects of video games and video game play that influence the specific effects likely to occur. The *Risk and Resilience* perspective reminds us that the effects of video game play—prosocial,

antisocial, and other—take place within a complex set of social and biological factors, each of which contribute to development of the individual's thoughts, feelings, and behaviors.

General Aggression Model and General Learning Model

The dominant models of social behavior in developmental, personality, and social psychology are all social-cognitive models. Along with numerous colleagues, we developed the General Aggression Model (GAM) to integrate and simplify a wide range of more specific social-cognitive models of aggression (e.g., Anderson & Bushman, 2002; Anderson & Carnagey, 2004; Anderson et al., 2007; Anderson & Huesmann, 2003; DeWall & Anderson 2011). Briefly, GAM is a dynamic biosocial cognitive-developmental model that provides an integrative framework for domain-specific aggression theories. It includes situational, personological, and biological variables. GAM draws heavily on social-cognitive and social-learning theories that have been developed over the past 40 years by social, personality, cognitive, and developmental psychologists (e.g., Bandura, 1977; Berkowitz, 1989, 1993; Crick & Dodge, 1994; Dodge, 1980, 1986; Geen, 2001; Huesmann, 1982, 1988, 1998; Mischel, 1973; Mischel & Shoda, 1995). These perspectives paved the way for understanding the learning and developmental processes involved in shaping aggressive behavior and how such processes contribute to the development and change of personality. Figure 13.1 presents an overview of the model. (For more detailed views and descriptions, see the works cited earlier.)

To understand aggression, or any social behavior, we must understand how such behavior in general depends on cognitive, affective, and arousal factors within the individual. Note that in Figure 13.1 no specific reference is made to aggressive behavior. One implication is that the model can be applied to other types of social behavior, such as helping other people. This generalization is the essence of

Figure 13.1 The General Aggression Model, Overview

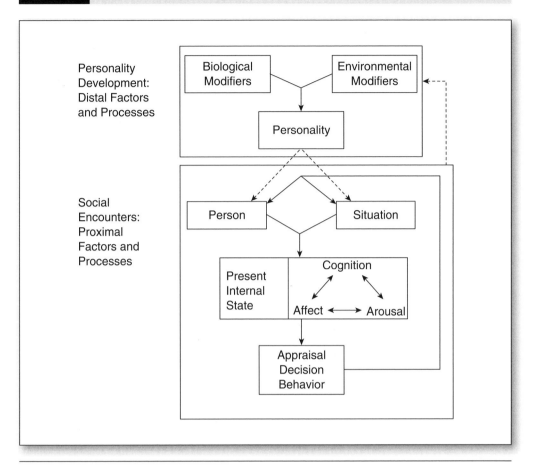

Source: Adapted from *Violent Evil and the General Aggression Model* (pp. 168–192), by C. A. Anderson and N. L. Carnagey, 2004. In A. Miller (Ed.), *The social psychology of good and evil*. New York: Guilford.

what has become known as the General Learning Model (for more details, see Barlett & Anderson, in press; Buckley & Anderson, 2006; Gentile et al., 2009).

In any specific social encounter (lower portion of Figure 13.1), social behavior depends on how an individual perceives and interprets his or her environment and the people therein—on expectations regarding the likelihood of various outcomes, on knowledge and beliefs about how people typically respond in certain situations, and on efficacy beliefs about the ability to respond to the ongoing events. By understanding these perceptions and cognitions, researchers have a basis for understanding both within-person cross-situational stability across time (because people show stability in how they perceive their social world over time), between person variability within the same situations (because different people perceive situations differently), and between person similarity within the same or similar situations (because situations frequently impose realistic demands that limit the number of options regarding how people can construe the situation). Furthermore, such social-cognitive models also account for variability in aggression across time, people, and contexts because different knowledge structures develop and change and different situational contexts prime different knowledge structures. The three main keys to these models involve discovering (1) what the person brings with him or her to the situations (knowledge structures, such as attitudes, beliefs, scripts, perceptual biases), (2) what types of knowledge structures are primed or activated by the features of the current situation, and (3) how various life experiences combine with biological predispositions to create and change personality, conceived of here as the person's set of operative knowledge structures.

GAM focuses heavily on how the development and use of knowledge structures influences both early (e.g., basic visual perception) and downstream (e.g., judgments, decisions, behaviors) psychological processes (e.g., Bargh, 1996; Collins & Loftus, 1975; Fiske & Taylor, 1991; Higgins, 1996; Wegner & Bargh, 1998). Of particular interest from cognitive psychology are findings showing that through repeated practice and exposure, complex judgments and choices become automatized, requiring little or no mental effort or conscious awareness (Bargh & Pietromonaco, 1982). With practice, one can learn to automatically scan the environment for threat, to perceive threat even in ambiguous situations, and to respond to threat with aggressive action. Alternatively, one can learn to automatically look for people in need of help, to perceive such needs quicker or more frequently than others, and to respond to this perception by offering help. Indeed, it is possible that both of these sets of knowledge structures could be well learned (automatized) within the same person.

The learning processes involved include all of the well-studied processes of classical conditioning, instrumental conditioning, imitation, and higher order forms of learning. These learning processes, which result from discrete social encounters, affect what we think of as *personality*, illustrated by the dashed line linking the proximal portion of Figure 13.1 to the distal portion. In this way, the present event influences the future.

The past influences the present by affecting what the person brings with them to the situation (e.g., knowledge structures) and by influencing the kinds of situations the person is likely to encounter. Figure 13.2 illustrates one way in which repeated exposure to a specific type of environmental modifier—media violence—creates an aggressive personality, which in turn increases the likelihood of aggressive behavior in a specific situation. A similar figure could be produced to illustrate how repeated exposure to prosocial media can increase an altruistic personality and prosocial behavior.

Repeated exposure to media violence, such as playing violent video games, increases the accessibility of a host of aggression-related knowledge structures while simultaneously decreasing feelings of empathy for victims of violence and decreasing negative emotional reactions to violent thoughts, images, and scripts. In essence, such exposure increases the aggressive personality. When an ambiguous provocation of some kind occurs (e.g., getting bumped in a cafeteria or bar), the increased accessibility of aggressive schemata increases the likelihood that a hostile attribution for the event will be made. This increases the likelihood that aggressive response options will be generated and that they will be selected for action. In short, the person becomes more likely to retaliate. That retaliation itself produces an outcome that influences one's expectations and beliefs about the future. The dashed line indicates that such learning has an impact (small) on further personality development. The victim's response, very likely an aggressive one, sets the stage for the next episodic cycle of this social interaction event.

Again, keep in mind that the same type of dynamic process occurs with repeated exposure to prosocial media. Of course, in this case more prosocial thoughts, feelings, and shifts in personality are instigated by the media exposure, resulting in more prosocial behavior under the right circumstances.

Five Dimensions of Video Game Effects

Gentile and his colleagues (Gentile, 2011; Gentile & Stone, 2005; Khoo & Gentile, 2007)

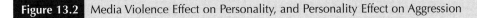

Figure 13.2 Media Violence Effect on Personality, and Personality Effect on Aggression

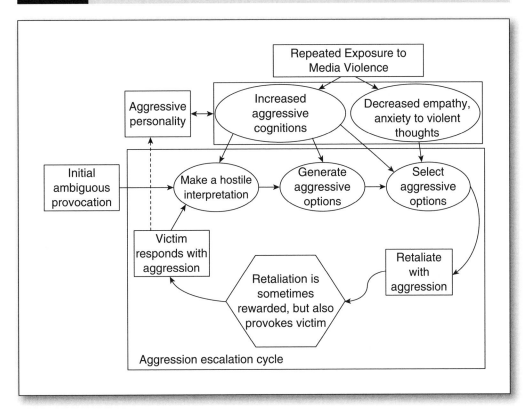

have proposed five dimensions along which video games can have effects—the *amount, content, context, structure,* and *mechanics.* This approach explains how research findings that initially appear contradictory are actually congruent. Games and the ways people interact with them are multidimensional, and each dimension is likely to be associated with specific types of effects.

The *amount* of time that people spend on recreational games can have effects on them, regardless of specific game features. Studies have demonstrated that amount of time playing games predicts poorer school performance (see later section). Theoretically, this effect is likely due to displacement of other academically beneficial activities. Other studies have demonstrated a relationship between amount of sedentary gaming and obesity (Berkey et al., 2000; Laurson et al., 2008; Vandewater, Shim, & Caplovitz, 2004). Again, it is likely that

sedentary games displace other more physically active activities, and children may also snack more while gaming than they otherwise would. Amount of gaming has also been implicated in repetitive stress disorders (Brasington, 1990), and in video game addiction (see later section).

Most of the research on video game effects has focused on the *content* dimension, with the bulk of that research focused on violent content. It should be no surprise that people learn the content of whatever games they play. If they play educational games, they learn the educational content and can apply it to their schoolwork (Murphy et al., 2002); if they play games designed to teach health content, they learn those concepts and apply them to their lives (Beale, Kato, Marin-Bowling, Guthrie, & Cole, 2007; Lieberman, 2001); if they play violent games, they learn the violent content and may apply it to their lives (see sections that follows).

The *context* of game play may produce differential effects, but this is the dimension with the least research at this time. Context can be defined within the game or outside of the game. One type of within-game context can be seen in violent games that allow for either team-based or free-for-all modes of play. Both may be equally violent, but playing in an everyone-for-oneself mode might lead to greater aggressive thoughts, lower empathy, and greater desensitization. If the in-game context requires players to cooperate to achieve goals, this might also teach teamwork and social coordination skills. Furthermore, the social context outside of the game may matter. Playing a violent game in a room with other friends (virtual or real) might increase the aggression effect because players are giving each other social support for aggression. It might actually reduce the aggression effect, however, if one's motivations are prosocial (to help your friends). To our knowledge, no studies have yet tested these hypotheses.

How the game is structured and displayed on the screen can also have effects. This screen *structure* provides information that is learned, similar to how we learn to perceive other visual information (Gibson, 1979). Perceptual skills can be improved through practice, as has been shown in several studies (Green & Bavelier, 2003, 2006a, 2006b, 2007; Greenfield, DeWinstanley, Kilpatrick, & Kaye, 1994). Other studies have demonstrated an improved ability to get three-dimensional information from flat screens (Greenfield, Brannon, & Lohr, 1994) or improved mental rotation skills (Cherney, 2008) after playing games that require those skills.

Finally, the *mechanics* dimension refers to what can be learned from practice with different types of game controllers. Depending on the type of controller, several different skills could be improved, including fine motor skills (e.g., by using a thumb controller), gross motor skills (e.g., by swinging the Wii remote like a golf club), or balance skills (e.g., using the Wii balance board). These effects can be used intentionally, such as in physical therapy (Deutsch, Borbely, Filler, Huhn, & Guarrera-Bowlby, 2008) or to improve dynamic balance control after brain surgery (Betker, Szturm,

Moussavi, & Nett, 2006). The intersection of structure and mechanics is the continuous feedback loop that is often referred to as hand-eye coordination.

One benefit of noting the dimensions on which games can have effects is that it allows us to recognize that the dichotomous question of whether games are good or bad is too simplistic. Games have multiple effects at multiple levels of analysis, some of which may be beneficial and some of which may be harmful, even within the same game.

Research Designs and Scientific Causality

Scientists use three main types of research designs to test theoretical models. Each type has characteristic strengths and weaknesses. No single study is thought of as conclusive, though some are stronger than others. Because no single empirical study can be wholly conclusive, researchers create and test theories using multiple studies and multiple study designs in order to *triangulate* on the clearest answer to the research question. Different designs are used to test various plausible alternative hypotheses. By ruling out such alternatives, the main causal hypothesis gains strength. If a plausible alternative explanation remains viable, then additional empirical tests or a modification of the theory is required. In sum, it is the total picture of combined studies that answers the question of whether or not a particular variable (e.g., violent video game exposure) is a causal factor for a particular outcome (e.g., aggressive behavior).

The three major types of studies are experimental, cross-sectional correlational, and longitudinal studies. Experimental studies randomly assign participants to different groups: for example, playing either a violent or non-violent video game. A major result of random assignment is that individual differences among the participants should be equally distributed between the groups, creating groups that are equivalent (more or less) at the outset—even on individual differences that have not been measured. The experimenter measures the outcome variable after the experimental manipulation takes place. If the groups differ on the outcome variable, the researcher can conclude with confidence that the manipulated variable caused the obtained difference in outcome. This is the great strength of experimental studies. The major weakness is that one frequently cannot use strong real-world measures of the conceptual outcome variable. For example, it would be unethical to actually allow study participants to physically harm each other; therefore, more ethical measures must be used. In such cases, researchers use ethically appropriate measures that faithfully represent the conceptual outcome variable. Ideally, though not necessarily, one would use measures that also predict or are predicted by more extreme real-world measures. For example, the competitive reaction time task frequently used to measure physical aggression in the lab has repeatedly shown high external validity.

Cross-sectional correlational studies allow researchers to get beyond the outcome variable limitation of experimental studies. In a cross-sectional study, for example, researchers might survey children about the video games they play and about several real-world types of aggressive behavior, such as how many physical fights they have had. The major weakness of cross-sectional studies is that claims of causality are more risky, especially from a single study. For example, it might be that playing violent games causes aggressive behavior, or that aggressive children are more likely to play violent games, or that some third variable causes both (such as poor impulse control). Cross-sectional studies are strong where experimental studies are weak and vice versa. According to the triangulation notion, if both types of studies show similar results, researchers can be reasonably comfortable in assuming that they have discovered a real causal effect on important, real outcomes. And of course, many plausible alternative explanations can be tested using cross-sectional designs.

Longitudinal studies document changes over a longer period of time. For example, one might measure children's video game habits and their aggressive behaviors at two points in time separated by 6 months. One can then test whether children who play violent games at the beginning of the study *change* to become relatively more aggressive by the end of the study. This design, when used properly, allows some causal conclusions and use of real world outcome variables. The major limitations of longitudinal studies are that they are difficult and expensive.

The strongest case for establishing that a hypothesized effect is causal arises when the same conceptual results are obtained regardless of the research design—and when plausible alternative explanations have been tested and ruled out. In the video game domain, such variables might include sex, personality trait hostility, parental education level, and parental monitoring of media, among others. Experimental studies by their very nature control for such individual difference variables, even if the variables haven't been measured. So do longitudinal studies, at least to some extent. Cross-sectional studies have no inherent control for such potential confounds, but if such variables are measured, then they can be statistically controlled.

Scientific Causality, Risk, and Resilience

It is important to note what scientifically established causality means and does not mean, as this often creates confusion for the public. Modern scientific causality is not the "necessary and sufficient" causality of old. Instead, it is probabilistic. For example, "smoking causes lung cancer" means that repeated smoking of tobacco products increases the likelihood that one will contract lung cancer. It does not mean that all smokers get lung cancer or that only smokers get it. Similarly, "media violence causes aggression" means that exposure to violent media increases the likelihood of later aggressive behavior. It does not mean that all violent game players will behave aggressively, or that only violent game players behave aggressively. The probabilistic nature of modern causality results from the fact that human health and behavior is multicausal. This approach to understanding the multicausality of behavior is sometimes known as *the risk and resilience approach* (Gentile & Sesma, 2003).

Years of study have documented scores of variables that individually increase the likelihood of concurrent or future aggression. These include variables at many different levels of analysis, including poverty, having been bullied, taking drugs, genetic risk for aggression, poor parenting, and media violence (Surgeon General, 2001). Each of these individually is a risk factor for aggression—that is, each increases the risk of current or future aggressive behavior. But no single factor alone is sufficient to elicit more extreme forms of aggression. This does not mean that we can ignore any of them—each is important, and steps could be taken to minimize them.

In addition, there are factors that help lower the risk of aggression: These are *protective factors*. These also include variables at many different levels of analysis (e.g., having prosocial peers, having highly involved parents, being female, and certain genetic/biological factors). To predict and understand which people will behave aggressively, therefore, we need to understand the risk and protective factors that each individual has. Each additional risk factor increases the risk, whereas each protective factor decreases the risk. Not every risk and protective factor has the same effect size; some are more important than others (Anderson et al., 2003; Surgeon General, 2001). Furthermore, some risk factors may interact, increasing their effects more together than they would individually, although much more research is needed in this area. Ultimately, it is important to understand that when scientific psychological research documents a causal effect of violent games on aggression, for example, this means that violent games are one risk factor increasing the likelihood of aggressive behaviors, not that they are the only cause of aggressive behavior. In order for a child to behave seriously violently, he or she would need to have multiple risk factors and few protective factors (Gentile & Sesma, 2003).

Violent Video Game Effects

Much research over several decades has documented how witnessing violence and aggression leads to a range of negative outcomes for children. Negative outcomes result both from witnessing real violence (e.g., Osofsky, 1995)

as well as from viewing media violence (Anderson et al., 2003; Gentile, 2003). Unfortunately, many parents who take great pains to keep children from witnessing real violence in the home and neighborhood often do little to keep them from viewing large quantities of violence on television, in movies, and in video games. This lack of parental concern about media violence is perplexing given the research on its harmful effects, the large number of national reviews of the research that have publicized these effects, and the strong critique of media violence by pediatricians. We do not mean to suggest that there is no controversy over how to interpret the results of studies. What appear to us to be overreactions happen in both directions, from some people claiming that violent games are training a generation of killers to others claiming there is no effect at all. For example, attorney (now disbarred) Jack Thompson stated on ABC's *World News Now* program (March 23, 2000): "In every school shooting, we find that kids who pull the trigger are video gamers." On the other extreme, psychologist Christopher Ferguson claimed that the existing research is largely "pseudoscience" (2009) and that researchers are attempting to create a "moral panic" (2008; 2010). Neither of these claims seems reasonable to us. The most recent comprehensive review of the overall media violence literature (including television, movies, and video games) documents the ". . . unequivocal evidence that media violence increases the likelihood of aggressive and violent behavior in both immediate and long-term contexts" (Anderson et al., 2003, p. 81). Interestingly, a 2004 survey of pediatricians found that over 98% believed that the media affect childhood aggression (Gentile, Oberg et al., 2004). But somehow this message has not been convincingly delivered to, or always understood by, average Americans (Dill, 2009a).

A Recent Meta-Analysis

In this section, we review the available research on the effects of playing violent video games. Six outcome variables have received sufficient research attention to warrant inclusion in a recent comprehensive meta-analytic review: aggressive behavior, aggressive cognition, aggressive affect, physiological arousal, prosocial behavior, desensitization/low empathy (Anderson et al., 2010). This meta-analysis is considerably larger than any prior meta-analysis of the violent video game effects literature (e.g., Anderson, 2004; Anderson & Bushman, 2001) for two primary reasons: (1) It included a large number of previously unavailable studies from Japan; and (2) there has been an explosive growth in research on this topic in recent years. Specifically, 381 effect sizes were obtained from 136 research reports involving over 130,000 participants. In the following sections, all reported meta-analytic results are from this new meta-analysis, and all are based on the sample of studies that met all best practices criteria (the "Best Raw" sample in Anderson et al., 2010). This sample included 221 effect sizes involving over 61,000 participants.[1]

Main Findings

The main findings can be succinctly summarized: Playing violent video games causes an increase in the likelihood of physically aggressive behavior, aggressive thinking, aggressive affect, physiological arousal, and desensitization/low empathy. It also decreases helpful or prosocial behavior. With the exception of physiological arousal (for which there are no cross-sectional or longitudinal studies), all of the outcome variables showed the same effects in experimental, cross-sectional, and longitudinal studies. The main effects occurred for both males and females, for participants from low-violence collectivistic type Eastern countries (e.g., Japan), and from high-violence individualistic type Western countries (e.g., United States, Europe). Table 13.1 displays the major findings of the meta-analyses.

| **Table 13.1** | Average Effect Size of Violent Video Game Play. (Results from the "Best Raw" data, Anderson et al., 2010.) |

Design	*Total N*	*K*	*Avg. Effect (r+)*	*Z*
Physical Aggression				
Experimental	2513	27	.210	10.512**
Longitudinal	4526	12	.203	13.787**
Cross-Sectional	14,642	40	.262	32.291**
Aggressive Cognition				
Experimental	2887	24	.217	11.695**
Longitudinal	3408	8	.115	6.728**
Cross-Sectional	9976	27	.183	18.445**
Aggressive Affect				
Experimental	1454	21	.294	11.289**
Longitudinal	2602	5	.075	3.836**

(Continued)

---

[1]Note that the other two samples—the Full Sample (N = 130,296) and the Best Partials Sample (N = 53,034)—yielded essentially the same results. That is, in each sample, the average violent video game effect sizes were significant.

Table 13.1 (Continued)

Design	Total N	K	Avg. Effect (r+)	Z
Cross-Sectional	5135	11	.101	7.227**
Prosocial (helping) Behavior				
Experimental	633	4	−.182	−4.599**
Longitudinal	2778	5	−.114	−6.022**
Cross-Sectional	3495	7	−.093	−5.506**
Empathy/Desensitization				
Experimental	249	1	−.138	−2.175*
Longitudinal	2421	4	−.184	−9.147**
Cross-Sectional	3910	10	−.203	−12.845**

Source: Results from the "Best Raw" data from Anderson, C. A., Shibuya, A., Ihori, N., Swing, E. L., Bushman, B. J., Sakamoto, A., Rothstein, H. R., & Saleem, M. (2010). Violent video game effects on aggression, empathy, and prosocial behavior in Eastern and Western countries. *Psychological Bulletin, 136,* 151–173. American Psychological Association.

Notes: Total N is the total number of participants in all of the summarized studies. K is the number of different studies. The Average Effect (r+) is the weighted average effect size, expressed as an r value. Z is the Z test of whether the effect is significantly different from zero.

* $p < .05$. ** $p < .001$.

Additional Findings

From a triangulation perspective, the results of the meta-analysis seem clear. There is strong evidence that playing violent video games increases aggression and affects a host of relevant outcome variables in theoretically expected ways. The violent game effect occurs in both the immediate situation (experimental studies) and across time (cross-sectional and longitudinal studies). The triangulation notion applies not only to using multiple research designs, but to using multiple methods and participant populations within each design. The findings were quite consistent in these ways as well, showing that the main findings held across culture, age, and sex. The range of measures used in these studies was also impressive. For example, physical aggression measures included standard laboratory measures, self-reports of fights at school, peer reports, teacher reports, and reports of truly violent behavior.

Overall, the basic question of whether violent games are a potential risk factor for increased aggressive thoughts, feelings, and behaviors appears to have been answered. Research is beginning to move into potentially more interesting questions, such as whether some children are more vulnerable to the effects than others. Markey and Markey (2010), for example, provide data suggesting that children with certain personality features (e.g., high neuroticism, low agreeableness, and low conscientiousness) may be the most vulnerable to violent game effects. Although other studies have not found a profile that strongly suggests increased vulnerability for some groups (e.g., boys, highly aggressive individuals, etc.), this is a promising area of research.

Prosocial Video Game Effects

There has been little research on the effects of prosocial, nonviolent video games. There are few nonviolent games that have lots of prosocial content—that is, games in which the main character's primary task is to help other game characters in nonviolent ways. Although some might argue that games in which the player's character is a hero killing "bad guys" and saving other "good" characters are prosocial, the large research literature on TV and film violence effects clearly demonstrates that such heroic violence increases later aggression, not helping behaviors. The paucity of studies of wholly prosocial video games is at least partly the result of a lack of appropriate games. Nonetheless, there have been a few recent studies.

Gentile et al. (2009) reported three studies, one of each design type. The experimental study had American elementary school students play certain scenes from a randomly assigned children's game with prosocial nonviolent content (*Chibo Robo, Super Mario Sunshine*), violent content (*Ty2, Crash Twinsanity*), or nonviolent nonsocial content (*Pure Pinball, Super Monkeyball Deluxe*). Later, they were each given an opportunity to help or to hurt another child's chances of winning a gift certificate. Those who had played one of the prosocial games were significantly more helpful than those in the violent or nonsocial conditions. The longitudinal study assessed the video game habits and prosocial behavior of a large sample of Japanese 5th, 8th, and 11th graders at two points in time about 3 to 4 months apart. A maximum likelihood model revealed that exposure to prosocial video games at Time 1 led to a relative increase in prosocial behavior at Time 2, even after controlling for prosocial behavior at Time 1. The cross-sectional study assessed the video game habits of a large sample of Singaporean secondary school children, along with several prosocial measures. After statistically controlling for sex, age, and violent game play, amount of prosocial game play was positively related to helping behavior, cooperation and sharing, and empathy. Interestingly, amount of violent game play was positively related to hostile attribution bias, and negatively related to helping behavior. Figure 13.3 displays some of the key results.

| **Figure 13.3** | Effects of Prosocial and Violent Video Game Play on Helping Behavior and Hostile Attribution Bias. |

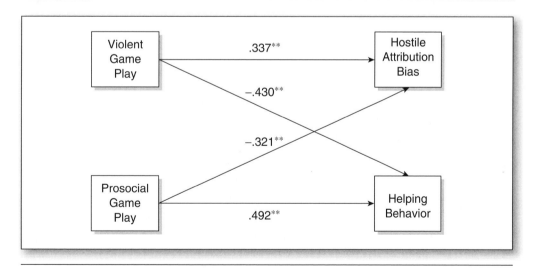

Source: Based on data from Study 1, Gentile et al., 2009.

Similar research by Greitemeyer and Osswald (2009) reported two experiments in which brief play of a prosocial video game led to a decrease in both hostile expectation bias and in accessibility of antisocial thoughts. In sum, the tiny research literature on prosocial game effects mirrors the huge literature on violent game effects, supporting the idea that the same basic social-cognitive processes underlie both phenomena.

Video Game Character Portrayals and Effects

There is a growing body of research on video game character portrayals and the effects of exposure to these representations. Theoretically, these studies—primarily content analyses and experiments—dovetail with the violent video game effects research because they have focused on portrayals of aggression and related themes such as power, dominance, objectification, and degradation. What is perhaps most substantively interesting about this work is that it is, in essence, a social psychological analysis of how stereotyping and prejudice relate to aggression. For example, this research has begun to analyze discrimination toward stereotyped group members (e.g., sexual harassment of women) as an aggressive outcome measure, which is distinct from the way aggression is measured in most previous video game violence effects studies (Dill, 2009a).

Content Analyses of Video Games

Gender

Content analyses of gender have found that White, male adults are the most common and most central game characters; women and nonwhites are underrepresented and often stereotyped (Beasley & Standley, 2002; Burgess, Stermer, & Burgess, 2007; Dill, Gentile, Richter, & Dill, 2005; Dill & Thill, 2007; Scharrer, 2004; Williams, Martins, Consalvo, & Ivory, 2009). This is true regardless of whether the source of content studied included game play, cover art, magazine articles, advertisements, or print or digital and Internet images. Male characters are commonly depicted as hypermasculine, powerful, dominant, muscular, and aggressive, whereas female characters are commonly portrayed as hypersexual (with an emphasis on breasts), scantily clad, thin, and attractive and are objectified (Beasley & Standley, 2002; Dill & Thill, 2007; Jansz & Martis, 2007; Miller & Summers, 2007; Robinson, Callister, Clark, & Phillips, 2008; Scharrer, 2004). For example, in a content analysis of popular video game websites, males outnumbered females 3 to 1, 80% of female characters were depicted as thin or very thin, and about a third of female characters had voluptuous breasts (Robinson et al., 2008).

In a related study (Dill & Thill, 2007, Study 2), researchers asked young men and women to describe their schemas for typical male and female video game characters. Results mirrored previous content analytic findings. Schemas for male video game characters focused on aggression, power, and dominance, whereas schemas for female video game characters focused on sexualization, attractiveness, the thin, busty body type, and to a lesser extent on aggressiveness.

Exposure to the vision of women as sex objects activates what has been called the "whore" (Rudman & Borgida, 1995) or "vamp" (Fox & Bailenson, 2009) schema, which increases negative attitudes toward women and Rape Myth Acceptance, whereas exposure to nonstereotypical female avatars does not (Fox & Bailenson, 2009). Interestingly, in addition to being sexualized, research has shown that female game characters are also more likely to be depicted as helpless, needing rescue, and innocent (Dietz, 1998; Miller & Summers, 2007). This dichotomy actually conforms to the predictions of Ambivalent Sexism Theory (Fiske & Glick, 1995; Glick & Fiske, 1996, 2001), which proposes that stereotypes about women incite two categories: benevolent sexism (e.g., the helpless woman) or hostile sexism (e.g., the vamp).

Experimental Studies on Gender in Games

Two studies measured the effects of exposure to sexually objectified female video game avatars and sexual harassment of women. In one study (Yao, Mahood, & Linz, 2010), males played either a video game that sexually objectified women (*Leisure Suite Larry: Magna Cum Laude*) or a control game (*The Sims*). Males exposed to the sexually objectified women self-reported a greater likelihood to sexually harass women and a greater accessibility of a women-as-sex-object schema compared to controls.

In another study, Dill and colleagues (Dill, Brown, & Collins, 2008) found that men, but not women, exposed to sex-typed female (sexualized) and male (aggressive) video game characters made more lenient judgments toward a perpetrator in a real-life case of sexual harassment and advocated more lenient punishment of the perpetrator than did controls who had seen non-objectified females and males. The men who saw the sex-typed characters also felt less sorry for the female victim of sexual harassment and tended to blame the victim to a greater extent than control participants. Similarly, Dill (2009b) found that violent video game play is positively correlated with Rape Myth Acceptance and negative attitudes toward women.

When asked their opinion about the harmfulness of sexualized and aggressive game content, women are more likely than men to think sex-stereotypical and violent content is inappropriate. Men and frequent-gamers are less likely to think game content influences behavior and more likely to categorize negative content as "just harmless entertainment" (Brenick, Henning, Killen, O'Connor, & Collins, 2007).

Race and the Race/Gender Intersection

Women and non-Whites (Blacks, Asians, Latinos, Native Americans) are underrepresented in video games, sending the message that members of these groups are viewed as less important and powerful than White males (Burgess, Dill, Stermer, Burgess, & Brown, in press; Williams et al., 2009). Women of color are almost invisible in video games (Burgess et al., in press). In a content analysis of gender and race in video games, Dunlop (2007) found that characters of color were rare and that few to no characters of color were playable avatars; rather, they were agents controlled by computer algorithms. Furthermore, both Dunlop (2007) and Burgess and colleagues (in press) found that Black male characters were often represented as either street criminals and thugs or athletes. Burgess and colleagues also found that Black male characters were underrepresented as engaging in military or justified violence.

Middle Eastern men have been portrayed disproportionately as targets of violence and have been portrayed by European and American game designers as terrorists specifically and as "the enemy" and "the other" generally (Dill et al., 2005; Sisler, 2008). However, the exception to this rule comes from the serious games movement and from emerging Middle Eastern game makers attempting to introduce "digital dignity" into Arab representations (Sisler, 2008).

Character Aggression

Research indicates that the aggression carried out by video game characters is usually portrayed as justified, retributional, necessary to complete the game, rewarded, and followed by unrealistic consequences (Dietz, 1998; Dill et al., 2005; Haninger, Ryan, & Thompson, 2004; Lachlan, Smith, & Tamborini, 2005; Robinson et al., 2008; Smith et al., 2004; Smith, Lachlan, & Tamborini, 2003). The overall level and realism of violent depictions, the use of guns, and the likelihood of being killed by a gun has risen substantially over time. In addition, female victims and police officer victims have risen significantly across time (Miller, 2009).

Avatars and Agents

As avatars have become more diverse and common, and as technological capabilities have improved, research has appeared that details the psychological ramifications of avatar and agent exposure and manipulation. Avatars and agents can appear in games as well as other venues, such as virtual worlds like Second Life. Yee and Bailenson (2007) labeled the effect of avatar characteristics on the player as the *Proteus effect*. Research on the Proteus effect has found that playing characters wearing black or aggressive clothing primes aggression, resulting in greater aggressive behaviors in-game (Peña, Hancock, & Merola, 2009; Yee & Bailenson, 2007). Furthermore, Fischer, Kastenmuller, and Greitemeyer (2010) found that playing a violent video game with a personalized avatar increased aggression, arousal, and self-activation in players. These results are consonant with findings that identification with game characters enhances imitation (Konijn, Bijvank, & Bushman, 2007).

Avatar attractiveness also influences players' related thoughts and feelings. According to some research, playing as an attractive avatar increases in-game social competence (Yee & Bailenson, 2007). Other research (Barlett & Harris, 2008; Chandler, Konrath, & Schwarz, 2009), however, has indicated that playing as an avatar with an idealized figure increases negative self-thoughts. For example, Barlett and Harris (2008) assigned male and female participants to play a video game with an avatar with an idealized figure. For males, this was a hypermuscular wrestler, for females, a hypersexual beach volleyball player. After playing as the idealized avatar, both male and female players felt significantly worse about their bodies.

Finally, avatar experiences can influence the person's behavior, thoughts, and feelings while in-game or in-world, but they also can carry over to real life. For example, Cabiria (2008) found that gay and lesbian people improved negative identity issues by coming out or seeking authentic connections with other gay and lesbian avatars in Second Life. Furthermore, these in-world experiences often translated to more authentic and positive experiences with gay and lesbian identity in real life.

Video Game Addiction

Many researchers have begun studying the concept of video game addiction, often defined by dysfunctional tendencies surrounding video games, computers, and the Internet. Although there is still considerable debate about how to define it (Shaffer, Hall, & Vander Bilt, 2000; Shaffer & Kidman, 2003; Shaffer et al., 2004), most researchers studying the pathological use of computer or video games have defined it similarly to how pathological gambling is defined—based on damage to family, social, school, occupational, and psychological functioning. Scientific studies using DSM-style criteria to investigate pathological computer or video gaming were first reported in the mid-1990s (Fisher, 1994; Griffiths & Dancaster, 1995; Griffiths & Hunt, 1998); the pace of studies has increased greatly in the past decade. Overall, the studies demonstrate good reliability and validity. That is, the construct of video game addiction can be measured reliably, and people who would be classified as pathological or addicted also demonstrate the patterns of problems and comorbid disorders that we would expect if it was similar to other addictions.

There currently is no medical diagnosis for video game\computer\Internet addiction in the United States. In 2007, the American Medical Association (AMA) released a report on the "addictive potential" of video games (American Medical Association [AMA], 2007). The report concluded with a recommendation

that the "AMA strongly encourage the consideration and inclusion of 'Internet/video game addiction' as a formal diagnostic disorder in the upcoming revision of the *Diagnostic and Statistical Manual of Mental Disorders*-IV" (p. 7). The American Psychiatric Association, which drafts diagnostic criteria for the DSM-V, added a new category of "behavioral addictions," but gambling will initially be the sole disorder. Internet addiction was considered for this category, but work group members decided there was insufficient research data to include it. Instead, they recommended that it be included in the manual's appendix, with the goal of encouraging additional study of Internet/video game addictions (American Psychiatric Association, 2005). New studies are needed to document how large a problem this is, who is most at risk, the etiology of the disorder, how long it lasts, what the outcomes are, whether treatment is needed, and what types of treatment are most effective before it would be accepted as a recognized mental health disorder.

Studies have begun working on this list. At the time of this writing, several studies in several countries have begun documenting the prevalence of people who are at a dysfunctional level. The most comprehensive study to date in the United States used a national sample of over 1,100 youth aged 8 to 18, in which 8.5% of video game players were classified as pathological (Gentile, 2009). In Europe, 11.9% of 7,069 computer gamers fulfilled the diagnostic criteria of computer game addiction (Grüsser, Thalemann, & Griffiths, 2007). A Norwegian study involving 3,237 adolescents between 12 and 18 years of age reported the pathological Internet use rate to be 4%, with an additional 18% showing at-risk use (Johansson & Götestam, 2004a). In the same sample, the prevalence of pathological video game use among video game players was 4%, with an additional 15.5% showing at-risk use (Johansson & Götestam, 2004b). A Chinese study reported a prevalence rate of 10.32% among 503 college students in mainland China (Peng & Li, 2009). In Taiwan, 7.5% of the 517 adolescents in a study were classified as "Internet addicts" (Ko, Yen, Yen, Lin, & Yang, 2007), among whom 42.9% played games online. Among 2,998 Singaporean children, 8.7% met the criteria for pathological video gaming (Choo et al., in press). The percentage of youth who could be considered to be addicted seems remarkably similar across cultures, demonstrating that (1) this is not a problem that is specific to one country, and (2) it is not a trivial number of people who are suffering damage to their lives because of their game play. More research in this area is clearly warranted.

School Performance

Several studies have documented a negative relation between amount of time playing video games and school performance among children, adolescents, and college students (Anderson & Dill, 2000; Anderson et al., 2007; Chan & Rabinowitz, 2006; Chiu, Lee, & Huang, 2004; Cordes & Miller, 2000; Gentile, 2009; Gentile, Lynch, Linder, & Walsh, 2004; Harris & Williams, 1985; Roberts, Foehr, Rideout, & Brodie, 1999; Sharif & Sargent, 2006). The displacement hypothesis, which states that games displace time on other activities, is the most typical explanation for this relation. It could be argued, however, that the relation might be due to the children themselves, rather than to game time. It is highly likely that children who perform more poorly at school are likely to spend more time playing games, where they may feel a sense of mastery that eludes them at school. Nevertheless, each hour a child spends playing entertainment games (in contrast to educational games, which have been demonstrated to have educational benefits) is an hour not spent on homework, reading, exploring, creating, or other things that might have more educational benefit. Some evidence has been found to support the displacement hypothesis. In one nationally representative U.S. sample of 1,491 youth between the ages of 10 and 19, gamers spent 30% less time reading and 34% less time doing homework (Cummings & Vandewater, 2007).Therefore, even if poor school performance tends to cause increases in time playing video games, large amounts of video game play are likely to further hurt school performance.

Visual-Spatial Skills

As mentioned earlier, a number of cross-sectional (e.g., Green & Bavelier, 2003) and a few experimental studies (e.g., Okagaki & Frensch, 1994) have found positive associations between video game play and a wide array of visual/spatial skills. Basically, games that require the player to practice extracting spatial information from the screen appear to improve that specific skill. Furthermore, other tasks that require that practiced skill appear to benefit from the practice. (For a review of this area, see Bailey, West, & Anderson, 2011.) For example, Gopher, Weil, and Bareket (1994) compared the flight performance of Israeli Air Force cadets who had been trained on *Space Fortress II* and an untrained group. They found that trained cadets performed better in almost all aspects of flight performance, resulting in the military adopting the game as a part of its training program. Many (but not all) of these studies used the fast-paced violent games known to increase aggression, thereby demonstrating the point that the same game can produce many types of effects, some of which are generally thought to be positive (e.g., improved visuospatial skills) and others which are generally seen as negative (increased aggression).

Executive Function, Cognitive Control, And Attention Deficits

Although the enhanced visuospatial skills discussed in the previous section have sometimes been misinterpreted—especially by the video game industry and the popular press—to promote the claim that violent video games improve attention in general, an emerging line of research suggests very different conclusions. A number of studies have found a positive association between amount of time using screen media (TV, video games) and various types of attention deficits (for reviews, see Bailey et al., 2001; Swing, Gentile, Anderson, & Walsh, 2001). Several studies have reported that the amount of video game experience is positively correlated with attention deficits, impulsivity, and hyperactivity. For example, Gentile (2009) observed that adolescents reporting pathological video game consumption (about 8.5% of the sample) were 2.77 times more likely to be diagnosed with Attention Deficit Disorder or Attention Deficit Hyperactivity Disorder than were adolescents who reported nonpathological video game consumption. Similar findings have been reported for TV consumption for over a decade (e.g., Christakis, Zimmerman, DiGiuseppe, & McCarty, 2004; Levine & Waite, 2000), leading the American Academy of Pediatrics to recommend that parents dramatically reduce children's screen time.

Recently, the first longitudinal study to specifically test the effects of video game use (Swing et al., 2011) found that even after statistically controlling for the effect of TV exposure, earlier attention problems, and gender, the amount of time spent playing video games by elementary school children predicted increases in teacher-assessed attention problems 13 months later. This study provides the strongest evidence to date that the association between video game play and attention problems is causal, not coincidental. The study also found that the effect of video game play on attention problems was stronger than the effect of TV viewing. What this study did not do, however, was distinguish between different types of video games. There are theoretical reasons to believe that slower paced games that require more controlled thought and planning (whether violent or not), and that some types of fast paced games that require high use of proactive control (e.g., *Rock Band, Guitar Hero*), may not have the same harmful effects as fast paced action games that require primarily reactive action by the player. Such findings have occurred in the TV literature.

A number of studies have examined the relation between video game experience and cognitive control using various versions of the Stroop interference task. In the original version of the Stroop task, participants were shown a series of words one at a time, presented in various colors, with instructions to name the color. Some of the words were color words (*red*). On some trials, a color word was presented in the same color (e.g., the word *red* printed in red), whereas on other trials it was presented in a different color (e.g., *red* printed in green). In general, naming the color is easier (faster) when a color word appears in the same color, and harder (slower) when it appears in a different color. Many variants of this task have been used for decades to assess various types of cognitive control.

Kronenberger et al. (2005) found that adolescents who spend a lot of time watching violent TV and playing violent video games performed more poorly on the Stroop interference task than those who seldom consumed violent media. The high-violence consumers also scored higher on a measure of ADHD. These two media violence effects remained significant even after total screen media time was statistically controlled, suggesting that there is something unique about violent media that contributes to attention problems. Complementing this finding, a study using fMRI found that high video game players failed to recruit anterior cingulate and lateral prefrontal cortex on incongruent trials during performance of the Stroop task, whereas these brain structures were recruited by low video game players (LVGs) (Mathews et al., 2005). This finding led the authors to suggest that video game experience is associated with a disruption in the ability to engage the cognitive control network (Mathews et al., 2005).

One limitation of these Stroop-based studies is that the task design made it impossible to determine whether there was a general effect of video game experience on cognitive control or whether the influence was limited to one or more specific control processes. Bailey et al. (2010) recently addressed this question using both behavioral (i.e., Stroop performance) and event-related brain potential (ERPs) measures to examine the influence of video game experience on proactive and reactive cognitive control. Proactive control represents a future-oriented form of control that serves to optimize task preparation; reactive control represents a just-in-time form of control that serves to resolve conflict within a trial (Braver, Gray, & Burgess, 2007). Bailey et al. (2010) compared performances of high versus low or no video gaming male college students.[2] They found that the conflict adaptation effect (a behavioral measure of proactive control) was attenuated (poorer) in high gamers relative to low or no gamers when there was a long delay between trials. Furthermore, this effect was associated with an attenuation of the ERP indicators of medial frontal negativity and frontal slow wave (ERP indices of proactive control) in high gamers. In other words, both behavioral and brain wave indicators showed that the high gamers were poorer at proactive control. In contrast, there was no difference between high and low gamers on either the behavioral or neural indices of reactive control.

On the whole, these findings complement evidence of an association between playing video games and attention deficits/hyperactivity and lead to the suggestion that video game experience may have a selective effect on proactive cognitive control processes that serve to maintain optimal goal-directed information processing. Of course, additional research using experimental and longitudinal designs is required to establish the causal nature of the effect of video game experience on cognitive control.

Exergames

Past research has usually categorized video game use as a sedentary activity, and this accurately reflected the games of the time. Only in recent years have games with physical activity, often called exergames, become available and popular. The exergaming trend has attracted attention from the general public and those interested in improving public health, especially for youth.

Popular exergames include dancing games such as the series of *Dance, Dance Revolution (DDR)* games and Wii's *Just Dance*. Exergames such as *Wii Fit* translate traditional forms of exercise like yoga and aerobics into an interactive format. Some games include cameras or other equipment designed to give direct feedback in response to players' movements, thus supplying operant conditioning and thereby acting as an interactive trainer.

While past studies have consistently found the majority of top-selling games and children's favorite games to be violent (Buchman & Funk, 1996; Dietz, 1998; Dill et al., 2005; Henry J. Kaiser Family Foundation, 2002), there is a positive trend in game content that has recently emerged. In 2009, of the top 10 console or handheld video games sold in the United States, 4 were exergames or movement games (*Wii Sports Resort, Wii Fit, Wii Fit Plus*, and *Wii Play*) (npd.com, 2010). Three games (*Halo 3* and two versions of *Call of Duty*), including the top-selling game, featured violence as the main action. Seven of the top 10 games were E-rated Nintendo games (6 Wii and 1 DS game). All 10 of the current (May, 2010) top 10 best selling games on Amazon.com's "Kids & Family" video games are Nintendo games (7 Wii, 3 DS). Five of those are exergames, with the best selling being the highly rated Wii game *Just Dance*.

Advocacy organizations have also noticed the popularity of physically active video games. Part of the *Serious Games Initiative*, a group called *Games for Health* (gamesforhealth.org) was founded in 2004. At their annual conference, researchers, health-care professionals, trainers, and others meet to discuss all the ways gaming can improve health. Topics covered include exergaming, biofeedback, training, disease management, and behavior modification. *Games for Health* is affiliated with the Robert Wood Johnson Foundation, which has offered sizable grants to several labs studying applications of gaming to health.

Research on exergames is just appearing and has focused on three main areas: energy expenditure, activity time, and activity preference. Given the recent popular emergence of physically active video games, future research should no longer classify video game play *de facto* as a sedentary activity, but it should categorize game play as either sedentary (such as most traditional violent games) or active, such as exergames like the *Wii Fit*.

---

[2]Although not specifically selected on the basis of violent game play, it should be noted that high gamers typically spend most of their gaming time playing violent games.

Energy Expenditure

Energy expenditure studies have generally found that exergames can be considered a viable form of exercise, though energy output varies by game and gaming experience. For example, Sell et al. (2008) found that college males who were experienced *DDR* players met the American College of Sports Medicine guidelines for moderate physical activity while playing the game, compared to non-players whose play was considered very light activity. Graf, Pratt, Hester, and Short (2009) found that energy expenditure when playing *DDR* and Wii boxing was similar to moderate-intensity walking. In a study of children in Hong Kong (Mellecker & McManus, 2008), those who played an active game involving walking, running, and jumping showed significantly higher energy expenditure and heart rate compared to baseline and to a less active game.

Activity Time and Preference

Because motivation and enjoyment are important factors in whether and how long people exercise, these variables have been studied in relation to exergaming. Studies have used age groups ranging from children to older adults. Findings indicate that people of a variety of ages prefer exergames to other physical activities such as dancing or using an exercise bike, treadmill, or elliptical trainer (McDonough, 2008; Ni Mhurchu et al., 2008; Rhodes, 2008; Rhodes et al., 2009).

During a 12-week intervention, children given an active video game engaged in more physical activity and less inactive video game play than did control children (Mellecker & McManus, 2008). College students had a positive attitude toward exergames in general and thought of exergaming more as entertainment than as exercise. Furthermore, those with low exercise efficacy thought they would be more likely to exercise with an exergame than to do traditional exercise (Klein & Simmers, 2009).

In a study by Rosenberg et al. (2010), community-dwelling senior citizens showed improvement in subsyndromal depression and health-related quality of life after a 12-week intervention where they played Wii sports. Although at first nervous about learning how to play, the seniors were generally highly satisfied with game playing: They enjoyed the challenge and found the games to be fun.

Conclusions

The recent explosion in research on video game effects has greatly improved our understanding of how this medium affects its consumers. Several conclusions can be drawn. First, there are many different effects of playing video games on the player. Some of these are short-term, whereas others are long-term. Second, the specific effects depend on a host of factors, including the content, structure, and context of the game. Third, the same game can have multiple effects on the same person, some of which may be generally beneficial whereas others may be detrimental. Fourth, playing violent video games is a causal risk factor for a host of detrimental effects in both the short- and the long-term, including increasing the likelihood of physically aggressive behavior.

A number of additional conclusions are less well established, and they require further empirical tests. For example, there is a small literature suggesting that playing video games that are both nonviolent and prosocial can lead to increases in short-term and long-term prosocial behavior, and possibly to decreases in aggressive behavior. Also, there is evidence that games with stereotyped images and storylines increase beliefs and behaviors congruent with the stereotypes. Most of this research has focused on gender and race issues. Furthermore, there is emerging evidence that exergames are more attractive to some users than other forms of exercise, that they can improve physical activity levels, and that they are among the most popular games sold today. Video game (and Internet) addiction appears to be a real phenomenon that affects a proportion of gamers. Finally, there is growing evidence that high levels of gaming might create or exacerbate certain types of attention problems. Given the large proportion of people who play games, this could have huge repercussions not only for individual lives, but for the economic welfare of modern society.

References

American Medical Association. (2007). *Emotional and behavioral effects, including addictive potential, of video games* (CSAPH Report 12-A-07). Retrieved on May 27, 2010, from www.ama-assn.org/ama1/pub/upload/mm/467/csaph12a07.doc

American Psychiatric Association. (2005). *DSM-V development*. Retrieved on May 27, 2010, from http://www.dsm5.org/Pages/Default.aspx

Anderson, C. A. (2004). An update on the effects of violent video games. *Journal of Adolescence, 27,* 133–122.

Anderson, C. A., Berkowitz, L., Donnerstein, E., Huesmann, R. L., Johnson, J., Linz, D., et al. (2003). The influence of media violence on youth. *Psychological Science in the Public Interest, 4,* 81–110.

Anderson, C. A., & Bushman, B. J. (2001). Effects of violent video games on aggressive behavior, aggressive cognition, aggressive affect, physiological arousal, and prosocial behavior: A meta-analytic review of the scientific literature. *Psychological Science, 12,* 353–359.

Anderson, C. A., & Bushman, B. J. (2002). Human aggression. *Annual Review of Psychology, 53,* 27–51.

Anderson, C. A., & Carnagey, N. L. (2004). Violent evil and the general aggression model. In A. Miller (Ed.), *The social psychology of good and evil* (pp. 168–192). New York: Guilford Publications.

Anderson, C. A., & Dill, K. E. (2000). Video games and aggressive thoughts, feelings, and behavior in the laboratory and in life. *Journal of Personality & Social Psychology, 78,* 772–791.

Anderson, C. A., Gentile, D. A., & Buckley, K. E. (2007). *Violent video game effects on children and adolescents: Theory, research, and public policy.* New York: Oxford University Press.

Anderson, C. A., & Huesmann, L. R. (2003). Human aggression: A social-cognitive view. In M. A. Hogg & J. Cooper (Eds.), *Handbook of social psychology* (pp. 296–323). London: Sage.

Anderson, C. A., Shibuya, A., Ihori, N., Swing, E. L., Bushman, B. J., Sakamoto, A., et al. (2010). Violent video game effects on aggression, empathy, and prosocial behavior in Eastern and Western countries. *Psychological Bulletin, 136,* 151–173.

Bailey, K., West, R., & Anderson, C. A. (2010). A negative association between video game experience and proactive cognitive control. *Psychophysiology, 47,* 34–42.

Bailey, K., West, R., & Anderson, C. A. (2011). The influence of video games on social, cognitive, and affective information processing. In J. Decety & J. Cacioppo (Eds.), *Handbook of social neuroscience* (pp. 1001–1011). New York: Oxford University Press.

Bandura, A. (1977). *Social learning theory.* New York: Prentice Hall.

Bargh, J. A. (1996). Automaticity in social psychology. In E. T. Higgins & A. W. Kruglanski (Eds.), *Social psychology: Handbook of basic principles* (pp. 169–183). New York: Guilford Press.

Bargh, J. A., & Pietromonaco, P. (1982). Automatic information processing and social perception: The influence of trait information presented outside of conscious awareness on impression formation. *Journal of Personality & Social Psychology, 43,* 437–449.

Barlett, C. P., & Anderson, C. A. (in press). Examining media effects: The general aggression and general learning models. In E. Scharrer (Ed.), *Media effects/media psychology.* Hoboken, NJ: Blackwell-Wiley.

Barlett, C. P., Anderson, C. A., & Swing, E. L. (2009). Video game effects—Confirmed, suspected and speculative: A review of the evidence. *Simulation & Gaming, 40,* 377–403.

Barlett, C. P., & Harris, R. J. (2008). The impact of body emphasizing video games on body image concerns in men and women. *Sex Roles, 59,* 586–601.

Beale, I. L., Kato, P. M., Marin-Bowling, V. M., Guthrie, N., & Cole, S. W. (2007). Improvement in cancer-related knowledge following use of a psychoeducational video game for adolescents and young adults with cancer. *Journal of Adolescent Health, 41*(3), 263–270.

Beasley, B., & Standley, T. C. (2002). Shirts vs. skins: Clothing as an indicator of gender role stereotyping in video games. *Mass Communication & Society, 5,* 279–293.

Berkey, C. S., Rockett, H. R. H., Field, A. E., Gillman, M. W., Frazier, A. L., Camargo, C. A., et al. (2000). Activity, dietary intake, and weight changes in a longitudinal study of preadolescent and adolescent boys and girls. *Pediatrics, 105,* 1–9.

Berkowitz, L. (1989). Frustration-aggression hypothesis: Examination and reformulation. *Psychological Bulletin, 106,* 59–73.

Berkowitz, L. (1993). *Aggression, its causes, consequences, and control.* New York: McGraw-Hill.

Betker, A. L., Szturm, T., Moussavi, Z. K., & Nett, C. (2006). Video game-based exercises for balance rehabilitation: A single-subject design. *Archives of Physical Medicine and Rehabilitation, 87*(8), 1141–1149.

Brasington, R. (1990). Nintendinitis. *New England Journal of Medicine, 322(20),* 1473–1474.

Braver, T. S., Gray, J. R., & Burgess, G. C. (2007). Explaining the many varieties of working memory variation: Dual mechanisms of cognitive control. In A. Conway, C. Jarrold, M. Kane, A. Miyake, & J. Towse (Eds.), *Variation in working memory* (pp. 76–106). New York: Oxford University Press.

Brenick, A., Henning, A., Killen, M., O'Connor, A., & Collins, M. (2007). Social evaluations of stereotypic images in videogames: Unfair, legitimate, or "just entertainment"? *Youth & Society, 38*(4), 395–419.

Buchman, D. D., & Funk, J. B. (1996). Video and computer games in the 90s: Children's time commitment & game preference. *Children Today, 24*(1), 12.

Buckley, K. E., & Anderson, C. A. (2006). A theoretical model of the effects and consequences of playing video games. In P. Vorderer & J. Bryant (Eds.), *Playing video games— Motives, responses, and consequences* (pp. 363–378). Mahwah, NJ: LEA.

Burgess, M. C. R., Dill, K. E., Stermer, S. P., Burgess, S. R., & Brown, B. P. (in press). Playing with prejudice: The prevalence and consequences of racial stereotypes in videogames. *Media Psychology.*

Burgess, M. C. R., Stermer, S. P., & Burgess, S. R. (2007). Sex, lies, and videogames: The portrayal of male and female characters on videogame covers. *Sex Roles, 57,* 419–433.

Cabiria, J (2008). Virtual world and real world permeability: Transference of positive benefits. *Journal of Virtual Worlds Research, 1*(1). Retrieved May 6, 2010, from http://journals.tdl.org/jvwr/article/view/284

Chan, P. A., & Rabinowitz, T. (2006). A cross-sectional analysis of video games and attention deficit hyperactivity disorder symptoms in adolescents. *Annals of General Psychiatry, 5,* 16.

Chandler, J., Konrath, S., & Schwarz, N. (2009). Online and on my mind: Temporary and chronic accessibility moderate the influence of media figures. *Media Psychology, 12*(2), 210–226.

Cherney, I. (2008). Mom, let me play more computer games: They improve my mental rotation skills. *Sex Roles, 59*(11–12), 776–786.

Chiu, S.-I., Lee, J.-Z., & Huang, D.-H. (2004). Video game addiction in children and teenagers in Taiwan. *CyberPsychology and Behavior, 7,* 571–581.

Choo, H., Gentile, D. A., Sim, T., Li, D., Khoo, A., & Liau, A. K. (in press). Pathological video-gaming among Singaporean youth. *Annals of the Academy of Medicine,* Singapore.

Christakis, D. A., Zimmerman, F. J., DiGiuseppe, D. L., & McCarty, C. A. (2004). Early television exposure and subsequent attentional problems in children. *Pediatrics, 113,* 708–713.

Collins, A. M., & Loftus, E. F. (1975). A spreading activation theory of semantic processing. *Psychological Review, 82,* 407–428.

Cordes, C., & Miller, E. (2000). *Fool's gold: A critical look at computers in childhood.* College Park, MD: Alliance for Childhood.

Crick, N., & Dodge, K. (1994). A review and reformulation of social information-processing mechanisms in children's social adjustment. *Psychological Bulletin, 115,* 74–101.

Cummings, H. M. M., & Vandewater, E. A. P. (2007). Relation of adolescent video game play to time spent in other activities. *Archives of Pediatric and Adolescent Medicine, 161*(7), 684–689.

Deutsch, J. E., Borbely, M., Filler, J., Huhn, K., & Guarrera-Bowlby, P. (2008). Use of a low-cost, commercially available gaming console (Wii) for rehabilitation of an adolescent with cerebral palsy. *Physical Therapy, 88*(10), 1196–1207.

DeWall, C. N., & Anderson, C. A. (2011). The general aggression model. Washington, DC: American Psychological Association.

Dietz, T. L. (1998). An examination of violence and gender role portrayals in video games: Implications for gender socialization and aggressive behavior. *Sex Roles, 38,* 425–442.

Dill, K. E. (2009a). *How fantasy becomes reality: Seeing through media influence.* New York: Oxford University Press.

Dill, K. E. (2009b). Violent video games, rape myth acceptance, and negative attitudes towards women. In E. Stark & E. S. Buzawa (Ed.), *Violence against women in families and relationships* (Vol. 4, The Media and Cultural Attitudes, pp. 125–140). Westport, CT: Praeger.

Dill, K. E., Brown, B. P., & Collins, M. A. (2008). Effects of exposure to sex-stereotyped video game characters on tolerance of sexual harassment. *Journal of Experimental Social Psychology, 44,* 1402–1408.

Dill, K. E., Gentile, D. A., Richter, W. A., & Dill, J. C. (2005). Violence, sex, age and race in popular video games: A content analysis.

In E. Cole & J. Henderson-Daniel (Eds.), *Featuring females: Feminist analyses of media.* Washington, DC: American Psychological Association.

Dill, K. E., & Thill, K. P. (2007). Video game characters and the socialization of gender roles: Young people's perceptions mirror sexist media depictions. *Sex Roles, 57,* 851–864.

Dodge, K. A. (1980). Social cognition and children's aggressive behavior. *Child Development, 51,* 620–635.

Dodge, K. A. (1986). A social information processing model of social competence in children. *The Minnesota Symposium on Child Psychology, 18,* 77–125.

Dunlop, J. C. (2007). The U.S. video game industry: Analyzing representation of gender and race. *International Journal of Technology and Human Interaction, 3*(2), 96–109.

Escobar-Chaves, S. L., & Anderson, C.A. (2008). Media and risky behaviors. *Future of Children, 18,* 147–180.

Ferguson, C. J. (2008). The school shooting/violent video game link: Causal link or moral panic? *Journal of Investigative Psychology and Offender Profiling, 5,* 25–37.

Ferguson, C. J. (2009). Violent video games: Dogma, fear, and pseudoscience. *Skeptical Inquirer, 33,* 38–43.

Ferguson, C. J. (2010). Blazing angels or resident evil: Can violent video games be a force for good? *Review of General Psychology, 14,* 68–81.

Fischer, P., Kastenmuller, A., & Greitemeyer, T. (2010). Media violence and the self: The impact of personalized gaming characters in aggressive video games on aggressive behavior. *Journal of Experimental Social Psychology, 46,* 192–195.

Fisher, S. (1994). Identifying video game addiction in children and adolescents. *Addictive Behaviors, 19,* 545–553.

Fiske, S. T., & Glick, P. (1995). Ambivalence and stereotypes cause sexual harassment: A theory with implications for organizational change. *Journal of Social Issues, 51*(1), 97–115.

Fiske, S. T., & Taylor, S. E. (1991). *Social cognition* (2nd ed.). Reading, MA: Addison-Wesley.

Fox, J., & Bailenson, J. N. (2009). Virtual virgins and vamps: The effects of exposure to female characters' sexualized appearance and gaze in an immersive virtual environment, *Sex Roles 61,* 147–157.

Geen, R. G. (2001). *Human aggression.* Philadelphia, PA: Open University Press.

Gentile, D. A. (Ed.). (2003). *Media violence and children.* Westport, CT: Praeger.

Gentile, D. A. (2009). Pathological video-game use among youth ages 8 to 18: A national study. *Psychological Science, 20,* 594–602.

Gentile, D. A. (2011). The multiple dimensions of video game effects. *Child Development Perspectives.*

Gentile, D. A., & Anderson, C. A. (2003). Violent video games: The newest media violence hazard. In D. A. Gentile (Ed.), *Media violence and children* (pp. 131–152). Westport, CT: Praeger Publishing.

Gentile, D. A., Anderson, C. A., Yukawa, S., Ihori, N., Saleem, M., Ming, L. K., et al. (2009). The effects of prosocial video games on prosocial behaviors: International evidence from correlational, experimental, and longitudinal studies. *Personality and Social Psychology Bulletin, 35,* 752–763.

Gentile, D. A., Lynch, P. J., Linder, J. R., & Walsh, D. A. (2004). The effects of violent video game habits on adolescent hostility, aggressive behaviors, and school performance. *Journal of Adolescence, 27*(1), 5–22.

Gentile, D. A., Oberg, C., Sherwood, N. E., Story, M., Walsh, D. A., & Hogan, M. (2004). Wellchild exams in the video age: Pediatricians and the AAP guidelines for children's media use. *Pediatrics, 114,* 1235–1241.

Gentile, D. A., & Sesma, A. (2003). Developmental approaches to understanding media effects on individuals. In D. A. Gentile (Ed.), *Media violence and children: A complete guide for parents and professionals* (pp. 19–38). Westport, CT: Praeger.

Gentile, D. A., & Stone, W. (2005). Violent video game effects on children and adolescents: A review of the literature. *Minerva Pediatrica, 57,* 337–358.

Gibson, J. J. (1979). *The ecological approach to visual perception.* Boston: Houghton Mifflin.

Glick, P., & Fiske, S. T. (1996). The ambivalent sexism inventory: Differentiating hostile and benevolent sexism. *Journal of Personality and Social Psychology, 70*(3), 491–512.

Glick, P., & Fiske, S. T. (2001). An ambivalent alliance: Hostile and benevolent sexism as complementary justifications for gender inequality. *American Psychologist, 56*(2), 109–118.

Gopher, D., Weil, M., & Bareket, T. (1994). Transfer of skill from a computer game trainer to flight. *Human Factors, 36,* 387–405.

Graf, D. L., Pratt, L. V., Hester, C. N., & Short, K. R. (2009). Playing active video games increases energy expenditure in children. *Pediatrics, 124*(2), 534–540.

Green, C. S., & Bavelier, D. (2003). Action video game modifies visual selective attention. *Nature, 423,* 534–537.

Green, C. S., & Bavelier, D. (2006a). Effect of action video games on the spatial distribution of visuospatial attention. *Journal of Experimental Psychology: Human Perception & Performance, 32,* 1465–1478.

Green, C. S., & Bavelier, D. (2006b). Enumeration versus multiple object tracking: The case of action video game players. *Cognition, 101,* 217–245.

Green, C. S., & Bavelier, D. (2007). Action-video-game experience alters the spatial resolution of vision. *Psychological Science, 18,* 88–94.

Greenfield, P. M., Brannon, C., & Lohr, D. (1994). Two-dimensional representation of movement through three-dimensional space: The role of video game expertise. *Journal of Applied Developmental Psychology, 15*(1), 87–103.

Greenfield, P. M., DeWinstanley, H., Kilpatrick, H., & Kaye, D. (1994). Action video games and informal education: Effects on strategies for dividing visual attention. *Journal of Applied Developmental Psychology, 15,* 105–123.

Greitemeyer, T., & Osswald, S. (2009). Prosocial video games reduce aggressive cognitions. *Journal of Experimental Social Psychology, 45,* 896–900.

Griffiths, M. D., & Dancaster, I. (1995). The effect of Type A personality on physiological arousal while playing computer games. *Addictive Behaviors, 20*(4), 543–548.

Griffiths, M. D., & Hunt, N. (1998). Dependence on computer games by adolescents. *Psychological Reports, 82,* 475–480.

Grüsser, S. M., Thalemann, R., & Griffiths, M. D. (2007). Excessive computer game playing: Evidence for addiction and aggression? *CyberPsychology & Behavior, 10,* 290–292.

Haninger, K. M., Ryan, S., & Thompson, K. M. (2004). Violence in teen-rated video games. *Medscape General Medicine, 6*(1), 1.

Harris, M. B., & Williams, R. (1985). Video games and school performance. *Education, 105*(3), 306–309.

Henry J. Kaiser Foundation. (2002, Fall). *Key facts: Children and video games* [Electronic version]. Menlo Park, CA: Author. Retrieved December 20, 2010, from http://www.kff.org/entmedia/3271-index.cfm

Higgins, E. T. (1996). Knowledge activation: Accessibility, applicability, and salience. In E. T. Higgins & A. W. Kruglanski (Eds.), *Social psychology: Handbook of basic principles* (pp. 133–168). New York: Guilford Press.

Huesmann, L. R. (1982). Information processing models of behavior. In N. Hirschberg & L. Humphreys (Eds.), *Multivariate applications in the social sciences* (pp. 261–288). Hillsdale, NJ: Lawrence Erlbaum.

Huesmann, L. R. (1988). An information processing model for the development of aggression. *Aggressive Behavior, 14,* 13–24.

Huesmann, L. R. (1998). The role of social information processing and cognitive schemas in the acquisition and maintenance of habitual aggressive behavior. In R. G. Geen & E. Donnerstein (Eds.), *Human aggression: Theories, research, and implications for policy* (pp. 73–109). New York: Academic Press.

Jansz, J., & Martis, R. G. (2007). The Lara phenomenon: Powerful female characters in video games, *56,* 141–148.

Johansson, A., & Götestam, K. G. (2004a). Internet addiction: Characteristics of a questionnaire and prevalence in Norwegian youth. *Scandinavian Journal of Psychology, 45,* 223–229.

Johansson, A., & Götestam, K. G. (2004b). Problems with computer games without monetary reward: Similarity to pathological gambling. *Psychological Reports, 95,* 641–650.

Khoo, A., & Gentile, D. A. (2007). Problem based learning in the world of games. In O. S. Tan & D. Hung (Eds.), *Problem-based learning and e-learning breakthroughs* (pp. 97–129). Singapore: Thomson Publishing.

Klein, M. J., & Simmers, C. S. (2009). Exergaming: Virtual inspiration, real perspiration. *Young Consumers, 10,* 35–45.

Ko, C., Yen, J., Yen, C., Lin, H., & Yang, M. (2007). Factors predictive for incidence and remission of Internet addiction in young adolescents: A prospective study. *CyberPsychology & Behavior, 10,* 545–551.

Konijn, E. A., Bijvank, M. N., & Bushman, B. J. (2007). I wish I were a warrior: The role of wishful identification in the effects of violent video games on aggression in adolescent boys. *Developmental Psychology, 43,* 1038–1044.

Kronenberger, W. G., Matthews, V. P., Dunn, D. W., Wang, Y., Wood, E. A., Giauque, A. L., et al. (2005). Media violence exposure and executive functioning in aggressive and control adolescents. *Journal of Clinical Psychology, 61,* 725–737.

Lachlan, K. A., Smith, S. L., & Tamborini, R. (2005). Models for aggressive behavior: The attributes of violent characters in popular video games. *Communication Studies, 56*(4), 313–329.

Laurson, K. R., Eisenmann, J. C., Welk, G. J., Wickel, E. E., Gentile, D. A., & Walsh, D. A. (2008). Combined influence of physical activity and screen time recommendations on childhood overweight. *Journal of Pediatrics, 153*(2), 209–214.

Lenhart, A., Kahne, J., Middaugh, E., Macgill, E. R., Evans, C., & Vitak, J. (2008, September 16).

Teens, video games, and civics. Washington, DC: Pew Internet & American Life Project.

Levine, L. E., & Waite, B. M. (2000). Television viewing and attentional abilities in fourth and fifth grade children. *Journal of Applied Developmental Psychology, 21,* 667–679.

Lieberman, D. A. (2001). Management of chronic pediatric diseases with interactive health games: Theory and research findings. *Journal of Ambulatory Care Management, 24,* 26–38.

Markey, P. M., & Markey, C. N. (2010). Vulnerability to violent video games: A review and integration of personality research. *Review of General Psychology, 14,* 82–91.

Mathews, V. P., Kronenberger, W. G., Wang, Y., Lurito, J. T., Lowe, M. J., & Dunn, D. W. (2005). Media violence exposure and frontal lobe activation measured by functional magnetic resonance imaging in aggressive and nonaggressive adolescents. *Journal of Computer Assisted Tomography, 29,* 287–292.

McDonough, S. (2008). *Comparison of an interactive dance video game and traditional exercise equipment relative to use preferences and energy expenditure in adolescent females ages 16–18.* Doctoral dissertation, The University of Mississippi, 2008). Retrieved May 4, 2010, from Dissertations & Theses: Full Text. (Publication No. AAT 3361189).

Mellecker, R. R., & McManus, A. M. (2008). Energy expenditure and cardiovascular responses to seated and active gaming in children. *Archives of Pediatric and Adolescent Medicine, 162*(9), 886–891.

Miller, M. K. (2009). Content analysis of the 18-year evolution of violence in video game magazines. *Journal of Criminal Justice and Popular Culture, 16*(1), 81–102.

Miller, M. K., & Summers, A. (2007). Gender differences in video game characters' roles, appearances, and attire as portrayed in video game magazines. *Sex Roles, 57,* 733–742.

Mischel, W. (1973). Toward a cognitive social learning reconceptualization of personality. *Psychological Review, 80,* 252–283.

Mischel, W., & Shoda, Y. (1995). A cognitive-affective system theory of personality: Reconceptualizing situations, dispositions, dynamics, and invariance in personality structure. *Psychological Review, 102,* 246–268.

Murphy, R. F., Penuel, W., Means, B., Korbak, C., Whaley, A., & Allen, J. E. (2002). *A review of recent evidence on the effectiveness of discrete educational software.* Washington, DC: Planning and Evaluation Service, U.S. Department of Education.

Ni Mhurchu, C., Maddison, R., Jiang, Y., Jull, A., Prapavessis, H., & Rodgers, A. (2008). Couch potatoes to jumping beans: A pilot study of the effect of active video games on physical activity in children. *International Journal of Behavioral Nutrition and Physical Activity, 5,* 1–8.

Npd.com. (2010). *2009 U.S. video game industry and PC game software retail sales reach $20.2 billion.* Retrieved May 27, 2010, from http://www.npd.com/press/releases/press_100114.html

Okagaki, L., & Frensch, P. A. (1994). Effects of interactive entertainment technologies on development. *Journal of Applied Developmental Psychology, 15,* 33–58.

Osofsky, J. D. (1995). The effects of exposure to violence on young children. *American Psychologist, 50,* 782–788.

Peña, J., Hancock, J. T., & Merola, N. A. (2009). The priming effects of avatars in virtual settings. *Communication Research, 36,* 838–856.

Peng, L. H., & Li, X. (2009). A survey of Chinese college students addicted to video games. *China Education Innovation Herald, 28,* 111–112.

Rhodes, A. (2008, July). Legislative efforts to combat childhood obesity. *Journal for Specialists in Pediatric Nursing, 13,* 223–225.

Rhodes, R. E., Warburton, D. E. R., & Bredin, S. S. D. (2009). Predicting the effect of interactive video bikes on exercise adherence: An efficacy trial. *Psychology, Health & Medicine, 14*(6), 631–640.

Roberts, D. F., Foehr, U. G., Rideout, V. J., & Brodie, M. (1999). *Kids & media @ the new millennium.* Menlo Park, CA: Kaiser Family Foundation.

Robinson, T., Callister, M., Clark, B., & Phillips, J. (2008). Violence, sexuality, and gender stereotyping: A content analysis of official video game web sites. *Web Journal of Mass Communication Research, 13,* 1–17.

Rosenberg, D., Depp, C. A., Vahia, I. V., Reichstadt, J., Palmer, B. W., Kerr, J., Norman, G., & Jeste, D. V. (2010). Exergames for subsyndromal depression in older adults: A pilot study of a novel intervention. *American Journal of Geriatric Psychiatry, 18,* 221–226.

Rudman, L. A., & Borgida, E. (1995). The afterglow of construct accessibility: The behavioral consequences of priming men to view women as sexual objects. *Journal of Experimental Social Psychology, 31,* 493–517.

Scharrer, E. (2004). Virtual violence: Gender and aggression in video game advertisements. *Mass Communication & Society, 7,* 393–412.

Sell, K., Lillie, T., & Taylor, J. (2008). Energy expenditure during physically interactive video game playing in male college students with different playing experience, *Journal of American College Health, 56,* 505–511.

Shaffer, H. J., Hall, M. N., & Vander Bilt, J. (2000). "Computer addiction": A critical consideration. *American Journal of Orthopsychiatry, 70,* 162–168.

Shaffer, H. J., & Kidman, R. (2003). Shifting perspectives on gambling and addiction. *Journal of Gambling Studies, 19,* 1–6.

Shaffer, H. J., LaPlante, D. A., LaBrie, R. A., Kidman, R. C., Donato, A. N., & Stanton, M. V. (2004). Toward a syndrome model of addiction: Multiple expressions, common etiology. *Harvard Review of Psychiatry, 12,* 367–374.

Sharif, I., & Sargent, J. D. (2006). Association between television, movie, and video game exposure and school performance. *Pediatrics, 118*(4), e1061–1070.

Sisler, V. (2008). Digital Arabs: Representation in video games. *European Journal of Cultural Studies, 11*(2), 203–219.

Smith, S. L., Lachlan, K., Pieper, K. M., Boyson, A. R., Wilson, B. J., Tamborini, R., et al. (2004). Brandishing guns in American media: Two studies examining how often and in what context firearms appear on television and in popular video games. *Journal of Broadcasting & Electronic Media, 48*(4), 584–606.

Smith, S. L., Lachlan, K., & Tamborini, R. (2003). Popular video games: Quantifying the presentation of violence and its context, *Journal of Broadcasting & Electronic Media, 47,* 58–76.

Surgeon General. (2001, April 11). *Youth violence: A report of the surgeon general.* Washington, DC: United States Surgeon General.

Swing, E. L., Gentile, D. A., Anderson, C. A., & Walsh, D. A. (2011). Television and video game exposure and the development of attention problems. *Pediatrics.*

Taylor, L. N. (2006). Positive features of video games. In N. Dowd, D. G. Singer, & R. F. Wilson (Eds.), *Handbook of children, culture and violence* (pp. 247–265). Thousand Oaks, CA: Sage.

Vandewater, E. A., Shim, M., & Caplovitz, A. G. (2004). Linking obesity and activity level with children's television and video game use. *Journal of Adolescence, 27,* 71–85.

Wegner, D. M., & Bargh, J. A. (1998). Control and automaticity in social life. In D. Gilbert, S. Fiske, & G. Lindzey (Eds.), *The handbook of social psychology* (pp. 446–496). New York: McGraw-Hill.

Williams, D., Martins, N., Consalvo, M., & Ivory, J. D. (2009). The virtual census: Representations of gender, race and age in video games. *New Media & Society, 11,* 815–834.

Yao, M. Z., Mahood, C., & Linz, D. (2010). Sexual priming, gender stereotyping, and likelihood to sexually harass: Examining the cognitive effects of playing a sexually-explicit video game. *Sex Roles, 62,* 77–88.

Yee, N., & Bailenson, J. N. (2007). The Proteus effect: The effect of transformed self-representation on behavior. *Human Communication Research, 33,* 271–290.

CHAPTER 14

Research on Sex in the Media

What Do We Know About Effects on Children and Adolescents?

Paul J. Wright
Indiana University

Neil M. Malamuth
University of California, Los Angeles

Ed Donnerstein
University of Arizona

This chapter examines scientific theory and research regarding the effects of sexual content in the mass media on children's and adolescents' sexual beliefs, attitudes, and behaviors. Research on sexual media has often been divided into two categories. The first may be referred to as "embedded sexual content." Here the sexual content is embedded within a larger context that includes considerable nonsexual content; the primary purpose is not to sexually arouse the consumer, although this may be one of the varied effects of exposure. Such content would be illustrated by a soap opera in which some of the scenes, although typically not a majority, include references to or actual portrayals of sexual interactions. The second category— "sexually explicit media"—consists of materials that primarily depict nudity and simulated or actual sexual acts (e.g., intercourse, fellatio) not embedded or interwoven with much nonsexual content. The primary function of such portrayals for consumers is to view nudity or sex, often as a stimulant for sexual arousal. We refer to such content as pornography, without any pejorative meaning intended. We acknowledge that the distinction between embedded and explicit sexual content is not always clear. Nevertheless, there are still some meaningful distinctions that may be made between these two types of media that will help frame our discussion.

Our primary focus is research on "embedded sexual content," but we also consider some relevant findings on sexually explicit media. Although concentrating on the first category, and considering as much as possible research in which the participants have been below the age of 18, we also describe studies of young adults. We include these studies because there are sound theoretical and empirical reasons to assume that the effects found with young adults would occur for younger individuals as well. Findings related to youths' experience with sex on the Internet are also reviewed. Finally, we will take a look at various solutions that might be considered in mitigating any undesirable effects from exposure to sexual media content.

Embedded Sexual Content

This section summarizes research on embedded sexual content in mainstream entertainment mass media. Both the extent and nature of embedded sexual depictions are assessed. Additionally, the most current data on children's and adolescents' mass media consumption patterns are outlined. Finally, the effects of exposure to embedded sexual content on young people's sexual beliefs, attitudes, and behaviors are explored.

Extent and Nature of Embedded Sexual Depictions

Television, feature-length films, and lifestyle magazines have been the three mainstream media most commonly analyzed for embedded sexual content. Our recent review of this literature (Wright, 2009a) reveals four important themes. To start, the mass media environment in general and the mass media vehicles preferred by young people in particular feature a good deal of sexual content. Kunkel, Eyal, Finnerty, Biely, and Donnerstein (2005) compared the finding from their analysis of 2004–05 television programs with the findings from a previous analysis of programs taped in 2001–02 (Kunkel et al., 2003) and their first analysis of programs taped in 1997–98 (Kunkel et al., 1999). The amount of sexual content on television appears to have

increased in recent years. In 2004–05, 70% of programs had sexual content. In contrast, less than 65% of programs had sexual content in 2001–02 and 56% of programs had sexual content in 1997–98 (see Figure 14.1). Programs popular with adolescents are even more likely to feature sexual depictions than television programs industrywide. In 2001–02, 83% of adolescents' favorite programs contained sexual content, compared to 64% of programs across the entire television landscape. Similarly, in 2004–05, teens' favorite programs averaged 6.7 sexual scenes per hour while the average number of sexual scenes industrywide was 5.0. About one-third of the PG and PG-13 films in Bufkin and Eschholz's (2000) sample of top-grossing films contained a sex scene and 57% of R-rated pictures contained a sexual scene. Likewise, 23 out of the 25 PG-13 and R-rated movies in Dempsey and Reichert's (2000) study of frequently rented films contained at least one instance of sexual behavior. Lifestyle magazines for older adolescent females (McMahon, 1990; Prusank, Duran, & DeLillo, 1993), younger adolescent females (Duffy & Gotcher, 1996; Evans, Rutberg, Sather, & Turner, 1991), and adolescent males (Taylor, 2005a) also feature numerous sexual accounts and descriptions.

Second, messages about the risks of sexual activity (e.g., pregnancy, STIs) and sexual responsibility (e.g., condom use) are infrequent on television, in films, and in lifestyle magazines targeting adolescent males. Only 14% of shows with sexual content across the entire television landscape and only 10% of teen preferred programs with sexual content contained a risk or responsibility reference in 2004–2005 (see Figure 14.2; Kunkel et al., 2005). In films, references to contraception are rare (Abramson & Mechanic, 1983; Greenberg et al., 1993; Gunasekera, Chapman, & Campbell, 2005) and mentions of HIV or other STIs are even more infrequent (Gunasekera et al., 2005). Taylor (2005a) did not find a single article with a primary focus on issues such as pregnancy, AIDS, or safe sex in his review of male magazines such as *Maxim* and *Stuff*. On the other hand, about 1 in 2 articles with sexual content in female lifestyle magazines mention issues such as contraception and unplanned pregnancy (Walsh-Childers, Treise, & Gotthoffer, 1997).

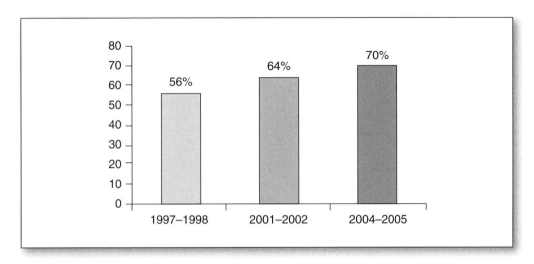

Figure 14.1 Percent of Television Shows With Sexual Content, Over Time

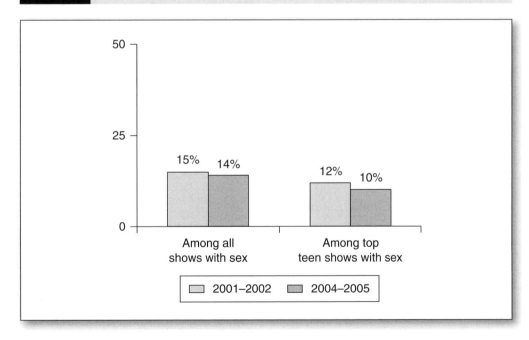

Figure 14.2 Percent of Television Shows With Sexual Content That Also Include Sexual Risk and Responsibility Messages, Over Time

Third, embedded media sex is often recreational and infrequently involves married couples. Across the entire television landscape, 15% of intercourse scenes involve people who have just met and 47% of intercourse scenes involve people who have no established or decipherable relationship (Kunkel et al., 2005). Ward (1995) found that the characters in teens' favorite prime-time programs view sex as a casual, recreational behavior that is often separate from relational commitments and rarely paired with procreational concerns. A consistent finding in film studies is that sex is the province of the unmarried and newly acquainted. More than 8 out of 10 sexual acts coded in Dempsey and Reichert's (2000) study occurred between unmarried partners. The ratio of unmarried intercourses to married intercourses was 32:1 in Greenberg and colleagues' (1993) study of R-rated films popular with young audiences. Gunasekera and company (2005) found that sex in popular films primarily occurs between persons who have only recently met, and Bufkin and Eschholz (2000) report a similar pattern. Although messages in women's magazines are often contradictory, a common theme "seems to be to enjoy sex for its physical pleasure . . . without concern for a long term relationship" (Prusank et al., 1993, p. 312). Sex before marriage is assumed in teen magazines: the only questions are "where, when, and with whom" (Garner, Sterk, & Adams, 1998, p. 73).

Finally, sexual portrayals in mainstream media are stereotypical and highly gendered. Much of the "humor" that takes place on prime-time programs is sexual, at females' expense, and could be classified as sexual harassment (Grauerholz & King, 1997). Males on adolescents' favorite television programs are preoccupied with females' physical appearance, obsessed with sex, and derive a sense of self from their sexual conquests. Females on adolescents' favorite programs often participate in their own sexual objectification and commonly desire males for their wealth, power, and status (Kim et al., 2007; Ward, 1995). Teen and women's magazines instruct females that they can exchange beauty and sex for male companionship (Duffy & Gotcher, 1996; Durham, 1996). Male-oriented periodicals support this idea, as scantily clad, provocatively posed females fill the pages of magazines targeting adolescent males (Taylor, 2005a).

Exposure Patterns

Do traditional media such as television, films, and magazines still play a prominent role in young people's lives in the modern-day media environment? The answer provided by the latest Kaiser Family Foundation study of United States 8- to 18-year-olds' media use is "absolutely" (Rideout, Foehr, & Roberts, 2010). When all of the various delivery platforms are considered (e.g., laptops, cell phones, iPods, actual TV sets), in 2009, young

people spent about 31.5 hours watching television a week. In 1999, they spent 26.5 hours a week watching television. In 2009, children and adolescents spent more than 6.5 hours a week watching films in and out of theaters. In 1999, they spent less than 5.5 hours a week watching films. Youthful magazine readers spend about the same amount of time reading magazines in print today as they did a decade ago, but they now also have the opportunity to read their favorite magazines online. In sum, it seems that "one of the main roles 'new' communication technologies play is to bring more 'old' media content into young people's lives" (Rideout et al., 2010, p. 15).

Effects of Exposure

Barren for some time, the mass media sexual effects research landscape has produced significant bounty in recent years (see Table for 14.1 for a list and summary of United States studies). The following subsections highlight studies of the effects of embedded sexual content on young people. Studies are organized by outcome (belief, attitude, behavior), by design (correlational, experimental), and by their linkage with the content themes reviewed (sexual risks and responsibilities, sexual permissiveness, and sexual stereotyping).

Beliefs. Beliefs are cognitions without valence (e.g., "Many teens in relationships have sex") and should be the sexual outcome variable most amenable to media influence. As the content findings presented previously would suggest, mass media exposure is correlated with naivety about the risks associated with having sex. High school students who are soap opera viewers are more likely than nonviewers to believe that unmarried teen mothers finish college, have healthy babies, male friends who help with child-rearing, and better-than-minimum-wage jobs (Larson, 1996). Junior high and high school-aged youth who view more sexual television are less likely than their peers who view less sexual television to believe that they would experience negative consequences from having intercourse such as contracting HIV or being involved in a pregnancy. On the other

(Text Continued on page 283)

Table 14.1	Summary of Studies Assessing United States Youths' Exposure to Entertainment Mass Media and Sexual Beliefs, Attitudes, and Behaviors

Method	*Year and author*	*Sample*	*Outcome*	*Major finding*
Cross-sectional survey	1976a. Baran	Young adults	2	Seeing media sex as real and perceiving that media characters are sexually satisfied negatively correlated with virginity satisfaction
Cross-sectional survey	1976b. Baran	Adolescents	2	Perceiving that media characters are more sexually capable and experienced negatively correlated with sexual satisfaction
Cross-sectional survey	1981. Buerkel-Rothfuss & Mayes	Young adults	1	Soap opera viewing positively correlated with estimates of real world sexual phenomena, including affairs
Cross-sectional survey	1985. Carveth & Alexander	Young adults	1	Soap opera viewing positively correlated with estimates of the number of children conceived outside of marriage
Cross-sectional survey	1987. Fabes & Strouse	Young adults	2, 3	Perceiving that media models are sexually responsible positively correlated with frequency of sexual intercourse
Cross-sectional survey	1987. Strouse & Buerkel-Rothfuss	Young adults	2, 3	Music TV and soap opera viewing positively correlated with number of lifetime sexual partners
Cross-sectional survey	1988. Solderman, Greenberg, & Linsangen	Adolescents	3	Pregnant teens watched more sexual TV and R-rated films than non-pregnant teens
Cross-sectional survey	1990. Potter and Chang	Adolescents	1, 2	TV and film viewing positively correlated with estimates of extramarital affairs
Cross-sectional survey	1991. Signorielli	Adolescents	2	TV viewing positively, but very weakly, associated with permissive premarital and extramarital sex attitudes
Cross-sectional survey	1993. Buerkel-Rothfuss & Strouse	Young adults	1	TV viewing negatively correlated with estimates of the number of people who remain sexually abstinent until marriage
Cross-sectional survey	1994. Olson	Young adults	1, 2	Soap opera viewers reported less need for contraception use than nonviewers
Cross-sectional survey	1994. Strouse, Goodwin, & Roscoe	Adolescents	2	Music video exposure positively correlated with acceptance of behaviors indicative of sexual harassment

(Continued)

Table 14.1 (Continued)

Method	Year and author	Sample	Outcome	Major finding
Cross-sectional survey	1995. Mullin & Linz	Young adults	1	Viewing "slasher" films positively correlated with belief in rape myths
Cross-sectional survey	1995. Peterson & Kahn	Adolescents	3	Exposure to music TV and other "antisocial" media positively correlated with sexual experience (including coitus)
Cross-sectional survey	1995. Strouse, Buerkel-Rothfuss, & Long	Adolescents	2, 3	Exposure to music TV positively correlated with having had coitus among adolescents from unsatisfactory family environments
Cross-sectional survey	1996. Larson	Adolescents	1	Soap opera viewing positively correlated with unrealistic beliefs about teenage motherhood
Cross-sectional survey	1998. Davis & Mares	Adolescents	1, 2	Talk show viewing positively correlated with estimates of teenage sex and extramarital affairs
Cross-sectional survey	1999. Haferkamp	Young adults	2	TV viewing positively correlated with unrealistic sexual expectations (i.e., "sexual perfectionism")
Cross-sectional survey	1999. Ward & Rivadeneyra	Young adults	1, 2, 3	TV viewing positively correlated with females' level of sexual experience
Cross-sectional survey	2002. Ward	Young adults	1, 2	TV viewing positively correlated with the belief that females are sex objects and estimates of peers' sexual experience
Cross-sectional survey	2003. Aubrey, Harrison, Kramer, & Yellin	Young adults	1	The more TV males watch the more sexual variety they expect; the more TV females watch, the earlier they expect sex in relationships
Cross-sectional survey	2004. Hatoum & Belle	Young adults	2	Magazine and film consumption positively correlated with the view that plump women cannot be sexually attractive
Cross-sectional survey	2004. Kim & Ward	Young adults	1, 2	Reading female targeted magazines positively correlated with stereotypical sexual beliefs and recreational attitudes towards sex
Cross-sectional survey	2005. Pardun, L'Engle, & Brown	Adolescents	2, 3	Exposure to a variety of media positively correlated with light and heavy sexual activity and sexual intentions

Method	Year and author	Sample	Outcome	Major finding
Cross-sectional survey	2005. Ward, Hansbrough, & Walker	Adolescents	1, 2	Music video consumption positively correlated with stereotypical sexual beliefs
Cross-sectional survey	2006a. Chia	Young adults	1, 2	Perceptions of media influence on peers positively correlated w/ perceptions of peer sexual permissiveness; perceptions of peer permissiveness positively correlated w/ casual sex intentions
Cross-sectional survey	2006b. Chia	Young adults	1, 2	Perceptions of media influence on peer sexual norms positively related to adolescents' own sexual attitudes; own sexual attitudes positively correlated w/ casual sex intentions
Cross-sectional survey	2006. Taylor	Young adults	1, 2, 3	Reading male-targeted magazines positively correlated with permissive sexual attitudes
Cross-sectional survey	2006. Ward & Friedman	Adolescents	1, 2, 3	Music video and talk show viewing positively correlated with sexual experience (including coitus)
Cross-sectional survey	2006. Ward, Merriwether, & Caruthers	Young adults	1, 2	Exposure to popular men's magazines positively correlated with masculine ideologies (e.g., sexual objectification of women)
Cross-sectional survey	2006. Zurbriggen & Morgan	Young adults	1, 2, 3	Relationship between viewing reality dating TV and sexual beliefs and attitudes mediated by viewing motivations
Cross-sectional survey	2007. Kaestle, Halpern, & Brown	Adolescents	2	Music video & pro-wrestling exposure positively correlated with date rape acceptance for males
Cross-sectional survey	2008. DuRant, Neiberg, Champion, Rhodes, & Wolfson	Adolescents	3	Watching pro-wrestling negatively correlated with birth control use
Cross-sectional survey	2008. Zhang, Miller, & Harrison.	Young adults	1, 2	Music video exposure positively correlated with both permissive sexual attitudes and stereotypical sexual beliefs
Cross-sectional survey	2009. Bleakley, Hennessy, Fishbein, & Jordan	Adolescents	1	Getting sexual information from movies and magazines positively correlated with belief that coitus without birth control is possible
Cross-sectional survey	2009. Fisher et al.	Adolescents	3	Watching cable TV positively correlated with having had coitus and oral sex

(Continued)

Table 14.1 (Continued)

Method	Year and author	Sample	Outcome	Major finding
Longitudinal survey	1991. Brown & Newcomer	Adolescents	3	T3 sexual TV exposure positively related to T3 coital status; T2 sexual experience unrelated to T3 sexual TV exposure
Longitudinal survey	1991. Peterson, Moore, & Furstenberg	Adolescents	3	Males who watched TV away from their parents at T1 were more likely to have had coitus by T2
Longitudinal survey	1993. Walsh-Childers & Brown	Adolescents	1	T1 TV viewing primarily unrelated to T2 sexually stereotyped beliefs
Longitudinal survey	2003. Collins, Elliot, Berry, Kanouse, & Hunter	Adolescents	1	Viewers of a show w/ a condom scene more likely at T2 than nonviewers to state that condoms are 95% to 100% effective
Longitudinal survey	2003. Wingood et al.	Adolescents	3	T1 rap video exposure positively related to number of lifetime sexual partners and contracting an STI at T2
Longitudinal survey	2004. Collins et al.	Adolescents	3	T1 TV exposure positively associated with having had coitus at T2
Longitudinal survey	2005. Martino, Collins, Kanouse, Elliot, & Berry	Adolescents	1, 3	Safe-sex self-efficacy, perceived peer norms, & outcome expectations mediate the over time association between TV exposure & coital debut
Longitudinal survey	2006. Ashby, Arcari, & Edmonson	Adolescents	3	T1 TV exposure positively associated with having had coitus at T2
Longitudinal survey	2006. Brown et al.	Adolescents	3	T1 media exposure positively associated with having had coitus at T2
Longitudinal survey	2007. Aubrey	Young adults	1	T1 TV viewing negatively related to T2 sexual-self concept (i.e., perception of one's qualities in the sexual domain)
Longitudinal survey	2008. Bleakley, Hennessy, Fishbein, & Jordan	Adolescents	3	T1 media exposure positively associated with T2 sexual experience; T1 sexual experience positively associated with T2 media exposure
Longitudinal survey	2008. Chandra et al.	Adolescents	3	T1 TV viewing positively associated with pregnancy involvement by either T2 or T3
Longitudinal survey	2009. Hennessy, Bleakley, Fishbein, & Jordan	Adolescents	3	White youths' sexual media exposure and sexual experience levels positively covaried over time

Method	Year and author	Sample	Outcome	Major finding
Experiment	1981. Malamuth & Check	Young adults	1	Males who saw sexual violence in feature films more likely to believe in rape myths
Experiment	1983. Greenberg, Perry, & Covert	Children	1	Viewing educational programming about sex enhanced children's sexual knowledge
Experiment	1983. Silverman-Watkins & Sprafkin	Adolescents	1	Older adolescents understood sexual innuendos on TV better than younger adolescents
Experiment	1986. Greeson & Williams	Adolescents	2	Exposing adolescents to MTV videos led to more positive attitudes towards premarital sex
Experiment	1988. Hansen and Hansen	Young adults	1	Watching sexually stereotypical music videos led to expectations that females should reciprocate males' sexual advances
Experiment	1988. Linz, Donnerstein, & Penrod	Young adults	1, 2	Repeated exposure to "slasher" films desensitized males to the degrading portrayals of women in these films
Experiment	1988. Sigal, Gibbs, Adams, & Derfler	Young adults	1	Exposure to "flirtatious" film clips did not affect judgments of a coed's behavior
Experiment	1993. Calfin, Carroll, & Shmidt	Young adults	2	Exposure to music videos led to more liberal sexual attitudes
Experiment	1993. Greenberg et al.	Adolescents	1	Exposure to a peculiar choice of experimental stimuli (prostitution/married sex vs. homosexual sex/unmarried sex) produced very few differences between conditions
Experiment	1994. Bryant & Rockwell	Adolescents	2	Family values, family communication, and critical viewing mitigated the effects of sexually licentious TV
Experiment	1994. Hansen & Krygowski	Young adults	1	The effects of sexually objectifying music videos on judgments are enhanced by physiological arousal
Experiment	1995. Johnson, Adams, Ashburn, & Reed	Adolescents	2	Exposure to sexist rap videos led to less negative attitudes towards teen dating violence among females
Experiment	1995. Weisz & Earls	Young adults	1, 2	Males' belief in rape myths more affected by sexual violence in films than females' belief in rape myths

(Continued)

Table 14.1 (Continued)

Method	Year and author	Sample	Outcome	Major finding
Experiment	1997. Gan, Zillman, & Mitrook	Young adults	1	Whites' exposure to sexually provocative Black female rappers led to negative sexual evaluations of Black women
Experiment	1999. Kalof	Young adults	1	Exposure to sexually stereotypical music videos led to heightened adversarial sexual beliefs
Experiment	2002. Mazur & Emmers-Sommer	Young adults	2	Exposure to a film with homosexual themes led to more positive attitudes towards non-traditional sexualities
Experiment	2002. Ward	Young adults	1, 2	Exposing females to sexual TV increased their belief that men are sex driven, that dating is a game, and that women are sexual objects
Experiment	2005. Ferguson, Berlin, & Noles	Young adults	1	Exposure to promiscuous women on talk shows led to desensitized views of sexual harassment
Experiment	2005b. Taylor	Young adults	1, 2	Realism perceptions enhanced the effects of exposure to sexual TV on content congruent attitudes and beliefs
Experiment	2005. Ward et al.	Adolescents	1	Exposure to sexist music videos enhanced sexual stereotypes
Experiment	2006. Emmers-Sommer, Pauley, Hanzal, & Triplett	Young adults	1	Females' rape myth acceptance lowered by showing them a film that depicted rape
Experiment	2006. Farrar	Young adults	2	Exposure to TV dramas w/ condom depictions improved females' attitudes towards safe sex
Experiment	2006. Ward & Friedman	Adolescents	1	Exposure to TV sitcoms and dramas increased sexually objectified beliefs about women
Experiment	2008. Eyal & Kunkel	Young adults	2	Exposure to TV shows that portrayed negative sexual consequences led to more negative attitudes towards premarital intercourse
Experiment	2008. Nabi & Clark	Young adults	2	Showing episode specific negative sexual consequences on TV may not lead to sexual inhibition if viewers believe the protagonist will ultimately be unaffected in the long run
Experiment	2008. Taylor	Young adults	2	Reading women's magazine articles with different sexual frames affects readers' mate preferences

Note: For outcome: 1 = sexual beliefs, 2 = sexual attitudes, 3 = sexual behavior.

hand, they are more likely to believe that having intercourse would lead to positive consequences such as making them feel grown up or gaining social status (Fisher et al., 2009).

Correlational studies also show that mass media exposure is associated with beliefs about promiscuity and recreational sex. College students who watch more soap operas believe that more men and women have affairs than college students who watch fewer soap operas (Buerkel-Rothfuss & Mayes, 1981). High school students' beliefs about the prevalence of extramarital sex positively covaries with their talk show viewing habits (Davis & Mares, 1998). Similarly, college students who watch more television programming known for its sexual content make higher estimates of the number of people who have sex without love and lower estimates of the number of people who remain sexually abstinent until marriage (Buerkel-Rothfuss & Strouse, 1993). Experimentally, Taylor (2005b) demonstrated that college students' beliefs about the sexual activity of their female peers can be affected by exposing them to sexual television that they perceive as realistic.

The effects of the mass media on stereotypical sexual beliefs have also been studied. The more female college students read teen magazines and the more they read women's magazines for advice, the more likely they are to believe that males are sex driven and fear commitment (Kim & Ward, 2004). The more male college students read popular men's magazines, the more likely they are to believe in stereotypical masculine views such as "men think about sex all the time" and "men love a challenge and often choose to pursue the seemingly unattainable women" (Ward, Merriwether, & Caruthers, 2006, p. 707). Watching music videos and believing in different sexual standards for men and women (Zhang, Miller, & Harrison, 2008) and reality television viewing and believing that male–female relationships are inherently adversarial (Zurbriggen & Morgan, 2006) are also correlated among youth. Experimental studies have found similar patterns. Exposing college students to gendered music videos strengthens their adversarial sexual beliefs (Kalof, 1999). Exposing high school students to sexual television increases their belief that sexually objectified views of women have real-world veracity (Ward & Friedman, 2006).

Attitudes. Attitudes are valenced cognitions (e.g., "There is nothing wrong with two teens in a relationship having sex") and should be more resistant to media influence than beliefs. Nevertheless, the power of the media to influence young people's sexual attitudes has been suggested or demonstrated by many studies. Hust, Brown, and L'Engle's (2008) study of the infrequent sexual health messaging in adolescents' favorite mainstream media found that safe-sex behavior is depicted as the province of females, not males. It is not surprising, then, that an experimental study using television programs with or without condom depictions had an effect on female but not male college students' positive attitudes toward safe sex (Farrar, 2006).

Several studies have explored the relationship between mass media exposure and young people's sexually permissive attitudes. Reading male-targeted magazines is associated with higher levels of premarital sexual permissiveness among male college students (Taylor, 2006), and reading women's magazines is positively associated with recreational attitudes toward sex among female college students (Kim & Ward, 2004). Other correlational studies have generated parallel results for television viewing and sexual permissiveness among both college (Ward & Rivadeneyra, 1999) and high school students (Strouse, Buerkel-Rothfuss, & Long, 1995). Experimental work has found that music video exposure leads to more acceptance of premarital sex (Greeson & Williams, 1986) among middle and high school students and more liberal sexual attitudes among college students (Calfin, Carroll, & Shmidt, 1993). Bryant and Rockwell (1994) showed that exposing young teenagers to television programming with recreational sex themes inures them to sexually licentious behavior. Similar findings have accrued from sexual stereotyping studies. For instance, the more male college students read male-targeted magazines and watch movies, the more likely they are to hold the attitude that plump women cannot be sexually attractive (Hatoum & Belle, 2004), and exposing high school students to sexist music videos exacerbates their sexually stereotyped attitudes (e.g., that males who exercise sexual restraint are abnormal; Ward, Hansbrough, & Walker, 2005).

Behaviors. Beliefs and attitudes are predictors but not perfect determinants of behavior (Hale, Householder, & Greene, 2002). Consequently, it is important for studies to explore associations between media exposure and actual behavior in addition to beliefs and attitudes. In the 2000s, several sophisticated longitudinal studies have demonstrated the powerful over time effect of the mass media on adolescents' sexual behavior. Given the economic (Maynard, 1997) and public health ramifications (Kirby, Lepore, & Ryan, 2005) of precocious youth sex, these studies have focused on outcomes such as coital debut, pregnancy, and STI contraction. Other studies have been conducted, but these recent efforts are so compelling that they deserve our exclusive attention.

Collins and colleagues (2004) and Brown and colleagues (2006) studied coital debut and the extent of noncoital sexual behavior among children and adolescents. Collins's team (2004) surveyed a national sample of youth in 2001 and 2002. Participants were between 12 and 17 years old at Wave 1. Sexual media exposure was measured by assessing how frequently participants viewed 23 popular prime-time programs analyzed for sexual content by coders employed in Kunkel and company's (2003) *Sex on TV 3* study. Probability analyses showed that "watching the highest levels of sexual content effectively doubled the next-year likelihood of initiating intercourse" (Collins et al., 2004, p. 287). Controlling for Wave 1. noncoital behavior, sexual television exposure at wave one also predicted advances in Wave 2 noncoital behavior (e.g., oral sex), and the magnitude of this effect rivaled the magnitude of the intercourse initiation effect.

Brown and company (2006) gathered two-wave data from more than 1,000 North Carolinian teenagers who were aged between 12 and 14 at Wave 1 and 14 and 16 at Wave 2. Sexual media exposure was assessed by examining each participant's "sexual media diet," a composite measure that gauges the sexual content of each popular television show, music album, movie, and magazine used frequently by the participant, as well as the frequency of exposure to each medium. Higher sexual media exposure scores at Wave 1

predicted intercourse initiation for both Black and White participants after controlling for a number of covariates, but the effect remained only for Whites in the full model. Probability analyses for Whites revealed that "white adolescents who were in the top exposure quintile to sexual content in the media were at 120% greater risk, or 2.2 times as likely, to have initiated sexual intercourse than white adolescents who were in the lowest exposure quintile" (Brown et al., 2006, p. 1025). Brown's team's (2006) results for noncoital behavior paralleled their results for coital status. By controlling for Wave 1 coital status and noncoital behavior, Collins's group (2004) and Brown's group (2006) make selective exposure explanations for these associations highly improbable. In concert with these more methodologically sound studies, Ashby, Arcari, & Edmonson (2006) used secondary data and also found a positive prospective association between media exposure (number of hours of television viewed per day) and intercourse initiation among a national sample of middle and high school students.

Bleakley, Hennessy, Fishbein, and Jordan (2008) were interested in the role of the mass media in young people's overall sexual experience. They surveyed high school-aged youth from the greater Philadelphia area in 2005 and 2006. Exposure to a variety of popular media content analyzed for sexual depictions at wave one predicted higher levels of sexual experience (e.g., petting, oral sex, vaginal sex) at Wave 2.

Given the paucity of sexual risk messages in the mass media attended to by youth, it is not surprising that recent studies have also documented prospective associations between media exposure, pregnancy involvement, and STI contraction. Chandra and colleagues (2008) found that exposure to sexual television at an earlier time period predicted male impregnation and female pregnancy status at a later time period among a national sample of youth even after controlling for intentions to have a child before the age of 22. In comparison to the 10th exposure percentile, being in the 90th percentile doubled the likelihood of pregnancy involvement. Wingood and colleagues (2003) found that Black female adolescents who watched more rap music videos at Wave 1 were 1.5 times more likely than their peers who watched fewer videos to have contracted chlamydia, trichomoniasis, or gonorrhea over the next 12 months.

While theoretically possible, it seems unlikely that an unmeasured third variable explains the media sex–sexual behavior associations demonstrated by these studies (Wright, in press). Nonmedia predictors of youth sexual behavior have been investigated for many years, and the studies reviewed controlled for a long list of potential confounds (e.g., age, having mostly older friends, household structure, parental education, parental monitoring, academic achievement, mental health, sensation-seeking tendencies, engaging in deviant behavior, gender, socioeconomic status, pubertal status, valence of relationship with mother, parenting styles, parents' disapproval of sex, religiosity, school connectedness, permissive peer sexual norms, unsupervised time at home, peers' approval of sex, physical development, relationship status, employment status, family's receipt of public assistance, involvement in extracurricular activities). That the most methodologically sound studies have found strong prospective associations between mass media consumption and sexual behavior after controlling for these (and other) third variables gives significant credence to the hypothesis that exposure to embedded media sex is a causal influence on youth sexual behavior.

Sexually Explicit Media (Pornography)

Introduction

An extensive scientific literature has developed over the past 30 or more years investigating the effects of exposure to sexually explicit media specifically designed to sexually arouse the consumer (i.e., pornography). This body of work has almost exclusively focused on adults. In keeping with the theme of this volume, we will focus on findings that have implications for younger individuals.

Explosive Growth

Over the past two decades in particular, production and distribution of pornography has been a vastly growing multibillion-dollar business. With Internet use becoming very common, what has dramatically changed most has been the accessibility of pornography. It used to be that most pornographic magazines and books were kept under lock and key at convenience stores and access was largely restricted to some adults. Of course, with sufficient effort, youth could still get access to various sexual images by some means, but it was often not easy to do so and the materials were typically not very explicit and the images static. Today, however, as described in greater detail in the section below focusing specifically on the Internet, anyone with an Internet connection can easily, anonymously, and without any cost frequently watch even extreme pornographic movies with virtually every imaginable theme that would have been much more difficult to access in previous generations or even a decade ago.

The Content of Pornography

Although some content analyses actually claim to show that the majority of current popular pornography now includes verbal and/or physical aggression (e.g., Bridges, Wosnitzer, Scharrer, Sun, & Liberman, in press; Sun, Bridges, Wosnitzer, Scharrer, & Liberman, 2008), the definition of aggression used in such research included acts such as slapping buttocks, causing gagging, and calling a person names such as "bitch." Such acts, without the clear intention to do harm, may not qualify as aggression or violence by commonly used definitions of aggression (e.g., Geen, 1990). Such pornographic content, however, appears frequently in the "common fare" of pornography most sexually arousing to heterosexual males (Glascock, 2005) and seems likely to be defined by most observers as intentional acts of sexual domination or even degradation (Cowan & Dunn, 1994).

Summary of Research Findings on Negative Effects

It is not necessarily the case that pornography exposure has negative effects for all or even for most consumers. In fact, many people report that pornography has had either neutral or positive effects on their sex life and life in general (e.g., Hald & Malamuth, 2008). Nevertheless, there is a great deal of both experimental and correlational research focusing on what most would agree are the potential negative effects of pornography exposure, particularly as such exposure relates to sexual aggression against women. Such studies have converged to show that pornography consumption, particularly in large quantities, can be a risk factor for sexually aggressive outcomes (e.g., attitudes and behaviors). However, these studies indicate such risk only for males who are predisposed to sexual aggression (for meta-analyses and reviews, see Hald, Malamuth, & Yuen, 2010; Kingston, Malamuth, Fedoroff, & Marshall, 2009; Seto, Maric, & Barbaree, 2001; Vega & Malamuth, 2007). In other words, this research has highlighted an interaction effect in which individuals classified as relatively low risk for antisocial behaviors, particularly sexual aggression, demonstrated no or a small association between frequency of pornography use and sexual aggression in correlational studies and virtually no significant effect in experimental studies, whereas high-risk men showed a large association or effect between pornography and sexually aggressive responses (e.g., attitudes, fantasies, and behaviors). Moreover, the findings suggest that even for men at relative risk for sexual aggression, it is the consumption of large amounts of pornography that is of particular concern and that certain types of pornography (e.g., violent pornography) show stronger associations than pornography use generally. Such research suggests the need for an increased emphasis on individual differences as fundamental in understanding effects of pornography consumption and a move away from "across the board" sweeping generalizations about the negatives of pornography consumption.

Although most of the research summarized above has used college students, Kingston, Federoff, Firestone, Curry, and Bradford (2008) demonstrated a similar pattern in the longitudinal prediction of recidivism in a sample of 341 child molesters. Specifically, it was found that a high rate of pornography consumption was predictive of recidivism among men who were at higher risk to re-offend, whereas frequency of pornography consumption had little predictive value for men assessed to be at lower risk for sexual aggression. Interestingly, a significant main effect was revealed for type of content, but no statistical interaction was evident. In other words, individuals who viewed deviant pornography, defined as images depicting children and/or violence, were more likely to recidivate when compared to individuals who did not view deviant pornography; however, this difference was consistent across levels of risk. In sum, the Kingston group's (2008) study found that frequency of pornography use (irrespective of content) was a significant risk factor for recidivism for the higher-risk individuals only, whereas all individuals, regardless of risk level, were negatively impacted by the use of deviant pornography.

Theoretical Mechanisms

While in the next section of this chapter the topic of theoretical mechanisms underlying media effects is discussed extensively, we briefly discuss here the individual differences in findings described above in the context of such mechanisms. The difference between males who are at risk for sexual aggression and those who are not[1] may be that the former group have "negative" scripts (i.e., cognitive, arousal, and emotional psychological mechanisms) that may be primed by pornography exposure, whereas the latter group have very different scripts primed by the same pornography exposure. "At-risk" males are relatively

---

[1]Although for the purpose of explication we discuss this difference as a dichotomy, it is clearly more appropriate as a continuum. Most men would not be considered at risk for sexual aggression, but many would (e.g., see Malamuth et al., 2000).

more likely to already hold sexually aggressive schemata (e.g., Berkel, Vandiver, & Bahner, 2004; Lonsway & Fitzgerald, 1995; Milburn, Mather, & Conrad, 2000) and to view women in relatively dichotomized categories such as "whores" vs. "madonnas" (Bargh, Raymond, Pryor, & Strack, 1995; Edelman, 2008; McKenzie-Mohr & Zanna, 1990; Zurbriggen, 2000). In keeping with Newell's classic unified theory of cognition (Newell, 1990), we suggest that cognitive mechanisms occur within an overall "embedded architecture" that results in the activation not only of the cognitions the individual brings to the "pornography experience" but also of associated motives and affective states that may impact behaviors.

A Theoretical Explanation for the Influence of Sexual Media on Behavior

This section presents an acquisition, activation, application conceptualization of mass media effects on sexual behavior (see Wright, in press, for a more detailed description). The perspective draws on the work of many theorists, but primarily on the script theory of Huesmann (1986, 1988, 1998). As alluded to above, scripts provide people with both general and specific behavioral options and forecast particular interaction outcomes. Young people may acquire sexual scripts from sexual media, and sexual scripts they already possess may be activated by sexual media. Stimuli other than sexual media may cue sexual scripts, but all scripts must be activated in order to guide behavior. Activation and application are not synonymous, however. In certain instances, activated scripts will be deemed inappropriate and discarded. Variables that can moderate or lessen the likelihood of exposure effects are identified at each stage. By and large, however, the theory and research that were drawn upon to develop the model support the idea that exposure to sexual media should generally have a facilitating effect on young people's sexual behavior (see Figure 14.3).

Acquisition

A number of content and audience variables should influence the acquisition of behavioral scripts from sexual media. The primary importance of content variables has to do with the ability of various portrayals to catch and retain the attention of receivers. Behaviors that do not attract at least a modest level of attention cannot be encoded (Bandura, 2001).

Attention should be enhanced when behaviors have arousal value, are simple, salient, functional, portrayed in realistic ways by attractive models, and prevalent. Sexually explicit depictions have obvious arousal value, but embedded sexual portrayals may also be arousing for some audiences (Gunter, 2002). Most sexual behaviors that are suggested, shown, and described in sexual media should not be difficult for adolescents to understand (although younger children may not understand subtler sexual messages; Silverman-Watkins & Sprafkin, 1983). It is axiomatic to say that sex is salient to adolescents (Diamond & Savin-Williams, 2009). Learning about sex is quite functional because of the dramatic rewards (e.g., intimacy, orgasm) that are associated with being sexual. Males and females may have evolved different ideas about the functionality of particular sexual scripts, however. Males perceive that short-term sexual scripts are most functional; females perceive that long-term sexual scripts are most functional (Malamuth, 1996). When young females are exposed to casual sex scripts, though, they may develop more liberal sexual attitudes (Aubrey, Harrison, Kramer, & Yellin, 2003; Ward & Rivadeneyra, 1999). Findings such as these support Bandura's (2001) assertion that humans have evolved particular psychological predilections but also have a certain amount of "plasticity" (p. 266).

While heightened perceptions of media sex realism do appear to facilitate socialization effects (Olson, 1994; Taylor, 2005b; Ward et al., 2006), they may not be a necessary requirement (Aubrey, Harrison, Kramer, & Yellin, 2003; Davis & Mares, 1998). Effects may occur in the face of more implausible portrayals due to a lack of criticality at the time of encoding (Wyer & Radvansky, 1999) and because distinguishing "fantastic" from

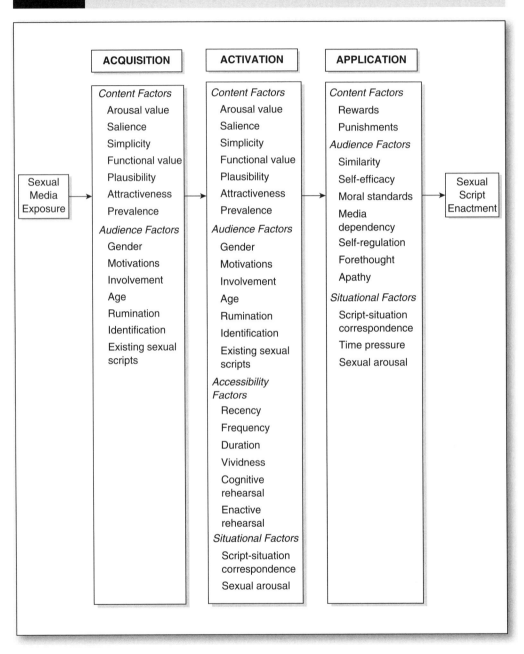

Figure 14.3 An Acquisition, Activation, Application Perspective on Mass Media Sexual Behavior Effects

"real" modeling events was unimportant in the environment of evolutionary adaptedness. Finally, young people perceive that the models in their preferred media are attractive (Milkie, 1999), and the more prevalent a behavior is (and sex in the media is highly prevalent), the more likely it is to be noticed, understood (McGuire, 1969), and, under certain conditions, liked (Zajonc, 1968).

In addition to age and gender, receivers' motivations, involvement level, propensity for rumination, degree of identification, and existing sexual beliefs should also moderate the acquisition of sexual scripts provided by mediated sources. Uses and gratifications scholars have often argued that audiences' motivations for media consumption impact what they learn from the media (Rubin, 2002). For example, audiences may have diversionary motives or may attend to media content for information acquisition. The latter motivation is expected to enhance effects, a supposition supported by several sexual socialization studies (Aubrey et al., 2003; Kim & Ward, 2004; Ward, 2002; Ward et al., 2006). Audience involvement can increase or decrease the likelihood of learning about sex from the media. High levels of attention and enthusiasm should have a catalyzing effect (Rubin, 2002). As evidence, the more college students actively view and talk about sexual television, the more likely they are to hold sexually objectified beliefs about women (Ward, 2002). Skeptical, incredulous approaches should inhibit learning (Rubin, 2002). For example, young teenagers who view sexual television with a critical eye become less desensitized to its permissive portrayals than their peers who are less critical (Bryant & Rockwell, 1994).

At least three other audience variables may be important. First, the propensity to ruminate and fantasize about sexual media content may increase the likelihood of script encoding due to increased comprehension and increased opportunity for abstract modeling (Bandura, 2001; Huesmann, 1986). Second, the more youth identify with sexual media models, the more likely they should be to pay attention to and retain the scripts for behavior suggested by the materials to which they have been exposed. Evidence for this core social learning concept is provided by Ward and colleagues (2005), who found that identification with music video personas enhanced the effect of sexist music videos on Black adolescents' sexual stereotypes in an experimental study. Other studies by Ward and her associates also point to the importance of identification for sexual script acquisition (Ward, 2002; Ward & Friedman, 2006; Ward et al., 2006). Finally, sexual mass media scripts should be more readily encoded when they are at least somewhat compatible with existing sexual scripts. To illustrate, the sexual values espoused by mass media models often contradict those

espoused by families (Zillmann, 1994). If content–value incongruity hinders script acquisition, it would be expected that living in a family with an open communication style and clearly defined values would buffer youth from the sexual scripts available for adoption in the mass media. Evidence in support of the mitigating effects of family values is provided by Bryant and Rockwell (1994). Because most religions emphasize relational and procreational sexual values, high levels of religiosity may also discourage the internalization of sexual scripts provided by the mass media (Strouse & Buerkel-Rothfuss, 1987).

Activation

Activation effects occur when already-acquired scripts are cued in memory by media messages or other environmental stimuli. The process of script activation is generally referred to as "priming" (Huesmann, 1998, p. 81). During the time scripts are activated, they may color perceptions and alter behavior. There are three types of moderating variables in the priming process: (1) variables that increase the likelihood that exposure will generate the force required to activate scripts, (2) variables that increase the accessibility of scripts in memory, and (3) variables that increase the likelihood that particular scripts will be activated in a given situation.

Media messages can only act as primes if audiences attend to them, so the content factors that were mentioned in the acquisition delineation also apply here. Depictions with attractive models that have arousal and functional value, are salient, simple, realistic, and prevalent should be most likely to activate sexual scripts. The audience variables also apply. For example, a certain level of decoding ability, cogitation, involvement, and character identification may be required for media primes to have an activation effect.

Several variables are thought to increase the accessibility of scripts in memory. Foremost among these are recency of activation and frequency of activation (Roskos-Ewoldsen, Roskos-Ewoldsen, & Dillman Carpentier, 2009). The more recently and frequently a script is activated, the more accessible it becomes. To the extent that recent and frequent media experiences activate sexual scripts, sexual media exposure increases sexual script accessibility. Additionally, the longer people are exposed to a particular set of related messages, the more likely it may be that the messages increase the accessibility of related scripts in memory (Roskos-Ewoldsen, Klinger, & Roskos-Ewoldsen, 2007). A content factor that may increase the accessibility of sexual scripts is vividness (Shrum, 2009). A number of authors have commented on the increasing vividness of sexual portrayals in the mass media (Brown & Steele, 1995; Huston, Wartella, & Donnerstein, 1998; Wingood et al., 2003). It seems reasonable to assume that the average adolescent has recently and frequently been exposed to vivid sexual mass media for considerable periods of time, given the media use and sexual content data reviewed earlier. Last, cognitive and enactive rehearsal (e.g., deliberation, fantasizing, masturbation) are audience behaviors that should increase the accessibility of sexual scripts primed by mediated sources (Bandura, 2001; Huesmann, 1986; Lyons, Anderson, & Larson 1994).

Huesmann (1988, 1998) identifies two situational cues that can impact the activation of sexual scripts: script–situation correspondence and arousal. All other factors being equal (e.g., accessibility), the script activated in a given situation will be the one that has the most overlap with current environmental factors. The variety of sexual scenarios presented in the mainstream mass media alone is impressive (e.g., extrarelationship sex, one-night stands, tit-for-tat sex; Greenberg & Hofschire, 2000; Wright, 2009a), not to mention the innumerable scripts acted out in sexually explicit fare. Thus, a youth who attends to a variety of sexual media may possess a script available for activation in nearly every sexual situation. Arousal plays a role in script activation in two ways. First, arousal shrinks the capacity of working memory and restricts memory searching, which increases the likelihood that the most accessible script will be the one activated in a given situation (Huesmann, 1998). An adolescent who is both sexually aroused and a heavy media consumer may find it difficult to access sexual scripts other than those provided by the media. The second way arousal plays a part in script activation is through "encoding specificity." *Encoding specificity* refers to the fact that cues and emotions present when information is first encoded become "associated with the encoded information and can trigger its activation in memory" (Huesmann, 1998, p. 83). If youth are sexually aroused when they encode a sexual script, arousal and the script become associated and the script is likely to be triggered in subsequent sexually arousing situations.

Application

The activation of a script increases the probability it will be employed but does not guarantee it. The script evaluation process involves an "effortful, controlled appraisal of the situation," a "thoughtful consideration of various behavioral alternatives to the situation," and a decision that can "correct or override the primary appraisal" (Roskos-Ewoldsen et al., 2009, p. 82).

A number of factors determine whether an activated script is applied. Since most scripts are learned vicariously (Bandura, 2001), the consequences that accompany models' behavior should weigh heavily in the decision-making process. Rewards should prompt behavioral matching; punishments should inhibit matching behaviors (Martino, Collins, Kanouse, Elliot, & Berry, 2005). Perceptions of similarity to media models should moderate the impact of portrayed rewards and punishments. For example, a model may be rewarded, but because of perceived dissimilarities, an observer may not believe she would experience the same positive outcomes. Behavioral matching is most likely when observers see themselves as similar to models and when models experiences positive consequences for their actions. Similarity leads to heightened self-efficacy; rewards lead to behavioral motivation. Even if observers perceive similarity between themselves and models and models experiences positive consequences for their behavior, however, observers may still decide to suppress the script in question if their internal moral standards proscribe against it (Bandura, 2001). That being said, exposure to sexual media predicts premarital sexual behavior even after the effects of variables such as religiosity and parental disapproval of unmarried sex are considered (Brown et al., 2006; Collins et al., 2004).

Finally, script contemplators should place more emphasis on the consequences that a model experienced when their situation corresponds closely with the model's situation.

Whether or not the filtering process results in the selection of a script learned from a source other than the mass media depends on whether the filterer has another script she can select. According to Rubin (2002), dependence on the mass media for behavioral guidance "results from an environment that restricts the availability of functional alternatives" (p. 536). Parents (Wright, 2009b), educators (Brown, Steele, & Walsh-Childers, 2002), and medical professionals (Schuster, Bell, Peterson, & Kanouse, 1996) are typically reluctant sexual communicators. Consequently, the role of the mass media in adolescent sexual decision making may represent a classic media dependency situation (Rubin & Windahl, 1986).

Recall that the script evaluation process involves an "effortful, controlled appraisal of the situation" and a "thoughtful consideration of various behavioral alternatives to the situation" (Roskos-Ewoldsen et al., 2009, p. 82). When such systematic processing takes place, secondary appraisals may indeed be dependent on the factors just outlined. But processing in many social situations is "automatic" (Bargh & Chartrand, 1999). Automatic processing "occurs very rapidly, without using many cognitive resources and without any conscious executive decisions made about the process" (Huesmann, 1998, pp. 80–81).

Systematic processing is inhibited when people lack the ability or motivation to engage in systematic behavioral analysis (Shrum, 2009). Some individuals' capacity for systematic processing may always be limited due to an inherent lack of self-regulation and forethought capacity (Bandura, 2001). Other individuals possess these capacities but are indifferent to the negative outcomes an inappropriate script will generate for themselves and others (Huesmann, 1988). Time pressure (Shrum, 2007) and sexual arousal (Huesmann, 1998) are situation-specific factors that should decrease the likelihood of systematic processing. Time pressure decreases the ability to process systematically; sexual arousal should decrease both the motivation and the ability to process systematically. Since spontaneity and sexual arousal are part and parcel to sexual

passion and intrigue, it seems likely that a good deal of sexual script processing is automatic, irrespective of innate individual differences in forethought and self-regulation capacity. Automatic processing should increase the likelihood of sexual media influence.

The Internet

Unlike traditional media such as TV and film, there are relatively few studies on the impact of exposure to sexual materials on the Internet. We believe special emphasis on these studies is warranted, however, because the prevalence and availability of sexual materials on the Internet almost certainly means that some youth are accessing and learning from online sexual sources (Malamuth, Linz, & Yao, 2005). It is interesting to note the recent commentary of researchers about the potential and far-reaching influences of this "newer" technology on sexual socialization:

> Mass media play an important role in the sexual socialization of American youth and given its expanding nature and accessibility, the Internet may be at the forefront of this education. (Braun-Courville & Rojas, 2009, p. 156)
>
> Teens have access to a variety of adult-oriented Web sites on the Internet. Chat rooms, pornography sites, adult-video sites, and romance/dating services are but a few of the many and easily accessible "adult-oriented" materials to be found. (Escobar-Chaves, Tortolero, Markham, Low, Eitel, & Thickstun, 2005, p. 319)
>
> Adolescents' increasing access to, and use of, sexually explicit Internet material—material that is not meant for minors—has led to concerns about whether youth are able to make sense of the reality depicted in that material. (Peter & Valkenburg, 2008, p. 584)

The Internet becomes the medium in which traditional media like TV, film, and video games can be downloaded, viewed, and processed. The most recent survey of children and adolescent media use by Rideout and colleagues (2010) indicated that the amount of time viewing TV content had increased over the last decade, but this increase is accounted for primarily by the viewing of such programming over the Internet and mobile devices.

Consequently, unlike traditional media such as TV, the Internet and these new technologies (e.g., mobile devices) give children and adolescents access to just about any form of content they can find (e.g., Livingstone & Haddon, 2009). For the first time, young people will be able (often with little effort) to view almost any form of sexual behavior, producing both positive and negative effects (Donnerstein, 2009; Strasburger, Jordan, & Donnerstein, 2010). Unlike years past, this can be done in the privacy of their own room with little supervision from their parents. Tarpley (in this volume) and Subrahmanyam, Kraut, Greenfield, and Gross (2001) discuss this new technology in more detail. The amount of usage of the Internet and newer technologies by youth is substantial. Studies by the Pew Internet and American Life Project (2009) revealed that 93% of youth aged 12 to 17 are online sometime during the day, and 71% have cell phones. Whether it's watching videos (57%), using social networking sites (65%), or playing video games (97%), children and adolescents have incorporated new technology into their daily lives. These frequencies are also observed across 21 different countries within Europe. The EU Kids Online Project found that in 2005, on average, 70% of 6- to 17-year-olds used the Internet. By 2008, it was at 75%, with the largest increase occurring among younger children (6–10), of which 60% were now online (Livingstone & Haddon, 2009).

More significant are findings that indicate substantial viewing of sexually explicit materials by youth on the Internet. In one large-scale survey, Salazar, Fleischauer, Bernhardt, and DiClemente (2009) gathered data suggesting that 17% of websites visited by teens were X rated (sexually explicit) and at least 6% contained sexual violence. Other studies have shown unwanted and accidental exposure between 50% and 65% for teens (Braun-Courville & Rojas, 2009; Wolak, Mitchell, & Finkelhor, 2007).

There are several reasons to expect effects from Internet exposure. Malamuth et al. (2005) have provided a perspective on Internet violence, and their theoretical discussion applies just as equally to the Internet and sex. According to these authors, the Internet provides motivational, disinhibitory, and opportunity aspects that make it somewhat different than traditional sexual media in terms of its potential impact.

With regard to motivation, the Internet is "ubiquitous" in that it is always on and can easily be accessed, thus leading to high levels of exposure. Sexual content on the Internet is available to almost everyone; there is no "family-viewing hour." And as many researchers have noted, online sexual content can be interactive and more engaging. From a disinhibitory aspect, the content is unregulated. Studies suggest that extreme forms of sexual content are more prevalent on the Internet than in other popular media (e.g., Strasburger et al., 2010). Participation is private and anonymous, such that individuals can search out materials they normally would not. There is the suggestion that finding such materials could increase social support for these images and messages. Malamuth and colleagues (2005) note a content analysis of Internet-related rape sites as an example. Finally, online media exposure is much more difficult for parents to monitor than media exposure in traditional venues. Opportunity aspects play a more important role in the area of child sexual exploitation (which we discuss later). Potential victims are readily available, and the identity of the "aggressor" is often disguised (as is often the case with pedophiles).

Given the above perspective, there is ample reason to expect effects from Internet exposure. As noted earlier, however, there are few studies on the impact of Internet exposure, particularly in areas such as e-mail and instant messaging. The few studies that have examined Internet sites are strongly suggestive of an association between Internet exposure and sexual attitudes and behaviors. Two large-scale, longitudinal surveys of youth conducted in the Netherlands (Peter & Valkenburg, 2008, 2009) found that more frequent intentional exposure to sexually explicit Internet material was associated with greater sexual uncertainty and more positive attitudes toward uncommitted sexual exploration (i.e., sexual relations with casual partners/friends or with sexual partners in one-night stands). Additionally, adolescents' exposure to Internet sex appeared to be both a cause and a consequence of their belief that women are sex objects. More frequent exposure predicted stronger beliefs that women are sex objects, while at the same time, stronger beliefs that women are sex objects predicted more frequent exposure to such materials.

Braun-Courville and Rojas (2009) looked at the sexual behaviors of adolescents in a cross-sectional study in New York. More than 50% of the participants had visited sexually explicit websites. Analyses revealed that adolescents exposed to these types of sites were more likely to (a) have multiple lifetime sexual partners, (b) have had more than one sexual partner in the last 3 months, (c) used alcohol or other substances at last sexual encounter, and (d) have engaged in anal sex. Furthermore, adolescents who visit these sites displayed higher sexual permissiveness scores compared with those who had never been exposed. It is difficult to disentangle causality in this study, but we can certainly assume that Internet exposure is at minimum reinforcing already existing attitudes and behaviors.

In a study with Taiwanese adolescents, Lo and Wei (2005) also found that Internet exposure was associated with greater acceptance of sexual permissiveness and a greater likelihood of engaging in sexually permissive behavior. Of interest was the finding in this study that exposure to Internet pornography had a stronger impact on sexual attitudes than exposure to such content in traditional media.

The above studies, while somewhat limited in design and generalizability, do suggest that the Internet can be an influence on adolescents' sexual attitudes and behaviors. Besides the fact that traditional media (which we have already acknowledged as an influence) can easily be obtained via the Internet, more explicit and potentially riskier materials are readily available to youth online. As Brown and L'Engle (2009) note in their longitudinal study of adolescents,

> By the end of middle school many teens have seen sexually explicit content not only on the Internet but in more traditional forms of media as well. Such exposure is related to early adolescents' developing sense of gender roles, sexual relationships, and sexual behavior, including perpetration of sexual harassment. (p. 148)

As children and adolescents move further away from traditional media channels to newer technologies, it will become increasingly important for researchers to explore the extent and nature of online sexual social influence.

Sexual Exploitation

We would be remiss in our discussion of the Internet if we did not acknowledge the potential for the sexual exploitation of children and adolescents. The sending of sexual information over e-mail or postings on bulletin boards by those targeting children has been an ongoing research issue. Perhaps the most comprehensive series of studies on these issues has come from the Crimes Against Children Research Center at the University of New Hampshire. These studies (see Wolak, Finkelhor, Mitchell, & Ybarra, 2008) involved a random national sample of 1,500 children ages 10 to 17 interviewed in 2000 and then an additional sample of 1,500 interviewed in 2005. This procedure allowed the researchers to look at changes in youths' experiences with the Internet. The major findings from this study can be summarized as follows:

1. There was a 9% increase over the 5-year period (25% to 34% of respondents) in exposure to unwanted sexual materials. It is interesting to note that this increase occurred in spite of the fact that more families were using Internet filtering software (more than 50%) during this period.

2. Fifteen percent of all of the youth reported an unwanted sexual solicitation online in the previous year with 4% reporting an incident on a social networking site specifically. Perhaps more important, about 4% of these were considered "aggressive" in that the solicitor attempted to contact the user offline. These are the episodes most likely to result in actual victimizations.

3. Additionally, in this study 4% of those surveyed were asked for nude or sexually explicit pictures of themselves.

4. Four percent said they were upset or distressed as a result of these online solicitations. These are the youth most immediately harmed by the solicitations themselves.

We can look at these small percentages and say that broad claims of victimization may not seem justified. The problem with this interpretation is that these are large-scale national surveys, so even if the percentages are small, the number of youth impacted is actually quite substantial. Researchers are correct in asserting that more research is needed in this area, however, mainly "because Internet-initiated sex crimes are a relatively new phenomenon, [and] it may take some time before there is enough information to understand their role and relationship to juvenile sexual victimization overall" (Wolak et al., 2008, p. 125).

Solutions: Can We Mitigate the Effects of Exposure?

We take the position that the negative effects of sexual content in the mass and other media can be mitigated (see Chapters 21, 33, and 34 in this volume). The most effective approach is one that is multifaceted and involves all constituents, from parents to the industry, who can play a role in children's exposure, understanding, and reactions to sexual media. In their discussion of the mass media and health effects, Strasburger and colleagues (2010) consider six groups who are important in working with children and adolescents with regard to the effects of mass media exposure. We believe that at least with respect to sexual content, these groups are essential if we are to have an impact on the effects of mass media sex on youth.

Parents

The American Academy of Pediatrics (AAP) has recommended that parents limit the amount of screen time for children while also monitoring and coviewing content with their children. Additionally, the AAP has a website that deals specifically with Internet safety issues (http://safetynet.aap.org). The research on parental coviewing has shown it to be effective in reducing the impact of both violent and sexual content (e.g., Cantor & Wilson, 2003). As an example, a recent study by Fisher and colleagues (2009) found that parents' imposition of limits on program content and hours of viewing for youth in the 12 to 16 age range was effective in reducing

the negative behavioral outcomes of exposure to televised sexual content. Likewise, parental discussions of content were also effective in countering media depictions.

Additionally for parents, we can recommend the following:

- Be aware of the potential risks associated with viewing televised portrayals of sex.
- Consider the context of sexual depictions in making viewing decisions for children.
- Consider a child's developmental level when making viewing decisions.

Schools

Strasburger and colleagues (2010) have strongly suggested that comprehensive sex education and media literacy programs are essential given the vast amount of exposure children and adolescents have to sexualized media. Both children and adolescents can be taught "critical viewing skills" in schools so that they learn to better interpret what they see in the media (e.g., Huston, Wartella, & Donnerstein, 1998). For example, children can learn to distinguish between fictional portrayals and factual presentations. In addition, they can be taught to recognize ways in which sexual behaviors may be portrayed unrealistically (e.g., when sex is portrayed without any negative consequences). Children can also learn to think about alternatives to those portrayals. Komaya (this volume) discusses the effects of media literacy programs as a vehicle for empowering youth as they confront the vast array of media content available today. With respect to sexual media, the issues go beyond just exposure to "risky" sexual content but also to behaviors and decisions within the sexual realm encountered in social networking sites and other forms of digital communication (i.e., sexting).

A recent study by Pinkleton, Austin, Cohen, Chen, and Fitzgerald (2008) is an example of these types of programs. The study focused on a peer-led media literacy curriculum about sexual portrayals in the media. The lessons were interactive and discussed the health risks associated with sexual activity. It also incorporated a social cognitive model in that students were also responsible for creating parts of the curriculum, a technique that has been used in successful media violence literacy approaches. The results of the study were quite encouraging in that the participants were less likely to overestimate sexually activity in teens, more likely to think they could delay sexual behavior, more aware of myths about sex, and less likely to consider sexual media imagery desirable. Research (Moreno et al., 2008) has also demonstrated that teens can be responsive to educational messages about potential risks of new technologies, such as the dangers of posting sexual references in their profiles on social networking sites, and will subsequently change their online behavior.

Entertainment Industry

A number of chapters in this book examine the role of the media industry in confronting the negative health-related effects from certain media content, and we will not review these here. We can, however, offer a number of suggestions with respect to our specific review, which is sexual content. For the media industry, the following can be recommended:

- Produce more programs that show positive sexual content like learning to say no in a difficult sexual situation or talking to your partner about safe sex.
- Be creative in showing:
  o sexual behavior that may have consequences (e.g., sexually transmitted diseases).
  o depictions that focus on nonrisky sexual behaviors (e.g., use of condoms).
  o reduction in the relationship between sex and violence.
- Ensure that ratings for sexuality on television and in the movies take into account the context of the portrayals.

Practitioners

Strasburger and colleagues (2010) strongly suggest that clinicians, particularly pediatricians who see children, need to understand that discussing children's media use is as important as other health-related issues. They suggest that two questions should be asked of the parent: (1) How much time per day does the child or teen spend with entertainment media? (2) Is there a TV set or Internet connection in the child's bedroom? Hopefully the start of this discussion will encourage parents to follow more closely the recommendations of the American Academy of Pediatrics on media use and parental involvement in their children's interactions with the media.

Researchers

As we have seen in this chapter, there has been a significant increase in research on media use and sexual behaviors since the first version of this chapter a decade ago. It is important for researchers to continue to assess the role and contribution of media exposure to the development of sexual behaviors and attitudes among youth. We should add that the contribution of the media needs to be looked at for all types of risk-related behaviors such as drug use, obesity, and eating disorders. It is encouraging to see the accumulation of longitudinal studies with children and adolescents reviewed in this chapter. We need to have further studies on diverse populations as well as longitudinal research to examine the causal relationships between sexual media and behavior for a variety of groups. Finally, research on expanding platforms like mobile phones and virtual game environments as well as peer-to-peer exchanges need to be examined as children and adolescents become more proficient and turn to these new media for sexual information.

Government

There are a number of chapters in this volume that articulate the role of the government (Congress and the FCC). In considering those who recommend and make policy in the area of the mass media, we can suggest the following with respect to sexual content:

- Continue to monitor the nature and extent of sexuality on television.
- Recognize that context is an essential aspect of media depictions of sex, and rely on scientific evidence to identify the context features that pose the most risk.
- Ensure that television program ratings accurately convey to parents the risks associated with different types of sexual portrayals.

Summary and Conclusions

The primary goal of this chapter was to review what we know about the impact of exposure to sexual media content on children's and adolescents' thoughts, attitudes, and behaviors. The research shows that viewing embedded sexual content can have a considerable influence on adolescents' sexual learning and attitudes toward sex. Moreover, recent studies have strongly suggested that exposure to embedded media sex is a causal influence on youth sexual behavior (Wright, in press). There are, without question, both individual and environmental differences in these effects. We have offered a broad theoretical model that we believe can articulate the content, viewer, and environmental variables that may influence the impact of sexual content on children and adolescents.

Much has changed in the 10 years since the first version of this chapter was presented. Not only do we have a more comprehensive set of data (experimental and longitudinal), but the acquisition of sexual media for youth has also moved from the traditional realms of TV and film to the Internet and mobile technologies. While the research on these new technologies is limited, we have offered our analysis and concerns about these new media for children's and adolescents' exposure to both mainstream and explicit sexual content.

This chapter (like many others in this book) would certainly lead us to conclude that the mass media are contributors to a number of antisocial behaviors and health-related problems in children and adolescents. We discussed in the previous section a number of ways in which these negative effects might be mitigated. We consider these to be viable and realistic recommendations because they are based upon a knowledge base supported by scientific research. We suggest that stronger reliance be placed on educational and media interventions specifically directed to changing beliefs about sexuality. Our ever-increasing knowledge of media effects, attitude formation and change, child development, and human behavior positions researchers as an important force in the solution to the problem of exposure to mass media sexual content.

References

Abramson, P. R., & Mechanic, M. B. (1983). Sex and the media: Three decades of best-selling books and major motion pictures. *Archives of Sexual Behavior, 12*, 185–206.

Ashby, S. L., Arcari, C. M., & Edmonson, M. B. (2006). Television viewing and risk of sexual initiation by young adolescents. *Archives of Pediatrics & Adolescent Medicine, 160*, 375–380.

Aubrey, J. S. (2007). Does television exposure influence college-aged women's sexual self-concept? *Media Psychology, 10*, 157–181.

Aubrey, J. S., Harrison, K., Kramer, L., & Yellin, J. (2003). Variety versus timing. Gender differences in college students' expectations as predicted by exposure to sexually oriented television. *Communication Research, 30*, 432–460.

Bandura, A. (2001). Social-cognitive theory of mass communication. *Media Psychology, 3*, 265–299.

Baran, S. J. (1976a). How TV and film portrayals affect sexual satisfaction in college students. *Journalism Quarterly, 53*, 468–473.

Baran, S. J. (1976b). Sex on TV and adolescent self-image. *Journal of Broadcasting, 20*, 61–68.

Bargh, J. A., & Chartrand, T. L. (1999). The unbearable automaticity of being. *American Psychologist, 54*, 462–479.

Bargh, J. A., Raymond, P., Pryor, J. B., & Strack, F. (1995). Attractiveness of the underling: An automatic power–sex association and its consequences for sexual harassment and aggression. *Journal of Personality and Social Psychology, 68*, 768–781.

Berkel, L. A., Vandiver, B. J., Bahner, A. D. (2004). Gender role attitudes, religion and spirituality as predictors of domestic violence attitudes in White college students. *Journal of College Student Development, 45*, 119–133.

Bleakley, A., Hennessy, M., Fishbein, M., & Jordan, A. (2008). It works both ways: The relationship between exposure to sexual content in the media and adolescent sexual behavior. *Media Psychology, 11*, 443–461.

Bleakley, A. Hennessy, M., Fishbein, M., & Jordan, A. (2009). How sources of information relate to adolescents' beliefs about sex. *American Journal of Health Behavior, 33,* 37–48.

Braun-Courville, D., & Rojas, M. (2009). Exposure to sexually explicit web sites and adolescent sexual attitudes and behaviors. *Journal of Adolescent Health, 45,* 156–162

Bridges, A., Wosnitzer, R., Scharrer, E., Sun, C., & Liberman, R. (in press). Aggression and sexual behavior in best-selling pornography videos: A content analysis update. *Violence Against Women.*

Brown, J. D., & L'Engle, K. L. (2009). X-rated: Sexual attitudes and behaviors associated with U.S. early adolescents' exposure to sexually explicit media. *Communication Research, 36,* 129–151.

Brown, J. D., L'Engle, K. L., Pardun, C. J., Guo, G., Kenneavy, K., & Jackson, C. (2006). Sexy media matter: Exposure to sexual content in music, movies, television, and magazines predicts black and white adolescents' sexual behavior. *Pediatrics, 117,* 1018–1027.

Brown, J. D., & Newcomer, S. F. (1991). Television viewing and adolescents' sexual behavior. *Journal of Homosexuality, 21,* 77–91.

Brown, J. D., & Steele, J. R. (1995). *Sex and the mass media.* Menlo Park, CA: Kaiser Family Foundation.

Brown, J. D., Steele, J. R., & Walsh-Childers, K. (2002). *Preface.* In J. Brown, J. R. Steele, & K. Walsh-Childers (Eds.), *Sexual teens, sexual media* (pp. xi–xiv). Mahwah, NJ: Lawrence Erlbaum.

Bryant, J., & Rockwell, S. C. (1994). Effects of massive exposure to sexually oriented prime-time television programming on adolescents' moral judgment. In D. Zillman, J. Bryant, & A. C. Huston (Eds.), *Media, children, and the family: Social scientific, psychodynamic, and clinical perspectives* (pp. 183–195). Hillsdale, NJ: Lawrence Erlbaum.

Buerkel-Rothfuss, N. L., & Mayes, S. (1981). Soap opera viewing: The cultivation effect. *Journal of Communication, 31,* 108–115.

Buerkel-Rothfuss, N. L., & Strouse, J. S. (1993). Media exposure and perceptions of sexual behaviors: The cultivation hypothesis moves to the bedroom. In B. S. Greenberg, J. D. Brown, & N. L. Buerkel-Rothfuss (Eds.), *Media, sex, and the adolescent* (pp. 225–247). Creskill, NJ: Hampton Press.

Bufkin, J., & Eschholz, S. (2000). Images of sex and rape: A content analysis of popular film. *Violence Against Women, 6,* 1317–1344.

Calfin, M. S., Carroll, J. L., & Shmidt, J. (1993). Viewing music-videotapes before taking a test of premarital sexual attitudes. *Psychological Reports, 72,* 475–481.

Cantor, J., & Wilson, B. J. (2003). Media and violence: Intervention strategies for reducing aggression. *Media Psychology, 5,* 363–403.

Carveth, R., & Alexander, A. (1985). Soap opera viewing motivation and the cultivation process. *Journal of Broadcasting & Electronic Media, 29,* 259–273.

Chandra, A., Martino, S. C., Collins, R. L., Elliott, M. N., Berry, S. H., Kanouse, D. E., et al. (2008). Does watching sex on television predict teen pregnancy? Findings from a national longitudinal survey of youth. *Pediatrics, 122,* 1047–1054.

Chia, S. C. (2006a). How media contribute to misperceptions of social norms about sex. *Mass Communication & Society, 9,* 301–320.

Chia, S. C. (2006b). How peers mediate media influence on adolescents' sexual attitudes and sexual behavior. *Journal of Communication, 56,* 585–606.

Collins, R. L., Elliott, M. N., Berry, S. H., Kanouse, D. E., & Hunter, S. B. (2003). Entertainment television as a healthy sex educator: The impact of condom-efficacy information in an episode of *Friends. Pediatrics, 112,* 1115–1121.

Collins, R. L., Elliott, M. N., Berry, S. H., Kanouse, D. E., Kunkel, D., Hunter, S. B., et al. (2004). Watching sex on television predicts adolescent initiation of sexual behavior. *Pediatrics, 114,* 280–289.

Cowan, G., & Dunn, K. F. (1994). What themes in pornography lead to perceptions of the degradation of women? *Journal of Sex Research, 31,* 11–21.

Davis, S., & Mares, M. L. (1998). Effects of talk show viewing on adolescents. *Journal of Communication, 48,* 69–86.

Dempsey, J. M., & Reichert, T. (2000). Portrayal of married sex in the movies. *Sexuality & Culture, 4,* 21–36.

Diamond, L. M., & Savin-Williams, R. C. (2009). Adolescent sexuality. In R. M. Lerner and L. Steinberg (Eds.), *Handbook of adolescent psychology* (pp. 479–523). New York: Wiley.

Donnerstein, E. (2009). The role of the Internet. In V. Strasburger, B. Wilson, & A. Jordan. *Children, adolescents and the media* (2nd ed.; pp. 471–498). Thousand Oaks, CA: Sage.

Duffy, M., & Gotcher, J. M. (1996). Crucial advice on how to get the guy: The rhetorical vision of power and seduction in the teen magazine *YM. Journal of Communication Inquiry, 20,* 32–48.

DuRant, R. H., Neiberg, R., Champion, H., Rhodes, S., & Wolfson, M. (2008). Viewing professional wrestling on television and engaging in violent and other health risk behaviors by a national sample of adolescents. *Southern Medical Journal, 101,* 129–137.

Durham, M. (1996). The taming of the shrew: Women's magazines and the regulation of desire. *Journal of Communication Inquiry, 20,* 18–31.

Edelman, S. (2008). *Computing the mind.* New York: Oxford.

Emmers-Sommer, T. M., Pauley, P., Hanzal, A., & Triplett, L. (2006). Love, suspense, sex, and violence: Men's and women's film predilections, exposure to sexually violent media, and their relationship to rape myth acceptance. *Sex Roles, 55,* 311–320.

Escobar-Chaves, S., Tortolero, S., Markham, C., Low, B., Eitel, P., & Thickstun, P. (2005). Impact of the media on adolescent sexual attitudes and behaviors. *Pediatrics, 116,* 303–326.

Evans, E. D., Rutberg, J., Sather, C., & Turner, C. (1991). Content analysis of contemporary teen magazines for adolescent females. *Youth and Society, 23,* 99–120.

Eyal, K., & Kunkel, D. (2008). The effects of sex in television drama shows on emerging adults' sexual attitudes and moral judgments. *Journal of Broadcasting & Electronic Media, 52,* 161–181.

Fabes, R. A., & Strouse, J. (1987). Perceptions of responsible and irresponsible models of sexuality: A correlational study. *Journal of Sex Research, 23,* 70–84.

Farrar, K. M. (2006). Sexual intercourse on television: Do safe sex messages matter? *Journal of Broadcasting & Electronic Media, 50,* 635–650.

Ferguson, T., Berlin, J., & Noles, E. (2005). Variation in the application of the "promiscuous female" female stereotype and the nature of the application domain: Influences on sexual harassment judgments after exposure to the *Jerry Springer Show. Sex Roles, 52,* 477–487.

Fisher, D. A., Hill, D. L., Grube, J. W., Bersamin, M. M., Walker, S., & Gruber, E. L. (2009). Televised sexual content and parental mediation: Influences on adolescent sexuality. *Media Psychology, 12,* 121–147.

Gan, S. L., Zillmann, D., & Mitrook, M. (1997). Stereotyping effect of Black women's sexual rap on White audiences. *Basic and Applied Social Psychology, 19,* 381–399.

Garner, A., Sterk, H. M., & Adams, S. (1998). Narrative analysis of sexual etiquette in teenage magazines. *Journal of Communication, 48,* 59–78.

Geen, R. G, (1990). *Human aggression.* Belmont, CA: Thomson.

Glascock, J. (2005). Degrading content and character sex: Accounting for men and women's differential reactions to pornography. *Communication Reports, 18,* 43–53.

Grauerholz, E., & King, A. (1997). Prime time sexual harassment. *Violence Against Women, 3,* 129–148.

Greenberg, B. S., & Hofschire, L. (2000). Sex on entertainment television. In D. Zillmann & P. Vorderer (Eds.), *Media entertainment* (pp. 93–111). Hillsdale, NJ: Lawrence Erlbaum.

Greenberg, B. S., Linsangan, R., & Soderman, A. (1993). Adolescents' reactions to television sex. In B. S. Greenberg, J. D. Brown, & N. L. Buerkel-Rothfuss (Eds.), *Media, sex, and the adolescent* (pp. 196–224). Creskill, NJ: Hampton Press.

Greenberg, B. S., Perry, K. L., & Covert, A. M. (1983). The body human: Sex education, politics and television. *Family Relations, 32,* 419–425.

Greenberg, B. S., Siemicki, M., Dorfman, S., Heeter, C., Stanley, C., Soderman, A., & Linsangan, R. (1993). Sex content in R-rated films viewed by adolescents. In B. S. Greenberg, J. D. Brown, & N. Buerkel-Rothfuss (Eds.), *Media, sex, and the adolescent* (pp. 45–58). Cresskill, NJ: Hampton Press.

Greeson, L. E., & Williams, R. A. (1986). Social implications of music videos for youth: An analysis of the content and effects of MTV. *Youth and Society, 18,* 177–189.

Gunasekera, H., Chapman, S., & Campbell, S. (2005). Sex and drugs in popular movies: An analysis of the top 200 films. *Journal of the Royal Society of Medicine, 9,* 464–470.

Gunter, B. (2002). *Media sex.* Mahwah, NJ: Lawrence Erlbaum.

Haferkamp, C. J. (1999). Beliefs about relationships in relation to television viewing, soap opera viewing, and self-monitoring. *Current Psychology, 18,* 193–204.

Hald, G. M., & Malamuth, N. M, (2008). Self-perceived effects of pornography consumption. *Archives of Sexual Behavior. 37,* 614–625.

Hald, G. M., Malamuth, N. M., & Yuen, C. (2010). Pornography and attitudes supporting violence against women: Revisiting the relationship in nonexperimental studies. *Aggressive Behavior, 36,* 14–20.

Hale, J. L., Householder, B. J., & Greene, K. L. (2002). The theory of reasoned action. In J. P. Dillard & M. Pfau (Eds.), *The handbook of persuasion* (pp. 259–286). Thousand Oaks, CA: Sage.

Hansen, C. H., & Hansen, R. (1988). How rock music videos can change what is seen when boy meets girl: Priming stereotypic appraisal of social interactions. *Sex Roles, 5,* 287–316.

Hansen, C. H., & Krygowski, W. (1994). Arousal-augmented priming effects: Rock music videos and sex object schemas. *Communication Research, 21,* 24–47.

Hatoum, I. J., & Belle, D. (2004). Mags and abs: Media consumption and bodily concerns in men. *Sex Roles, 7,* 397–407.

Hennessy, M., Bleakley, A., Fishbein, M., & Jordan, A. (2009). Estimating the longitudinal association between adolescent sexual behavior and exposure to sexual media content. *Journal of Sex Research, 46,* 1–11.

Huesmann, L. R. (1986). Psychological processes promoting the relations between exposure to media violence and aggressive behavior by the viewer. *Journal of Social Issues,* 42, 125–139.

Huesmann, L. R. (1988). An information processing model for the development of aggression. *Aggressive Behavior, 14,* 13–24.

Huesmann, L. R. (1998). The role of social information processing and cognitive schema in the acquisition and maintenance of habitual aggressive behavior (pp. 73–109). In R. G. Geen & E. Donnerstein (Eds.), *Human aggression: Theories, research, and implications for policy.* New York: Academic Press.

Hust, S. J., Brown, J. D., & L'Engle, K. L. (2008). Boys will be boys and girls better be prepared: An analysis of the rare sexual health messages in young adolescents' media. *Mass Communication & Society, 11,* 3–23.

Huston, A. C., Wartella, E., & Donnerstein, E. (1998). *Measuring the effects of sexual content in the media.* Menlo Park, CA: Kaiser Family Foundation.

Johnson, J., Adams, M. S., Ashburn, L., & Reed, W. (1995). Differential gender effects of exposure to rap music on African American adolescents' acceptance of teen dating violence. *Sex Roles, 33,* 597–605.

Kaestle, C. E., Halpern, C. T., & Brown, J. D. (2007). Music videos, pro wrestling, and acceptance of date rape among middle school males and females: An exploratory analysis. *Journal of Adolescent Health, 40,* 185–187.

Kalof, L. (1999). The effects of gender and music video imagery on sexual attitudes. *Journal of Social Psychology, 139,* 378–385.

Kim, J. L., Sorsoli, C. L., Collins, K., Zylbergold, B. A., Schooler, D., & Tolman, D. L. (2007). From sex to sexuality: Exposing the heterosexual script on primetime network television. *Journal of Sex Research, 44,* 145–157.

Kim, J. L., & Ward, L. M. (2004). Pleasure reading: Associations between young women's sexual attitudes and their reading of contemporary women's magazines. *Psychology of Women Quarterly, 28,* 48–58.

Kingston, D. A., Federoff, P., Firestone, P., Curry, S., & Bradford, J. M. (2008). Pornography among sexual offenders. *Aggressive Behavior, 34,* 341–351.

Kingston, D. A., Malamuth, N.M., Fedoroff, P., & Marshall, W. L. (2009). The importance of individual differences in pornography use: Theoretical perspectives and implications for treating sexual offenders. *Journal of Sex Research, 46,* 216–232.

Kirby, D., Lepore, G., & Ryan, J. (2005). *Sexual and risk protective factors: Factors affecting teen sexual behavior, pregnancy, childbearing and sexually transmitted disease: Which are important? Which can you change?* National Campaign to Prevent Teen Pregnancy. Washington, DC: ETR Associates.

Kunkel, D., Biely, E., Eyal, K., Cope-Farrar, K. M., Donnerstein, E., & Fandrich, R. (2003). *Sex on TV 3: A biennial report to the Kaiser Family Foundation.* Menlo Park, CA: Kaiser Family Foundation.

Kunkel, D., Cope, K. M., Farinola, W. M., Biely, E., Rollin, E., & Donnerstein, E. (1999). *Sex on TV: A biennial report to the Kaiser Family Foundation.* Menlo Park, CA: Kaiser Family Foundation.

Kunkel, D., Eyal, K., Finnerty, K., Biely, E., & Donnerstein, E. (2005). *Sex on TV 4: A biennial report to the Kaiser Family Foundation.* Menlo Park, CA: Kaiser Family Foundation.

Larson, M. S. (1996). Sex roles and soap operas: What adolescents learn about single motherhood. *Sex Roles, 35,* 97–110.

Linz, D. G., Donnerstein, E., & Penrod, S. (1988). Effects of long-term exposure to violent and sexually degrading depictions of women. *Journal of Personality and Social Psychology, 55,* 758–768.

Livingstone, S., & Haddon, L. (2009). *EU Kids Online: Final report.* LSE, London: EU Kids Online.

Lonsway, K. A., & Fitzgerald, L. F. (1995). Attitudinal antecedents of rape myth acceptance: A theoretical and empirical reexamination. *Journal of Personality and Social Psychology, 68,* 704–711.

Lo, V., & Wei, R. (2005). Exposure to Internet pornography and Taiwanese adolescents' sexual attitudes and behavior. *Journal of Broadcasting & Electronic Media, 49,* 221–237.

Lyons, J. S., Anderson, R. L., & Larson, D. B. (1994). A systematic review of the effects of aggressive and nonaggressive pornography. In D. Zillman, J. Bryant, & A. C. Huston (Eds.), *Media, children, and the family: Social scientific, psychodynamic, and clinical perspectives* (pp. 271–310). Hillsdale, NJ: Lawrence Erlbaum.

Malamuth, N. (1996). Sexually explicit media, gender differences, and evolutionary theory. *Journal of Communication, 46,* 8–31.

Malamuth, N., & Check, J. (1981). The effects of mass media exposure on acceptance of violence against women: A field experiment. *Journal of Research in Personality, 15,* 436–446.

Malamuth, N. M., Addison, T., & Koss, M. (2000). Pornography and sexual aggression: Are there reliable effects and can we understand them? *Annual Review of Sex Research, 11,* 26–91.

Malamuth, N., Linz, D., & Yao, M. Z. (2005). The Internet and aggression: Motivation, disinhibitory and opportunity aspects. In Y. Amichai-Hamburger (Ed.), *The social net: Human behavior in cyberspace* (pp. 163–191). New York: Oxford University Press.

Martino, S. C., Collins, R. L., Kanouse, D. E., Elliot, M., & Berry, S. H. (2005). Social cognitive processes mediating the relationship between exposure to television's sexual content and adolescents' sexual behavior. *Journal of Personality and Social Psychology, 89,* 914–924.

Maynard, R.A. (1997). *Kids having kids: Economic costs and social consequences of teen pregnancy.* Washington, DC: Urban Institute.

Mazur, M. A., & Emmers-Sommer, T. M. (2002). The effect of movie portrayals on audience attitudes about nontraditional families and sexual orientation. *Journal of Homosexuality, 44,* 157–178.

McGuire, W. J. (1968). The nature of attitudes and attitude change. In G. Lindzey & E. Aronson (Eds.), *Handbook of social psychology* (2nd ed., pp. 136–314). Reading, MA: Addison-Wesley.

McKenzie-Mohr, D., & Zanna, M. (1990). Treating women as sexual objects: Looking to the (gender schematic) male who has viewed pornography. *Personality and Social Psychology Bulletin, 16,* 296–308.

McMahon, K. (1990). The *Cosmopolitan* ideology and the management of desire. *Journal of Sex Research, 27,* 381–396.

Milburn, M. A., Mather, R., & Conrad, S. D. (2000). The effects of viewing R-rated movie scenes that objectify women on perceptions of date rape. *Sex Roles, 43,* 645–664.

Milkie, M. A. (1999). Social comparisons, reflected appraisals and mass media: The impact of pervasive beauty on black and white girls' self-concepts. *Social Psychology Quarterly, 62,* 190–210.

Moreno, M. A, VanderStoep, A., Parks, M. R, Zimmerman, F. J., Kurth, A., & Christakis, D.C. (2008). A randomized pilot intervention to reduce at-risk adolescents' online risk behavior display on a social networking web site. *Archives of Pediatrics and Adolescent Medicine, 163,* 27–34.

Mullin, C. R., & Linz, D. (1995). Desensitization and resensitization to violence against women: Effects of exposure to sexually violent films on judgments of domestic violence victims. *Journal of Personality and Social Psychology, 69,* 449–459.

Nabi, R. L., & Clark, S. (2008). Exploring the limit of social cognitive theory: Why negatively reinforced behaviors on TV may be modeled anyway. *Journal of Communication, 58,* 407–427.

Newell, A. (1990). *Unified theories of cognition.* Cambridge, MA: Harvard University Press.

Olson, B. (1994). Soaps, sex, and cultivation. *Mass Communication Review, 21,* 106–113.

Pardun, C. J., L'Engle, K. L., & Brown, J. D. (2005). Linking exposure to outcomes: Early adolescents' consumption of sexual content in six media. *Mass Communication & Society, 8,* 75–91.

Peter, J., & Valkenburg, P. M. (2008). Adolescents' exposure to sexually explicit Internet material, sexual uncertainty, and attitudes toward uncommitted sexual exploration: Is there a link? *Communication Research,* 35, 579–602.

Peter, J., & Valkenburg, P.M. (2009). Adolescents' exposure to sexually explicit internet material and notions of women as sex objects: Assessing causality and underlying processes. *Journal of Communication,* 59, 407–433.

Peterson, R. A., & Kahn, J. (1995). Media preferences of sexually active and inactive youth. *Sociological Imagination, 32,* 29–43.

Peterson, J. L., Moore, K. A., & Furstenberg, F. F., Jr. (1991). Television viewing and early initiation of sexual intercourse: Is there a link? *Journal of Homosexuality, 21,* 93–118.

Pew Foundation. (2009). *The Pew Internet & American Life Project.* Philadelphia, PA: The Pew Charitable Trusts.

Pinkleton, B. E., Austin, E. W., Cohen, M., Chen, Y., & Fitzgerald, E. (2008). Effects of a peer-led media literacy curriculum on adolescent knowledge and attitudes regarding sexual behavior and media portrayals of sex. *Health Communication, 23,* 462–472.

Potter, W. J., & Chang, I. C. (1990). Television exposure measures and the cultivation hypothesis. *Journal of Broadcasting & Electronic Media, 34,* 313–333.

Prusank, D., Duran, R. L., & DeLillo, D. A. (1993). Interpersonal relationship in women's magazines: Dating and relating in the 1970s and 1980s. *Journal of Social and Personal Relationships, 10,* 307–320.

Rideout, V. J., Foehr, U. G., & Roberts, D. F. (2010). *Generation M²: Media in the lives of 8- to 18-year-olds*. Menlo Park, CA: Kaiser Family Foundation.

Roskos-Ewoldsen, D. R., Klinger, M. R., & Roskos-Ewoldsen, B. (2007). Media priming: A meta-analysis. In R. W. Preiss, B. M. Gayle, N. Burrell, M. Allen, & J. Bryant (Eds.), *Mass media effects research: Advances through meta-analysis* (pp. 53–80). New York: Lawrence Erlbaum.

Roskos-Ewoldsen, D. R., Roskos-Ewoldsen, B., & Dillman Carpentier, F. R. (2009). Media priming. An updated synthesis. In J. Bryant & M. B. Oliver (Eds.), *Media effects: Advances in theory and research* (pp. 74–93). New York: Psychology Press.

Rubin, A. M. (2002). The uses-and-gratifications perspective on media effects. In J. Bryant & D. Zillmann (Eds.), *Media effects: Advances in theory and research* (pp. 525–548). Mahwah, NJ: Lawrence Erlbaum.

Rubin, A. M., & Windahl, S. (1986). The uses and dependency model of mass communication. *Critical Studies in Mass Communication, 3,* 184–189.

Salazar, L., Fleischauer, P. J., Bernhardt, J. M., & DiClemente, R. (2009). Sexually explicit content viewed by teens on the Internet. In A. Jordan, D. Kunkel, J. Manganello, & M. Fishbein. *Media messages and public health: A decision approach to content analysis* (pp. 116–136). New York: Routledge.

Schuster, M. A., Bell, R. M., Peterson, L. P., & Kanouse, D. E. (1996). Communication between adolescents and physicians about sexual behavior and risk prevention. *Archives of Pediatrics and Adolescent Medicine, 150,* 906–913.

Seto, M. C., Maric, A., & Barbaree, H. E. (2001). The role of pornography in the etiology of sexual aggression. *Aggression and Violent Behavior, 6,* 35–53.

Shrum, L. J. (2007). The implications of survey methods for measuring cultivation effects. *Human Communication Research, 33,* 64–80.

Shrum, L. J., (2009). Media consumption and perceptions of social reality: Effects and underlying processes. In J. Bryant & M. B. Oliver (Eds.), *Media effects: Advances in theory and research* (pp. 50–73). New York: Psychology Press.

Sigal, J., Gibbs, M., Adams, B., & Derfler, R. (1988). The effect of romantic and nonromantic films on perception of female friendly and seductive behavior. *Sex Roles, 19,* 545–554.

Signorielli, N. (1991). Adolescents and ambivalence toward marriage: A cultivation analysis. *Youth and Society, 23,* 121–149.

Silverman-Watkins, L. T., & Sprafkin, J. N. (1983). Adolescents' comprehension of televised sexual innuendos. *Journal of Applied Developmental Psychology, 4,* 359–369.

Solderman, A. K., Greenberg, B. S., & Linsangan, R. (1988). Television and movie behaviors of pregnant and non-pregnant adolescents. *Journal of Adolescent Research, 3,* 153–170.

Strasburger, V. C., Jordan, A. B., & Donnerstein, E. (2010). Health effects of media on children and adolescents. *Pediatrics, 125,* 756–767.

Strouse, J. S., & Buerkel-Rothfuss, N. L. (1987). Media exposure and the sexual attitudes and behaviors of college students. *Journal of Sex Education and Therapy, 13,* 43–51.

Strouse, J. S., Buerkel-Rothfuss, N. L., & Long, E. C. (1995). Gender and family as moderators of the relationship between music video exposure and adolescent sexual permissiveness. *Adolescence, 30,* 505–521.

Strouse, J. S., Goodwin, M. P., & Roscoe, B. (1994). Correlates of attitudes toward sexual harassment among early adolescents. *Sex Roles, 31,* 559–577.

Subrahmanyan, K., Kraut, R., Greenfield, P., & Gross, E. (2001). New forms of electronic media: The impact of interactive games and the Internet on cognition, socialization, and behavior. In D. Singer & J. Singer (Eds.), *Handbook of children and the media* (pp. 73–99). Thousand Oaks, CA: Sage.

Sun, C., Bridges, A., Wosnitzer, R., Scharrer, E., & Liberman, R. (2008). A comparison of male and female directors in popular pornography: What happens when women are at the helm? *Psychology of Women Quarterly, 32,* 312–325.

Taylor, L. D. (2005a). All for him: Articles about sex in American lad magazines. *Sex Roles, 3,* 153–163.

Taylor, L. D. (2005b). Effects of visual and verbal sexual television content and perceived realism on attitudes and beliefs. *Journal of Sex Research, 42,* 130–137.

Taylor, L. D. (2006). College men, their magazines, and sex. *Sex Roles, 55,* 693–702.

Taylor, L. D. (2008). Cads, dads, and magazines: Women's sexual preferences and articles about sex and relationships. *Communication Monographs, 75,* 270–289.

Vega, V., & Malamuth, N. M. (2007). Predicting sexual aggression: The role of pornography in the context of general and specific risk factors. *Aggressive Behavior, 33,* 104–117.

Walsh-Childers, K., & Brown, J. D. (1993). Adolescents' acceptance of sex-role stereotypes and television viewing. In B. S. Greenberg, J. D. Brown, & N. L. Buerkel-Rothfuss (Eds.), *Media, sex, and the adolescent* (pp. 117–133). Creskill, NJ: Hampton Press.

Walsh-Childers, K., Treise, D., & Gotthoffer, A. (1997). *Sexual health coverage in women's, men's, teen, and other specialty magazines.* Menlo Park, CA: Kaiser Family Foundation.

Ward, L. M. (1995). Talking about sex: Common themes about sexuality in the prime-time television programs children and adolescents view most. *Journal of Youth & Adolescence, 24,* 595–615.

Ward, L. M. (2002). Does television exposure affect emerging adults' attitudes and assumptions about sexual relationships? Correlational and experimental confirmation. *Journal of Youth and Adolescence, 31,* 1–15.

Ward, L. M., & Friedman, K. (2006). Using TV as a guide: Associations between television viewing and adolescents' sexual attitudes and behavior. *Journal of Research on Adolescence, 16,* 133–156.

Ward, L. M., Hansbrough, E., & Walker, E. (2005). Contributions of music video exposure to black adolescents' gender and sexual schemas. *Journal of Adolescent Research, 20,* 143–166.

Ward, L. M., Merriwether, A., & Caruthers, A. (2006). Breasts are for men: Media, masculinity ideologies, and men's beliefs about women's bodies. *Sex Roles, 55,* 703–714.

Ward, L. M., & Rivadeneyra, R. (1999). Contributions of entertainment television to adolescents' sexual attitudes and expectations: The role of viewing amount versus viewer involvement. *Journal of Sex Research, 36,* 237–249.

Weisz, M. G., & Earls, C. M. (1995). The effects of exposure to filmed sexual violence on attitudes towards rape. *Journal of Interpersonal Violence, 10,* 71–84.

Wingood, G. M., DiClemente, R. J., Bernhardt, J. M., Harrington, K., Davies, S. L., Robillard, A., & Hook, E. W. (2003). A prospective study of exposure to rap music videos and African American female adolescents' health. *American Journal of Public Health, 93,* 437–439.

Wolak, J., Finkelhor, D., Mitchell, K. J., & Ybarra, M. L. (2008). Online "predators" and their victims: Myths, realities, and implications for prevention and treatment. *American Psychologist, 63,* 111–128.

Wolak J., Mitchell, K. J., & Finkelhor, D. (2007). Unwanted and wanted exposure to online pornography in a national sample of youth Internet. *Pediatrics, 119,* 247–257.

Wright, P. J. (2009a). Sexual socialization messages in mainstream entertainment mass media: A review and synthesis. *Sexuality & Culture, 4,* 181–200.

Wright, P. J. (2009b). Father–child sexual communication in the United States: A review and synthesis. *Journal of Family Communication, 4,* 1–18.

Wright, P. J. (in press). Mass media effects on youth sexual behavior: Assessing the claim for causality. *Communication Yearbook, 35.*

Wyer, R. S., & Radvansky, G. A. (1999). The comprehension and validation of social information. *Psychological Review, 106,* 89–119.

Zajonc, R. B. (1968). Attitudinal effects of mere exposure. *Journal of Personality and Social Psychology Monographs, 9,* 1–27.

Zhang, Y., Miller, L. E., & Harrison, K. (2008). The relationship between exposure to sexual music videos and young adults' sexual attitudes. *Journal of Broadcasting & Electronic Media, 52,* 368–386.

Zillmann, D. (1994). Erotica and family values. In D. Zillman, J. Bryant, & A. C. Huston (Eds.), *Media, children, and the family: Social scientific, psychodynamic, and clinical perspectives* (pp. 183–195). Hillsdale, NJ: Lawrence Erlbaum.

Zurbriggen, E. L. (2000). Social motives and cognitive power–sex associations: Predictors of aggressive sexual behavior. *Journal of Personality and Social Psychology, 78,* 559–581.

Zurbriggen, E. L., & Morgan, E. M. (2006). Who wants to marry a millionaire? Reality dating television programs, attitudes towards sex, and sexual behaviors. *Sex Roles, 54,* 1–17.

CHAPTER 15

Media and Identity Development

NINA HUNTEMANN
Suffolk University

MICHAEL MORGAN
University of Massachusetts Amherst

> *"The media we use and the stories they tell help to make us who we are."*
>
> (Mastronardi, 2003, p. 89)

Media and communication technologies play a critical and increasingly complex role in the process of identity development for children and adolescents. Media have made the experience and meaning of childhood and adolescence fundamentally different from what they were in previous generations. The dominant media of the early-middle 20th century—motion pictures, radio, comic books, magazines—provided popular models of behavior and style and also helped imbue young people with a sense of shared identities as members of "taste cultures." Later, the rise of television revolutionized the process of socialization;

for decades now, children have grown up in households in which the television is on for many hours a day, every day, and the parents (and even many of the grandparents) of today's children and adolescents have never known a world without TV. The massive flow of images, representations, and symbolic models disseminated by television profoundly shapes what young people think about the world and how they perceive themselves in relation to it.

In the 21st century, the implications of media for identity development are being dramatically transformed in ways we are just beginning to understand. Television and other traditional media still play significant roles—indeed, the amount of time children and adolescents spend watching television continues to increase—but the entire process of identity development has become far more intricate, multilayered, permeable, and complex with the explosion of new digital media.

The pervasiveness of the media and the extent to which their images and stories permeate family life, peer interaction, and the entire process of growing up means that young people today have far more vicarious (yet vivid and "realistic") experiences of other people and roles than ever before. Media provide an extraordinary quantity of examples of different types of people behaving in different types of ways in different types of situations. Yet just under the surface of this vast flow of images lie systematic patterns of inclusion and exclusion, of conventions and stereotypes, reflecting ideology and social power.

Media offer attractive avenues to ease the difficult and disturbing tensions of this developmental stage. They offer signposts for identities through broadly shared definitions of taste, style, values, models of personalities, and roles, whether specifically manufactured for and targeted to young audiences or as part of the general culture. The fact that what they provide are *mediated representations* is not in itself especially important in this context; it matters little whether young people perceive such images as true or false, as realistic or fictional. Every exposure to every media model provides a potential guide to behavior or attitude, a potential source of identification, a human exemplar that adolescents (and adults, for that matter) may use—whether in accordance with the model or explicitly contrary to it, and whether consciously or not—to define and construct identity. Moreover, as Rivadeneyra, Ward, and Gordon (2007) note, "Adolescents may also be more vulnerable to media messages because they are in a critical stage of self-evaluation and self-definition . . . . During this period, an individual's self-concept is unstable and often vacillates due to the challenges of identity exploration" (p. 266). This makes the media's impact on identity development during childhood and adolescence especially delicate and multifaceted.

While consumption of traditional media presents a vast array of potential models for identity, engagement with new interactive media practically forces young people to actively define themselves. The very use of new technologies now literally mediates the ways in which children and adolescents relate to each other; that is, media now provide powerful and dynamic mechanisms for peer interaction and self-presentation. New mobile and personal media (such as iPods and cell phones) are less extensions of our senses than they are parts of our physical beings, aspects of how young people show themselves to the world and relate to each other. The role played by peers in the process of identity development is now itself shaped by and enacted through media.

All this has significant implications for young people struggling to forge a sense of identity. Since its invention in the 19th century, "adolescence" has never been an easy period, emotionally, socially, or physically; arguably, it is now more complex and challenging than ever before. According to Erikson (1959, 1968), the successful transition from adolescence to adulthood depends on the formation of a coherent sense of identity, which is not an easy task. In varying ways, media can facilitate—or complicate—that process.

What Is Identity?

Before we can consider the media's contribution to identity development, we should first discuss just what we mean by *identity*. "Identity" is by no means a new concept, but in recent years, it has taken on new levels of social, political, and psychological importance and complex new layers of meaning. When we use the term *identity* in everyday conversation, the word seems reasonably clear and unambiguous. As with so many concepts, on the other hand, when it's placed under the lens of academic scrutiny, it becomes a slippery, problematic, and even contradictory notion. (Unfortunately, the term is notably absent from Raymond Williams's 1976 book, *Keywords*, an exploration of the diverse social and cultural meanings that swirl around such "simple, everyday" words as *behavior, family, critical, individual, personality,* and many others.)

Commonly, we tend to think of "identity" as something that resides somewhere within an individual, some profound and all-encompassing sense of the self that remains relatively fixed and stable once it is attained, recognized, or discovered. One may "discover" one's identity by maturation, deep introspection, "soul searching." Yet, somewhat paradoxically, identity may be externally and socially defined; one may "adopt" an identity by virtue of identification with a person or group. There is thus a curious tension between the personal and social aspects of identity, as it is partly informed by elements of both personality and social role. Although it is assumed that identity constitutes what makes someone unique (every identity is presumably different from every other identity; it is seen as something deep and ineffable and personal), it can be powerfully associated with our membership (or lack of membership) in some group, religion, or nationality. Along these lines, Tajfel (1978) developed an elaborate theoretical framework for studying "social identity" as something distinct from one's "personal identity" based on traits, appearance, and so on (see also Robinson, 1996). Identity therefore requires both individuation and social relatedness (Josselson, 1980).

There are familiar images from fables and myths, as well as examples from everyday life, of being "in search of" one's identity, trying to solve the puzzle of "who I really am." Succeeding in this quest is defined as essential; being "without" an identity, or having an "identity crisis" (an allegedly common ailment during adolescence), is an unenviable status. Yet this is by no means easy to resolve. As Ezra Pound put it,

> The real meditation is . . . the meditation on one's identity. Ah, voilà une chose!! You try it. You try finding out why you're you and not somebody else. And who in the blazes are you anyhow? Ah, voilà une chose! (Andrews, 1993, p. 438)

Identity is coveted and contested; we demand the right to determine our own. When Susan Faludi argues that feminism "asks that women be free to define themselves—instead of having their identity defined for them, time and again, by their culture and their men" (1991, p. xxiii), she is drawing on a notion of identity as a mechanism of social control. For one group to impose "identity" on another, in effect forcing a group to internalize others' demands for their exploitation, constitutes an extraordinarily powerful form of hegemony. On the other hand, those who resist such domination are often accused of engaging in "identity politics."

Ultimately, "identity"—as a sense of our subjective personhood—is not a fixed, internal phenomenon. Rather, it is a dynamic, shifting, continuous, socio-cultural *process*. Identity is fluid, partly situational, and thus constantly under construction, negotiation, and modification. As a process, it is actively constructed as it is expressed—and vice-versa.

Thus, identity is multidimensional; it is defined, shaped, and transformed by a vast range of factors: physical, sexual, emotional, religious, racial, ethnic, institutional, familial, and more. At some time or place, it may privilege personal descriptors or qualities: "fat," "funny," "clever," "unartistic," "nervous," "sociable," "athletic," or thousands more. It may be strongly shaped by diverse socio-demographic characteristics (some of which are more straightforward, stable, or changeable than others), including gender, age, class, religion, ethnicity, nationality, or race. It may also overlap with whatever social role we happen to be playing at any given moment—mother, nephew, student, shopper, team member, stamp collector, airline passenger, voter, and so on.

Components of identity are actively formed and reformed in social interactions with family, friends, peers, authorities, and others, as well as on the basis of media images and values. Indeed, since the media influence how other people treat us, as clusters of demographic and cultural characteristics, social interactions are in part informed by the shared understandings or stereotypes about people that the media provide. This influence is not, of course, literal or simple. Identity can be defined in opposition to or coherence with popular or vivid media stereotypes. The lack of a precise translation, as with many areas of media effects research, makes the task of understanding how media influence identity development a complex one.

Media and Identity

The significance of media in the daily lives of children cannot be overstated. Television alone occupies 4 hours of a child's day. Every year a child sees 20,000 TV commercials, and over his or her youth will spend more time watching TV than in school. Although no one image or program or activity will necessarily alter a child's consciousness or directly influence behavior, the quantity and redundancy of media images accumulate as part of the overall childhood experience. As Comstock (1993) states,

> . . . the influence of the medium (television) resides not in affecting how people behave but in what they think about. The medium (television) becomes a socio-cultural force not because people are what they see, but because what they see and talk about are important parts of their experience. (p. 118)

This accumulated experience contributes to the cultivation of a child's values, beliefs, dreams, and expectations, which shape the adult identity a child will carry and modify throughout his or her life. The potential contribution of the media to identity development is immense (Swidler, 1986).

Yet the importance of media in forming a child's identity is never constant. At a very young age, children gain most of their sense of self from their parents. A child sees herself as an extension of her parents during the first few years of life. Over time, other factors, such as peers and nonfamily authority figures, influence identity development. During adolescence, the presence and direct influence of parents, siblings, and other family members diminishes as teenagers search for independence and autonomy. It is during this time that young people search for ways to define themselves outside of their parents and family unit (Steinberg & Silverberg, 1986); the ubiquity of media and their immersion in it means they don't have to search very far. Overall media usage of 8- to 18-year-olds is approaching 8 hours a day, and the time they spend with every type of medium (except reading) increased steadily between 1999 and 2009 (Rideout, Foehr, & Roberts, 2010). Interpretations of media content and the implications of that content for identity development vary systematically with age and developmental stage (Granello, 1997).

The research reviewed below overviews childhood identity development in relation to media with a primary focus on adolescents, since the contours of a child's autonomous sense of self become more meaningful and distinct in early adolescence. Adolescents' values and beliefs are becoming uniquely their own, separate from and perhaps even contrary to the values of parents. In a broad variety of ways, media contribute to this process.

Multidirectional Patterns

The media play a reciprocal and multifaceted role in the ongoing process of identity development among young people. Indeed, this is an area in which concerns about media uses, functions, impacts, and reception all intersect in dynamic ways.

Teens are a critical target audience for numerous media—radio, television, movies, magazines, websites, and more. Young "hip" characters dominate TV programs and films, in large part due to attempts by producers to attract the lucrative youth market. Young audience members learn many lessons from the portrayals that result from these commercial imperatives, as media figures, celebrities, stars, and characters become icons for emulation. These media models provide not only countless elements of style, outlook, and value that can be incorporated into one's own identity, but they define and perpetuate common social categories as well. A viewer, for example, may learn the social definition of what it means to be a young Black female or a working-class White male. Moreover, these elements may guide our schemas and expectations in dealing with different types of people, which may then indirectly contribute to others' sense of identity. Young people may accept or reject these representations, but they cannot avoid having to deal with them.

The stories of television and other media—in both fictional and "reality" formats—demonstrate modes of problem solving with lessons of what works and what does not and for whom. These stories illustrate what "popular kids" are like, who is successful, and who is not. They offer modes of behaving, of engaging in social interaction, and of thinking about oneself, in terms of what kind of "self" one chooses to construct. The most urgent and compelling stories of all—that is, those of advertising—promote a sense of self and identity that can only be constructed meaningfully through consumption. Indeed, perhaps the dominant message of commercial media is that the actualization of the self depends on what products we buy. Consumption not only satisfies our deepest desires and solves almost any problem, it is also how we (and others) know who we are.

Yet, it is not simply that media *affect* young people's identity development through the establishment and glorification of role models and commodities (although the extent of this particular impact should not be underestimated; cf. Shaw, Kleiber, & Caldwell, 1995). It is important to stress that young people also actively *use* and *create* media to define themselves, and that media can help children and adolescents make sense of their lives, as a form of self-socialization. Indeed, Arnett (1995) casts "identity formation" as one of the five dominant uses of media by adolescents (the others being entertainment, high sensation, coping, and youth culture identification).

Moreover, media choices and behaviors "can be a personal expression of adolescent identity development" (Huston, Wartella, & Donnerstein, 1998, p. 11). Media preferences constitute a kind of badge of identity that young people use to define themselves, to themselves as well as to others. These preferences and habits signify membership in various taste cultures that unite (and divide) teens in subcultures, distinct from children and adults. These may be oppositional subcultures, as in the case of "media delinquents" (Roe, 1995), or they may be the result of carefully structured and efficient marketing strategies. Either way, media usage itself functions as a commodity, as a signal of group membership, style, and values. Music, for example, is "important to adolescents because it helps define their public self outside the family" (Larson, 1995, p. 543). Similarly, co-viewing certain programs can foment group identity (Granello, 1997), and personalizing one's profile page on a social networking site is a form of identity management (boyd, 2008). Beyond providing a coin of exchange in everyday conversation, the specific media choices children and adolescents make represent an integral aspect of self-definition—both for the self and

for others. It is this extremely wide range of ways in which media can impact young people's sense of identity that makes this influence so complex and so important.

Methodological Approaches

The first step in understanding how media influence the identity development of children and adolescents is that something needs to be known about the content of the media, particularly the images and representations portrayed that may contribute to young people's conceptions of themselves and others. Content analysis represents the overwhelming bulk of this scholarship. This is both a strength and a limitation of existing research. Literally an assessment of the messages of media, content analysis studies have included the examination of Saturday morning cartoons (Thompson & Zerbinos, 1995), prime-time television programs (Elasmar, Hasegawa, & Brain, 1999; Ward, 1995), horror films (Cowan & O'Brien, 1990; Weaver, 1991), Sunday comics (Brabant & Mooney, 1999), television commercials (Bretl & Cantor, 1988), children's television advertising (Smith, 1994), teen magazines (Evans, Rutberg, Sather, & Turner, 1991), music videos (Seidman, 1992), soap operas (Greco Larson, 1991), video games (Haninger & Thompson, 2004), and much more. From these content analyses, a general inventory is developed of the most common images and representations in media. This inventory is categorized into themes such as sex roles; the depiction of race, gender, class, and sexuality; and portrayals of work, politics, and citizenship.

In order to make the connection between the content of media and its influence on the identity development of children, researchers move beyond the media text—the collection of television programs, magazines, music lyrics, and so forth—to the child audience and ask the question, how do media influence a child's self-concept? Methods employed here include self-administered surveys and media reporting (Larson, 1995), one-on-one interviews (Steele & Brown, 1995), participant observation (Milkie, 1994), or a combination of these and additional ethnographic approaches (Ito, 2009). The purpose is to investigate the evasive and complex relationship between childhood and media. How is media content integrated into children's lived experience—that is, the practices and experiences of their everyday life—and how does that experience, in turn, shape their understanding of themselves and the world in which they live?

It is a difficult process to parse out the influence of peers, parents, and community from media. In a sense, a complete disconnect does not reflect the wedded relationship in which peers, parents, and community are likewise exposed to media. Parents, for example, also derive conceptions about the world partly from media and integrate those conceptions into their ideas and practices about parenting as well as into their relationships with their children. To cleanse the research subject of any influence other than media is not only impossible but also undesirable if we wish to grasp the fullness of identity.

Gender: Masculinity and Femininity Role Learning

A well-studied area of children's identity development and the media is the analysis of gender-role learning. Whether a child is a boy or girl is, perhaps, the most significant aspect of self that a child develops within the first few years of life. Taking cues from parents, other children and adults, and the media, a child quickly learns what it means to be a girl or a boy and how that difference dictates behavior. As a child will discover at a very young age, transgressing socially constructed gender expectations can invite painful alienation and ridicule. As a result, children observe carefully the particulars about being masculine or feminine. Toward this task, media provide a constant source of information about gender distinctions and a nonstop flood of normative models of male and female behavior.

Countless content analyses have examined the roles for girls, boys, women, and men portrayed in the media, particularly television programming and advertising. Common findings observe that, despite some progress, men outnumber women two or three to one in prime-time television, women are younger than men, and women are typically cast in traditional and stereotyped roles (Signorielli, 1989). Although the overall number of women on television may have increased over the decades, women's gains are limited mainly to minor roles (Elasmar, Hasegawa, & Brain, 1999), and conventional portrayals dominate. Being female continues to be equated with vulnerability (Stabile, 2009) and women are still defined primarily in terms of romance and family (Lauzen, Dozier, & Horan, 2008). The world of video games, in which 85% of characters are male, only exacerbates these patterns (Williams, Martins, Consalvo, & Ivory, 2009). Even in virtual world games, such as World of Warcraft, where players can create a character—or avatar—and choose its gender, male avatars (65%) still outnumber female avatars (35%; Yee, 2005).

Sex role research finds that children will replicate the role expectations seen in the media when asked about appropriate chores for boys and girls (Signorielli & Lears, 1992). Television can also strengthen the consistency between adolescents' gender-based attitudes about chores and their actual behavior in the family (Morgan, 1987). The medium's contributions to the endorsement and maintenance of traditional gender roles have been observed over time in longitudinal data and in diverse cultural contexts (Morgan, 1982, 1990). Ethnographic work (Milkie, 1994) has shown how teens make meanings from media content in terms of conventional gender roles; boys reproduce gendered meanings by "appropriating scenes . . . that embody traditional male culture, identifying with the models of masculinity available through media content and imputing stereotypical notions of gender to the mass media" (p. 354).

As children mature, television use decreases, but other media, magazines and music in particular, increase in use and significance for the young adult's navigation of gender identity. Duke and Kreshel (1998) found that young adolescent girls used teen magazines to develop their notions of femininity, of what it means to be a woman. Femininity was largely defined in the magazines as based on physical appearance and a girl's success at relationships with other girls and boys. In addition, the magazines provided insights into the needs and wants of boys and how girls can fulfill those desires. These messages about beauty, relationships, and the desires of boys and men are replicated on the websites of popular teen and women's magazines, where an increasing number of girls are turning for advice and information about how to be a woman (Labre & Walsh-Childers, 2003). Girls negotiate the meanings of femininity offered in the magazines with the expectations and values of their peers. The imprint of teen magazine gender roles is not universally or uniformly accepted, but their representations serve to reproduce dominant gender trajectories that readers must either conform to or deviate from; they thus contribute to a cultural context within which girls tend to identify their role as women as determined in part by how they please men and by their ability to look physically appealing.

Sexuality

Media have potentially vast impacts on the development of children's and adolescents' perceptions of their sexual identities. Young people are immensely curious about the subject of sex—not only its biological and physical aspects but also its emotional and social implications—and parents and schools are inconsistent in providing adequate information. This leaves peers and media as crucial sources almost by default (Brown, Walsh-Childers, & Waszak, 1990; Huston, Wartella, & Donnerstein, 1998). Television and other media may thus play a key role in the emergence and definitions of sexual perceptions, assumptions, and behaviors (Singletary, Ziegler, Reid, & Milbourne, 1990), especially as it normalizes culturally defined modes of gender and sexuality (Williams, 1996).

The bulk of existing research consists of content analyses rather than studies of the media's effects, although the latter are increasing. Research on music videos (Arnett, 2002; Seidman, 1992), soap operas (Greenberg & Busselle, 1996; Olson, 1995), daytime talk shows (Greenberg & Smith, 2002), prime-time television (Kunkel & Cope-Farrar, 2002; Lowry & Shidler, 1993), television advertising

(Kuriansky, 1996; Signorielli, McLeod, & Healy, 1994), women's and teen-oriented magazines (Walsh-Childers, 1997) and movies (Greenberg, Brown, & Buerkel-Rothfuss, 1993; Weaver, 1991) has substantiated what casual observation suggests: There has been a steady increase in the representation of sex in the media (implicit and explicit, verbal and visual) from the 1970s onward. In 2005, the Kaiser Family Foundation released a comprehensive content analysis of television from the late 1990s to the early 2000s, confirming the continued increase in sexual content but also noting for the first time a slight increase in representations of safer sexual practice and abstinence (Kunkel, Eyal, Finnerty, Biely, & Donnerstein, 2005).

Teenagers who watch more sexual content on television are more likely to have had physically intimate relations and/or intercourse (Brown & Newcomer, 1991; Brown, White, & Nikopoulou, 1993; Collins, et al., 2004; Ward & Rivadeneyra, 1999), although there is evidence that parents can mediate this association (Fisher, Hill, Grube, Bersamin, Walker, & Gruber, 2009). Moreover, teenage viewers of music videos are more likely than nonviewers to be accepting of premarital sex (Greeson & Williams, 1987; Strouse, Buerkel-Rothfuss, & Long, 1995). Bleakley, Hennessy, Fishbein, & Jordan (2008) present longitudinal data (based on 14- to 16-year-olds) that indicate a reciprocal "feedback loop" over time: "the more sexual activity in which adolescents engaged, the more likely they are to be exposed to sex in media, and the more they are exposed to sex in media, the more likely they are to have progressed in their sexual activity" (p. 458). Whatever one's moral position on media sex, these tendencies are worrisome given that the consequences of sex, such as pregnancy and sexually transmitted diseases (STDs), are rarely addressed.

One pervasive media lesson is that physical and sexual attractiveness is a critical asset (Ward, 1995). This invites (and even demands) self-image comparisons with the media-defined "ideal" body. These comparisons will be favorable for few teens. The perfect bodies that populate the media—print and electronic, programs and commercials, across all genres—are a key element in marketing strategies that use the body (especially the female body) to attract audiences and sell goods. The images can contribute to feelings of inadequacy, isolation, and self-rejection, especially among young people who feel vulnerable and insecure about the many physical and social changes taking place. They can also contribute to dangerous eating disorders. Girls, especially overweight girls, may be more susceptible to these kinds of consequences. Of course, as in any other area of media effects, such outcomes are neither automatic nor uniform but depend on a wide variety of personal and social factors (Henderson-King & Henderson-King, 1997).

Content studies reveal not merely a great deal of sexual content but very specific patterns of portrayals. "Sex in the media" largely means heterosexual sex between unmarried partners. This is by far the most frequent type of sexual representation. Accordingly, although the assumption of heterosexuality is a deeply ingrained cultural habit, the media play a major role in perpetuating such an assumption (Herek, 1992). This puts nonheterosexual teens in a situation similar to members of certain ethnic minority groups (see below): They are invisible, disempowered, and with few role models to look toward to help structure identity (Gross, 1994).

Few groups in society experience such strong tensions over sexuality as do gay and lesbian teens. In a cultural climate that is still largely hostile to homosexuality, the paucity of positive role models in the media is disturbing. As Kielwasser and Wolf (1994) note, "Gay and lesbian youth are not only excluded from representation on television, they are also never addressed as members of the audience" (p. 66). These authors also point out that although gay and lesbian adults may "subversively deconstruct" heterosexist media texts, young gay people may not have the developmental skill or world knowledge to do so.

Representations of gay characters on television increased dramatically in the 1990s (Becker, 2006). Following the much-publicized coming out of the title character on the situation comedy *Ellen* in 1998, program producers and advertisers began to be less apprehensive that gay characters would cause viewer outrage and lost profits (Wilke, 1998).

The Gay & Lesbian Alliance Against Defamation (GLAAD), which tracks gay, lesbian, and transgender characters on cable and broadcast channels in its annual Network Responsibility Index, has reported a steady increase in portrayals, but continues to find that LGBT characters are rarely cast in starring roles (2009). Cable channels, particularly premium subscription-based networks like HBO and Showtime, consistently include more, and more diverse, LGBT roles, which suggests that advertising-dependent broadcast channels are still skittish about risking ratings and ad revenue.

Since the coming out of Ellen DeGeneres, both as a lesbian actress and as a lesbian character on the TV sitcom *Ellen*, the narratives available to LGBT characters on television have opened up as well. The once-staple story, popular on shows such as *Beverly Hills 90210* and daytime soap operas, of a lone gay male dying of AIDS in a cold hospital room or the young teenager coming out to his homophobic parents, has receded. Richer storylines about gay couples in committed relationships often with adopted children (*Six Feet Under*, *Modern Family*) have replaced the one-off "gay friend episodes" of 1990s sitcoms like *Friends*. With the rise in the 1990s and 2000s of reality-based television programming, LGBT characters are increasingly seen in a variety of contexts, including as professionals in the style trades (*Queer Eye for the Straight Guy*, *Project Runway*) and as contestants on game shows (*Survivor*, *Amazing Race*). While the vast majority of these portrayals focus on the lives of adult characters, adolescent audiences are at least seeing professionally successful and socially accepted gay men on television. Unfortunately, mirroring the more general tendencies in the portrayal of women and minorities, these nonheterosexual characters are almost exclusively White and male; lesbians and gay people of color remain largely invisible (GLAAD, 2009). Thus, representations relevant to sexual identity are closely interwoven with many other layers of media portrayals, and it is these complex but coherent multidimensional clusters that must be taken into account in trying to understand the media's role in adolescent identity development. The

FOX television musical drama *Glee* is a notable exception to the otherwise invisible teen gay or lesbian character.

Race/Ethnicity: Alienation vs. Integration

Racial and ethnic stereotypes persist despite decades of attempts to eradicate them, from the civil rights movement through more recent initiatives to promote multiculturalism. The perseverance of stereotypes is one of the ways in which dominant groups can maintain their position in the hierarchy and impose their will on others (recall the Faludi quote above about women "having their identity defined for them"). One reason they persist is that group members enhance their self-esteem by favorably comparing themselves with relevant others (Harwood, Giles, & Ryan, 1995). The media rarely create these stereotypes; most have deep historical roots. Yet the media play a significant role in repeating, normalizing, and perpetuating many negative images of specific groups, and this can have crucial implications for how minority children and adolescents view themselves.

One of the most powerful mechanisms of keeping power away from a group is to render its members invisible. In the case of the media, those who are not represented do not exist; invisibility indicates the absence of social power (Gross, 1994). Children and adolescents who do not see characters "like themselves" in the media are learning a fundamental lesson about their group's (and their own) importance in society. Daily, they are being sent a loud and clear message that they do not count for very much.

While there have been substantial gains in the number of African-Americans in the media, other racial and ethnic minorities, particularly Latinos, remain greatly underrepresented and, when they are present, they are often negatively portrayed (Mastro & Behm-Morawitz, 2005; Mastro & Stern, 2003). Typically, ethnic minorities are associated with crime, violence, alcohol and drug abuse, and unemployment. They are generally not shown in cross-ethnic interactions or relationships unless involved with authority figures

and institutions (Coltrane & Messineo, 2000; Huston et al., 1992). White privilege is maintained even if racial and ethnic minorities are included in more positive, non-crime-related roles. One of the ways in which this occurs is in portrayals of the workplace where minority characters hold less prestigious occupations than White characters (Signorielli, 2009). Children's programming and commercials are highly segregated. White and non-White children rarely play together (Bang & Reece, 2003; Barcus, 1983; Maher, Herbst, Childs, & Finns 2008). The underrepresentation of minority characters, including women, is also found in the digital worlds of video and computer games (Williams, Martins, Consalvo, & Ivory, 2009). In the context of video games, the lack of diverse character choices often forces minority children and girls to accept and play identities in the form of avatars that do not look like themselves. When children have the opportunity to create virtual-world characters, such as in multiuser domains (MUDs) and massively multiplayer online role-playing games (MMORPGs), they construct avatars that reflect "real-life properties of themselves" (Calvert, Mahler, Zehnder, Jenkins, & Lee, 2003). This suggests that interactive environments that do not provide diverse representations hinder the potential for self-expression and self-exploration.

Based on this near invisibility, unattractive portrayals and socially segregated programming, Palmer, Smith, and Strawser (1993) found that minority children who watch more television experience lowered self-concept, feel alienated, and are uninterested in being part of life outside their immediate community. These researchers concluded that "the television tool through which (minorities) sought socialization and integration in the final analysis segregate(d) them" (p. 145).

Similarly, Allen (1993) states that the distorted view of African heritage in the media and public education system has "miseducated African-American children to believe they have no African heritage of which they should be proud" (p. 155). Instead, minority children are ashamed and may reject any associations with non-White, non-European heritage. For example, Allen found that the "African-American child may feel ambivalent about his or her racial identity and often will prefer characters on television that do not resemble themselves" (p. 170).

Still, minority children and adolescents often prefer to watch programs portraying members of their own ethnic groups (Greenberg & Brand, 1994), just as viewers would rather watch characters of their own age (Harwood, 1997). This attraction to characters with similar social identities is especially pronounced among those who more strongly identify themselves as members of specific social groups, and the desire to bolster social identity may drive viewing choices (Harwood, 1999). Thus, identity development can be especially precarious and the role of media especially significant in the case of those minority groups who remain nearly invisible in the world of television, such as Latinos, Asians, and Native Americans. Young people who belong to these and other neglected groups search in vain to find programs featuring characters like themselves and thus have ample opportunity to absorb the message that the majority culture does not value them very highly. The few programs featuring minority characters that do exist are often on networks that capture the smallest overall audience (UPN and WB in the 1990s, and BET). As a result, as Brown and Pardun (2004) note, "young people grow up in an increasingly segregated media world while the world in which they are living is increasingly diverse" (p. 276).

Learning the lesson that "society devalues my ethnicity," whether through media or other means, can have at least three potential (and not necessarily exclusive) outcomes: (1) the child may infer that if it is undesirable to be a member of that group, that minority status implies some personal deficiency, with negative repercussions on personal ethnic identity; that is, simply, "being a member of that group is bad, so I am bad"; (2) if membership in that ethnic group is undesirable, then denying that membership offers a solution; that is, "being a member of that group is bad, so I will try to look, act, and think of myself as a non-member of that group" (of course, this is easier for some minority groups than for others); and (3) the social undercutting of that minority status can *increase* frustration with and rejection of majority culture, intensifying

attachment to the minority culture and making identification with it even stronger; that is, "the people I know and love are members of that group, so society is wrong and unjust, and my allegiance to that group is stronger." In other words, resentment may serve paradoxically to raise consciousness, creating a backlash effect in which invisible minorities demand greater rights and representations.

A critical challenge for future research is to determine which of these three is most likely, for whom, and under what circumstances. It is worth noting that the only scenario of these three that positively *strengthens* ethnic identity is the third one, the one that involves rejecting dominant social values. Thus, although television and other popular media often function as social and cultural homogenizers (Morgan, 1986), their role in generating a backlash that foments "identity politics" and increases alienation and fragmentation should not be overlooked. Indeed, this is a plausible but markedly underresearched media effect.

New Media and Identity

The explosion of computer technology, like television before it, is transforming the experience of adolescence. New media offer new modes of both self-presentation and social interaction along with new opportunities for experimentation, exploration, and testing limits. These may help resolve—or intensify—the ongoing tensions between the personal and social dimensions of "identity." How new media technologies can influence adolescents' understanding of themselves and the world in which they live is important uncharted territory, just beginning to be explored.

Early work in this area looked toward postmodern theory for understanding the ways in which we experience identity online (e.g., Haraway, 1991). Some suggested that cyberspace challenges our reliance on embodied communication, fixed gender, sexual, class, and racial and other identities and allows us to experience the fluidity and multiplicity of identity construction. Turkle (1995, p. 26) observed that "We are using life on computer screens to become comfortable with new ways of thinking about evolution, relationships, sexuality, politics, and identity."

When chat rooms first began to emerge, many were taken by the fact that they offered the ability to play with or disguise identity in ways never before possible. Popular media accounts sensationalize the extent to which adolescents pretend to be someone they are not when online. Research suggests that this is not, in fact, a common activity; when it does occur, youth mainly tend to present themselves as older than they actually are (Gross, 2004). Pretending to be someone of another gender or sexual identity is quite rare and more often done as a joke among friends than as a serious attempt to be taken for someone else.

When not a joke, adolescents undertake identity experiments online primarily for purposes of self-exploration—"to explore how others react" (Valkenburg, Schouten, & Peter, 2005). Girls and younger adolescents engage in these behaviors more often. In contrast, older adolescents mainly spend their time online interacting with close personal friends.

"Exploring possibilities" of identity is a hallmark of adolescence, and new media do allow such explorations on an unprecedented scale, not only in chat rooms but also in the construction of home pages, Web journals and blogs (Huffaker & Calvert, 2005; Stern, 2004).

Home pages constitute a comparatively safe space where experimentation can take place within the privacy of one's bedroom or at a computer station. Yet simultaneously, they offer the unusual prospect of a large audience. Subsequently, authors can receive feedback from their home-page visitors, helping them to fashion their identities in much the same way Erikson claimed social interaction facilitates identity construction offline (Stern, 2004, p. 220).

New media such as social networking websites reshape the ways in which adolescents interact with their peers as well as give them vast new resources for defining themselves to others (and for easily and thoroughly revising their presentations of self). This means that new media represent critical mechanisms of identity formation (Goldman, Booker, & McDermott, 2008; Ito et al., 2008).

The very technology that offers easy editing and modification of visual and audio features also provides a way for—and may encourage—adolescents to "repeatedly reinvent themselves" (Stern, 2004, p. 222). They may "try on" entirely different personalities to see how they "fit" as often as they wish. Even the very choice of what site or service to use for these purposes (e.g., MySpace vs. Facebook vs. Twitter) sends a powerful message about self-presentation to others.

Younger and older adolescents differ in the ways in which they construct their online identities. Livingstone (2008) observes that "While younger teenagers relish the opportunities to recreate continuously a highly-decorated, stylistically-elaborate identity, older teenagers favour a plain aesthetic that foregrounds their links to others, thus expressing a notion of identity lived through authentic relationships" (p. 393). As adolescents mature, identity as a form of display "is replaced gradually by the mutual construction among peers of a notion of identity through connection" (p. 402).

Social networking sites thus have implications for both personal and social identity; users "may post material that relates to personal predilections but also include content that acts as a group marker" (Barker, 2009, p. 209). In a larger sense, these media can be used to both perpetuate and resist dominant power structures. For example, Gajjala (2007) found that Mexican-American teens use the social networking site MySpace.com to construct identities "that both reproduce and contest stereotypes about Mexican-Americans" (p. 1).

The Internet provides adolescents with a wide range of opportunities to explore sexual issues as well as unprecedented access to sexually explicit images and materials. They use online chat "to air adolescent concerns about sexuality and to develop creative strategies to exchange identity information with their peers" (Subrahmanyam, Greenfield, & Tynes, 2004, p. 651). Peter and Valkenburg (2008) examined the connection between adolescents' exposure to sexual content on the Internet and sexual socialization from an identity development framework. Their study of Dutch adolescents found that those who are more exposed to sexually explicit Internet materials are both more sexually uncertain (less likely to feel their sexual beliefs and values are fixed) and more favorable toward uncommitted sexual exploration. The Internet may play an especially important role in the exploration of sexual identity among lesbian, gay, and bisexual adolescents (Bond, Hefner, & Drogos, 2009).

Conclusions and Further Research

Media play a significant role in terms of how adolescents come to view themselves in relation to the larger world according to gender, sexuality, body image, race, ethnicity, and more. Television continues to provide an unending stream of models and a massive flow of vivid lessons about different social types. These lessons contribute to how children and adolescents define themselves as well as to how they are treated by others. Clearly, the media/identity relationship is not a one-way street; media content contributes to identity, but identity also shapes how we select and respond to media content (Cohen, 1991; Davis & Gandy, 1999).

After more than half a century of living with (and studying) television, we know quite a bit about what stereotypes, conventional models, and dominant roles persist. Updated content analyses should continue to monitor media representations of gender, race, class, occupation, sexuality, age, physical ability, and the like. Some may consider this old news, but the continued monitoring of the symbolic environment is essential to understanding media effects; despite the emergence of new media, television viewing by children and adolescents continues to increase, often *through* new media (e.g., online streaming and mobile video).

Beyond the extensive research that exists on content patterns, the connection between how different groups are represented in the media and how that translates into self-concept and identity development requires far more theoretical and methodological attention than has been brought to bear to date. There is a tendency in this research to investigate the identity development of nondominant populations—women and girls, people of color, and gay men and lesbians. While there is a

great deal of scholarship on the development of feminine, racial minority, and homosexual identity (both in content analysis and effects research), research on the construction of masculinity, whiteness, and heterosexuality is less prevalent.

There was a time in media effects research when representations of nondominant populations were ignored, and the consumption and influence of media among minority children were assumed to be like the majority: that is, White, middle-class boys. Now, with the recognition that children's relationships to media messages vary, we have, perhaps, the opposite situation (see Asamen & Berry in this collection for a discussion of television and multicultural awareness). Attention to nondominant children can have the effect of "normalizing" dominant identities, suggesting that a tangible "identity" only belongs to those *different* from the assumed majority. Without the comparable investigation of dominant and nondominant audiences and media messages, we cannot understand how boys and girls construct their gender identity *in relationship with* masculine and feminine media representations, their racial identity from images of both White people and people of color, or their sexual development as dependent on both straight and gay depictions of sexuality. That being said, it is also critical to recognize that these categories of gender, race, and sexuality oversimplify what are, in fact, complex continua rather than simple dichotomies.

As if the impact of "traditional" media was not enough, new media are extending and deepening the role of communication technology in adolescents' lives by reshaping their modes of participation in immediate social groups, especially in terms of their peers. Social networking websites also allow adolescents to construct and revise their public identities with ease.

Many, if not all, of the communicative functions of computers are now available on cell phones. Cell phones have become the new e-mail for adolescents, and they use them far more often for texting friends than for actually speaking with them. At the start of 2009, teens in the United States were sending and receiving an average of nearly 3,000 text messages a month—nearly 100 a day—compared to less than 200 monthly voice calls (Nielsen, 2009). Contemporary cell phones allow adolescents to engage in a broad range of mediated interactions with peers—now, from virtually anywhere, at any time—thus producing both a shared youth culture and group identity based on technological fluency and offering more frequent and mobile opportunities to construct both personal and social identity. Through forms of use (from texting to sexting—an activity that 20% of teens are alleged to have engaged in) and a growing range of applications (including Web browsing, music, photography, watching downloaded video, GPS, and much more), cell phones have become a sine qua non of adolescence, an indispensable accouterment that an adolescent effectively needs in order to interact socially or to be a member of a social group.

Livingstone argues that "for today's teenagers, self actualization increasingly includes a careful negotiation between the opportunities (for identity, intimacy, sociability) and risks (regarding privacy, misunderstanding, abuse) afforded by internet-mediated communication" (2008, p. 407). This now applies to the cell phone as well. By its very mobility and the privacy (and relative immunity from supervision) it offers, both the opportunities and the risks may be vastly magnified.

As we noted at the start of this chapter, identity is an active process, as is the negotiation of symbolic media messages into the everyday life of children and adults. Also, it is vital to recall that the media/identity relationship is not a one-way street; identity also shapes how we respond to media content (Cohen, 1991; Davis & Gandy, 1999; Durkin & Nugent, 1998), setting up complex dynamics that will vary by developmental stage and a vast range of other factors.

Meanwhile, technology is developing so quickly that even recent research goes out of date quickly. The emphasis on adolescent use of chat rooms and MUDS of just a few years ago has been replaced by research on social networking sites such as MySpace and Facebook and even newer applications such as Twitter and Chatroulette. One can barely imagine the changes the next decade or two will bring.

Understanding these critical processes will require creative syntheses of the entire spectrum of methodological approaches. Ethnographic methods such as one-to-one interviews and participant observation can provide thick descriptions of daily life, allowing for the messy and complex connections between identity and culture. Large-scale survey research can uncover broad patterns of associations between media exposure and beliefs about self and others, such as pride in group membership, self-esteem, endorsement of nontraditional roles, and so on, for different groups of children and adolescents. Focus group research can shed light on how young people make sense and meaning out of various types of portrayals and representations, and how they define themselves and interact with others through media. Most important, theoretical work is needed to give us richer and more meaningful conceptualizations of "identity" as a dynamic and complex interplay of personal, social, and cultural influences. From there, we may hope to shed a little more light on how children and adolescents integrate and negotiate symbolic messages and media technologies with the various and intertwined daily influences on their conceptions of who they are in relation to the world in which they live. This theoretical work is vital; the task of understanding the role of media in identity development is only going to become more challenging in the future.

References

Allen, R. L. (1993). Conceptual models of an African-American belief system. In G. L. Berry & J. K. Asamen (Eds.), *Children & television: Images in a changing sociocultural world* (pp. 155–176). Newbury Park, CA: Sage.

Andrews, R. (1993). *The Columbia dictionary of quotations*. New York: Columbia University Press.

Arnett, J. (1995). Adolescents' uses of media for self-socialization. *Journal of Youth and Adolescence, 25,* 519–534.

Arnett, J. (2002). The sounds of sex: Sex in teens' music and music videos. In Brown, J. D., Steele, J. R., & Walsh-Childers, K. (Eds.), *Sexual teens, sexual media: Investigating media's influence on adolescent sexuality* (pp. 253–264). Mahwah, NJ: Lawrence Erlbaum.

Bang, H., & Reece, B. B. (2003). Minorities in children's television commercials: New, improved, and stereotyped. *Journal of Consumer Affairs, 37*(1), 42–67.

Barcus, F. E. (1983). *Images of life on children's television*. New York: Praeger.

Barker, V. (2009). Older adolescents' motivations for social network site use: The influence of gender, group identity, and collective self-esteem. *Cyberpsychology & Behavior, 12*(2), 209–213.

Becker, R. (2006). *Gay TV and straight America*. New Brunswick, NJ: Rutgers University Press.

Bleakley, A., Hennessy, M., Fishbein, M., & Jordan, A. (2008). It works both ways: The relationship between exposure to sexual content in the media and adolescent sexual behavior. *Media Psychology, 11*(4), 443–461.

Bond, B. J., Hefner, V., & Drogos, K. L. (2009). Information-seeking practices during the sexual development of lesbian, gay, and bisexual individuals: The influence and effects of coming out in a mediated environment. *Sexuality & Culture, 13,* 32–50.

boyd, d. (2008). Why youth (heart) social network sites: The role of networked publics in teenage social life. In D. Buckingham (Ed.), *Youth, identity, and digital media* (pp. 119–142). Cambridge, MA: MIT Press.

Brabant, S., & Mooney, L. A. (1999). The social construction of family life in the Sunday comics: Race as a consideration. *Journal of Comparative Family Studies, 30,* 113–114.

Bretl, D. J., & Cantor, J. (1988). The portrayal of men and women in U.S. television commercials: A recent content analysis and trends over 15 years. *Sex Roles, 18,* 595–609.

Brown, J. D., & Newcomer, S. F. (1991). Television viewing and adolescents' sexual behavior. *Journal of Homosexuality, 21,* 77–92.

Brown, J. D., & Pardun, C. J. (2004). Little in common: Racial and gender differences in adolescents' television diets. *Journal of Broadcasting & Electronic Media, 48*(2), 266–278.

Brown, J. D., Walsh-Childers, K., & Waszak, C. S. (1990). Television and adolescent sexuality. *Journal of Adolescent Health Care, 11,* 62–70.

Brown, J. D., White, A. B., & Nikopoulou, L. (1993). Disinterest, intrigue, resistance: Early adolescent girls' use of sexual media content. In B. S. Greenberg, J. D. Brown, & N. L. Buerkel-Rothfuss (Eds.), *Media, sex and the adolescent* (pp. 183–195). Hillsdale, NJ: Lawrence Erlbaum.

Calvert, S. L., Mahler, B. A., Zehnder, S. M., Jenkins, A., & Lee, M. S. (2003). Gender differences in preadolescent children's online interactions: Symbolic modes of self-presentation and self-expression. *Applied Developmental Psychology, 24*(6), 627–644.

Cohen, J. R. (1991). The "relevance" of cultural identity in audiences' interpretations of mass media. *Critical Studies in Mass Communication, 8,* 442–454.

Collins, R. L., Elliott, M. N., Berry, S. H., Kanouse, D. E., Kunkel, D., Hunter, S. B., & Miu, A. (2004). Watching sex on television predicts adolescent initiation of sexual behavior. *Pediatrics, 114*(3), 280–289.

Coltrane, S., & Messineo, M. (2000). The perpetuation of subtle prejudice: Race and gender imagery in 1990s television advertising. *Sex Roles, 42*(5–6), 363–389.

Comstock, G. (1993). The role of television in American life. In G. L. Berry & J. K. Asamen (Eds.), *Children & television: Images in a changing sociocultural world* (pp. 117–131). Newbury Park, CA: Sage.

Cowan, G., & O'Brien, M. (1990). Gender and survival vs. death in slasher films: A content analysis. *Sex Roles, 23,* 187–196.

Davis, J .L., & Gandy, O. (1999). Racial identity and media orientation. *Journal of Black Studies, 29,* 367.

Duke, L. L., & Kreshel, P. J. (1998). Negotiating femininity: Girls in early adolescence read teen magazines. *Journal of Communication Inquiry, 22*(1), 48–71.

Durkin, K., & Nugent, B. (1998). Kindergarten children's gender-role expectations for television actors. *Sex Roles, 38,* 387–402.

Elasmar, M., Hasegawa, K., & Brain, M. (1999). The portrayal of women in U.S. prime time television. *Journal of Broadcasting & Electronic Media, 43,* 20–33.

Erikson, E. H. (1959). *Identity and the life cycle*. New York: International Universities Press.

Erikson, E. H. (1968). *Identity: Youth and crisis*. New York: Norton.

Evans, E. D., Rutberg, J., Sather, C., & Turner, C. (1991). Content analysis of contemporary teen magazines for adolescent females. *Youth & Society, 23*(1), 99–120.

Faludi, S. (1991). *Backlash: The undeclared war against women*. New York: Crown.

Fisher, D., Hill, D., Grube, J., Bersamin, M., Walker, S., & Gruber, E. (2009). Televised sexual content and parental mediation: Influences on adolescent sexuality. *Media Psychology, 12*(2), 121–147.

Gajjala, R. (2007, May). *Race and ethnicity in MySpace: Producing identity as interface.* Paper presented at the annual meeting of the International Communication Association, San Francisco, CA. Retrieved April 1, 2010, from http://www.allacademic.com/meta/p169173_index.html.

GLAAD. (2009). *Network responsibility index: Primetime programming, 2008–2009.* New York: Author. Retrieved April 1, 2010, from http://www.glaad.org/Page.aspx?pid=831.

Goldman, S., Booker, A., & McDermott, M. (2008). Mixing the digital, social, and cultural: Learning, identity and agency in youth participation. In D. Buckingham (Ed.), *Youth, identity, and digital media* (pp. 185–206). Cambridge, MA: MIT Press.

Granello, D. H. (1997). Using *Beverly Hills, 90210* to explore developmental issues in female adolescents. *Youth & Society, 29,* 24–54.

Greco Larson, S. (1991). Television's mixed messages: Sexual content on *All My Children. Communication Quarterly, 39*(2), 156–163.

Greenberg, B. S., & Brand, J. E. (1994). Minorities and the mass media: 1970s to 1990s. In J. Bryant & D. Zillman (Eds.), *Media effects: Advances in theory and research* (pp. 273–314). Hillsdale, NJ: Lawrence Erlbaum.

Greenberg, B. S., Brown, J., & Buerkel-Rothfuss, N. L. (Eds.). (1993). *Media, sex, and the adolescent.* Cresskill, NJ: Hampton Press.

Greenberg, B. S., & Busselle, R. W. (1996). Soap operas and sexual activity: A decade later. *Journal of Communication, 46,* 153–160.

Greenberg, B. S., & Smith, S. W. (2002). Daytime talk shows: Up close and in your face. In Brown, J. D., Steele, J. R., & Walsh-Childers, K. (Eds.), *Sexual teens, sexual media: Investigating media's influence on adolescent sexuality* (pp. 79–94). Mahwah, NJ: Lawrence Erlbaum.

Greeson, L. E., & Williams, R. A. (1987). Social implications of music videos for youth: An analysis of the content and effects of MTV. *Youth & Society, 18,* 177–189.

Gross, E. F. (2004). Adolescent Internet use: What we expect, what teens report. *Journal of Applied Developmental Psychology, 25,* 633–649.

Gross, L. (1994). What is wrong with this picture? Lesbian women and gay men on television. In R. J. Ringer (Ed.), *Queer words, queer images: Communication and the construction of homosexuality* (pp. 143–156). New York: New York University Press.

Huffaker, D. A., & Calvert, S. L. (2005). Gender, identity, and language use in teenage blogs. *Journal of Computer-Mediated Communication, 10*(2). Retrieved May 10, 2010, from http://jcmc.indiana.edu/vol10/issue2/huffaker.html.

Haninger, K., & Thompson, K. M. (2004). Content and ratings of teen-rated video games. *Journal of the American Medical Association, 291,* 856–865.

Haraway, D. (1991). A cyborg manifesto: Science, technology, and socialist-feminism in the late twentieth century. In *Simians, cyborgs and women: The reinvention of nature* (pp. 149–181). New York: Routledge.

Harwood, J. (1997). Viewing age: Lifespan identity and television viewing choices. *Journal of Broadcasting and Electronic Media, 41,* 203–213.

Harwood, J. (1999). Age identification, social identity gratifications, and television viewing. *Journal of Broadcasting & Electronic Media, 43,* 123–133.

Harwood, J., Giles, H., & Ryan, E. B. (1995). Aging, communication, and intergroup theory: Social identity and intergenerational communication. In J. F. Nussbaum & J. Coupland (Eds.), *Handbook of communication and aging research* (pp. 133–159). Hillsdale, NJ: Lawrence Erlbaum.

Henderson-King, E., & Henderson-King, D. (1997). Media effects on women's body esteem: Social and individual difference factors. *Journal of Applied Social Psychology, 27,* 399–417.

Herek, G. M. (1992). The social context of hate crimes: Notes on cultural heterosexism. In G. Herek & K. Berril (Eds.), *Hate crimes: Confronting violence against lesbians and gay men* (pp. 89–104). Newbury Park, CA: Sage Publications.

Huston, A. C., Donnerstein, E., Fairchild, H., Feshbach, N. D., Katz, P. A., Murray, J. P., Rubinstein, E. A., Wilcox, B., & Zuckerman, D. (Eds.). (1992). *Big world, small screen: The role of television in American society.* Lincoln: University of Nebraska Press.

Huston, A. C., Wartella, E., & Donnerstein, E. (1998, May). *Measuring the effects of sexual content in the media: A report to the Kaiser family foundation.* Menlo Park, CA: Kaiser Family Foundation.

Ito, M. (2009). *Hanging out, messing around, geeking out: Kids living and learning with new media.* Cambridge, MA: MIT Press.

Ito, M., Horst, H., Bittanti, M., boyd, d., Herr-Stephenson, B., Lange, P. G., Pascoe, C. J., & Robinson, L. (2008). *Living and learning with new media: Summary of findings from the Digital Youth Project*. Chicago: The MacArthur Foundation.

Josselson, R. (1980). Ego development in adolescence. In Adelson, J. (Ed.), *Handbook of adolescent psychology* (pp. 140–167). New York: Wiley.

Kielwasser, A. P., & Wolf, M. A. (1994). Silence, difference, and annihilation: Understanding the impact of mediated heterosexism on high school students. *High School Journal, 77,* 58–79.

Kunkel, D., & Cope-Farrar, K. (2002). Sexual messages in teens' favorite prime-time television programs. In Brown, J. D., Steele, J. R., & Walsh-Childers, K. (Eds.), *Sexual teens, sexual media: Investigating media's influence on adolescent sexuality* (pp. 59–78). Mahwah, NJ: Lawrence Erlbaum.

Kunkel, D., Eyal, K., Finnerty, K., Biely, E., & Donnerstein, E. (2005). *Sex on TV: 2005.* Menlo Park, CA: The Henry J. Kaiser Family Foundation.

Kuriansky, J. (1996). Sexuality and television advertising: An historical perspective. *SIECUS Report, 24,* 13.

Labre, M. P., & Walsh-Childers, K. (2003). Friendly advice? Beauty messages in web sites of teen magazines. *Mass Communication & Society, 6*(4), 379–396.

Larson, R. (1995). Secrets in the bedroom: Adolescents' private use of media. *Journal of Youth and Adolescence, 24*(5), 535–550.

Lauzen, M., Dozier, D., & Horan, N. (2008). Constructing gender stereotypes through social roles in prime-time television. *Journal of Broadcasting & Electronic Media, 52*(2), 200–214.

Livingstone, S. (2008). Taking risky opportunities in youthful content creation: Teenagers' use of social networking sites for intimacy, privacy and self-expression. *New Media & Society, 10*, 393–411.

Lowry, D. T., & Shidler, J. A. (1993). Prime time TV portrayals of sex, "safe sex" and AIDS: A longitudinal analysis. *Journalism Quarterly, 70,* 628–637.

Maher, J. K., Herbst, K. C., Childs, N. M., & Finn, S. (2008). Racial stereotypes in children's television commercials. *Journal of Advertising Research, 48*(1), 80–93.

Mastro, D. E., & Behm-Morawitz, E. (2005). Latino representation on primetime television. *Journalism & Mass Communication Quarterly, 82*(1), 110–130.

Mastro, D. E., & Stern, S. R. (2003). Representations of race in television commercials: A content analysis of prime-time advertising. *Journal of Broadcasting & Electronic Media, 47*(4), 638–647.

Mastronardi, M. (2003). Adolescence and media. *Journal of Language & Social Psychology, 22*(1), 83–93.

Milkie, M. A. (1994). Social world approach to cultural studies: Mass media and gender in the adolescent peer group. *Journal of Contemporary Ethnography, 23*(3), 354–380.

Morgan, M. (1982). Television and adolescents' sex-role stereotypes: A longitudinal study. *Journal of Personality and Social Psychology, 43,* 947–955.

Morgan, M. (1986). Television and the erosion of regional diversity. *Journal of Broadcasting & Electronic Media, 30,* 123–139.

Morgan, M. (1987). Television, sex-role attitudes, and sex-role behavior. *Journal of Early Adolescence, 7,* 269–282.

Morgan, M. (1990). International cultivation analysis. In N. Signorielli & M. Morgan (Eds.), *Cultivation analysis: New directions in media effects research* (pp. 225–247). Newbury Park, CA: Sage.

Nielsen, A. C. (2009, June). *How teens use media: A Nielsen report on the myths and realities of teen media trends.* Retrieved September 14, 2009, from http://blog.nielsen.com/nielsenwire/reports/nielsen_howteensusemedia_june09.pdf.

Olson, B. (1995). Sex and soaps: A comparative content analysis of health issues. *Journalism Quarterly, 71,* 840–850.

Palmer, E. L., Smith, K. T., & Strawser, K. S. (1993). Rubik's tube: Developing a child's television worldview. In G. L. Berry & J. K. Asamen (Eds.), *Children & television: Images in a changing sociocultural world* (pp. 143–154). Newbury Park, CA: Sage.

Peter, J., & Valkenburg, P. M. (2008). Adolescents' exposure to sexually explicit Internet material, sexual uncertainty, and attitudes toward uncommitted sexual exploration: Is there a link? *Communication Research, 35*(5), 579–601.

Rideout, V. J., Foehr, U. G., & Roberts, D. F. (2010.) *Generation M²: Media in the lives of 8- to 18-year-olds.* Menlo Park, CA: The Henry J. Kaiser Family Foundation. Retrieved April 1, 2010, from http://www.kff.org/entmedia/upload/8010.pdf.

Rivadeneyra, R., Ward, M. L., & Gordon, M. (2007). Distorted reflections: Media exposure and Latino adolescents' conceptions of self. *Media Psychology, 9*(2), 261–290.

Robinson, W. R. (Ed.). (1996). *Social groups and identities: Developing the legacy of Henri Tajfel.* Boston, MA: Butterworth Heinemann.

Roe, K. (1995). Adolescents' use of socially disvalued media: Toward a theory of media delinquency. *Journal of Youth and Adolescence, 25,* 617–629.

Seidman, S. A. (1992). An investigation of sex-role stereotyping in music videos. *Journal of Broadcasting, 36,* 209–216.

Shaw, S. M., Kleiber, D. A., & Caldwell, L. L. (1995). Leisure and identity formation in male and female adolescents: A preliminary examination. *Journal of Leisure Research, 27,* 245–264.

Signorielli, N. (1989). Television and conceptions about sex-roles: Maintaining conventionality and the status quo. *Sex Roles, 21,* 337–356.

Signorielli, N. (2009). Race and sex in prime time: A look at occupations and occupational prestige. *Mass Communication & Society, 12*(3), 332–352.

Signorielli, N., & Lears, M. (1992). Children, television, and conceptions about chores: Attitudes and behaviors. *Sex Roles, 27,* 157–170.

Signorielli, N., McLeod, D., & Healy, E. (1994). Gender stereotypes in MTV commercials: The beat goes on. *Journal of Broadcasting & Electronic Media, 38,* 91–101.

Singletary, M. W., Ziegler, D., Reid, K., & Milbourne, C. (1990, June). *Media use and high school students perceptions of sexual behavior: A cultivation analysis.* Paper presented at the annual meeting of the International Communication Association, Dublin, Ireland.

Smith, L. J. (1994). A content analysis of gender differences in children's advertising. *Journal of Broadcasting and Electronic Media, 38,* 323–337.

Stabile, C. (2009). "Sweetheart, this ain't gender studies": Sexism and superheroes. *Communication & Critical/Cultural Studies, 6*(1), 86–92.

Steele, J. R., & Brown, J. D. (1995). Adolescent room culture: Studying media in the context of everyday life. *Journal of Youth and Adolescence, 24*(5), 551–576.

Steinberg, L., & Silverberg, S. B. (1986). The vicissitudes of autonomy in early adolescence. *Child Development, 57,* 841–851.

Stern, S. R. (2004). Expressions of identity online: Prominent features and gender differences in adolescents' World Wide Web home pages. *Journal of Broadcasting and Electronic Media, 48,* 218–243.

Strouse, J., Buerkel-Rothfuss, N., & Long, E. C. (1995). Gender and family as moderators of the relationship between music video exposure and adolescent sexual permissiveness. *Adolescence, 30,* 505–521.

Subrahmanyam, K., Greenfield, P. M., & Tynes, B. (2004). Constructing sexuality and identity in an online teen chat room. *Applied Developmental Psychology, 24,* 651–666.

Swidler, A. (1986). Culture in action: Symbols and strategies. *American Sociological Review, 51,* 273–286.

Tajfel, H. (1978). Social categorization, social identity, and social comparison. In H. Tajfel (Ed.), *Differentiation between social groups: Studies in the social psychology of intergroup relations* (pp. 61–76). London: Academic Press.

Thompson, T. L., & Zerbinos, E. (1995). Gender roles in animated cartoons: Has the picture changed in 20 years? *Sex Roles, 32,* 651–674.

Turkle, S. (1995). *Life on the screen: Identity in the age of the internet.* New York: Simon & Schuster.

Valkenburg, P. M., Schouten, A. P., & Peter, J. (2005). Adolescents' identity experiments on the Internet. *New Media and Society, 7,* 383–402.

Walsh-Childers, K. (1997). *A content analysis: Sexual health coverage in women's, men's, teen and other specialty magazines.* Menlo Park, CA: Kaiser Family Foundation.

Ward, M. L. (1995). Talking about sex: Common themes about sexuality in the prime-time television programs children and adolescents view most. *Journal of Youth and Adolescence, 24*(5), 595–615.

Ward, M. L., & Rivadeneyra, R. (1999). Contributions of entertainment television to adolescents' sexual attitudes and expectations: The role of viewing amount versus viewer involvement. *Journal of Sex Research, 36*(3), 237–249.

Weaver, J. B. (1991). Are "slasher" horror films sexually violent? A content analysis. *Journal of Broadcasting and Electronic Media, 35,* 385–392.

Wilke, M. (1998, June 22). *Ellen* legacy: Gay TV roles are more acceptable, but number drops for fall season. *Advertising Age, 69,* 25, 31.

Williams, D., Martins, N., Consalvo, M., & Ivory, J. (2009). The virtual census: Representations of gender, race and age in video games. *New Media & Society, 11*(5), 815–834.

Williams, J. P. (1996). Biology and destiny: The dynamics of gender crossing in *Quantum Leap. Women's Studies in Communication, 19,* 273–290.

Williams, R. (1976). *Keywords: A vocabulary of culture and society.* New York: Oxford University Press.

Yee, N. (2005). WoW gender-bending. *The Daedalus project: The psychology of MMORPGs.* Retrieved May 10, 2010, from http://www.nickyee.com/daedalus/archives/001369.php.

CHAPTER 16

Television's Gender-Role Images and Contribution to Stereotyping

Past, Present, Future

NANCY SIGNORIELLI
University of Delaware

Gender-role socialization has been a critical element in the study of mass communication since the late 1960s. Most of the research and attention on the socialization of gender roles have focused on television and how its images have become one of the most important agents of socialization in today's society.

As we progress in the 21st century, the screen we watch the most is television (Blair, 2009). The way we watch, however, has changed substantially from decades of watching ABC, CBS, NBC (the "big 3"), and maybe PBS. Today, television programming has become an on-demand medium and we are no longer tied to the time-bound schedules of broadcast television or cable channels. Nielsen (2009) reports that viewing statistics are stable and have been rising. At the end of 2009, the average person watched TV at home for about 35 hours a week. Children's media use and television viewing are also extremely high. The Kaiser Family Foundation's recent survey of 2,000 youngsters between 8 and 18 found that media use averaged more than 7.5 hours a day that expanded to almost 11 hours a day when multitasking was taken into account (Rideout, Foehr, & Roberts, 2010).

Given the continued high levels of viewing, television's role as the central and most pervasive mass medium in American culture has not changed. Television still plays a distinctive and historically unprecedented role as our nation's most common, constant, and vivid learning environment. Television, whether we watch on a traditional set, on our mobile phone, or on the Internet, is still our primary storyteller, telling most of the stories to most of the people most of the time. These stories, however, are the product of a few multinational and centralized commercial institutions. Television's stories show and tell us about life—its people, places, power, and fate as well as how things work and how to solve problems. Characterizations represent the good and bad, the happy and sad, successes and failures, and show who's on the top and who's on the bottom of the economic and social ladder and/or pecking order.

Understanding and examining the images and stereotypes that pervade characterizations has been the goal of numerous research studies since the 1950s. This line of research has proliferated during the past 60 years, and it is important now to step back and take stock of what we have done and what we have found and to think about where we should go in the future.

The Research Question in Retrospect

The study of the mass media can be viewed as a three-step process: (1) examining the images in the media, (2) ascertaining what impact or effects these images may have, and (3) understanding the institutional processes that create these images and ensure their success and/or failure. All three steps are interconnected; without understanding the nature of the images, we cannot understand the nature of their effects or the institutional forces involved in their success. Consequently, a major research question asks how different kinds of people are portrayed in the media.

Research on this topic began in the mid-1950s (Head, 1954; Smythe, 1954). Interest was particularly stimulated by the forces that impacted the country during the late 1960s, notably national turmoil, civil rights, and the women's movement. Two national commissions were appointed to uncover the dynamics of these forces on society, and the agendas of these commissions set the stage for research on media images.

The national turmoil that rocked the country after the assassinations of Martin Luther King and Bobby Kennedy increased concern about violence in society and in the media. In 1968, the National Commission on the Causes and Prevention of Violence was appointed to examine violence in society, including violence on television (see Baker & Ball, 1969). Then, in 1969, before the report of the National Commission on the Causes and Preventions of Violence was released, Congress appropriated $1 million and set up the Surgeon General's Scientific Advisory Committee on Television and Social Behavior (1972). Although interest in television violence faded somewhat during the 1980s, congressional concern about media violence again increased during the 1990s, culminating in the development of ratings for television programs and the inclusion of V-chip technology in television sets.

Concern with civil rights during the late 1960s and early 1970s contributed to the proliferation of studies on minority images. The Kerner Commission, appointed by President Johnson to investigate racial disturbances in many of our cities, charged that these disturbances could be traced to the U.S. mass media industry's failure to serve and adequately represent minority interests (Kerner Commission, 1968).

Finally, the events and increased consciousness that marked the late 1960s also led to a "new beginning" for the women's movement and concern for how women were presented in the media. Scores of studies documenting the underrepresentation and negative images of women on television and in advertising were undertaken despite the lack of a national commission to provide funding for research. This body of research has continued, with concern about the media's, particularly television's, influence on gender-role stereotypes as high on the research agenda today as it was during the early 1970s. Today, this research continues as part of the ongoing research programs of scholars in communication with funding sometimes provided from foundations such as the Geena Davis Institute on Gender in Media (see www.thegeenadavisinstitute.org).

Most of the early studies were concerned with determining baseline measures (how much violence, how many minorities, how many women), particularly in prime-time network dramatic programming. Later research examined the representation of women in relation to topics, such as age, marital status, and occupations, as well as differences across program genres and delivery systems. This chapter will discuss the theoretical orientations of research on gender stereotypes and summarize the findings of this research, with emphasis on the studies conducted during the first decade of the 21st century, looking in particular at the author's ongoing study of fall prime-time programming broadcast between 2000 and 2009.[1]

Theoretical Orientations

Socialization is the way people learn about their culture and acquire its values, beliefs, perspectives, and social norms. It is an ongoing process; we are socialized and resocialized throughout the life cycle. Traditionally, parents, peers, teachers, and the clergy have had the major responsibility for socialization. Numerous studies have found, however, that the mass media are important in the socialization process (Berry & Mitchell-Kerman, 1982; Roberts & Bachen, 1981; Roberts & Maccoby, 1985). Stereotypes, in particular, play an important part in television's role as an agent of socialization. Stereotypes are conventional or standardized images or conceptions; they are generalizations or assumptions that are often based on misconceptions. Stereotypes typically lack originality. They fall back upon commonly known and often one-dimensional elements of portrayal. They appeal to people's emotions rather than to their intellects. Television programs with limited time to devote to character development often resort to stereotypes. The concern is that viewers, especially children, continually exposed to television's stereotyped roles may develop conceptions and perceptions about people that reflect the stereotypical images they see in the media.

The actual processes of media socialization are different from those used by more traditional agents of socialization. Media socialization does not permit face-to-face social interaction and may lack some of the seductive or coercive powers of traditional agents who have the tools of interpersonal communication at their disposal (Wright, 1986). Nevertheless, the media have their own brand of seductiveness, and much of the socialization through the media may involve observational and/or social learning.

Social or observational learning theory (Bandura & Walters, 1963) examines the role of modeling in a child's social development. It posits that viewers, especially children, imitate the behavior of television characters in much the same way they learn social and cognitive skills by imitating their parents, siblings, and peers (Lefkowitz & Huesmann, 1980). Bandura's (1986, 2009) extension of cognitive processing to social learning theory (social cognitive theory) adds rules and strategies to the traditional why, what, and when of behavior change. Television provides not only specific responses but also the strategies and rules viewers may use to copy what they observe (Comstock, 1989). Television's stereotypes are particularly suited to the processes of social learning/cognitive theory because they provide simplistic, often one-dimensional models of behaviors, strategies, and rules that appear regularly in many different genres of programs.

A second theoretical orientation relevant to the media's role as an agent of socialization is cultivation theory (Morgan, Shanahan, & Signorielli, 2009). This theory explores the general hypothesis that the more time viewers spend with television, the more likely their conceptions about the world and its people will reflect what they see on television. Thus, in order to understand the effects of television on attitudes, beliefs, and behavior, television must be studied as a collective symbolic environment of messages with an underlying pattern or formulaic structure. Due to commercial constraints, television presents a common worldview and common stereotypes through a relatively restrictive set of images and messages that cut across all programs in all delivery systems.

Images on Television

The world of television drama with its ongoing schedule changes gives the illusion of constant change. Yet the hundreds of content

---

[1]Data were collected in each fall between 2000 and 2009 except for the fall of 2007, when the author was on sabbatical. The methods used in these analyses are the same as those used in Signorielli and Bacue, 1999, and Signorielli and Kahlenberg, 2003.

analyses examining media images present a very different picture. In short, the world of television, its themes, characterizations, and stereotypes exhibits considerable and remarkable stability.

Certain key aspects of television's portrayals have undergone little overall change in the past 60 years. The underrepresentation of women is one of these elements. In study after study, men have outnumbered women in prime-time dramatic programming (Greenberg & Worrell, 2007; Signorielli, 1985; Signorielli & Bacue, 1999). The earliest studies of network television broadcast during the early 1950s (e.g. Head, 1954; Smythe, 1954) found three male characters for every female. Most of the studies conducted during the 1970s and early 1980s found a high degree of consistency in the television world's demography, with men typically outnumbering women by 3 to 1 (see Signorielli, 1985). Change in representation began in the mid-1980s, and by the end of that decade, the proportion of females in samples of prime-time broadcast programs increased to about one-third of the major characters. Since the mid-1990s, the percentage of females has remained steady at 40% of the major characters (Signorielli & Bacue, 1999). Greenberg and Worrell (2007), examining the demography in new network prime-time programs using *TV Guide's* fall preview issues published between 1993 and 2004, found that women made up 39% of the new characters each season and that there was never a season in which the characters were equally distributed between the men and women. The author's ongoing research shows that between 1967 and 2009, there has been a statistically significant linear trend ($F = 132.6$, $df = 1,40$, $p = .000$) in the numbers of female characters. The proportion of women increased significantly and steadily between 1967 and 2009, moving from 24% of the characters in 1967 to 41% in the fall of 2009. Nevertheless, the distribution of men and women in prime-time network programs still does not come close to parity with the U.S. population (51% female and 49% male).

Past research has also shown that program genre often determines the male–female distribution. Action-adventure programs broadcast from the late 1960s until the end of the 20th century had the fewest female characters, while situation comedies have the most egalitarian distribution of men and women. Dramas overrepresented male characters until the 1990s, when the distribution became 54% male and 46% female (Signorielli & Bacue, 1999). Similarly, Lauzen and Dozier (1999) found that women were underrepresented in all genres of programs, with the least underrepresentation in situation comedies and the most in action-adventure programs.

These patterns have continued during the first decade of the 21st century. The author's ongoing analysis finds representation still dependent upon program genre, but given the recent constraints on the economics of broadcasting, the distribution of programs by genre has changed. Today, there are fewer situation comedies, while there are more action programs and low-cost reality programs. The most recent gender distributions show that, by genre, situation comedies are 56% male and 44% female and action programs are 67% male and 33% female, while dramas are 55% male and 45% female. Reality programs, however, overrepresent males and have a 60% to 40% male–female distribution.

Similar patterns are found in cable programming even though cable, because of its numerous channels, has been heralded for its likelihood to provide greater diversity in programming. Gerbner (1993), comparing the demography of network and cable programming, found that the patterns of underrepresentation in broadcast programming were also prevalent in samples of cable TV. Kubey, Shifflet, Weerakkody, and Ukeiley's (1995) analysis of programming on 32 cable channels throughout the day found that males outnumber females by about 2.5 to 1 across all channels, with more underrepresentation on nonbroadcast channels.

Portrayals and Behind-the-Scenes Personnel

The male–female distribution is also related to the gender makeup of writers, directors, producers, and other behind-the-scenes personnel. Glascock (2001) found a positive relationship between the number of female major characters and the number of female producers and/or writers. First, during the 1996 to 1997 network prime-time season, males who created, produced, and directed television shows outnumbered females in similar roles by 3.6 to 1. Second, among the characters, males outnumbered females by almost 2 to 1. Similarly, in 1996, Lauzen and Dozier (1999) found that male characters outnumbered female characters and that men were three-quarters and women one-quarter of the behind-the-scenes personnel. The women behind the scenes also did not have prestigious positions; they were the assistant directors or associate producers compared to the men, who were producers or directors. Interestingly, there were more female characters when women were in more powerful behind-the-scenes positions (executive producers and producers).

The sex distribution of behind-the-scenes personnel is related to other aspects of male–female portrayals in prime-time programs. Female characters in programs with women executive producers were more verbal (spoke, interrupted, used more powerful language, and had the last word in a discussion or argument) than female characters in programs with male executive producers (Lauzen & Dozier, 1999; Lauzen, Dozier, & Hicks, 2001). Interestingly, when women were the writers or creators, both male and female characters appeared in interpersonal (home, family, romance) roles. When men were the writers and creators, both male and female characters were often seen in work-related roles (Lauzen, Dozier, & Horan, 2008).

Age, Body Type, and Occupations

The world of television has consistently presented stereotyped images of both men and women. A meta-analysis of eight content analyses (Herrett-Skjellum & Allen, 1996) found strong evidence of gender-typed stereotypes on television. In particular, studies have consistently found that women in prime time are likely to be younger than men (Signorielli, 2004; Vernon, Williams, Phillips, & Wilson, 1990); are cast in traditional and stereotypical roles (Signorielli, 1989); and are more likely to have blond or red/auburn than black or brown hair (Davis, 1990). This is not to say that

change has not occurred or that nontraditional women do not appear on television; it is just that these images are not found consistently. Most of us can easily cite many examples of women who are not stereotyped, and much of the research examining nonstereotyped roles has focused upon small and select groups/samples of programs (see, for example, Atkin, 1991; Reep & Dambrot, 1987). Moreover, in programs such as *Providence, Law & Order,* and the *CSI* series many of the female characters who break with the stereotypes on one dimension of their portrayal (for example, their occupation) fall back upon traditional stereotypes when involved in or dealing with a romantic relationship (Signorielli & Kahlenberg, 2001).

Television places great value on youthfulness. Women typically are cast as younger than men (Lauzen & Dozier, 1999; Signorielli & Bacue, 1999). Study after study shows that the world of prime-time network broadcast television overrepresents young adult and middle-aged characters while underrepresenting children, adolescents, and the elderly. At the end of the first decade of the 21st century, the message is still that a woman's value is in her youthfulness. Signorielli (2004), in an analysis of samples of prime-time programs broadcast between 1993 and 2002, found more females than males were classified as young adults, while more males than females were portrayed as middle aged. At the same time, the proportion of older characters on television remained very small, and women age faster than men. Men between 50 and 64 were often seen as vibrant and categorized as middle aged, and 8 out of 10 were still seen in the work environment. Women of this age, however, were more likely to be categorized as elderly, and only half had jobs outside the home. Consequently, at the end of the first decade of the 21st century, television programs are still populated by those age groups advertisers most want to reach: young adults and the middle-aged.

Along with images of youthfulness, the media, particularly television, present very stereotyped images of women's and men's bodies that do not reflect general population statistics. Women on television typically have thin and almost perfect bodies; their weight is judged as average or below average, and very few (less than 1 in 10) are even somewhat overweight (Fouts & Burggraf, 1999). Characters, particularly those who are quite thin, often hear positive comments about their bodies and how they look, while overweight women on television are often insulted (Fouts & Burggraf, 2000). Similarly, Greenberg, Eastin, Hofschire, Lachlan, and Brownell (2003) found, in the 1999 to 2000 season, that 30% of the women and 12% of the men were very thin and that only 13% of the women and 24% of the men were overweight. Once again, heavier female characters were portrayed less positive; they were not likely to be involved romantically and had fewer positive social interactions. Finally, the author's ongoing analysis of programs broadcast between the fall of 2000 and the fall of 2009 found close to 1 in 4 women are thin and fewer than 1 in 10 is overweight, while only 1 in 10 men is thin and 15% are overweight (Signorielli, ongoing).

Another set of stereotypes is found in occupational portrayals. On television, occupations, while varied, are stereotyped and often gender typed. In fact, Herrett-Skjellum and Allen's (1996) meta-analysis found the most evidence for stereotypes in occupational portrayals. The early studies of prime-time programming found that women's employment possibilities were limited, with clerical work the most common job (Signorielli, 1984, 1993; Vande-Berg & Streckfuss, 1992). Today, more women on television are presented as employed outside the home, and their jobs are a little more prestigious than 30 years ago (Signorielli & Bacue, 1999). For example, the percentage of women cast in the professions increased from the 1970s to the 1990s. Whereas in the 1970s women were often depicted in traditional female occupations such as teachers, nurses, secretaries, and clerks, during the 1980s and 1990s, fewer women were cast in these jobs while more women appeared in traditional male or gender-neutral jobs. Men, on the other hand, appear most frequently in traditional male occupations, and very few are found in traditional female jobs.

Signorielli and Kahlenberg (2001) found that the world of work on television is determined by dramatic rather than educational considerations. Television programs revolve around those jobs that help tell a good story. The work of doctors, lawyers, police, and forensic specialists is more interesting and exciting than the everyday work of laborers and bus or truck drivers. Overall, fewer women than men were categorized as having an occupation: only 6 out of 10 females compared to three-quarters of the male characters. But women were not always cast in traditional female jobs. By the end of the 20th century, women were just as likely as men to be cast as professionals (doctors, lawyers, teachers, etc.) and in white-collar (managers, clerical) jobs.

Since the turn of the century, the author's ongoing analysis shows that fewer women than men are still seen as having a specific job: Three-quarters of the men but only 6 out of 10 women are portrayed in an occupation (Signorielli, ongoing). At the same time, only 1 in 5 women is cast in a traditionally female job, while about one-third have traditional male jobs and another third have gender-neutral jobs. Half of the males, on the other hand, have traditional male jobs, 1 in 3 has a gender-neutral job, and less than 5% have traditionally female jobs. Women were as likely as men to be cast as professionals, but while 1 in 5 men was cast in law enforcement, only 1 in 10 of the women was so employed.

Television, thus, continues to overrepresent glamorous and more exciting jobs (doctors, lawyers, police, crime scene investigators), but work typically appears to be easy and exciting, and characters are almost always successful. The more mundane jobs, in which most people spend their work lives, are rarely found. Moreover, the world of work on television does not present work or occupations very realistically because we rarely see characters actually working. For example, recent and very popular crime-scene programs (*CSI, Law & Order*) present these jobs as more glamorous and exciting than they actually are; the mundane day-to-day but important tasks are often overlooked (Houck, 2006).

Finally, the world of work on television is tied to race and marital status. Signorielli and Kahlenberg (2001) found that, compared to men, women's marital status was often identified. Married women on television were less likely than single or formerly married women to be shown working outside the home. But there were differences by race. Proportionally more married women of color, compared to married White women, were cast in a specific occupation. On the other hand, more White than women of color portrayed as single or formerly married were seen in specific occupations. Overall, married women, particularly White married women, were presented as having reduced options because they were not cast as both married and employed; employment outside the home was more often delegated to single women or those no longer married. Similarly, Glascock's (2003) analysis of network programs broadcast in the fall of 2001 found that while the proportions of Blacks and Whites portrayed as working were similar, Blacks were seen in a greater variety of jobs. Likewise, Hunt's (2005) analysis of a sample of programs broadcast in 2002 found Black and White characters in high-status jobs while Latino characters had low-status occupations.

Children's Programming, Movies, and Commercials

Women are especially shortchanged and underrepresented on children's programs. In cartoons, studies consistently find that men outnumber women by 4 or 5 to 1 (Signorielli, 1985, 2008). Thompson and Zerbinos (1995) found that female cartoon characters of the 1990s were more assertive, intelligent, independent, and likely to show leadership qualities than the characters of the 1970s and 1980s. Nevertheless, female characters were also more likely than male characters to be portrayed in traditional stereotypes (emotional, romantic, affectionate, and domestic). Male cartoon characters of the 1990s were presented as more intelligent, more technical, more aggressive, and they asked and answered more questions. Finally, in the cartoons of the 1990s, male characters typically had recognizable jobs while the females were often cast as caregivers. There were also differences by cartoon type. The fewest female lead characters were

found in chase and pratfall cartoons (*Tom and Jerry*), followed by continuing adventure cartoons (*Teenage Mutant Ninja Turtles*) and teachy-preachy cartoons (*Smurfs*).

Cartoons broadcast at the start of the 21st century continued to be stereotyped. Leaper, Breed, Hoffman, and Perlman (2002) found that male characters outnumbered female characters by 4 to 1 in traditional adventure cartoons (*Spiderman*), 2 to 1 in comedy cartoons (*Animanics*), and 1.5 to 1 in educational/family cartoons (*Carmen Sandiego, The Magic School Bus*). There was, however, an almost equal representation of males and females in nontraditional adventure cartoons (*Sailor Moon, Gargoyles*). At the same time, males were more physically aggressive, particularly in the traditional adventure cartoons, than the females. Overall, females were more fearful, more supportive, more polite, and more interested in romance. Similarly, an analysis of children's programs on network, public stations, and cable outlets seen in 2005 (Smith & Cook, 2008) found that male characters appeared more often than female characters, particularly in programs rated TVY or TVY7 (see Chapter 30 in this volume for definitions of ratings). Finally, males outnumbered females in all types of children's programs cartoons, particularly adventure cartoons (*Teenage Mutant Ninja Turtles*), seen on Saturday mornings during February 2007 except those geared toward teens (*Hannah Montana, That's So Raven*; Signorielli, 2008).

Superheroes are particularly stereotyped. K. Baker and Raney (2007) found that two-thirds of the superheroes were very muscular males, and one-third were average-sized females. Female superheroes were more emotional, attractive, concerned about their personal appearance, and asked questions, while the male superheroes were more likely to exhibit angry behavior. Although all of the superheroes were physically aggressive and powerful, female superheroes were more stereotyped because they often worked under a mentor, while the male superheroes had positions of leadership and operated independently.

Gender stereotypes are also found in educational and informational (E/I) programming. Barner's (1999) analysis of social/emotional

E/I programs (e.g., *Sweet Valley High, Bobby's World, Ghostwriter*) aired in the summer of 1997 found that a majority of the programs had males as central characters and included a boy's name in the title. On the other hand, no programs had a female in the central role or a girl's name in the program's title. Males outnumbered females 58% to 42% among major characters. Males exhibited 2.1 behaviors per scene compared to 1.5 behaviors per scene for females. These behaviors, moreover, were often gender stereotyped. Males made and carried out plans, sought attention and were more aggressive, dominant, and active—behaviors that elicited consequences. Female behaviors, on the other hand, were deferential, nurturing, and dependent—behaviors that typically did not result in consequences for the character.

Movies have consistently underrepresented female characters and perpetuate gender stereotypes. Lauzen and Dozier's (2005) analysis of the top films of 2002 found a male–female distribution of three-quarters male to one-quarter female with men cast as older (in their 30s and 40s) than the women (usually in their 20s and 30s). Males, particularly those older than 40, were often seen in powerful and leadership roles, while older women were largely invisible, very negatively stereotyped, and perceived as less attractive, less friendly, and less intelligent (Bazzini, McIntosh, Smith, Cook, & Harris, 1997).

In comparison, the top teen movies distributed between 1995 and 2005 (e.g., *Clueless, Mean Girls, She's All That*) had more female than male characters—55% female to 45% male. But there were few, if any, adult characters; 99% of the characters were high school or college students (Behm-Morawitz & Mastro, 2008). Although socially cooperative behaviors appeared more often than socially aggressive behaviors and were not gender related, female characters were significantly more likely than male characters to engage in socially aggressive behaviors. The socially aggressive behaviors (e.g., illustrating the mean girl), however, were typically not punished and were often rewarded.

Smith and Cook's (2008) analyses of films released between 1990 and 2006 found in the 100 top-grossing G-rated movies that only 28% of the speaking characters were women and that more than 8 in 10 narrators were males. Similarly, the analysis of 400 G-, PG-, PG-13-, and R-rated films found that only one-quarter of the characters were women, with no change in male–female distributions during this 16-year time span. Finally, females were portrayed either traditionally (parents, nurturing, etc.) or as hypersexualized (very attractive, thin, alluring attire, etc.).

Disney movies, a staple of children's viewing repertoire, are very gender stereotyped. Dundes (2001) notes that one modern Disney heroine, *Pocahontas*, is defined both by her romantic relationship and her nurturing role. Similarly, Ariel in *The Little Mermaid* shows both her romanticism and her willingness to embrace life as a human in order to marry the prince. Finally, Tanner, Haddock, Zimmerman, and Lund (2003) note that Disney films typically stereotype male–female relationships by presenting couples (mothers and fathers, for example) in traditional gender stereotypes.

Commercials are also sex typed and stereotyped on numerous dimensions (Courtney & Whipple, 1983). Strong links typically are made between attractiveness and the presentation of women (Downs & Harrison, 1985; Lin, 1997) as well as placing women in domestic settings advertising products for the home (Bretl & Cantor, 1988; Craig, 1992a). Males outnumber females in all but commercials for beauty or health/household domestic products (Bartsch, Burnett, Diller, & Rankin-Williams, 2000; Ganahl, Prinsen, & Netzley, 2003). In particular, women are much more likely than men to be found in commercials for over-the-counter medications and typically presented as the experts in home health care (Craig, 1992b). Research consistently shows that a woman's voice is rarely used as a voice-over and that men are presented as authoritative, even for products used primarily by women (Allan & Coltrane, 1996; Bretl & Cantor, 1988; Lovdal, 1989).

A study of national commercials portraying domestic chores in prime-time network broadcast programming found that almost two-thirds of those seen doing domestic chores were women, typically mothers, who performed child-care-related activities, cooked, or cleaned (Scharrer, Kim, Lin, & Liu, 2006). Men's performance of domestic chores was often presented humorously, sending the message that men are not capable of really helping around the house. Overall, most of the chores were stereotyped in terms of who did them. In addition, Stern and Mastro (2004) found that in commercials, females were most underrepresented as children and in middle age and least underrepresented as teenagers.

Commercials in children's cartoons are also gender stereotyped (Browne, 1998). Boys were more likely to illustrate how to use the product, even when the products were gender neutral. Adult women and men were seen in very gender-typed roles with the women as homemakers and the men working outside the home. Interestingly, a study of images on cereal boxes (Black, Marola, Littman, Chrisler, & Neace, 2009) found evidence of considerable gender-role typing. Males outnumbered females by 2 to 1 and were more often portrayed as animals (e.g., Tony the Tiger) or adults, while females were children or adolescents.

Overview

There has been some but not much improvement in the presentation of women on television during the past 50 years. First, the proportion of women on prime time has gone from 25% to 40% of all characters—a statistically significant if small increase. Nevertheless, the number of female characters depends upon program genre. Women make up half of the characters in situation comedies but only a quarter of characters in action-adventure programs. Second, women are still cast as younger than men and are often seen in interpersonal roles (home, family, romance). Finally, women's work roles have improved, with more women presented in "typically male" or gender-neutral occupations. We thus find that at the end of the first decade of the 21st century that media, particularly television images, have not undergone many changes in terms of gender-role stereotypes.

Impact of Stereotyping on Viewers

The description of television images is an important and necessary first step in understanding the role of television in society.

Clearly, one cannot assess effects without knowing what people see. Consequently, as awareness of the images of men and women on television and in other media became widespread, research turned to examining the impact of these images. Interestingly, except for research on body image and sexuality, in recent years, less attention has been paid to the overall effects of gender-stereotyped content than to the nature of the content itself.

Viewers, particularly children, are aware of and expect to find stereotyped images on television (Reeves & Greenberg, 1977). Thompson and Zerbinos (1997), for example, found that children perceived stereotyped cartoon characters—boys were active and violent while girls were concerned with appearances and seen more often in domestic settings. Similarly, Wroblewski and Huston (1987) found that children were aware of television's stereotyped occupational images. Moreover, children as young as kindergarten age are aware of television's gender stereotypes and are able to predict whether men or women, boys or girls, would be found in these activities on television (Durkin & Nugent, 1998). More recently, however, Ogletree, Mason, Grahmann, and Raffeld (2001), looking at two cartoons produced during the late 1990s, found that elementary school children perceived the cartoon *Powerpuff Girls* as more aggressive than *Johnny Bravo*. At the same time, even though the *Powerpuff Girls* were seen as more androgynous, the girls giggled often, and the children noticed that they sometimes resorted to typically stereotypical female behaviors (e.g., kisses) to achieve their goals. Although viewers, particularly children, perceive the existence of gender stereotypes on television, the more important question is how these stereotypes influence attitudes and behaviors, looking specifically at identification with television characters and the cultivation of gender-role attitudes.

Identification

Identification with characters in the media is influenced by gender-role stereotypes (see Chapter 15 in this volume for more information about identification). Children continue to identify with television characters. As was true in the 1960s and 1970s (e.g., Reeves &

Greenberg, 1977), boys are still more likely to name only a male as their favorite character, while girls are equally likely to name both males and females as favorite characters. Hoffner (1996) extended this effect to what she calls wishful identification—wanting to be like characters, particularly those characters perceived as successful or attractive. This line of research finds that girls select female characters when they are physically attractive and select male characters who are intelligent and/or exhibit typical masculine traits such as physical strength. Hoffner's interviews with 7- to 12-year-old children show that wishful identification is more pronounced with same-sex characters and more pronounced for boys than girls. Interestingly, girls who choose males as favorite characters see them as "pseudofriends" rather than role models and perceive them as intelligent. At the same time, the girls show more parasocial interaction with same-sex favorite characters, usually selected because they are attractive.

Aubrey and Harrison's (2004) study of first- and second-grade children found that the boys who preferred stereotyped content and male cartoon characters said they valued the traits of humor and hard work. Girls who indicated they preferred male characters (in both stereotyped or counterstereotyped roles) did not identify with or were not attracted to female characters. On the other hand, those girls who said they preferred female characters cast in gender-neutral roles were attracted to and identified with female characters.

Identification continues into young adulthood. Undergraduates who watched more teen movies (e.g., *Mean Girls*, *10 Things I Hate About You*) expressed greater identification with the characters in these movies (Behm-Morawitz & Mastro, 2008). Moreover, college women who said they identified with female action heroes (e.g., Buffy the Vampire Slayer) believed that they had traits such as confidence and assertiveness in common with these female action heroes. These women also perceived that female action heroes were smart, confident, powerful, and attractive (Greenwood, 2007). In addition, Hoffner, Levine, and Toohey (2008) found that while male college freshmen's favorite characters were males, only half of the freshmen women

chose a female television character as their favorite. These students said that they liked characters portrayed with good-paying and higher-status jobs and did not particularly identify with characters whose jobs required a higher level of intelligence or skill.

Cultivation of Gender-Role Images

The influence of the mass media, especially television, upon conceptions relating to gender roles is an important area of investigation. This research differs from research relating to perceptions of gender roles (stereotyping) in programming or identification with (wanting to be like) specific characters because it examines how the media may be shaping people's and especially children's views of what it means to be a man or a woman. This, in turn, may aid or abet those goals (occupational, educational, personal) a person may set out to achieve. Clearly the evidence points to the fact that society's notions of appropriate roles for men and women have changed (Signorielli, 1989). We still must determine whether the media, notably television, have helped or hindered this process.

Studies of television's impact or effects are generally hampered because it is almost impossible to find control groups who are not exposed to television. Moreover, those who do not watch television tend to be a small but quite eclectic group (Jackson-Beeck, 1977). Finally, nontraditional or nonsexist portrayals of male and female roles have only recently appeared with some regularity. Consequently, the overall effects of many of these studies are small because even light viewers watch several hours of television a day and experience many of the same things as those who watch more television (Morgan et al., 2009).

The research generally points to the existence of a relationship between television viewing and having more stereotypic conceptions about gender roles. Meta-analyses have found support for this relationship. Herrett-Skjellum and Allen (1996) examined 19 nonexperimental and 11 experimental studies dealing with television and gender-role stereotypes and found an average effects size of .101. They found all positive relationships and no age-related patterns, concluding that these studies, particularly those using nonexperimental designs, seem to indicate that television viewing is particularly related to conceptions about occupations. Similarly, Morgan and Shanahan's (1997) meta-analysis of all published studies relating to cultivation theory found an average effects size of .102 in the analysis of 14 cultivation studies relating to gender roles. Hearold's (1986) meta-analysis of 230 studies found that television viewing had a strong effect on role stereotyping. Finally, Oppliger (2007) examined 31 primarily nonexperimental studies, finding a positive and statistically significant relationship ($r = .117$) between exposure to gender-role stereotypes and gender-typed behaviors and/or attitudes between both adults and children. Moreover, the correlations were similar for both males and females and were somewhat stronger for measures of behavior than attitudes. Overall, then, meta-analyses have shown considerable support for the idea that media images influence people's, particularly children's, conceptions about gender roles.

Nonexperimental Studies

Beuf (1974), in a study of 3- to 6-year-old children, found that those children who watched more television were more likely to stereotype occupational roles. This research also found that preschool-aged boys were unable to say "what they would be when they grew up" if they were a girl, while the girls always had a response to this question. Gross and Jeffries-Fox (1978), in a panel study of 250 8th-, 9th-, and 10th-grade children, found that television viewing was related to giving sexist responses to questions about the nature of men and women and how they are treated by society. Rothschild (1984) reported that third- and fifth-grade children who watch more television were more likely to exhibit traditional sex-role stereotypes for gender-related qualities (independence, warmth) and gender-related activities (playing sports or cooking). Finally, Katz and Coulter (1986) found more gender stereotyping among children who watched a lot of television compared to children who spent a lot of time reading.

Additional support for the notion that television viewing contributes to children's perceptions about appropriate male and female behaviors is found in two studies. Frueh and McGhee (1975), in a study of children in kindergarten through sixth grade, found that those who spent more time watching television exhibited greater sex typing than those who spent less time watching television. McGhee and Frueh (1980), similarly, found that heavy viewers had more stereotyped perceptions of gender roles than light viewers. For male stereotypes, there was an interaction effect indicating that among light viewers, the perception of male stereotypes declined with age, while among heavy viewers, male stereotypes remained with increasing age. An interaction was not found for the perception of female stereotypes. Studies by Morgan (1982, 1987) and Morgan and Rothschild (1983) also indicate that television cultivates gender-role attitudes among adolescents, while Morgan and Harr-Mazar (1980) found that television seems to cultivate attitudes about when to form a family and how many children to have. Morgan and Rothschild (1983) also found that children who watch more television were more likely to endorse traditional divisions of labor between the sexes.

Morgan (1982), in a 3-year panel study of sixth- through eighth-grade children, found that levels of sexism were higher among all boys and lower-class girls and that television cultivates notions such as "women are happiest at home raising children" and "men are born with more ambition than women." Among girls, the amount of television viewing was significantly associated with scores on an index of gender-role stereotypes 1 year later, over and above the influence of demographics and earlier scores on this same index; there was no evidence that gender-role stereotyping leads to more television viewing. For boys, the patterns were reversed: There was no relationship between viewing and gender-role attitudes, but greater sexism was related to more viewing 1 year later. Overall, this study reveals that television viewing is most likely to make a difference among those who are otherwise least likely to hold traditional views of gender roles, a concept cultivation theory refers to as "mainstreaming."

In a second study of 287 adolescents using measures taken at two points in time, Morgan (1987) found that television viewing made an independent contribution to adolescents' gender-role attitudes over time, but television viewing was not related to some of their specific behaviors in relation to seven specific chores. Signorielli and Lears (1992), in a cross-sectional replication of this analysis with a sample of children in the fourth and fifth grades, also found statistically significant relationships between viewing and having gender-typed attitudes toward chores but no relationship between viewing and actually doing gender-stereotyped chores. Moreover, attitudes toward gender-stereotyped chores and actually doing "girl" or "boy" chores were related but gender specific. Children, particularly those who said they watched more television, who had more stereotyped ideas about who should do which chores were more likely to do those chores traditionally associated with their gender.

In addition, Signorielli (1991) found that high school students' conceptions about marriage reflected the ambivalent presentation of marriage in prime-time network programming. Television viewing was positively related to high school students saying they probably would get married, have children, and stay married to the same person. At the same time, there was a positive relationship between viewing and expressing the opinion that one sees so few good or happy marriages that one could question marriage as a way of life.

Television cultivates more sexist attitudes in specific race/ethnically defined subgroups. Rivadeneyra and Ward (2005) examined the relationship between gender-role attitudes and television viewing among Latino high school students in the Los Angeles area. Using a checklist of English-language and Spanish-language prime-time programs, soap operas, and talk shows, students' average monthly viewing was determined. Two measures of viewer involvement, motivation for viewing, and identification with 16 specific television characters were also collected. Gender-role attitudes were measured by a three-item feminism scale that included items such as "the husband should make all

the important decisions in the marriage" and "a wife should do whatever her husband wants" (p. 462).

In general, Latino youth watch more television than European-American youngsters, and in this sample, the Latino girls watched more television than the boys. Those girls who watched more television, especially talk shows and situation comedies, were more likely to endorse more traditional gender-role stereotypes. In addition, watching more Spanish-language programs contributed to the expression of more traditional gender-role attitudes. Finally, perceived realism and viewer involvement were also related to expressing more gender-role stereotyped attitudes. The boys in the sample did not show the same degree of stereotyping, perhaps because they did not watch as much television as the girls, particularly those programs with more overall stereotyping. Moreover, the authors suggest that more stereotyped views for the boys were not found because the boys began with more traditional attitudes, and findings may not have emerged because of existing ceiling effects.

One area in which we continue to find relationships between viewing and conceptions about sex roles is in relation to occupations. While family and friends play a large role in children's socialization about work, television's images have consistently made important contributions because television characters are seen frequently and are attractive role models. As noted above, however, television presents a rather limited picture of occupations, particularly for women and minorities, that overrepresents exciting jobs and shows few characters actually working.

Wroblewski and Huston (1987) found that fifth- and sixth-grade children knew about jobs they typically encountered on television as well as experienced in real life. Occupations on television, however, were seen as more sex stereotyped than jobs in real life. The children had more negative attitudes about men holding television's typically feminine jobs than men having jobs that women typically hold in real life. The girls in this sample were particularly positive about television's typically masculine jobs.

Signorielli (1993) found that high school students' conceptions about work reflected two contradictory views about work that often appear on television. Television viewing was related to (1) adolescents' wanting to have high-status jobs that would also give them a chance to earn a lot of money and (2) wanting to have jobs that were relatively easy with long vacations and time to do other things in life. Hoffner and colleagues (2008), in a study of college freshmen, found that parents' views and the types of jobs their parents held as well as television contributed to these students' attitudes and aspirations about work. Those youngsters whose favorite characters had an "easy" job also said that they would like to have a job that was easy; in short, they wanted to be like characters who were rarely seen working.

Similarly, Levine and Hoffner (2006) found that high school students got information about working and job requirements from parents and having a part-time job. At the same time, they cited the mass media, although with some skepticism about the degree of accuracy, as providing information about work. The students said that dramas presented more negative views about work and gave the impression that work was difficult and stressful but that situation comedies provided positive information but mostly that work was easy and enjoyable.

Watching other media is also related to having more gender-role stereotyped views. Behm-Morawitz and Mastro's (2008) study of undergraduates found that those who watched and enjoyed teen movies (e.g., *Mean Girls*) saw female friendships in more stereotyped ways and did not have very favorable attitudes toward women. Moreover, watching and liking these movies led to the perception that being more socially aggressive may increase popularity with peers. Studies have also found relationships between watching music videos, especially rap videos, and conceptions about gender roles. Music videos tend to present very gender-stereotypical behaviors, with rap videos often presenting women as sex objects (Arnett, 2001). Bryant (2008) found that greater exposure to rap videos was related to Black adolescents' having more adversarial ideas about male–female relationships and agreeing with the negative images of men and women in these videos. Interestingly, those

youngsters who expressed higher levels of spirituality were less likely to accept the negative images of women, men, and male–female relationships portrayed in these videos. Studies have shown that while younger African Americans do not necessarily like the way women are presented in rap music videos, at the same time, they are not necessarily opposed to these portrayals (Kitwana, 2002).

Ward, Hansbrough, and Walker (2005) that found African American high school students who watched more music videos and more sports programming had more traditional gender-role stereotyped attitudes and said that attributes such as being cool, athletic, rich, and attractive were important. On the other hand, viewing prime-time situation comedies, dramas, and movies was not related to more gender-role stereotyped views.

There are only a few studies examining the relationship between conceptions about gender roles and television viewing among adults. Volgy and Schwartz (1980), in a study of registered voters in a southwestern city, found a positive relationship between viewing entertainment programs and the acceptance of traditional sex roles. Pingree, Starrett, and Hawkins (1979), using a small sample of women in Madison, Wisconsin, found a positive relationship between viewing daytime serial dramas and supporting traditional family values and family structures. Ross, Anderson, and Wisocki (1982), using a sample of 78 college students and a group of 19 older adults, found that the amount of sex-role stereotyping in self-descriptions was positively correlated with amount of viewing of stereotyped television programs.

Finally, Signorielli (1989), in an analysis of the NORC General Social Surveys (GSS) fielded between 1975 and 1986, found support for a general hypothesis that those who watch more television will have more sexist views and a mainstreaming hypothesis that certain groups of respondents who espouse very different views when they are light viewers will have more similar outlooks in regard to women's role in society as heavy viewers. This analysis found that even though there was a decrease in the number of respondents who agreed with sexist statements between the 1970s and 1980s, television viewing was related to the maintenance of notions of more limited roles for women in society, particularly in regard to politically oriented issues.

A recent reexamination of this hypothesis using data from the GSS fielded between 2000 and 2006 (Shanahan, Signorielli, & Morgan, 2008), however, found that this relationship had diminished. The authors suggest several reasons for this finding. First and maybe most important, the GSS questions used to create the dependent measure in the two analyses are different because the questions asked between 1975 and 1986 in the GSS were no longer part of the questionnaire fielded between 2000 and 2006. Hence, the second analysis used different questions relating to gender roles. Second, people's conceptions about gender roles may have reached the ceiling, because today most people are cognizant of real-life demographics that have pushed more women into jobs, choosing smaller families, lower marriage rates, and so on. While television is slowly catching up to social reality, it is not surprising that cultivation relationships have diminished or disappeared in all but a few groups. Moreover, there is also some evidence that television may cultivate acceptance of nontraditional families such as unmarried women having children (Morgan & Shanahan, 1997).

Experimental Studies

Further evidence comes from a number of experiments conducted both in the laboratory and in the field. Atkins and Miller (1975) found that children who viewed commercials in which females were cast in typically male occupations were more likely to say that this occupation was appropriate for women. Another laboratory experiment was designed to determine the effects of exposure to beauty commercials "on the perceived importance of beauty commercial themes in social relations on adolescent female viewers" (Tan, 1979, p. 284). The results revealed that high school girls exposed to beauty commercials rated beauty characteristics significantly more important for the role "to be popular with men" than girls who saw neutral commercials. Those girls exposed to beauty commercials also rated beauty as

personally more important than those who saw neutral commercials. In addition, Geis, Brown, Walstedt, and Porter (1984) indicated that women who viewed traditionally sex-typed commercials, compared to men and women who saw reversed role commercials, emphasized homemaking rather than achievement themes in an essay imagining what their lives would be like in 10 years. Ward and colleagues (2005) found African American high school students who saw clips of music videos with very stereotypical portrayals of both men and women expressed more stereotyped and traditional views about sexual relationships and gender.

Pike and Jennings (2005) found that gender-role stereotypes may be influenced by commercials. First- and second-grade students were placed in one of three conditions: (1) *traditional*, who saw toy commercials in which boys played with gender-neutral toys (e.g., Harry Potter Legos and Playmobile Airport Set), (2) *nontraditional,* who saw the same commercials with the boys' faces digitally replaced by very feminine girls' faces, and (3) a *control group,* who saw nontoy commercials (e.g., Chucky Cheese Restaurants and Lucky Charms). The results indicated that those children, particularly boys, in the nontraditional group were likely to say both boys and girls could play with gender-neutral toys while those in the traditional group said that only boys should play with these gender-neutral toys.

Finally, one of the very few studies having natural control groups of children who had very little, if any, exposure to television (Williams, 1986) revealed changes in conceptions about gender roles after television became available to the control groups. In this study girls, in NOTEL (town without television) and girls in UNITEL (town with very limited television) had weaker gender-typed views than girls in MULTITEL (town with greater television availability). Two years after the introduction of television into NOTEL and an increase of television's availability in UNITEL, the girls in NOTEL had become significantly more sex typed and the views of both these girls and the girls in UNITEL were similar to the views of the girls in MULTITEL. Similar results were found for boys in these towns except for anomalous high scores for the UNITEL boys in the first phase of the study (Kimball, 1986).

Conclusions

This review has explored gender-role socialization from a communication research perspective. Overall, research examining the presentation of gender roles on television reveals a stable image, especially in relation to physical appearance and marriage. While occupational portrayals have exhibited some change, those women most likely to work outside the home are single or formerly married. Thus, the consistent image is that the woman who is married cannot mix marriage, child rearing, and working outside the home. Moreover, women who do not fit stereotypical molds on one dimension of their characterization, such as their occupation, often revert to very traditional gender-role stereotypes in relation to their interpersonal relationships with men. These images serve to support the notion that women should not outshine men, particularly those to whom they are married and/or have an ongoing romantic relationship (IMHI, 1997).

Research on the impact of such images in regard to conceptions about sex roles points to the existence of a relationship between television viewing and having more stereotypic conceptions about gender roles. These relationships exist at all stages of the life cycle. There is evidence in samples of preschoolers, middle and high school students, and college students, as well as adults. Support has also been found in both experimental and nonexperimental settings. In essence, television may be contributing to the maintenance of notions of more limited roles for women in society because the images seen on television typically foster the maintenance of the status quo vis-á-vis male and female roles in society.

Continued research in this area is crucial. Future research, however, must be grounded in the content-effects-institutional analysis paradigm noted at the beginning of this chapter. We need up-to-date content studies to assess whether there is change in character portrayals

and the nature of that change. Then these findings can provide the background data needed to design studies of television effects. It is only when we have information about the images to which people are exposed that we can start to assess their impact. Finally, we need to conduct studies of the institutions that produce these messages to understand why women have not made greater inroads in joining the ranks of those involved in television and film production as writers, directors, and producers. Above all, it is critical to ascertain how to get better representation of women and people of color in the industry that makes pictures and tells the stories.

We know where the deficiencies lie and we have some idea of how to eliminate them. Continued research can only facilitate this process and prevent us from becoming complacent about what we see on TV. Finally, our research on effects is just beginning to make inroads in understanding the powerful impact of this medium on our lives. This research, however, must be driven by specific information on what people see when they watch television, not what we think they see. We have come a long way in the past 50 years. We cannot forget, nevertheless, that we still have a long way to go.

References

Allan, K., & Coltrane, S. (1996). Gender displaying television commercials: A comparative study of television commercials in the 1950s and 1980s. *Sex Roles, 35*(3/4), 185–203.

Arnett, J. J. (2001). *Adolescence and emerging adulthood: A cultural approach.* Upper Saddle River, NJ: Prentice Hall.

Atkin, D. (1991). The evolution of television series addressing single women, 1966–1990. *Journal of Broadcasting & Electronic Media, 35*(4), 517–523.

Atkins, C., & Miller, M. (1975). *The effects of television advertising in children: Experimental evidence.* Paper presented to the Mass Communication Division, International Communication Association, Chicago.

Aubrey, J. S., & Harrison, K. (2004). The gender-role content of children's favorite television programs and its links to their gender-related perceptions. *Media Psychology, 6*(2), 111–146.

Baker, K., & Raney, A. A. (2007). Equally super? Gender-role stereotyping of superheroes in children's animated programs. *Mass Communication & Society, 10*(1), 25–41.

Baker, R., & Ball, S. (Eds.). (1969). *Violence and the media.* Washington, DC: U.S. Government Printing Office.

Bandura, A. (1986). *Social foundations of thought and action: A social cognitive theory.* Englewood Cliffs, NJ: Prentice Hall.

Bandura, A. (2009). Social cognitive theory of mass communication. In J. Bryant & M. B. Oliver (Eds.), *Media effects: Advances in theory and research* (3rd ed., pp. 94–124). New York: Routledge.

Bandura, A., & Walters, R. H. (1963). *Social learning and personality development.* New York: Holt, Rinehart & Winston.

Barner, M. R. (1999). Sex-role stereotyping in FCC-mandated children's educational television. *Journal of Broadcasting & Electronic Media, 43*(4), 551–564.

Bartsch, R. A., Burnett, T., Dinner, T. R., & Rankin-Williams, E. (2000). Gender representation in television commercials: Updating an update. *Sex Roles, 43*(9/10), 735–743.

Bazzini, D. G., McIntosh, W. D., Smith, S. M., Cook, S., & Harris, C. (1997). The aging woman in popular film: Underrepresented, unattractive, unfriendly, and unintelligent. *Sex Roles, 36*(7/8), 531–543.

Behm-Morawitz, E., & Mastro, D. E., (2008). Mean girls? The influence of gender portrayals in teen movies on emerging adults' gender-based attitudes and beliefs. *Journalism & Mass Communication Quarterly, 85*(1), 131–146.

Berry, G., & Mitchell-Kerman, C. (Eds.). (1982). *Television and the socialization of the minority child.* New York: Academic Press.

Beuf, A. (1974). Doctor, lawyer, household drudge. *Journal of Communication, 24*(2), 142–154.

Black, K. A., Marola, J. A., Littman, A. I., Chrisler, J. C., & Neace, W. P. (2009). Gender and form of cereal box characters: Different medium, same disparity. *Sex Roles, 60*, 882–889.

Blair, E. (2009, Dec. 31). *In this decade, every room is a screening room.* NPR. http://www .npr.org/templates/story/story.php?storyId= 122068037.

Bretl, D. J., & Cantor, J. (1988). The portrayal of men and women in U.S. television commercials: A recent content analysis and trends over 15 years. *Sex-Roles, 18*(9–10), 595–609.

Browne, B. A. (1998). Gender stereotypes in advertising on children's television in the 1990s:

A cross-national analysis. *Journal of Advertising, 27*(1), 83–96.

Bryant, Y. (2008). Relationships between exposure to rap music videos and attitudes toward relationships among African American youth. *Journal of Black Psychology, 34*, 356–380.

Comstock, G. (1989). *The evolution of American television.* Newbury Park, CA: Sage.

Courtney, A. E., & Whipple, T. W. (1983). *Sex stereotyping in advertising.* Lexington, MA: Lexington Books.

Craig, R. S. (1992a). The effect of television day part on gender portrayals in television commercials: A content analysis. *Sex Roles, 26*(5–6), 197–211.

Craig, R. S. (1992b). Women as home caregivers: Gender portrayal in OTC drug commercials. *Journal of Drug Education, 22*(4), 303–312.

Davis, D. M. (1990). Portrayals of women in prime-time network television: Some demographic characteristics. *Sex Roles, 23*(5/6), 325–332.

Downs, A. C., & Harrison, S. K. (1985). Embarrassing age spots or just plain ugly? Physical attractiveness stereotyping as an instrument of sexism on American television commercials. *Sex Roles, 13*(½), 9–19.

Dundes, L. (2001). Disney's modern heroine Pocahontas: Revealing age-old gender stereotypes and role discontinuity under a facade of liberation. *Social Science Journal, 38,* 353–365.

Durkin, K., & Nugent, B. (1998). Kindergarten children's gender-role expectations for television actors. *Sex Roles, 38*(5/6), 387–402.

Fouts, G., & Burggraf, K. (1999). Television situation comedies: Female body images and verbal reinforcements. *Sex Roles, 40*(5/6), 473–481.

Fouts, G., & Burggraf, K. (2000). Television situation comedies: Female weight, male negative comments and audience reactions. *Sex Roles, 42*(9/10), 925–932.

Frueh, T., & McGhee, P. (1975). Traditional sex-role development and amount of time spent watching television. *Developmental Psychology, 11,* 109.

Ganahl, D. J., Prinsen, T. J., & Netzley, S. B. (2003). A content analysis of prime time commercials: A contextual framework of gender representation. *Sex Roles, 49*(9/10), 546–551.

Geis, F. L., Brown, V., Walstedt, J. J., & Porter, N. (1984). TV commercials as achievement scripts for women. *Sex Roles, 10*(7/8), 513–525.

Gerbner, G. (1993). *Violence in cable-originated television programs.* Philadelphia, PA: The Annenberg School for Communication.

Glascock, J. (2001). Gender roles on prime-time network television: Demographics and behaviors. *Journal of Broadcasting & Electronic Media, 45*, 656–669.

Glascock, J. (2003). Gender, race and aggression in newer TV networks; prime time programming. *Communication Quarterly, 51*(1), 90–100.

Greenberg, B. S., Eastin, M., Hofshire, L., Lachlan, K., & Brownell, K. D. (2003). Portrayals of overweight and obese individuals on commercial television. *American Journal of Public Health, 93*(8), 1342–1348.

Greenberg, B. S., & Worrell, T. R. (2007). New faces on television: A 12-season replication. *Howard Journal of Communications, 18,* 277–290.

Greenwood, D. N. (2007). Are female action heroes risky role models: Character identification, idealization and viewer aggression. *Sex Roles, 57,* 725–732.

Gross, L., & Jeffries-Fox, S. (1978). What do you want to be when you grow up, little girl? In G. Tuchman, A. K. Daniels, & J. Benet (Eds.), *Hearth and home: Images of women in the mass media* (pp. 240–265). New York: Oxford University Press.

Head, S. (1954). Content analysis of television drama programs. *Quarterly of Film, Radio, and Television, 9, 175–194.*

Hearold, S. (1986). A synthesis of 1043 effects of television on social behavior. In G. Comstock (Ed.), *Public communication and behavior, Vol. 1.* Orlando, FL: Academic Press.

Herrett-Skjellum, J., & Allen, M. (1996). Television programming and sex stereotyping: A meta-analysis. In B. R. Burleson (Ed.), *Communication Yearbook 19* (pp. 157–185), Thousand Oaks, CA: Sage Publications.

Hoffner, C. (1996). Children's wishful identification and parasocial interaction with favorite television characters. *Journal of Broadcasting & Electronic Media, 40*, 389–402.

Hoffner, C. A., Levine, K. J., & Toohey, R. A. (2008). Socialization to work in late adolescence: The role of television and family. *Journal of Broadcasting & Electronic Media, 52*(2), 282–302.

Houck, M. M. (2006), CSI: Reality. *Scientific American, 295*(1), 84–89.

Hunt, D. (2005). Making sense of Blackness on television. In D. Hunt (Ed.), *Channeling Blackness: Studies on television and race in America* (pp. 1–24). New York: Oxford University Press.

IMHI. (1997). Women's work: Will it ever be done? *Dialogue, 5*(1), 1–4.

Jackson-Beeck, M. (1977). The non-viewers: Who are they? *Journal of Communication, 27*(3), 65–72.

Katz, P. A., & Coulter, D. K. (1986). *Progress report: Modification of gender: Stereotyped behavior in children.* (Grant No. BNS-8316047). Washington, DC: National Science Foundation.

Kerner Commission (1968). *Report of the national advisory commission on civil disorders.* Washington, DC: U.S. Government Printing Office.

Kimball, M. M. (1986). Television and sex-role attitudes. In T. M. Williams (Ed.), *The impact of television: A natural experiment in three communities.* New York: Academic Press.

Kitwana, B. (2002). *The hip hop generation: Young Blacks and the crisis in African American culture.* New York: Basic Books.

Kubey, R., Shifflet, M., Weerakkody, N., & Ukeiley, S. (1995). Demographic diversity on cable: Have the new cable channels made a difference in the representation of gender race and age? *Journal of Broadcasting & Electronic Media, 39*(4), 459–471.

Lauzen, M. M., & Dozier, D. M. (1999). Making a difference in prime time: Women on screen and behind the scenes in the 1995–96 television season. *Journal of Broadcasting & Electronic Media, 43*(1), 1–19.

Lauzen, M. M., & Dozier, D. M. (2005). Recognition and respect revisited: Portrayals of age and gender in prime-time television. *Mass Communication & Society, 8*(3), 241–256.

Lauzen, M. M., Dozier, D. M., & Hicks, M. V. (2001). Prime-time players and powerful prose: The role of women in the 1997–98 season. *Mass Communication & Society, 4*(1), 39–59.

Lauzen, M. M., Dozier, D. M., & Horan, N. (2008). Constructing gender stereotypes through social roles in prime-time television. *Journal of Broadcasting & Electronic Media, 52*(2), 200–214.

Leaper, C., Breed, L., Hoffman, L., & Perlman, C. A. (2002). Variations in the gender-stereotyped content of children's television cartoons across genres. *Journal of Applied Social Psychology, 32*(8), 1653–1662.

Lefkowitz, M. M., & Huesmann, L. R. (1980). Concomitants of television violence viewing in children. In E. L. Palmer & A. Dorr (Eds.), *Children and the faces of television: Teaching, violence, selling* (pp. 163–181). New York: Academic Press.

Levine, K. J., & Hoffner, C. A. (2006). Adolescents' conceptions of work: What is learned from different sources during anticipatory social-ization? *Journal of Adolescent Research, 21*, 647–669.

Lin, C. A. (1997). Beefcake versus cheesecake in the 1990s: Sexist portrayals of both genders in television commercials. *Howard Journal of Communications*, *8*(3), 237–249.

Lovdal, L. T. (1989). Sex role messages in television commercials: An update. *Sex Roles*, *21*(11/12), 715–724.

McGhee, P. E., & Frueh, T. (1980). Television viewing and the learning of sex-role stereo-types. *Sex Roles*, *6*(2), 179–188.

Morgan, M. (1982). Television and adolescents' sex-role stereotypes: A longitudinal study. *Journal of Personality and Social Psychology*, *43*(5), 947–955.

Morgan, M. (1987). Television, sex-role attitudes, and sex-role behavior. *Journal of Early Adolescence*, *7*(3), 269–282.

Morgan, M., & Harr-Mazar, H. (1980). *Television and adolescents' family life expectations*. Unpublished manuscript, The Annenberg School of Communications, Philadelphia, PA.

Morgan, M., & Rothschild, N. (1983). Impact of the new television technology: Cable TV, peers, and sex-role cultivation in the electronic envi-ronment. *Youth and Society*, *15*(1), 33–50.

Morgan, M., & Shanahan, J. (1997). Two decades of cultivation research: An appraisal and meta-analysis. In B. R. Burleson (Ed.), *Commu-nication yearbook, 20* (pp. 1–46). Thousand Oaks, CA; Sage.

Morgan, M., Shanahan, J., & Signorielli, N. (2009). Growing up with television: Cultivation pro-cesses. In J. Bryant & M. B. Oliver (Eds.), *Media effects: Advances in theory and research* (3rd ed., pp. 34–49). New York: Routledge.

Nielsen, A. C. (2009). *Three screen report, vol. 7, 4th quarter*. http://blog.nielsen.com/nielsen wire/wp-content/uploads/2010/03/3Screens_ 4Q09_US_rpt.pdf.

Ogletree, S. M., Mason, D. V., Grahmann, T., & Raffeld, P. (2001). Perceptions of two televi-sion cartoons: *Powerpuff Girls* and *Johnny Bravo*. *Communication Research Reports, 18*, 307–313.

Oppliger, P. A. (2007). Effects of gender stereo-typing on socialization. In R. W. Press, B. M. Gayle, N. Burrell, M. Allen, & J. Bryant (Eds.), *Mass media effects research: Advances through meta-analysis* (pp. 199–214). Mahwah, NJ: Lawrence Erlbaum.

Pike, J. J., & Jennings, N. A. (2005). The effects of commercials on children's perceptions of gender appropriate toy use. *Sex Roles, 52*(1/2), 83–91.

Pingree, S., Starrett, S., & Hawkins, R. (1979). *Soap opera viewers and social reality*. Unpublished manuscript, Women's Studies Program, University of Wisconsin–Madison.

Reep, D. C., & Dambrot, F. H. (1987). Television's professional women: Working with men in the 1980s. *Journalism Quarterly*, *64*(2/3), 376–381.

Reeves, B., & Greenberg, B. (1977). Children's perceptions of television characters. *Human Communication Research*, *3*(2), 113–127.

Rideout, V. J., Foehr, U. G., & Roberts, D. F. (2010). *Generation M^2: Media in the lives of 8- to 18-year-olds*. Menlo Park, CA: Kaiser Family Foundation.

Rivadeneyra, R., & Ward, L. M. (2005). From Ally McBeal to Sabado Gigante: Contributions of television viewing to the gender role attitudes of Latino adolescents. *Journal of Adolescent Research, 20*, 453–475.

Roberts, D. F., & Bachen, C. M. (1981). Mass communication effects. *American Review of Psychology*, *32*, 307–356.

Roberts, D. F., & Maccoby, N. (1985). Effects of mass communication. In G. Lindzey & E. Aronson (Eds.), *Handbook of social psy-chology* (3rd ed., Vol. II, pp. 539–598). Reading, MA: Addison-Wesley.

Ross, L., Anderson, D. R., & Wisocki, P. A. (1982). Television viewing and adult sex-role attitudes. *Sex Roles*, *8*(6), 589–592.

Rothschild, N. (1984). Small group affiliation as a mediating factor in the cultivation process. In G. Melischek, K. E. Rosengren, & J. Stappers (Eds.), *Cultural indicators: An international symposium*. Vienna: Osterreichischen Akademie der Wissenschaften.

Scharrer, E., Kim, D. D., Lin, K., & Liu, Z. (2006). Working hard or hardly working? Gender, humor, and the performance of domestic chores in television commercials. *Mass Media & Society, 9*(2), 215–238.

Shanahan, J., Signorielli, N., & Morgan, M. (2008). *Television and sex roles 30 years hence: A retrospective and current look from a cultural indicators perspective*. Paper presented at the annual conference of the International Commu-nication Association, Montreal, Quebec, Canada**.**

Signorielli, N. (1984). The demography of the tele-vision world. In G. Melischek, K. E. Rosengren, & J. Stappers (Eds.), *Cultural indicators: An international symposium*. Vienna: Osterreich-ischen Akademie der Wissenschaften.

Signorielli, N. (1985). Role portrayal on televi-sion: *An annotated bibliography of studies relating to women, minorities, aging, sexual behavior, health, and handicaps.* Westport, CT: Greenwood Press.

Signorielli, N. (1989). Television and conceptions about sex-roles: Maintaining conventionality and the status quo. *Sex Roles, 21*(5/6), 341–360.

Signorielli, N. (1991). Adolescents and ambivalence toward marriage: A cultivation analysis. *Youth & Society, 23*(1), 121–149.

Signorielli, N. (1993). Television and adolescents' perceptions about work. *Youth & Society, 24*(3), 314–341.

Signorielli, N. (2004). Aging on television: Messages relating to gender, race, and occupation in prime time. *Journal of Broadcasting & Electronic Media, 48*(2), 279–301.

Signorielli, N. (2008). *Children' programs 2007: Basic demography and violence.* Paper presented at the annual conference of the National Communication Association. San Diego, CA.

Signorielli, N. (ongoing). Ongoing content analyses. University of Delaware.

Signorielli, N., & Bacue, A. (1999). Recognition and respect: A content analysis of prime-time television characters across three decades. *Sex Roles, 40*(7/8), 527–544.

Signorielli, N., & Kahlenberg, S. (2001). Television's world of work in the nineties. *Journal of Broadcasting & Electronic Media, 45*(1), 1–19.

Signorielli, N., & Lears, M. (1992). Children, television and conceptions about chores: Attitudes and behaviors. *Sex Roles, 27*, 157–170.

Smith, S. L, & Cook C. A. (2008). *Gender stereotypes: An analysis of popular films and TV.* CA: The Geena Davis Institute on Gender and Media.

Smythe, D. W. (1954). Reality as presented by television. *Public Opinion Quarterly, 18*, 143–154.

Stern, S. R., & Mastro, D. E. (2004). Gender portrayals across the life span: A content analytic look at broadcast commercials. *Mass Communication & Society, 7*(2), 215–236.

Surgeon General's Scientific Advisory Committee on Television and Social Behavior. (1972). *Television and growing up: The impact of televised violence.* Washington, DC: U.S. Government Printing Office.

Tan, A. S. (1979). TV beauty ads and role expectations of adolescent female viewers. *Journalism Quarterly, 56*(2), 283–288.

Tanner, L. R., Haddock, S. A., Zimmerman, T. S., & Lund, L. K. (2003). Images of couples and families in Disney feature-length animated films. *American Journal of Family Therapy, 31*(5), 355–373.

Thompson, T. L., & Zerbinos, E. (1995). Gender roles in animated cartoons: Has the picture changed in 20 years? *Sex Roles, 32*(9/10), 651–673.

Thompson, T. L., & Zerbinos, E. (1997). Television cartoons: Do children notice it's a boy's world? *Sex Roles, 37*(5/6), 415–432.

Vande-Berg, L., & Streckfuss, D. (1992). Prime-time television's portrayal of women and the world of work: A demographic profile. *Journal of Broadcasting & Electronic Media, 36*(2), 195–208.

Vernon, J. A., Williams, J. A., Jr., Phillips, T., & Wilson, J. (1990). Media stereotyping: A comparison of the way elderly women and men are portrayed on prime-time television. *Journal of Women & Aging, 2*(4), 55–68.

Volgy, T. J., & Schwartz, J. E. (1980). Television entertainment programming and sociopolitical attitudes. *Journalism Quarterly, 57*(1), 150–155.

Ward, L. M., Hansbrough, E., & Walker, E. (2005). Contributions of music video exposure to Black adolescents' gender and sexual schemas. *Journal of Adolescent Research, 20*(2), 143–166.

Williams, T. M. (1986). *The impact of television: A natural experiment in three communities.* New York: Academic Press.

Wright, C. W. (1986). *Mass communication: A sociological perspective* (3rd ed.) New York: Random House.

Wroblewski, R., & Huston, A. C. (1987). Televised occupational stereotypes and their effects on early adolescents: Are they changing? *Journal of Early Adolescence, 7*, 283–298.

CHAPTER 17

Media and the Family

ROBERT KUBEY
Rutgers University

SMITA C. BANERJEE
Memorial Sloan-Kettering Cancer Center

BARNA WILLIAM DONOVAN
St. Peter's College

"If we are forced, at every hour, to watch or listen to horrible events, this constant stream of ghastly impressions will deprive even the most delicate among us of all respect for humanity," writes one critic. "Then shall we simply allow our children to listen to any story anyone happens to make up, and so receive into their minds ideas often the very opposite of those we shall think they ought to have when they are grown up?" writes another.

With the state of the family structure and the welfare of children always at the flash point of political and social discourse, studies of the media are ever more challenged to probe and understand the familial use of mass media products and the impact this behavior has on the structure, function, and mind-set of the family. As we begin the 21st century, the two critics quoted above would seem to be referring to a media environment of confrontational,

salacious talk shows, sexually graphic and violent dramas, random and senseless killings in the news media, or a dose of in-your-face professional wrestling. The sources of such criticism might be anyone from Pat Robertson to William Bennett or Tipper Gore. Yet the writers are, respectively, Cicero, writing of the Roman theater in the first century BCE, and Plato, writing in the *Republic* more than 2,300 years ago. The fears have been the same for more than two millennia, and the rhetoric hardly changes.

Recent decades have seen the state of the family as it relates to the media at the center of political debate. The controversy ignited by Dan Quayle's 1992 criticism of a character deciding to become a single mother on the situation comedy *Murphy Brown* still resonates today (Morgan, Leggett, & Shanahan, 1999). In an age of communication technology explosion, where cable and satellite channels increase the range and amount of content,

341

where high-definition television increases the quality of the televised image, where digital video recorders (DVRs) ensure the unremitting availability of television programs, and where the Internet and the World Wide Web massively increase the available sources of information, the impact of the electronic media on the family needs to be studied as much now as ever.

Media in the Home

Observations in the early 1950s held that the television set froze the natural order of family interaction—talking, joking, arguing, catching up on the disparate experiences of each family member (Bronfenbrenner, 1973; Maccoby, 1951). When the TV is on, there is "more privatization of experience; the family may gather around the set, but they remain isolated in their attention to it" (Maccoby, 1951, pp. 428–429). Frankfurt School scholars argued that the socializing role of the family had been supplanted by the mass media, advertisers, and celebrities (Horkheimer & Adorno, 1972; Marcuse, 1964). Indeed, for scores of critics, the family's role in instilling values and standards of behavior has been usurped by the media industries and their motivation to instill consumerist values.

When Holman and Jacquart (1988) indicated that marriages might stay stronger if spouses were involved in leisure-time activities, thereby increasing interpersonal communication rather than quietly watching TV, the popular press quickly declared that less television was a key to improved marriages and stable families. But television also brings families together. Television's unifying effect on the family was observed as early as 1949; the medium acted as a catalyst in bridging generational gaps (Riley, Cantwell, & Ruttiger, 1949). Among those who wished to increase contact with the family, television use was actually preferred to the use of other media (Friedson, 1953). Recent research confirms that television use is the most commonly used leisure activity (e.g., Beck & Arnold, 2009; Turtiainen, Karvonen, & Rahkonen, 2007). Other scholars who have pointed out that

greater family solidarity may be achieved via television-induced interaction and conversation include Brody, Stoneman, and Sanders (1980); Faber, Brown, and McLeod (1979); Fine (1952); Foley (1968); Katz and Foulkes (1962); Katz and Gurevitch (1976); Lull (1980); and Lyle (1972).

But the experience of television in the family context has also been shown to be complex beyond the arguments citing mere divisive or unifying effects. As Coffin argued in 1955, television viewing can often do both. Television can be "credited with increasing the family's fund of common experience and shared interests and blamed for decreasing conversation and face-to-face interaction" (p. 634). Indeed, Rosenblatt and Cunningham (1976) suggested that television viewing can also serve as a means to avoiding tense interaction in crowded homes where conflict avoidance through spatial separation is impossible.

At this point, McLeod, Fitzpatrick, Glynn, and Fallis's (1982) call for a broader definition of the positive and negative effects media use may have on families in the National Institute of Mental Health's report still needs to be heeded. As is the case generally in media effects research, data prompting researchers to draw conclusions rarely explain clear cause-and-effect relationships. Illustrating this dilemma is Chaffee and Tims's (1976) study on viewing content determined by companions around the TV set. Junior and senior high school students in the study regularly watched different programs depending on whether they watched with parents or with siblings. The direction of cause and effect was complex at best, meaning that one cannot know without clear study—and even then—if the choice of programming was adapted to one's coviewers or if the children watching TV selected their coviewers for a particular program. In the same way, easy conclusions cannot be reached about whether the atmosphere in a family is fostered by TV use or whether family members use television in ways that accommodate an already existing family orientation or mood. Generally speaking, the direction of causality in such situations is at the very least two way and mutually reinforcing. One cannot really separate the chicken from the egg, and the assumptions of clean cause–effect relationships are just that, assumptions.

Time and Experience With Television

Adding a new and significant dimension has been the proliferation of new media technologies and the subsequent increase in the sheer volume of information and entertainment available. Much of the earliest research questioning whether television inhibited family interaction or promoted it was done in households with only one TV set. As television technology improved and became ever more affordable, the households added first one and then another TV set, coupled with radio, CD players, VCRs, and Internet-connected computers, all of them capable of individualized use.

One of the early and notable significant changes in family life that attended the growing ubiquity of a new medium of communication occurred with radio. For much of a decade, the American family gathered around a singular living room radio, but as the sets became less expensive, radios began to occupy space in multiple rooms in the home, permitting family members to break away into different locales.

This trend was repeated even more dramatically over the first 15 years of television's arrival on the national scene. And this time, the eventual effect on program content was unmistakable. Once families moved from having a singular living room set where they often watched TV together to having multiple sets in the family room, dens, bedrooms, and kitchens, programmers began developing more niche programming driven by the demographics of age.

The most telling sign was the demise of the family variety show by the mid-1970s. Families in the 1950s and 1960s had religiously gathered together to view CBS's Ed Sullivan program almost every Sunday night with its very intergenerational provision of an older comedian for grandma and grandpa, a middle-aged crooner for the parents, a rock group for the teens, and Topo Gigio, a cute puppet mouse for the children. Some of these performers were designed to appeal to more than one age group (e.g., a circus performer spinning dishes atop tall sticks for the whole family). But with the family members attracted to age-niche programming in different rooms, ratings for the family variety show fell, and it has been a nearly nonexistent form of American television for more than 20 years now. Among the precious few current network programs that a whole family might watch and enjoy together are the funniest home video programs and the new revival of the prime-time high-stakes quiz shows.

According to the 1999 Kaiser Family Foundation report, children's media use then totalled an entire full-time workweek, often using several media at the same time. The same research shows that children are exposed to heavy doses of media fare at a very early age. Children between the ages of 2 and 7 are already using media for 3.5 hours each day. A third of them have a TV in their bedroom, 16% have a VCR, and 13% have a video game console in their bedroom. As children grow older, substantially more of them are likely to have electronic media in their bedrooms. Of children 8 years old and older, 65% have a TV in their room and 21% have a computer.

These findings are noted in the light of the American Academy of Pediatrics, Committee on Public Education (1999) recommendation that children under the age of 2 should not be exposed to television programs and a daily limit of 1 to 2 hours of quality programming for older children. More recent studies have found that 74% (Rideout, Vandewater, & Wartella, 2003) to 100% (Weber & Singer, 2004) of children watch television before the age of 2. In fact, today, the median age at which children begin to regularly watch television is approximately 9 months (Zimmerman, Christakis, & Meltzoff, 2007).

The most noteworthy finding of the Kaiser Family Foundation report, for the purposes of this chapter, is that so much of children's media use is unsupervised; this is especially notable in light of findings dating back more than two decades that watching and talking with children helps them view more actively and intelligently (Singer & Singer, 2005). Almost half of the children in the Kaiser Foundation survey reported having no rules governing their TV watching. Diaries kept by the children in the study revealed that those older than 7 almost never watch TV with their parents. Parents of children between 2 and 7 report that 81% of the time, they are doing something else while their children watch television.

The most recent report by the Kaiser Family Foundation (2010) states that "young kids and teens today are part of a plugged-in, media friendly generation" (p. 4). The Kaiser Family Foundation conducted a survey of 2,002 kids between October 2008 and May 2009. The results showed startling increases in media use as compared to the 1999 and 2004 reports, when similar surveys were conducted. According to the report, kids are switched on to media almost from the time they wake up to the time they go to bed. Eight- to 18-year-olds spend an average of 7 hours and 38 minutes a day with media using computers, televisions, MP3 players, and other media. TV is still the top-most media activity for most kids and teens. Children watch television for an average of nearly 4.5 hours a day. However, there has been a dramatic shift in terms of viewing habits. More children are turning away from watching TV on televisions. What is preferred instead is watching the same program on other media and having more technology available. About 59% of young people's TV viewing consists of watching shows when they are broadcast. The rest of the viewing is done online or using DVRs, mobile devices, or DVD players. The Kaiser survey results show that young people today spend more time listening to music, playing games, and watching TV on their cell phones than talking on them. What is even more intriguing is that teenagers are masters at "media multi-tasking," or using more than one medium at a time. The report documents that 39% of teens say they use computers, read, play video games, text, or listen to music "most of the time" while watching TV.

Other research groups echo similar findings. Bridge Ratings and Research report that an average American teen/young adult (15–24 years old) spends about 11 hours per day using some form of media including television, radio, Internet, magazines, cell phones, newspapers, and MP3 players. Most time spent on the Internet includes watching video on such sites as YouTube, Yahoo!, and MySpace or streamed replays of prime-time shows on TV network websites (Bridge Ratings, 2007).

These findings take on another character when considered in light of our own studies of media use relying on the experience sampling method (ESM). We examined how people use and experience television at home and with their families, as well as how media use is related to the use of time and experience in non-TV settings. In ESM research, subjects are given paging devices (beepers) and small booklets of self-report forms. Each time the respondents are randomly signaled—usually six to eight times each day for a week—they fill out a report form telling us where they are, what they are doing, and how they feel on a set of very simple psychological measures. This way, behavioral reports are generated as people actually engage in media use, allowing for a comparison between media use and all the other things people do on a daily basis.

One of the things we found that people do when they watch television with others is talk. Talking occurred 21% of the time adults viewed with their family members. When adults were with family members but not watching television, they talked 36% of the time, more than with TV but not as much more as many had thought (Kubey & Csikszentmihalyi, 1990). In other words, the early arguments that television completely froze interaction, that the viewing experience was purely "parallel," were almost certainly an artifact of the very early novelty of the medium when Maccoby made her observation in 1951. But the conclusion still holds that television watching is a less active form of family interaction than is almost anything else a family finds to do together. And the research jury is still out on the potential beneficial effects of parents and children playing video games together.

Partly because they talk a good deal when they view television, respondents' ESM reports show that familial television viewing is a significantly more challenging activity than viewing alone. Respondents also report feeling more cheerful when viewing TV with the family than when viewing alone. However, much larger experiential differences are observed between family time *without* TV and family time *with* TV. Without TV, adult respondents reported time spent with the family as being more challenging and significantly more psychologically and physically activating, but significantly less relaxing than time spent with the family with television.

The dose of individuals' media intake has also been shown to be related to the quality of family life they experience. At home, heavy television viewers are likely to spend more time alone (Kubey, 1994), but they do not report particularly negative experiences with their families. In fact, heavy viewers report feeling significantly more "free" (vs. constrained) during non-TV activities with family members than do light viewers. Furthermore, heavy viewers are no more likely to be "alienated from the family," as measured on Maddi's Alienation Index (Kubey & Csikszentmihalyi, 1990; Maddi, Kobasa, & Hoover, 1979).

ESM research also shows that television is usually experienced passively. Viewing involves little concentration but does elicit feelings of relaxation. Not surprisingly, in the instance of family group viewing, the experience is more sedate when compared with TV-free family activities. For heavy TV viewers, the whole of family life beyond viewing is perceived as being less active.

Besides the ESM approach, ethnographic studies also provide data that complement the work on time and experience with television (e.g., Beck & Arnold, 2009; Broege, Owens, Graesch, Arnold, & Schneider, 2007). In these studies, typically, the researchers observe and film family times spent on weekdays and weekends. These observations are supplemented by self-reports. Beck and Arnold (2009) found that home leisure consists primarily of television viewing in the family room or living room. In fact, their study shows that television is the dominant leisure activity experienced by the heterosexual couples they studied. Not only does television allow parents to rest while children are quiet and occupied, it was an activity preferred over crafts or games, which require more energy than parents may have at the end of a working day. Participants in their study reported that television viewing was an enjoyable activity that "sometimes brings together family members" (Beck & Arnold, 2009, p. 139).

Marriage and having children generally reorient people from social lives focusing on friends to time spent at home with each other and the children, and television viewing is often a pleasurable homebound experience for families. Time spent watching television is often the compromise activity that families choose and, after a time, almost automatically and habitually do together (Kubey, 1996).

To summarize, there is as much evidence in the research literature to show that television brings family members together as there is that it rends them apart. More time spent viewing is correlated with more time spent with the family. Television, after all, is in many ways a conservative medium attempting to gather and hold the largest audiences possible. As a result, a lot of content, particularly through the first two decades of the medium's history in the United States, is articulated particularly well with conventional family interests and values.

This relationship is particularly telling among children and adolescents (Kubey, 1990). Indeed, one marker of becoming adolescent in contemporary society is a movement *away* from television and many hours spent with the family and *toward* more time spent outside the home with friends and listening to music (Larson, Kubey, & Colletti, 1989). It is interesting to note that adolescents who watch more television report feeling better during time spent with the family and relatively worse with friends, whereas adolescents who listen to more music feel worse with the family and better with friends (Larson & Kubey, 1983).

Film and Television Content and Family Values

The rise of the mass media has constituted an alteration in the frequency with which certain kinds of messages about what is to be valued in society are communicated. Prior to the rise of the mass media, there were three primary societal institutions charged with the responsibility of socializing the young and moving them toward particular ideals of what they should know about and value on reaching their majority. These three institutions were the church, the family, and the school. The mass media that rose up in the first three decades of the 20th century constituted a new fourth voice heard by the young. But this fourth institution, unlike the others, is only marginally responsible for formal socialization. Yet it *does* socialize.

The mass media, particularly as they are constituted in the United States, are operated by individuals and corporations who stand to profit by attracting and holding the attention of audiences. Their prime responsibility is to themselves and to stockholders, and only secondly, at best, do they operate in the public interest and to the varying and often minimal requirements of the Federal Communications Commission or Congress.

Although qualitative research on media creators has demonstrated that there are television and film performers and creators who adhere to strict personal standards (Gitlin, 1983) the popular media have also revealed many entertainment personalities who don't see themselves as role models. And although it is the case that many of the messages promulgated on television are conservative, in the mainstream, and supportive of family values, it is also the case that other messages may either directly or indirectly controvert processes and orientations that are critical to sustaining families. As Albada (2000) notes, "In fact, television is probably more conservative in its presentation of family than in any other area" (p. 81).

The social cognitive theory (Bandura, 1986, 2001) came out of the quantitative research tradition and contends that human behavior is a triadic, dynamic, and reciprocal interaction of personal factors, behavior, and the environment. According to this theory, an individual's behavior is uniquely determined by each of these three factors. Observational learning occurs when a person watches the actions of another person and the reinforcements that the person receives (Bandura, 1997). Whereas such learning through observation can include simple imitation of behavior, it typically goes beyond simple imitation to involve the adoption of attitudes, values, aspirations, and other characteristics observed in others (Hoffner, Levine, & Toohey, 2008). Examples of social learning may include children learning about daily chores, role plays,

and relationships by observing parents and other family members. However, television is also an important factor in young people's lives and provides many additional salient and attractive role models (Albada, 2000; Hoffner, 2008; Signorielli & Kahlenberg, 2001). Research evidence indicates that young people learn from the values, beliefs, and behaviors exhibited by television characters (e.g., Valkenburg, 2004).

The creation of what is seen, read, and heard in the media, however, must be understood within the context of broader social trends. It is an undeniable fact that TV, film, and radio producers cannot create successful content that does not, in some way, reflect already existing social realities. Arguments of the inherent conservatism of the media state that mass media industries are reluctant to present ideas that truly conflict with too many people's values too much of the time lest audiences turn away and advertising revenue dry up (Gitlin, 1972, 1983). Thus, the racy and violent images that critics regularly excoriate and public opinion polls denounce must appeal to sizable audiences.

From a family perspective, the most notable shifts in the 1950s and 1960s media were the rise of rock 'n roll—still the art form of choice for adolescents as they begin to rebel and make their break from identifying with the family to the peer group—and youth culture movie stars such as Marlon Brando and James Dean, whose films chronicled youth angst, delinquency, and, notably, significant problems of the family unit.

In 1950s America, the film industry, even in the wake of Senator McCarthy's attacks, no longer needed to churn out only optimistic visions of the American way of life, as it had done in a time of war. Film entertainment began to take on edgier subjects (Schrader, 1986). It could move from teenage Andy Hardy (late 1930s and early 1940s) making his way through the trials of adolescence with the guidance of a benevolent adult to a tormented James Dean in *Rebel Without a Cause* (1955), failed by the family and by adult society.

The film and music sectors of the mass media quickly learned to capitalize on teenage rebellion because it was profitable. Referring to a mix of conservative values and material appealing to more base, antisocial, and hedonistic instincts, Daniel Bell (1976) articulates how the rise in images of sexuality and violence constituted "cultural contradictions of capitalism."

Relative to film and music, television would take longer to change, but when it did, it changed because of similar social and economic forces. While James Dean and Marlon Brando on the big screen made parents nervous in the 1950s, the TV images of that same time were generally so benign that they still make many today nostalgic. Others, however, argue that such images were both *benign and misleading,* at considerable variance with the realities of family life in that decade.

The change of television from an orderly landscape, one of intact nuclear families, to one of shifting, relativistic values and varying and often conflicting points of view has been argued to be a result of the late-20th-century shift from a universalist worldview of enlightenment values to the quicksand-like world of postmodernity. As Elkind (1993) writes, "The assumptions that societies, as they become progressively civilized, educated and cultured, also become more humanitarian and less savage is no longer tenable" (p. 601).

In the 1950s, TV showed an ideal world to which, it was incorrectly assumed, everyone aspired. Families were together (almost exclusively White), they loved each other, they lived in safe neighborhoods, and kids could count on adults to help them through the trials and tribulations of adolescence. But not only were those images something very difficult to live up to, they were also often unrealistic and overly sentimental. Television producers increasingly dispelled the myths of middle-American perfection, as well as the myth of a singular desirable way of life. In the postmodern television landscape, the chaos of the world is depicted more frequently in the medium's fictional offerings. The once-sacred nuclear family's role as a haven against the threats and disorder of the world is questioned and alternatives are sometimes considered. In fact, Morgan et al. (1999) analyzed data from 1988 and 1994 General Social Surveys (GSS) and reported that "television viewing is indeed contributing to the fraying of traditional family values" (p. 58). They found

that heavy viewers in their study were more accepting of single parenthood and having children out of wedlock.

Although the image of the family has changed on TV, the industry's reliance on the family in programs and plots and on family viewership and patronage of advertised goods has not. Not all TV genres can easily accommodate families or family themes. Police or action-adventure shows, for example, glorify single males and bachelorhood (Cantor, 1990). In police dramas, single life is preferred, with fewer than 1 out of 5 major characters being married (Signorielli, 1991). Living the single life in this genre has the advantage over marriage and domesticity. Single men on television are more effective and powerful, concludes Signorielli (1982). Shows promising story lines of crime fighting and investigation cannot be weighed down by domesticity. This, of course, is a general trend but not an absolute rule. In the 1980s, Don Johnson's *Miami Vice* character was married in a highly publicized sweeps month episode, then his wife was killed off in the following episode. As TV critics remarked, macho sex symbol Johnson couldn't very well drive around Miami with a baby seat in his Ferrari Testarossa.

This trend is somewhat changed today, with more shows categorized as "family entertainment programs." To name a few, there is *Nanny 911*, in which American families with unmanageable children are reformed by English nannies. More family relationships are unraveled in *The Secret Life of the American Teenager*, with focus on the relationships between families and friends and how they deal with the unexpected teenage pregnancy, juggling motherhood and high school, and relationship challenges. *Make It or Break It* takes family entertainment to competitive heights with lives of teen gymnasts who strive to make it to the Olympic Games. No discussion of family shows can be complete without the mention of *7th Heaven*, which tells the story of a Protestant minister's family living in the fictional town of Glen Oak, California. Each episode in the series deals with a lesson based in morality or a controversial theme that the family handles either directly or indirectly. More religious feelings were stirred with *Touched by an Angel*, where people at crossroads in their lives or difficult junctures are helped by angels and messages from God.

But, from the earliest days of TV, family-oriented story lines often dominated evening lineups (Gerbner, Gross, Morgan, & Signorielli, 1980; Greenberg, 1982; Head, 1954; Signorielli, 1985; Smythe, 1954). Situation comedies and soap operas are the perfect vehicles to deal with the family, and it is hard to imagine these genres without family life at the center. The major comedy format *is* the family sitcom. Its mise-en-scene is the family home, its main sets the living room and the kitchen. Here, both implicitly and explicitly, the internal world of a family sitcom is one of the most desirable places one could hope to inhabit.

Traditionally, the sitcom world is one in which the most disturbing behaviors of contemporary society and the rest of the TV world—murder, rape, domestic violence, marital breakup, and child abuse—do not take place, and certainly not directly to the central characters. Although on rare occasions "very special episodes" of such shows do deal with the darker side of life (e.g., *All in the Family's* Edith Bunker nearly raped or threatened by breast cancer), violence is not a regular staple of the sitcom landscape—indeed, it is nearly nonexistent. In this sense, just as most of us like to think of our own families as safe havens away from the turmoil of the world beyond, so too does the family sitcom serve as an oasis amid the often cruel flotsam and jetsam found elsewhere on the small screen.

Content analyses of general situation comedy and family drama behavior abound, and this is significant because the type of behavior these programs represent may be more readily imitated by viewers given the sheer identifiability of the settings of the shows (Comstock & Strzyzewski, 1990). Abelman (1986) concludes that, although there exists a "relatively equal amount of antisocial and prosocial behavior on television, prosocial fare is not as visually stimulating or identifiable in the context of a program as is antisocial fare" (p. 55). Conflict, after all, is the very nature of conventional drama. Without it, no drama, no entertainment vehicle, exists. However, as writers and TV and film producers have come to learn, antisocial plot resolutions can sometimes be as

popular as prosocial resolutions. The vanquishing of a particularly heinous villain or getting the upper hand on a romantic rival in a relationship-oriented drama does not always sell as well if it is done in a cozy, prosocial manner. And television research has long been concerned that individuals may learn of and model undesirable ways to deal with social and familial situations by supplementing their observations of the real world with messages from television (Bandura, 1971; Dail & Way, 1985; Gerbner, Gross, Morgan, & Signorielli, 1980, 1986; Greenberg, Hines, Buerkel-Rothfuss, & Atkin, 1980).

Certainly, compared with police and action shows, characters on situation comedies engage in more prosocial behavior (Greenberg, Atkin, Edison, & Korzenny, 1977). In fact, Cantor (1990) argues that the world of domestic dramas may easily be regarded as a fantasy world, where life and people are better than what is most often encountered in the real world. Certainly, in the early days of the sitcom, parents often gave their children advice and the children often took it (Fisher, 1974). The communicative behaviors among family members are, for the greater part, positive in the family program (Skill & Wallace, 1990).

The family unit that has steadily transformed from the prototypical 1950s "perfect" middle-class nuclear family of *Leave It to Beaver, The Donna Reed Show,* or *Father Knows Best* has been classified by Chesebro (1979) and Steenland (1985) under a number of specific categories encompassing programs from various decades. They identify the childless couples (*The Honeymooners, Mad About You* [for four seasons]); communal families (*Gilligan's Island, The Mary Tyler Moore Show, Friends, Lost, The Office, Scrubs*); geriatric families (*The Golden Girls*); unmarried men *(Bachelor Father, Diff'rent Strokes, Full House)* and women *(Julia, One Day at a Time, Grace Under Fire, Gilmore Girls)* as parents; aggregate or "blended" families *(Drake and Josh, Life with Derek, The Brady Bunch, Step by Step, Sister Sister, Modern Family);* and trial or probationary marriages *(Ned and Stacey).* Although these "familial" arrangements deviate, often radically, from the nuclear family structure—a "hook" selling these shows is the question of "how can they make it work?"—the programs, nevertheless, exist in an idealized world where positive, prosocial behaviors achieve positive results. Indeed, the characters *can* make it "work." Jerry Seinfeld's vigorous insistence that the characters in his program experience "no learning, no growing, no hugging" indicates the "feel good" state of general affairs in the rest of the sitcom world.

Situation comedies are mostly set in middle-class households—after all, the largest sector of the audience must be reached—but the lives of families across the socioeconomic spectrum, from working and middle classes to the upper middle and upper classes, have been depicted within the genre (Cantor, 1990). Working-class comedies have been seen as some form of a feminist ideal, according to Cantor (1990). Classic programs, from *The Life of Riley* and *I Remember Mama* to *All in the Family,* enact a world of diminished male supremacy. The typical blue-collar sitcom family is one ostensibly ruled over by a buffoonish, clueless, yet good-hearted and lovable man (even if he's a bigot, as in the case of *All in the Family)* and a sensible and strong woman. The father figure of the working-class family tries to enjoy his society-granted status as ruler of the family, the king of his castle. But he's often a blowhard and a loudmouth, and the programs suggest that neither he nor the marriage nor the family itself would last long without the level-headed intelligence and common sense of his wife. The loudmouth, blowhard blue-collar guy of the sitcom, however, is never abusive; he's not an alcoholic or ever unfaithful. In fact, underneath his macho blustering, he has a heart of gold neither his wife and family nor the audience can help but love.

No sitcom is sunnier in disposition than that of the middle-class family (Cantor, 1990). Here, husbands and wives are nearly equal, and their skill at managing the family and raising kids is laudable. Conflict between spouses is rare, although when it happens it is often resolved using affiliative communication techniques (Comstock & Strzyzewski, 1990). And the conflicts are resolved quickly. In the middle-class television sitcom families, fathers do sometimes know best. The roles of women in these sitcoms have expanded: Many of them are professionals, such as Claire Huxtable (Phylicia Rashad) of *The Cosby Show,* Elise Keaton (Meredith

Baxter) of *Family Ties,* and Maggie Seaver (Joanna Kerns) of *Growing Pains* in the 1980s. In fact, by the 2000s, it has become virtually impossible to find any sitcom—or any family-centric show—where a family is unproblematically run by a working father and a stay-at-home mom. Where television women do nothing more than stay at home and watch after the house and children, the shows tend to be dark satires of domesticity. One example is the long-running *Desperate Housewives* on ABC. Another stay-at-home TV mom is Carmella Soprano on the ground-breaking HBO series *The Sopranos.* But the nuclear family of *The Sopranos* is also a twisted, monstrous parody of the American family, with a murderous sociopath of a father and a mother who chooses to be blind to his criminality as long as he can provide a luxurious, upper-class life.

Although conflicts in family programs nearly doubled over the late 1970s and the late 1980s across the socioeconomic spectrum, again they were almost always successfully resolved using affiliative, prosocial communication techniques (Heintz, 1992). Conflicts children face in latter-day sitcoms are also greater in scope and intensity, more realistic than in the classic perfect-family sitcoms (Larson, 1991)—problems ranging from drugs or alcohol to cheating in school, pressure to have sex, or even problems of violence involving guns, date rape, or child abuse in "very special episodes"—but the solutions are nearly as idealized as the rest of existence in the programs' universe.

Even though the problems and the makeup of the families have changed, becoming more complex or unconventional, these fictional worlds still operate according to internal rules adhering close to the Golden Rule. While television has turned somewhat more ambiguous since the 1970s and the postmodern worldview crisis of the post-Vietnam and post-Watergate era, that segment of the world inside the tube focusing on the family has remained the most desirable still. In medical dramas, by contrast, beloved protagonist doctors make mistakes. In the world of crime and punishment, lawyers like Perry Mason, or his 1980s/1990s reincarnation, Matlock, who only defended innocent clients, have given way to *The Practice* and *Boston Legal,* in which the heroic defense lawyers routinely release criminals back to the streets. On critically acclaimed police dramas such as *NYPD Blue,* the various entries in the *CSI* and *Law & Order* franchises, or *Homicide,* crime often does pay, the guilty are not always punished, the innocent suffer, and justice is denied. In this TV landscape, however, the programs dealing with families are more orderly and idealized. Children, more often than not, are taught, and they believe, that the universe has a just order to it. Honesty is the best policy, good people are eventually rewarded, and family members can reach positive solutions to interpersonal problems.

Throughout the 1990s, another "youth quake" of aggressively spending teens made up a vigorous consumer market, with youth-themed films and TV shows in frantic production. Many of them present a worldview of youth supremacy and adult obsolescence. Lauded by critics, the TV program *Buffy the Vampire Slayer* is an allegory of modern teen life—one replete with violent threats facing teenagers in such traditionally safe environments as the middle-class suburb and high school. All but one of the adult characters is completely oblivious to the dangerous world of the teens, leaving children to survive evil among doltish and useless adults, a vision comparable to Elkind's (1993) postmodern analysis:

> The concept of wise, mentoring adults who impart their knowledge, skills, and values to the innocent, naive, next generation has also become blurred. . . . These children, from an early age, live independent lives outside the home, and this independence helps to break down the distinction between parents and children. (p. 602)

Of course, this sort of youth-oriented program in which children fend for themselves is not recent. The signature film of this "genre" is *Rebel Without a Cause* (1955), in which James Dean, Natalie Wood, and Sal Mineo, all miserably failed by their inept or absent parents, form their own new nuclear family, right down to settling into an abandoned home with Dean and Wood playing parents to Mineo's child. Twelve years later, *The Graduate* (1967) served up two affluent

suburban families, lost and dysfunctional and badly out of touch with the needs and worldviews of their 21-year-old offspring. In the 1980s, a number of highly popular feature films operated on the premise of children having to solve dangerous problems that adults had created but were unable or unwilling to deal with. In *WarGames* (1983), a high school computer hacker saves the world from nuclear annihilation. In *Red Dawn* (1984), high school students form the resistance against foreign invaders. A teenager steals a fighter jet and rescues his father held hostage in a Middle Eastern dictatorship in *Iron Eagle* (1986). The operating formula in youth-oriented entertainment is power and autonomy to children.

Other interesting variations on the traditional landscape of idealized TV families have included a recent series of controversial cartoon parodies of situation comedies. The Fox network's *Family Guy, American Dad!,* and *The Cleveland Show* have not merely depicted humorously imperfect families, but they aggressively—even mean-spiritedly—lampoon the happy-ending world of sitcoms and their inherent conservatism. Although these cartoons have their roots in such adult-oriented, satirical fare as *The Flintstones* and *The Simpsons*, they are more critical and disrespectful of the family-friendly genre than anything seen before. On *Family Guy,* for example, the family's evil infant has repeatedly planned on murdering his family. *American Dad!*'s titular main character is a CIA agent and far-right-wing zealot, and the show's sight gags have drawn parallels between "family values" and Nazism. Both shows have also been the frequent targets of the conservative Parents Television Council for advertiser-boycott campaigns.

Immediate Gratification and the Family

Although filled with idealized notions of what a family or a marriage should be like, the commercial considerations of the media impress a format of presentation on programming that might well have undesirable effects on its viewers. The immediacy and speed of information, the immediacy of stimuli and gratifications, is one such dubious trait of media programming.

The orientation toward immediate gratification so common to contemporary media and quick solutions to problems is in conflict with many of the basic commitments and slow, gradual processes necessary to sustain the family, a social arrangement that one hopes will endure for at least the 18-odd years that a child lives with his or her parents.

What might this mean for the family? First, a single parent often heads sitcoms. Why? So that the parent can also play out story lines with romantic and sexual possibilities, spicing up the plot and holding viewers' attention. *Bachelor Father* is perhaps the most notable of these from the mid-1950s, followed by a host of others, some just as vapid (e.g., *My Three Sons, The Courtship of Eddie's Father*) and some more socially relevant such as *One Day at a Time*. Even the intact marital unit has become more sexualized and available for sexual hijinks (e.g., *Married . . . With Children*). With ads promising quick solutions and with the propensity to convey information quickly, the commercial electronic media may well contribute to an expectation that we should obtain gratification immediately and that solutions should come easily and quickly.

But this brings us to question the gratifications obtained from the latest trend of paranormal television shows and even the genre's occasional subversion of the traditional *one-hour-solution* format of most episodic television. The term "paranormal" encompasses a wide range of extraordinary phenomena including such things as ESP (extrasensory perception), haunted houses, ghosts, devils, spirits, reincarnation, telekinesis (the ability of the mind to move or bend objects just by thinking), UFOs (unidentified flying objects), astrology, and astral projection (one's spirit leaving the body, traveling some distance, and then returning; Sparks, Nelson, & Campbell, 1997). The television industry has tapped into the public beliefs about the paranormal by catapulting the wide range of shows under this genre. For instance, to name a few, there are *The X-Files, Beyond Reality, Roswell, Charmed, Touched by an Angel, Buffy the Vampire Slayer, Lost, Invasion,* *Heroes, FlashForward, Ghost Whisperer, Fringe,* and *V.*

It is notable that many of the most recent paranormal-themed television series either have families and family issues at their core, or they involve the formation of familial groups. For example, perhaps the most iconic paranormal series of the 2000s, ABC's *Lost,* traces a six-season-long emergence of a surrogate family among a group of island castaways. In the wake of *Lost*'s breakout success, all of the major broadcast networks premiered a number of shows founded on a paranormal or science-fictional premise, with all of the shows balancing family melodramas with their hauntings, possessions, alien invasion, and superpowers. For example, *Invasion* has a divorced couple dealing with an alien takeover in the midst of very familiar family issues like shared-custody problems and teen angst. On *Heroes,* families are strained by several main characters' budding superpowers. *FlashForward* has an FBI agent tasked with unraveling a sinister global conspiracy all the while struggling to save his troubled marriage. *Ghost Whisperer* challenges a newlywed woman with helping ghosts resolve their last earthly (and mainly family) problems while she balances the demands of her marriage. *Fringe* foregrounds a troubled father-and-son relationship in the midst of interdimensional warfare. On *V,* an FBI agent and single mother must organize a resistance movement against alien invaders, all the while contending with her troubled son's rebelliousness and resentment of her divorce.

But an interesting aspect of many of these recent paranormal family programs is their continuous story line format (only *Ghost Whisperer* has most of its "stand-alone" episodes occasionally interwoven with an ongoing "mythology" story-arc of a town's deep, dark secrets). These ongoing stories, similar to a soap opera's story structure, demand a greater investment of attention than the traditional episodic television. Viewers had to watch week after week to get any kind of a clear sense for where the characters of *Heroes* got their powers or who caused the blackout of *FlashForward,* and they had to wait years to find out the meaning of the numbers on the hatch, who the Others were, and what was the true nature of the island itself on *Lost.* Thus, while on the one hand these programs challenged their viewers to expand their attention span and suffer through delayed gratification until major questions were answered, the success rates of these shows were also spotty. Programs like *Invasion* and *FlashForward* were cancelled after a single season. Even the ratings of powerhouse shows like *Lost* and *Heroes* declined when fans indicated their frustration with a dearth of answers to long, ongoing mysteries.

Immediate gratification with the television cannot be discussed without the mention of reality television. The last 5 years have put reality TV as one of the most popular genres of television programming (Ferris, Smith, Greenberg, & Smith, 2007). With its filming of real people as they live out events in their lives (see Nabi, Biely, Morgan, & Stitt, 2003), reality TV brings something to the screen that other fictional TV programs could not (e.g., Nabi, Stitt, Halford, & Finnerty, 2006). In order to examine the desires and gratifications, Reiss and Wiltz (2004) explored the association between 16 human desires and values with reality TV viewing and concluded that the motivation to feel self-important was most strongly associated with reality TV consumption. In fact, "personal utility" has been suggested as the latest gratification obtained from viewing reality television (Barton, 2009). One possible explanation for the higher level of gratifications obtained may be that "as reality programs have become more individualized and specific in terms of content, they no longer appeal to the wider audience they did at their inception" (Barton, 2009, p. 474). With the creation of a niche market for reality television, viewers may be using reality television to obtain gratification at a more personal level. Finally, it will be futile not to discuss the simplest explanations for the boom of reality television, as Nabi and colleagues (2003) report that reality TV allows viewers to take a peek into other people's lives, and this gratification makes reality TV enjoyable. However, the nature of these instant gratifications may present some basic, inherent problems for the viewers at large.

If people have been conditioned to expect quick and easy solutions, if they are impatient and not prepared to persist and to endure difficult times, complexity, and uncertainty from time to time, then being a husband or wife, and especially a parent, may well be roles that they are not prepared to successfully enact.

Because holding attention is the sine qua non of the commercial media, other things happen as well. Sound bites in television and in radio must be short, and scenes must change rapidly lest the audience grow bored or change the channel (Adatto, 1990; Hallin, 1992). The advertising that supports the media also suggests to us that we should never feel bad for too long. After all, there is one nostrum or another for almost anything that ails us, and these medications, as often as not, are positioned within the context of one family member helping another quickly gain the fast relief promised. However, the landscape of television and television advertising has changed. Consumers have more options for controlling their exposure to advertising messages. While some may turn the television on and passively watch the programming and advertising coming across the airwaves, many consumers actively control their viewership via technologies such as TiVo and DVRs (Kwak, Andras, & Zinkhan, 2009). The emphasis in much advertising on products that can make one feel better almost immediately may well be related to some of our culture's problems with drug abuse. And given that drug abuse can seriously disturb a family's life, this may be another way that the form, style, and content of the commercial mass media indirectly contribute to familial problems.

In a review on the effects of television on scholastic performance written for the U.S. Department of Education, one of the few consistent findings cited across many studies was that children who viewed television heavily, especially violent programming, had more difficulties in impulse control, task perseverance, and delay of gratification (Anderson & Collins, 1988; see also Singer & Singer, 2005). Recent research also suggests that television viewing before the age of 3 is associated with cognitive delays, attentional problems, and sleep disorders (e.g., Christakis & Zimmerman, 2009; Thompson & Christakis, 2005; Zimmerman & Christakis, 2005). In a case study of three middle school students that assessed the influence of self-reflection on general academic performance, limiting the use of television resulted in improved academic performance, albeit this case study is reflective of one person's experience only (Williams, 2006). One of the requirements of participation in the study was that for 2 months, participants limited TV, computer and video games, music, and telephone time to 30 minutes per day. It is interesting (though, not surprising) that two of the participants dropped out of the study within 2 weeks, stating that they could not bear the lack of electronic activities. That such children grow into adults is unquestionable. Whether these problems are sustained into adulthood is not clear.

In other research, self-labeled television "addicts" scored significantly higher than "nonaddicted" viewers on measures of mind wandering, distractibility, boredom, and unfocused daydreaming (McIlwraith, 1990; Smith, 1986). Whether television itself can be held directly responsible remains unclear. But it seems plausible that some of the people who spend 4 and 5 hours almost every day over decades watching television may be less practiced in directing their own attention, in entertaining themselves, and in maintaining psychological equilibrium when left to their own devices than those who are infrequent viewers (Kubey, 1986). And if self-control is a problem for a parent, there are almost certainly going to be repercussions for the family as a whole.

Commercial pressures in the mass media, along with the general speed of technological development, also result in an emphasis on "the new." Products, programs, fashions—things are better if they are new. Not only is the family not new, but such an orientation may contribute to older extended members of the family, such as grandparents, being more easily deemed obsolete, not "with it," or even useless (Kubey, 1980). Grandparents may not know a lot about the World Wide Web, how to program a DVR, or about CD players or the latest rap group, but they may well be wise about life.

Competing for Attention

One area of concern rarely, if ever, examined concerns family members who feel that they must compete with the people on television for the attention of other family members. This is not an insignificant problem, yet there is virtually no research that bears on it.

It is undeniably the case that, from time to time, and in some families frequently, people are neglected or ignored by other family members because of television viewing or other media involvement. The image of the father who comes home from work to find that his children can barely greet him with a hello because they are watching *American Idol* is legion in film, and, although fictionalized, such images retain a basis in reality. Our society even has the term *football widow* to describe a woman who feels neglected by her husband because he watches so many football games on television over his 2 days at home with her each fall weekend.

Most problematic of all are cases in which the emotional and physical needs of children are neglected because of a parent's extreme involvement with television. Although very inconclusive and counterintuitive, one study has indicated that hyperactive and attention deficit hyperactivity disorder (ADHD) children do not watch more television than nonhyperactive children do. Instead, this research found that the *parents* of ADHD children watch *more* television than do the parents of non-ADHD children (Shanahan & Morgan, 1989). One of the researchers' unusual speculations is the possibility that some children may actually be mimicking television's kinetic nature in an attempt to be as exciting as the tube in order to win parental attention. There may well be more sound interpretations, but this one is especially disturbing even to consider.

On the other hand, recent studies have concluded that television viewing is, in fact, an exacerbating, if not causal, factor in the development of ADHD symptomatology (e.g., Christakis, Zimmerman, DiGiuseppe, & McCarty, 2004; Geist & Gibson, 2000; Levine & Waite, 2000). However, these studies have actually been conducted on children without the disorder, so inferences may be questionable (Acevedo-Polakovich, Lorch, & Milich, 2007).

The increasing ubiquity of Internet access at home raises another potentially problematic trend, one that remains understudied to date. Much has been written on how home and work are merging, with more workers on flexible time and with communication technologies enabling them to work from home. But what does it do to the processes of family life when Mom or Dad is furiously drafting an important e-mail memo to all the staff at work just 10 feet from where the children are playing in the adjacent room? Speaking from the first author's personal experience, the sense of urgent immediacy of responding to and sending e-mail memos, drafts of coauthored articles, and grant proposals while at home *does* interfere with a more consistent family atmosphere in the home (and my children will attest to this). Yet it seems difficult as a contemporary academic—and this is no doubt true of other occupations as well—to *not* stay in touch with work concerns late into the evening, during weekends, and even over the holidays. When the children 10 feet away come into the study asking for attention, to play, for a drink or a cookie, the hardworking parent may not be in a family frame of mind. If the child is young, parents feel that they must do what the child wants, and when they're that young, one easily surrenders to the cute child's request. Some parents may have to delay for a bit until they finish something that is under deadline or send an e-mail critical to the smooth functioning of the workplace.

Of course, well before the arrival of the Internet, parents did work at home via phone, legal pad, and computer, but there is little question that the Internet has added a new and more immediate means of communication into the home, one that was largely absent only 5 years earlier. Our contemporary communications technologies have changed the way we work and live, right down to *where* and *when* we work. These changes are clearly affecting the ebb and flow of family life, but no research that we have located to date solidly confirms measurable effects. Yet, no doubt, they exist.

Parents are not the only family members hooked up to the newer media technologies of video games, computers, and the Internet. Although children and adolescents still spend proportionately more time with traditional media (56% of their media use time is devoted to TV, movies, and videos; 22% to CDs and the radio; and only 5% each spent on video games and computers), the computer and Internet mystique has a very strong hold on young people (Kaiser Family Foundation, 1999). According to the Kaiser study, if the children surveyed were forced to choose between media, a majority (33%) would pick a computer with Internet access.

Devaluation of Spouses and Monogamy

Never before in the history of the human species has there been such a form of distraction in the home as television wherein the most beautiful, interesting, and engaging people that a culture can find are presented incessantly in full "living" color. Television and film—and increasingly the World Wide Web—are thick with extremely attractive young adults, as well as intense love scenes, in large part, once again, because of the commercial domination of these media and the goal of attracting and holding audiences.

The question arises whether this constant barrage of attractive opposite-sex celebrities on television brings any new pressures to a marriage. One or another mate may feel that they are somehow missing something if their spouse is not as young, as beautiful, or as svelte as the people on television. It seems that there is more pressure on women in our culture to compete with the thousands of attractive women who appear on television. (The same phenomenon goes on for men as well, but its effects are likely to be less pervasive if for no other reason than that women have been historically valued for their appearance more than men have been).

We might also ask whether film and television overromanticizes the intensity of love and passion between men and women, thereby making it more likely for some people who have been married or involved for a number of years to feel that the reduced intensity of their own romance and lovemaking pales by comparison. Put another way, does television leave some people thinking to themselves, "Am I missing something"? The possibility arises that some people may be more likely to look outside the marriage for romantic and/or sexual satisfaction to get for themselves that *something* that they are more intensely aware they are missing precisely because of what they see routinely in the media. And it is no accident that, on average, women on TV are roughly 10 years younger than men (Kubey, 1980; Signorielli & Gerbner, 1978).

Galician (2004) found that mass media images of romance in television, movies, and advertisements affect or reinforce unrealistic ideals about romantic relationships. In fact, Galician (2004) states that television images may influence romantic partners to have negative perceptions about their romantic relationships, possibly to the point of terminating their relationships. This fear is heightened by Bachen and Illouz (1996), who report that mass media images affect children's perceptions of romance. Media influence children's perception of romance to an extent of excessive or grandiose expectations about relationships. Exposure to sexual content on television also presents another problem for the youth, namely teen pregnancy. Recent research supports the notion that frequent exposure to sexual content on television predicts early initiation of sex (e.g., Collins et al., 2004; Kunkel et al., 2007; Martino, Collins, Kanouse, Elliott, & Berry, 2005) and early pregnancy (Chandra et al., 2008).

Although a clear directional cause is not established, evidence does exist that viewers of pornography are more dissatisfied with their spouses (Zillmann & Weaver, 1989). A growing yet still relatively small body of research on pornography and its effects on attitudes toward marriage, sex, relationships, and the general human worth and welfare of others gives cause for concern with the breakneck-paced proliferation of new technologies. After all, many new media technologies are quickly harnessed for the dissemination of pornography. The Internet and World Wide Web's ability to reach into homes and unleash a mass of unregulated images is especially troubling given the Kaiser Family Foundation's (1999) report of how adept even relatively young children are at computer use and how little supervision they experience. And, for more than 15 years now, DVDs have substantially increased the availability of pornography for home viewing—if not in your home, then perhaps at the neighbor's house down the street where your children play.

Potential damage to young viewers, as well as to family and marriage-sustaining value systems, is illustrated by research pointing to a coldness and indifference to human worth (especially that of women) after nonusers are exposed to pornography. As Zuromskis (2007) writes, "The 'corrosive' element in pornography that threatens cinematic traditions of narrative and aesthetic distance is bolstered by what is imagined to be the 'real world' component to the degraded excesses on-screen" (p. 5). Here, the Zillmann and Weaver (1989) sexual callousness model suggests how prolonged pornography use could lead to a climate of misogyny, aggressiveness, and violence toward women. Pornography frequently depicts indiscriminately voracious sexual appetites among women and, in certain genres, their "enjoyment" of abuse, rape, and degradation (Brownmiller, 1984, p. 42). Research demonstrating significant correlations between pornography use and sex crimes (Baron & Strauss, 1984; Court, 1984; Kutchinsky, 1973), the use of pornography by child molesters before and during their attacks (Marshall, 1988), and the ambivalence of pornography users toward the punishment of sex crimes (Weaver, 1987; Zillmann & Weaver, 1989) indicates some of the potential threats such media products pose, even as researchers still cannot perfectly disentangle cause from effect and as theoretical and policy debates continue about how a civilized society should deal with pornography in its midst.

As Zillmann (1994) draws a comparison between the value systems repeated in erotic and pornographic media and family values, he argues that they are inherently antithetical to the value systems needed to sustain a healthy, safe, and nurturing family environment. As we have argued earlier, the family is essentially a relationship founded on long-term commitment. For Zillmann, and for us, it consists of parents' commitments to each other, to the long-term intellectual, moral, and economic well-being of the family unit, and, above all, the commitment to the day-to-day welfare of their children. Long-term commitment, however, is the antithesis of pornography. The scenarios depend on casual meetings between strangers, quick sexual gratification that's approached as the satisfaction of a physical need alone with no emotional investment, then a parting of these strangers apparently never to interact again. Pornography treats promiscuity and transience in relationships as normal and desirable. Physical gratification is valued above all other concerns—such as the emotional, spiritual, or intellectual investment in an interpersonal relationship—and pornography suggests that relationships between people need to last only as long as the physical satisfaction is sustained in ever more novel and exotic ways.

Almost as disturbing as the implication of the devaluation of women is Zillmann's (1994) work indicating an indifference to having children exhibited by both young male and female research subjects exposed to pornography in an experimental setting. The desire to have children—especially girls—was shown to diminish among these research subjects, at least in their self-reports on a questionnaire administered 1 week after the experimental exposure. Evidence of a reduced interest in an enduring family unit is suggested.

Media Courtship Behavior as Preparation for Marriage and Family

Married couples and families are members of an audience. Indeed, for many married couples and in many families, the majority of time spent together is as an audience. This is an important fact that, to our knowledge, has never been dealt with in research. A question develops: How critical in courtship and the decision to marry have similar leisure orientations and film and television tastes become?

In contemporary times, an increasing number of people meet their future spouses through shared leisure activities. Consider the period of courtship in which a couple spends a huge percentage of its time together on dates, at movies and concerts, or watching TV. Modern courtship could be increasingly thought of as a testing period for a lifetime of sharing entertainment and being members of an audience together. Presumably, some relationships break down in the early courtship stage partly because the two people's tastes

in leisure activities and in film and television vary severely.

Certainly in previous centuries, similar tastes for entertainment had to be of far less import to the nature and experience of courtship, if for no other reason than that so much less time was spent being entertained. Today, in contrast, millions of married couples spend 10 to 20 hours almost every week, week in and week out, over decades, receiving entertainment and information together as audience members. Viewed in this way, there may be extraordinary impacts of the media on family life that are much greater and more pervasive than we typically think, impacts that are extraordinarily difficult to observe or measure as they speak to very gradual changes in the ways that the relationships themselves are formed and maintained.

Avenues for Action

As for what can be done, first, parents need to exercise greater control and become more vigilant with regard to what their children are being exposed to and for how long. With the new modes of delivery and the greater diversity of what is now available, especially via cable, DVDs, and the Internet, the challenge to parents is greater than it has ever been, but many parents exercise very little control over what their young children view or are unaware of potential problems that the media pose (Kaiser Family Foundation, 1999; Kubey, 1991). For example, some parents permit their young children to watch horrific and graphically violent material on TV. Other parents are unaware that their adolescents are watching hardcore pornography at the neighbor's house or late at night via cable or the Internet.

There is also a role for the government, as well as for political action groups, and for citizens working with one another or alone. There will always be disagreements over the precise effects of different kinds of content and different media on both individuals and families. Because in most cases we cannot predict precisely what the effects might be, many researchers are reluctant to prescribe solutions. But some solutions involve common sense.

Children should not be exposed to excessively graphic violence or pornography (Kubey, 1987). We also do not need to wait for definitive social science research findings to set policy in these areas. We should be urging the media industries to more effectively regulate themselves and exercise greater restraint. And we should be urging the government to bring greater pressure on media industries to better serve the public interest. One avenue is for parents and educators to use the Children's Television Act to encourage local TV stations to provide more programs of value to children. And there is a myriad of media public action groups that one can join and participate in.

Families need to be encouraged to use the media together and, especially, to use the media more critically. To accomplish this, we must encourage media literacy training and critical viewing skills to be taught formally in our school systems (Kubey, 1991; Singer & Singer, 1998). Media education is now called for in some form in 48 states (Kubey & Baker, 1999) but is not delivered as widely as it is mandated. Meanwhile, both Canada and Australia call for media education nationwide, and media education is increasingly developed in England, Scotland, and many European countries.

Media education is important because parents cannot do the job entirely by themselves, and some parents will not do the job regardless. The commercial media industries are also not likely to change the practices that they employ to attract and hold attention, and the FCC or the government is not likely to significantly alter the commercial dominance of the media in our society. What we can do is better prepare children and parents to analyze and think more critically about what they view, read, and listen to, and the family and our society will be better for the effort.

References

Abelman, R. (1986). Children's awareness of television's prosocial fare: Parental discipline as an antecedent. *Journal of Family Issues, 7,* 51–66.

Acevedo-Polakovich, I. D., Lorch, E. P., & Milich, R. (2007). Comparing television use and reading in children with ADHD and non-referred children across two age groups. *Media Psychology, 9,* 447–472.

Adatto, K. (1990). *Sound bite democracy: Network evening news presidential campaign coverage, 1968 and 1988* (Research Paper R-2). Cambridge, MA: Harvard University, Joan Shorenstein Barone Center.

Albada, K. F. (2000). The public and private dialogue about the American family on television. *Journal of Communication, 50,* 79–110.

American Academy of Pediatrics, Committee on Public Education (1999). Media education. *Pediatrics, 104,* 341–343.

Anderson, D., & Collins, P. (1988). *The impact on children's education: Television's influence on cognitive development.* Washington, DC: U.S. Department of Education.

Bachen, C. M., & Illouz, E. (1996). Imagining romance: Young people's cultural models of romance and love. *Critical Studies in Mass Communication, 13,* 297–308.

Bandura, A. (1971). *Social learning theory.* New York: General Learning Press.

Bandura, A. (1986). *Social foundations of thought and action.* Englewood Cliffs, NJ: Prentice Hall.

Bandura, A. (1997). *Self-efficacy: The exercise of control.* New York: Freeman.

Bandura, A. (2001). Social cognitive theory of mass communication. *Media Psychology, 3,* 265–299.

Baron, L., & Strauss, M. A. (1984). Sexual stratification, pornography, and rape in the United States. In N. M. Malamuth & E. Donnerstein (Eds.), *Pornography and sexual aggression* (pp. 185–209). Orlando, FL: Academic Press.

Barton, K. M. (2009). Reality television programming and divergent gratifications: The influence of content on gratifications obtained. *Journal of Broadcasting and Electronic Media, 53,* 460–476.

Beck, M. E., & Arnold, J. E. (2009). Gendered time use at home: An ethnographic examination of leisure time in middle-class families. *Leisure Studies, 28,* 121–142.

Bell, D. (1976). *The cultural contradictions of capitalism.* New York: Basic Books.

Bridge Ratings. (2007). *Bridge Ratings Youth Audience Media Use Study 2007.* Glendale, CA: Bridge Ratings. Retrieved on April 21, 2010, from http://www.bridgeratings.com/.

Brody, G. H., Stoneman, Z., & Sanders, A. (1980). Effects of television viewing on family interactions: An observational study. *Family Relations, 29,* 216–220.

Broege, N., Owens, A., Graesch, A. P., Arnold, J. E., & Schneider, B. (2007). Calibrating measures of family activities between large- and small-scale data sets. *Sociological Methodology, 37,* 119–149.

Bronfenbrenner, U. (1973). In J. Clayre (Ed.), *The impact of broadcasting.* London: Compton Russell.

Brownmiller, S. (1984, November). The place of pornography: Packaging eros for a violent age [Comments to a forum held at the New School for Social Research in New York City moderated by L. H. Lapham]. *Harper's* pp. 31–39, 42–45.

Cantor, M. G. (1990). Prime-time fathers: A study in continuity and change. *Critical Studies in Mass Communication, 7,* 275–285.

Chaffee, S. H., & Tims, A. R. (1976). Interpersonal factors in adolescent television use. *Journal of Social Issues, 32,* 98–115.

Chandra, A., Martino, S. C., Collins, R. L., Elliott, M. N., Berry, S. H., Kanouse, D. E., et al. (2008). Does watching sex on television predict teen pregnancy? Findings from a National Longitudinal Survey of Youth. *Pediatrics, 122,* 1047–1054.

Chesebro, J. W. (1979). Communication, values, and popular television series: A four-year assessment. In G. Gumpert & R. Cathcart (Eds.), *Inter/media: Interpersonal communication in a media world* (pp. 528–560). New York: Oxford University Press.

Christakis, D. A., & Zimmerman, F. J. (2009). Young children and media: Limitations of current knowledge and future directions for research. *American Behavioral Scientist, 52,* 1177–1185.

Christakis, D. A., Zimmerman, F. J., DiGiuseppe, D. L. & McCarty, C. A. (2004). Early television exposure and subsequent attentional problems in children. *Pediatrics, 113,* 708–713.

Coffin, T. (1955). Television's impact on society. *American Psychologist, 10,* 634.

Collins, R. L., Elliott, M. N., Berry, S. H., Kanouse, D. E., Kunkel, D., Hunter, S. B., et al. (2004). Watching sex on television predicts adolescent initiation of sexual behavior. *Pediatrics, 114,* 280–289.

Comstock, J., & Strzyzewski, K. (1990, Summer). Interpersonal interaction on television: Family conflict and jealousy on primetime. *Journal of Broadcasting and Electronic Media, 34*(3), 263–282.

Court, J. H. (1984). Sex and violence: A ripple effect. In N. M. Malamuth & E. Donnerstein (Eds.), *Pornography and sexual aggression* (pp. 143–172). Orlando, FL: Academic Press.

Dail, P. W., & Way, W. L. (1985). What do parents observe about parenting from prime-time television? *Family Relations, 34,* 491–499.

Elkind, D. (1993, October). Adolescents, parenting, and media in the twenty-first century. *Adolescent Medicine: State of the Art Reviews, 4,* 599–606.

Faber, R. J., Brown, J. D., & McLeod, J. M. (1979). Coming of age in the global village: Television and adolescence. In E. Wartella (Ed.), *Children communicating: Media and development of thought, speech, and understanding* (pp. 215–249). Beverly Hills, CA: Sage.

Ferris, A. L., Smith, S. W., Greenberg, B. S., & Smith, S. L. (2007). The content of reality dating shows and viewer perceptions of dating. *Journal of Communication, 57,* 490–510.

Fine, B. J. (1952). *Television and family life: A survey of two New England communities.* Boston: Boston University, School of Public Relations.

Fisher, C. (1974). Marital and familial roles on television: An exploratory sociological analysis (Doctoral dissertation, Iowa State University, 1974). *Dissertation Abstracts International, 35,* 599A.

Foley, J. M. (1968). *A functional analysis of television viewing.* Unpublished doctoral dissertation, University of Iowa.

Friedson, E. (1953). The relation of the social situation of contact to the media in mass communication. *Public Opinion Quarterly, 17,* 230–238.

Galician, M. (2004). *Sex, love, and romance in the mass media.* Hillsdale, NJ: Lawrence Erlbaum.

Geist, E. A., & Gibson, M. (2000). The effect of network and public television programs on four- and five-year-olds' ability to attend to educational tasks. *Journal of Instructional Psychology, 27,* 250–262.

Gerbner, G., Gross, L., Morgan, M., & Signorielli, N. (1980). *Media and the family: Images and impact.* Paper presented at the National Research Forum on Family Issues, White House Conference on Families, Washington, DC.

Gerbner, G., Gross, L., Morgan, M., & Signorielli, N. (1986). Living with television: The dynamics of the cultivation process. In J. Bryant & D. Zillmann (Eds.), *Perspectives on media effects.* Hillsdale, NJ: Lawrence Erlbaum.

Gitlin, T. (1972). Sixteen notes on television and the movement. In G. White & C. Newman (Eds.), *Literature in revolution* (pp. 335–366). New York: Holt, Rinehart & Winston.

Gitlin, T. (1983). *Inside prime time.* New York: Pantheon.

Greenberg, B. (1982). Television and rote socialization: An overview. In B. Pearl, L. Bouthilet, & J. Lazar (Eds.), *Television and behavior: Ten years of scientific progress and implications*

for the eighties (pp. 179–190). Washington, DC: U.S. Government Printing Office.

Greenberg, B., Atkin, C., Edison, N., & Korzenny, F. (1977). *Pro-social and anti-social behaviors on commercial television in 1976–1977* [Report by Michigan State University, Department of Communication]. Washington, DC: U.S. Office of Child Development.

Greenberg, B. S., Hines, M., Buerkel-Rothfuss, N., & Atkin, C. K. (1980). Family role structure and interactions on commercial television. In B. S. Greenberg (Ed.), *Life on television: Content analyses of U.S. TV drama* (pp. 149–160). Norwood, NJ: Ablex.

Hallin, D. C. (1992). Sound bite news: Television coverage of elections, 1968–1988. *Journal of Communication, 42,* 5–24.

Head, S. W. (1954). Content analysis of television drama programs. *Quarterly of Film, Radio, and Television, 9,* 175–194.

Heintz, K. E. (1992, Fall). Children's favorite television families: A descriptive analysis of role interactions. *Journal of Broadcasting and Electronic Media,* 443–451.

Hoffner, C. A. (2008). Parasocial and online social relationships. In S. L. Calvert & B. J. Wilson (Eds.), *Handbook of children, media, and development* (pp. 309–333). Boston, MA: Wiley-Blackwell.

Hoffner, C. A., Levine, K. J., & Toohey, R. A. (2008). Socialization to work in late adolescence: The role of television and family. *Journal of Broadcasting and Electronic Media, 52,* 282–302.

Holman, T. B., & Jacquart, M. (1988). Leisure-activity patterns and marital satisfaction: A further test. *Journal of Marriage and the Family, 50,* 69–77.

Horkheimer, M., & Adomo, T. W. (1972). The culture industry: Enlightenment as mass deception. In M. Horkheimer &. T. Adorno (Eds.), *The dialectics of enlightenment* (pp. 120–167). New York: Seabury Press.

Kaiser Family Foundation. (1999). *Kids and media at the new millennium: A comprehensive analysis of children's media use.* Menlo Park, CA: Author.

Kaiser Family Foundation. (2010). *Generation M²: Media in the lives of 8- to 18-year-olds.* Menlo Park, CA: The Henry J. Kaiser Family Foundation. Retrieved April 21, 2010, from www.kff.org.

Katz, E., & Foulkes, D. (1962). On the use of the mass media as "escape": Clarification of a concept. *Public Opinion Quarterly, 26,* 377–383.

Katz, E., & Gurevitch, M. (1976). *The secularization of leisure, culture, and communication in Israel.* Cambridge, MA: Harvard University Press.

Kubey, R. (1980). Television and aging: Past, present, and future. *Gerontologist, 20,* 16–35.

Kubey, R. (1986). Television use in everyday life: Coping with unstructured time. *Journal of Communication, 36,* 108–123.

Kubey, R. (1987, June 24). *Testimony on Senate Bill 844, 100th Congress: A television violence antitrust exemption* [Hearing before the Subcommittee on Antitrust, Monopolies, and Business Rights of the Committee on the Judiciary, U.S. Senate, Serial No. J-1OO-27]. Washington, DC: U.S. Government Printing Office.

Kubey, R. (1990). Television and family harmony among children, adolescents, and adults: Results from the experience sampling method. In J. Bryant (Ed.), *Television and the American family* (pp. 73–B8). Hillsdale, NJ: Lawrence Erlbaum.

Kubey, R. (1991, March 6). The case for media education. *Education Week, 10,* 27.

Kubey, R. (1994). Media implications for the quality of family life. In D. Zillmann, J. Bryant, & A. C. Huston (Eds.), *Media, children, and the family: Social scientific, psychodynamic, and clinical perspectives.* Hillsdale, NJ: Lawrence Erlbaum.

Kubey, R. (1996). Television dependence, diagnosis, and prevention: With commentary on video games, pornography, and media education. In T. MaeBeth (Ed.), *Tuning in to young viewers: Social science perspectives on television* (pp. 221–260). Thousand Oaks, CA: Sage.

Kubey, R., & Baker, F. (1999, October 27). Has media literacy found a curricular foothold? *Education Week, 19,* 56.

Kubey, R., & Csikszentmihalyi, M. (1990). *Television and the quality of life: How viewing shapes everyday experience.* Hillsdale, NJ: Lawrence Erlbaum.

Kunkel, D., Eyal, K., Donnerstein, E., Farrar, K. M., Biely, E., & Rideout, V. (2007). Sexual socialization messages on entertainment television: Comparing content trends 1997–2002. *Media Psychology, 9,* 595–622.

Kutchinsky, B. (1973). Eroticism without censorship. *International Journal of Criminology and Penology, 1,* 217–225.

Kwak, H., Andras, T. L., & Zinkhan, G. M. (2009). Advertising to "active" viewers: Consumer attitudes in the U.S. and South Korea. *International Journal of Advertising, 28,* 49–75.

Larson, M. S. (1991, Fall). Sibling interactions in the 1950s versus 1980s sitcoms: A comparison. *Journalism Quarterly, 68,* 381–387.

Larson, R., & Kubey, R. (1983). Television and music: Contrasting media in adolescent life. *Youth and Society, 15*, 13–31.

Larson, R., Kubey, R., & Cotletti, J. (1989). Changing channels: Early adolescent media choices and shifting investments in family and friends. *Journal of Youth and Adolescence, 18*, 583–599.

Levine, L. E., & Waite, B. M. (2000). Television viewing and attentional abilities in fourth and fifth grade children. *Journal of Applied Developmental Psychology, 21*, 667–679.

Lull, J. (1980). Family communication patterns and the social uses of television. *Communication Research, 7*, 319–334.

Lyle, J. (1972). Television in daily life: Patterns of use. In E. Rubinstein, G. Comstock, & J. Murray (Eds.), *Television and social behavior: Vol. 4. Television in day-to-day life: Patterns of use* (pp. 1–32). Washington, DC: U.S. Government Printing Office.

Maccoby, E. (1951). Television: Its impact on school children. *Public Opinion Quarterly, 15*, 421–444.

Maddi, S. R., Kobasa, S., & Hoover, M. (1979). An alienation test. *Journal of Humanistic Psychology, 19*, 73–76.

Marcuse, H. (1964). *One dimensional man.* Boston: Beacon.

Marshall, W. L. (1988). The use of sexually explicit stimuli by rapists, child molesters, and nonoffenders. *Journal of Sex Research, 25*, 267–288.

Martino, S. C., Collins, R. L., Kanouse, D. E., Elliott, M., & Berry, S. H. (2005). Social cognitive processes mediating the relationship between exposure to television's sexual content and adolescents' sexual behavior. *Journal of Personality & Social Psychology, 89*, 914–924.

McLeod. J. M., Fitzpatrick, M. A., Glynn, C. J., & Fallis, S. (1982). Television and social relations: Family influences and consequences for interpersonal behavior. In D. Pearl, L. Bouthilet, & J. Lazar (Eds.), *Television and behavior: Ten years of scientific progress and implications for the eighties* (Vol. 2, pp. 272–286). Washington, DC: U.S. Government Printing Office.

McIlwraith, R. D. (1990, August). *Theories of television addiction.* Talk given to the American Psychological Association, Boston.

Morgan, M., Leggett, S., & Shanahan, J. (1999). Television and family values: Was Dan Quayle right? *Mass Communication & Society, 2*, 47–63.

Nabi, R. L., Biely, E. N., Morgan, S. J., & Stitt, C. R. (2003). Reality-based television programming and the psychology of its appeal. *Media Psychology, 5*, 303–330.

Nabi, R. L., Stitt, C., Halford, J., & Finnerty, K. (2006). Emotional and cognitive predictors of the enjoyment of reality-based and fictional television programming: An elaboration of the uses and gratifications perspective. *Media Psychology, 8*, 421–447.

Reiss, S., & Wiltz, J. (2004). Why people watch reality TV. *Media Psychology, 6*, 363–378.

Rideout, V. J., Vandewater, E. A., & Wartella, E. A. (2003). *Zero to six: Electronic media in the lives of infants, toddlers, and preschoolers.* Menlo Park, CA: Kaiser Family Foundation.

Riley, J., Cantwell, R., & Ruttiger, K. (1949). Some observations on the social effects of television. *Public Opinion Quarterly, 13*, 223–224.

Rosenblatt, P., & Cunningham, M. (1976). Television watching and family tensions. *Journal of Marriage and the Family, 31*, 105–111.

Schrader, P. (1986). Notes on film noir. In B. K. Grant (Ed.), *Film genre reader* (pp. 170–182). Austin: University of Texas Press.

Shanahan, J., & Morgan, M. (1989). Television as a diagnostic indicator in child therapy: An exploratory study. *Child and Adolescent Social Work, 6*, 175–191.

Signorielli, N. (1982). Marital status in television drama: A case of reduced options. *Journal of Broadcasting, 26*, 585–597.

Signorielli, N. (1985). *Role portrayal and stereotyping on television: An annotated bibliography of studies relating to women, minorities, aging, sexual behavior, health, and handicaps.* Westport, CT: Greenwood.

Signorielli, N. (1991). Adolescents and ambivalence toward marriage: A cultivation analysis. *Youth and Society, 23*, 121–149.

Signorielli, N., & Gerbner, G. (1978). The image of the elderly in prime time television drama. *Generations, 3*, 10–11.

Signorielli, N., & Kahlenberg, S. (2001). Television's world of work in the nineties. *Journal of Broadcasting & Electronic Media, 45*, 4–22.

Singer, D. G., & Singer, J. L. (1998). Developing critical viewing skills and media literacy in children. In K. H. Jamison and A. B. Jordan (Eds.), *The annals* (pp. 164–179). Philadelphia, PA: American Academy of Political and Social Science.

Singer, D. G., & Singer, J. L. (2005). *Imagination and play in the electronic age.* Cambridge, MA: Harvard University Press.

Skill, T., & Wallace, S. (1990, Summer). Family interactions on primetime television: A descriptive analysis of assertive power interactions.

Journal of Broadcasting & Electronic Media, 34, 243–262.

Smith, R. (1986). Television addiction. In J. Bryant & D. Zillmann (Eds.), *Perspectives on media effects* (pp. 109–128). Hillsdale, NJ: Lawrence Erlbaum.

Smythe, D. W. (1954). Reality as presented by television. *Public Opinion Quarterly, IB,* 143–156.

Sparks, G. G., Nelson, C. L., & Campbell, R. G. (1997). The relationship between exposure to televised messages about paranormal phenomena and paranormal beliefs. *Journal of Broadcasting & Electronic Media, 41,* 345–359.

Steenland, S. (1985). *Prime time kids: An analysis of children and families on television.* Washington, DC: National Commission on Working Women.

Thompson, D. A., & Christakis, D. (2005). The association between television viewing and irregular sleep schedules among children less than 3 years of age. *Pediatrics, 116,* 851–856.

Turtiainen, P., Karvonen, S., & Rahkonen, O. (2007). All in the family? The structure and meaning of family life among young people. *Journal of Youth Studies, 10,* 477–493.

Valkenburg, P. M. (2004). *Children's responses to the screen: A media psychological approach.* Hillsdale, NJ: Lawrence Erlbaum.

Weaver, J. B. (1987). Effects of portrayals of female sexuality and violence against women on perceptions of women (Doctoral dissertation, Indiana University, Bloomington, 1988).

Dissertation Abstracts International, 48(10), 2482–A.

Weber, D. S., & Singer, D. G. (2004). The media habits of infants and toddlers: Findings from a parent survey. *Zero to Three, 25,* 30–36.

Williams, J. D. (2006). Why kids need to be bored: A case study of self-reflection and academic performance. *RMLE Online: Research in Middle Level Education, 29(5),* 1–17.

Zillmann, D. (1994). Erotica and family values. In D. Zillmann, J. Bryant, & A. C. Huston (Eds.), *Media, children, and the family: Social scientific, psychodynamic, and clinical perspectives* (pp. 199–213). Hillsdale, NJ: Lawrence Erlbaum.

Zillmann, D., & Weaver, J. B. (1989). Pornography and men's sexual callousness toward women. In D. Zillmann & J. Bryant (Eds.), *Pornography: Research advances and policy considerations* (pp. 95–125). Hillsdale, NJ: Lawrence Erlbaum.

Zimmerman, F. J., & Christakis, D. A. (2005). Children's television viewing and cognitive outcomes: A longitudinal analysis of national data. *Archives of Pediatrics and Adolescent Medicine, 159,* 619–625.

Zimmerman, F. J., Christakis, D. A., & Meltzoff, A. N. (2007). Television and DVD/video viewing in children younger than 2 years. *Archives of Pediatric & Adolescent Medicine, 161,* 473–479.

Zuromskis, C. (2007). Prurient pictures and popular film: The crisis of pornographic representation. *Velvet Light Trap, 59,* 4–14.

CHAPTER 18

Television, Children, and Multicultural Awareness

Comprehending the Medium in a Complex Multimedia Society

Joy Keiko Asamen
Pepperdine University

Gordon L. Berry
University of California, Los Angeles

A very narrow view of the fields of biology and anthropology informs us that humans are bipedal and belong to the species *Homo sapiens*. Although biology and many other scholarly disciplines understand that very early humans engaged in some forms of individual and group communication, the development of many of their speech processes is still not fully understood. It is likely, however, that complex languages only began when the Cro-Magnon group (*Homo sapiens*) appeared sometime around 40,000 years ago, give or take a few thousand years (Dennis & DeFleur, 2010). Language enabled humans to think about the past and the future, and it is the essential medium through which we share vision, knowledge, meaning, and identity (Potts & Sloan, 2010).

What we do know is that the modern-day offspring of the early humans use many forms of communication processes represented by sophisticated language, speech, and technically based devices as the foundation for transmitting a variety of culturally diverse beliefs and ideas about themselves and others. Equally important, the various types of communication devices created today are overtly and, at times, imperceptibly at the

core of the socialization processes so important to developing children in society today. These are the same children who are growing and developing in an ever-changing multimedia and broadly based multicultural world.

This chapter is conceptualized through a type of multicultural prism where many of the principles of child development and self-identity are discussed within a framework of group portrayals that are communicated through the medium of television and a host of related media. Selected principles of child development, the perspectives of multicultural thought, and the power of television to provide role models all converge in this chapter to show how they affect the teaching and learning of children. This means that much of the psychosocial development of children is taking place today just as some of the past and present print and electronic media, many of which grew out of the medium of television, are also converging to create a set of dynamic technical platforms that will contain images and portrayals of cross-cultural and intercultural content. Through the same prism, the foci of this chapter are also on an examination of research and evaluation paradigms employed to understand both the positive and negative impact of television content in a world of converging media and its implications for the multicultural attitudes of developing children and early adolescents in an ever-changing, culturally diverse society.

The converging media and the transformations taking place in society due to the rapid advancements in the types of technologies that produce new forms and ways of communicating are not make-believe *Star Wars*- or *Avatar*-type cinematic images. Nor are the changing technologies simply metaphors that tend to illustrate and stimulate new ways of thinking about a changing society. We are simply, in the world and the United States, shaping vast and interlocking multimedia systems that will not only increase new scientific knowledge but also drive popular culture. Our challenges from the present and emerging technologies that are fueling the advances in new forms of electronic and print media are not based on whether we—the men, women, and children—can cognitively process, interpret, absorb, and handle them.

Rather, a part of the challenge turns on whether we, as a people, can exploit these new multimedia and communication reservoirs so that they can be a source of supply for creating informed citizens and the needed elements of social capital for building and maintaining a more just, humane, and civil society. These challenges from a media-rich environment are also coming at a time when American society is going through a social transformation in terms of a shifting demographic landscape that will ultimately define the country's cultural and ethnic makeup.

Television and Its Multimedia Relatives in a Changing Multicultural Society

The nexus involving our emerging technologies and multimedia with the changing multicultural landscape of the country offers both opportunities and challenges. Among the opportunities is the potential for the new technologies to foster a greater understanding and civil dialogue about cultural pluralism that is at the heart of a culturally diverse country. This type of diversity recognizes that the multicultural landscape in the country has changed through the impact of present immigration and differential fertility rates (Chisman, 1998; Stantrock, 2007). That is to say, as we move into the 21st century, one-third of all school-age children fall into the category of being African American, Latino, Native American, and Asian American. If this present trend continues, projections indicate that there will be more Latino children and adolescents in the United States than non-Hispanic White children and adolescents (Stantrock, 2007). For example, in some states, Latinos represent a significant presence, and a recent estimate concluded that 1 out of every 5 people who reside in the states of Arizona, California, Texas, and New Mexico speaks Spanish (Liang, Salcedo, Rivera, & Lopez, 2009). The diversification of the United States can be seen more dramatically by data showing that the population is increasingly

aging, people with disabling conditions and special needs are rightfully seeking more opportunities, and women represent one of the growing groups entering the labor force, as well as the colleges and universities (Berry, 2008). Thus, it is safe to say that urban and rural life, media, business, and the schools have been influenced by the level of ethnic diversity present in the United States (Maton, Kohout, Wicherski, Leary, & Vinokurov, 2006).

The changing demographics of the country toward a new type of landscape mean that our educational, religious, political, economic, and familial institutions will need to be oriented to reach out to and understand a type of cultural diversity at the very foundation of the belief system of a people, a worldview requiring

> (a) a central consciousness of diversity and global citizenship; (b) an attitude of inclusion; (c) an assumption that difference is not deviance but is to be valued, honored, and affirmed; (d) a view of people of all cultures as fully human with dignity and the right to self-determination; (e) an awareness of social and economic asymmetries that confer privilege based on social location; and (f) a belief in the power of the independencies and interconnectedness across cultures. (Harrell & Gallardo, 2008, pp. 115–16)

The perspectives put forth by Harrell and Gallardo suggest that a number of social, economic, and political characteristics are associated with multicultural beliefs and practices. Within this framework, it is important for students of behavior and others to understand the value of openness to cultural beliefs. This does not mean, however, that some cross-cultural views are immune from commentary, analysis, and scholarly review.

Multicultural, *cross-cultural*, *cultural diversity*, and *cultural pluralism*, while they have some differences in terms of their strict meanings, are used interchangeably in this chapter. These terms are used with a full recognition that the issues associated with the broad notions of multiculturalism as an ideal or a concept are not foreign to our thinking or our history because they involve the ability to recognize, understand, and appreciate the cross-cultural

nature of American society. And yet, American society is not unique in its concerns and struggles over multicultural ideals, principles, and goals. Within the framework of understanding and appreciating the scope of multicultural communities, we believe that they should represent individuals of diverse backgrounds, including age, appearance, class, disabilities, ethnicity/race, gender, national origin, political views, religion/spirituality, and sexual orientation (Council of Counseling Psychology Training Programs, Association of Counseling Center Training Agencies, and Society of Counseling Psychology, 2009).

Some of the classic work in multicultural thought has been advanced by Derald Wing Sue and others as they tried to evolve both philosophical and working definitions for this dynamic and complicated concept. While Sue and colleagues (1998) offered what are now early concepts of multiculturalism, its characteristics are still timely and have scholarly vigor today:

1. Multiculturalism values cultural pluralism and acknowledges our nation as a cultural mosaic rather than a melting pot. It teaches the valuing of diversity rather than negation or even toleration.

2. Multiculturalism is about social justice, cultural democracy, and equity. It is consistent with the democratic ideals of the Declaration of Independence, the U.S. Constitution, and the Bill of Rights. Although these documents have been intended for only an elite few at our nation's birth, multiculturalism seeks to actualize these ideals for all groups.

3. Multiculturalism is about helping all of us to acquire the attitudes, knowledge, and skills needed to function effectively in a pluralistic democratic society and to interact, negotiate, and communicate with peoples from diverse backgrounds.

4. Multiculturalism is reflected in more than just race, class, gender, and ethnicity. It also includes diversity in religion, national origin, sexual orientation, ability and disability, age, geographic origin, and so forth.

5. Multiculturalism is about celebrating the realistic contributions and achievements of our and other cultures. It also involves our willingness to explore both the positive

and negative aspects of our group's behavior over time. It appreciates the complexity of lived experience.

6. Multiculturalism is an essential component of analytical thinking. It is not about advocating an orthodoxy or dogma, but rather about challenging us to study multiple cultures, to develop multiple perspectives, and to teach our children how to integrate broad and conflicting bodies of information to arrive at sound judgments.

7. Multiculturalism respects and values other perspectives, but is not value neutral. It involves an activist orientation and a commitment to change social conditions that deny equal access and opportunities (social justice).

8. Multiculturalism means "change" at the individual, organizational, and societal levels. It encourages us to begin the process of developing new theories, practices, policies, and organizational structures that are more responsive to all groups.

9. Multiculturalism may mean owning up to painful realities about oneself, our group, and our society. It may involve tension, discomfort, and must include a willingness to honestly confront and work through potentially unpleasant conflicts.

10. Multiculturalism is about positive individual, community, and societal outcomes because it values inclusion, cooperation, and movement toward mutually shared goals. (pp. 5–6)

Recent researchers in the field of counseling psychology emphasized the vitality of the early work by Sue and his colleagues by pointing out that this discipline must be rooted in the ideals, principles, and philosophical beliefs that multiculturalism is about social justice and cultural diversity (DeBlaere, Brewster, Sarkees, & Moradi, 2010; Leung & Chen, 2009). Jean Lau Chin (2010) suggests that the social justice movements of the 20th century (e.g., the women's, civil rights, and gay pride movements) ushered in a commitment to cultural diversity in our nation's institutions and communities. She further suggested that research in psychology requires a paradigm shift so that it will not remain silent on the issues of equity, diversity, and social

justice (Chin, 2010). Moreover, Beverly Greene (2009) argues that the present discourse in psychology and other fields needs to move beyond a focus on ethnoracial issues and concerns of people of color as the core to multicultural and diversity studies to include a broader definition of the construct to include issues of age, class, disabilities, gender, religion/spirituality, and sexual orientation, as well as other socially marginalized groups.

While technically everyone in a pluralistic society is multicultural to some degree, our broad-based focus looks at this complicated issue using as our reference racial/ethnic, religious, gender/women, social class, the elderly, and individuals with disabilities, as well as gay, lesbian, bisexual, and transgender groups. Recognizing the difficulties inherent in the scope of this multicultural perspective, however, we will tend to focus on the media and women and ethnic/racial groups. We would also include under the multicultural umbrella the emerging immigrant groups and new Americans who are a part of the country and who bring with them their special religions and languages, as well as some established White Americans of the underclass. These are, we would argue, the groups of people who have often been excluded, misrepresented, victimized, and marginalized in our society. Thus, placing groups and cross-cultural concepts in perspective, it is safe to say that multicultural studies aim to promote social justice, understanding, inclusion, affirmation, and harmony in a pluralistic world (Fowers & Davidov, 2006; Greene, 2009).

The challenges that arise between an emerging multimedia environment and that of the dynamic changes in cultural diversity are related, in part, to the ability of the country to maintain its First Amendment media-related creative freedoms while understanding the role, power, and responsibilities of the new technologies. To understand the multicultural context of this chapter means to be mindful of the historical and present-day cultural images, cultural representations, and stereotypic hegemonic presentations that have, at times, purposely and unfairly characterized many of the ethnic, gender, religious, class, and social role portrayals in the electronic and print media. To understand from a

multimedia perspective is to comprehend the roles that various media presently play or can play in a democratic society. These media, for the purpose of our discussion, are broadcast television, cable television, radio, recorded music, advertising through these various media, Internet services, World Wide Websites, direct-broadcast satellite services, video and electronic games, and other emerging forms of mass communication. Dennis and DeFleur (2010) classified selected media using the following three areas: (a) publishing to include books, magazines, and newspapers; (b) film to principally include motion pictures; and (c) electronic media, which was represented mainly by radio, television, and several associated forms such as cable television and DVDs. Levinson (2009) uses the term *new new media* to include what is generally known as social media. These social media utilize written words as the primary mode of communication, such as blogging, MySpace, Facebook, Twitter, and others. These new media and emerging technologies are also capable of having individuals and groups create messages, images, and audio tracks that can carry cross-cultural content from which positive and negative concepts are learned. Kevin Clark (2008), drawing on past research, notes that technology can successfully support the multicultural development of children by helping them become familiar with the traditions of their own culture, increase their awareness of self and self in relation to others, and foster empathy for others through the recognition of similarities and an appreciation of differences.

While this chapter uses television as a primary medium of focus, it is clear that it has been the doorway through which some of the so-called new media have stepped. Young children, drawing on the common experiences of television and their media-rich environment, can simply move into the new phase of their technological learning process and absorb the cross-cultural and multicultural content available to them.

All of the new and emerging technologies that are creating our multimedia environment will continue to have profound psychosocial effects on the multicultural understanding of children and adults in this country and the world. Of all of the various types of media, it is the medium of television that will, in one form or another, continue to exercise a major influence related to the way we see ourselves and others in a growing culturally diverse country. Indeed, the entire digital revolution, which is a part of television, only symbolizes the new wave of power and influence of this medium. Digital television can deliver high-definition pictures and CD-quality audio to create a true home theater. Telecasters, through digital technology, are able to target specific messages to different individual receivers and send audio, video, and text simultaneously (Dennis & DeFleur, 2010; Firestone & Garner, 1998).

The medium of television revolutionized the way the world has been entertained and informed. Television is also the connecting link to other technologies that have emerged and those planned for the future. Even with the emergence of the new media, however, television viewing continues to dominate media consumption (Rideout, Foehr, & Roberts, 2010). Kubey (2007) noted that people throughout the industrialized world typically devote about 3 hours a day to watching television and, in many societies, this easily constitutes half of all a person's leisure time. For 8- to 18-year-old young people in the United States, television continues to dominate their media diets, averaging 2 hours 39 minutes a day for regularly scheduled programming watched on a television set, plus another 1 hour 50 minutes a day that is either recorded or watched on such other platforms as computers, DVDs, cell phones, or iPods, for a total of 4 hours 29 minutes of television content in a day (Rideout et al., 2010). Rideout and colleagues (2010) of the Kaiser Family Foundation reported some demographic differences in television viewing that we felt were important to cite here because of the gender, age, and ethnic elements associated with features of this chapter. In their research, they found that media exposure per day was higher among boys than girls by about an hour, primarily due to console video games; youth in the 11- to 18-year-old age range were higher than children 8 to 10 years old by about 8 hours; and Black and Hispanic youth were higher than White youth by nearly 4.5 hours. The Kaiser Family Foundation research demonstrates the

ubiquitous nature and power of television as well as its ability to still engage young people who live in a multimedia environment where audiovisual and technical devices compete for their time, attitudes, beliefs, and values.

Television, Developing Children, and Learning in a Multicultural and Multimedia Society

A variety of publics associated with television and other electronic media express a great many concerns related to their positive and negative impact on young viewers. Most of the concerns have been, of course, about the perceived negative effects on children related to whether the nature of the content had the ability to influence attitudes, values, violent behavior, and learning. Clearly, it is not inconsistent or surprising that the established and emerging media forms would attract so much attention from adults. After all, adults are charged with the socialization of the young, and the medium of television and its emerging multimedia relatives deserve detailed analysis and constructive criticism— the type of constructive criticism and analysis one would give to any social force that intrudes into the socialization process of children and wraps its messages and content around the core of their psychosocial thought. As Firestone and Garmer (1998) suggested a number of years ago, one is hard pressed to think of any other common experience that binds Americans together more than television, with its pervasive reach into both the American home and its psyche.

Television is, by itself, also a natural medium of concern because few, if any, social scientists, broadcasters, educators, parents, and child advocacy groups would deny the ability of its content to teach. The developing child can be uniquely susceptible to the power and presence of the characters and images and the accompanying formal features that serve to highlight television's content. Fact or fiction, real or unreal, television programs create cognitive and affective environments that describe and portray people, places, and things that carry profound general and specific cross-cultural learning experiences for the child and early adolescent who is growing and developing in a media-rich digital age.

Television, as a part of this digital age, remains a major player in the sociopsychological attitudinal equation that helps to decide how the young people in U.S. society acquire, process, interpret, and act toward the cross-cultural portrayals and social roles of people that are culturally similar to and different from them. A key phrase in the previous sentence is *helps to decide* because we take the position that the child is not simply an observer when looking at television or merely a passenger on the "digital highway" but a cognitively active viewer and participant when engaged in television and related audiovisual media forms.

The digital age, with its new forms of media, just as with television, will carry into the future many of their distinctive features that will play a role in the types of learning experiences provided to young viewers. For example, we know from the research that television derives some of its distinctiveness for children and adolescents because of its ability to combine pictures, print, sound (speech), sound effects, music, and simply the range and kinds of programming it is able to make available (Berry, 2003). Equally important, the use of formal features such as pacing, zooms, and action sequences all can interact with program content to influence children's attention, comprehension, and interpretation (Huston, Brickham, Lee, & Wright, 2007).

The distinctiveness of the medium of television and the special ways in which it might advance gender, multiethnic, and cross-cultural images and portrayals becomes important because of the cognitive activity generated by the viewer when processing the audiovisual elements of televised content. That is, children watching television acquire a certain amount of practice and familiarity with the structure and form of the medium that makes it continually easier for them to master and process its audiovisual conventions or principles. Indeed, as children

develop, both the amount and content of their television viewing habits change; their cognitive abilities, structural elements in their lives, and personal preferences combine to determine the duration of viewing and program choices (Huston et al., 2007). All of these factors combine to suggest that the more viewers participate in the audiovisual environment of television and the older they get, the greater their ease in learning and processing the content from the medium. When the content being processed is related to cross-cultural themes, researchers are not always clear how children acquire social attitudes, stereotypical beliefs, and prejudices related to race and gender. Social scientists have known for some time, however, that children learn social, racial, and religious prejudices in the course of observing and being influenced by the existence of patterns in the culture in which they live (Berry, 2007; Chin, 2010; Graves, 2008). Huston and colleagues (2007) addressed the child's culture and her or his television viewing patterns by seeing them within the ecological context of the family, and this is, in turn, affected by the social and cultural institutions surrounding the family.

Researchers have, over the years, also become interested in what happens as people learn by watching or observing others. This line of inquiry, pioneered by Albert Bandura and originally called observation learning, is also known today as social cognitive theory (Bandura, 1986; Schultz & Schultz, 2009). Social cognitive theory is important to our discussion of how and what cross-cultural attitudes young viewers acquire from television, because central to this concept is the idea that people learn through interacting with and observing each other. The primary mechanism in this process is modeling, and this refers to changes in people that result from observing the actions of others. As an illustration of how mass media can influence us, Dennis and DeFleur (2010) noted the following:

> These [depictions] can show ways of speaking, smoking, relating to members of the opposite sex, dressing, walking, or virtually any form of meaningful action. These depictions can serve as "models" of behavior that can be imitated, and people who see such actions depicted may adopt them as part of their own behavior repertoire. (p. 366)

Acquiring a repertoire of behavior can even be learned through vicarious reinforcement by observing the actions and behavior of others and anticipating the reward for behaving in the same way (Schultz & Schultz, 2009). In this connection with acquiring the behavior of the model, three factors that influence modeling are: the model's characteristics, the observer's characteristics, and the behavior's reward consequences (Schultz & Schultz, 2009). Indeed, the models that individuals create in their minds from television and various forms of media, the family, and the peer group, as well as educational and religious institutions, help them to process information about people, places, and things they encounter in real life (Berger, 2009; Feldman, 2007; Murray, 1993). They can even use these models to process information about people and cultural groups with whom they have had little or no contact except through the various media and other forms of popular culture. Thus, one small part of the complicated cognitive processing matrix relates to a number of stored categories, bits of information, and images that assist the learner in understanding her or his environment. These stored categories and bits of information are referred to as schemas. Although there can be some disagreement among specialists in learning theory as to their meaning, schemas can be seen as complex knowledge structures that serve as guides for action, mental plans, and cognitive frameworks for the interpretation of information (Myers, 2010; Reber, Allen, & Reber, 2009).

Television and other media can play a role in the development of schemas, especially for children and early adolescents. Brickman, Rhodes, and Bushman (2007) noted that schemas are thought to be formed by repeated exposure to consistent information, and traditional messages about gender and ethnic stereotypes can cause young viewers to develop faulty attitudes. These same three researchers pointed out that schemas serve as

a type of shortcut during the processing of information, and they do so through the following processes:

> (a) guide attention by orienting individuals toward information that is relevant to them; (b) processing, by providing a framework for understanding information in a way that is consistent with prior beliefs; and, (c) remembering, by providing a link with information already stored in memory. (Brickman et al., 2007, p. 733)

Schemas can also guide the behavior of a child. One type of schema is a script. Scripts involve a process of sequencing activities and plans as the individual goes about solving problems (Ciccarelli & White, 2009; Eggen & Kauchak, 1997). Scripts as a type of schema, we would argue, also can play a part in the way in which individuals perceive the ethnic, gender, social class, and religious social roles of others they experience in their daily activities and in the multimedia world.

The concept of social roles, naturally, comes into play at this point in our discussion of the impact of various media on the multicultural views of the child and developing adolescent. Social roles, in this context, are based on the principle that each individual tends to occupy or is perceived to be in a position in groups to which she or he belongs, and other people tend to behave and agree on certain expectations concerning her or his behavior (Adler & Rodman, 2009). Social psychologists would, for example, suggest that the position the individual occupies is termed her or his social role, and the attitudes and behaviors associated with that category are termed role expectations or role behaviors. Social roles become important whether you select the social descriptors yourself or have them thrust on you. Any social system can be viewed as a group of roles where they are defined by reference to others, related roles, or counterpositions and the rights and obligations that each role possesses in the social system (Berry, 2007; Goldenson, 1994). A social role can also be more or less a set of stereotypes if a person is expected by others to act or perform a certain way in a given social situation. There are, to be sure,

general and specific social-role attitude consequences that children can acquire from portrayals on television and other forms of the media. Berry (2007), drawing on some of the early work of Blocher (1987), identified four kinds of assumptions that can cause television and other audiovisual media program content to reflect systematic negative social role portrayals. These assumptions are the following: (a) "social pathology or deviance" that condemns a given culture as the root of its own problems, (b) "social disorganization" that explains differences between majority and minority groups as due to failure within the minority group, (c) "cultural deficit" that accounts for differences between majority and minority cultures as due to deficiencies in the heritage of the minority group members, and (d) "genetic deficiency" that explains intellectual differences between cultural groups as due to genetics (Berry, 2007, pp. 94–95). These four assumptions reflected in social role portrayals, when coupled with attractive models that actually perform certain actions and behaviors, are potentially able to alter cognitions, aspirations, expectations, and beliefs (Asamen & Berry, 2003; Comstock & Scharrer, 2005). Faulty social-role understandings can be especially troublesome for children and maturing adolescents who have limited experiences and are in the process of developing a type of worldview about themselves and others.

It is the world of television today and its vast new multimedia spin-offs of tomorrow from which developing children construct a part of their positive and negative attitudes about people and cultures that are similar to and different from their own. Glaubke and Miller (2008) suggested that parents and caregivers should actively search for media content for their children's early preschool years that offers quality portrayals of a diverse and multicultural array of characters and contexts. Acceptable multicultural content would include culturally diverse characters engaged in diverse occupations, cast characters of color in nonstereotypical roles and leading roles, and portray a more balanced view of racial/ethnic group members. More acceptable and balanced racial/ethnic portrayals become important when we note

what some researchers have found related to the attitudes that can be formed by children who watch television programs. For example, a national study involving 1,200 children aged 10 to 17 conducted by the policy organization Children Now (1998) found that across all races, children were more likely to associate positive characteristics with White characters (e.g., having lots of money and being well educated), and negative characteristics with minority characters (e.g., breaking the law and acting goofy). These points were reinforced in later work by Graves (2008), with the general conclusion that television does influence the racial knowledge, attitudes, and behavior of children as a result of stereotyping in some ethnic portrayals in programs.

Television is the medium that authorizes the people and ideas it selects to advance on the screen. It is also the springboard for other media in the present and future because it learned very early how to tell stories, show pictures, select popular characters, and provide sound from screens of various sizes. We know that what children can learn from the content and formal features of television, and the new or emerging media will depend on an entire range of psychosocial and developmental factors that converge to comprise what will eventually be their cross-cultural attitudes and worldview. Realizing the complicated nature and unanswered issues about child and adolescent learning patterns related to race, ethnicity, class, religion, gender, disabilities, age, and other misrepresented social roles, we have thus far argued that, when they are distorted or inaccurate, television can potentially harm the social development of children. We are also aware that there is some evidence that television and other media, with the appropriately crafted content, can assist children toward a better level of cross-cultural understanding. One of the best ways to summarize the impact of television and other media on developing children and our culture is to quote an early but classic statement from Douglas Kellner (1995). Kellner wrote the following:

> Radio, television, film and other products of media culture provide materials out of which we forge our very identities, our sense of selfhood; our notion of what it means to be male and female; our sense of class, of ethnicity and race, of nationality, or sexuality of "us" and "them." (p. 5)

Television, we argue, has made important and attractive audiovisual footprints through which other media have stepped as they supplied both overt and subtle stimuli from which developing children and adolescents can craft messages as a part of their processes of learning. In order to better understand some of the evidence related to the ability of television and some of the related media to teach children to learn about their multicultural world, we will now explore some of the research paradigms that might serve to address these issues.

Research Paradigms for Studying Complex Multimedia Questions in a Multicultural Society

Studying how television and other media forms influence the social behavior and worldview of developing children who interact with these media has challenged social scientists for over half a century. Research that targets the nexus of multimedia and multicultural considerations in the development of children raises unique methodological issues that bear reflection. For example, Hunt and James (2008) argue that our understanding of children of color and media is divided between those studies that focus on the "effects" of watching television and studies that examine how children make meaning of their viewing encounters. By not bringing together the findings gained from both these types of studies, our knowledge of children of color and media "is riddled with theoretical, methodological, and empirical gaps" (Hunt & James, 2008, p. 369). In other words, it is important to take into account the interaction between the message and the viewer of the message to fully comprehend what children learn from their television encounters about race/ethnicity, gender, and other cultural considerations.

For the most part, social scientists divide research methods into two philosophical camps, positivistic/postpositivistic and phenomenological/interpretive, also known broadly as quantitative and qualitative methods, respectively. The former includes a range of methodological exemplars such as experimental and quasiexperimental designs in which the researcher manipulates conditions to discern their effects to descriptive or observational models in which the researcher studies the nature of variables or the associations among variables. Typically, these investigations involve the collection of quantitative data for which value is based on achieving statistical significance. In contrast, the qualitative researcher is rooted in a constructivist perspective that is mindful of the social context in which participants exist in order to understand their behavior, what Anderson (1998) refers to as "hermeneutic empiricism" (p. 206). That is to say, the reality constructed by the participant to explain her or his behavior takes salience over the researcher's hypotheses about the participant's behavior. Examples of methods in this camp include case study, ethnography, critical studies, cultural studies, phenomenological and ethnomethodological research, and textual analysis.

Researchers tend to lean either in the direction of being predominately postpositivists or constructivists in their preferred research paradigm, depending on what they value in research, how they view the nature of reality and knowledge, and their methodological preferences in conducting research. But today, as the merger of the quantitative and qualitative perspectives is viewed as complementary rather than incompatible, the "purist" approach to conducting research has less of a hold on the research enterprise while engaging in mixed-methods investigations is gaining in popularity. In other words, the assets that each perspective brings to the investigation enhance both the scientific validity and contextual relevance of the study results. The merits of engaging in the use of mixed methods for studying the development of children and the related multicultural concepts have been deemed vital by a number of researchers (Leong, Qin, & Huang, 2008). An excellent illustration of this methodological

integration is a media study by D. Singer, J. Singer, and Bellin (2008) in which they collected both quantitative and qualitative data from samples of low-income, preschool-age children who were predominately African American and Latino and their parents, teachers, and home care providers to assess the efficacy of the *Magic Story Car* program that uses electronic media to foster emergent literacy skills. Outcome was recorded using three instruments that generated ratings of emergent literacy skills, frequency of engagement with the program games, and ratings of program usefulness, while qualitative data were collected through focus groups conducted with the adult participants. These data were then analyzed and triangulated to derive the study findings.

Still another research paradigm that is less discussed but worthy of inclusion and certainly relevant to the study of children, media, and multiculturalism is what Mertens (2010) refers to as transformative. Methodologically, this paradigm might approach inquiry through the use of qualitative, quantitative, or mixed methods, but it is distinguished from postpositivists and constructivists along axiological, ontological, and epistemological grounds (Mertens, 2010). The philosophical underpinnings of a transformative paradigm go beyond the participant's construction of reality, although different versions of reality are acknowledged, but reality is based on the interplay of one's construction within the context of an oppressive power structure that privileges some members of society while marginalizing others. Researchers who subscribe to a transformative paradigm emphasize the importance of both social and historical contexts in designing, conducting, and interpreting their study findings, which are certainly relevant considerations for understanding the influence of media within a multicultural context.

When the desire is to understand what and how developing children learn about themselves and others from media, collaboration among social scientists from diverse research perspectives, we propose, is the most efficacious means of furthering our current understanding. On one hand, there are clearly some generalizations that can be applied to all children, regardless of their ethnicity,

gender, religion, social class, and physical condition. It is in this arena that quantitative research paradigms excel. On the other hand, we must also acknowledge that there does not exist a "universal" child; therefore, understanding a child within her or his socio-cultural context is also relevant to our understanding of how children process the values and images portrayed on television and its media relatives. The need for conducting studies that result in contextually relevant findings favors the qualitative research paradigms. The integration of knowledge gained from the perspective of postpositivists and constructivists ensures our forward movement in media research.

We propose a schema for achieving the integration of knowledge to which we refer by delineating some philosophical dimensions along which we believe researchers are guided in their inquiry process, whether consciously or unconsciously. These philosophical dimensions include: (a) etic and emic, (b) reality and relativity, and (c) objective and relational. These dimensions, if taken as opposites, tend to fall into a quantitative–qualitative dichotomy, but we advance the notion that the dichotomy can be dispensed with in favor of "research pluralism." Rather than an "either/ or" standpoint, we propose to view research from an "and" perspective. Like cultural pluralism, we believe research pluralism allows us to achieve wholeness by drawing on the strengths of diverse perspectives to arrive at answers to complex multimedia questions that challenge social scientists in a multicultural society.

Etic and emic. Berry (2008) argues the need for a "sociocultural narrative" that considers both the emic and the etic (p. xxii)—that is to say, what knowledge is unique to a culture (emic) versus knowledge that is universal and cuts across cultures (etic). Researchers are making a similar decision depending on the favored research paradigm. Quantitative researchers strive for generalizability that favors a more etic-oriented research philosophy, while qualitative researchers endeavor to particularize over generalize, which is clearly more emic in its orientation. We maintain that etic and emic perspectives need

to be preserved in conducting multimedia research that serves the needs of children from culturally diverse walks of life. An illustration of the importance of the etic and the emic comes out of the work of Christenson and ter Bogt (2008) on the implications of popular music usage among youth. In discussing the crossover popularity of music between racial/ ethnic groups and nationalities, these researchers make the point that "the motivations, the meaning, and the impact" of music preferences differ for groups of listeners. In other words, youth globally are "border crossing" in their music preferences, but personal meaning is particular to the listener.

When we rely solely on what is universal rather than balance what surfaces as typical against that which is unique, we run the risk of propagating ethnocentric notions that are then used to guide decisions that potentially devalue rather than celebrate multiculturalism. We believe the enlightened researcher who studies multimedia phenomena and their pervasive influence on our diverse society and world would consider the contributions of both etic and emic perspectives in the design of her or his own study. To not balance the etic and emic, we maintain, is to act with a type of methodological narrowness that limits cultural awareness.

Reality and relativity. When research paradigms are generically described, we often see the description of "one reality" when characterizing quantitative research, while the existence of "multiple realities" is used to describe qualitative research (Creswell, 2007; Mertens, 2010). From the quantitative perspective, the researcher selects the variables to study, proposes a hypothesis as to the nature of the relationship for the variables selected, designs a study that tests the hypothesized relationship that controls for environmental influences and participant variability that may confound the study results, and moves from data collection to data analysis to interpretation. This description implies that there is a single reality, that of the researcher, that explains what might be observed among study participants. If the researcher has been thoughtful about issues of validity in the design and execution of the investigation and finds statistically significant

results, a compelling argument can be made for supporting the researcher's reality.

A qualitative researcher, on the other hand, looks at phenomena holistically by allowing the participants themselves to identify the salient variables rather than imposing what she or he believes is important on the participants. Furthermore, the researcher is as interested, perhaps even more so, in generating hypotheses as in testing hypotheses and is not wanting to disturb the natural context in which the participants exist so that what is observed preserves the integrity of the participants' own life experiences. Data collection-analysis-interpretation, as a package, is dialectical, not linear, so until "theoretical saturation" is achieved, the cycle does not come to an end. The presence of participant input is evident throughout the course of this type of investigation. What results moves away from that which is typical to reflect the diverse social constructions that exist in a culturally diverse society. To further superimpose a transformative perspective takes into account the societal and historical contexts that intersect with and influence the construction of participants.

A socially responsible multimedia researcher values the contribution of both reality *and* relativity when designing and conducting studies in a multicultural context. The value placed on television as a medium of entertainment and an educational tool is a reality, with a vast majority of American households owning television sets, and it is a reality that television influences behavior and attitude formation of children, including intergroup interactions and racial/ethnic attitudes about self and others (Graves, 2008). We have a number of quantitative investigations that have supported these observations. But how and why the medium is so influential is best studied by taking into account the full range of contexts that influence the development of children. In other words, to understand how children understand their media consumption, one must consider the interplay of their needs, activities, and behaviors in which they engage in their media encounters and the people who are present during these encounters (Hunt & James, 2008). Based on the complex interplay of these elements and the fact that no two

children are the same, we maintain that a balance between what is real and what is relative is essential to the study of children in a multicultural and multimedia world.

Objective and relational. In quantitative investigations, the researcher strives for a dispassionate relationship with the study participants. The researcher controls the experimental setting, manipulates the experience of the participants, and defines and measures behavior using objective forms of measurement. Emphasis is placed on the value of impartiality achieved through minimizing contact between researcher and participants. There is a great deal of wisdom in taking this rigorous approach in the design and execution of research studies. Eliminating counterinterpretations makes a stronger case for a precise cause–effect relationship. If the researcher remains in the background, less criticism may result as to the unintentional (or intentional) influence she or he might have exerted over the participants, hence threatening the validity of the study.

In comparison, qualitative researchers embrace the investigator–participant "interactive link" (Mertens, 2010, p. 11), and the researcher becomes still another aspect of the cultural context inhabited by study participants. It is explicitly acknowledged that the researcher holds some level of influence over the study participants, and this potential influence is factored into the design and execution of the study. With this method of study, researchers can obtain a more profound understanding of the thoughts, beliefs, and feelings of study participants. The relationship that has developed between researcher and participant allows the researcher access to information about the participant that might be otherwise off limits if the researcher was to maintain a more objective, aloof demeanor during data collection. This research approach certainly opens the researcher up to criticisms regarding the validity of her or his study. To counter these criticisms, verification or confirmatory procedures (e.g., triangulation of data, multiple sources of evidence) are introduced into the design of qualitative studies to contend with these potential threats.

We hold that a responsible multimedia researcher who is studying phenomena in a

multicultural context integrates both objective *and* relational perspectives into the design of her or his research study. The rigor of research paradigms that emphasize objectivity in combination with the richness of research paradigms that are relational in nature allows us to understand what a person might think, believe, and feel as well as why she or he thinks, believes, and feels this way. We know children learn about themselves and others from television and its electronic kin (Clark, 2008; Graves, 2008; Kelley, 2008; Thomas, Day, & Ward, 2008), but we also want to know how television might be used to encourage children to behave in a prosocial manner or to adopt a worldview that embraces diversity rather than tolerating, fearing, or denying its existence.

Children in a Multicultural and Multimedia Society: Future Perspectives

This chapter began with a series of concepts that argued about the important role television and the emerging media serve and will serve in a postmodern society and world in which multiculturalism plays a significant role. An impressive assemblage of electronic and print media has the potential to carry messages and images that can shape the worldview of developing children. Television and its electronic kin of the future can influence children's values and beliefs about the nature of equality, equity, and social justice through what journalists report, what network executives choose to air, what fictional characters and assumptions about human existence writers invent, and the games computer programmers design. These highly attractive communication vehicles set the psychosocial context for the multicultural views many children and adolescents will hold as they grow and develop.

Our chapter argues forcibly that television and other media have contributed toward the negative perception of the social contribution made by ethnic minorities, women, religious groups, social and economic groups, and a variety of other cultural groups, especially for those individuals who do not have access to or are unwilling to seek diverse experiences in their lives. These inaccurate representations can become a part of the individual's schema about others and could result in serving as the basis for faulty beliefs about others, prejudiced thinking, and subtle and not-so-subtle stereotypes. We also hope that we have successfully balanced our reservations about these media with the important contribution television and other media forms have made to communicating positive multicultural views and building cultural bridges. We must recognize the benefit developing and growing children have derived from these electronic tools. To further complicate our understanding of the power and potential of television and other media as purveyors of both positive and negative views, we must be mindful of how a child's development influences her or his learning experience and the acquisition of social role understanding.

As we continue to strive for answers to questions about how television and other electronic media influence the values and beliefs of developing children, we are also faced with electronic "concepts" that we have yet to experience. With the ever-changing demographics of our society that parallel the fast pace with which we are being introduced to new forms of technology, social scientists are facing a significant challenge in both the identification of issues and the best approach to seeking resolutions for these issues. We have proposed that socially responsible researchers need to be pluralistic in their research approach to meet the demands of our rapidly changing multicultural and multimedia society.

References

Adler, R. B., & Rodman, G. (2009). *Understanding human communication.* New York: Oxford University Press.

Anderson, J. A. (1998).Qualitative approaches to the study of the media: Theory and methods of hermeneutic empiricism. In J. K. Asamen & G. L. Berry (Eds.), *Research paradigms, television, and social behavior* (pp. 205–236). Thousand Oaks, CA: Sage.

Asamen, J. K., & Berry, G. L. (2003). The multicultural worldview of children through the lens of

television. In E. L. Palmer & B. M. Young (Eds.), *The faces of televisual media teaching, violence, selling to children* (pp. 107–123). Mahwah, NJ: Lawrence Erlbaum.

Bandura, A. (1986). *Social foundations of thought and action: A social cognitive theory.* Upper Saddle River, NJ: Prentice Hall.

Berger, K. S. (2009). *The developing person through childhood and adolescence.* New York: Worth.

Berry, G. L. (2003). Developing children and multicultural attitudes: The systemic psychosocial influences of television portrayals in a multimedia society. *Cultural Diversity & Ethnic Minority Psychology, 9,* 360–366. doi: 10.1037/1099-9809.9.4.360.

Berry, G. L. (2007). Television, social roles, and marginality: Portrayals of the past images for the future. In N. Pecora, J. P. Murray, & E. A. Wartella (Eds.), *Children and television: Fifty years of research* (pp. 85–107). Mahwah, NJ: Laurence Erlbaum.

Berry, G. L. (2008). Introduction: The interface of child development, multiculturalism, and media within a worldview framework In J. K. Asamen, M. L. Ellis, & G. L. Berry (Eds.), *The SAGE handbook of child development, multiculturalism, and media* (pp. xvii–xxvii). Thousand Oaks, CA: Sage.

Blocher, D. H. (1987). *The professional counselor.* New York: Macmillan.

Brickman, D. W., Rhodes, M., & Bushman, B. J. (2007). Schema theory. In J. J. Arnett (Ed.), *Encyclopedia of children, adolescents, and the media* (Vol. 2, pp. 733–734). Thousand Oaks, CA: Sage.

Children Now. (1998). *A different world: Children's perceptions of race and class in media.* Oakland, CA: Author.

Chin, J. L. (2010). Introduction to the special issue on diversity and leadership. *American Psychologist, 65,* 150–156. doi: 10.1037/a0018716.

Chisman, F. P. (1998). Delivering on diversity: Serving the media needs and interests of minorities in the twenty-first century. In A. K. Garmer (Ed.), *Investing in diversity: Advancing opportunities for minorities and the media* (pp. 1–30). Washington, DC: Aspen Institute.

Christenson, P., & ter Bogt, T. (2008). In J. K. Asamen, M. L. Ellis, & G. L. Berry (Eds.), *The SAGE handbook of child development, multiculturalism, and media* (pp. 277–311). Thousand Oaks, CA: Sage.

Ciccarelli, S. K., & White, N. (2009). *Psychology.* Upper Saddle River, NJ: Prentice Hall.

Clark, K. (2008). Educational settings and the use of technology to promote the multicultural development of children. In J. K. Asamen, M. L. Ellis, & G. L. Berry (Eds.), *The SAGE handbook of child development, multiculturalism, and media* (pp. 411–417). Thousand Oaks, CA: Sage.

Comstock, G., & Scharrer, E. (2005). *The psychology of media and politics.* Boston: Elsevier Academic Press.

Council of Counseling Psychology Training Programs, Association of Counseling Center Training Agencies, and Society of Counseling Psychology. (2009). Counseling psychology model training values statement addressing diversity. *The Counseling Psychologist, 37*(5), 641–643. doi: 10.1177/0011000009331930.

Creswell, J. W. (2007). *Qualitative inquiry and research design* (2nd ed.). Thousand Oaks, CA: Sage.

DeBlaere, C., Brewster, M.E., Sarkees, A., & Moradi, B. (2010). Conducting research with LGB people of color: Methodological challenges and strategies. *The Counseling Psychologist, 38,* 331–362. doi: 10.1177/0011000009335257.

Dennis, E. E., & DeFleur, M. L. (2010). *Understanding media in the digital age: Connections for communication, society, and culture.* New York: Allyn & Bacon.

Eggen, R. M., & Kauchak, D. (1997). *Educational psychology: Windows on classroom.* Upper Saddle River, NJ: Prentice Hall.

Feldman, R. S. (2007). *Child development.* Upper Saddle River, NJ: Prentice Hall.

Firestone, C. M., & Garmer, A. K. (Eds.). (1998). Foreword. *Digital broadcasting and the public interest.* Washington, DC: Aspen Institute.

Fowers, J., & Davidov, B. J. (2006). The virtue of multiculturalism: Personal transformation, character, and openness to the other. *American Psychologist. 61,* 581–594. doi: 10.1037/0003-066X.61.6.581.

Glaubke, C. R., & Miller, P. (2008). The role of parents and caregivers in creating a healthy multicultural media environment for children. In J. K. Asamen, M. L. Ellis, & G. L. Berry (Eds.), *The SAGE handbook of child development, multiculturalism, and media* (pp. 433–442). Thousand Oaks, CA: Sage.

Goldenson, R. M. (1994). *The encyclopedia of human behavior: Psychology, psychiatry, and mental health.* New York: Doubleday.

Graves, S. B. (2008). Children's television programming and the development of multicultural attitudes. In J. K. Asamen, M. L. Ellis, & G. L. Berry (Eds.), *The SAGE handbook of child development, multiculturalism, and media* (pp. 213–232). Thousand Oaks, CA: Sage.

Greene, B. (2009). The use and abuse of religious beliefs in dividing and conquering between socially marginalized groups: The same-sex marriage debate. *American Psychologist, 8,* 698–709. doi: 10.1037/a0017214.

Harrell, S. P., & Gallardo, M. E. (2008). Sociopolitical and community dynamics in the development of a multicultural worldview. In J. K. Asamen, M. L. Ellis, & G. L. Berry (Eds.), *The SAGE handbook of child development, multiculturalism, and media* (pp. 113–1270). Thousand Oaks, CA: Sage.

Hunt, D., & James, A. (2008). Making sense of kids making sense: Media encounters and multicultural methods. In J. K. Asamen, M. L. Ellis, & G. L. Berry (Eds.), *The SAGE handbook of child development, multiculturalism, and media* (pp. 365–378). Thousand Oaks, CA: Sage.

Huston, A. C. Bickham, D. S., Lee, J. H., & Wright, J. C. (2007). From attention to comprehension: How children watch and learn from television. In N. Pecora, J. P. Murray, & E. A. Wartella (Eds.), *Children and television: Fifty years of research* (pp. 41–63). Mahwah, NJ: Lawrence Erlbaum.

Kelley, V. A. (2008). Children and television news broadcasting: An intercultural communication analytic approach. In J. K. Asamen, M. L. Ellis, & G. L. Berry (Eds.), *The SAGE handbook of child development, multiculturalism, and media* (pp. 249–260). Thousand Oaks, CA: Sage.

Kellner, D. (1995). Cultural studies, multiculturalism, and media culture. In G. Dines & J. M. Humez (Eds.), *Gender, race, and class in media* (pp. 5–17). Thousand Oaks, CA: Sage.

Kubey, R. (2007). Television. In J. J. Arnett (Ed.), *Encyclopedia of children, adolescents, and the media.* (Vol. 2, pp. 798–801). Thousand Oaks CA: Sage.

Leong, F. T. L., Qin, D. B., & Huang, J. L. (2008). Research methods related to understanding multicultural concepts. In J. K. Asamen, M. L. Ellis, & G. L. Berry (Eds.), *The SAGE handbook of child development, multiculturalism, and media* (pp. 63–80). Thousand Oaks, CA: Sage.

Leung, S. A., & Chen, P. H. (2009). Counseling psychology in Chinese communities in Asia: Indigenous, multicultural, and cross-cultural considerations. *The Counseling Psychologist, 37,* 944–966. doi: 10.1177/0011000009339973.

Levinson, P. (2009). *New new media.* New York: Allyn & Bacon.

Liang, T. H., Salcedo, J., Rivera, A. L. Y., & Lopez, M. J. (2009). A content and methodological analysis of 35 years of Latino/a-focused research. *The Counseling Psychologist, 37*(8), 1116–1148.

Maton, K. I., Kohout, J. L., Wicherski, M., Leary, G. E., & Vinokurov, A. (2006). Minority students of color and the psychology graduate pipeline: Disquieting and encouraging trends, 1989–2003. *American Psychologist, 61,* 117–131. doi: 10.1037/0003-066X .61.2.117.

Mertens, D. M. (2010). *Research and evaluation in education and psychology* (3rd ed.). Thousand Oaks, CA: Sage.

Murray, J. P. (1993). The developing child in a multimedia society. In G. L. Berry & J. K. Asamen (Eds.), *Children and television: Images in a changing sociocultural world* (pp. 9–22). Newbury Park, CA: Sage.

Myers, D. G. (2010). *Psychology.* New York: Worth.

Potts, R., & Sloan, C. (2010). *What does it mean to be human?* Washington, DC: National Geographic Society.

Reber, A. S., Allen, R., & Reber, E. S. (2009). *Penguin dictionary of psychology.* New York: Penguin Books.

Rideout, V. J., Foehr, U. G., & Roberts, D. F. (2010, January). *Generation M²: Media in the lives of 8- to 18-year-olds.* Menlo Park, CA: Henry J. Kaiser Foundation.

Schultz, D. P., & Schultz, S. E. (2009). *Theories of personality.* Belmont CA: Wadsworth.

Singer, D. G., Singer, J. L., & Bellin, H. F. (2008). Electronic media and learning through imaginative games for urban children. In J. K. Asamen, M. L. Ellis, & G. L. Berry (Eds.), *The SAGE handbook of child development, multiculturalism, and media* (pp. 313–331). Thousand Oaks, CA: Sage.

Stantrock, J. W. (2007). *Children.* New York: McGraw-Hill.

Sue, D. W., Carter, R. T., Casas, J. M., Fouad, N. A., Ivey, A. E., Jensen, M., . . . Vazquez-Nutall, E. (1998). *Multicultural counseling competencies: Individual and organizational development.* Thousand Oaks, CA: Sage.

Thomas, K. A., Day, K. M., & Ward, L. M. (2008). Multiculturalism and music videos: Effects on the socioemotional development of children and adolescents. In J. K. Asamen, M. L. Ellis, & G. L. Berry (Eds.), *The SAGE handbook of child development, multiculturalism, and media* (pp. 297–311). Thousand Oaks, CA: Sage.

CHAPTER 19

Children's Media Use in a Global Perspective

CECILIA VON FEILITZEN
Södertörn University
University of Gothenburg

I n mid-2010, the world population is getting near to 7 billion. If we—in keeping with the UN Convention on the Rights of the Child—mean all persons under the age of 18, children constitute more than one third of the total world population. This proportion varies between countries. In what is called by the UN "more developed regions," children under 18 make up less than a quarter of the population, while in some of the "least developed countries," about half of the population is children. This also means that of the 2 to 2.5 billion children in the world, only a small minority is living in "more developed regions," while the overwhelming majority are growing up in "less developed regions."

Such facts are easy to disregard when reflecting upon the rapidly changing international media landscape and when dealing with research on children, youth, and media. According to such research, there are in the richer parts of the world often several TV sets in young people's homes, and many children and adolescents have a TV set, a computer, and a mobile phone of their own, often accessible in their own bedrooms. These children have also become used to multitasking: that is, using more than one medium at the same time (for example, socializing gaming on the Internet, having the television on for checking possible items of interest, and texting messages to friends on the mobile phone).

Can research give a fair picture of the relations among children, adolescents, and media in the some 200 states on the globe? Literature by local experts is only partly written and only partly collected. What this chapter can do, therefore, is to give some fragmentary

glimpses of a few topics on children, youth, and media. It will be limited primarily to some different aspects of young people's media access and media use. To a certain extent, the chapter will also comment on the deceptive concept of media globalization. An abundance of research has theorized about this phenomenon, above all on the globalization of leisure—through media entertainment flowing over borders in the form of TV series, soap operas, films, and music, through social media used by hundreds of millions on the Internet, as well as through traditional and new forms of advertising products and brands recognized by inhabitants in a wealth of countries, such as certain soft drinks, candy, fast food, snacks, sport articles, fashion, toys, and media electronics. There is also literature on the globalization of news—international TV news channels, new journalism practices on the Internet, and youth finding their information on the Internet instead of via traditional media. Certain changes of (school) work and languages have also been discussed. However, there is not much *empirical* research on media globalization, especially not when it comes to children, youth, and media.

A Growing International Awareness of Children and Media

During the 1990s and 2000s, the international debate on children, adolescents, and the media intensified: Which risks are associated with the accelerated stream of transnational satellite TV channels, electronic games, the Internet, and advertising? How do all new kinds of more latent, intertwined marketing via the Internet, games, and mobile phones affect children? (Montgomery & Chester, 2007). Do media contribute to or reinforce aggression, biased gender roles, excessive sexualization, distorted body images, stereotypes of ethnic groups and other cultures, cyber bullying, materialistic values, and impaired physical and mental health? How can good programming and other quality media content for children be supported? In which forms can education for media literacy

be realized? How do we guarantee freedom of expression for both children and adults? And how can media be a resource for education and democratic participation, when, as will be discussed, they are so unevenly distributed in the world?

Even if the producers of children's media content often are aware that children need special consideration, many richer countries lack the political will or simply the ability to resist commercial media pressures and, at best, restrict themselves to creating a subsidized space for children's media, although children from early on use adult media content as well. In many poorer countries, on the other hand, media professionals often work under more difficult circumstances, since the countries are burdened by graver issues (e.g., providing shelter, water, food, health services, electricity, and other basic necessities for the population).

There are numerous ways of trying to improve the children's media situation and counteract the resignation often felt concerning solutions of problems experienced with the media. Many media contents now are transnational and cannot be regulated in the ways that were possible when the media output was national in the main. There are also numerous examples of such personal, local, regional, and international activities. Some international activities are long standing, such as the PRIX JEUNESSE Foundation established in 1964 and working for high-quality child television.[i] During the last two decades, however, international activities focusing on children and media have increased markedly. This increase can be regarded as a direct response to the spread of media content beyond national borders and influence. An essential support in this regard has been the UN Convention on the Rights of the Child from 1989. Some activities have been initiated by the UN, UNESCO, and UNICEF. Other activities have consisted of international and regional meetings and declarations to promote children's access to media, as well as better production conditions for and diversity and quality in children's programming, games, websites, and social networking sites. Meetings and activities on media education, media literacy, and children's participation in media production, in order to facilitate

their competence as media users, have also been multiplying. Still other activities have been research conferences and seminars on children and media striving at making children's voices heard.

Concurrently with the spreading of media, more and more media research is, naturally, carried out in more and more countries. Nevertheless, media research with children and adolescents is still much more comprehensive and has a longer tradition in richer countries/ regions such as Australia and New Zealand, Europe, Japan, and other well-to-do countries in Asia, as well as in North America, while such research is less common in other countries, at places even nonexistent. At the same time, findings on media reception, influences of the media, and so forth can often not be generalized across borders, which is why there is a great need for research in most countries. This research should be performed both on each country's own conditions and in the relevant social, political, economic, cultural, and religious contexts of children and adolescents. Besides the need of local research, there is great need of internationally comparative research as well.

Media in the World

Statistics giving a comparative and updated picture of the spread of all media worldwide are lacking if by *media* we mean the printed media (books, newspapers, magazines, journals), the audio media (radio, audiobooks, CDs, MP3, iPhones, and other means for recorded music), the video media (film, television, video/DVD, digital games), and the multimedia platform of the Internet with mobile phones and smart phones as its extended arms. Some recent overall figures on the spread of and access to media are available, though, especially for the screen media. Regarding television, there was, together with the development of satellite television during the late 1980s and first half of the 1990s, a 100% increase of channel expansion, hours of television watched, and television possessed by households over the world. In 1996, 7 out of 10 households worldwide were estimated

to own a TV set, several times more than had a telephone (Lamb, 1997). After that, the increase of television has slowed down. In 2009, the proportion of households with a TV set was estimated at 79% (ITU, 2010a).

Television has gradually worked its way up to a position similar to that of radio. Radio, however, is more widespread and is still more essential than television in large rural areas in Africa, Asia, and Latin America where electricity and infrastructure are less advanced. In 2008, the proportion of inhabitants living in urban areas had increased to 50% in the world (WHO, 2010).

Internet users are considerably fewer than radio listeners and TV viewers. The Internet users were, in the end of 2009, estimated to be 27% of the world's population—67% of persons living in the "developed countries" and 18% of persons living in the "developing countries." An *Internet user* is, in this estimation, a person who has available access to an Internet connection point and the basic knowledge required to use Web technology (Internet World Stats, 2010; ITU, 2010b). This is a broader definition than the amount of Internet access subscribers and includes Internet connections shared by many individuals, for example, Internet cafés. The definition is also tricky because it does not say anything about how often the Internet is used. Paying for Internet use is, for many people, both at home and at Internet cafés, still too expensive for regular use. Before broadband is extended and use of the Internet becomes cheaper, the overall percentage of Internet users is not expected to increase much (Internet World Stats, 2010). And even if the proportion of Internet users might be larger among adolescents compared to the overall average, a qualified guess is that the Internet is nevertheless used regularly by a minority of the world's youths.

Much more revolutionary than the Internet on the world scene is the mobile cellular phone, which is cheaper and easier to use than the Internet and requires less complicated infrastructure. In the end of 2009, the International Telecommunication Union (ITU) estimated that there were 68% mobile cellular telephone subscriptions per 100 habitants in the world (with 115 mobile

cellular subscriptions per 100 habitants in the "developed regions" and 58 per 100 inhabitants in the "developing regions"; ITU, 2010c). Experts hope that mobile devices can be a short cut to the Internet for the majority in the future.

In sum, it is easy to understand that the television explosion since the late 1980s has given rise to much literature on media globalization—possibilities to watch the same news, TV series, soap operas, children's programs, and commercials over the world. Besides hope for increased enlightenment and democracy, possible negative consequences of this viewing for cultures and identities has also been reflected upon (e.g., homogenization, heterogenization, exclusion, and conflict).

It is quite common in discussions in richer parts of the world to use the concept of media globalization in a positive sense, implying that all people now are on equal communication terms. But even if television reaches the majority of households, it may not be introduced in all of them, and the exchange of programs and commercials is, as we will see, dominated by certain world regions. The previous statistics also show that there are new, big inequalities in the world when it comes to digital media's spread and access. These raw figures call the notion of media globalization in question.

How Much Do Children Use the Media?

Naturally, statistics on access to media in the world do not tell how much children and adolescents use them. For example, how many young people internationally watch television on an ordinary day, and how long a time do they devote to it in different population groups (according to age, gender, parents' income, and so on)? The answer is that no such comparative, quantitative data for children (or adults) across the different continents exist. The figures, which are available only for certain countries, vary heavily because of different methods of collecting data (e.g., by face-to-face interviews, telephone interviews, postal inquiries, group

inquiries, diaries, and so on), and because of the way in which questions are formulated (e.g., about yesterday or about habits). To be able to generalize findings statistically to a larger population, probability samples and low nonresponse rates are also necessary requirements. (For a more detailed discussion of the next paragraphs, see also von Feilitzen, 2010.)

Of the few existing comparative academic studies performed in several countries, one survey in the late 1990s approached, for example, more than 5,000 12-year-olds in 23 countries in the world's regions.[ii] The same standardized questionnaire was filled in at school (Groebel, 1998). Although the survey gives valuable information on cultural similarities and differences in children's relations to media violence—which was the object of the study—the children's self-reported amounts of TV viewing (on average 3 hours a day) are not generalizable. Statistics from that time show that considerable proportions of children in several of the countries studied did not attend school more than 5 years, and some did not go to school at all (Bellamy, 1997). Lower socioeconomic strata of the child populations, not least girls, were thus excluded.

Of polls carried out by private institutes, one example deals with Internet behavior in 14 countries in different continents[iii] (Symantec Corporation, 2010). In this case, children 8 to 17 years of age and their parents who spent 1 or more hours online each month were sampled. Considering the uneven spread of the Internet in the world, the fact that Internet use starts spreading among high-educated persons and the circumstance that persons in the different countries have had access to the Internet during varying numbers of years, it becomes meaningless to talk, as the report does, about differences in Internet behavior among *countries*.

Although cross-country comparative studies seldom yield statistically generalizable figures, they can nevertheless, if they are well performed, give an idea of relative distributions or distinct tendencies and can, above all, be used in order to study relations among different variables. This can lead to theoretical generalizations: that is, attempts

to explain why matters stand as they do (Petrov & von Feilitzen, 2005).

Child Audience Ratings

But what about the audience ratings wherein the media themselves are investing substantial amounts? Over the years, a discontent has developed within the media branch, precisely because different samples, nonresponse rates, and methods, as well as different data collection firms and institutes in the same country (the so-called institutional effect; see Petrov, 2009), lead to different results. A comparison of radio audience ratings, for instance, found that the differences between radio listening in different countries could be explained more by differences in methods than in cultures (Meneer, 1994). For a long time, therefore, out of a common wish from the media, a so-called harmonization of audience ratings has been in progress, hitherto realized above all for television. Since the beginning of the 1980s, quite a number of countries have successively changed to measuring the audience by means of a people meter system in order to get greatest possible comparability.[iv]

With an augmenting growth of the same TV contents across frontiers, international comparability of the audience ratings is, from a commercial viewpoint, more and more desirable. The aim of audience ratings for commercial channels is, in the first place, not to get genuine knowledge about the audience but to strengthen the channel's competitiveness and to settle the prices of commercials, which are more expensive when the audience in a certain desired segment is larger. The people meter method, however, does not build on the probability theory and, with that, does not live up to the bases of statistical generalization. The panel that has accepted a people meter at home is a nonrandom quota sample.[v] It is also a minority of persons asked who want to participate in a people meter panel. Furthermore, people meter data on TV viewing do not exist in all countries. The Nielsen Company, based in the United States, says it measures more than 40% of the world's TV-viewing behavior (2010). Eurodata TV Worldwide, describing itself as the international data bank for TV

transmissions and TV programs, sells audience ratings obtained by people meter in 70 "territories" (2010).

Comparing the ratings for children involves still more complications. For one thing, different countries start the measurements at different minimum ages (e.g., 2 years or 8 years) and then categorize the children into completely different age groups according to national wants. Another disparity is that the samples sometimes are drawn from the whole country but, in several countries, only from the capital or big cities. Consequently, not only homeless children but also children in smaller cities, in the countryside, and within lower socioeconomic strata are omitted. The size of the panels and the criteria of the quota samples also vary among nations (von Feilitzen, 1999).

Thus, people meter data do not compare how much children watch television in different countries. Figures from the late 1990s for varying countries or cities where there was television and before the Internet was spread (another platform for watching) varied between averages in different countries/cities of 1.5 and about 3 hours for younger children and, for the average school-aged child (up to the early teens), between about 1.5 and 3.5 hours. However, because of methodological biases, such as those described above, the figures cannot indicate in which countries children watch more or less. Naturally, average figures also hide large individual variations—from very light to very heavy viewers (von Feilitzen, 2007).

From a cross-country comparative view, people meter figures for the child audience are without mutual consistency and meaning—figures that, however, have purport for advertisers, since the audience ratings primarily aim at the more well-to-do people. It is in less affluent countries that the sample only covers the capital.

In sum, international audience ratings for television are a distinct expression of the kind of media "globalization" prevailing in the world: This globalization is not valid for all countries and/or areas outside the big cities, because it is focusing on consumers with spending power, driven by economic profit.

Simultaneously, the ratings reveal another power relation in that they are more cursory for children's viewing than for adults' viewing.

With the "three screens" (television, the Internet, mobile phones), Nielsen and corresponding companies are nowadays busy expanding their measurements to comprise TV viewing at different places (also outside home) and via different platforms. Naturally, other online behaviors are also studied. With the unevenly distributed digital platforms in the world, comparative international measures will be even more difficult to achieve.

A Few Ad Hoc Findings

In light of the lack of statistically comparative studies, comparisons of ad hoc and case studies on children, young people, and media can sometimes give insight. The following few glimpses from studies and articles about children's media use give a faint idea of differences between countries, cities, and the countryside in varying economic circumstances.

According to a survey in 2009, 8- to 18-year-olds in the whole of the United States, on average, spent about 7.5 hours on media an ordinary day. And since they devoted much time to media multitasking (using more than one medium at the same time), they succeeded in compressing a total of 10 hours and 45 minutes of media use into these 7.5 hours. The figures indicate a huge increase in media use among young people in the United States compared to 5 years earlier. Moreover, use of the "same" medium had spread over platforms. For instance, about 2.5 hours were devoted to "live TV," while 2 hours' more TV viewing occurred via other means (Rideout, Foehr, & Roberts, 2010).

In India it is true that the media environment in the bigger cities has changed drastically during the past two decades with the introduction of hundreds of national and international cable and satellite channels and broadband Internet in the middle-class homes. At the same time, the media environment of millions of children in most small towns and villages across the country has not changed. There, it is a question of some radio, occasional cassette music, little access to television, rare sightings of a computer in the village school or at the center of the nongovernmental organization, no access to the Internet or cinema, hardly any leisure time, and no possibility of discussing or experimenting with any kind of media production (Banaji, 2008).

In Chile, most families have access only to open TV (no cable or satellite). In 2006, 2- to 5-year-olds in the capital, Santiago de Chile, watched television on average 3.5 hours a day with 1 hour more in low-income groups and 1 hour less among children who attended preschool/school. Toddlers under 2 years of age watched more than 2 hours a day (but less if the mother worked outside the home). Economic growth, increased democracy, media globalization, and technology had contributed to changes within the family. For instance, preschoolers had increasingly got media devices of their own (e.g., TV set, computer) and children in lower-income groups even more often than children in higher-income groups (National Television Council, 2007).

Of children 7 to 11 years of age living in extremely poor economic circumstances in Buenos Aires, the capital of Argentina, the vast majority watched television more than 5 hours a day in the late 1990s (compared to 3 hours and 50 minutes for the average child in primary school in Argentina). Television—generally situated in the center of the often only room in the house—had many functions for these children, among others a family-unifying function and a compensating function, because watching TV was one of the few entertaining activities in which these children participated. Television was also often seen as a learning source by the children, and they watched all kinds of programs without guilt (Morduchowicz, 2002).

A survey in 16 countries across the world[vi] indicates that the major free-time activity among children aged 1 to 12 years is watching television. Furthermore, in the "newly industrialized" and "developing" countries studied, it was, on average, more common among children of these ages to watch television "often" than it was in the "developed" countries. This may reflect that children in the "developed" countries have more other

activities that occupy them after school. For instance, using electronic games "often" was, on average, more usual in the latter countries (Singer, Singer, D'Agostino, & DeLong, 2009).

Kibera in Nairobi, Kenya, is regarded as the largest slum settlement in Africa, and the majority of the population living there consists of children and youth. Of all media, radio was, in 2003, the most important source of news on current events. However, the use of mobile phones was growing fast and facilitated contacts, business, and everyday life for the dwellers (Warah, 2006).

Factors Affecting the Amount of Media Use

With so different media scenes, conclusions about factors affecting the amount of media use are difficult to draw outside the single country. Research studies point tentatively to the following factors, among others:

Access to more and more media and platforms increases media use.

In countries or areas with few media, children of low-income parents often use the media less because they do not have access to them. In countries or areas with many media, children of low-income parents devote more time to television (and video/DVD and digital games) than children of high-income parents. Children of high-educated parents use print media, computers, and the Internet more often than children of low-educated parents. However, in the few places in the world where practically all children have access to computers and the Internet, such as in Sweden, there seems on the whole to be no difference in the amount of use of these platforms among adolescents in families with different education and economy (von Feilitzen & Petrov, 2011).

Besides media access, income, and education, the age (or development) of the child influences the amount of media use in general so that the older the child, the longer the time s/he uses media in total. However, there seems to be a difference among preschoolers: In countries or areas with many media and

where the majority of children go to preschool, watching television appears, on average, to be lower than in media-rich areas, where preschoolers stay at home with their mothers/fathers.

There do not seem to be any big and consistent differences between boys' and girls' amount of media use across countries, with the exception of boys' more intensive playing of digital games on TV consoles, computers, and the Internet. However, the situation may be different in countries where girls' activities outside the home are restricted. Gender differences are otherwise more noticeable as regards choice of media contents (see below).

Parents' own media behavior often stands out as a model of how their child/ren will use media. In addition, in families where parents actively mediate (regulate) their children's use by co-using, rule setting, and talking about the contents, something that is more common in middle-class than in working-class families, children often spend less time on the media, and influences of the media are also often modified.

With more and more television channels, computers, and other media apparatuses in the home, media use is becoming more individualized, and parents then have less idea about their child's media use. This is especially valid for teens' Internet use, in which parents in several countries are not especially involved. In other regions and cultures of the world, media use can be more of a collective activity.

What Media Contents Do Children Use?

Amount of media use is one thing, the media contents used, another. Internet use in richer countries has continuously nestled down among children in preschool age (3- to 5-year-olds). The children's first contact with the Internet is usually websites aimed at children (but such sites do not always exist even in well-to-do countries) where they can play games and watch videos that are often familiar from TV programs and

films (e.g., Findahl, 2010; Rideout, Vandewater, & Wartella, 2003). Later, when children can read, chat and instant messaging play an increasing role besides games. With even older age, being in social networks, visiting communities, watching video clips, listening to music, and searching for information (often about amusements and products but also for schoolwork) become important, as well.

What this implies in the long run is too early to prophesy. However, Swedish research indicates that while a relatively large number but still a minority of youths also read Internet tabloids and blogs, watching traditional TV news among young people has diminished drastically during the last decade. An important question is if the more opinion-based news on the Internet can compensate for professional journalism (Carlsson, 2010).

At the same time, while Swedish youths, both those attending theoretical and practical study programs, respectively, use the Internet for socializing with other people, for entertainment, and for handling everyday business, the "theoretical" teens search more often for societal information (e.g., politics, science, law). They have a corresponding interest outside the Internet—societal information is something relevant to them due to their background and (imagined) future position in society. Information and communication technology per se is not a factor that appears to counteract the social structures that give rise to inequalities between different population groups but seems instead to reinforce the different dispositions, values, and activities that users bring to it (von Feilitzen & Petrov, 2011).

As for television, children do not, as mentioned previously, watch only children's programs. Especially in countries with a small media offer aimed at children, as well as in child groups who use television a lot, children also watch adult programming from an early age (e.g., Goonasekera, 2000). In countries with a diverse child TV output of good quality, shown at times when most children can watch, younger children readily choose these programs, and their viewing of adult programming is more a consequence of the child's wish to be with the family in front of the television. However, even in countries with a rich supply of children's programming, an interest in adult programs, mainly entertainment and fiction, appears when children begin to orient themselves more toward the peer group, often around the age of 8 or 9. Boys are generally more interested in sports, "nasty" comedies, and action (and, when a little older, in pornography), whereas girls are more interested in relationship dramas (e.g., soap operas, reality TV shows) and "calmer amusement" (e.g., von Feilitzen, 2007). Attractive programs directed specifically at somewhat older children also find their viewers.

Imported Child Programming

It is in relation to media contents that globalization mostly has been discussed. How much of international child and adult TV programs, films, music, Internet contents, advertising, products, brands, and so forth reach children and adolescents in the world? In the media violence study from the late 1990s mentioned before, about 90% of the more than 5,000 12-year-olds in the 23 countries were acquainted with Arnold Schwarzenegger as the *Terminator* (Groebel, 1998). There are many icons, blockbusters, and ubiquitous products we can refer to—but no all-embracing research telling about their global reach. However, two recent studies illustrate the specific situation of children's programs internationally and can serve as examples not of use but of the quantity of imported programs.

One study applies to Asia, where more than half of the world's population lives. It surveyed children's programs on popular TV channels[vii] in 20 Asian countries[viii] during 2 weeks in 2009 and showed that, on average, the commercial/subscription channels offered about four fifths of all child programming and national public broadcasters about one fifth. Furthermore, about four fifths of all children's programs were bought in from other countries, while about one fifth were produced in-country. Of the minority of children's programs broadcast on public television, the in-country proportion was higher (PRIX JEUNESSE Foundation, 2009).

Moreover, the analysis demonstrated that half of all children's programs in the Asian countries studied came from North America and one third from Asia, particularly Japan. Regarding bought-in programs only, the proportion of U.S.-produced programs was higher.

The other study, a content analysis of children's programming on popular TV channels[ix] in 24 countries[x] in all continents during a month in 2007 (Götz et al., 2008a; Götz et al., 2008b), completes the picture. The overwhelming majority of all children's programs were fiction. Considering only public providers, however, the proportion of fictional programs was clearly smaller and the proportion of documentaries, school TV, and mixed formats explicitly higher than in the commercial/subscription channels. Of the fiction shows, almost all were animation and produced outside the country. This study evinced, as well, that the biggest export region of children's TV programs in the 24 countries was North America, with 60% of the worldwide production, followed by Europe with 30% and Asia with 9%.

The Case of Animation

To buy broadcast rights for programs produced abroad is, on average, much cheaper than to produce one's own programs, especially fiction and drama. As the company Screen Digest expressed it on the website when it introduced its report *The Business of Children's Television* in 1999:

> Children's television sells. Animation is one of the most exportable genres of programming [. . . and] shift millions of licensed products from the selves of retailers [. . .] [. . .] the main supporters of children's television—generalist broadcasters—are reducing their spending on the genre as their audiences fragment and the battle for prime-time audiences intensifies [. . .]. (Screen Digest, 1999, p. 1)

From the perspective of the media industry, animation is, thus, an "attractive investment" (Screen Digest, 2001), these words presenting Screen Digest's 2001 report *Animation: The Challenge for Investors*. In that report, one can read that the animation market dramatically increased during the 1990s for both television and film. One reason given is that such children's films and programs sell all over the world. The figures are imaginary, and their settings are less culturally bound than characters and environments in live-action programs. Animation is also easier to translate linguistically (supply with voice-over, dub, subtitle). In addition, animated programs have a long life because they can be repeated more often than any other TV genre (since children grow up). Animated programs can also, if they become popular, create big extra income through films, print media, toys, clothes, gadgets, and other licensed products and activities. Furthermore, the report says that animation is fitting ideally on the Internet (Westcott, 2001).

As mentioned, viewing children's programming does not make up more than a part of children's total media use. The example is nevertheless pertinent as it clearly sheds light on the interests of the transnational media industry. The ownership of media conglomerates, mostly based in the United States, has continuously been concentrated. The development of satellite television and the marketability of animation (interspersed with other traditional commercials), together with its additional licensed products, also went hand in hand with reports, particularly since the 1990s, that children in several areas in the world, besides their own spending, have great purchasing power and influence on family spending (e.g., McNeal, 1999).

That children also prefer animated programs is an argument from the media industry and a belief among many adults. Even if we have not worldwide counterevidence, much points, instead, to the circumstance that children like animated programs of good quality and at least as much live action of good quality. At the same time they reject programs—both animated and live action—of low quality. The reason for viewing is, consequently, not live action or animation as such. This research finding comes from Swedish audience ratings and children's answers in qualitative interviews (von Feilitzen, 2004a). Research from certain countries indicates, too, that children, on average, prefer high-quality programs

produced in their own country (Rydin, 2000). However, the (unusual) condition for such choices among children among live action, animation, domestically produced, and bought-in programs, respectively, is a sufficient and varied output of all these different kinds of children's programs broadcast at times when children can watch. What "quality" of child programs means varies according to different cultural contexts. Media professionals', parents', and children's views, respectively, also differ partly in this respect (Nikken, 2000; *Televizion,* 2009).

According to the 24-country study above, and unlike in the other countries, more than four fifths of the children's programs in the United States were domestic productions. In sum, animated children's programs over the world—of which the United States exports the majority but imports very few children's programs itself—is a manifestation of the prevailing *one-sided* kind of "globalization." These "globalized" productions in many countries become a too-narrow substitute for the needed diversity of children's programs that strengthen children's own cultural identities.

Cultural Variations

These common trends in child programming over the world also conceal large cultural variations. For example, the Asian survey in 20 countries indicates that in some places studied, the national public channels offered more children's programs than the commercial/subscription ones did, namely in Japan, South Korea, Thailand, and Vietnam. On the other hand, children's programming existed only on commercial channels/subscription channels (and not on the national ones) in Bhutan, Brunei, Fiji, and the Philippines (and, as mentioned, commercial/subscription channels are often those with much bought-in production and a considerable proportion of United States programs). In Bangladesh, on the third hand, all children's programs during the period studied were produced in-country. Other Asian countries studied with a high overall share of domestically produced programming during the 2 weeks were China, Mongolia, and Nepal (PRIX JEUNESSE Foundation, 2009).

The content analysis of child programming in 24 countries from all continents also revealed large variations. While the U.K., besides the United States, had a big share of domestic productions, there were a few countries in the study that had no or almost no domestically produced programs for children at all, only imported ones. There were, on the other hand, also countries that did not import as big proportions of U.S. productions as the others did. Examples were the European countries in the study (Belgium, Germany, Netherlands, Norway, Slovenia, and U.K.) and also Egypt. These countries broadcast children's programs from a broader range of countries (Götz et al., 2008a; Götz et al., 2008b).

We also know that national and regional children's TV channels have been established in, for example, several European countries and in Qatar as countermeasures to the children's channels emanating from the United States (e.g., Cartoon Network, Disney, Nickelodeon with channels and "feeds" in numerous countries).

It would be essential to further analyze the economic, political, social, cultural, and religious conditions, as well as the regulation and other policy decisions, that contribute to different situations of child programming. Research on such media economy and media policy (although partly valid for other countries than in the two studies above, e.g., Banerjee & Seneviratne, 2006; Goonasekera, 2000; Pecora, Osei-Hwere & Carlsson, 2008; Westcott, 2002) indicates, among other things, that a conscious child programming policy—quality programming, a decent share of domestic productions, a diverse and careful import, and so on—cannot be realized without economic means deposited for this purpose. But often, child programming is given less priority than adult programming when money is scarce and high ratings are what count in a competitive TV market.

Reception of Media Content

Even if the majority of the world's children (and adults) have television in the household, all do not have subscription channels or extra channels via cable and satellite besides the national ones. A large supply of

channels is more common among well-to-do families in bigger cities. Marketable TV series and films are, however, often available on video/DVD and reach a greater number of children in this way.

In addition, media use does not only imply amount of use in general and of different kinds of media contents. It also includes the deeper reception of media content in the sense of understanding, interpreting, experiencing, and interacting with it, as well as the role of media in the individual's everyday life, lifestyle, and cultural context. Several studies point at the process of "glocalization," namely that children, while appropriating certain global or universal values (e.g., concerning relationships, human emotions, interpersonal conflicts), also impose local meanings to the media content (Lemish, 2002). Children in Denmark and Ethiopia interpret, thus, Disney films partly differently (Drotner, 2003; Workalemahu, 2008). And hybrid cultures sometimes grow, for example, when adolescents create new music or fashion with both global and local ingredients.

Qualitative studies in different parts of the world[xi] demonstrate in a similar vein that what children and adolescents find in or ascribe to soap operas and reality TV shows depends on a complex of factors: the specific programs; the culture in which they are produced and transmitted; the child's age, gender, sociocultural background, previous experiences, personal needs, and interests; and the specific reception context. But in many of these studies, the similar result has also emerged that children and youth learn and get ideas, tips about, and insight into life and people from these series, especially when it comes to human relations. Young people experience this kind of information as useful now and for how they will handle their lives in the future (von Feilitzen, 2004b).

Child Participation in the Media

All media messages contain values and ideologies. Repeated studies prove that violence is common in child and adult fiction, in video/computer games, and on the Internet.

There are also latent structures of other symbolic oppression in the form of great inequalities between the representations of boys and girls, men and women, and persons belonging to different ethnic groups and cultures—both when it comes to how often and in what ways they are represented.

There is also research about the *media's* use of children, indicating a constant and heavy underrepresentation of them in the media output in general. Two exceptions are in media contents aimed directly at children—and, in many countries, in advertising, where child images are common.

When children and teens are represented in the media output in general, two usual but opposing pictures stand out: On the one hand, there is, above all in advertising, the image of the sweet, innocent, and (in certain countries) more and more sexualized child. On the other hand, several studies from different countries[xii] point out that when children and adolescents are represented in the news, they are, to an unreasonable extent, related to crime and accidents, as victims and perpetrators, and their voices are seldom heard (e.g., Naidoo, Meyer, & Bird, 2009).

The fact that children seldom are portrayed in media output in general may be regarded as an indication that they are, in many respects, attributed a low value (not for the family but) in society, for example, as participants in decision processes. However, the exception of advertising is with all probability a sign of children's comparatively high economic consumption value in society—as present and future consumers and as selling concepts and advertising strategies for products, values, and lifestyles.

There are several indications over the years that young people feel negative about the way the media present them. A few of the several recurrent themes in these viewpoints are that children want to be taken seriously and that they want to be allowed to speak for themselves. A recent example is the campaign elaborated by the Global Youth Media Council at the 6th World Summit on Media for Children and Adolescents in 2010 with young people representing 20 countries,[xiii] saying, among other things, that the representation of children and young people in the

media must be more balanced and that children and young people should be more involved in decision making.

This mirrors yet another aspect of the power relation between the media industry and young people. A way to achieve more equality in this relation is not only to implement existing ethical guidelines on how to report on and portray children and youth in the media but also to let children express themselves by giving them possibilities to participate in different ways in media production. This is, thus, a further definition of children's media use. Many such efforts over the world have been carried out in research contexts, in schools, among nongovernmental organizations, and others. It can be about writing wall papers among working children in India, producing video films about their own stories in Canada or Japan, making radio programs in Ghana, Burkina Faso, or Spain in a local community, producing music in a multicultural school fraught with conflict in Australia, making animated film in Egypt, or contributing to sites and blogs on the Internet. The consequences of these child and youth media productions have often been very positive and, within the young people, contributed to: pride, increased self-esteem, and a feeling of being able to influence; strengthened cultural identity; critical understanding of the media and increased media competence; knowledge and interest in the local community; and inspiration to action—and with that, a step toward increased democracy. There are also examples of somewhat older youths over the world who are engaged in various media projects, including on the Internet, in order to communicate for social change (Tufte & Enghel, 2009).

Concluding Words

Children's media use varies strongly in different parts of the world. In richer countries and areas, young people devote most of their leisure time (and some of their school time) to the Internet, mobile phones, and television (and some reading). In other parts of the world, there is, above all, television. In still other large areas, radio is what counts; however, to an increasing degree, it is also supplemented by mobile phones.

Besides access to the media and time devoted to them, the concept of media use has other facets—for example, the use of different media content; preferences for or interest in varying content; interpretation, meaning making, and interaction regarding content; and participation in and production of content.

In many ways, children and adolescents look upon the media as social, entertaining, informative, and practical resources. But research shows that the relations between children, adolescents, and the media in several respects are a question of disregard, oppression, and exploitation of children. Children are substantially underrepresented in media output in general: that is, are seldom seen, heard, or talked about, and when they are there, they are often stereotyped as consumers or as victims or threats, in the main deprived of joint community discussion. Even the child audience ratings are more superficial than those for adults. Children are also seldom participating in the media production processes, something that would empower them and contribute to understanding of how the media function. Yet children have the right to freedom of expression through any media of the child's choice (Article 13, UN Convention on the Rights of the Child, 1989).

Also when focusing on media content aimed at children, it is, as are children's needs, prioritized less than content for (and needs of) adults. In many countries, the media afford a certain amount of home-produced children's programs, websites, and so on— but in many more countries where there are few or no domestically produced alternatives, children are, besides their use of adult contents, referred most often to U.S. (i.e., "globalized") animation with attendant and surrounding extra products.

Apart from the fact that there are big inequalities in terms of media access and amount of media use in a global perspective, there are, thus, stark streams of one-sidedly transmitted media content and products. In sum, the so-called media globalization covers different parts of the globe asymmetrically—in places

not at all. The current "media globalization" means different things depending on location in the global economy.

It is true that during the past decades, the economic situation has changed rather strikingly in some "developing" countries; economic indicators point to an economic rise. But these indicators often conceal great differences between bigger cities and the countryside. Even audience ratings—for television, the Internet, and mobile phones—cover only those regions and cities deemed by the media industry to be sufficiently well-to-do for further consumption. And it is in affluent areas that marketers are interested in portraying children and adolescents in advertising, since they influence the family's purchasing habits.

Since the prevailing media globalization, to a great extent, is a one-sided economic process, a symptom of the economic power relations in the world, "media globalization" is an embellishing concept that glosses over the simple fact that the main aim of the industry in the present market economy is to sell. Commercial media are financially dependent on advertising and are the auxiliary engine of the advertisers' inescapable need to encourage consumption. Therefore, most of the commercial media are, by definition, reinforcing consumer values. Possible negative consequences are exaggerated consumerism and an overemphasizing of material values, laying more stress on "clientship" and less stress on citizenship, equality, human rights, health, care for environment, and sustainability.

Notes

i. The PRIX JEUNESSE Foundation is working for television that meets children's needs within their own culture and arranges workshops and screenings over the world, as well as a festival and competition for children's and youth television programs every second year. It also supports research activities (www.prixjeunesse.de).

ii. Angola, Argentina, Armenia, Brazil, Canada, Costa Rica, Croatia, Egypt, Fiji, Germany, India, Japan, Mauritius, Netherlands, Peru, Philippines, Qatar, South Africa, Spain, Tajikistan, Togo, Trinidad & Tobago, Ukraine

iii. Australia, Brazil, Canada, China, France, Germany, India, Italy, Japan, New Zealand, Spain, Sweden, U.K., U.S.

iv. People meter is an electronic box applied to the TV sets in the homes and that reads, in principle every second, which channel is on and who in the household are viewing—each member of the household shall log in and out on a remote control when she is in the TV room. Data are collected each night and delivered to the paying TV channels next morning.

v. The quotas can be related to gender, age, household composition, economy, and so forth (but are not the same in all countries)—and therefore we do not know if the sample is representative in other respects.

vi. Argentina, Brazil, China, France, India, Indonesia, Ireland, Morocco, Pakistan, Portugal, South Africa, Thailand, Turkey, U.K., U.S., Vietnam

vii. That is, children's programs on TV channels that had at least a 5% market share among the child audience in the country, both public broadcasters and private broadcasting networks.

viii. Bangladesh, Bhutan, Brunei, Cambodia, China, Fiji, India, Indonesia, Japan, Malaysia, Maldives, Mongolia, Nepal, Pakistan, Philippines, Singapore, South Korea, Sri Lanka, Thailand, Vietnam

ix. This study also built on samples of all children's programs on channels beyond a market share of approximately 5%, both public broadcasters and private broadcasting networks.

x. Argentina, Australia, Austria, Belgium, Brazil, Canada, China, Cuba, Egypt, Germany, Great Britain, Hong Kong, Hungary, India, Israel, Kenya, Malaysia, Netherlands, New Zealand, Norway, Slovakia, South Africa, Syria, U.S.

xi. Australia, Brazil, Chile, Europe, Hong Kong, Nigeria, South Africa, South Korea

xii. Countries in Asia, Australia, Portugal, Sweden, South Africa, U.S.

xiii. Australia, Bolivia, Cambodia, China, Colombia, Egypt, Gambia, India, Ireland, Malaysia, Mexico, Nepal, Nigeria, Qatar, Slovakia, South Africa, Sweden, U.K., U.S., Zambia

References

Banaji, S. (2008). Children's media encounters in contemporary India: Exclusion, leisure and learning. *Newsletter on Children, Youth and Media in the World, 12*(2). Retrieved December 23, 2008, from http://www.nordicom.gu.se/cl/publ/letter.php?id=106.

Banerjee, I., & Seneviratne, K. (2006). Money, ratings and the kid: Children's television in Asia. In U. Carlsson & C. von Feilitzen (Eds.), *In the service of young people? Studies and reflections on media in the digital age* (pp. 159–166). Yearbook 2005/2006. University of Gothenburg: The International Clearinghouse on Children, Youth and Media, Nordicom.

Bellamy, C. (1997). *The state of the world's children 1997*. New York: UNICEF.

Carlsson, U. (2010). *Nordicom-Sveriges mediebarometer 2009* (Nordicom-Sweden's media barometer 2009). Medienotiser nr 1. Göteborgs universitet: Nordicom.

Drotner, K. (2003). *Disney i Danmark: At vokse op med en global mediegigant* (Disney in Denmark: Growing up with a global media giant). København: Høst og Søn.

Eurodata TV Worldwide (2010). General website information. Retrieved May 15, 2010, from www.tvfrance-intl.com/en/annuaire/forms/societe/fichesociete.php?fsv_id=44.

Findahl, O. (2010). Preschoolers and the Internet in Sweden. In M. D. Souza & P. Cabello (Eds.), *The emerging media toddlers* (pp. 35–38). University of Gothenburg: The International Clearinghouse on Children, Youth and Media, Nordicom.

Goonasekera, A. (2000). Introduction. In A. Goonasekera et al., *Growing up with TV: Asian children's experience* (pp. 1–11). Singapore: Asian Media Information and Communication Centre (AMIC).

Götz, M., Hofmann, O., Dobler, S., Scherr, S., & Bulla, C. (2008a). *Children's television worldwide: Gender representation in total. Statistical analysis and report*. München: International Central Institute for Youth and Educational Television (IZI) & The PRIX JEUNESSE Foundation. Retrieved May 16, 2010, from http://www.prixjeunesse.de/childrens_tv_worldwide/studies/CTV_WW_00_total_IZI_PG_2008.pdf.

Götz, M., Hofmann, O., Brosius, H.-B., Carter, C., Chan, K., Donald, St. H., et al. (2008b). Gender in children's television worldwide: Results from a media analysis in 24 countries. *Televizion, 21,* 4–9.

Groebel, J. (1998). Media access and media use among 12-year-olds in the world. In C. von Feilitzen & U. Carlsson (Eds.), *Children and media: Image, education, participation* (pp. 61–67). Yearbook 1998. University of Gothenburg: The UNESCO International Clearinghouse on Children and Violence on the Screen, Nordicom.

Internet World Stats. (2010). Retrieved June 6, 2010, from http://www.internetworldstats.com/stats.htm.

ITU. (2010a). Proportions of households with a TV set, 2009. Retrieved June 6, 2010, from http://www.itu.int/ITU-D/ict/statistics/index.html.

ITU. (2010b). Internet users per 100 inhabitants, 2009. Retrieved June 6, 2010, from http://www.itu.int/ITU-D/ict/statistics/material/graphs/Internet_users_98-08.jpg.

ITU. (2010c). Mobile cellular subscriptions per 100 inhabitants, 2009. Retrieved June 6, 2010, from http://www.itu.int/ITU-D/ict/statistics/material/graphs/Mobile_cellular_98-08.jpg.

Lamb, R. (1997). *The bigger picture: Audio-visual survey and recommendations*. New York: UNICEF.

Lemish, D. (2002). Between here and there: Israeli children living cultural globalization. In C. von Feilitzen & U. Carlsson (Eds.), *Children, young people and media globalisation* (pp. 125–134). Yearbook 2002. University of Gothenburg: The International Clearinghouse on Children, Youth and Media, Nordicom.

McNeal, J. U. (1999). *The kids market: Myths and realities*. Ithaca, NY: Paramount Market.

Meneer, P. (1994). Radio audiences: Figures to be taken at face value? Paper for the ESOMAR Athens seminar November 30–December 3, 1994. Claygate: Peter Meneer.

Montgomery, K. C., & Chester, J. (2007). Food advertising to children in the new digital marketing ecosystem. In K. M. Ekström & B. Tufte (Eds.), *Children, media and consumption: On the front edge* (pp. 179–193). Yearbook 2007. University of Gothenburg: The International Clearinghouse on Children, Youth and Media, Nordicom.

Morduchowicz, R. (2002). The meanings of television for underprivileged children in Argentina. In C. von Feilitzen & U. Carlsson (Eds.), *Children, young people and media globalisation* (pp. 135–148). Yearbook 2002. University of Gothenburg: The International Clearinghouse on Children, Youth and Media, Nordicom.

Naidoo, R. with editing by Meyer, M., & Bird, W. (2009). *Children's views are not in the news: Portrayal of children in South African print media 2009*. Parkhurst, South Africa: Media Monitoring Africa, retrieved March 2, 2010, from http://www.mediamonitoringafrica.org/images/uploads/ChildrensReport_WEB.pdf.

National Television Council (CNTV). (2007). *Informe 0-5. Pre-escolares toons chilenos* (Report 0 to 5: Chilean preschoolers/toons). Santiago de Chile: National Television Council, Research Department. Retrieved May 17,

2010, from http://www.cntv.cl/informe-0-5-pre escolares-toons-chilenos-2007 .

The Nielsen Company. (2010). Television measurement. Retrieved April, 21 2010, from http://www.nielsen.com/us/en/measurement/ television-measurement.html.

Nikken, P. (2000). Standards for children's television programs: TV professionals more liberal about TV violence than kids and mothers. *News From ICCVOS, 4*(2), 14–15.

Pecora, N., Osei-Hwere, E., & Carlsson, U. (Eds.). (2008). *African media, African children.* Yearbook 2008. University of Gothenburg: The International Clearinghouse on Children, Youth and Media, Nordicom.

Petrov, P. (2009). *Kvantitativa frågeundersökningar: Produktionsvillkor, vetenskaplighet, spridning i medierna* (Quantitative surveys: Production conditions, scientific bases, spread in the media). Umeå universitet: Institutionen för kultur- och medievetenskaper.

Petrov, P., & von Feilitzen, C. (2005). *Virtuellt rum och socialt rum: Om IT i vardagslivet* (Virtual space and social space: On IT in everyday life). Huddinge: Södertörns högskola.

PRIX JEUNESSE Foundation. (2009). *Situation of children's TV in Asia.* München. Retrieved May 7, 2010, from http://www.prixjeunesse.de.

Rideout, V. J., Foehr, U. G., & Roberts, D. F. (2010). *Generation M²: Media in the lives of 8- to 18-year-olds.* Menlo Park, CA: Henry J. Kaiser Family Foundation.

Rideout, V. J., Vandewater, E. A., & Wartella, E. A. (2003). *Zero to six: Electronic media in the lives of infants, toddlers and preschoolers.* Menlo Park, CA: Henry J. Kaiser Family Foundation.

Rydin, I. (2000). Children's TV programs on the global market. *News From ICCVOS, 4*(1), 17–23.

Screen Digest. (1999). Website presentation of the report *The Business of Children's Television.* Retrieved January 15, 2001, from http://www.screendigest.com/rep_bchild.htm (URL now defunct), cited in von Feilitzen, C. (2004a), p. 28. (The 4th edition of *The Business of Children's Television* in 2010 is announced at http://www.screendigest.com/ reports/2010101a/10_10_key_childrens_tele vision_players_stay_in_the_game/view.html, retrieved November 15, 2010).

Screen Digest. (2001). Website presentation of the report *Animation. The challenge for investors.* Retrieved October 29, 2001, from http://www .screendigest.com/rep_animation.htm (URL now defunct), cited in von Feilitzen, C. (2004a), p. 31.

Singer, D. G., Singer, J. L., D'Agostino, H., & DeLong, R. (2009). Children's pastimes and play in sixteen nations: Is free-play declining? *American Journal of Play, 1*(3), 283–312.

Symantec Corporation. (2010). *Norton online family report: Global insights into family life online.* Retrieved June 2, 2010, from http:// www.symantec.com/content/en/us/home_ homeoffice/media/pdf/nofr/Norton_Family-Report-UK_June9.pdf.

Televizion. (2009). *What is quality in children's television?* München: Internationales Zentralinstitut für das Jugend- und Bildungsfernsehen (IZI), No. 22.

Tufte, T., & Enghel, F. (Eds.). (2009). *Youth engaging with the world: Media, communication and social change.* Yearbook 2009. University of Gothenburg: The International Clearinghouse on Children, Youth and Media, Nordicom.

von Feilitzen, C. (1999). Children's amount of tv viewing: Statistics from ten countries. In C. von Feilitzen & U. Carlsson (Eds.), *Children and media: Image, education, participation* (pp. 69–73). Yearbook 1999. Göteborg University: The UNESCO International Clearinghouse on Children and Violence on the Screen, Nordicom.

von Feilitzen, C. (2004a). *Mer tecknat . . . ? Animerade TV-program: marknad, utbud, barn, föräldrar* (More cartoons . . . ? Animated TV programs: Market, output, children, parents). Nr 31. Stockholm: Våldsskildringsrådet.

von Feilitzen, C. (Ed.) (2004b). *Young people, soap operas and reality TV.* Yearbook 2004. Göteborg University: The International Clearinghouse on Children, Youth and Media, Nordicom.

von Feilitzen, C. (2007). Television, child variables and use of. In *Encyclopedia of children, adolescents, and the media, Vol. 2* (pp. 803–806). Thousand Oaks, CA: Sage.

von Feilitzen, C. (2010). Komparativa studier om barn, unga och medier: Anteckningar från The International Clearinghouse on Children, Youth and Media (Comparative studies on children, youth and media: Notes from The International Clearinghouse on Children, Youth and Media). In T. Broddason, U. Kivikuru, B. Tufte, L. Weibull, & H. Østbye (Eds.), *The Nordic Countries and the world: Perspectives from research on media communication* (pp. 75–85). Göteborgs universitet: Göteborgs studier i journalistik och masskommunikation.

von Feilitzen, C. & Petrov, P. (2011). New media and social divides: A comparative analysis of Stockholm and St. Petersburg. In C. von Feilitzen & P. Petrov (Eds.) *Use and views of media in Sweden & Russia* (pp. 53–100).

Huddinge: Södertörn University, Södertörn Academic Studies 44.

Warah, R. (2006). Divided city: Information poverty in Nairobi's slums. In U. Carlsson & C. von Feilitzen (Eds.), *In the service of young people? Studies and reflections on media in the digital age* (pp. 101–115). Yearbook 2005/2006. University of Gothenburg: International Clearinghouse on Children, Youth and Media, Nordicom.

Westcott, T. (2001). *Animation: The challenge for investors.* London: Screen Digest Ltd.

Westcott, T. (2002). Globalisation of children's TV and strategies of the "big three." In C. von Feilitzen & U. Carlsson (Eds.), *Children, young people and media globalisation* (pp. 69–76). Yearbook 2002. University of Gothenburg: The International Clearinghouse on Children, Youth and Media, Nordicom.

WHO. (2010). Part II. Global Health Indicators, p. 166. Retrieved May 28, 2010, from http://www.who.int/whosis/whostat/EN_WHS10_Part2.pdf.

Workalemahu, T. (2008). Disney kids: Ethiopian children's reception of a transnational media mogul. In N. Pecora, E. Osei-Hwere, & U. Carlsson (Eds.), *African media, African children* (pp. 82–99). Yearbook 2008. University of Gothenburg: The International Clearinghouse on Children, Youth and Media, Nordicom.

CHAPTER 20

Children and Advertising

Content, Comprehension, and Consequences

Dale Kunkel and Jessica Castonguay
University of Arizona

Ten years ago, the chapter on children and advertising in this handbook focused exclusively on television because that medium completely dominated commercial marketing efforts targeted at youth. Since then, a significant shift has transpired. The media environment has experienced unprecedented growth in the number and diversity of technologies, channels, and venues, and this shift has led to an increasing emphasis on niche audiences (Turow, 2006). One of the niche groups that has proven popular for numerous media outlets is children.

Children are now attracted to a host of new media including the Internet, interactive games, and cell phones, as well as the more traditional television environment. Most of these new media incorporate child-targeted advertising into their content mix, and the result is that children are now exposed to unprecedented levels of marketing efforts. Indeed, several recent books (Linn, 2004; Schor, 2004; Thomas, 2007) have documented the depth and diversity of commercial messages that children encounter on an everyday basis. Susan Linn (2004), for example, observes that "the explosion of marketing aimed at kids today . . . is more pervasive and intrusive than ever before" (p. 5).

Another important change in the environment involves children's easy access to a broad range of electronic media. An average child in the United States lives in a home with 3.8 TVs, 2.8 DVD/VCR players, 2.3 video game consoles, and 2.0 computers, among other devices (Rideout, Foehr, & Roberts, 2010). Media have also migrated to young people's bedrooms, enabling them to spend even more time indulging electronic messages while unsupervised by parents. More than half (54%) of 8- to 10-year-olds have a TV in their bedroom, as do more than three-quarters (76%) of 11- to 18-year-olds (Rideout et al., 2010). In addition, one third (33%) of 8- to 18-year-olds have a computer with Internet access in their bedroom (Rideout et al., 2010).

The implications of these trends are that young people spend more time with media than ever before, they are exposed to more child-targeted commercial messages than in the past because of the increase in niche targeting, and they are more likely to experience marketing messages on their own in the privacy of their bedrooms.

Given these developments, it is clear that the issue of advertising to children remains vitally important, though more complex to understand and more challenging to address with policies to protect young people. Do youngsters recognize commercial messages in new media as readily as they do television ads? Does spending time playing an interactive game based on a toy or food item create more desire for the product than watching a traditional television commercial? Disappointingly, we don't yet have answers to most such questions regarding advertising to children in the new media environment. Indeed, scholarly research has lagged in investigating the topic of advertising to children in new media contexts.

A search using the *PsychInfo* database to identify empirical studies of children and advertising published between 2001 and 2010[1] using the terms *children*, *advertising*, and *television* yielded 50 citations between 2001 to 2005, compared to just four cites for *children*, *advertising*, and *Internet*. The ratio improved somewhat between 2006 and 2010, with 56 studies of television identified, compared to 16 for the Internet. Yet if research on children and advertising in new-media environments is finally beginning to develop, such evidence is dwarfed by the vast literature that has accrued over many decades examining children and television advertising. Thus, it is unavoidable that this chapter will still rely primarily on television-based research in addressing key issues involving children and advertising.

While it certainly would be beneficial to gain more knowledge about children and advertising in new-media environments, the emphasis on television research is hardly a serious shortcoming. Even in an era when new technologies such as the Internet and interactive games have dramatically reshaped the media landscape, children continue to spend more time with "television content"

(albeit sometimes delivered by other platforms) than with all other forms of media combined, and this pattern is especially true for younger children (Foehr, 2006; Rideout et al., 2010; Roberts & Foehr, 2004). Because television viewing is typically a child's first media experience, and regular viewing begins before 1 year of age (Zimmerman, Christakis, & Meltzoff, 2007), children inevitably encounter TV advertising messages much sooner than they develop the ability to effectively recognize such content as commercial persuasion. Consequently, television remains an important focus for researchers examining children's developing cognitive abilities and assessing how these skills influence the comprehension and effects of advertising throughout early childhood.

In this chapter, we survey the full range of evidence regarding children's exposure to media advertising, the nature of the advertising environment targeted at children, the developmental differences that occur in children's comprehension of advertising, and findings regarding the influence of advertising on children. For a discussion of the governmental regulations and industry self-regulatory policies that protect children in this realm, we refer the reader to Chapter 28 in this volume, which addresses that topic at length in the context of an overall analysis of children and media policy.

Children's Exposure to Advertising

Early estimates of children's exposure to television advertising were calculated by multiplying the average amount of time spent viewing with the average level of commercial content aired per hour. Using this technique, a research team funded by the National Science Foundation (NSF) estimated that children viewed about 20,000 television commercials per year in the 1970s (Adler et al., 1977). Others subsequently used this same tactic to estimate that children viewed roughly 30,000 commercials in the 1980s (Condry, Bence, & Scheibe, 1988) and 40,000 product ads in the 1990s (Kunkel & Gantz, 1992). The accuracy

of such estimates, however, is difficult to gauge because of numerous complications. For example, the fact that most children spend part of their television time with non-commercially supported networks (e.g., PBS, HBO); that advertising levels vary across different genres viewed by young people (e.g., prime-time shows vs. children's programming); and that the average length of advertising messages (e.g., 60 seconds vs. 30 seconds vs. 15 seconds) has changed over time all present confounds for such calculations.

In an effort to empirically validate the level of children's television advertising exposure, the Federal Trade Commission (FTC) conducted its own analysis of commercial viewing based upon Nielsen audience estimate data from 2004 (Holt, Ippolito, Desrochers, & Kelley, 2007). According to their analysis, children aged 2 to 5 years saw an average of 24,939 television ads per year, while children aged 6 to 11 years saw 26,079 ads, and those aged 12 to 17 saw 31,188 ads annually. Another large-scale study sponsored by the Kaiser Family Foundation (Gantz, Schwartz, Angelini, & Rideout, 2007) used a different methodology and produced somewhat different findings. Gantz and colleagues (2007) linked detailed data from previous children's media use studies with content analysis of digitally recorded commercials in 2005 to estimate children's annual advertising exposure. This study concluded that 2- to 7-year-olds see an average of 13,904 television commercials yearly, compared to 30,155 for 8- to 12-year-olds and 28,655 for 13- to 17-year-olds.

Although the age groups used for the Kaiser research vary from the categories employed by the FTC, the findings clearly diverge for younger children but are generally consistent for older children. While both studies provide informative data, neither is definitive. Nielsen estimates of time spent watching television do not always conform with other measures of children's TV exposure (Anderson, Lorch, Field, Collins, & Nathan, 1986; Roberts & Foehr, 2004), and thus the FTC's findings are not necessarily any more accurate than other empirical estimates. The only clear conclusion that can be drawn is that children see several tens of thousands of television commercials annually, with at least 30,000 ads representing a common ceiling.

Among that large volume of commercial exposure, a significant proportion of television ads are devoted to food products. Children's exposure to food advertising has recently been identified as a risk factor contributing to childhood obesity (Institute of Medicine, 2006), and thus efforts have also been pursued to identify the overall volume of food advertising seen by children. That goal was the primary concern of the FTC report examining children's advertising exposure (Holt et al., 2007), which found that children aged 2 to 17 saw roughly 5,500 televised food ads a year in 2004, or about 15.1 food ads per day, with little variability across age groups. In contrast, the Kaiser Family Foundation study (Gantz et al., 2007) estimated that 2- to 7-year-olds saw 4,427 televised food ads per year (12.1/day), compared to 7,609 for 8- to 12-year-olds (20.8/day) and 6,098 for 13- to 17-year-olds (16.7/day). A more recent analysis of 2007 Nielsen data by researchers at the University of Illinois at Chicago (Powell, Szczypka, & Chaloupka, 2010) found that exposure to televised food ads was down somewhat, with 2- to 5-year-olds exposed to 11.5 food ads per day, 6- to 11-year-olds 13.1 per day, and 12- to 17-year-olds 13.6 per day. This reduction is almost certainly linked to political interests and pressures calling for food marketers to limit advertising of unhealthy foods to children (Brownell & Warner, 2009; Sharma, Teret, & Brownell, 2010).

While the precise details continue to be debated, there is no question that children see a tremendous volume of advertising messages during their time spent viewing television. But, in addition to television, children today regularly encounter advertising messages in a host of other new-media environments. In an average week, children spend more than 3 hours on their cell phones, more than 8 hours playing video games, and more than 10 hours on the computer (Rideout et al., 2010). Attracted to these new audiences of children, marketers deliver advertising on websites (Moore, 2004), in video games (McCarthy, 2005), and even via cell

phones (Marketplace, 2008). No metric has yet been designed to calculate children's cumulative exposure to advertising in these new media, but there is little doubt that it is quite substantial. In the following section, we explicate the nature of the advertising messages targeted at children on television, as well as in new-media environments such as the Internet.

The Nature of the Advertising Environment Targeting Children

Once past the preschool years, a substantial amount of children's time spent viewing television is devoted to programs intended for general audiences (Lyle & Hoffman, 1972; Roberts & Foehr, 2004). The advertising on such programs is generally less salient for young people. Indeed, several studies demonstrate reduced levels of influence on children after watching adult-oriented advertising as compared to child-oriented commercials (Gorn & Florsheim, 1985; Mizerski, 1997). Thus, the emphasis here is on advertising targeted specifically at children, for it is these ads that are most likely to attract children's attention (Greer, Potts, Wright, & Huston, 1982) and to have the most immediate effects on young viewers (Comstock & Scharrer, 2007).

The most recent data assessing the amount of advertising that appears during children's television programs (Kunkel, McKinley, & Wright, 2009) indicate an average of roughly 10.5 minutes of commercials are shown per hour, representing a significant increase over recent years (see Table 20.1). More than 25 commercial messages are presented in an average hour of children's programming. Research in the 1990s found that children's programs on cable television channels had lower levels of advertising than on broadcast channels (Kunkel & Gantz, 1992), but this situation has now been reversed. An average hour of children's programming on cable television included 10:45 of commercials in 2009, compared to 9:52 per hour on broadcast channels (Kunkel, et al., 2009).

Products and Pitches. The content of children's television advertising has been studied actively since the 1970s, when F. Earle Barcus (1971, 1972, 1975a, 1975b, 1978) conducted a series of studies commissioned by a leading public interest advocacy organization of the time, Action for Children's Television (ACT). In a summary of that body of work, Barcus (1980) observed that more than 80% of all advertising to children falls within four product categories: toys, cereals, candies, and fast food restaurants. Research in subsequent decades has underscored the remarkable stability of this pattern first identified in the 1970s (Kunkel & McIlrath, 2003).

Another long-standing pattern is the seasonal variation in product advertising that occurs each year in the pre-Christmas months. During this period, toy commercials gain a larger share of the market, increasing from their normal rate of roughly 1 in every 5 or 6 commercials to half or more of all ads in children's programs (Atkin & Heald, 1977; Barcus, 1976; Condry et al., 1988; Kunkel & Gantz, 1994). This increase in toy advertising

---

Table 20.1	Amount of Advertising in Children's Programming Across Channel Type, 2005–2009

	Broadcast			*Cable*			*Overall*		
	2005	*2007*	*2009*	*2005*	*2007*	*2009*	*2005*	*2007*	*2009*
Ads per hour	24.2[a]	21.5[a]	24.1[a]	23.2[a]	23.8[a]	26.3[b]	23.7[a]	23.3[a]	25.8[b]
Minutes per hour devoted to ads	9:45[a]	8:49[a]	9:52[a]	9:52[a]	9:45[a]	10:45[b]	9:51[a]	9:32[a]	10:34[b]

Source: Kunkel, McKinley, & Wright, 2009.

Note: Findings with different superscripts are significantly different at $p < .05$.

generally displaces commercials for cereals and candies, which then resurface after the holidays in their normal volume. However, no new data reconfirming this pattern have been reported in more than a decade, and thus one should be cautious in presuming this practice still persists.

The most common theme or appeal (i.e., persuasive strategy) employed in advertising to children is associating the product with fun and happiness rather than conveying any factual product-based information (Atkin & Heald, 1977; Barcus, 1980; Folta, Goldberg, Economos, Bell, & Maltzer, 2006; Kunkel & Gantz, 1992). For example, a commercial featuring Ronald McDonald dancing, singing, and smiling in McDonald's restaurants without any mention of the food products available there would be categorized as employing a fun/happiness theme. Although ads for food products employ taste/flavor appeals most often (Gantz et al., 2007; Warren, Wicks, Wicks, Fosu, & Chung, 2008), fun/happiness themes are typically second in frequency for this category of commercials and first in all others.

Disclosures/disclaimers. A common feature of advertising to children is the use of product disclosures and disclaimers such as "batteries not included" or "each part sold separately" (Stern & Harmon, 1984). Studies make clear that young children do not comprehend the intended meaning of the most widely used disclaimers (Liebert, Sprafkin, Liebert, & Rubinstein, 1977; Stern & Resnik, 1978; Stutts & Hunicutt, 1987). Fewer than 1 in 4 kindergarten through second-grade children could grasp the meaning of "some assembly required" when shown a commercial, but the use of child-friendly language, such as "you have to put it together," more than doubled the proportion of children who correctly understood the message (Liebert et al., 1977).

The phrase "part of a balanced breakfast" is another frequent disclosure that is included in most cereal commercials ostensibly to convey the message that cereal alone is not a nutritionally adequate meal. Atkin and Gibson (1978) found that, consistent with the data on toy disclaimers, fewer than 1 in 3 4- to 7-year-olds had any idea what the term

"balanced breakfast" meant. Rather than informing young viewers about the importance of a nutritious breakfast, this common disclaimer actually leaves many children with the misimpression that cereal alone is sufficient for a meal (Palmer & McDowell, 1981). Although this evidence has been clearly established for several decades, it has been consistently ignored by the food marketing industry. In a recent sample of 138 cereal ads examined by Kunkel and colleagues (2009), 88% still employed the standard disclosure that highly sugared cereals are "part of a balanced breakfast."

Food Marketing to Children. Advertising of food products to children has long been a staple of the commercial environment (Gamble & Cotugna, 1999; Palmer & Carpenter, 2006), but the growing concern with childhood obesity that has surfaced in recent years has triggered much closer examination of this topic (Institute of Medicine, 2005). In decades past, researchers would typically focus strictly on analyzing which product types (e.g., sugared cereals, salted snacks) were advertised. Unfortunately, this approach requires inferences to be drawn about the nutritional value of various food product categories. In some cases, such as ads for sugared cereals, those inferences may be sound; but in others, such as tallying ads for fast food restaurants, they can be problematic. A contemporary commercial for a fast food restaurant could be devoted to a fruit salad offering just as well as a hamburger-and-fries meal. While either of these examples would hold dramatically different implications regarding nutritional quality, both would simply be classified as a fast food ad if content analysis measurement was limited strictly to product type.

Studies in recent years have more carefully scrutinized the nutritional quality of the advertised foods, and the findings establish a compelling conclusion. Most food commercials targeted at children promote what nutritionists label as "low-nutrient, calorie-dense" products (Larson & Story, 2008; Powell, Szczypka, Chaloupka, & Braunschweig, 2007; Story & French, 2004), or what the lay public generally terms "junk food." Two out of every three (66%) cereals advertised to children fail to

meet national nutrition standards, particularly with regard to added sugar (Schwartz, Vartanian, Wharton, & Brownell, 2008). Nearly all (98%) food advertisements viewed by children and 89% viewed by adolescents are for products high in fat, sugar, or sodium (Powell et al., 2007). A related finding is that genuinely healthy foods that should be a part of a regular diet are almost never advertised to children (Gantz et al., 2007; Powell et al., 2007; Stitt & Kunkel, 2008). Less than 1% of a sample of more than 500 food ads aired on children's programs in 2009 featured products such as fruits, vegetables, whole grain breads, or other healthy items recommended for a child's daily diet (Kunkel et al., 2009).

The emphasis on advertising of nonnutritious foods prevails across most all genres of programming viewed by youth, including prime-time shows on broadcast networks and cable channels popular with young people (Harrison & Marske, 2005), as well as Saturday morning children's shows (Batada, Seitz, Wootan, & Story, 2008; Byrd-Bredbenner, 2002). Despite claims by the food marketing industry that it has pursued significant reforms to improve the nutritional quality of foods marketed to children (Peeler, Kolish, & Enright, 2009), few meaningful improvements have yet been identified (Harris et al., 2010; Kunkel et al., 2009; Warren, Wicks, Wicks, Fosu, & Chung, 2007). This outcome, coupled with increasing evidence that the marketing of unhealthy food products is disproportionately targeted at ethnic minority children (Bell, Cassady, Culp, & Alcalay, 2009; Grier & Kumanyika, 2010; Henderson & Kelly, 2005), raises significant policy concerns about the efficacy of reliance on industry self-regulation to ameliorate the problems in this area (Ludwig & Nestle, 2008).

Tobacco and Alcohol Advertising. Commercials for unhealthy food products are not the only type of advertising to threaten children's health. Though alcohol and tobacco cannot legally be used by children, advertising for these products has had a long and controversial history because of concern about its impact on young people.

Smoking remains the leading cause of preventable death and disease in the United States, causing 438,000 deaths per year (Centers for Disease Control, 2009). In 1964, the Surgeon General released a landmark report linking cigarette smoking with lung cancer and emphysema (U.S. Department of Health, Education, & Welfare, 1964), which ultimately led Congress to ban all cigarette advertising on radio and television in 1971. Advertising persisted in print and other media, prompting a voluntary code among tobacco companies stating they would not target advertising to young people, although historical analysis reveals this pledge was repeatedly violated (Glantz, Slade, Bero, Hanauer, & Barnes, 1996; Richards, Tye, & Fischer, 1996). When research revealed that more than 90% of 6-year-old children recognized Old Joe, the animated Camel tobacco spokes-character (Fischer, Schwartz, Richards, Goldstein, & Rojas, 1991), political pressure against the tobacco industry mounted (Derthick, 2005).

Developments ultimately led to a 1998 legal action to restrict marketing practices explicitly targeted at children. Known as the Master Settlement Agreement (MSA), Attorney Generals from 46 states settled claims with the four largest U.S. tobacco companies for health damages from smoking, accepting significant monetary compensation as well as a legally binding commitment to prohibit any future advertising aimed at initiating, maintaining, or increasing youth smoking (Attorney General of California, 1998).

One area of advertising expressly targeted by the MSA was public billboards. Prior to the agreement, nearly 20% of billboards promoted tobacco products, 74% of which were estimated to be within 2,000 feet of schools (Luke, Esmundo, & Bloom, 2000). The MSA eliminated all such promotions. However, no restrictions were placed on depictions of smoking in movies (Sargent, Gibson, & Heatherton, 2009) or advertising in retail stores (Slater, Chaloupka, Wakefield, Johnston, & O'Malley, 2007). Advertising also continues in general-audience magazines, which carry roughly two cigarette advertisements in every issue (Landrine et al., 2005). Thus, it seems that tobacco advertising continues to contribute to underage smoking despite the MSA.

Like tobacco, alcoholic beverages are illegal for children. Nevertheless, the U.S.

Surgeon General estimates that approximately 5,000 persons under age 21 die annually from injuries involving underage drinking (U.S. Public Health Service, 2007). This is but one of many statistics that underscore the risks of early alcohol consumption (Institute of Medicine, 2003).

The alcohol industry has several self-regulatory codes that restrict advertising in media venues with a substantial proportion of the audience (typically above 30%) under the legal drinking age (Federal Trade Commission, 2008). However, extensive placement of alcohol advertising on television programs with a youth audience slightly under 30% ensures that commercials "intended" for adult viewers are seen by large numbers of young people on a daily basis (Center on Alcohol Marketing and Youth, 2008). According to one estimate, an average 12- to 20-year-old sees roughly 300 television commercials and 90 print ads for alcohol products yearly (Center on Alcohol Marketing and Youth, 2007). Promotional merchandise featuring alcohol brands is another youth-oriented marketing tactic (Austin, Chen, & Grube, 2006), with an estimated 3 million adolescents owning alcohol-branded merchandise (McClure, Stoolmiller, Tanski, Worth, & Sargent, 2009).

Such practices raise concern because of evidence documenting the impact of alcohol advertising on youth (Atkin, 2003). Early research in this realm established that children's ability to recall a recently viewed beer advertisement predicted favorable beliefs about drinking (Grube & Wallack, 1994), while more recent studies have consistently found a dose-response relationship between advertising exposure and underage drinking (Anderson, P., Bruijn, Angus, Gordon, & Hastings, 2009; Collins, Ellickson, McCaffrey, & Hambarsoomians, 2007; Snyder, Milici, Slater, Sun, & Strizhakova, 2006).

As the U.S. Surgeon General recently noted, the alcohol industry has a public responsibility to market its products cautiously, given that its use is illegal for more than 80 million underage Americans (U.S. Public Health Service, 2007). While companies air some commercials with messages advocating responsible drinking, young people are 20 times more likely to see an alcohol ad simply promoting the product than to see

an ad with a responsible consumption theme (Center on Alcohol Marketing and Youth, 2008). Leading scholars (Jernigan, Ostroff, & Ross, 2005) have proposed that alcohol marketing should be limited to audiences with no more than 15% underage youth, which is roughly the percentage of 12- to 20-year-olds in the population of those aged 12 and above. Despite its intuitive appeal and increasing evidence of alcohol advertising effects on youth, no serious effort has yet been pursued to formally adopt such a policy.

New Media Advertising to Children. Given that 84% of children can access the Internet from their homes and that an average child spends more than an hour a day online (Rideout et al., 2010), it is hardly surprising that child-oriented websites are a fast-growing area of media content (Calvert, 2008). A 2001 survey found that 98% of children's websites permitted advertisements, and more than two thirds relied on advertising as their main source of revenue (Neuborne, 2001). More recently, Cai and Zhao (2010) reported that 87% of a large sample of children's most popular websites included some form of advertising. Websites not only contain traditional billboard or banner-style advertising but also include advergames that engage children in entertaining activities while immersing them in a product-related environment (Moore & Rideout, 2007). Annual spending on advergames and related content was estimated at $217 million in 2007 (Schiller, 2008), and advergames were included in 63% of children's websites (Weber, Story, & Harnack, 2006).

Advergames are one of the clearest examples of increased blurring of the boundaries between commercial and noncommercial content that occur in new media such as the Internet, as compared to traditional media such as television (Dahl, Eagle, & Baez, 2009). Another angle on blurring of commercial boundaries in new media is that some companies maintain children's websites that are, in essence, comprised entirely of advertising content. For example, postopia.com and millsberry.com are sites maintained by cereal marketers that offer an extensive array of advergames popular with children, particularly

younger age groups. Television ads are often used to promote such product-related websites to children (Gantz et al., 2007; Kunkel et al., 2009; Stitt & Kunkel, 2008).

Labels called "ad breaks" are sometimes applied to Internet advertising to children, ostensibly to help youngsters recognize commercial messages. These markers use terms such as *ad*, *advertisement*, or *commercial* in a bar set atop a box devoted to advertising content on a Web page. This practice vaguely parallels the use of separators before and after commercial breaks during children's television programs, which are meant to help youngsters discriminate between commercial and noncommercial matter. But only 18% of ads on children's websites in one study (Moore, 2006) and 29% in another (Cai & Zhao, 2010) applied such labels. A recent study (An & Stern, 2011) indicates that ad breaks do not help 8- to 11-year-olds identify Internet advertising. Similarly, studies of program–commercial separators on television indicate clearly that such devices do not increase children's ability to identify advertising messages (Butter, Popovich, Stackhouse, & Garner, 1981; Palmer & McDowell, 1979; Stutts, Vance, & Hudleson, 1981).

Although toys and media products are among the most common types of items advertised to children online (Folta et al., 2006), content-based research has increasingly focused on food and beverage marketing in recent years. The food brands most heavily advertised on television are also featured prominently online (Moore, 2006). Not surprisingly, it appears that the broad-based pattern of marketing primarily nonnutritious foods to children on television is being replicated on the Internet (Alvy & Calvert, 2008; Chester & Montgomery, 2007; Lingas, Dorfman, & Bukofzer, 2009). Most online food ads are for candy, cereal, soda, salty snacks, and other foods low in nutritional value (Jones, Wiese, & Fabrianesi, 2008).

In some ways, food marketing on the Internet is similar to television in that banner or billboard ads most often use appeals based on fun/happiness or "great taste" in promoting advertised products (Moore, 2006; Weber et al., 2006). But Chester and Montgomery (2007) make a compelling case that innovative interactive advertising techniques targeted at youth are more engaging than television commercials and therefore more likely to exert influence on child audiences. These tactics include personalizing commercial messages to increase interest and appeal and using viral marketing strategies that reward children for promoting products to peers, among other factors.

Another concern with interactive advertising involves privacy protections related to the information collected online from minors (Montgomery, 2007; Schwartz & Solove, 2009). Cai and Zhao (2010) report that 87% of children's websites collect personal information from users. A law known as the Children's Online Privacy Protection Act (COPPA) requires that any website must obtain parental consent before obtaining personally identifiable information from those below age 13 (www.coppa.org). Studies show that problems with compliance continue to persist (Cai, 2008; Cai & Gantz, 2000; Cai & Zhao, 2010; Chester & Montgomery, 2007). Enforcement of the law is delegated to the Federal Trade Commission (2007).

If the Internet predominates among new media in advertising to children, there are nonetheless many other venues for conveying commercial messages to youth. The integration of advertising into video games has become so routinized that it has spawned a new acronym, IGA, for "in-game advertising," which is now a common term in industry parlance (Vitka, 2005; Wikipedia, 2010). Although few studies explore print advertising to children, Cowburn and Boxer (2007) reported an average of 28 ads per 100 pages in a broad sample of children's magazines. Extensive advertising to children occurs in the schools (Molnar, 2001; U.S. Government Accountability Office, 2004). And product placement occurs in movies popular with children (Auty & Lewis, 2004; Sutherland, MacKenzie, Purvis, & Dalton, 2010) as well as in many other media contexts (Cohen, 2006; McCarty, 2004).

In sum, unprecedented increases and innovations have occurred in the marketing messages that electronic media deliver to youth audiences. Many use the term *commercialization of childhood* to describe these developments when voicing concern about

the implications of this trend, including such public health organizations as the American Academy of Pediatrics (Committee on Communications, 2006) and American Psychological Association (Kunkel et al., 2004). To appreciate those implications, it is important to examine how children comprehend advertising messages as well as how they are affected by them. Thus, we turn next to analysis of the information-processing tasks involved when children encounter media advertising.

Children's Comprehension of Advertising

At what point do children perceive advertising as a type of message that is separate and distinct from noncommercial content such as a television program or an online encyclopedia entry? When do children begin to apply skepticism to their understanding of advertising claims and appeals? Researchers in the 1970s and 1980s devoted great attention to these and related questions focusing on children's comprehension of television advertising, in part because of the importance public policy makers have placed on such evidence as they seek to enforce legal protections related to fairness in advertising (Kunkel & Roberts, 1991; Pomeranz, 2010).

Children must acquire two key information-processing skills to achieve mature comprehension of advertising messages. First, they must be able to discriminate at a perceptual level commercial from noncommercial content, and second, they must be able to attribute persuasive intent to advertising and to adjust their interpretation of commercial messages consistent with that knowledge. Each of these capabilities develops over time, largely as a function of cognitive growth and development rather than the accumulation of any particular amount of experience with commercial messages.

Program/Commercial Discrimination. Given the similarity of production conventions and featured characters found in both children's television programs and commercials, it is not surprising that very young children experience

difficulty distinguishing between these two types of content. Numerous investigations of children's program/commercial discrimination ability document confusion on the part of a substantial proportion of children below the age of about 4 to 5 years.

Research using direct verbal questioning to measure children's ability to discriminate programs from commercials indicates that children first recognize this difference based upon either affective ("commercials are more funny than programs") or perceptual ("commercials are short and programs are long") cues (Blatt, Spencer, & Ward, 1972; Ward, Reale, & Levinson, 1972). These studies report that a majority of children below age 5 exhibit "low awareness of the concept of commercials, frequently explaining them as part of the show" (Ward et al., 1972, p. 486).

In addition, techniques that avoid dependence on children's language skills have also been used to explore this issue. For example, Palmer and McDowell (1979) showed kindergarten and first-grade children (approximately 5–7 years old) videotapes of children's shows with commercials included. At predetermined points, the tape was stopped and children were asked whether what they had just watched was "part of the show" or "a commercial." The findings indicate that children correctly identified a commercial 64% of the time in one program and 55% of the time in the other, both of which are only slightly above chance for a dichotomous measure.

Even once children can correctly apply the label "a commercial" to advertising, they do not necessarily understand that such content is separate and conceptually distinct from the adjacent program material. One study found that although 91% of 3- to 5-year-olds could correctly apply the term *commercial* to an ad inserted in a program, only 31% recognized that a commercial just viewed was not part of the story in the adjacent program material (Kunkel, 1988). This suggests that children's initial use of the concept of a commercial does not reflect the understanding that such content is independent and disconnected from the adjacent entertainment material that surrounds it.

To summarize, the evidence is clear that a substantial proportion of young children below age 5 do not consistently discriminate

between television program and commercial content. By about age 5, however, the majority of children have developed the ability to distinguish between these two quite well at a perceptual level. Yet such differentiation is only the first of two key information-processing tasks involved in children's comprehension of advertising messages.

Recognition of Persuasive Intent. The primary purpose of media advertising is to influence the attitudes and subsequent behavior of the audiences for such messages. For adults, the recognition that a given piece of television content is a commercial triggers a cognitive filter that takes into account the following factors: (a) The source of the message has other perspectives and other interests than those of the receiver; (b) the source intends to persuade; (c) persuasive messages are biased, and; (d) biased messages demand different interpretive strategies than unbiased messages (Roberts, 1982). When these considerations are understood and applied in a child's cognitive processing of commercial messages, then that child can be said to have developed mature comprehension of advertising.

The cognitive development of children below the age of approximately 7 to 8 years is typically described as highly egocentric, and thus they experience difficulty in taking the perspective of another person (Kurdek & Rodgon, 1975; Selman, 1980; Warren & Tate, 1992). Youngsters in this age range are also characterized by perceptual boundedness (Bruner, 1965, 1966; Piaget, 1954; Springer, 2001), which is a tendency to focus on concrete objects and their surface characteristics to the detriment of devoting attention to abstract and conceptual dimensions of situations and experiences. This suggests that comprehension of an advertiser's motives or intentions in conveying commercial messages poses a mental challenge that children below roughly 8 years of age are poorly equipped to handle. A younger child is more likely to focus on the product featured in an advertisement as opposed to thinking about the company that produced it or the abstract concept of their economic interests.

Recent psychological research into children's development of cynicism is also relevant

here. Mills and Keil (2005) conducted two experiments in which they read stories to children and evaluated the believability of statements by characters who either were or were not motivated by self-interest. In Study 1, 8- and 10-year-old children thought self-interested characters were less believable than disinterested characters, while 6-year-old children showed the opposite pattern. That is, the younger children attributed greater believability to statements aligned with a character's self-interest. In Study 2, a similar pattern emerged, but this time only 10-year-olds could take into account the bias of a character's situation in evaluating the truthfulness of a claim. The authors concluded that it is not until age 10 that children consistently use information about a speaker's self-interest to adjust their interpretations of that speaker's message. This research is consistent with long-standing evidence that younger children have limited ability at perspective taking as they try to make sense of the social world (Flavell, 1977; Shantz, 1975).

Given these basic findings regarding children's cognitive skills, one should expect that comprehension of the persuasive intent of advertising would be rather limited before roughly age 8 and that such ability might emerge and consolidate in the several years that follow. A substantial body of empirical evidence confirms this expectation.

Numerous television-based studies conducted in the 1970s and 1980s produced comparable findings that age is positively related with an understanding of commercials' persuasive intent, with a majority of children demonstrating such ability by about age 8 (Blosser & Roberts, 1985; Donahue, Meyer, & Henke, 1978; Robertson & Rossiter, 1974; Rossiter & Robertson, 1974; Ward & Wackman, 1973; Ward, Wackman, & Wartella, 1977). Consistent with theoretical expectations, children's skill at role taking was the best predictor for comprehension of advertising's persuasive intent (Faber, Perloff, & Hawkins, 1982).

Following the emergence of these studies, some raised objections that younger children's limited ability to verbalize their thoughts might be suppressing scores on question/answer measures of persuasive intent attribution and masking their true level of knowledge (Donahue, Henke, & Donahue, 1980; Macklin, 1983).

This "children know more than they can tell" argument led some researchers to employ nonverbal measurement techniques and to argue for their greater validity. For example, one study asked 3- to 6-year-old children to choose between two pictures (one of a mother and child buying cereal at a supermarket and one of a child watching television) to indicate what the commercial they had just seen wanted them to do (Donahue et al., 1980). Results indicated that about 80% of the subjects picked the supermarket picture, an outcome that the authors interpreted as indicating an understanding of advertising's persuasive intent. However, several attempts to replicate these findings proved unsuccessful (Ballard-Campbell, 1983; Kunkel, 1988; Macklin, 1985), and this line of argument was largely abandoned. Comstock and Scharrer (2007) summarize as follows:

> We would not take choosing a picture of a child in a supermarket (from one or more alternatives) as the goal of a commercial as evidence of comprehension among very young children as Donahue, Henke, and Donahue (1980) and Macklin (1985) have . . . Instead, we would consider these and similar outcomes as more evidence that very young children associate characters and elements of commercials with marketed products. (p. 173)

Studies conducted since the 1980s have often (Bijmolt, Claasen, & Brus, 1998; Oates, Blades, & Gunter, 2002; Wilson & Weiss, 1992) though not always (Andronikidis & Lambrianidou, 2010; Batada & Borzekowski, 2008; Rozendaal, Buijzen, & Valkenburg, 2010) corroborated the finding that children's understanding of persuasive intent in television advertising develops at about age 8. Still, reviewers in this area have consistently drawn the conclusion that persuasive intent attribution develops at roughly this age (Calvert, 2008; Committee on Communications, 2006; John, 1999; Strasburger, Wilson, & Jordan, 2009; Young, 2008).

Comprehension of Internet Advertising. Efforts have finally begun to examine children's understanding of the nature and purpose of Internet advertising. We identified a small handful of studies that provide initial insight into children's comprehension of Web advertising.

In one study, researchers showed printed copies of child-oriented Web pages that included advertisements, and asked more than 400 children ages 6, 8, 10, and 12 to point to whatever they thought was an advertisement (Ali, Blades, Oates, & Blumberg, 2009). Six-year-olds recognized a quarter of the ads, 8-year-olds recognized half, and 10- and 12-year-olds recognized about three-quarters of the ads. In contrast, a sample of adults correctly identified 98% of the ads in the study. These data indicate that children's ability to discriminate commercial from noncommercial material on the Internet may be a more difficult task than on television.

McIlrath (2006) conducted an experiment in which 185 children explored a website where they encountered three types of Internet advertising: banner ad, pop-up ad, and advergame. Younger children aged 5 to 7 years ($M = 6.08$) correctly identified 2.56 of 5 ads, compared to 3.53 for children aged 9 to 12 years ($M = 11.1$). Older children performed significantly better than younger children at identifying all three types of ads, as well as in their overall ability. This study also examined children's understanding of persuasive intent for Internet advertising, classifying performance as either low, medium, or high comprehension. Among 5- to 7-year-olds, 84% expressed a low level of understanding of persuasive intent, while 9- to 12-year-olds did significantly better, with only 40% judged to possess low understanding and 38% categorized as having high understanding.

Two small-scale studies by Henke (1999; Henke & Fontenot, 2007) also investigated children's understanding of Internet advertising. In the first, twenty-three 9- to 11-year-olds identified their favorite Internet site (e.g., Toys R Us, Ben & Jerry's), and then were asked about the purpose of the site. Most said it was for entertainment, while 13% said it was to advertise (Henke, 1999), indicating very modest comprehension. The more recent study interviewed 39 9- to 11-year-olds and asked them to assess the purpose of six specific websites (Henke & Fontenot, 2007). Children performed remarkably better in this study, with large majorities correctly identifying

"advertising" as the purpose of websites for Toys R Us (97%) and Sony (77%) and similar proportions correctly identifying "information" as the primary purpose of websites for the CIA (91%), CNN (91%), and the Boston Museum of Science (66%). The authors reported that 89% correctly identified "entertainment" as the primary purpose of the Nickelodeon website, although the accuracy of that judgment strikes us as questionable given the commercial nature of Nickelodeon's entire enterprise. This situation underscores the more complicated challenge of commercial and noncommercial line drawing in the Internet environment. No explanation was offered to account for the varying outcomes of the two studies, which provide quite differing perspectives on this age group's ability to comprehend the purpose of a website as opposed to the purpose of a given piece of content.

While this overall base of evidence is modest, the two large-scale studies (Ali et al., 2009; McIlrath, 2006) are remarkably complementary in their findings on commercial recognition. They suggest that children's ability to discriminate commercial content develops more slowly for the Internet than for television, a conclusion that fits well with the fact that there is greater blurring of the boundaries between entertainment and advertising on the Internet. The existing data are too scant to venture even a tentative conclusion about children's understanding of persuasive intent in Internet advertising, but the preliminary findings hint at the prospect that a similar pattern may emerge for this variable as well.

Does Comprehension of Advertising Moderate Effects?

A long-standing, if implicit, assumption has held that the development of a mature understanding of advertising's persuasive intent should function as a moderator of effects. That is, once child viewers can apply a skeptical eye to an ad, the ability to recognize exaggeration and bias should make them less susceptible to commercial persuasion. As has been previously noted, researchers have largely overlooked careful examination of the linkage between comprehension and effects for several decades (Kunkel et al., 2004).

Livingstone and Helsper (2006) have engaged this issue with an elaborate examination of the existing body of evidence exploring the effects of food advertising on children. In their analysis, they examine more than 50 studies, comparing advertising efficacy across three age groups: 2- to 6-year-olds; 7- to 11-year-olds, and 12- to 16-year-olds. They observe that "mixed or weak findings are more common for the youngest age group, whereas among 7- to 12-year-olds and especially among teenagers, research is more likely to find evidence of advertising effects" (p. 567). While acknowledging that artifactual explanations may account for this pattern, they nonetheless conclude that different models of persuasion should be considered beyond mere information processing capabilities (e.g., persuasive intent attribution) to fully understand the process by which advertising influences children. Such advice should resonate with anyone who might ponder why, despite mature comprehension capabilities, advertising often successfully influences adults.

Another significant review, also focused on the topic of children and food marketing (Harris, Brownell, & Bargh, 2009), makes the same general point, noting that "traditional models used to explain advertising effects have overemphasized the importance of children's understanding of persuasive intent . . . to defend against direct marketing attempts" (p. 217). Indeed, several recent studies demonstrate explicitly that knowledge of persuasive intent alone does not moderate advertising effects, both in the context of exposure to television ads (Chernin, 2007, 2008) and Internet advergames (Mallinckrodt & Mizerski, 2007). Harris and colleagues (2009) recommend that increasing attention should be devoted to emotional factors, priming influences, and social elements such as peer norms to more adequately explain the process of advertising effects on youth. One critical implication of this new perspective is that adolescents may also be highly vulnerable to commercial persuasion to an extent that warrants policy protections previously afforded only to children (Harris et al., 2009; Montgomery &

Chester, 2009; Nairn & Fine, 2008; Pechmann, Levine, Loughlin, & Leslie, 2005).

To conclude on this topic, it is important to note that the critiques that call for an expanded perspective in the study of advertising effects on youth do not advocate dismissing the role that comprehension of persuasive intent may play; rather, they simply point out that it alone is an insufficient explanation and that it is essential to incorporate other factors as well. Thus, it is important to consider one final point related to understanding of persuasive intent.

It has recently been argued that the large majority of studies that examine this variable limit their measurement of the concept strictly to children's *understanding of selling intent* (i.e., that ads intend to sell a product), omitting entirely the complementary dimension of *understanding of source bias* (i.e., that ads tend to exaggerate and embellish; Kunkel, 2010). As specified earlier, this latter element is an essential part of the conceptual definition of persuasive intent attribution, though it has largely been overlooked in empirical investigations. Thus, it may well be the case that the widely held conclusion that children develop mature understanding of advertising's persuasive intent by age 8 is in fact erroneous. Kunkel (2010) argues that the few studies that include more comprehensive measures encompassing understanding of source bias indicate that children develop such capability only at older ages, as late as 12 years old. This argument, which remains to be resolved by subsequent research, holds important implications for understanding the extent to which children's understanding of persuasive intent serves as a moderator of advertising effects.

Effects of Advertising on Children

One way of conceptualizing the impact of television advertising on children is to distinguish the intended from the unintended effects of exposure. For example, a cereal ad may have the intended effect of generating product purchase requests and increasing product sales, but it may also contribute to unintended outcomes such as misperceptions about proper nutritional habits, parent–child conflict when purchase influence attempts are rejected, and weight gain from regular consumption. We use the framework of intended and unintended effects to help organize our review of the influence of advertising on children.

The most noteworthy development in research on children and advertising over the past decade has been the extraordinary attention devoted to investigating the effects of food marketing on children. Many dozens of studies on the topic have been published from a broad range of scholarly perspectives, including communication, psychology, child development, marketing, nutrition, public health, and pediatric medicine. As the examples above indicate, these contributions to knowledge may fall into either of the two categories of influence we examine here.

Intended Effects. Advertisers are interested in outcomes such as the viewers' recall for the product, their attitude toward the product, and—depending on the age of the child—either purchase-influence attempts or actual purchase of the product. Although some commercial campaigns certainly are more successful than others, studies have documented the general effectiveness of advertising across all of these areas.

When experiments measure recall of television advertisements immediately following viewing, at least half of the children studied tend to remember ads for youth-oriented products such as toys and snacks (Gorn & Goldberg, 1980; Zuckerman, Ziegler, & Stevenson, 1978). Recall of ads can be influenced by the adjacent program environment, with animated commercials attaining better recall by children when viewed during animated program content (Gunter, Baluch, Duffy, & Furnham, 2002).

Numerous experiments demonstrate short-term advertising effects on children's attitudes toward food products and their product preferences (for reviews, see Gunter, Oates, & Blades, 2005; Hastings et al., 2003; Institute of Medicine, 2006). For example, Macklin (1994) found that half of 4- to 6-year-old children ($M = 5.0$ years) could recall a fictional cereal product unaided after three exposures to a 25-second advertisement for it. When participants were shown the cereal box featured in the commercial, as might occur at a supermarket, recall increased to 80%. Showing children

the cereal box increased their positive attitude toward the product and their intent to ask their mother to buy it. But even without cuing of the product, children reacted very positively on measures of attitude and purchase influence intention. Borzekowski and Robinson (2001) found a significant effect on product preferences from just a single exposure to an ad among preschoolers.

Naturalistic field experiments have also been reported, such as one conducted by Goldberg and Gorn (1978) at a summer camp. The researchers manipulated the television advertising seen by 5- to 8-year-olds over a 2-week period and then tracked children's actual food consumption in the camp cafeteria. They found that the foods children ate were significantly influenced by the ads they had viewed. This outcome corresponds with survey research demonstrating that the amount of children's exposure to television significantly predicts their subsequent volume of requests for advertised foods and drinks (Chamberlain, Wang, & Robinson, 2006).

"Branding" of products is an important element of the advertising process that assists children's recall and enhances persuasive effects (Harris et al., 2009). Whether accomplished by logos, slogans, or spokes-characters, brand associations are reinforced every time an ad is viewed (Connor, 2006). Indeed, amount of television exposure is positively associated with children's ability to correctly identify product brands (Valkenburg & Buijzen, 2005) and with their consumption of advertised brands (Buijzen, Schuurman, & Bomhof, 2008). Use of spokes-characters to assist with building brand identity is common (Callcott & Lee, 1994) and generates high levels of attention, character recognition and liking, and product recognition and liking (Mizerski, 1997; Neeley & Schumann, 2004; Pine & Nash, 2003).

Perhaps the most powerful demonstration of branding effects involves a clever study in which the researchers provided identical foods to children aged 3 to 5 years ($M = 4.6$), but half of the participants received the items in McDonald's packaging while the other half were served the food in plain wrappers (Robinson, Borzekowski, Matheson, & Kraemer, 2007). For all items tested, including carrots (which McDonald's

does not offer), the children preferred the branded foods.

If it is clear that noninteractive television advertising targeted at children is effective at generating recall, positive attitudes, and strong product preferences, there is certainly reason to believe that Internet advertising and other interactive marketing tactics are likely to lead to similar persuasive outcomes (Chester & Montgomery, 2007). To date, however, scant empirical evidence corroborates that expectation.

One large-scale study of 5- to 8-year-old children ($N = 295$) compared those who played a Fruit Loops advergame on an Internet website with a control group that had no such exposure (Mallinckrodt & Mizerski, 2007). The researchers found that advergame playing led children to prefer Fruit Loops over other cereal choices and also to prefer cereal to other food categories, as compared to the control. However, no effects were observed regarding purchase influence requests. McIlrath's (2006) experiment, described earlier in the section on *Comprehension of Internet Advertising*, found that children who saw three different types of Internet advertising reported strong liking of the featured product and moderate purchase influence intent following exposure, although no control group was employed so no firm conclusions about effects can be drawn. However, few other studies of Internet advertising effects on children exist at this point, and thus there is not yet sufficient evidence to draw any empirically based conclusions. Given the significant role of the Internet and interactive media in children's lives, that is indeed a disappointment. The need for future research in this realm is urgent.

Our caveat about the effects of Internet advertising notwithstanding, the overall conclusion that "advertising to children works" is still clear if unremarkable. What does that mean in practical terms? In an ideal world, perhaps parents would ignore all of children's requests for lavish toys and unhealthy snack foods, but in fact, research is clear that parents have a high rate of yielding to children's purchase-influence requests (Atkin, 1978; Wilson & Wood, 2004). Moreover, most children begin to receive their own spending money as young as 8 years of age, and one of the earliest products they are allowed to buy

without explicit parental consent is snack foods (Chaplin, 1999; Dotson & Hyatt, 2005). By age 13 to 15 years, nearly half (43%) of young people have made purchases of their own on the Internet (Thomson & Laing, 2003). Thus, we can conclude that advertising succeeds not only in prompting children's desires but also in shaping their product consumption, just as advertisers intend.

Unintended Effects. Although an individual ad may have as its primary purpose promoting the sales of its featured product, the cumulative effect of children's exposure to large quantities of advertising may exert other types of influences with significant social implications.

Early research on children and television advertising in the 1970s identified parents' denial of children's frequent purchase influence attempts as a significant source of parent–child conflict (Atkin, 1978; Goldberg & Gorn, 1978; Robertson, 1979; Sheikh & Moleski, 1977; Ward & Wackman, 1972). Given the volume of advertising to which children are exposed, as well as evidence of its general efficacy, it is inevitable that parents must refuse a large number of children's product requests. These denials then place strain on parent–child interaction, often resulting in arguments and intemperate behavior and, at times, aggressiveness by the child.

Subsequent studies have confirmed this general pattern (Isler, Popper, & Ward, 1987; Stoneman & Brody, 1981), and more recent research has advanced knowledge at a theoretical as well as practical level. Buijzen and Valkenburg (2003) modeled the process by which parent–child conflict occurs, identifying significant pathways between children's advertising exposure and their purchase requests, as well as between purchase requests and parent–child conflict. Related studies by the same authors determined that concept-oriented parental mediation is more effective at ameliorating parent–child conflict than socio-oriented mediation strategies (Buijzen, 2009; Buijzen & Valkenburg, 2005). Concept-oriented communication involves active discussion with children about consumer matters, whereas socio-oriented communication involves promoting obedience and harmony.

It has also been suggested that children's cumulative exposure to advertising contributes to increased materialism (Goldberg & Gorn, 1978; Moschis & Moore, 1982). Materialism is generally defined as the view that products and their acquisition are the basis for determining one's personal worth, which distills to "you are what you buy." Several early studies found correlations between amount of viewing and materialistic values (Adler et al., 1977; Greenberg & Brand, 1993), and more recent investigation has identified the strength of that linkage in a path model as $B = .22$ (Buijzen & Valkenburg, 2003). While other factors such as parents' values help to foster materialism in children, it now appears that advertising exposure is a contributor as well (Kasser & Kanner, 2004).

By far the most heavily studied topic within the realm of advertising's unintended effects is the role that food marketing plays in shaping children's nutritional knowledge, eating habits, and weight status. Research shows that heavy exposure to televised food advertising is associated with nutritional misperceptions; that is, the greater the exposure to food advertising, the greater the likelihood that unhealthy items will be judged as healthy and nutritious (Harrison, 2005; Signorielli & Lears, 1992; Signorielli & Staples, 1997). This outcome is particularly problematic because eating habits formed during childhood often persist throughout life (Birch & Anzman, 2010; Institute of Medicine, 2006).

The most pernicious effect of children's exposure to food marketing is its role in contributing to the growing epidemic of childhood obesity. More than 100 studies have examined this issue since a seminal report by Dietz and Gortmaker (1985) initiated investigation of this topic. That body of evidence is best summarized by the Institute of Medicine (2006) of the National Academies of Science. A congressionally mandated report delivered by a panel of 16 scientific experts included a systematic review of all existing research examining the effects of food advertising on children. A total of 123 empirical studies were evaluated quantitatively on the strength of their methods and findings. Among the key conclusions of the IOM report was that (a) there is strong evidence that advertising influences the short-term food consumption of children 2 to 11 years of age; (b) there is moderate evidence that advertising influences

the regular diet of children 2 to 5 years and weak evidence that it influences children 6 to 11 years of age; and (c) there is strong evidence that exposure to advertising is associated with adiposity in children 2 to 11 years and teens 12 to 18 years of age.

While acknowledging that food marketing to children is only one of multiple factors that contribute to childhood obesity, the report concluded that "Food and beverage marketing practices geared to children and youth are out of balance with healthful diets, and contribute to an environment that puts their health at risk" (Institute of Medicine, 2006, p. 374). Further evidence published since the IOM report strengthens the indictment against food marketing as the likely causal mechanism underlying the relationship between television exposure and childhood obesity. For example, Zimmerman and Bell (2010) statistically controlled for children's exercise and eating while watching and still observed significant correlations between television viewing and weight status. The conclusion that marketing unhealthy food products contributes to childhood obesity is now widely drawn. The final report of the White House Task Force on Childhood Obesity (2010) incorporates this perspective, asserting that "new or revised rules to limit advertising during children's programming may be helpful or even necessary to fully address the childhood obesity epidemic" (p. 31).

Conclusion

In 1955, the Mattel toy company launched one of the first significant television advertising campaigns targeted at children. That campaign propelled the company's annual revenues from $500,000 to $12 million almost overnight (Jennings, 1970, as cited in Liebert, Neale, & Davidson, 1973). More than a half-century later, the tactic that Mattel innovated has grown to be a billion-dollar business. According to a 2008 report, total U.S. expenditures on marketing to children are estimated at $15 to 17 billion (Shah, 2008). It is hard to imagine (and certainly difficult to estimate) the total economic stakes involved for businesses that depend upon child purchases and child

influence on parental spending. Those stakes are seemingly the catalyst that has driven the increasing commercialization of childhood.

In an era of evolution in electronic media, child-targeted advertising has taken on new forms and is migrating from television to the Internet and other new venues, as we have described above. There is already some indication that increased blurring of the boundaries between commercial and noncommercial messages in these new media makes it more difficult for children to recognize the nature and purpose of advertising. Much more research is needed, however, before any firm conclusions can be drawn.

Although the lack of scholarly research on Internet advertising to children is disappointing, it is not surprising. Television entered the American household in the 1950s, but it was roughly 20 years before meaningful academic studies began to provide knowledge about how advertising in that medium impacted children. The pace of Internet-based research is moving somewhat faster than that, but the ongoing innovation in that medium means the gap may not be closing much between new advertising practices and scholars' knowledge of their implications for children.

The most fruitful development in the study of children and advertising over the past decade has been the growth of research on food marketing to youth. The overall base of evidence is now strong and the convergence of findings across differing measures, methods, and samples affords strong confidence in a number of key conclusions that not only advance knowledge but also hold practical implications for parents and policy makers. Given the profound threat to public health posed by the childhood obesity crisis, this area of research should certainly remain vibrant in years to come.

The last several decades of empirical investigation chronicled here have taught us much about children and advertising, yet researchers still face challenges such as theorizing the process by which children are persuaded and devising intervention strategies to best enhance children's advertising literacy. The success of those efforts holds broad implications for children, families, and society. Those stakes ensure that research on children and advertising will continue to thrive in years to come, just as it has been such a prolific area in the past.

Note

1. The search was conducted on July 1, 2010. The search produced citations that included essays and other non-data-based studies that were excluded from our count. The numbers we report reflect empirical studies only.

References

Adler, R., Friedlander, B., Lesser, G., Meringoff, L., Robertson, T., Rossiter, J., et al. (1977). *Research on the effects of television advertising to children: A review of the literature and recommendations for future research.* Washington, DC: U.S. Government Printing Office.

Ali, M., Blades, M., Oates, C., & Blumberg, F. (2009). Young children's ability to recognize advertisements in web page designs. *British Journal of Developmental Psychology, 27*(1), 71–83.

Alvy, L. M., & Calvert, S. L. (2008). Food marketing on popular children's websites: A content analysis. *Journal of the American Dietetic Association, 108*(4), 710–713. doi: 10.1016/j.jada.2008.01.006.

An, S., & Stern, S. (2011). Mitigating the effects of advergames on children: Do advertising breaks work? *Journal of Advertising, 40*(1), 43–56.

Anderson, D. R., Lorch, E. P., Field, D. E., Collins, P. A., & Nathan, J. G. (1986). Television viewing at home: Age trends in visual attention and time with TV. *Child Development, 57*(4), 1024–1033.

Anderson, P., Bruijn, A., Angus, K., Gordon, R., & Hastings, G. (2009). Impact of alcohol advertising and media exposure on adolescent alcohol use: A systematic review of longitudinal studies. *Alcohol and Alcoholism, 4*(3), 229–243. doi:10.1093/alcalc/agn115.

Andronikidis, A. I., & Lambrianidou, M. (2010). Children's understanding of television advertising: A theory approach. *Psychology & Marketing, 27,* 299–322.

Atkin, C. (1978). Observation of parent–child interaction in supermarket decision-making. *Journal of Marketing, 42,* 41–45.

Atkin, C. (2003). Media intervention impact: Evidence and promising strategies. In Institute of Medicine (Ed.), *Reducing underage drinking: A collective responsibility.* Washington, DC: National Academies Press.

Atkin, C., & Gibson, W. (1978). *Children's nutrition learning from television advertising.* East Lansing: Michigan State University, Department of Communication.

Atkin, C., & Heald, G. (1977). The content of children's toy and food commercials. *Journal of Communication, 27*(1), 107–114.

Attorney General of California (1998). *Master settlement agreement.* Sacramento, CA: Office of The Attorney General. Retrieved July 1, 2010, from http://ag.ca.gov/tobacco/pdf/1msa.pdf.

Austin, E. W., Chen, M., & Grube, J. (2006). How does alcohol advertising influence underage drinking? The role of desirability, identification and skepticism. *Adolescent Health, 38*(4), 376–384.

Auty, S., & Lewis, C. (2004). Exploring children's choice: The reminder effect of product placement. *Psychology & Marketing, 21*(9), 697–713.

Ballard-Campbell, M. (1983). *Children's understanding of television advertising: Behavioral assessment of three developmental skills.* Unpublished doctoral dissertation, University of California, Los Angeles.

Barcus, F. E. (1971). *Saturday children's television: A report of TV programming and advertising on Boston commercial television.* Newtonville, MA: Action for Children's Television.

Barcus, F. E. (1972). *Network programming and television in the Saturday children's hours: A June and November comparison.* Newtonville, MA: Action for Children's Television.

Barcus, F. E. (1975a). *Television in the after-school hours.* Newtonville, MA: Action for Children's Television.

Barcus, F. E. (1975b). *Weekend children's television.* Newtonville, MA: Action for Children's Television.

Barcus, F. E. (1976). *Pre-Christmas advertising to children.* Newtonville, MA: Action for Children's Television.

Barcus, F. E. (1978). *Commercial children's television on weekends and weekday afternoons.* Boston: Boston University School of Public Communications.

Barcus, F. E. (1980). The nature of television advertising to children. In E. Palmer & A. Dorr (Eds.), *Children and the faces of television* (pp. 273–285). New York: Academic Press.

Batada, A., & Borzekowski, D. (2008). Snap! Crackle! What? Recognition of cereal advertisements and understanding of commercials' persuasive intent among urban, minority children in the U.S. *Journal of Children and Media, 2,* 19–36.

Batada, A., Seitz, M. D., Wootan, M., & Story, M. (2008). Nine out of 10 food advertisements shown during Saturday morning children's programming are for foods high in fat,

sodium, or added sugars, or low in nutrients. *Journal of the American Dietetic Association, 108,* 673–678.

Bell, R. A., Cassady, D. C., Culp, J. C., & Alcalay, R. (2009). Frequency and types of foods advertised on Saturday morning and weekday afternoon English- and Spanish-language American television programs. *Journal of Nutrition Education and Behavior, 41*(6), 406–413.

Bijmolt, T. H. A., Classen, W., & Brus, B. (1998). Children's understanding of TV advertising: Effects of age, gender, and parental influence. *Journal of Consumer Policy, 21,* 171–194.

Birch, L., & Anzman, S. (2010). Learning to eat in an obesogenic environment: A developmental systems perspective on childhood obesity. *Child Development Perspectives, 4*, 138–143.

Blatt, J., Spencer, L., & Ward, S. (1972). A cognitive developmental study of children's reactions to television advertising. In G. Comstock & E. Rubinstein (Eds.), *Television and social behavior (Vol. 4).* Washington, DC: U.S. Government Printing Office.

Blosser, B., & Roberts, D. (1985). Age differences in children's perceptions of message intent: Responses to TV news, commercials, educational spots and public service announcements. *Communication Research, 12,* 455–484.

Borzekowski, D. L. G., & Robinson, T. N. (2001). The 30-second effect: An experiment revealing the impact of television commercials on food preferences of preschoolers. *Journal of the American Dietetic Association, 101,* 42–46.

Brownell, K., & Warner, K. E. (2009). The perils of ignoring history: Big tobacco played dirty and millions died. How similar is big food? *Milbank Quarterly, 87*(1), 259–294.

Bruner, J. S. (1965). The growth of mind. *American Psychologist, 20,* 1007–1017.

Bruner, J. S. (1966). On cognitive growth. In J. S. Bruner, R. R. Olver, & P. M. Greenfield (Eds.), *Studies in cognitive growth* (pp. 1–67). New York: Wiley.

Buijzen, M. (2009). The effectiveness of parental communication in modifying the relation between food advertising and children's consumption behaviour. *British Journal of Developmental Psychology, 27,* 105–121. doi: 10 .1348/026151008X334719.

Buijzen, M., Schuurman, J, & Bomhof, E. (2008). Associations between children's television advertising exposure and their food consumption patterns: A household diary-survey study. *Appetite, 50,* 231–239.

Buijzen, M., & Valkenburg, P. (2003). The unintended effects of television advertising. *Communication Research, 30,* 483–503.

Buijzen, M., & Valkenburg, P. (2005). Parental mediation of undesired advertising effects.

Journal of Broadcasting & Electronic Media, 49, 153–165.

Butter, E., Popovich, P., Stackhouse, R., & Garner R. (1981). Discrimination of television programs and commercials by preschool children. *Journal of Advertising Research, 21*(2), 53–56.

Byrd-Bredbenner, C. (2002). Saturday morning children's television advertising: A longitudinal content analysis. *Family and Consumer Science Research Journal, 30,* 382–403.

Cai, X. (2008). Advertisements and privacy: Comparing for-profit and non-profit web sites for children. *Communication Research Reports, 35*(1), 67–75. doi:10.1080/08824090 701831826.

Cai, X., & Gantz, W. (2000). Online privacy issues associated with web sites for children. *Journal of Broadcasting & Electronic Media, 44*(2), 197–214.

Cai, X., & Zhao, X. (2010). Click here kids! Online advertising practices on children's websites. *Journal of Children and Media, 4*(2), 135–154. doi:10.1080/17482791003629610.

Callcott, M., & Lee, W. (1994). A content analysis of animation and animated spokes-characters in television commercials. *Journal of Advertising, 23*(4), 1–12.

Calvert, S. (2008). Children as consumers: Advertising and marketing. *The Future of Children, 18*(1), 205–234.

Center on Alcohol Marketing and Youth. (2007). *Youth exposure to alcohol advertising on television and in national magazines, 2001 to 2006.* Washington, DC: Center on Alcohol Marketing and Youth.

Center on Alcohol Marketing and Youth. (2008). *Youth exposure to alcohol advertising on television, 2001 to 2007.* Washington, DC: Center on Alcohol Marketing and Youth.

Centers for Disease Control. (2009). The WorkLife initiative: Protecting and promoting worker health and well-being. (DHHS Publication No. 2009-146). Retrieved July 1, 2010, from http://www.cdc.gov/niosh/worklife/pdfs/ worklifesummary8.pdf.

Chamberlain, L. J., Wang, Y., & Robinson, T. N. (2006). Does children's screen time predict requests for advertised products? *Archives of Pediatric and Adolescent Medicine, 160,* 363–368.

Chaplin, H. (1999). Food fight. *American Demographics, 21*(6), 64–65.

Chernin, A. (2007). *The relationship between children's knowledge of persuasive intent and persuasion: The case of televised food marketing* (Doctoral dissertation). Retrieved July 1, 2010, from http://repository.upenn.edu/disser tations/AAI3292015.

Chernin, A. (2008). The effects of food marketing on children's preferences: Testing the

moderating roles of age and gender. *The ANNALS of the American Academy of Political and Social Science, 615,* 102–120. doi: 10.1177/0002716207308952.

Chester, J., & Montgomery, K. C. (2007). *Interactive food and beverage marketing: Targeting children and youth in the digital age.* Berkeley, CA: Berkeley Media Studies Group. Retrieved July 1, 2010, from http://digitalads.org/reports.php.

Cohen, N. (2006, 23 February). Virtual product placement infiltrates TV, film, games. *E-Commerce Times.* Retrieved July 1, 2010, from http://www.ecommercetimes.com/story/48956.html.

Collins, R., Ellickson, P., McCaffrey, D. & Hambarsoomians, K. (2007). Early adolescent exposure to alcohol advertising and its relationship to underage drinking. *Journal of Adolescent Health, 40,* 527–534.

Committee on Communications. (2006). Children, adolescents and advertising. *Pediatrics, 118*(6), 2563–2569. doi:10.1542/peds.2006-2698.

Comstock. G., & Scharrer, E. (2007). *Media and the American child.* Burlington, MA: Elsevier.

Condry, J., Bence, P., & Scheibe, C. (1988). Non-program content of children's television. *Journal of Broadcasting, 32,* 255–270.

Connor, S. M. (2006). Food-related advertising on preschool television: Building brand recognition in young viewers. *Pediatrics, 118*(4), 1478–1485.

Cowburn, G., & Boxer A. (2007). Magazines for children and young people and the links to Internet food marketing: A review of the extent and type of food advertising. *Public Health Nutrition, 10,* 1024–1031. doi:10.1017/S1368980007666658.

Dahl, S., Eagle, L., & Baez, C. (2009). Analyzing advergames: Active diversions or actually deception. An exploratory study of online advergames content. *Young Consumers, 10*(1), 46.

Derthick, M. (2005). *Tobacco politics* (2nd ed.). Washington, DC: CQ Press.

Dietz, W. H., & Gortmaker, S. L. (1985). Do we fatten our children at the television set? Obesity and television viewing in children and adolescents. *Pediatrics, 75,* 807–812.

Donahue, T., Henke, L., & Donahue, W. (1980). Do kids know what TV commercials intend? *Journal of Advertising Research, 20,* 51–57.

Donahue, T., Meyer, T., & Henke, L. (1978). Black and White children: Perceptions of television commercials. *Journal of Marketing, 42,* 34–40.

Dotson, M. J., & Hyatt, E. M. (2005). Major influence factors in children's consumer socialization. *Journal of Consumer Marketing, 22*(1), 35–43.

Faber, R., Perloff, R., & Hawkins, R. (1982). Antecedents of children's comprehension of television advertising. *Journal of Broadcasting, 26,* 575–584.

Federal Trade Commission. (2007). *Implementing the children's online privacy act: A report to Congress.* Report of the Federal Trade Commission. Retrieved July 1, 2010, from http://www.ftc.gov/reports/coppa/07COPPA_Report_to_Congress.pdf.

Federal Trade Commission. (2008). *Marketing food to children and adolescents: A review of industry expenditures, activities, and self-regulation.* Report of the Federal Trade Commission. Retrieved July 1, 2010, from www.ftc.gov/os/2008/07/P064504foodmktingreport.pdf.

Federal Trade Commission. (2008). *Self-regulation in the alcohol industry.* Report of the Federal Trade Commission. Retrieved July 1, 2010, from http://www.ftc.gov/os/2008/06/080626alcoholreport.pdf.

Fischer, P. M., Schwartz, M. P., Richards, J. W., Goldstein, A. O., & Rojas, T. H. (1991). Brand logo recognition by children aged 3 to 6 years: Mickey Mouse and Old Joe the Camel. *Journal of the American Medical Association, 266*(22), 3145–3148.

Flavell, J. (1977). *Cognitive development.* Englewood Cliffs, NJ: Prentice Hall.

Foehr, U. (2006). *Media multitasking among American youth: Prevalence, predictors and pairings.* Menlo Park, CA: Kaiser Family Foundation. Retrieved July 1, 2010, from http://www.kff.org/entmedia/upload/7592.pdf.

Folta, S. C., Goldberg, J. P., Economos, C., Bell, R., & Meltzer, R. (2006). Food advertising targeted at school-age children: A content analysis. *Journal of Nutrition Education and Behavior, 38*(4), 244–248.

Gamble, M., & Cotugna, N. (1999). A quarter century of TV food advertising targeted at children. *American Journal of Health Behavior, 23,* 261–267.

Gantz, W., Schwartz, N., Angelini, J., & Rideout, V. (2007). *Food for thought: Television food advertising to children in the United States.* Menlo Park, CA: Kaiser Family Foundation. Retrieved July 1, 2010, from http://www.kff.org/entmedia/7618.cfm.

Glantz, S., Slade, J., Bero, L., Hanauer, P., & Barnes, D. (1996). *The cigarette papers.* Berkeley: University of California Press.

Goldberg, M., & Gorn, G. (1978). Some unintended consequences of TV advertising to children. *Journal of Consumer Research, 5,* 22–29.

Gorn, G., & Florsheim, R. (1985). The effects of commercials for adult products on children. *Journal of Consumer Research, 11,* 962–967.

Gorn, G., & Goldberg, M. (1980). Children's responses to repetitive television commercials. *Journal of Consumer Research, 6,* 421–424.

Greenberg, B., & Brand, J. (1993). Television news and advertising in schools: The "Channel One" controversy. *Journal of Communication, 43,* 143–151.

Greer, D., Potts, R., Wright, J., & Huston, A. (1982). The effects of television commercial form and commercial placement on children's social behavior and attention. *Child Development, 53,* 611–619.

Grier, S. A., & Kumanyika, S. (2010). *Annual Review of Public Health, 31,* 349–369. doi:10.1146/annurev.publhealth.012809.103607.

Grube, J., & Wallack, L. (1994). Television beer advertising and drinking knowledge, beliefs and intentions among schoolchildren. *American Journal of Public Health, 94,* 254–259.

Gunter, B., Baluch, B., Duffy, L., & Furnham, A. (2002). Children's memory for television advertising: Effects of programme-advertisement congruency. *Applied Cognitive Psychology, 16*(2), 171–190.

Gunter, B., Oates, C., & Blades, M. (2005). *Advertising to children on TV: Content, impact, and regulation.* Mahwah, NJ: Lawrence Erlbaum.

Harris, J. L., Brownell, K. D., & Bargh, J. A. (2009). The food marketing defense model: Integrating psychological research to protect youth and inform public policy. *Social Issues and Policy Review, 3*(1), 211–271.

Harris, J. L., Weinberg, M. E., Schwartz, M. B., Ross, C., Ostroff, J., & Brownell, K. D. (2010). *Trends in television food advertising: Progress in reducing unhealthy marketing to young people?* New Haven, CT: Yale University.

Harrison, K. (2005). Is "fat free" good for me? A panel study of television viewing and children's nutritional knowledge and reasoning. *Health Communication, 17,* 117–132.

Harrison, K., & Marske, A. L. (2005). Nutritional content of foods advertised during the television programs children watch most. *American Journal of Public Health, 95,* 1568–1574.

Hastings, G., Stead, M., McDermott, L., Forsyth, A., MacKintosh, A. M., Raynre, M., et al. (2003). *Review of research on the effects of food promotion to children.* Glasgow, Scotland: Center for Social Marketing.

Henderson, V. R., & Kelly, B. (2005). Food advertising in the age of obesity: Content analysis of food advertising on general market and African American television. *Journal of Nutrition Education and Behavior, 37*(4), 191–196.

Henke, L. (1999). Children, advertising, and the Internet: An exploratory study. In D. Schumann & E. Thorson (Eds.), *Advertising and the World Wide Web* (pp. 73–83). Mahwah, NJ: Lawrence Erlbaum.

Henke, L., & Fontenot, G. (2007). Children and Internet use: Perceptions of advertising, privacy, and functional displacement. *Journal of Business & Economics Research, 5*(11), 59–66.

Holt, D., Ippolito, P., Desrochers, D., & Kelley, C. (2007). *Children's exposure to TV advertising in 1977 and 2004: Information for the obesity debate.* Federal Trade Commission Bureau of Economics Staff Report. Retrieved July 1, 2010, from http://www.ftc.gov/os/2007/06/cabecolor.pdf.

Institute of Medicine (IOM). (2003). *Reducing underage drinking: A collective responsibility.* Washington, DC: National Academies Press.

Institute of Medicine. (IOM). (2005). *Preventing childhood obesity: Health in the balance.* Washington, DC: National Academies Press.

Institute of Medicine (IOM). (2006). *Food marketing to children and youth: Threat or opportunity?* Washington, DC: National Academies Press.

Isler, L., Popper, E., & Ward, S. (1987). Children's purchase requests and parental responses: Results from a diary study. *Journal of Advertising Research, 27*(5), 28–39.

Jennings, R. (1970). *Programming and advertising practices in television directed to children.* Boston: Action for Children's Television.

Jernigan, D. H, Ostroff, J., & Ross, C. (2005). Alcohol advertising and youth: A measured approach. *Journal of Public Health Policy, 26*(3), 312–325.

John, D. R. (1999). Consumer socialization of children: A retrospective look at twenty-five years of research. *Journal of Consumer Research, 26,* 183–213.

Jones, S. C., Wiese, E., & Fabrianesi, B. (2008). Following the links: Food advertising and promotion on children's magazine websites. *Journal of Nonprofit and Public Sector Marketing, 20*(2), 165–190.

Kasser, T., & Kanner, A. (2004). *Psychology and consumer culture.* Washington, DC: American Psychological Association.

Kunkel, D. (1988). Children and host-selling television commercials. *Communication Research, 15*(1), 71–92. doi: 10.1177/009365088015001004.

Kunkel, D. (2010). Mismeasurement of children's understanding of the persuasive intent of advertising. *Journal of Children and Media, 4,* 109–117.

Kunkel, D., & Gantz, W. (1992). Children's television advertising in the multichannel environment. *Journal of Communication, 42,* 134–152.

Kunkel, D., & Gantz, W. (1994, July). *Children's television advertising at Christmas time.* Paper presented at the annual conference of

the International Communication Association, Sydney, Australia.

Kunkel, D., & McIlrath, M. (2003). Message content in advertising to children. In E. Palmer & B. Young (Eds.), *Faces of televisual media: Teaching, violence, selling to children* (pp. 287–300). Mahwah, NJ: Lawrence Erlbaum.

Kunkel, D., McKinley, C., & Wright, P. (2009). *The impact of industry self-regulation on the nutritional quality of foods advertised on television to children.* Oakland, CA: Children Now.

Kunkel, D., & Roberts, D. (1991). Young minds and marketplace values: Research and policy issues in children's television advertising. *Journal of Social Issues, 47*(1), 57–72.

Kunkel, D., Wilcox, B., Cantor, J., Palmer, E., Linn, S., & Dowrick, P. (2004). Psychological issues in the increasing commercialization of childhood. Washington, DC: American Psychological Association. Retrieved July 1, 2010, from http://www.apa.org/pi/families/resources/advertising-children.pdf.

Kurdek, L., & Rodgon, M. (1975). Perceptual, cognitive and affective perspective taking in kindergarten through sixth-grade children. *Developmental Psychology, 11,* 643–650.

Landrine, H., Klonoff, E. A., Fernandez, S., Hickman, N., Kashima, K., Parekh, B., et al. (2005). Cigarette advertising in Black, Latino, and White magazines, 1998–2002: An exploratory investigation. *Ethnic Disparities, 15*, 63–67.

Larson, N., & Story, M. (2008). The adolescent obesity epidemic: Why, how long, and what to do about it. *Adolescent Medicine: State of the Art Reviews, 19*(3), 357–379.

Liebert, R. M., Neale, J. M., & Davidson, E. S. (1973). *The early window: Effects of television on children and youth.* Elmsford, NY: Pergamon Press.

Liebert, D., Sprafkin, J., Liebert, R., & Rubinstein, E. (1977). Effects of television commercial disclaimers on the product expectations of children. *Journal of Communication, 27*(1), 118–124.

Lingas, E., Dorfman, L., & Bukofzer, E. (2009). Nutrition content of food and beverage products on web sites popular with children. *American Journal of Public Health, 99*(7), 1–10.

Linn, S. (2004). *Consuming kids: The hostile takeover of childhood.* New York: New Press.

Livingstone, S., & Helsper, E. (2006). Does advertising literacy mediate the effects of advertising on children? A critical examination of two linked research literatures in relation to obesity and food choice. *Journal of Communication 56,* 560–584.

Ludwig, D. S., & Nestle, M. (2008). Can the food industry play a constructive role in the obesity epidemic? *Journal of the American Medical Association, 300*(15), 1808–1811.

Luke, D., Esmundo, E., & Bloom Y. (2000). Smoke signs: Patterns of tobacco billboard advertising in a metropolitan region. *Tobacco Control, 9,* 16–23. doi:10.1136/tc.9.1.16.

Lyle, J., & Hoffman, H. R. (1972). Children's use of television and other media In E. A. Rubinstein, G. A. Comstock, & J. P. Murray (Eds.), *Televisions and social behavior: Volume 4. Television in day-to-day life: Patterns of use* (DHEW Publication No. HSM 72-9059, pp. 129–256). Washington, DC: U.S. Government Printing Office.

Macklin, M. C. (1983). Do children understand TV ads? *Journal of Advertising Research, 23*(1), 63–70.

Macklin, M. C. (1985). Do young children understand the selling intent of commercials? *Journal of Consumer Affairs, 19,* 293–304.

Macklin, M. C. (1994). The effects of an advertising retrieval cue on young children's memory and brand evaluations. *Psychology & Marketing, 11*(3), 291–311.

Mallinckrodt, V., & Mizerski, D. (2007). The effects of playing an advergame on young children's perceptions, preferences, and requests. *Journal of Advertising, 36*(2), 87–100. doi: 10.2753/JOA0091-3367360206.

Marketplace. (2008, February 6). Cell phone advertising to get specific. *American Public Media.* Retrieved July 1, 2010, from http://marketplace.publicradio.org/display/web/2008/02/06/cell_phone_advertising/.

McCarthy, M. (2005, January 17). Disney plans to mix ads, video games to target kids, teens. *USA Today.* Retrieved July 1, 2010, from http://www.usatoday.com/money/media/2005-01-17-disney-advergaming_x.htm.

McCarty, J. (2004). Product placement: The nature of the practice and potential avenues of inquiry. In L. J. Shrum (Ed.), *The psychology of entertainment media* (pp. 45–61). Mahwah, NJ: Lawrence Erlbaum.

McClure, A. C., Stoolmiller, M., Tanski, S. E., Worth, K. A., & Sargent, J. D. (2009). Alcohol-branded merchandise and its association with drinking attitudes and outcomes in US adolescents. *Archives of Pediatrics and Adolescent Medicine, 163*(3), 211–217.

McIlrath, M. (2006). *Children's cognitive processing of Internet advertising.* Unpublished doctoral dissertation, University of California, Santa Barbara. Retrieved July 1, 2010, from http://gradworks.umi.com/32/45/3245951.html.

Mills, C., & Keil, F. C. (2005). The development of cynicism. *Psychological Science, 16*(5), 385–390.

Mizerski, R. (1997). The relationship between cartoon trade character recognition and attitude toward product category in young children. *Social Marketing Quarterly, 4*(1), 6–29. doi: 10.1080/15245004.1997.9960983.

Molnar, A. (2001). *Giving kids the business: The commercialization of American schools.* Dunmore, PA: Westview Press.

Montgomery, K. C. (2007). *Generation digital: Politics, commerce, and childhood in the age of the Internet.* Cambridge, MA: MIT Press.

Montgomery, K. C., & Chester, J. (2009). Interactive food and beverage marketing: Targeting adolescents in the digital age. *Journal of Adolescent Health, 45*(3, Suppl.), S18–S29. doi:10.1016/j.jadohealth.2009.04.006.

Moore, E. S. (2004). Children and the changing world of advertising. *Journal of Business Ethics, 52,* 161–167.

Moore, E. S. (2006). *It's child's play: Advergaming and the online marketing of food to children.* Menlo Park, CA: Kaiser Family Foundation. Retrieved July 1, 2010, from http://www.kff.org/entmedia/upload/7536.pdf.

Moore E. S., & Rideout, V. (2007). The online marketing of food to children: Is it just fun and games? *Journal of Public Policy & Marketing, 26*(2), 202–220.

Moschis, G., & Moore, R. (1982). A longitudinal study of television advertising effects. *Journal of Consumer Research, 9,* 279–286.

Nairn, A., & Fine, C. (2008). Who's messing with my mind? The implications of dual-process models for the ethics of advertising to children. *International Journal of Advertising, 27*(3), 447–470.

Neeley, S., & Schumann, D. W. (2004). Using animated spokes-characters in advertising to young children. *Journal of Advertising, 33*(3), 7–23.

Neuborne, E. (2001, August 13). For kids on the web, it's an ad, ad, ad, ad world. *Business Week,* 108–109.

Oates, C., Blades, M., & Gunter, B. (2002). Children and television advertising: When do they understand persuasive intent? *Journal of Consumer Behaviour, 1*(3), 238–245.

Palmer, E., & Carpenter, C. F. (2006). Food and beverage marketing to children and youth: Trends and issues. *Media Psychology, 8*(2), 165–190.

Palmer, E., & McDowell, C. (1979). Program/commercial separators in children's television programming. *Journal of Communication, 29*(3), 197–201.

Palmer, E., & McDowell, C. (1981). Children's understanding of nutritional information presented in breakfast cereal commercials. *Journal of Broadcasting, 25,* 295–301.

Pechmann, C., Levine, L., Loughlin, S., & Leslie, F. (2005). Impulsive and self-conscious: Adolescents' vulnerability to advertising and promotion. *Journal of Public Policy and Marketing, 24*(2), 202–211.

Peeler, C. L., Kolish, E., & Enright, M. (2009). *The children's food and beverage advertising initiative in action: A report on compliance and implementation during 2008.* Arlington, VA: Council of Better Business Bureaus, Inc. Retrieved July 1, 2010, from http://cms-admin.bbb.org/storage/0/Shared%20Documents/finalbbbs.pdf.

Piaget, J. (1954). *The construction of reality in the child.* New York: Ballantine.

Pine, K. J., & Nash, A. (2003). Barbie or Betty? Preschool children's preference for branded products and evidence for gender-linked differences. *Journal of Developmental & Behavioral Pediatrics, 24*(4), 219–224.

Pomeranz, J. (2010). Television food marketing to children revisited: The Federal Trade Commission has the constitutional and statutory authority to regulate. *Journal of Law, Medicine, and Ethics, 38,* 98–116.

Powell, L. M., Szczypka, G., & Chaloupka, F. J. (2010). Trends in exposure to television food advertisements among children and adolescents in the United States. *Archives of Pediatric and Adolescent Medicine, 164*(9), 1–9. doi: 10.1001/archpediatrics.2010.139.

Powell, L. M., Szczypka, G., Chaloupka, F. J., & Braunshweig, C. L. (2007). Nutritional content of television food advertising seen by children and adolescents in the United States. *Pediatrics, 120*(3), 576–583. doi: 10.1542/peds.2006-3595.

Richards, J. W., Tye, J. B., & Fischer, P. M. (1996). The tobacco industry's code of advertising in the United States: Myth and reality. *Tobacco Control, 5,* 295–311.

Rideout, V., Foehr, U., & Roberts, D. (2010). *Generation M²: Media in the lives of 8- to 18-year-olds.* Menlo Park, CA: Henry J. Kaiser Family Foundation. Retrieved July 1, 2010, from http://www.kff.org/entmedia/mh012010pkg.cfm.

Roberts, D. F. (1982). Children and commercials: Issues, evidence, interventions. *Prevention in Human Services, 2,* 19–35.

Roberts, D. F., & Foehr, U. G. (2004). *Kids and media in America.* Cambridge, UK: Cambridge University Press.

Robertson, T. (1979). Parental mediation of advertising effects. *Journal of Communication, 29*(1), 12–25.

Robertson, T., & Rossiter, J. (1974). Children and commercial persuasion: An attribution theory

analysis. *Journal of Consumer Research, 1,* 13–20.

Robinson, T., Borzekowski, D., Matheson, D., & Kraemer, H. (2007). Effects of fast food branding on young children's taste preferences. *Archives of Pediatric and Adolescent Medicine, 161*(8), 792–797.

Rossiter, J., & Robertson, T. (1974). Children's television commercials: Testing the defense. *Journal of Communication, 24*(4), 137–144.

Rozendaal, E., Buijzen, M., & Valkenburg, P. M. (2010). Comparing children's and adults' cognitive advertising competences in the Netherlands. *Journal of Children and Media, 4,* 77–89. doi: 10.1080/17482790903407333.

Sargent, J. D., Gibson, J., & Heatherton, T. F. (2009). Comparing the effects of entertainment media and tobacco marketing on youth smoking. *Tobacco Control, 18,* 47–53. doi:10.1136/tc.2008.026153.

Schiller, G. (2008, February 12). Brand spending grows nearly 15%. *Hollywood Reporter.* Retrieved July 1, 2010, from http://www.hollywoodreporter.com/news/brand-spending-grows-15-104609 [requires fee].

Schor, J. B. (2004). *Born to buy: The commercialized child and the new consumer culture.* New York: Scribner.

Schwartz, M. B., Vartanian, L. R., Wharton, C. M., & Brownell, K. D. (2008). Examining the nutritional quality of breakfast cereals marketed to children. *Journal of the American Dietetic Association, 108*(4), 702–705. doi:10.1016/j.jada.2008.01.003.

Schwartz, P., & Solove, D. (2009). *Privacy: The FTC's role in privacy protection: Implications for food & beverage marketing.* Berkeley Media Studies Group. Retrieved July 1, 2010, from http://digitalads.org/reports.php.

Selman, R. (1980). *The growth of interpersonal understanding.* New York: Academic Press.

Shah, A. (2008). Children as consumers. Retrieved July 1, 2010, from http://www.globalissues.org/article/237/children-as-consumers.

Shantz, C. (1975). The development of social cognition. In H. Hetherington (Ed.), *Review of child development research (Vol. 5).* Chicago: University of Chicago Press.

Sharma, L., Teret, S., & Brownell, K. D. (2010). The food industry and self-regulation: Standards to promote success and to avoid public health failures. *American Journal of Public Health, 100,* 240–246.

Sheikh, A., & Moleski, M. (1977) Conflict in the family over commercials. *Journal of Communication, 27*(1), 152–157.

Signorielli, N., & Lears, M. (1992). Television and children's conceptions of nutrition: Unhealthy messages. *Health Communication, 4,* 245–257.

Signorielli, N., & Staples, J. (1997). Television and children's conceptions of nutrition. *Health Communication, 9,* 289–301.

Slater, S., Chaloupka, F., Wakefield, M., Johnston, L., & O'Malley, P. (2007). The impact of retail cigarette marketing practices on youth smoking uptake. *Archives of Pediatrics and Adolescent Medicine, 161*(5), 440–445.

Snyder, L. B., Milici, F. F., Slater, M., Sun, H., & Strizhakova, Y. (2006). Effects of alcohol advertising exposure on drinking among youth. *Archives of Pediatrics and Adolescent Medicine, 160,* 18–24.

Springer, K. (2001). Perceptual boundedness and perceptual support in conceptual development. *Psychological Review, 108,* 691–708.

Stern, B., & Harmon, R. (1984). The incidence and characteristics of disclaimers in children's television advertising. *Journal of Advertising, 13*(2), 12–16.

Stern, B., & Resnik, A. (1978). Children's understanding of a televised commercial disclaimer. In S. Jain (Ed.), *Research frontiers in marketing: Dialogues and directions* (pp. 332–336). Chicago: American Marketing Association.

Stitt, C., & Kunkel, D. (2008). Food advertising during children's television programming on broadcast and cable channels. *Health Communication, 23,* 573–584.

Stoneman, Z., & Brody, G. (1981). The indirect impact of child-oriented advertisements on mother–child interactions. *Journal of Applied Developmental Psychology, 2,* 369–376.

Story, M., & French, S. (2004). Food advertising and marketing directed at children and adolescents in the US. *International Journal of Behavioral Nutrition and Physical Activity, 1*(3), 1–17. doi:10.1186/1479-5868-1-3.

Strasburger, V. C., Wilson, B. J., & Jordan, A. B. (2009). *Children, adolescents, and the media.* Thousand Oaks, CA: Sage.

Stutts, M., & Hunnicutt, G. G. (1987). Can young children understand disclaimers in television commercials? *Journal of Advertising, 16*(1), 41–46.

Stutts, M., Vance, D., & Hudleson S. (1981). Program-commercial separators in children's television: Do they help a child tell the difference between Bugs Bunny and the Quik Rabbit? *Journal of Advertising, 10,* 16–25.

Sutherland, L., Mackenzie, T., Purvis, L., & Dalton, M. (2010). Prevalence of food and beverage brands in movies: 1996–2005. *Pediatrics, 125*(3), 468–474. doi:10.1542/peds.2009-0857.

Thomas, S. G. (2007). *Buy, buy baby: How consumer culture manipulates parents and harms young minds.* New York: Houghton Mifflin.

Thomson, E. S., & Laing, A. W. (2003). The net generation: Children and young people, the

Internet and online shopping. *Journal of Marketing Management, 19,* 491–512.

Turow, J. (2006). *Niche envy.* Cambridge, MA: MIT Press.

U.S. Department of Health, Education and Welfare. (1964). *Smoking and health: Report of the advisory committee to the Surgeon General of the Public Health Service.* (DHEW Publication No. 1103). Washington, DC: U.S. Government Printing Office.

U.S. Government Accountability Office (2004). *Commercial activities in schools: Use of student data is limited and additional dissemination of guidance could help districts develop policies.* Washington, DC: United States Government Accountability Office. Retrieved July 1, 2010, from http://www.gao.gov/new.items/d04810.pdf.

U. S. Public Health Service. (2007). *The Surgeon General's call to action to prevent and reduce underage drinking.* Rockville, MD: United States Department of Health and Human Services. Retrieved July 1, 2010, from http://www.surgeongeneral.gov/topics/underagedrinking/.

Valkenburg, P. M., & Buijzen, M. (2005). Identifying determinants of young children's brand awareness: Television, parents, and peers. *Applied Developmental Psychology, 26,* 456–468.

Vitka, W. (2005, 16 July). *In-game advertising: IGA worldgroup leads the pack and they might be getting it just right.* Retrieved July 1, 2010, from http://www.cbsnews.com/stories/2005/07/15/tech/gamecore/main709467.shtml.

Ward S., & Wackman, D. (1972). Children's purchase influence attempts and parental yielding. *Journal of Marketing Research, 9,* 316–319.

Ward, S., & Wackman, D. (1973). Children's information processing of television advertising. In P. Clarke (Ed.), *New models for mass communication research.* Beverly Hills, CA: Sage.

Ward, S., Reale, G., & Levinson, D. (1972). Children's perceptions, explanations, and judgments of television advertising: A further exploration. In G. Comstock & E. Rubinstein (Eds.), *Television and social behavior (Vol. 4).* Washington, DC: U.S. Government Printing Office.

Ward, S., Wackman, D., & Wartella, E. (1977). *How children learn to buy: The development of consumer information processing skills.* Beverly Hills, CA: Sage.

Warren, A. R., & Tate, C. (1992). Egocentrism in children's telephone conversations. In R. Diaz & L. Berk (Eds.), *Private speech: From social interaction to self-regulation* (pp. 245–264). Hillsdale, NJ: Lawrence Erlbaum.

Warren, R., Wicks, J. Wicks, R., Fosu, I., & Chung, D. (2007). Food and beverage advertising to children on US television: Did national food advertisers respond? *Journalism and Mass Communication Quarterly, 84*(4), 795–810.

Warren, R., Wicks, J. Wicks, R., Fosu, I., & Chung, D. (2008). Food and beverage advertising to children on US television: A comparison of child-targeted versus general audience commercials. *Journal of Broadcasting & Electronic Media, 52*(2), 231–246. doi: 10.1080/08838150801992037.

Weber, K., Story, M., & Harnack, L. (2006). Internet food marketing strategies aimed at children and adolescents: A content analysis of food and beverage brand web sites. *Journal of the American Dietetic Association, 106,* 1463–1466. doi:10.1016/j.jada.2006.06.014.

White House Task Force on Childhood Obesity. (2010). *Solving the problem of childhood obesity within a generation. Report to the President.* Washington, DC: Executive Office of the President of the United States. Available at http://www.letsmove.gov/whitehouse-task-force-childhood-obesity-report-president.

Wikipedia. (2010). *In-game advertising.* Retrieved July 1, 2010, from http://en.wikipedia.org/wiki/In_game_advertising.

Wilson, B. J., & Weiss, A. J. (1992). Developmental differences in children's reactions to toy advertisement linked to toy-based cartoon. *Journal of Broadcasting & Electronic Media, 36,* 371–394.

Wilson, G., & Wood, K. (2004). The influence of children on parental purchases during supermarket shopping. *International Journal of Consumer Studies, 28*(4), 329–336.

Young, B. (2008). Media and advertising effects. In S. Calvert & B. Wilson (Eds.), *The handbook of children, media and development.* Malden, MA: Blackwell.

Zimmerman, F. J., & Bell, J. F. (2010). Associations of television content type and obesity in children. *American Journal of Public Health, 100,* 334–340.

Zimmerman, F. J., Christakis, D. A., & Meltzoff, A. N. (2007). Television and DVD/video viewing in children younger than 2 years. *Archives of Pediatrics and Adolescent Medicine, 161,* 473–479.

Zuckerman, P., Ziegler M., & Stevenson, H. (1978). Children's viewing of television and recognition memory of commercials. *Child Development, 49,* 96–104.

Children, Adolescents, Drugs, and the Media

Victor C. Strasburger
University of New Mexico

The Marlboro Man emanated in 1954 from the minds of Chicago admen Leo Burnett and John Benson, who were trying to devise a more macho pitch for Philip Morris' filter-tip cigarette and agreed that the "most masculine figure in America" was the cowboy. In the next 40 years, the smoking cowboy traveled the world (and 2 actors who played him died of lung cancer).

W. Nugent (1999)

A cigarette in the hands of a Hollywood star onscreen is a gun aimed at a 12- or 14-year-old.

Screenwriter Joe Eszterhas (2004)

How about that powerful anti-drug commercial paid for by the U.S. government? It aired right between the seventh and eighth Budweiser commercials.

David Letterman,
CBS's *Late Show*,
on the 2002 Super Bowl
commercials (*TV Guide*, 2002)

My 6 year-old daughter turned to me and said, "What's a 4-hour erection?" said Kelly Simmons, executive vice president at Tierney Communications in Philadelphia. "How do you explain it?"

www.bettydodson.com/
potencyads.htm

W hile the "War on Drugs" and "Just Say No" campaigns have been waged since the 1980s, children and teenagers have been exposed to more than $20 billion worth of cigarette, alcohol,

and prescription drug advertising annually that has worked very effectively to get them to just say yes to smoking, drinking, and other drugs (see Figure 21.1; American Academy of Pediatrics, 2006; Federal Trade Commission, 2009; Strasburger, Wilson, & Jordan, 2009). In addition, content analyses show that television programs, movies, and popular music all contain appreciable drug content (see Figure 21.2). Up until recently, correlational studies found a significant connection between exposure to advertising and to drug content but not a cause-and-effect impact. But increasing evidence now exists that exposure to drug advertising and to scenes of smoking or drinking in movies may be one of the leading causes—if not *the* leading cause—of early adolescent experimentation with cigarettes and alcohol (Strasburger, Jordan, & Donnerstein, 2010).

Adolescent Drug Use

Illegal drugs certainly take their toll on society; but tobacco and alcohol—two legal drugs—pose a far greater danger to children and teenagers. Every year, more than 400,000 Americans die from tobacco-related causes—more than from AIDS, car crashes, murder, and suicide combined (American Academy of Pediatrics, 2009a). Tobacco is the only known legal drug that kills when used as directed. And each day in the United States, approximately 4,000 adolescents try their first cigarette (Centers for Disease Control, 2008).

With increased globalization, concerns are emerging about the impact of American tobacco exports on worldwide smoking rates (Prokhorov et al., 2006). More than 1.1 billion people currently smoke worldwide, resulting in 4 million deaths per year. Nearly 100,000 young people begin smoking *daily* (Tanski, Prokhorov, & Klein, 2004). If this trend continues, a billion people will die prematurely of smoking-related causes during this century (World Health Organization, 2008). Secondhand smoke has also become an important problem in developing countries. The World Health Organization (WHO) reports that 700 million children are exposed to environmental smoke annually, especially in countries like India, China, Indonesia, Pakistan, and Russia

Figure 21.1

Figure 21.2 a Substance appearance in popular movies and songs. Note that movies far exceed songs as a source of drug depictions.

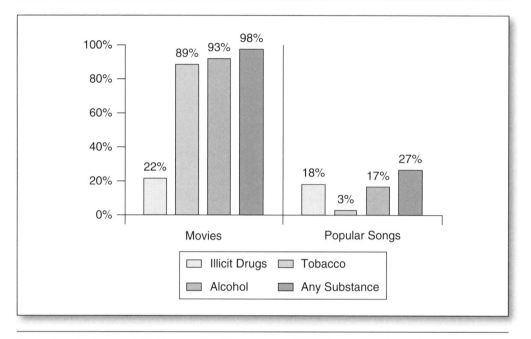

Source: From Christenson, P. G., Henriksen, L., & Roberts, D. F. (2000). Substance use in popular prime-time television. Washington, DC: Office of National Drug Policy Control.

Figure 21.2 b Substance Use in Television

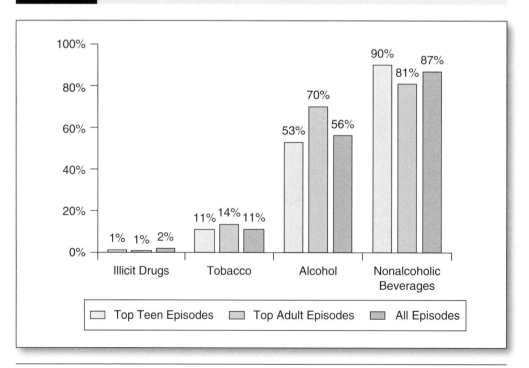

Source: From Christenson, P. G., Henriksen, L., & Roberts, D. F. (2000). Substance use in popular prime-time television. Washington, DC: Office of National Drug Policy Control.

(Prokhorov et al., 2006). The United States is the leading producer of cigarettes, exporting three times as many as any other country, and American tobacco companies are increasingly turning overseas as the U.S. market tightens (Womach, 2003). While most of the dangers of smoking and of second-hand smoke are well understood (e.g., lung cancer, other cancers, heart disease, respiratory illness, infertility, etc.), new research is finding additional concerns for young people. Smoking may cause damage to lung cell DNA that produces physiological changes that persist despite quitting smoking (Wiencke et al., 1999). Tobacco use may also be a marker for depression and anxiety disorders in adolescence (Sims and Committee on Substance Abuse, 2009).

Alcohol is the most commonly abused drug by young people ages 12 to 17 years and may account for as many as 100,000 deaths annually, including 5,000 people under 21 years (U.S. Department of Health and Human Services, 2007). In the United States alone, alcohol accounts for 28,000 unintentional injury deaths, 17,000 traffic deaths, 300,000 traffic injuries, and 1.4 million emergency department injury visits annually (Hingson & Zha, 2009). The risk of an injury increases ninefold among patients consuming five to six drinks in the few hours before the injury (Hingson & Zha 2009; Vinson, Maclure, Reidinger, & Smith, 2003). It is the most commonly abused drug by 12- to 17-year-olds. In fact, underage drinkers account for about 20% of all alcohol consumption (Foster, Vaughan,

Figure 21.3 Trends in Lifetime Prevalence of Various Illicit Drugs Among 12th Graders, 1975–2009

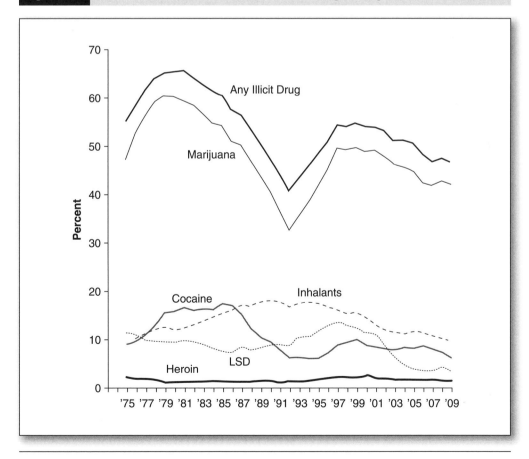

Source: Used with permission of Monitoring the Future Study Survey. University of Michigan.

| Table 21.1 | Adolescent Drug Use, 2009 (n = 13,700 12th graders) (in percentages) |

Drug	Ever Used	Used During Past Year
Any illicit drug	47	37
Any illicit drug other than marijuana	24	17
Alcohol	72	66
Ever been drunk	57	47
Cigarettes	44	—
Marijuana	42	33
Smokeless tobacco	16	—
Amphetamines	10	7
Inhalants	10	3
Hallucinogens	7	5
Ecstasy	7	4
Tranquilizers	9	6
Cocaine	6	3
Steroids	2	2
Heroin	1	1
OxyContin	—	5
Vicodin	—	10

Source: Adapted from Johnston, O'Malley, Bachman, & Schulenberg, 2010.

| Table 21.2 | Trends in 12th Graders' Perception of Drugs as Harmful (in percentages) |

How Much Do You Think People Risk Harming Themselves If They	1975	1990	2009
Try marijuana once or twice	15	23	19
Smoke marijuana occasionally	18	37	27
Smoke marijuana regularly	43	79	52
Try LSD once or twice	49	45	37
Try cocaine once or twice	43	59	53
Try MDMA once or twice	—	—	53
Try one or two drinks of an alcoholic beverage	5	8	9
Have five or more drinks once or twice each weekend	38	47	48
Smoke one or more packs of cigarettes per day	51	68	75

Source: Adapted from Johnston, O'Malley, Bachman, & Schulenberg, 2010.

Foster, & Califano, 2003) and for one-third of all alcohol industry revenues (Foster, Vaughan, Foster, & Califano, 2006). Physicians who treat teenagers know that alcohol can contribute significantly to the three leading causes of death among teens—accidents, homicides, and suicides—which together account for 75% of their mortality rate (Kulig & the Committee on Substance Abuse, 2005; Swahn, Bossarte, & Sullivent, 2008; Thompson, Sims, Kingree, & Windle, 2008). Increasing research is discovering that alcoholism begins young: Nearly half of all alcoholics are diagnosable before age 21 (Brown et al., 2008; Hingson, Heeren, & Winter, 2006). Globally, alcohol consumption causes 1.8 million deaths (3.2%) annually and is the leading risk factor for morbidity in many developing countries (WHO, 2002).

The best data regarding adolescent drug use come from the University of Michigan Monitoring the Future Study (MTF), which surveys nearly 45,000 students annually in the 8th, 10th, and 12th grades at more than 430 public and private schools across the country (www.monitoringthefuture.org). Funded by the National Institute on Drug Abuse (NIDA), this study has been conducted annually since the mid-1970 data is so extensive over so long a period of time. The next best source of data is the Youth Risk Behavior Survey (YRBS), conducted by the Centers for Disease Control (CDC) every 2 years in nearly every state (http://www.cdc.gov/mmwr/pdf/ss/ss5905 .pdf). The 2009 survey included more than 16,000 9th–12th graders.

Highlights of the 2009 MTF survey and the 2009 YRBS include:

- Continued decreases in smoking levels, which reached a peak in 1996 to 1997, according to the MTF. While 49% of 8th graders in 1996 had ever tried cigarettes, in 2009, only 20% had. Those reporting cigarette use in the month prior to being surveyed decreased from 21% of 8th graders in 1996 to 7% in 2009, from 30% of 10th graders in 1996 to 13% in 2009, and from 37% of 12th graders in 1996 to 20% in 2009. Interestingly, more than 80% of 8th and 10th graders and 75% of 12th graders said that they "would prefer to date people who don't smoke."
- At the same time, the YRBS found that nearly half of all teenagers had tried smoking cigarettes at some time, down from a high of 71% in 1995 but still an alarming figure.
- A leveling off in alcohol use rates. Nearly three-fourths of 12th graders have tried alcohol at least once, down from a peak of 88% in 1991. More than one third of 8th graders have tried alcohol at least once. More worrisome are the figures for binge drinking and ever being drunk. Eight percent of 8th graders report having consumed five or more drinks of alcohol in the 2 weeks prior to being surveyed, 17% of 10th graders, and one fourth of all high school seniors. More than 17% of 8th graders, one third of 10th graders, and one-half of 12th graders report having ever been drunk.
- In the YRBS, 42% of high school students report having had at least one drink of alcohol and nearly one fourth report binge drinking during the previous 30 days. Although athletes are ordinarily less likely to use illicit drugs other than anabolic steroids (Kulig, Brener, & McManus, 2003), male athletes may be more likely to use alcohol (Fisher, Miles, Austin et al., 2007).
- Levels of illicit drug use among teenagers have remained relatively stable over the past several years. Use peaked at 66% in 1981 and declined to a low of 41% in 1992. Currently, nearly half of all seniors report having used an illicit drug, more than one-third of sophomores, and 1 in 5 8th graders. One fourth of seniors have used an illicit drug other than marijuana.
- A leveling off in marijuana use among teenagers. Marijuana use peaked in 1979, when 60% of high school seniors reported having ever tried it. Now, just over 40% of seniors say that they have tried marijuana.
- Marijuana, cocaine, heroin, and MDMA ("ecstasy") use bottomed out in the early 1990s, began rising in the mid- to late 1990s, and now has slowly decreased again.
- For all drugs, it is important to understand that young adults and older adults have higher rates of smoking and alcohol use, and young adults have the highest rates of illicit drug use. But the onset of alcohol and tobacco use is during adolescence in the majority of cases.

The United States is not unique in having an adolescent drug problem. More than half of all female 15-year-olds in Greenland smoke daily, 85% of Scottish 11-year-olds have tried alcohol at least once, more than half of Welsh 15-year-olds consume alcohol at least weekly, and more than 70% of Danish 15-year-olds have been drunk at least twice (Currie,

Hurrelmann, Settertobulte, Smith, & Todd, 2000). In the United Kingdom, 10 to 12% of 15-year-olds report having used marijuana in the month prior to being surveyed (Brooks et al., 2009).

Determinants of Child and Adolescent Drug Use

Adolescents use drugs for a variety of different reasons, including poor self-image, low religiosity, poor school performance, alienation from parents, family dysfunction, physical and emotional abuse, and self-medication (Briones, Wilcox, Mateus, & Boudjenah, 2006; Fisher, Miles, Austin, Camargo, & Colditz, 2007; Schydlower & Arredondo,

2006; Shrier, Harris, Kurland, & Knight, 2003). Media can play an important role as well, making substance use seem like "normative" behavior, especially smoking and drinking. Reviews of adolescent substance use often fail to mention media influence as an etiologic agent for young people initiating drug use (Strasburger, 1998), and researchers typically neglect to ask media-related questions when they are surveying teens for substance use (Strasburger, 2009a).

Peers. Peer pressure may play one of the most important roles in early drug use among young teens (Bahr, Hoffmann, & Yang, 2005), but it may also be a key factor in teens abstaining from drugs as well. Teens who see their friends using drugs are more likely to do so themselves; teens who believe their friends

Figure 21.4

Drawn for Broadcasting by Sidney Harris

"All right, it's a deal. The four-letter words are in, the drug lyrics are out."

Source: ScienceCartoonsPlus.com.

are antidrug are more likely to abstain (Robin & Johnson, 1996). (Another possible and as yet untested hypothesis is that teens prone to drug use or to abstaining search out like-minded peers.) Mapping the social networks of nearly 8,500 adolescents has shown that the likelihood of marijuana use may increase if "friends" are known to use drugs (Mednick, Christakis, & Fowler, 2010).

In many ways, the media can function as a "super-peer," making it seem as if "everyone" is using alcohol, tobacco, or other drugs (Figure 21.4; Strasburger et al., 2009). Because teens always want to be doing what is "normal" and "current" for their peer group (Olds, Thombs, & Tomasek, 2005), the media may represent one of the most powerful influences on their behavior. Media also are a leading source of health information for teens. One study of nearly 800 5th- through 12th-grade students found that television was the leading source of information about smoking (Kurtz, Kurtz, Johnson, & Cooper, 2001).

Family. Parents represent an important influence on whether teens use drugs or not. Depending on the circumstances, parents can be a significant risk factor or a significant protective factor (Bahr et al., 2005; Briones et al., 2006; Halpern-Felsher & Cornell, 2005). Abused children are at greater risk for drug use, for example. Similarly, a "coercive" parenting style can lead to greater substance use and even delinquency (McMahon, 1994). Genetically, alcoholic parents are two to nine times more likely to produce biological children who are alcoholic (Belcher & Shinitzky, 1998). This inherited risk may extend to other drug abuse as well (Comings, 1997). Alternatively, nurturing parents with good communication skills represent a major protective factor (Fisher et al., 2007).

Media have sometimes been called "electronic parents," and if parents and schools fail to give children appropriate information about drugs, the media may fill the void with unhealthy information or cues. For example, latchkey children are more prone to substance use, perhaps because they are unsupervised and have unrestrained access to a variety of potentially unhealthy media (Chilcoat & Anthony, 1996). Likewise, teens who have TV sets in their own bedrooms are more likely to watch more TV and to engage in risky behaviors like sex and using tobacco, marijuana,

and alcohol (Gruber, Wang, Christensen, Grube, & Fisher, 2005; Strasburger & the Council on Communications and Media, 2010b).

Personality. In general, adolescents can be notorious risk takers. Part of the explanation for this probably comes from new research on brain development that shows that the key areas of the frontal cortex (involved in judgment) do not mature until the early to mid-20s (Giedd, 2008; Walsh & Bennett, 2005). MRI studies of teens with alcohol problems show that areas of the brain involved in drug craving and reward (e. g., the limbic system) light up more when shown pictures of alcoholic beverages than in controls (Tapert et al., 2003). Areas of the brain involved in motivating behavior are also different in teenagers (Bjork et al., 2004; White & Swartzwelder, 2004). Both tobacco and alcohol can be considered "gateway drugs" as well, meaning that their use may lead to more worrisome drugs later. For example, teens who smoke are 3 times more likely to use alcohol than nonsmokers, 8 times more likely to use marijuana, and 22 times more likely to use cocaine (U.S. Public Health Service, 2004). Alcohol is often the first drug to be experimented with and may lead to lower grades and to other risk-taking behaviors like premature sexual intercourse and experimentation with other drugs (Brown et al., 2008; Champion et al., 2004; Tapert, Aarons, Sedlar, & Brown, 2001).

Biology. Adolescents' developing brains may make them more susceptible to nicotine addiction and require fewer cigarettes smoked to establish addiction compared to adults (Prokhorov et al., 2006). New research shows that the nicotine in cigarettes can become addictive after only a few puffs (Sims & Committee on Substance Abuse, 2009). A small number of adolescents with psychiatric disorders may also use substances like marijuana or alcohol to try to regulate their mood disorders (U.S. National Drug Control Policy, 2008).

Impact of Advertising on Children and Adolescents

Tobacco and alcohol represent two hugely profitable industries that require the constant recruitment of new users. With the death of

1,200 smokers a day and with thousands more trying to quit, the tobacco industry must recruit new smokers to remain profitable. Inevitably, these new smokers come from the ranks of children and adolescents, especially given the demographics of smoking—50% of smokers begin by age 13, and 80% before age 18 (American Academy of Pediatrics, 2009a; U.S. Department of Health and Human Services, 1994). Worldwide, this amounts to nearly 100,000 young people starting smoking daily (American Academy of Pediatrics, 2009a). Big Tobacco has engaged in a systematic campaign to attract underage smokers for decades and then lied to Congress about it (Glantz, Slade, Bero, Hanauer & Barnes, 1996; Kessler, 2001). The industry continues to resist any Congressional attempts to regulate it (Nocera, 2006). Similarly, the alcohol industry has targeted minority groups and the young for years, particularly through promotion of sports and youth-oriented programming (Gerbner, 1990). Because 5% of drinkers consume 50% of all alcoholic beverages (Gerbner, 1990), new recruits are a must for the alcohol industry as well, preferably heavy drinkers. For underage drinkers, more than 90% of the alcohol consumed is done so as binge drinking (Jernigan, 2006).

Celebrity endorsers are commonly used, and older children and teenagers may be particularly vulnerable to such ads (American Academy of Pediatrics, 2006; Gunter, Oates, & Blades, 2004). Many commercials for alcohol employ some combination of rock music, young attractive models, humor, or adventure. "Beach babes," frogs, lizards, and dogs are all commonly seen in beer commercials. Humor is particularly effective with adolescents (Salkin, 2007). Production values are extraordinary: Costs for a single 30-second commercial may easily exceed those for an entire half-hour of regular programming, and 30 seconds' worth of advertising during the 2010 Super Bowl cost close to $3 million. In 2007, Anheuser-Busch bought 5 entire minutes of advertising during the Super Bowl (Sutel, 2007). Recently, a new form of alcoholic beverage has been dubbed "learner drinks for kids"—so-called "hard" lemonades, which contain about 5% alcohol. They, too, use fictitious cool guys such as "Doc" Otis and One-Eyed Jack and "make a mockery of the industry's claim that it doesn't market to kids," according to one

expert (Cowley & Underwood, 2001). Similarly, tobacco companies are now marketing flavored cigarettes with names like "Beach Breezer," "Kuai Kolada," "Twista Lime," and "Mandarin Mints," despite the 1998 Master Settlement Agreement that included a promise not to market to children (Harris, 2005).

A variety of studies have explored the impact of advertising on children and adolescents (see Figure 21.5). Nearly all have shown advertising to be extremely effective in increasing youngsters' awareness of and emotional responses to alcohol products, their recognition of certain brands, their desire to own or use the products advertised, and their recognition of the advertisements themselves (Borzekowski & Strasburger, 2008). There are, however, some researchers who disagree and feel that children have become increasingly sophisticated about the intent of advertising in general and therefore more media resistant to alcohol advertising specifically. They cite the fact that older meta-analyses find a much larger effect size than more recent ones (Desmond & Carveth, 2007). Nevertheless, two recent studies confirm an association: One analysis involved seven prospective cohort studies involving 13,255 subjects and found at least modest effects (Smith & Foxcroft, 2009); a second analysis examined 13 longitudinal studies involving more than 38,000 young people and concluded that "alcohol advertising and promotion increases the likelihood that adolescents will start to use alcohol, and to drink more if they are already using alcohol" (Anderson, de Bruijn, Angus, Gordon, & Hastings, 2009, p. 229).

Although the research is not yet considered to be scientifically "beyond a reasonable doubt," there is a preponderance of evidence that cigarette and alcohol advertising is a significant factor in adolescents' use of these two drugs (Borzekowski & Strasburger, 2008; Federal Trade Commission, 1999; Grube & Waiters, 2005; Jernigan, 2006; Snyder, Milici, Slater, Sun, & Strizhakova, 2006; Strasburger et al., 2009). The 1999 Federal Trade Commission report on the alcohol industry concluded, "While many factors may influence an underage person's drinking decisions, including among other things parents, peers and the media, there is reason to believe that advertising also plays a role" (Federal Trade Commission, 1999). For alcohol, advertising may account for as much as 10% to 30% of adolescents' usage (Atkin,

Figure 21.5

Source: © British American Tabacco; © R. J. Reynolds Tobacco Company. All rights reserved; © 2007 Suaaza Tequilla Import Company, Deerfield, IL; ©2008 James B. Beam Distilling Co., Clermont, KY.

1995). Interestingly, one study of students' use of cigarette promotional items found that a similar figure applies to cigarettes as well: Approximately one third of adolescents' cigarette use could be predicted by their purchase or ownership of tobacco promotional gear (Pierce, Choi, Gilpin, Farkas, & Berry, 1998). Nevertheless, as one group of researchers notes,

> To reduce the argument regarding the demonstrable effects of massive advertising campaigns to the level of individual behavior is absurdly simplistic. . . . Rather, what we are dealing with is the nature of advertising itself. Pepsi Cola, for example, could not convincingly prove, through any sort of

defensible scientific study, that particular children or adolescents who consume their products do so because of exposure to any or all of their ads. (Orlandi, Lieberman, & Schinke, 1989, p. 90)

Although there is some legitimate debate about how much of an impact such advertising has on young people and their decisions whether to use cigarettes or alcohol, advertising clearly works—or else companies would not spend millions of dollars a year on it. This leaves American society with a genuine moral, economic, and public health dilemma: Should advertising of unhealthy products be allowed when society then has to pay for the disease,

disability, and death that these products cause? (Kunkel, 2007; Strasburger et al., 2009). Tobacco companies and beer manufacturers claim that they are simply influencing "brand choice," not increasing overall demand for their products. Moreover, they claim that because it is legal to sell their products, it should be legal to advertise them as well, and any ban represents an infringement on their First Amendment rights of commercial free speech. Recently, a conservative U.S. Supreme Court seems to agree with them (Bayer & Kelly, 2009; Gostin, 2009).

Public health advocates counter that tobacco companies and beer manufacturers are engaging in unfair and deceptive practices by specifically targeting young people, using attractive role models and youth-oriented messages in their ads, and making smoking and drinking seem like normative behavior (Borzekowski & Strasburger, 2008; Brown & Moodie, 2009; Grube & Waiters, 2005; U.S. Department of Health and Human Services, 1994). For alcohol, teens are exposed to 48% more beer advertising, 20% more advertising for hard liquor, and 92% for ads for sweet alcoholic drinks in magazines than adults of legal drinking age (Center on Alcohol Marketing and Youth, 2005; Garfield, Chung, & Rathouz, 2003). Of the 10 most popular teen magazines, only *Seventeen, Teen,* and *YM* refuse alcohol advertising (Garfield et al., 2003). Teen girls are actually more likely to be exposed to alcohol advertising than women in their 20s or 30s (Jernigan, Ostroff, Ross, & O'Hara, 2004). The fact that alcohol and tobacco manufacturers are trying to get adolescents to "just say yes" to cigarettes and beer at a time when society is trying to get them to "just say no" to drugs seems like a situation straight out of *Alice in Wonderland* (Strasburger, 2010). As we shall see, the available data strongly support the public health viewpoint.

Cigarettes

Impact of Cigarette Advertising

More money is spent on the advertising and promotion of tobacco—nearly $13 billion a year—than on alcohol ($5 billion/year) or prescription drugs ($4 billion/year; American Academy of Pediatrics, 2010; Federal Trade Commission, 2009). Most youth in the United States are exposed to protobacco messages in the media. In a sample of as many as 33,000 6th through 12th graders, 85% had seen tobacco ads in stores and half had seen ads in newspapers and magazines (Duke et al., 2009). Cigarette advertising appears to increase teenagers' risk of beginning to smoke by glamorizing both the act of smoking and smokers themselves (Borzekowski & Strasburger, 2008; National Cancer Institute, 2008). Attractive celebrities smoke; and smokers are portrayed as being independent, healthy, youthful, unconventional, and adventurous. By contrast, the adverse consequences of smoking are almost never shown. Nearly 20 years ago, the U.S. Surgeon General concluded, "Cigarette advertising appears to affect young people's perceptions of the pervasiveness, image, and function of smoking. Since misperceptions in these areas constitute psychosocial risk factors for the initiation of smoking, *cigarette advertising appears to increase young people's risk of smoking*" (U.S. Department of Health & Human Services, 1994, p. 195, emphasis added).

The history of cigarette advertising on TV is one of the more remarkable public health stories on record. In June 1967, the Federal Communications Commission ruled that the "fairness doctrine" applied to cigarette advertisements, which were being broadcast for 5 to 10 minutes per day. That meant that TV stations would be required to air antismoking ads for free to "balance" the number of smoking ads. The FCC decision was subsequently upheld by the courts. The industry volunteered to remove their ads from TV and radio, but Congress refused to permit tobacco companies to discuss it among themselves, claiming it would be a violation of antitrust law. Gradually, as the number of antismoking ads rose, the industry decided it was wise not to oppose the Public Health Cigarette Smoking Act of 1970, which then banned tobacco ads altogether. The upshot of supporting the legislation was that antismoking ads then had to compete with all other public service announcements (PSAs) and quickly diminished in quantity dramatically. In addition, the tobacco industry used the money saved on TV and radio ads for other forms of marketing and promotion (Fritschler & Hoefler, 2006; Warner, personal communication, 2010).

To this day, some of the industry's advertising strategies are nearly Orwellian in their sophistication. Litigation originally brought by the U.S. Attorney General uncovered the fact that tobacco companies have specifically targeted teenage smokers as young as age 13 in an attempt to regain market share (Weinstein, 1998); and a federal judge ruled in 2006 that the tobacco industry has been deceiving the public for five decades about the risks of smoking (Editorial, 2006). In November 2003, the tobacco industry did agree to cease advertising in school library editions of four magazines with large youth readership (*Time, People, Sports Illustrated,* and *Newsweek*); (ConsumerAffairs.com, 2005); but the industry continued for a while to target youth with ads in adult magazines with high youth readership (Alpert, Koh, & Connolly, 2008). Recently, the two largest tobacco companies stopped advertising major brands in many magazines— Philip Morris (e.g., Marlboro) in 2005 and R. J. Reynold (e.g., Camel) in 2008 (Newman, 2009). At the same time, the industry has begun publishing lifestyle magazines like *Unlimited* and *CML*, both of which feature "under-the-radar" strategies like attractive brand imagery that targets young adults (Cortese, Lewis, & Ling, 2009). New marketing strategies also include targeting teen girls and young women with new brands and packages like Camel No. 9 that comes in shiny black boxes with hot pink and teal borders and ads with wording like "light and luscious," "now available in stiletto" running in women's magazines like *Vogue, Glamour,* and *Cosmopolitan* (Campaign for Tobacco-Free Kids, 2009a; Pierce et al., 2010). Researchers estimate that the Camel No. 9 campaign may have attracted as many as 170,000 new female teenage smokers in just a few years (Pierce et al., 2010). The few studies that have been published that do not find an association between tobacco marketing and teen use have been secretly underwritten by the industry itself (DiFranza et al., 2006). More recently, the industry has attempted to deflect criticism by introducing "youth smoking education and prevention" programs worldwide. The programs stress that smoking is an "adult choice," children begin smoking because of peer pressure and lack of guidance from their parents, and buying cigarettes is illegal for teens. The programs do *not* mention the fact that nicotine is addictive, smoking causes

disease, or that marketing increases smoking. In addition, the research done for such programs allows the tobacco industry to collect valuable demographic data on teenagers and their habits (Landman, Ling, & Glantz, 2002). Finally, Lewis Carroll might have admired the fact that R. J. Reynolds is reportedly in talks to acquire Niconovum, a Swedish company that makes nicotine gum and other nicotine-replacement devices to wean smokers off of cigarettes (Gomstyn, 2009). Perhaps, as a result, 40% of eighth graders do not believe that smoking a pack of cigarettes a day represents a health risk (Johnston et al. 2009). Tobacco advertising may even undermine the impact of strong parenting practices (Pierce et al., 2002).

As of 2008, the magazine landscape has changed. Ads for smokeless tobacco in magazines with large youth readership have actually increased (Morrison, Krugman, & Park, 2008). Magazine advertising currently represents only about 1% of the total nearly $13 billion spent annually on marketing and promotion (Alpert et al., 2008). The major companies could decide to resume print advertising at any time, of course, depending on their business needs (Alpert et al., 2008). The new FDA Tobacco law, passed in 2009, also will be a crimp in future promotional efforts (see Table 21.3; Wilson, 2009).

Beginning in the early 1990s, some classic research has more clearly delineated the impact of cigarette advertising on young people. In 1991, two studies examined the impact of the Old Joe the Camel advertising campaign. In one, 6-year-olds were as likely to recognize Old Joe as the famous Mouseketeer logo for the Disney Channel (Fischer, Schwartz, Richards, Goldstein, & Rojas, 1991). Even at age 3, 30% of children could still make the association between the Old Joe Camel figure and a pack of cigarettes. In the second study, more than twice as many children as adults reported exposure to Old Joe. Not only were children able to recognize the association with Camel cigarettes, but they found the ads to be appealing as well (DiFranza et al., 1991). Not coincidentally, in the 3 years after the introduction of the Old Joe campaign, the preference for Camel cigarettes increased from 0.5% of adolescent smokers to 32%. During the same time period, the sale of Camels to minors increased from $6 million to $476 million,

Table 21.3	Some Provisions of the New FDA Law

Tobacco Law (signed into law by the President on June 22, 2009)

- All advertising for cigarettes and smokeless tobacco must be black text on white background only (effective 6/22/10)
- No advertising in magazines with more than 15% or 2 million youth readers (effective 6/22/10)
- No outdoor advertising within 1,000 feet of schools, parks, or playgrounds (effective 6/22/10)
- No branded sponsorships of athletic or cultural events by cigarette manufacturers (effective 6/22/10)
- FDA must issue regulations to prevent the sale of tobacco products to youth via the Internet or mail-order (effective 10/1/12)
- FDA must issue regulations addressing the marketing and promotion of tobacco products on the Internet (effective 4/1/13)

Source: American Academy of Pediatrics, Office of Government Affairs, Washington, DC, 2010.

Table 21.4	How Good Is the Research Linking Tobacco Marketing to Onset of Adolescent Smoking?

Research Question	*# of Studies*	*# of Subjects Studied*
Are nonsmoking children exposed to and more aware of tobacco promotion?	4 prospective 12 cross-sectional	37,649
Does exposure to promotions increase the risk of initiation?	12 prospective 14 cross-sectional 2 time-series	349,306
Does a dose—response relationship exist?	2 prospective 7 cross-sectional	25,180

Source: Adapted from DiFranza et al., 2006.

Table 21.5	Does the Research on Tobacco Marketing and Onset of Smoking Fulfill the Hill Criteria[a] for Causality?

YES.

1. Children are exposed to tobacco marketing before they begin smoking.
2. Exposure to marketing increases the risk for initiation of smoking.
3. A dose–response relationship does exist: Increased exposure results in higher risk.
4. The association between exposure and increased risk is well substantiated with a variety of research methodologies and populations.
5. Cohesive theories can explain the relationship.
6. No other explanation other than causality can explain the relationship.

Source: Adapted from DiFranza et al., 2006.

[a]Hill, A. B. (1965). The environment and disease: Association or causality? *Proceedings of the Royal Society of Medicine, 58*, 295–300.

representing one quarter of all Camel sales and one third of all illegal cigarette sales to minors (DiFranza et al., 1991).

Since then, the research has been clear and convincing that tobacco marketing and promotion are highly effective in influencing young people to begin smoking. There are at least four dozen cross-sectional and longitudinal studies (see Table 21.4). The Hill criteria for causality have been fulfilled (Hill, 1965), although the size of the effect remains arguable (see Table 21.5). Some of the most notable or more recent studies include:

- Numerous studies show that children who pay closer attention to cigarette advertisements, who are able to recall such ads more readily, or who own promotional items are more likely to view smoking favorably and to become smokers themselves (Biener & Siegel, 2000; Sargent, Dalton, & Beach, 2000; Sargent, Gibson, & Heatherton, 2009). Teens who smoke are also more likely to believe messages in print ads for cigarettes (Hawkins & Hane, 2000). Among teenage girls, smoking rates increased dramatically around 1967, exactly the same time that women were being targeted by such new brands as Virginia Slims (Pierce, Lee, & Gilpin, 1994).
- Comprehensive 3-year and 6-year longitudinal studies of 1,752 California adolescents who never smoked found that one-third of all smoking experimentation in California between 1993 and 1996 could be attributed to tobacco advertising and promotions (Pierce et al., 1998; Gilpin, White, Messer, & Pierce, 2007). This was the first study of its kind to use longitudinal correlational data that could yield cause-and-effect conclusions.
- Adolescent brand preference follows closely the amount of money that tobacco companies spend on advertising. Marlboro, Camel, and Newport are the brands of choice for 87% of high school smokers (see Table 21.6; Centers for Disease Control, 2009). Similarly, in England, the most popular brands of cigarettes (Benson & Hedges, Silk Cut, Embassy, and Marlboro) are likewise the mostly heavily advertised (Vickers, 1992).
- Sargent and colleagues (2000) actually found a dose–response relationship between the number of cigarette promotional items owned by adolescents and their smoking behavior.
- A recent meta-analysis of 51 separate studies found that exposure to tobacco marketing and advertising more than doubles the risk of a teenager beginning to smoke (Wellman, Sugarman, DiFranza, & Winickoff, 2006).

This is hardly an American phenomenon, however. In the United Kingdom, a survey of 1,450 students ages 11 and 12 years found that awareness of cigarette advertising correlated with smoking (While, Kelly, Huang, & Charlton, 1996), as did a survey of nearly 2,000 students who were exposed to so-called passive cigarette advertising during an India–New Zealand cricket series televised in India. The message conveyed was "you become a better cricketer if you smoke," and the risk for initiation of smoking in nonsmoking youth tripled if they believed this message (Vaidya, Vaidya, & Naik, 1999). In Germany, a recent cross-sectional survey of 3,415 schoolchildren ages 10 to 17 years also found a two- to three-times increased risk of new-onset smoking with exposure to cigarette ads and a dose–response relationship (Hanewinkel, Isensee, Sarent, & Morgenstern, 2010).

Unlike the United States, other countries have been more aggressive in banning cigarette advertising. In New Zealand, consumption fell

Table 21.6	Is Cigarette Advertising Effective?	
Advertising in $ Millions	Adolescent Brand Preference	Adult Brand Preference
1. Marlboro ($75)	1. Marlboro (60.0%)	1. Marlboro (23.5%)
2. Camel ($43)	2. Camel (13.3%)	2. Winston (6.7%)
3. Newport ($35)	3. Newport (12.7%)	3. Newport (4.8%)

Source: Data from CDC (1994) and Pollay et al. (1996). From Strasburger and Donnerstein (1999). Copyright American Academy of Pediatrics. Reprinted with permission.

Table 21.7	Some Features of the 1998 Tobacco Master Settlement Agreement

Payment of $206.4 billion from the tobacco industry to the states over the next 25 years, including $1.5 billion to fund research to reduce teen smoking

A ban on the use of cartoon characters in the advertising, promotion, or labeling of tobacco products

A prohibition on targeting youth in advertising, promotions, or marketing

A ban on all outdoor advertising, including billboards and signs in stadiums

A ban on the sale of merchandise with brand-name logos, such as T-shirts or backpacks

A ban on payments to producers of TV and movies for product placements

Source: Adapted from *AAP News, 15*(1): 4 January 1999.

after a complete ban on cigarette advertising (Vickers, 1992). In Norway, the prevalence of 13- to 15-year-old smokers decreased from 17% in 1975 to 10% in 1990 after an advertising ban was imposed (Vickers, 1992). In fact, an analysis of factors influencing tobacco consumption in 22 countries revealed that since 1973, advertising restrictions have resulted in lower rates of smoking (Laugesen & Meads, 1991).

In 1998, the U.S. Attorney General negotiated what may be a remarkable settlement with the tobacco industry, calling for the payout of more than $206 billion to the states over the next 25 years, along with severe restrictions on marketing and advertising to children (see Table 21.7). Critics point to the fact that this figure represents a mere 8% of the $2.5 trillion that the federal government will lose over the same 25 years in health care costs related to smoking (Jackson, 1998). In addition, according to the Federal Trade Commission (FTC), the tobacco industry actually spent more money on advertising and promotions immediately after the lawsuits were settled: $8.2 billion in 1999, a 22% increase from 1998 (Journal Wire Reports, 2001). Nevertheless, the now-substantial cigarette advertising research is hardly "moot" and may certainly have implications for alcohol advertising as well. For example, will there be future lawsuits by the Attorney General to recover health care costs? In addition, the research may come back into play if the Attorney General settlement is overturned by a federal court decision or by a Congress that has traditionally

been heavily influenced by tobacco money. What may replace the concerns about advertising and promotion is increasing alarm over the depictions of tobacco use in movies, music videos, and television programs—in a sense, the new "advertising" arena for tobacco companies.

Cigarettes in Television Programming, Music and Music Videos, Movies, and the Internet

A report from the National Cancer Institute in 2008 concluded that "the total weight of evidence from cross-sectional, longitudinal, and experimental studies indicates a causal relationship between exposure to depictions of smoking in movies and youth smoking initiation" (National Cancer Institute, 2008, p. 12). Although the amount of smoking in movies may now be decreasing, new research shows that it may be one of the leading factors in adolescents' decision whether to smoke (National Cancer Institute, 2008; Sargent et al., 2009; Titus-Ernstoff, Dalton, Adachi-Mejia, Longacre, & Beach, 2008).

Hollywood seems to use cigarette smoking as a shorthand for troubled or antiestablishment characters, but the smoking or nonsmoking status of the actors themselves is also influential in whether their characters will smoke on screen (Shields, Carol, Balbach, & McGee, 1999). Smoking among male characters is associated with violent behavior and dangerous acts; among

females, it is associated with sexual affairs, illegal activities, and reckless driving (Heatherton & Sargent, 2009). Movie depictions also tend to be very prosmoking, with only 14% of screen time dealing with adverse health effects (Stockwell & Glantz, 1997). Of the 100 top-grossing films of 2002, less than 1% of the smoking incidents depicted the fatal consequences of smoking (Dozier, Lauzen, Day, Payne, & Tafoya, 2005).

Teenagers constitute 26% of the movie-going audience but only 16% of the U.S. population (Rauzi, 1998). For many years, content analyses have found that a large proportion of American movies contained cigarette smoking. For example, in a study of the 100 top-grossing films from 1996 to 2004, researchers found that half of all R-rated movies (26% of PG-13 and 17% of PG movies) contained tobacco use (Tickle, Beach, & Dalton, 2009). From 1998 to 2004, nearly three-quarters of the top 100 box office hits contained smoking, and each movie had been seen by 25% of the 6,500 teenagers surveyed nationwide. That adds up to billions of smoking images overall and 665 per 10- to 14-year-old (Sargent, Tanski, & Gibson, 2007). Another content analysis found that 80% of children's smoking exposure actually occurred via G, PG, or PG-13 films, not R-rated films (see Figure 21.6; Titus-Ernstoff et al., 2008). Even G-rated movies can contain tobacco use (see Table 21.8; Goldstein, Sobel, & Newman, 1999; Yakota & Thompson, 2001). However, two recent analyses—of the 25 top-grossing movies each year from 1990 to 2007 and the 30 top-grossing movies from 1950 to 2006—have found that as smoking occurrences decrease, so does the prevalence of smoking among adolescents (Jamieson & Romer, 2010; Sargent & Heatherton, 2009).

A number of correlational and longitudinal studies have confirmed that exposure to smoking in the media is one of the key factors prompting teenagers to smoke (Strasburger & Council on Communications and Media, 2010). It may account for up to one-third of smoking initiation in young teenagers (Dalton et al., 2002). Public health advocates estimate that smoking portrayals in movies lead 300,000 adolescents to begin smoking each year, resulting in nearly $1 billion profit for the tobacco industry (Alamar & Glantz, 2006; Charlesworth & Glantz, 2005). In fact, exposure

Table 21.8 Tobacco or Alcohol Content of G-Rated Children's Films

Film	Tobacco Use/ Exposure (Seconds)	Alcohol Use/ Exposure (Seconds)
The Three Caballeros	Yes (548)	Yes (8)
101 Dalmations	Yes (299)	Yes (51)
Pinocchio	Yes (22)	Yes (80)
James & the Giant Peach	Yes (206)	Yes (38)
All Dogs Go to Heaven	Yes (205)	Yes (73)
Alice in Wonderland	Yes (158)	No
Great Mouse Detective	Yes (165)	Yes (414)
The Aristocats	Yes (11)	Yes (142)
Beauty & the Beast	No	Yes (123)

Source: Adapted from Goldstein, Sobel, and Newman (1999).

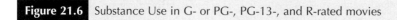

Figure 21.6 Substance Use in G- or PG-, PG-13-, and R-rated movies

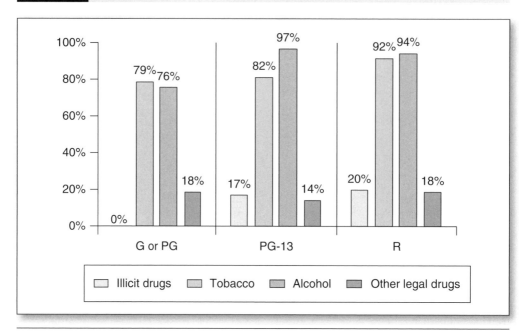

Source: From DuRant, R. H., Rome, E. S., Rich, M., Allred, E., Emans, S. J., & Woods, E. R. (1997). Tobacco and alcohol use behaviors portrayed in music videos: A content analysis. *American Journal of Public Health, 87*:1131–1135.

to movie smoking may even trump parents' smoking status as being the key factor in adolescents' initiation of smoking (Titus-Ernstoff et al., 2008):

- A prospective study of more than 3,500 teenagers found that exposure to R-rated movies doubles the risk of smoking, even when controlling for all other known factors, while exposure to R-rated movies alone doubles the risk (Dalton et al., 2002). Even exposure to movie trailers in movie theaters or on TV may increase the lure of cigarettes (Hanewinkel, 2009).
- A sample of 735 12- to 14-year-olds, with a 2-year follow-up, found that exposure to R-rated movies and having a TV set in the bedroom significantly increased the risk of smoking initiation for White teens but not for Black teens (Jackson, Brown, & L'Engle, 2007). This is now the third longitudinal study documenting the risk of R-rated movies (Dalton et al., 2003; Jackson, Brown, & L'Engle 2007; Sargent et al., 2005).
- Four other longitudinal studies have documented the risk of seeing smoking in movies of all ratings (Sargent, Stoolmiller, Worth, Gibson. & Gibbons, 2007) in German preteens

and teens (Hanewinkel & Sargent, 2007, 2009) and for elementary schoolchildren (Titus-Ernstoff et al., 2008).

The most comprehensive content analyses that examined substance use on television and in the movies are now 10 years or more old (see Figure 21.2; Christenson, Henriksen, & Roberts, 2000; DuRant et al., 1997). Self-reported exposure to protobacco messages in various media then declined from 2000 to 2004, except on the Internet. Still, 81% of 6th through 12th graders reported seeing images of smoking on TV or in movies (down from 90% previously), and 33% saw tobacco ads on the Internet (up from 22%) in three very large longitudinal samples (Duke et al., 2009). Reality shows like *The Osbournes* frequently feature drug content in which tobacco use is endorsed (Blair, Yue, Singh, & Bernhardt, 2005). On British TV, one content analysis found smoking-related scenes occurring at 3.4 instances per hour (Cumberbatch & Gauntlett, 2005). But generally, tobacco portrayals on TV are outnumbered by alcohol and illicit drugs: On prime-time TV, 16% of all episodes studied in one analysis featured smoking,

29% illicit drug use, but one third featured alcohol (Murphy, Hether, & Rideout, 2008).

Only one study has examined the impact of TV on adult smoking—a unique 26-year longitudinal study in New Zealand that followed an unselected cohort of 1,000 individuals from birth. Researchers found that heavy TV viewing in childhood correlated with smoking at age 26 and that 17% of adult smoking might be attributable to the influence of excessive TV viewing during childhood (Hancox, Milne, & Poulton, 2004).

In music videos, smoking seems to have taken a backseat to more illicit substances (Gruber, Thau, Hill, Fisher, & Grube, 2005b). Similarly, an analysis of the 279 most popular songs from 2005 found that only 3% contained mentions of tobacco use, versus 24% alcohol use and 14% marijuana use (Primack, Dalton, Carroll, Agarwal, & Fine, 2008).

On the Internet, tobacco may not be as much of a problem. A study involving 346 teenagers viewing 1.2 million Web pages found that less than 1% contained tobacco content, much of which was antitobacco anyway. However, more than half of the content was from social networking sites, especially MySpace (Jenssen, Klein, Salazar, Daluga, & DiClemente, 2009). For many years teenagers could purchase cigarettes easily online (Bryant, Cody, & Murphy, 2002). The PACT Act (Preventing Illegal Internet Sales of Cigarettes & Smokeless Tobacco) would prevent that and was recently passed by Congress (Campaign for Tobacco-Free Kids, 2010; Cruz & Deyton, 2010). The recently signed FDA Tobacco Law also contains provisions that would address this by 2012 (see Table 21.3).

Alcohol

Research on Alcohol Advertising

Although the research on alcohol advertising is not quite as compelling as that on tobacco advertising, children and teenagers are a uniquely vulnerable audience. In particular, beer ads seem custom made to appeal to preteens and teens: images of fun-loving, sexy, successful young adults having the time of their lives (Borzekowski & Strasburger, 2008; Chen, Grube, Bersamin, Waiters, & Keefe, 2005). Who wouldn't want to indulge, especially when the ads make it seem as if everyone drinks (drinking as normative behavior; see Table 21.9)? Alcohol ads frequently feature sexual and social stereotypes that target teenagers (Austin & Hust, 2005). Youth aged 12 to 20 are 22 times more likely to see a product advertisement for alcohol than an alcohol-industry-funded "responsibility" message (Center on Alcohol Marketing and Youth, 2008).

The density of alcohol ads and exposure of children and teens to them is a major concern: The average young person in the United States sees nearly 2,000 annually on TV alone (Jernigan, 2006; Strasburger, 2006)—more than adults see (Center on Alcohol Marketing and Youth, 2004a). Similarly, in Australia, teens' overall exposure to alcohol advertising exceeds adults' exposure (Winter, Donovan, & Fielder, 2008). Often, this advertising is concentrated in teen shows or sports programming. All of the top 15 teens shows contain alcohol ads (Center on Alcohol Marketing and Youth, 2004b). Ads are also frequently embedded in sports programming—on banners, scoreboards, or emblazoned on race cars (Nicholson & Hoye, 2009). Even hard liquor is now being advertised for the first time in years (Semuels, 2009).

For many years, alcoholic beverages popular with underage drinkers were disproportionately advertised in magazines with higher youth readership (King et al., 2009). However, in recent years, magazine advertising has been curtailed by the industry's voluntary standard that now restricts ads in media where the youth audience exceeds 30%. Consequently, youths' exposure has dropped significantly (Centers for Disease Control, 2007). But on the radio—the second most popular medium for teenagers—young people hear more alcohol ads than adults (Center on Alcohol Marketing and Youth, 2004c). A CDC study found that half of all the nearly 70,000 alcohol ads in 104 major markets around the country were airing in programming with a predominantly adolescent audience (Centers for Disease Control, 2006).

Table 21.9	Seven Myths That Alcohol Advertisers Want Children and Adolescents to Believe

1. Everyone drinks alcohol.

2. Drinking has no risks.

3. Drinking helps to solve problems.

4. Alcohol is a magic potion that can transform you.

5. Sports and alcohol go together.

6. If alcohol were truly dangerous, we wouldn't be advertising it.

7. Alcoholic beverage companies promote drinking only in moderation.

Source: Adapted from Kilbourne (1993).

Digital advertising and social networking sites have also come to the forefront (Montgomery & Chester, 2009; Moreno, Briner, Williams, Walker, & Christakis, 2009). In just a 6-month period during 2003, teenagers made nearly 700,000 in-depth visits to 55 alcohol websites (Center on Alcohol Marketing and Youth, 2004). According to one survey, more than 3 million teens have a friend who has bought alcohol online, and more than half a million have done so themselves (Hitti, 2006). A study of 500 MySpace profiles of 18-year-olds found that 41% referenced substance use (Moreno, Parks, Zimmerman, Brito, & Christakis, 2009). Another, similar study of 400 17- to 20-year-olds' profiles found that 56% contained references to alcohol (Moreno et al., 2010).

Several studies have found significant associations between exposure to alcohol advertising and subsequent consumption (Borzekowski & Strasburger, 2008; Jernigan, 2006, 2009). Seven cohort studies involving 13,000 young people have found modest associations (Smith & Foxcroft, 2009). Teenagers who obtain alcohol-branded merchandise are more likely to begin drinking (McClure, Stoolmiller, Tanski, Worth, & Sargent, 2009). In one large longitudinal study of more than 1,000 6th through 8th graders, those who had never tried alcohol but were receptive to alcohol marketing were 77% more likely to initiate drinking a year later than those who were unreceptive (Henriksen, Feighery, Schleicher, & Fortmann, 2008).

Alcohol in Television Programming, Music and Music Videos, and Movies

Several content analyses have been done recently that show that alcohol remains prevalent in mainstream American media:

- From 2004 through 2006, one third of the top 10 primetime shows featured alcohol, with only 6% showing negative consequences (Murphy et al., 2008).
- An average of 9.1 drug messages were featured in the first season of the reality show *The Osbournes.* Two thirds implied approval for alcohol (Blair et al., 2005).
- A recent analysis of 50 episodes of children's shows, 50 episodes of "tween" programs (9- to 14-year-old target audience), 40 episodes of soap operas, and 50 episodes of prime-time shows during the 2003 season found as much alcohol content in the tween shows (37%) as in the soaps (33%) and the adult shows (38%) (Greenberg, Rosaen, Worrell, Salmon, & Volkman, 2009). On *The OC*, a show popular with preteens and teens, most of the drinking was done by adult women; but one-third did involve adolescents (Van den Bulck, Simons, & Van Gorp, 2008).
- In an analysis of 359 music videos broadcast in 2001, nearly half contained depictions of alcohol (Gruber et al., 2005b).
- Of the 279 most popular songs of 2005, nearly one-quarter contained references to alcohol use. Rap music had the most

alcohol references, with 53% of the songs studied (Primack et al., 2008). A separate study found that references to alcohol increased five-fold from 1979 to 1997, and the author speculates that this is because of commercial pressures and the marketing of alcoholic beverages (Herd, 2005).

- In the UK, the top 10 programs watched by 10- to 15-year-olds in 2004 contained 12 alcohol-related scenes per hour (Cumberbatch & Gauntlett, 2005). In New Zealand, a study of 98 hours of prime-time TV programs from 2004 found one scene every 9 minutes, with positive portrayals of alcohol outnumbering negatives ones by a 12-to-1 margin (McGee, Ketchel, & Reeder, 2007).

- An analysis of the 100 top-grossing films for each year from 1996 through 2004 found that half of all R- and PG-13-rated movies and one fourth of PG movies contained alcohol use (Tickle et al., 2009). A 2006 study found that 92% of a random sample of 601 contemporary movies contained alcohol use (Sargent, Wills, Stoolmiller, Gibson, & Gibbons, 2006).

As with cigarette portrayals, alcohol portrayals seem to have an impact on actual use among adolescents (Sargent et al., 2006; Tanski, Dal Cin, Stoolmiller, & Sargent, 2010; Wills, Sargent, Gibbons, Gerrard, & Stoolmiller, 2009). A survey of more than 1,200 Pittsburgh high school students found that exposure to movies was independently associated with alcohol use (Primack, Kraemer, Fine, & Dalton, 2009). Similarly, a longitudinal study of more than 2,700 German students ages 10 to 16 years found that exposure to movie depictions of alcohol use was an independent predictor of alcohol initiation (Hanewinkel & Sargent, 2009). Most recently, a longitudinal study of 2,406 fifth- through eighth-grade students who had never used alcohol found that exposure to R-rated movies tripled the risk of their using alcohol when resurveyed 1 to 2 years later (Tanski et al., 2010). A review of seven cohort studies involving more than 13,000 young people found modest but significant effect sizes between alcohol portrayals and subsequent consumption (Smith & Foxcroft, 2009). An even larger study—of 13 longitudinal

studies involving more than 38,000 young people—also concluded that exposure to media and commercial depictions involving alcohol is associated consistently with an increased likelihood of starting to drink and increased alcohol consumption among teens already drinking (Anderson et al., 2009). One creative lab experiment actually exposed young adults to various movies with and without alcohol depictions and observed what they drank while watching. Movies with alcohol content and alcohol commercials resulted in more alcohol being consumed while watching (Engels, Hermans, van Baaren, Hollenstein, & Bot, 2009).

Illicit Drugs in TV Programming, Music and Music Videos, and Movies

Illicit drugs are rarely seen on TV (Christenson et al., 2000) with the exception of programs like Showtime's *Weeds* and *Californication* and HBO's *Entourage*. Drug scenes are more common in movies (22% of movies in one study contained drug scenes), where more than half of the time no harmful consequences are shown (Roberts & Christenson, 2000). Marijuana is the most frequent drug seen in movies and seems to be making a comeback in R-rated movies like *Harold and Kumar Go to White Castle* (2004), *Harold & Kumar Escape From Guantanamo Bay* (2008), *Totally Baked* (2008), *The Pineapple Express* (2008), and *The Wackness* (2009; Halperin, 2008). A Columbia study found that viewing R-rated movies was associated with a sixfold increased risk of trying marijuana (see Figure 21.7; National Center on Addiction and Substance Abuse, 2005). Hollywood filmmakers do not seem to understand that humor tends to undermine normal adolescent defenses against drugs and legitimizes their use (Borzekowski & Strasburger, 2008). Increased consumption of popular music is also associated with marijuana use (Primack, Douglas, & Kraemer, 2010; Primack et al., 2009).

| Figure 21.7 | Percentage of Teens Who Have Tried Cigarettes, Alcohol, or Marijuana, According to Their Viewing of R-Rated Movies |

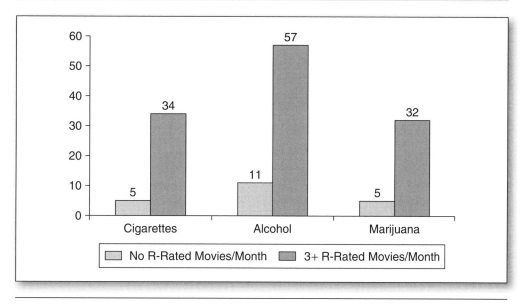

Source: The National Center on Addiction and Substance Abuse at Columbia University. Reprinted with permission.

In rap music, the prevalence of drug mentions and behavior has increased six-fold over the past several decades, with marijuana predominating (two thirds of instances). Drug use in rap music has come to signify wealth and sociability, and attitudes toward drugs have changed from negative to positive (Herd, 2008). In one study, 77% of rap songs contained portrayals of substance use (Primack et al., 2008). Teens may hear as many as 84 drug references daily in popular songs (see Figure 21.4; Primack et al., 2008). Music videos have paralleled that trend, with rap and hip-hop videos containing two to three times more alcohol and illicit substance mentions than other genres (American Academy of Pediatrics, 2009b). Overall, nearly half of music videos examined in one study contained alcohol, tobacco, or other drugs of abuse, with alcohol present in 35%, tobacco in 10%, and illicit drugs in 13% (Gruber et al., 2005b).

Teens with TVs in their own bedrooms have a far greater likelihood of engaging in risky health behaviors like sexual activity or using tobacco, marijuana, or alcohol (Gruber et al., 2005; Hanewinkel & Sargent, 2009).

A Word About Prescription and Nonprescription Drugs

Nearly $30 billion is spent annually on promotion of prescription drugs (Donohue, Cevasco, & Rosenthal, 2007), including $4.4 billion on advertising (Rubin, 2009). In 2000, Merck spent more money advertising Vioxx ($161 million) than Dell, Budweiser, Pepsi, or Nike spent (Rosenthal, Berndt, Frank, Donohue, & Epstein, 2002). Drug companies now spend more than twice as much money on marketing and promotion as they do on research and development, and studies show that the marketing efforts pay off (Rosenthal et al., 2002): A survey of physicians found that 92% of patients had requested an advertised drug (Thomaselli, 2003). Direct-to-consumer advertising has remained controversial since the FDA first approved of it in 1997 (Frosch, Grande, Tarn, & Kravitz, 2010; Gellad & Lyles, 2007). American TV viewers see as many as 16 hours of prescription drug ads per year (Frosch et al., 2007). Emotional appeals are almost universal, and the ads provide only limited educational information (Frosch et al.,

2007). Children and teenagers get the message that there is a pill to cure all ills and a drug for every occasion, including sexual intercourse (Borzekowski & Strasburger, 2008). In the first 10 months of 2004, drug companies spent nearly half a billion dollars advertising Viagra, Levitra, and Cialis (Snowbeck, 2005). Yet the advertising of condoms, birth control pills, and emergency contraception is haphazard and rare and remains controversial (American Academy of Pediatrics, 2010b).

Solutions

In the past three decades, when "just say no" has become the watchword for many parents, school-based drug prevention programs, and Federal drug-prevention efforts, unprecedented amounts of money are being spent to induce children and adolescents to "just say yes" to tobacco and alcohol.

Table 21.10	Newspapers and Magazines That Refuse Cigarette Advertising (partial listing)

Newspapers

The Christian Science Monitor

The New York Times

Parade magazine

Magazines (adult)

American Baby

Business Week

Consumer Reports

Good Housekeeping

The New Yorker (does accept cigar ads)

Parenting

Reader's Digest

Scientific American

Magazines (youth)

Boy's Life

Mad Magazine

Seventeen

Perhaps, as one group of researchers has suggested, the "discussion [should] be *elevated* from the scientific and legal arenas to the domain of ethics and social responsibility" (see Table 21.10; Orlandi et al., 1989, p. 92, emphasis added). Below are eight possible approaches that could very well result in significant reductions in adolescent cigarette, alcohol, and drug use.

1. *A ban on cigarette advertising in all media and new restrictions on alcohol advertising.* Any product as harmful as tobacco should have severe restrictions placed on it (American Academy of Pediatrics, 2009a, 2010a; Kunkel, 2007). An increasing number of countries are banning all tobacco advertising in all media (Prokhorov et al., 2006). On the other hand, a total ban on all alcohol advertising would be both impractical and unproductive. Unlike cigarettes, alcohol may have legitimate uses when consumed in moderation. But restricting alcohol advertising to programming with youth audiences of less than 15% would be an easily achievable and significant step (Center on Alcohol Marketing and Youth, 2007) that would result in alcohol manufacturers being able to reduce their advertising costs by 8% and teens' exposure to alcohol ads being reduced by 20% (Jernigan, 2006; Jernigan et al., 2005). In turn, reducing adolescents' exposure to alcohol ads could reduce their alcohol consumption by as much as 25% (Saffer & Dave, 2006). Alternatively, beer and wine manufacturers could be restricted to so-called "tombstone ads" (an industry term for ads that show only the product, not the sexy beach babes or funny talking animals; Chen et al., 2005; Strasburger et al., 2009). A ban on direct-to-consumer prescription drug marketing should be considered as well (Stange, 2007). Only the U.S. and New Zealand allow it.

2. *Higher taxes on tobacco and alcohol products.* Taxes have a direct and immediate effect on the consumption of products, particularly by teenagers (Centers for Disease Control, 2008). For cigarettes, every 10% increase in the price will reduce underage smokers by 6 to 7% (Campaign for Tobacco-Free Kids, 2009b).

3. *More aggressive counteradvertising.* Counteradvertising has been shown to be effective, but only if it is intensive, thoughtfully planned, and uses a variety of different media (Figure 21.8; Flynn et al., 2007; Ibrahim & Glantz, 2007; Noar, 2006). For example, a 4-year, $50 million campaign in Massachusetts resulted in 50% reduction in the new onset of smoking by young teens (Siegel & Biener, 2000). Antismoking ads may be particularly effective for young children (Nixon, Mansfield, & Thoms, 2008). For current smokers, new brain-imaging technology (functional magnetic resonance imaging) has found that low-key antismoking ads may actually be preferable to attention-grabbing ads (Langleben et al., 2009). However, the biggest hurdle is that rarely if ever does counteradvertising ever come close to the occurrence rate of regular advertising.

The two best-known counteradvertising campaigns have been the Partnership for a Drug-Free America (PDFA) and the Truth campaign. A study of the former found that more than 80% of nearly 1,000 public school students ages 11 through 19 could recall such ads, and half of the students who had tried drugs reported that the ads actually convinced them to decrease or stop using drugs (Reis, Duggan, Adger, & DeAngelis, 1992). However, a more recent study questioned the effectiveness of PDFA ads. A nationally representative sample of more than 5,000 9- to 18-year-olds was surveyed four times between 1999 and 2004. Although substantial exposure to antidrug advertising was achieved—94% of youths reported exposure to one or more ads per month, with a media frequency of about two to three per week—there was no change in prevalence of

Figure 21.8 Examples of Provocative and Potentially Effective Antidrug Advertising

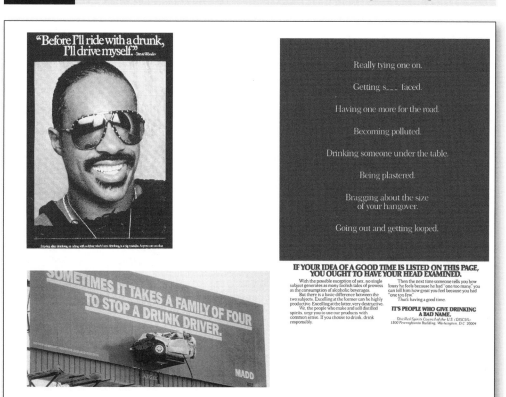

Source: Partnership for a Drug-Free America.

marijuana use and some evidence for a possible boomerang effect (Hornik, Jacobsohn, Orwin, Piesse, & Kalton, 2008). Unfortunately, not a single Partnership ad has ever aired that targets either tobacco or alcohol. This may be due to the fact that the advertising firms that volunteer to do PDFA ads often receive large sums of money from the tobacco and alcohol industries. Similarly, Congress has funded the federal government's Office of National Drug Policy Control (ONDCP) for nearly $1 billion for the National Youth Anti-Drug Media Campaign, which has included partnering with the PDFA (Hornik et al., 2008); but so far not a single ad has targeted tobacco or alcohol—a remarkable finding, given that tobacco and alcohol represent the two most significant drug threats to children and adolescents (Strasburger, 2010).

As part of the tobacco industry's $246 billion Tobacco Master Settlement Agreement (see Table 21.7), the nonprofit American Legacy Foundation was established, which produces the "Truth" ads. Such ads often try to expose the tobacco industry as being manipulative and deceptive. In one ad, two teenagers carry a lie detector into Philip Morris's New York headquarters and announce that they want to deliver it to the marketing department. In another, a group of teens in a large delivery truck pull up in front of the headquarters and begin unloading body bags. One teen shouts through a megaphone, "Do you know how many people tobacco kills every day?" (Bryant, 2000). The ads are so hard hitting that Philip Morris actually insisted that two be withdrawn. Yet in Florida, they accounted for one fourth of the decline in the prevalence of teen smoking from 25% in 1999 to 18% in 2002 (Farrelly, Davis, Haviland, Messeri, & Healton, 2005). By contrast, ads made by Philip Morris as part of its $100 million campaign cautioning teens to "Think. Don't smoke" are ineffectual and may be a "sham" ("Big Tobacco's Promises," 2006; Henriksen, Dauphinee, Wang, & Fortmann, 2006; Paek & Gunther, 2007). "Citizens and policymakers should reject any 'educational' programs by the tobacco industry. If the tobacco industry were sincere in its stated desire to contribute to reducing youth smoking, it would stop opposing policies and programs that have been demonstrated to be effective" (Landman et al., 2002, p. 925).

Recently, the Motion Picture Association of America agreed to put an antismoking ad on all new DVDs (Serjeant, 2008). Airing antismoking ads just before big Hollywood movies that feature a lot of smoking would also be effective (Edwards, Harris, Cook, Bedford, & Zuo, 2004; Edwards, Oakes, & Bull, 2007) but is not currently being done. The 15-minute period prior to movie previews is actually under the control of local theater owners, not Hollywood, so this would be feasible (Heatherton & Sargent, 2009). Hollywood filmmakers need to stop using smoking as a short-hand device for an evil or conflicted character, and film school students need to be educated about the health effects of what they produce (Chapman, 2008). In 2007, Disney actually vowed to discontinue all smoking in its movies (ABC News, 2007).

4. Increased sensitivity and awareness of the entertainment industry to the health-related issues of smoking, drinking, and other drug use in TV programming, movies, music and music videos, and video games. Ideally, people in the entertainment industry would understand that with the billions of dollars they make each year comes a public health responsibility; sadly, most of the time they do not (Strasburger, 2009b). There are exceptions, however: The old *Beverly Hills 90210* was conscientious in avoiding gratuitous drug use and showing the consequences instead. *Ferris Bueller's Day Off* was intentionally smoke free in 1986, and so was *The Devil Wears Prada* in 2006. In the UK, old cartoons such as *Tom and Jerry, The Flintstones, The Jetsons,* and *Scooby Doo* are now being edited to eliminate smoking scenes (Associated Press, 2006). Prosocial content does not have to interfere with story lines, and it can contribute significantly to young people's notions about health (Hogan & Strasburger, 2008; Kaiser Family Foundation, 2004). The idea that being drunk is funny is a myth that needs to be seriously reexamined by the entertainment industry and could easily be contributing to the high rates of binge drinking among teens (see Figure 21.8; Miller, Naimi, Brewer, & Jones, 2007). Rock music lyrics and music videos could avoid glamorizing drinking or drug use (American Academy of Pediatrics, 2009b). Teen-oriented shows and channels like MTV and BET could lead the way by developing more prosocial programming and by airing antismoking and anti-alcohol PSAs. Of course, according to one group of researchers, there may not be a problem to begin with—TV characters use drugs less often than the actual U.S. population does (Long, O'Connor, Gerbner, & Concato, 2002)!

5. *Revision of the ratings systems for both television and movies.* Several studies show that parents would prefer a universal ratings system that would apply to movies, TV, and video games, one that would be more specific and content based (Greenberg, Rampoldi-Hnilo, & Mastro, 2000; Walsh & Gentile, 2001). A recent survey of more than 3,000 adults nationwide found that 70% support an R rating for movies that depict smoking (see Figure 21.9) and two-thirds would like to see antismoking PSAs before any film that depicts smoking (McMillen, Tanski, Winickoff, & Valentine, 2007). In May 2007, the MPAA announced that it would consider cigarette smoking in its ratings scheme (Motion Picture Association of America, 2007), but it is unclear how exactly this will play out in the future (Pupillo, 2007).

6. *Increased sensitivity to media effects and increased media literacy.* A century ago, to be "literate" meant that you could read and write. In the year 2011, to be literate means that you can successfully understand and "decode" a dizzying array of different media and media messages (Rich & Bar-on, 2001). Ideally, parents need to begin this process

Figure 21.9

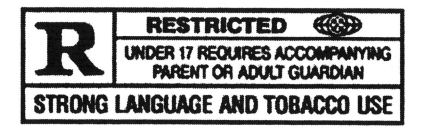

"R" FOR RESPONSIBLE. The MPAA claims the First Amendment is the reason it won't rate smoking "R." But it R-rates offensive but perfectly legal language now. Surely it doesn't consider its own age-classification system censorship? After all, the First Amendment prohibits the government from banning movies, not voluntary, responsible rating choices by the studio-controlled MPAA.

Source: Copyright Smokefreemovies.org. Reprinted with permission.

Note: Some critics have proposed that an R-rating be given by the MPAA for any tobacco use in films. But this has been opposed both on First Amendment grounds and because some tobacco use (e.g., by historical figures) may be necessary. An alternative solution would be to have all movie sets declared smoke-free zones because secondhand smoke is an occupational health hazard.

early with their children and understand that a child who watches TV 4 hours or more a day has a five-fold increased risk of smoking, for example, compared to one who watches less than 2 hours per day (Gidwani, Sobol, DeJong, Perrin, & Gortmaker, 2002). Similarly, young children exposed to PG-13 and R-rated movies at young ages are at increased risk for both smoking and drinking (Dalton et al., 2006; Dalton et al., 2009; Sargent et al., 2004; Tanski et al., 2009; Tanski et al., 2010; Thompson & Gunther, 2007). A study of more than 6,500 preteens and teens found that, on average, 12.5% of them had seen each of 40 R-rated movies (Worth, Chambers, Nassau, Rakhra, & Sargent, 2008). According to the American Academy of Pediatrics, parents need to avoid screen time for children less than 2 years old, limit total entertainment screen time to less than 2 hours per day, coview with their children, carefully monitor what media their child use and watch, and avoid letting young children see PG-13 and R-rated movies (Strasburger & Council on Communications and Media, 2010a); Longacre et al., 2009). Schools can help as well. Certain drug-prevention programs—ones that incorporate media literacy—have been shown to be extremely effective in reducing levels of teen drug use, but such programs must go far beyond the DARE (Drug Abuse Resistance Education) approach that is currently in 70% of public schools across the country (Botvin & Griffin, 2005). The United States is unique among Western nations in not requiring some form of media literacy for its students (Brown, 2007). Several studies now indicate that successful drug prevention may be possible through this unique route (Austin & Johnson, 1997; Austin, Pinkleton, Hust, & Cohen, 2005; Kupersmidt, Scull, & Austin, 2010; McCannon, 2009; Potter, 2010; Primack, Fine, Yang, Wickett, & Zickmund, 2009; Primack, Gold, Land, & Fine, 2006; Primack, Sidani, Carroll, & Fine, 2009; Slater et al., 2006). In addition, there are now media education programs that can reduce adolescents' displays of risky behaviors on social networking websites (Moreno et al., 2009).

7. More research. Considering how significant the impact of the media is on young people, it seems astounding that more financial resources are not being devoted to media research (Christakis & Zimmerman 2006; Strasburger et al., 2010). According to the most recent Kaiser report, children and teens spend more than 7 hours per day with a variety of different media (Rideout, 2010), yet the Federal government funds only a handful of studies. Currently, no foundation funds any media research (the Kaiser Family Foundation announced in February 2010 that it was discontinuing its Program for the Study of Media and Health, which has produced some of the best media research in the past 15 years). New studies of how different teens process drug content in different media are needed, as are continuing studies of the impact of the Internet and of social networking sites. Understanding how media affect audiences differently is critical to better-focused intervention efforts (Austin, Chen, & Grube, 2006; Ringel, Collins, & Ellickson, 2006; Ward, Day, & Thomas, 2010). For example, African-American youth are known to be relatively resistant to tobacco advertising, but why this is true is unclear (Centers for Disease Control, 2006; West, Romero, & Trinidad, 2007). Existing research needs to be more widely disseminated as well. A new Surgeon General's report or National Institute of Mental Health (NIMH) report might prove to be extremely useful to researchers, health professionals, parents, and policy makers and could provide the impetus for increasing funding of research. The last NIMH report on children and media was in 1982, well before the Internet, DVRs, cell phones, digital advertising, and social networking sites!

8. Campaign finance reform in Congress. This recommendation may seem strange in a chapter about the effects of media on young people, but three major groups arguably control much of what is media related in congress—the National Rifle Association (NRA), beer and wine manufacturers, and the tobacco industry—and none have the best interests of the nation's children and adolescents at heart. Congress can control the media and help to make them healthier, but until it is liberated from its dependence on these special interest groups, American media will remain unhealthy for young people.

References

ABC News. (2007, July 16). Up in smoke: Disney bans cigarettes. Retrieved August 12, 2009, from http://abcnews.go.com/print?id=3416434.

Alamar, B., & Glantz, S. A. (2006). Tobacco industry profits from smoking images in the movies (letter). *Pediatrics, 117,* 1462.

Alpert, H. R., Koh, H. K., & Connolly, G. N. (2008). After the Master Settlement Agreement: Targeting and exposure of youth to magazine tobacco advertising. *Health Affairs* (Millwood), *27,* w503–w512.

American Academy of Pediatrics. (2006). Children, adolescents, and advertising. *Pediatrics, 118,* 2563–2569.

American Academy of Pediatrics. (2009a). Tobacco use: A pediatric disease. *Pediatrics, 124,* 1474–1487.

American Academy of Pediatrics. (2009b). Impact of music, music lyrics, and music videos on children and youth. *Pediatrics, 124,* 1488–1494.

American Academy of Pediatrics. (2010). Media education. *Pediatrics, 126*(5), 1012–1017.

Anderson, P., de Bruijn, A., Angus, K., Gordon, R., & Hastings, G. (2009). Impact of alcohol advertising and media exposure on adolescent alcohol use: A systematic review of longitudinal studies. *Alcohol and Alcoholism, 44,* 229–243.

Associated Press. (2006, August 30). British channel bans smoking cartoons. Retrieved August 30, 2006, from http://www.usatoday.com/life/television/news/2006-08-22-cartoon-smoking_x.htm.

Atkin, C. K. (1995). Survey and experimental research on effects of alcohol advertising. In S. Martin (Ed.), *Mass media and the use and abuse of alcohol* (pp. 39–68). Rockville, MD: National Institute on Alcohol Abuse and Alcoholism.

Austin, E. W., Chen, M. J., & Grube, J. W. (2006). How does alcohol advertising influence underage drinking? The role of desirability, identification and skepticism. *Journal of Adolescent Health, 38,* 376–384.

Austin, E. W., & Hust, S. J. T. (2005). Targeting adolescents? The content and frequency of alcoholic and nonalcoholic beverage ads in magazine and video formats November 1999–April 2000. *Journal of Health Communication, 10,* 769–785.

Austin, E. W., & Johnson, K. K. (1997). Effects of general and alcohol-specific media literacy training on children's decision making about alcohol. *Journal of Health Communication, 2,* 17–42.

Austin, E. W., Pinkleton, B. E., Hust, S. J. T., & Cohen, M. (2005). Evaluation of an American Legacy Foundation/Washington State Department of Health Media Literacy Study. *Health Communication, 18,* 75–95.

Bahr, S. J., Hoffmann, J. P., & Yang, X. (2005). Parental and peer influences on the risk of adolescent drug use. *Journal of Primary Prevention, 26,* 529–551.

Bayer, R., & Kelly, M. (2010). Tobacco control and free speech—an American dilemma. *New England Journal of Medicine, 362,* 281–283.

Belcher, H. M. E., & Shinitzky, H. E. (1998). Substance abuse in children: Prediction, protection, and prevention. *Archives of Pediatrics & Adolescent Medicine, 152,* 952–960.

Biener, L., & Siegel, M. (2000). Tobacco marketing and adolescent smoking: More support for a causal inference. *American Journal of Public Health, 90,* 407–411.

Big Tobacco's promises to reform go up in smoke [Editorial]. (2006, September 12). *USA Today,* p. 14A.

Bjork, J. M., Knutson, B., Fong, G. W., Caggiano, D. M., Bennett, S. M., & Hommer, D. W. (2004). Incentive-elicited brain activation in adolescents: Similarities and differences from young adults. *Journal of Neuroscience, 24,* 1793–1802.

Blair, N. A., Yue, S. K., Singh, R., & Bernhardt, J. M. (2005). Sex, drugs, and rock and roll: Depictions of substance use in reality television: A content analysis of *The Osbournes. British Medical Journal, 331,* 1517–1519.

Borzekowski, D. L. G., & Strasburger, V. C. (2008). Tobacco, alcohol, and drug exposure. In S. Calvert & B. J. Wilson (Eds.), *Handbook of children and the media* (pp. 432–452). Boston: Blackwell.

Botvin, G. J., & Griffin, K. W. (2005). Models of prevention: School-based programs. In J. H. Lowinson, P. Ruiz, R. B. Millman, et al. (Eds.), *Substance abuse: a comprehensive textbook* (4th ed., pp. 1211–1229). Philadelphia: Lippincott Williams & Wilkins.

Briones, D. F., Wilcox, J. A., Mateus, B., & Boudjenah, D. (2006). Risk factors and prevention in adolescent substance abuse: A biopsychosocial approach. *Adolescent Medicine: State of the Art Reviews, 17,* 335–352.

Brooks, F., van der Sluijs, W., & Klemera, E., et al. (2009). *Young people's health in Great Britain and Ireland—findings from the Health Behaviour in School-Aged Children (HBSC) Survey, 2006.* Edinburgh, Scotland: University of Edinburgh.

Brown, A., & Moodie, C. (2009). The influence of tobacco marketing on adolescent smoking intentions via normative beliefs. *Health Education Research, 24,* 721–733.

Brown, J. D. (2007). Media literacy has potential to improve adolescents' health. *Journal of Adolescent Health, 39,* 459–460.

Brown, S. A., McGue, M., & Maggs, J., et al. (2008). A developmental perspective on alcohol and youths 16 to 20 years of age. *Pediatrics, 121*(Suppl. 4), S290–S310.

Bryant, A. (2000, March 20). In tobacco's face. *Newsweek,* 40–41.

Bryant, J. A., Cody, M. J., & Murphy, S. (2002). Online sales: Profit without question. *Tobacco Control, 11,* 226–227.

Campaign for Tobacco-Free Kids. (2009a). *Deadly in pink: Big Tobacco steps up its targeting of women and girls.* Washington, DC: Author. Retrieved March 4, 2010, from www.tobacco freekids.org.

Campaign for Tobacco-Free Kids. (2009b). *Raising cigarette taxes reduces smoking, especially among kids (and the cigarette companies know it).* Washington, DC: Author. Retrieved March 18, 2010, from http://tobaccofreekids .org/research/factsheets/pdf/0146.pdf.

Campaign for Tobacco-Free Kids. (2010, January 12). The PACT Act (fact sheet). Washington, DC: Author. Retrieved March 4, 2010, from www.tobaccofreekids.org.

Center on Alcohol Marketing and Youth (CAMY). (2004). *Clicking with kids: Alcohol marketing and youth on the Internet.* Washington, DC: Author.

Center on Alcohol Marketing and Youth (CAMY). (2004a, April 21). *Georgetown study finds number of alcohol ads bombarding teens rose in 2002* (press release). Retrieved September 30, 2005, from http://www1.georgetown.edu/ explore/news/?ID=783.

Center on Alcohol Marketing and Youth (CAMY). (2004b). *Alcohol advertising on television 2001 to 2003: More of the same.* Washington, DC: Author.

Center on Alcohol Marketing and Youth (CAMY). (2004c). *Youth exposure to radio advertising for alcohol—United States, summer 2003.* Washington, DC: Author.

Center on Alcohol Marketing and Youth (CAMY). (2005). *Youth overexposed: Alcohol advertising in magazines, 2001 to 2003.* Washington, DC: Author.

Center on Alcohol Marketing and Youth (CAMY). (2007). *Alcohol advertising and youth.* Washington, DC: Author.

Center on Alcohol Marketing and Youth (CAMY). (2008). *Youth exposure to alcohol advertising on television, 2001 to 2007.* Washington, DC: Author.

Centers for Disease Control. (2006). Racial/ ethnic differences among youths in cigarette smoking and susceptibility to start smoking—United States, 2002–2004. *Morbidity and Mortality Weekly Report, 55,* 1275–1277.

Centers for Disease Control. (2007). Youth exposure to alcohol advertising in magazines—United States, 2001–2005. *Morbidity and Mortality Weekly Report, 56,* 763–767.

Centers for Disease Control. (2008). *Tobacco use and the health of young people.* U.S. Department of Health and Human Services. Retrieved February 3, 2010, from http://www.cdc.gov/ HealthyYouth/Tobacco/facts.htm.

Centers for Disease Control. (2009). Cigarette brand preference among middle and high school students who are established smokers—United States, 2004 and 2006. *Morbidity and Mortality Weekly Report, 58,* 112–115.

Champion, H. L., Foley, K. L., DuRant R. H., Hensberry, R., Altman, D., & Wolfson, M. (2004). Adolescent sexual victimization, use of alcohol and other substances, and other health risk behaviors. *Journal of Adolescent Health, 35,* 321–328.

Chapman S. (2008). What should be done about smoking in movies? *Tobacco Control, 17*(1), 363–367

Charlesworth, A., & Glantz, S. A. (2005). Smoking in the movies increases adolescent smoking: A review. *Pediatrics, 116,* 1516–1528.

Chen, M.-J., Grube, J. W., Bersamin, M., Waiters, E., & Keefe, D. B. (2005). Alcohol advertising: What makes it attractive to youth? *Journal of Health Communication, 10,* 553–565.

Chilcoat, H. D., & Anthony, J. C. (1996). Impact of parent monitoring on initiation of drug use through late childhood. *Journal of the American Academy of Child & Adolescent Psychiatry, 35,* 91–100.

Christakis, D. A., & Zimmerman, F. J. (2006). Media as a public health issue. *Archives of Pediatrics & Adolescent Medicine, 160,* 446–447.

Christenson, P. G., Henriksen, L., & Roberts, D. F. (2000). *Substance use in popular prime-time television.* Washington, DC: Office of National Drug Policy Control.

Comings, D. E. (1997). Genetic aspects of childhood behavioral disorders. *Child Psychiatry & Human Development, 27,* 139–150.

ConsumerAffairs.com. (2005, June 20). Tobacco ads will be removed from school magazines. Retrieved March 1, 2010, from http://www .consumeraffairs.com/news04/2005/tobacco_ schools.html.

Cortese, D. K., Lewis., M. J., & Ling, P. M. (2009). Tobacco industry lifestyle magazines targeted to young adults. *Journal of Adolescent Health Care, 45,* 268–280.

Cowley, G., & Underwood, A. (2001, February 19). Soda pop that packs a punch: Are the new alcoholic lemonades aimed at kids? *Newsweek,* p. 45.

Cruz, M. L., & Deyton, L. R. (2010). A new regulatory challenge: Youth and tobacco. *Pediatrics.* Retrieved April 19, 2010, from www.pediatrics.org.

Cumberbatch, G., & Gauntlett, S. (2005). Smoking, alcohol and drugs on television: A content analysis. Retrieved March 4, 2010, from http://stakeholders.ofcom.org.uk/binaries/research/radio-research/smoking.pdf.

Currie, C., Hurrelmann, K., Settertobulte, W., Smith, R., & Todd, J. (2000). *Health behaviour in school-aged children: A WHO cross-national study.* Copenhagen, Denmark: Author.

Dalton, M. A., Adachi-Mejia, A. M., & Longacre, M. R., et al. (2006). Parental rules and monitoring of children's movie viewing associated with children's risk for smoking and drinking. *Pediatrics, 118,* 1932–1942.

Dalton, M. A., Ahrens, M. B., Sargent, J. D., et al. (2002). Correlation between use of tobacco and alcohol in adolescents and parental restrictions on movies. *Effective Clinical Practice, 1,* 1–10.

Dalton, M. A., Beach, M. L., Adachi-Mejia, A. M., et al. (2009). Early exposure to movie smoking predicts established smoking by older teens and young adults. *Pediatrics, 123,* e551–e558.

Dalton, M. A., Sargent, J. D., Beach., M. L., et al. (2003). Effect of viewing smoking in movies on adolescent smoking initiation: A cohort study. *Lancet, 362,* 281–285.

Desmond R., & Carveth, R. (2007). The effects of advertising on children and adolescents: A meta-analysis. In R. W. Preiss, B. M. Gayle, N. Burrell, M. Allen, & J. Bryant (Eds.), *Mass media effects research: Advances through meta-analysis* (pp. 169–179). Mahwah, NJ: Lawrence Erlbaum.

DiFranza, J. R., Richards, J. W., Paulman, P. M., et al. (1991). RJR Nabisco's cartoon camel promotes Camel cigarettes to children. *Journal of the American Medical Association, 266,* 3149–3153.

DiFranza, J. R., Wellman, R. J., Sargent, J. D., et al. (2006). Tobacco promotion and the initiation of tobacco use: Assessing the evidence for causality. *Pediatrics, 117,* e1237–e1248.

Donohue, J. M., Cevasco, M., & Rosenthal, M. B. (2007). A decade of direct-to-consumer advertising of prescription drugs. *New England Journal of Medicine, 357,* 673–681.

Dozier, D. M., Lauzen, M. M., Day, C. A., Payne, S., & Tafoya, M. (2005). Leaders and elites: Portrayals of smoking in popular films. *Tobacco Control, 14,* 7–9.

Duke, J. C., Allen J. A., Pederson, L. L., Mowery, P. D., Xiao, H., & Sargent, J. D. (2009). Reported exposure to pro-tobacco messages in the media: Trends among youth in the United States, 2000–2004. *American Journal of Health Promotion, 23,* 195–202.

DuRant, R. H., Rome, E. S., Rich, M., Allred, E., Emans, S. J., & Woods, E. R. (1997). Tobacco and alcohol use behaviors portrayed in music videos: A content analysis. *American Journal of Public Health, 87,* 1131–1135.

Editorial. (2006, September 12). Big Tobacco's promises to reform go up in smoke. *USA Today,* p. 14A. Retrieved March 20, 2010, from http://www.usatoday.com/news/opinion/editorials/2006-09-11-our-view_x.htm.

Edwards, C. A. Harris, W. C., Cook, D. R., Bedford, K. F., & Zuo, Y. (2004). Out of the smokescreen: Does an anti-smoking advertisement affect young women's perception of smoking in movies and their intention to smoke? *Tobacco Control, 13,* 277–282.

Edwards, C., Oakes, W., & Bull, D. (2007). Out of the smokescreen II: Will an advertisement targeting the tobacco industry affect young people's perception of smoking in movies and their intention to smoke? *Tobacco Control, 16,* 177–181.

Engels, R. C. M. E., Herman, R., van Baaren, R. B., Hollenstein, T., & Bot, S. M. (2009). Alcohol portrayal on television affects actual drinking behaviour. *Alcohol and Alcoholism, 44,* 244–249.

Eszterhas, J. (2004). *Hollywood animal.* New York, Knopf.

Farrelly, M. C., Davis, K. C., Haviland, M. L., Messeri, P., & Healton, C. G. (2005). Evidence of a dose–response relationship between "truth" antismoking ads and youth smoking prevalence. *American Journal of Public Health, 95,* 425–431.

Federal Trade Commission. (1999). *Self-regulation in the alcohol industry: A review of industry efforts to avoid promoting alcohol to underage consumers.* Washington, DC: Author.

Federal Trade Commission. (2009). *Federal Trade Commission cigarette report for 2006.* Washington, DC: Author. Retrieved March 3, 2010, from http://ftc.gov/os/2009/08/090812cigarettereport.pdf.

Fisher, L. B., Miles, I. W., Austin, S. B., Camargo, C. A. Jr., & Colditz, G. A. (2007). Predictors of initiation of alcohol use among US adolescents: Findings from a prospective cohort study. *Archives of Pediatrics & Adolescent Medicine, 161,* 959–966.

Fischer, P. M., Schwartz, M. P., Richards, J. W., Goldstein, A. O., & Rojas, T. H. (1991). Brand logo recognition by children aged 3 to 6 years: Mickey Mouse and Old Joe the Camel. *Journal of the American Medical Association, 266,* 3145–3153.

Flynn, B. S., Worden, J. K., Bunn, J. Y., Dorwaldt, A. L., Connolly, S. W., & Ashikaga, T. (2007). Youth audience segmentation strategies for smoking-prevention mass media campaigns based on message appeal. *Health Education & Behavior, 34,* 578–593.

Foster, S. E., Vaughan, R. D., Foster, W. H., & Califano, J. A. Jr. (2003). Alcohol consumption and expenditures for underage drinking and adult excessive drinking. *Journal of the American Medical Association, 289,* 989–995.

Foster, S. E., Vaughan, R. D., Foster, W. H., & Califano, J. A. Jr. (2006). Estimate of the commercial value of underage drinking and adult abusive and dependent drinking to the alcohol industry. *Archives of Pediatrics & Adolescent Medicine, 160,* 473–478.

Fritschler, A. L., & Hoefler, J. M. (2006). *Smoking & politics: Policy making and the federal bureaucracy* (6th ed.). Upper Saddle River, NJ: Prentice Hall.

Frosch, D. L., Grande D., Tarn, D. M., & Kravitz, R. L. (2010). A decade of controversy: Balancing policy with evidence in the regulation of prescription drug advertising. *American Journal of Public Health, 100,* 24–32.

Frosch, D. L., Krueger, P. M., Hornik, R. C., Cronholm, P. F., & Barg, F. K. (2007). Creating a demand for prescription drugs: A content analysis of television direct-to-consumer advertising. *Annals of Family Medicine, 5,* 6–13.

Garfield, C. F., Chung, P. J., & Rathouz, P. J. (2003). Alcohol advertising in magazines and adolescent readership. *Journal of the American Medical Association, 289,* 2424–2429.

Gellad, Z. F., & Lyles, K. W. (2007). Direct-to-consumer advertising of pharmaceuticals. *American Journal of Medicine, 120,* 475–480.

Gerbner, G. (1990). Stories that hurt: Tobacco, alcohol, and other drugs in the mass media. In H. Resnik (Ed.), *Youth and drugs: Society's mixed messages* (pp. 53–129). OSAP Prevention Monograph-6. Rockville, MD: Office for Substance Abuse Prevention.

Gidwani, P. P., Sobol, A., DeJong, W., Perrin, J. M., & Gortmaker, S. L. (2002). Television viewing and initiation of smoking among youth. *Pediatrics, 110,* 505–508.

Giedd, J. N. (2008). The teen brain: Insights from neuroimaging. *Journal of Adolescent Health, 42,* 335–343.

Gilpin, E. A., White, M. M., Messer, K., & Pierce, J. P. (2007). Receptivity to tobacco advertising and promotions among young adolescents as a predictor of established smoking in young adulthood. *American Journal of Public Health, 97,* 1489–1495.

Glantz, S. A., Slade, J., Bero, L. A., Hanauer, P., & Barnes, D. E. (1996). *The cigarette papers.* Berkeley: University of California Press.

Goldstein, A. O., Sobel, R. A., & Newman, G. R. (1999). Tobacco and alcohol use in G-rated children's animated films. *Journal of the American Medical Association, 281,* 1131–1136.

Gomstyn, A. (2009, November 12). Buying cigarettes and quit-smoking aids from the same company? ABCNews.com. Retrieved March 18, 2010, from http://abcnews.go.com/print?id=9057261.

Gostin, L. O. (2009). FDA regulation of tobacco: Politics, law, and the public's health. *Journal of the American Medical Association, 302,* 1459–1460.

Greenberg, B. S., Rampoldi-Hnilo, L., & Mastro, D. (2000). *The alphabet soup of television program ratings.* Cresskill, NJ: Hampton Press.

Greenberg, B. S., Rosaen, S. F., Worrell, T. R., Salmon, C. T., & Volkman, J. E. (2009). A portrait of food and drink in commercial TV series. *Health Communication, 24,* 295–303.

Grube, J. W., & Waiters, E. (2005). Alcohol in the media: Content and effects on drinking beliefs and behaviors among youth. *Adolescent Medicine: State of the Art Reviews, 16,* 327–343.

Gruber, E. L., Thau, H. M., Hill, D. L., Fisher, D. A., & Grube, J. W. (2005b). Alcohol, tobacco and illicit substances in music videos: A content analysis of prevalence and genre. *Journal of Adolescent Health, 37,* 81–83.

Gruber, E. L., Wang, P. H., Christensen, J. S., Grube, J. W., & Fisher, D. A. (2005). Private television viewing, parental supervision, and sexual and substance use risk behaviors in adolescents (abstract). *Journal of Adolescent Health, 36,* 107.

Gunter, B., Oates, C., & Blades, M. (2004). *Advertising to children on TV.* Oxford, UK: Routledge.

Halperin, S. (2008, April 18). Going to pot. *Entertainment Weekly,* 38–41.

Halpern-Felsher, B. L., & Cornell, J. L. (2005). Preventing underage alcohol use: Where do we go from here? *Journal of Adolescent Health, 37,* 1–3.

Hancox, R. J., Milne, B. J., & Poulton, R. (2004). Association between child and adolescent television viewing and adult health: A longitudinal birth cohort study. *Lancet, 364,* 257–262.

Hanewinkel, R. (2009). Cigarette smoking and perception of a movie character in a film trailer. *Archives of Pediatrics & Adolescent Medicine, 163,* 15–18.

Hanewinkel, R., Isensee, B., Sargent, J. D., & Morgenstern, M. (2010). Cigarette advertising and adolescent smoking. *American Journal of Preventive Medicine, 32*(6), 466–473.

Hanewinkel, R., & Sargent, J. D. (2007). Exposure to smoking in popular contemporary movies and youth smoking in Germany. *American Journal of Preventive Medicine, 32,* 466–473.

Hanewinkel, R., & Sargent, J. D. (2009). Longitudinal study of exposure to entertainment media and alcohol use among German adolescents. *Pediatrics, 123,* 989–995.

Harris, D. (2005, November 2). Is big tobacco sweet-talking kids into smoking? ABCNews.com. Retrieved March 20, 2010, from http://abcnews.go.com/WNT/QuitToLive/story?id=1274643.

Hawkins, K., & Hane, A. C. (2000). Adolescents' perceptions of print cigarette advertising: A case for counteradvertising. *Journal of Health Communication, 5,* 83–96.

Heatherton, T. F., & Sargent, J. D. (2009). Does watching smoking in movies promote teenage smoking? *Current Directions in Psychological Science, 18,* 63–67.

Henriksen, L., Dauphinee, A. L., Wang, Y., & Fortmann, S. P. (2006). Industry sponsored anti-smoking ads and adolescent reactance: Test of a boomerang effect. *Tobacco Control, 15,* 13–18.

Henriksen, L., Feighery, E. C., Schleicher, N. C., & Fortmann S. P. (2008). Receptivity to alcohol marketing predicts initiation of alcohol use. *Journal of Adolescent Health, 42,* 28–35.

Herd, D. (2005). Changes in the prevalence of alcohol use in rap song lyrics, 1979–97. *Addiction, 100,* 1258–1269.

Herd, D. (2008). Changes in drug use prevalence in rap music songs, 1979–1997. *Addiction Research and Theory, 16,* 167–180.

Hill, A. B. (1965). The environment and disease: Association or causality? *Proceedings of the Royal Society of Medicine, 58,* 295–300.

Hingson, R. W., Heeren, T., & Winter, M. R. (2006). Age at drinking onset and alcohol dependence. *Archives of Pediatric & Adolescent Medicine, 160,* 739–747.

Hingson, R. W, & Zha, W. (2009). Age of drinking onset, alcohol use disorders, frequent heavy drinking, and unintentionally injuring oneself and others after drinking. *Pediatrics, 123,* 1477–1484.

Hitti, M. (2006, August 11). Teens buying alcohol online. *WebMD Medical News.* Retrieved March 17, 2010, from http://www.webmd.com/parenting/news/20060811/teens-buy-alcohol-online.

Hogan, M. J., & Strasburger, V. C. (2008). Media and prosocial behavior in children and adolescents. In L. Nucci & D. Narvaez (Eds.), *Handbook of moral and character education* (pp. 537–553). Mahwah, NJ: Lawrence Erlbaum.

Hornik, R., Jacobsohn, L., Orwin, R., Piesse, A. N., & Kalton, G. (2008). Effects of the National Youth Anti-Drug Media Campaign on youths. *American Journal of Public Health, 98,* 2229–2236.

Ibrahim, J. K., & Glantz, S. A. (2007). The rise and fall of tobacco control media campaigns, 1967–2006. *American Journal of Public Health, 97,* 1383–1396.

Jackson, D. Z. (1998, November 23). Big tobacco's chump change, *Liberal Opinion Week,* p. 23.

Jackson, C., Brown, J. D., & L'Engle, K. L. (2007). R-rated movies, bedroom televisions, and initiation of smoking by White and Black adolescents. *Archives of Pediatrics & Adolescent Medicine, 161,* 260–268.

Jamieson P. E., & Romer, D. (2010). Trends in U.S. movie tobacco portrayal since 1950: A historical analysis. *Tobacco Control.* Published online April 15, 2010. Retrieved April 26, 2010, from http://tobaccocontrol.bmj.com/content/early/2010/04/14/tc.2009.034736.short?q=w_tobaccocontrol_ahead_tab.

Jenssen, B. P., Klein, J. D., Salazar, L. R., Daluge, N. A., & DiClemente, R. J. (2009). Exposure to tobacco on the Internet: Content analysis of adolescents' Internet use. *Pediatrics, 124,* e180–e186.

Jernigan, D. H. (2006). Importance of reducing youth exposure to alcohol advertising. *Archives of Pediatrics & Adolescent Medicine, 160,* 100–102.

Jernigan, D. (2009). Alcohol-branded merchandise: The need for action. *Archives of Pediatrics & Adolescent Medicine, 163,* 278–279.

Jernigan, D. H., Ostroff, J., Ross, C. et al. (2005). Alcohol advertising and youth: A measured approach. *Journal of Public Health Policy, 26,* 312–325.

Jernigan, D. H., Ostroff, J., Ross, C., & O'Hara, J. A. (2004). Sex differences in adolescent exposure to alcohol advertising in magazines. *Archives of Pediatrics & Adolescent Medicine, 158,* 629–634.

Johnston, L. D., O'Malley, P. M., Bachman, J. G., & Schulenberg, J. E. (December 14, 2009). "Smoking continues gradual decline among U.S. teens, smokeless tobacco threatens a comeback" (press release). University of Michigan News Service: Ann Arbor, MI. Retrieved March 1, 2010, from http://www.monitoringthefuture.org.

Journal Wire Reports (2001, March 15). Advertising rose after tobacco suits. *Albuquerque Journal,* p. A4.

Kaiser Family Foundation. (2004). *Entertainment education and health in the United States.* Menlo Park, CA: Author.

Kessler, D. (2001). *A question of intent: A great American battle with a deadly industry.* New York: Public Affairs.

King, C. III, Siegel, M., Jernigan, D. H., et al. (2009). Adolescent exposure to alcohol advertising in magazines: An evaluation of advertising placement in relation to underage youth readership. *Journal of Adolescent Health, 45,* 626–633.

Kulig, J. W., & the Committee on Substance Abuse (2005). Tobacco, alcohol, and other drugs: The role of the pediatrician in prevention, identification, and management of substance abuse. *Pediatrics, 115,* 816–821.

Kulig, K., Brener, N. D., & McManus, T. (2003). Sexual activity and substance use among adolescents by category of physical activity plus team sports participation. *Archives of Pediatrics & Adolescent Medicine, 157,* 905–912.

Kunkel, D. (2007). Inching forward on tobacco advertising restrictions to prevent youth smoking. *Archives of Pediatrics & Adolescent Medicine, 161,* 515–516.

Kupersmidt, J. B., Scull, T. M., & Austin, E. W. (2010). Media literacy education for elementary school substance use prevention: Randomized efficacy study of Media Detective. *Pediatrics, 126*(3), 525–531.

Kurtz, M. E., Kurtz, J. C., Johnson, S. M., & Cooper, W. (2001). Sources of information on the health effects of environmental tobacco smoke among African-American children and adolescents. *Journal of Adolescent Health, 28,* 458–464.

Landman, A., Ling, P. M., & Glantz, S. A. (2002). Tobacco industry youth smoking prevention programs: Protecting the industry and hurting tobacco control. *American Journal of Public Health, 92,* 917–930.

Langleben, D. D., Laughead, J. W., Ruparel, K. et al. (2009). Reduced prefrontal and temporal processing and recall of high "sensation value" ads. *NeuroImage, 46,* 219–225.

Laugesen, M., & Meads, C. (1991). Tobacco advertising restrictions, price, income and tobacco consumption in OECD countries, 1960–1986. *British Journal of Addiction, 86,* 1343–1354.

Long, J. A., O'Connor, P. G., Gerbner, G., & Concato, J. (2002). Use of alcohol, illicit drugs, and tobacco among characters on prime-time television. *Substance Abuse, 23,* 95–103.

Longacre, M. R., Adachi-Mejia, A. M., Titus-Ernstoff, L., Gibson, J. J., Beach, M. L., & Dalton, M. A. (2009). Parental attitudes about cigarette smoking and alcohol use in the Motion Picture Association of America rating system. *Archives of Pediatrics & Adolescent Medicine, 163,* 218–224.

McCannon B. (2009). Media literacy/media education: Solution to Big Media? A review of the literature. In V. C. Strasburger, B. J. Wilson, & A. B. Jordan, *Children, adolescents, and the media* (2nd ed., pp. 519–569). Thousand Oaks, CA: Sage.

McClure, A. C., Stoolmiller, M., Tanski, S. E., Worth, K. A., & Sargent, J. D. (2009). Alcohol-branded merchandise and its association with drinking attitudes and outcomes in U.S. adolescents. *Archives of Pediatrics & Adolescent Medicine, 163,* 211–217.

McGee, R., Ketchel, J., & Reeder, A. I. (2007). Alcohol imagery on New Zealand television. *Substance Abuse Treatment, Prevention, and Policy.* Retrieved March 20, 2010, from http://www.substanceabusepolicy.com/content/2/1/6.

McMahon, R. L. (1994). Diagnosis, assessment and treatment of externalizing problems in children: The role of longitudinal data. *Journal of Consulting & Clinical Psychology, 62,* 901–917.

McMillen, R. C., Tanski, S., Winickoff, J., & Valentine, N. (2007). *Attitudes about smoking in the movies.* Retrieved March 8, 2007, from http://www.socialclimate.org/pdf/smoking-attitudes-movies.pdf.

Mednick, S. C., Christakis, N. A., & Fowler, J. H. (2010). The spread of sleep loss influences drug use in adolescent social networks. *PloS One, 5,* e9775.

Miller, J. W., Naimi, T. S., Brewer, R. D., & Jones, S. E. (2007). Binge drinking and associated health risk behaviors among high school students. *Pediatrics, 119,* 76–85.

Montgomery, K. C., & Chester, J. (2009). Interactive food and beverage marketing: Targeting adolescents in the digital age. *Journal of Adolescent Health, 45,* S18–S29.

Moreno, M. A., Briner, L. R., Williams, A., Brockman, L., Walker, L., & Christakis, D. A. (2010). A content analysis of displayed alcohol references on a social networking Web site. *Journal of Adolescent Health.* Retrieved March 22, 2010, from http://download.journals.elsevierhealth.com/pdfs/journals/1054-139X/PIIS1054139X10000200.pdf.

Moreno, M. A., Briner, L. R., Williams, A., Walker, L., & Christakis, D. A. (2009). Real use or "real cool": Adolescents speak out about displayed alcohol references on social networking sites. *Journal of Adolescent Health, 45,* 420–422.

Moreno, M. A., Parks, M. R., Zimmerman, F. J., Brito, T. E., & Christakis, D. A. (2009). Display of health risk behaviors on MySpace by adolescents. *Archives of Pediatrics & Adolescent Medicine, 163,* 27–34.

Moreno, M. A., VanderStoep, A., Parks, M. R., et al. (2009). Reducing at-risk adolescents' display of risk behavior on a social networking web site. *Archives of Pediatrics & Adolescent Medicine, 163,* 35–41.

Morrison, M. A., Krugman, D. M., & Park, P. (2008). Under the radar: Smokeless tobacco advertising in magazines with substantial youth readership. *American Journal of Public Health, 98,* 543–548.

Motion Picture Association of America. (2007, May 10). *Film rating board to consider smoking as a factor* [press release]. Los Angeles, CA: Motion Picture Association of America.

Murphy, S. T., Hether, H. J., & Rideout, V. (2008). *How healthy is prime time? An analysis of health content in popular prime time television programs.* Menlo Park, CA: Kaiser Family Foundation.

National Cancer Institute. (2008). *The role of the media in promoting and reducing tobacco use.* Smoking and tobacco control monograph No. 19. NIH Pub. No. 07-6242, June 2008. Available at http://cancercontrol.cancer.gov/tcrb/monographs/19/m19_complete.pdf.

National Center on Addiction and Substance Abuse. (2005). *National Survey of American Attitudes on Substance Abuse IX: Teens and Parents.* New York: National Center on Addiction and Substance Abuse.

Newman, A. A. (2009, September 21). A different camel is back in the glossies. *New York Times,* Retrieved March 18, 2010, from http://www.nytimes.com/2009/09/22/business/media/22adco.html.

Nicholson, M., & Hoye, R. (2009). Reducing adolescents' exposure to alcohol advertising and promotion during televised sports. *Journal of the American Medical Association, 301,* 1479–1482.

Nixon, C. L., Mansfield, P. M., & Thoms, P. (2008). Effectiveness of antismoking public service announcements on children's intent to smoke. *Psychology of Addictive Behaviors, 22,* 496–503.

Noar, S. M. (2006). A 10-year retrospective of research in health mass media campaigns: Where do we go from here? *Journal of Health Communication, 11,* 21–42.

Nocera, J. (2006, June 18). If it's good for Philip Morris, can it also be good for public health? *New York Times Magazine,* pp. 46–53, 70, 76–78.

Nugent, W: (1999). *Into the West.* New York: Knopf.

Olds, R. S., Thombs, D. L., & Tomasek, J. R. (2005). Relations between normative beliefs and initiation intentions toward cigarette, alcohol and marijuana. *Journal of Adolescent Health, 37,* e75.

Orlandi, M. A., Lieberman, L. R., & Schinke, S. P. (1989). The effects of alcohol and tobacco advertising on adolescents. In M. A. Orlandi, L. R. Lieberman, & S. P. Schinke (Eds.), *Perspectives on adolescent drug use* (pp. 77–97). Binghamton, NY: Haworth Press.

Paek, H.-J., & Gunther, A. C. (2007). How peer proximity moderates indirect media influence on adolescent smoking. *Communication Research, 34,* 407–432.

Pierce, J. P., Choi, W. S., Gilpin, E. A., Farkas, A. J., & Berry, C. (1998). Industry promotion of cigarettes and adolescent smoking. *Journal of the American Medical Association, 279,* 511–515.

Pierce, J. P., Choi, W. S., Gilpin, E. A. et al. (2002). Does tobacco marketing undermine the influence of recommended parenting in discouraging adolescents from smoking? *American Journal of Preventive Medicine, 23,* 73–81.

Pierce, J. P., Lee, L., & Gilpin, E. A. (1994). Smoking initiation by adolescent girls, 1944 through 1988: An association with targeted advertising. *Journal of the American Medical Association, 271,* 608–611.

Pierce, J. P., Messer, K., James, L. E., White, M. M., Kealey, S., Vallone, D. M., & Healton, C. G. (2010). Camel No. 9 cigarette-marketing campaign targeted young teenage girls. *Pediatrics, 125*(4), 619–626.

Potter, W. J. (2010). *Media literacy* (5th ed.). Thousand Oaks, CA: Sage.

Primack, B. A., Dalton, M. A., Carroll, M. V., Agarwal, A. A., & Fine, M. J. (2008). Content analysis of tobacco, alcohol, and other drugs in popular music. *Archives of Pediatrics & Adolescent Medicine, 162,* 169–175.

Primack, B., Douglas, E., & Kraemer, K. (2010). Exposure to cannabis in popular music and cannabis use among adolescents. *Addiction, 105,* 515–523.

Primack, B. A., Fine, D., Yang, C. K., Wickett, D., & Zickmund, S. (2009). Adolescents' impressions of antismoking media literacy education: Qualitative results from a randomized controlled trial. *Health Education Research, 24,* 608–621.

Primack, B. A., Gold, M. A., Land, S. R., & Fine, M. J. (2006). Association of cigarette smoking and media literacy about smoking among adolescents. *Journal of Adolescent Health, 39,* 465–472.

Primack, B. A., Kraemer, K. L., Fine, M. J., & Dalton, M. A. (2009). Media exposure and marijuana and alcohol use among adolescents. *Substance Use and Misuse, 44,* 722–739.

Primack, B. A., Sidani, J., Carroll, M. V., & Fine, M. J. (2009). Associations between smoking and media literacy in college students. *Journal of Health Communication, 14,* 541–555.

Prokhorov, A. V., Winickoff, J. P., Ahluwalia, J. S., et al. (2006). Youth tobacco use: A global perspective for child health care clinicians. *Pediatrica*, *118*, e890–e902.

Pupillo J. (2007). Hot air: AAP experts skeptical of movie industry's commitment to curb smoke-filled images in youth-rated films or add R-ratings. *AAP News, 28*, 16–17.

Rauzi, R. (1998, June 9). The teen factor: Today's media-savvy youths influence what others are seeing and hearing. *Los Angeles Times*, p. F1.

Reis, E. C., Duggan, A. K., Adger, H., & DeAngelis, C. (1992). The impact of anti-drug advertising on youth substance abuse (abstract). *American Journal of Diseases of Children, 146,* 519.

Rich, M., & Bar-on, M. (2001). Child health in the information age: Media education of pediatricians. *Pediatrics*, *107*, 156–162.

Rideout, V. (2010). *Generation M²: Media in the lives of 8- to 18-year-olds.* Menlo Park, CA: Kaiser Family Foundation.

Ringel, J. S., Collins, R. L., & Ellickson, P. L. (2006). Time trends and demographic differences in youth exposure to alcohol advertising on television. *Journal of Adolescent Health, 39*(4), 473–480.

Roberts, D. F., & Christenson, P. G. (2000). *"Here's looking at you, kid": Alcohol, drugs and tobacco in entertainment media.* Menlo Park, CA: Kaiser Family Foundation.

Robin, S. S., & Johnson, E. O. (1996). Attitude and peer cross pressure: Adolescent drug and alcohol use. *Journal of Drug Education, 26,* 69–99.

Rosenthal, M. B., Berndt, E. R., Frank, R. G., Donohue, J. M., & Epstein, A. M. (2002). Promotion of prescription drugs to consumers. *New England Journal of Medicine, 346,* 498–505.

Rubin, A. (2009, November 19). *Prescription drugs and the cost of advertising them.* Retrieved March 8, 2010, from http://www.therubins.com/geninfo/advertise2.htm.

Saffer, H., & Dave, D. (2006). Alcohol advertising and alcohol consumption by adolescents. *Health Economics*, *15,* 617–637.

Salkin, A. (2007, February 11). Noir lite: Beer's good-time humor turns black. *New York Times*, WK, p. 3.

Sargent, J. D., Beach, M. L., Adachi-Mejia, A. M., et al. (2005). Exposure to movie smoking: Its relation to smoking initiation among U.S. adolescents. *Pediatrics*, *116,* 1183–1191.

Sargent, J. D., Dalton, M., & Beach, M. (2000). Exposure to cigarette promotions and smoking uptake in adolescents: Evidence of a dose–response relation. *Tobacco Control, 9,* 163–168.

Sargent, J. D., Dalton, M., & Beach, M. et al. (2004). Effect of parental R-rated movie restriction on adolescent smoking initiation. *Pediatrics*, *2004,* 149–156.

Sargent J., Gibson J., & Heatherton, T. (2009). Comparing the effects of entertainment media and tobacco marketing on youth smoking. *Tobacco* Control, *18,* 47–53.

Sargent, J. D., & Heatherton, T. F. (2009). Comparison of trends for adolescent smoking and smoking in movies, 1990–2007. *Journal of the American Medical Association, 301,* 2211–2213.

Sargent, J. D., Stoolmiller, M., Worth, K. A., Gibson, J., & Gibbons, F. X. (2007). Exposure to smoking depictions in movies: Its association with established adolescent smoking. *Archives of Pediatrics & Adolescent Medicine, 161,* 849–856.

Sargent, J. D., Tanski, S. E., & Gibson, J. (2007). Exposure to movie smoking among U.S. adolescents aged 10 to 14 years: A population estimate. *Pediatrics, 119,* e1167–e1176.

Sargent, J. D., Wills, T. A., Stoolmiller, M., et al. (2006). Alcohol use in motion pictures and its relation with early onset teen drinking. *Journal of Studies of Alcohol, 67,* 54–65.

Serjeant, J. (2008, July 11). Some U.S. DVDs to carry anti-smoking ads. *Reuters*. Retrieved August 12, 2009, from http://www.reuters.com/article/entertainmentNews/idUSN1134673320080711.

Schydlower, M., & Arredondo, R. M. (Eds.). (2006). Substance abuse among adolescents. *Adolescent Medicine State of the Art Reviews, 17,* 259–504.

Semuels, A. (2009, February 13). Alcohol, sex ads get prime TV time. *Los Angeles Times*. Retrieved March 20, 2010, from http://articles.latimes.com/2009/feb/13/business/fi-ads13.

Shields, D. L., Carol, J., Balbach, E. D., & McGee, S. (1999). Hollywood on tobacco: How the entertainment industry understands tobacco portrayal. *Tobacco Control, 8,* 378–386.

Shrier, L. A., Harris, S. K., Kurland, M., & Knight, J. R. (2003). Substance use problems and associated psychiatric symptoms among adolescents in primary care. *Pediatrics, 111,* e699–e705.

Siegel, M., & Biener, L. (2000). The impact of an antismoking media campaign on progression to established smoking: Results of a longitudinal youth study. *American Journal of Public Health, 90,* 380–386.

Sims, T. H., & Committee on Substance Abuse, American Academy of Pediatrics. (2009). Technical report—tobacco as a substance of abuse. *Pediatrics, 124,* e1045–1053.

Slater, M. D., Kelly, K. J., Edwards, R. W., et al. (2006). Combining in-school and community-based media efforts: Reducing marijuana and alcohol uptake among younger adolescents. *Health Education Research, 21,* 157–167.

Smith, L. A., & Foxcroft, D. R. (2009). The effect of alcohol advertising, marketing and portrayal on drinking behaviour in young people: Systematic review of prospective cohort studies. *BMC Public Health,* 9, published online February 6, 2009 at doi:10. 1186/1471-2458-9-51.

Snowbeck, C. (2005, April 19). FDA tells Levitra to cool it with ad. *Post-Gazette.* Business News Section. Retrieved March 8, 2010, from http://www.postgazette.com/pg/05109/490334-28.stm.

Snyder, L. B., Milici, F. F., Slater, M., Sun, H., & Strizhakova, Y. (2006). Effects of alcohol advertising exposure on drinking among youth. *Archives of Pediatrics & Adolescent Medicine, 160,* 18–24.

Stange, K. C. (2007). Time to ban direct-to-consumer prescription drug marketing. *Annals of Family Medicine, 5,* 101–104.

Stockwell, T. F., & Glantz, S. A. (1997). Tobacco use is increasing in popular films. *Tobacco Control, 6,* 282–284.

Strasburger, V. C. (1998). Adolescents, drugs, and the media (letter). *Archives of Pediatrics & Adolescent Medicine, 153,* 313.

Strasburger, V. C. (2006). Risky business: What primary care practitioners need to know about the influence of the media on adolescents. *Primary Care: Clinics in Office Practice, 33,* 317–348.

Strasburger, V. C. (2009a). Why do adolescent health researchers ignore the impact of the media? *Journal of Adolescent Health, 44,* 203–205.

Strasburger, V. C. (2009b). Media and children: What needs to happen now? *Journal of the American Medical Association, 301,* 2265–2266.

Strasburger, V. C. (2010, February 24). Is there a conspiracy against teenagers? *Liberal Opinion Week,* p. 26.

Strasburger, V. C., & Council on Communications and Media. (2010a). Children, adolescents, substance abuse, and the media. *Pediatrics, 126*(4), 791–799.

Strasburger, V.C., & Council on Communications and Media. (2010b). Sexuality, contraception, and the media. *Pediatrics, 126*(3), 576–582.

Strasburger, V. C., Jordan, A. B., & Donnerstein, E. (2010). Health effects of the media on children and adolescents. *Pediatrics, 126*(4), 756–767.

Strasburger, V. C., Wilson, B. J., & Jordan, A. B. (2009). *Children, adolescents, and the media* (2nd ed.), Thousand Oaks, CA: Sage.

Sutel, S. (2007, January 26). Watching the ads. *Albuquerque Journal* (Associated Press), p. B4.

Swahn, M. H., Bossarte, R. M., & Sullivent, E. E. 3rd. (2008). Age of alcohol use initiation, suicidal behavior, and peer and dating violence victimization and perpetration among high-risk, seventh-grade adolescents. *Pediatrics, 121,* 297–305.

Tanski, S. E., Dal Cin, S., Stoolmiller, M., & Sargent, J. D. (2010). Parental R-rated movie restriction and early onset alcohol use. *Journal of Studies of Alcohol and Drugs, 71,* 452–459.

Tanski, S. E., Prokhorov, A. V., & Klein, J. D. (2004). Youth and tobacco. *Minerva Pediatrica, 56,* 553–565.

Tanski, S. E., Stoolmiller, M., Dal Cin, S., Worth, K., Gibson, J., & Sargent, J. D. (2009). Movie character smoking and adolescent smoking: Who matters more, good guys or bad guys? *Pediatrics, 124,* 135–143.

Tapert, S. F., Aarons, G. A., Sedlar, G. R., & Brown, S. A. (2001). Adolescent substance abuse and sexual risk-taking behavior. *Journal of Adolescent Health, 28,* 181–189.

Tapert, S. F., Cheung, E. H., Brown, G. G. et al. (2003). Neural response to alcohol stimuli in adolescents with alcohol use disorder. *Archives of General Psychiatry, 60,* 727–735.

Thomaselli, R. (2003, January 14). 47% of doctors feel pressured by DTC drug advertising. *Advertising Age.* Retrieved March 20, 2010, from http://adage.com.

Thompson, E. M., & Gunther, A. C. (2007). Cigarettes and cinema: Does parental restriction of R-rated movie viewing reduce adolescent smoking susceptibility? *Journal of Adolescent Health, 40,* e1–e6.

Thompson, M. P., Sims, L., Kingree, J. B., & Windle, M. (2008). Longitudinal associations between problem alcohol use and violent victimization in a national sample of adolescents. *Journal of Adolescent Health, 42,* 21–27.

Tickle, J. J., Beach, M. L., & Dalton, M. A. (2009). Tobacco, alcohol, and other risk behaviors in film: How well do MPAA ratings distinguish content? *Journal of Health Communication, 14,* 756–767.

Titus-Ernstoff, L., Dalton, M. A., Adachi-Mejia, A. M., Longacre, M. R., & Beach, M. L. (2008). Longitudinal study of viewing smoking in movies and initiation of smoking by children. *Pediatrics, 121,* 15–21.

TV Guide. (2002, February 23)."Cheers & Jeers."

U.S. Department of Health and Human Services. (1994). *Preventing tobacco use among young people: report of the Surgeon General*. Washington, DC: U.S. Government Printing Office.

U.S. Department of Health and Human Services. (2007). *The Surgeon General's call to action to prevent and reduce underage drinking*. Rockville, MD: U.S. Department of Health and Human Services.

U.S. National Drug Control Policy. (2008, May 10). Teen 'self medication' for depression leads to more serious mental illness, new report reveals. *Science Daily*. Retrieved February 22, 2010, from http://www.sciencedaily.com/releases/2008/05/080509105348.htm.

U.S. Public Health Service, Office on Smoking and Health. (2004). *The health consequences of smoking: A report of the Surgeon General*. Rockville, MD: U.S. Department of Health and Human Services.

Vaidya, S. G., Vaidya, J. S., & Naik, U. D. (1999). Sports sponsorship by cigarette companies influences the adolescent children's mind and helps initiate smoking: Results of a national study in India. *Journal of the Indian Medical Association, 97,* 354–356.

Van den Bulck, H., Simons, N., & Van Gorp, B. (2008). Let's drink and be merry: The framing of alcohol in the prime-time American youth series *The OC. Journal of Studies of Alcohol and Drugs, 69,* 933–940.

Vickers, A. (1992). Why cigarette advertising should be banned. *British Medical Journal, 304,* 1195–1196.

Vinson, D. C., Maclure, M., Reidinger, C., & Smith, G. S. (2003). A population based case-crossover and case-control study of alcohol and the risk of injury. *Journal of Studies on Alcohol and Drugs, 64,* 358–366.

Walsh, D., & Bennett, D. (2005). *WHY do they act that way? A survival guide to the adolescent brain for you and your teen*. New York: Free Press.

Walsh, D., & Gentile, D. A. (2001). A validity test of movie, television, and video-game ratings. *Pediatrics, 107,* 1302–1308.

Ward, L. M., Day, K. M., & Thomas, K. A. (2010). Confronting the assumptions: Exploring the nature and predictors of Black adolescents' media use. *Journal of Broadcasting & Electronic Media, 54,* 69–86.

Weinstein, H. (1998, January 15). Papers: RJR went for teens. *Los Angeles Times*, p. A1.

Wellman, R. J., Sugarman, D. B., DiFranza, J., & Winickoff, J. P. (2006). The extent to which tobacco marketing and tobacco use in films contribute to children's use of tobacco. *Archives of Pediatrics & Adolescent Medicine, 160*(12), 1285–1296.

West, J. H., Romero, R. A., & Trinidad, D. R. (2007). Adolescent receptivity to tobacco marketing by racial/ethnic groups in California. *American Journal of Preventive Medicine, 33,* 121–123.

While, D., Kelly, S., Huang, W., & Charlton, A. (1996). Cigarette advertising and onset of smoking in children: Questionnaire survey. *British Medical Journal, 313,* 398–399.

White, A. M., & Swartzwelder, H. S. (2004). Hippocampal function during adolescence: A unique target of ethanol effects. *Annals of the New York Academy of Sciences, 1021,* 206–220.

Wiencke, J. K., Thurston, S. W., Kelsey, K. T. et al. (1999). Early age at smoking initiation and tobacco carcinogen DNA damage in the lung. *Journal of the National Cancer Institute, 91,* 614–619.

Wills, T. A., Sargent, J. D., Gibbons, F. X., Gerrard, M., & Stoolmiller, M. (2009). Movie exposure to alcohol cues and adolescent alcohol problems: A longitudinal analysis in a national sample. *Psychology of Addictive Behaviors, 23*(1), 23–25.

Winter, M. V., Donovan, R. J., & Fielder, L. J. (2008). Exposure of children and adolescents to alcohol advertising on television in Australia. *Journal of Studies on Alcohol and Drugs, 69,* 676–683.

Wilson D. (2009, June 13). Congress passes measure on tobacco regulation. *New York Times*. Retrieved November 12, 2009, from http://www.nytimes.com/2009/06/13/business/13tobacco.html.

World Health Organization. (2002). *World health report*. Retrieved March 20, 2010, from http://www.who.int/whr/2002/chapter4/en/index6.html.

Womach, J. (2003). *U.S. tobacco production, consumption, and export trends: A report to Congress*. Washington, DC: Congressional Research Service, Library of Congress.

World Health Organization. (2008). *WHO report on the global tobacco epidemic, 2008*. Geneva, Switzerland: Author.

Worth, K. A., Chambers J. G., Nassau, D. H., Rakhra, B. K., & Sargent, J. D. (2008). Exposure of U.S. adolescents to extremely violent movies. *Pediatrics, 122,* 306–312.

Yakota, F., & Thompson, K. M. (2001). Depiction of alcohol, tobacco, and other substances in G-rated animated films. *Pediatrics, 107,* 1369–1374.

CHAPTER 22

Food Marketing

Targeting Young People in a Toxic Environment

KATHERINE BATTLE HORGEN
Yale University

JENNIFER L. HARRIS
Yale University

KELLY D. BROWNELL
Yale University

An Australian study reported that more than half of 9- to 10-year-old children believe that Ronald McDonald knows best what is good for children to eat (Food Commission, 1997). This occurs at a time when "the prevalence of overweight and obesity is increasing worldwide at an alarming rate . . . in children as well as in adults" (World Health Organization [WHO] Consultation on Obesity, 1997). From 1980 to 2002, overweight prevalence tripled for U.S. children and adolescents aged 6 to 19 (Ogden et al., 2006); today, more than one-third of young people in the United States are overweight (Ogden, Carroll, Curtin, Lamb, & Flegal, 2010). The incidence of obese children (i.e., those with body mass index [BMI]

at the 95th percentile and above) is even more disturbing: More than 12% of preschoolers (ages 2 to 5 years) and 17% of older children and adolescents are obese. Although obesity results from an imbalance of physical activity and caloric consumption, increasing empirical evidence demonstrates that the ready availability of inexpensive energy-dense, nutrient-poor foods and beverages is a significant contributor to this epidemic (Frieden, Dietz, & Collins, 2010; Goldberg & Gunasti, 2007; Harris, Pomeranz, Lobstein, & Brownell, 2008).

Childhood obesity takes a major toll on health care costs and coverage in the United States. One study analyzed hospital admissions and found that obesity-related hospital visits nearly doubled from 1999 to 2005 and associated costs increased from $125.9 million to $237.6 million (Trasande, Liu, Fryer, & Weitzman, 2009). In addition to monetary costs, obesity has serious long-term health consequences, including increased risk of cardiovascular disease, type 2 diabetes, high cholesterol and blood pressure, and other diseases (Centers for Disease Control, 2009; McGinnis, Gootman, & Kraak, 2006) and has been linked to premature mortality (Flegal, Graubard, Williamson, & Gail, 2005). As a result of obesity-related diseases, children today may be the first generation to live shorter lives than their parents (Olshansky et al., 2005). Psychosocial risks include social discrimination that leads to psychological stress and other negative health and social outcomes, such as decreased academic performance and depression among children and adults (Puhl & Heuer, 2009).

If unhealthy foods are the wares of a toxic food environment, marketing is the peddler. Given the impact of diet on health and well-being and the documented impact of advertising on attitudes and eating behaviors, it is unfortunate how little oversight there is of food advertising. This chapter will review the impact of food marketing on diet and make policy recommendations for monitoring and limiting unhealthy marketing practices directed at children and adolescents.

Advertising Pervasiveness

In the past 5 years, media use among young people (ages 8 to 18) increased by more than 1 hour per day: from 6 hours and 21 minutes in 2004 to 7 hours and 38 minutes daily in 2009, nearly a full day of work for a typical adult (Rideout, Foehr, & Roberts, 2010). Due to multitasking (i.e., consuming more than one media at a time), young people are exposed to on average 10 hours and 45 minutes of media content daily. Television remains their primary form of media: "The typical child spends more time watching television than doing anything else except sleeping and adolescents spend more time watching television each year than they do in school" (Avery, Mathios, Shanahan, & Bisogni, 1997, p. 217).

Increasingly, much of young people's television viewing does not occur in front of a TV set. Viewing of regularly scheduled television programming decreased by 25 minutes a day for the first time in 2009, but the amount of time watching TV programming increased to almost 4 hours per day due to a variety of new ways to watch television, including on the Internet, cell phones, and iPods (Rideout et al., 2010). The average young person also spends 1.75 hours per day listening to music, more than 1 hour using the computer, and 49 minutes playing video games.

As young people consume large amounts of media, they are also exposed to massive doses of food advertising. Twenty-four of the top 100 advertising campaigns of the 20th century endorsed food products (Klein & Donaton, 1999a). Each day, children view an average of 15 food ads on television (Federal Trade Commission [FTC], 2007). Among ads targeted at children, food is one of the two largest categories, the other being toys (Williams, Achterberg, & Sylvester, 1993). An American study comparing food ads on networks targeting English- and Spanish-speaking youth reported that one fifth of the commercials were for food, and that food ads were especially prevalent during Saturday morning cartoons and on children's networks (Bell, Cassady, Culp, & Alcalay, 2009). An analysis of 27.5 hours of children's television revealed that 49% of the advertisements were for food (Seitz, Wootan, & Story, 2008).

Yet only 46% of the $1.6 billion that the food industry spends peddling their wares to children and adolescents is devoted to traditional television advertising (FTC, 2008). Increasingly, food companies target young people with advertising in other forms of media, including radio, the Internet, and other digital media. Nearly two thirds of food companies reported having child-directed Internet activities online. One popular food company advergaming website, Millsberry.com from General Mills, attracts 767,000 unique youth visitors every month who spend an average of 66 minutes on the site; and nearly all 167 pages on the site include branded content to promote high-sugar cereals (Harris et al., 2009c). Food companies also embed marketing messages within other media content, making them more appealing and difficult to identify. Examples of embedded marketing techniques include product placements in television, movies, music lyrics, and video games and advergames on company-owned websites. A recent examination of product placements in movies showed that 69% of the most popular movies from 1996 to 2005 included at least one food, beverage, or restaurant product placement (Sutherland, MacKenzie, Purvis, & Dalton, 2010). Finally, food companies target young people with extensive marketing programs in other nonmedia venues including schools, supermarkets and convenience stores, child-targeted product packaging, and event sponsorships. These forms of marketing represent almost 30% of food companies' marketing budgets and are disproportionately used to target young people (FTC, 2008).

Increasingly, food companies integrate their marketing messages across multiple media to increase their reach and effectiveness (Garretson & Burton, 2005; Naik & Raman, 2003). For example, 20% of children's TV advertisements also promoted a website (Gantz, Schwartz, Angelini, & Rideout, 2007). Similarly, 50% of packages for child-targeted cereals include a URL to direct young people to advergaming websites, and many include codes needed to unlock special features on the website (Harris et al., 2009c). Even friends have become a marketing tool. Digital media contain numerous viral features that encourage young people to send marketing messages to their friends, such as invitations to play an advergame, advertisements that can be forwarded via YouTube, and "e-cards" (Chester & Montgomery, 2008). Viral features were found on 74% of child- and adolescent-targeted food company websites (Moore & Rideout, 2007). More recently, the use of social media, such as Facebook and Twitter, to promote food products has skyrocketed (Lenhart, Purcell, Smith, & Zickuhr, 2010). Examples of these new technology-based marketing techniques include a mobile marketing by 7-Eleven in which consumers send a text message to receive free beverages, including Slurpees and Big Gulp (i.e., 32-oz.) soft drinks (Brandweek, 2009) and invitations to parties to try the new UltraViolet Mountain Dew distributed via Twitter and Facebook (Hein, 2009). Parents who diligently monitor and attempt to limit their children's media consumption find it nearly impossible to shield them from massive amounts of food marketing exposure. In total, Americans view an estimated 3,000 marketing messages every day (Klein, 1999), and food products represent approximately 10% of all advertising spending (The Nielsen Company, 2010).

Targeting a Vulnerable Audience

This level of media exposure combined with the malleability of children's beliefs translates into a fruitful target population for advertisers. Advertisers began to view children as a separate advertising market in the 1960s (Kunkel & Roberts, 1991) and found the rewards were great. Children and adolescents spend (or influence the spending of) nearly $200 billion annually, much of which is spent on food products (McGinnis et al., 2006). McNeal (*Kids as Customers: A Handbook of Marketing to Children*, 1992) strongly encourages businesses to include children in their marketing strategies, citing examples in which children were excluded from strategic planning to the industry's detriment. As McNeal notes, "Kids are the most unsophisticated of all consumers: they have the least and therefore want the most. Consequently, they are in a perfect position to be taken" (p. 19). He encourages safeguards to promote ethical marketing to this vulnerable group, but the implication is clear: Children are easy targets for advertisers.

A large body of consumer behavior research documents young children's inherent vulnerability to advertising (see IOM, 2006; John, 1999; Kunkel et al., 2004). Until the age of 8 years, children do not possess the cognitive ability to understand that advertising presents a biased point of view; they view advertising as simply another source of information about the world around them. Accordingly, the American Academy of Pediatrics (2006) and the American Psychological Association (Kunkel et al., 2004) support complete bans on advertising to young children. When surveyed, even businesspeople in the youth marketing industry agree that it is inappropriate to market to children under age 7 (Geraci, 2004).

More recent psychological research demonstrates that older children and adolescents are also extremely susceptible to the influence of food marketing. Until the age of 14 years, children do not automatically access their knowledge about the misleading tactics and appeals used by advertisers when viewing commercials (John, 1999). As a result, older children are also unlikely to critically process the advertising messages they encounter. In addition, although adolescents express high levels of skepticism and mistrust about advertising in general (Boush, Friestad, & Rose, 1994), marketers have identified techniques that effectively persuade in subtle ways that do not activate defensive responses to marketing information, including "covert" forms of marketing and marketing techniques that take advantage of their unique developmental needs (Harris, Brownell, & Bargh, 2009).

Examples of covert marketing techniques commonly used by food companies include humorous advertising that entertains without providing rational product benefits, brand messages embedded within entertainment content (e.g., product placements and advergames), and brand logo placement at entertainment and sporting events (Petty & Andrews, 2008; Sprott, 2008). Many of these practices are used disproportionately by food marketers to target adolescents (FTC, 2008). Social and viral marketing and messages that promote products as "cool" and socially desirable appeal to older children and adolescents' strong desire to fit in with their peers and separate from their parents (Valkenburg & Cantor, 2001). Image advertising, celebrity endorsements, and sponsorships also encourage unhealthy food consumption as a means to convey a desired image; these messages have powerful appeal to young people who are actively attempting to establish their own identities (Chaplin & John, 2005; Russell, Norman, & Heckler, 2004; Snyder & DeBono, 1985).

When the products that advertisers promote can damage their health in the future but may be especially hard to resist in the short term (e.g., alcohol, tobacco, and junk food), adolescents are also much more susceptible than adults (Leslie, Levine, Loughlin, & Pechmann, 2009; Pechmann, Levine, Loughlin, & Leslie, 2005). Resisting the appeal of highly desirable foods that should be consumed only in small quantities requires self-regulatory abilities to inhibit impulsive behaviors and resist immediate gratification for long-term benefits. However, these skills do not fully develop until a person is in his or her early 20s. Even many adults are unable to resist the immediate appeal of junk food marketing (Harris, Bargh, & Brownell, 2009).

A market research company advises its clients, "Clearly, the early to mid-teenage years are ones where brands need to be investing in brand building. As consumers enter their 20's, brand preferences are established and they seek more rational support for choices they have already made" (Harris Interactive, 2004, p. 4). If advertisers can reach young people often enough, before their judgment and decision-making skills are fully developed, those young people will become loyal life-long customers.

Content of Food Advertisements

If these advertisements promoted nutritious products and provided positive health messages, food marketing would not be a significant threat to public health. Unfortunately, 97% of television food advertisements viewed by children in the United States and 89% of those viewed by adolescents are for foods high in fat, sugar, and/or sodium (Powell, Szczypka, Chaloupka, & Braunschweig, 2007). Of the foods promoted on Saturday-morning cartoons, 91% were low in nutrients and/or high in fat, sodium, and added sugar (Seitz et al., 2008). Sugared cereal and cereal bars represented the largest food advertisement category with 27% of all food ads, followed by restaurants with a 19% share and snack foods with an 18% share. Outside the United States, Consumers International reviewed advertisements in 23 countries in Europe and Asia and found that the most commonly advertised foods were sweetened cereals, fast foods, confectionary, savory snacks, and soft drinks (Consumers International, 1996, 1999, 2004). Advertising to children in the United States and around the world focuses on unhealthy food and beverages, and the situation has not improved.

As with television advertising, calorie-dense, nutrient-poor foods and beverages predominate in all forms of youth-targeted marketing. Carbonated beverage companies spend almost $500 million targeting children and adolescents (FTC, 2008). Together with restaurants and breakfast cereals, these three categories make up 63% of all food marketing to children and adolescents. Sugar-sweetened beverages and restaurant foods may be among the worst contributors to rising obesity. Consumption of sweetened beverages is positively associated with increased energy intake, BMI, and diet-related health issues in both childhood and adolescence (Fiorito, Marini, Francis, Smiciklas-Wright, & Birch, 2009; Malik, Schulze, & Hu, 2006; Vartanian, Schwartz, & Brownell, 2007). Similarly, fast food consumption is associated with greater caloric intake and poor diet among children and likely contributes to childhood obesity (Bowman, Gortmaker, Ebbeling, Pereira, & Ludwig, 2004). Although consumption of breakfast cereal has positive health outcomes (Albertson et al., 2009; Williams, O'Neil, Keast, Cho, & Nicklas, 2009), the cereals marketed to children contain 2.5 to 3 teaspoons of sugar per 28- to 30-gram serving; 32 to 44% of all calories in these products consist of refined sugar (Harris et al., 2009c).

Child and nutrition advocates also raise concerns that the messages in children's food ads do not promote healthy habits. Gussow (1973) concluded that few advertisements even hint at proper eating but, on the contrary, encourage poor eating habits. Another study found that snacking was shown in commercials more often than breakfast, lunch, and dinner combined (Harrison & Marske, 2005). Even promotional spots during preschool programming on public television predominantly promote fast food and associate it with fun and happiness (Connor, 2006). The way in which an unhealthy diet is advertised is also disturbing. An analysis of stories in 92 television food ads aimed at children found that the ads contained violence (62%), conflict (41%),

achievement (24%), mood alteration (23%), trickery (20%), enablement (18%), and dependence (8%; Rajecki et al., 1994). A cluster analysis found that 64% of the ads were characterized by some combination of violence, conflict, and trickery (Rajecki et al., 1994).

Food advertisers promote their unhealthy products using techniques specifically designed to appeal to young people. For example, advertisements targeting children often utilize licensed characters or easily recognizable animated celebrities to capture children's attention. Licensed characters are often used to market fast food meals specially designed for children, such as McDonald's Happy Meal. In a recent analysis, fast food restaurants spent $360 million on licensed character and other toys distributed with children's meals (FTC, 2008). An examination of the cross-promotions with youth appeal on packaging in the supermarket revealed that 71% included licensed characters and only 18% of the products met accepted nutrition standards for food sold to youth (Harris, Schwartz, & Brownell, 2010).

Some companies have invented their own "spokescharacters" (FTC, 2008), which often appear in ads, on Internet games, on packaging, and even as toys or on branded clothing. These figures take on a disturbing power in the lives of the children. A 1990 study of 8-year-olds found that Ronald McDonald and Tony the Tiger were more popular than the child's father, teacher, or grandparents when asked, "Who would you like to take you out for a treat?" (Dibb, 1994). Seven of the top 10 advertising icons of the 20th century represented the food industry, including Ronald McDonald, the Pillsbury Doughboy, and Tony the Tiger. Ronald McDonald was rated as the #2 ad icon, second only to the Marlboro Man in effectiveness and worldwide impact (Klein & Donaton, 1999b). Even abroad, of 68 Japanese children from the 3rd to 6th grade, all recognized the image of Ronald McDonald. The children claimed "they liked Ronald because he was funny, gentle, kind, and—several added—he understood children's hearts" (Watson, 1997, p. 64).

Leiber (1996) showed that the use of licensed and spokescharacters effectively aids product recall in children. She showed still, color images of characters from TV including the Budweiser frogs, Tony the Tiger, and Bugs Bunny. Two hundred twenty-one children 9 to 11 years of age were asked to recall the slogan associated with the characters and to identify the product the character advertised. Ninety-four percent of the children said "cereal" when asked what product Tony the Tiger sells, and 81% knew that frogs sell beer. Bugs Bunny's "What's up, Doc?" slogan was the most recognized (80%), followed by the "Bud-weis-er" frogs' slogan (73%) and Tony's "They're Grrrreat!" slogan (57%). In an e-poll ranking likability, the M&M's characters were cited as the favorite spokescharacter, with Mrs. Butterworth and Aunt Jemima coming in fourth and fifth (Pomerantz & Rose, 2010).

Impact of Advertisements on Attitudes and Behavior

The impact of this mass marketing on children's attitudes and, more importantly, behavior, is predictable and powerful. The IOM (2006) conducted a comprehensive review of existing research on effects of food marketing and confirmed that "food marketing works." They found strong evidence that exposure to television food advertising increases children's preferences, choices, and requests to parents for advertised brands. Another comprehensive review conducted for the U.K. Food Standards Agency concluded that advertising also affects children's preferences for the unhealthy categories of food most commonly promoted (Hastings et al., 2003). These reviews also noted that relatively few studies had examined the impact of food advertising on broader health-related outcomes, effects of newer forms of marketing, and effects on adolescents and very young children. Within the past 5 years, researchers have made significant progress to address these gaps in the literature; numerous recent studies confirm that food advertising has a profound negative impact on the health of children today from preschool through adolescence.

Research consistently demonstrates that amount of television viewing by children is related to snacking, unhealthy food preferences, and higher BMI (Bolton, 1983; Coon, Goldberg, Rogers, & Tucker, 2001; Crespo et al., 2001; Danner, 2008; Lumeng, Rahnama, Appugliese, Kaciroti, & Bradley, 2006; Signorelli & Staples, 1997; Taras, Sallis, Patterson, Nader, & Nelson, 1989; Wiecha et al., 2006). Recent research highlights the critical causal link between exposure to food advertising and increased caloric consumption, eliminating other potential explanations for this relationship such as sedentary behavior or permissive parenting. For example, a randomized controlled trial to assess the impact of reduced screen time showed that less television viewing immediately resulted in lower caloric intake but not reduced sedentary behavior (Epstein et al., 2008). Similarly, preschoolers who watch more TV are more overweight than those who watch less, but that relationship is not mediated by physical activity (Jackson, Djafarian, Steward, & Speakman, 2009). The researchers attributed the link to television's impact on food intake. Exposure to television food advertising, as opposed to other forms of advertising, increases consumption of any available snack food during and immediately following exposure (Halford et al., 2004, 2007; Harris et al., 2009). Exposure to both regular and diet soft drink advertising increases sugar-sweetened beverage consumption among children (Andreyeva, Kelly, & Harris, 2011).

Research also demonstrates longer-term effects of exposure to food advertising on reduced fruit and vegetable consumption 5 years later (Barr-Anderson, Larson, Nelson, Neumark-Sztainer, & Story, 2009) and on taste preferences for commonly advertised categories of foods (Harris & Bargh, 2009). Furthermore, exposure to fast food advertising specifically increases obesity rates among children (Chou, Rashad, & Grossman, 2008). In addition, the link between obesity and television viewing is found only with commercial television; viewing of public television (without advertising) and videos or DVDs was not related to higher rates of obesity in children (Zimmerman & Bell, 2010).

Although the majority of research on effects of food marketing has focused on television advertising, recent studies also demonstrate similar effects of other forms of marketing. A product placement of a Pepsi bottle in a movie scene led to increased choice of Pepsi over Coke, even when children did not remember they had seen the Pepsi bottle (Auty & Lewis, 2004). Playing a Froot Loops advergame increased children's preference for Froot Loops over another cereal (Mallinckrodt & Mizerski, 2007). Likewise, radio ads for soft drinks increased adolescents' intent to purchase the product and preference for the brand (Bao & Shao, 2002). Although relatively few studies have examined direct effects of food marketing on adolescents, the food industry's $1.1 billion annual investment in marketing targeted to adolescents (FTC, 2008) suggests that it likely has a significant effect.

Marketers' investment in advertising to preschool children is especially troubling. As discussed, advertising to very young children is inherently deceptive. Yet marketers express their intent to create "product identities that penetrate our limbic brains" by targeting children (Urbick, 2008). Their efforts to "imprint" brand meaning in the minds of young children are extremely successful. Even before they can read, 2-year-olds recognize brand logos on product packaging (Valkenburg & Buijzen, 2005); preschoolers can recall brand names seen on television (Macklin, 1996); and as many as 90% of preschoolers recognized child-targeted fast food and snack food brand logos and were able to match the logos with their associated products (McAlister & Cornwell, 2010). Preschoolers exposed to children's cartoons with commercials chose more advertised foods than did their counterparts who did not see the commercials (Borzekowski & Robinson, 2001). Preschool children preferred French fries in a McDonald's package over the same fries in a plain package (Robinson, Borzekowski, Matheson, & Kraemer, 2007). Similarly, the common use of licensed characters on packaging for unhealthy food increases preschoolers' preferences for those foods (Roberto, Baik, Harris, & Brownell, 2010). Children were more likely to choose a snack in a package with Dora the Explorer, SpongeBob, or Shrek on it and liked the taste of the food more than the same food in a plain package. Unfortunately, these effects were stronger for unhealthy foods such as gummy fruit snacks than for carrots.

Food Advertising in Schools and Communities

Children are not protected from food advertising in their schools. Food companies spend nearly 11% of their advertising budget ($186 million) on in-school advertising, and 90% of that spending goes to beverage marketing (FTC, 2008). Richards, Wartella, Morton, and Thompson (1998) reviewed commercial marketing in schools and cited numerous examples of corporate presence including advertisements in gymnasiums, on school buses, in bathroom stalls, and even on sports teams' warm-up suits. Classroom materials sent to teachers promote food products as learning tools, from counting Tootsie Rolls to determining which brand of tomato sauce is thicker. Competitive foods, or foods and beverages sold at school that are not part of the school lunch program, are common at all grade levels (Larson & Story, 2010). These foods are commonly sold to students through school stores or snack bars, vending machines, and a la carte in school cafeterias. Three-quarters of schools also sell competitive foods for fundraising. Nearly all competitive food programs in schools offer low-nutrient, energy-dense foods. Shaul (2000) identified four main avenues of school advertising: product sales, direct advertising, indirect advertising, and market research. Other research has focused on incentive programs, exclusive product sales agreements, appropriation of school space, and fundraising efforts at school (Molnar, Boninger, Wilkinson, & Fogarty, 2009). McDonald's hosts "McTeacher nights, where teachers can serve McDonald's food and children draw pictures of McDonald's characters, all in the name of making money (McTeachers Night, 2002; Memrick, 2010; Molnar et al., 2009). Pizza Hut sponsors the "Book It" program, offering children free pizza as a reward for reading (Center for Science in the Public Interest (CSPI), 2009a). In early 2010, Pizza Hut introduced a program called the RED ZONE, an online interactive program purported to encourage reading in young children. Ironically, the slogan reads, "It's Never Too Early to Start" (Pizza Hut online, 2010). In one Florida public school system, McDonald's coupons were included on the envelope of the report cards for children with good grades, behavior, or attendance, with a note stating "Reward yourself with a Happy Meal" (Deardoff, 2007).

PBS, on the other hand, has designed a classroom program called the "Play with your Produce Classroom Challenge," which encourages kindergarten through sixth-grade classroom teachers to create classroom activities centered on healthy eating. Teachers can win prizes for innovative ways to spur children to eat more fruits and vegetables (ProduceforKids.org, 2010).

Children cannot escape television advertising even within the classroom. Channel One, a 10-minute news program with 2 minutes of commercials, is broadcast daily into the classroom in exchange for TVs, VCRs, and a satellite dish for the school (Consumers Union, 1996). More than 8 million middle and high school children watch the program in 12,000 schools (Mifflin, 1998). Advertisers pay $175,000 for the opportunity to target 40% of American teenagers for 30 seconds on Channel One (Coeyman, 1995). Researchers note that the 12-minute daily broadcast time of Channel One costs the schools nearly $158,000 per year, which is far greater than the value of the video equipment (Sawicky & Molnar, 1998).

Brand and Greenberg (1994) evaluated the effects of advertising on Channel One. In a 4-week period, 31 (69%) of the 45 commercials shown on Channel One were for food products including gum, soft drinks, fast food, candy, and snack chips. The study also showed that advertising on Channel One affects adolescents' cognitions about advertised products, produces positive affect toward products advertised, enhances their consumer orientations, and adds to their intentions to purchase the advertised products compared to adolescents who do not view Channel One. However, the study reported that students at schools with Channel One are no more likely than their nonviewing peers to report actual purchases of those products. After financial struggles, Alloy, Inc.

bought Channel One from Primedia, Inc. in 1997. Alloy continues to promote Channel One as a marketing tool for teachers in the classroom but has pledged it will not show junk food ads (ChannelOne.com, 2010; CommercialAlert. org, 2010b).

BusRadio, a commercial radio station that airs only on school buses, has been billed as a "Channel One for school buses" (Molnar et al., 2009, p. 12). Because BusRadio does not have a broadcasting license, it is not subject to the Federal Communications Commission's (FCC) rules. Nevertheless, the FCC criticized the website in its September 2009 review (Molnar et al., 2009). As of September 28, 2009, BusRadio had ceased its operations on buses. The website remained but was not being updated. This may be an example of a success story by watchdog groups.

Numerous studies show that children in schools that restrict the sale of unhealthy competitive foods have better diets (Larson & Story, 2010); but there has been little published scientific evaluation of the effects of other forms of in-school marketing. A rationale for allowing advertising in the schools is that children will be bombarded with marketing messages anyway, so schools may as well get something in return (money, supplies, equipment). Also, school administrators claim that in choosing to ally themselves with certain marketing programs, they actually have more control over the content and quality of the messages delivered, thereby protecting the children. Some companies deny that the materials they give to schools are advertisements, citing their educational purposes or their need to give back to the community. Others, however, admit that reaching children and adolescents early is a valuable advantage, as children may form brand allegiance that could last a lifetime (Richards et al., 1998).

Marketing to children as a captive audience in schools raises several ethical concerns, among them forced exposure to advertising, lack of parental consent and/or knowledge, and potential confusion with educational content (Shaul, 2000). Critics argue that these advertising programs endanger the quality of education, send mixed messages, and result in the equivalent of school endorsements of unhealthy products. Through Channel One, the schools are also modeling a sedentary behavior—watching television. The practice of selling and promoting unhealthy foods in schools also undermines parents' ability to teach their children healthy eating habits. When a 7-year-old child comes home from school and tells her parent that she had Froot Loops for breakfast today at school and asks for them at home, it takes considerable determination for the parent explain to her that Froot Loops are bad for her, the school is wrong to serve them, and the parent does not want them in the house.

Beyond the media and schools, young people are inundated with commercial messages that promote unhealthy products in their local communities. The food industry spends $195 million on marketing targeted to young people in stores and on product packaging and $99 million on marketing at local events, totaling 18% of their youth marketing budgets (FTC, 2008). KFC has been unusually creative in its community marketing efforts. It paid two communities in Indiana $7,500 to promote its "fiery" wings on fire hydrants (*USA Today*, 2010) and similarly paid to fill potholes in Louisville, Kentucky, in exchange for placing the KFC logo on the covers (York, 2009). An especially intrusive marketing effort to promote the "Got Milk" campaign used chocolate chip cookie-scented advertisements at bus shelters (Cuneo, 2006). The campaign was quickly discontinued by order of the City of San Francisco. Billboards that promote fast food and sugared beverages appear seven to nine times as often in low-income Latino and African-American communities than they do in White and high-income communities (Yancey et al., 2009). Energy-dense snack foods are also widely available in retail stores whose primary business is not food, including pharmacies, gas stations, and general merchandise retailers (Farley, Baker, Futrell, & Rice, 2009). Candy and other sweet and salty snacks are most commonly placed within reach of the cash register line to encourage purchase. Young people cannot escape these highly appealing messages that continually tempt them to consume calorie-dense, nutrient-poor foods.

How to Protect Young People From Unhealthy Food Marketing

In response to growing concerns about this massive level of exposure to unhealthy food marketing, the public health community has proposed many potential solutions to counteract its harmful effects. These solutions fall into two broad categories: individual-focused approaches to teach young people how to resist the influence of exposure to unhealthy food marketing messages and environmental-level approaches to significantly reduce the number of marketing messages to which they are exposed in the first place. Approaches that attempt to educate young people about the biased nature of marketing and the long-term benefits of physical activity and good nutrition are broadly supported (Barry, Brescoll, Brownell, & Schlesinger, 2009; Brescoll, Kersh, & Brownell, 2008). Examples commonly proposed include media literacy programs in schools, public service announcements (PSAs) to promote healthy behaviors, and marketing to promote nutritious foods (Harris & Bargh, 2009). Unfortunately, there is little evidence that understanding marketers' intent or the harmful effects of consuming energy-dense, low-nutrient foods can effectively counteract the unhealthy influence of food marketing.

Media literacy education in schools is commonly proposed to teach children to defend against advertising influence by increasing critical viewing skills and skepticism about media and marketing (AAP, 2006). However, no published studies have systematically evaluated the media literacy curricula used in elementary schools (Brown, 2001; Kunkel et al., 2004), and a few recent studies demonstrate that understanding the intent of food marketing (as taught in media literacy programs) does not reduce its influence (e.g., Chernin, 2007; Livingstone & Helsper, 2006; Mallinckrodt & Mizerski, 2007). Exposure to media literacy curricula regarding food advertising may even *increase* preferences for the advertised foods presented (Chernin, 2007).

Similarly, there is no evidence that unhealthy food consumption is caused by inaccurate beliefs about the nutrition of either healthy or unhealthy foods in children or adults (Glanz, Basil, Maibach, Goldberg, & Snyder,1998; Harris & Bargh, 2009; IOM, 2006; Neumark-Sztainer, Wall, Perry, & Story, 2003). In fact, much of the appeal of consuming junk food for young people may be due to their knowledge that adults would not approve (Schor & Ford, 2007). Therefore, nutrition education and PSAs are unlikely to offset the effects of unhealthy food marketing. Even if they were proven to be effective, PSAs and advertising for nutritious foods cannot begin to offset the $1.6 billion spent to promote primarily unhealthy messages in food advertising (FTC, 2008). Wallack and Dorfman (1992) found that, of 20 hours of randomly selected TV over a 3-week period, none of the PSAs addressed diet, although diet is one of the three leading behavioral risk factors for poor health. In 52.5 hours of Saturday-morning television, there were 10 nutrition-related PSAs compared to 564 advertisements for food (Kotz & Story, 1994).

Due to the increasingly sophisticated psychological techniques employed by food marketers to influence preferences and eating behaviors, effectively resisting their unhealthy influence at all times may be almost impossible at any age (Harris et al., 2009). The food marketing defense model proposes four conditions that are necessary to effectively resist the influence of unhealthy food marketing (see Figure 22.1): (a) *Every time a young person encounters a food marketing message, she or he must consciously notice the message and understand that it is intended to persuade.* As discussed, very young children cannot understand the persuasive intent of advertising, and even older children and adolescents may not fully comprehend the intent of newer, more sophisticated forms of marketing. Additionally, covert forms of marketing are often designed to blend in with the entertainment content of media and thus may be difficult to recognize. Given the immense number of marketing messages encountered daily, it would be virtually impossible to attend to every one. (b) *An individual must know how the marketing message affects him or her and know how to

effectively resist.* Increasingly, companies employ subtle psychological techniques in their marketing to create positive attitudes about their products and prime behaviors outside of individuals' conscious awareness. These types of influence are extremely difficult to counteract, and most adults are not aware of how these techniques influence them. (c) *Young people must have the cognitive maturity to be able to effectively resist, and cognitive resources must also be available at the time the stimulus is encountered.* As discussed, greater self-regulatory abilities are needed to resist the influence of highly tempting but unhealthy products, and these abilities do not fully develop until early adulthood. Additionally, self-regulatory resources can become depleted, for example at the end of a long day or when one is distracted, making it virtually impossible to resist at all times. (d) *An individual must be motivated enough to want to resist.* Food companies have discovered powerful ways to appeal to the unique developmental needs of young people such as having fun, fitting in with peers, and creating their own self-image; these techniques can effectively counteract any motivation to resist. The odds are overwhelmingly stacked against young people and make it virtually impossible for them to resist the powerful influence of marketing for calorie-dense, nutrient-poor, but highly appealing foods and beverages.

The only effective means to protect young people from the unhealthy influence of food marketing, therefore, may be to limit their exposure to these marketing messages. Reducing young people's exposure to commercial television is an important first step. The American Academy of Pediatrics recommends no more than 2 hours of screen time per day for children (Shifrin, 2005). European researchers created a mathematical simulation model to estimate potential effects of reducing television exposure of American 6- to 12-year-olds on obesity and overweight. The investigators estimate that one in three to seven cases of obesity in American children could be prevented in the absence of unhealthy food advertising on television (Veerman, Van Beeck, Barendregt, & Mackenbach, 2009). As cited earlier, Epstein and colleagues (2008) found that reducing children's screen

| Figure 22.1 | The Food Marketing Defense Model (Harris, Brownell & Bargh, 2009) |

Necessary conditions to effectively defend against unhealthy food marketing influence:

Awareness

- Attend to marketing stimuli
- Comprehend persuasive intent

Understanding

- Understand underlying processes and outcomes (i.e., how and what is affected)
- Understand how to effectively resist

Ability

- Cognitive ability to effectively resist
- Available cognitive resources

Motivation

- Interest and desire to resist

their schools and communities. Additionally, few parents are aware of the amount or wide variety of techniques used by food marketers to target children (Speers, Goren, Harris, Schwartz, & Brownell, 2009; Ustjanauskas et al., 2010). As marketers continue to find ways to incorporate their messages into the latest technological advances, it is unlikely that most parents will be able to keep up with the new and creative ways that food marketers find to target their children. As a result, public health advocates in the United States and around the world increasingly call for environmental interventions to reduce young people's exposure to food marketing (IOM, 2006; Swinburn et al., 2008; World Health Assembly, 2007).

Environmental Intervention: The Unrealized Potential of Policy

The public health debate has shifted dramatically from the time we first published this chapter. Ten years ago, researchers were asking, "Does food marketing negatively impact young people's health?" Today, the more common question is, "Will food industry self-regulation effectively reduce young people's exposure to unhealthy food marketing, or is government intervention required?" Although many barriers exist to direct regulation of food marketing to young people, numerous initiatives have begun to increase the advisory role of governments and to implement restrictions at the local level.

Food Industry Self-Regulation

In an effort to demonstrate that it can be part of the solution, the food industry has sponsored 24 different pledges to reduce unhealthy food marketing to children around the world (Hawkes & Harris, in press). The pledges involve 50 different food companies, including 11 who have issued global pledges to reduce child-targeted marketing worldwide.

use resulted in a gradual reduction in BMI for children in the 75th or higher BMI percentile due entirely to reduced calorie consumption; the intervention had no effect on overall sedentary behavior.

As discussed throughout, television advertising is only one form of food marketing that young people encounter every day. Even parents who diligently monitor and control their children's television viewing cannot shield them from the barrage of marketing messages that promote primarily calorie-dense, low-nutrient foods at friends' houses and in

The remaining pledges have been instituted in seven individual countries and one region (the European Union). In the United States, the Council of Better Business Bureaus (CBBB) established The Children's Food and Beverage Advertising Initiative (CFBAI) in 2006 to "shift the mix of advertising messaging directed to children under 12 to encourage healthier dietary choices and healthy lifestyles," (CBBB, 2006). Currently, 16 food companies including Coca-Cola, Kellogg's, General Mills, Post, Nestle USA, and McDonald's have implemented pledges (Peeler, Kolish, & Enright, 2009). Together, these companies account for 80% of food marketing to children on television. Participating companies have agreed to either market only healthier foods in child-targeted advertising (including television, radio, print, or Internet) or to refrain from advertising to children under the age of 12 altogether. The pledges also limit marketing to children in elementary schools and to using licensed characters on television or in product placements (Peeler et al., 2009).

These efforts by the food industry clearly indicate that they recognize public concerns about unhealthy food marketing to children. Many public health advocates argue, however, that food industry self-regulation is intended primarily as a means to generate favorable public relations and deflect potentially stricter government regulations (Harris et al., 2008; Hawkes, 2007; Sharma, Teret, & Brownell, 2009). Two important caveats in the CFBAI pledges, as well as pledges in other countries, limit the likelihood that they will result in meaningful changes to the unhealthy food marketing environment that surrounds young people. First, participating food companies have each developed their own definitions of healthier dietary choices that can be marketed to children, euphemistically referred to as "better-for-you" products. Examination of the list of products defined as "better for you" reveals many foods and beverages whose consumption should, in fact, be severely limited, including fruit snacks and fruit-flavored beverages that consist of almost 100% added sugar, canned pasta and convenience meals with up to 840 mg of sodium per serving size, and some fast food products that contain trans fats and high sodium levels (CBBB, 2011.) Second, companies have agreed only to

limit "advertising primarily directed to children under 12" according to definitions that they, again, created themselves. As a result, most companies continue to advertise extensively on popular television programs that are viewed by a wide audience (e.g., *American Idol* and sports programming), promote licensed characters and toy giveaways on product packaging and kids' meals at fast food outlets, and provide branded materials and sell competitive foods in schools. In addition, food marketers place no limitations on their marketing targeted to youth ages 12 years and older. As a result, the Children's Food and Beverage Advertising Initiative pledges actually apply to less than one third of the $1.6 billion in youth-targeted marketing expenditures that food companies reported to the FTC (2008).

As each company has created its own definition of success, it is not surprising that evaluations of pledge implementation by self-regulatory groups demonstrate close to 100% compliance (Peeler et al., 2009; World Federation of Advertisers, 2009). Yet independent evaluations of food marketing to children following implementation of the CFBAI pledges in the United States demonstrate that food companies continue to aggressively target children with marketing for calorie-dense, nutrient-poor foods. For example, nearly three fourths of all foods advertised on children's television in 2008 were for products in the poorest nutrition category (Kunkel, McKinley, & Wright, 2009). Similarly, cereals advertised directly to children in 2008 on television, on the Internet, and in the supermarket contained 85% more sugar, 65% less fiber, and 60% more sodium than those marketed to adults (Harris et al., 2009c). The use of licensed characters and other cross-promotions on packaging in the supermarket that appeal to young people increased by 78% from 2006 through 2008 (Harris et al., 2010).

Increasing Calls for Government Intervention

Given the evidence that current food industry self-regulatory efforts are not likely to significantly improve the unhealthy marketing environment surrounding young people, there are signs of increased support worldwide for government intervention of various forms. Proposed policy interventions include establishment of government-sponsored guidelines (to replace industry self-defined guidelines), statutory regulations and restrictions on specific forms of marketing at the national level, restrictions in school settings and other community venues, and litigation against individual companies (see Harris et al., 2008).

Government bodies have begun to develop their own guidelines for food marketing to young people to replace food industry self-defined marketing and nutrition guidelines. In 2007, the World Health Assembly (2007) of the United Nations declared that the World Health Organization (WHO) should develop "recommendations on marketing of foods and nonalcoholic beverages to children." To lay the groundwork for these recommendations, an international working group of obesity experts developed the Sydney Principles to define responsible food and beverage marketing practices targeted to children (Swinburn et al., 2008). More than 200 public health and marketing experts, including food industry representatives, reviewed and supported these recommendations. The WHO has released its recommendations, which were presented and voted upon at the World Health Assembly in May 2010 (WHO, 2009). In the United States, an Interagency Working Group comprised of representatives from the FTC, Food and Drug Administration (FDA), CDC, and U.S. Department of Agriculture (DOA) has requested public comments on preliminary "standards for the marketing of food when such marketing targets children who are 17 years or younger" and definitions of "the scope of the media to which such standards should apply" (Interagency Working Group on Food Marketed to Children, 2011). They were directed to report their recommendation to Congress by July 15, 2010 (HR 1105). Although compliance with these standards will be voluntary, the establishment of independent standards set by government bodies with the primary goal of improving young people's health and well-being represents an important first step to implementing more responsible food company marketing practices.

Most countries continue to rely on industry self-regulation to reduce unhealthy food marketing; however, a few have implemented regulatory bans on some forms of marketing to young people. Both Quebec and Sweden ban all forms of advertising targeted to children under 12 or 13 years old; bans such as these are driven primarily by ethical considerations due to young children's greater vulnerability to marketing influence (Hawkes, 2007). In 2008, the United Kingdom banned marketing on children's television stations and programming targeted to children under 16 years old for foods that do not meet government-defined nutrition standards (Ofcom, 2006). In the United States, enactment of government regulations to limit marketing faces additional barriers due to commercial speech protections afforded by the First Amendment (Pomeranz, 2010). The FTC does have the power to ban advertising that is considered to be misleading and deceptive; however, it may be reluctant to do so due to its experience with KidVid in the 1970s. At that time, the FTC ruled that advertising to children is unfair, but Congress intervened and terminated the FTC's authority to regulate advertising to children as unfair. Additional government initiatives suggest potential for increased regulation of other forms of marketing. For example, the FCC commissioner has called for a ban on interactive advertising targeted to children (Eggerton, 2008) and the FCC is considering rules to require disclosure of sponsorships and product placements on children's television (FCC, 2008).

In the United States, there are more options for regulations that can be enacted at the state and local level. Many school districts have implemented nutrition standards for competitive foods sold in elementary schools and increasingly in middle and high schools (Larson & Story, 2010). Maine is the first to enact a ban on food marketing in schools at the state level (State of Maine, 2009); however, many school districts have implemented such bans as part of their school wellness policies and public advocacy groups have developed "toolkits" to advise other districts who wish to take similar measures (California Project LEAN, 2007; NPLAN, 2009a). One municipality in California is testing a local statute to require nutrition standards for children's meals in fast food restaurants that include a giveaway

(NPLAN, 2009b). Other local initiatives that are likely to withstand First Amendment tests include limitations on the placement of unhealthy foods in prime locations in retail establishments and other restrictions on marketing to children near schools, in restaurants, and in other community facilities (see CSPI, 2009b).

The fight for regulation of food advertising has been compared to campaigns against the marketing of cigarettes to youth (Brownell & Warner, 2009; Williams et al., 1993). Ultimately, the ban on tobacco advertising to children required multiple lawsuits against the tobacco industry. In 1998, as part of the $206 billion tobacco industry Master Settlement Agreement, cigarette makers agreed to: (a) make marketing changes including a cessation of billboard advertising; (b) finance educational campaigns intended to stop young people from starting to smoke; (c) stop sponsorship of sports teams, stadiums, or events where participants are underage; and (d) pay for research intended to help smokers quit (Meier, 1999). Similar actions have begun to appear in the food marketing arena. In 2006, the Center for Science in the Public Interest (CSPI) filed a lawsuit against the Kellogg Company that resulted in its adoption of nutrition standards for foods marketed to children (CSPI, 2007). More recently, the mere threat of a lawsuit by the Connecticut Attorney General's office resulted in the discontinuation of the industry-wide Smart Choices front-of-pack labeling program (State of Connecticut Office of the Attorney General, 2009). The program had been widely criticized for allowing nutritionally questionable products such as Froot Loops cereal and mayonnaise to boast the Smart Choices label (Neuman, 2009).

Public Pressure

As is true of all publicly held companies, the food industry is primarily responsible to its customers and stockholders. Regardless of whether government regulation to limit food marketing to children is enacted or lawsuits take a significant financial toll, food marketers will change their practices if they feel enough

pressure from the public to do so. Parents have the most incentive (and the purchasing power) to force food companies to change. However, as discussed, parents greatly underestimate the amount and scope of food marketing their children encounter every day and express more concern about other media issues (e.g., tobacco and alcohol advertising and sexual images and thin ideals in the media; Speers et al., 2009). Recent research suggests a significant opportunity to educate parents about the scope of food marketing targeted to their children, as well as its negative impact, to increase public pressure on the food industry to change (Goren, Harris, Schwartz, & Brownell, 2010). During focus groups, many parents became outraged enough to demand food industry change after being shown only a few examples of child-targeted marketing practices that they were not aware of including advergaming websites, mobile phone marketing, and examples of "better-for-you" foods that food companies claim to be nutritious options that should be marketed to children (Ustjanauskas et al., 2010).

Framing the issue becomes critical to effectively increase parental support for reducing food marketing. For example, conservatives were equally supportive of food marketing regulation as liberals when positioned as an issue of undermining parents' authority to decide what to feed their children (Goren et al., 2010). Similarly, parents expressed greater support for regulations when they understood that they would not restrict the foods they could buy but only the foods that could be promoted directly to children on television and other forms of marketing (Ustjanauskas et al., 2010). The recent publication of the Cereal FACTS report provides a case study in the power of public opinion to change food industry marketing practices (Harris et al., 2009c). The report documented the full scope of cereal company marketing practices and the high sugar content of all cereals marketed directly to children. Shortly after the report was published and received considerable media attention (Rochman, 2009), General Mills announced that it would reduce the sugar content of its cereals marketed to children by as much as 25% (General Mills, 2009).

Avenues for Future Intervention

As reviewed earlier in the chapter, studies have indicated that pronutritional messages can counter the impact of advertisements for unhealthy foods. Perhaps sanctions similar to those passed to address tobacco advertisement could be imposed. The Fairness Doctrine Act, effective from 1968 through 1970, required that one antismoking advertisement be aired for every four prosmoking advertisements on television and radio. In 1971, the U.S. Broadcast Advertising Ban was imposed, eliminating all cigarette advertising from television and radio (Tremblay & Tremblay, 1999).

The government could require food companies to provide money for equal air time for healthy choices to balance the messages aimed at children. It would be difficult to completely ban advertising to children. Industries as well as individuals have free speech guarantees under the First Amendment, and an advertising ban could represent an infringement upon that right. Scheraga and Calfee (1996) suggest that the 1971 advertising ban, which also ended free antismoking messages, was counterproductive because its net effect was to reduce competition in the marketplace but not to reduce smoking. Similarly, it is possible that a ban on advertising unhealthy foods to children would decrease competition while consumption patterns remain constant. Finally, it is possible that food companies, in the absence of TV advertising, might find more cost-effective means of marketing.

Joe Camel, the cartoon mascot advertising smoking to children, was retired along with apparel with tobacco logos (Golway, 1998). It is reasonable to ask whether it would be beneficial to public health if similar action were taken against icons such as Ronald McDonald, Tony the Tiger, and products like Coke apparel.

The political machinery that drives the food industry is incredibly complex, and much larger than the tobacco industry (Rocawich, 1994). As of 2010, there were more than 200 lobbying groups and trade associations organized to protect the varied interests within the food industry (Opensecrets.org, 2010). If the food industry is not included as a full partner in any policy efforts, any endeavors at systemic change are likely to be unsuccessful (Sims, 1998). When the economic advantage of the industry coincides with public health benefits, changes that are mutually beneficial can be achieved. For example, Ippolito and Mathios (1991) indicate how policy affects how consumers process new information into altered behavior. Although the health effects of fiber were known from the 1970s, health advertising regulations did not allow health claims to be included in advertising messages. The advertising ban prevented widespread awareness of fiber's health benefits. In 1984, however, the FDA suspended the ban on health claims while new regulations were being determined.

Fiber cereal consumption increased significantly after the ban was lifted and producers were able to advertise the health features of the products. Adult cereals introduced after health advertising began contained significantly more fiber than cereals introduced before health advertising. Producers also decreased the sodium and fat content of the high-fiber cereals. Interestingly, the healthfulness of child cereals did not improve with the new advertising campaigns (Ippolito & Mathios, 1991). This example demonstrates the economic and public health ramifications of advertising policies. When provided with sufficient economic incentive, the food industry can market healthier foods.

The tobacco and alcohol industries provide other possible examples for interventions. One target area could be the tax deductions that businesses receive for advertising expenses. The tax code allows "reasonable advertising expenses" to be deductible business expenses (Publication 535, 1998, p. 66). The 1998 Proposed Tobacco Bill contained an amendment to prohibit tax deductions for tobacco advertising that violated FDA regulations (Senate Records, 1998). While the 1998 Tobacco Bill did not ultimately become law, such deductions could be a target for policy change (Torry, 1998). Tax deductions for advertising of unhealthy foods could be eliminated, or tax deductions might be increased for healthy foods advertised. Modifying tax deductions would give the food industry economic incentive to advertise more healthy products and possibly provide revenue for other public health initiatives.

Less restrictive interventions targeting tax deductions or equal time advertising are more likely to be favored by the public. A questionnaire completed by mothers of schoolchildren in first through sixth grade indicated that parents wished that there were more direct appeals to children to be nutrition conscious (Grossbart & Crosby, 1984). In a survey of community attitudes toward public policies to control alcohol, tobacco, and high-fat food, interventions designed to protect children and youths were most strongly endorsed, followed by restrictions on advertising. However, support for regulatory controls on high-fat food was given less often than that for alcohol and tobacco, with those reporting the least personal use of high-fat foods most in favor of control policies (Jeffery et al., 1990). This may be due in part to the general perception that obesity is not a serious public health issue. However, recent estimates that nearly 68% of adults in America are overweight or obese (Flegal, Carroll, Ogden, & Curtin, 2010; Mendes, 2010) and that annual obesity-related health care costs total well over $100 billion (CDC, 2009; Wolf & Colditz, 1998) indicate otherwise.

In addition to government regulation, it may also prove worthwhile to harness the interest shown by parents in counteracting promotion of unhealthy foods. Ward (1971) suggests that the family mediates the influence of television and advertising on buying behavior. In fact, a promising corollary to the Bolton (1983) study was that parental influence could have a stronger long-term effect than food advertising, suggesting a potential pathway for combating the toxic environment.

Conclusions

Food advertising is a highly profitable segment of the marketing world, and children are easy targets. Research reveals the power of the media and other forms of marketing to influence attitudes and increase desire for advertised products. Increasingly, research also demonstrates the unhealthy impact of marketing for calorie-dense, low-nutrient foods on broader health-related beliefs and behaviors, as well as the difficulty for young people to effectively resist influence or for parents to shield their children.

Although the food industry has pledged to reduce unhealthy marketing directed at children, these efforts appear unlikely to significantly reduce young people's exposure. As marketers continue to find even more creative and effective ways to reach young people, the need for regulation and other forms of government intervention grows. One can only assume that expansion of covert forms of marketing and attempts to integrate marketing into every aspect of young people's lives will worsen the situation.

With the rate of obesity continuing to spiral upward, exposing the population to earlier onset of obesity-related diseases and public health costs, action is critical. Intervention at the environmental level, where children are often unwitting targets of heavily financed persuasion, is imperative. If the environment remains unchanged, we cannot expect the outcome to differ.

References

Albertson, A. M., Affenito, S. G., Bauserman, R., Holschuh, N. M., Eldridge, A. L., & Barton, B. A. (2009). The relationship of ready-to-eat cereal consumption to nutrient intake, blood lipids, and body mass index of children as they age through adolescence. *Journal of the American Dietetic Association, 109*(9), 1557–1565.

American Academy of Pediatrics, C. o. C. (2006). Children, adolescents, and advertising. *Pediatrics, 118*(6), 2563–2569.

Andreyeva, T; Kelly, I. R.; Harris, J. L. *Exposure to food advertising on television: Associations with children's fast food and soft drink consumption and obesity,* Economics and Human Biology *9*(3): 221–233, July 2011.

Auty, S., & Lewis, C. (2004). Exploring children's choice: The reminder effect of product placement. *Psychology and Marketing, 21,* 697–713.

Avery, R., Mathios, A., Shanahan, J., & Bisogni, C. (1997). Food and nutrition messages communicated through prime-time television. *Journal of Public Policy & Marketing, 16,* 217–233.

Bao, Y., & Shao, A. T. (2002). Nonconformity advertising to teens. *Journal of Advertising Research, 42*(3), 56–65.

Barr-Anderson, D. J., Larson, N. I., Nelson, M. C., Neumark-Sztainer, D., & Story, M. (2009). Does television viewing predict dietary intake five years later in high school students and young adults? *International Journal of Behavioral Nutrition and Physical Activity, 6,* 7.

Barry, C. L., Brescoll, V. L., Brownell, K. D., & Schlesinger, M. (2009). Obesity metaphors: How beliefs about the causes of obesity affect support for public policy. *Milbank Quarterly, 87*(1), 7–47.

Bell, R. A., Cassady, D., Culp, J., & Alcalay, R. (2009). Frequency and types of foods advertised on Saturday morning and weekday afternoon English- and Spanish-language American television programs. *Journal of Nutrition Education and Behavior, 41*(6), 406–413.

Bolton, R. N. (1983). Modeling the impact of television food advertising on children's diets. *Current Issues and Research in Advertising, 6*(1), 173–199.

Borzekowski, D. L, & Robinson, T. N. (2001). The 30-second effect: An experiment revealing the impact of television commercials on food preferences of preschoolers. *Journal of the American Dietetic Association, 101*(1), 42–46.

Boush, D. M., Friestad, M., & Rose, G. M. (1994). Adolescent skepticism toward TV advertising and knowledge of advertising tactics. *Journal of Consumer Research, 21,* 165–175.

Bowman, S. A., Gortmaker, S. L., Ebbeling, C. B., Pereira, M. A., & Ludwig, D. S. (2004). Effects of fast-food consumption on energy intake and diet quality among children in a national household survey. *Pediatrics, 113*(1), 112–118.

Brand, J., & Greenberg, B. (1994, Jan.). Commercials in the classroom: The impact of Channel One advertising. *Journal of Advertising Research, 34,* 18–23.

Brandweek. (2009, December 11). *7-Eleven launches mobile marketing test.* Retrieved March 19, 2010, from www.brandweek.com/fdcp?12691 07330463.

Brescoll, V. L., Kersh, R., & Brownell, K. D. (2008). Assessing the feasibility and impact of federal childhood obesity policies. *The Annals of the American Academy of Political and Social Science, 615*(January), 178–194.

Brown, J. A. (2001). Media literacy and critical television viewing in education. In D. G. Singer & J. L. Singer (Eds.), *Handbook of children and the media* (pp. 681–697). Thousand Oaks, CA: Sage.

Brownell, K. D., & Warner, K. E. (2009). The perils of ignoring history: Big Tobacco played direct and millions died. How similar is Big Food? *Millbank Quarterly, 87*(1), 259–294.

California Project LEAN. (2007). *Marketing in schools.* Retrieved March 19, 2010, from http://www.californiaprojectlean.org/doc.asp?id=178.

Center for Science in the Public Interest. (2007). *Kellogg makes historic settlement agreement, adopting nutrition standards for marketing foods to children.* Press release June 14, 2007. Retrieved March 19, 2010, from http://www.cspinet.org/new/200706141.html.

Center for Science in the Public Interest. (2009a). *Food industry seeks to maintain junk-food marketing in schools.* Retrieved January 3, 2010, from http://www.cspinet.org/new/20090 9221.html.

Center for Science in the Public Interest. (2009b). *Food marketing to children: State and local options.* Retrieved March 19, 2010, from http://cspinet.org/new/pdf/state_and_local_policy_options_09.pdf.

Centers for Disease Control and Prevention. (2009). *Childhood overweight and obesity.* Retrieved November 18, 2009, from http://www.cdc.gov/obesity/childhood/prevalence.html.

ChannelOne.com. (2010). *About Channel One News: Who are we?* Retrieved January 22, 2010, from channelone.com.

Chaplin, L. N., & John, D. R. (2005). The development of self-brand connections in children and adolescents. *Journal of Consumer Research, 31,* 119–129.

Chernin, A. (2007). *The relationship between children's knowledge of persuasive intent and persuasion: The case of televised food marketing.* Dissertation, University of Pennsylvania, Philadelphia.

Chester, J., & Montgomery, K. (2008). *Interactive food & beverage marketing: Targeting children and youth in the digital age.* An update. Retrieved January 22, 2010, from www.digital ads.org.

Chou, S.-Y., Rashad, I., & Grossman, M. (2008). Fast-food restaurant advertising on television and its influence on childhood obesity. *Journal of Law and Economics, 51,* 599–618.

Coeyman, M. (1995, July 20). Follow the customer: New media ventures may help marketers target a market. *Restaurant Business, 94*, 36.

CommercialAlert.org. (2010a). *Channel One stumbles due to financial woes, old tv's and opposition.* Retrieved January 22, 2010, from http://www.commercialalert.org/issues/education/channel-one.

CommercialAlert.org. (2010b). *Commercial Alert comment on Alloy Inc's acquisition of Channel One.* Retrieved January 22, 2010, from http://www.commercialalert.org/issues/education/channel-one.

Connor, S. M. (2006). Food-related advertising on preschool television: Building brand recognition in young viewers. *Pediatrics, 118*, 1478–1485.

Consumers International. (1996). *A spoonful of sugar—television food advertising aimed at children: An international comparative survey.* London: Author. Retrieved May 3, 2011, from http://www.consumersinternational.org.

Consumers International. (1999). *Easy targets—a survey of food and toy advertising to children in four Central European countries.* London: Author. Retrieved May 3, 2011, from http://www.consumersinternational.org/news-and-media/publications/easy-targets-survey-of-television-and-toy-advertising-to-children-in-four-central-european-countries.

Consumers International. (2004). *The junk food generation—a multi-country survey of the influence of television advertisements on children.* Retrieved May 3, 2011, from http://www.consumersinternational.org/news-and-media/publications/the-junk-food-generation-a-multi-country-survey-of-the-influence-of-television-advertisements-on-children.

Consumers Union. (1996). *Selling America's kids: Commercial pressures on kids of the >90s.* Yonkers, NY: Consumers Union Educational Services Department. Retrieved May 3, 2011, from http://www.consumersunion.org/other/sellingkids/index.htm..

Coon, K. A., Goldberg, J., Rogers, L., & Tucker, K. L. (2001). Relationships between use of television during meals and children's food consumption patterns. *Pediatrics, 107*(1), e7. Retrieved January 13, 2010, from http://pediatrics.aappublications.org/cgi/content/abstract/107/1/e7.

Council of Better Business Bureaus. (2006). *New food, beverage initiative to focus kids' ads on healthy choices; Revised guidelines strengthen CARU's guidance to food advertisers.* Retrieved August 16, 2007, from http://www.bbb.org/alerts/article.asp?ID=728.

Council of Better Business Bureaus. (2011, April). BBB children's food and beverage advertising initiative: Food and beverage products that meet participants' approved nutrition standards. Retrieved May 3, 2011, from http://www.bbb.org/us/storage/0/Shared20%Documents/April%202011.pdf.

Crespo, C. J., Smit, E., Troiano, R. P., Bartlett, S. J., Macera, C. A., & Andersen, R. E. (2001). Television watching, energy intake, and obesity in U.S. children. *Archives of Pediatric and Adolescent Medicine, 155*(3), 360–365.

Cuneo, A. Z. (2006, December 6). Milk Board forced to remove outdoor scent strip ads. *Advertising Age.* Retrieved March 22, 2009, from http://adage.com/article?article_id=113643.

Danner, F. W. (2008). A national longitudinal study of the association between hours of TV viewing and the trajectory of BMI growth among U.S. children. *Journal of Pediatric Psychology, 33*(10), 1100–1107.

Deardoff, J. (2007, Dec. 16). *Fast food gets greasy hands on report cards.* Chicago Tribune, Retrieved January 22, 2010, from http://archives.chicagotribune.com/2007/dec/16/health/chi-1216dcardorffdec16.

Dibb, S. (1994, November). *Advertising. Witnesses. Statement of advertising researcher, witness for defence.* Retrieved May 3, 2011, from http://www.mcspotlight.org/people/witnesses/advertising/dibb_sue.html.

Eggerton, J. (2008, June 11). Adelstein: FCC must give parents more content control. *Broadcasting & Cable.* Retrieved May 3, 2011, from http://www.broadcastingcable.com/article/print/114119-Adelstein_FCC_Must_Give_Parents_More_Content_Control.php.

Epstein, L. H., Roemmich, J. N., Robinson, J. L., Paluch, R. A., Winiewicz, D. D., Fuerch, J. H., et al. (2008). A randomized trial of the effects of reducing television viewing and computer use on body mass index in young children. *Archives of Pediatric and Adolescent Medicine, 162*, 239–245.

Farley, T. A., Baker, E. T., Futrell, L., & Rice, J. C. (2009). The ubiquity of energy-dense snack foods: A national multicity study. *American Journal of Public Health, 100*(2), 306–311.

Federal Communications Commission. (2008, June 13). *Sponsorship identification rules and embedded advertising.* MB Docket No. 08-90.

Federal Trade Commission. (2007). *Bureau of Economics staff report: Children's exposure to TV advertising in 1977 and 2004.* Retrieved October 22, 2007, from http://www.ftc.gov.

Federal Trade Commission. (2008). *Marketing food to children and adolescents. A review of industry expenditures, activities, and self-regulation. A report to Congress.* Retrieved September 20, 2008, from www.ftc.gov.

Fiorito, L. M., Marini, M., Francis, L. A. Smiciklas-Wright, H., & Birch, L. (2009). Beverage intake of girls at age 5 y predicts adiposity and weight status in childhood and adolescence. *American Journal of Clinical Nutrition, 9,* 935–942.

Flegal, K., Carroll, M., Ogden, C., & Curtin, L. (2010). Prevalence and trends in obesity among US adults, 1999–2008. *Journal of the American Medical Association, 303*(3), 235–241.

Flegal, K. M., Graubard, B. I., Williamson, D. F., & Gail, M. H. (2005). Excess deaths associated with underweight, overweight, and obesity. *Journal of the American Medical Association, 293*(15), 1861–1867.

Food Commission. (1997, Jan./Mar.). Advertising to children: UK the worst in Europe. *Food Magazine.*

Frieden, T. R., Dietz, W., & Collins, J. (2010). Reducing childhood obesity through policy change: Acting now to prevent obesity. *Health Affairs, 29*(3), 357–363.

Gantz, W., Schwartz, N., Angelini, J., & Rideout, V. (2007). Food for thought: Television food advertising to children in the United States. Menlo Park, CA: The Henry J. Kaiser Family Foundation. Retrieved November 28, 2009, from http://www.kff.org/entmedia/upload.7618.pdf.

Garretson, J. A. & Burton, S. (2005). The role of spokescharacters as advertisement and package cues in integrated marketing communications. *Journal of Marketing, 69,* 118–132.

General Mills. (2009). *General Mills to reduce sugar in cereals.* Press release, December 9, 2009. Retrieved March 19, 2010, from http://www.generalmills.com/en/Media/NewsReleases/Library/2009/December/sugar_reduced_in_cereals.aspx.

Geraci, J. C. (2004). What do youth marketers think about selling to kids? *Advertising & Marketing to Children,* (April–June), 11–17.

Glanz, K., Basil, M., Maibach, E., Goldberg, J., & Snyder, D. (1998). Why Americans eat what they do: Taste, nutrition, cost, convenience and weight control concerns as influences on food consumption. *Journal of American Dietetic Association, 98,* 1118–1126.

Goldberg, M. E., & Gunasti, K. (2007). Creating an environment in which youth are encouraged to eat a healthier diet. *Journal of Public Policy & Marketing, 26*(2), 162–181.

Golway, T. (1998, Dec. 12). Life in the 90s: Youth, smoking and the tobacco settlement. *America,* 6.

Goren, A., Harris, J. L., Schwartz, M. B., & Brownell, K. D. (2010). Predicting support for restricting food marketing to youth. *Health Affairs, 29*(3), 419–424.

Grossbart, S. L., & Crosby, L. A. (1984). Understanding the bases of parental concern and reaction to children's food advertising. *Journal of Marketing, 48*(3), 79–92.

Gussow, J. (1973). It even makes milk a dessert: A report on the counternutritional messages of children's television advertising. *Clinical Pediatrics, 12*(2), 68–71.

Halford, J. C. G., Gillespie, J., Brown, V., Pontin, E. E., & Dovey, T. M. (2004). Effect of television advertisements for foods on food consumption in children. *Appetite, 42,* 221–225.

Halford, J. C. G., Boyland, M. J., Hughes, G., Oliveira, L. P., & Dovey, T. M. (2007). Beyond-brand effect of television (TV) food advertisement/commercials on caloric intake and food choice of 5- to 7-year-old children. *Appetite, 49,* 263–267.

Harris Interactive. (2004). *Trends & tudes, 3*(11). Retrieved November 5, 2005, from http://www.harrisinteractive.com/newsroom/Newsletters/TrendsTudes/aspx.

Harris, J. L., & Bargh, J. A. (2009). Television viewing and unhealthy diet: Implications for children and media interventions. *Health Communication, 24*(7), 660–673.

Harris, J. L., Bargh, J. A., & Brownell, K. D. (2009). Priming effects of television food advertising on eating behavior. *Health Psychology, 28*(4), 404–413.

Harris, J. L., Brownell, K. D., & Bargh, J. A. (2009). The food marketing defense model: Integrating psychological research to protect youth and inform public policy. *Social Issues and Policy Review, 3,* 211–271.

Harris, J. L., Pomeranz, J. L., Lobstein, T., & Brownell, K. D. (2008). A crisis in the marketplace: How food marketing contributes to obesity and what can be done. *Annual Review of Public Health, 30,* 5.1–5.15.

Harris, J. L., Schwartz, M. B., & Brownell, K. D. (2010). Marketing foods to children and youth: Licensed characters and other promotions on packaged foods in the supermarket. *Public Health Nutrition, 13*(3), 409–417.

Harris, J. L., Schwartz, M. B., Brownell, K. D., Sarda, V., Weinberg, M. E., Speers, S., et al. (2009c). *Cereal FACTS: Evaluating the nutrition quality and marketing of children's cereals.* Retrieved May 3, 2011, from www.cerealfacts.org.

Harrison, K., & Marske, A. (2005). Nutritional content of foods advertised during the television programs children watch most. *American Journal of Public Health, 2005, 95*(9), 1568–1574.

Hastings, G., Stead, M., McDermott, L., Forsyth, A., MacKintosh, A., Rayner, M., et al. (2003). *Review of research on the effects of food promotion to children.* Retrieved February 20, 2006, from http://www.food.gov.uk/multimedia/pdfs/promofoodchildren.exec.pdf.

Hawkes, C. (2007). Regulating food marketing to young people worldwide: Trends and policy drivers. *American Journal of Public Health, 97,* 1962–1973.

Hawkes, C., & Harris, J. L. (in press). An analysis of the content of food industry pledges on marketing to children. *Public Health Nutrition.*

Hein, K. (2009, Aug. 5). Mountain Dew goes ultraviolet. *AdWeek.* Retrieved March 19, 2009, from http://www.adweek.com/aw/content_display/news/client/e3i9a9104a5cd264656974ebcb535970dd2.

Institute of Medicine. (2006). *Food marketing to children and youth: Threat or opportunity?* Washington, DC: National Academies Press.

Interagency Working Group on Food Marketed to Children (2011). Preliminary proposed nutrition principles to guide industry self-regulatory efforts. Retrieved June 6, 2011, from www.ftc.gov/os/2011/04/110428foodmarketproposedguide.pdf.

Ippolito, P., & Mathios, A. (1991). Information, advertising, and health choices: A study of the cereal market. *Economics of Food Safety.* New York: Elsevier Science Publishing, 211–246.

Jackson, D. M., Djafarian, K., Stewart, J., & Speakman, J. R. (2009). Increased television viewing is associated with elevated body fatness but not with lower total energy expenditure in children. *American Journal of Clinical Nutrition, 89,* 1031–1036.

Jeffrey, R. W., Forster, J. L., Schmid, T. L., McBride, C. M., Rooney, B. L., & Pirie, P. L. (1990). Community attitudes toward public policies to control alcohol, tobacco, and high-fat food consumption. *American Journal of Preventive Medicine, 6*(1), 12–19.

John, D. R. (1999). Consumer socialization of children: A retrospective look at twenty-five years of research. *Journal of Consumer Research, 26,* 183–213.

Klein, D., & Donaton, S. (Eds.). (1999a) The advertising century: Top 100 advertising cmpaigns. *Advertising Age.* Retrieved May 3, 2011, from http://adage.com/century/campaigns.html.

Klein, D., & Donaton, S., (Eds.). (1999b) The advertising century: Top 10 advertising icons. *Advertising Age.* Retrieved May 3, 2011, http://adage.com/article/news/top-10-advertising-icons/62929/

Klein, N (1999). *No logo: Taking aim at the brand bullies.* New York: Picador.

Kotz, K., & Story, M. (1994, November) Food advertisements during children's Saturday morning television programming: Are they consistent with dietary recommendations? *Journal of the American Dietetic Association, 94,* 1296–1300.

Kunkel, D., & Roberts D. (1991). Young minds and marketplace values: Issues in children's advertising. *Journal of Social Issues, 47*(1), 57–72.

Kunkel, D., McKinley, C., & Wright, P. (2009). *The impact of industry self-regulation on the nutritional quality of foods advertised on television to children.* Retrieved January 10, 2010, from www.childrennow.org/uploads/documents/adstudy_2009.pdf.

Kunkel, D., Wilcox, B. L., Cantor, J., Dowrick, P., Linn, S., & Palmer, E. (2004). Report of the APA task force on advertising and children. Retrieved November 22, 2004, from http://www.apa.org/pi/families/resources/advertising-children.pdf.

Larson, N., & Story, M. (2010). Are "competitive foods" sold at schools making our children fat? *Health Affairs, 29*(3), 430–435.

Leiber, L. (1996). *Commercial and character slogan recall by children aged 9 to 11 years.* Berkeley, CA: Center on Alcohol Advertising.

Lenhart, A., Purcell, K., Smith, A., & Zickuhr, K. (2010). *Social media and mobile Internet use among teens and young adults*: Pew Research Center. Retrieved April 22, 2010, from www.pewinternet.org/Reports/2010/social-media-and-young-adults.

Leslie, F. M., Levine, L. J., Loughlin, S. E., & Pechmann, C. (2009). *Adolescents' psychological and neurobiological development: Implications for digital marketing.* Paper presented at the Second NPLAN/BMSG Meeting on Digital Media and Marketing to Children. Retrieved May 3, 2011, from www.digitalads.org/documents/Leslie_et_al_NPLAN_BMSB_memo.pdf.

Livingstone, S., & Helsper, E. J. (2006). Does advertising literacy mediate the effects of advertising on children? A critical examination of two linked research literatures in relation to obesity and food choice. *Journal of Communication, 56,* 560–584.

Lumeng, J. C., Rahnama, S., Appugliese, D., Kaciroti, N., & Bradley, R. H. (2006). Television exposure and overweight risk in preschoolers. *Archives of Pediatrics & Adolescent Medicine, 160*(4), 417–422.

Macklin, M. C. (1996). Preschoolers' learning of brand names from visual cues. *Journal of Consumer Research 2*(4), 304–319.

Malik, V. S., Schulze, M. B., & Hu, F. B. (2006). Intake of sugar-sweetened beverages and weight gain: A systematic review. *American Journal of Clinical Nutrition, 84*(2), 274–288.

Mallinckrodt, V., & Mizerski, D. (2007). The effects of playing an advergame on young children's perceptions, preferences, and request. *Journal of Advertising, 36*, 87–100.

McAlister, A. R., & Cornwell, T. B. (2010). Children's brand symbolism understanding: Links to theory of mind and executive functioning. *Psychology & Marketing, 27*(3), 203–228.

McGinnis, J. M., Gootman, J., & Kraak, V. I. (Eds.). (2006). *Food marketing to children and youth: Threat or opportunity?* Washington, DC: National Academies Press.

McNeal, J. (1992) *Kids as customers: A handbook of marketing to children.* Lexington, MA: Lexington Books.

McTeachersNight. (2002). Retrieved November 18, 2009, from http://mcteachersnight.com.

Meier, E. (1999, Jan.). The tobacco settlement and 1999 forecasts. *Nursing Economics, 17,* 53.

Memrick, A. (2010, October 5). McTeacher's Night serves up dollars for local schools. *Gaston Gazette.*

Mendes, E. (2010, Feb. 9). *Six in 10 overweight or obese in U.S., more in '09 than in '08.* Retrieved May 26, 2010, from http://www.gallup.com/poll/125741/six-overweight-obese.aspx.

Mifflin, L. (1998, Dec. 28). Nielsen to research Channel One's audience. *New York Times,* C6.

Molnar, A., Boninger, F., Wilkinson, G., & Fogarty, J. (2009). *Click: The twelfth annual report on schoolhouse commercialism trends: 2008–2009.* Boulder and Tempe: Education and the Public Interest Center & Commercialism in Education Research Unit. Retrieved November 18, 2009, from http://epicpolicy.org/publication/School house-commercialism-2009.

Moore, E. S., & Rideout, V. J. (2007). The online marketing of food to children: Is it just fun and games? *Journal of Public Policy and Marketing, 26*(2), 202–220.

Naik, P. A., & Raman, K. (2003). Understanding the impact of synergy in multimedia communications. *Journal of Marketing Research, XL,* 375–388.

Neuman, W. (2009, September 4). For your health, Froot Loops. *New York Times.* Retrieved March 19, 2010, from http://www.nytimes.com/2009/09/05/business/05smart.html.

Neumark-Sztainer, D., Wall, M., Perry, C., & Story, M. (2003). Correlates of fruit and vegetable intake among adolescents: Findings from Project EAT. *Preventive Medicine, 37,* 198–208.

The Nielsen Company. (2010). *Advertising spending by major product category.* Unpublished data.

NPLAN. (2009a). *District policy restricting food and beverage advertising on school grounds.* Retrieved March 19, 2010, from http://www.nplanonline.org/nplan/products/district-policy-restricting-food-and-beverage-adver tising-school-grounds.

NPLAN. (2009b). *Model California ordinance regulating chain restaurant giveaways with children's meals.* Retrieved May 3, 2011, from http://www.nplanonline.org/sites/phlpnet.org/files/ToyGiveawayOrd_FINAL_20100817 .pdf.

Ofcom. (2006, November 17). *New restrictions on the television advertising of food and drink products to children.* Retrieved April 26, 2010, from http://www.ofcom.org.uk/media/news/2006/11/nr_20061117.

Ogden, C. L., Carroll, M. D., Curtin, L. R., Lamb, M. M., & Flegal, K. M. (2010). Prevalence of high body mass index in U.S. children and adolescents. *JAMA, 303*(3), 242–249.

Ogden, C. L., Carroll, M. D., Curtin, L. R., McDowell, M. A., Tabak, C. J., & Flegal, K. M. (2006). Prevalence of overweight and obesity in the U.S., 1999–2004. *JAMA, 295*(13), 1549–1555.

Olshansky, S. J., Passaro, D. J., Hershow, R. C., Layden, J., Carnes, B. A., Brody, J., et al. (2005). A potential decline in the life expectancy in the United States in the 21st century. *New England Journal of Medicine, 352,* 1138–1145.

Opensecrets.org. (2010). *Lobbying: Food industry. Annual number of clients lobbying on food industry.* Retrieved May 25, 2010, from http://www.opensecrets.org/lobby/issuesum .php?lname=Food+Industry&year=.

Pechmann, C., Levine, L., Loughlin, S., & Leslie, F. (2005). Impulsive and self-conscious: Adolescents' vulnerability to advertising and promotion. *Journal of Public Policy and Marketing, 24*(2), 202–221.

Peeler, C. L., Kolish, E. D., & Enright, M. (2009). *The children's food and beverage advertising initiative: A report on compliance and implementation during 2008.* Retrieved from http://www.bbb.org/us/Storage/0/shared%20Documents/finalbbs1.pdf.

Petty, R. D., & Andrews, J. C. (2008). Covert marketing unmasked: A legal and regulatory guide for practices that mask marketing messages. *Journal of Public Policy & Marketing, 27*(1), 7–18.

Pizza Hut online. (2010). Retrieved January 13, 2010, from http://www.bookitprogram.com.

Pomerantz, D., & Rose, L (2010). *America's most loved spokescreatures*. Retrieved April 1, 2010, from www.forbes.com/2010/03/18/tony-tiger-woods-doughboy-cmo-network-spokescreatures.html.

Pomeranz, J. L. (2010). Television food marketing to children revisited: The Federal Trade Commission has the constitutional and statutory authority to regulate. *Journal of Law, Medicine and Ethics* (Spring), 98–116.

Powell, L. M., Szczypka, G., Chaloupka, F. J., & Braunschweig, C. L. (2007). Nutritional content of television food advertisements seen by children and adolescents in the United States. *Pediatrics, 120*(3), 576–583.

ProduceForKids.org. (2010). Retrieved January 13, 2010, from http://www.produceforkids.org/teachers/play_with_your_produce_winners

Publication 535. (1998) *Business expenses*. Internal Revenue Service, catalogue no. 15065Z, Department of the Treasury.

Puhl, R. M., & Heuer, C. A. (2009). The stigma of obesity: A review and update. *Obesity, 17*, 941–964.

Rajecki, D. W., McTavish, D. G., Rasmussen, J. L., Schrueders, M., Byers, D. C., & Jessup, K. S. (1994). Violence, conflict, trickery, and other story themes in TV ads for food for children. *Journal of Applied Social Psychology, 24*(19), 1685–1700.

Richards, J. I., Wartella, E. A., Morton, C., & Thompson, L. (1998). The growing commercialization of schools: Issues and practices. *Annals of the American Academy of Political and Social Science, 557*, 148–163.

Rideout, V. J., Foehr, U. G., & Roberts, D. F. (2010, January). *Generation M²: Media in the lives of 8- to 18-year-olds*. A Kaiser Family Foundation Study. Retrieved May 3, 2011, from http://www.kff.org/entmedia/upload/8010.pdf.

Roberto, C., Baik, J. J., Harris, J. L., & Brownell, K. D. (2010). The influence of licensed characters on children's taste and snack preferences. *Pediatrics, 126*(1), 88–93.

Robinson, T. N., Borzekowski, D. L., Matheson, D. M., & Kraemer, H. C. (2007). Effects of fast food branding on young children's taste preferences. *Archives of Pediatric & Adolescent Medicine, 161*, 792–797.

Rocawich, L. (1994, Sept.) Michael Jacobson; director of the Center for Science in the Public Interest; Interview. *The Progressive, 58*, 30.

Rochman, B. (2009). Sweet spot: How sugary-cereal makers target kids. *Time Magazine*, November 2, 2009. Retrieved March 19, 2010, from http://www.time.com/time/magazine/article/0,9171,1931730,00.html.

Russell, C. A., Norman, A. T., & Heckler, S. E. (2004). The consumption of television programming: Development and validation of the connectedness scale. *Journal of Consumer Research, 31*, 150–161.

Sawicky, M. B. & Molnar, A. (1998, April). *The hidden costs of Channel One: Estimates for the fifty states*. Milwaukee, WI: Center for the Analysis of Commercialism in Education. University of Wisconsin–Milwaukee.

Scheraga, C., & Calfee, J. (1996). The industry effects of information and regulation in the cigarette market: 1950–1965. *Journal of Public Policy & Marketing, 15*, 216–220.

Schor, J. B., & Ford, M. (2007). From tastes great to cool: Children's food marketing and the rise of the symbolic. *Journal of Law and Medical Ethics*, 10–21.

Seitz, B. A., Wootan, M. G., & Story, M. (2008). Nine out of 10 food advertisements shown during Saturday morning children's television programming are for foods high in fat, sodium, or added sugars, or low in nutrients. *Journal of the American Dietetic Association, 108*(4), 673–678.

Senate Records. (1998, June 15). Tobacco Bill/FDA Regulations and Advertising Tax Deduction. 105th Congress, 2nd Session, Vote No. 159. Retrieved June 5, 2000, from http://www.senate.gov/~rpc/rva/1052/1052159.htm.

Sharma, L. L., Teret, S. P., & Brownell, K. D. (2009). The food industry and self-regulation: Standards to promote success and to avoid public health failures. *American Journal of Public Health, 100*, 240–246.

Shaul, M. S. (2000). *Public education: Commercial activities in schools*. Report to Congressional Requesters. Washington, DC. United States General Accounting Office. ED 444 752. Retrieved May 3, 2011, from http://www.education.com/print/Ref_Commercialism.

Shifrin, D. (2005, July 14–15). Remarks at Federal Trade Commission Workshop. *Perspectives on Marketing, Self-Regulation and Childhood Obesity*. Washington, DC. Retrieved November 14, 2005, from http://www.aap.org/advocacy/Washing/Testimonies-Statements-Petitions/dr_%20Shifrin_remarks.htm.

Signorelli, N., & Staples, J. (1997). Television and children's conception of nutrition. *Health Communication, 9*(4), 289–301.

Sims, L. (1998). *The politics of fat: Food and nutrition policy in America*. Armonk, NY: ME Sharpe.

Snyder, M., & DeBono, K. G. (1985). Appeals to image and claims about quality: Understanding the psychology of advertising. *Journal of Personality and Social Psychology, 49,* 586–587.

Speers, S., Goren, A., Harris, J. L., Schwartz, M., & Brownell, K. D. (2009). Public opinions about food marketing to youth. *Rudd Report.* Retrieved April 22, 2010, from www.yaleruddcenter.org.

Sprott, D. E. (2008). The policy, consumer, and ethical dimensions of covert marketing: An introduction to the special section. *Journal of Public Policy and Marketing, 27*(1), 4–6.

State of Connecticut Office of the Attorney General (2009). *Attorney General announces all food manufacturers agree to drop Smart Choices logo.* Press release on October 29, 2009. Retrieved March 19, 2010, from http://www.ct.gov/AG/cwp/view.asp?A=3673&Q=449880.

State of Maine. (2009). Public Law, Chapter 230 LD 1183, item 1, 124th Maine State Legislature. An act to prevent predatory marketing practices against minors.

Sutherland, L. A., MacKenzie, T., Purvis, L. A., & Dalton, M. (2010). Prevalence of food and beverage brands in movies: 1996–2005. *Pediatrics, 125*(3), 468–474.

Swinburn, B. S., G., Lobstein, T., Rigby, N., Baur, L. A., Brownell, K. D., Gill, T., et al. (2008). The "Sydney Principles" for reducing the commercial promotion of foods and beverages to children. *Public Health Nutrition, 11,* 881–886.

Taras, H. L., Sallis, J. F., Patterson, T. L., Nader, P. R., & Nelson, J. A. (1989). Television's influence on children's diet and physical activity. *Journal of Developmental & Behavioral Pediatrics, 10*(4), 176–180.

Torry, S. (1998, Oct. 30). Tobacco's lobbying outlays soared in '98. *Washington Post,* A10.

Trasande, L., Liu, Y., Fryer, G., & Weitzman, M. (2009). Effects of childhood obesity on hospital care and costs, 1999–2005. *Health Affairs, 28*(4). w751–w760.

Tremblay, C., & Tremblay, V. (1999, Feb. 1) Reinterpreting the effect of an advertising ban on cigarette smoking. *International Journal of Advertising, 18,* 41.

USA Today. (2010, January 6). *KFC markets "fiery" wings on fire hydrants.* Retrieved April 26, 2010, from http://www.usatoday.com/money/advertising/2010-01-06-kfc-ads-on-hydrants_N.htm.

Urbick, B. (2008). Make a big impression on kids. *Brand Strategy, 224,* 46–47.

Ustjanauskas, A., Eckman, B., Harris, J. L., Goren, A., Schwartz, M. B., & Brownell, K. D. (2010). *Focus groups with parents: What do they think about food marketing to their kids?* Rudd Report. Retrieved April 22, 2010, from www.yaleruddcenter.org.

Valkenburg, P. M., & Buijzen, M. (2005). Identifying determinants of young children's brand awareness: Television, parents, and peers. *Journal of Applied Developmental Psychology, 26*(4), 456–468.

Valkenburg, P. M., & Cantor, J. (2001). The development of a child into a consumer. *Applied Developmental Psychology, 22,* 61–72.

Vartanian, L., Schwartz, M. B., & Brownell, K. D. (2007). Effects of soft drink consumption on nutrition and health: A systematic review and meta-analysis. *American Journal of Public Health, 97*(4), 667–675.

Veerman, J. L., Van Beeck, E. F., Barendregt, J. J., & Mackenbach, J. P. (2009). By how much would limiting TV food advertising reduce childhood obesity? *European Journal of Public Health, 19*(4), 365–369.

Wallack, L., & Dorfman, L. (1992). Health messages on television commercials. *American Journal of Health Promotion, 6*(3), 190–196.

Ward, S. (1971). Television advertising and the adolescent. *Clinical Pediatrics, 10*(8), 462–464.

Watson, J. (Ed.) (1997) *Golden Arches East: McDonald's in East Asia.* Stanford University Press: Stanford, CA.

Wiecha, J. L., Peterson, K. E., Ludwig, D. S., Kim, J., Sobol, A., & Gortmaker, S. L. (2006). When children eat what they watch. *Archives of Pediatrics and Adolescent Medicine, 160*(4), 436–442.

Williams, B. M., O'Neil, C. E., Keast, D. R., Cho, S. & Nicklas, T. A. (2009). Ready-to-eat breakfasts are associated with improved nutrient intake and dietary adequacy but not body mass index in Black adolescents. *American Journal of Lifestyle Medicine, 3*(6), 500–508.

Williams, J. O., Achterberg, C., & Sylvester, G. P. (1993). Targeting marketing of food products to ethnic minority youths. In C. L. Williams and S. Y. S. Kimms (Eds.), Prevention and treatment of childhood obesity. *Annals of the New York Academy of Sciences. Vol. 699,* pp. 107–114. New York: New York Academy of Sciences.

Wolf, A. M., & Colditz, G. A. (1998). Current estimates of the economic cost of obesity in the United States. *Obesity Research, 6,* 97–106.

World Federation of Advertisers. (2009). *EU pledge 2009 monitoring report. September 09.* Retrieved June 28, 2010, from http://markenverband.de/kompetenzen.

World Health Assembly. (2007). *Resolution WHA60.23 Prevention and control of non-communicable diseases: Implementation of the global strategy, item 2 (6).* 60th World Health Assembly. Geneva, Switzerland. Retrieved May 2007 from http://www.who.int.

World Health Organization (2009, November 26). *Prevention and control of noncommunicable diseases: implementation of the global strategy.* Report by the Secretariat. Retrieved March 22, 2010, from apps.who.int/gb/ebwha/pdf_files/EB126/B126_12-en.pdf.

World Health Organization Consultation on Obesity (1997, June 3–5). *Obesity: Preventing and managing the global Epidemic* (Report, p. 17). Geneva, Switzerland: Author.

Yancey, A. K., Cole, B. L., Brown, R., Williams, J. D., Hillier, A., Kline, R. S. et al. (2009). A cross-sectional prevalence study of ethnically targeted and general audience outdoor obesity-related advertising. *Milbank Quarterly, 87*, 155–184.

York, E. B. (2009, March 25). Need a pothole filled in your city? Call KFC. *Advertising Age.* Retrieved March 22, 2010, from http://adage.com/article?article_id=135534.

Zimmerman, F. J., & Bell, J. F. (2010). Associations of television content type and obesity in children. *American Journal of Public Health, 100*(2), 334–340.

CHAPTER 23

Popular Music

The Soundtrack of Adolescence

DONALD F. ROBERTS
Stanford University

PETER G. CHRISTENSON
Lewis and Clark College

lmost a quarter century ago, Keith Roe wrote: "in terms of both sheer amount of time devoted to it and the meanings it assumes, it is music, not television, that is the most important medium for adolescents" (Roe, 1987, pp. 215–216). Research continues to support this contention. Music listening time reaches parity with television viewing by mid-adolescence (Nippold, Duthie, & Larsen, 2005; Rideout, Foehr, & Roberts, 2010; Roberts & Foehr, 2004; Roberts, Foehr, & Rideout, 2005; Roberts & Henriksen, 1990) and possibly as early as fifth or sixth grade (Christenson, 1994). In terms of its *importance* to adolescents, music undoubtedly surpasses other media content. Roberts and Henriksen (1990) found that when asked which single medium they would take with them to a desert island, more than

80% of a sample of 7th to 11th graders placed music in the top three. Music, moreover, was the *first* choice of nearly half—indeed, by the 11th grade, music was selected first over television by a margin of two to one. Although the picture has become somewhat more complicated with the emergence of digital media, nothing about new technology threatens popular music's central place in adolescent life: Indeed, recent work confirms its preeminence (Rentfrow & Gosling, 2003; Rideout, et al., 2010; Roberts, Foehr, Rideout, & Brodie, 1999).

Given such empirical data, it is perplexing that critics, parents, and media researchers concerned with the role of popular culture in young people's lives generally view television as the center-stage medium. The imbalance, perhaps, is due to the fact that television has pictures and popular music (aside from music videos) does not—that is, as Tennyson put it, "things seen are mightier than things heard." One could argue that it was popular music's "visibility" in the form of music videos that stimulated both general concern (often to the point of outrage) and research attention to the role popular music plays in the lives of today's youth. Whether it is the pictures, the words, or, for that matter, the on- and off-stage behavior of the musicians themselves, there is plenty in the messages and images of today's popular music to direct attention to the potential impact of music exposure on adolescents.

Most readers will be aware of the many recent condemnations of pop music, especially heavy metal and rap/hip-hop, for their reputed misogyny, sexual explicitness, violence, racism, and glorification of drugs and alcohol, to name but a few of the complaints. Such condemnations have a long history, of course, but the current strain can be traced back to the anti-"porn rock" crusade spearheaded by Tipper Gore, a movement that in 1985 culminated in hearings before the Senate Commerce Committee and ultimately pressured the industry to adopt a system of "parental advisories" on albums with potentially offensive lyrics. A decade later, the Senate Juvenile Justice Committee aired a similar set of concerns from a contingent of citizens outraged by "gangsta rap," and in 1998 the Senate Commerce Committee revisited the arena to examine the efficacy of "parental advisory" labels on music lyrics. Popular music has even been accused of instigating school shootings (it appears that several of the shooters have shared a taste for "death metal" music.)

Many of the concerns and accusations surrounding popular music's most raunchy, outrageous side are oversimplified and needlessly alarmist. In fact, as we will describe below, for the vast majority of today's young people, popular music is not a problem but a pleasure. They are engaged with music, but they are not controlled by it. Rather, adolescents *actively use* popular music to orchestrate their lives; music is, as suggested by the title of this piece, the very "soundtrack of adolescence." Whether the focus is on the negative or the positive, however, there is a growing

awareness of popular music's important role in the process of adolescent development and a growing body of empirical work describing that role.

Amount of Music Exposure

It is a complicated task to measure listening time, and we suspect most studies tend to underestimate music exposure. Music listening is often a secondary or background activity. A teenager may be driving to school while chatting with a friend, all the while "listening" to music on a car stereo. Or a teen may be simultaneously writing a paper on a computer, instant messaging with a friend, and listening to background music from an iPod. Music's tendency to slip between foreground and background and the common practice of media multitasking (Foehr, 2006) raise questions about what kind of "listening" should be counted as true *exposure*. We believe background listening matters, and for those who might disagree, we offer this challenge: Turn off the "background" music when adolescents are studying, chatting, or partying and observe their responses.

Assessments of music listening based only on one or two dominant platforms also consistently underestimate exposure. For example, several earlier studies focusing only on radio listening (e.g., Brown, 1976; Greenberg, Ku, & Li, 1989; Lyle & Hoffman, 1972) produced lower figures than surveys with additional questions about records, tapes, or CD playback. And the problem persists. Although items concerning music exposure via MP3 players have begun to appear in surveys of young people's media use, we have located only a few studies that specifically ask about streaming music via computers and only two that include questions about music exposure via smart phones (Nielsen, 2007; Rideout et al., 2010). In short, research covering all platforms and including background as well as foreground listening reveals levels of music exposure equal to TV time by the late middle school years and considerably higher in late adolescence (see, for example, Rideout et al., 2010; Roberts et al., 2005; Roberts & Henriksen, 1990; Wartella, Heintz, Aidman, & Mazzarella, 1990).

Some of the most informative current data regarding young people's music exposure comes from a series of three national sample surveys of 8- to 18-year-olds spanning the period from 1999 to 2009, a decade that has produced dramatic technology-assisted changes in how young people access and consume music, especially through the conjunction of Internet connectivity and MP3 music listening platforms such as the iPod (Rideout et al., 2010; Roberts & Foehr, 2004; Roberts et al., 2005: Roberts et al., 1999). The 1999 study measured music listening with questions on the dominant platforms of that time—radio, CDs, and tapes. In 2004, MP3 players were added to the list, and by 2009, music listening via computers and cell phones had joined the mix. That same period saw young people's personal ownership of iPods and other MP3 players climb from essentially zero in 1999 to 18% in 2004 and 76% by 2009, and of cell phones from 39% to 66%. So-called "Smart phones" such as the Blackberry and the iPhone entered the mix largely post–2005.

The same period saw youth ownership of radios decline from 86% in 1999 to 75% in 2009 and CD players from 88% to 66% (Rideout et al., 2010). These statistics are accompanied by industrywide declines in album sales and increases in the use of Napster-style file-sharing applications, the frequency of downloading "free" music (Jones & Lenhart, 2004; Madden, 2009), and the use of commercial Internet music sources such as iTunes. In short, the music-listening environment is changing dramatically and rapidly, with implications not only for the sheer amount of time young people's ears are exposed to music but also for the types of music listened to and how music is used in adolescent lifestyles.

It seems quite clear that the new technologies have increased music exposure. In 1999 and 2004, 8- to 18-year-olds reported about 1.75 hours of daily music listening. In 2009, listening had jumped to 2.5 hours, an increase of three-quarters of an hour and 43% above the earlier level. Among older adolescents (15–18 years), music listening increased from roughly 2.5 hours daily (2:34 in 1999 versus 2:24 in 2004) to 3:33 in 2009—up a remarkable full hour or 66%. The latest report (Rideout et al., 2010) concludes that the

increase is due to the emergence of the new music platforms—computers, MP3 players, Smart phones—that either did not exist or were just emerging 10 years earlier. Indeed, between 2004 and 2009, both radio and CD listening went down. Clearly, then, time spent with the new platforms more than offset the decreases in time spent with the old. The 2010 report does not hedge in its conclusion: "Changes in media technology—the development of the iPod and other MP3 players, and being able to listen on a cell phone or a laptop—have enabled young people to spend more time with music than ever" (Rideout et al. 2010, p. 28).

Not all adolescents pay equal attention to popular music. Although popular music listening often begins in early grade school (Christenson, DeBenedittis, & Lindlof, 1985; Nippold et al., 2005), music exposure increases through the middle school years and is substantially higher among older adolescents (Greenberg et al., 1989; Rideout et al., 2010; Roberts et al., 1999, 2005; Roberts & Henriksen, 1990). Race also predicts amount of music listening. African-American youths listen the most, followed by Hispanic youths, then by Whites (Brown, Childers, Bauman, & Koch, 1990; Rideout et al., 2010; Roberts et al., 1999, 2005). Most studies have found higher levels of listening among girls than boys (cf. Christenson & Roberts, 1998; Greenberg et al., 1989; Roberts et al., 1999, 2004; Roberts & Henriksen, 1990). Rideout and her colleagues (2010) note, however, that this gender gap is on the wane and may well disappear, given the absence of gender differences in the use of new digital music listening platforms.

Finally, despite the considerable attention given to music videos by critics and researchers, music video viewing occupies relatively little time compared with music listening. Most published reports set average daily viewing at between 15 and 30 minutes (Christenson, 1992; Kubey & Larson, 1989; Leming, 1987; Wartella et al., 1990). The Kaiser studies found that fewer than 10% of 8- to 18-year-olds watch music videos on any given day (Rideout et al., 2010; Roberts et al., 1999, 2005). Interestingly, youths' interest in music videos seems to peak early in adolescence, dropping off slightly into the high school years (Roberts & Henriksen, 1990), even as overall involvement in music continues to rise. This decrease in attention to music videos, of course, parallels a similar decrease in attention to television in general. We have found no data that speaks to whether the easy access to videos on the Internet (e.g., YouTube) may be stimulating increased levels of exposure, though that outcome seems likely.

Popular Music Uses and Gratifications

In his 1962 essay "Popular Songs and the Facts of Life," S. I. Hayakawa wrote about the role of blues music in the African-American community of the time:

> I am often reminded by the words of blues songs of Kenneth Burke's famous description of poetry as "equipment for living." In the form in which they developed in Negro communities, the blues are equipment for living humble, laborious, and precarious lives of low social status or no social status at all—nevertheless, they are valid equipment . . . (Hayakawa, 1962, p. 161).

Contemporary popular music is an equally valid piece of equipment for living the life of an American adolescent. In fact, one could argue that of all media content, music meshes best with the needs and desires of youth. Its dominant themes—love, sex, partying, individual and social identity, relationships with peers and parents—fit squarely with the adolescent agenda, and its ability to slip between foreground and background as needed allows it to be incorporated into a myriad of settings and situations, both solitary and social. Music can relieve tension, provide escape or distraction from problems, relieve loneliness, fill the time when there is nothing much to do, ease the drudgery of repetitive, menial tasks and chores, fill uncomfortable silence, provide topics of conversation, make parties livelier, impart new vocabulary, articulate political attitudes, and even act as a sleep aid (Eggermont & Van den Bulck, 2006). Music listening is, in other words, an extremely versatile tool.

Affective Uses

It is important to keep in mind that, despite the concentration in the research on deviant adolescents and music styles, listening to popular music is most properly seen as a natural and largely benign part of growing up in contemporary Western society. At the simplest, most global level, children, adolescents, and young adults listen to music because, above all, it gives them pleasure. For adolescents, especially, the pleasure of music can be powerful and is often associated with the most intense, "peak" experiences of life. As Lull (1992) put it: "Music promotes experiences of the extreme for its makers and listeners, turning the perilous emotional edges, vulnerabilities, triumphs, celebrations, and antagonisms of life into hypnotic, reflective tempos that can be experienced privately or shared with others" (Lull, 1992, p. 1).

Overall, research on popular music uses and gratifications points to a principle we call "the primacy of affect" (Christenson & Roberts, 1998). That is, for most young people, music use is driven primarily by the motivation to control mood and enhance emotional states. When young people want to be in a certain mood, when they feel lonely, when they seek to work through or divert attention from troubles, music tends to be the medium they choose (Brown, 1976; Christenson & Roberts, 1998; Larson, Kubey, & Colletti, 1989; Lyle & Hoffman, 1972, Miranda & Claes, 2009; Roe, 1985). The emotional work of music can be performed in private or in the company of others, but it is worth noting that a good deal (by some accounts, most) of the use of music for mood management takes place in solitude. By late grade school, listening typically occurs alone in the bedroom. Christenson (1994) found that about 40% of third and fourth graders and 70% of fifth and sixth graders said they were usually alone when they listened to music, compared to 10% who said they were usually with friends. The importance of solitary listening strengthens into middle and late adolescence (Larson & Kubey, 1983). Because new technologies are altering some of these patterns by making it possible to listen to music anytime and anywhere, it has been suggested that the effect may be to increase the overall proportion of "alone" listening (North, Hargreaves, & Hargreaves, 2004). Moreover, we would suggest that miniaturization and portability of the iPod and its ilk, along with the increasingly unobtrusive "earbuds" through which they are listened, make it more possible than ever to listen *privately* even when in the company of others. If anything, such listening constitutes an attempt to create a personal "bubble" in otherwise social contexts.

Most listening, whether in the background or the foreground, functions in a simple (though important) way to enhance the moment. One's favorite music sounds good, and it is a rewarding presence. But music is also used in more direct, instrumental ways to address or deal with the problems and stressors confronted by listeners. Miranda and Claes (2009) examined the relationship between adolescents' depression levels and their use of music for coping. They distinguished three processes of music use. In one process, problem-focused coping, music and its embedded social messages may be used deliberately to work through (understand) current problems—for example, to reflect on what one's favorite songs might have to say about the breakup of a romantic relationship. The second process is emotion-focused coping: Here, for example, an adolescent might listen to happy, upbeat music to counter a somber mood state. A third process consists of avoidance/disengagement, in which music consumption serves to help one avoid problems—for example, to divert attention from conflicts with parents or the pressure of an impending exam.

Miranda and Claes (2009) found that adolescents use all three mechanisms, but the results vary by gender. Problem-oriented coping is associated with lower depression levels among females but not among males, suggesting that females may be more effective at using music adaptively in dealing with negative emotions. Emotion-oriented coping, on the other hand, is associated with higher levels of depression among males but not girls, suggesting that boys may be more prone than girls to maladaptive emotional-oriented coping. That is, boys may be more likely to engage in "emotional venting"—such as listening to

angry music when one is angry, the result being to make them even angrier (Miranda & Claes, 2009). Other studies have found males more likely than females to use music as a tool to increase their energy level and seek stimulation—to get "pumped up" or "psyched up;" females are more likely to use music to lift their spirits when they're down or lonely, or even to dwell on a somber mood (Arnett, 1991a; Larson et al., 1989; Roe, 1985; Wells, 1990). Larson and his colleagues wrote:

> For girls, whose listening tastes are more often directed toward ballads and love songs, music is not elevating, but rather is associated with sadness, depression and sometimes anger. While boys appear to use music to pump themselves up, young adolescent girls' use of music may be driven more by a need to both explore and cope with new concerns and worries that accompany this age period, perhaps especially those surrounding intimate relations that are so often the themes of these songs. (Larson et al., 1989: p. 596)

Social Uses

Some scholars contend that, important though certain affective gratifications may be, the social uses and meanings of popular music provide the real key to understanding its niche in the lives of young people (Frith, 1981; Lull, 1987; Roe, 1984, 1985). We propose three divisions within the broad category of social uses: quasisocial, socializing, and cultural. *Quasisocial* refers to listening that occurs alone but still serves goals and needs related to social relationships. A good example of quasisocial use is when music replaces or invokes the presence of absent peers, thus relieving feelings of loneliness. Gantz and his colleagues reported that two-thirds of a sample of college respondents listened either "somewhat" or "very frequently" to "make me feel less alone when I'm by myself" (Gantz, Gartenburg, Pearson, & Schiller, 1978). This and other studies also suggest that the use of music to relieve loneliness—that is, to provide the sense of company when one is alone—is significantly more common for girls than for boys (Larson et al., 1989; Roe, 1984). Solitary music listening may also prepare adolescents for *future* peer interactions and relationships. To a large extent, adolescents who know nothing about pop culture or current music trends are relegated to the periphery of teen culture. Conversely, pop music "experts" tend to have more friends and enjoy enhanced status in the adolescent social structure (Adoni, 1978; Brown & O'Leary, 1971; Dominick, 1974).

Popular music almost always functions as a crucial element of the milieu when adolescents get together to *socialize*. In romantic dyads, music accompanies courtship and sexual behavior. In larger gatherings, such as parties, dances, or clubs, music reduces inhibitions, attracts attention and approval, provides topics for conversation, and encourages dancing. Perhaps the best evidence of the importance of the socializing uses of music is the virtual impossibility of envisioning a teen party without it. In general, though, music's socializing uses derive from its ability to create atmosphere—in a sense, this could be called "collective mood management."

Adolescents differ in the extent to which they incorporate popular music into social interactions. Females are somewhat more likely than males to use music in social settings (Carroll et al., 1993; Gantz et al., 1978), and on average, females report more interest in dancing (Roe, 1985; Wells, 1990). African-American youths are not only more involved with music generally than Whites but are also more involved in dancing and more likely to view the ability to dance skillfully as an important personal attribute (Kuwahara, 1992; Lull, 1992). The use of music in social contexts also varies according to music taste and subcultural membership. An ethnographic study on social behavior in music clubs revealed quite different patterns of interaction between "metalheads," who engaged in relatively little cross-sex communication of any kind, and a crowd referred to as "yuppies" or "preppies," who were much more likely to engage in boy–girl chatting and dancing (Kotarba & Wells, 1987).

The third type of social use—cultural—concerns the role of music taste in the organization of adolescent culture. Music often provides a basis for initiating friendships, and agreement on music is an important predictor of friendship success and longevity

(Christenson & Roberts, 1998; Lull, 1987). The prominence of information about favorite bands, songs, and genres in social networking profiles indicates that this applies in the online world of social networking as well as the "real world." At a different level, music functions to define and publicize various "us–them" distinctions that differentiate the adolescent social world. Music taste says much about one's patterns of affiliation, whether clique, crowd, or subculture. For many groups and subcultures, music allegiance is the *central pillar* of group identity, and the members often use music quite consciously to express group pride and solidarity. For example, Kuwahara (1992) found that rap music provided Black students in a predominantly White university an important focus of resistance against the dominant culture.

The Uses of Lyrics

Although children and adolescents usually say it is the "sound" that attracts them to their favorite music, significant numbers mention lyrics as a primary gratification, and most identify lyrics as a secondary gratification (Gantz et al., 1978; Roe, 1985). Rosenbaum and Prinsky (1987) reported that 17% of young males (12–18 years) and nearly 25% of females said they liked their favorite song " . . . because the words express how I feel." When Cleveland-area high school students ranked music against several other possible sources of moral and social guidance (e.g., parents, teachers, friends, church leaders, coworkers), 16% placed music in the top three sources of moral direction, and 24% placed music in the top three for information on social interaction (Rouner, 1990). For better or worse, then, lyrics are often attended to, processed, discussed, memorized, even taken to heart.

Two general patterns seem to emerge from the research on attention to lyrics. First, the more *important* music is to an adolescent, the more importance he or she places on lyrics relative to other elements of music gratification. Second, attention to lyrics is highest among fans of *oppositional* or controversial music, whether it be 1960s protest rock or the heavy metal and rap of today. In other words, the more defiant, alienated, and threatening to the mainstream a music type is, the more closely fans follow the words (Christenson & Roberts, 1998). Given the long-standing controversies surrounding heavy metal and hip-hop lyrics, it is interesting to note that heavy metal and hip-hop fans report considerably higher levels of interest and attention to lyrics than other adolescents (Arnett, 1991a; Kuwahara, 1992).

Music Preferences and Taste

To most adults, contemporary popular music all sounds pretty much the same: If distinctions are made at all, they are typically between "rock" and the two most visible and controversial current pop music genres, heavy metal and rap. A close look at youth culture, however, reveals a boggling variety of popular music genres. *Billboard* magazine currently reports listening data for well over 20 different music genres, including pop, adult contemporary, hip-hop, rap, rock, alternative, independent, Latin, regional Mexican, tropical, Christian, gospel, world, and new age. These distinctions, however, do not begin to scratch the surface of the many genres and subgenres recognized by contemporary youth culture. A current inventory of popular music types might include, in addition to the above, soft rock, folk, indie rock, classic rock, grunge, progressive rock, swamp rock, reggae, industrial rock, college rock, funk, soul, alternative country, salsa, house, ska, Afropop, high life, rave, techno, folk, synthpop, death metal, trash metal, and thrash punk. Such a list could go on at length, and indeed many of the genres listed above are broken down into several more or less distinct subgenres, most of which would be quite recognizable to the majority of adolescents and college students.

To be sure, not all of these genres matter equally. Some types are really the same thing by a different name, others are very closely related musically and culturally, and still others (e.g., bluegrass or new age) don't really figure very much into adolescent culture. Factor analytic research, moreover, indicates

that a deeper structure of taste underlies the apparent profusion; when the relationships and similarities among all the genres and subgenres are taken into account, much of the variation in music taste can be reduced to a handful of "metagenres" clustered around: pop music, hard rock/heavy metal, "high brow" (classical and jazz), and Afro-American forms (hip-hop, R&B, soul) (Christenson & Roberts, 1998; Rentfrow & Gosling, 2003; Ter Bogt, Raaijmakers, Vollebergh, Van Vel, & Sikkema, 2003). The key point is that young people do not simply listen to "rock" or "popular" music but gravitate toward certain *types* of music. The diversity of music and the selectivity of audience taste matter for two reasons. First, assuming for the moment that music listening may have some impact on adolescents, this impact ought to depend on the specific type they choose. Three hours a day of death metal is a different thing than 3 hours a day of soft rock ballads, and the effects of the two ought to be different. Second, as we have noted already, distinctions in music preference matter because of their linkage with individual and group identity: They tell us something about who adolescents think they are and how they function in their society. Differences in music preference, then, relate to a variety of social background variables, peer group patterns, and behavioral and psychological characteristics.

Of all the demographic and background predictors of music taste, race and ethnicity may be the most powerful (Christenson & Roberts, 1998; Denisoff & Levine, 1972). Entire genres of popular music are linked unambiguously and proudly with their racial and ethnic roots—R&B, soul, and hip-hop with African-American culture, salsa with Hispanics, reggae with its Jamaican heritage, for example. Racial differences in taste emerged quite strongly in the Kaiser Family Foundation's 2005 national survey of childhood and adolescent media use (Roberts et al., 2005). The study asked respondents to indicate which of 14 genres they had listened to the previous day. Overall, the highest percentage was for rap/hip-hop at 65%, followed by alternative rock at 32%, hard rock/heavy metal at 27%, and ska/punk at 23%. These overall percentages, however, mask several dramatic differences based on race. Following are some of those differences:

Rap/hip-hop: Whites 60%, Blacks 81%

Alternative rock: Whites 38%, Blacks 9%

Hard rock/heavy metal: Whites 33%, Blacks 7%

Ska/punk: Whites 29%, Blacks 6%

Reggae: Whites 9%, Blacks 24%

R&B/soul: Whites 5%, Blacks 33%

The results indicate the high level of popularity enjoyed by rap/hip-hop, which was by far the top-rated genre for both Whites and Blacks. Clearly, multitudes of White youth are "crossing over" to a form with strong roots in urban African-American culture. Aside from that phenomenon, however, the 8- to 18-year-olds in this study tend to stay home with their music affiliation. Whites listened much more often than African-Americans to the "White" sounds of alternative rock, hard rock/heavy metal, and ska/ punk, while African-Americans listened more often than Whites to hip-hop and much more often to reggae and R&B, all three of which are strongly identified with Black culture.

Gender is nearly as powerful a predictor as race. Two primary gender differences emerge from the research on music preferences. The first and most fundamental musical gender gap is the separation between pop (female) and rock (male) tastes. Whatever the historical era and whatever the population being studied, females exhibit greater attraction to the softer, more romantic, more mainstream forms (pop, disco, soft rock, Top 40), while males gravitate to the harder-edged rock forms (heavy metal, hard rock, punk, grunge, psychedelic rock). Second, males are more likely than females to adopt nonmainstream, fringe or "progressive" music affinities (Christenson & Peterson, 1988; Christenson & Roberts, 1998; Dykers, 1992; Roberts et al., 2005; Tanner, 1981; Wells, 1990).

These gender differences in music taste have proven so robust that it is reasonable to speculate on what might explain them. As we noted earlier, females tend to use music in different ways and for different reasons than males, and these disparities imply different music preferences. Dancing, for example, tends to be more important to girls and so "danceability" becomes for them a more important criterion of music taste than for boys. In addition, it would seem logical for girls to avoid music with reputations for misogynist or macho-aggressive messages, such as hard rock, heavy metal, and gangsta rap. More broadly, it is undeniable that girls are encouraged to be popular, deferent, romantic, nurturing, and to fit in, while boys are expected to be independent, aggressive, competitive, and to stand out. These conventional social expectations likely help to explain boys' preference for powerful, aggressive, defiant, "on-the-edge" forms of music and girls' inclination toward romantic, acceptable, mainstream music (cf. Christenson & Roberts, 1998).

The research also reveals a close connection between music preference and where adolescents stand in their peer culture. "Music style"—that is, the adoption of a certain type of music and a personal style to go with it—is one of the most powerful identifying markers in the school crowd structure. Indeed, some groups (e.g. "metalheads") are identified and labeled primarily on the basis of music affiliation (Christenson & Roberts, 1998). Keith Roe's (1984) research on Swedish adolescents is particularly informative on the relationship between school variables and music preference. Roe argued that the connection between school orientation and popular music taste springs from the process of academic evaluation, which inevitably creates an "in-group," who are popular with other youth and share the dominant values and goals of the school structure, and an "out-group" of youth, who operate on the margin and harbor antischool, antiadult feelings. Roe hypothesized that it is would be quite natural for the in-group to pursue relatively nonthreatening, mainstream music and the out-group to gravitate toward defiant genres, and that is precisely what he found. More successful, pro-school youth tended to prefer classical music, jazz, and mainstream pop, while those with lower levels of commitment to school and lower academic achievement sought out "disapproved" and "oppositional" music forms such as hard rock and punk. These patterns applied regardless of social class. Studies conducted in the

United States and Canada find essentially the same pattern. In a 1992 survey of more than 2,800 high school students in the Southeast, only 1 in 10 heavy metal fans expressed certainty that they would attend college, compared to 25% of pop and rock fans (Dykers, 1992). Similarly, Hakanen and Wells (1993) found adolescents' school grades to be strongly related to music taste, more strongly even than parental education.

Popular music taste also correlates with a number of psychological and behavioral factors. A number of studies have looked at how music preference relates to these sorts of variables. For example, research has revealed positive relationships between:

- heavy metal preference and assertiveness, aggressiveness, indifference to the feelings of others, moodiness, pessimism, impulsivity, feelings of rejection, and disconnectedness (cf. Baker & Bor, 2008; Rubin, West, & Mitchell, 2001), with suicidal ideation (Burge, Goldblat, & Lester, 2002; Lester & Whipple, 1996) and with reckless behavior (Arnett, 1991b);
- pop preference with being overly responsible, role conscious, conforming and struggling with peer acceptance (Swartz & Fouts, 2003);
- rap/hip-hop preference with extraversion (Swartz & Fouts, 2003);
- rap/hip-hop preference with alcohol and marijuana use and aggressive tendencies (Chen, Miller, Grube, & Waiters, 2006);
- in Canada, French rap with violence, gang membership, and drug use (Miranda & Claes, 2004);
- jazz and R&B with psychoticism scores (Swartz & Fouts, 2003);
- blues, jazz, folk, and heavy metal with levels of civic activism (Leung & Kier, 2008); and
- "nonmainstream forms" (e.g., punk and reggae) with substance use (Mulder et al., 2009).

Rentfrow and Gosling (2003) conducted a particularly interesting study of the relationship between music preferences and adolescent behavior/attitudes. They analyzed data on adolescents' taste for various genres, placing respondents into one of four taste groups (or genre clusters) that were labeled using terms that seemed to capture their distinctive thematic and/or musical qualities. They found

that: (a) attraction to "reflective and complex" music (classical, jazz, blues) correlated positively with openness to new experiences, self-perceived intelligence, and political liberalism; (b) a taste for "intense and rebellious" (rock/heavy metal) went with openness to new experiences, risk-taking, and athleticism; (c) "upbeat and conventional" taste (country, pop) was positively associated with extraversion and conservatism; and (d) a preference for "energetic and rhythmic" (hip-hop, R&B) music correlated positively with extraversion and liberalism.

Is There a Heavy Metal Syndrome?

Much of the research on music preferences has focused on heavy metal fans, and the findings confirm that there is something different about this group of adolescents. With regard to school, heavy metal fans report more conflict with teachers and other school authorities and perform less well academically than those whose tastes run more to the mainstream (Christenson & van Nouhuys, 1995; Hakanen & Wells, 1993). They tend to be distant from their families (Martin, Clarke, & Pearce, 1993) and are often at odds with their parents. When relationships with parents are described as satisfactory, it is usually because the parents let the children go their own way (Arnett, 1991a). At the same time, there is no evidence that heavy metal fans see themselves as socially isolated. They are just as satisfied as nonfans with the quality of their peer relationships (Arnett, 1991a). If anything, the peer group exerts a more powerful influence on heavy metal fans than on most other adolescents (Gordon, Hakanen, & Wells, 1992).

According to Arnett (1991a, 1991b), hardcore heavy metal fans tend to be driven by a generalized tendency to seek sensation and thrills and a need to engage in a variety of risky behavior—more or less "to see what it would be like." In accord with this thesis, he reported differences between heavy metal fans and nonfans not only in their expression of sensation-seeking motivations generally but also in their self-reports of specific reckless behaviors, including drunk driving, casual sex, and marijuana and cocaine use (also see Mulder et al., 2009 on the connection to substance use). Wass and her colleagues (Wass, Miller, & Reditt, 1991) report that youth in juvenile detention were three times more likely than regular high school students to be heavy metal fans (see also Epstein, Pratto, & Skipper, 1990; Tanner, 1981).

The research also suggests a connection between a preference for heavy metal music and sexual behavior. In one study, 54% of a group of high school-age heavy metal fans said they had had sex with a casual acquaintance, compared to 23% of nonfans (Arnett, 1991b); another found a correlation between a taste for heavy metal and approval of premarital sex (Yee, Britton, & Thompson, 1988). More relevant to the specific nature of heavy metal music's treatment of women, Hansen and Hansen (1991a) found that the amount of time college students listened to heavy metal was correlated with a "macho" personality. Specifically, exposure to heavy metal correlated positively with "male hypersexuality" (as indicated by the levels of agreement with idea that "young men need sex even if some coercion of females is required to get it") and negatively with general respect for women. Christenson and van Nouhuys (1995) found a connection between heavy metal and interest in other-sex contact as early as 11 or 12 years.

Concern has also been expressed over the potential impact of heavy metal music's often dismal, depressed view of the world and of its depiction of depression and suicide (e.g., Litman & Farberow, 1994). Arnett writes:

> One can hear an echo in (heavy metal themes) of concerns with social issues from the music of the 1960's, but with this difference: the songs of the sixties often lamented the state of the world but promised a brighter future if we would mend our ways; heavy metal songs often lament the state of the world but do not provide even a hint of hope for the future. Hopelessness and cynicism pervade the songs. (Arnett, 1991a: 93)

Data from more than 200 Australian high school students showed that those who preferred heavy metal or hard rock music reported feelings of depression, suicidal thoughts, and deliberate infliction of self-harm more frequently than others in the sample (Martin, Clarke, & Pearce, 1993). For instance, 20% of the males and more than 60% of the female heavy metal/hard rock fans reported having deliberately tried to kill or hurt themselves in the prior 6 months, compared to only 8% and 14%, respectively, of the pop fans. Although the research is not entirely unequivocal on this issue (see, e.g., Stack, 1998), most other studies have concluded that a preference for heavy metal may indicate higher suicidal risk among teens (Scheel & Westefeld, 1999).

Do these various findings, however, support the construct of a "heavy metal syndrome?" Is there a constellation of related traits with heavy metal at the focal point? Probably not. If there is a "syndrome" at work here, it is more properly considered a "troubled youth syndrome." Setting aside for the moment the question whether popular music exercises any influence on adolescents' values and behavior (and we think it probably does), it is not the consumption of heavy metal that brings together the various "at-risk," "troubled," or "alienated" characteristics with which heavy metal fandom tends to be associated. The best way to phrase the relationship is this: White adolescents who are troubled or at risk gravitate strongly toward a style of music that provides the most support for their view of the world and meets their particular needs . . . heavy metal.

The point can be further clarified, perhaps, by juxtaposing these statements: (a) Most heavy metal fans are not particularly troubled or at risk; but (b) adolescents who are troubled or at risk tend overwhelmingly to embrace heavy metal. In other words, whatever percentage one uses to estimate the proportion of heavy metal fans in the total adolescent population, they surely number in the tens of millions. Most of these young people are not on drugs, not in jail, not failing in school, not depressed, perhaps not even particularly at odds with their parents (except maybe when it comes to music). Arguing the other way, however, if we know a youth is White, male, 15 years old, drug involved, and in trouble with the law, then the odds are *very high* indeed that his music of choice will be some sort form of hard rock or heavy metal.

Our rejection of the idea of a true heavy metal syndrome should not be taken to imply that heavy metal music plays only a peripheral role in the lives of heavy metal fans, who are indeed an especially committed, devoted audience. Those who love heavy metal are highly absorbed in their musical identity, in terms of both listening time (Wass, Miller, & Stevenson, 1989) and a variety of other music-related behaviors. High school students who describe themselves as "metalheads" spend more than twice as much on albums, concerts, and music equipment than a comparison group of nonmetal fans (Arnett, 1991a). They also express very high levels of personal identification with their favorite performers, are more likely to say lyrics are important to them, claim a deeper understanding of lyrics, and are more likely than other youth to adopt their favorite musicians as role models. In sum, heavy metal plays a crucial role in the lives of the alienated and disaffected youth who seek it out: For many such youth, listening to heavy metal is what matters to them most (Arnett, 1991a; Wass, Miller, & Stevenson, 1989).

Making Sense of Popular Songs

Much of the criticism aimed at current popular music and music videos stems from assumptions that "content"—that is, the attitudes, values, and behaviors portrayed in lyrics and music video images—influences how young listeners think and act. Not surprisingly, such concern emphasizes the negative. Public anxiety is fueled by trends toward greater sexual explicitness and clear increases in lyric treatments of such topics as violence, misogyny, racism, suicide, Satanism, and substance use (Carey, 1969; Christenson & Roberts, 1998; Christenson, Roberts, & Bjork, in press; Fedler, Hall, & Tanzi, 1982; Roberts, Henriksen, & Christenson, 1999). It is doubtful whether nearly as much attention would be paid to popular music if teens were listening to hymns or traditional folk songs.

Claims that popular song lyrics pose a danger implicitly assume that young listeners interpret songs in much the same way that adult critics do. That is, for sexually explicit lyrics to promote teenage sexual activity or for substance use portrayals to encourage experimentation with illicit drugs, young audiences presumably must find sexual and/or substance-related messages in the songs. Indeed, to be truly "influenced," youngsters probably need to go a step further and connect such messages to their own lives. The problem with such assumptions is that several decades of communication research show quite clearly that message interpretation as much a process of construction as of recognition or discovery. The sense youngsters make of popular songs depends not only on what the lyric or video brings to them but also on what they bring to the lyric or video.

Research on comprehension of song lyrics and music videos typically takes one of three approaches: (1) It compares understanding of particular songs to some "definitive" interpretation; (2) it compares and contrasts interpretations of the same song given by different groups of youngsters; (3) it examines how adolescents think about and relate popular songs to their own lives. Each approach provides different insights on how youngsters make sense of lyrics and music videos. In studies of the first type, the standard for comparison is typically an adult "expert" reading of the text, where "expert" ranges from songwriters (Denisoff & Levine, 1971) to teachers and parents (Leming, 1987) and to the judgments of the researchers themselves (Greenfield et al., 1987; Robinson & Hirsch, 1972; Rosenbaum & Prinsky, 1987). Assuming such readings set a valid standard, studies of this type find relatively low levels of lyric comprehension—that is, substantial numbers of youths fail to produce responses matching the researchers' criteria for correctness. Denisoff and Levine (1971), for example, found that only 14% of San Francisco Bay Area college students understood the 1965 protest rock hit "Eve of Destruction" in terms of the songwriter's intent—namely, the threat of nuclear destruction. Another 45% showed partial understanding, and 41% showed none. When Patricia Greenfield and colleagues (1987) asked 4th-, 8th-, 12th-grade, and college students to explain such terms as *hometown jam* and *yellow man* from Bruce Springsteen's "Born in the USA" ("Got in a little hometown jam so they put a rifle in my hand/Sent me off to a foreign land to go and kill the yellow man"), a good deal of misunderstanding emerged, especially among the younger participants. Only 20% of the 4th graders and 60% of the 8th graders correctly identified "hometown jam" as some kind of dilemma the singer encountered in the place where he grew up; only 10% of 4th graders, 30% of 8th graders and 50% of 12th graders understood "yellow man" to refer to a North Vietnamese soldier. Most striking, however, is how few listeners of any age understood what the researchers saw as the song's general message of "despair, disillusionment, and resentment." No 4th graders, 30% of 8th graders, 40% of 12 graders, and just half the college students interpreted the song in these terms. Rather, many seemed simply to take the upbeat title and catch phrase of the refrain at face value.

Of course, if we assume a particular lyric has just one correct meaning, a great many adults don't get the message either. Ronald Reagan, for example, invoked "Born in the USA" as a patriotic and optimistic view of America during his 1984 presidential campaign, and the New York City affiliate of Planned Parenthood called Madonna's "Papa Don't Preach" a potent message about the "glamour of sex, pregnancy and childbearing" even as the California chapter of Feminists for Life in America labeled it a positive, prolife song (cited in Brown & Schulze, 1990). James Leming (1987) attempted to establish the "correct" meaning of various rock lyrics for his study of adolescent comprehension by asking public school teachers to decide what different songs meant. Although fair consensus emerged for some of the songs (e.g., most interpreted Olivia Newton John's "Physical" as suggesting casual sex), on others he found substantial levels of disagreement. Half of the group understood "I Want a New Drug" by Huey Lewis and the News as a metaphor for a search for love, but the other half took it literally as a quest for a drug with no side effects.

The point is that to presume a single, correct meaning for a song ignores the constructive nature of interpretation (not to mention centuries of honest debate over what particular poems, plays, or paintings "mean"). It also runs the risk of overlooking information that

may be embedded in the nature of young listeners' "misinterpretations." Right or wrong, the fact that a significant group of young adolescents in Leming's 1987 study understood "Physical" as a call to aerobic exercise tells us something. More broadly, it can be argued that a more interesting question than whether a set of interpretations is correct or incorrect is what explains the variation.

Studies comparing different groups' interpretations to one another rather than to some objective criterion demonstrate that variation in interpretation can often be predicted on the basis of differing cognitive abilities, social backgrounds, and personal experiences. Some differences are attributable to the developmental progression from concrete to abstract cognitive operations. Greenfield and her colleagues (1987) found 4th graders' misinterpretations of "Born in the USA" tended to be quite concrete (" . . . a man who fell in yellow paint") whereas college students erred at a more abstract level ("A yellow man is any kind of Communist!"). Similar age differences were found in response to Madonna's plaint from "Like a Virgin": "Made it through the wilderness, somehow I made it through/ Didn't know how lost I was until I found you. . . ." Many younger listeners interpreted the song as describing a perilous wilderness trek, while high school and college students were more likely to read "rough times" and "emotional loneliness" into the phrase. So, too, with interpretation of music videos. Christenson (1992) compared 9- and 10-year-olds' and 12-year-olds' descriptions of the major theme of Billy Ocean's music video, "Get Outta My Dreams, Get Into My Car." Most of the older group made sense of the video in relatively abstract terms, focusing on the male–female relationship ("It's about a guy who likes a girl and wants to know her better"). The younger children, however, spoke about concrete events and details ("It's about a guy who wants to take a girl for a ride in his car"). Some simply said it was about a guy and his car.

Differential expectations related to social background play a role in the interpretation process. Robinson and Hirsch (1972) found that middle-class adolescents interpreted the vocalist of the rock hit "Green Light" as wanting a date with a girl, while those from working-class homes said "he wanted the girl to go all the way." Race and gender also related to how young people interpret lyrics. Noting evidence associating race and gender with different sexual norms, attitudes, and behaviors among U.S. adolescents, Brown and Schulze (1990) reasoned that these differences might play a role in the process of interpreting music videos. Some of their most interesting results came in response to Madonna's controversial "Papa Don't Preach" video, which depicts a young woman struggling to tell her father that she is pregnant. While more than half of the White participants understood the video as being primarily about teen pregnancy, only 40% of African-American females and 21% of African-American males saw this as the central theme. Rather, African-American youths tended to view the father–daughter relationship as the video's central issue. Gender also played a role, interacting with race: White males were most likely to mention the possibility of marriage in the future (65%), and Black males least likely (21%). Interestingly, the direction of the gender difference depended on race: White females were less likely than males to mention marriage, whereas African-American females were more likely. Cultural and personal experiences relate strongly to interpretations of popular music content—so strongly, in fact, that "Papa Don't Preach" could be seen as anything from "a commercial for teenage pregnancy" (Goodman, 1986) to an anthem for female independence. There can be substantial and valid variations in how youngsters interpret songs.

Clearly, then, interpretations are neither random nor idiosyncratic. Youths from similar backgrounds or with similar experiences agreed on roughly similar interpretations. Christine and Ranald Hansen (1991b) have argued that although listeners may vary in interpretations of *specific elements in particular lyrics*, a good deal of similarity prevails in perceptions of general themes. They found that even when circumstances made it difficult for college students to agree about specific elements in a particular song lyrics (e.g., when lyrics were garbled or overpowered by the sound of the instruments in the song), there was still a great deal of consensus on

general themes. Students' popular music-related schemas—for instance, for certain music genres—produced high levels of agreement as to overall themes on the basis of a few sketchy cues. Taking a specific example from the study, listeners' schems for "heavy metal" music produced agreement on a song's central theme (e.g., suicide), even though there was considerable disagreement as to the meaning, or even the existence, of a particular phrase in the lyrics (e.g., "suicide is slow with liquor").

Thompson, Walsh-Childers, and Brown (1993) distinguish between two kinds of mental structures that may play a role in how listeners make sense of lyrics. "Content-specific" structures refer to personal knowledge (or schemas) related to the particular subject matter of a song. For example, depending on experience, some kids approach a song about male–female relationships with fairly elaborated mental schemas of sexual activity, others with relatively meager conceptualizations. "Generic" structures, on the other hand, relate to how individuals typically deal with new information regardless of topic. Some individuals absorb new information uncritically, while others test, evaluate, and elaborate; some focus on message source, others on message content; some seek cognitive conflict, others avoid it.

Both kinds of mental structures influenced high school students' responses to the "Papa Don't Preach" video (Thompson et al., 1993). In terms of content-specific structures, girls with more sexual and pregnancy experience and more complex teen pregnancy schemas interpreted the video more personally, making more connections to their own lives than did girls with less experience and less elaborated schemas. (Among boys, however, no relationship emerged between content-specific schemas and responses to the video, a gender difference that the authors explain on the basis of the song's focus on a young woman.) At the generic level, the findings indicated that both boys and girls processed the video differently depending on their "family communication environment"—that is, whether they came from family backgrounds that stressed the maintenance of interpersonal harmony or from families emphasizing the exploration and testing of new ideas (see Chaffee & McLeod, 1972; Ritchie, 1991). For example, girls from families that emphasized the maintenance of social harmony drew more inferences about the video and made more connections between the video and their own lives than did girls from families that placed little emphasis on social harmony. In short, both content-specific schems and generic information processing structures interacted with the content of the video to shape the nature, complexity, and intensity of students' responses.

In sum, we find: First, that variant readings of popular songs are more common than many observers and critics of contemporary popular music assume; and second, the variance is related in predictable ways to group and individual differences. It seems that when it comes to interpreting popular music, it is not so much a case of "you are what you hear" as "you hear what you are" (Christenson & Roberts, 1998, p. 179).

The Effects of Popular Music and Music Videos

Popular music's effects on young people's beliefs, attitudes, behaviors, and abilities have been examined in several domains, including social interactions, school work, hearing, mood and emotion, body image (see Ashby & Rich, 2005; Christenson & Roberts, 1998), and, more recently, prosocial behavior (Greitemeyer, 2009a, 2009b). It is fair to say, however, that most of the concern about the effects of contemporary popular music has focused on the impact of its more extreme messages—that is, those related to violence, drugs, and sexual behavior (see, for example, Allen et al., 2007; Gentile, Roberts, & Christenson, 2003; Timmerman, Allen, Jorgensen, Herrett-Skjellum, Kramer, & Ryan, 2008). It is not surprising, perhaps, that a generation raised on the Everly Brothers' 1958 line "When I want you in my arms, all I have to do is dream" ("Dream," 1958) becomes concerned when it finds its children listening to 2 Live Crew's 1990 title line "Hey, we want some pussy" and its grandchildren immersed in Li'l Wayne's "And that

pussy in my mouth had me lost for words/ Told her back it up like erp erp/And I made that ass jump like jerk, jerk/And that's when she lick me like a lollipop (oh yeah I like that)" ("Lollipop," 2008). Nonetheless, even though a minority of popular songs and music videos really push the edge on topics such as sex, violence, racism, misogyny, Satanism, and suicide, those that do not only attract a good deal of press, they often raise legitimate questions about the role popular music plays in the socialization of youth. The fundamental concern is that because music is so important to them, some may adopt beliefs, attitudes, and/or behaviors articulated in at least some of these songs.

A number of studies report positive associations between exposure to various types of popular music and a variety of troublesome attitudes and behaviors. As we reported earlier in the section on music preferences, exposure to rock, heavy metal, rap, hip-hop, and "sexy" or "edgy" music in general has been shown to relate to such problematic outcomes as drunk driving, experimentation with marijuana and cocaine, conflict with parents, school, and legal authorities, antiestablishment attitudes, Satanic beliefs, low levels of trust in others, aggressive behavior, permissive sexual attitudes, acceptance of casual sex, and early initiation of sexual behavior (e.g., Arnett, 1991a, 1991b; Chen et al., 2006; Christenson & van Nouhuys, 1995; Gordon et al., 1992; Hansen & Hansen, 1991a; Martin et al., 1993; Pardun, L'Engle, & Brown, 2005; Primack, Douglas, Fine, & Dalton, 2009; Robinson, Chen, & Killen, 1998; Scheel & Westefeld, 1999; Wass, Miller, & Stevenson, 1991; Wingood et al., 2003; Zhang, Miller, & Harrison, 2008).

Although the relationships reported in most of these studies are relatively robust, surveys do not allow the inference that music exposure *produced* any of the various outcomes listed. That is, the causal arrow might run from exposure to the presumed outcome variable, or from the outcome variable to exposure, or some third variable might produce both exposure and outcome. However, several more recent studies that have controlled for an array of possible third variables and/or that report longitudinal data speak to the issue of causality a bit more fully. For example, Primack and colleagues (2009) found that urban adolescents who listened to high levels of "degrading" sexual lyrics engaged in substantially higher levels of sexual behavior than those who listened less, even after controlling for nine other variables (age, gender, race, maternal education, school grades, demanding parenting, responsive parenting, sensation seeking, and rebelliousness) that were related to sexual behavior. In other words, exposure to degrading sexual lyrics was shown to be related to sexual behavior independent of an array of third variables that were also related to sexual behavior.

Two studies have employed an over-time panel design to examine the "prospective" relationship between music exposure and various outcomes. Robinson, Chen, and Killen (1998) gathered baseline information about amount of music video exposure and alcohol use from a large sample of ninth graders and follow-up data 18 months later. By dividing the baseline sample into drinkers and nondrinkers, then relating baseline music video exposure to drinking onset at Time two, the researchers were able to demonstrate that music exposure preceded the initiation of drinking, adding plausibility to a possible causal relationship. They also found that an increase of 1 hour in daily music video exposure at Time one was associated with a 31% increase in the risk of starting to drink over the next 18 months. Combining both longitudinal and multivariate analytic procedures, Martino and his colleagues (Martino et al., 2006) gathered data on sexual knowledge, attitudes, and behavior, and an array of demographic and psychosocial variables known to predict either sexual behavior or media use from a national sample of teenagers in 2001 and again in 2002 and 2004. Overall music exposure, exposure to sexual lyrics, and exposure to "degrading" sexual lyrics were also assessed at Time two. This design allowed testing not only the prospective effect of music exposure on sexual behavior (i.e., the relationship between exposure at Time two and sexual behavior at Time three) but also examination of the degree to which sexual attitudes and experience at Time one influenced teens' selection of music content at Time two while controlling for a number of other possible confounding variables. Results indicated that teens who listened to more degrading sexual lyrics (but not those who listened to nondegrading

sexual lyrics or to music in general) at Time two were more likely to progress to more advanced levels of noncoital sexual activity and to initiate intercourse by Time three. Moreover, these relationships withstood controls for 18 respondent characteristics that might otherwise explain those linkages. It appears, then, that evidence for a causal relationship between exposure to at least some kinds of some music lyrics and outcomes related to those lyrics is beginning to mount, even in correlational studies.

Of course, causality is more convincingly demonstrated with experimental research. Experiments on the effects of popular music typically involve high school or undergraduate college students viewing various types of music videos (rather than audio exposure alone), followed by postexposure assessment of attitudes and beliefs. For example, Greeson and Williams (1986) found that 7th and 10th graders who viewed 30 minutes of music videos with high concentrations of sex, violence, and antiestablishment themes showed higher approval of premarital sex than did similar participants who viewed 30 minutes of videos randomly taped off the air. Exposure to the treatment videos also reduced disapproval of violence among 10th graders. Peterson and Pfost (1989) showed that undergraduate males exposed to violent videos scored higher than those exposed to nonviolent videos on measures of negative affect and "antagonistic orientation toward women." Unfortunately, since participants completed the dependent measures immediately after viewing and since those measures were highly reflective of the content of the experimental treatment, participants may have formed hypotheses about the intent of the research which, in turn, may have influenced responses.

Several more recent experiments have incorporated better disguises, typically engineering situations in which participants hear music under the guise of one kind of activity but respond to dependent measures as part of what they perceive to be a second, unrelated activity. Johnson, Jackson, and Gatto (1995), for example, showed 11- through 16-year-old lower-income African-American adolescents either violent or nonviolent rap videos, ostensibly as part of a study of memory. After completing the "memory test," participants moved on to a second study concerned with "decision-making skills," in which they answered questions about two brief stories. These questions served as measures of whether the videos influenced the young viewers/ listeners. Participants' responses clearly indicated an effect of videos on both approval of violence and academic aspirations. Youths who viewed the violent videos were more likely than those who saw nonviolent videos (or than a no-video control group) to condone violence and to express substantially lower academic aspirations and expectations.

Other studies using this sort of two-phase experimental design also find that music video content can alter viewers' subsequent assessments of other people and their behavior. Viewing "antisocial" rock videos increased college students' subsequent acceptance of what they presumed to be real-life rude and defiant behavior (Hansen & Hansen, 1990). Exposure to highly gender-stereotyped music videos affected students' evaluation of the behavior of presumed "real" men and women in subsequent, realistically staged situations (Hansen & Hansen, 1988). Watching various types of "sexy" music videos influenced students to rate men and women in subsequently viewed nonsexy television commercials as more attractive, sexier, and generally similar to the actors portrayed in the videos (Hansen & Krygowski, 1994). Gan, Zillmann, and Mitrook (1997) had White undergraduates record their impressions of both White and Black women subsequent to watching (ostensibly unrelated) videos in which a Black female artist presented rap lyrics that were either sexually titillating or that expressed devoted love. They found that exposure to sexual rap resulted in a downgrading of positive traits and an upgrading of negative traits of the Black women portrayed in the photo array.

Finally, Zillmann and his colleagues (Zillmann et al., 1995) used an elaborate experimental procedure to examine the effect of politically radical rap music on race-related political attitudes. First, under the impression that their task was to evaluate music videos, White and African-American high school students saw one of three sets of music videos: popular rock videos, nonpolitical rap videos, or radical political rap videos. Later, the students participated in a presumably unrelated study of student politics in which they responded to one of six ostensible candidates for student office, three of whom were White and three African-American. Within each race, these candidates were portrayed as espousing one of three political stances: racially liberal, racially radical, or neutral. The videos had no effect on the political attitudes of African-American adolescents. White participants, however, were influenced. Exposure to radical political rap videos dramatically increased White listeners' support for the message of racial harmony advocated by an African-American candidate and decreased their acceptance of a conservative White candidate arguing against affirmative action. The authors note that this finding not only shows an effect of music video exposure but an effect that runs contrary to the frequently voiced claim that radical rap makes White adolescents more racially defensive.

With few exceptions, experimental studies of the effects of pop music *lyrics* (as opposed to lyrics embedded in music videos) are relatively recent. One early study found no difference in college students' expressions of hostility after hearing aggressive music (Wanamaker & Reznikoff, 1989). Another found that male undergraduates who heard either sexually violent heavy metal or Christian heavy metal were more likely than those who listened to classical music to express negative attitudes toward women (St. Lawrence & Joyner, 1991), perhaps indicating that the "sound" of heavy metal matters at least as much as the verbal message contained in the lyrics. One recent study focusing on popular music lyrics (Carpentier, Knobloch-Westerwick, & Blumhoff, 2007) exposed university students to either four "sexually charged" or four nonsexual songs as part of a "break" between two studies asking them to evaluate various Internet platforms. Subsequent to the musical break, participants completed an evaluation of personal ads in an online dating service, rating individuals portrayed in the ads. Results indicated that the sexually provocative songs acted as a prime, influencing respondents who listened to the more sexual songs to evaluate the target individuals with a substantially heavier emphasis on attributes associated with sex appeal (i.e., sexy; desirable). Fischer and Greitemeyer (2006) also found that exposure to "sexual-aggressive" songs increased aggression-related thoughts, emotions, and behavior. A series of five experiments in which college students listened to songs with either violent or nonaggressive lyrics found that those who heard violent lyrics reported more hostile feelings and more aggressive thoughts than those who heard nonaggressive lyrics (Anderson, Carnagey, & Eubanks, 2003). Finally, a recent meta-analysis of 23 experimental and survey studies examining a relationship between music exposure and some measure of social belief or action found substantial support for the proposition that exposure to music increases antisocial beliefs and actions, with the caveat that there is also evidence for the existence of a moderator variable (Timmerman et al., 2008). This finding, while not surprising, is likely as much a result of the kinds of content likely to be examined (i.e., presumed problematic content dealing with such issues as violence, sex, drugs, and the like), as of any negative bias inherent in *all* music.

In a long overdue change of focus, Greitemeyer (2009a, 2009b) conducted a series of experiments focused on *positive outcomes* following exposure to prosocial music lyrics. His procedure was to expose university students to either prosocial songs (e.g., the Beatles' "Help," Michael Jackson's "Heal the World") or neutral songs (e.g., the Beatles' "Octopus's Garden," Michael Jackson's "On the Line") under the guise of one task (e.g., a survey of music preferences), then to measure prosocial responses during a second, presumably unrelated task (e.g., helping an experimenter who spills a cup of pencils while preparing to administer a second survey). Using various permutations of this basic design, Greitemeyer has shown that compared to listening to neutral lyrics, exposure to prosocial lyrics increases students' accessibility of positive thoughts, empathy, and prosocial behaviors such as helping, donating, and cooperation. This work also affords tests of Buckley and Anderson's (2006) General Learning Model of media effects and indicates that the important mediator of prosocial behavior subsequent to exposure to prosocial lyrics is affective (i.e., arousal of empathy) as opposed to cognitive (i.e., increased accessibility of prosocial thoughts).

Greitemeyer's demonstration of the importance of music's influence on affective responses brings us to a final topic that must be acknowledged in any discussion of the effects of popular music: public concern with whether popular music influences teen suicide. Does angry, nihilistic music promote angry, nihilistic thoughts and behavior? Most professionals concerned with the causes of suicide point to a broad array of conditions unrelated to popular culture (depression, access to guns, substance abuse, "conduct disorders," and so on) as necessary precursors of such drastic acts, and empirical work does indeed show that these conditions have characterized most of the incidents at issue in the recent debates over popular music's role (e.g., Berman & Jobes, 1991; Egan, 1998; Levy & Deykin, 1989; Scheel & Westefeld, 1999).

The importance of such contributing conditions, however, does not necessarily absolve popular music from also playing a role in at least some suicides and other violent incidents. As noted earlier, one of the more important functions of popular music is mood management (Christenson & Roberts, 1998). Teenagers frequently acknowledge the direct, profound impact music has on their emotional states (Arnett, 1991a), and other work suggests what might be called an "amplification effect," a strong tendency for music to heighten whatever emotional state a listener brings to a listening situation—including anger and depression (Gordon et al., 1992; Scheel & Westefeld, 1999; Wells, 1990). In light of substantial evidence that adolescents who are depressed, angry, alienated, experiencing suicidal thoughts, having family problems, abusing drugs or alcohol, and so on are particularly drawn to the sort of angry, nihilist music that celebrates these "troubled" states and traits, there seems to be legitimate cause for concern. It is reasonable to propose that if a preoccupation with heavy metal is carried to an extreme by troubled and at-risk teens, the music is more likely to deepen the problem than alleviate it. For that small minority who are, for whatever reason, already alienated and disturbed, extreme music may be another risk factor.

It seems to us that the important inference to draw from both the survey and experimental work reviewed above is that exposure to certain types of content—whether prosocial or antisocial—does influence subsequent thoughts and behaviors. Music is important to young listeners; they pay attention to it and are influenced by their interpretation of it, just as they pay attention to and are influenced by other salient influences such as parents, schools, churches, peers, and other media content.

Coda

Does all this mean that the booming bass and screeching guitars parents hear behind their adolescent offspring's bedroom doors or the green-haired, leathered, and pierced dervish whirling across the music video screen are turning young people into monsters? Generally not. As we have said, for most adolescents, most of the time, music is a source of pleasure. They listen not to analyze lyrics and learn about the world, not to sort out emotions and feelings, not to facilitate social interaction, but simply because they like it. To be sure, popular music does teach them things, does help them to sort out emotions and feelings, does facilitate social interaction. It is the medium that matters most to adolescents, not least because it addresses issues that are central to them—love, sex, loyalty, independence, friendship, authority—with a directness they often do not get from adults. Although many teenagers will discuss sensitive personal issues with the significant adults in their lives, just as many will avoid such discussions, opting instead for what they perceive as more legitimate sources—their peers, to be sure, but also the culture of youth. For most of today's adolescents, popular music functions not just as equipment for living but as *essential* equipment for living. Most will survive it . . . just as their parents did.

References

Adoni, H. (1978). The functions of mass media in the political socialization of adolescents. *Communication Research, 6,* 84–106.

Allen, M., Jorgenson, J., Ryan, D. J., Herrett-Skjellum, J., Kramer, M. R., & Timmerman, L. (2007). Effects of music. In R. W. Preiss, B. Gayle, N. Brurell, M. Allen, & J. Bryant (Eds.), *Mass media effects research: Advances through meta-analysis* (pp. 263–278). Mahwah, NJ: Lawrence Erlbaum.

Anderson, C. A., Carnagey, N. L., & Eubanks, J. (2003). Exposure to violent media: The effects of songs with violent lyrics on aggressive thoughts and feelings. *Journal of Personality and Social Psychology, 84,* 960–971.

Arnett, J. (1991a). Adolescence and heavy metal music: From the mouths of metalheads. *Youth and Society, 23*(1), 76–98.

Arnett, J. (1991b). Heavy metal music and reckless behavior among adolescents. *Journal of Youth and Adolescence, 20,* 573–592.

Ashby, S. L., & Rich, M. (2005). Video killed the radio star: The effects of music videos on adolescent health. *Adolescent Medicine, 16,* 371–393.

Baker, F., & Bor, W. (2008). Can music preferences indicate mental health status in young people? *Australian Psychiatry, 16*(4), 284–288.

Berman, A. L., & Jobes, D. A. (1991). *Adolescent suicide: Assessment and intervention.* Washington, DC: American Psychological Association.

Brown, J. D., Childers, K., Bauman, K., & Koch, G. (1990). The influence of new media and family structure on young adolescents' television and radio use. *Communication Research, 17,* 65–82.

Brown, J. D., & Schulze, L. (1990). The effects of race, gender, and fandom on audience interpretations of Madonna's music videos. *Journal of Communication, 40,* 88–102.

Brown, J. R. (1976). Children's uses of television. In R. Brown (Ed.), *Children and television* (pp. 116–136). Beverly Hills, CA: Sage.

Brown, R., & O'Leary, M. (1971). Pop music in an English secondary school system. *American Behavioral Scientist, 14,* 401–413.

Buckley, K. E., & Anderson, C. A. (2006). A theoretical model of the effects and consequences of playing video games. In P. Vorderer and J. Bryant (Eds.), *Playing video games: Motives, responses, and consequences* (pp. 363–378). Mahwah, NJ: Lawrence Erlbaum.

Burge, M., Goldblat, C., & Lester, D. (2002). *Death Studies, 26,* 501–504.

Carey, J. (1969). Changing courtship patterns in the popular song. *American Journal of Sociology, 4,* 720–731.

Carpentier, F. D., Knobloch-Westerwick, S., & Blumhoff, A. (2007). Naughty versus nice: Suggestive pop music influences on perceptions of potential romantic partners. *Media Psychology, 9,* 1–17.

Carroll, R., Silbergleid, M., Beachum, C., Perry, S., Pluscht, P., & Pescatore, M. (1993). Meanings of radio to teenagers in a niche-programming era. *Journal of Broadcasting and Electronic Media, 37*(2), 159–176.

Chaffee, S. H., & McLeod, J. M. (1972). Adolescent television use in the family context. In G. A. Comstock & E. A. Rubinstein (Eds.), *Television and social behavior: Vol. 3. Television and adolescent aggressiveness* (pp. 149–172). Washington, DC: U.S. Government Printing Office.

Chen, M. J., Miller, B. A., Grube, J. W., & Waiters, E. D. (2006). Music, substance use and aggression. *Journal of Studies on Alcohol, 67,* 373–381.

Christenson, P. (1992). Preadolescent perceptions and interpretations of music videos. *Popular Music and Society, 16*(3), 63–73.

Christenson, P. (1994). Childhood patterns of music use and preferences. *Communication Reports, 7*(2), 136–144.

Christenson, P., DeBenedittis, P., & Lindlof, T. (1985). Children's use of audio media. *Communication Research, 12,* 327–343.

Christenson, P., &. Peterson, J. (1988). Genre and gender in the structure of music preferences. *Communication Research, 15*(3), 282–301.

Christenson, P., & Roberts, D. F. (1998). *It's not only rock and roll: Popular music in the lives of adolescents,* Cresskill, NJ: Hampton Press.

Christenson, P., Roberts, D. F., & Bjork, N. (in press). Booze, drugs, and pop music: Trends in substance portrayals in the Billboard Top 100—1968–2008. *Substance Use and Misuse,* in press.

Christenson, P., & van Nouhuys, B. (1995, May). *From the fringe to the center: A comparison of heavy metal and rap fandom.* Paper presented at the annual meeting of the International Communication Association, Albuquerque, NM.

Denisoff, R. S., & Levine, M. H. (1971). The popular protest song: The case of "Eve of Destruction." *Public Opinion Quarterly, 35,* 119–124.

Denisoff, R. S., & Levine, M. H. (1972). Youth and popular music: A test of the taste culture hypothesis. *Youth and Society, 4*(4), 237–255.

Dominick, J. (1974). The portable friend: Peer group membership and radio usage. *Journal of Broadcasting, 18*(2), 164–169.

Dykers, C. (1992, May). *Rap and rock as adolescents' cultural capital at school.* Paper presented at the annual meetings of the International Communication Association, Miami, FL.

Egan, T. (1998, June 14). From adolescent angst to shooting up schools. *New York Times,* p. 1.

Eggermont, S., & Van den Bulck, J. (2006). Nodding off or switching off? The use of popular music as a sleep aid in secondary-school children. *Journal of Paediatrics and Child Health, 42*(7/8), 428–433.

Epstein, J., Pratto, D., & Skipper, J. (1990). Teenagers, behavioral problems, and preferences for heavy metal and rap music: A case study of a Southern middle school. *Deviant Behavior, 11,* 381–394.

Fedler, F., Hall. J., & Tanzi, L. (1982). Popular songs emphasize sex, de-emphasize romance. *Mass Communication Review, 9,* 10–15.

Fischer, P., & Greitemeyer, T. (2006). Music and aggression: The impact of sexual-aggressive song lyrics on aggression-related thoughts, emotions and behavior toward the same and the opposite sex. *Personality and Social Psychology Bulletin, 32,* 1165–1176.

Foehr, U. G. (2006). *Media multitasking among American youth: Prevalence, predictors, and pairings.* Menlo Park, CA: Kaiser Family Foundation.

Frith, S. (1981). *Sound effects: Youth, leisure, and the politics of rock 'n' roll.* New York: Pantheon.

Gan, S., Zillmann, D., & Mitrook, M. (1997). Stereotyping effect of Black women's sexual rap on White audiences. *Basic and Applied Social Psychology, 19,* 381–399.

Gantz, W., Gartenberg, H., Pearson, M., & Schiller, S. (1978). Gratifications and expectations associated with popular music among adolescents. *Popular Music and Society, 6*(1), 81–89.

Gentile, D., Roberts, D. F., & Christenson, P. G. (2003). The effects of violent music on children and adolescents. In D. Gentile (Ed.), *Media violence and children* (pp. 153–170). Westport, CT: Praeger.

Goodman, E. (1986, September 20). Commercial for teen-age pregnancy. *Washington Post,* p. A–23.

Gordon, T., Hakanen, E., & Wells, A. (1992, May). *Music preferences and the use of music to manage emotional states: Correlates with self-concept among adolescents.* Paper presented at the annual meetings of the International Communication Association. Miami, FL.

Greenberg, B., Ku, L., & Li, H. (1989, June). *Young people and their orientation to the mass media: An international study. Study 2: United States.* East Lansing: Michigan State University, College of Communication Arts.

Greenfield, P. M., Bruzzone, L., Koyamatsu, K., Satuloff, W., Nixon, K., Brodie. M., et al. (1987). What is rock music doing to the minds of our youth? A first experimental look at the effects of rock music lyrics and music videos. *Journal of Early Adolescence, 7,* 315–329.

Greeson, L., & Williams, R. A. (1986). Social implications of music videos for youth: An analysis of the content and effects of MTV. *Youth and Society, 18,* 177–189.

Greitemeyer, T. (2009a). Effects of songs with prosocial lyrics on prosocial behavior: Further evidence and a mediating mechanism. *Personality and Social Psychology Bulletin, 35,* 1500–1511.

Greitemeyer, T. (2009b). Effects of songs with prosocial lyrics on prosocial thoughts, affect, and behavior. *Journal of Experimental Social Psychology, 45,* 186–190.

Hakanen, E., & Wells, A. (1993). Music preference and taste cultures among adolescents. *Popular Music and Society, 17*(1), 55–69.

Hansen, C., & Hansen, R. (1988). How rock music videos can change what is seen when boy meets girl: Priming stereotypic appraisal of social interactions. *Sex Roles, 79,* 287–316.

Hansen, C., & Hansen, R. (1990). The influence of sex and violence on the appeal of rock music videos. *Communication Research, 17,* 212–234.

Hansen, C., & Hansen, R. (1991a). Constructing personality and social reality through music: Individual differences among fans of punk and heavy metal music. *Journal of Broadcasting and Electronic Media, 35,* 335–350.

Hansen, C., & Hansen, R. (1991b). Schematic information processing of heavy metal lyrics. *Communication Research, 18,* 373–411.

Hansen, C. H., & Krygowski, W. (1994). Arousal-augmented priming effects: Rock music videos and sex object schemas. *Communication Research, 21,* 24–47.

Hayakawa, S. I. (1962). *The use and misuse of language.* Greenwich, CT: Fawcett.

Johnson, J. D., Jackson, L. A., & Gatto, L. (1995). Violent attitudes and deferred academic aspirations: Deleterious effects of exposure to rap music. *Basic and Applied Social Psychology, 16*(1/2), 27–41.

Jones, S., & Lenhart, A. (2004). Music downloading and listening: Findings from the Pew Internet and American Life Project. *Popular Music and Society, 27*(2), 185–199.

Kotarba, J., & Wells, L. (1987). Styles of adolescent participation in an all-ages, rock 'n' roll nightclub: An ethnographic analysis. *Youth and Society, 18*(4), 398–417.

Kubey, R., & Larson, R. (1989). The use and experience of the new video media among children and young adolescents: Television viewing compared to the use of videocassettes, video games, and music videos. *Communication Research, 17,* 107–130.

Kuwahara, Y. (1992). Power to the people, y'all: Rap music, resistance, and Black college students. *Humanity and Society, 16*(1), 54–73.

Larson, R., & Kubey, R. (1983). Television and music: Contrasting media in adolescent life. *Youth and Society, 15*(1), 13–31.

Larson, R., Kubey, R., & Colletti, J. (1989). Changing channels: Early adolescent media choices and shifting investments in family and friends. *Journal of Youth and Adolescence, 18*(6), 583–599.

Leming, J. (1987). Rock music and the socialization of moral values in early adolescence. *Youth and Society, 18,* 363–383.

Lester, D., & Whipple, M. (1996). Music preference, depression, suicidal preoccupation, and personality: A comment on Stack and Gundlach's papers. *Suicide and Life-threatening Behavior, 26,* 68–70.

Leung, A., & Kier, C. (2008). Music preferences and civic activism of young people. *Journal of Youth Studies, 11*(4), 445–460.

Levy, C. J., & Deykin, E. Y. (1989). Suicidality, depression, and substance abuse in adolescence. *American Journal of Psychiatry, 146,* 1462–1467.

Litman, R. E., & Farberow, N. L. (1994). Pop-rock music as precipitating cause in youth suicide. *Journal of Forensic Sciences, 39,* 494–499.

Lull, J. (1987). Listeners' communicative uses of popular music. In J. Lull (Ed.), *Popular music and communication* (pp. 140–174), Newbury Park, CA: Sage.

Lull, J. (1992). Popular music and communication: An introduction. In J. Lull (Ed.), *Popular music and communication* (2nd ed., pp. 1–32). Newbury Park, CA: Sage.

Lyle, J., & Hoffman, H. (1972). Children's use of television and other media. In E. Rubinstein, G. Comstock, & J. Murray (Eds.), *Television in day-to-day life: Patterns of use* (pp. 129–256). Washington, DC: U.S. Government Printing Office.

Madden, M. (2009, June). The state of music online: Ten years after Napster. Washington, DC: Pew Internet and American Life Project. Retrieved May 24, 2010, from www.pewinternet.org/Reports/2009/9-The-State-of-Music-Online-Ten-Years-After-Napster.aspx.

Martin, G., Clarke, M., & Pearce, C. (1993). Adolescent suicide: Music preference as an indicator of vulnerability. *Journal of the Academy of Child and Adolescent Psychiatry, 32*(3), 530–535.

Martino, S. C., Collins, R. L., Elliott, M. N., Strachman, A., Kanouse, D. E., & Berry, S. H. (2006). Exposure to degrading versus nondegrading music lyrics and sexual behavior among youth. *Pediatrics, 118,* 430–441.

Miranda, D., & Claes, C. (2004). Rap music genres and defiant behaviors in French-Canadian adolescents. *Journal of Youth and Adolescence, 33*(2), 113–122.

Miranda, D., & Claes, C. (2009). Music listening, coping, peer affiliation and depression in adolescence. *Psychology of Music, 37*(2), 215–233.

Mulder, J., Ter Bogt, T., Raaijmakers, Q., Gabhainn, S. N., Monshouwer, K., & Vollebergh, W. M. (2009). The soundtrack of substance use: Music preference and adolescent smoking and drinking. *Substance Use and Misuse, 44,* 514–531.

Nielsen (2007, December). Kids on the go; Mobile usage by U.S. teens and tweens—Q3 2007 study. New York: Nielsen Company. Retrieved May 24, 2010, from http://s3.amazonaws .com/thearf-org-aux-assets/downloads/cnc/ youth/2008-04-15_ARF_Resnick.pdf.

Nippold, M. A., Duthie, J. K., & Larsen, J. (2005). Literacy as a leisure activity: Free-time preferences of older children and young adolescents. *Language, Speech and Hearing Services in Schools, 36,* 93–102.

North, C. A., Hargreaves, D. J., & Hargreaves, J. J. (2004). Uses of music in everyday life. *Music Perception, 22*(1), 41–77.

Pardun, C. J., L'Engle, K. L., & Brown, J. D. (2005). Linking exposure to outcome: Early adolescents' consumption of sexual content in six media. *Mass Communication and Society, 8,* 75–91.

Peterson, D. L., & Pfost, K. S. (1989). Influence of rock videos on attitudes of violence against women. *Psychological Reports, 64,* 319–322.

Primack, B. A., Douglas, E. L., Fine, M. J., & Dalton, M. A. (2009). Exposure to sexual lyrics and sexual experience among urban adolescents. *American Journal of Preventive Medicine, 36*(4), 317–323.

Rentfrow, P. J., & Gosling, S. D. (2003). The do re mi's of everyday life: The structure and personality correlates of music preferences. *Journal of Personality and Social Psychology, 84*(6), 1236–1256.

Rideout, V. J., Foehr, U. G., & Roberts, D. F. (2010). *Generation M²: Media in the Lives of 8- to 18-year-olds.* Menlo Park, CA: Kaiser Family Foundation.

Ritchie, L. D. (1991). Family communication patterns: An epistemic analysis and conceptual reinterpretation. *Communication Research, 18,* 548–565.

Roberts, D. F., & Foehr, U. G. (2004). *Kids & media in America.* Cambridge, UK: Cambridge University Press.

Roberts, D. F., Foehr, U. G., Rideout, V. J., & Brodie, M. (1999). *Kids & media @ the new millennium.* Menlo Park, CA: Kaiser Family Foundation.

Roberts, D. F., Foehr, U. G., & Rideout, V. J. (2005). *Generation M: Media in the lives of 8- to 18-year-olds.* Menlo Park, CA: Kaiser Family Foundation.

Roberts, D. F., & Henriksen, L. (1990, June). *Music listening vs. television viewing among older adolescents.* Paper presented at the annual meetings of the International Communication Association, Dublin, Ireland.

Roberts, D. F., Henriksen, L., & Christenson, P. (1999, April). *Substance use in popular movies and music.* Washington, DC: Office of National Drug Control Policy.

Robinson, T. N., Chen, H. L., & Killen, J. D. (1998). Television and music video exposure and risk of adolescent alcohol use. *Pediatrics, 102,* e54–59.

Robinson, J. P., & Hirsch, P. M. (1972). Teenage response to rock and roll protest songs. In R. S. Denisoff & R. A. Peterson (Eds.), *The sounds of social change: Studies in popular culture* (pp. 222–231). Chicago: Rand McNally.

Roe, K. (1984, August). *Youth and music in Sweden: Results from a longitudinal study of teenagers' media use.* Paper presented at the meetings of the International Association of Mass Communication Research, Prague, Czech Republic.

Roe, K. (1985). Swedish youth and music: Listening patterns and motivations. *Communication Research, 12*(3), 353–362.

Roe, K. (1987). The school and music in adolescent socialization. In J. Lull (Ed.), *Popular music and communication* (pp. 212–230). Newbury Park, CA: Sage.

Rosenbaum, J., & Prinsky, L. (1987). Sex, violence, and rock 'n' roll: Youth's perceptions of popular music. *Popular Music and Society, 11*(2), 79–89.

Rouner, D. (1990). Rock music use as a socializing function. *Popular Music and Society, 14*(1), 97–107.

Rubin, A. M., West, D. V., & Mitchell, W. S. (2001). Differences in aggression, attitudes toward women, and distrust as reflected in popular music preferences. *Media Psychology, 3,* 25–42.

Scheel, K. R., & Westefeld, J. S. (1999). Heavy metal music and adolescent suicidality: An empirical investigation. *Adolescence, 34,* 253–273.

Stack, S. (1998). Heavy metal, religiosity, and suicide acceptability. *Suicide and Life-Threatening Behavior, 28,* 388–394.

St. Lawrence, J. S., & Joyner, D. J. (1991). The effects of sexually violent rock music on males' acceptance of violence against women. *Psychology of Women Quarterly, 15,* 49–63.

Swartz, K. D., & Fouts, G. T. (2003). Music preferences, personality style, and developmental issues of adolescents. *Journal of Youth and Adolescence, 32*(3), 205–213.

Tanner, J. (1981). Pop music and peer groups: A study of Canadian high school students' responses to pop music. *Canadian Review of Sociology and Anthropology, 18*(2), 1–13.

Ter Bogt, T., Raaijmakers, Q., Vollebergh, W., Van Vel, F., & Sikkema, P. (2003). Youngsters and their musical taste: Musical styles and taste groups. *Netherlands Journal of Social Sciences, 39*(1), 35–52.

Thompson, M., Walsh-Childers, K., & Brown, J. D. (1993). The influence of family communication patterns and sexual experience on processing of a music video. In B. Greenberg, J. D. Brown, & N. L. Buerkel-Rothfuss (Eds.), *Media, sex, and the adolescent* (pp. 248–262). Cresskill, NJ: Hampton Press.

Timmerman, L. M., Allen, M., Jorgensen, J., Herrett-Skjellum, J., Kramer, M. R., & Ryan, D. J. (2008). A review and meta-analysis of music content with sex, race, priming, and attitudes. *Communication Quarterly, 56,* 303–324.

Wanamaker, C. E., & Reznikoff, M. (1989). Effects of aggressive and nonaggressive rock songs on projective and structured tests. *Journal of Psychology, 123,* 561–570.

Wartella, E., Heintz, K., Aidman, A., & Mazzarella, S. (1990). Television and beyond: Children's video media in one community. *Communication Research, 17,* 45–64.

Wass, H., Miller, D., & Reditt, C. (1991). Adolescents and destructive themes in rock music: A follow-up. *Omega, 23*(2), 193–206.

Wass, H., Miller, D., & Stevenson, R. (1989). Factors affecting adolescents' behavior and attitudes toward destructive rock lyrics. *Death Studies, 13,* 287–303.

Wells, A. (1990). Popular music: Emotional use and management. *Journal of Popular Culture, 24*(1), 105–117.

Wingood, G., DiClemente, R., Bernhardt, J., Harrington, K., Davies, S. L., & Hook, E. W. (2003). A prospective study of exposure to rap music videos and African American female adolescents' health. *American Journal of Public Health, 93,* 437–439.

Yee, S., Britton, L., & Thompson, W. (1988, April). *The effects of rock music on adolescents' behavior.* Paper presented at the annual meeting of the Western Psychological Association, Burlingame, CA.

Zhang, Y., Miller, L. E., & Harrison, K. (2008). The relationship between exposure to sexual music videos and young adults' sexual attitudes. *Journal of Broadcasting & Electronic Media, 52,* 368–386.

Zillmann, D., Aust, C. F., Hoffman, K. D., Love, C. C., Ordman, V. L., Pope, J. T., Seigler, P. D., & Gibson, R. J. (1995). Radical rap: Does it further ethnic division? *Basic and Applied Social Psychology, 16,* 1–25.

PART II

Forging the Media Environment for the Future: The Media Industry and Its Technology

Preliminary Comments From the Editors

We began this handbook by looking carefully at child viewers and their experience confronting the media as well as their reactions to this confrontation. We now shift our perspective to the other side of the box. Where does the programming come from? Why do people make programs? What goals do they have? What content do they emphasize? What technology do they use to reach children and youth? What responsibilities do they bear if they are seeking to communicate with the youth of society?

Chapter 24 by J. Cory Allen introduces us to the dynamic impulse of the electronic media industry, its economic structure. In the United States, with the development of radio in the late 1920s, the Communications Act of 1934 acknowledged that the airwaves belonged to the people, but it licensed them to commercial broadcast stations with the understanding that some public-interest responsibility would be reflected in programming in order to sustain a license. When television began

to spread around the world in the 1950s, most governments controlled the one or two networks, and great initial emphasis was placed (in contrast to the United States) on educational or other public informational programming. This situation has changed drastically; commercial purposes now prevail worldwide in the electronic media industry. Allen's chapter and Chapter 25 by Alison Alexander spell out in considerable detail the objectives, methods, and effectiveness of the booming commercial electronic media industry. Whereas Allen focuses more on the economic and organizational issues, Alexander reviews the type of children's programming and the content of the commercial media, including television and computer approaches. Chapter 26 by Michel Cohen introduces us to public broadcasting in the United States and exemplifies how educational and entertaining children's programs are developed and disseminated. Cohen provides a research-based but practically oriented examination of how formative research can play a role in helping writers and producers develop and evaluate educational and entertaining children's programs.

The emphasis on the mixed blessings of new technology is examined in Chapter 27 by Nancy Jennings and Ellen Wartella, who focus on the applications of television and computer use in formal educational settings. What can be gained by school use of these new technologies? But also, what risks are there of commercialization and of children being distracted from formal engagements with their teachers? They summarize available research and point to new needed research.

How can we take advantage of the extensive research reported in Part I and the suggestions for producers that have emerged from the studies of *Sesame Street, Mister Rogers, Barney & Friends, Blues Clues,* and *SuperWhy?* It is our hope that industry workers in the commercial and public sectors will do much more careful planning and evaluative research for the new shows or their computer disks and Internet applications.

CHAPTER 24

The Economic Structure of the Commercial Electronic Children's Media Industries

J. Cory Allen
WGBH Educational Foundation

Economic Structure

Any parent, advocate, or academic who wants to maximize the enlightening potential or curb the undesired effects of children's electronic media must first understand the economic forces and incentives that shape these industries. This chapter will analyze the economic structure of the electronic commercial media, paying special attention to the distinct economic characteristics of the children's media industries. The chapter will use a production-centered definition of children's media in its analysis of industries, thereby focusing on media produced primarily for children age 2 to 12.

A number of steps must be taken to describe the economics that operate in these industries. The economics of the media products must be explained, such as the costs, risks, and rewards that companies negotiate to produce goods such as movies and television programs. Equally important, however, are the economics of the media distribution systems, the companies that own the infrastructure and pay production companies for content to deliver to the audience. This chapter will identify the pertinent economic arrangements and regulations particular to each media industry, as well as three economic concepts that operate throughout all media industries: *windowing*, *licensing*, and *ownership*.

Windowing, the sale of video products through multiple media outlets, and *licensing*, the sale of characters and images to any commercial outlet, will be analyzed individually. *Ownership* will be discussed throughout the chapter, both in terms of companies owning the rights to content and companies owning the systems that distribute content. Once the economic framework and operations of the industries are established, the chapter will assess the success of participants in complying with industry regulations and explore economic changes in the industries that the new media technologies will catalyze.

Windowing

Economically, video products demonstrate the properties of both private and public goods. Television programs are a public good because the viewers who consume them do not diminish their availability to potential viewers. A movie is also a public good in that the number of viewers does not affect its value, but it is a private good due to commercial applications imposed by the movie industry. Viewers who buy a ticket to see a movie are paying for a seat in the theater; thus the number of seats available for sale imposes a limitation on the number of potential consumers. Nonetheless, since an unlimited number of customers can consume video products, their owners have strong incentives to sell these products to as many people and for as many prices as consumers are willing to pay. This practice of selling video products through many different channels over different points in time to maximize audiences through price discrimination is known as "windowing."

Windowing has become a fundamental economic mechanism for the media industries. For example, film producers speculate how many people will pay a premium price to see their movie in a theater, how many will pay less to rent it on DVD (or more to own it on DVD), and how many will wait to watch it air on television. Windowing also influences production decisions, as economists Owen and Wildman (1992) explain. "Programs that are windowed generally have larger budgets than programs that are not windowed, and among windowed programs, budgets increase with the number of windows in which the programs are released" (Owen & Wildman, 1992, p. 48). This point becomes increasingly important as large media companies acquire multiple channels of distribution. These companies can invest more money in their video products because they own outlets that guarantee the products the opportunity to generate additional revenue. Producers assess the competitive conditions in all potential windows for their product and often alter its content and composition to improve its chance of success in these additional markets. Lastly, windowing is especially important in the children's media industries because of audience regeneration. Children's media products have the opportunity to enjoy extended commercial success, since every newborn baby represents a potential customer completely unexposed to every children's movie, television show, or DVD.

A window that merits separate analysis is the window of international video markets. International markets represent enormous profit centers for American media companies, due in large part to the fact that the English-language market is by far the largest in both income and population among free-market countries. U.S. companies receive 75 cents of every dollar of international television trade. More importantly, the "Hollywood majors" (Warner Bros., Disney, Paramount, 20th Century Fox, Universal, Columbia, and MGM/UA), the studios that produce most of America's film and television programs, receive anywhere from 60 to 67 cents of that amount (Segrave, 1998, p. 1).

In 1995, Michael Eisner, then-chairman and CEO of the Hollywood major Disney, provided insight into America's multimedia dominance. "More than 200 million people a year watch a Disney film or home video; 395 million watch a Disney TV show every week; 212 million listen or dance to Disney music, records, tapes or compact discs; 270 million buy Disney-licensed merchandise in 50 countries." He continued, "such figures would mean little in themselves except that they are similar to figures of other American entertainment companies, demonstrating the universal appeal of American culture" (Gardels, 1995, p. 8). Eisner noted that American films comprise only 10% of films produced worldwide every year, yet they garner 65% of the world's box office receipts. He did not, however, mention the economic realities that underwrite this dominance. Media companies of most countries can acquire American productions at a fraction of what it would cost them to produce domestically. U.S. media companies enjoy the ability to sell their products internationally at low prices, since they have often already recouped their production costs through the U.S. windows.

Licensing

Licensing is a contractual arrangement that allows copyright holders to loan out their intellectual property for another company to use. In the children's media industries, companies can license the characters and images of their media products to companies for a fee. The fee is typically 5 to 15% of the wholesale cost of the item that uses the license. The owners of children's movies and television programs enjoy the greatest profit potential from licensing of any media industry segment or subdivision, because these two forms of media are the most popular among children. Companies seek licensing deals with children's movies because these can be marketed into big commercial events, and they pursue licensing deals with children's television programs, since they entertain a child audience as frequently as every day of the week.

The toy industry has benefited the most from the character licensing of children's movies and television. In 2008, character products accounted for $5.8 billion in toy sales—27% of the toy industry total (Mahoney, 2008). Other industries have also realized the rewards of character licensing. Snack food companies, fast food restaurants, and clothing manufacturers are just a few of the businesses that recognize that incorporating popular characters into their products will increase the likelihood that children will buy them. Licensing benefits both the program owners and the manufacturers in numerous ways. Manufacturers enhance the appeal of their product among children, program owners earn revenue without having to risk capital or produce the goods themselves, and both the programs and the products provide free advertising for each other. For example, Disney's *The Lion King* generated $1.5 billion in the sale of licensed products, and Disney earned hundreds of millions of dollars without incurring any risks or costs but simply by contracting out the movie's characters and images (Morgan, 1998, p. 6).

The chapter will later discuss how toy companies demonstrated the profit potential

of character licensing through developing their own programs based on their own toys and action figures. The lessons were not lost on the producers of children's programming; character licensing became as important a revenue stream as the income generated from television or film distribution. More importantly, developments in the ownership of children's media companies have combined these revenue streams. These few large companies own both the programs and the channels that distribute them; thus advertiser, distribution, and licensing revenue flow back to the same source.

Broadcast Television

Almost 99% of the households in the United States receive broadcast television. This penetration rate is achieved in part through more than 1,200 commercial television stations broadcasting to their local communities. The broadcast signals are free, both for the viewers who watch them and for the stations that transmit them. Stations broadcast television signals through the electromagnetic spectrum, a national resource that the Federal Communication Commission (FCC) manages. Congress has empowered the FCC to regulate television broadcasting by licensing the spectrum in the "public interest, convenience and necessity." Therefore, stations must obtain a license from the FCC in order to broadcast. This is a renewable 8-year contract that is given for free to stations that comply with FCC regulations. Stations that do not comply with the "public interest" obligations of the FCC can have their licenses revoked. Moreover, Congress or the FCC can amend these requirements. As such, these regulations constitute the price stations pay to broadcast. For instance, when the FCC fortified the 1990 Children's Television Act in 1997 by requiring broadcasters to air 3 hours of educational children's television per week, it imposed, in effect, a new price for broadcasters to conduct business. The Self-Controls section will analyze other events that forced television companies to rein in economic motives to circumvent additional regulations. (See Chapter 29 on industry standards and practices in this volume.)

Broadcast television is free for viewers because they form its primary product. The business of broadcast television is to produce audiences to sell to advertisers. Companies pay money to have their products and services advertised in commercials during television programs. The price these companies pay for commercial time depends on the size and demographics of the audience that a program attracts. One ratings agency, Nielsen Media Research, monitors the viewing activities of the American population and provides the industry-accepted statistics on audience sizes and their demographic characteristics (i.e., age and gender of viewers).

The television industry uses numerous terms to analyze and sell its audiences. Programs are measured in rating and share points. A rating point is a numerical representation of the audience size of a program, defined as a percentage of the total market population in the United States. A national household rating point represents 1% of all television households, or 1,145,000 households of the 114.5 million households that had televisions in 2009. A share is the percentage of people watching a program among only the households or persons using television during the time the program is airing. Advertisers price the commercial time they buy in terms of cost per thousand (CPMs): the price they are paying for the commercial to reach 1,000 households (or 1,000 of the target demographic). Advertisers also measure the commercial time they buy in gross ratings points (GRPs). They calculate this figure as *reach* (the percentage of the households or target audience that potentially views their commercial over a certain amount of time) multiplied by *frequency* (the number of times their commercial airs over this time; Vogel, 1998, p. 159). Advertisers want to reach their target audience as efficiently as possible; therefore, they are extremely concerned with the demographics of the audiences that programs attract.

Sources of Broadcast Programming: Network, Syndication, and Local Network

Of the 1,200 commercial stations in the United States, approximately 800 are affiliated with one of the Big Four networks:

ABC, NBC, CBS, or Fox. The Big Three networks (ABC, NBC, and CBS) conduct business on a network-affiliate model that has been used for decades. Fox, however, implemented a different affiliate arrangement when it formed in 1986. The Big Three supply programs to their affiliates for free, but the networks retain most of the commercial time during these programs to sell to national advertisers. Stations sell some time during network programs to local advertisers, but the main financial dividend that affiliate stations receive is an annual payment from the network known as compensation. This fee is paid to compensate stations for clearing their schedule to air network programs, thereby allowing the programs to reach a national audience. Indeed, the network programs of the Big Four are the only ones that regularly reach a mass audience of several million viewers.

Network Program Supply Conditions

The networks pass their programs to the affiliates free of charge, but they rarely pay full price for them in the first place. When networks reach an agreement with a production company to place its series in the network lineup, the network pays the production company a negotiated license fee for each individual episode that it puts on the air. However, the license provides the network with the freedom to air each episode a number of times. Thus the time-honored practice of rerunning shows is simply a method for networks to maximize their investment in each episode.

The license fee that program suppliers receive from the network generally amounts to half the production cost of each episode. Program suppliers accept this deficit arrangement because programs that receive network distribution qualify for two larger economic incentives. First, if the show becomes a hit in America and stays in the network's lineup for a number of years, the accumulated episodes can be syndicated and sold to stations across the country. The production company will receive a great deal of income from the cash and commercial time that stations will pay to air the show. Second, a show that achieves network status, even if it fails to become a syndicated hit, can usually be sold to international television markets.

The economic factors that dictate the supply of network programming are similar to those that operate in the production and distribution of movies. This is not coincidental, since the major Hollywood studios are the major suppliers of network programming. These companies have been the predominant programming providers throughout the history of network television since the FCC prevented the networks from owning the programs they aired (a rule that is no longer in effect) and because the drama and comedy formats that these studios offered found favor with audiences.

The movie companies can thrive in the deficit production scenario of network television because they have the capital to absorb insufficient license fees and even the production costs of programs that failed to make a network lineup. They can endure these losses because one hit show pays for many failures and because they have unmatched experience and support in international sales and distribution. These companies can even derive revenue from shows that failed in the United States from block-booking their sales in international markets. In this practice, which, incidentally, is illegal in the United States, the companies sell their programs in packages, leaving foreign purchasers who want to buy popular American programs with little choice but to pay for failed programs as well.

Broadcast Network Children's Television

The indirect nature of the business of television—the fact that viewers are its products and not its purchasers—presents numerous implications. Broadcasters program to the lowest common denominator, favoring content and formats that attract the largest or most valuable audiences. Commercial concerns dictate programming decisions far more than the public interest obligations that broadcasters are licensed to represent. They serve the public interest by serving that which interests the public. Viewers have no consumer sovereignty in regard to television; they cannot vote with their dollars to influence programming decisions as they can in direct-purchase markets such as movies and home videos. Many have found this economic

reality especially troubling in children's television. However, since broadcast television is a regulated industry, consumers have often taken their protests about the content or commercialism of children's television to the FCC. Some of these protests convinced Congress and the FCC to monitor, lobby, or impose new regulations upon the children's television industry.

Turow (1981) traced the economic development of network children's television. Many facets of the current state of network children's television have remained unchanged since their development in the early 1960s. In the '60s, the broadcast networks realized that certain advertisers, such as snack food and toy companies, only wanted to reach a child audience. The networks also discovered that a block of children's programs was a profitable use of the Saturday morning time slot, when audience sizes, especially for adults, were near their lowest. Furthermore, color TV was introduced in this decade, and production companies such as Hanna-Barbera developed limited animation techniques that provided inexpensive color cartoons to the networks.

After the landscape of Saturday morning television was set, the networks soon discovered that children's television functioned as enormous profit centers. Saturday morning television had features that let them make and save money. For years, they set aside more commercial time per hour during Saturday morning shows than they did during their prime-time blocks. Even after they curbed this practice, they still saved on programming expenses, rerunning children's shows at a far greater frequency than prime-time fare and easily retiring the cost of the license fee that they paid for each episode. The networks did not, however, profit from licensing deals since they did not own the programs they aired. The production companies benefited from the income provided through licensing revenues on merchandise and the networks mainly profited from advertising. Turow concluded that in network children's television from the 1950s through the 1970s, "the dominant forces have clearly been the networks and their advertisers . . . their basic goal . . . has remained the same, namely, to bring an audience of youngsters to commercials on a cost-efficient basis. Government and public pressures have not blunted this goal" (Turow, 1981, p. 120).

Network children's television remained unchanged for much of the 1980s and 1990s, but competition in children's programming increased dramatically. Syndicated children's cartoons began airing on weekday afternoons, and the cable networks emerged, offering children's programming throughout their hours of operation. Consequently, the child audience grew increasingly divided, no longer a gathering unique to Saturday morning. These developments led one network, NBC, to replace children's programs with teen-oriented sitcoms. As Fox grew into a major network, however, one of its primary goals was to establish a successful block of children's programming on both Saturday morning and weekday afternoons. The WB and UPN both imitated this focus on children's television to an extent as their networks began operating. By the late 1990s, the corporations owning broadcast networks also owned children's cable networks, and this fueled a great deal of cross-branding and program sharing between the broadcast and cable networks. Viacom owned CBS and Nick, and CBS aired Nickelodeon programs in a Nick-branded block. Similar synergy occurred between Disney-owned ABC and Disney Channel and Time Warner-owned Cartoon Network and Kids WB.

Another major change in the business of network children's television was not a result of competition but a directive from the FCC. The FCC introduced a requirement for stations to air 3 hours of educational children's television a week. In response, all of the networks agreed to supply their affiliates with FCC-friendly educational programming—an indication that the networks accepted this new price for doing business in children's television. By 2006, much of the aforementioned corporate synergy had ebbed, with CBS splitting from Viacom, Fox divesting almost all of its children's programming operations, and the WB and UPN merging. Some networks stopped providing affiliates with programming to satisfy the Three Hour Rule, leading those stations to seek programming from syndicators.

Syndication

Syndicated programs are supplied to a station through a syndicator on a market-by-market basis, whereas networks supply programs to their affiliate stations on a national basis. The syndicator acts as a temporary distributor, selling the programming to stations with the goal of securing time slots in enough communities to comprise a national audience that can be sold to advertisers. Stations and syndicators engage in a practice known as barter sales in which stations receive the syndicated programming without paying any actual money but instead give the syndicator an allotment of commercial time during each episode of the program. This allows the syndicator to sell the commercial time during the show to advertisers.

Children's Syndicated Television and the Program-Length Commercials

These developments in the syndicated programming market, combined with a politically appointed, industry-friendly FCC that developed a deregulatory stance in the early 1980s, led to fundamental changes in children's television. The toy industry took advantage of these conditions: creating and licensing their own characters, making toy products and television shows about them, and earning money from the licensing fees that other manufacturers paid to capitalize on their creations. This reversed the traditional relationship between toys and television in that the toy industry no longer waited for the television industry to provide shows that could be licensed into toys. Furthermore, these programs functioned as their own commercials, portraying characters, settings, and vehicles that the company also manufactured as toys. The "program-length commercials" that the toy companies produced for themselves proved to be both a financial and popular success. In 1983, 14 such programs were on the air, and after 2 years, their numbers swelled to 40, with even more toy programs in development (Engelhardt, 1987, p. 78). Many advertisers supported these programs for reasons of cost efficiency, since these shows provided access to audiences of specific demographic compositions, as opposed to Saturday-morning network programs that delivered large audiences of assorted ages and both genders.

Pecora (1998) provides case studies into how far toy manufacturers entered into the business of children's television. The toy and production companies behind *He-Man*, the first major product designed as both a toy and a television show, collaborated on the production and distribution of the show and even convinced stations to carry the show every weekday afternoon. From this point on, children's television was no longer limited to the weekends. A few years later, the companies that developed *Thundercats* offered stations profit participation in either the show's distribution rights or in the toy's sales. Both of these examples signify the lengths that the toy companies, program producers, and television stations would go to in order to spread the economic risks among each other and minimize the possibilities of failure.

The FCC's inaction played a major role in the developments of these conditions. In 1969, ABC aired *Hot Wheels*, a cartoon based on the toy cars. Responding to complaints that this show constituted nothing more than advertisements for the toys, the FCC ruled that the show was undoubtedly a commercial for the *Hot Wheels* toys, and, as such, it exceeded the permissible amount of time allowed for commercials. The Commission added, "We find this pattern disturbing . . . for {it} subordinates programming in the interest of the public to programming in the interest of salability" (Engelhardt, 1987, p. 75). ABC subsequently removed the show from its lineup. In 1984, the FCC removed its regulations on the amount of commercial minutes permitted during children's programs. The production of program-length commercials began, and the FCC validated their presence on the airwaves in rejecting a complaint based on the Commission's 1969 *Hot Wheels* ruling (Engelhardt, 1987, p. 76).

Toy-based programs remain within children's programming blocks, but not in the numbers witnessed in the 1980s Many independent stations joined networks in the 1990s, and all networks provided their affiliates the programs to satisfy the Three Hour Rule (though some have now stopped doing so).

Local

A station can also produce or buy programming to show to its local community. Locally produced programs inflict economic risks on stations because they incur the production costs. The reward for the risk, however, is that the stations keep all of the advertising revenue the programs generate, whereas they have to share the advertising revenue they earn from network and syndicated programming. Locally produced children's programs were once a mainstay for many stations, but over time, most abandoned this type of programming for network or syndicated fare that demanded less direct investment. Melody (1973) notes that many of these local shows shared a similar format, comprised of a local personality who introduced old theatrical cartoons and pitched advertisers' products.

Cable

Cable Systems

The fundamental economic difference between broadcast and cable television is that people pay for cable. Nine out of 10 U.S. households pay for television. Six in 10 pay for cable television, and 3 in 10 pay for alternate systems such as satellite television. In terms of economic structure, there is little distinction between cable and satellite television; they have similar arrangements with the subscribers they serve and the networks they transmit. Households subscribing to cable are served by their local cable system, the company that installs and maintains the coaxial cable that runs through the community and into subscribers' television sets. Cable systems sell packages of cable networks to their subscribers. The cable system receives these network signals from satellites and distributes their signals through the cable to subscribers. Since cable television is not transmitted through the spectrum, and because it is a subscription service, the cable industry receives far less regulatory scrutiny from the FCC. In fact, the very infrastructure necessary for cable service generally allows cable systems to operate as natural monopolies. The local governments that permit the installation of cable generally negotiate for one cable system to provide service because they do not want multiple companies laying miles of cable throughout the community. This monopoly status provides cable systems with a great deal of economic power. There are more than 9,000 cable systems in the United States, though large companies known as multi-system operators (MSOs) own many of them. In fact, the 25 largest MSOs provide cable service to approximately 90% of the nation's subscribers (Donald, 1999, p. 8). Many MSOs own part or all of many of the cable networks they transmit. Beginning in the 1990s, cable systems entered into the digital distribution business in marketing a bundle of services: phone, Internet, and video.

Cable Networks

Unlike the broadcast networks, cable networks enjoy two revenue streams: advertising and subscription. Cable networks sell advertising during their programs and often give part of this time to cable systems for them to sell locally. The main revenue stream for networks is subscription; all cable systems pay fees to the networks that are distributed to their subscribers. Payments are made on a monthly per-subscriber basis, and the fee is arranged between the cable network and the cable system. Thus, more popular cable networks generally negotiate higher fees, such as a few dollars per subscriber, than the less popular ones, perhaps a few cents per subscriber. Most cable systems offer premium networks, such as HBO and Showtime, and these networks generally do not participate in the advertising revenue stream but do charge a great deal more for subscriptions to the channel. Program supply conditions to cable networks differ in a number of ways. Cable networks cannot compete with the broadcast networks in the price they offer for license fees due to smaller audiences. In fact, reruns of network programs comprise a significant portion of the programming of cable networks. Additionally, just as many MSOs own the cable networks they distribute, many cable networks own the programming they air.

Children's Cable Television

The biggest economic benefit cable networks offer to advertisers in comparison to broadcast network is cost-efficient advertising. The children's cable industry has grown because children's networks provide advertisers with excellent reach into their target audiences. Nickelodeon, the first children's cable network, began as a commercial-free network. Cable systems were nonetheless eager to include the network in their service as a "loss leader" to encourage subscribers. The systems realized that parents would pay for cable in part because it offered a quality channel for children to watch. As Nickelodeon grew in popularity, it quickly switched to selling commercial time. The Disney Channel launched in 1983 as a premium channel distributed only to subscribers who paid an additional fee. In the late 1990s, the channel migrated to the basic package that many cable systems offer in order to increase its presence in the child audience. The Cartoon Network and the Fox Family Channel entered the children's cable market in the 1990s. Fox Family Worldwide (the children's media company formed through a spin-off from parent company News Corporation and a merger with the Saban Entertainment production company) bought the Family Channel for $1.9 billion and changed it to Fox Family Channel. This price was essentially a distribution fee for the new children's cable network to gain immediate penetration into the 69 million homes that received the Family Channel. In 2001, Disney paid $2.9 billion for the channel and the Saban Entertainment production company and rebranded the channel ABC Family. Nickelodeon, Disney, and Cartoon Network produce or otherwise own a great deal of the content they deliver. The companies therefore realize profits not just through production and distribution but also through windowing and licensing.

Digital Cable

In the late 1990s, cable systems began offering digital cable, which provided many more channels and, in many cases, new services like video on demand and digital video recorders (DVRs). By 2010, over 4 in 10 U.S. households subscribed to digital cable. Digital cable networks received much less per-subscriber money from cable systems than basic cable networks. Some receive no subscriber money at all. Advertising is still available as a revenue source for digital networks. Many digital networks are owned by companies that also own basic cable networks, and in such situations, the company can bundle the networks to use as leverage in negotiating preferable subscriber fees and distribution with cable systems and in selling these additional audiences to advertisers. The digital networks can often serve as additional television windows for programs that originate on the basic cable network.

The children's cable networks were quick to extend their presence into the digital cable market. Disney launched Toon Disney (later reformatted into boys' network Disney XD) and Cartoon Network launched Boomerang, which airs an extensive library of older cartoons. Nickelodeon launched several digital networks, including Nicktoons, Nickelodeon Games and Sports, Noggin, and The N (the latter two rebranded Nick Jr. and Teen Nick). Just as the syndicated programming environment of the 1980s allowed for the toy-based program, the digital cable environment has given rise to the first toy-based network. In 2009, the toy company Hasbro paid $300 million for half of Discovery Kids, and the network will be rebranded The Hub.

Video on Demand

Video on demand is a feature cable systems provide that allows subscribers to select programs to view instantly. Cable networks and production companies can earn money from video on demand in a number of ways: from cable subscriber fees, from advertising accompanying the content, or from a direct fee they may charge for consumers to view the content. Comcast, the nation's largest MSO, reports that the kids' section is the most-viewed area in its On Demand system. In 2009, its customers ordered 25 million hours of children's content a month, and between 2005 and 2010, the views of On Demand children's shows increased almost 400% (Atkinson, 2010). The popularity of video-on-demand children's content is reminiscent of Nickelodeon's value to both cable systems and subscribers when

it launched as the first cable network just for children.

Movies

The movie industry is an oligopoly, since a handful of companies dominate the market. In 1998, movies generated $6.9 billion in ticket sales, and 90% of this box office total went to seven movie companies (Graves, 1999, p. 5). Six of these seven were among the aforementioned Hollywood majors, which also dominate the trade of international television. This figure is not atypical; the Hollywood majors generally account for at least 80% of the box office revenues. The Hollywood majors make most of their profit in the movie industry as the distributors of films. They are the companies that finance the production of films, arrange for them to be released into theaters throughout the country, and underwrite the advertising and promotional campaigns that accompany their release. Distributors are entitled to most of the revenue a film generates, regardless of whether the film is produced by the distributor's studio or a separate production company. Distributors receive the rental fee theater owners pay to show a film, which typically amounts to more than half of the ticket money the theater earned from the movie. Lastly, distributors often retain the rights to distribute the film into other video markets, such as home video and television.

The multiple rewards of distribution have been explained, but this business also involves a great number of risks. Most movies fail to earn back the money they cost to make. Movie companies therefore depend on a few hit films to pay for the majority of their failures. This business condition presents a tremendous barrier to entry. Competitive companies need vast sums of capital to produce a number of films in order to diversify their risks and increase the potential that a few of their films will be profitable. Moreover, the major movie distributors have long-standing working relationships with theater chains and companies. Such a track record can only be developed when a company proves it can consistently create, fund, and distribute films that people will pay to see.

Children's Movies

The market for children's movies contains additional barriers to entry because of licensing. For example, in Disney's *The Lion King* (McCarthy & Warner, 1994) and Viacom's *Rugrats* (Morgan, 1998), sizable portions of each company's production costs were recovered through licensing agreements arranged with companies before the films were even released. New companies in the children's film industry will probably not enjoy licensing fees subsidizing their films to such an extent, since they do not have the track record of success in appealing to children and providing licensed content that sells. This disadvantage can limit the production quality of their films, such as special effects and computer animation, which are major components of box office success.

Home Video

The home video market best exemplifies the potential for economic rewards in windowing a video product. Whereas people spent $7 billion to see movies in theaters in 1998, they spent more than $9 billion to rent them and $8 billion to buy them on videocassette or videodisc (Graves, 1999, p. 7). By 2006, the amount spent on home video purchases had doubled to $16.3 billion, and these purchases were estimated to account for up to 70% of a movie's profit (Grover, 2009). The introduction of the digital videodisc (DVD) format in 1997 fueled this growth. Within 10 years, 81% of homes owned a DVD player, surpassing the percentage of homes owning VCRs. Before the introduction of the DVD, the rental window was a major source of revenue for video products, except for children's videos—these had always been priced to sell directly to consumers. In the pre–DVD era, children's videos comprised an estimated 80% of the home videos sold directly to consumers (McCormick, 1996). Pecora (1998) explains that "children are a unique market for the industry," in that children's videos are purchased rather than rented, "because unlike adults, children are content to view a cassette multiple times—seldom tiring of a favorite story" (Pecora, 1998, p. 125).

The future of the DVD window is a major industry concern. Sales of DVDs have fallen since the peak in 2006, and it is not known how much of the decline is due to the global economic recession and how much is due to purchases made via new-media distribution systems. If new-media purchases are displacing DVD purchases, the economic impact is substantial, since producers realize less profit from these new-media windows than from the DVD window. According to an industry estimate, movie studios earn $10 for a DVD sold at retail but $7 for the same movie purchased on iTunes and only $3.50 when someone views it on demand via a cable system (Grover, 2009).

In 2010, movie studios made major adjustments to the DVD retail window. Several created an exclusive 28-day window in which a movie could be purchased but not rented. Disney strained its relationship with theater owners by shortening the time between the theatrical and home video release of *Alice in Wonderland* from 4 months to 3.

Internet

The Internet is a revolutionary medium because of a number of its characteristics. First, it can perform the functions of all the electronic media that preceded it. The Internet can transmit songs like a radio station or videos like a television network. Second, all content it distributes is digital, so it can be consumed on many platforms, such as television, computers, and mobile devices. Third, the barriers to entry for digital distribution are very low. Before the Internet, video content had to be transmitted through expensive infrastructures like broadcast stations or cable systems. Digital distribution via the Internet relies on far less expensive assets such as servers to host a website and the bandwidth required to serve visitors. Additionally, websites like YouTube allow any producer, professional or amateur, to upload video content for free distribution.

Content providers using digital distribution have a number of options regarding how to monetize their content. They can provide their content for free and sell the audience to advertisers, as broadcast networks do. They can charge a subscription fee for access to their content, as cable networks do. They can sell their content directly to consumers, as does the home video market. Additionally, a content provider can implement each of these arrangements and monetize the content across three windows, all within the Internet.

While the economic structure sounds straightforward, the question of how media companies can profit from the Internet remains unanswered for many. The digital distribution of content via the Internet has disrupted many existing media industries. The music industry faced many immediate challenges. Consumers began purchasing MP3s of individual songs instead of more expensive compact discs of multiple songs. Apple's iTunes became a major distributor of music and demanded a fee for all of the songs it sold. Most importantly, piracy of digital music exploded, costing companies a great deal of potential revenue. The print media also experienced disruptions. Newspapers and magazines could not sell their digital advertisements at as a high a price as their print advertisements. Furthermore, the price they could charge for print advertisements declined with subscription levels, as many of their subscribers switched from paying for print to reading online for free.

The video industries have had more time to adapt to digital distribution and extend their presence into the Web. This is especially true for the children's cable networks. Cartoon Network, Nickelodeon, and Disney all boast of extremely popular branded websites. These companies have also purchased popular children's websites. In 2005, Nickelodeon's parent company, Viacom, purchased virtual pet site Neopets for $160 million, and in 2007, Disney purchased the children's online community site Club Penguin for $350 million. Websites, as well as other digital platforms, offer tremendous economic opportunities for the networks. Nickelodeon reported that of its total advertising revenue in 2007 (approximately a billion dollars), one third was from digital platforms (Hampp, 2008).

As the importance of digital media grows for companies, it is important to note how companies characterize their relationship with the Web and digital distribution. In 1998, when Fox Kids was still a major presence, its parent company, News Corporation, stated in its Annual Report: "we are building an unrivaled platform but it is the performance that counts. Distribution for us is merely a means to an end—to ensure that we can market our real product—and that product is content" (News Corporation, 1998, p. 1). Over a decade later, Disney CEO Robert Iger expressed the same sentiment: "Our number one strategic priority is creating great content. And number two is the application of technology to improve our production's distribution" (Grover, 2006). Content is still king for these companies. Digital platforms are mainly new windows to market their content, be it on Web pages, mobile phones, or other digital devices.

Self-Controls

In his book *Children's Television*, Cy Schneider, a veteran children's advertising executive, stressed that "commercial television, even for children, is just another business," and in light of this fact, he argued, "is it fair to ask the television industry to be different from other businesses?" (Schneider, 1987, p. 5). This statement reveals a great deal about the attitude and behavior of companies in the children's media industries—economics and market competition guide their conduct until this course runs them into regulatory problems. *Self-control* is the term that describes the ability of these companies to maintain behavior in compliance with industry regulations. For instance, broadcasters failed to exercise appropriate self-control in serving the educational needs of children, as mandated by the 1990 Children's Television Act, so the FCC imposed the Three Hour Rule. Companies exercised self-control more successfully in complying with the advertising standards they established in the Children's Advertising Review Unit (CARU) and in providing labeling systems for their programs. Nonetheless, both cases forced companies to negotiate their business practices with regulatory and public policy pressures.

Children's Advertising Review Unit (CARU)

The National Advertising Division of the Council of Better Business Bureaus created CARU in 1974 during a time when the FCC had issued an unfavorable report on the state of children's television. Furthermore, the

Federal Trade Commission (FTC) was considering acting on the petitions of consumer groups to limit children's advertising on television and to prohibit all types of advertising to children under 8. With these public policy pressures, industry participants realized they needed to address these issues themselves before regulations altered business conditions. CARU established six basic principles for advertising to children, including some that reiterated FCC or FTC policies on deceptive advertising. CARU had the authority to respond to complaints or initiate its own investigation into possible violations, yet it was not endowed with enforcement powers other than the ability to refer violators to the FCC or FTC. Nonetheless, industry compliance with the CARU guidelines has been extremely high except for in its policies concerning the Internet. For the television industry, however, this compliance has prevented increased protests against advertising to children and preserved the idea that such advertising is a legitimate social and economic activity (See Kunkel & Wilcox, Chapter 28 in this volume).

Privacy

In 1997, CARU introduced guidelines for interactive electronic media that combined its existing rules of advertising to children with rules specifically addressing online sales and the collection of data from children. The FTC assessed the compliance with these guidelines and concluded that more than half of the children's websites violated rules on data collection. Sites were collecting information from children without parental consent, and some companies sold this data to third parties. Campbell (1999) reasoned that this low level of compliance as compared to that of advertisers on children's television was because "the number of companies offering Web sites to children, while including these same advertisers, appears to be much larger and diverse" (Campbell, 1999, p. 744). Regardless, the lack of self-control resulted in the implementation of the Children's Online Privacy Protection Act (COPPA) in 1998. The law focuses on regulations for commercial websites that collect personal information from children under 13. These sites must obtain prior parental consent before collecting information, the information that they request must be limited

in scope, and they must adhere to parental requests to review information collected about their child or to cease the collection and use of this information altogether. In 2001, the Federal Trade Commission approved CARU's self-regulatory program as a "safe harbor" program for COPPA, meaning that compliance with CARU guidelines would also mean compliance with COPPA and therefore keep program participants free from FTC scrutiny. The FTC designated CARU's program as safe harbor because its guidelines mirrored COPPA rules and it provided independent mechanisms to encourage and evaluate compliance (Federal Trade Commission, 2001).

Program Labels

The television industry agreed to design a ratings system for programs that would work in coordination with the V-chip, a device installed in television sets that offers parents more power in shielding their children from programs that they considered harmful. The television industry, however, designed a ratings system that addressed its own concerns about preserving advertisers instead of one that empowered and informed parents. The system provided only age recommendations for programs and not indicators of their content. Children's programs received one of two labels: "TV-Y: all children" and "TV-Y7: aimed at older children." The television industry changed the system shortly after its debut, in January 1997, in response to protest that it must contain content labels and out of fear that the FCC would design one for them. The new system provided labels such as V for violent content, S for sexual content, L for foul language, D for sexual innuendo, and FV for the fantasy violence in children's shows.

Economic Implications of New Media Technologies

Ownership

Despite the disruptive power of digital distribution, ownership is still a key factor in shaping the children's media industries. In many ways, the children's media industries remain in a period of economic concentration that began in the 1990s. In the last decade, four companies—Disney, Time Warner, News Corporation, and Viacom—own numerous forms of production and distribution systems for children's media (Schmuckler, 1997). These four corporations each owned a major Hollywood distributor, a broadcast network, and at least one children's cable network. Additionally, they all owned international content and distribution operations. By the early 2000s, concentration increased, with News Corporation selling off most of its children's media assets to Disney. Further into the decade, however, the presence of these corporations on broadcast networks declined, and their presence on digital cable networks expanded.

These corporations have all leveraged their children's brands into popular websites, and they have spent hundreds of millions of dollars acquiring popular children's websites. They also exercise tremendous economic power in determining how video content will be distributed digitally. Consider this quote from media analyst Craig Moffett: "Five companies—Time Warner, Disney, Viacom-CBS, Comcast–NBC Universal, Fox—control 85 percent of video viewing hours in America. At the end of the day this train ain't going anywhere that those five companies don't agree to" (Wolff, 2010). These corporations have taken some major steps to shape the digital distribution of video content. In 2007, Viacom sought to stop unauthorized distribution of its content—consumers uploading its video content to YouTube—by filing a $1 billion copyright lawsuit against Google, YouTube's parent company. Three of the five major corporations mentioned above—Fox, NBC-Universal, and Disney—own Hulu, a website in which they offer a great deal of their video content for online viewing. This popular site was free to viewers for its first 2 years of operation, but now offers the additional option of a monthly subscription for access to some of its content.

Free or Pay?

As the children's media industries adapt to digital distribution, a key concern from the consumer perspective is how much content remains free and how much comes at a cost? The same concern applies to the quality of the content as well. Can distribution systems that

are effectively free for consumers, like broadcast television and ad-supported websites, remain economically viable windows for children's content? Or will the economic structure thrive around closed systems, such as cable television and download-to-own services like Apple's iTunes and App Store, in which consumers pay a direct cost? The latter option, while perhaps an extreme scenario, suggests a society of digital haves and have-nots, segregated by spending power. The former option is more likely, since there should still be incentive for companies to distribute digital content across many windows and at a range of prices. That said, if the advertising-supported model cannot function as profitably as it did in the 20th century, new indirect costs might be applied to consumers, and these might push against the self-controls that the industry currently maintains in its interactions with the child audience.

Conclusion

In the 20th century, Hollywood production companies shaped the children's commercial electronic media industries. They had the financial, technological, and creative assets to produce expensive content and extract revenue from it across film, television, and home video markets domestically and internationally. Many companies experienced great financial success in these industries. However, digital distribution has disrupted how these industries produce, distribute, and monetize content. The economic structure of these industries in the 21st century remains uncertain. The Hollywood production companies have not yet been able to generate as much money from the new-media markets as they have from the old-media markets. New participants, unburdened by expensive 20th century distribution and production systems, might emerge as the most successful companies in the industries.

But as business models for production and distribution change, so may the costs demanded of the consumers. Consumers benefited in the 20th century structure since they received much of the content for "free," paying the indirect cost of receiving advertisements with the content. The new structure may ultimately demand more direct payments from consumers.

Another challenge is to maintain the industry self-controls and policies through these structural changes. New ways of doing business need not prevent the obligation to provide children a minimum of educational programming or the assurance that their privacy will be protected online.

References

Atkinson, C. (2010, March 1). Overcrowding a problem for kids. *Broadcasting & Cable*. Retrieved at the Broadcasting & Cable website on April 26, 2010, at http://www.broadcastingcable.com/article/449399-Overcrowding_A_Problem_For_Kids.php.

Campbell, A. (1999, May). Self-regulation and the media. *Federal Communications Law Journal, 51,* 711–772.

Donald, W. (1999, July 8). Broadcasting & cable. *Standard & Poor's Industry Surveys, 167*(27), 1–27.

Engelhardt, T. (1987). The Shortcake strategy. In T. Gitlin (Ed.), *Watching television*. New York: Pantheon Press.

Federal Trade Commission. (2001, January 26). Letter to children's advertising review unit (BBB) approving CARU program. Retrieved April 26, 2010, from http://www.ftc.gov/os/2001/02/caruletter.pdf.

Gardels, N. (1995). Planetized entertainment. *New Perspectives Quarterly, 12*(4), 8–10.

Graves, T. (1999, May 20). Movies and home entertainment. *Standard & Poor's Industry Surveys, 166* (20), 1–31.

Grover, R. (2006, February 21). Disney builds a better mousetrap. *BusinessWeek*. Retrieved from the BusinessWeek website on April 26, 2010, at http://www.businessweek.com/bwdaily/dnflash/feb2006/nf20060221_3337_db011.htm.

Grover, R. (2009, February 4). Hollywood DVD sales: Are the good times gone? *BusinessWeek*. Retrieved from BusinessWeek's website on April 26, 2010, at http://www.businessweek.com/technology/content/feb2009/tc2009024_458580.htm.

Hampp, A. (2008, February 25). Nickelodeon sees digital dollars surge on "multi-splatform" approach. *Advertising Age*. Retrieved from the *Advertising Age* website on April 26, 2010, at http://adage.com/kidsupfront2008/article?article_id=125295.

Mahoney, S. (2008, June 11). *What a character! Licensing revenues holding their own*. Retrieved April 26, 2010, from MediaPost website: http://www.mediapost.com/publications/index.cfm?fa=Articles.showArticle&art_aid=84392.

McCarthy, M., & Warner, F. (1994, March 21). Mane attraction: Marketers, Disney put $100 million on nose of Lion King. *Brandweek*, 35(12), 1–2.

McCormick, M. (1996, December 28). News-filled year in children's media; Disney dominates audio and video. *Billboard, 108*(52), 57–59.

Melody, W. (1973). *Children's television: The economics of exploitation*. New Haven, CT: Yale University Press.

Morgan, R. (1998, December 21). TV toys are making big noise. *Variety, 373*, 6.

News Corporation. (1998). *1998 Annual report*. New York: Author.

Owen, B., & Wildman, S. (1992). *Video economics*. Cambridge, MA: Harvard University Press.

Pecora, N. (1998). *The business of children's entertainment*. New York: The Guilford Press.

Schmuckler, E. (1997, January 27). A small world after all: The children's TV business now in the hands of only four companies. *Mediaweek, 7*(4), 30–36.

Schneider, C. (1987). *Children's television: The art, the business and how it works*. Lincolnwood, IL: NTC Business Books.

Segrave, K. (1998). American television abroad: Hollywood's attempt to dominate world television. Jefferson, NC: McFarland & Company, Inc.

Turow, J. (1981). *Entertainment, education and the hard sell*. New York: Praeger.

Vogel, H. (1998). *Entertainment industry economics: A guide for financial analysis* (4th ed.). New York: Cambridge University Press.

Wolff, M. (2010, March). Ringside at the Web fight. *Vanity Fair*. Retrieved from the Vanity Fair website on April 26, 2010, at http://www.vanityfair.com/culture/features/2010/03/wolff-201003?currentPage=2.

CHAPTER 25

The Children's Television Business

Programming and Structure

ALISON ALEXANDER
University of Georgia

With more than 98% of American homes having television and 90% with cable/satellite, the television business is clearly big business. More than 75% of television stations are commercial, and most of them are network affiliates, which assures them a steady stream of network programs, an identified brand, and a high profile with advertisers and viewers. Yet the "Big Four," ABC, CBS, NBC, and Fox, which once dominated television viewing, now share television time with other broadcast and cable networks. Viewing of cable services now accounts for more than half of U.S. viewing. Fueling these developments are the business synergies among production, distribution, cable, and broadcast business units that support media giants such as Time Warner, Walt Disney, Viacom, News Corporation, and NBCUniversal.

Within this larger picture, children's television is a very small piece of the pie. *Children's television* refers to programs targeted primarily to children and designed to attract a majority of viewers who are children. Children's television is only a small part of the total viewing of television by children. Shows broadcast between 8:00 and 9:00 PM have huge child and teen audiences. A popular prime-time situation comedy may attract many more child viewers than a "children's program" does despite the fact that it is not targeted primarily to children, and children are not a majority of the audience. As a result, most of the highest-rated programs for children 5 to 17 are prime-time programs.

In industry parlance, children are divided into three major age groups: 2 to 5 years old, 6 to 11, and 12 to 17, although teens are frequently discussed separately from the younger age groups. The increasingly popular "tween" market is 9 to 14. Typically, when the industry talks about children's television, it is referring to the 2-to-11 age group. These are important markets for advertisers and represent a substantial percentage of the total 2+ population of persons in U.S. television households.

517

The 2- to 11-year age range is estimated at more than 40 million children or 14% of the 2+ total; teens are estimated at close to 25 million and about 8% of the 2+ population (Marketers Guide, 2008). In focusing on the business of children's television, this chapter does not address public television, video games, the Internet, and other aspects of children's media environment that are reviewed in other chapters. In this chapter, the operation of children's television is explored. The goals are (a) to identify trends in programming and exposure to children's programs; (b) to trace the structure of children's television broadcast and cable; (c) to identify patterns of program development, production, and promotion; and (d) to identify financial patterns such as trends in profit and loss and sources of revenue.

Analyzing Trends in Programming and Exposure for Children

Early children's shows were designed to sell TV sets by enhancing television's appeal to the entire family. Because most households in the 1950s had only one television set, programs appealing to children as well as adults were seen as a way of attracting families. By 1951, the networks' schedules included up to 27 hours of children's programs. Like much of television programming, offerings for children continued radio's tradition of action-adventure themes and a pattern of later-afternoon and evening broadcasts. By the decade's end, children's programs had completed the migration from prime time to less valuable morning, early afternoon, or Saturday-morning hours.

During the 1960s, cartoons became synonymous with children's television. Reduced costs resulting from limited-action animation techniques and the clear appeal of cartoons to children transformed scheduling, and the institutionalization of the Saturday-morning cartoon became complete—an unexpectedly lucrative time slot for the networks. The 1970s continued the Saturday animation trend with 60- or 90-minute shows that incorporated a number of segments under umbrella labels such as *The New Super Friends Hour*

or *Scooby Laff-a-Lympics*. These extended shows were designed to increase audience flow across the entire morning.

The 1980s brought a revolution to broadcast, as cable and VCR penetration began to erode the network audience and international coventures began to change the production process. Cartoons remained the standard children's fare, but cable networks such as Nickelodeon that targeted children began to experiment with different types of programming for children. For the cabled home, access to children's programming increased dramatically over the 1980s and 1990s.

Based on the rationale that other outlets were adequately serving the child audience and that diversity of programming for the child was greater than ever before, many of the broadcast networks were getting out of the children's television business as the 1990s began. But with the legislative requirement of the 1990 Children's Television Act (CTA) as interpreted by the Federal Communications Commission (FCC) for broadcast stations, the major networks now provide their affiliates with the required 3 hours of educational/informational (E/I) programming a week. Currently, ABC's linkage with parent Disney has paid off on Saturday morning, with a 3-hour lineup of shows from Disney-owned studios. CBS has a Saturday-morning lineup of shows produced by Cookie Jar Entertainment and NBC's programming is produced by QUBO. FOX no longer provides a Saturday-morning block of children's programming to its affiliates. CW, a young broadcast network formed by the merger of UPN and WB in 2006, is offering a 4-hour Saturday morning lineup produced by 4Kids Entertainment.

But the biggest news of the 1980s and 1990s was that the networks were no longer the major player in children's television. Those decades saw a dramatic shift in children's viewing patterns, where children's viewing went from 98% broadcast to 15% with the advent of cable with its targeted children's programs and networks (Petrozzello, 1998). The shift to cable has fragmented the children's television market. In the United States, child-oriented fare accounts for more than 1,000 hours of airtime a week on network and cable channels (Jackson, 1999), and viewing is widely distributed across that large set of offerings. Nickelodeon garners more than 60% of child viewing, followed by the Cartoon Network and the Disney Channel. Newcomers Disney DX and the Hub may further fragment the child cable audience. While these figures can change dramatically with program popularity, the overall tendency to small network and large cable channel viewership seems stable. These are percentages of total viewing and are influenced by the more extensive children's offerings on cable, but ratings of individual dayparts also show the larger audiences attracted by the cable networks. Saturday-morning average ratings for major network children's shows ran between 1.2 and 1.4 in the four quarters of 2006 (*Marketer's Guide*, 2008). These ratings indicate that, of the slightly more than 112 million television households, about 1.5 million households are watching. Recent Saturday-morning programming on the broadcast networks showed average ratings of children's programming ranging from .2 to .6, with cable children's channels ranging from .8 to 4.6 (Turner, June 11, 2010).

For many years, industry and academic researchers have been examining children's television. Much of the industry research on children's programming is in the hands of the network research departments. Most networks' research departments work to identify appealing programs and to provide information to advertisers.

Extensive academic research looks at television programming and children, as is seen in this volume. However, little research examines the specific linkages between individual commercial broadcast programs and their consequences. As researchers begin to demonstrate the linkage between E/I programming and child viewers, such studies should begin to enter the research arena.

Analyzing Industry Structure

The broadcast television business is a complex industry. For most viewers, their linkage with this industry is through their viewing of the local network affiliates in their market. Local affiliates run the shows provided by the networks. Networks profit from affiliate viewers, who cumulatively provide the national mass audience that advertisers desire. In return, the networks provide children's programming for the affiliates with some advertising space available for local sales; this programming also fulfills the regulatory requirement for broadcast stations. In the past, affiliates were paid by the networks to exhibit their programming, a procedure called "compensation." Compensation has almost entirely vanished, and some networks are floating the idea of charging affiliates for their programming. Whatever the conflict over compensation, networks and stations are supported primarily by advertising revenue. Local children's ads are not particularly lucrative because of the relatively small audience. Costs for a Saturday-morning ad in many markets may be only a few hundred dollars and, in smaller markets, could be significantly less than $100. At the local affiliate level, the program director generally oversees children's programming in addition to managing all station production, community relations, and promotions. There is a long history of affiliates providing local origination children's programs. Most markets offer a high school "quiz bowl." Many do local public affairs specials targeted to older children, dealing with social issues such as drugs, violence, safe driving, smoking, or racism. Some provide magazine-format shows that can be wide ranging in content: Some are news programs, many focus on local events, and others have an adventure focus. Many of these include children on air or even as writers, producers, and directors.

Networks provide the programs that fill much of the affiliate schedule: prime time, network news, soaps, sports, quiz shows, talk shows, and children's shows. Vice presidents in charge of daytime or vice presidents for children's programs manage the network scheduling of children's programming. Promotion departments, research departments, and community-relations departments become involved. In the current regulatory environment, networks, except Fox, are providing the required 3 hours of educational and informational programming. Their goals are to meet the regulation, to be able to point with pride to their program content, and to meet the competition within their time slot. With the increased competition from smaller networks and cable, these programmers realize that regaining large numbers is unlikely. Thus, for most local stations, children's programming has moved from being seen as a modest profit center to a public service obligation.

This simplified picture of local/network affiliate stations obscures larger issues of ownership. All networks possess a certain number of owned and operated (O & O) stations, which form powerful station groups. Ion, Trinity, and Univision are companies that own a number of stations. These groups can exert considerable pressure on the networks and act in concert in the purchase of nonnetwork syndicated fare.

Cable and satellite profit from a dual revenue stream in which advertising and subscriber fees are available. Cable involves distributing a number of channels from a central location to subscribers in a community through a network of coaxial or fiber cable. Satellite television is delivered by means of a communications satellite and received by a satellite dish and set-top box. For convenience, I will refer throughout the chapter to both systems as *cable*. Cable channels generally fall into four categories: local broadcast stations, superstations, basic cable services, and premium channels. Cost is based on the package chosen and may include DVR, Internet, and telephone access. Cable systems pay a per-subscriber carriage fee for the most popular channels. The most successful children's cable channels are Nickelodeon, Cartoon Network, and Disney—the last is the only nonadvertising-supported channel of the three. Disney reportedly costs $.86 per subscriber, Nickelodeon $.44, and Cartoon Network $.17 ("Growing Nickelodeon," 2010). Both cable systems and cable channels are valuable properties. Many corporations are interested in owning the fiber link to the home for the delivery of multimedia services. Similarly, the horizontal integration of production has motivated the acquisition of cable programming entities by larger entertainment industry organizations. In a twist on usual patterns of acquisition, in 2009 Comcast, the largest cable company in the United States, inked an agreement to acquire NBC Universal (Stelter, Arango, Carr, & Carter, December 7, 2009). Clearly, cable and broadcast have substantially different business models. Ironically, this difference is invisible to the viewing audience. For children and many adults, the difference between cable and broadcast is irrelevant to their viewing.

Business Models for Children's Television: Patterns of Program Development, Distribution, and Promotion

Structuring Program Supply, Development, and Production

There are three basic ways in which a TV station can acquire programs: network, syndication, and local origination. As indicated previously, *network programming* refers to original programming funded by, produced by or for, and distributed by the networks. *Syndication* refers to TV programming sold by distribution companies to local TV stations (and cable services). *Local origination* refers to programs produced by local TV stations for viewers in their own communities.

The network programming process seems simple, but the work of program producers and distributors quickly becomes very complex. Some now-outdated rules shaped the original programming process. Under the financial interest and syndication rules (known as fin-syn), the Federal Communications Commission (FCC) rules limited network participation in the ownership of programs produced for them and in the subsequent syndication. Rather than buying shows outright or producing their own, networks paid license fees to production companies. After the network run, the shows were sold into syndication, with the networks barred from reaping any financial reward. Now the fin-syn rules have been abandoned, allowing networks to own their own shows and to sell them in syndication. Nonetheless, many programming practices that evolved under fin-syn remain.

The networks are now actively engaged in producing their own programs, as witnessed by the plethora of reality and game shows on prime time. Now it is much easier for media conglomerates to take advantage of horizontal and vertical integration wherein they own both movie and television production companies as well as cable and broadcast outlets (networks and stations).

A cable channel or network has a simpler method of acquisition. It can develop shows that are produced within its own company or it can purchase programming from independent studios, large and small. Thus, programming can be in the form of new shows owned and produced by the parent corporation, new shows licensed from independent studios, joint-venture programming in which it was part of the funding and development team, programs repurposed from the parent corporation such as Disney Channel programs moving to ABCKids, and programming of older shows from syndication.

The production of children's programming is dominated by major studios, a few independents, and, increasingly, international producers and coproductions. Almost all of the major television studios are well known. Some of the major media giants include Time Warner, which owns children's entertainment firms such as Warner Brothers, Warner Brothers Animation, and Turner Entertainment, which owns Cartoon Network; Walt Disney, which owns Walt Disney Studios, Disney Animation, and Pixar as well as ABC; Viacom, which owns Paramount, Nickelodeon, and MTV; News Corporation, which owns Fox Animation, 20th Century Fox, the Fox network, and multiple cable channels; and General Electric/Comcast, which own NBC Universal, which owns NBC Entertainment, as well as cable channels such as Bravo and AMC. There are hundreds of independent production firms including 4Kids, Cookie Jar, Discovery, Marvel, Nelvana, Scholastic, and Sesame Workshop, to name a few. There are many more that are less well known. Ironically, ongoing viable independents are hard to identify because, despite their number, a larger corporation may quickly acquire the successful ones; the others tend to disappear. To identify the current state of this shifting mass, one must look for the names at the ends of children's programming. You will see that most are of the form "Produced by XXX (a firm you have never heard of) and YYY (a big name)." This represents the pattern of

the industry. Small firms pitch ideas to networks or production companies and exchange some control over the production process for funding to produce their program content and production credit. Such a pattern of "joint venturing" is now widely recognized as an efficient organizational form for maximizing the synergy from combining the "comparative advantages" of large firms with extensive financial resources and the creativity of smaller entities with creative owners involved in operations. Increasingly, international programs and producers have gained entry into the U.S. market through these joint ventures.

What is the process by which program series make it to the air? Television production is a complex business, dependent on artistic, political, and economic factors. Most series begin with a program pitch to a production company, program distributor, or network. Pitches begin with a concept or a short narrative known as a treatment and move to a storyboard or pilot. If the program is chosen for further development, the network or studio will provide development money in return for some measure of control over content. Networks generally require varying amounts of control over script, casting, and directing The individual or company making the pitch will also seek merchandise licensing and coproduction arrangements to fund the costs of production and generally retains additional licensing and rerun syndication rights. Unlike adult series, pilots are not commonly produced. Most networks order 26 episodes for an initial season. These will often run in multiple time slots. This rerun practice is possible because younger audiences do not object and turn over quickly.

The barriers to program entry into the children's television market are enormous. One only has to prowl the aisles of the annual convention of the National Association of Television Program Executives (NATPE) to see many creative children's program ideas. At NATPE, companies without distribution outlets try to make deals and find financial support by selling to networks or to syndicators or put together international production and coproduction deals. The international scope of children's television is seen at Marché International des Films et des Programmes (MIPCOM), a yearly trade event at Cannes.

MIP Junior is the children's programming element of this conference where buying, selling, and financing deals are made. More than 100 distributors of multicultural, U.S., and/or international offerings offer their children's series for global distribution. With the proliferation of cable and satellite offerings internationally, children's programming has developed a wide and lucrative international market. National and international coventures are increasingly an important part of program creation, as national and international licensing, tax credits, and coventure capital are sought to fund program creation for multiple markets. An extensive analysis of the differing business models for program funding can be found in Cahn, Kalagian, and Lyon, 2008.

Deep pockets are a necessity. Cost for individual episodes ranges from $100,000 to several hundred thousand dollars (Cahn et al., 2008). Production companies retain ownership of the shows, although networks are now allowed to have some financial interest in the program. These business organizations operate on a near-term deficit-financing model, anticipating that aftermarket sales and merchandising agreements will create ultimate profitability. Networks pay a licensing fee to air the program, which is typically significantly less than the show costs to produce. The fragmentation of the current audience means less money to individual companies, so license fees, which for children's programs were once in the range of $250,000 to $500,000 per episode (Jackson, 1999), now range from $10,000 to $60,000 in the United States (Cahn et al., 2008).

Networks, station groups, or individual stations want to buy from a reputable firm, someone they can trust to deliver what is promised. They would like to know that they are dealing with professionals who have been successful in similar endeavors in the past. But the children's television market is expanding with the new networks and cable services. How does it all come together in completed programs?

Patterns of Distribution

Production. After network programming, the largest program providers are syndicators: the companies that sell directly to TV stations and cable services. Local stations may purchase syndicated programs to fill slots where there is no network programming provided. Fox stations, because of their decision not to provide a children's block, will purchase from syndicators. Syndication companies sell two kinds of shows for kids: off-network series (series that have appeared on networks and are being rerun by local stations) and first-run shows that are expressly produced for syndication. Off-network series are packaged so that broadcast stations or cable channels pay for the right to play a certain number of episodes a specified number of times with a time frame. For a children's show, the accumulation of 65 episodes allows for repeatability and makes the show salable beyond its initial run to other outlets. Programs are frequently scheduled to run daily Monday through Friday, a process called stripping. Frequently, syndicated programming is purchased on a barter basis. In barter syndication, the producer provides the programming free or at a reduced cost but keeps some of the advertising slots in the show. The syndicator can place its own ads into the show or sell them to major advertisers. The key is market clearance. The more stations the syndicated program plays in, the larger the audience that can be offered to advertisers. First-run syndication, where syndicators sell shows expressly produced for syndication, blurs the line between production and syndication. Thus, some argue that syndication is a dying business. It may simply be that the distinction between syndication and other forms of program acquisition is vanishing within the children's market, with companies increasingly branding themselves as "acquiring and developing programming for distribution" rather than as syndicators.

With vertical integration and network consolidation, most major networks own production studios and prefer programming from that studio or license a block of programming from an independent. Thus, the majority of local affiliates' time devoted to children's television is produced by one studio or from studios under the same ownership as the network.

Advisory boards have become an important component of the production process. Developmental psychologists, educators, mass communication scholars, advocates, and others meet to discuss program acquisition and development. These boards offer advice on strategy and tactics within the network or production decision processes.

Nonprogram Content: Promotions and Public Service

Building a successful program or lineup does not end with program completion. The process of promotion is central to encouraging child audiences to sample, or indeed to eagerly anticipate, a new program. Channels and networks use internal program promotions as well as cross-media promotions and website tie-ins. For example, Nickelodeon uses promotions, games, websites, and media tie-ins to promote its brand and its programming lineup. Part programming and part promotion, another popular strategy is a wraparound segment that has its own characters and interstitial material. These wraparounds include common characters, promote upcoming programs, and contain short sketches.

External promotion is an increasingly important part of the promotion process. Some marketing initiatives tie in to local businesses. Cookie Jar Entertainment is partnering with Hardee's for Johnny Test-themed children's meal promotions. In an example of brand promotion, Nickelodeon is promoting themed Norwegian Line cruises.

An often-overlooked segment of nonprogram content is the public service announcement (PSA). The Advertising Council, which is an advertising industry group designed to provide social advocacy campaigns, produces many of the PSAs that audiences see or hear. This group donates advertising space and creative talent to these campaigns, many of which are targeted to teens as well as the larger adult market. A recent publication of the Advertising Council highlighted the availability of TV, radio, or print campaigns targeting children and young adults in the areas of antidiscrimination, crime prevention, fire safety, forest fire prevention, math, and youth fitness. Highlighted was a Shrek-themed campaign for children designed to get kids out of doors and reconnected with nature. Networks and cable channels also devote resources to their own campaigns. One of the best known is the long-running NBC campaign called "The More You Know," which

features media celebrities talking about issues of interest to children. The environment, nutrition, and physical activity are recent PSA topics.

Educational outreach, including educational resources, Web tie-ins, and distance learning, is discussed elsewhere in this handbook. Each of the networks offers a site for its child viewers or youth offerings. Most are interactive in some fashion, and some connect to other sites, some of which are educational in nature. Rarely can basic information such as production company, target age, educational objectives, or the E/I symbol be found. Most do include advertising.

All of this is about branding, the process whereby a product or service is seen to stand for something and to be qualitatively different from similar products or services. Branding is an outgrowth of the integrated marketing perspective that advocates the integrated use of all marketing tools to produce a brand. All networks try to create a brand for their entire service and can be embodied in their tag lines: Nickelodeon, "putting kids first"; Cartoon Network, "having fun with toons."

Identifying Financial Patterns

Inescapably, local station revenues come chiefly from the sale of time to advertisers. Individual broadcast stations, particularly in large markets, were historically very profitable, with annual profit margins in the 35 to 50% range. Yet networks have not been particularly profitable business units in recent years, as audiences erode and program costs climb. Nonetheless, media giants are gobbling up available broadcast stations, and the 1990s saw the advent of more than three additional networks. Why this seeming contradiction? The answer lies in the amortization of program costs by program content creators (major studios, independents, and international firms) and networks in the ancillary and aftermarkets. Ancillary markets include, among other things, international sales and merchandise licensing. Aftermarkets, sometimes called the back end, refer to post–first-run sales of the program.

The program costs vary widely, depending on longevity, stars, and quality. Nonetheless, children's programs are significantly less expensive to produce than prime-time programs. A dramatic series averages between $2 and $4 million per week, a situation comedy between $1 and $2 million. Children's television programs tend to average $100,000 and up per half-hour episode (cf. Cahn et al., 2008). Although the profit on children's programs is smaller than on adult series, their ancillary and aftermarket potential is vast. It seems clear that part of any pitch is a potential merchandising link and international sales. Thus, the deficit per episode (the cost per episode minus the licensing fee paid by the network) is to be made up in the ancillary and aftermarket. Concurrently with the program run, the show can be marketed internationally. Similarly, licensing and merchandising for successful children's shows can be a multibillion-dollar activity. This internationalization is helping production companies weather decreasing ratings for children's shows in the U.S. market.

It is this concentration of business activities that is the key to profitability. Chan-Olmsted (1996) concluded that the children's television market is moderately concentrated and on the verge of becoming highly concentrated as major players such as Disney and Fox consolidate their activities. She notes that network-syndication ownership is a critical combination for gaining market control.

Merchandise licensing refers to an agreement that allows the right to use a name or image in exchange for a royalty fee, generally 5 to 15% of the cost of the item (Pecora, 1998). Toys, games, clothing, lunchboxes, and the many other licensed products afford the manufacturer a recognizable character with ongoing "promotion" when the program airs, increasing product visibility and demand. The entertainment industry profits from the promotion of the product and the additional source of corporate revenue. Increasingly, production companies and product manufacturers have agents to manage these contractual negotiations.

The worldwide sale of licensed merchandise was $187.5 billion in 2008 (Lisanti, 2009). Character and brand licensing are major components of that total. Disney is the No. 1 top licensor worldwide. For the toy industry,

television- and movie-themed products help to introduce some stability to a volatile marketplace. For the entertainment industry, the royalties are an important source of income. Hanna-Barbera was grossing $40 to $50 million from licensed products in the 1970s; royalty fees for Mattel totaled $10 million in 1985 (Pecora, 1998, p. 57). These agreements seem to extend the life cycle of both the toy and the program.

The toy/program tie-in can come at any time in the process. Children's films and merchandised products usually hit the market at about the same time. For television, licensed toys that can be purchased during the Christmas rush quickly follow the September premiere. Some programs evolve in popularity, and product lines emerge after that. For example, *Barney & Friends* products appeared after that show gained popularity. A few were popular toys before they become programs; *Strawberry Shortcake* and *My Little* Pony are two examples.

Despite the impact of program resale and merchandise licensing, the foundation of the children's television business is advertising. Sales for children's television ads during the upfront season passed the $1 billion mark in 1998, despite a trend that sees children watching less television. This can be compared to the $44.5 billion total advertising volume for television and cable together (Turner, 2010). Nationally, the children's television market is divided into two time periods. Upfront selling usually occurs in April, when advertisers make the bulk of their buys for the upcoming season, locking up the "prime" advertising real estate. What remains is bought up throughout the year on what is called the scatter market.

Whatever choices they make, advertisers buy gross ratings points (GRPs), the sum of all ratings for all programs in a schedule of buys. This is the most frequently used measure of audiences for the advertising community. Of course, these buys must be made at an appropriate cost per thousand (CPM), which is the cost to reach 1,000 people or homes. Another frequently used measure is the cost per rating point (CPP), which is the cost to deliver a single rating point. The *Marketer's Guide* (1998) reports an average CPM cost of network children's programming (cable and broadcast combined) of $5.92 in 1997 to 1998. This can be compared to a CPM cost in prime time of $11.93. One cable channel—Nickelodeon—controls more than 60% of the available children's gross ratings points (which is the same as saying it accounts for 60% of all of children's viewing). Cable as a whole controls 80% of children's GRPs. However, these GRPs are very fragmented, and it is not easy to reach children efficiently (*Marketer's Guide*, 1998, 2008).

Traditionally, the major advertisers on children's television have been toy and food companies such as Hasbro, Mattel, Kraft, General Foods, and Kellogg's. The variety of companies' spending on children's television is increasing. In 1994, toys and cereals accounted for 56% of total children's ad dollars; in 1998, that figure was only 36%. Now two additional categories are emerging as major advertisers to children ("Food for thought," March 2007). The first is advertising for media products, with advertisements for video games, movies, magazines, and videos. A second category is for entertainment, particularly for amusement parks and vacation spots. With children's programming proliferating, particularly on cable, some worry that a surplus of advertising time will be created, driving profits down. The number of choices creates significant audience fragmentation and gives ad buyers more alternatives for where to place their ad dollars. Whatever the outcome, children's viewing has become a very fragmented demographic, raising serious questions about how to effectively reach them.

There are self-regulatory groups within the advertising industry that strive to oversee advertising. One of these is a part of the Better Business Bureau, the National Advertising Review Council's Children's Advertising Review Unit (CARU). Part of a comprehensive self-regulatory process of the NARC, CARU's goal is to work with the industry to ensure that advertising to children is truthful and fair. Like the larger review unit, CARU investigates complaints, recommends modifications or discontinuance of offending claims, and may refer the matter to appropriate government agencies. The major federal agency that deals with deceptive or untrue advertising is the Federal Trade Commission (FTC), which has, in its, time responded to numerous complaints about advertising practices to children, many filed by the former organization Action for Children's Television (ACT).

Conclusion

Several important observations emerge from this analysis of the children's broadcast television business. First, the proliferation of content in children's programming is significantly fragmenting the child audience. Most viewing of children's programming is now via cable services. With the regulation of children's television, local stations executives' perception of children's television increasingly places it in the arena of public service rather than entertainment programming. The traditional Big Three (ABC, CBS, NBC) are not generating major profits from their children's television over-the-air offerings; newer broadcast and cable networks that more centrally target children are doing much better. But the real profit in children's television is in the production/distribution arena, where ancillary marketing, aftermarkets, international coventures, and distribution are a multibillion-dollar industry. With the increasing integration of media corporations, all are sharing in these profits.

The body of television content emerging from these economic and industrial practices has been a central component of "childhood" since the 1950s. Because children are seen as a special "group" of both citizens and viewers, great concerns for the role of television in the lives of children have accompanied the development of the medium. As a result, issues surrounding children and television have often been framed as "social problems," issues of central concern to numerous groups. Large-scale academic research enterprises have been mounted to monitor, analyze, and explain relationships between television and children. Congress, regulatory agencies, advocacy groups, and the television networks have struggled continuously over research findings, public responsibility, and popular response.

The regulatory decisions of the 1990s transformed children's television. We are only beginning to assess the consequences of these transformations.

References

Cahn, A., Kalagian, T., & Lyon, C. (2008). Business models for children's media. In S. L. Calvert & B. J. Wilson (Eds.), *Handbook of children, media and development* (pp. 27–48). Chichester, Sussex, United Kingdom: Blackwell.

Chan-Olmsted, S. (1996). From *Sesame Street* to Wall Street: An analysis of market competition in commercial children's television. *Journal of Broadcasting & Electronic Media, 40* (1), 30–44.

Food for thought: Food advertising to children in the United States (2007, March). Kaiser Family Foundation. Retrieved May 10, 2011, from http://www.kff.org/entmedia/upload/7618 .pdf.

Growing Nickelodeon subscriber fees important for Viacom's stock. (2010, March 8). Retrieved May 10, 2011, from http://www.trefis.com/ articles/12706/growing-nickelodeon-subcriber-fees-important-for-viacoms-stock/2010-03-08.

Jackson, W. (1999, April 12). Viewer's call. *Variety, 37,* 46.

Lisanti, T. (2009, October 1). *Licensing industry annual report: The future looks brighter.* Retrieved May 10, 2011, from http://www .licensemag.com/licensemag/Home/Licensing-I ndustry-Annual-Report-The-Future-Looks-/ ArticleStandard/Article/detail/631632?context CategoryId=47729&searchString=2008%20 annual%20report.

Marketer's guide to media, 1998 (Vol. 21). New York: ASM Communications.

Marketer's guide to media, 2008 (Vol. 31). New York: ASM Communications.

Pecora, N. (1998). *The business of children's entertainment.* New York: Guilford.

Petrozzello, D. (1998, July 27). Cable competition for kids intensities. *Broadcasting and Cable,* 27–28.

Stelter, B., Arango, T., Carr, D., & Carter, B. (2009, December 7). NBC-Comcast deal puts broadcast TV in doubt. *New York Times,* 1.

Turner, C. (2010, June 11). *Cynopsis: Kids.* Retrieved May 10, 2011, from www.cynopsis.com/editions/ kids/061110.

CHAPTER 26

The Role of Research and Evaluation in Educational Media

MICHAEL COHEN
Michael Cohen Group LLC

Introduction: The Research, Education, and Media Landscape

This chapter offers an updated description of the role of applied and evaluative research in the development and assessment of a wide range of children's educational media. In recent years, all the elements involved—research, education, and media—have undergone rapid transformation and require new descriptions and redefinitions. The range of available media content and technology is vast and now includes laptop and netbook computers, the Internet and high-speed broadband access, iPads, tablets, apps, search engines, interactive video games, and sophisticated gaming systems, Web-based virtual worlds, social networking, cell phones, Smart phones, handheld devices, and texting—all in addition to television. The digital revolution can be characterized by the extraordinary introduction, availability, and increased use of a variety of media in our lives. We commonly accept that this has behaviorally transformed the way we communicate, work, and play. Importantly, all of these media technologies are now utilized (or are being considered) in the service of education, both formally in the classroom and informally in the home.

Similarly, the fields of education and research have also undergone significant change. In order to appreciate the role of research now, it is helpful to understand these changes in historical context. The curious relationship between research and the educational media industry began in the 1960s with the birth of *Sesame Street*. In order to provide context, this chapter presents a brief overview of these 40-plus years with an intense focus on recent developments of the past 10.

During this past decade, research (defined as knowledge derived from studies and experiments conducted by psychologists and other social scientists) has had an increasingly visible and expanded role in the creation of children's media. The role of applied research has historically been twofold (Palmer, 1988; Palmer & Dorr, 1980). (1) Research informs the creation of educational media products by providing ongoing feedback to the content creators. The feedback is based directly on children's experiences accessed via research activity including their perceptions, attitudes, and behaviors regarding the educational products in development. (2) Research evaluates the media product's educational effectiveness. Were the stated educational goals successfully met? This role has greatly expanded over the past decade as a result of the emphasis on effectiveness and the use of student performance as its measure.

Additionally, as a result of other developments in education and media (discussed in Section 2), researchers are currently functioning in new capacities requiring expertise in a variety of areas, including knowledge of standardized assessment measures and the use of scientific trials to determine educational efficacy; mastery of the new data available in the form of digital tracking of student activity; fluency in methodologies for inquiry both in and out of the classroom; a technical knowledge of new and emerging technologies and content; mastery of the entire range of core academic curriculum; an equal mastery of the range of effective pedagogy; and the communication skills necessary for optimal knowledge dissemination to multiple audiences. How these roles emerged and operate is discussed in detail in Section 3.

Mastering these multiple content areas and acquiring these skills is a daunting task, but in the field of education, the need is not unusual. Similar to other disciplines, notably teaching, the function of research has evolved—and although not unrecognizable, it now looks quite different than its 10-years-younger self.

Structure of the Chapter

This chapter explores the current role of research in educational media within the context of recent developments in the fields of education and media. **Section 1** presents a brief overview of educational media, primarily television, from the mid-1960s to 2000. **Section 2** presents the significant and recent changes in education and media that have

occurred during the decade of 2000 to 2010. **Section 3** presents a description of the current role of research. **Section 4** presents several illustrative research case studies. **Section 5** offers a brief conclusion. Within these sections, there are highlighted discussions of several critical areas, not limited to, and including: (1) the impact of government policy, legislation, and funding; (2) the theoretical and methodological foundations of research; (3) the various stages of media product production at which research is used; (4) the emergence of a new form of evidence and assessment derived from the tracking of student digital activity and user logs; and (5) case studies illustrating several of the dynamics discussed. The overall goal is to provide a concise, clear, and accurate description of applied research in the service of educational media.

The rate of change in the social environment has been increasing, and any description risks a resemblance to a snapshot of a landscape taken from the window of a moving bullet train. By the time the shutter closes, the scene is gone. Ten years ago, research in educational media concerned itself primarily with educational television. Since then, research, media, technology, and education have undergone extraordinary change occurring at a staggering pace, and there are no indications that this process is subsiding. In this context, a description of the role of research, by definition, risks being out of date even as it is being created and before it is ever presented.

Section 1. The Historical Context: The Beginnings: Educational Television From the Mid-1960s Through 2000

An exceptional situation occurred when the formal and academic discipline of applied research became a critical component in the creation and marketing of commercial products. This phenomenon developed in the 1940s and 1950s when the research methods employed by the social sciences—surveys, interviews, and observations—were first utilized to identify and understand consumers' preferences, needs, and expectations. Labeled market research, the methodology essentially borrowed from the social sciences, including a new field of consumer psychology.

TV and the Vast Wasteland

One might argue that television, from its inception in the late 1940s, has always educated the public. Only a handful of prior technologies, including the printing press, photography, film, recordings, and radio had ever opened such vast vistas to so many. Television, arguably, had a particularly powerful effect, exposing many to worlds far away and people different from themselves. In this sense, television programs—showing animals in distant jungles, people in foreign cities, or the private lives of strangers who live next door—have always offered viewers a certain amount of de facto education. And this education often took the form of information. However, early broadcast television was commercial and not explicitly educational and quickly developed to be a medium of pure entertainment. The goal was to attract the most viewers in order to demand high rates from advertisers. Television producers did not, nor were they expected to, create curriculum for their shows. Education was neither an explicit nor an implicit goal, and during television's first decade, the novelty of form, content, and entertainment were openly embraced.

The initial collective vision of television as a pure and benign form of entertainment, however, vanished in the mid-1960s. Giving voice to the widespread and growing concern with television's potential harmful effects, Newton N. Minnow, chairman of the Federal Communications Commission (FCC), labeled it "a vast wasteland" (Palmer, 1988). Much serious critical debate over media's (television's) role ensued. The shared understanding of this wasteland was that television had become an intellectual desert. Its identifying feature was the absence of any positive information or educational content, particularly for children. The perceived harmful consequence was a nation of young, empty, and thoughtless minds, "glued to the tube" (Zillman, Bryant, & Huston, 1994).

In response, it was believed that television's enormous power could be directed for other than commercial interest, and more than mindlessly entertain, it could educate. The result was the beginning of what is now defined as educational television for children— that is, television programs with formally articulated, explicit curricular goals and educational content integrated within. The airing of the first episode of *Sesame Street* in the late 1960s marked the symbolic beginning of a new form: programming that intentionally married entertainment and education.

In the 1970s, educational television flourished as *The Electric Company*, *Zoom*, *3-2-1 Contact*, and other series joined the ranks, continuing the mission of entertaining children while teaching specific skills (Montgomery, 1989). During this time, the curriculum was comprised primarily of early cognitive and academic skills, including preliteracy (letters and alphabet); prenumeracy (numbers and counting); primary colors; and spatial orientation (distinguishing right from left, up from down, etc.). One extraordinary exception was *Mister Rogers' Neighborhood*, in which the emphasis was on imagination and social and emotional development.

Television—the Evil Force

During the 1980s, however, there was a change in America's concerns regarding television and media. The fear shifted to children's moral degeneration. Parents and educators voiced concern that television made children "evil"—insensitive to violence, violent themselves, and incapable of making appropriate moral and ethical decisions (Cantor, 1998; Davies, 1997; Gunter, McAleer, & Clifford, 1991; Jamieson & Romer, 2008; Von Feilitzen & Carlsson, 1999). Television was now perceived to be imparting values that were, at best, callous and disrespectful, and, at worst, antisocial, exploitative, sexist, and racist— and at the most extreme, sociopathic (Carlsson & von Feilitzen, 1998).

Such fears, of course, did not arise ex-nihilo (Washington & Andreas, 1998). As a result of the profound changes in the American family and the economy that included a rising divorce rate, an increase of single-parent families, and women entering the workforce in record numbers, children's relationship to television was necessarily transformed. Once just a source of entertainment and skill acquisition, television was perceived, perhaps accurately, as having become our children's babysitter, caretaker, and interlocutor (Levin, 1998). Additionally, television became more ubiquitous in America—more accessible and containing more content. Regardless of income, by 1980, most Americans owned a TV set, and cable television was expanding channel access.

Television's Response— the Second Wave

In response to the new anxieties over television's negative influence, educational television turned its attention to young children's social/ emotional and moral/ethical development. Along with cognitive and academic content, explicit educational curriculum included moral tales, the modeling of good manners, positive social values, and interpersonal skills such as being polite, taking turns, and sharing. Prior to the 1980s, Americans strongly held the cultural belief that it was the responsibility of parents, the extended family, and the immediate religious community to transmit such values and skills to children. By the 1980s, however, parents no longer felt confident undertaking this task on their own. Television and media had assumed a large and influential role in their children's lives and seemed too powerful to combat alone. Educational television, again, set out to combat the new evils of commercial television (Buckingham, 1993; Steyer, 2002).

Basically, the definition of *educational* had changed. Curriculum remained, but the accepted content had broadened and now included socioemotional development. This shift led to the creation and acceptance of series such as *Barney & Friends*, in which social development comprised a substantial portion of the stated curriculum. This was well documented in 10 studies of *Barney & Friends* by Jerry and Dorothy Singer (Singer & Singer, 1998). It is important to note the significance of this shift in the definition of education—by the late 1990s, a formal overview of the television landscape showed that the vast majority of educational television was explicitly devoted to social and emotional curricula.

Education and Entertainment

Educational television's definition of education was changing in response to needs in the social environment. What remained constant, however, was the challenge of providing curricular content while maintaining appeal and entertainment value. For public television, the quest for ratings was as heightened as for the commercial networks. Essential revenue from corporate sponsorship and member/viewer contributions depended on ratings, and the pressure to achieve high ratings coexisted with the demand of providing effective educational content. Integrating education and entertainment has always posed a considerable challenge, and high-quality programs of this genre are historically very difficult to create. This is where research has made a significant contribution from the late 1960s on.

It is important to note that educational television competes for children's attention against content solely designed as entertainment. As a result, it is essential that educational television content be highly appealing and engaging; otherwise it will never be viewed. Additional challenges are inherent to educational television: (1) Programming reaches young children in an informal space—their home—a space not explicitly organized for learning; (2) the learning experience is non-mediated—there's no teacher present; (3) there is no predetermined order in which a child will view episodes. Sequencing lessons becomes quite impossible when the order in which children will view episodes cannot be determined as it is in a classroom.

In light of all the constraints and challenges, by 2000, public broadcasting's achievement regarding television content for children ages 2 through 7 cannot be overstated. Educational television had accepted the challenge of creating content with integrated curriculum and continually outperformed commercial entertainment properties on ratings and appeal. Importantly, the Public Broadcasting Service (PBS) had set the standard for what was acceptable television for young children and had determined the criteria for how educational television would be evaluated. For 30 years, PBS had been presenting television to young children that was highly appealing, free of gratuitous violence, and commercial free; modeled positive values; and included explicit learning goals integrated into the programming. Parents, the gatekeepers of young children's viewing, came to demand nothing less, raising the bar for viable content. Viacom and Disney understood these market requirements and created their branded media environments accordingly. Nick Jr. and Playhouse Disney joined PBS in creating high-quality television programming for young children.

It was at this time, and as a result of extraordinary technological advances and innovation, that the world of educational media expanded far beyond TV. Educational media, in an astonishingly brief time frame, came to include every available technology and platform. Educational media entered the classroom, and television now represents only a fraction of its scope. Significantly, educational media are viewed by a vocal group of educators and observers as nothing less than the key to revitalizing public education, effectively delivering core academic curriculum from a new central position in the classroom. No longer playing an ancillary role as the counter to the wasteland of television, educational media are poised to be essential components of education reform in the United States. In order to appreciate the current role of research, an examination of the past decade at closer range is necessary. Understanding the significant current dynamics within the fields of education and media provides the needed context.

Section 2. The Context: The New Millennium: Education and Media 2000 Through 2010

Crisis in American Education and the Achievement Gap

A comprehensive overview of the current challenges and dynamics of U.S. public education requires volumes. The goal of this section is a brief presentation of the significant trends, dynamics, and policies that are characteristic of the contemporary education landscape and have the greatest direct impact on educational media and research. Perhaps the defining dynamic underlying an understanding of the current landscape is the ongoing crisis facing education in the United States. Simply, the public education system is failing to educate a large portion of students. A sizable percentage of young children are not acquiring developed language skills, literacy, math abilities, and higher-order thinking skills. Many of the youngest generation are not learning to read.

A disproportionate number of these non-learners live in poverty or the lower economic strata of our society (Knight, Roosa, & Umana-Taylor, 2009). Additionally, the percentage of nonlearners is also disproportionately greater for disadvantaged populations. As a consequence of the high correlation between race, ethnicity, and economic status (Natriello, McDill, & Pallas, 1990), African-Americans and Hispanics face overwhelming obstacles. In spite of extraordinary activity and investment to address this issue, the achievement gap has continued to grow.

In 2003, the nation's report card for educational progress showed that 37% of all fourth graders did not achieve the minimum reading standards (National Assessment of Educational Progress [NAEP], 2003). The crisis was far worse for lower-income, historically disadvantaged children with limited English proficiency: 55% of fourth graders from low-income families, 60% of African-American and Hispanic children, and 70% of children with limited English proficiency did not achieve minimum national standards (NAEP, 2003). At that time, it had been more than 20 years since the landmark education study "A Nation at Risk" (1983), and evidence indicated that little progress had been made.

Education has received an extraordinary amount of attention over the past decade, taking its place in the public dialogue alongside war, the economy, and the environment. A bipartisan Congress passed the No Child Left Behind (NCLB) legislation in 2001, and 8 years later, more than one hundred billion dollars of the federal stimulus package was directed to education. Despite these and many other efforts, American school performance remains poor, and the situation appears static over time. Simply, there has not been substantial improvement. Reading scores are, at best, unchanged after years of investment. In 2005, at least 17,929 schools across the nation had failed to meet "adequate yearly progress," and a greater number of schools had been found to be "in need of improvement" than in 2004 (NAEP, 2005). In the absence of new and effective approaches, it has been estimated that 70% of first-grade children at risk for reading failure will become adults without basic literacy skills (Lyon & Fletcher, 2001).

Literacy is not the only academic area of concern. In 2009, fully 61% of U.S. fourth graders failed to achieve basic proficiency in mathematics (National Center for Education Statistics [NCES], 2009). Overall, American students' achievement in mathematics and numeracy is mediocre compared to their peers worldwide (National Assessment of Educational Progress [NAEP], 2009). Children from China, Japan, and Korea outperform their American counterparts in mathematics achievement as early as kindergarten and continue to do so throughout their entire school careers.

From an educational policy perspective, the ramifications for our nation's future are profound and bleak (Boyer, 1991). The policy logic unfolds as follows. Failing to acquire literacy and mathematics skills, unable to read, unable to engage in critical thought, and unskilled for employment in technology and science, members of the U.S. labor force will be unable to engage in lifelong learning, to assume their roles as informed citizens in the democratic process, or to take their place as responsible family members. Regarding employment specifically, it is estimated that the percentage of jobs requiring literate, technically skilled workers has increased from 20% to 65% since 1950 (National Cyber Summit on 21st Century Skills, 2009) and will continue to do so. An illiterate and unlearned population weakens the workforce, threatens global standing, engenders national vulnerability, and squanders the nation's achievements and potential. As a result, educational policy is focused on the importance of early effective instruction, prevention, and remediation.

At the same time that the demand for educational effectiveness, higher standards, and the closing of the achievement gap is increasing, education is faced with the harsh reality that money and resources are significantly decreasing. Teachers' pay, evaluation, and retention

are controversial issues at a historical moment when schools do not have the money to even maintain the status quo. Literal financial survival haunts many districts nationwide. As smaller class size and higher teacher–student ratios are called for, the reality for most schools will be exactly the opposite. The educational crisis is the critical dynamic shaping the landscape. However, several other developments of the past decade are important and deserve a brief articulation.

New Knowledge in Child Development

During this period of ongoing educational crisis, there has been a parallel and counterbalancing phenomenon. Over the past decade, there has occurred an unprecedented and extraordinary advance in our knowledge regarding the workings of the human brain, infant and child development, and learning. Advances in the fields of neuroscience, developmental psychology, education, psychiatry, and pediatrics have all contributed to this knowledge explosion. Importantly, the focus of a considerable amount of this scholarly research is infancy and early childhood from birth through the preschool years. Studies have investigated a variety of topics, including: how infants and children learn; what they know; how they think; how their minds and brains develop; how they acquire cognitive, emotional, and social skills; and, specifically, how they acquire early literacy and numeracy (Bronson & Merryman, 2009; Carr, 2010; Collins & Halverson, 2009; Galinsky, 2010; Guernsey, 2007; Hart, 2002; Hirsh-Pasek & Golinkoff, 2003; Jenkins, 2006; Jensen, 2005; Medina, 2008; Posner & Rothbart, 2007; The Jossey-Bass Reader, 2008; Wolf, 2007) .

In a recent article, Gopnik, a contributing scholar to this new base of knowledge, summarized that " . . . scientists have discovered that even the youngest children know more than we have ever thought possible . . . Since about 2000, researchers have started to understand the underlying . . . mechanisms that underpin these remarkable early abilities" (Gopnik, 2010, p. 76). It is now accepted that very young children are involved in abstract and symbolic thinking and capable of learning at a very early age. Additionally, educators now have a grasp of the dynamics of remediation as well as an appreciation for the critical contribution of parent/caregiver involvement in early learning and achievement. Our new knowledge also emphasizes constructivist learning and the importance of play in early life (Zigler, Singer, & Bishop-Josef, 2004). Young children learn by *doing*. Simply, through the active process of trial and error, formulating hypotheses, and trying out different courses of action, children are actively constructing their understanding and knowledge of the world. And for young children, unstructured and creative play is the fertile activity in which constructivist learning occurs (Gopnik, 2010; Gopnik, Meltzoff, & Kuhl, 1999).

This new understanding has led to a dramatic rethinking of previously accepted ideas and assumptions about young children and their education. The recent formulation that very young children are capable of learning the abstract symbol systems of language and mathematics—letters, words, and numbers—has resulted in the current view of young children as early learners. A broad national consensus, first articulated in the early 1990s, identified U.S. children as unprepared to enter school at age 5, lacking the basic skills, maturity, and required knowledge. The subsequent Ready to Learn Initiative was conceived to prepare children with the basic prerequisites for school success. For many educators, this goal of preparing young children for learning has transformed and expanded into the goal of actively engaging young children as early learners.

Prior to 1990, the primary focus of kindergarten was socialization and the acquisition of the prerequisite skills leading to reading, math, and academic readiness. Today, the kindergarten curriculum in many states is composed of specific academic goals and lessons. Additionally, the standardized assessment of kindergarten children's reading and numeracy skills has become common practice. Classroom instruction, in general, now emphasizes cognitive skill acquisition and student performance in an attempt to simultaneously improve academic achievement and eliminate the achievement gap (Zigler & Bishop-Josef, 2004). There have been many other significant developments in the human sciences. Our knowledge of learning, development, and maturation continues to

expand and deepen and shows no signs of slowing down.

Education and Parents

Parents' and caregivers' perceptions and attitudes about education have changed over the past decade. An important social phenomenon observed throughout the developed world is the growing concern on the part of parents regarding their children's ability to achieve future economic and social success. Perceiving the world as highly competitive, with limited and fixed resources, parents desire to provide their children with every possible advantage. In the United States, and with varying degrees of awareness, parents are responding to the reality that their children may be part of the first American generation whose opportunity and standard of living—economic and social—will neither equal nor exceed those of the generation that preceded them.

For many parents, their child's education is the primary variable that provides an advantage and determines future success or failure. Academic performance, school prestige, and technological skills are perceived advantageous for the 21st century when their grown children will be competing for college admissions, jobs, pay, and, by extension, overall social standing and standard of living. In the context of the increasingly competitive process of college admission, the pressure for many parents, and by extension their children, begins at preschool and kindergarten (Ravitch, 2010).

Over the course of the past decade, parents embraced the new perspective of their young children as prime for explicit learning. The intensified focus on education meshed perfectly with the new perspective on young children as early learners. The advocates of early explicit learning found a huge support and a vibrant market for educational products among parents. Combined with the increasing numbers of young children attending day care or preschool, a significant percentage of U.S. children ages 3 and younger are now receiving regular explicit formal and informal educational instruction (Cohen et al., 2009). Another related and significant social trend is the increasingly scheduled and structured quality of young children's lives. As a result of many factors, including perceived lack of safety and participation in organized team sports, parents are now managing their children's lives very carefully, scheduling and filling free time with beneficial activities to ensure that "no time is wasted." As a result, children spend considerably less time engaged in creative free play. It is estimated that preschool-age children have lost more than 12 hours of free time a week during the past decade alone. Eight hours of this time had previously been allocated to unstructured play—and opportunities for constructivist learning (Elkind, 2007).

The emphasis on more rigorous teacher-led instruction in the classroom and parent-organized, after-school beneficial experiences has resulted in children spending most of their time in highly structured activities. This dynamic is in direct contradiction to the research discussed earlier indicating the critical importance of play and constructivist learning for children's cognitive and social development. Creative play allows for the acquisition of a range of skills and capabilities, including language skills, problem solving, representational skills, creativity, collaboration, turn taking, empathy, and motivation (Zigler & Bishop-Josef, 2004). Again, research findings emphasize the need for creative playtime and child-initiated learning opportunities in order that young children develop their abilities to think creatively and work collaboratively—exactly the skills identified as important to achieving academic and social success in the 21st century.

Another trend is the increase in the quality and quantity of educational toys and games that are standard fare in homes with young children. Leap Frog, Fisher-Price, and others, thumbs firmly pressed to the pulse of the parent consumer, responded to the call for educating children early. With parents acutely preoccupied with their children's academic performance, learning-oriented products, including electronic games, toys, and media devices, have flooded stores and entered homes. The presence and popularity of these products is the manifestation of yet another and larger transformation: Education now takes place at home as well as in school. Furthermore, both schools as well as parents

have been trading children's playtime for study time. Homework assignments are now common even in the earliest grades and require more time for completion at all grade levels. After-school programs, homework help, test preparation, and online courses available 24/7 comprise a multibillion-dollar industry and further blur the line separating school and home.

The Role and Impact of Government Policy and Initiatives

During the past 10 years, government policy, initiatives, and changes in law have had a powerful impact on education and research. These governmental perspectives and activities are broad based, emanating from the president's office, Congress, and the U.S. Department of Education. Again, a comprehensive review of this topic alone merits an entire volume. The immediate goal here is to highlight only several activities viewed as having the most significant impact on the activity of research in educational media.

The first is the passage of the No Child Left Behind (NCLB) legislation by Congress in 2001. A complex and far-reaching act, its execution has been the topic of never-ending controversy, critique, and praise and will not to be taken up again here. There are several features to NCLB, however, that have radically altered the world of educational media and the role of research. Arguably, the most important dimension of NCLB for this discussion is the introduction and central position of *outcome* in education. In the simplest terms, NCLB has determined the following: that every child has the right to an effective and successful education and that the evaluative criteria for determining educational effectiveness and school success is *outcome*—outcome exclusively in the form of student academic performance (NCLB, 2001).

Applied to educational media, the implications are far reaching and profound. The child's experience, the product's level of appeal, commercial success, parental appreciation, and so forth may all be important but are not considered evidence of its educational value. Rather, the question is specific and direct: Were the stated educational goals achieved?

Did the child learn or not? And learning and achievement are determined exclusively by student academic performance. Parent, teacher, or child self-reports of learning that did or did not occur do not constitute evidence of achievement. The student subjective experience of the learning process is not a proxy for outcome. Educational media, for historical reasons, had been primarily focused on process—both the process of making the educational media product and the process of young children using the media product. Research inquiry was focused on level of appeal and comprehension as well as the child's intent to view (Galinsky, 2010; Hirsh-Pasek & Golinkoff, 2003; Zhao, 2009).

Restricted by law, NCLB does not identify for the individual U.S. states what academic skills and achievements are to be assessed or what assessment measures should be utilized. The individual states, left to their own resources, developed a national morass of standardized assessment tests and an accompanying tunnel-vision focus on test scores. Therein lies the core of a good deal of the controversy and the critique that U.S. schools now "teach to the test." Educational media, often created with vague and/or ever-changing educational objectives, were now faced with a variation of the question "against what specific educational goals are we evaluating our performance?"

A second important feature of NCLB is the determination by the U.S. Department of Education Institute of Educational Sciences as to what research methodologies are considered scientifically valid and yield "strong evidence" in an assessment of educational effectiveness (What Works Clearinghouse, http://ies.ed.gov/ncee/wwc). The methodology identified is a scientific evidence-based random-control trial (RCT). An RCT (defined in detail in the next section) is rigorous, often difficult to execute, and as compared to other applied research methodologies, large scale and labor intensive. Offering descriptive power at the expense of explanatory power, prior to NCLB, this method was rarely utilized in the assessment of educational media effectiveness. Results can describe, definitively, if learning occurred, and one can attribute *cause* as to why learning occurred. Simply, "student learning did or did not occur

and it was the use of this educational product, and not the result of any other variable, that caused, or failed to cause, such learning to occur." An explanation as to why or how learning did or did not occur is not an objective of an RCT, and other research methodologies are utilized to explore these questions.

In sum, although the impact from NCLB is multifaceted, one feature of the legislation—the introduction of *educational outcome with student academic performance as its measure*—stands out as having had a particularly profound effect on the practice of assessment and evaluation.

Ready to Learn

The attention and resources committed to educational media and technology at the U.S. Department of Education are vast. A brief discussion of a specific initiative, however, is particularly relevant to our discussion. The Ready to Learn Television grant has funded educational media projects, primarily educational television and accompanying websites, since 1995. Conceived as a contributor to the overall national Ready to Learn activities, the grant's central premise was to enlist educational media, which in 1995 was educational television, in the service of preparing young children for kindergarten. Preparation consisted of engendering the acquisition of a wide range of cognitive, intrapsychic, and interpersonal skills as well as exposing preschoolers to age-appropriate general knowledge. Awarded exclusively to PBS for 10 years, funds from the Ready to Learn grant contributed to the production of many of the educational series that air on public television (Cohen, 2004).

During the past decade, as the media landscape developed and NCLB became law, the Department of Education responded and, in the view of many observers, presciently took actions that redirected the educational media industry toward the future. These actions included: (1) a call for funded projects to use multiple media platforms along with television, (2) a call for an expanded utilization of research, and (3) a call for new partnerships to be formed that included the public, nonprofit, and private sectors. The U.S. Department of Education, in its proposal requests for the Ready to Learn grant, required grantees to utilize research to both inform the creation of an educational media product (formative research) and to assess its educational effectiveness (summative research), utilizing RCT methodology with student performance as its outcome measure. In doing so, policy has placed research in a prominent, vital, and essential role.

The Department of Education Technology Plan

In addition to NCLB and RTL, the U.S. Department of Education's current perspective on educational technology and media impacts the future of research. As articulated in the 2010 National Educational Technology Plan published by the Office of Educational Technology, U.S. Department of Education, digital media and technology have central roles to play in the transformation of U.S. education. This vision offers a segue into a discussion on overall media developments.

At its core, the NAEP identifies the challenge to be that education needs to utilize new knowledge that has come from the learning sciences as well as advances in modern technology in order to mirror the reality of students' lives in regard to technology and media.

> . . . students' lives today are filled with technology that gives them mobile access to information . . . , enables them to create multimedia content . . . , allows them to participate in online social networks . . . (and) pursue their passions in their own way and at their own pace . . . (National Educational Technology Plan, 2010, pp. 4–5)

Media and Educational Media 2000–2010

The explosion of digital media—both technology and content—during the past 10 years is the subject of books, articles, and endless conversation. Additionally, each of us has our own experience and vantage point from which we both participate in and observe the resultant impact. The goal here is to briefly identify several developments in digital media and technology that are most relevant to our discussion.

The basic connective tissue of the digital world is, of course, the Internet. Conceived at the Department of Defense during the cold war, the Internet Society was chartered in 1992, the same year the World Wide Web was released (Internet Timeline, http://www.cc.utah.edu/~jay/history.html). In 1995, there were 16 million Internet users worldwide; today there are more than two billion. The number of websites is estimated to be somewhere between two hundred billion and one trillion (http://news.netcraft.com/,http://www.all aboutmarketresearch.com/internet.htm). Computer ownership in the United States now approaches a one-to-one correlation with high-speed Internet access. Computers in the United States, as of 2010, remain the primary technology for accessing the Internet and available digital content. However, the increasing sophistication and power of handheld devices and Smart phones may well make the preceding statement out of date in a very short time frame.

Certainly the extraordinary phenomenon of search engines is transforming education and research as well. Individuals now have the ability to locate knowledge at a speed and in volume that were literally unthinkable 10 years ago. This has already affected a core function of library service and transformed one aspect of the research industry. Individuals now have the capability to search and locate information far more efficiently than trained researchers did 15 years ago. Similarly, other industries have undergone transformative change. Surveys and polling can now be conducted online, reaching more respondents and at less cost than telephone surveys. This development has placed an entire research subindustry—survey phone banks—on the brink of extinction.

The development of video games during the past decade is of particular interest. In relationship to educational media, video games are to this decade what television was in the 1960s, 1970s, and 1980s. Controversy abounds. Fears of harmful effects, addiction to playing, gratuitous violence, overt sexual content, and the interactive nature of the involvement are all combined with a new dynamic. Parents, as nonplayers, have no access and remain ignorant of the actual play and content. Critics hold video games responsible for society's ills and consider tragedies such as the Columbine massacre to be the consequence of gaming (Collins & Halverson, 2009).

Gaming, like television 40 years earlier, is "where the kids are." More than 90% of U.S. children have a video game system in their homes (Cohen et al., 2009; Lenhart, 2009). Additionally, academic interest is high and the domain of video gaming has received the most attention as compared to other media forms. Findings from studies on video games offer a promising view of their employment for education; however, the nature of these investigations often makes it difficult to generalize from the findings. The challenge is to take video games and *turn them on their heads,* similar to what *Sesame Street* did with TV in the 1960s. The goal is to create video-games that are instructional and educational without losing the compelling and appealing qualities that drive their commercial success (Gee, 2007; Jenkins, 2006).

Academics and educators see video games as a template and tool for powerful learning (Gee, 2007; Jenkins 2006). Currently, the educational video game movement is strong, and academic programs such as the NYU Games for Learning Institute attract students, educators, and other practitioners who continue the work of creating educational games. The video game equivalent of *Sesame Street*, however, has proven to be elusive.

At present, similar to earlier controversy regarding television, a debate ensues in the public dialogue about the effects of children's media consumption in general. In a Joint Statement (2000) before the Congressional Public Health Summit, a number of American medical associations, including the American Medical Association, American Academy of Pediatrics, and American Psychological Association, strongly cautioned parents about violent content in the media and its negative effects on children. Their report stated that exposure to media violence could elevate aggressive thoughts and feelings and that these effects could be long term. Likewise, critics of video games cite research suggesting that violent games have a more negative and dramatic influence on children's behavior than television (Bushman & Anderson, 2002; Gentile & Anderson, 2003; see also Chapters 12 and 13 in this volume) and contribute to a decline in academic performance (Rideout, Foehr, & Roberts, 2010). Critics explicitly compared the current computer and video game landscape to the "vast wasteland"

of television in the 1960s, arguing that media "screen time" squeezes out time for real-world play with adverse health consequences, including obesity and diabetes.

Nonetheless, children's exposure to media and digital technology in the home has increased steadily (Cohen et al., 2009). Children ages 2 to 8 now spend a minimum of 21 hours a week engaged with media on multiple platforms, including television, computers, and video games (Cohen et al., 2009). Children's multimedia consumption increases with age; 8- to 18-year-olds now devote more than 53 hours a week to a multitude of different media and technologies (Lenhart, 2009).

In sum, digital media are ubiquitous in children's lives. New technologies and content have altered the social, economic, and political landscapes in a very brief time frame. They have transformed almost every arena including health care, travel, media, finance, national defense, and private lives. Interestingly, education, in desperate need of reform, has not yet been transformed by the digital revolution.

Educational Media

Recent research indicates that educational media games and other products are powerful learning tools for teaching specific skills and engendering cognitive development (Buckleitner, 2008; Linebarger & Walker, 2005). These findings, along with evidence of children's increasing involvement with media, have underscored the need to leverage the positive potential of digital media content and related technologies in the service of education (Gee, 2007; Klopfer, Osterweil, & Salen, 2009). Over the past decade, children's use of media has increased, and research findings highlight the importance of the home environment in shaping their experience with technology (Cohen et al., 2009). Although the digital divide, in terms of media ownership, is now more accurately identified as a digital continuum, a new divide has emerged, identified as the participation gap. It is defined as the unequal access to the opportunity, experience, skill, and knowledge that prepare youth for full participation in the digital culture. According to educators, these skills together comprise an essential foundation for success in the 21st century

(Jenkins, 2006). Media and technologies are increasingly available to actively engage children as early learners, yet parents often do not know how to use media for educating their children.

Digital Tracking and Assessment

As the crisis in education continues, educators and academics look to technology for solutions. As noted, recent innovations in media technology and an explosion of digital content have changed the way young children and their families play, work, and communicate. In response, interest in leveraging the powerful appeal of the new digital universe has increased. Media and technology now have prominent roles in educational policy and as part of proposed strategies for strengthening our preschool and early K–12 school-age students' education. Increasingly, media content is designed for explicit educational use and has entered both the classroom and the home. At the national policy level, media and technology are held as essential components in the positive transformation of the educational system.

As part of this overall vision, the National Educational Technology Plan also articulates the role envisioned by the U.S. Department of Education for research and assessment. The promise of authentic child-centered and child-directed educational experience rests on the shoulders of media technology. The NAEP envisions " . . . an integrated system that provides real-time access to learning experiences tuned to the levels of difficulty and . . . incorporates self-improving features that enable it to become increasingly effective . . . " (National Educational Technology Plan, 2010, pp. 4–5). This educational system produces a new form of data, which is the students' digital input. These digital logs allow for

> . . . better ways to measure what matters, diagnose strengths and weaknesses in the course of learning, . . . technology-based assessments can provide data to drive decisions . . . that will lead to continuous improvement . . . When combined with learning systems, technology-based assessments can be used formatively to diagnose

and modify the conditions of learning and instructional practices while at the same time determining what students have learnt for grading and accountability purposes. Furthermore, systems can be designed to capture students' inputs and collect evidence of their knowledge and problem solving abilities as they work. Over time, the system "learns" more about students' abilities and can provide increasingly appropriate support . . . (National Educational Technology Plan, 2010, pp.4–5)

This vision represents a significant shift in thinking regarding the role for media and technology. What accounts for this extraordinary envisioned role? Two characteristics of digital media provide important elements of the answer. (1) Digital media are interactive: We view television; however, we *use* media. Television is, behaviorally, a passive experience. Interactive digital media require and invite compelling behavioral involvement. (2) Interaction with digital media gives rise, literally, to a new kind of data in the form of a digital log or tracking of the user's input. The ability to use a student's digital record for assessment purposes—evaluative and diagnostic—is unprecedented and powerful.

The use of digital media and technology for education presents new challenges for researchers. After 30 years of television research, further investigation into basic viewing behavior was no longer necessary. Simply, it is understood how, why, and when television is viewed. However, in regard to digital media, these basic questions represent an uncharted frontier. A description at even a basic behavioral level of *how* people interact with digital media, as well as *when* and *with whom,* is unfolding in real time and remains unknown. Additionally, there is only a small body of literature focused on the *why* and the meaning of digital experience at both an individual and societal level (Ito, 2009; van Oostendorp, Breure, & Dillon, 2005).

Overall, although there is considerable interest on the part of educators, researchers, academics, and the general public, there is limited scientific literature—exploratory or descriptive—focused on young children's engagement with and use of digital interactive media. This includes a lack of knowledge of children's increasing use of multiple media platforms and their involvement with multi-tasking. This small overall body of research is the result of several barriers, including research challenges intrinsic to the subject at hand as well as the speed at which new technology and media enter the social environment.

Section 3. The Role of Research in Educational Media

These developments of the past 10 years represent the context for an updated description of the role of research in educational media. Research, generally, is often categorized as either basic/scientific or applied. Basic/scientific research refers to scientific inquiry conducted with the goal of adding to the body of human knowledge. Applied research is conducted for the explicit purpose of solving a particular problem. Educational media, primarily, make use of applied research. Understanding and knowledge derived from research findings are *applied* to the development and evaluation of effective educational media products.

Educational media researchers utilize several types of applied inquiry, including market research, particularly in the development phase—when the educational media product is being created. Market research, arising in the 1950s, initially responded to corporate America's need to successfully influence the American consumer. Connected to the emerging discipline of consumer psychology, it provided consumer feedback to product developers and advertisers. Activities included testing product concepts, products in development, marketing concepts, and strategies for packaging and advertising. Market research quickly became a valuable tool in the creation of products, services, and the design of effective communications strategies (i.e., marketing and advertising). By the 1960s and 1970s, market research expanded to provide consumer and public opinion feedback for public relations, corporate branding, public policy, and political election campaigns (Bryant & Roskos-Ewoldson, 1999). All products, services, and communications, whether originating from the private, public,

or nonprofit sectors, became legitimate topics for market research. Within this context, television became an arena for applied market research activity.

The following definition is from ESOMAR, the preeminent global association of professional market researchers (http://www.esomar.org/index.php/codes-guidelines.html).

> Market research, which includes social and opinion research, is the systematic gathering and interpretation of information about individuals or organizations using the statistical and analytical methods and techniques of the applied social sciences to gain insight or support decision making. The identity of respondents will not be revealed to the user of the information without explicit consent and no sales approach will be made to them as a direct result of their having provided information.

Since the late 1960s, professional researchers (psychologists, educators, and marketing professionals) have played a significant part in the development of educational television. The Children's Television Workshop (CTW) pioneered the integration of research in its initial development of *Sesame Street*. The Venn diagram below is a representation of the CTW model (Children's Television Workshop, 1989). Moving clockwise, the first ring, Production, represents the creative content of an educational media product—its premise, characters, storyline, and visuals. The second ring, Content, represents the educational curriculum and pedagogy. The third ring is research.

Figure 26.1

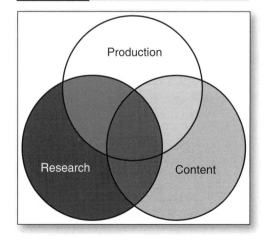

Research gives voice to children's experience of the product's appeal and children's response to the educational content and curriculum. By providing ongoing feedback to the product's creators in the form of findings from studies with children, research informs the successful integration of curriculum and entertainment, helping to merge two realms that are often at odds. This model elevated research to an equal role with other disciplines and has provided the blueprint for educational media research for more than 40 years. This model continues to be relevant and currently and effectively serves the new media landscape.

As stated, for educational media in the form of television, a primary challenge continues to be the integration of curriculum and entertainment. Consequently, a focus of research activity continues to be product appeal as well as children's development and learning. As we have seen, change has occurred and additional dynamics and issues are also the focus of research. Media products are now in the classroom delivering core curriculum, and issues of appeal have yielded to issues of usability and engagement. Additionally, the emphasis on outcomes has heightened the focus on summative research—the evaluation and assessment of educational effectiveness. Furthermore, the new realm of technology-based assessment provides a new dimension for research activities.

Formative Research

Formative research accounts for the majority of the studies undertaken on behalf of a media product. It is typically considered alongside its counterpart, *summative research*. Basically, *formative research* refers to all research activity that informs the *creation* and *development* of a media product and *summative research* refers to the assessment of the educational effectiveness of media product after its completion. Importantly, *formative* refers to the function of the research—how it is used—and not the methodology employed. Formative research is a neutral category in regard to research methodology—all types of research are potentially formative dependent on how the findings are utilized. As such,

formative research is composed of the wide range of research methodologies taken from the social sciences. These include in-depth group interviews; phone, online, and pencil-and-paper surveys; clinical interviews; and observations—conducted in the lab (the research facility) and in natural settings (schools, homes, playgrounds, etc.).

Research can be also characterized by a combination of methodology and the type of findings produced—and placed into one of two groups—*qualitative* and *quantitative*. *Qualitative research* is typically defined by specific characteristics of the findings that are textured, offering an explanatory comprehensive understanding of what, why, and how people think, feel, and behave as they do. It is typically associated with a methodology—the in-depth individual or group interview. *Quantitative research* differs in that it yields findings that are expressed numerically. Quantitative research is also associated with specific methodologies, in this case, surveys and questionnaires. Both qualitative and quantitative research can be used for formative purposes, informing product development.

Qualitative Research

The objectives of qualitative inquiry are varied; however, two overarching goals characterize a majority of qualitative studies. (1) Findings from qualitative research allow us to understand what perceptions and attitudes exist in a social environment. (2) They provide an in-depth understanding of how and why these perceptions and attitudes exist and developed. As stated, the methodology most typically associated with qualitative research is an in-depth, open-ended interview conducted with either an individual or a small group. Qualitative research is often the methodology of choice when working with children and is valuable in that it allows the researcher enormous freedom. During the interview, the researcher or moderator is free to change direction, to follow new lines of questioning in order to delve deeply into the topic at hand. Specific techniques employed with children include: direct and indirect questioning, ethnographies (interviews and observations conducted in homes, schools, etc.), clinical interviews, observations, and various projective techniques (developed by psychologists).

The most common form of qualitative research is the focus group. Widely used in market research, the focus group refers to an interview and discussion with a group of people (ranging in number from 3 to 10), moderated by a trained researcher. Equipped with a predetermined set of questions in the service of obtaining the relevant data, the moderator has the freedom to direct the discussion by asking questions, probing, and using play activities. Qualitative research yields findings that accurately identify perceptions and attitudes that exist in the social environment. Qualitative research does not and cannot yield data that will tell us at what frequency these perceptions exist. Shirley articulated the contribution of qualitative research.

> The value of qualitative research—in terms of the depth of insight and understanding it engenders—cannot be overstated. The nature of a qualitative interview yields data that is uniquely detailed and nuanced. The process facilitates an understanding of the larger context (social, cultural, economic or institutional) in which an issue or problem exists. Because the research data is used to formulate actual strategies or solutions, it is imperative to understand the issues and problems, not in a vacuum, but in the real world in which consumers develop their attitudes toward and expectations of specific products and services, and in which they actually make decisions about selecting products and services. (Shirley, 1998, p. 3)

Quantitative Research

Quantitative research yields results that are represented and expressed numerically. The general public's most common experience with quantitative research is in the form of public opinion and marketing surveys, election polls, and TV popularity votes, typically conducted by phone and reported by the press in newspapers and on TV and the Internet. Quantitative research, at its most basic, provides important information about the *quantity, distribution,* and *frequency* of perceptions, attitudes, and behaviors in society.

Simply, quantitative research provides answers to such questions as *how many, what percentage,* and *among whom.*

As stated earlier, its counterpart, qualitative research, is used to identify the perceptions and attitudes that exist in the social environment about a political candidate, a government policy, or a soft drink. Quantitative research is often used to confirm these findings but also to tell us what percentage of the population holds the same opinion—or, stated in research terminology, the *frequency* at which the opinion is held. Additionally, quantitative findings are *projectable.* The findings derived from a sampling of a population (the sample size determined by statistics) can be projected onto an entire population with extraordinary accuracy. For example, in the aftermath of the 9/11 attacks, qualitative research revealed that young children in NYC were at risk for several mental health disorders. It was the use of quantitative research that revealed the percentage, the *frequency* of children at risk—thereby quantifying the mental health impact (Cohen, 2002).

Researchers commonly conduct quantitative research using a survey instrument conducted with a large-size sample. The large-scale survey, developed by sociologists, social psychologists, economists, and political scientists, is designed for a specific set of statistical analyses to be applied to the data. It is the use of carefully constructed questions and surveys combined with the appropriate analytic tools that yield projectable results that identify the amount, frequency, and distribution of the perceptions, attitudes, and behaviors of interest.

In the context of formative research for educational media development, the processes for qualitative and quantitative studies share critical elements. The first phase of a research endeavor is to clearly communicate a study's objectives. In the absence of a clear understanding of the producers' needs, the research will veer off and explore topics that have no bearing on the actual challenge or problem to be solved. Once objectives are clear, both survey instruments and interview guidelines (for in-depth interviews) are developed, often in close consultation with the product producers and creators.

In quantitative research, survey instruments can be designed to include measurements of any number of variables—demographic and psychographic. The following is only a partial list of variables and includes: levels of content acquisition; unaided and aided awareness of other products; attitudes toward learning and specific content; levels of parental involvement; levels of motivation; levels of comfort with media and technology; navigational ease or frustration with product use; prior technology experience; preferences and attitudes; comprehension of content levels; ranking of product attributes; and the entire range of student demographic information. Analyses of the relationships between these variables allow researchers to understand the key determinants of children's media behaviors as well as their attitudes and preferences.

Additionally, the identification and measurement of demographic and psychographic variables form the basis of another unique contribution of quantitative research. The use of a variety of statistical analyses can reveal the existing interactions and correlations between variables. These analyses identify the naturally occurring and often counterintuitive relationships between variables. By extension, results identify naturally occurring subgroups within the sample, allowing for a projectable and accurate segmentation of the larger population. Analyses include a variety of multivariate analytical techniques: cross-tabulations; multiple regression; path analyses; principle components and factor analyses; structural modeling; and multidimensional scaling.

Sample sizes for the majority of quantitative studies range from 300 to 1,200 respondents. For research with children, it is critical to have a sample size large enough in order to ensure (1) that the diversity of the overall current population is represented and (2) the analytical power required to detect subtle meaningful differences across subgroups or segments. Simply, larger sample sizes allow for greater subgroup findings.

The value of quantitative research is the dependable, accurate, and projectable findings it yields. These findings often confirm and quantify qualitative research results as well as identify the scope and frequency of relevant perceptions, attitudes, and behaviors.

In addition, quantitative findings identify key segments in a population based on attitudinal, behavioral, and demographic data.

An Integrated Model

An integrated program that utilizes a combination of qualitative and quantitative research is considered highly effective for the purposes of applied research. Findings derived from integrated research have provided the basis for four decades of accurate, insightful, and actionable feedback to the producers of educational media.

Summative Research

Summative research, in general, refers to the range of studies and experiments designed to evaluate and assess a wide scope of products, services, and initiatives. Summative research, in the context of our discussion, refers to the evaluation of the effectiveness of educational media products. The goal of a summative evaluation is to provide an independent assessment of the effectiveness of media products' educational impact on target-age children and students.

Summative evaluations have been conducted throughout the entire history of educational media development (Fisch & Truglio, 2001; Guernsey, 2007). However, until recently, summative evaluations were conducted infrequently and assessed only a small fraction of educational media products, resulting in a limited body of research focused on this topic (Steyer, 2002). Within this limited literature, several evaluations met rigorous scientific standards and are referred to as seminal studies in the field. Other evaluations were flawed in several ways, characterized by research designs and methodology that did not meet scientific standards, sample sizes that were too small, inappropriate assessment measures, and lack of clarity regarding curriculum goals (Fisch & Truglio, 2001). Producers of media products, however, issued continuous positive statements and claims regarding educational value. These claims were based on a variety of sources, including professional and expert reviews of the product as well as teacher and parent testimonials

(Cohen, 1995). There was no industry agreement regarding evaluative criteria for effectiveness. Furthermore, the educational media universe was legitimately focused on the difficult process of creating the product, and the integration of educational curriculum alone was considered a success.

The introduction of the NCLB legislation in 2002, as discussed earlier, heightened the focus on accountability and effectiveness as a foundation for education reform. NCLB identified rigorous, evidence-based research as satisfying scientific criteria. Today, well-designed and well-implemented controlled trials, including random assignment of subjects to either intervention or control conditions, are considered the "gold standard" for yielding strong evidence in the evaluation of educational effectiveness (http://ies.ed.gov/ncee/wwc).

Federal funding has been critical to the vibrancy of the industry, and, by extension, the NCLB legislation has had a profound impact on educational media in general. The criteria for determining effectiveness and its measurement are clear. In order to successfully compete for federal funding, a scientific and rigorous evaluation plan yielding strong evidence of outcome, in the form of student academic performance, tested in a random controlled trial by a third-party independent evaluator, is required.

In order to meet all of the Institute of Educational Science criteria for demonstrating strong evidence, a study design needs to satisfy several conditions, including the random assignment of children to a treatment or control condition; the use of standardized and documented intervention procedures to enable study replication; the collection and comparison of baseline data prior to the intervention (e.g., achievement test scores) to confirm equivalence across conditions in order to control for differences not removed by random assignment; the use of well-validated, standardized measures whenever possible; sample sizes large enough to provide adequate statistical power in order to detect treatment or impact effects; the use of multiple sites in order to maximize external validity; and appropriate pretest and posttest assessment of all subjects (http://ies.ed.gov/ncee/wwc).

There is a reason for the attention and focus on the "random assignment to treatment or control group" component of this type of study. The process of randomly assigning a large number of students to either a treatment group (sometimes called an intervention or experimental group) or a control group ensures, with a high degree of confidence, that the only difference between the two is that the treatment group is exposed to the media product and the control group is not. Therefore (assuming the trial is properly conducted), at the close of the trial, a difference in the outcome—that is, a difference in student performance as measured by standardized assessment between the treatment group and the control group—can be attributed exclusively to the exposure and use of the educational media product. As discussed earlier, the strength and value of a random controlled study allow for reporting results that indicate a causal relationship between the use of an educational media product and student learning, skill acquisition, and development.

Analytics, Digital Tracking, and Technology-Based Assessment

A new form of data has come into existence as digital educational products enter schools and homes. This new form of evidence is the record of students' input when interacting with digital technology and media-based learning systems. It is a foundation for an accurate description of the interaction with the educational product and is used to identify changes over time. It is the basis for ongoing real-time assessment of student learning and progress. The information it provides is both evaluative and diagnostic and, as such, valuable for the student, the product creators, educators, teachers, parents/caregivers, and others (Brunner & Tally, 1999; Collins & Halverson, 2009; Gibson, Aldrich, & Prensky, 2007; Jenkins, 2006; Tancer, 2008; van Oostendorp et al., 2005).

The vision of a future where technology-based learning systems seamlessly incorporate real-time assessment of student learning was quoted and discussed earlier. This arena is fertile ground for researchers, who now need to master an entirely new form of data and analysis. Additionally, conducting meaningful formative research and evaluation of the educational effectiveness of technology and media-based learning systems poses new challenges. Educational products based on the use of multiple media platforms confront researchers with several formidable methodological challenges. Fortunately, the very same conditions that create these challenges offer opportunities and provide the needed solution.

Multiple Media Platforms and Research—Making the Invisible Visible

The first of the methodological challenges concerns constructing a behavioral account of students' interaction with digital content. TV viewing and listening to audio hold few behavioral secrets regarding what children are doing when watching TV or listening to recorded music. During viewing, researchers can observe time viewed and level of attention as well as channel surfing and other behaviors. Eye-tracking tools to measure more subtle eyes-on-screen time are readily available. However, in the context of the interactive digital world, a child's mouse, keyboard, and joystick usage are at best difficult to observe and describe for even the briefest time frame. The data are invisible. A description of use over time is impossible to record by in-person observation, and user self-reports of possibly thousands of movements at the keyboard are obviously not an option.

The solution is to make the invisible (student behavior when involved with interactive digital material) visible (available as data). It is provided in the form of an ongoing digital record of the student's activity, accomplished by including a tracking ability in the educational property itself. This digital record provides valuable data and describes exactly what the student is doing. It provides the data for an assessment of student progress as well a new form of feedback to a variety of stakeholders, including the project creators, teachers, parents, and caregivers.

The second methodological challenge in evaluating an educational multimedia experience is intrinsic to student involvement with multiple platforms working in concert. It becomes an important research objective to determine the level of synergy when different platforms work together as well as to differentiate the effect of exposure to individual platforms.

The third challenge arises from the difficulty in identifying a multiple media experience that is identical for all users. By definition, an educational multiple media experience is characterized by the absence of a standardized exposure and experience across students. It is by design that no two students will share the same experience. Although learning goals may be standardized, exposure to content is not. The challenge for researchers is to design appropriate interventions utilizing multiple media interventions for treatment conditions in a summative evaluation.

Research—When Is It Used?

Research contributes at four different stages in the "life" of an educational media product: (1) the concept phase; (2) the formative or development phase; (3) the summative or evaluation phase; and (4) an ongoing phase of technology-based assessment.

1. *Concept stage.* At the concept stage, prior to a media property being developed, research with target-age children provides feedback and informs the decision-making process of determining which concepts to move forward for development. Once a concept is chosen for development, research with target-aged students can evaluate concept appeal, age appropriateness, and student expectations prior to exposure.

2. *Formative or development stage.* A majority of research in educational media occurs during the formative stage when the product is in development. During the formative stage, ongoing research with target-age students measuring levels of engagement, comprehension, awareness, and involvement informs every aspect of product creation.

3. *The summative or evaluation phase.* Evaluation of educational effectiveness occurs only when a product is completed. However, research involvement starts much earlier. Identifying the appropriate standardized measures and field organization need to be completed and in place. Early clarity in regard to the educational objectives is

essential in order to ensure that the media product is assessed against its curriculum.

4. *Analytics.* Ongoing technology-based assessment is the historically newest research activity, and involvement begins early with product design in order to ensure the best use of digital tracking data.

Section 4. Relevant Case Studies

Three case studies have been selected to highlight the range of applied research conducted in the development and evaluation of educational media.

*A. Understanding the culture of children's lives and the role of media: An ongoing **Kids Panel** with boys and girls 7 and 8 years old.*

An important role for research is to provide feedback to educational product developers in the form of both a rich description of the reality of children's daily life and an understanding of the child's world from a developmental perspective. The immediate challenge: Digital media and technology have transformed children's lives, and the educational media producers do not know what the current social culture is for 7- and 8-year-olds. As a result, developers risk a serious misstep in the product's creative execution. This case study presents a research project designed to address this challenge by exploring and describing school-age children's lives with media.

As part of the evaluation activities funded by the U.S. Department of Education Ready to Learn Media grant, an ongoing year-long research study (2009) with children age 7 and 8 years old explored the use, meaning, and impact of media and technology in daily life. As stated, the explicit objective was to provide feedback in the form of a description of children's lives to product producers actively involved in the development of entertainment-oriented educational media products.

Thirty boys and girls, age 7 and 8, participated in the research study. The study was designed as a *research panel*, characterized by multiple meetings over time with the same participants. At the initial meeting, the children were all introduced to each other and were then assigned to a boys' or girls' group. Once assigned, membership was stable and the same children stayed together in that group, meeting regularly for a full calendar year. Periodically, the boys' and girls' groups would meet together. Each group was led by a same-sex researcher/moderator who stayed with the group over the course of the year and was present at every meeting.

Meetings occurred monthly on Saturday afternoons for several hours. Led by the researcher/moderator, a variety of media-related topics were discussed and explored. The children presented examples and media content brought from home to discuss. Additionally, media products were supplied in order to engender response. In order to gain additional perspective on the children's use of media and technology, parents/caregivers participated in several surveys and attended focus groups held at midpoint in the year.

The findings: Children reported going online every day; surfing the Web had become part of their daily routine. Children also played video games on a regular, often daily, basis, using a computer, console, and/or a handheld gaming device. Several had been gaming since they were 3 years old. Their knowledge of available Web and game content was considerable. Additionally, they expressed sophisticated expectations relative to design and graphics and rejected digital content with rudimentary graphics, favoring 3-D images and "textured" appearance. Extended dialogue or large blocks of text on screen were experienced as boring. Games without challenge and purpose were less appealing and engaging than games requiring teamwork and more intense interactivity in order to achieve a specific goal. Children clearly divided their media experiences between "in school" and "outside of school." Overall, they were considerably more passionate and animated about the media and technology they used outside of school. School, characterized by limited Internet access and software and CD-ROM use, was perceived to be out of date. Attitudes toward computer lab classes at school were negative. Children universally agreed that they already knew more than their teachers about media and technology.

Their parents/caregivers reported that their children preferred to go online or play a video game rather than view television. Additionally, they reported that their 7- and 8-year-olds surfed the Web or played games frequently and for extended periods of time—typically two to three times a week at minimum, for 45 minutes to an hour each session. The 7- and 8-year-olds actively sought out additional media platforms when exploring content or stories and moved easily from one device to another.

The value for media producers from this study was multileveled. The significant and most apparent impact was a profound reorientation, on the part of the content producers to the target age group, specifically regarding the extent and sophistication of children's media use.

*B. Evaluating educational effectiveness: **A randomized controlled trial to assess the effects of viewing WordWorld on preschool children's early literacy acquisition.***

As discussed, a critical role for research is evaluation—providing an assessment of the educational effectiveness of a media product. This second case study presents a recent large-scale randomized controlled trial conducted to assess the effectiveness of *WordWorld*, a preschool, animated television series that airs on PBS and is designed to engender early literacy skill acquisition.

WordWorld features WordFriends and WordThings, animals and objects physically made from the letters that make up the word and the object they represent (e.g., the character DOG is made from D-O-G, C-A-K-E looks like a cake, etc.). *WordWorld* also visually depicts letters coming together to form new words as well as depicting the letters that make up words. Story lines are constructed to explicitly integrate sound and letter recognition in order to engender phonemic awareness as well as word building and word recognition. All episodes share certain features that run through the entire series. The narrative for each episode includes *WordWorld* characters creating a new word and invites the viewer to participate by saying the letters out loud, accompanying the characters. As part of each narrative, *WordWorld* characters search for and find these individual

letters, and word creation occurs as the letters and word "morph" into the object they represent. For example, the narrative requires a table, the WordFriends find the letters t, a, b, l, and e in order to create the word *table*, and the word *table* then morphs into a table (the object). The overarching curriculum goals address a variety of cognitive skills integral to early and emergent literacy, including phonemic awareness, letter–sound correspondence, oral vocabulary, print awareness, letter recognition, and word recognition.

Production of the *WordWorld* television series began in 2005 and the series aired in 2007. Extensive and ongoing formative research was conducted to inform the series development throughout all stages of production. This case study focuses on the methodology and results of the evaluation of the series educational effectiveness (Cohen, Hadley, & Rosen, in press).

In order to produce results that would meet criteria for strong evidence, the study design includes a robust sample size and multiple sites. Approximately 800 children in 104 prekindergarten classrooms at 84 preschools located at five geographically diverse sites participated in the study. Sites included California, Texas, Mississippi, North Carolina, and New York.

Random assignment was conducted at the classroom level. Preschool classes were assigned to either a treatment or control condition. Children in classes assigned to the treatment condition would view one episode of *WordWorld* every day, Mondays through Fridays, for 6 weeks—for a total of 30 viewings. These 30 WordWorld viewings were composed of five different episodes, randomly repeated. Simply, children would view each one of five different episodes six separate times over the course of the study. Children in classes assigned to the control group did not view *WordWorld* and continued with preschool as usual.

All children were administered a pretest interview consisting of a battery of assessments designed to measure preliteracy and emergent skills. The assessment instrument included standardized measures for English-language vocabulary, fluency, concepts of print, phonemic awareness, letter recognition, and word recognition, as well as knowledge of the specific content presented in the *Word-World* episodes (e.g., specific written letters and words as well as oral vocabulary).

The random controlled trial lasted 6 weeks, during which children assigned to the treatment group completed their *WordWorld* viewing. At the end of the 6 weeks, all children were administered a posttest interview utilizing the same instrument that had been used in the pretest.

Overall, the evaluation provided strong evidence indicating that *WordWorld* was effective in achieving several of its stated educational goals. There were significant main effects for two educational goals. Children in pre–K classes assigned to the treatment condition benefited significantly in learning oral vocabulary featured in *WordWorld* ($p < .001$) and in reading and recognizing written words featured in *WordWorld* ($p < .001$) as compared to children in classes assigned to the control condition.

Additionally, results indicated significant moderator effects for subgroups of children. Children age 4 years and 10 months and older, assigned to the treatment condition, demonstrated significantly greater gains in reading written words featured in the series ($p < .02$), as did preschoolers living in rural areas ($p < .05$) and preschoolers with higher (top one third of the group) pretest PPVT scores (oral vocabulary) who were assigned to the treatment condition. Results also indicated significant moderator effects for gains in phonemic awareness for preschoolers assigned to the treatment condition whose parents/caregivers' highest achieved level of education was high school or less ($p < .05$) and for preschoolers whose PPVT scores were in the lowest third of the group ($p < .05$), as compared to children assigned to the control condition.

In sum, *WordWorld* is effective as an educational intervention in achieving some— not all—of its goals, and several subgroups of children benefit more than others. These findings have been used by the producers to plan future seasons and refine their educational objectives.

C. The Digital Continuum: Tracking media technology ownership and use across the income spectrum.

The rapid introduction of digital media and technology discussed earlier has transformed the landscape of contemporary daily life. Another critical role of research is providing an accurate and timely description of the ownership and usage of media and technology by families with young children. The third case study presents a recent large-scale benchmark and tracking study designed to identify and measure media ownership for families at all income levels as well as describe changes in media ownership over time. This study was conducted in order that educational media product creators were current in their understanding of what media their target students had access to and used.

In 2006, a large-scale survey of the ownership and use of media by young children and their caregivers in the United States was conducted. The survey included all income levels but focused on households living at or below poverty level. This benchmark survey represented phase one of a multiyear investigation, primarily designed to address the significant gaps in knowledge regarding media use in U.S. households with 2- to 8-year-old children. The survey was conducted with a nationally representative sample of primary caregivers of children between ages 2 and 8. A total of 1,601 caregivers were surveyed. This total number included an oversampling of lower-income and disadvantaged households.

The results provide a detailed description of the media technologies present in the households with young children. These data also provide an initial description of specific aspects of children's and caregivers' media use, including time allocation, content preference, and functions served. Importantly, the study served as a benchmark, allowing for change to be measured for years to come. Researchers' perspective was that identifying change over time in media ownership and use as well as content preferences would provide an invaluable tool for media producers, policy makers, educators, and others.

Several key findings emerged from this 2007 research.

1. Households at all income levels participated in media ownership. For example, among caregivers with annual household

incomes below $25,000, nearly three-quarters subscribed to cable TV, two thirds had DVD players, over half had mobile phones, more than one third had computers, and one-quarter had home access to the Internet.

2. Access equaled ownership. For most, access to media technology translated into ownership of that technology. For instance, while Internet access may be found in places outside of the home (work, libraries, etc.), most individuals who accessed the Internet did so from home.

3. Participation in a range of media content and technologies occurred at all income levels. Variation in ownership by income differed depending on the technology. However, all technologies were represented in at least some households at all income levels.

4. There were substantial differences in the incidence of ownership by income level for many media. In particular, more expensive and emerging media technologies were less commonly found at lower income levels. For instance, ownership of wireless hand-held devices ranged from 8% of those with incomes of less than $25,000 to 50% of those with incomes of greater than $75,000.

5. Other technologies enjoy near-universal penetration. The least variation was found for a mature technology: television (95% of households earning less than $25,000 a year and 99% of those earning more than $75,000 a year own television). Cable service, radios, and CD players were also found in most homes at all income levels.

6. Ownership and involvement in media and technology involved both affordability and perceived value; not everyone necessarily wanted all media. For instance, video game ownership topped out at 58% of households earning $75,000 a year or more, and, overall, there was only slight variation by income in frequency of ownership of this technology.

7. In addition to ownership of media technology hardware, most individuals subscribed to additional services that deliver a wide range of media content. Specifically, the vast majority of households with televisions also had cable service; those with computers also had Internet access (dial-up or broadband).

8. Once a technology is owned, the ways in which caregivers used the technology are nearly identical at all income levels. Some differences existed; home computer usage rates in computer-owning low-income households exceeded overall usage rates in such key areas as work and professional tasks (68% compared to 55%) and for adult study (45% compared to 38%).

Overall, the results of this study provided a robust description of media and media technology in the lives of young children and their caregivers. Certainly these data confirmed the collective perception that media are increasingly integral to family and personal life. If there was any doubt that there is a great deal of media in young children's lives, these findings confirmed their increasingly common presence for even the youngest children.

These findings also painted a complex portrait of the relationship between income and media technology use and ownership. The portrait illustrated the incredible reach of multiple technologies into homes at all income levels while at the same time making evident the real differences in access and ownership by income; many technologies that are ubiquitous for those at higher income levels are far less common at lower levels. In short, some of these findings suggested that financial barriers to media and technology ownership are being lowered and that the motivations to use media technologies are increasing, while other findings indicated that there continue to be real differences by income in ownership and use, particularly for more expensive and emerging technologies. In fact, both are accurate. Regardless of how one assessed the current state, it is clear that, given the proliferation and increased affordability of media technologies, the metaphor of the "digital divide" no longer adequately characterized the complex relationship between income and ownership of media technology. The current state is perhaps best described as a digital continuum.

In 2009, a follow-up survey of 1,204 caregivers of children age 2 to 8 years old was conducted in order to examine changes in media and technology usage and ownership since 2007. The sample was stratified by annual household income level: 602 participating caregivers represented families living at or below the poverty level (as established by 2008 Department of Health and Human Services guidelines); and 602 caregivers represented families living above the poverty level. The distribution of race, ethnicity, and geography represented the overall U.S. population. Respondent selection ensured an equal distribution of gender and age of children from ages 2 to 8.

Findings in 2009 confirmed the results of the earlier benchmark survey. Families of children ages 2 to 8 participated in the ownership of the full range of available media technology, and ownership of specific media technologies was no longer correlated with economic status. Differences in incidence of specific media technologies had decreased. In fact, in 2009, media technology ownership by lower-economic-status households had reached the 2006 levels of media technology ownership by higher-economic-status households. Additionally, results indicated a one-to-one correspondence between ownership of television and cable/satellite access and between computers and Internet access. Again, media and technology usage, including coviewing and couse by caregivers and children, was similar in kind across all income levels.

This multiyear study described the extraordinary amount of media in young children's lives at all income levels and indicated the need for a shift to the metaphor of a digital continuum to describe media ownership.

Section 5. Conclusions

Describing a complex system is challenging. The role of applied research and researchers in educational media is evolving in real time and at an unprecedented pace. Technological advances and innovations basically guarantee ongoing profound transformations for some time to come. Knowledge obtained through systematic inquiry has become integral and essential to the process of creating educational media and assessing its impact. Researchers are currently problem solvers, consultants, authorities on, and sources of expert knowledge, and perhaps most importantly, an honest and accurate voice for the end user—the student. It is exciting to be involved in research during this unusual and extended moment in contemporary history. Behaviorally, our lives have changed as a result of media and digital technology. The impact on our psychic lives and on the nature of our relationship with ourselves and others is unfolding.

References

A nation at risk: The imperative for educational reform. (1983). A report to the Nation and the Secretary of Education, United States Department of Education. National Commission on Excellence in Education. Washington, D.C.

Boyer, E. L. (1991). *Ready to learn: A mandate for the nation.* Princeton, NJ: Carnegie Foundation for the Advancement of Teaching.

Bronson, P., & Merryman, A. (2009). *Nurtureshock: New thinking about children.* New York: Twelve Hachette Book Group.

Brunner, C., & Tally, B. (1999). *The new media literacy handbook: An educator's guide to bringing new media into the classroom.* New York: Anchor.

Bryant, J., & Roskos-Ewoldson, D. (1999). *Media psychology.* Mahwah, NJ: Lawrence Erlbaum.

Buckingham, D. (1993). *Children talking television.* London, England: Falmer Press.

Buckleitner, W. (2008, June 12). So young, and so gadgeted. [Electronic version]. *The New York Times.* Retrieved August 3, 2010, from http://www.nytimes.com/2008/06/12/technology/personaltech/12basics.html?_r=2&em&ex=1213761600&en=10ad107a6e1221f4&ei=5087%0A.

Bushman, B., & Anderson, C. (2002). Violent video games and hostile expectations: A test of the general aggression model. *Personality and Social Psychology Bulletin, 28,* 1679–1686.

Cantor, J. (1998). *Mommy, I'm scared.* San Diego: Harcourt Brace.

Carlsson, U., & von Feilitzen, C. (Eds.). (1998). *Children and media violence.* Gothenburg, Sweden: UNESCO International Clearinghouse on Children and Violence on the Screen. Nordicom.

Carr, N. (2010). *The shallows: What the Internet is doing to our brains.* New York: W.W. Norton.

Children's Television Workshop. (1989). *Sesame Street research: A 20th anniversary symposium.* New York: Children's Television Workshop.

Cohen, M. (1995). *Creating an educational children's network.* New York: Noggin.

Cohen, M. (2002). *Effects of the World Trade Center attack on New York City public school students.* Invited talk, the New York City Board of Education.

Cohen, M. (2004). *The future is changing the present.* Invited talk, Media-Jeunes 2004, Montreal.

Cohen, M. et al. (2009). *Children, families, and media: Media technology in U.S. households with children ages 2 to 8: Phase II: Media technology ownership and usage tracking study.* New York: Michael Cohen Group.

Cohen, M., Hadley, M., & Rosen, C. (in press). *Effects of viewing the WordWorld television program on pre-kindergartners' literacy-related skills.* Manuscript submitted for publication.

Collins, A., & Halverson, R. (2009). *Rethinking education in the age of technology: The digital revolution and schooling in America.* New York: Teachers College Press.

Davies, M. M. (1997). *Fake, fact and fantasy.* Mahwah, NJ: Lawrence Erlbaum.

Elkind, D. (2007). *The power of play: Learning what comes naturally.* Philadelphia: Perseus Books Group.

Fisch, S. M., & Truglio, R. T. (2001). *"G" is for growing: Thirty years of research on children and Sesame Street.* Mahwah, NJ: Lawrence Erlbaum.

Galinsky, E. (2010). *Mind in the making: The seven essential life skills every child needs.* New York: HarperCollins.

Gee, J. P. (2007). *What video games have to teach us about learning and literacy.* New York: Palgrave Macmillan.

Gentile, D. A., & Anderson, C.A. (2003). Violent video games: The newest media violence hazard. In D. A. Gentile (Ed.), *Media violence and children.* Westport, CT: Praeger.

Gibson, D., Aldrich, C., & Prensky, M. (2007). *Games and simulations in online learning: Research and development frameworks.* Hershey, PA: Idea Group.

Gopnik, A. (2010, July). How babies think. *Scientific American,* 76.

Gopnik, A., Meltzoff, A. N., & Kuhl, P. K. (1999). *The scientist in the crib.* New York: HarperCollins.

Guernsey, L. (2007). *Into the minds of babes: How screen time affects children from birth to age five.* New York: Basic Books.

Gunter, B., McAleer, J., & Clifford, B. (1991). *Children's views about television.* Aldershot, UK: Avebury.

Hart, L. (2002). *Human brain and human learning* (3rd ed.). Covington, WA: Books For Educators.

Hirsh-Pasek, K., & Golinkoff, R. (2003). *Einstein never used flash cards.* New York: Holtzbrink Publishers.

Ito, M. (2009). *Engineering play: A cultural history of children's software.* Cambridge, MA: MIT Press.

Jamieson, P., & Romer, D. (2008). *The changing portrayal of adolescents in the media since 1950.* New York: Oxford University Press.

Jenkins, H. (2006). *Convergence culture: Where old and new media collide.* New York: New York University Press.

Jensen, E. (2005). *Teaching with the brain in mind* (2nd ed.). Alexandria, VA: Association for Supervision and Curriculum Development.

Joint Statement. (2000). Congressional Public Health Summit, July 26, 2000. Retrieved in 2005 from http://www.aap.org/advocacy/releases/jstmtevc.htm.

Klopfer, E., Osterweil, S., & Salen, K. (2009). *Moving learning games forward.* Cambridge, MA: Education Arcade.

Knight, G., Roosa, M., & Umana-Taylor, A. (2009). *Studying ethnic minority and economically disadvantaged populations: Methodological challenges and best practices.* Washington, DC: American Psychological Association.

Lenhart, A. (2009, April 10). *Teens and social media. An overview.* Pew Internet & American Life Project. Retrieved in 2010 from http://www.pewinternet.org/.

Levin, D. E. (1998). *Remote control childhood?* Washington, DC: National Associates for the Education of Young Children.

Linebarger, D., & Walker, D. (2005). Infants' and toddlers' television viewing and language outcomes. *American Behavioral Scientist, 48*(5, January), 624–645. London: Sage.

Lyon, G., & Fletcher, J. (2001). *The diagnosis and management of learning disabilities. Annales Nestle, 59,* 112–120.

Medina, J. (2008). *Brain rules.* Seattle, WA: Pear Press.

Montgomery, K. C. (1989). *Target: Prime time.* New York: Oxford University Press.

National Assessment of Educational Progress (NAEP). (2003). *The nation's report card: Reading highlights 2003.* Institute of Education Sciences, U.S. Department of Education, Washington, D.C. Retrieved in 2005 from http://nces.ed.gov/nationsreportcard/pdf/main2003/2004452.pdf.

National Assessment of Educational Progress (NAEP). (2005). *The nation's report card: Reading 2005.* Institute of Education Sciences, U.S. Department of Education, Washington, D.C. Retrieved in 2010 from http://nces.ed.gov/nationsreportcard/pdf/main2005/2006451.pdf.

National Assessment of Educational Progress (NAEP). (2009). *The nation's report card: Math highlights 2009.* Institute of Education Sciences, U.S. Department of Education, Washington, D.C.

National Center for Education Statistics (NCES). (2009). *The nation's report card: Mathematics*

2009 (NCES 2010-451). National Center for Education Statistics, Institute of Education Sciences, U.S. Department of Education, Washington, DC.

National Cyber Summit on 21st Century Skills. (2009, June 12). *The mile guide. Milestones for improving learning & education.* Partnership for 21st Century Skills. Washington, D.C.

National Educational Technology Plan (NETP). (2010). Retrieved in 2010 from (http://ies.ed.gov/ncee/wwc). Washington, DC: U.S. Department of Education.

No Child Left Behind Act of 2001 (NCLB), Public Law 107–110, 2002. 107th Congress.

Natriello, G., McDill, E., & Pallas, A. (1990). *Schooling disadvantaged children: Racing against catastrophe.* New York: Teachers College Press.

Palmer, E. L. (1988). *Television and America's children.* New York: Oxford University Press.

Palmer, E. L., & Dorr, A. (1980). *Children and the forces of television.* New York: Academic Press.

Posner, M., & Rothbart, M. (2007). *Educating the human brain* (2nd ed.).Washington, DC: American Psychological Association.

Ravitch, D. (2010). *The death and life of the great American school system: How testing and choice are undermining education.* New York: Basic Books.

Rideout, V., Foehr, U. G., & Roberts, D. F. (2010). *Generation M²: Media in the lives of 8- to 18-year-olds.* Washington, DC: Kaiser Family Foundation.

Shirley, D. (1998). *ARC: A capabilities presentation.* New York: ARC internal document.

Singer, J. L., & Singer, D. G. (1998). *Barney & Friends* as entertainment and education: Evaluating the quality and effectiveness of a television series for preschool children. In J. Asamen & G. Berry (Eds.), *Research paradigms in the study of television and social behavior* (pp. 305–367). Thousand Oaks, CA: Sage.

Steyer, P. (2002). *The other parent.* New York: Atria Books.

Tancer, B. (2008). *Click: What millions of people are doing online and why it matters.* New York: Hyperion.

The Jossey-Bass reader on the brain and learning. (2008). San Francisco: Jossey-Bass.

Van Oostendorp, H., Breure, L., & Dillon, A. (2005). *Creation, use, and deployment of digital information.* London, England: Lawrence Erlbaum.

Von Feilitzen, C., & Carlsson, U. (1999). *Children and media.* Gothenburg, Sweden: UNESCO International Clearinghouse on Children and Violence on the Screen, Nordicom.

Washington, V., & Andrews, J. D. (1998). *Children of 2010.* Washington, DC: NEA.

Wolf, M. (2007). *Proust and the squid: The story and science of the reading brain.* New York: HarperCollins.

Zhao, Y. (2009). *Catching up or leading the way: American education in the age of globalization.* Alexandria, VA: Association for Supervision and Curriculum Development.

Zigler, E. F., & Bishop-Josef, S. J. (2004). The current attack on play. In E. F. Zigler, D. G. Singer, & S. J. Bishop-Josef (Eds.), *Children's play: The roots of reading.* Washington, DC: Zero to Three Press.

Zigler, E. F., Singer, D. G., & Bishop-Joseph, S. J. (2004). *Children's play: The roots of reading.* Washington, DC: Zero to Three Press.

Zillman, D., Bryant, J., & Huston, A. C. (1994). *Media, children and the family.* Hillsdale, NJ: Lawrence Erlbaum.

CHAPTER 27

Hazards and Possibilities of Commercial Media in the Schools

NANCY A. JENNINGS
University of Cincinnati

ELLEN A. WARTELLA
Northwestern University

Corporate involvement in schools and education continues to be a contentious intersection between business motives and educational philosophy. In the United States, schools are faced with a need to support educational endeavors with limited funding from federal agencies. According to the U.S. Department of Education, 89.5% of funding for elementary and secondary level education comes from nonfederal sources including state, local, and private sources (U.S. Department of Education, 2010). Corporations can fill that gap through altruistic philanthropy or through strategic self-interests, and educators struggle with the hazards and possibilities of each corporate initiative, program, and donation.

In the educational environment, corporate involvement includes public and private interests of companies and their employees. Mickelson (1999) suggests a typology of corporate involvement that identifies the types

of actors, motives, and nature of their involvement with schools. Of the six types of involvement, Mickelson posits that four types serve an altruistic motive. These include the following: (1) Type I: Large, independent foundations that donate millions through grants, (2) Type III: mid-level executives and small business owners that serve to establish collaborative task forces between business and education, (3) Type IV: corporate employees and hourly wage earners working in ongoing reform programs who volunteer in classrooms as tutors, mentors, and guest speakers, and (4) Type V: corporate leaders as state actors who are elected or appointed status in a federal bureaucracy or educational association. The other two types have strategic self-interests in schools. These include Type II: elite corporate heads, individual firms, and business organizations that donate corporate resources to schools, and Type VI: for-profit firms as reform, which manage and provide school services and products for purchase by schools. These last two types are of particular concern in terms of the commercialization of the school environment and will be the focus of this chapter.

Children compose a huge consumer market, and schools provide a place where they can all be gathered together and separated into age groups. James McNeal, a leading scholar in children's consumer behavior, calculates that children between the ages of 4 and 12 years spent almost $40 billion of their own money and had a direct influence on their parents to spend $350 billion in 2005 (McNeal, 2007). It is estimated that teens in 15 countries worldwide constitute $592 billion in spending power (TRU, 2009). Moreover, public education in the United States brings together 49.8 million members of this consumer market (Snyder & Dillow, 2010). It is no surprise, then, that the size and importance of the youth market has enticed new kinds of marketers to attend to children and youth and that the most cost-effective manner to reach them would be through their schools. Indeed, in 2000, nearly 70% of school districts engaged in some form of business partnership, resulting in an estimated $2.4 billion investment in schools (Council for Corporate and School Partnerships, 2001).

Corporate involvement and marketing to youth in American schools will be examined in this chapter. First, we will look at the categorization of commercial practices in schools. Second, we will examine one of the most controversial marketing practices in light of the current childhood obesity epidemic, marketing and selling of unhealthy food products to children in schools. Third, we will examine the state of public policy in this arena and the prevalence of this phenomenon around the world.

Marketing Practices Used in Schools

Since 1998, Alex Molnar has been tracking trends in commercial practices in schools. Over time, he has identified seven categories of marketing activities including the following: (1) sponsorship of school programs and activities, (2) exclusive agreements, (3) sponsorship of incentive programs, (4) appropriation of space on school property, (5) sponsorship of supplementary educational materials, (6) fundraising, and (7) digital marketing, previously called "electronic marketing" (Molnar, Boninger, Wilkinson, & Fogarty, 2009). In 2000, the United States General Accounting Office created a broader organizing structure of four types for commercial activities in schools that incorporate Molnar's more specific categories (USGAO, 2000). An integrated model with contemporary examples can be found in Table 27.1.

Direct advertising is the most obvious and visual marketing practice in school. This type of commercial practice includes Molnar's categories of electronic marketing and appropriation of space. Molnar (2005) defines electronic marketing as "the provision of electronic programming or equipment in return for the right to advertise to students or their families and community members in school or when they contact the school or district" (p. 24). This would include media-based advertising such as that offered by Channel One—video equipment and news programming in exchange for 2 minutes of daily advertising. Appropriation of space provides for the allocation of school space on which companies and corporations may place their logos or advertising messages (Molnar, 2005). This would include advertising in school facilities, on school buses, on team uniforms, and in school publications. The USGAO report would also include the corporate giving of free samples to members of the school community as direct advertising.

A variation on direct advertising is the growth of product sales through school fundraising activities, cash or credit rebate programs, and exclusive agreements. In a study of 1,000 principals of elementary schools, 94% of the principals indicated they use fundraisers to generate revenue to pay for school equipment and supplies and that 76.1% conducted one to five fundraisers per year (Krueger, 2007). According to Molnar (2005), fundraising includes programs that link schools or school-affiliated volunteer groups with companies to sell products or services in order to generate funds for the schools. This strategy is particularly problematic as it encourages children to become the sales force. Some of these

Table 27.1 Organizing structure and contemporary examples of in-school marketing practices

USGAO (2000)	Molnar et al. (2009)	Examples
Direct Advertising • Advertising in schools, in school facilities, and on school buses; • advertisements in school publications; • media-based advertising; • samples	Electronic marketing	• BusRadio's wired radios for buses with four minutes of advertising per hour (Hu, 2008) • Ads on school websites (Martin, 2010)
	Appropriation of space	• Nike sponsorship of high school football uniforms (Stein & Encina, 2008) • Future Shop sponsorship of computer labs in exchange for painting the lab the colors of the company logo (Weeks, 2009)
Product Sales • Product sales benefiting a district, school, or student activity; • cash or credit rebate programs; • fundraising activities	Fundraising	• Tickets for school musical productions (Klein, 2010) • Sale of Christmas trees (Krueger & Zayas, 2005)
	Incentive programs	• Free McDonald's Happy Meals for good report cards (York, 2007). • "Ford Drive For Your School" program where Ford Motor Company donates $20 for each test dive (Lawrence, 2009)
	Exclusive agreements	• New York City School's 5-year exclusive agreement with Snapple to allow the company exclusive rights to sell their product in schools (Day, 2003)
Indirect Advertising • Corporate-sponsored educational materials; • corporate-sponsored teacher training; • corporate-sponsored contests and incentives; • corporate grants or gifts	Sponsorship of educational materials	• "Elf" study guide by New Line Cinema and Ohio Art distributed prior to the release of the film (McClintock, 2005) • Armour All's curriculum on "clean living" (Thomson, 1998)
	Sponsorship of school programs or activities	• Target Field Trip Grants awards up to $800 to 5,000 schools nationally for various school field trips (Wegner, 2009) • Toshiba's contest featuring ways everyday people use laptops for $15,000 in Toshiba laptops for the district of the winning community (Ford, 2009)
Market Research • Surveys or polls; • internet panels; • internet tracking		• Elementary school students take part in Internet panels to answer questions using school computer (Tabor, 1999) • Elementary school students doing taste tests of sports drinks (Farber, 1999)

fundraising activities cross borders as incentive programs described by Molnar (2005) as corporate programs that provide funds, goods, or services in exchange for the participation of students, parents, or staff in specified activities with the corporation such as collecting product labels or cash register receipts from particular stores or restaurants. Recently, some incentive programs have gone digital with Internet-based purchasing plans where schools get a portion of online purchases made by family and friends and by linking corporate cards such as Target's Red Card to designated schools in order that the school receive a portion of all sales from that card. Finally, some schools have made exclusive agreements with corporations that give the corporation the right to sell and promote its goods or services exclusively in the school or school district (Molnar, 2005). These exclusive agreements have been heavily criticized, leading to voluntary changes by some companies toward schools. For example, Coca-Cola no longer encourages local bottlers to require exclusive beverage contracts with school districts, advocates to offer more juices, water, and sugar-free, caffeine-free and calcium-rich beverages, reduce the commercial signage on vending machines in schools, and urges bottlers to "unconditionally honor" the wishes of schools to refrain from beverage sales at certain times during the day or in certain locations (Unger & Paul, 2001).

Thus far, the types of practices have been very overt forms of commercialization. More subtle forms of commercialization come in the form of indirect advertising. Although perhaps less striking than the giving of free products, indirect advertising can be equally powerful. Indirect advertising takes the form of the sponsorship of educational materials and the sponsorship of school programs and activities. Curriculum materials provided by corporations that claim to have instructional value are what Molnar (2005) describes as the sponsorship of educational materials. This becomes particularly problematic when the corporate agenda is attached to the educational lesson. A second form of indirect advertising (sponsorship of school programs and activities) involves corporations that subsidize school events in exchange for associating their name with the activity. This has been carried as far as selling the naming rights of school buildings and rooms (Keen, 2006).

One form of marketing practices that Molnar does not discuss is market research. According to the USGAO Report (2000), few schools allow corporations to conduct market research in their school in exchange for funds, and few examples of market research have been found in the popular press and research literature. Although there is indication that firms such as Education Market Resources have been established to make connections in schools and conduct market research for corporations, very little current information can be found concerning these practices.

Commercials on the Screen and in the Air

Beginning in the 1990s, Whittle Communications' Channel One marked a watershed moment in the commercialization of the classroom and set into motion other companies to follow in their footsteps. Whittle Communications offered hardware—a satellite dish, VCRs, and television monitors for all classrooms in the school and all wiring and maintenance facilities—in exchange for a captive audience to watch its 12-minute newscast with 2 minutes of advertisements. In 2009, Channel One claimed to reach nearly 6 million teens in 8,000 middle and high schools in the United States (Channel One Network, 2009).

Criticism rose not only concerning the commercial practices of Channel One but also the nature of the schools targeted by Whittle Communication. In a study of 17,000 school districts, Morgan (1993) found that Channel One was more likely to reach schools in an urban setting, with a high proportion of African-American and Latino students compared to Anglos and Asian-American students, and in schools with lower student expenditures (6 of 10 schools that spend $2,600 or less per student use Channel One compared to 1 in 10 schools that spend $6,000 or more per student).

Channel One has also faced controversy regarding the integrity of its news coverage.

A report by Fairness and Accuracy in Reporting (FAIR) criticized Whittle for a lack of breaking news stories, oversimplification of political news, and too much of a focus on consumption rather than other economic issues (Jayson, 1997). Since then, however, Channel One has won numerous awards for its news coverage, including a Gold Hugo from the Chicago International Television Awards in March 2003 and a George Foster Peabody Award in 2005 (Channel One Network, 2009).

Other corporations have followed the Whittle Communication model. Founded in 1997, ZapMe! offers to install computer labs in exchange for on-screen advertising (Braun, 2000). As part of the contract, the computers come with a preloaded permanent interface known as "netspace" that features a 2-inch border around the screen. Ads appear in the box in the lower left-hand corner (Bazeley, 1999). Inside the netspace, students can link to multiple educational websites and enter chat rooms or use message boards that are provided and monitored by ZapMe! (Cearley, 1999). Similarly to Channel One, their practices have generated both concerns and praise. Some educators feel that this offer provides an opportunity to close the gap between the haves and the have-nots of computer technology and Internet access (Cearley, 1999). Yet others consider the exposure to the advertisements and the tracking of students' online behavior detrimental to children and "borderline child abuse" (Walters, 1998, p. D3). Ultimately, ZapMe! left this line of business to pursue other adventures.

Despite the failure of ZapMe!, at least one other company has ventured into the territory of media-based advertising. BusRadio, a start-up company in Massachusetts, set its sights on providing radios and radio programming for school buses while providing 4 minutes of advertising (Hu, 2008). In just 2 years since its startup in 2006, BusRadio had wired 10,000 buses in 24 states (de Vise, 2008). Like its predecessors, BusRadio fueled the fire again concerning media-based advertising in schools. And, like ZapMe!, BusRadio met its demise in 2009 (Illescas, 2009).

While media-based advertising raises concerns about exploitation of the child audience, food marketing in schools has become a growing area of debate and unease.

Schools and Food Marketing

In 2005, the Institute of Medicine (IOM) released its report *Preventing Childhood Obesity Health in the Balance* (Koplan, Liverman, & Kraak, 2005). This report called to national attention the "critical public health threat" of the childhood obesity crisis in this country. Between the 1970s and mid-2000s, the obesity rate among children and adolescents soared, more than doubling among preschool children aged 2 to 5 years, tripling for children aged 6 to 9 years, and doubling among adolescents aged 12 to 19 years. According to a January 2010 report from the Centers for Disease Control (Belluck, 2010), obesity rates leveled off over the past decade, but they are at alarmingly high rates of obesity for children. Approximately 17% of American children are obese, defined as having a body mass index of 30 or higher, and one third of American children are considered overweight with a body mass index of 25 or higher (Belluck, 2010). While we may have stopped the increasing rate of obesity among children, nonetheless, an alarmingly high percentage of children is obese or at risk of becoming obese. And as the IOM report points out, childhood obesity is associated with a wide range both of physical and psychological health issues, such as increased risk for cardiovascular disease, diabetes, metabolic syndrome, and a variety of psychological issues including low self-esteem and potential eating disorders (Koplan et al., 2005).

The report called for national attention to the issue of childhood obesity with recommendations for what parents, communities, and schools might do to reverse the trends. Schools were scrutinized especially for three reasons: (1) the downward trends in physical education programs and recess in the younger grades; (2) the increase in competitive foods or foods sold via vending machines, school stores, and school fundraisers outside of the school lunch programs; and (3) the presence of food marketing messages on the school grounds. The latter two issues are relevant for this discussion.

In addition to the 2005 IOM report on childhood obesity, the IOM conducted a separate study of the role of food marketing in the obesity crisis (McGinnis, Gootman, & Kraak, 2007; see also Chapters 20 and 22 in this volume). This report noted that children's diets are high in calories and fat and low in nutrients necessary for healthy growth. Further, there is an imbalance in the sorts of foods marketed via the media and promoted in fast food restaurants, with an emphasis on foods that are high in calories, added sugars, fats, and salt. Moreover, after a systematic review of the literature on the relationship between food advertising and children's food preferences, food choices, diets, and adiposity (fatness), the 2007 IOM report concluded that food marketing indeed influenced children's food preferences and purchase requests, children's food choices, and, for children aged 2 to 11, their dietary health. There were too few studies to draw conclusions regarding food marketing's impact on the health of adolescents. In short, food marketing practices were found to be out of balance with healthful diets for children and adolescents. The two IOM reports brought concerns about food marketing via traditional advertising and food sales in schools to national attention. Furthermore, in 2004, the Child Nutrition and WIC Reauthorization Act of 2004 (P.L. 108-265, Section 204) requires local educational agencies (LEAs) participating in federally subsidized programs such as the National School Lunch Program, Breakfast Program, and other child nutrition programs to implement a child wellness policy that must include an assurance that school meal nutrition guidelines meet the minimum federal school meal standards and that established guidelines for competitive foods sold in schools. In short, since 2004, there has been substantial attention to foods marketed and sold to children in schools as a consequence of the rising public awareness of childhood obesity. School-related food marketing involves both the foods sold in schools and more traditional forms of advertising and marketing associated with schools and school activities.

First, consider the nutritional standards of foods sold in schools. There are two basic foods provided in American schools: foods in the school lunch programs and competitive foods. Competitive foods are foods sold outside of the traditional cafeteria lunch program.

For many schools, competitive foods offer opportunities to raise money for a variety of school activities (sports teams, for instance) and also to help subsidize the cafeteria lunch program. Since 1946, the federal government has subsidized school lunch programs (as well as breakfast programs) for children from low-income families; approximately 29 million children participate in these programs daily (Stallings & Yaktine, 2007). Nutritional standards have been scrutinized over the past several years, and an IOM study in 2007 found that the typical high school lunch program is too high in sugar, sodium, and saturated fat and offers too few vegetables and fruits. The IOM report recommended that no more than 35% of total calories in the lunch should come from fat, no trans fats, and less than 10% of calories from saturated fats; only 35% from total calories should come from sugars; and restrictions on sodium content to 200 mg or less per portion. In 2009, the Robert Wood Johnson Foundation released the report as part of its Bridging the Gap program and found that by the beginning of the 2007–08 school year, most school districts had established a wellness program that included the acceptance of federal guidelines on food nutrition, and 50% of students nationwide were in a school district meeting the more stringent 2005 dietary guidelines (Chriqui, Schneider, Chaloupka, Ide, & Pugach, 2009). The establishment of national standards for school lunch programs has improved the nutritional makeup of these food choices for school students. However, such foods aren't the only ones available to most schoolchildren; competitive food sales have increased substantially over the past several decades and are the current focus of concern of nutritionists.

Competitive foods are a large part of foods available to children in school. In the 2004–05 school year, two thirds of elementary school children and 90% of middle and high school children were in a school that sold ala carte foods and beverages outside of the school lunch program; as well, 25% of elementary school students, 87% of middle school students, and 98% of high school students had access to vending machines at school. And as the Bridging the Gap report notes, there is an association between access to competitive foods in school and increased student consumption of soft drinks, other sugar-sweetened beverages, and foods low in nutrients and high in fat and calories (such as chips, cakes, and candy). Accordingly, since there currently are no national nutritional standards for competitive foods in schools, the IOM 2007 report recommended the establishment of nutritional guidelines for competitive foods, limited sugar, calories, fat, and sodium comparable to school lunches.

According to the Bridging the Gap report, there has been limited progress in improving the nutritional quality of the competitive foods available to children: Only 25% of students were enrolled in a school district with a policy that discouraged or prohibited the marketing of unhealthy foods and beverages in schools. Yet the public concern about childhood obesity and the role that competitive foods in schools play in this has led to some voluntary efforts. In early 2010, PepsiCo announced that it would remove all sugary drinks from schools around the world by 2015. PepsiCo, along with other food and beverage companies, is reformulating its products to reduce fat, added sugars, and sodium ("Taking the Challenge," 2010).

The marketing of foods in schools is clearly a focus of concern as well. The Bridging the Gap report found that the marketing of food and beverages in public schools had increased in the past decade as a result of both the companies' interest in increasing revenue and acquiring youth to develop brand loyalty at a young age and the school districts' interest in the revenue generated for the schools through such practices. Food marketing in schools is similar to other marketing practices discussed in this chapter; it includes logos displayed on athletic fields, gyms, scoreboards, textbook covers, screensavers, and direct advertising on vending machines. Increasingly, advocacy groups such as Center for Science in the Public Interest are recommending that school districts remove all food marketing from the schools in the wake of the obesity crisis (Center for Science in the Public Interest, 2007). Policies regarding food marketing in schools will be a target of advocacy activities as part of an attempt to not just stop the rise in childhood obesity but to reduce the incidence overall.

Public Policy and Commercial Practices in U.S. Schools

Despite the growing concerns regarding commercialism in the schools, public policy often falls behind public practice. At the time of the first USGAO report in 2000, no federal laws specifically pertained to commercial activities in schools; only general federal laws that apply to all businesses or that govern school finance would apply to commercial practices in schools (USGAO, 2000). Nineteen states had statutes or regulations that address specific commercial activities in schools (see Table 27.2). Of these 19 states, 18 states have regulations covering direct advertising, 7 states cover product sales, and only 2 states address indirect advertising in schools such as curricular involvement (USGAO, 2000). However, it should be recognized that some statutes and regulations prohibit particular practices while others permit the same practice. For example, a regulation in Virginia prohibits advertising on and in school buses whereas a statute and a regulation in New Mexico permit the same activity (USGAO, 2000). Moreover, it should also be noted that in 2000, state educational codes did not address market research activities in schools specifically. Privacy of the students was protected under general privacy laws, but nothing specifically as student activities would relate to market research activities.

Since 2000, some changes have occurred at both the federal and state level concerning public policies on in-school commercial activities. At the federal level as a part of the No Child Left Behind Act (NCLBA) of 2001, Congress mandated new protections regarding the collection, disclosure, and use of student data for marketing or selling purposes. Specifically, the NCLBA changed the Protection of Pupil Rights Amendment (PPRA) of 1994 such that school districts are now required to have a policy concerning the collection, disclosure, and use of personal student data including requirements for parental notification and consent (USGAO, 2004).

In 2004, the U.S. General Accounting Office conducted a second analysis of public

| Table 27.2 | States With Statutes and Regulations Concerning Commercial Activities in Schools |

States	Statutes and Regulations in 2000	Statutes and Regulations in 2004
Alabama		Statute
Alaska		Statute
Arizona	Statute	Statute
Arkansas		Statute
California	Regulation and Statute	Statute
Colorado		Regulation
Connecticut		Regulation
Florida	Statute	Regulation and Statute
Georgia		Regulation
Hawaii		Statute
Illinois	Statute	Regulation and Statute
Indiana		Statute
Kansas	Statute	Statute
Kentucky		Regulation
Louisiana	Statute	Regulation
Maine	Statute	Statute
Maryland	Statute	Statute
Massachusetts		Regulation and Statute
Minnesota	Statute	Statute
Mississippi	Statute	Regulation and Statute
Nevada	Statute	Statute
New Hampshire		Regulation and Statute
New Jersey		Regulation
New Mexico	Regulation and Statute	Regulation and Statute
New York	Regulation	Regulation and Statute
North Carolina	Statute	Regulation and Statute
North Dakota	Statute	Statute
Rhode Island	Statute	Statute
Tennessee	Regulation and Statute	Regulation and Statute
Texas	Regulation	Regulation and Statute
Virginia	Regulation	Regulation and Statute
West Virginia		Regulation

Source: USGAO, 2000, and USGAO, 2004.

policies concerning commercial activities to see to what extent public policies had changed given a new federal mandate and to see what types of proposed legislation were at hand. By 2004, 13 more states had established statutes, regulations, or both that specifically addressed commercial activities in schools (see Table 27.2). Six states passed legislation that directly affects market research practices in schools, an area that had been neglected prior to 2004 (USGAO, 2004). Moreover, as of February 2004, at least 25 states were proposing legislation regarding in-school commercial activities, primarily regarding the sale of food and beverages (USGAO, 2004). Finally, in an analysis of 61 district policies concerning the privacy of student information, the USGAO reports that few district policies address the new provisions of the PPRA. Indeed, only 11 districts created comprehensive policies compliant with PPRA, and 8 other districts had policies, but they did not adequately cover the provisions of PPRA (USGAO, 2004). Once again, most of the decisions and policies concerning commercial activities, then, reside at the local level in the hands of the school board, superintendent, or principal.

Commercialism in Schools: A Global Concern

Corporate involvement in schools is not exclusive to the United States. A 1999 report of the European Commission indicates that examples of direct advertising can be found in schools in Germany, Austria, and France (Ray, 2001). Indirect advertising including Nestlé's sponsorship of the Key Skills in Context educational materials for schools and a media literacy initiative sponsored by Mars and Kellogg's has been reported in the UK (Milmo, 2003). Product sales through incentive programs including Cadbury's commitment to provide sports equipment to schools based on the number of chocolate wrappers the school collects have also been found in the UK (Milmo, 2003).

European countries are not alone in the global commercialization of schools. A survey of commercial practices in 2004 reveals that Canadian schools also have a wide variety of marketing practices. Of the 3,105 schools responding to a survey on school commercialism, 32% reported the presence of advertising in or on the school, 27% maintained exclusive marketing agreements with soft drink companies, 30% had incentive programs, and fundraising was abundant (Froese-Germain, Hawkey, Larose, McAdie, & Shaker, 2006). Moreover, Canadian teachers were exposed through their professional magazines to hundreds of advertisements by companies offering free, branded materials for classroom use (Gidney & Gidney, 2008). In this instance, the teachers are then persuaded to use these corporate-sponsored materials in their classrooms. Gidney and Gidney (2008) suggest that the framing the appeals used in the advertisements capitalized on the social and educational concerns of the time, including (1) the promotion of the Canadian identity, (2) a contribution to school health, (3) ease of use to reduce the teacher's workload, (4) lively lessons that will keep the students motivated to learn, and (5) special attention to the importance of linking school to "real life" as part of the rhetoric of progressive education.

Marketing practices in schools can be found in New Zealand as well. Results from a survey of schools in six regions of New Zealand indicate that 83% of primary/intermediate schools and 85% of secondary/area schools engage in some form of marketing practices (Richards, Darling, & Reeder, 2005). The most prevalent activities among the primary/intermediate schools were sponsored programs and events (53%) and incentive programs (52%). While very few (3%) of primary/intermediate schools had exclusive agreements, almost half (41%) of the secondary/area schools did. Almost a third of the schools (32% of primary/intermediate schools and 30% of secondary/area schools) receive sponsored educational materials (Richards et al., 2005). These may include the teaching resources created by Chelsea Sugar, a well-known sugar refinery in New Zealand, which contain lessons that address "Sugar and its role in a healthy diet" (Barnett, 2006). Other schools have been involved in the allocation of space in exchange for corporate sponsorship such as a South Auckland primary school that legally changed its name to include the corporate sponsor, Baird's Mainfreight Primary School, and painted the halls in Mainfreight's corporate colors of red and blue (Barnett, 2006).

Interestingly, many of these countries face a similar situation to that of the United States in regard to public policies on commercial practices in schools. As indicated, few regulations exist in the United States concerning marketing in schools, and decisions are often left in the hands of the school administration. This also seems to be the case in a several other countries. In Canada, many regional governments including Ontario, Alberta, British Columbia, Nova Scotia, Saskatchewan, and the Northwest Territories have explicitly left these decisions to be made by individual school boards or districts (Froese-Germain et al., 2006). In New Zealand, even though 91% of primary/intermediate schools reported participating in fundraising activities where they sell products, less than a quarter (23%) had any policy or process to guide participation (Richards et al., 2005). This is particularly problematic regarding food marketing in schools. According to the World Health Organization, two thirds (49 of 73 countries reviewed) do not have any specific regulations on in-school marketing (Hawkes, 2004).

Decision Making About Marketing in Schools: Finding a Balance

Given that the decision-making power resides in the hands of local authorities, an examination of the moral and socioeconomic implications of commerce in schools provides insight into the decision-making process administrators and teachers endure to weigh the hazards and possibilities of in-school marketing practices. Domine (2007) identified four dominant perspectives—protectionist, celebrant, cultural critic, and educated consumer— to assess the power of commerce in an educational setting. She constructed these perspectives along the two dimensions of the moral and socioeconomic implications of commerce in schools. Only one of these perspectives, protectionist, would not accept marketing practices in schools. Grounded in the belief that media do more harm than good, especially for young people, a protectionist would censor, filter, and suppress commercial and corporate messages, particularly in a school setting. The inverse of the protectionist, the celebrant, embraces the new technologies that commerce in schools allows

and sees these new technologies as forms of motivation and inspiration for students. A celebrant would welcome new technologies at the price of commercialism, believing that the benefits far outweigh any negative consequences. In between these two extremes, Domine (2007) suggests we find the cultural critic and the educated consumer. Both of these perspectives would accept marketing practices in the schools, but under a different guise. The cultural critic is wary of the strength of commercial media institutions and would be opposed to exclusive advertising rights and agreements or anything that would prohibit educators and students from speaking critically of a particular product or corporation. Therefore, marketing practices would be permissible as long as they were not exclusive or stifled open expression. Finally, the educated consumer is a savvy media consumer and accepts media and technologies as a means for improvement and knowledge. To this end, the educated consumer is selective in what commercial activities are permitted based on the value of the choices available.

School administrators must decide what they value, what the community expects, and what the students need. Interestingly, in a study of school principals, few (17.7% of 91 principals) had a negative opinion on the effect of marketing in school, and even fewer (2.2%) had a negative opinion about fundraising activities at school (Feuerstein, 2001). Principals were particularly supportive and valued the effect of fundraising and corporate-sponsored events on the academic and extracurricular programs at their schools. Moreover, many principals perceived school board members to be supportive of various marketing activities, particularly fundraising, exclusive agreements, and corporate-sponsored events. Feuerstein (2001) suggests that in the eyes of the principals, the desire for increased resources for the children outweighs their concern for the potential harm of the marketing practice. To this extent, then, the principals seem to operate from the perspective of the educated consumer or perhaps even as a celebrant.

The main difference in these perspectives focuses on the beliefs of the presumed effects of commercial media on children and whether the benefits outweigh the potential harm. Domine (2007) calls for another perspective on commercial practices in schools based in social constructionism, symbolic interaction, and media education. As such, commercial media and corporate practices may be a facilitator of meaning making between the media text and the social structures in which they operate. Therefore, through media education, these marketing practices may be deconstructed within the class setting to equip students with tools necessary to participate in society. Indeed, media literacy training has been found to create critical viewers. A recent study examined the effect of media education training on seventh- and eight-grade viewers of Channel One (Austin, Chen, Pinkleton, & Johnson, 2006). Results suggest that students who received media literacy training recalled program content and were more skeptical of advertisers than students who did not receive the training. Students who received the media literacy training, however, also recalled more ads. However, it is unclear why the students recalled more of both ads and news. Austin and her colleagues (2006) speculate that the increased recall may be a result of the training and the discussion of the program and the ads in the class. Therefore, they recommend that until this can be better understood, students would benefit from media literacy training as a way to better understand and interrupt Channel One and its ads.

Conclusion

Marketing to youth is growing throughout the globe and across cultural boundaries. Through direct sales, advertising, promotions, curricular materials, and various forms of corporate sponsorship of school activities, corporate involvement continues to reside in the school environment. The reasons for this are clear: Youth represent a multibillion-dollar market for products today and schools provide a setting to capture the eyes, ears, and hearts of their current and future consumers as they influence family purchases along the way. American schools look for resources from corporations to fill a gap left by ever-shrinking budgets and increasing demand for enhanced educational performance (Molnar, 1996).

Administrators and teachers seem to be able to parse the good and bad experiences they have with corporate marketing strategies. Parents and consumer advocates have been developing an awareness of commercialization of schools in the past decade, but slowly.

The childhood obesity epidemic has ripped open the debate again concerning marketing practices in schools. However, this time, the perceived threat may actually shorten the lives of our youth. Therefore, new strategies must be developed to change the trajectory of the health and well-being of contemporary youth. Media education can provide hope for a better future. More research should be conducted to better understand the role of media education in the lives of youth. Far too little has been done to clearly understand the effects, both short term and longer term, of in-school marketing practices on children's consumer knowledge, attitudes, and behaviors. How can the goals of public education be harnessed to transform corporate involvement in schools? Does commercialization in the classroom influence youth to be consumers or critics of commercial practices? To what extent can public policy direct the future of commercial practices in schools? These questions leave us with the uncertainty of the strength of commercialism in schools and the power of education and public policy. Future research should provide an answer to achieve a better tomorrow for today's youth.

References

Austin, E. W., Chen, Y. Y., Pinkleton, B. E., & Johnson, J. Q. (2006). Benefits and costs of Channel One in a middle school setting and the role of media-literacy training. *Pediatrics, 117*(3), e423-e433. doi: 10.1542/peds.2005-0953.

Barnett, T. (2006, April 12). Soft sell easy as ABC when corporate sponsor schools. *New Zealand Herald.* Retrieved May 4, 2011, from http://www.nzherald.co.nz/nz/news/article.cfm?c_id =1&objectid=10377052.

Bazeley, M. (1999, March 21). ZapMe! school role debated: Students get computers; advertisers get a market! *Silicon Valley News,* p. 1A.

Belluck, P. (2010, January 14). Obesity rates hit plateau in US, data suggest. *New York Times.*

Retrieved May 4, 2011, from http://www .nytimes.com/2010/01/14/health/14obese .html?scp=2&sq=obesity&st=cse.

Braun, M. Z. (2000, November 3). Firm ends its plan for free computers for schools a Calif. Company says it doesn't have the money for the equipment. It had come under fire for ads in its system. *Philadelphia Inquirer,* p. C01.

Cearley, A. (1999, January 7). ZapMe! package has been delivered; schools get computers, the firm gets ad time. *San Diego Union-Tribune,* p. B-1.

Center for Science in the Public Interest. (2007). Marketing of low-nutrition foods and beverages in schools: Reading, writing and a candy ad? Retrieved May 4, 2011, from http://www .cspinet.org/nutritionpolicy/schoolfoodmar ketingfacts.pdf.

Channel One Network (2009). About Channel One News: Who are we? Retrieved May 10, 2010, from http://www.channelone.com/about/.

Chriqui, J. F., Schneider L., Chaloupka, F. J., Ide, K., & Pugach, O. (2009). *Local wellness policies: Assessing school district strategies for improving children's health. School years 2006–07 and 2007–08.* Chicago: Bridging the Gap Health Policy Center, Institute for Health Research and Policy, University of Illinois at Chicago.

Council for Corporate and School Partnerships. (2001). *Guiding principles for business and school partnerships.* Retrieved May 10, 2010, from http://www.corpschoolpartners.org/pdf/ guiding_principles.pdf.

Day, S. (2003, September 12). Sizing up Snapple's drink deal with New York City. *New York Times,* p. 2.

de Vise, D. (2008, December 11). School bus radio service no music to some parents' ears. *Washington Post,* p. B01.

Domine, V. (2007). Commerce in US schools: Four dominant perspectives. *Society and Business Review, 2*(1), 98–120. doi: 10.1108/17465 680710725290.

Farber, P. J. (1999, October 25). Market researchers turn classrooms into test labs. *Advertising Age,* p. 24.

Feuerstein, A. (2001). Selling our schools? Principals' views on schoolhouse commercialism and school-business interactions. *Educational Administration Quarterly, 37*(3), 322–371.

Ford, M. A. (2009, May 16). Selling Toshiba: Normal to help market laptops. *Pantagraph,* p. A1.

Froese-Germain, B., Hawkey, C., Larose, A., McAdie, P., & Shaker, E. (2006). *Commercialism in Canadian schools: Who's calling the shots?* Retrieved May 7, 2010, from http://www.policyalternatives.ca/sites/default/ files/uploads/publications/National_Office_ Pubs/2006/Commercialism_in_Canadian_ Schools.pdf.

Gidney, C., & Gidney, R. D. (2008). Branding the classroom: Commercialism in Canadian schools, 1920–1960. *Histoire social/Social history, 41*(82), 345–379. doi: 10.1353/his.0.0041.

Hawkes, C. (2004). *Marketing food to children: The global regulatory environment.* Retrieved May 7, 2010, from http://whqlibdoc.who.int/ publications/2004/9241591579.pdf.

Hu, W. (2008, April 17). Radio on the bus fosters quiet, but not peace. *New York Times*, p. 1.

Illescas, C. (2009, September 30). School buses jettison piped-in radio BusRadio—fought for years by child-advocacy group for its ads— apparently has signed off. *Denver Post*, p. B-04.

Jayson, S. (1997, January 22). Study out today details content of school TV news. *Austin American-Statesman*, pp. B1, B6.

Keen, J. (2006, July 28). Wis. schools find corporate sponsors; Cafeterias, gyms, more renamed to nab easy cash. *USA Today,* p. 3A.

Klein, M. (2010, January 10). Inqlings: School musical worthy of a Tony. *Philadelphia Inquirer*, p. B02.

Koplan, J. P., Liverman, C. T., & Kraak, V. (Eds.) (2005). *Preventing childhood obesity: Health in the balance.* Washington, DC: National Academies Press.

Krueger, C., & Zayas, A. (2005, December 2). Extra green for greenery. *St. Petersburg Times*, p. 1B.

Krueger, J. (2007). Controlling your school's "fundraising noise." *Principal*, 46–50. Retrieved May 4, 2010, from http://www.naesp.org/ resources/2/Principal/2007/S-Op46.pdf.

Lawrence, K. (2009, November 22). Ford promotion helps DCHS. *Messenger-Inquirer*, p. 1.

Martin, J. (2010, March 18). Schools consider adding ads to websites; more need new sources of money. *USA Today*, p. 3A.

McClintock, P. (2005, June 20). Kids get muscled by marketers. *Variety*, p. 8.

McGinnis, M., Gootman, J., & Kraak, V. (Eds.). (2007). *Food marketing and the diets of children and youth.* Washington, DC: National Academies Press.

McNeal, J. U. (2007). *On becoming a consumer: Development of consumer behavior patterns in childhood.* Burlington, MA: Elsevier.

Mickelson, R. A. (1999). International business machinations: A case study of corporate involvement in local educational reform. *Teachers College Record, 100*(3), 476–512.

Milmo, C. (2003, June 17). Toilet tissue firm accused over children's books ploy. *Independent*, p. 7.

Molnar, A. (1996). *Giving kids the business: The commercialization of America's schools.* Boulder, CO: Westview Press.

Molnar, A. (2005). *School commercialism: From democratic ideal to market commodity.* New York: Routledge.

Molnar, A., Boninger, F., Wilkinson, G., & Fogarty, J. (2009). *Click: The twelfth annual report on schoolhouse commercialism trends: 2008–2009.* Retrieved May 4, 2011, from http://epicpolicy. org/files/RS-CommTrends-FINAL2.pdf.

Morgan, M. (1993). *Channel One in the public schools: Widening the gaps.* Research report for UNPLUG. ED 366 688.

Ray, A. (2001, October 18). New guidelines for marketing to schools call for activity to have "clear educational benefit." What will this mean for brands, asks Alastair Ray. *Marketing,* p. 26.

Richards, R., Darling, H., & Reeder, A. I. (2005). Sponsorship and fund-raising in New Zealand schools: Implications for health. *Australian and New Zealand Journal of Public Health, 29*(4), 331–336.

Snyder, T. D., & Dillow, S. A. (2010). *Digest of education statistics 2009* (NCES 2010-013). National Center for Education Statistics, Institute of Education Sciences, U.S. Department of Education, Washington, DC.

Stallings, V., & Yaktine, A. (Eds.). (2007). *Nutrition standards for foods in school.* Washington, DC: National Academies Press.

Stein, L., & Encina, E. A. (2008, March 9). Sports branding hits high schools. *St. Petersburg Times,* p. 1B.

Tabor, M. B. (1999, April 5). Schools profit from offering pupils for market research. *New York Times,* p. A1.

Taking the challenge: The giant drinks and snacks firm attempts to wean itself off sugar, salt and fat. (2010, March 25). *Economist,* p. 15.

Thomson, G. (1998, June 27). Is public schooling to be a PR exercise?: Business hijacking curriculum, book warns. *Gazette,* p. J4.

TRU. (2009). *The TRU study: 2009 global teen edition.* Retrieved May 4, 2010, from http:// www.wpp.com/NR/rdonlyres/1D4ECC1D -7F9F-497F-9356-79BB01FA68D2/0/Global Glance.pdf.

Unger, H., & Paul, P. C. (2001, March 14). Coca-Cola learns a lesson in schools; Nutrition is in, exclusivity is out in strategy shift. *Atlanta Journal and Constitution,* p. 1A.

U.S. Department of Education. (2010). *Overview: The federal role in education.* Retrieved May 7, 2010, from http://www2.ed.gov/about/over view/fed/role.html?src=ln.

U.S. General Accounting Office. (2000). *Public education: Commercial activities in schools.* Retrieved September 17, 2002, from http://www .gao.gov/new.items/he00156.pdf.

U.S. Government Accountability Office. (2004). *Commercial activities in schools: Use of student data is limited and additional dissemination of guidance could help districts develop policies.* Retrieved April 21, 2010, from http:// www.gao.gov/new.items/d04810.pdf.

Walters, J. (1998, December 30). ZapMe! stirs up educators: Controversial program supplies cash-strapped school boards with free computers in return for running advertisements and monitoring students. *Gazette (Montreal),* p. D3.

Weeks, C. (2009, April 15). A lesson in breeding brand loyalty. *Globe and Mail,* p. L1.

Wegner, N. (2009, February 26). Out of the class, onto the ice; DBA pupils strap on skates to learn laws of motion. *Post-Standard,* p. 3.

York, E. B. (2007, December 10). McDonald's latest ad platform: Report cards; despite industry history of promos, fast feeder get an F from watchdogs. *Advertising Age,* p. 26.

PART III

Policy Issues and Advocacy

Preliminary Comments From the Editors

Because the electronic media enter the home and are susceptible to extensive viewing by the youngest children, concerns among parents, child advocates, and even public officials have been prominent for 40 years. Understanding children and the media, therefore, calls for an examination of how government agencies, industry, and new emergent advocacy groups have combined efforts to cope with the hazards so vividly outlined in Part I in the subsections: Fears, Aggression, and Sexual Attitudes; Personality, Social, and Cultural Variations; and Health Issues.

The chapters in Part III also point to ways we can foster the potential benefits of these media, as suggested in Part I in the Cognitive Functions and School-Readiness Skills section.

When we and other early workers in television research began our efforts more than 40 years ago, we felt that we were working in relative isolation. Our first goals were to establish in reasonably scientific fashion what the evidence was for positive or negative television effects. Parent advocacy groups such as Action for Children's Television took a strong role even before the great bulk of the data were in. By the early 1990s, we all began to see results in our efforts as Congress passed new legislation and as public debate about children and television entered

political campaigns. We were pleased to be able to prepare a report to Congress for the Corporation for Public Broadcasting outlining the concept of a Ready to Learn line-up of preschool children's shows. This plan has been implemented by the Public Broadcasting Network (see Chapter 26).

We turn first in this part of our handbook to Chapter 28 by Dale Kunkel and Brian Wilcox on the legal and governmental approaches to children's media. These authors lay out the legislative steps and Federal Communications Commission rulings that have reshaped national policy in the last decade. They also call attention to relevant research studies that support or question government policy decisions and actions. Of special importance for our handbook is the attention they pay to the cognitive and emotional developmental levels of the children for whom policy actions are taken. Chapter 29, by Karen Hill Scott, provides a useful overview of how the television industry responded to the federal policy actions of the 1990s. We learn not only about network and cable companies' in-house "standards and practices" responses but also about research and programming efforts that are under way.

Chapter 30 by Bradley Greenberg and Lynn Rampoldi-Hnilo uses the new age-based and

567

content-based rating systems now applied to programming as a kind of case study. Can parents use these systems, and with what effect? Useful research in this area has already appeared, and the authors examine the strengths, limitations, and possible modifications necessary if parents are to "take back" their home leadership roles with respect to what their children watch. The issue of parent empowerment, as well as child safety and family security, is carried even further in Chapter 31 by Kathryn Montgomery, who focuses on the computer use spreading rapidly to millions of American homes. What impact on children can already be discerned from their use of the highly commercialized Internet? What safeguards against child exploitation are necessary, and what forms of advocacy must come into play to avoid the hazards of cyberspace?

In Chapter 32, Amy Jordan moves a step back from public policy and regulation to looking within the home. What can parents do to ensure their children's benign use of television and the Internet? What steps must one take within the home to control media reliance by children, and what role can industry or education play to help them along? Marjorie J. Hogan carries this emphasis on parents or other caregiving adults further in Chapter 33. She draws on research and case material to provide a series of practical guidelines to adults for how to monitor, coview, discuss, and limit children's television viewing or other media use. She points out ways

that parents can make their beliefs known to television stations and appropriate policy makers through advocacy groups. Still another form of empowerment of the home viewer is through using a variety of educational resources to make media literacy and critical viewing a feature of both child and adult education. In Chapter 34, Mami Komaya offers numerous definitions of the concept of media literacy, reviews the available research literature, and outlines plans for incorporating critical analyses of one's TV viewing or computer use into the general educational curriculum.

We would like to think that the vast review of the research literature and social issues raised in this volume can yield some specific practical outcomes. Our closing Chapter 35, written by Laurie Trotta, provides a history and clearly organized categorization of advocacy efforts and groups in the field of children and the media. She leads us step by step to the present and future possibilities of child advocacy in the electronic world. Her chapter ends with an impressive outline that encompasses 20 media advocacy groups and their philosophies working today in the United States (one is focused internationally). The organizations are organized by approach, methodology, and the audiences they primarily serve, although great overlap exists. If one takes the findings reported in this handbook seriously, the list may offer many readers an opportunity to move from indignation or hope toward action.

CHAPTER 28

Children and Media Policy

Historical Perspectives and Current Practices

DALE KUNKEL
University of Arizona

BRIAN L. WILCOX
Center on Children, Families, and the Law,
University of Nebraska

Media are a central aspect of the everyday environment of childhood. It is well established that children are shaped and influenced by media in meaningful ways, just as they are shaped by other agents of socialization such as the family, peers, and educational institutions. Media effects on children may be detrimental, as with the case of exposure to heavy doses of televised violence or advertising for unhealthy food products. Conversely, media effects may also be beneficial, as occurs when children learn valuable lessons from viewing educational television programs. In this chapter, we examine the public policy efforts that have been employed to address media effects on children from both of these perspectives, enhancing the positive elements while reducing or ameliorating the negative aspects.

Since the advent of electronic media in the early 20th century, policy makers have voiced concerns about the negative effects of media on children (Wartella & Reeves, 1985). Motion pictures and television attracted the greatest scrutiny in the past, while video games and the Internet have been the focus of more recent attention. Concerns center mostly on particular types of content that may exert harmful influence on children, such as depictions of realistic, graphic violence, which occur in films, television programs, and video games, among other media. Yet interestingly, the policies that have emerged in response to these concerns are not grounded simply in terms of message content *per se*; rather, much of the regulatory framework in the realm of children and media policy is shaped by the nature of each medium's delivery mechanism. That is, the regulations applied to the same *type* of content vary from one medium to another, as we explain below.

The Importance of Media Delivery Systems

For a parent or child viewer who turns on an electronic screen to obtain some particular content such as a half-hour video program, it probably matters little whether the mechanism delivering it is a broadcast station, a cable program network, or an Internet site. In fact, the delivery mechanism is a key element in determining the applicable regulatory framework.

Broadcast television encompasses stations that transmit their signal over the air, a technology that uses the publicly owned airwaves and hence requires a license granted by the Federal Communications Commission (FCC). The FCC is the independent regulatory body created by Congress in 1934 that is charged with responsibility for administering the licensing process. Notwithstanding modest administrative fees, broadcast licenses are granted by the FCC free of charge, although not free of burden. Those accepting licenses must agree to serve the public interest, convenience, and necessity in return for receiving their license. The Commission has the power to create rules and regulations that stipulate specific public-interest obligations for broadcast licensees.

In contrast, cable and other nonbroadcast technologies are not bound by any obligation to serve the public interest because they do not use the broadcast airwaves to distribute their content. Consequently, cable and the Internet tend to be relatively free from governmental regulation of message content. At one level, this makes little sense. If, for example, there is concern about the harmful effects of televised violence, it should not matter whether the programming is delivered by broadcast or other means because the material's influence on a child will not vary according to how the signal reaches the screen. Yet at another level, such as the legal issues related to First Amendment protections, technological factors such as the scarcity of

the broadcast media (i.e., it is a finite resource, only one user can occupy a given frequency at a time, and there are more who wish to use this resource than can be accommodated) have made differential regulation of the mass media a well-established political reality.

The debate over children's media policy has been carried out largely in the context of broadcast regulatory battles because broadcast television has been the principal medium attracting children's attention over the last 60 years. Even though children spend significant amounts of time with new technologies, they still spend more time with traditional television content than with any other medium (Hofferth, 2010; Rideout, Foehr, & Roberts, 2010). Thus, we devote the bulk of our analysis in this chapter to three primary areas of children's television policy that have each received significant attention over many years: (1) policies intended to protect children from adverse effects of exposure to television content; (2) policies designed to promote educational programming for children; and (3) policies designed to protect children from unfair advertising practices.

We conclude by discussing the implications of the increasing trend toward media convergence for shaping policy to protect children's interests in the future.

Protecting Children From Harmful Content

With rare exception, media exist to make profit for their owners and investors. Those profits derive from attracting large audiences, and one of the surest ways to attract large audiences is to include sex and/or violence in the content conveyed (Bartholow, Dill, Anderson, & Lindsay, 2003; Hamilton, 1998; Wirth, Baldwin, & Zenaty, 1984). Even though most media content containing such material may be intended for adults, it is often seen by large numbers of children, raising concern about harmful effects on youth. Across all of the issues addressed in this chapter, none has drawn more consistent public and political scrutiny than concern regarding exposure to media violence and sexual content, the two topics upon which we focus in this section.

Regulation of Media Violence

Concern with the effects of violent programming on children dates to the earliest years of television. Congressional interest in the topic first surfaced during a 1954 hearing by the Senate Subcommittee on Juvenile Delinquency (U.S. Senate, 1956), long before any empirical evidence on the subject was available to inform policy makers. Across subsequent decades, Congress continued to devote significant attention to television violence, albeit without ever pursuing any formal regulation until reaching the 1990s (Cooper, 1996).

Throughout the years, social science research examining the effect of violent portrayals has played an important role in the debate about this topic. In the late 1960s, the Congress directed the U.S. Surgeon General to conduct a major program of research on the effects of television violence. The Surgeon General's report (Surgeon General's Scientific Advisory Committee on Television and Social Behavior, 1972) drew clear connections between exposure to violence and subsequent aggressive behavior, yet it presented many caveats involving mediating variables. The complexity of the qualifications led to misunderstanding by the press and the public, with some news stories erroneously indicating that the Surgeon General's report absolved the TV industry of responsibility for contributing to real-world violence and aggression (Cater & Strickland, 1975).

Following the release of the Surgeon General's report, numerous Congressional hearings were held, and the controversy they generated led to a tremendous surge in media violence research. As evidence mounted, further hearings were conducted throughout the 1970s. Although Congress considered no formal legislation on the topic during this period, the hearings nonetheless generated some impacts. Murray (1980) found a reduction in the amount of violence presented during prime-time network programming in the years immediately following each series of major hearings on the topic; and in 1975, the television industry adopted a self-regulatory policy known as the "Family Hour," which pushed programs containing violence and other sensitive material later into the evening, leaving the first hour of prime time (8:00–9:00 PM for most of the country) devoted solely to content judged appropriate for family viewing (Cowan, 1979). The Family Hour policy proved short lived, however, as the courts judged it to be unconstitutional due to strong governmental pressure exerted on the industry to take such action (Edwards & Berman, 1995).

By the early 1980s, research in the area had grown so significantly that the National Institute of Mental Health (NIMH) undertook a major new review of the overall accumulated evidence (Pearl, Bouthilet, & Lazar, 1982). With a stronger base of findings upon which to draw, the NIMH report concluded much more firmly than had the Surgeon General that viewing televised violence was causally related to children's aggressive attitudes and behaviors, as well as a contributor to desensitization and fear. This report might have prompted a stronger response from policy makers had it not been issued at exactly the time that a new regulatory philosophy was sweeping the country, that of reliance on the marketplace rather than governmental rules and regulations to ensure the public interest was served (Derthick & Quirk, 1985; Fowler & Brenner, 1982). Consequently, attention to the topic of televised violence waned for several years until Senator Paul Simon decided to champion it as an important cause.

Senator Simon sponsored legislation adopted by Congress in 1990 granting the industry an antitrust exemption allowing all parties to meet jointly for the purpose of discussing strategies to reduce violence on television. Technically speaking, the legislation required nothing of the industry; rather, it simply created the opportunity for programmers to respond to the problem should they choose to do so without fear of antitrust litigation, which they had often argued prohibited such efforts in the past (Simon, 2003).

The industry declined to take any steps in response to Senator Simon's initiative for several years. During that time, the level of consensus in the scientific community about the effects of televised violence began to consolidate in important ways. In the early

1990s, such organizations as the American Medical Association (1996), the American Psychological Association (1993), the Centers for Disease Control (1991), and the National Academy of Sciences (Reiss & Roth, 1993) all issued reports drawing the same strong conclusion: Viewing televised violence poses a risk of harmful effects on children. Public opinion followed closely in step with these conclusions, with a strong majority holding the view that media violence is harmful to children and that there is too much violence on television (Guttman, 1994; Times Mirror Center for People and the Press, 1993; Welkos, 1995).

The Advent of the V-Chip

In a political context shaped by strong scientific consensus about the harms of violent portrayals, and equally solid public opinion against media violence, U.S. Representative Edward Markey introduced his V-chip legislative proposal. The technology of the V-chip is relatively simple. It is an electronic filtering device that parents can use to block the reception of programming they do not want their children to see because it contains violence or other sensitive material.

Following President Clinton's endorsement of the V-chip in his 1996 State of the Union address, Congress quickly adopted Markey's legislative proposal, adding it as an amendment to the omnibus Telecommunications Act of 1996. The only firm requirement in the law was that all television sets sold in the U.S. must be equipped with a V-chip device that would facilitate program-blocking capabilities. While the blocking technology cannot function effectively unless programs are rated in some way, the law did not mandate any particular rating system out of deference to First Amendment concerns raised by the industry (Spitzer, 1998). Thus, rating of programs by the industry is technically voluntary, although refusal to do so would have been a highly volatile gesture that almost certainly would have backfired politically.

In 1997, the industry proposed a set of age-based advisory categories for use with the V-chip blocking technology (Albiniak, 1997). A major controversy ensued about the adequacy of these rating categories, and the debate was heavily influenced by relevant social science findings. Research conducted at the University of Wisconsin as part of the National Television Violence Study (1997) found that children reacted differently to various types of program ratings. While content labels (e.g., contains certain levels of violent content) did not increase children's interest in programs, age-based advisories (e.g., parental discretion advised for children under a certain age) did (Cantor & Harrison, 1997). Thus, the age-based ratings employed by the industry posed the risk of a boomerang effect by attracting children's attention to the very programs the rating system indicates pose cause for concern.

Following extensive coverage in the press and a Congressional hearing focused on the controversy (U.S. Senate, 1997), the industry quickly agreed to amend the V-chip rating framework to incorporate content-specific categories to complement the age-based advisory labels (Farhi, 1997; Gruenwald, 1997). More than a decade after it was introduced, the V-chip system remains largely unchanged. Program ratings are applied by each television network without any effective public or governmental oversight, despite the fact that questions have been raised about the validity of many rating judgments (Gentile, 2008; Kunkel et al., 2002; Walsh & Gentile, 2001).

Passage of the V-chip legislation was the first, and to date only, substantive governmental policy to address the issue of media violence. The impact of the initiative has been modest largely because of the relatively low level of parental awareness and use of the system. Surveys conducted by the Kaiser Family Foundation (2001; Rideout, 2004, 2007) found that a modest percentage of parents report using the technology, despite other data indicating that large majorities of parents continue to report strong concern about TV violence.

Recent Developments

Other initiatives to address the problem of media violence have been pursued in recent years by federal regulatory agencies such as the Federal Communications Commission and Federal Trade Commission (FTC).

At the request of President Clinton, the FTC issued a report in 2000 examining the marketing of violent entertainment to children, with a primary focus on movies and videos, music, and video games. The report concluded that all of these industries engaged in youth-oriented marketing practices promoting violent media content that is clearly labeled as inappropriate for children (FTC, 2000). The FTC found numerous examples of promotions for PG-13-rated films linked to foods, toys, and other products clearly oriented to younger age groups. For example, Burger King offered Kids' Meals featuring a character from the *Ironman* movie, while Batman toys were offered inside boxes of Cheerios. The M-rated violent video game *Halo 3* was heavily promoted on 7-Eleven Slurpee cups and Burger King food and drink packaging. In sum, the FTC determined that the very industries responsible for developing rating systems they claimed would help parents protect their children from inappropriate media content were in fact engaging in the hypocritical act of marketing that same media content directly to children. Though underscoring a serious problem, the report offered no proposed regulatory solutions, instead recommending that industry self-regulation should be pursued to prevent problematic practices.

At the direction of the Senate Commerce Committee, the FTC conducted six follow-up assessments in this realm between 2001 and 2009. These reports tracked the industry commitments and initiatives employed to address the concerns raised, as well as scrutinized compliance with the voluntary standards on advertising and retail sales recommended in the FTC's initial report.

While compliance with recommended efforts to reduce the marketing of violent entertainment media to children increased substantially in some areas, the overall rate of marketing such content to children remained high throughout this 10-year period. For example, the FTC had children between the ages of 13 and 16 attempt to purchase R-rated movie tickets, R-rated and unrated DVDs, CDs with Parental Advisory Labels, and M-rated video games. In 2009, 28% of these

youth successfully bought R-rated movie tickets, 54% purchased R-rated DVDs, and 58% purchased unrated DVDs without being challenged, all in violation of industry self-regulatory initiatives (FTC, 2009). In addition, 20% were able to purchase M-rated video games, while 72% successfully purchased explicit-content music CDs without being challenged. These findings clearly identify the limitations of self-regulatory initiatives that run counter to the industry's economic interests, although the FTC currently lacks authority to implement any direct regulation of practices in this area. Congressional action would be required for any formal governmental regulation limiting the marketing of violent media products to young people.

Reflecting their disappointment with the apparent lack of impact from the V-chip and dissatisfaction with the industry's efforts to decrease violent content, 39 members of the House Commerce Committee sent a request to the FCC in 2004 asking it to undertake a broad review of policy options on the topic of television violence (FCC, 2007a, p. 7930). The Commission's report embraces the conclusion that exposure to television violence can cause harm to children, establishing a potential foundation for government action (FCC, 2007a). It also concludes that the V-chip system, including the voluntary rating framework and efforts to inform consumers about it, has been an ineffective policy response. According to the Commission, "we believe that the evidence clearly points to one conclusion: the V-chip is of limited effectiveness in protecting children from violent programming" (FCC, 2007a, p. 7942).

Of particular importance, the FCC also asserts in the report that Congress could successfully craft restrictions on broadcast violence without violating the First Amendment, a position initially adopted by Attorney General Janet Reno in the 1990s (Reno, 1993). According to the FCC's analysis, Congress must ground its regulation in the compelling governmental interest of reducing children's exposure to material known to be linked to harmful effects; craft a definition of violence consistent with social science evidence about harmful effects that is not overly broad; and also devise its regulation using the least restrictive means that would still allow adults who wish to view violent portrayals reasonable access to such material.

Since the FCC's report was released, members of Congress have introduced modest legislative proposals regarding television violence, but none of these bills has received serious attention. No significant proposal has yet surfaced to formally restrict televised violent portrayals, at least in part because of criticism from legal scholars who disagree with the FCC report's conclusion that such a policy could be implemented without violating broadcasters' First Amendment rights (Corn-Revere, 2007; Edwards & Berman, 1995; Sparr, 2008).

Violent Video Games

The video game industry is based upon a different economic model than advertiser-supported television, selling its products directly to consumers; and it is also subject to a different regulatory environment, lacking any of the public-interest obligations associated with over-the-air television channels. Like television, however, a substantial body of research evidence documents the risks of increased aggression associated with young people's video game use (Anderson, Gentile, & Buckley, 2007; Anderson et al., 2010; see Chapters 12 and 13 in this volume). Indeed, the American Psychological Association (2005) issued a policy statement concluding that violent video games have serious detrimental effects on youth and recommended a number of steps to address these harms.

Based upon concerns raised by the relevant research, several state and local jurisdictions have adopted restrictions on the sale of violent video games to minors, including Illinois (Entertainment Software Association v. Blagojevich, 2005), Minnesota (Entertainment Software Association v. Swanson, 2008), and Louisiana (Entertainment Software Association v. Foti, 2006). All of these ordinances were quickly overturned in federal court as violations of the First Amendment free speech rights of video game makers.

A similar law adopted by the California state legislature in 2005 banned the sale or rental to minors of games considered excessively violent. This law (Assembly Bill 1179, 2005) initially met the same fate as that of the earlier ordinances. Immediately following its approval, the U.S. District Court for the Northern District of California granted an injunction blocking implementation of the act and later overturned the law (Video Software Dealers Association v. Schwarzenegger, 2005). California appealed the ruling, and the 9th U.S. Circuit Court of Appeals upheld the lower court ruling (Video Software Dealers Association v. Schwarzenegger, 2009), relying upon two key arguments.

First, the appeals court judged that existing research did not establish that video game exposure represents a clear danger of harmful effects on children. Second, the court held that the law violates the First Amendment rights of those selling and renting video games since less restrictive means could be designed to limit children's exposure to violent video content.

Given that the court rulings on the California law were similar to all of the previous efforts to regulate violent video games, most observers expected the Court of Appeals judgment to be the end of the line for this case. It is not. The U.S. Supreme Court granted certiorari, and the State of California's arguments to uphold the law were heard in late 2010. Legal pundits have puzzled about why the Supreme Court would agree to hear this case if its predilection was simply to uphold the lower court's ruling (Orland, 2010; Rovello, 2010), but it is impossible to predict an outcome in advance. The Supreme Court's decision is expected in mid–2011 and will certainly represent a landmark.

Future Prospects for Media Violence Policy

If past precedent holds true, the issue of media violence is likely to be re-engaged most actively in the future as a by-product of some cataclysmic violent event that threatens the nation's social fabric, as occurred in the aftermath of a wave of school shootings in West Paducah, Kentucky; Jonesboro, Arkansas; Springfield, Oregon; and Littleton, Colorado, in the late 1990s (Newman, 2004). In several of these instances media violence, generally, and video game violence, specifically, were cited as possible causative factors triggering the outbursts. In the absence of such a catalyst, however, it seems unlikely that any new and strong governmental regulation will be adopted, despite all of the evidence documenting the harmfulness of media violence. Over the half-century that the nation's policy makers have debated this issue, the V-chip initiative remains the only substantive policy yet adopted by the government in this area.

Regulating Exposure to Indecent Material

The government has traditionally played a far more active role in the regulation of indecency than violence, although most of the involvement in this realm has stemmed from actions involving the FCC and the courts rather than Congress. Indecency is defined by the FCC as "language or material that depicts or describes, in terms patently offensive as measured by contemporary community standards for the broadcast medium, sexual or excretory activities or organs" (Carter, Franklin, & Wright, 1999, p. 246). In other words, while indecency consists of words or pictures that are strongly offensive, not just any offensive material can qualify as indecent; to be defined as such, it is essential that the material be associated with sexual and/or excretory elements. This means, for example, that a highly graphic portrayal of violence that most people would judge as offensive could not be deemed indecent under current law.

The "Pacifica" Precedent

In perhaps the FCC's most visible enforcement effort throughout its long history, the agency took action in the 1970s against a station for airing comedian George Carlin's "Filthy Words" skit, which ironically enough was a tirade against the FCC's indecency policy. In the skit, Carlin utters "the seven words you can't say on the broadcast airwaves" to a chorus of uncontrolled laughter from a live audience. When the FCC attempted to punish the station involved in airing the skit, the broadcaster appealed on First Amendment grounds, claiming indecency restrictions were unconstitutional.

In a landmark ruling, the Supreme Court upheld the right of the FCC to prohibit indecent material during times of day when children are likely to be in the audience (FCC v. Pacifica Foundation, 1978). In reaching its decision, the Court had to strike a balance between (a) the First Amendment rights of broadcasters and listeners in general who wished to have access to indecent content, and (b) the rights of parents who wished to protect their children from exposure to material they deemed inappropriate and/or potentially harmful. The Court considered the protection of children to be a compelling governmental interest. Because the FCC enforced its indecency restriction only from 6 AM to 10 PM, the time when children were judged most likely to be in the audience, the policy met the Supreme Court's "least restrictive means" test and was therefore considered constitutional.

In the late 1980s, the Congress adopted legislation extending the FCC's indecency restriction to 24 hours a day, but subsequent court rulings held that this policy was unconstitutional because the new law failed the court's "least restrictive means" test (Action for Children's Television v. FCC, 1988; 1991). Following its return to the "safe harbor" approach, which allows the broadcast of indecent material between 10 PM and 6 AM, the courts have consistently judged the FCC's indecency policy constitutional. However, a recent set of developments, including shifts in enforcement action at the FCC along with a major court ruling regarding these tactics, has changed the regulatory landscape.

The FCC Steps Up Indecency Enforcement

Following the Supreme Court's ruling in *Pacifica*, the FCC for many years pursued a restrained enforcement policy. Consistent with the Supreme Court's judgment that its decision did not "speak to cases involving the isolated use of a potentially offensive word . . . " (FCC v. Pacifica, 1978, pp. 760–761), the FCC did not act on indecency complaints based upon an isolated word or utterance that met the definition of indecency. This posture changed, however, in 2004. During the broadcast of the Golden Globe Awards program, an honoree used an unusually strong but isolated vulgarity in expressing his pleasure at receiving a top award. Reversing decades of precedent, the FCC ruled that this single use of a highly offensive expletive was indecent and sought to fine the stations that had aired it (FCC, 2004b).

This reflected a significant shift in policy (Barron, 2010), with the FCC indicating that "fleeting expletives" would, in the future, be subject to scrutiny and fines. All prior decisions in which the use of an isolated word was held *per se* not indecent were overruled. Primary among the reasons offered for this shift was what became known as the "first blow" policy—that children can be harmed by their first, brief exposure to an indecent utterance or image. The FCC offered no empirical support for this claim.

This ruling was part of a series of indecency enforcement actions by the FCC against broadcasters, including the infamous "wardrobe malfunction" involving Janet Jackson at the 2004 Super Bowl, during which her breast was briefly exposed. Congress expressed its support for the FCC's posture by increasing the fines for indecency violations tenfold, from $32,500 to $325,000 per violation. As a result of these changes, the fines by the FCC for broadcast indecency increased from $440,000 in 2003 to $7.9 million in 2004 (FCC, 2006).

Predictably, broadcasters objected to the new policy and appealed in the courts to overturn it. A three-justice panel of the 2nd Circuit Court of Appeals ruled (2–1) that the FCC had failed to adequately establish a basis for its shift in policy, as required under the Administrative Procedures Act whenever a federal agency adopts new rules, effectively blocking the policy (Fox Television Stations v. FCC, 2007).

The FCC appealed the ruling, and the Supreme Court reversed (5–4) the 2nd Circuit Court's decision (FCC v. Fox Television Stations, 2009), holding that the agency's fleeting expletive policy was reasonable and justified rather than arbitrary and capricious. In weighing the risk of harm from children's exposure to indecency, the court observed that despite an absence of supporting evidence, "it suffices to know that children mimic the behavior they observe . . . " and that "if enforcement had to be supported by empirical data, the ban would effectively be a nullity" (FCC v. Fox Television Stations, 2009, p. 1813).

This decision represents another in a long string of industry challenges to indecency enforcement that have largely failed to rein in the government. It is noteworthy, however, that this latest Supreme Court decision was based solely on a challenge to administrative aspects of the law. Indeed, the lower court ruling had accepted without comment that it was constitutional for the FCC to restrict indecency, based on the long-standing Pacifica precedent. While upholding the FCC's administration of the law, the Supreme Court declined to address the broadcasters' complaint that the indecency policy was unconstitutional, noting that the lower court had not yet considered that question and observing that the high court is "one of last review and not of first view" (FCC v. Fox Television Stations. 2009, p. 1819).

With the case remanded to them for reconsideration, the 2nd U.S. Circuit Court of Appeals addressed the constitutional question and ruled (3–0) that the FCC's indecency policy as a whole, not just its fleeting expletive policy, is unconstitutionally vague (Fox Television Stations v. FCC, 2010). The justices argued that by adopting a flexible definition of indecency, the FCC had created an indiscernible standard that could not be fairly anticipated by broadcasters. The result, according to the ruling, is a chilling effect by which broadcasters must self-censor speech that is protected by the First Amendment because of fear it might be judged indecent by the FCC (Campbell, 2010).

In the latest development, the FCC has appealed this decision. If the full 2nd Circuit Court declines to revisit the case, the U.S. Supreme Court will quite likely hear it. If it does, it will be the first time since 1978 that the Supreme Court has weighed a First Amendment challenge to the FCC's indecency policy. Whatever ruling is issued will set the precedent on this question for many decades to come. Whether the court will shift its stance on the constitutionality question is impossible to predict.

Harmful Content: A Summary

Contrasting the differing outcomes of efforts to regulate violent and indecent television content, one is struck by the substantial restrictions on indecency and the more laissez faire approach to regulating violence. The contrast is particularly ironic if one bears in mind the empirical research on the effects of exposure to indecent versus violent material. As noted above, there is a substantial body of evidence indicating that television violence contributes significantly to the aggressive attitudes and behaviors of many children and adolescents. In contrast, there is no comparable body of data to support serious concern about any harmful effects of children's exposure to indecent content. While research in the area may be difficult due to ethical concerns, some researchers have applied relevant theory to argue against the expectation of any substantial effects from children's exposure to such material. Donnerstein, Wilson, and Linz (1992) assert there is "no reason to conclude any risk of harm should be associated with [children's] exposure to broadcast indecency" (p. 116). Interestingly, this absence of empirical validation has not yet discouraged the courts from upholding the constitutionality of the government's restriction on indecency.

The fact that the general public finds greater offense in displays of indecency in the media than they do in depictions of violence is almost certainly a critical factor underlying the different approaches to policy in these two areas. Indeed, it is important to keep in mind that the courts have viewed violence and indecency in entirely different ways. In the instance of exposure to indecent content, the courts have focused on the issue of offensiveness and have held that despite any evidence of harm resulting from exposure, they are willing to accept as a matter of common sense that indecent material is offensive to and inappropriate for children. In contrast,

the courts (and the regulating agencies) have expressed interest in questions about the psychological harm resulting from exposure to violence but have not raised major concerns regarding the offensiveness of such material (American Amusement Machine Association v. Kendrick, 2001; Video Software Dealers v. Schwarzenegger, 2009). Their assumption has been that if there is a major market for such content, it must not be highly offensive.

Notwithstanding a possible shift in the Supreme Court's views about the constitutionality of indecency regulation, no fundamental policy changes seem likely in either of these realms in the immediate future. Still, it is noteworthy that scholars have begun to mine this terrain in search of new perspectives. Law professor Kevin Saunders (1996, 2003) has argued that some forms of violence might be appropriately treated in the same way as indecency, while Harvard philosopher Sisella Bok (1998) has questioned why the First Amendment should prevail over other competing rights when conflict occurs. These viewpoints challenge conventional thinking grounded in the policies of the past and may ultimately yield new and unique policy perspectives for the future in a changing media environment.

Educational Programming for Children

Public-interest advocacy groups first came to prominence as a political force in the 1960s, led by Ralph Nader's campaign to require seat belts and other consumer safety features in automobiles (Nadel, 1971; Schuck, 1977). Consistent with that trend, advocacy groups also began to pressure the FCC to adopt new rules to ensure that television stations served the public interest. In 1969, an advocacy organization known as Action for Children's Television (ACT) petitioned the FCC to require at least an hour a day of children's educational programming as part of each broadcast television station's obligation to serve the public interest (Cole & Oettinger, 1978; Kunkel & Watkins, 1987). That development instigated a long-standing policy battle that still persists today regarding the adequacy of industry programming efforts to serve the needs of children.

The battle results from a clash between two distinct viewpoints, one forwarded by child advocates and the other the response of the broadcast industry. The advocates observe that children of different ages vary in their information-processing skills and learning capabilities. Thus they argue that stations should be required to provide educational programming that is tailored to a narrow target age group, with curricular goals appropriate for that particular segment of the overall child population.

It is well established that children learn best from television content designed specifically for a narrow age range of youth (Bickham, Wright, & Huston, 2001; Rice, Huston, & Wright, 1982). Just as one would not expect all children from ages 2 to 12 to be able to learn effectively from the same book, one should not expect children across that entire age span to comprehend equally well a given television program. Different approaches in terms of the learning goals addressed, the vocabulary used, and the production techniques employed have proven more or less effective for children of different ages (Fisch, 2004; Fisch & Truglio, 2001; Kirkorian & Anderson, 2008; Linebarger & Piotrowski, 2010). Without age-specific targeting, advocates argue that programming for children is unlikely to achieve meaningful educational outcomes.

In contrast, the television industry argues that a wide variety of program content that appeals to a diverse range of viewers can nonetheless be considered educational and hence fulfill a station's obligation to children. This position has surfaced in varying political contexts, at times during battles regarding the adoption of policies governing broadcasters' responsibilities to children, as well as in debates regarding efforts to hold the industry accountable for compliance with existing regulations (Calvert, 2008). The tension between these two positions underlies more than 40 years of controversy regarding the adequacy of the educational programming efforts that television provides for children.

In the first round of this battle, ACT's petition to require television stations to provide educational programming for children proved only partially successful. After investigating the issue for several years, the FCC ruled in 1974 that the industry's efforts at children's programming were deficient and that improvements were essential. More specifically, the FCC stated that stations must air children's programs at diverse times of the day and week, not just on Saturday mornings; that the amount of programs for children should be significantly increased; and that the educational content of programs should be more carefully tailored to specific age groups within the overall child population (FCC, 1974). However, none of these policies were adopted as formal rules that required absolute compliance to avoid penalties. Rather, these criteria were established as license-renewal processing guidelines that would be weighed at the time each station applied to renew its license along with all other evidence regarding its service to the public during the licensing period. Since only an overall pattern of deficiencies and violations can lead to sanctions during the renewal process, and only a handful of stations have ever been denied their license renewal, this situation created little pressure for compliance (Levi, 2010).

Subsequent research conducted in the late 1970s by both the FCC and independent scholars established clearly that these initial policy guidelines had virtually no impact on the amount of children's programming offered, the diversity of program scheduling, or the educational quality of the shows presented (FCC, 1979; Palmer, 1988; Turow, 1981). This outcome led the FCC to propose the adoption of formal rules to mandate minimum amounts of age-specific educational programming for children as part of each station's public-interest obligations (FCC, 1980). However, given the slow pace with which regulatory proposals move through the process toward approval, it soon became apparent that such a policy clashed with a new direction in governmental policy that was being embraced at the time.

Deregulation of Children's Programming Policies

In the 1980s, most agencies of the federal government shifted their political philosophy from an emphasis on regulation to achieve public goals to a reliance on market-place competition to best serve the public's interest (Derthick & Quirk, 1985; Fowler & Brenner, 1982). The conceptual foundation of this strategy is that government rules tend to interfere with marketplace competition, and hence the new philosophy dictated that existing rules should be deregulated when-ever possible and new rules should be avoided, except in clear cases of demon-strated marketplace failure. Thus, it is hardly surprising that the FCC chose to reject the pending proposal to require stations to air minimum amounts of children's educational programming (FCC, 1984a).

Marketplace proponents at the FCC noted that broadcast television was not the only source of children's educational program-ming available to families. Arguing that alter-natives such as subscribing to cable networks or purchasing educational videos were avail-able, the FCC (1984a) rejected the new regu-lation that would have required every broadcaster to provide programs of value to children. At the same time, the agency also deregulated the previously established licens-ing guidelines, ruling that broadcast stations had no obligation to provide children's pro-gramming in communities where cable or other alternative technologies delivered video programming for children. This led to dra-matic reductions in the amount of children's shows delivered on broadcast channels (Kerkman, Kunkel, Huston, Wright, & Pinon, 1990; Wartella, Heintz, Aidman, & Mazzarella, 1990), and the cancellation of long-standing educational programs such as *Captain Kangaroo* (Barnouw, 1990).

These developments triggered signifi-cant criticism of the FCC, with *Time Magazine* terming the situation a "national disgrace" (Waters, 1983). One of the key points of criticism was the FCC's failure to consider the equity of access to nonbroad-cast technologies, which typically require some form of direct payment to obtain and that many families simply cannot afford. The new policy reflected a clear socioeco-nomic bias. While children from middle- and upper-class families that could afford to pay for alternative sources of children's programming such as cable television and videotapes might be well served by the new deregulatory policy, the needs of children from lower-class families were seemingly overlooked.

Congress Approves the Children's Television Act

Disappointed with the FCC's action, Congress soon pursued its own effort to regu-late in this area. A protracted political debate ensued, leading to a presidential veto of the initial Children's Television Act adopted by Congress in 1988 (Kunkel, 1991). But in the following session, Congress adopted a sec-ond version that became law, establishing a landmark statutory framework for children's television policy. The law is called the Children's Television Act (CTA) of 1990.

The linchpin of the law is its requirement that every broadcast television station must provide programming "specifically designed" to serve the educational and informational needs of children. Ironically, the Congress left the implementation of the law directly in the hands of the FCC, the agency that had consis-tently avoided children's television regulation over the past several decades. Although the CTA established a basic conceptual frame-work, it was left up to the FCC to determine what programming would qualify as educa-tional, when it must be shown, and how much would be enough to adequately fulfill the requirement.

The FCC first adopted rules to administer the law in 1991, establishing what it called a flexible definition of educational program-ming. It specified that stations could fulfill the law by offering content "that furthers the positive development of the child in any res-pect, including the child's cognitive/intellectual or social/emotional needs" (FCC, 1991, p. 2114). No limitations were initially placed on when the programming must be aired, and no guidance was provided to specify how much educational content each station was expected to provide.

Despite touting the use of educational con-sultants and an earnest commitment to improve children's programming (Hill-Scott, 2001; Stipp, Hill-Scott, & Dorr, 1987), many seg-ments of the television industry failed to take the law seriously at the outset. Rather than offering new educational programs to fulfill the CTA requirements, many stations simply reported that their existing children's entertainment-oriented shows qualified as "educational." Although this practice did not come to public light until several years later when license renewal forms were filed, frivolous claims to the FCC about the educational value of children's shows were widespread (Center for Media Education, 1992; Kunkel & Canepa, 1994; Kunkel & Goette, 1997). Programs such as *The Flintstones* were claimed to teach important history lessons, while *The Jetsons* were said to teach about new technologies. One station in Pennsylvania claimed that *Yogi Bear* was educational and described its learning goal as teaching children not to do stupid things or be willing to pay the consequences (Kunkel & Goette, 1997).

Embarrassed by the results of its lax enforcement efforts, the FCC in 1996 adopted a much more stringent set of rules to implement the Children's Television Act (Hundt & Kornbluh, 1996). These new rules include a minimum standard of 3 hours per week for each station's educational programming for children, a more strict definition of what content qualifies as educational, and a mandate that all educational shows be clearly labeled as such at the time they are broadcast (FCC, 1996).

Under this new policy framework, which reflects the current state of the law, programs that fulfill the CTA obligations must: (1) have education as a significant purpose; (2) specify the educational goal and target audience in quarterly reports to the FCC, which are available for public inspection; (3) be aired between 6:00 AM and 11:00 PM on a regular basis; and (4) be identified as children's educational content at the time the show is aired (Calvert, 2008).

The rating designation "EI" (for educational/informational) is used to identify programs that stations claim to comply with the CTA requirements. An "EI" must remain on screen during the entire time the program is aired to comply with the FCC's policy. The requirement that programs be labeled in this fashion has two purposes. At the most obvious level, such information may help parents to identify worthwhile shows for their children to view, which could benefit both families and broadcasters if it increases the audience for educational children's shows. In addition, the rating requirement discourages stations from making exaggerated claims of educational value, as occurred in the past when viewers had no real-time knowledge about what shows were claimed as educational. Unfortunately, few parents understand the meaning of the E/I ratings (Rideout, 2004; Stanger, 1997), and thus labeling programs as educational has had little actual impact.

Evaluating the Educational Quality of E/I Programs

Following the adoption of these new FCC rules, Dr. Amy Jordan and colleagues at the Annenberg Public Policy Center of the University of Pennsylvania conducted several annual studies evaluating the educational quality of the E/I programs aired by commercial broadcast stations (Jordan, 1998, 2000; Schmitt, 1999). The findings indicated that program quality was strongest shortly after the new FCC rules were adopted, with roughly a third of all E/I programs rated as "highly educational" in 1997–1998 (29%) and 1998–1999 (33%).

After those initial years, the industry's efforts then diminished in quality. In 1999–2000, only 20% of 41 series examined were judged to be "highly educational," while nearly a quarter (23%) were rated in the lowest category, "minimally educational." Some of the minimally educational programs, such as *NBA Inside Stuff* and *NFL Under the Helmet,* seemed intended for adults as much as for children, and others that were more distinctly child oriented were judged to be deficient in effectively conveying any educational message. Although Calvert and Kotler (2003) have demonstrated that actual learning outcomes do sometimes occur as a result of viewing E/I shows, the bulk of the evidence clearly suggests widespread deficiencies in such programming (see Chapter 26 in this volume for a discussion of the research on effects of educational programming).

Since the completion of the last Annenberg Center study in 2000, several developments suggest that the quality of the E/I programming on commercial television may have suffered even further. In 2004, two Washington, DC-area broadcast stations had their license renewals challenged by public-interest advocacy groups on the basis of serious inadequacies in their children's educational programming efforts (Office of Communication of the United Church of Christ and Center for Digital Democracy, 2004). The petitioners assert that numerous programs claimed to be educational for children failed to include legitimate content with meaningful learning goals and failed to tailor the material to specific target age groups (Calvert, 2008; Kunkel, 2007). For example, one station relied almost entirely on two heavily violent, animated programs for all of its E/I compliance for several years, while another aired only a single series entitled *Miracle Pets* that experts judged to be primarily intended for adults. At the end of 2010, the FCC had yet to rule on the merits of the license challenges, an unusually long and callous delay in discharging its administrative responsibilities.

In a separate case decided in 2007, the FCC applied a record fine of $24 million to the Spanish-language broadcast network Univision for significant shortcomings in the children's educational programming on its 24 stations (FCC, 2007b). Univision had claimed that youth-oriented soap operas, or so-called *telenovelas*, were educational when in fact the episodes appeared to be no different than common entertainment-oriented dramas (Ahrens, 2007). The fine averages out to roughly $8,600 per station per violation (i.e., each airing of a noncompliant program), with the size of the overall penalty underscoring the long-standing nature of the deficient practice. In describing the FCC's action, *The New York Times* characterized it as an unusual rebuke to the industry "after years of permissive oversight in this area" (Labaton, 2007).

Finally, the most recent study to evaluate the commercial broadcast industry's efforts at children's programming (Wilson, Kunkel, & Drogos, 2008) reported that only one of every eight episodes claimed as E/I was rated as highly educational (13%), whereas a larger proportion of shows (23%) were judged to be only minimally educational (23%). Most programs (63%) fell into the moderately educational category. In terms of curriculum, 67% of all E/I shows addressed basic social/emotional lessons such as sharing or getting along with others; in contrast, only 3% conveyed lessons about art, only 3% addressed nutrition and health topics, and only 1% devoted attention to mathematics. Collectively, these findings suggest that E/I programs suffer not only from poor quality but also from a limited range and diversity of subject material that is important for youth.

The late Edward Palmer, founding research director of Children's Television Workshop (now Sesame Workshop), advocated for adoption of the Children's Television Act. He argued that the United States needs "to take sensible advantage of the most cost-efficient—but still the most neglected—form of . . . educational technology ever invented" (Palmer, 1988, p. xviii). That same sentiment is echoed in another volume coauthored by former FCC Chairperson Newton Minow, entitled *Abandoned in the Wasteland: Children, Television, and the First Amendment* (Minow & Lamay, 1995). Reflecting frustration with the government's timidity in holding the broadcast industry responsible for serving the public interest, Minow and Lamay (1995) observed, "If we can't figure out what the public interest means with respect to [children] . . . , then we will never figure out what it means anywhere else" (p. 5).

More than 20 years following enactment of the Children's Television Act by Congress, however, it seems increasingly clear that the law has failed to transform the landscape of commercial broadcast programming for children into something beneficial for youth (Levi, 2010). Alternative sources of children's programming such as public broadcast channels (Linebarger, Kosanic, Greenwood, & Doku, 2004; Simensky, 2007; Wilson et al., 2008) and cable networks (Anderson, Bryant, Wilder, Santomero, & Williams, 2000; Linebarger & Walker, 2005) tend to provide better-quality educational content in their shows. In the absence of more stringent enforcement efforts by the FCC to hold the industry accountable for compliance, it seems unlikely that the current policy will prove any more successful in the future.

Fairness of Television Advertising to Children

The fundamental policy concerns in the realm of advertising to children revolve around issues of fairness. Are young children fair targets for television advertisers? Is it fair to allow unrestricted advertising to children, or are some limits appropriate? Does fairness require special safeguards to constrain certain types of advertising strategies directed to children? While the answers to these questions require value judgments that can only be reached as part of the political process of constructing public policy, social science research provides an abundance of evidence to help inform those who must answer these questions.

Examining children's ability to recognize and defend against televised commercial persuasion has been the focus of extensive research efforts since the early 1970s. Consistent findings establish that most children experience difficulty discriminating between programs and commercials until about 4 to 5 years of age; and age is positively correlated with an understanding of advertising's persuasive intent, with such ability typically emerging in its earliest form at about 7 to 8 years of age (see Chapters 20 and 22 in this volume for a more detailed discussion).

From a policy perspective, these findings are significant because it is often argued that if young children are unaware of persuasive intent, then commercial practices aimed at them may be considered inherently unfair and deceptive (Pomeranz, 2010). This principle derives in part from the premise that all advertising must be clearly identifiable as such to its intended audience, a concept embodied in such statutes as the Communications Act of 1934 (see Section 317).

There are two types of regulations currently applied to television advertising shown during children's programs: (1) policies that maintain a clear separation between program and commercial content; and (2) policies restricting the amount of time that may be devoted to commercials.

Program/Commercial Separation Policies

In the 1950s and 1960s, commercial messages during children's shows were often seamlessly woven into the program material. *Romper Room,* a popular show that began airing in 1953, frequently focused on the promotion of its branded line of toys (Inglis, 2003). Each episode featured a schoolteacher

and children who would play with toys such as a punch ball, after which the teacher would praise the product and implore children to ask their parents to buy it for them. Similarly, the animated *Rocky and Bullwinkle Show* would depict Rocky the Squirrel flying circles around the cereal products that were offered by the company that sponsored the program.

Based on evidence of children's limited comprehension of advertising, the FCC issued policy guidelines in 1974 that halted such practices. The agency specified that commercial messages must be clearly separated from entertainment content during programs targeted at audiences aged 12 and under (FCC, 1974). There are three applications of this separation principle. They include:

1. *Bumpers*—Program/commercial separation devices, known in the industry as bumpers, are required during children's programs. These devices are roughly 5-second segments shown before and after commercial breaks that say something like, "And now a word from our sponsor."

2. *Host-selling*—Program characters or hosts are prohibited from promoting products during commercials adjacent to their shows. For example, a *Flintstones* cereal commercial featuring Fred and Wilma would not be allowed to air during a break in the *Flintstones* cartoon program in which these same characters appear.

3. *Program-length commercials (PLCs)*—Program-length commercials targeted at children are prohibited. The current definition of a PLC, which was significantly narrowed by the FCC in 1991, is "a program associated with a product in which commercials for that product are aired" (FCC, 1991, p. 2117).

The program-length commercial policy originated in 1969, when one of the broadcast networks collaborated with Mattel Toys to produce a program called *Hot Wheels*, a cartoon show based entirely on the company's new line of toy cars (Kunkel, 1988). The FCC (1969) ruled at the time that such a program constituted commercial matter and would exceed existing limits on the amount of commercial time allowed. Immediately following the ruling, the network canceled the program.

This precedent was expanded in 1974 as part of the "clear separation" policy, when the FCC defined a PLC as a program with a primary purpose of promoting products to children (FCC, 1974). However, the FCC deregulated its prohibition of children's program-length commercials in 1984, arguing that such strategies represent "an innovative technique to fund children's programming," while observing that "we have no reason to believe product-related considerations will come to dominate children's programming" (FCC, 1984b, p. 26). In fact, the FCC's decision irreversibly transformed the economics of the children's television business. Revenues from the sale of licensed products related to popular children's shows became so lucrative that product-related programming soon dominated the airwaves, including shows such as *He-Man and Masters of the Universe*, *Strawberry Shortcake*, and *Teenage Mutant Ninja Turtles* (Kunkel, 1988; Pecora, 1998).

Child advocates soon complained about the overtly commercial nature of children's programming (Hendershot, 1998), and the Congress responded by ordering the FCC to reconsider its decision to deregulate the PLC policy by including a provision to that effect in the Children's Television Act of 1990. The deregulatory-minded FCC responded creatively, ostensibly reinstating the prohibition on PLCs but in fact revising the definition of a program-length commercial in a manner that allowed all of the existing product-related programming to remain on the air.

Under the revised policy, which still remains in effect, programs may be product based so long as no traditional spot commercials for the program-related products appear during breaks in the show. The FCC justified this stance by arguing that it feared it might harm the quality of children's shows if it were to "jeopardize the additional revenue streams generated by product merchandising needed by many children's programs" (FCC, 1991, para. 42). Indeed, media executives today argue that in the absence of government subsidies that sometimes accompany public broadcast productions, licensed product revenues are an essential aspect of successful children's programming (Cahn, Kalagian, & Lyon, 2008). In sum, current policy does little to discourage the use of full-length programs as merchandising vehicles targeting children.

Policies Restricting the Amount of Advertising to Children

Time limits on advertising to children were originally established in 1974, when the FCC adopted existing industry self-regulation as appropriate public policy (Kunkel & Watkins, 1987). At that time, the FCC specified clearly that stations could air advertising to children only in order to generate revenues roughly commensurate with their expenditures on children's program efforts. More specifically, the FCC (1974, p. 39400) stated:

> Although advertising should be adequate to insure that the station will have sufficient revenues with which to produce programming that will serve the children of its community meaningfully, the public interest does not protect advertising that is substantially in excess of that amount.

That posture changed significantly in the 1980s amid an overall shift to emphasize marketplace competition rather than governmental regulation to best serve the public interest. The FCC (1984b) abandoned all of its policies limiting the amount of advertising to audiences of adults as well as children, arguing that market forces would ensure stations do not air excessive commercial content. When this decision was challenged by child advocates, the federal court rejected as untenable the FCC's argument that market forces would limit advertising to children and ordered the agency to reconsider this aspect of its policy (Action for Children's Television v. FCC, 1987). Before the FCC could respond to the court's ruling, the issue was rendered moot when Congress stepped in and reinstated specific limits on commercial time during children's shows as part of the Children's Television Act of 1990.

The Children's Television Act includes a statutory provision limiting the amount of commercial time allowed during children's programming to no more than 12 minutes per hour on weekdays and 10.5 minutes per hour on weekends.

Because statutory law adopted by Congress supersedes administrative law implemented by regulatory agencies such as the FCC, this policy is now firmly established and subject to change only by a vote of Congress.

Interestingly, the CTA's advertising time limits were extended to cable television networks as well as broadcast stations. Because cable lacks the public-interest obligations of the broadcast industry, only Congress and not the FCC has the authority to establish rules limiting advertising on cable networks. When the limits on cable advertising to children were proposed, industry leaders agreed to accept the restriction willingly. Acceding to the policy helped the cable industry in its overall relations with Congress (Kunkel, 1991) and was relatively painless because the levels of commercial time for most children's shows on cable were well within the new regulatory limits (Kunkel & Gantz, 1992). Compliance with the time restrictions appears generally strong; audits conducted by the FCC indicate that more than 90% of the networks and stations surveyed fall at or below the limits allowed, although fines for occasional violations are applied.

Advertising Industry Self-Regulation

Since the 1970s, the advertising industry has maintained self-regulatory policies administered by the Children's Advertising Review Unit (CARU) of the National Council of Better Business Bureaus. These voluntary guidelines place constraints on the advertising practices deemed appropriate for commercials that target child audiences. For example, guidelines address such areas as product presentations and claims, sales pressure, disclosures/disclaimers, and safety concerns.

Within each area, guidelines specify practices to be either avoided or required. Some of these standards are fairly specific, such as the requirement that "advertisements should demonstrate the performance and use of a product in away [sic] that can be duplicated by a child for whom the product is intended" (CARU, 2009, p. 7). Others are more vague and general, such as the admonition that "claims should not unduly exploit a child's imagination" (CARU, 2009, p. 7).

According to an independent study conducted in the early 1990s, compliance with CARU guidelines was relatively high, with just 4% of commercials found to include a violation (Kunkel & Gantz, 1993). However, no subsequent investigation along these lines has been undertaken. Follow-up research is clearly overdue, given that self-regulation typically functions to inoculate industries from more stringent governmental consumer-protection policies (Brownell & Warner, 2009).

Should Advertising to Children Be Allowed at All?

The passages above address the law regarding children and television advertising as it has unfolded over time. In fact, however, another perspective has been seriously proposed, although never adopted in the United States. Many child advocates argue that all advertising to children is inherently unfair and that the practice of directing commercial messages to child audiences should be entirely banned.

In 1978, the Federal Trade Commission formally proposed such a ban for advertising targeted at children too young to recognize persuasive intent in commercial messages (Kunkel & Roberts, 1991). The regulatory proposal triggered an enormous political controversy, with industry interests arguing that the government was running amok and trying to create a nanny state (Foote & Mnookin, 1980). The Congress was sympathetic to such complaints and responded by revoking the FTC's authority to establish trade regulation rules regarding advertising to children, effectively killing the proposal (Westen, 2006).

Despite that history, ethical questions continue to persist about the propriety of allowing advertising to young children. The research evidence documenting young children's limited ability to comprehend the nature and purpose of advertising has grown over time and clearly establishes that children below age 8 cannot understand the selling intent of commercials. Moreover, recent analysis in this realm suggests that an understanding of advertising's persuasive intent may not fully develop until as late as age 12 (see Chapter 20 in this volume).

Given this evidence, organizations such as the American Academy of Pediatrics (Committee on Communications, 2006), American Psychological Association (Wilcox et al., 2004), and Institute of Medicine (2005) have adopted policy recommendations that support a ban or severe restrictions on television advertising to children. As Harris, Brownell, and Bargh (2009) note, these recommendations are also consistent with strong public opinion in the United States in support of restrictions on advertising to children, as well as bans that have been adopted in several other countries worldwide. The counterpoint that is commonly offered in opposition to a ban is that media content for children would be seriously diminished without revenues from advertising.

Concern About Unhealthy Food Marketing to Children

The most recent development in children and advertising policy is grounded in sobering statistics that document the growing epidemic of childhood obesity (Institute of Medicine, 2005). For the first time in modern history, the current generation of children may face a life expectancy that is shorter than that of their parents due to the wide range of medical complications associated with obesity. Although many elements contribute to this epidemic, food marketing to children has been identified as a significant risk factor (Institute of Medicine, 2006).

This conclusion is based upon extensive research documenting the prevalence of obesogenic foods in television advertising targeted at children (Palmer & Carpenter, 2006; Story & French, 2004), coupled with systematic evidence that establishes the effects of

advertising on children's attitudes toward food products, their purchase influence requests, and actual diet (Institute of Medicine, 2006). Consequently, numerous countries worldwide have already adopted regulatory policies to limit advertising of obesogenic foods to children (Hawkes, 2007), including a particularly stringent restriction on televised junk food commercials in the United Kingdom (OFCOM, 2007).

Hoping to forestall what many see as inevitable government regulation in the United States (Darwin, 2009; Harris, Brownell, & Bargh, 2009; Sharma, Teret, & Brownell, 2010), the food marketing industry has established a self-regulatory effort known as the Children's Food and Beverage Advertising Initiative, or CFBAI (Kolish & Peeler, 2008; Peeler, Kolish, & Enright, 2009). With participation from more than a dozen of the nation's largest food conglomerates, the CFBAI is a pledge program whereby each company offers a commitment to advertise foods to children only if they meet its own unique nutritional criteria for defining healthful products.

The initiative has been criticized for its lack of a uniform nutrition standard (White House Task Force on Childhood Obesity, 2010), which allows products classified as "healthy" by one company to fall short of standards set by another, potentially confusing consumers. Moreover, recent research has demonstrated that industry self-regulation has failed to significantly improve the overall nutritional quality of foods marketed to children industrywide. More than a year after the CFBAI was implemented, nearly three fourths (72.5%) of all foods advertised on television to children were classified in the poorest nutritional category (Kunkel, McKinley, & Wright, 2009).

The issue of unhealthy food marketing to children combines fundamental concern about the fairness of advertising to children, which applies to all merchandise, with a public-health orientation that is focused on a particular type of product that cannot be consumed safely in abundance. This nexus creates multiple foundations to justify governmental intervention. Given the high stakes involved with the obesity crisis and the ineffectiveness to date of industry self-regulation, the prospects for future government restrictions on food marketing to children appear relatively strong.

Technological Innovations in Advertising to Children

Advertising to children using interactive media is revolutionizing the process of youth-oriented commercial persuasion. Innovative tactics include viral marketing, individually targeted advertising of particular products choreographed according to a user's previously cached browsing history, and so-called advergames, which embed products within interactive games that appeal to children (Cai & Zhao, 2010; Chester & Montgomery, 2007). No governmental restrictions apply to the amount of advertising that may be contained on a children's website, nor is there any requirement for separation between entertainment and commercial content on the Internet.

While it is obvious that children today encounter unprecedented levels of advertising messages via the Internet and other interactive media, scholarly research lags far behind in documenting the implications of these developments. Barely a handful of studies have yet examined how children understand and are influenced by Internet advertising. Given the well-established efficacy of noninteractive advertising to children, however, such evidence is hardly essential to raise concerns.

An unlikely development occurred in this realm in 2004, when the FCC was first establishing policies for interactive television service that is only now on the near horizon. The transition to digital television that occurred in 2009 brings with it the potential for interactivity by which viewers can control and manipulate content in a manner akin to the experience of networked computing, such as occurs in browsing the Internet. Once interactivity is functional, viewers who see something that interests them will be able to "learn more about it" by signaling their television set with a remote command that will trigger access to some supplementary material. One such application might be to enhance the value of educational programs by allowing child viewers to obtain more information about an intriguing concept presented in a program. Another obvious application of this new capability is to facilitate interactive advertising, which might occur in many different forms including impulse purchasing that can be accomplished with a single click, a particularly problematic prospect for children.

In 2004, in response to requests from a coalition of child advocacy groups led by Children Now, the FCC issued a preliminary judgment that interactive television advertising targeted at children is contrary to the public interest (Kunkel, 2007). More specifically, the FCC has stated that it will "prohibit interactivity during children's programming that connects viewers to commercial matter" (FCC, 2004a, para. 72). The implications of this development are difficult to gauge until the FCC pursues further steps to specify the operational details of the conceptual foundation it has laid. Nonetheless, this is a rare case in which child advocates have landed a successful policy beachhead in advance of media industry innovations that potentially threaten child welfare. Upon taking office as FCC Chairperson in 2009, Julius Genachowski announced that his agenda included following up to ensure that this preliminary policy was formally adopted, but to date no action has yet been pursued to accomplish that goal.

Future Regulatory Challenges

The three major sections of this chapter have all dealt with the history of children's media policy, which is grounded largely in terms of broadcast regulation. In the future, broad approaches to policy making that encompass multiple delivery systems will be increasingly important. Broadcasting was the dominant medium in children's lives until the 1990s, when it faced serious competition from cable. By the year 2000, Internet use was another significant competitor for children's time spent with media. In the future, media convergence is likely to occur such that a single wire (or wireless signal) and one video screen will deliver all of the content that users previously associated with individual media received via multiple devices. This scenario underscores the importance of shifting policy makers' focus away from delivery mechanisms and directing it toward the consideration of children's interests relative to the content in question.

Consider how such an approach might work in the area of advertising to children. Under present law, an advertiser is not allowed to employ host-selling tactics in a television commercial aired on children's programming delivered by broadcast television. In contrast, host-selling technically is legal on cable networks because the policy restricting the practice applies solely to broadcast channels. With websites for children now growing in popularity, many advertisers already have developed sites that feature the same popular characters involved in games and entertainment content as well as in marketing messages clearly meant to promote product sales (Chester & Montgomery, 2007). In other words, these websites intermingle rather than clearly separate commercial from noncommercial content. Of course, there is currently no government policy restricting such tactics on Internet sites.

An alternative approach would be for a governmental agency such as the Federal Communications Commission or the Federal Trade Commission to establish a fundamental set of policy guidelines that would apply across all media that deliver advertising directed to children. One such policy might involve broad application of the "separation principle," which holds that advertisers should take steps to clearly distinguish between commercial and noncommercial content, regardless of the media delivery system involved.

It is axiomatic that communication technologies move faster than the rules and regulations that govern them, and the changing media environment certainly presents many new puzzles to be solved. Any effort to establish a broad policy framework extending beyond the reach of individual media would have to be authorized by new legislation coming from Congress. Yet there is an important counterpoint to such a proposal. The growth and international reach of new media such as the Internet actually raise the question

of how much longer individual countries can effectively govern electronic communication at all. If content that is regulated in one country is unregulated in another region of the world, then how effective can any regulatory policies be when every home with a computer can access any point on the globe via the World Wide Web?

These are the conundrums that policy makers must face as they grapple with the future of children and media policy. The stakes are the same as they have always been in the past: to employ the nation's resources—the media among them—for the benefit of children and to ensure the protection of the nation's youth. In an era of significant change in the media environment, there remains a single constant: the need to consider the lives of children in framing our future media policies.

References

Action for Children's Television v. FCC, 821 F.2d 741 (D.C. Cir. 1987).

Action for Children's Television v. FCC, 932 F.2d 1504 (D.C. Cir. 1991).

Action for Children's Television et al. v. FCC, 852 F 2d. 1332 (D.C. Cir. 1988).

Ahrens, F. (2007, February 25). FCC expected to impose record $24 million fine against Univision. *Washington Post.* Retrieved August 1, 2010, from http://www.washingtonpost.com/wp-dyn/content/article/2007/02/24/AR2007022401453.html.

Albiniak, P. (1997, July 14). Ratings get revamped: Networks except for NBC, agree to add content labels. *Broadcasting and Cable,* p. 4.

American Amusement Machine Association v. Kendrick, 244 F. 3d 572 (7th Cir. 2001).

American Medical Association. (1996). *Physician's guide to media violence.* Chicago, IL: American Medical Association.

American Psychological Association. (1993). *Violence and youth: Psychology's response.* Washington, DC: Author.

American Psychological Association. (2005). *Resolution on violence in video games and interactive media.* Washington, DC: Author. Retrieved August 1, 2010, from http://www.apa.org/pubs/journals/releases/resolutiononvideoviolence.pdf.

Anderson, C. A., Gentile, D. A., & Buckley, K. E. (2007). *Violent video game effects on children and adolescents: Theory, research, and public policy.* New York: Oxford University Press.

Anderson, C. A., Shibuya, A., Ihori, N., Swing, E. L., Bushman, B. J., Sakamoto, A., Rothstein, H. R., & Saleem, M. (2010). Violent video game effects on aggression, empathy, and prosocial behavior in Eastern and Western countries. *Psychological Bulletin, 136,* 151–173.

Anderson, D. R., Bryant, J., Wilder, A., Santomero, A., & Williams, M. (2000). Researching *Blue's Clues*: Viewing behavior and impact. *Media Psychology, 2,* 179–194.

Assembly Bill 1179, CA Civil Code §§ 1746–1746.5 (2005).

Barnouw, E. (1990). *Tube of plenty: The evolution of American television.* New York: Oxford University Press.

Barron, J. A. (2010). *FCC v. Fox Television Stations* and the FCC's new fleeting expletive policy. *Federal Communication Law Journal, 62*(3), 567–585.

Bartholow, B. D., Dill, K. E., Anderson, K. B., & Lindsay, J. J. (2003). The proliferation of media violence and its economic underpinnings. In D. Gentile (Ed.), *Media violence and children: A complete guide for parents and professionals* (pp. 1–18). Westport, CT: Praeger.

Bickham, D. S., Wright, J. C., & Huston, A. C. (2001). Attention, comprehension, and the educational influences of television. In D. Singer & J. Singer (Eds.), *Handbook of children and the media* (pp. 101–120). Thousand Oaks, CA: Sage.

Bok, S. (1998). *Mayhem: Violence as public entertainment.* Reading, MA: Addison-Wesley.

Brownell, K., & Warner, K. E. (2009). The perils of ignoring history: Big Tobacco played dirt and millions died. How similar is Big Food? *Milbank Quarterly, 87*(1), 259–294.

Cahn, A., Kalagian, T., & Lyon, C. (2008). Business models for children's media. In S. L. Calvert & B. J. Wilson (Eds.), *The handbook of children, media, and development* (pp. 27–48). Malden, MA: Blackwell Publishing.

Cai, X., & Zhao, X. (2010). Click here kids! Online advertising practices on children's websites. *Journal of Children and Media, 4*(2), 135–154. doi:10.1080/17482791003629610.

Calvert, S. (2008). Children as consumers: Advertising and marketing. *Future of Children, 18(1),* 205–234.

Calvert, S. (2008). The Children's Television Act. In S. L. Calvert & B. J. Wilson (Eds.), *The handbook of children, media, and development*

(pp. 455–478). Malden, MA: Blackwell Publishing.

Calvert, S., & Kotler, J. (2003). Lessons from children's television: The impact of the Children's Television Act on children's learning. *Applied Developmental Psychology, 24,* 275–335.

Campbell. A. J. (2010). Pacifica reconsidered: Implications for the current controversy over broadcast indecency. *Federal Communications Law Journal, 63*(1), 195–260.

Cantor, J., & Harrison, K. (1997). Ratings and advisories for television programming. In *National television violence study* (Vol. 1). Thousand Oaks, CA: Sage.

Carter, T., Franklin, M., & Wright, J. (1999). *The First Amendment and the fifth estate: Regulation of electronic mass media* (5th ed.). New York: Foundation Press.

Cater, D., & Strickland, S. (1975). *TV violence and the child: The evolution and fate of the Surgeon General's Report.* New York: Russell Sage Foundation.

Centers for Disease Control. (1991). *Position papers from the Third National Injury Conference: Setting the national agenda for injury control in the 1990s.* Washington, DC: Department of Health and Human Services.

Center for Media Education. (1992). *A report on station compliance with the Children's Television Act.* Washington, DC: Georgetown University Law Center.

Chester, J., & Montgomery, K. C. (2007). *Interactive food and beverage marketing: Targeting children and youth in the digital age.* Berkeley, CA: Berkeley Media Studies Group. Retrieved August 1, 2010, from http://digitalads.org/documents/digiMarketingFull.pdf.

Children's Advertising Review Unit. (2009). *Self-regulatory program for children's advertising.* New York: Council of Better Business Bureaus. Retrieved August 1, 2010, from http://www.caru.org/guidelines/index.aspx.

Cole, B., & Oettinger, M. (1978). *Reluctant regulators: The FCC and the broadcast audience.* Reading, MA: Addison-Wesley.

Committee on Communications. (2006). Children, adolescents, and advertising. *Pediatrics, 118,* 2563–2698.

Cooper, C. (1996). *Violence on television: Congressional inquiry, public criticism and industry response.* Lanham, MD: University Press of America.

Corn-Revere, R. (2007). *FCC television violence report: A conclusion in search of an analysis.*

Retrieved August 1, 2010, from http://www
.firstamendmentcenter.org/fcc-television-
violence-report-a-conclusion-in-search-of-
an-analysis.

Cowan, G. (1979). *See no evil: The backstage battle
over sex and violence on television.* New York:
Simon and Schuster.

Darwin, D. (2009). Advertising obesity: Can the
US follow the lead of the UK in limiting
television marketing of unhealthy foods to
children? *Vanderbilt Journal of Transnational
Law, 42,* 317–350.

Derthick, M., & Quirk, P. (1985). *The politics of
deregulation.* Washington, DC: Brookings
Institute.

Donnerstein, E., Wilson, B., & Linz, D. (1992).
On the regulation of broadcast indecency to
protect children. *Journal of Broadcasting and
Electronic Media, 36,* 111–117.

Edwards, H. T., & Berman, M. N. (1995). Regulating violence on television. *Northwestern
University Law Review, 89,* 1487–1565.

Entertainment Software Association v. Blagejovich,
404 F. Supp. 2d 1051 (N.D. Ill. 2005).

Entertainment Software Association v. Foti, 451 F.
Supp 2d 823 (M.D. La. 2006).

Entertainment Software Association v. Swanson,
519 F. 3d 768 (8th Cir. 2008).

Farhi, P. (1997, July 10). TV ratings agreement
reached. *Washington Post,* pp. A1, A16.

Federal Communications Commission. (1969). In
re: Complaint of Topper Corporation concerning American Broadcasting Company and
Mattel Inc. *Federal Communications Commission Reports, 21*(2nd series), 148–149.

Federal Communications Commission. (1974).
Children's television programs: Report
and policy statement. *Federal Register, 39,*
39396–39409.

Federal Communications Commission. (1979).
*Television programming for children: A
report of the Children's Television Task Force*
(NTIS No. PB 81-108722).Washington, DC:
Federal Communications Commission.

Federal Communications Commission. (1980).
Children's television programming and advertising practices: Notice of proposed rulemaking. *Federal Register, 45,* 1976–1986.

Federal Communications Commission. (1984a).
Children's television programming and adver-
tising practices: Report and order. *Federal
Register, 49,* 1704–1727.

Federal Communications Commission. (1984b).
Revision of programming and commercialization policies, ascertainment requirements,
and program log requirements for commercial

television stations. *Federal Register, 49,*
33588–33620.

Federal Communications Commission. (1991).
Policies and rules concerning children's television programming: Memorandum opinion
and order. *Federal Communications Commission Record, 6,* 2111–2127.

Federal Communications Commission. (1996). In
the matter of policies and rules concerning
children's television programming: Report
and order. *Federal Communications Commission Record, 11,* 10660–10778.

Federal Communications Commission. (2004a).
Children's television obligations of digital
television broadcasters: Report and order and
further notice of proposed rulemaking. *Federal
Communications Commission Record, 19,*
22943–22996.

Federal Communications Commission. (2004b).
In re: Complaints against various broadcast
licensees regarding their airing of the "Golden
Globes Award" program, *Federal Communications Commission Report, 19,* 4975–4794.

Federal Communications Commission. (2006).
Indecency complaints and NALs: 1993–2006.
Retrieved August 1, 2010, from http://www
.fcc.gov/eb/oip/ComplStatChart.pdf.

Federal Communications Commission. (2007a).
In the matter of violent television programming and its impact on children: Report.
*Federal Communications Commission Record,
22,* 7929–7968.

Federal Communications Commission. (2007b).
Memorandum opinion and order: Shareholders
of Univision Communications Inc. (trans-
feror) and Broadcasting Media Partners
(transferee). *Federal Communications Commission Record, 22,* 5842.

Federal Communications Commission v. Fox
Television Stations, 129 S. Ct. 1800 (2009).

Federal Communications Commission v. Pacifica
Foundation, 438 U.S. 726 (1978).

Federal Trade Commission. (2000). *Marketing
violent entertainment to children: A review of
self-regulation and industry practices in the
motion picture, music recording and electronic game industries.* Retrieved August 1,
2010, from http://www.ftc.gov/reports/violence/
vioreport.pdf.

Federal Trade Commission. (2009). *Marketing
violent entertainment to children: A sixth
follow-up review of industry practices in the
motion picture, music recording and electronic game industries.* Retrieved August 1,
2010, from http://www.ftc.gov/os/2009/12/
P994511violententertainment.pdf.

Fisch, S. M. (2004). *Children's learning from educational television:* Sesame Street *and beyond.* Mahwah, NJ: Lawrence Erlbaum.

Fisch, S., & Truglio, R. (2001). Why children learn from *Sesame Street.* In S. M. Fisch & R. T. Truglio (Eds.), "G" is for growing: Thirty years of research on children and Sesame Street (pp. 234–244). Mahwah, NJ: Lawrence Erlbaum.

Foote, S. B., & Mnookin, R. H. (1980). The "kid vid" crusade. *The Public Interest, 61,* 90–105. Retrieved August 1, 2010, from http://www .aeforum.org/aeforum.nsf/3deac671ffcb0cc7 80256c5100355eb5/fd6f719ad103835b8025 67b6003de968/$FILE/Okid0011.pdf.

Fowler, M., & Brenner, D. (1982). A marketplace approach to broadcast regulation. *Texas Law Review, 60,* 207–257.

Fox Television Stations v. FCC, 489 F. 3d 444 (2nd Cir. 2007).

Fox Television Stations v. FCC, 613 F. 3d 317 (2nd Cir. 2010).

Gentile, D. A. (2008). The rating systems for media products. In S. L. Calvert & B. J. Wilson (Eds.), *The handbook of children, media, and development* (pp. 527–551). Malden, MA: Blackwell Publishing.

Gruenwald, J. (1997, February 15). Critics say TV ratings system doesn't tell the whole story. *Congressional Quarterly, 55*(7), 424–425.

Guttman, M. (1994, May 9). Violence in entertainment: A kinder, gentler Hollywood. *U.S. News and World Report,* 39–46.

Hamilton, J. (1998). *Channeling violence: The economic market for violent television programming.* Princeton, NJ: Princeton University Press.

Harris, J. L., Brownell, K. D., & Bargh, J. A. (2009). The food marketing defense model: Integrating psychological research to protect youth and inform public policy. *Social Issues and Policy Review, 3*(1), 211–271.

Hawkes, C. (2007). Regulating food marketing to young people worldwide: Trends and policy drivers. *American Journal of Public Health, 97,* 1962–1973.

Hendershot, H. (1998). *Saturday morning censors: Television regulation before the V-chip.* Durham, NC: Duke University Press.

Hill-Scott, K. (2001). Industry standards and practices: Compliance with the Children's Television Act. In D. Singer & J. Singer (Eds.), *Handbook of children and the media* (pp. 605–620). Thousand Oaks, CA: Sage.

Hofferth, S. L. (2010). Home media and children's achievement and behavior. *Child Development, 81,* 1598–1619.

Hundt, R., & Kornbluh, K. (1996). Renewing the deal between broadcasters and the public: Requiring clear rules for children's educational television. *Harvard Journal of Law and Technology, 9, 11*–23.

Inglis, R. (2003). *The window in the corner: A half-century of children's television.* London, UK: Peter Owen Ltd.

Institute of Medicine. (2005). *Preventing childhood obesity: Health in the balance.* Washington, DC: National Academies Press.

Institute of Medicine. (2006). *Food marketing to children and youth: Threat or opportunity?* Washington, DC: National Academies Press.

Jordan, A. (1998). *The 1998 state of children's television report: Programming for children over broadcast and cable television.* Washington, DC: Annenberg Public Policy Center of the University of Pennsylvania.

Jordan, A. (2000). *Is the three-hour rule living up to its potential?* Philadelphia, PA: Annenberg Public Policy Center of the University of Pennsylvania. Retrieved August 1, 2010, from http://www.annenbergpublicpolicycenter.org/ NewsDetails.aspx?myId=145.

Kaiser Family Foundation. (2001). *Parents and the V-chip 2001.* Retrieved August 1, 2010, from http://www.kff.org/entmedia/3158-V-Chip-release.cfm.

Kerkman, D., Kunkel, D., Huston, A., Wright, J., & Pinon, M. (1990). Children's television programming and the "free market" solution. *Journalism Quarterly, 67,* 147–156.

Kirkorian, H. L., & Anderson, D. R. (2004). Learning from educational media. In S. L. Calvert & B. J. Wilson (Eds.), *The handbook of children, media, and development* (pp. 188–213). Malden, MA: Blackwell Publishing.

Kolish, E., & Peeler, L. (2008). *Changing the landscape of food and beverage advertising: The Children's Food and Beverage Advertising Initiative in action.* Arlington, VA: Council of Better Business Bureaus. Retrieved August 1, 2010, from http://www .bbb.org/us/children-food-beverage-advertising-initiative/.

Kunkel, D. (1988). From a raised eyebrow to a turned back: The FCC and children's product-related programming. *Journal of Communication, 38*(4), 90–108.

Kunkel, D. (1991). Crafting media policy: The genesis and implications of the Children's Television Act of 1990. *American Behavioral Scientist, 35*(2), 181–202.

Kunkel, D. (2007). Kids' media policy goes digital: Current developments in children's television regulation. In J. A. Bryant (Ed.), *The *children's television community* (pp. 203–228). Mahwah, NJ: Lawrence Erlbaum.

Kunkel, D., & Canepa, J. (1994). Broadcasters' license renewal claims regarding children's educational programs. *Journal of Broadcasting and Electronic Media, 38,* 397–416.

Kunkel, D., Farinola, W., Cope-Farrar, K., Donnerstein, E., Biely, E., & Zwarun, L. (2002). Deciphering the V-chip: An examination of the television industry's program rating judgments. *Journal of Communication, 52,* 112–138.

Kunkel, D., & Gantz, W. (1992). Children's television advertising in the multi-channel environment. *Journal of Communication, 42*(3), 134–152.

Kunkel, D., & Gantz, W. (1993). Assessing compliance with industry self-regulation of television advertising to children. *Journal of Applied Communication Research, 21,* 148–162.

Kunkel, D., & Goette, U. (1997). Broadcasters' response to the Children's Television Act. *Communication Law and Policy, 2,* 289–308.

Kunkel, D., McKinley, C., & Wright, P. (2009). *The impact of industry self-regulation on the nutritional quality of foods advertised on television to children.* Oakland, CA: Children Now. Retrieved August 1, 2010, from http://www.childrennow.org/index.php/learn/reports_and_research/article/576.

Kunkel, D., & Roberts, D. (1991). Young minds and marketplace values: Research and policy issues in children's television advertising. *Journal of Social Issues, 47*(1), 57–72.

Kunkel, D., & Watkins, B. (1987). Evolution of children's television regulatory policy. *Journal of Broadcasting & Electronic Media, 31,* 367–389.

Labaton, S. (2007, February 24). Record fine expected for Univision. *New York Times,* p. C1.

Levi, L. (2010). A "pay or play" experiment to improve children's educational television. *Federal Communication Law Journal, 62*(2), 275–341.

Linebarger, D. L., Kosanic, A. Z., Greenwood, C. R., & Doku, N. S. (2004). Effects of viewing the television program *Between the Lions* on the emergent literacy skills of young children. *Journal of Educational Psychology, 96,* 297–308.

Linebarger, D. L., & Piotrowski, J. T. (2010). Structure and strategies in children's educational television: The role of program type and learning strategies in children's learning. *Child Development, 81,* 1582–1597.

Linebarger, D. L., & Walker, D. (2005). Infants' and toddlers' television viewing and relations to language outcomes. *American Behavioral Scientist, 46,* 624–645.

Minow, N., & LaMay, C. (1995). *Abandoned in the wasteland: Children, television, and the First Amendment.* New York: Hill and Wang.

Murray, J. (1980). *Television and youth: 25 years of research and controversy.* Boys Town, NE: Boys Town Center for the Study of Youth Development.

Nadel, M. V. (1971). *The politics of consumer protection.* New York: Bobbs-Merrill.

National television violence study (Vol. 1). (1997). Thousand Oaks, CA: Sage.

Newman, K. S. (2004). *Rampage: The social roots of school shootings.* New York: Basic Books.

OFCOM (2007, February 22). *Television advertising of food and drink products to children: Final statement.* London, England: Author. Retrieved August 1, 2010, from http://stakeholders.ofcom.org.uk/binaries/consultations/foodads_new/statement/statement.pdf.

Office of Communication of the United Church of Christ and Center for Digital Democracy. (2004). *Petition to deny the license renewal of WPXW and WDCA.* Before the Federal Communications Commission, Washington, DC. FCC File No. BRCT-20040527AGS.

Orland, K. (2010, October 7). Lead counsel in SCOTUS violent games case lays out arguments. *Game Politics.* Retrieved August 1, 2010, from http://www.gamepolitics.com/2010/10/07/lead-counsel-scotus-violent-games-case-lays-out-arguments.

Palmer, E. L. (1988). *Television and America's children: A crisis of neglect.* New York: Oxford University Press.

Palmer, E., & Carpenter, C. F. (2006). Food and beverage marketing to children and youth: Trends and issues. *Media Psychology, 8*(2), 165–190.

Pearl, D., Bouthilet E., & Lazar, J. (Eds.). (1982). *Television and behavior: Ten years of scientific progress and implications for the eighties* (Vol. 2). Rockville, MD: National Institute of Mental Health.

Pecora, N. (1998). *The business of children's entertainment.* New York: Guilford Press.

Peeler, C. L., Kolish, E., & Enright, M. (2009). *The children's food and beverage advertising initiative in action: A report on compliance and implementation during 2008.* Arlington, VA: Council of Better Business Bureaus, Inc. Retrieved August 1, 2010, from http://cms-admin.bbb.org/storage/0/Shared%20Documents/finalbbbs.pdf.

Pomeranz, J. (2010). Television food marketing to children revisited: The Federal Trade Commission has the constitutional and statutory authority to regulate. *Journal of Law, Medicine, & Ethics, 38,* 98–116.

Reiss, A., & Roth, J. (Eds.). (1993). *Understanding and preventing violence.* Washington, DC: National Academy Press.

Reno, J. (1993, October 20). *Statement concerning violent television programming.* Hearings before the U.S. Senate Committee on Commerce, Science & Transportation.

Rice, M., Huston, A., & Wright, J. (1982). The forms of television: Effects on children's attention, comprehension, social behavior. In D. Pearl, E. Bouthilet, & J. Lazar (Eds.) *Television and behavior: Ten years of scientific progress and implications for the eighties,* (Vol. 2). Rockville, MD: National Institute of Mental Health.

Rideout, V. (2004). *Parents, media, and public policy: A Kaiser Family Foundation survey.* Menlo Park, CA: Kaiser Family Foundation. Retrieved August 1, 2010, from http://www .kff.org/entmedia/7156.cfm.

Rideout, V. (2007). *Parents, children and media: A Kaiser Family Foundation survey.* Menlo Park, CA: Kaiser Family Foundation. Retrieved August 1, 2010, from http://www.kff.org/ entmedia/7638.cfm.

Rideout, V., Foehr, U., & Roberts, D. (2010). *Generation M^2: Media in the lives of 8- to 18-year-olds.* Menlo Park, CA: Henry J. Kaiser Family Foundation. Retrieved August 1, 2010, from http://www.kff.org/entmedia/mh 012010pkg.cfm.

Rovello, J. (2010, July 8). 131 million reasons the Supreme Court could censor video games. *Huffington Post.* Retrieved August 1, 2010, from http://www.huffingtonpost.com/jessica-rovello/131-million-reasons-the-s_b_639054 .html.

Saunders, K. (1996). *Violence as obscenity: Limiting the media's First Amendment protection.* Durham, NC: Duke University Press.

Saunders, K. (2003). *Saving our children from the First Amendment.* New York: New York University Press.

Schmitt, K. L. (1999). *The Three-Hour Rule: Is it living up to expectations?* Philadelphia, PA: Annenberg Public Policy Center of the University of Pennsylvania. Retrieved August 1, 2010, from http://www.annenbergpublicpolicy center.org/NewsDetails.aspx?myId=146.

Schuck, P. H. (1977). Public interest groups and the policy process. *Public Administration Review, 37*(2), 132–140.

Sharma, L., Teret, S., & Brownell, K. D. (2010). The food industry and self-regulation: Standards to promote success and to avoid public health failures. *American Journal of Public Health, 100,* 240–246.

Simensky, L. (2007). Programming children's television: The PBS model. In J. A. Bryant (Ed.), *The children's television community* (pp. 131–146). Mahwah, NJ: Lawrence Erlbaum.

Simon, P. (2003). *Our pandering culture.* Carbondale: Southern Illinois University Press.

Sparr, F. (2008). The FCC's report on regulating broadcast violence: Is the medium the message? *Loyola of Los Angeles Entertainment Law Review, 28*(1), 1–25.

Spitzer, M. (1998). A first glance at the constitutionality of the V-chip rating system. In J. T. Hamilton (Ed.), *Television violence and public policy,* pp. 335–383. Ann Arbor: University of Michigan Press.

Stanger, J. (1997). *Television in the home: The 1997 survey of parents and children.* Washington, DC: Annenberg Public Policy Center of the University of Pennsylvania.

Stipp, H., Hill-Scott, K., & Dorr, A. (1987). Using social science to improve children's television: An NBC case study. *Journal of Broadcasting & Electronic Media, 31,* 461–473.

Story, M., & French, S. (2004). Food advertising and marketing directed at children and adolescents in the US. *International Journal of Behavioral Nutrition and Physical Activity, 1*(3), 1–17. doi:10.1186/1479-5868-1-3.

Surgeon General's Scientific Advisory Committee on Television and Social Behavior. (1972). *Television and growing up: The impact of televised violence.* Report to the Surgeon General, United States Public Health Service, Washington, DC: U.S. Government Printing Office.

Times Mirror Center for People and the Press. (1993). *TV violence: More objectionable in entertainment than in newscasts.* Washington, DC: Times/Mirror Center for People and the Press.

Turow, J. (1981). *Entertainment, education, and the hard sell: Three decades of network children's television.* New York: Praeger.

U.S. Senate, Committee on the Judiciary. (1956, January 16). *Television and juvenile delinquency: Investigation of juvenile delinquency in the United States.* (84th Congress, 2nd session, Report # 1466). Washington, DC: U.S. Government Printing Office.

U.S. Senate, Committee on Commerce, Science, and Transportation. (1997, February 27). *Hearing on television rating system.* (105th Congress, 1st session, Document #105157). Washington, DC: U.S. Government Printing Office.

Video Software Dealers Association v. Schwarzenegger, 401 F. Supp. 2d 1034 (N.D. Cal. 2005).

Video Software Dealers Association v. Schwarzenegger, 556 F. 3d 950 (9th Cir. 2009).

Walsh, D. A., & Gentile, D. A. (2001). A validity test of movie, television, and video-game ratings. *Pediatrics, 107,* 1302–1308. doi: 10.1542/peds.107.6.1302.

Wartella, E., Heintz, K., Aidman, A., & Mazzarella, S. (1990). Television and beyond: Children's video media in one community. *Communication Research, 17,* 45–64.

Wartella, E., & Reeves, B. (1985). Historical trends in research on children and the media: 1900–1960. *Journal of Communication, 35*(2), 118–133.

Waters, H. (1983, October 17). Kidvid: A national disgrace. *Newsweek,* pp. 82–83.

Welkos, R. (1995, June 14). The *Times* poll: Public echoes Dole view on sex, violence. *Los Angeles Times,* p. A1, A24–25.

Westen, T. (2006). Government regulation of food marketing to children: The Federal Trade Commission and the kid-vid controversy. *Loyola of Los Angeles Law Review, 39,* 79–91. Retrieved August 1, 2010, from http://llr.lls.edu/volumes/v39-issue1/docs/westen.pdf.

White House Task Force on Childhood Obesity. (2010). *Solving the problem of childhood obesity within a generation. Report to the president.* Washington, DC: Executive Office of the President of the United States. Retrieved August 1, 2010, from http://www.letsmove.gov/white-house-task-force-childhood-obesity-report-president.

Wilcox, B. L., Cantor, J., Dowrick, P., Kunkel, D., Linn, S., & Palmer, E. (2004). *Report of the APA Task Force on Advertising and Children: Recommendations.* Washington, DC: American Psychological Association. Retrieved August 1, 2010, from http://www.apa.org/news/press/releases/2004/02/children-ads.aspx.

Wilson, B. J., Kunkel, D., & Drogos, K. L. (2009). *Educationally insufficient? An analysis of the availability and educational quality of children's E/I programming.* Oakland, CA: Children Now. Retrieved August 1, 2010, from http://www.childrennow.org/index.php/learn/reports_and_research/article/211.

Wirth, M. O., Baldwin, T. F., & Zenaty, J. (1984). Demand for sex-oriented cable TV in the USA. Community acceptance and obscenity law. *Telecommunications Policy,* 314–320.

CHAPTER 29

Television Broadcaster Practices

Compliance With the Children's Television Act

KAREN HILL-SCOTT
Consultant

Introduction

In the first edition of the *Handbook of Children and the Media* (Singer & Singer, 2001), this chapter opened with a description of the explosive changes taking place in the broadcast, satellite, and cable television industries. That pace of change has only accelerated in this decade with significant impacts on children's television as a whole. The structural context that gave rise to the Children's Television Act has completely shifted. The broadcast networks are no longer the primary providers of children's television content. Children's access to other content providers (PBS and cable/satellite providers) has increased; close to 85% of all homes have cable or satellite television. In addition, the economics of producing children's television content has changed. Front-end financing is dependent upon projected short-term revenues from television advertising, and more importantly, back-end revenues from product merchandising and program syndication. Without all three, financing of new content, and especially educational content, is very difficult to obtain.

The purpose of this chapter is to review how the national networks have adapted to the changes in the structure of the industry over a 20-year period, especially as their "property values" decreased and regulation increased. After reviewing these practices, the chapter will also consider what the economic and organizational context foretells for compliance with the CTA. Additionally, some suggestions are offered for leveraging the intent and the constructive potential of the CTA even as its detractors declare it is obsolete.

Policy Context of the Children's Television Act: 1990–2000

When Congress passed the Children's Television Act (CTA) of 1990, the Federal Communications Commission (FCC) developed regulations to guide implementation of the Act (FCC, PL 101-437, 1990). Broadcasters were required to air programming specifically designed to meet the educational and informational needs of children up to age 16. The CTA required advertising limits, quarterly reporting, and a FCC review of compliance at the time television stations applied for license renewal. Within a year after the law was passed, it became apparent that abuses of the policy were a problem, and by 1993, the FCC issued a Notice of Inquiry designed to hear comments on the implementation of the Act. An *en banc* hearing followed, and in 1995, the FCC issued a Notice of Proposed Rule Making (NPRM) to refine the rules regarding implementation. There was an overwhelming response from academics, advocates, and parent and religious organizations to make the CTA more specific and to use much clearer criteria for compliance.

The result of the NPRM was that the CTA was augmented by collateral regulations, the Children's Television Rules (the Rules) of 1996 (FCC, Vol.73.671, 1996). The Rules established a more specific definition of educational and informational (E/I) content and required a minimum 3 hours per week of regularly scheduled programming for children ages 16 and under, broadcast in half-hour shows between the hours of 7:00 AM and 10:00 PM. The CTA also required that an E/I icon be shown on screen during the time the program is aired. The Rules also continued limits on advertising and pre-emptions, separation of programs and commercials, and restrictions on host-selling. It specified quarterly reporting requirements for individual stations and maintenance of a public inspection file documenting the educational content of the programs. In addition to reviewing license renewal applications, the FCC would levy financial penalties against stations not in compliance with any aspect of the CTA.

Ironically, when the Rules went into effect, less than a decade after the passage of the CTA, the audience it was intended to serve had shrunk considerably. While some in the industry might have grumbled that the E/I requirement was the cause, the truth was that children were migrating to cable and satellite channels. There children's television content was offered on approximately 15 channels, with five cable networks completely devoted to children's programming. Despite their entitlement under the Federal Communications Act of 1934 to broadcast free of charge if they served the public interest, the three major networks were seriously undermined by the cable upstarts that charged user fees to consumers. Not surprisingly, children in homes with cable/satellite services preferred to watch age-related programming that was cycled through 24-hour-a-day, 7day-a-week schedules. E/I content was reaching significantly smaller audiences than ever imagined when the CTA was passed. Compared to the ubiquity of cable offerings, the E/I content required by the CTA was, practically speaking, lost on the 3-hour island of Saturday morning.

New Rules, New Challenges: 2000–2010

In 2000, the pending launch of digital channels signaled to advocates that they needed to redouble efforts if the provisions of the CTA were to extend to the new technology. This conversion from analog to digital would permit free broadcasters to multicast on six channels simultaneously, and advocates wanted to ensure that E/I programming would be required on these new channels. In response, the FCC issued the first Order of proposed rule making for digital broadcasters in 2004 (FCC 04-221). However, specific aspects of these Rules were challenged and in 2006, after much negotiation, the Joint Proposal of Industry and Advocates on Reconsideration of the Children's Television Rules (FCC 06-33) was submitted to the FCC. After consideration of the Joint Proposal, the FCC issued the Second Order of Reconsideration and Second Report and Order (FCC 06-143) to resolve issues related to rules for the digital channels.

The September 2006 Rules retained all the provisions of the CTA's 1996 Rules for a single-channel broadcast. However, for multicasting, advertising, and website labeling, the FCC made several nuanced requirements. For example, the E/I time requirement would increase proportionate to the amount of free programming per week offered on multicast channels. For each 28-hour increment of free programming on secondary digital channels, an additional half-hour of E/I content must be provided to the main or multicast digital stream. If a secondary digital channel offers 168 hours of free programming, it therefore has an obligation to offer 3 hours of children's educational programming.

Another important rule is that at least 50% of the core programming not be repeated during the same week on the same channel in order to qualify for meeting the 3-hour core requirement. However, the entire schedule can be time-lifted and repeated on a secondary channel. Other rules include letting stand the four-pronged criteria for channel-related children's websites—the primary intent must be noncommercial, primary content is program related, landing page is not commercial, and menu pages are clearly labeled to distinguish commercial from non-commercial sections. Finally, the rules on character use and host-selling on websites were refined.

In the background, as the advocates and broadcasters wrangled over digital broadcasting, the competition for the children's viewing audience was decisively won by the cable industry. More than 77% of children's television viewing was on cable, 15% on networks, and 8% to syndicated providers (Alexander & Owers, 2007). In the 10 years since the first edition of the *Handbook* was published, the number of cable channels focused exclusively on children's programming also doubled, from 6 to 12 (see Table 29.1).

Table 29.1 Growth in Number of Children's Cable Channels 2000–2010

Kids Only Cable/Satellite Channels		*Mass Market Broadcast Channels With Kids Programs*	
2000	2010	2000	2010
Disney Channel (1983)	Disney Channel	ABC	ABC
	Disney XD	CBS	CBS
Toon Disney (1998)		FOX	
	Disney Junior (2012)	NBC	NBC (QUBO)
		UPN	The CW
Discovery Kids (1996)	Discovery Kids/ The Hub TV (2010)	The WB	
		6	4
Cartoon Network (1992) Boomerang (2000)	Cartoon Network Boomerang	**Mass Market Cable/Satellite Channels With Kids Programs**	
	Baby TV	Fox Family Channel (1977, 1998) sold to	ABC Family (2001)

(Continued)

Table 29.1 (Continued)

Kids Only Cable/Satellite Channels		Mass Market Broadcast Channels With Kids Programs	
Nickelodeon (1977,1979)	Nickelodeon Nick Jr.	HBO Family	HBO Family
	Teen Nick Nick Toons	Animal Planet	Animal Planet
	Sprout (2005)	PBS	PBS
		National Geographic	National Geographic
			Hallmark (2001)
6	12	5	6

Amid today's competition, the national networks' Saturday-morning block has low ratings, which results in low advertising revenues. The daypart is more a cost center than a revenue producer that can finance the cost of producing new shows (Cahn, Kalagian, & Lyon, 2008). Cable networks, in contrast to free broadcast networks, have two streams of revenue that go toward the funding base: advertising and subscriber fees. For cable networks, the aggregate subscriber fees for children's television alone are estimated at more than $1 billion per year (Blumenthal & Goodenough, 2006). Advertising fees layer revenue onto the base. Merchandising revenues and resale or licensing fees from distribution to other markets complete the backend stream of income, yielding even larger profits. In contrast, the networks, which have progressively lost audience share over the past 15 years against 12 cable channels solely dedicated to children's programming, do not have the same leverage. The base audience has not simply been partitioned into narrow segments with the network as one segment. With cable, children effectively have access to their own networks, their own shows, their own brands all day, every day of the year. As Jordan stated in her report on broadcast-industry insider perspectives, a prescient national broadcaster would probably drop children's programming altogether were it not for the Children's Television Act (Jordan, 1999).

During the past decade, a spate of mergers and acquisitions to aggregate cable, broadcast, and other media assets under one corporate umbrella also had an impact on E/I programming. In September 1999, CBS and Viacom merged, bringing children's E/I asset Nick Jr. to CBS Saturday morning (Goldman & Johnson, 1999).[1] In 2001, ABC bought Fox Family from Rupert Murdoch's News Corporation to create Disney Family (Britt & Wilkerson, 2001). Disney immediately began incorporating its own programming into the channel and used content from the cable channels in the Saturday-morning daypart. In September 2005, NBC Universal acquired an ownership interest in ION Media Networks, the largest hybrid and independent network of 59 local television stations, cable, and satellite distribution systems in the country (Ionpress.com, 2010). Six months later, NBC with Ion assembled a consortium of content providers—Corus Entertainment, Scholastic, and Classic Media/Big Idea—to launch the QUBO children's network, which furnishes programming to Ion and NBC (redOrbit, 2006). Within 3 years of this deal, NBC Universal, the first television broadcaster in America, was sold to Comcast Corporation, the largest cable company in the United States (Arango, 2009). These mergers and acquisitions cemented the secondary role of the free broadcaster to cable and satellite

---

[1]This was an insignificant part of the deal, but nonetheless important for the children's daypart.

television and had a trickle-down impact on children's programming.

If the cable company had high-quality children's assets, the broadcaster could benefit. Multiplatform media corporations could air their own E/I shows on their cable and broadcast outlets, doubling and/or intensifying the audience exposure. One schedule could support the other as long as the compliance rules were observed. Disney was first to use its vertical alignment of multiplatform media by furnishing ABC Saturday morning with selected episodes of the Disney Kids' library for E/I programming. Viacom's Nick Jr. did the same thing for CBS before the two were legally separated as corporate entities in late 2005 (Alfano, 2006). With these corporate sister relationships, there would be a lot of repetition of the E/I content across platforms. Repetition would not necessarily be a bad thing if program quality was good and conveyed strong educational content. Basically, the business relationship could provide some synergy with the educational goals of the CTA. However, by the end of the decade, only ABC had continued to use the cross-platform arrangement. Another approach to meeting the E/I requirement emerged: leasing or outsourcing the E/I daypart to an outside producer.

Forty years ago, networks financed independent production companies to develop original programming for the schedule. A 1970 law prevented networks from having any long-term syndication or financial interest in the programming they purchased. In 1995, when the FCC abolished the "fin-syn" rules, networks modified the outsourcing model to co-own or own programming outright and then benefit from the long tail of syndication revenues (Blumenthal & Goodenough, 2008; McAllister, 2004). As stated earlier, with the ascent of cable, the potential for back-end revenue basically closed for Saturday-morning television, and that changed the model for outsourcing children's programs. What is different about the model today is that the vendor shoulders much of the responsibility for the daypart and the network acts as a pass-through, making the programming available to its affiliate stations. A lot of the content that networks license from vendors is existing content, not original programming designed

for an E/I schedule. While each network and vendor relationship has unique terms, outsourcing typically includes cobranding, in which the vendor is identified as the provider of content and the network is the home where that content resides. Other differences from the direct-management model are that the vendor may be responsible for generating the advertising revenue and in some cases may even furnish the underlying documentation for the FCC reports.

E/I packaging through cobranding arrangements was used by The WB and UPN shortly after the 1996 Rules went into effect (Hill-Scott, 2001). NBC used a variant on the outsourcing model with Discovery Communications from 2002 through 2006. However, most of the content was original, designed as E/I, and the FCC production support and documentation was managed by the network. After the separation from Viacom, CBS established an arrangement with DIC Entertainment to provide its E/I block, and NBC cobranded with QUBO in 2006. The most important feature of outsourcing and cobranding is the financial synergy it provides both the broadcaster and the vendor. The network pays a license fee on previously produced content, and the lower cost reduces the gap between the expense of the content against the advertising income generated by the daypart (Alexander & Owers, 2007). A big benefit for the outside vendor is that doing business with the network increases the redistribution potential of the content library. The value of being on the air in the United States is one key to leveraging repeat business for the same material in the global marketplace (Cahn et al., 2008). The big question is whether those synergies truly extend a benefit to the dissemination of high-quality E/I content. Some of the outsourced content is original E/I programming. However, the existing libraries of content were originally designed for entertainment. If the content is not modified to conform to an E/I standard, a compliance issue could emerge, resulting in fines for the individual stations that relied on the programs to fulfill their E/I obligations.

The preceding review of the policy and business context should convey how the business of network television is one stratum in a multilayered, multiplatform industry that is crisscrossed by complex business transactions. Children's television is quite a small parcel of real estate in the scheme of things but not so insignificant that the CTA can be ignored. While broad strategic business needs typically eclipse the specific concerns of how to best serve children's interests, the goals of the CTA still have to be met and met completely. Networks will do their due diligence, and the FCC has shown through enforcement that it will back up the tenets of the CTA. In 2010, eight stations were fined for violations of the advertising rules (FCC-NALF, 2010), but fines can be levied for any violation of the CTA, including inadequate content. In fact, the largest fine ever levied by the FCC was a $24 million penalty against Univision (Labaton, 2007) for misrepresenting a *telenovela* as an educational program for children.

Current Industry Practices to Meet the E/I Compliance Standards

This section of the chapter will review industry practices to comply with the CTA that were in force at the end of the first quarter 2010 (March 31). The review is not a survey of multiple stations in multiple markets; instead, it takes a case study approach, focusing on the network decision making that determines what content will be available in those markets.

Method

The documentation of approaches to meeting the E/I requirement was gathered in interviews with executives and consultants attached to either the network or the production company supplying content. All interview participants were forthcoming and provided narrative commentary on the issues from their perspective but mainly focusing on the challenges programmers and content developers face in getting any new children's

television production financed. The interviews were especially important for clarifying questions about the business context. The starting point analyzing the practical impact of network decisions was the FCC Form 398 for the first quarter of 2010 for the Los Angeles market. The local stations are network owned and operated (O&O), and their document represents what each affiliate station was provided for their local programming. It is case material and reflects the central decision making for the network regardless of local station decisions to run all or part of the offered schedule. The overall approach to E/I compliance was compared to the type of approach each network offered 10 years ago when this handbook was first published. To be consistent, the presentation of findings for each network follows the same format: the current approach for complying with the CTA, the target age group, and the amount of time for E/I programming. Summary tables encapsulate relevant information from the FCC compliance form.

Findings Overview

In 2010, four networks provided uniform national coverage of children's E/I offerings: ABC, CBS, NBC, and The CW[2]. The Fox network withdrew from direct management of a children's schedule in fall 2009 and directed its affiliates to obtain or produce their own programming. Fox provides one 30-minute program for just part of the calendar year to its affiliate stations. Each affiliate licenses or produces additional content and manages the daypart and the FCC filing independently. For this chapter, the Los Angeles Fox affiliate report was reviewed as an exemplar of what an independent station might provide. Beyond the networks, independent station groups around the country provide the remainder of other free-broadcast E/I programming. They may license programming from existing libraries and may have access to locally developed programming. Each station, whether or not it is a network affiliate, must file its own reports

---

[2]The CW is the new network created as a joint venture of CBS (owner of UPN) and Time Warner (owner of the WB) from the remains of UPN and The WB, both of which folded in 2006.

with the FCC. The station must also maintain an onsite public inspection file that documents the validity of the E/I content in each episode of a program.[3]

Table 29.2 summarizes some of the key content made available in the quarterly FCC filings. Based on the first-quarter FCC filing for 2010, it is possible to see each network's overall children's programming, target age group, and the quantity of programming aired for E/I content. The FCC Form 398 does not require the network to disclose how it determined the content was E/I, but the educational inputs strategy is included here for purposes of comparison across networks.

Three of the four networks, CBS, The CW, and NBC, used external consultants to validate E/I compliance on the content. The narrative discussion of each network will describe how the broadcaster compliance process worked to meet a good-faith standard

of educational content within each broadcaster's offerings. As can be seen in Table 29.2, each broadcaster met the minimum standard of 3 hours of content. Two networks, ABC and CBS, exceeded the minimum. The target age group varied by program and hour of the day, and each show was a half-hour in length.

Network Findings

The schedule for CBS, The CW, NBC, and the local Fox station was outsourced, while ABC relied on its Disney parent content library. Of all the programs aired during the first quarter 2010, just two programs were original productions or developed for first run on the schedule: *Turbo Dogs* and *Shelldon* for NBC/QUBO. There is a mix of animation and live action programming on ABC and The CW. Both networks also have split-day programming. ABC has a 3-hour

Network	Total Shows	Total Weekly Hours	Target Audience	Total E/I Hours	Total E/I Shows	Educational Inputs Strategy
ABC	7	4	8–11 8–12 10–13 11–13 (13–16)	3 (1)	5 (2)	Internal Review
CBS	3	3	3–6 3–7 7–12	3	3	Producer's Consultant* External Consultant
The CW	3	3.5	6–11 13–16	3.5	3	External Consultant
NBC	8**	3.0	4–8	3.0	8	External Consultant
FOX [LA]	4	3	13–16	3	4	Internal Review

Table 29.2 Reported Compliance With the CTA FCC Form 398 March 31, 2010

*A producer's or external consultant is an independent third party retained to evaluate and validate if content meets an E/I standard.

**More than six shows are reported due to schedule changes during the quarter.

( ) Additional noncore but educational/informational programming.

[3]The reports can be found at http://licensing.fcc.gov/KidVid/public/report/9/index.faces.

Table 29.3 Network Programming March 31, 2010, Main Channel

SATURDAY MORNING SCHEDULE

Network	7:00	7:30	8:00	8:30	9:00	9:30	10:00	10:30	11:00	11:30
ABC Kids					That's So Raven	That's So Raven	Hannah Montana	The Suite Life of Zack and Cody	Emperor's New School	The Replacements
CBS	Busytown Mysteries	Noonbory and the Super Seven	Busytown Mysteries	Sabrina: The Animated Series	Busytown Mysteries	Noonbory and the Super Seven				
The CW (KTLA)	Winx Club	Winx Club								
NBC			Zula Patrol (1) / Turbo Dogs (11)	My Friend Rabbit (1)/ Shelldon (12)	Willa's Wild Life (1)/ 3-2-1 Penguins (12)	Babar	Shelldon (1) / Willa's Wild Life (7)	Jane and the Dragon		
Fox (KTTV)	Awesome Adventures	Awesome Adventures	The Real Winning Edge	Whaddyado	Saved By the Bell	Saved By the Bell				

SATURDAY AFTERNOON SCHEDULE

Network	12:00 PM	12:30	1:00	1:30	2:00	2:30	3:00	3:30	4:00	5:00
ABC Kids			Animal Exploration with Jarod Miller				Teen Kids News			
CBS										
The CW (KTLA)	Degrassi: Next Generation (until 1/16/10)/ Edgemont	Degrassi: Next Generation (until 1/16/10)/ Edgemont	Degrassi: Next Generation (until 1/16/10)/ Edgemont	Degrassi: Next Generation (until 1/16/10)/ Edgemont	Eco Company					
NBC										
Fox (KTTV)										

children's block in the morning and airs two live-action reality-based programs for teens in the afternoon. The CW has a 1-hour mini-block for young children in the morning and a 2.5-hour live-action teen block in the afternoon. NBC and CBS offer an all-animation schedule. The local Fox station airs licensed live-action content, with 2 hours in a documentary format and 1 hour for a comedy.

Following is a summary description of each network's approach to programming the main channel daypart.

ABC

In 2001, ABC began airing content from its (cable) sister network, the Disney Channel. The live-action shows were broadly prosocial, aimed at the "tween" audience, and filtered for episodes that met E/I compliance by both the Standards and Practices Division of the network and any educational consultants who were attached to the shows. The content on the air in 2010 follows the same model and consists of reruns from live-action *That's So Raven, Hannah Montana,* and *The Suite Life of Zack and Cody* augmented by reruns of *The Emperor's New School* and new episodes of *The Replacements,* both animated shows. The afternoon schedule is filed on the Form 398 as noncore programming, but both programs, *Teen News* and *Animal Exploration,* are live-action news/documentary shows. ABC also airs syndicated content for its digital channels, offering 6 additional hours of E/I programming.

CBS

From 2000 to 2005, Nick Jr., the CBS cable sister, provided the Saturday-morning schedule. Cobranding the daypart began in 2006 when DIC Entertainment signed a deal with CBS to launch *KOL Secret Slumber Party* on CBS. DIC had its own educational consultant working on content, and CBS used an external consultant to support the network in reviewing content. In 2008, DIC was merged with and later purchased by Cookie Jar Entertainment. The daypart is now cobranded as *Cookie Jar TV* (Bell, 2008). Cookie Jar is a global children's entertainment

company that owns a library of nearly 6,000 episodes of animated and live-action content, including E/I and entertainment properties. The programming for CBS includes three licensed animated series: *Busytown* and *Noonbory* and *Sabrina: The Animated Series* from the Cookie Jar library.

The CW

In 2008, The CW outsourced its daypart to 4Kids, a global entertainment and brand-management company that is known for re-versioning Japanese anime for the U.S. market. 4Kids owns properties such as *Pokemon, Yu-gi-oh,* and *The Cabbage Patch Kids.* It also produces educational content through *WordWorld,* an animated television show funded in part by the U.S. Department of Education. In the past, 4Kids has engaged a consultant/educator to edit episodes that need to be strengthened to clearly communicate E/I content. It will manage The CW daypart as *TheCW4Kids* until 2013. The content for the 2009 to 2010 schedule contains one original show, the *Eco Company. The Winx Club* is a girl-oriented Italian animated action series for children 5 to 13, and the balance of the schedule is reruns from the teen-oriented *DeGrassi: The Next Generation* and *Eco Company,* a live-action news magazine format featuring teens who explore all aspects of ecological conservation. The CW is also multicasting five shows for 3 hours of content on one of its digital channels.

FOX (Local Station KTTV-Los Angeles)

Because Fox affiliates are on their own, each develops a schedule that will work in the local community. The Los Angeles affiliate licensed content for four live-action series serving teens ages 13 to 16. Three of the four shows follow a news magazine format: travel throughout the world (*Awesome Adventures*), case studies of teens overcoming adversity (*The Real Winning Edge*), and teens taking action to help others (*Whattyado*). The last show is the "vintage" prosocial teen comedy *Saved by the Bell,* originally produced by NBC.

NBC

At NBC, the outsourcing model was introduced in 2002 when the network made its exit from producing or financing content for children's programming. Discovery Kids leased Saturday morning from NBC, supplied original E/I content, and secured the advertising to support the daypart. In 2006, the cobranded block *QUBO on NBC* furnished original and licensed content for the daypart. For the 2009 to 2010 schedules, four of the eight animated shows on this quarter's schedule are original programming: *Shelldon*, *My Friend Rabbit*, *Turbo Dogs*, and *3-2-1-Penguins!* One of the remaining shows, *The Zula Patrol,* is a former PBS property, and *Willa, Jane and the Dragon*, and *Babar* are existing shows that have been edited and/or repurposed to feature the inherent educational content. The author is the external consultant for NBC. NBC/QUBO is also multicasting 6 hours of digital content that consists of seven different shows from different sources.

Discussion

From 2001 to 2010, there were three things that distinguished these schedules from those of the previous decade. First, there are fewer national broadcasters involved in children's programming. UPN no longer exists and Fox pulled out of the market in the 2009 to 2010 season altogether, leaving the individual broadcast stations to figure out how to manage the E/I requirement. Since the penalties for noncompliance fall to the individual stations, Fox has offloaded the responsibility and the possible penalties. Other broadcasters may follow suit in future years. Second, there is not as much original programming created specifically for the E/I daypart. Based on a study of the E/I content aired during the fourth quarter 2007 (Wilson, Kunkel, & Drogos, 2008), there were 40 E/I shows aired (including PBS). This author researched the production dates on each show and found that 19 had ceased production on or before the year of the research. Some of these were long-standing E/I shows in recirculation, and others were E/I shows developed from existing content. On this

2010 schedule, of the four original productions on QUBO, *Shelldon* continued production in Asia; the other three have ended production. Based on the consultant interviews, both the licensing companies and the networks made investments in culling the strongest episodes from the libraries and even editing and modifying footage to bring out the educational lesson embedded in the existing content. Third, the programming is not as focused on drawing a single core target audience. Certainly, the CTA does not require that all the programming on one channel serve one age group, and some consultants seem to favor airing different types of programming for different-aged target audiences. However, neither audience size nor attachment to the channel will occur if the block does not have a developmental identity. CBS has a preschool schedule punctuated in the middle with a program that is very popular among girls ages 7 to 12. The CW maintains a split schedule with a 2-hour morning block for young children and 1 hour for teens in the afternoon. ABC also has an interesting transitional schedule. The morning begins with a younger target audience for the first hour and a somewhat older one for the later part of the morning; however, the ages are probably close enough for the programming to serve all children ages 8 to 13. Like The CW, ABC does offer two noncore E/I shows to older teens and airs them on Saturday afternoon.

Another dimension of children's programming that is different from the beginning of the decade is that the multicast digital channels are up and running. Based on the Form 398, three of the broadcasters—ABC, The CW, and NBC—are multicasting. From the reporting form, it is difficult to discern the E/I value of the offerings. An independent review of the content would be very useful for consumers. All of the multicast content appears to be outsourced, and there is a narrative snapshot of each schedule at the end of this section.

In summary, each broadcaster has aired the minimum 3 hours of E/I programming, all on Saturday morning, and where applicable has aired the minimum hours on the multicast. Both ABC and The CW, respectively, aired an additional hour and a half hour of E/I content. There is no daily programming, which is typical of the broadcasters, though Fox and UPN did air a daily strip in the late 1990s.

Clearly, the broadcasters are looking for cost-effective ways to put E/I content on the air and support affiliates' abilities to comply with the CTA. Based on the interviews, the networks, without exception, feel caught in a zero-sum situation. The child audience has gone to cable, and what used to be a small audience (in numbers) is a big audience today. In Table 29.4, for example, we see the impact that multiple channels could have on audience partitioning. The peak Saturday-morning audience hits about 16% of the total potential audience of about 34 million children ages 2 to 11 in the United States. This number from the census is within the range of Nielsen's documentation of TV households. When there were just three networks, the successful network would have had at least a million viewers or close to 2 million viewers if it pulled 25% from each of its competitors.[4]

Today, with 18 channels, the networks are lucky to pull in very low six figures for their programming blocks, especially since Table 29.4 does not further partition by age group. With limitations on advertising and not a single branded program with merchandising potential or current backend, executives report that the daypart operates at a loss.

On the other hand, cable is in a healthier position, and in 2010, one show, *SpongeBob SquarePants,* is the brand to beat. SpongeBob has an impact similar to what the networks got when there was no cable competition. Based on a public relations release from the *PR Newswire* (2009), Nickelodeon was the number-one children's channel for the 59th straight quarter, a period of almost 15 years, ironic since this was the same year the 1996 Rules for the CTA were announced. The channel averaged 2.2 million viewers, including 1.2 million children ages 2 to 11, right in the range of the peak size audience for the "old" network scenario in Table 29.4. Its top animated show, *SpongeBob SquarePants,* had its highest numbers recorded at 4.8 million for a special episode in November of 2009. Clearly, with ratings like this, it is not just the networks that are suffering; Nickelodeon has managed to break through the clutter and hold on to a large audience despite both cable and free broadcast challengers.

Table 29.4	Impact of Multiple Channels on Audience Size and Ratings

Population Base Ages 2–11	% of Audience	Raw Number in Audience at x%	Audience per Channel @ 5 networks	Audience per Channel @ 12 Channels	Audience per Channel @ 18 Channels (Network, Cable, PBS)
34,285,714	12%	4,114,286	822,857	374,026	228,571
	14%	4,800,000	960,000	400,000	266,667
Peak Size Saturday	16%	5,485,714	1,097,143	457,143	304,762
	18%	6,171,429	1,234,286	514,286	342,857
	20%	6,857,143	1,371,429	571,429	380,952

Source: Based on data compiled from the U.S. Census 2008 American Community Survey Table #SO901.

---

[4]This figure is not adjusted for actual audience size then vs. now.

Digital Content

Given the reality check of a changed marketplace, the starting point for the digital channels is completely licensed content. Across all three networks, the offerings are very diverse. The 15 hours a week of content ranges from didactic lesson plans set to hip-hop rhymes to a teen news program developed by the creator of the Eyewitness News format. In contrast, there are other shows in the qualifying lineup where one offers a primer on how to break into the music business and another covers clips and commentary on extreme sports.

The following section of this chapter provides a cursory review of the coverage, including a few ratings of program quality for shows that were on E/I broadcast schedules in 2008 and are now recycled in the digital lineup for 2009 to 2010.

ABC

ABC has licensed syndicated digital content that is for the 13- to 16-year-old target audience (Table 29.5). All the shows are live-action magazine/reality/documentary format.

NBC

The NBC digital listings cover weekday mornings and weekends (Table 29.6). The programming is skewed toward teens and is all live action except for two shows for young children on early Saturday morning.

The CW

Digital programming on The CW is a mix of animated and live-action shows, and each show has a different target audience (Table 29.7).

Table 29.5 ABC Digital Channel Broadcast

ABC Digital Channel (6 hours)					
Title	Target Audience	Day/Time Program Airs	Number of Hours	Program Type	External Rating where applicable
Jack Hanna's Animal Adventure	13–16	Saturday 8:00–10:30 AM	2.5	Live Action	Moderate
Aqua Kids	13–16	Saturday 10:30 AM and 12:20 PM	1.0	Live Action	
Teen Kids News	13–16	Saturday 11:00–11:30 AM	.5	Live Action	High
Animal Exploration with Jarod Miller	13–16	Saturday 11:30 AM–12:00 PM	.5	Live Action	Moderate
B In-Tune TV	13–16	Saturday 12:00–12:30 PM	.5	Live Action	
Dragonfly TV	13–16	Saturday 1:00–1:30 PM	.5	Live Action	
Swap TV	13–16	Saturday 1:30–2:00 PM	.5	Live Action	

Table 29.6	The NBC Digital Broadcast

NBC Digital Channel (6 Hours)					
Title	Target Audience	Day/Time Program Airs	Number of Hours/Day	Program Type	External Rating where applicable
Safari Tracks	13–16	Mon-Tues-Wed 7:00, 7:30 AM	1	Live Action	Moderate
Planet X	13–16	Mon-Tues-Wed 7:00–9:00 AM Feb 1–Feb 10	2	Live Action	
Planet X	13–16	Mon-Tues-Wed 7:00, 7:30 AM Mar 1–Mar 31	1	Live Action	
The Kids Block	3–5	Saturday 7:00–7:30 AM	.5	Live, Puppet, Animation	
Zodiac Island	5–8	Saturday 7:30–8:00 AM	.5	Animated	
Aqua Kids	13–16	Saturday 8:00, 10:00 AM	1	Live Action	
B In-Tune Rewind	13–16	Saturday 8:30–9:00 AM	.5	Live Action	
My Parents, My Sister and Me	13–16	Saturday 9:00–9:30 AM	.5	Live Action	

Table 29.7	The CW Digital Broadcast

The CW Digital Channel (3 hours)					
Title	Target Audience	Day/Time Program Airs	Number of Hours/Day	Program Type	External Rating where applicable
The Country Mouse and the City Mouse Adventures	4–9	Saturday 8:00 AM	.5	Animation	
Wimzie's House	2–5	Saturday 7:30 AM	.5	Animation	
Green Screen Adventures	7–9	7:00 AM	.5	Live Action	
Horseland	9–11	Saturday 8:30 AM	.5	Animation	Moderate
Liberty's Kids	7–12	Saturday 9:00, 9:30 AM	1	Animation	

Summary

This review of network practices reveals that at this stage, without a competitive edge or appetite for deficit financing to make a bold foray into the children's market, network television is relying primarily on licensing mostly previously aired content to meet its public-interest obligation. To fill the content void, this material is culled, repurposed, and recycled into content that can meet E/I criteria. Where financially possible, some original programming was developed by QUBO and the Eco-Company to meet the requirements of the CTA. ABC also ran an "echo" of new content from the Disney Channel. In short, the network response to fulfilling the quantitative requirements of the CTA is very pragmatic. But reruns and recycled and repurposed content are short-term solutions. There are other issues that loom over future years.

First is the issue of program quality, when much of the content in existing libraries may be inadequate to the E/I standard. A related issue to quality is accountability for compliance and how to achieve it. Second is the problem of a sustaining a content pipeline, particularly as the additional digital channels are launched. Every 128-hour increment of digital programming will require an additional 3 hours of E/I programming. This could result in 18 hours of content per network, essentially the equivalent of a new children's channel. Third is the issue of developing organizational/institutional financing models that will lead to new E/I content generation.

In the next section of this chapter, a review of data from a 2008 study of E/I compliance will reveal whether the first concern about quality is warranted. Then the closing of this chapter will offer some ideas for approaches to address the remaining concerns: the need to create new content for increased requirements and organizational/institutional approaches to financing that could lead to new content production.

Program Quality and Compliance

Over the course of 5 years, from 1996 to 2000, the Annenberg Public Policy Center evaluated the qualitative extent of compliance with the CTA (Jordan, 1996, 1998, 2000; Jordan & Woodard, 1997; Woodard, 1999). At an annual press conference, audience members, including network executives, listened anxiously to find out which shows aired the previous season had high, moderate, or low E/I value.

Based on a summary of these reports performed by Calvert (2008), quality went up in the year after the 1996 Rules were passed, and the proportion of highly educational programs was the highest of all years, about 42% of the total. Soon, however, the highly educational shows began to decline and the moderately educational shows became a larger proportion of the total. By 2000, the highly educational programs had dropped to about 22% of the total. On the positive side, minimally educational shows, which were almost 40% of the total before the rules, dramatically dropped by half after the Rules and have hovered around the 20 to 25% mark ever since (Calvert, 2008).

In 2008, the most recent report on compliance with the CTA, published by Children Now, is modeled after the Annenberg analyses. There are a few changes to the scoring system, with two additional criteria and what appears to be a higher cutoff point separating high from moderate (Wilson et al., 2008). The study looked at and rated E/I programs that were aired during the fall 2007 quarter and sampled 24 media markets in four market groups defined by population size (television households). Wilson and colleagues found that the quality of programming had degraded since the last Annenberg report in 2000. Only 13% of sampled programs were scored as *highly educational*, the lowest proportion ever, while the proportion that was *minimally educational* remained at the perennial 20 to 25%.

During the 2000 to 2008 period, the moderately educational category ballooned from about half of all content to 63% of all content. This finding could be an artifact of the new scoring approach, which was more stringent than Annenberg, or because a lot of the programs were not designed around the E/I Requirement or the specific criteria of the study. But in the end, we see that this study corroborates the Annenberg findings of 2000; a large majority the E/I content is adequate but not exceptional in quality (see Table 29.8).

The 2008 report also provided comparison between commercial and public television

| Table 29.8 | Shifts in Quality Over 10 Years |

Year	Level of Educational Quality		
	Minimal	Moderate	High
1997–1998	21%	35%	42%
1998–1999	21%	46%	33%
2007–2008	23%	63%	13%

Source: Based on data from Wilson et al., *Educationally Insufficient*, Children Now, 2008

programs, finding the public programs were rated both higher in quality and lower on aggression for both social/emotional messaging and intellectual/informational content.

It is interesting to note, though, that of the top eight E/I programs on the air in 2008, half were commercially produced and half were from public broadcasting. The issue of quality is not the source of material as much as it is the purpose of the show at the point of origination. All of the commercially developed shows in the top group were designed to convey a message of value to the audience, as were the PBS series. Also, six of the eight shows were in production the year they were evaluated. Only two shows were drawn from archival material, *Beakman's World* and *Between the Lions*. Since these two shows were designed to be E/I, being archival clearly does not inherently translate to lower educational value. These shows are inherently high-quality content even if recycled (see Table 29.9).

Overall, the Annenberg and Children Now reports are very useful markers for commenting on program compliance. When analyzed against the overall landscape of children's television and media use, these reports are highly useful for creating a sense of how the CTA is being upheld and in what areas it might be compromised. If one understands the underlying methodology of each study, the work can help trigger ideas for improving the efficacy of the CTA and for reconsidering what variables are really most important for a compliance study.

| Table 29.9 | Top-Scoring Programs in 2008 |

Title	Score	Public	Commercial	Source
Sesame Street	11.3	Yes		Original Programming
Beakman's World	10.7		Yes	Library
Between the Lions	10.7	Yes		Library
3-2-1 Penguins!	10.3		Yes	Original Programming
Cyberchase	10.3	Yes		Original Programming
Suite Life of Zack and Cody	10.3		Yes	Original Programming
Fetch! w/ Ruff Ruffman	10.0	Yes		Original Programming
Teen Kids News	10.0		Yes	Original Programming

Source: Based on Wilson et al. (2008). *Educationally Insufficient*. Children Now.

On the level of policy compliance, the content of this chapter and the much larger work scope of the Annenberg and Children Now studies relied on the Form 398 for base data regarding compliance with the letter of the law. After reviewing and writing material for several years' worth of forms, it is evident that there is a compelling need for Form 398 to be structurally revised. In effect, the form is really only a data collection point and does not constitute a fully functioning reporting system. The FCC, as the regulatory agency, should be vested with the responsibility to provide an accessible and easily understood public accountability regarding implementation of the CTA.

By converting the data collection function into an automated data reporting function, several benefits would accrue to the agency and to the community, and, certainly, to external researchers. Currently the forms are electronic but not formatted for use as an automated database. Each station takes an idiosyncratic approach to completing the form, and errors are bound to occur. Anyone aiming for a consolidated glance at efforts to comply with the CTA must construct a database or develop tables by hand. Automation is a modest proposal but way overdue considering the number of years the CTA has been in effect. Also, if networks were to follow Fox's lead and opt out of centralized programming for the children's market, there will be no centralized nodes of program consistency. With more than 1,200 television stations in the United States, the starting point for reviewing practices and compliance will be at the molecular level—half-hour by half-hour, station by station—until a national picture is constructed.

Data compilation can be automated at the agency level, and the quarterly reports filed by the stations could be treated as a quarterly census, downloadable into a database. The Form 398 database could produce an *accountability dashboard* for each station. One could aggregate data by different variables so local and national statistics could be easily compiled. Such an investment in automation would be consistent with the current federal efforts to increase transparency and accountability to the public through agencywide interactive websites. Web-based interactive tools would make it easier to report and much easier for the public to understand how responsive their broadcasters are to children's needs and fulfilling the public interest.

The Policy-to-Practice Conundrum

Based on the practices of today, there are compelling financial reasons the E/I void is filled with licensed content that can meet an E/I standard. However, the content pipeline is a genuine concern because as more hours for E/I content become available through digital broadcasting, more content will be needed. The current base of content is already compromised, as evidenced by the small proportion of programs in the "highly educational" category. Though the libraries may appear to be numerically deep with programs, the content is not E/I; in fact, what is on the air today may be the best of what can be adapted for E/I purposes.

The conundrum is that while the number of E/I required hours will likely increase over time due to the increase of digital channels, there may not be an adequate source of E/I content to fulfill the demand. This conundrum is explored by Cahn and colleagues (2008) in their chapter on models of children's media financing in different countries. In the United States, without a sister channel from cable as a first-run or rebroadcast platform, broadcasters will simply continue to rely on licensing existing content as a pragmatic and cost-effective way to fulfill the requirement (Blumenthal & Goodenough, 2006).

Congress passed the Telecommunications Act of 1996 with the express intent that broadcasters fulfill their obligation to serve the public interest (Kunkel, 2003), and the FCC has pursued claims of noncompliance and enforced penalties (FCC, 2010). But the carrot/stick approach will not change the qualitative dimension of content unless there is a way to guarantee profitability. As is evident from this chapter, the wide range and frequency of business transactions in the media sector are not driven by a concern for the CTA but for the overall financial health and competitive position of the media corporations. Perhaps a pathway out of the conundrum is to give some thought to creating a new approach to financing that specifically addresses the requirements of the CTA.

Research and Content Alignment

One starting point would be to examine a different approach to creating E/I content. As an entry point (or soft sell to the broadcast industry), it would actually be useful to develop a forum or similar type of process where strategically important research findings are repurposed and packaged for dissemination to the creative or content-producing community. As Anderson points out (2003), we know from research that the CTA has shown benefits to programming and that E/I television has an impact on children's learning. Calvert and Kotler (2003a), in a very interesting study, have documented a variety of ways programming has had a positive impact on children. They have described age and gender differences in viewing behavior that run counter to the creative community's conventional wisdom. For example, an unwritten axiom of television writers is that girls will watch boys as lead characters, but boys will not watch female lead characters. The Calvert and Kotler research clearly explains how and why this does not hold true using *The Wild Thornberrys* as an example. If a research-to-practice forum were held, it would have to be done in a unique way, so the content from the research community resonates to the interests and priorities of the creative community while still being compelling on its own merit. Certainly, some advocates and researchers may feel an effort around communication is pointless, and information-sharing events have been tried with little result. But it also takes continuous work to shift beliefs about the ineffectiveness of E/I television. There are a few persistent myths about children's preferences and viewing behaviors that need to be dispelled, using interesting and surprising data from different sectors of the research community.

The children's television sector would benefit from some E/I (encouragement and inspiration) of its own to take what it perceives

to be a risk and develop E/I content within entertainment properties. At minimum, many entertainment vehicles could be imbued with E/I content if it is planned for during script development. *The Suite Life of Zack and Cody,* which received a "highly educational" rating in the 2008 study cited earlier, was not designed to be an E/I vehicle. But the writing often embedded a lesson into the plot itself, resulting in an educational theme being carried throughout the episode. If the academic community had a nurtured but informal means of communicating and packaging insights about children's interests and abilities to the industry, it might be more attainable to genuinely have a E/I impact on story development. For example, the Calvert and Kotler study (2003a) on the impact of the CTA on children's learning is very rich in the nature and breadth of its findings. Even the stories children wrote about what they learned from television episodes are fascinating. That boys liked girl heroes will surprise most writers and producers, as will the findings that demonstrate how interest in E/I programming changes with age and the format (live action vs. animation). This kind of scholarly work could actually inform decisions about character development and program format.

The platform has yet to be built for good independent research to regularly and constructively inform the children's entertainment arena (Calvert & Kotler, 2003b). Perhaps if that loop were closed a bit more often, we would witness some discernable results of a positive impact on children's television (Wilcox, 2003). Television history is replete with examples—beginning with the work of Gerald Lesser, Edward Palmer, and others on *Sesame Street* (Fisch & Truglio, 2001; Lesser, 1974). At the launch of Nick Jr., Dan Anderson had a substantial impact on *Blue's Clues* (Anderson, Bryant, Wilder, Santomero, Williams, & Crawley, 2000; Crawley, Anderson, Santomero, Wilder, Williams, Evans, & Bryant, 2002). Jerome and Dorothy Singer's classic works on early aggression (Singer & Singer, 1981) and media literacy (Desmond, Singer, Singer, Calam, & Colimore, 1985; Singer & Singer, 1998) have had a substantial impact on framing the child's developmental context and capacity for truly understanding television. Most recently, the latest Kaiser Foundation Study on media usage by children (Rideout, Foehr, & Roberts, 2010) literally stunned researchers. The study revealed that assumptions about children's engagement with media grossly underestimated multitasking and actual usage. Indeed, the Nielsenwire report for the third quarter 2009 (McDonough, 2009) presaged the Kaiser Study as television viewing among children was reported at an 8-year high. Perhaps now is as good a time as any to consider the feasibility of a scholar-engagement model to catalyze fresh thinking about E/I content, how to communicate groundbreaking research with the creative community, and to stream new ideas based on research into the conversation about the E/I content conundrum. With an annual meeting and periodic publications of succinctly presented findings relevant to production and content, the distance between academe and the research community could possibly be bridged.

A Few vs. Many New Channels

One issue that is getting very little discussion but that must be a background concern to the financing issue is how many channels can be absorbed by television audiences. When the CTA was conceived, there was certainly no expectation that families would have hundreds of channels to easily choose from to provide for their entertainment and information needs. And in the present circumstance, one has to question "how many is enough" before the human brain ceases to successfully differentiate among all the choices.

One strategy for dealing with children's content needs, and with the E/I programming in particular, emerged during the early 1980s when the CTA was first under discussion. Again, 25 years ago, one must be reminded that the networks had the ability to reach the most people and PBS stations were often on a frequency that was hard to receive even in major markets. Equity of access to entertainment, education, and information was a big concern underlying the discussion. At the time, the broadcasters were attempting to float an idea that could not get any traction. The proposal was that the networks and

affiliate stations would meet their public-interest obligation by contributing resources to a superfund that would support programming on a children's E/I channel perhaps operated by PBS or through a public–private entity. This proposal, fully fleshed out, might still be controversial, and in a tight economic market, the original proposers may be reluctant to float the idea again. But the kernel of truth behind it is that adequate resources focused on high-quality educational content for children would be a lot better than diffuse resources being spent to recycle benign entertainment that may not be up to par for the E/I standard.

Conclusion

Whatever pathway emerges out of the conundrum of 2010—where rapid change in technology, the media industries, and consumer behavior has created a new media reality for children and adults—the underlying intent of the CTA should be preserved. What Congress had in mind when the Telecommunications Act of 1996 was passed was for broadcasters to fulfill their commitment to serve the public interest through creative, inspiring and educational television (Kunkel, 2003). After all, a high-quality E/I show is typically designed with an overarching goal in mind—that is, to engage the audience's attention, draw them into continuous observation of the content, and transition them into active reflection about the meaning of what they saw and its relevance to their lives. A tall order, to be sure, and one not easily translated into operational steps for content development. But it is completely analogous to the very best structure of entertaining storytelling. The two goals of education and entertainment need not be so far apart in the expression of ideas for children's media content.

References

Alexander, A., & Owers, J. (2007). The economic infrastructure of children's television. In J. A. Bryant (Ed.), *The children's television community* (pp. 57–74). Mahwah, NJ: Routledge.

Alfano, S. (2006, January 3). CBS, Viacom formally split. *CBS News*. Retrieved May 9, 2010, from http://www.cbsnews.com/stories/2006/01/03/business/main1176111.shtml.

Anderson, D. R. (2003). The Children's Television Act: A public policy that benefits children. *Journal of Applied Developmental Psychology, 24*(3), 337–340.

Anderson, D. R., Bryant, J., Wilder, A. Santomero, A., Williams, M., & Crawley, A. M. (2000). Researching *Blue's Clues*: Viewing behavior and impact. *Media Psychology, 2,* 179–194.

Arango, T. (2009, December 7). G.E. makes it official: NBC will go to Comcast. *New York Times*. Retrieved May 10, 2011, from http://www.nytimes.com/2009/12/04/business/media/04nbc.html?scp=1&sq=december%204,%202009&st=Search.

Bell, R. (2008, June 20). Cookie Jar, DIC Merge. *Animation Magazine*. Retrieved May 11, 2011, from http://www.animationmagazine.net/tv/cookie-jar-dic-merge/.

Blumenthal, H. J., & Goodenough, O. R. (2006). *This business of television: The standard guide to the television industry*. New York: Billboard Books.

Britt, R., & Wilkerson, D. B. (2001, July 23). Disney to buy Fox Family Worldwide. *Wall Street Journal, MarketWatch*. Retrieved May 11, 2011, from http://www.marketwatch.com/story/disney-snares-fox-family-for-53-bln.

Cahn, A., Kalagian, T., & Lyon, C. (2008). Business models for children's media. In S. L. Calvert & B. J. Wilson (Eds.), *The handbook of children, media, and development* (pp. 27–48). West Sussex, UK: Blackwell.

Calvert, S. L. (2008). The Children's Television Act. In S. L. Calvert & B. J. Wilson (Eds.), *The handbook of children, media, and development* (pp. 455–478). West Sussex, UK: Blackwell.

Calvert, S. L., & Kotler, J. A. (2003a). Lessons from children's television: The impact of the Children's Television Act on children's learning. *Journal of Applied Developmental Psychology, 24,* 275–335. doi: 10.1016/S0193-3973(03)00060-1.

Calvert, S. L., & Kotler, J. A. (2003b). The Children's Television Act: Can media policy make a difference? *Journal of Applied Developmental Psychology, 24*(3), 375–380.

Crawley, A. M., Anderson, D. R., Santomero, A., Wilder, A., Williams, M., Evans, M. K., & Bryant, J. (2002). Do children learn how to watch television? The impact of extensive experience with *Blue's Clues* on preschool children's television viewing behavior. *Journal of Communication, 52,* 264–280.

Desmond, R. J. , Singer, J. L., & Singer, D. G. (1985). Family mediation patterns and television viewing. *Journal of Human Communication Research, 11*(4), 461–480.

Federal Communications Commission. (1990, October 18). *Children's Television Act of 1990* (Pub. L. No. 101–437). Washington, DC: U.S. Government Printing Office.

Federal Communications Commission. (1996, August 8). *Children's television rules* (Vol. 73.671). Washington, DC: U.S. Government Printing Office.

Federal Communications Commission. (2004). *Report and order and further notice of proposed rule making: In the matter of Children's Television Obligations of Digital Television Broadcasters* (MM Docket No: 00–167). Retrieved May 11, 2011, from http://hraunfoss.fcc.gov/edocs_public/attachmatch/FCC-04-221A1.pdf.

Federal Communications Commission. (2006). Joint proposal of industry and advocates on reconsideration of children's television rules. (MM Docket No. 00-167). Retrieved May 11, 2011, from http://hraunfoss.fcc.gov/edocs_public/attachmatch/FCC-06-33A2.pdf.

Federal Communications Commission (2006). Second Order on Reconsideration and Second Report and Order: In the Matter of Children's Television Obligations Of Digital Television Broadcasters (MM Docket No: 00-167). Retrieved May 11, 2011 from http://hraunfoss.fcc.gov/edocs_public/attachmatch/FCC-06-143A1.pdf.

Federal Communications Commission. (2010). Notices of apparent liability for forfeiture 2010. Retrieved May 11, 2011, from http://www.fcc.gov/Document_Indexes/Media/2010_index_MB_NALF.html.

Fisch, S., & Truglio, R. (Eds.). (2001). *G is for growing: Thirty years of research on children and* Sesame Street. Mahwah, NJ: Lawrence Erlbaum.

Goldman, M. C., & Johnson, T. (1999, September 7). Viacom tunes into CBS. *CNN*. Retrieved May 11, 2011, from http://money.cnn.com/1999/09/07/deals/cbs/.

Hill-Scott, K. (2001). Industry standards and practices: Compliance with the Children's Television Act. In D. G. Singer & J. L. Singer (Eds.), *Handbook of children and the media* (pp. 605–620). Thousand Oaks, CA: Sage.

Ionpress.com. (2005). Ion pressroom: Brandon Burgess executive bio. Retrieved May 10, 2010, from http://www.ionpress.com/execbios.php.

Jordan, A. (1996). *The state of children's television: An examination of quantity, quality and industry beliefs*. (Rep. No. 2). Philadelphia: Annenberg Public Policy Center of the University of Pennsylvania.

Jordan, A. (1998). *The 1998 state of children's television report: Programming for children over broadcast and cable television.* Report No. 23. Philadelphia, PA: University of Pennsylvania, Annenberg Public Policy Center.

Jordan, A. (2000). *Is the Three-Hour Rule living up to its potential? An analysis of educational television for children in the 1999/2000 broadcast season.* (Report No. 34). Philadelphia: Annenberg Public Policy Center of the University of Pennsylvania.

Jordan, A. B. (1999). *The Three-Hour Rule: Insiders' perspectives.* Report No. 29. Philadelphia, PA: University of Pennsylvania, Annenberg Public Policy Center.

Jordan, A., & Woodard, E. (1997). *The 1997 state of children's television report: Programming for children over broadcast and cable television.* Report No. 14. Philadelphia: University of Pennsylvania, Annenberg Public Policy Center.

Kunkel, D. (2003). The truest metric for evaluating the Children's Television Act. *Journal of Applied Developmental Psychology, 24*(3), 347–353.

Labaton, S. (2007. February 24). A record fine expected for Univision. *New York Times.* Retrieved May 9, 2011, from http://www.nytimes.com/2007/02/24/business/24fcc.html.

Lesser, G. (1974). *Children and television: Lessons from* Sesame Street. New York: Vintage Books/Random House.

McDonough, P. (2009, October 26). TV viewing among kids at an eight-year high. *Nielsenwire.* Retrieved May 10, 2011, from http://blog.nielsen.com/nielsenwire/media_entertainment/tv-viewing-among-kids-at-an-eight-year-high/.

McAllister, M. (2004). The financial interest and syndication rules: U.S. Broadcasting Regulations. In the *Encyclopedia of television,* Section F. Retrieved May 11, 2011, from http://www.museum.tv/eotvsection.php?entrycode=financialint.

PR Newswire. (2009, December 22). Nickelodeon is 2009's top-ranked cable network. Retrieved July 4, 2010, from http://www.prnewswire.com/news-releases/nickelodeon-is-2009s-top-ranked-cable-network-79920022.html.

redOrbit. (2006, May 8). ION Media Networks, Scholastic, NBC Universal, Corus Entertainment, and Classic Media/Big Idea unite to launch groundbreaking multi-platform network for children. Retrieved May 11, 2011, from http://www.redorbit.com/news/technology/495875/ion_media_networks_scholastic_nbc_universal_corus_entertainment_and_classic/.

Rideout, V. J., Foehr, U. G., & Roberts, D. F. (2010). *Generation M²: Media in the lives of 8- to 18-year olds.* Retrieved May 10, 2011, from http://www.kff.org/entmedia/mh012010pkg.cfm.

Singer, J. L., & Singer. D. G. (1981). *Television, imagination, and aggression: A study of preschoolers.* Hillsdale, NJ: Lawrence Erlbaum.

Singer, D. G. & Singer, J. L. (1998). Developing critical viewing skills and media literacy in children. *Annals of the American Academy of Political and Social Science, 557*(1), 164–179.

Singer, D. G., & Singer, J. L. (Eds.). (2001). *Handbook of children and the media.* Thousand Oaks, CA: Sage.

Wilcox, B. L. (2003). The research/policy nexus: The Children's Television Act as a case in point. *Journal of Applied Developmental Psychology, 24*(3), 367–373.

Wilson, B. J., Kunkel, D., & Drogos, K. L. (2008). Educationally/insufficient? An analysis of the availability & educational quality of children's E/I programming. *Children Now.* Retrieved May 11, 2011, from http://www.childrennow.org/index.php/learn/reports_and_research/article_search/eireport_2008/.

Woodard, E. (1999). *The 1999 state of children's television report: Programming for children over broadcast and cable television.* Report No. 28. Philadelphia, PA: University of Pennsylvania, Annenberg Public Policy Center.

CHAPTER 30

Child and Parent Responses to the Age-Based and Content-Based Television Ratings

BRADLEY S. GREENBERG
Michigan State University

LYNN RAMPOLDI-HNILO
Oracle

In 2010—13 years after age-based and content-based ratings first appeared on America's TV screens—they remain unchanged. Yes, they're still there, typically in the upper corner of your screen at the beginning of each show and every half hour. But a large plurality of viewers doesn't understand them and/or doesn't pay attention to them. Research conducted since the first edition of this volume has been added to this chapter.

Providing warning labels and content advisories to mass media products has long been a conundrum among congressional policy makers, parents, media industry leaders, and child activists. Although it may have begun long ago with book banning by church officials, it became explicit in the 20th century with the labeling of motion pictures. A half-century after television sets became commonplace in American homes, the debate over providing viewers with advance information about some kinds of content in television shows has been actualized. In 1993, four broadcast networks—ABC, NBC, CBS, and Fox—presented the following warning in front of those shows of their choice: Due to some violent content, parental discretion advised (Mandese, 1993). Although this warning conveyed some information to assist in judging the appropriateness of program content, it was more a precaution than a description of the content. Parent and child groups and political leaders marshaled their dissatisfaction. After a series of congressional hearings, the 1996 Telecommunication Act included a mandate to the television industry. It had until January 1997 to create and implement its own rating system or the Federal Communications Commission (FCC) would create its own version.

Earlier, Cantor, Stutman, and Duran (1997) conducted a survey with a nationwide random sample of PTA members in the United States. Cantor and colleagues (1997) investigated what format would be most useful to parents—one that was more content based or one that was more of a summary rating like those coming from the Motion Picture of America Association. They found that parents overwhelmingly (4 to 1) preferred ratings that were more content specific (tell them what is in a program), as compared to a single summary rating involving age-based guidance like that of the movies. Parents wanted to make decisions based on knowledge, not be given advice on what they should do. One respondent from California wrote, "I don't want to be told if it's appropriate for my child. I want to know what's in it so I can judge myself" (Cantor et al., 1997). The majority of parents in that study were in favor of having a TV ratings system, with 89% indicating that a rating system was either very important (62%) or moderately important (27%). Importance did not vary as a function of the child's age or gender.

Ignoring the ratings format preference identified in this national survey, and to comply with the congressional mandate, the U.S. television industry agreed to visually display information at the start of each show to inform viewers about the show's appropriateness for different age groups. Appropriateness was to be based on the show's inclusion of violent content, sexual content, and/or strong language. A two-tier rating system was developed. The first tier created a dichotomy of children's shows for children under 7 (TV-Y) and those 7 and older (TV-Y7), without any clear rationale why that age division was the chosen one. The second tier relied on the Motion Picture Association of America (MPAA) movie ratings (Stern, 1996). It focused on programming for the entire family. The labels specified that a TV show was intended for all audiences (TV-G), that parental guidance was advised (TV-PG), that the young viewer should be at least 14 (TV-14), or that the show was intended for a distinctly more mature audience (TV-MA).

This rating and labeling system came under rapid and intense criticism for lacking content-specific information (Hepburn, 1997).

New negotiations between public activist groups and the new ratings oversight committee, which then consisted entirely of industry representatives, resulted in an extension of show labeling information. Content information about each show began to be added in October 1997. One label was added to the children's tier of programs to indicate fantasy violence (FV) among TV-Y7 shows, and five labels were made available for the adult tier—for violence (V), profane language (L), sexual behavior (S), adult dialogue (D), and fantasy violence (FV). This industry-modified version of the program ratings was accompanied by an agreement from the government to permit the system to be tested without further modification for some indefinite time. Two networks of interest chose not to comply. NBC provides age-based ratings but not content ratings, and Black Entertainment Television (BET) provides neither. In contrast, the Public Broadcasting System opted not to adopt the original rating system but joined in using the combined age-content option. This particular ratings scheme has not changed from its inception in 1997 through 2010, giving some parameters to the government's offer of an "indefinite" time frame for testing.

Implementation of this rating system provided a rare and rich opportunity to examine the responses of parents and children. Most of the research was conducted while the system was still relatively new. Survey studies done early can provide a baseline for follow-up studies after the system has been in place for some period of time. Experimental studies add a component to the system as it has been implemented, with a "what if this had been done?" emphasis. This chapter brings together both those bodies of research, focusing as directly as possible on the users for whom the system was designed to provide an informational function. Unfortunately, little follow-up research has occurred in the past decade.

In addition to the intended users of the ratings information, the research also can inform those involved with the advocacy, creation, and policing of the ratings. Much of the research tends to examine similar outcome variables, as laid out in the original proposal funded by the National Association of Broadcasters: Who is aware of and pays attention to the ratings? Who understands and is knowledgeable about the ratings? What general and specific use is made of the ratings? What misuse is made of the ratings? What attitudes exist toward them? Answers to these kinds of questions should contribute to the evolution of the system. This chapter provides an overview of the findings associated with these kinds of questions from multiple studies.

Parental Mediation and Responses to the Ratings System

This review begins with parents. Although it is anticipated that older children may make more independent decisions about their television choices, a primary reason for the implementation of the ratings system was to provide additional information about television programs to parents, especially parents of younger children. Here, we review a portion of the literature on parental mediation of children's television behavior prior to and after the implementation of the ratings system.

As children age, parental monitoring and mediating of children's television behavior generally declines (i.e., parents mediate television more with younger children). This finding is robust and begins with parents more likely to restrict the television viewing of 3-year-olds than 5-year-olds (St. Peters, Fitch, Huston, Wright, & Eakins, 1991). Next, parents of elementary school-age children used more positive guidance (recommendations and use of media as reward) and negative guidance (recommending against specific shows and withholding media as punishment) than parents of middle school students (Mohr, 1979). In a survey of 7th and 10th graders, Lin and Atkin (1989) found that television-viewing mediation was negatively related to the child's age, and these findings were replicated in a later study with 5th and 10th graders and their parents (Atkin, Greenberg, & Baldwin, 1991).

Similar concerns about parental mediation exist for such television-related technologies as cable, pay movie channels, and video choices. Concurrent with these TV enhancements, there has been a continuing concern

with how these technologies may have influenced parental mediation. Atkin, Heeter, and Baldwin (1989) investigated the degree to which parental mediation of child TV viewing (including restrictions and discussion regarding content) varied across pay, basic, and noncable households. Although they found that children with cable were exposed to more PG and R movies than those in noncable homes, in general, there were low levels of mediation and no significant differences among the three groups. Similarly, Atkin and colleagues (1991) found that having or not having cable played only a small role in predicting television viewing and parental mediation in their sample of 5th and 10th graders. That study also included an assessment of the impact of the videocassette recorder (VCR) at the time when the VCR was considered to be the new electronic babysitter. VCR ownership was unrelated to restrictive parental mediation but was related positively to viewing R-rated movies. In a prior study, Lin and Atkin (1989) found that there was a significant correlation between parental mediation and rule making for those children if there was a home VCR and that mediation decreased as the child grew older. Overall, the extent of parental mediation with these technologies has been low.

Although several researchers have investigated parental mediation of television (Abelman & Petty, 1989; Austin, 1993; Desmond, Singer, Singer, Calam, & Colimore, 1985) and the influences of related technologies (Atkin et al., 1989; Lindlof & Shatzer, 1990), few studies have focused on parental mediation with advisories and/or ratings. Krcmar and Cantor (1997) found that parents made negative comments about programs that contained advisories or PG-13 ratings and discouraged their children from viewing these programs. Most ratings or advisory research has focused on the influence of labels in persuading or dissuading viewers' choices directly and not as mediated by others (Bushman, 1997; Cantor & Harrison, 1996b). The ratings were created to aid parents in deciding what is appropriate for their children to watch. Now with the full-scale implementation of the ratings system, we wish to know if the information it provides is being used to inform parents' decisions about their children's viewing.

To be a useful information source for parents and others in the viewing audience, a system should provide consistent and accurate content criteria. Studies have shown, however, that program content and TV ratings are far from precise and too often do not match each other. Research by Kunkel and colleagues (2002) demonstrated further that 60% of children's shows contained violence and averaged 5.6 violent scenes per episode. The presence, level, and intensity of violence were all higher in the TV-Y7 shows, as compared to TV-Y. This symmetry in the children's ratings was reflected in the age-based adult ratings; that is, as the rating designated an older viewer, there was more violence, more sex, and so forth.

The key findings, however, from this elaborate research effort showed strong and consistent discrepancies between the presence of content descriptors and the content of the shows. The researchers concluded that *most* programs that contain violence, sex, adult language, and sexual dialog do not have content descriptors. They " . . . conclude that the industry's performance at applying content ratings is disappointing. Parents who might rely solely on the content-based categories to block their children's exposure to objectionable portrayals would be making a serious miscalculation . . ." (Kunkel et al., 2002, p. 136).

Content analyses also indicate inconsistent application of the ratings. Greenberg, Eastin, and Mastro (2000b) found that one of every four programs that should have had a rating identified in *TV Guide* did not have one during a 2-month sampling among eight major broadcast and cable networks. Whether no rating existed or the rating information came too late for the publication deadline is irrelevant; it was not there in advance of airtime. Moreover, 75% of the shows that did receive an age-based rating had no content descriptors. Should parents assume that the dialogue and the images in all those programs warranted no content warnings? The two most prominent content labels were the symbol D, indicating adult dialogue (38% of all content labels), and V for violence (33%); the S for sexual content was used least. Cantor and colleagues (1997) had identified sexual content

as one of the primary concerns for parents, regardless of their child's age or gender.

With respect to the age-based ratings, TV-PG was the most common rating (40%), followed by TV-G (28%), TV-14 (16%), TV-Y7 (9%), and TV-Y (7%). TV-MA was absent. There also were significant differences in the distribution of ratings between the broadcast and cable networks studied. Broadcast networks were more adult oriented (28% of their shows were TV-14), and cable networks oriented to more family programming (38% were TV-G).

Pursuing the accuracy question, Greenberg, Eastin, and Mastro (2000a) directly compared the ratings that appeared on the shows and the ratings as they had been published in *TV Guide*. In this study, one third of all shows that should have had ratings printed did not. Only half the shows listed in *TV Guide* matched their on-air rating. For those that did not, viewers who read *TV Guide* (or other published outlets with a similar advance deadline) were likely to think that a program had a lower age rating or less problematic content than was actually shown. The published information indicated more general family-oriented programming than was actually available; 90% of the shows rated differently had a more stringent rating on-air than had been published. In a strange twist, shows intended for older audiences had more ratings information matched for age and content than did shows targeted for the youngest age groups.

Kaye and Sapolsky (2001, 2004) examined discrepancies in offensive language. First, they compared the presence of offensive language in prime-time television between 1994 and 1997 (before and after the introduction of the ratings). The rate per hour across all language categories, for example, sexual, excretory, dropped from 7.3 to 4.7 per hour. Four years later, they replicated their study. The drop reported in 1997 was replaced by a surge in offensive words that brought it back fully to the prelabeling level (7.6 per hour). All foul language categories increased. Programs marked with an L contained significantly more offensive language than programs not so marked (7.6 vs. 4.3 per hour)—meaning that unlabeled shows contained ample amounts. The Fox network was the runaway winner, generating 11.6 per hour.

One more indicator of the difference between what is and is not rated comes from Linder and Gentile (2009). They looked at the favorite shows of 10- and 11-year-old girls. They determined that shows with a TV-Y7 rating had significantly more physical aggression than any other age-based rating, that 67% of shows without a V or FV content rating contained at least one act of physical aggression, and that there was an average of 4.1 aggressive acts in shows without a content label.

Given these findings, likely unknown to the potential users of the ratings system, what then have parents been doing with this information? Here we examine parents' awareness, use, knowledge, concerns, and recommendations about the ratings system. *Are the ratings helpful to parents in mediating television with their children?*

To begin, a set of 9 focus groups (4–12 parents in each) and 20 whole-family interviews were conducted with Latino and Caucasian parents during late 1997 and early 1998 (Gregg, 2000; Mastro, 2000). All parents and families interviewed had a child between the ages of 6 and 10. Parents were asked to describe their awareness and use of the ratings system and give their opinions about it. They also answered questions about their parenting style, their children's knowledge of the ratings, how they dealt with their offspring regarding television, and their general concerns with television.

A primary concern among all parents was with what the ratings actually mean. Parents, especially Latina mothers, were troubled by the criteria used to rate the programs, the differences between ratings, and the accessibility of the ratings. One Latina parent responded to a question about trusting the ratings with, "I would still have to watch the program, maybe my idea of TV-Y7 is different from their [TV raters'] idea of TV-Y7. Maybe I would be stricter or maybe I would be more lenient." Parents varied greatly when asked what was and was not acceptable television content for their offspring. One Caucasian parent stated, "They're not allowed to watch *The Simpsons,* because Bart is rude to his parents. Most of the shows play the parents as dumb and the kids as smart and funny." Instead of relying on the ratings system, most of

these parents indicated much more active parental mediation—coviewing with their children, explaining programs, and actively permitting or forbidding individual shows. In general, these parents supported the television ratings system and what it was attempting to do but were confused about the system and considered it ineffective for themselves. Collectively, these parents suggested that the system would be more useful if the ratings (a) were displayed throughout the show, (b) were on the screen longer, (c) were verbally presented, (d) were larger in size, and (e) were displayed after each commercial break.

To provide more substantial evidence about issues raised in the focus groups and interviews, a sample of Latina and Caucasian mothers in Michigan with a child between the ages of 6 and 10 was interviewed (Greenberg, Rampoldi-Hnilo, & Mastro, 2000; Rampoldi-Hnilo & Greenberg, 2000) about 18 months after the ratings system had started. Approximately 30% of these mothers were not aware of the ratings at all. They were somewhat older and distinctly lower in average family income, and only 30% of them had more than one child. Of those aware of the ratings, they rated the clarity of the ratings below the midpoint of the scale used. These mothers considered the ratings more accurate than inaccurate, but few were strongly convinced about the accuracy. Latina mothers were most likely to let their children watch shows with these ratings: TV-G (75%), TV-PG (67%), TV-Y7 (58%), and TV-Y (42%). Caucasian mothers said they would let their children watch TV-G (78%), followed by TV-Y (69%), TV-Y7 (64%), and TV-PG (47%). Not many would allow their children to watch programs rated TV-14 or TV-MA. Thus, the shows designated especially for young viewers (TV-Y and TV-Y7) were not judged as acceptable as TV-G shows, indicating a clear lack of understanding of those ratings.

These mothers could identify that the "V" rating indicated violence, but the other content labels fared less well among the mothers who were aware of the ratings system. One-third did not understand the "L," 45% did not know that sexual content would be labeled, 58% believed the ratings would indicate if the show was scary, and 74% thought nudity would be identified.

Few mothers used the ratings to choose shows for themselves, only half used them to choose shows for their children, and one mother in six said she did so "every so often." Instead, their mediation consisted of (a) having bedtime rules on school nights; (b) using the VCR for alternative programming; (c) changing the channel when inappropriate content appeared; (d) discussing TV content to help their children understand; (e) coviewing with their children, especially at night; and (f) vetoing unacceptable shows.

The Kaiser Family Foundation conducted a nationwide survey in 1998 with 1,358 parents of a child between 2 and 17 years of age to determine attitudes, claimed use, perceived benefits, and their knowledge of the ratings system (Foehr, Rideout, & Miller, 2000b). Parents reported being concerned "a great deal" with the amount of sexual content (67%), violence (62%), and adult language (59%) on television. In this sample, nearly one fifth (18%) of parents were unaware of the TV ratings system. In the aware group, although 9 out of 10 thought that the ratings were a good idea, only half stated that they use the system "often" or "sometimes" in guiding their children's viewing. African-American (72%) and Latino parents (73%) were less likely to be aware of the system than Caucasian parents (85%), as were older parents, those with less education, and single parents. There were few ethnic differences in use and understanding of the system.

Most parents claimed to have a good working knowledge of the icons and labels used, but an independent assessment of actual knowledge did not support those claims. With the knowledge questions used in the Kaiser survey, 14% were "very well informed" and 40% were "fairly well informed." Parents did somewhat better in understanding the age-based ratings than they did the content descriptors, and those who actually understood the ratings preferred the content descriptors. Large proportions of the parents, however, did not know what the ratings meant. Parents with children under 10 were

not much better informed about TV-Y and TV-Y7 symbols than were parents of older children. Parents who claimed direct exposure to information about the TV ratings system—4 in 10 of the aware parents—had a better understanding of the system. With respect to the V-chip technology itself, few parents said they would actively pursue buying a TV set equipped with the chip but will wait until their current set malfunctions. Primary advocated changes in the ratings system were for more detail and information on the shows' content, more frequent display of the symbols, and a better explanation of what the ratings mean.

One year after its first survey, the Kaiser Family Foundation repeated it (Kaiser Family Foundation, 1999). Their findings illuminate the fate of the ratings system with a parallel group of parents after another year of experience. The bottom line is that very little change occurred in that 12 months, and those changes that did occur can be characterized as lack of support for the ratings system. One fifth were still unaware that there was such a system, one-half had "ever" used it, but 9% less than before were "often" using it. Five percent less (43%) knew that the system provided both age and content information, 5% less (only 36%) knew that children's shows "like *Sesame Street* and Saturday-morning cartoons" were rated, 5% less knew that prime-time dramas such as *ER* were rated, and 8% less knew that situation comedies such as *Frasier* were rated. Only one fourth knew that the ratings originated with the television industry itself.

As for knowledge of the ratings, only 10% of parents with children under 10 (down from 17%) could correctly recall any one of the specific ratings used in children's shows. Then, when asked what a TV-Y or TV-Y7 rating meant, one-third of these parents responded correctly in both the 1998 and 1999 studies. They did much better in correctly identifying the adult television program age ratings, except for TV-MA. But understanding of the content symbols was abysmal in both studies. Two percent were correct as to what D means, 3% for FV, 34% for S (down from 44% a year earlier), 40% for L, and 54% for V. Yet two of every three parents said it was the content-based ratings alone that provided the most useful information! If anything, the second survey provided evidence for a drop in use and understanding.

Abelman (2000) focused on profiling parents who were most likely and least likely to use the age-based ratings and to adopt the system in their decision-making and home regulation of television. Findings suggest that parents who need mediation assistance the least are the ones most likely to use the ratings information in discussing TV with their children. These parents were classified as high mediators. Their primary mediation methods are working together to create and enforce rules about television, interacting frequently with their children, and using reasoning, explanation, and appeals to the child's pride and achievements as disciplinary techniques, while avoiding coercive strategies. Their children were low to moderate consumers of television, high academic achievers, and primarily female. These parents, who are characterized by strong communication practices and low external force with their children, are unlikely to use the V-chip to block TV programs because that restrictive technique would be uncharacteristic of their mediation approach.

Parents and children in greatest need of the ratings information were least likely to use the ratings, Abelman concludes. These parents create rules without consulting each other and do not offer explicit supervision or direct discipline in child rearing, particularly in monitoring television. They do not believe that television has strong impacts on their children. Their children, mostly boys, were heavy television viewers. Because this parental mediation style is relatively unfocused, in that there is not much parent–child discussion or punishment, Abelman predicts that these parents will not use the rating system.

The third profile of families was those who engaged in restrictive forms of television mediation. These parents restrict their children's consumption of objectionable content, and it was expected that they would be heavy users of the ratings, but they were not. They were found to be moderate mediators who limit the number of viewing hours and

ban specific programs. These parents will likely use the ratings as a way to justify their restrictive mediation style.

In sum, this array of studies of parents indicates that parents are perplexed. Violent and sexual content and coarse language are significant concerns. In general, their attitude toward the ratings is supportive, indeed quite positive, but behaviors that would correspond with this attitude are largely absent. Use is quite marginal. Claims of understanding exceed actual understanding. How does one use a system that is not well understood? There also is the issue of accuracy. Many parents remain unsure of the television raters' judgments of a program's content and what age range is appropriate to view it, as compared with their own ideas of what they think their children can handle. Most are relying on their established modes of oversight, with a significant minority adding the ratings to their mediation repertoire. But those doing so may be least in need of doing so. Add the 20% of parents who admit they are still totally unaware of the ratings and the magnitude of the problem of an uninformed or disinterested public is better framed. What could have been attributed to the newness of this innovation and the need for greater familiarization seems unlikely based on the lack of or even regression of response differences between the two Kaiser Family Foundation surveys of parents.

In 2004, the Kaiser Family Foundation (2004) sponsored a nationally representative survey of 1,001 parents with children from 2 to 17. Thirty-four percent of parents were most concerned about inappropriate content on TV, with 60% "very" concerned about the amount of sex and 53% "very" concerned regarding the amount of violence (53%) their children are exposed to on TV. Half (50%) of all parents have used the TV ratings to help guide their children's viewing, with approximately 25% who have said they use them "often" (2004), proportions that did not vary substantially from the earlier Kaiser studies. Of the parents who use the TV ratings, 38% have found them "very" useful and 50% said they were somewhat useful. While more than half (52%) say that most TV shows are rated accurately, 39% disagree and say most are not. This study found that many parents do not understand what the various ratings mean. For example, TV-Y7 was correctly interpreted by 28% of parents, but the opposite and incorrect meaning was cited by 13% of the parents—7 years after the ratings were introduced.

A parallel sample in 2007 yielded similar results (Kaiser Family Foundation, 2007). Half the parents said they've used the ratings, and one in four have "often" used them to help make program choices for their children. But the report concludes, "Most parents don't understand the TV ratings system. . . . Even among those who say they've heard of the ratings, most don't understand what they mean" (p. 8). Thirty percent of parents with children 2 to 6 could name any of the ratings used for children's shows. For the label FV, 11% knew it had something to do with violence, while 9% thought it meant Family Viewing! Half knew that V is for violence, 26% knew that S goes with sexual content, and just 2% knew that D indicates suggestive dialogue.

Youth Responses to the Ratings System

Young children and adolescents are active viewers. Many make the majority of their own viewing choices, although it is likely that some restrictions exist in terms of either total viewing time or content options. Here, we address the studies that consider how aware and attentive young viewers are to the ratings, what they understand about the ratings, and if and how they use the ratings to select or reject TV shows.

The first major study was conducted in the spring of 1997, when only the original age-based ratings were available and had been available for less than 6 months (Greenberg, Rampoldi-Hnilo, & Hofschire, 2000). Across 4th, 8th, and 10th graders in a mid-Michigan urban center, the key results showed that attention to the ratings was low and attitudes about the system were marginally positive. These young people seldom used the ratings, their level of understanding of the ratings

labels and the kinds of television programs rated was close to chance, and perceived misuse (using the ratings to choose shows they were not supposed to watch) was believed to be low. Along the age dimension, older students had more knowledge, but the younger claimed to pay more attention (although the average attention score was near the scale's midpoint), made more general use (60% more than the older groups), and perceived more misuse. Gender was not a predictor of any of their responses to the ratings system. There was equal attention, similar attitudes, and equivalent knowledge, understanding, and use between boys and girls in all the age groups. Among other predictor variables examined in the study, it was found that greater parental mediation (as identified by the youngsters), larger family sizes, and the presence of sibling influence were all contributors to increased attention, more positive attitudes, and more use, but they were not related to knowledge or understanding.

Would the addition of content labels and another year make a difference? A subsequent study a year later answered that question. Findings were quite consistent between the two studies (Greenberg & Rampoldi-Hnilo, 2000). Students continued to report little attention, a middle-of-the-road attitude, and not much use or predicted misuse. Knowledge of what gets rated or what the age-based ratings mean did not improve. Knowledge of the content ratings was low for fantasy violence (FV) and adult dialogue (D) and highest for sexual content (i.e., they knew or could better guess that S indicated sex, and at a far higher level than did parents in the studies reported earlier). Here, we will compare the two studies on some of the key outcome variables: knowledge, use, and misuse.

Knowledge

Twelve items asked what content was identified in the ratings and which shows contained ratings. In the first study, the youth answered 6.2 correctly and in the second year answered 6.9 correctly. This difference is significant ($p < .001$), but the magnitude of the change is less than one additional item correctly answered a year later. Here we identify what they knew and did not know:

	Percentage Correct	
Content Area	*Year 1*	*Year 2*
Do the ratings tell if there is:		
Sex	52	60
Scary content	—	33
Violence	70	78
Bad language	70	73
Are there ratings for:		
TV shows at night	50	52
Soaps	24	29
Commercials	76	78
Game shows	12	16
Cartoons	47	57
Talk shows	43	66
News	59	66
TV movies	78	85

Greater recognition that there are ratings on talk shows and on cartoons but not the news accounts for most of the change, along with moderate increases in understanding that sex and violence are described in the ratings. Because the entire set of content symbols had been in place for several months at the time of this study, the lack of larger shifts in understanding that sex, language, and violence are flagged in the ratings should be noted.

The youth also were asked to correctly match the meaning of five of the six ratings. To minimize the effect of sheer guessing, we omitted the G rating, which was nearly identical to its movie ratings meaning. The samples averaged 3.4 in the first study and 3.5 in the second, or no difference. Here is how they fared:

% Correctly Matched	*Year 1*	*Year 2*
TV-Y	52	58
TV-Y7	77	75
TV-PG	64	55
TV-14	80	82
TV-MA	71	69

They did best with symbols that contained a specific age designation (7 or 14).

Respondents in the second study were asked to match four of the five possible symbols (V, S, D, L, and FV) with appropriate definitions, omitting V.

"Which rating means the show contains sexual content?" 73% chose S.

"Which rating means the show contains bad language or swearing?" 56% chose L.

"Which rating means the TV show has cartoons with violence in them?" 25% chose FV.

"Which rating means the TV show has adults talking about topics that should not be heard by children?" 25% chose D.

Alternative questions might have led to more correct responses, but to the extent these questions are objective, the symbols were not understood very well, except for sex.

Interpreting the Ratings

Respondents also were asked to interpret a sample set of on-air labels. For this, the format was very similar to what would appear on screen. For example, a small box framed a TV-14 symbol with labels V and D beneath it. The respondents were asked four questions about each of three boxed sets of symbols. For the TV-14, V, D label, they were asked whether the show had violence (93% correct), sex (67% correct), and swearing or bad language in it (36% correct), as well as whether the show was meant to be watched by children under 14 (85% correct). Generally, the youth answered questions better in this form than in the others. This suggests that young viewers may actually do better when asked to decipher the individual symbols in a comprehensive context.

General Use of the Ratings

This scale assessed the sample's orientation to use the ratings in choosing shows to watch or not watch. In the first sample, the average (with a scale midpoint of 12.5) was 8.8, and in the second sample, it was 9.7. Although a significant increase ($p < .001$), it continues to reflect an average response between "not at all" and "not much." Nevertheless, self-reported general use of the ratings for program selection increases.

Specific Use of the Ratings

Respondents reported how often they watched shows with the six different age-based ratings. The rate was no different between the two years, and the average scores of 14.4 and 14.6 were at the scale's midpoint of 15. Here are their responses:

Percentage Who Said Often or Very Often	Year 1	Year 2
TV-Y	31	37
TV-Y7	29	38
TV-G	36	38
TV-PG	54	54
TV-14	46	49
TV-MA	35	32

These findings are problematic. For example, in each year, about one third of the youth said that they "often" or "very often" watch TV shows with MA ratings, just about the same proportion who watch Y-, Y7-, and G-rated shows. However, an entire season of broadcast and cable television contains very few shows with an MA rating. When they respond about their frequency of viewing, they may be indicating what they would watch or what they have watched, or they may be confused by the ratings. From this study, it is not possible to sort through these alternative explanations, but it should serve as a caution in making any literal interpretation of what they (or their parents) report, in a context of incomplete or inadequate understanding of the ratings system.

Misuse of the Ratings

In both studies, the average response was essentially that the ratings were not being used for inappropriate purposes. The modal response was "never" for such purposes by "others" in elementary, middle, or high school.

Fourth graders claimed more use and anticipated more misuse, reported more attention, and offered more positive opinions. As for knowledge about the ratings, the grade groups did not differ in their knowledge of what gets rated, but the oldest group consistently scored highest on the other three measures of knowledge identifying the age ratings, identifying the content ratings, and interpreting the replicas of the on-air icons. The eighth graders were not far behind, and the fourth graders were the least knowledgeable. In the follow-up study, males were more knowledgeable about what was rated and could better identify the age-based ratings. The key predictors for the ratings system outcome variables were age of the respondent, television influence from siblings, independence in decision making, parental mediation, and overall television exposure.

Concurrent with the second Michigan State study, the Kaiser Family Foundation surveyed a nationally representative sample of 446 children between 10 and 17 years old (Foehr, Rideout, & Miller, 2000a). Of these young people, 80% said they were aware of the TV ratings system, and 45% of the aware group said they chose not to watch a particular show because of its rating. The ratings most likely to be a deterrent to their interest in viewing were S (44%), D (33%), TV-Y7 (28%), TV-MA (27%), and L (26%). But the largest group of children (from 44 to 70%) reported that the ratings had no effect on their interest in what they chose to watch.

Four in 10 young people said their parents were using the ratings to make decisions about television viewing, a level of use that was not reflected in any of the direct studies of parents reported earlier. Almost all report no restrictions on shows with TV-Y7 or TV-PG designations, whereas from 10 to 15% report restrictions for S, V, FV, L, D, and TV-14 labels, and 21% for MA. Younger children (10–13) and girls were more likely to be dissuaded from watching a program based on its rating than were their older and male counterparts, especially if there was an S label. Younger children in this study also perceived more misuse, in this case their own. They more often reported watching a show they weren't supposed to because they were curious about it based on its rating (Foehr et al., 2000a).

Children claim a better understanding of the ratings than they actually demonstrate when tested directly on what the ratings mean. Consistent with the parent studies, they were better at correctly defining the age-based ratings than the content descriptors. Only 18% of the children could correctly identify the four age-based ratings (TV-G, TV-PG, TV-14, and TV-MA) asked about, and 25% answered none or only one of them correctly. Regarding the content descriptors, 52% could not correctly define any one of them, and only 2% could correctly identify all five of them. Even those who had received an explanation of the system and were more likely to say they understood the system "very well" demonstrated no better knowledge than those who had received no explanation (Foehr et al., 2000a).

In sum, young viewers are somewhat aware of the ratings but have little understanding of what they represent. At the time of these studies, the youth were more knowledgeable about the age-based than the content descriptors. Findings are mixed in terms of use, with some reporting very little use and others a bit more, but overall it cannot be considered substantial use. Those who were younger and female claimed greater use of the ratings, but, at least for the younger children, acquiescence to these questions (i.e., saying what they perceive they should be saying) may have been a factor.

Related Experimental Research

Work preceding these surveys of the actual television ratings system has been largely experimental and has focused on the specific issue of potential abuse and misuse of the ratings information. The conceptual framework most often posed has been a variation of the "forbidden fruit hypothesis" (Christenson, 1992). This hypothesis proposes that the ratings may influence viewers to increase their viewing of inappropriate shows rather than refrain from viewing such programs. Thus, it

posits a potential boomerang effect of the ratings on viewing behaviors whether they be movie ratings (Austin, 1980), TV warning labels (Bushman, 1997), or TV ratings systems (Krcmar & Cantor, 1997). This conception is based on the theory of psychological reactance (Brehm, 1966), which predicts that those who perceive their behavioral freedom to be threatened or restricted will be motivated to restore their freedom by engaging in the restricted behavior. Therefore, content may be more attractive to children, young people, or anyone else if parents (or other authorities) restrict or forbid viewing. An alternative conception is, of course, the "tainted fruit" possibility—being informed that a show is for older viewers or bears content that is unacceptable will be a turnoff to viewing.

Three experiments for media other than television—films with high school students, films with college undergraduates, and music albums with middle school students—produced no support for the forbidden fruit hypothesis (Austin, 1980; Bank, 1998; Christenson, 1992). Then a series of experiments using television advisories and/or labels began. Cantor's experiments began by attaching either a parental advisory or parental violence advisory to fictitious and actual shows. Boys chose more reality-based crime shows with a parental advisory than girls did, and they chose those same shows more so overall when such an advisory was attached than when it was not. Randomly assigning different ratings to a movie did not affect the children's interpretation of the clip. The older youth better understood the advisories used (Cantor & Harrison, 1996b). In a follow-up study, Cantor, Harrison, and Nathanson (1997) had children rate their interest in fictitious TV program titles that had different ratings attached. Younger boys were more interested in programs with a parental discretion advisory than were young girls (5–9), with no differences among the older children (10–15). But the older ones were more interested in shows with more severe ratings than in those with G ratings.

Bushman and Stack (1996) tested made-for-television movies with and without labels and found that movies with labels were preferred. In a second experiment, they specifically tested whether these labels induced reactance and found that high-reactance subjects wanted to watch the TV films with labels more than the low-reactance subjects did. Finally, Bushman (1997) gave 600 subjects descriptions of six violent and six nonviolent programs that had a warning label, an information label, or no label. Across all age groups (9–21+), there was greatest preference for the programs with the warning label, and this preference was keenest in the 9- to 11-year-old age group.

Thus, the findings are mixed. Most have used ratings systems similar but not identical to that actually now in place (Hofschire, 2000). Some find support for the forbidden fruit notion that programs will be more attractive if they carry labels that are elevated, while others find evidence that "stronger" labels may deter viewing. However, the weight of the studies' evidence is that restrictive ratings attract viewers more so than not (Bushman, 1997; Bushman & Stack, 1996; Cantor & Harrison, 1996a), particularly males (Cantor & Harrison, 1996a; Chen, 1998) and older youth (Cantor & Harrison, 1996a). The tainted fruit effect has been found more with younger, female children (Cantor & Harrison, 1996a; Cantor et al., 1997) and when a parent–child dyad is making joint viewing decisions (Krcmar & Cantor, 1997). The field studies reviewed in this chapter indicated that the perceived normative level of misuse would be low, but higher occurrence levels were judged to be likely among younger viewers, and they themselves were more likely to report doing so.

Conclusions and Recommendations

The initial field studies by the Kaiser Family Foundation and Michigan State University, and the more recent Kaiser studies, certainly document the diffusion of the television ratings system. At best, understanding, adoption, and application of the system by parents are tepid, even among those with young children. And for the youth themselves, the television ratings appear unlikely to be a serious criterion for determining what shows they choose to watch.

We recognize that between 1997 and 2010, the media world of young people has changed drastically. Today's youth are spending more time with media than ever before. The most recent Kaiser Family Media study (2009) indicates that daily time spent with media has increased from 6 hours 21 minutes in 2004 to 7 hours 38 minutes in 2009—an increase of 1 hour 17 minutes a day. Further, youth are spending more time "media multitasking" (simultaneously using multiple media at one time), so the 7.5 hours of media content use becomes 10 hours 45 minutes of multitasking. African-American and Hispanic children consume even more media daily. Total media exposure for Hispanics and African-Americans in this Kaiser study was estimated at 13 hours a day, while the Caucasian level was 8 hours 36 minutes. While TV ratings were not addressed in the study, it would be of value to understand how well known and useful the ratings are for youth in this changed media environment. This study also finds that most parents (7 out of 10) have no rules regarding how much time their children can spend with TV, video games, and the computer.

In the meantime, we offer our opinion as to why responses have been as these studies indicated. First, if these field studies somehow would assess which parents (or children) are in greater or lesser need of such a system (Abelman, 2000), we would expect to find that the ratings system provides a useful supplement to the in-home mediation activities of the latter. Further, we anticipate that those parents who do not provide much mediation are unlikely to use this new tool to do so. Selectivity is operative in this process. Parents who already monitor their children's television can point to the age designation or content labels as supportive of their own judgment and thereby reinforce their monitoring activities. Parents who do not find television much of a concern are unlikely to assimilate this information for any functional use. It also is noted that information and influence might run in the other direction; that is, many parents have suggested that they found out about the ratings from their children

(Mastro, 2000). Some of the effort now aimed at informing parents might be refocused directly at their offspring. The older children are more aware of what TV has to offer in all its forms. Perhaps learning about the age and content ratings at an early age will be a precursor of use later in life.

Recent research finds a lack of parental rules on amount of TV viewing (Kaiser Family Foundation, 2009) and a lack of understanding what the ratings mean 7 years after the ratings were introduced (Kaiser Family Foundation, 2004). These primary outcomes from both young people and their parents, little use of the ratings, marginal attention to them, and not knowing what they mean have substantial support from multiple studies. Alternative modes of informing about media programs/content should be considered.

Second, the credibility of the television ratings system information is in question among many parents. This factor was clearly evident in the focus group outcomes (Gregg, 2000; Mastro, 2000) and was not well addressed in the field studies. Today, after a more extended period of ratings availability, it would be possible to determine how often parents have found themselves disagreeing with the designated rating for a show and how often they have been snake-bit by believing a show was acceptable for their child and then seeing that it was not. Or, more fairly, has the credibility of the ratings improved or faltered as they have been applied to more and more shows over a longer period of time? Has the public come to better assess the consistency or lack of consistency in ratings that are created by an unknown host of raters without hard criteria? Or do parents use different criteria not incorporated into the ratings system?

Third, the ratings system may be too confusing in its combining of age and content designations. The MPAA ratings for movies appear to be well understood, although the addition of an NC-17 category may have clouded even that system a bit. The television ratings have two tiers, one for children and one for all viewers, and then the content designations mean different things within different age ratings. And some age ratings do not carry content labels. One can only ponder what such a system might have looked like if fewer political interests had to be accommodated in the final version. Hofschire (2000) describes operative and planned systems in other English-speaking countries that may be simpler to understand; however, there is a dearth of research on those systems, including whether they are well understood. Because those systems have a single rating body, the combination of ratings consistency and greater ease in understanding would suggest an enhanced credibility. That, in turn, may lead to greater acceptance and implementation.

Finally, we pose the third-person effect as an appropriate phenomenon to consider here. The strongest expression of opinion in these studies is the need for a system that identifies what age viewer the show is appropriate for and whether it has content that may be offensive in terms of violence, sex, or language. The request for a ratings system is strong and prevalent. But who is it that needs the system to facilitate the choice of appropriate television shows? *You do. He does. She does. Their children do. But I'm OK. I know what's good and what's bad for my own children. It's all those others out there who are confused. I'm not.* Under such a rubric, the perceived imposition of this system from the outside, from very partial interests, and/or the lack of a perceived personal need may relegate the ratings to a minor personal role.

We prefer some information to none and urge the ratings system to plug at least one large hole over which it has complete control—to make the ratings information more consistent and reliable across shows and across networks. The raters and their staffs could network with each other to arrive at a more common set of definitions for the relatively few variables with which they deal. If those definitions do not satisfy the operational criteria of social scientists, so be it. Let those definitions at least be used in common in the television industry, and make those definitions available. We can agree to disagree over them, but having them out there might go a long distance to upgrade their believability. As long as raters operate with their individual brand of professional wisdom, and that wisdom differs from one network to the next, what's a parent to do but ignore the in-fighting and rely on her or his own experience and values.

References

Abelman, R. (2000). Profiling parents who do and don't use the TV advisory ratings. In B. S. Greenberg, L. Rampoldi-Hnilo, & D. Mastro (Eds.), *The alphabet soup of television program ratings.* Cresskill, NJ: Hampton Press.

Abelman, R., & Petty, G. (1989). Child attributes as determinants of parental television-viewing mediation. *Journal of Family Issues, 10*(2), 251–266.

Atkin, D., Heeter, C., & Baldwin, T. (1989). How presence of cable affects parental mediation of TV viewing. *Journalism Quarterly, 66*(3), 557–563.

Atkin, D. J., Greenberg, B. S., & Baldwin, T. F. (1991). The home ecology of children's television viewing: Parental mediation and the new video environment. *Journal of Communication, 41*(3), 40–52.

Austin, B. A. (1980). The influence of MPAA's film-rating system on motion picture attendance: A pilot study. *Journal of Psychology, 106,* 91–99.

Austin, E. W. (1993). Exploring the effects of active parental mediation of television content. *Journal of Broadcasting & Electronic Media, 37*(2), 147–158.

Bank, C. M. (1998). Descriptions of sexual content and ratings of movie preference. *Psychological Reports, 82,* 367–370.

Brehm, J. (1966). *A theory of psychological reactance.* New York: Academic Press.

Bushman, B. J. (1997). *Effects of warning labels on attraction to television violence in viewers of different ages.* Paper presented as part of an invited colloquium at the Telecommunication and Policy Research Conference, Alexandria, VA.

Bushman, B. J., & Stack, A. D. (1996). Forbidden fruit versus tainted fruit: Effects of warning labels on attraction to television violence. *Journal of Experimental Psychology: Applied, 2*(3), 207–226.

Cantor, J., & Harrison, K. (1996a). Ratings and advisories for television programming. In *National Television Violence Study scientific papers 1994–95* (pp. III-2–III-26). Studio City, CA: Mediascope.

Cantor, J., & Harrison, K. (1996b). Ratings and advisories for television programs. In *National Television Violence Study* (Vol. 1, pp. 361–409). Thousand Oaks, CA: Sage.

Cantor, J., Harrison, K., & Nathanson, A. (1997). Ratings and advisories for television programming. In *National Television Violence Study year 2* (pp. 267–322). Thousand Oaks, CA: Sage.

Cantor, J., Stutman, S., & Duran, V. (1997). *What parents want in a television rating system: Results of a national survey* [Online]. Retrieved from http://yourmindonmedia.com/wp-content/uploads/parent_survey.pdf.

Chen, H. L. (1998). *Young adolescents' responses to television ratings and advisories.* Unpublished doctoral dissertation, Stanford University, Stanford, CA.

Christenson, P. (1992). The effect of parental advisory labels on adolescent music preferences. *Journal of Communication, 42*(1), 106–113.

Desmond, R. J., Singer, J. L., Singer, D. G., Calam, R., & Colimore, K. (1985). Family mediation, mediation patterns, and television viewing: Young children's use and grasp of the medium. *Human Communication Research, 11*(4), 461–480.

Foehr, U. G., Rideout, V., & Miller, C. (2000a). Children and the TV ratings system: A national study. In B. S. Greenberg, L. Rampoldi-Hnilo, & D. Mastro (Eds.), *The alphabet soup of television program ratings.* Cresskill, NJ: Hampton Press.

Foehr, U. G., Rideout, V., & Miller, C. (2000b). Parents and the TV ratings system: A national study. In B. S. Greenberg, L. Rampoldi-Hnilo, & D. Mastro (Eds.), *The alphabet soup of television program ratings.* Cresskill, NJ: Hampton Press.

Greenberg, B. S., Eastin, M., & Mastro, D. (2000a). Comparing the on-air ratings with the published ratings: Who to believe? In B. S. Greenberg, L. Rampoldi-Hnilo, & D. Mastro (Eds.), *The alphabet soup of television program ratings.* Cresskill, NJ: Hampton Press.

Greenberg, B. S., Eastin, M., & Mastro, D. (2000b). The ratings distribution in 1998, according to *TV Guide.* In B. S. Greenberg, L. Rampoldi-Hnilo, & D. Mastro Eds.), *The alphabet soup of television program ratings.* Cresskill, NJ: Hampton Press.

Greenberg, B. S., & Rampoldi-Hnilo, L. (2000). Young people's responses to the content-based ratings. In B. S. Greenberg, L. Rampoldi-Hnilo, & D. Mastro (Eds.), *The alphabet soup of television program ratings.* Cresskill, NJ: Hampton Press.

Greenberg, B. S., Rampoldi-Hnilo, L., & Hofschire, L. (2000). Young people's responses to the age-based ratings. In B. S. Greenberg, L. Rampoldi-Hnilo, & D. Mastro (Eds.), *The alphabet soup of television program ratings.* Cresskill, NJ: Hampton Press.

Greenberg, B. S., Rampoldi-Hnilo, L., & Mastro, D. (Eds.). (2000). *The alphabet soup of television program ratings.* Cresskill, NJ: Hampton Press.

Gregg, J. (2000). Field studies of the reactions of Caucasian parents to the new television ratings. In B. S. Greenberg, L. Rampoldi-Hnilo, & D. Mastro (Eds.), *The alphabet soup of television program ratings.* Cresskill, NJ: Hampton Press.

Hepburn, M. A. (1997). A medium's effects under scrutiny. *Social Education, 61*(5), 244–249.

Hofschire, L. (2000). Media advisories and ratings: What the experimental research tells us. In B. S. Greenberg, L. Rampoldi-Hnilo, & D. Mastro (Eds.), *The alphabet soup of television program ratings.* Cresskill, NJ: Hampton Press.

Kaiser Family Foundation. (1999). *Parents and the V-chip: A Kaiser Family Foundation survey* [Online]. Retrieved November 1999 from http://www.kff.org/entmedia/1477-index.cfm.

Kaiser Family Foundation. (2004). *Parents, media and public policy: A Kaiser Family Foundation Survey* [Online]. Retrieved April 2010 from http://www.kff.org/entmedia/upload/Parents-Media-and-Public-Policy-A-Kaiser-Family-Foundation-Survey-Report.pdf.

Kaiser Family Foundation. (2007). *Parents, children & media: A Kaiser Family Foundation Survey* [Online]. Retrieved April 2010 from http://www.kff.org/entmedia/7638.cfm.

Kaiser Family Foundation. (2009). *Generation M²: Media in the lives of 8- to 18-year-olds.* [Online]. Retrieved April 2010 from http://www.kff.org/entmedia/mh012010pkg.cfm.

Kaye, B. K., & Sapolsky, B. S. (2001). Offensive language in prime-time television: Before and after content ratings. *Journal of Broadcasting & Electronic Media, 45*(2), 303–319.

Kaye, B. K., & Sapolsky, B. S. (2004). Offensive language in prime-time television: Four years after television age and content ratings. *Journal of Broadcasting & Electronic Media, 48*(4), 554–569.

Krcmar, M., & Cantor, J. (1997). The role of television advisories and ratings in parent–child discussion of television viewing choices. *Journal of Broadcasting & Electronic Media, 41,* 393–411.

Kunkel, D., Farinola, W. J. M., Farrar, K., Donnerstein, E., Biely, E., & Zwarun, L. (2002). Deciphering the V-chip: An examination of the television industry's program rating judgments. *Journal of Communication, 52*(1), 112–138.

Lin, C. A., & Atkin, D. J. (1989). Parental mediation and rulemaking for adolescent use of television and VCRs. *Journal of Broadcasting & Electronic Media, 33*(1), 53–67.

Linder, J. R., & Gentile, D. A. (2009). Is the television rating system valid? Indirect, verbal and physical aggression in programs viewed by fifth-grade girls and associations with behavior. *Journal of Applied Developmental Psychology, 30,* 286–297.

Lindlof, T. R., & Shatzer, M. J. (1990). VCR usage in the American family. In J. Bryant (Ed.), *Television and the American family* (pp. 89–112). Hillsdale, NJ: Lawrence Erlbaum.

Mandese, J. (1993). Marketers on TV warnings: Yawn. *Advertising Age, 64*(28), 1–3.

Mastro, D. (2000). Reactions of Hispanic parents to the new television ratings. In B. S. Greenberg, L. Rampoldi-Hnilo, & D. Mastro (Eds.), *The alphabet soup of television program ratings.* Cressbill, NJ: Hampton Press.

Mohr, P. J. (1979). Parental influence of children's viewing of evening television programs. *Journal of Broadcasting, 23*(2), 213–228.

Rampoldi-Hnilo, L., & Greenberg, B. S. (2000). A poll of Latina and Caucasian mothers with 6- to 10-year-old children. In B. S. Greenberg, L. Rampoldi-Hnilo, &. D. Mastro (Eds.), *The alphabet soup of television program ratings.* Cresskill, NJ: Hampton Press.

Stern, C. (1996). TV makes history at the White House. *Broadcasting & Cable, 126*(10), 5–8.

St. Peters, M., Fitch, M., Huston, A. C., Wright, J. C., & Eakins, D. J. (1991). Television and families: What do young children watch with their parents? *Child Development, 62,* 1409–1423.

CHAPTER 31

Safeguards for Youth in the Digital Marketing Ecosystem

KATHRYN C. MONTGOMERY
American University

In 2008, McDonald's transformed its popular Happy Meal website into a new online virtual world. The company worked with a number of digital advertising "hot shops" to create an immersive environment filled with an array of interactive elements designed to attract and engage young visitors. On the Happy Meal site, for example, children were encouraged to create their own customized avatars, play with virtual pets, and interact with characters from movies, comic books, and TV shows. They could also connect with their friends on the site's social networking platform. Through mobile applications, they could take the virtual world with them wherever they went. And even offline, in the real world, special codes printed on Happy Meal boxes, bags, and toys lured children back online to play interactive games, enter contests, and receive online coupons for McDonald's products. Visitors to the site could save their favorite activities in a customized "My Happy Meal" profile, enabling the company to gather valuable data for targeted advertising ("McDonald's Launching Virtual World," 2008; "McDonald's New Virtual World," 2008). According to its research, the user-generated content (UGC) campaign produced a "purchase intent" rate of 67% and engaged 5 million individuals in more than 100 countries over a 6-month period (Chang, 2009).

McDonald's online "McWorld" is emblematic of the new global "media and marketing ecosystem" that is transforming how corporations do business with young people in the Digital Age. Broadband networks and Web 2.0 technologies are creating an interactive media culture that is increasingly participatory, pervasive, and mobile. This rapid expansion of digital media is ushering in a new set of behaviors, especially for youth, who marketers are monitoring closely (Montgomery, 2007).

In many ways, children and teens are the defining users of this new culture, the quintessential "early adopters" of new technology, eagerly embracing a host of digital tools, integrating them into their daily lives, and forging a new set of cultural practices that are quickly moving into the mainstream. Youth are especially enthusiastic participants in online social networks such as MySpace and Facebook, which are among the fastest-growing platforms (Owyang, 2010). Seventy-three percent of online youth between the ages of 12 and 17 use social networking sites (Lenhart, Purcell, Smith, & Zickuhr, 2010; Williamson, 2008). These digital media are playing an increasingly important role in the socialization of youth. The features of interactive media are especially appealing to young people because they tap into such key developmental needs as identity exploration, self-expression, peer relationships, and independence (John D. and Catherine T. MacArthur Foundation, 2006; MIT Press, 2007; Subrahmanyam & Greenfield, 2008).

However, powerful commercial forces are also shaping this new interactive media culture, where advertising is not restricted to discrete commercial messages but, rather, woven through the online experience. The forms of advertising, marketing, and selling to children that are emerging as part of the new media depart in significant ways from the more familiar commercial advertising and promotion in children's television. The interactive media are ushering in an entirely new set of relationships, breaking down the traditional barriers between "content and commerce," and creating unprecedented intimacies between children and marketers. Because marketing to children is already a well-established, profitable industry, its imperatives are influencing the design of digital content and services for children and teens in fundamental ways. These developments raise serious questions that need to be addressed by researchers, policy makers, health professionals, and parents.

The Rise of "Digital Kids"

Several trends have converged to make young people such a powerful target for marketers in the Digital Age. One of the most important is the exponential rise in spending by children and teens during the last three decades of the 20th century, which doubled between the years 1960 and 1980 and tripled in the '90s (Schor & Ford, 2007). In 2002, children aged 4 to 12 spent $30 billion in direct purchases, nearly five times as much as they spent in 1989 (Committee on Prevention of Obesity in Children and Youth, 2005). Between 1999 and 2004 alone, teenage spending increased nearly

40%, from $122 billion to $169 billion ("Teens Cash In," 2005). Experts point to a number of demographic and economic trends that contributed to this dramatic increase. Not only did the number of children and teens in the United States grow, but the divorce rate also rose, forcing more parents to work outside the home. This, in turn, meant that more children were responsible for shopping decisions that once were strictly the domain of parents (Linn, 2004; McNeal, 1992, 1999; Schor, 2004). Nor do children and teens simply spend their own money; they also influence purchases by their parents, in many cases having significant sway over such major items as family vacations, household appliances, and automobiles ("Advergaming," 2006; Nestle, 2003, pp. 173–196). Marketers have developed an entire set of strategies for stimulating this practice, known in the industry as "kidfluence" (Linn, 2004; Schor, 2004)

Children's media culture also expanded dramatically during the past several decades. The rise of "kidvid" TV channels—such as Nickelodeon, Disney, and the Cartoon Network—increased both the number of outlets and the amount of programming available for children, offering marketers a variety of new opportunities for directly reaching this lucrative demographic group (Montgomery, 2007, pp. 11–34). With the launch of the World Wide Web in 1993, these networks began expanding their franchises onto the Internet and across a proliferating array of new digital platforms, joined by hundreds of new-media ventures aimed specifically at children and teens.

Because the digital media emerged in the midst of a highly commercialized youth culture, a large infrastructure of market research firms and ad agencies was already studying how children and teens engage with media. With the growth of the Internet and other new technologies, a host of boutique consultants, trend-analysis companies, and digital strategists moved into place, making today's young people the most intensely analyzed demographic group in the history of marketing (Jacobson & Mazur, 1995; Linn, 2004; Montgomery, 2007, pp. 11–34; Schor, 2004).

These young people are valuable to marketers not only because of their own spending power and ease with technology but also because of their role as trendsetters in the new media environment. Researchers have coined a variety of labels to define this powerful target group of users—from *Generation Y* to the *N-Geners* to the *New Millennials* to *Digital Natives*. As one marketing trade article explained, "Gen Yers are 'influencers' by nature . . . . New devices and services will be bought by/for them, they will encourage older populations to 'get with it' and join them, and they will be emulated by younger generations trying to be like them" (Dickey & Sullivan, 2007).

Market researchers employ the expertise of an increasingly diverse array of specialists in sociology, psychology, and anthropology to explore youth subcultures and conduct motivational research (Schor, 2004, pp. 99–118). A considerable amount of contemporary market research is focused on identifying ways to tap into the critical developmental stages of childhood (Harter, 1990; Lippe, 2001; Marcus & Nurius, 1986). Researchers are both tracking how children are integrating digital technologies into their lives and identifying social and psychographic subcategories based on sophisticated new data-gathering and -analysis techniques. For example, the "tween" demographic, which was introduced by marketers during the 1980s, has become a key focus of research on digital media (Kantrowitz & Wingert, 1999; Romano, 2004).

Among the many youth market research initiatives is the Advertising Research Foundation's Council on Youth Marketing, whose role is to "expand industry knowledge of how to best communicate with, and market to, children and teens," to "review and stimulate research to measure youth's media consumption patterns, and to relate these to effective marketing communications" (Advertising Research Foundation, 2006). More generally, the youth market research industry sponsors dozens of seminars, conferences, and trade shows every year. With catchy names like "Digital Kids," "Teen Power," "Kidscreen Summit," these high-priced events pay homage to the value and influence of the child and youth demographic. Eager marketers fork out thousands of dollars to attend these meetings and tens of thousands more for the steady stream of specialized trade publications and reports offering strategies, secrets, and success stories from the front lines of the children's marketplace. A joint study by Yahoo! and OMD in 2005, for example— "Truly, Madly, Deeply Engaged"—involved more than 5,000 interviews in 11 countries with youth between the ages of 13 and 24, providing "a roadmap for reaching the My Media Generation, by showing where they are and what devices and media they are using for a wide variety of tasks" (Yahoo & OMD, 2005, p. 28).

The interactive nature of digital technologies makes it possible for market research to be woven into the content of new media, offering marketers the opportunity to remain in constant contact with children and teens, effectively creating a feedback system for the refinement of marketing techniques. Sulake (2009), for example, the Finnish online entertainment company, conducts an annual Global Youth Survey that draws on the user base of its popular virtual world, Habbo.com. The most recent month-long survey in 2009 included 112,000 youth between the ages of 11 and 19 in more than 30 countries, yielding information and insights on media usage patterns and brand preferences for fast food, beverages, mobile services, and other products.

Digital Marketing Paradigm

All of these trends are ushering in a new digital marketing paradigm, rooted in the steady stream of ongoing research and designed to take advantage of the unique capacities of interactive media to forge strong, continuous, emotional relationships between brands and individual consumers. With marketing integrated throughout the new media culture, it is difficult to isolate advertising as a separate form of communication, comparable to the 30-second television commercial. (Even in television, advertising and content have merged, with product placement now a common practice.) However, it is possible to identify a number of practices that are among the defining features of marketing in the Digital Age. These are not discrete techniques but, rather, a constellation of new strategies that are often combined in digital marketing campaigns. Some are extensions of long-standing practices in the advertising industry that have been further refined and enhanced through the use of new technologies; others are recent innovations that depart quite dramatically from conventional business practices. Taken together—and viewed against the backdrop of the major changes taking place in the worlds of media, advertising, and market research—they constitute a new direction that is fundamentally different from the ways in which advertising and marketing were conducted in the past.

This chapter will briefly outline the key features of digital marketing, provide illustrations of the major techniques that are employed to target children and youth in contemporary media, and discuss the need for effective safeguards for young people that can guide the growth and development of the digital media culture.

Ubiquitous Connectivity

Today's youth are growing up in an "always-on," 24/7 media environment that is accessible to them wherever they go throughout the day, creating an internalized expectation of constant connectivity to technology. Marketers design their campaigns to take advantage of young people's fluid media experiences, dependency on technology, and multitasking behaviors. Major media companies have restructured their marketing and sales operations to facilitate cross-platform strategies, where, in a single buy, advertisers can target customers across a company's properties and affiliates, online and off (New Media Age, 2008). Marketers not only tap into these patterns of behavior but also purposely cultivate them, designing campaigns that can "drive" young consumers from one medium to the next (Chester & Montgomery, 2007, pp. 36–37). Increasingly, advertisers are taking advantage of what is known as the "three-screen" viewing environment, with ad campaigns running simultaneously on television, the Web, and mobile devices (Nielsen, 2009).

Accordingly, the "360-degree strategy" is one of the core principles of today's youth

marketing, aimed at reaching individuals repeatedly through multiple "touchpoints" (Covino, 2006). For example, Sprite created an "alternate reality game (ARG)" called "Lost Experience," based on the highly popular ABC television series, *Lost.* As reported in the trade press, the venture provided viewers "a way to further their pursuit of the show's mystery while inadvertently engaging in a Sprite-branded website." Marketers began by creating a "faux-commercial" that aired during an episode of the TV series in order to "leak" a special Web address—"Sublymonal.com" (now defunct) to viewers. Once online, site visitors were invited to participate in a scavenger hunt with "DJ podcasts, videos and hidden memos." Codes were also hidden in print ads that ran in *Entertainment Weekly* and *People* magazine, which enabled players to "unlock even more online content." The campaign was highly successful:

> As fan excitement about the ARG grew, so did Sprite's Web traffic (up 400 percent) and average visit time (up 275 percent). In total, more than 500,000 of the hidden codes were entered into the site. . . . By providing viewers with something valuable—information about the characters and the show—they were able to drive them to the Sprite website. (Sernovitz & Stairhime, 2007, para. 5)

Time Warner's Cartoon Network, similarly, offers advertisers "custom promotions and powerful multiplatform sponsorships that reach kids everywhere." The network has commissioned 2-minute episodes of some of its popular programs "and put them on every digital platform going" (Cartoon Network, 2006, p. M14). Among the many marketing opportunities for brands are music videos targeting kids 6 to 11; an online "Video Broadband Channel" featuring "download-ables," video clips, and "character bios" from the network's various programs; and a "Funk Box," enabling 6- to 11-year-olds to "Mix your own funky beats" with the popular cast of the *Class of 3000* show. Advertisers are informed that they can be exclusive sponsors of "games, episodes and show content via display and video ads." Companies can also buy ads in Cartoon Network podcasts and/ or reach children through various features available on the new "Cartoon Network Mobile," where children who "Text CTOON" receive theme song ringtones and download-able clips on their cell phones, along with targeted ads on the tiny screens (Cartoon Network, 2006).

Mobile Marketing

As Web-enabled cell phones become more popular, such advertising is becoming more common. Combining text messaging, mobile video, and other new applications, mobile marketing is one of the fastest-growing digital commerce platforms throughout the world and a particularly effective way to reach and engage youth (Burns, 2009). "By age 10, roughly half of children own a mobile phone. . . . By age 12, fully three-fourths of all children have their own mobile phone" (Blackshaw, 2009, para. 10). According to a 2010 Kaiser Family Foundation study,

> Over the past five years, there has been a huge increase in [cell phone] ownership among 8- to 18-year-olds: from 39% to 66%. . . . During this period, cell phones. . . have become true multi-media devices: in fact, young people now spend more time listening to music, playing games, and watching TV on their cell phones (a total of :49 daily) than they spend talking on them (:33). (Kaiser Family Foundation, 2010, para. 4)

As one media executive commented, the mobile phone is "the ultimate ad vehicle . . . the first one ever in the history of the planet that people go to bed with" (Klaassen, 2008, para. 19).

Mobile technology enables marketers to directly target users based on such information as previous purchase history, geographic location, and other profiling data. Mobile marketing is expected to become one of the major forms of advertising and marketing in the Digital Age (Nielsen, 2010; Schonfeld, 2010). People are becoming dependent on Internet-connected cell phones and other wireless devices to access essential information,

learn about entertainment, participate in community events, and shop, not to mention the downloading of games and music, already a major pastime for young consumers. Through "location targeting," ads on mobile phones can reach consumers when they are near a particular business and offer electronic pitches and discount coupons (Johannes, 2005).

Young people are an especially coveted target for such messages. Not only is mobile device ownership widespread among children, studies show that minors are especially susceptible to mobile advertising. According to Harris Interactive, mobile marketing has a great deal of potential to influence young mobile consumers and "can gain a foothold among this large and growing group," if the advertising is both "unobtrusive" and "targeted" (Harris Interactive, 2008).

Behavioral Targeting

Digital technologies and ad industry innovations provide digital marketers with an unprecedented ability to target not only demographic groups but also individual consumers. Behavioral targeting—a form of database or "customer relationship marketing" (CRM)—enables companies to develop unique, long-term relationships with individual customers. Through ongoing data collection and tracking, marketers can create personalized marketing and sales appeals based on a customer's unique preferences, behaviors, and psychological profile (Hallerman, 2008).

Advances in behavioral advertising enable marketers to predict and influence user behavior even more accurately. So-called "predictive behavioral targeting" combines data from a number of different sources and makes inferences about how users are likely to behave in their response to marketing messages. Increasingly, behavioral profiles incorporate information from outside databases (Acxiom, 2010). Behavioral targeting has also made its way onto social media platforms (24/7 Real Media, 2008; Acxiom, 2009; ValueClick Media , 2008). Through *online ad exchanges* and *real-time auctioning*, marketers can buy access to specific consumers. In addition, so-called *smart ads* can deliver highly personalized messages to individuals, with the "ad creative" altered to respond to consumer behaviors on an instantaneous basis. These developments further the concept of personalization for digital advertising—interactive marketing that is tailored to reflect what consumers have "watched, read, experienced and shared" (Ramsey, 2009).

Ad networks represent a collection of different websites, enabling marketers to deliver their messages across a variety of online locations. Through "behavioral retargeting," advertisers can track users across all the websites affiliated with a network, permitting an ongoing campaign for a specific product or service on a site that may not have any connection with the initial one that "served" the ad. These networks also monitor users' online navigation patterns, combining this information with a wealth of other data. The ad network Tribal Fusion (n.d.), for example, offers access to online teens at a cost of $4 per thousand, enabling advertisers to "target users based on specific behaviors, and retarget those consumers that have already expressed an interest in their offering during a past session on the network" (Meskauskas, 2006, para. 7).

Branded Entertainment

Since the beginning of the World Wide Web, one of the defining features of digital marketing has been the complete integration of advertising and content. Thousands of corporations have created their own online branded entertainment sites, seamlessly weaving a variety of interactive content with product pitches (Moore, 2006). Such sites are designed to encourage young consumers to engage playfully with products over long periods of time. Many offer "free" content or allow users to create their own content in a fully branded setting. With the advent of broadband networks, these digital playgrounds have evolved into highly sophisticated interactive online experiences, offering games, contests, branded merchandise, and endless replays of television commercials (Chester & Montgomery, 2007). For example, General Mills' Cinnamon Toast Crunch's CTCMix site featured an "AudioMixer," where visitors could get free music downloads (CTC Music Mixer, 2010). M&M candies offers downloadable PC "wallpaper" featuring product "spokescharacters" (M&M, 2010). The Coca-Cola Company is a "founding sponsor" of new hip-hop video-on-demand (VOD) channel run by music artist Russell Simmons (Lieb, 2007). Google's YouTube—the leading online video service with more than 80 million monthly users—has been working to increase revenues by forging "branded entertainment" channels with advertisers (Barnes, 2008; Morrissey, 2009). Industry research suggests, moreover, that far from being annoyed by the intrusion of brands into their programming of choice, younger Internet users actually seek out such content (Microsoft Advertising, 2008).

Alcohol beverage companies have been especially aggressive in the area of branded entertainment, with such experiments as the BudTV "online entertainment network," Dos Equis beer's MOJO HD cable channel, Malibu Rum's online "Radio Maliboom Boom," and Chivas scotch's "This Is The Life" online channel developed in partnership with Microsoft's MSN (Berens, 2006; Chivas Regal, 2007; Mojo, 2009; Straczynski, 2009). Coupled with the thousands of branded widgets and Smart phone apps that are now available, it is clear that digital entertainment and advertising are now thoroughly intertwined.

Advertisers are also using social networks to blur the lines between advertising and content, embedding their messages in social network conversations and encouraging users to interact with brands as if they were "friends." MySpace, for example, actively encourages marketers to create "branded profiles" for their products. "Essentially," explains Pete Lerma (2006, para. 7) of the Click Here ad agency, "you can set up a page for a brand with all the same features as individual profiles and more. By doing this, you create a mini-social network in which users interact with the brand just as they would with other profiles. MySpace's standard branded page functionality includes product information, videos, wallpaper, a friends' network, forums, comments, and more."

Social Media Marketing

For years, companies have purposefully sought out the most influential young "connectors" within their social groups and encouraged them to promote brands among their friends (Montgomery, 2007). With the growth of digital media, peer-to-peer marketing (sometimes called "buzz," "word-of-mouth," or "viral" marketing) has become a staple among youth advertisers (Buzz Marketing, 2010; Hughes, 2005; Lindstrom & Seybold, 2003; Rosen, 2000). A 2006 report entitled "Tapping into the Super Influencer: What You Need to Know to Engage the Elusive Young Consumer" found that "word of mouth driven by technology has greater impact than ever before" (Elkin, 2006; Starcom Mediavest Group, 2006, p. 32). The ethnographic study of more than 10,000 young people was conducted by the Digital Connections Unit at Starcom Mediavest Group (MediaVest, 2007, 2008). A "small but significant portion of respondents"—between 15 and 20%—fell into a category dubbed "Brand Sirens." These "super-influential" individuals can "have a profound network effect on marketing through their ability to influence friends and family via word-of-mouth, viral video and applications such as instant messaging and blogs," among other media (Elkin, 2006, para. 1). While these youth could be somewhat skeptical about "marketing and corporations," they also "appreciated brands." Among the Sirens' key attributes is their ability and interest to take "information in" (via books, friends, the Internet, TV, etc.) and then send it "out" using "texting, blogging, MySpace, IM-ing" as well as videos and pictures. With the right approach, they "can be a marketer's **strongest** voice in a seemingly fragmented media landscape" (Starcom Mediavest Group, 2006, p. 14). The study explored a variety of techniques for reaching out to these influential youth, including Internet search sites; online coupons; text messaging from a brand to a cell phone or PDA; as well as brand-sponsored,

Web-based entertainment and Internet ads. "Insert your brand in a conversation" across platforms, marketers were advised, using "touchpoints that can deliver both emotional and rational messages" (Starcom Mediavest Group, 2006, p. 41).

With the widespread adoption of social networking software, the practice of *social media marketing* is becoming even more sophisticated, tapping into an ever-expanding array of new platforms—from YouTube to Facebook to Twitter—to spread the word about product brands among young people. Social networks provide unique spaces where youth can explore their own identities, form communities, and negotiate their social relationships (boyd, 2007). A study by the Kaiser Family Foundation (2010) documented the continued rise in social media use by youth, as "[t]hree-quarters (74%) of all 7th-12th graders say they have a profile on a social networking site," where they spend on average 22 minutes a day. Because of the peer-to-peer nature of these online networks, they are ready-made vehicles for viral marketing. As one trade publication observed, MySpace is able to leverage its online community into a "peer recommendations framework for leads on everything and anything," from

> the best children's playgrounds in Los Angeles to the best concert seats in Madison Square Garden to the best steakhouse in Dallas. Such peer recommendations provide a gentle seaway into targeted, fine-tuned behavioral marketing for national and local advertisers wanting to reach MySpace's 15–34 core user. (Mermigas, 2006)

MySpace's media kit offers advertisers a range of digital marketing opportunities for "Viral Networking" and "Digital Word of Mouth," including sophisticated software that can track the number of users viewing a branded ad, as well as "direct/brand interaction," "amplification of message," and "reposts in bulletins" (MySpace, 2008).

Like many of the digital marketing strategies targeted at young people, social network marketing purposely takes advantage of the identity-exploration process that is such an essential part of adolescent development. "Millions of people are defining what they are there," explained a MySpace executive, "and for young people especially, getting feedback and evolving themselves. For advertisers, it's the potential for a level of intimacy that they could never have dreamed of 20 years ago. . . . It's word-of-mouth on steroids" (Bulik, 2006, paras. 9, 16).

Online Video

Viewing video online has become a regular routine for almost 117 million Americans, more time than is currently spent on blogs and social networking sites. It is a particularly popular pastime for young people, with 82% of older teens routinely sharing their favorite videos through social networks, e-mail, and instant messaging (eMarketer, 2009b). The growing role of advertising will help transform the online video medium itself, with long-form content earning most of the ad revenues (eMarketer, 2009a). "Watching a video ad on YouTube alone significantly increases ad recall and attribution," according to Google advertising research, "up to 14% higher than watching the same ad on TV" (YouTube , 2009, p. 2).

Short online videos are an increasingly popular way of promoting brands among youth, who like to consume these "quick snacks of media" and forward the links along to their friends through IM, text messaging, and blogs (Piper Jaffray, 2007, p. 75). With the growth of broadband, streaming video has become pervasive throughout the Internet, migrating to cell phones and other mobile devices as well. In a 2007 report, investment analysts at Piper Jaffray called video advertising the new "killer app of the Web," which is "supplementing or taking over most other forms of content." As the report explained, "In today's Internet, the advertiser must actively engage the user in order to create a brand impression, and video ads allow brand advertisers to create an emotional connection with a user similar to the dynamic in TV advertising" (Piper Jaffray, 2007, p. 223).

The potential of such advertising first became apparent in 2004, when Burger King launched its "Subservient Chicken" campaign, pioneering a new marketing technique. Created by ad agency Crispin Porter + Bogusky to promote the fast-food restaurant's new chicken sandwich, this interactive "viral video," featuring a man dressed in a bizarre-looking chicken costume, was programmed to allow users to control the "subservient" chicken. Echoing the Burger King slogan, "Have it your way," the ad instructed visitors to "Get chicken just the way you like it. Type in your command here." Along with links, TV clips, and photos, the video offered a downloadable chicken mask. Backed by "online buzz marketing," the ad "took the blogosphere by storm, moving from obscurity to an astounding 46 million visits in the first week," according to Nielsen Buzz Metrics (Blackshaw & Nazzaro, 2006, p. 10). Hailing it as a "trail-blazing" effort," Nielsen noted that it "was one of the first-online campaigns fueled almost entirely by consumers, bloggers and others willing to pass it digitally around the Internet because of its uniqueness" (Blackshaw & Nazzaro, 2006, p. 10; Kuperman, 2006; "Subservient Chicken," 2004).

User-Generated Advertising

Many youth are not only fueling such viral campaigns by forwarding videos to their friends and embedding them on their social network pages, they are also creating their own advertising on behalf of their favorite brands and products. The growth in popularity of digital video cameras and online video sharing sites such as YouTube has made it very easy for young people to create and distribute their own videos. To take advantage of this trend, marketers are encouraging young consumers to "co-create" and promote commercials for their favorite brands. The strategy is designed to foster powerful emotional connections between consumers and products, tap into a stable of young creative talent willing to offer their services for free, and produce a new generation of "brand advocates" (DoubleClick, 2009; Meez, 2010; Studiocom, 2006). These practices turn the conventional model of advertising on its head, transforming children from passive viewers of commercials into ad producers and distributors.

While some industry observers have expressed concern over consumers gaining too much control and creating videos that may undermine rather than enhance a brand's image, most marketers have figured out how to make the boom in user-generated content work for them. For example, the Coca-Cola Company initially played down the phenomenal success of the unauthorized viral video—viewed by millions on YouTube—in which Mentos candy is dropped into a Diet Coke, triggering a chemical explosion. Officials told *The Wall Street Journal* that while the video was "entertaining," it didn't "fit with the brand personality." However, the company subsequently decided to build consumer-generated content into its Coke.com site, tempering unfettered online expression with a carefully calculated campaign. "We give the structure, we try to give the guidance," one official explained, "but we're looking for consumers to fill it with content that's relevant to them rather than us talking to them" (Armano, 2006, para. 8). In August 2006, the website began featuring a series of monthly challenges that encourage people around the world to create videos in response to a theme. The first challenge on the site, "The Essence of You," asks, "If you could bottle the essence of you and share it with the world, what story would you tell?" Visitors can vote on each other's work, and the winner is awarded about $5,000 worth of video equipment and editing software. "We're bringing a global creative community together," explained a Coke spokesperson. "It's not just the U.S. creative teenagers uploading their videos. It's going to be everyone around the world, and you're going to see everybody's [stuff]" (Rodgers, 2006, para. 6).

Pepsi has made a similar commitment to such marketing, and its Mountain Dew DEWmocracy campaign is a prime example of how brands can take advantage of the many social networking features to engage and enlist users as brand advocates. The brand utilized Facebook and other social networking platforms to create a multilayered effort combining a variety of digital techniques, with users invited to help determine the flavor, color, packaging, and name of new Mountain Dew products. In addition to

the dedicated social network, the campaign includes a presence on Facebook and Twitter, as well as an online contest, a video social networking channel, a video streaming distribution service (USTREAM), and a branded YouTube channel (Cirillo, 2010).

In-Game Advertising and Three-Dimensional Virtual Worlds

Interactive games remain one of the fastest-growing forms of entertainment, surpassing even the movie box office in earnings (Thomson, 2010). Gaming takes place across many digital platforms in addition to the Internet—from consoles to hand-held devices such as Nintendo to mobile phones. According to a Kaiser Family Foundation study, video game playing has increased significantly over the past 5 years, primarily because of an increase in cell phones and handheld playing. Sixty percent of young people play video games. Hispanics and African Americans are particularly avid game players, spending significantly more time across all platforms than White youth (Kaiser, 2010).

Advertising is now seen as an important revenue source for game companies. Marketing through interactive games has become such a profitable business that it has spawned a new generation of companies specializing in the creative integration of brands into interactive games. In-game advertising is a highly sophisticated, finely tuned strategy that combines product placement, behavioral targeting, and viral marketing to foster deep, ongoing relationships between brands and individual gamers. Through "dynamic product placement," advertisers not only incorporate their brands into the game's story line but also respond to a player's actions in real time, changing, adding, or updating advertising messages to tailor their appeal to that particular individual (Gaudiosi, 2007; Shields, 2006).

Marketing is already shaping how new games are designed. At a conference on interactive advertising, software developers explained how they purposefully create games to make them "in sync with the brand," ensuring that images players see in the game are similar to what "they see in the supermarket aisle. . . [and on TV] Saturday morning." Games must always be "addictive," and should include a "viral component" as a "persistent navigation element" that is always a part of the experience, thus giving players "the opportunity to contact friends and urge them to play." The more rooms built into a game, the more opportunities players will have to "interact with the brand," enabling the game to foster "deeper engagement with users" (MIXX Conference, 2006). Finally, games need to be designed in such a way that they can be "continually updated" and facilitate ongoing data collection and analysis so that companies can know which "elements are being used" (MIXX Conference, 2006).

The next generation of interactive games could be even more powerful vehicles for engaging young people with brands. Recent innovations such as augmented reality, which deliberately blurs the lines between the real world and the virtual world, have made games more compelling, intense, and realistic. Through the use of virtual, computer-generated imagery alone or integrated with real images, augmented reality can create a vivid interactive experience that can be personalized for individual users (Barrett, 2010).

Three-dimensional virtual worlds are another important vehicle for marketing to children. These extensions of online "multi-player" games enable hundreds of players to interact in real time on the Internet. In recent years, virtual worlds have become complex, multilayered enterprises that combine many of the most popular online activities—such as instant messaging, interactive gaming, and social networking—into elaborate three-dimensional settings designed to engage users for long periods of time. According to a 2009 report by the Federal Trade Commission, "there may be as many as 200 youth-oriented live, planned, or beta virtual worlds, with these numbers expected to grow in the coming years." These immersive sites are very popular with children and youth, especially pre-teens (Federal Trade Commission, 2009).

One of their most powerful appeals is the ability for individuals to create their own online identities through avatars, which can then form relationships with other avatars in the virtual spaces (Bryant & Akerman, 2009). The use of avatars and other online identities is by no means new; scholars such as MIT's Sherry Turkle (1997) have been writing about these extensions of self into cyberspace for more than a decade (Wolf & Perron, 2003). But only recently have these various digital forms of identity and the worlds they inhabit figured so prominently in the strategies of marketers, who are seizing them as "a dream marketing venue" (Hemp, 2006). A growing infrastructure of consultants, ad agencies, and academic experts has moved into place to help companies take advantage of this commercial bonanza. "Once the stuff of science fiction," explains the website for the new-media ad agency Millions of Us (2007), "virtual worlds are becoming central to the future of marketing, technology, entertainment and brand-building." Indeed, these online spaces are increasingly being shaped by the imperatives of the marketplace, designed to serve as powerful vehicles for brand promotion and financial transactions. Buying and selling virtual "goods and services" has already become big business, with more than $1 billion being spent on them in 2006 (Hemp, 2006).

New Metrics

In response to all of these developments, the advertising industry has produced an array of "new metrics" to further refine the nuances of interactions between users and advertising. Specialized companies are routinely measuring responses to online videos, for example. "Audience interactions (views, stops, rewinds, sharing)," explained one firm, "are gauged by the millisecond and response can be measured, in real numbers. Advertisers who can combine that data with behavioral or demographic profiling, to reach exact targets, get amazing results" (RockYou, 2009).

A fundamental goal of interactive advertising is to foster *engagement,* which refers to the "subtle, subconscious process in which consumers begin to combine the ad's messages with their own associations, symbols and metaphors to make the brand more personally relevant" (Advertising Research Foundation, 2008; Nail, 2006). The concept of engagement is being operationalized into a measurable set of responses, which will enable marketers to precisely assess and further refine their strategies for influencing individual consumer behaviors. Described as "a marketing strategy that directly engages consumers and invites and encourages consumers to participate in the evolution of a brand" (Engagement Marketing, 2010, para. 1), the goal is not simply to expose consumers to a particular product or service but to create an environment in which they are actually interacting with the brand, befriending the product, and integrating it into their personal and social relationships. Through "cost-per-engagement" metrics (a form of performance marketing), marketers are paid through a fee structure based on quantifying "relevant, meaningful interactions" with brands through such consumer actions as "content creations or entries, reviews, votes, shares and plays of brand-focused content" (Brickfish, 2010).

The tools of neuroscience have also been adapted for advertising, creating a variety of *neuromarketing* techniques for measuring such responses as "degrees of attention, emotional engagement, and memory retention that consumers experience at the deep subconscious level of the brain," and to assess how "specific patterns of brain activation predict purchasing," the potential "shopping centers in the brain," and the neurological basis of purchasing (Dagher, 2007; Dooley, 2007; Knutson, Rick, Wimmer, Prelec, & Lowenstein, 2007; Sensory Logic, 2010). Through functional magnetic resonance imaging (fMRI), eye-tracking studies, galvanic skin response, and electroencephalography (EEG), marketers can hone their engagement strategies for maximum impact. Neurofocus, the leading neuromarketing company, boasts that its metrics are drawn from clinical methods for diagnosing mental illness and learning disabilities. For example, measurement for "attention level" is "based on the science behind ADD/ADHD clinical diagnosis;" "emotion" is "based on the science behind mania & phobia clinical diagnosis;" and "memory retention" measures are

"based on the science behind Alzheimer's clinical diagnosis" (Bush & Padreep, 2009).

Promise and Peril in the Digital Age

Marketing has become a pervasive presence in the lives of children and adolescents, extending far beyond the confines of television, and even the Internet, into an expanding and ubiquitous digital media culture. Youth marketers are purposefully seeking to integrate their brands into every sector of a young person's experience. The techniques that have become central to digital marketing constitute a dramatic departure from traditional advertising. Such techniques as in-game advertising, viral marketing, and user-generated commercial messages have combined to change the face of modern marketing—and with it the environment, both online and off, in which young people come of age.

Market researchers and ad agencies are actively engaged in efforts to perfect these new techniques, largely under the radar of a public that no longer enjoys the protection of the barriers that traditionally separated programming from the commercial content of the sponsors of such programming. The "message from our sponsor," in short, is now suffused throughout the programming. Nor are such messages limited to traditional content. The insinuation of brands into social networking platforms, for example, where they now have their own "profiles" and networks of "friends"—is emblematic of the many ways in which contemporary marketing, having all but obliterated the boundaries between advertising and editorial content, is inserting itself into our conversations as well. The unprecedented ability of digital technologies to track and profile individuals across the media landscape, moreover, and engage in "micro" or "nano" targeting, raises the twin specters of manipulation and invasion of privacy.

There is no question that digital media are also playing a positive role in the lives of young people. With the Internet's unprecedented, instantaneous access to vast global resources, children and youth have been able to seek out information on any number of topics, find like-minded peers, and connect with online communities. Digital media have become indispensable allies in the quest for identity, training wheels for social interaction. Blogs, social networking software, and webcams enable new levels of self-reflection and documentation of young peoples' inner lives. Many youth have eagerly embraced the Web as an electronic canvas to showcase their writing, music, art, and other creations to the infinite audiences of cyberspace. Three-dimensional virtual worlds are among the most exciting innovations in the digital media, creating a host of new possibilities for furthering education, fostering innovative forms of e-commerce, and promoting citizenship. The U.S. Centers for Disease Control and Prevention, for example, has not only established a presence on the virtual world, Second Life, but also employs a full slate of social media campaigns and tools as vehicles for promoting health education (Centers for Disease Control and Prevention, 2010; Weinreich, 2006).

At both extremes, then—as a threat to privacy and as a boon to civic life—the dramatic changes in media distribution and advertising technologies require a comprehensive and systematic approach to academic research and public policy.

Research and Policy Agenda

The explosion in interactive marketing during the last decade has occurred within a tradition of limited government and industry oversight in the United States. In many other countries, children's advertising has been strictly regulated, especially in television, where government-run broadcasting systems established restrictions and, in some cases, complete bans on TV advertising aimed at this vulnerable group of consumers (Valkenburg, 2000). In the United States, however, advertisers have enjoyed considerable freedom to target children, with little interference by the government (Campbell, 1999; Kunkel, 2001; Kunkel & Wilcox, 2001). In recent years, consumer, health, and child advocacy groups have been able to institute some marketing safeguards for children in the digital media. The Children's Online Privacy Protection Act (COPPA), enacted in 1998, was the first federal law to regulate children's privacy on the Internet, the result of an intense advocacy campaign by the Center for Media Education and other consumer and privacy groups. (As president of the Center for Media Education, the author spearheaded the campaign that led to COPPA's passage.) That law gave the Federal Trade Commission the authority to develop and implement rules restricting commercial website operators' ability to collect "personally identifiable information" (e.g., e-mail, name, address) from children under the age of 13 (Federal Trade Commission, 1998, 2006). In a separate effort, several years later, a coalition of child advocates was able to persuade the Federal Communications Commission to establish a set of limited provisions on the amount and type of commercial content allowed on Web pages whose links are displayed in children's commercials (Kunkel, 2006).

But while these rules established an important framework for safeguarding our youngest consumers in the digital marketplace, adolescents have no such protections (Chester & Montgomery, 2009). They are being socialized into this new commercial digital culture, which resonates so strongly with many of their fundamental developmental tasks, such as identity exploration, social interaction, and autonomy (Harter, 1990; Hill, 1983; Subrahmanyam & Greenfield, 2008; Uhlendorff, 2004). Thus, they may be internalizing and normalizing the marketing practices that have been so integrally woven into their everyday actions and experiences.

Recent research within the fields of neuroscience, psychology, and marketing has identified key biological and psychosocial attributes of the adolescent experience that may make members of this age group particularly susceptible to interactive marketing and data collection techniques (Leslie, Levine, Loughlin, & Pechmann, 2009; Pechmann, Levine, Loughlin, & Leslie, 2005). A number of scholars have challenged the notion that cognitive defenses enable adolescents to resist advertising (particularly in new media) more effectively than younger children (Livingstone & Helsper, 2006). Rather than communicating rational or factual appeals, many digital marketing techniques are forms of "implicit persuasion" that promote "subtle affective associations," often circumventing a consumer's explicit persuasion knowledge (Nairn & Fine, 2008).

Although fully understanding the variety of ways that commercial practices influence young people may be a long-term process, academic researchers need to play an active role in the current public policy debates. An international effort could bring together scholars, advocates, advertisers, policy makers, and youth themselves to create a framework that could help guide policies in various countries and regions. These, in turn, could be implemented in a combination of government regulation and self-regulatory industry guidelines. Rather than try to institute wholesale advertising bans or specify an age below which there are rules and above which there are none, we should develop a set of *principles for fair marketing practices* in the digital marketplace. If informed by contemporary research on child and adolescent development, these principles could help articulate the ethical parameters for the emerging social compact that governs the relationship between marketers and young people in the digital environment. Because many of the new practices have not yet been fully instituted, there is an opportunity to forge some consensus on which techniques are appropriate and which are not. Some of these new techniques may violate existing laws (Campbell, 2006). At the very least, marketing practices and research methods should be clearly disclosed to the public. There is already some international cooperation in this area. For example, the Trans Atlantic Consumer Dialogue (2009), a consortium of consumer groups from the United States and EU countries, has issued a resolution on social networking, including privacy principles for youth.

Finally, as governments across the globe consider appropriate safeguards for youth, it will be important to position young people in ways that acknowledge their unique vulnerabilities to marketing (including those described above) while honoring and respecting their rights as active participants (and important influencers) in both the media culture and the larger society. Too often debates—in both scholarly and policy arenas—have taken a polarized view of children and youth, seeing them either as victims who need protection against harmful content in a dangerous new digital world or as powerful actors who can navigate these new waters with no safety measures in place at all. Commercial interests have portrayed youth as immune to the marketplace—cynical, savvy, elusive consumers who know very well how marketers are trying to manipulate them. This view has helped justify a marketing culture filled with an array of stealth techniques and ongoing surveillance of teen social interactions. Policy advocates have focused more on the vulnerable aspects of the youth media experience, with some calling for protective ad bans (Buckingham, 2007; Livingstone, 2007). If we are to make progress in our discussions of young people in the marketing arena, we will need to find some way to balance between these competing discourses and consider youth in all of their multiple dimensions, embracing their agency as well as their immaturity and safeguarding their health as well as their autonomy.

References

24/7 Real Media. (2008, April 28). *24/7 Real Media becomes first network to deploy psychographic targeting from Mindset Media.* Retrieved August 4, 2009, from http://www.mindset-media.com/aboutmm-press.php.

Acxiom. (2009). *Digital marketing services.* Retrieved June 7, 2009, from http://www.acxiom.com/products_and_services/agency_services/Pages/Direct%20Marketing%20Agency%20Services.aspx.

Acxiom. (2010). *About Acxiom.* Retrieved June 7, 2009, from http://www.acxiom.com/about_us/Pages/AboutAcxiom.aspx.

Advergaming: The future of marketing to kids online. (2006, September 5). *Online Branding Voodoo.* Retrieved March 26, 2007, from http://www.brandingvoodoo.com/2006/09/advergaming-future-of-marketing-to.html.

Advertising Research Foundation. (2006). *Council on Youth Advertising.* Retrieved March 27, 2007, from http://www.thearf.org/assets/youth-council.

Advertising Research Foundation (2008). *Engagement Council*. Retrieved June 7, 2009, from http://www.thearf.org/assets/engagement-council.

Armano, D. (2006, July 10). *Coke-creation. Logic + Emotion*. Retrieved May 17, 2010, from http://darmano.typepad.com/logic_emotion/2006/07/cokecreation.html.

Barnes, B. (2008, August 17). Serving 3 brands: Burger King, Google and Seth MacFarlane. *New York Times*. Retrieved August 5, 2009, from http://www.nytimes.com/2008/08/18/business/media/18burger.html.

Barrett, B. (2010, February 11). Gaming's augmented reality future is one terrifying trip. *Gizmodo*. Retrieved August 26, 2010, from http://gizmodo.com/5469796/gamings-augmented-reality-future-is-one-terrifying-trip.

Berens, B. (2006, September 12). Anheuser-Busch speaks! Execs talk Bud.TV. *iMedia Connection*. Retrieved September 12, 2006, from http://www.imediaconnection.com/content/11159.imc.

Blackshaw, P. (2009, November 2). A pocket guide to social media and kids. Nielsen Wire. Retrieved March 16, 2010, from http://blog.nielsen.com/nielsenwire/consumer/a-pocket-guide-to-social-media-and-kids/.

Blackshaw, P., & Nazzaro, M. (2006, Spring). *Consumer-generated media (CGM) 101: Word-of-mouth in the age of the web-fortified consumer* (2nd ed.). Retrieved March 29, 2007, from http://www.nielsen-online.com/downloads/us/buzz/nbzm_wp_CGM101.pdf.

boyd, d. (2007). Why youth (heart) social networks. In D. Buckingham (Ed.), *Youth, identity, and digital media* (pp. 119–142). Cambridge, MA: MIT Press.

Brickfish. (2010). *You only pay for engagement*. Retrieved September 12, 2009, from http://www.brickfish.com/Pages/Company/BFSolutionCPE.aspx.

Bryant, J. A., & Akerman, A. (2009). Finding mii: Virtual social identity and the young consumer. In N. T. Wood & M. R. Solomon (Eds.), *Virtual social identity and consumer behavior* (127–140). Armonk, NY: M.E. Sharpe.

Buckingham, D. (2007) Selling childhood? Children and consumer culture. *Journal of Children and Media, 1*(1), 15–24. doi:10.1080/17482790 60100501.

Bulik, B. S. (2006, June 5). How MySpace is like word-of-mouth marketing on steroids: Marketing VP Shawn Gold explains the brand value behind consumer empowerment. *Ad Age Digital*. Retrieved October 2, 2008, from http://content1.clipmarks.com/content/AD5B0EE8-8F84-44CB-B786-541AFF398BA5/.

Burns, E. (2009, February 25). U.S. mobile ad revenue to grow significantly through 2013. *ClickZ*. Retrieved August 4, 2009, from http://www.clickz.com/3632919.

Bush, J., & Padreep, A. K. (2009). *Maximizing message impact for Alcon Laboratories*. Presentation at the 2009 annual national conference of the PMRG, March 8–10, 2009.

Buzz Marketing. (2010). Retrieved March 29, 2007, from http://buzzmarketing.com/.

Campbell, A. (1999). Self regulation and the media. *Federal Communications Law Journal, 51*, 711–771.

Campbell, A. J. (2006). Restricting the marketing of junk food to children by product placement and character selling. *Loyola of Los Angeles Law Review, 39*(1), 447–506.

Cartoon Network. (2006, November 6). *Advertising Age 360° Media Guide*, M14.

Centers for Disease Control and Prevention. (2010). *Social media at CDC*. Retrieved April 17, 2010, from http://www.cdc.gov/socialmedia/.

Chang, R. (2009, March 30). AKQA embodies new digital-agency model. *Advertising Age*. Retrieved June 7, 2009, from http://adage.com/digitalalist09/article?article_id=135583.

Chester, J., & Montgomery, K. C. (2007). *Interactive food & beverage marketing: Targeting children and youth in the digital age*. Berkeley, CA: Berkeley Media Studies Group.

Chester, J., & Montgomery, K. C. (2009). Interactive food & beverage marketing: Targeting adolescents in the digital age. *Journal of Adolescent Health, 45*, S18–S29.

Chivas Regal embraces cutting edge technology to launch MSN TV channel. (2007). *Fine Expressions*. Retrieved September 26, 2009, from http://www.fineexpressions.co.uk/chivas_life.htm.

Cirillo, J. (2010, March 11). DEWmocracy 2 continues to buzz. *Beverage World*. Retrieved April 10, 2010, from http://www.beverageworld.com/index.php?option=com_content&view=article&id=37525&catid=34.

Committee on Prevention of Obesity in Children and Youth. (2005). *Preventing childhood obesity: Health in the balance*. Washington, DC: National Academies Press.

Covino, R. M. (2006, March). Tapping into kids' touchpoints. *Confectioner*. Retrieved April 25, 2007, from http://www.confectioner.com/content.php?s=CO/2006/03&p=9.

CTC Music Mixer. (2010). Retrieved April 17, 2010, from http://audiomixer-d.oddcast.com/php/ctc//.

Dagher, A. (2007). Shopping centers in the brain. *Neuron, 53*, 7–8.

Dickey, J., & Sullivan, J. (2007, February 12). Generational shift in media habits: Advertisers must embrace change in order to draw new audiences. *MediaWeek*. Retrieved March 26, 2007, from http://www.allbusiness.com/ser vices/business-services-miscellaneous-busi ness/4846005-1.html.

Dooley, R. (2007, January 5). Brain scans predict buying behavior. *Futurelab*. Retrieved October 2, 2008, from http://blog.futurelab .net/2007/01/brain_scans_predict_buying_beh .html.

DoubleClick. (2009). *DoubleClick rich media and video*. Retrieved May 16, 2010, from http:// www.doubleclick.com/products/richmedia/ index.aspx.

Elkin, T. (2006, September 26). Study: Some 13–34s show high brand loyalty. *Online Media Daily*. Retrieved October 2, 2008, from http://publications.mediapost.com/index .cfm?fuseaction=Articles.san&s=48721&Nid =23744&p=328566.

Engagement Marketing. (2010). *Wikipedia*. Retrieved May 16, 2010, from http://en.wikipedia.org/ wiki/Engagement_marketing.

eMarketer. (2009a). *Marketers eye online video for 2009*. Retrieved June 7, 2009, from http:// www.emarketer.com/Articles/Print.aspx? 1006848.

eMarketer. (2009b). *How people share online video*. Retrieved August 5, 2009, from http:// www.emarketer.com/Article.aspx?R=1007111.

Federal Trade Commission (1998). *Children's online privacy protection act of 1998*. Retrieved April 30, 2010, from http://www.ftc.gov/ogc/ coppa1.htm.

Federal Trade Commission (2006). *How to comply with the children's online privacy protection rule*. Retrieved April 30, 2010, from http:// business.ftc.gov/documents/bus45-how-comply-childrens-online-privacy-protection-rule.pdf.

Federal Trade Commission. (2009, December). *Virtual worlds and kids: Mapping the risks*. Retrieved August 26, 2010, from http://www .ftc.gov/os/2009/12/oecd-vwrpt.pdf.

Gaudiosi, J. (2007, March 20). Google gets in-game with Adscape. *Hollywood Reporter*. Retrieved October 2, 2008, from http://www .hollywoodreporter.com/hr/content_display/ business/news/e3i898ca0de1754206ae43b dbc6ee2d9ffd (subscription required).

Hallerman, D. (2008). *Behavioral targeting: Marketing trends*. New York: eMarkerter.

Harris Interactive. (2008, May 2). *New Harris Interactive study: During economic downturn, mobile advertising seen as key to reaching on-the-go consumers*. Retrieved December 10, 2008, from http://www.harrisinteractive.com/ news/allnewsbydate.asp?NewsID=1310.

Harter, S. (1990). Processes underlying the construction, maintenance and enhancement of the self-concept in children. *Psychological Perspective on the Self, 3,* 45–78.

Hemp, P. (2006, June). Avatar-based marketing. *Harvard Business Review*, 48–57. Retrieved August 5, 2009, from http://vhil.stanford.edu/ news/2006/hbr-avatar-based-marketing.pdf.

Hill, J. (1983). Early adolescence: A framework. *Journal of Early Adolescence, 3*(1), 1–21.

Hughes, M. (2005). *Buzzmarketing: Get people to talk about your stuff*. New York: Portfolio.

Interactive Advertising Bureau. (2007). *Game advertising platform status report: Let the games begin*. Retrieved May 13, 2011, from http:// www.iab.net/media/file/games-reportv4.pdf.

Jacobson, M., & Mazur, L. A. (1995). *Marketing madness: A survival guide for a consumer society*. Boulder, CO: Westview Press.

Johannes, A. (2005, October 26). McDonald's serves up mobile coupons in California. *PROMO Magazine*. Retrieved August 4, 2009, from http://promomagazine.com/incentives/mcds_ coupons_102605/.

John D. and Catherine T. MacArthur Foundation. (2006). Building the field of digital media and learning. Retrieved March 25, 2009, from http://digitallearning.macfound.org/site/ c.enJLKQNlFiG/b.2029199/k.94AC/Latest_ News.htm.

Kaiser Family Foundation. (2010, January 20). *Daily media use among children and teens up dramatically from five years ago*. Retrieved April 7, 2010, from http://www.kff.org/ entmedia/entmedia012010nr.cfm.

Kantrowitz, B., & Wingert, P. (1999, October 18). The truth about tweens. *Newsweek*, 62.

Klaassen, A. (2008, September 8). Why Google sees cellphones as the "ultimate ad vehicle." *Advertising Age*. Retrieved August 4, 2009, from http://adage.com/mobilemarketinggui de08/article?article_id=130697.

Knutson, B., Rick, S., Wimmer, G. E., Prelec, D., & Lowenstein, G. (2007). Neural predictors of purchases. *Neuron*, 53, 147–156.

Kunkel, D. (2001). Children and television advertising. In D. G. Singer & J. L. Singer (Eds.), *Handbook of children and the media* (pp. 375–393). Thousand Oaks, CA: Sage.

Kunkel, D. (2006). Kids media policy goes digital: Current developments in children's television regulation. In J. A. Bryant & J. Bryant (Eds.), *The children's television community: Institutional, critical, social systems, and network analyses* (pp. 203–228). Mahwah, NJ: Lawrence Erlbaum.

Kunkel, D., & Wilcox, B. (2001). Children and media policy. In D. G. Singer & J. L. Singer

(Eds.), *Handbook of children and the media* (pp. 585–604). Thousand Oaks, CA: Sage.

Kuperman, J. (2006, March 15). Is it all about chicken slavery? How the Subservient Chicken set the bar for online ads. *Adotas.* Retrieved March 29, 2007, from http://www.adotas.com/2006/03/is-it-all-about-chicken-slavery-how-the-subservient-chicken-set-the-bar-for-online-ads/.

Lenhart, A., Purcell, K., Smith, A., & Zickuhr, K. (2010, February 3). Social media and young adults. Pew Internet & American Life Project. Retrieved April 26, 2010, from http://www.pewinternet.org/Reports/2010/Social-Media-and-Young-Adults.aspx.

Lerma, P. (2006, July 25). Is MySpace an advertiser space? *ClickZ.* Retrieved March 29, 2007, from http://www.clickz.com/showPage.html?page=3622942.

Leslie, F. M., Levine, L. J., Loughlin, S. E., & Pechmann, C. (2009). *Adolescents' psychological & neurobiological development: Implications for digital marketing.* Retrieved April 27, 2010, from http://digitalads.org/documents/Leslie_et_al_NPLAN_BMSG_memo.pdf.

Lieb, R. (2007, February 9). When all media emulate the web. *ClickZ.* Retrieved March 28, 2007, from http://www.clickz.com/showPage.html?page=3624926.

Lindstrom, M., & Seybold, P. (2003). *BRANDchild.* London: Kogan.

Linn, S. (2004). *Consuming kids: The hostile takeover of childhood.* New York: New Press.

Lippe, D. (2001, June 25). It's all in creative delivery: Gurus in the teen universe build a track record by gauging where the market is going. *Advertising Age,* S8.

Livingstone, S. (2007). Do the media harm children? Reflections on new approaches to an old problem. *Journal of Children and Media, 1*(1), 5–14. doi:10.1080/17482790601005009.

Livingstone, S., & Helsper, E. J. (2006). Does advertising literacy mediate the effects of advertising on children? A critical examination of two linked research literatures in relation to obesity and food choice. *Journal of Communication, 56*(3), 560–584.

M&M. (2010). M&M fun & games: Downloads: Wallpapers. Retrieved April 17, 2010, from http://www.mms.com/us/fungames/downloads/wallpapers/.

Marcus, H., & Nurius, P. (1986). Possible selves. *American Psychologist, 41*(9), 954–969.

McDonald's launching virtual world. (2008, August 4). *Virtual Worlds News.* Retrieved June 7, 2009, from http://www.virtualworldsnews.com/2008/08/mcdonalds-launc.html.

McDonald's new virtual world: More platform than website. (2008, September 19). *Virtual Worlds News.* Retrieved June 7, 2009, from http://www.virtualworldsnews.com/2008/09/mcdonalds.html.

McNeal, J. (1992). *Kids as customers: A handbook of marketing to children.* New York: Lexington Books.

McNeal, J. (1999). *The kid's market: Myths and realities.* Ithaca, NY: Paramount Market.

MediaVest. (2007). *Our leadership.* Retrieved March 29, 2007, from http://www.mediavestww.com/.

MediaVest. (2008). *We deliver value.* Retrieved March 29, 2007, from http://www.mediavestww.com/.

Meez. (2010). *Advertise with us.* Retrieved October 2, 2008, from http://www.meez.com/help.dm?sect=8.

Mermigas, D. (2006, July 25). MySpace a launch-pad for next-gen media biz. *Hollywood Reporter.* Retrieved October 2, 2008, from http://www.hollywoodreporter.com/hr/search/article_display.jsp?vnu_content_id=1002878693&src=bchallenge (subscription required).

Meskauskas, J. (2006, January 23). Ad networks crib sheet. *iMedia Connection.* Retrieved August 4, 2009, from http://www.imediaconnection.com/content/7937.asp.

Microsoft. (2006, May 4). *Microsoft to acquire in-game advertising pioneer Massive Inc.* Retrieved March 29, 2007, from http://www.microsoft.com/presspass/press/2006/may06/05-04MassiveIncPR.mspx.

Microsoft Advertising. (2008, October 29). *Young adults eager to engage with brands online.* Retrieved September 23, 2009, from http://advertising.microsoft.com/research/young-adults-brand-engagement.

Millions of Us. (2007). Retrieved March 31, 2007, from http://www.millionsofus.com/about.php.

MIT Press. (2007). The John D. and Catherine T. MacArthur foundation series on digital media and learning. Retrieved April 29, 2009, from http://mitpress.mit.edu/catalog/browse/browse.asp?btype=6&serid=170.

MIXX Conference. (2006, September 25–26). Interactive Advertising Bureau, New York City. Author's personal notes.

Mojo. (2009, June 12). *Dos Equis and Mojo HD Channel collaborate to produce original TV series.* Retrieved September 17, 2009, from http://www.mojohd.com/press/view/31.

Montgomery, K. C. (2007). *Generation digital: Politics, commerce, and childhood in the age of the Internet.* Cambridge, MA: MIT Press.

Moore, E. S. (2006). *It's child's play: Advergaming and the online marketing of food to children.*

Retrieved October 2, 2008, from http://www
.kff.org/entmedia/upload/7536.pdf.

Morrissey, B. (2009, June 1). Carl's Jr. makes
new kind of network buy. *Adweek.* Retrieved
August 5, 2009, from http://www.adweek
.com/news/technology/carls-jr-makes-new-
kind-network-buy-99446.

MySpace. (2008). MySpace media kit.

Nail, J. (2006, October 13). The 4 types of engagement. *iMedia Connection.* Retrieved October 2,
2008, from http://www.imediaconnection
.com/content/11633.asp.

Nairn, A., & Fine, C. (2008). Who's messing with
my mind? The implications of dual-process
models for the ethics of advertising to children. *International Journal of Advertising,
27*(3), 447–470.

Nestle, M. (2003). *Food politics* (173–196).
Berkeley, CA: University of California Press.

New Media Age. (2008). *NMA marketing services
guide 2008.* Retrieved August 4, 2009, from
http://www.nma.co.uk (subscription required).

Nielsen. (2009). *Americans watching more TV
than ever; web and mobile video up too.*
Retrieved August 4, 2009, from http://blog
.nielsen.com/nielsenwire/online_mobile/
americans-watching-more-tv-than-ever/.

Nielsen, (2010, February 24). *U.S. ad spending
down nine percent in 2009, Nielsen says.*
Retrieved April 17, 2010, from http://blog
.nielsen.com/nielsenwire/wp-content/uploads/
2010/02/2009-Year-End-Ad-Spend-Press-
Release.pdf.

Owyang, J. (2010, January 19). A collection of
social network stats for 2010. Web Strategy.
Retrieved March 13, 2010, from http://www
.web-strategist.com/blog/2010/01/19/acollec
tion-of-social-network-stats-for-2010/.

Pechmann, C., Levine, L., Loughlin, S., & Leslie, F.
(2005). Impulsive and self-conscious: Adolescents' vulnerability to advertising and promotion. *Journal of Public Policy & Marketing,
24*(2), 202–221.

Piper Jaffray Investment Research. (2007). *The
user revolution: The new advertising ecosystem and the rise of the Internet as a mass
medium.* Retrieved October 1, 2008, from http://
people.ischool.berkeley.edu/~hal/Courses/
StratTech07/Lectures/Google/Articles/user-
revolution.pdf.

Ramsey, G. (2009, Dec. 14). Seven predictions
for 2010 from eMarketer's CEO. *eMarketer.*
Retrieved June 7, 2009, from http://www
.emarketer.com/Article.aspx?R=1007416.

RockYou. (2009, February 3). RockYou adds video
to its ad network. *RockYou Super Blog.* Retrieved
June 7, 2009, from http://blog.rockyouads
.com/?cat=20.

Rodgers, Z. (2006, July 31). Coca-Cola tries the
CGM side of life. *ClickZ.* Retrieved March 29,
2007, from http://www.clickz.com/showPage
.html?page=3623010.

Romano, A. (2004, April 19). Tween and mean.
Broadcasting & Cable, 17.

Rosen, E. (2000). *The anatomy of buzz: How to
create word of mouth marketing.* New York:
Doubleday.

Schonfeld, E. (2010, January 4). JPMorgan forecasts a 10.5 percent rebound in U.S. display
advertising in 2010. *Washington Post.* Retrieved
April 17, 2010, from http://www.washingtonpost
.com/wp-dyn/content/article/2010/01/05/AR20
10010500516.html.

Schor, J. B. (2004). *Born to buy: The commercialized
child and the new consumer culture.* New York:
Scribner.

Schor, J. B., & Ford, M. (2007). From tastes great to
cool: Children's food marketing and the rise
of the symbolic. *Journal of Law, Medicine &
Ethics,35*(1), 10–21. doi:10.1111/j.1748-720X.2007
.00110.x.

Sensory Logic. (2010). *Research.* Retrieved
August 4, 2009, from http://www.sensorylogic
.com/index.php/research.

Sernovitz, A., & Stairhime, S. (2007, February 8).
Chrysler, Coke: New brand buzz leaders. *iMedia
Connection.* Retrieved March 28, 2007, from
http://www.imediaconnection.com/content/
13526.asp.

Shields, M. (2006, April 12). In-game ads could
reach $2 bil. *Adweek.* Retrieved October 2,
2008, from http://www.adweek.com/news/
advertising/game-ads-could-reach-2-bil-84837.

Starcom Mediavest Group. (2006). *Tapping into
the super influencer: What you need to know
to engage the elusive young consumer.*
Retrieved March 29, 2007, from http://www
.brandsirens.com/presentation.pdf.

Straczynski, S. (2009, August 4). Malibu Rum
serves up online radio. *Brandweek.* Retrieved
September 13, 2009, from http://www.brand
week.com/bw/content_display/news-and-fea
tures/packaged-goods/e3ida14248896111f7c
3f31386f4e38f3bf.

Studiocom. (2006). *Immersive online experiences.*
Retrieved October 2, 2008, from http://www
.studiocom.com/godeep/.

Subrahmanyam, K., & Greenfield, P. (2008).
Online communication and adolescent relationships. *The Future of Children, Children
and the Electronic Media, 18*(1), 119–146.

Subservient Chicken. (2004). Retrieved March 29,
2007, from http://www.subservientchicken
.com/.

Sulake. (2009). *Global Habbo youth survey 2009
uncovers American teens' unique attitudes*

towards brands. Retrieved August 3, 2009, from http://www.prweb.com/releases/2009/06/prweb2493344.htm.

Teens cash in. (2005, August). Fiscal Notes. Retrieved March 26, 2007, from http://www.cpa.state.tx.us/comptrol/fnotes/fn0508/teens.html.

Thomson, J.(2010, August 2). Internet and interactive games tipped to drive media sector growth. *SmartCompany*. Retrieved May 13, 2010, from http://www.smartcompany.com.au/media/20100802-internet-and-interactive-games-tipped-to-drive-media-sector-growth.html.

Trans Atlantic Consumer Dialogue. (2009). *Safety and privacy must come first on social networks*. Retrieved August 7, 2009, from http://tacd.org/index.php?option=com_content&task=view&id=149&Itemid=43.

Tribal Fusion. (n.d.). *Teen channel*. Retrieved August 4, 2009, from http://www.tribalfusion.com/channels/teen/index.html.

Turkle, S. (1997). *Life on the screen: Identity in the age of the Internet*. New York: Touchstone.

Uhlendorff, U. (2004). The concept of developmental tasks. *Social Work & Society, 2*(1), 54–63.

Valkenburg, P. M. (2000). Media and youth consumerism. *Journal of Adolescent Health, 27*(2–S1), 52–56.

ValueClick Media. (2008, July 21). *ValueClick Media launches predictive behavioral targeting*. Retrieved April 29, 2009, from http://ir.valueclick.com/releasedetail.cfm?ReleaseID=539255.

Weinreich, N. K. (2006, November 1). The CDC's second life. *Spare Change*. Retrieved August 7, 2009, from http://www.social-marketing.com/blog/2006/11/cdcs-second-life.html.

Williamson, D. A. (2008). *Kids and teens: Communications revolutionaries*. New York: eMarketer. Retrieved March 23, 2009, from http://www.emarketer.com/Report.aspx?code=emarketer_2000539.

Wolf, M., & Perron, B. (Eds.). (2003). *The video game theory reader*. New York: Routledge.

Yahoo & OMD. (2005). *Truly, madly, deeply engaged: Global youth, media and technology*. Retrieved March 27, 2007, from http://us.yimg.com/i/adv/tmde_05/truly_madly_final_booklet.pdf.

YouTube. (2009). *Demonstrating the branding and engagement value of YouTube advertising*. Retrieved April 27, 2010, from http://robertoigarza.files.wordpress.com/2008/11/rep-demonstrating-the-branding-and-engagement-youtube-2009.pdf.

CHAPTER 32

Public Policy and Private Practice

Government Regulations and Parental Control of Children's Television Use in the Home

AMY B. JORDAN
*The Annenberg Public Policy Center,
University of Pennsylvania*

This chapter explores how information, technology, and the increasingly media-saturated home environment all serve to shape the ways in which parents direct their children's television use. It focuses on whether and how public policies and advocacy efforts designed to empower parents affect the type and frequency of oversight parents give in this realm. In reviewing research on parents' control of children's TV use, it lays out the most common mediation efforts parents employ. Finally, the chapter asks: Have changes in media policies and technologies affected parents' practices within the home? Data that have tracked the availability of media in the home, parents' concerns, family rules, and the place of television in the overall landscape of electronic media technologies are used to provide answers to these questions.

The Regulatory Environment of Children's Television

The year 1997 brought a new look to America's television screens. New regulations governing children's educational television and a newly implemented ratings system created a virtual explosion of letters, numbers, and symbols in the opening moments of a program. Regulations and voluntary labeling practices came as polls showed parents increasingly concerned about the amount of sex and violence in the media (Hart, 1996). In addition, the general public's worries over copycat crimes inspired by the media and the sense of escalating violence in society were blamed, in part, on excessive violence in the media (Richey, 1996). Advocates and policy makers contended that new regulations and guidelines would empower parents to more effectively guide their children's television choices and would ultimately diminish the impact of the medium's problematic elements (Cantor, 1998). Television executives, though resistant at first, acquiesced to public pressure to head off what they feared could be more severe infringements on their First Amendment rights (Sullivan & Jordan, 1999).

The V-Chip

Section 551 of the Telecommunications Act of 1996 requires broadcasters to provide parents with information about programs on the air. The Act required the establishment of an advisory committee to "recommend procedures for the identification and rating of video programming that contains sexual, violent or other indecent material about which parents should be informed before it is displayed to children" (p. 103–104). Moreover, the Act required that television sets be manufactured with a "feature designed to enable viewers to block display of all programs with a common rating" (p. 104). Thus, beginning in January 1997, all programs on broadcast and cable television, with the exception of news and sports, were required to display a "rating." The ratings system is designed to work in conjunction with the "V-chip"—a computer device that has been manufactured into TV sets since July 1999. Sets with the V-chip can be programmed by parents to block out any shows that contain material that may be offensive or considered problematic. Viewers without the technology can review a program's ratings by watching the opening moments of the program or referring to a television program guide.

The Three-Hour Rule

A second federal regulation affecting children's television requires commercial broadcasters to "serve the educational and informational needs of children" (FCC, 1996) by offering a minimum of 3 hours a week of educational television and by identifying educational programs with an on-air icon. To count toward the 3 hours, programs must air between the hours of 7:00 AM and 10:00 PM,

must have "education as a significant purpose," and must be specifically designed for children 16 and under (FCC, 1996). Broadcasters may air somewhat less than 3 hours a week, but they must then submit to a full license review and provide evidence that they are serving the child audience in other ways. Programmers began airing 3 hours a week of educational and informational (E/I) programming in the 1997–1998 season.

Nonregulatory Activities

The legislative efforts of Congress (led by Representative Ed Markey, D-MA) and the Executive Office (under the leadership of President Clinton and Vice President Gore) were catalyzed by advocates, who demanded a more responsible media industry (Jordan, 2008). Founder of Action for Children's Television (ACT). Peggy Charren argued for and ultimately gained passage of the Children's Television Act of 1990, which laid the groundwork for the Three-Hour Rule (Jordan, 2008). The Center for Media Education (CME) and the Parent–Teacher Association (PTA), concerned with the impact of violent television on children, also provided both pressure and expertise during the development of the ratings system (Cantor, 1998). Their input ultimately led to the inclusion of the content ratings indicating violence (V), fantasy violence (FV), sex (S), sexual dialogue, including innuendo (D), and harsh language (L). It is unlikely that legislative acts such as the Children's Television Act, the Three-Hour Rule, or the Telecommunications Act of 1996, which mandates the V-chip, would have garnered the attention and the bipartisan support they required to become law without the insistence and assistance of child advocacy groups such as ACT and the PTA.

The work of advocacy groups extends beyond the passage of legislation and regulations. Parents must learn about the new information available as a result of the regulations. Thus, advocacy groups such as the Center for Media Education, the Kaiser Family Foundation, and Children Now have created outreach projects. Additionally, groups try to raise parents' awareness of the role of media in children's lives. The Center for Screen-Time Awareness (www.screentime.org), for example, is a grassroots organization that provides parents, schools, and communities with an organizer's kit that encourages families to eliminate entertainment screen media for 1 week in order to reduce their overall screen media use and consider leisure-time alternatives. (See Chapter 35 in this volume for a description of advocacy groups.)

The Reasoning Behind the Activity

Legislators, advocates, and academics who support advances in technology (such as the V-chip) and increased information (such as the ratings) work under the assumption that parents have been limited in their ability to protect children from the media's deleterious effects. New devices and new information, they believe, will give parents the tools they need to better guide their children's choices. Also presumed is that the natural inclination of the market and audience taste is toward the negative, potentially harmful entertainment and away from positive, enriching fare. Such assumptions give rise to the question of whether parents want and need assistance and whether these are the resources they need to effectively control their children's media use. It is therefore important to consider how parents have traditionally influenced the choices children make about television.

Mediating Television: What the Research Says

A review of research on parents' guidance of children's television viewing indicates that parents can and do act as mediators in the home in three distinct ways: (1) setting explicit rules (including rules about *when* children can and cannot watch, *what* children can and cannot watch, and *how much time* children can spend with a medium); (2) making recommendations (encouraging the use of media or particular media content); and (3) coviewing (monitoring children's media use by watching together). This section briefly considers the mechanisms through which parents might

intervene and sets the context for an examination of current uses of television in the home.

Explicit Rules

Explicit mediation has emerged as an important type of mediation (Jordan, 1990; Mohr, 1979). In a 1997 national survey of those families with rules, 91.7% said they prohibited certain programs; 75% said they required homework and/or chores to be done before viewing; and 68.9% said they limit the number of hours children can watch (Stanger, 1997). It is not always clear how active parents are in enforcing these rules, however (Dorr, 1986; Jordan, Hersey, McDivitt, & Heitzler, 2006). In addition, parents may be inclined to falsely indicate to researchers that they have rules because this response may be seen as the socially acceptable response. In one early study, 40% of mothers reported having rules limiting viewing but only 19% of their first graders said they had such rules (Lyle & Hoffman, 1972). More recently, Schmitt (2000) found that parents do not actively seek out information about programming for their children but instead make judgments of appropriateness based on their own viewing and their children's reactions. And while parents and children of all ages indicate that there are rules in the home about television, the third- to ninth-grade children in Schmitt's study said they can easily get around their parents' TV rules.

Valkenburg, Krcmar, Peeters, and Marseille (1999) argue that parents who have rules about content are more likely to worry about the medium's effects on their school-age children than are those who do not. This Dutch study involving 519 parents of children between the ages of 5 and 12 suggests that parents with explicit rules (which they refer to as restrictive mediation) are more likely to have concerns about television-induced aggression and television-induced fright. They point out that "it is likely that these parents aim to minimize the negative impact of television and that for these parents restricting what their children watch is the simplest, most direct way of doing so" (p. 63).

Many of the restrictions parents have for children's viewing involve children's exposure to violent content. Krcmar and Cantor (1996) found that 70% of their sample of parents reported controlling what their children view, and close to 90% reported controlling their children's viewing when violent content was involved. However, Holz (1998) found an apparent discrepancy between what parents say they "protect" their children from and what children actually watch. Her focus group discussions with children revealed that though rules are in place, they are often not consistently enforced—a finding that may partially explain the consistently high ratings violent programs receive among children.

Viewing Recommendations

Children indicate that their parents sometimes positively direct their viewing; that is, they make specific recommendations for programs they should watch. In one study, nearly 42% of 10- to 17-year-old children said that there are specific programs their parents encourage them to watch. Interestingly, the programs they listed were often not targeted to children but were programs for a general audience or specific channels such as the Discovery Channel or PBS (Stanger, 1997). As Mohr (1979) once noted, "although parents offered little guidance overall about children's evening viewing, they offered nearly twice as much positive as negative guidance about family sitcoms" (p. 220). To make recommendations, parents need to know the content and schedule of appropriate programs. Many parents of school-age children, however, do not seem to know enough about what is on to be able to recommend specific programs. In one study, parents of preschool children could readily list enriching or educational programs for their very young children, but parents of older children had trouble naming even one "educational" programs for their school-age child. Many resorted to listing a channel (e.g., Nickelodeon or Discovery) or a preschool program such as *Sesame Street* (Hart, 1996).

Coviewing

Parents can monitor their children's viewing by watching programs together, a practice often referred to as coviewing. Advocates and researchers argue that parents should view programs with children to monitor their children's viewing, help them understand the medium and its content, enhance the child's learning, and diminish the effects of violent content (Nathanson, 1997; Singer & Singer, 1981; Warren, 2005; Wilson & Weiss, 1993). Although coviewing is encouraged, it is not clear how often it occurs (Nathanson, 2002). The previously mentioned Dutch study found coviewing to be more common than restrictive (explicit) guidance (Valkenburg et al., 1999). Other researchers, however, have argued that coviewing is fairly uncommon (Dorr, Kovarik, & Doubleday, 1989; Lin & Atkin, 1989). Lawrence and Wozniak (1989) found that families almost never watched together and that, when children watched television with another family member, it was generally with a brother or sister rather than a parent. Consistent in the literature is the finding that, when parents and children watch television together, they are much more likely to watch adult programming than children's programming (Huston, Donnerstein, Fairchild, Feshbach, & Zuckerman, 1992; Lin & Atkin, 1989). This conclusion is supported by Dorr and colleagues (1989), who found that "coviewing was more common with older children whose preferences should have been more similar to those of their parents but whose needs for parental involvement were less" (p. 48). Valkenburg and colleagues (1999) argue that social coviewing is unrelated to the concerns about the negative impact of television; rather, "parents sit down with their child merely to watch television as family entertainment or as a means of spending time together" (p. 63).

Though many researchers have found that coviewing leads to important socializing and socialization opportunities (see Jordan, 1990; Lull, 1980; Messaris, 1986), others report that there is generally little or no dialogue around program content when parents and children watch together (Himmelweit, Oppenheim, & Vince, 1958; Mohr, 1979). Austin (1993), for example, cites a 1989 Gallup poll that showed that parents were "seven times more likely to turn the channel or forbid a program than to actually discuss the offending content" (p. 148). Nathanson & Yang (2003), moreover, have found that not all coviewing is equally helpful for children, particularly when it comes to coviewing of violent content. Adult commentary of the content, which Nathanson and others have labeled "active mediation," must be tailored to the child's developmental needs in order to be useful (Nathanson, 2002; Nathanson & Yang, 2003).

Recent television regulations and technologies have the potential to enhance parents' current practices of restricting, encouraging, and coviewing. But do they translate into increased parental influence over children's media use? This section presents a review of research on the current media environment of the home, parents' current mediation practices, and parents' awareness and understanding of regulations regarding one very important medium in the home: the television.

Parents, Children, and Television

Research indicates that television remains the most predominant medium in the home. Though in the past decade, new media such as computers, video games, and cell phones have had an increasing presence in children's lives, children still spend more time watching television than they do with any other leisure-time activity (Kaiser Family Foundation, 2010).

The Availability of Media Within the Home

The average home today has four working television sets, and a majority of children have a television set in the bedroom (Jordan et al., 2006). Though the American Academy of Pediatrics recommends that children spend no more than 2 hours a day with screen media, the average time children spent watching television is well beyond that recommendation. A recent national survey shows that children between the ages of 8 and 18 watch television for approximately 3.5 hours per day (Kaiser Family Foundation, 2010). Given the plethora of media through which one can watch television programs (including on the computer, on an iPod, and through a DVD player), it is

perhaps not surprising that only about 59% of this viewing is done on a traditional television set (Kaiser Family Foundation, 2010).

Parents' Concerns About and Oversight of Television

A 2007 national survey of parents found that a majority say they are very concerned about the amount of sex, violence, and adult language in the media, and many believe that such content has a real impact on young people's behaviors (Kaiser Family Foundation, 2007). When parents are asked about the concerns they have regarding their children's media use, television consistently tops the list. In one Annenberg survey, nearly half (43.8%) of parents said the medium of most concern is television (Stanger, 1999). The Internet, however, has also become worrisome for many parents. The 1999 shooting at Columbine High School, in which the gunmen were allegedly influenced by computer games and the Internet, provided one of the many "focusing events" that made parents pay greater attention to non-television media.

Parents report being more concerned about what their children watch on television than how much their child watches (Jordan et al., 2006). These data are supported by children's reports of their parents' rules. The Kaiser Family Foundation reports that just under half of young people (46%) say they have rules about which shows they can watch compared to 28% who say they have time-related rules.

Most parents report that they supervise their children's viewing a great deal, and a majority say they have household rules about television viewing (Jordan et al., 2006; Stanger, 1999). Parents also say that they watch television with their children at least once in awhile (Stanger, 1999). How effective is this supervision? One quarter of parents say their child watches inappropriate programs "sometimes" or "a great deal," while 29.6% of 10- to 17-year-olds say they watch shows their parents wouldn't approve of (Stanger, 1999). Despite inconsistencies in the efficacy of particular rules, the Kaiser Family Foundation study of 8- to 18-year-olds suggests that "when parents set limits, children spend less time with media. Those young people who say their parents have some rules about their media are exposed to nearly three hours (2:52) less media content per day than those who say they don't have rules" (Kaiser Family Foundation, 2010, p. 36).

Parents' Awareness and Use of Information and Technologies— The Case of the V-chip

National surveys indicate that most parents are aware of the TV ratings system and that a significant number of their children are aware of the ratings as well. However, only about half (53%) of parents say they have ever used TV ratings to guide their children's viewing, and only 28% say they use them "often" to make decisions about what children can watch. Parents are far less likely to use TV ratings than they are to use movie ratings (Kaiser Family Foundation, 2007).

The television ratings were designed to be read by a blocking technology known as the V-chip. Prior to the implementation of the V-chip mandate, which required that all television sets manufactured after the year 2000 have the device built in, a clear majority of parents supported the idea. In 1999, 84% of parents of 2- to 17-year-olds said they "strongly" or "somewhat" favor the V-chip and 71.9% said they would use the V-chip if they had one. Only about 1 in 10 (11%) said they would never use the V-chip (Stanger, 1999).

From 1999 to 2001, researchers at the Annenberg Public Policy Center (APPC) of the University of Pennsylvania undertook an exploration of the utility of the V-chip mandate for families (Jordan & Woodard, 2003; Scantlin & Jordan, 2006). They sought to answer a fundamental question related to V-chip legislation: If parents of school-age children have access to a V-chip-equipped TV in their home, will they use it to control their children's viewing?

Researchers provided a sample of families with 7- to 10-year-old children with V-chip-equipped television sets and tracked their response to the device over a 1-year period from November 1999 (before the mandate went into effect) to November 2000 (after it had been in place for nearly a year). A subsample of these families subsequently participated in a month-long trial during which they committed to keeping their V-chips engaged. A total of 150 families were recruited and assigned to different conditions of the experiment through a random procedure. Families represented a variety of ethnic/racial backgrounds and were from the Philadelphia metropolitan area.

Three distinct groups were created to explore whether providing information and training about the V-chip and the TV ratings would influence V-chip use. In the High Information group, 58 families were given a 27-inch, V-chip-equipped RCA-model TV. Mothers were shown how to program the V-chip in their new TV and provided detailed information about the meanings of the TV ratings. In the Low Information group, 52 families received the same V-chip-equipped set as the High Information group, but they were not given special training in how to use the V-chip. They were shown a variety of features of the television set, including the parental controls menu (which contains the V-chip), color options, and the sleep timer. In the Control group, 40 families did not receive a television set but rather monetary compensation for their time. Families were followed over the same period to see whether they would acquire and use the V-chip on their own.

Each family was interviewed twice by phone and twice at home. In addition, mothers were asked to keep detailed logs about their own and their child's media use in the home at two different points in time. The true purpose of the study was masked by the researchers. At the end of the study, parents were asked what they thought the study was about; only 11% correctly guessed its true aim. Over the course of the year, only five families from the control group acquired a V-chip-equipped set and, of those families, only two realized they had it. None of those families used the V-chip feature of their new TVs. The data presented below, therefore, focus on those families who received a V-chip equipped television set as part of the APPC study (Jordan & Woodard, 2003).

Do Families Find the V-Chip Useful?

Overall, 33 out of the 110 families (30%) who received a V-chip-equipped television

Figure 32.1	V-Chip Use by Philadelphia Experiment Families

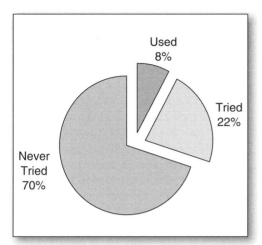

Obstacles to Families' Use of the V-Chip

As Scantlin and Jordan (2006) report, the overall low level of V-chip use makes it somewhat difficult to draw firm conclusions about the characteristics of the families who used the V-chip and those who did not. However, over the course of the year, families provided insight into why the V-chip may not have been more widely used. One significant obstacle to V-chip engagement was lack of knowledge. Initial telephone interviews with families indicated that several of the ratings were unclear to mothers. Only 7 out of the 110 families (6%) could name one of the ratings for children's programs (TV-Y, TV-Y7, or FV) and only five parents (4%) correctly identified the meaning of the D content rating (suggestive dialogue). Studies conducted by the Kaiser Family Foundation have found similarly low levels of understanding (Kaiser Family Foundation, 1998).

set programmed it during the course of the year. Of those families, nine families (8%) had the V-chip programmed and actively engaged when visited 1 year after receiving the TV. Twenty-four families (22%) tried out the device at some point during the year but did not have it on when researchers made their final home visit. Of these 24 families who tried the V-chip, 14 were successful in engaging it but opted to turn it off. The remaining 10 reported that they had tried to use the device but could not get it to work properly. Finally, 77 families (70%) reported that they never used the V-chip during the 1-year period (Jordan & Woodard, 2003).

Families who received detailed information about the meaning of the TV ratings and how to use their televisions' parental controls feature (the High Information condition) were significantly more likely to try the V-chip than families who did not. Thirty-six percent of the High Information-condition families tried the V-chip during the course of the year while 23% of the Low Information families tried it. None of the families in the Control condition that acquired a V-chip-equipped TV during the course of the study tried it.

Figure 32.2	V-Chip Use Across High- and Low-Information Conditions

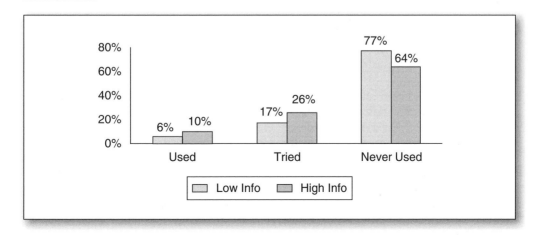

A second reason why many of the study families did not use the V-chip is because they did not realize they had one. More than a third of the families who received the sets (35%) reported that their TV could not block programs based on the ratings system, even though they were told during home visits that their TV had this option. In addition, programming the V-chip is a multistep and often confusing process. No fewer than five menus must be navigated and parents must move quickly or programming menus disappear. In addition, parents must be familiar with the symbols for the age-based and content-based codes. And, once the V-chip is programmed, the user must lock it with a password—a final step that several families missed (rendering their programming efforts useless, unbeknownst to them).

A final reason why parents did not program the V-chip in their new television sets was that many did not feel they needed it. Approximately one third (32%) of families who never tried to use the V-chip said that they felt they could supervise their children's viewing without the technology. Another 23% said they trust their children to make appropriate decisions about TV (Jordan & Woodard, 2003).

Changing the Landscape of Children's Television: The Case of the Three-Hour Rule

The task of monitoring children's media use can be daunting and frustrating. Parents say they have little time to closely supervise their children's media use. Moreover, the sheer quantity of media in the home can make it difficult to keep track of what children should and shouldn't be exposed to. Children with access to cable television can choose from dozens of channels and hundreds of programs specifically designed for them (Woodard, 2000).

The Children's Television Act (CTA) of 1990 was designed to increase the amount and quality of children's educational media available on commercial broadcast stations. It was introduced after a period in children's television history that saw the rise of the program-length commercial, and it aimed to encourage broadcasters to do a better job of serving the child audience with educational and informational content. Unfortunately, analyses of the broadcasters' offerings after the CTA's implementation found that stations were often relabeling existing cartoons and making dubious claims about their educational value. Kunkel and Canepa (1994) write, for example, that programs like *The Jetsons* were listed as educational and Jordan's (1996) analysis found that many of the most educational programs aired at times when few children were likely to be awake and in the audience. Ultimately, the CTA was found to do little to improve the overall landscape of children's television. By 1996, regulators were interested in clarifying their expectations of broadcasters, and the Federal Communications Commission spelled out what could count as "educational and informational" children's programming in a processing guideline known as the Three-Hour Rule. As with the original Children's Television Act, educational programming is defined as that which furthers the cognitive/intellectual and social/emotional development of children. With the new processing guideline, however, programs must now be labeled as educational on the air, must be specifically designed for children, have education as a significant purpose, be regularly scheduled and at least 30 minutes long, and air between 7 AM and 10 PM.

Has the Three-Hour Rule Helped Parents Mediate Children's Television Viewing?

According to a 2007 survey conducted by the Kaiser Family Foundation, parents tend to have a positive view of media's impact on children's educational development, and most are at least somewhat satisfied with the educational shows available to them (Kaiser Family Foundation, 2007). However, surveys with parents conducted in the years after the implementation of the Three-Hour Rule found that few parents were aware of the mandate for educational television, and virtually none recognized the on-air symbol indicating educational content for children (Schmitt, 2000; see Figure 32.3). Focus-group conversations with parents conducted by the Annenberg Public Policy Center found that parents were often working from a different definition of "educational" than broadcasters. Specifically, "prosocial" programs that emphasize getting along with others or self-esteem were not seen by

Educational/Informational
Programming

On-Air Symbol for

Figure 32.3

Source: From ABC's The Emperor's New School, 2010.

parents as educational per se, while school subject-themed programs that focused on math, literacy, or science were viewed as educational.

An analysis of the commercial broadcasters' educational offerings may provide insight into why so few parents are aware of the educational shows and why the parents don't direct their children to these shows. According to Wilson, Kunkel, and Drogos (2009), only 13% of E/I programs can be considered of high educational value, and nearly one quarter do not have any discernable educational value at all. In the years since the Three-Hour Rule went into effect, there have been fewer and fewer high-quality programs offered on the free airwaves. In addition, the majority of programs (67%) feature "social/emotional" lessons (which the parents don't define as "educational") rather than traditionally academic content. Finally, analyses of the 2009 season shows that violence is not uncommon in E/I programming—28% of the episodes were found to be high in aggressive content.

Connecting Public Policy to Private Practice

Increasing parents' involvement in their children's television use appears to require more than improving the overall landscape of children's television. Research described below

suggests several challenges to the use of appropriate technologies and information within the home environment. These challenges include: a general lack of public awareness of what's on for children; an overall low opinion of the value of the medium; and an ignorance or distrust of the information provided by broadcasters.

Parents Are Unaware of the Diversity of Options

Parents do not appear to know much about the quality of programming available once their children reach school age. They have difficulty naming any enriching shows for older children, and they do not recognize the E/I offerings (Schmitt, 2000; Stanger, 1999). One could argue that there are no quality offerings for children after the age of 5, but a recent content analysis by Wilson and colleagues (2009) suggests otherwise.

A study of industry insiders' and observers' perspectives on the challenges and opportunities of the Three-Hour Rule found that parents are not alone in their ignorance (Jordan, 1999). One of the most striking findings from interviews with industry personnel emerged when they were asked to name a commercial broadcaster's educational program for children of different target ages. The "experts" struggled and often could not think of an E/I show unless it was a program they worked on, one that had previously aired on PBS, or one that had been canceled.

The reasons for parents' unfamiliarity with programming are not completely clear, but they may be partially rooted in the increasingly complex media environment of the home. Not only do parents need to monitor their children's television use, many also feel the need to keep tabs on children's Internet activities and computer and video game choices (Jordan et al., 2006). What's more, recent surveys find that more than half of all children have their own bedroom TV sets, removing much of children's viewing from the visual oversight parents may informally provide (Kaiser Family Foundation, 2010). Thus, even though parents say they set up rules and at least occasionally coview with their children, children say they can go to their rooms when they want to watch shows their parents don't want them to watch (Holz, 1998; Schmitt, 2000).

Parents Have a Low Opinion of Television for Children

Despite the large quantity and vast array of programming available to children, parents have an overall low opinion of television for children. Woodard's (1999) analysis indicates that three-quarters of programs for preschoolers and more than one-quarter of programs for 6- to 16-year-olds are "high quality"—programs that contain some educational value and are devoid of potentially problematic content such as violence or stereotypes. Yet parents are correct in their perception that the majority of programming for children is little more than mindless entertainment. Two thirds of programming for older children was of "low" or "moderate" quality.

Parents may also be judging the overall quality of television based on what their children watch. Nielsen ratings reveal that children's favorite programs are not necessarily children's programs. Top-rated programs such as *Lost, 24*, and *Glee* have a sizable youth audience although the age and content ratings would suggest the need for adult guidance. Also popular with children are shows such as *The Simpsons* and *Family Guy*, which are animated programs meant for older teens and adults.

Parents May Not Trust or Understand Program Information

Analyses of the implementation of the Three-Hour rule and the program ratings for age appropriateness and content indicate that the information that parents receive may not always be trustworthy. Wilson, Kunkel, and Drogos's 2008 analyses of the educational strength of the commercial broadcasters' E/I programs reveals that, although many broadcasters have lived up to the letter of the law, there are still many shows that simply fail to convey anything educational whatsoever, even though they are touted as "FCC-friendly" programming. Schmitt's (2000) focus group interviews with parents indicate that few are willing to accept at face value the educational claims made by broadcasters. Similarly, analyses of program ratings suggest

a gap between what parents would define as suitable content for children and what the industry labels as age-appropriate. For example, Woodard's (1999) analysis of children's programs reveals that 75% of children's programs that contained "a lot" of violence did not carry the FV rating.

Conclusions

The research reviewed in this chapter indicates that, even though parents are concerned about the impact of media on their children, they have not yet effectively translated the new information and technologies available into greater parental supervision. To institute change at the household level, policy makers and advocates must provide more effective outreach to inform parents that the regulations do exist and can potentially be useful in the guidance of program choices. As important is conveying the information that parents have a right and responsibility to provide feedback to broadcasters who are not meeting their public interest obligations. If, for example, a parent does not believe that a program is meeting the educational and informational needs of children, this opinion must be passed on to the local broadcaster that airs the program, the network that provides the program, and the Federal Communications Commission that determines whether the station's license should be renewed.

It is also critical that producers and programmers of television for children become more reliable and consistent about the information they provide. Programs containing violence should be labeled appropriately. Parents and programmers together now need to play a more active role in promoting the high-quality, enriching fare. Not only should parents educate themselves about programming appropriate for children, but they should also take the time to watch these programs with their children. Broadcasters, for their part, should devote at least as much promotional time and money to their educational shows as they do to their violence-laden, toy-based properties. Perhaps then children will find and watch programs that are beneficial rather than potentially detrimental.

Finally, research must now begin to focus on the motivations parents have for mediating children's television use. There are now enough data to support many citizens' fears that television in its worst form can be harmful to children. Yet there is also accumulated evidence that most parents use a fairly light hand in guiding their children to and away from the set. It is, therefore, critical to understand the social, psychological, and structural obstacles that prevent a more careful and deliberate use of the medium. Only then can we truly maximize the value of this important agent in children's lives.

References

Austin, E. (1993). Exploring the effects of active parental mediation of television content. *Journal of Broadcasting and Electronic Media, 37*(2), 147–158.

Cantor, J. (1998). Ratings for program content: The role of research findings. *Annals of the American Academy of Political and Social Science, 557*, 54–69.

Dorr, A. (1986). *Television and children: A special medium for a special audience.* Beverly Hills, CA: Sage.

Dorr, A., Kovarik, P., & Doubleday, C. (1989). Parent–child coviewing of television. *Journal of Broadcasting and Electronic Media, 33*(1), 35–51.

Federal Communications Commission. (1996). *Policies and rules concerning children's television programming: Revision of programming policies for television broadcast stations* (MM Docket No. 93-48). Washington, DC: Author.

Hart, P. D. (1996). *Children/parents: Television in the home* (Survey No. 1). Philadelphia: University of Pennsylvania, Annenberg Public Policy Center.

Himmelweit, H. T., Oppenheim, A. N., & Vince, P. (1958). *Television and the child.* London: Oxford University Press.

Holz, J. (1998). *Measuring the child audience: Issues and implications for educational programming.* (Survey No. 3). Philadelphia: University of Pennsylvania, Annenberg Public Policy Center.

Huston, A., Donnerstein, E., Fairchild, H., Feshbach, N., & Zuckerman, D. (1992). *Big*

world, small screen: The role of television in American society. Lincoln: University of Nebraska Press.

Jordan, A. (1990). *The role of mass media in the family system: An ethnographic approach.* Unpublished doctoral dissertation, University of Pennsylvania, Philadelphia.

Jordan, A. (1999). *The Three-hour Rule: Insiders' perspectives* (Report No. 30). Philadelphia: University of Pennsylvania, Annenberg Public Policy Center.

Jordan, A. (1996). *The state of children's television: An examination of quantity, quality and industry beliefs.* (Rep. No. 2). Philadelphia: The Annenberg Public Policy Center of the University of Pennsylvania.

Jordan, A. (2008). Children's media policy. *The Future of Children, 18*(1), 235–253.

Jordan, A., Hersey, J., McDivitt, J., & Heitzler, C. (2006). Reducing children's television-viewing time: A qualitative study of parents and their children. *Pediatrics, 18*(5), e1303–1310.

Jordan, A., & Woodard, E. (2003). *Parents' use of the V-chip to supervise children's television use.* Philadelphia: University of Pennsylvania, The Annenberg Public Policy Center.

Kaiser Family Foundation. (1998). *Parents, children, and the television ratings system: Two Kaiser Family Foundation surveys.* Menlo Park, CA: Author.

Kaiser Family Foundation. (2007). *Parents, children & media.* Menlo Park, CA: Author.

Kaiser Family Foundation. (2010). *Generation M²: Media in the lives of 8- to 18-year olds.* Menlo Park, CA: Author.

Krcmar, M., & Cantor, J. (1996). *Discussing violent television: Parents, children, and TV viewing choices.* Paper presented at the annual conference of the International Communication Association. Montreal, Canada.

Kunkel, D., & Canepa, J. (1994). Broadcasters' license renewal claims regarding children's educational programming. *Journal of Broadcasting & Electronic Media, 38*, 397–416.

Lawrence, F., & Wozniak, P. (1989). Children's television viewing with family members. *Psychological Reports, 65*(2), 395–400.

Lin, C., & Atkin, D. (1989). Parental mediation and rulemaking for adolescent use of television and VCRs. *Journal of Broadcasting & Electronic Media, 33*(1), 53–67.

Lull, J. (1980). The social uses of television. *Human Communication Research, 6*(3), 197–209.

Lyle, J., & Hoffman, H. (1972). Children's use of television and other media. In E. A. Rubenstein, G. A. Comstock, & J. P. Murray (Eds.),

Television and social behavior: Vol. 4 Television in day-to-day life: Patterns of use. Washington, DC: U.S. Government Printing Office.

Messaris, P. (1986). Parents, children, and television. In G. Gumpert & R. Cathcart (Eds.), *Inter/media: Interpersonal communication in a media world.* New York: Oxford University Press.

Mohr, P. (1979). Parental guidance of children's viewing of evening television programs. *Journal of Broadcasting, 23*(2), 213–229.

Nathanson, A. (1997). *The relationship between parental mediation and children's anti- and pro-social motivations.* Paper presented at the annual meeting of the International Communication Association, Montreal, CA.

Nathanson, A. (2002). The unintended effects of parental mediation of antisocial television on adolescents. *Media Psychology, 4,* 207–230.

Nathanson, A., & Yang, M. (2003). The effects of mediation content and form on children's responses to violent television. *Human Communication Research, 29*(1), 111–134.

Richey, W. (1996, November 14). Group enlists parents to fight TV violence. *Christian Science Monitor,* p. 3.

Scantlin, R., & Jordan, A. (2006). Families' experiences with the V-chip: An exploratory study. *Journal of Family Communication, 6*(2), 139–159.

Schmitt, K. (2000). *Public policy, family rules, and children's media use in the home.* (Report No. 35). Philadelphia: University of Pennsylvania, Annenberg Public Policy Center.

Singer, D., & Singer, J. (1981). *Television, imagination, and aggression: A study of preschoolers.* Hillsdale, NJ: Lawrence Erlbaum.

Stanger, J. (1997). *Television in the home: The second annual survey of parents and children in the home* (Survey Series No. 2). Philadelphia:

University of Pennsylvania, Annenberg Public Policy Center.

Stanger, J. (1999). *Media in the home 1999: The fourth annual survey of parents and children.* (Survey series no. 5). Philadelphia: University of Pennsylvania, Annenberg Public Policy Center.

Sullivan, J., & Jordan, A. (1999). Playing by the rules: Impact and implementation of children's educational television regulations among local broadcasters. *Communication Law and Policy, 4*(4), 483–511.

Telecommunications Act of 1996, P.L., 104–104, 110 Stat. 56.

Valkenburg, P., Krcmar, M., Peeters, A., & Marseille, N. (1999). Developing a scale to assess three styles of television mediation: "Instructive mediation," "restrictive mediation," and "social coviewing." *Journal of Broadcasting and Electronic Media, 43*(1), 52–66.

Warren, R. (2005). Parental mediation of children's television viewing in low-income families. *Journal of Communication, 55*(4), pp. 847–863.

Wilson, B. J., Kunkel, D., & Drogos, K. L. (2009). *Educationally/Insufficient: An analysis of the availability and educational quality of E/I programming.* Oakland, CA: Children Now.

Wilson, B. J., & Weiss, A. J. (1993). The effects of sibling coviewing on preschoolers' reactions to a suspenseful movie scene. *Communication Research, 20,* 214–248.

Woodard, E. (1999). *The 1999 state of children's television report: Programming for children over broadcast and cable television* (Report No. 28). Philadelphia: University of Pennsylvania, Annenberg Public Policy Center.

Woodard, E. (2000). *Media in the home 2000: The fifth annual survey of parents and children.* (Survey Series No. 7). Philadelphia: University of Pennsylvania, Annenberg Public Policy Center.

CHAPTER 33

Parents and Other Adults

Models and Monitors of Healthy Media Habits

MARJORIE J. HOGAN
Hennepin County Medical Center

Parents' Role: Setting the Stage

Importance of the Parental Role

Parents and other caregivers of children and adolescents, whether grandparents, foster parents, community elders, or other adults in a parental role, are the most important models, monitors, and mediators of appropriate media use for children and adolescents. In our rapidly evolving modern society, churches and communities no longer are able or expected to be traditional cultural teachers for youth; the homogenized picture of American culture is provided through characters, plots, and commercials on screens and other media across the land. Years ago, respected researcher George Gerbner noted that our common cultural teacher was entertainment television, "a set of cultural indicators—symbolic representations of the power relations and human values of our culture" (as cited in Huston et al., 1992, p. 21).

Media messages and images are ubiquitous and penetrate deeply into the lives of children and adolescents. Over the past 5 years, the hours young people (8- to 18-year-olds) spend with entertainment media rose dramatically. On average, 7 hours 38 minutes daily are devoted to using a variety of media—a massive 53 hours every week. And, because these youth are skillful multitaskers, "they pack a total of 10 hours and 45 minutes worth of media into those 7½ hours" (Rideout, Foehr, & Roberts, 2010, p. 2). According to the detailed Kaiser Family Foundation study released in early 2010, over the past 10 years, use of every subtype of media, including television, video games, computers, and music, has increased except for reading. This leap in media use is fueled by an explosion in online and mobile media, notably cell phones, iPods, handheld video players, and laptops. Over the past 5 years, the percentage of children and teens owning an iPod or MP3 player has risen from 18 to 76% and laptop ownership from 12 to 29%. Of those between 8 and 18 years of age, 66% own a cell phone. Nearly all young people in this study (99%) report at least one television set in the home and a surprising 79% of these homes have three or more sets. Many children and teens (71%) have a television set in their bedroom, and a majority of these also report cable or satellite access (Rideout et al., 2010). And the youngest children? Those ages 2 to 5 years spend 32 hours weekly watching television. The slightly older 6- to 11-year-old age group, spending part of the day in school, still sit in front of the small screen for 28 hours every week (McDonough, 2010). Our children and youth live in a media world.

How do caring adults help youngsters navigate this media world? Parents can incorporate the lessons from their own experience, values, cultural traditions, and spiritual beliefs into a unique parenting style, providing balance with the barrage of media messages encountered by children. In our diverse American society, families from vastly different cultures, countries, and circumstances struggle to make sense of our shared media as they influence their lives and their children. In addition to being cultural teachers, parents know each individual child best. A parent understands the personality, the developmental path, and the special needs of a given child or adolescent. Children of different ages, distinctive temperaments, and diverse experience respond uniquely to media images and messages. For example, a preschool-age child who has recently lost an aging grandparent may be especially vulnerable to fears after watching a scary movie on DVD. A child living in a neighborhood rife with real-life violence from gunfire will likely feel more frightened after seeing stories about death on the news or watching a prime-time, violent, made-for-TV movie. Young people with learning disabilities may become more distractible after any time spent watching a rapidly paced action show; homework, or any task requiring attention and organization, suffers. Many young children enjoy a rich, creative imagination; savvy parents know that such children may have heightened fears after exposure to

media themes beyond their ken and control. Attuned parents provide guidance about and control over exposure to certain media offerings because they understand the strength and fragility unique to their own child (Cantor, 1998).

Parents are in a position to work with other partners invested in optimizing media for children and families. Many parents are integral members of PTA groups and can set the agenda for these influential local bodies. Parents and families form communities and, with collaboration and commitment, can generate neighborhood-based movements to sponsor "TV-Turnoff Weeks," alternative activities for children and adolescents, and letter-writing campaigns about good or bad media programs. Early Childhood Family Education programs offer ideal settings for parents of young children to converse about a myriad of topics, including strategies to approach media in the home and community.

For compelling reasons, parents are in the best position to guide children in appropriate and healthy media use habits:

- Parents can be cultural teachers for children, understanding the importance of family priorities and beliefs and how media messages and images affect the family.
- Parents know and have empathy for their own children's strengths and vulnerabilities.
- Parents can partner with others (parents, schools, and community groups) interested in optimizing media for children, including supporting media literacy in the classroom.
- Parents have the opportunity, through access and authority, to establish rules and guidance beginning in infancy and continuing through adolescence.

At Wichita State University in 1979, Philip Mohr reported that 85% of parents surveyed gave no guidance to their children about television viewing. He also found that, on Saturday mornings, 92% of parents provided no limits on television viewing, but 75% of parents established a cut-off time on school nights (Mohr, 1976, 1979). Two decades later, the Fourth Annual Annenberg Survey of Media in the Home found that 61% of parents supervised their children's television habits "a great deal," and 62% established household rules for TV viewing (Stanger & Gridina, 1999). In the Kaiser Family Foundation study in 2010, the majority of 8- to 18-year-olds report no parental rules about media content or time limits, with the exception of rules for computer use. Video games and music tend to be far less regulated than other forms of media. Sixteen percent of youth have absolutely no rules about media use, 26% report having some media rules that are enforced, and the largest group (39%) admits to parental rules about media content and time limits, but reports that the rules are not consistently enforced. Children and adolescents with some media rules are exposed to less media content than young people without media rules. The study also found that younger children, not surprisingly, are more likely to have parental media rules established and report that parents enforce the rules most of the time. Interestingly, parents tend to put limits on content (46%) rather than on media time (28%; Rideout et al., 2010).

The Kaiser study also analyzed the media environment in American homes, finding that many children and adolescents live in homes with an almost constant television presence. Whether anyone is watching or not, 64% of 8- to 18-year-olds report that the television is on during meals and 45% say that the television is left on "most of the time." Young people living in homes with television as an ever-present family member spend far more time watching live television (Rideout et al., 2010).

The Children's Television Act of 1990 mandated 3 hours per week of educational or informational (E/I) programming for children on broadcast networks; this seems fair, in that the networks enjoy free access to the public airwaves. Cautionary note to parents: The mandate has not been enforced, and networks take great liberties with the definition of "educational and informational." A Children Now study found that only 13% of E/I programs met criteria as highly educational, while 23% were rated minimally educational. Few programs featured positive health messages, and a substantial number (28%) included high levels of aggression (Wilson, Kunkel, & Drogos, 2008).

Brief Overview of the Effects of Media on Children

Parents and other advocates for children are becoming increasingly concerned about the potential negative impact of media. Understanding the existing research and experience regarding the effects of messages and images from various forms of media on children and adolescents reinforces the need for parental control and monitoring in the home. As Dr. Jerome Singer stated in the video program *On Television:*

> Parents have to realize that there is a stranger in your house. If you came home and you found a strange man . . . teaching your kids to punch each other, or trying to sell them all kinds of products, you'd kick him right out of the house. But here you are; you come in and the TV is on; and you don't think twice about it. (as cited in McGee, 1984)

Sometimes the impact of media exposure on young viewers is immediate and unmistakable (e.g., when a preschooler imitates violent karate moves seen on a favorite cartoon show or when children clamor for a certain sweetened cereal advertised heavily on network television). Usually, the effects of media on children and adolescents are cumulative, akin to a slowly growing stalagmite in a cave; over time, with repeated exposure to the same messages and images, attitudes and behaviors change.

Discussed in detail in other chapters in this book, several child and adolescent health and behavioral concerns may be associated with media use habits and choices (Christakis & Zimmerman, 2006; Committee on Public Education, 1999; Council on Communications and Media, 2010; Strasburger, Jordan, & Donnerstein, 2010; Strasburger, Wilson, & Jordan, 2009).

Numerous studies confirm that some heavy viewers of media violence learn to behave aggressively toward others, become desensitized to and accepting of violence, and tend to view the world as a scary, hostile place. In addition, violent scenes may provide scripts for imitative behavior and may increase a viewer's appetite for violence. The violent images and messages may be on television, video games, movies, computers, or any variety of media (Anderson et al., 2010).

Increasing concern also is being raised about the thousands of graphic, unhealthy sexual portrayals young people view yearly in the media. Only a few of these provide messages to vulnerable viewers about abstinence, safe and responsible sexual behavior, or the harmful consequences of casual sexual activity, including pregnancy and sexually transmitted diseases (Kunkel et al., 1999).

The rates of alcohol, tobacco, and marijuana use are disturbingly high for preteens and teens across the United States. Although many factors are at play, substance use and abuse are common themes in the media, as young viewers see characters smoking and drinking in advertisements, television shows, and movies. These images normalize and glamorize substance use; this is "cool" and "sexy" (not unhealthy) behavior.

Another example of a health risk associated with media use is the promotion and advertising of unhealthy foods (high in fat and salt, low in nutritional benefit) while telling young people that weight loss and thinness are important. Research associates heavy media use with the risk of obesity, and, clearly, hours in front of a screen means less time for physical activity.

Young people learn from watching the world around them and from the behavior of parents, siblings, other adults, and appealing characters in the media. Myths and stereotypes about gender, race and ethnicity, profession, and disability are commonly shown and reinforced in the media. How these issues are portrayed on the screen shapes children's beliefs about the real world, promotes schisms and differences, and defines success and influence.

With the well-founded concern about the harmful impact of media on the health of children and adolescents, the potential prosocial and educational aspects of media programs and products may be lost or ignored (Hogan & Strasburger, 2008). Public television, although grossly underfunded, features several high-quality educational programs for children of all ages. Selected programs for children, whether on cable channels or network television, also offer options for positive entertainment and

education. With parental or teacher supervision, children can explore new worlds and interests on the Internet, from pursuing hobbies to researching elusive topics to keeping current on international events. Software aimed at young girls is a burgeoning business, and similarly, several new teen magazines have arrived on the scene for girls. Rather than emphasizing dating and dieting, this new genre celebrates the many positive facets of being female: intelligence, athleticism, and self-confidence. When negative or harmful media products and programs are recognized and their impact minimized, we will be able to appreciate the untapped benefits and joys the mass media have to offer (Christakis & Zimmerman, 2006; Gentile et al., 2009).

Media Education Within the Family

The ubiquitous nature of media in our children's lives and the potential harm from exposure to media messages and images lead parents and other caregivers to turn to media education, or media literacy, as a simple and effective approach to managing media use in the home. More than schools, communities, or government mandates, parents are in a unique and powerful position to control, limit, and shape media use habits for their children through media education (McCannon, 2009). Parents can turn to respected, experienced organizations for assistance in understanding and incorporating media education into their homes and lives. The American Academy of Pediatrics introduced its national campaign for media education, Media Matters, in 1998 and has also published a policy statement on media education in 1999 (Committee on Public Education, 1999) and has an updated policy statement (Council on Communications and Media, 2010). Similarly, the National Parent Teacher Association offers helpful, relevant parent guides on its website in the form of specific tip sheets on various media topics (www.pta.org). The Center on Media and Child Health (CMCH) is a visionary nonprofit based in Boston aiming "to educate and empower children and those who care for them to create and consume media in ways that optimize children's health and development." The CMCH offers helpful articles on many media issues for all age groups, encourages readers to send media-related questions to the "Mediatrician," and publishes current research about media and children for both parents and professionals (www.cmch.tv).

For families, media education is the process of becoming selective, wise, and critical media consumers. Some of the components of media education, or media literacy, include the following (American Academy of Pediatrics, 1998; McCannon, 2009):

- People create (construct) media messages.
- Each form of media uses its own language and techniques.
- No two people experience media messages in the same way.
- Each media message has its own values and point of view.
- Mass media may be driven by powerful economic, social, and political forces.

Parents can teach and model these insights for children and ensure that media education permeates every aspect of life in a family. Media education is a lifelong skill that will make all of us better media consumers, whether we are enjoying a movie, reading a newspaper, listening to a political ad, or surfing the Internet. Children who are media educated should enter adolescence and adulthood with a healthy cynicism about media offerings. Is this movie worth the price of admission? Do I believe this political candidate's pledges? Why are young women's bodies being used to promote this brand of beer? How do I respond to this posting on my Facebook page?

Parents can and should use every opportunity to bring media education into the family conversation:

- Sitting around the dinner table discussing a newspaper article
- Planning to watch an educational TV show about Siberian tigers as a family
- Discussing a billboard advertising alcohol while driving to a family activity
- Coviewing a popular sitcom with young teens and their friends and "talking back" to the characters about their offensive dialogue

Media education, through filtering, questioning, and analyzing media images and messages, is fun and empowering for children and adults. Media education, when incorporated into everyday life, allows children to feel "smarter than the TV," savvy about advertising, and thus better able to evaluate products and be in control of misleading messages. Media education skills are also transferred between children; for example, if your child "talks back" to the TV about violence in a cartoon, this can have a powerful influence on a young friend visiting for the afternoon. When a child cries "Aha!" upon discovering the power of deconstructing a media message and passes that skill to family and friends, this is media education.

Basic media education principles for the family are simple and effective:

- Arrange your home to be a positive media environment.
- Establish clear, fair rules about media use for your family.
- Encourage active, critical viewing of media programs amplified by family discussions.

Pediatricians believe strongly that the home media environment is key to healthy media use and emphasize two simple points (that should also be asked by every pediatrician at every well child visit): Do you limit screen time in the home? Does your child have a TV set in his/her bedroom? (Hogan, 2010; Jordan, Hersey, McDivitt, & Heitzler, 2006; Strasburger, Jordan, & Donnerstein, 2010).

In addition to incorporating media education principles into the everyday life of a family, an understanding of the developmental needs and milestones of children and teens is essential to making positive media choices.

Infants and Children Under Age 2

This age group, according to the American Academy of Pediatrics (Committee on Public Education, 1999; Council on Communications and Media, 2010), should not watch TV; experts know that these very young children need positive, nurturing social time with adults and other children. Infants and young toddlers are exploring their world, forming attachments to the adults and other children in their lives, and learning through multisensory input. Experience tells us that reading with youngsters and providing them safe, stimulating environments to explore maximizes development. They need touching, tasting, manipulating, smiling (and receiving a smile in return), and kissing! Research and experience suggest that infants and very young children must securely attach to adults in their lives, benefit from exploring the real world around them, and need a variety of experiences, including playing with a variety of safe toys, exposure to books, physical exercise, and other multisensory, creative pastimes (Ginsburg & Jablow, 2006). Little ones require real-life experiences for brain development and for mastery of independent thinking. No accredited research is available about the positive benefits of TV for infants (although some producers tout television programming and even software aimed at this group). For these reasons, the American Academy of Pediatrics' policy statement on media education (Committee on Public Education, 1999; Council on Communications and Media, 2010) recommended no media exposure for infants and children under the age of 2 years—as early as 1999 (see Table 33.1).

New research shows the negative impact of media exposure on multiple domains of development of infants and very young children, including language, cognition, and attentional capacity (Christakis, 2009; Zimmerman & Christakis, 2005; Zimmerman, Christakis, & Meltzoff, 2007). Accordingly, the Baby Einstein video products produced and touted by Disney as educational for infants can now be returned for a full refund; the marketing was found to be false and deceptive, the videos potentially harmful for infant development (Campaign for a Commercial-Free Childhood, 2009; www.commercialfreechildhood.org). It seems prudent to provide little ones with the active loving and learning they need, not counting on figures on a screen to supplant parents and other adults.

Toddlers and Preschoolers

Parents should exercise caution with this group of children when it comes to media exposure. Toddlerhood is a developmentally fragile time when the business at hand is the emerging sense of selfhood, body integrity, separation, and individuation. Toddlers are susceptible to scary portrayals and cannot separate fantasy from reality: What they view on the screen is very real to them. Children in this age group need multisensory stimulation and a variety of activities. Encouraging imaginative play is far better for positive development than is the imitative play fostered by watching television (Singer & Singer, 2008). There can be some positive skills learned from carefully selected programming, notably on public television stations or on videotapes or DVDs.

Children in home-based day care are exposed to significantly more television than their peers in center-based child care settings (Christakis & Garrison, 2009). Parents should remember that in the 21st century, many children spend hours per day or week in homes and centers other than their own homes—media are present everywhere.

School-Age Children

The work of the child in school is challenging but rewarding, including the honing of language skills, thinking strategies, and study habits. Occupying too many hours with television or video games does not foster the literacy skills of reading and writing. Time spent with media steals important hours from interacting with friends, running and playing outside, and developing the skills to persevere at homework. Many young elementary-school-age children still do not distinguish fantasy from reality or understand the intent of advertising. And some children have special needs (children with vivid imaginations or fearfulness or those who lack consistent, loving adult attachments), making them more susceptible to negative impacts of excessive media exposure. Some recent studies reveal growing concern about the impact of heavy media use on children's cognitive skills, attentional skills, and self-reported school performance (Rideout et al., 2010; Strasburger et al., 2010; Zimmerman & Christakis, 2005).

Adolescents

Young adolescents trying to answer the central question "Who am I?" encounter

Table 33.1 AAP Media Education Policy Statement Recommendations

- Pediatricians should understand health risks of media exposure.

- Pediatricians should begin incorporating questions about media use into their routine visits. Advice to parents should include the following:

  - Encourage careful selection of programs to view.
  - Coview and discuss content with children and adolescents.
  - Teach critical viewing skills.
  - Limit and focus time spent with media.
  - Be good media role models.
  - Emphasize alternative activities.
  - Create an electronic-media-free environment in children's rooms,
  - Avoid the use of media as an electronic babysitter.
  - Urge parents to avoid TV for children under 2.

- Pediatricians should also

  - Serve as role models for appropriate media use
  - Alert and educate parents, children, teachers, and other professionals about media-associated health risks
  - Collaborate with other professionals, including parent–teacher, school, and community groups, to promote media education
  - Continue to monitor media and advocate for increased educational and prosocial programming and messages
  - Encourage state and federal governments to explore mandating and funding universal media education programs
  - Encourage government and private institutions to increase funding available for media education research

Source: Committee on Public Education (1999).

dubious role models and scripts for attitude and behavior online, in movies, through favorite song lyrics, and on television. Many teens acquire misinformation about sexuality and gender roles through media. Unfortunately, they may also define desirable body shapes and facial features by images on the screen and in magazines. As teens move through adolescence into higher levels of cognitive abilities, many still cannot separate fiction from reality on the screen. Socially, adolescents need face-to-face time with nurturing adults and peers. For some alienated youth, online companions or hours listening to music alone may take the place of real-life relationships. Although information on the Internet can greatly assist in finding information for school projects, and movies or video games can be the fulcrum for a social gathering, media should still be monitored and limited for adolescents. Adolescence is the time of transition from childhood to adulthood; the requirements for a successful journey are good physical health, challenge and success in school, the ability to negotiate and cooperate, and the presence of supportive, available adults (Ginsburg & Jablow, 2006).

New media—specifically online and mobile—play growing roles in "tween" and teen lives (Lenhart, Purcell, Smith, & Zickuhr, 2010; Strasburger et al., 2010). A startling 93% of adolescents are online (Rideout et al., 2010), and these youth stay connected with peers through texting on cell phones and updating social networking sites on Facebook and MySpace. Parents engage in a delicate balancing act between understanding these powerful, age-appropriate social norms and monitoring the potential downsides of social networking—bullying, sharing explicit sexual material, or isolation. A recent survey revealed that 4% of teens have sent sexually suggestive images by cell phone and 15% have received nude or nearly nude images (Lenhart, 2009). "Sexting" by cell phone or on social networking sites is best managed through family media education; one school district referred involved students for criminal prosecution, but appropriately, higher courts found this plan unconstitutional (*New York Times,* 2010). A recent study found that teens heeded online messages about the dangers of posting explicit sexual images in their social networking profiles; these teens altered their behavior (Moreno et al., 2009). Happily, savvy adolescents can glean important educational and psychosocial benefits online (Lenhart et al., 2010; Walsh, 2007) which include "developing cognitive skills . . . and perspective-taking skills" necessary for thriving in our complex society (Tynes, 2007).

Specific Roles Parents Play in Media-Educated Families

Keeping in mind the basic principles of media education, parents can play specific roles that work effectively within individual families. In becoming a media-educated (media-literate) family, flexibility, humor, and good communication are paramount. Media education is a process, and adults and children work together to optimize media use through the following guidelines.

Limit Time Spent With Media

For many years, the American Academy of Pediatrics (AAP) has recommended that children's and adolescents' media time be limited to 1 to 2 hours of quality programming daily, with no screen time for children less than 2. Each family, according to priorities, values, and interests, must define "quality."

Time spent with any form of media, high-quality or not, is time away from friends and family, active pursuits, creative play and hobbies, reading, and homework (Ginsburg & Jablow, 2006).

Media-educated parents and children can discuss establishing clear and consistent rules for media use, including finishing homework before watching TV, going online, or playing video games. Some families allow more flexibility with hours on weekends or during the summer, but well-enforced, respected limits on total screen time and on the kind of programs deemed appropriate are important bases of media education. Such limits are difficult to employ for the first time with an older child or adolescent; rules are best instituted and applied consistently when children are young. Parents should explain why specific media rules are instituted: "the violence in this program doesn't teach how to solve a problem;" "the language we hear on this program is very disrespectful to others;" or "there will be no video games until your homework is completed." This respectful approach to establishing guidelines for family media use teaches children and adolescents about parents' values and limits (McCannon, 2009).

Family ground rules for media should endeavor to maximize family time and optimize school performance. Individual families should determine guidelines appropriate for their home as follows:

- Establish media time limits for each family member, either on a per-day or per-week basis.
- Discuss the kinds of programs that are off limits.
- Homework and chores must be completed before TV or other media are turned on.
- Television should not be turned on before school or during mealtimes (or on school nights).
- Consider having "media-free days" once or twice each week (or "media-free weeks").
- Use a timer to help children remember when to turn off the television, computer, or video game.
- Avoid any screen time for children less than 2 years of age.

Choose Quality Programs

Whether television shows, films in the theater or on video, or computer software, choosing quality programs and products is an essential component of media education (Christakis & Zimmerman, 2006). Families should plan their media schedule actively and wisely (Walsh, 2007). If a program of interest to the family (e.g., a sporting event or a special on animals) is scheduled during the week, this show should be a planned, anticipated family event. Family media plans should reflect each family's value system, and guidelines for content should take into account ages and interests of family members. Some families may like to catch a weekly baseball game on television, while others eagerly await a nature show on public television. Another family may allot one half-hour weekly for a regularly enjoyed family comedy series. The salient concept is the "media plan" (DeGaetano & Bander, 1996).

- Why do we want to see this program?
- What will we get out of the experience?
- Is this program appropriate for family members?
- Are there activities we will forego?
- If more than one program is of interest, which will we choose?

Using a healthy diet as an analogy (Common Sense Media, www.commonsensemedia.org), parents decide which components of a "healthy media diet" will benefit their own children. Children and adolescents readily grasp this concept. We do not eat too many fat-laden foods because they are not good for our bodies, and similarly, too many violent or worthless programs are not conducive to healthy bodies and minds. To extend the analogy, excessive consumption of media (as seen in 45% of homes where the television is on most of the time) leads to an unhealthy amount of screen time (Rideout et al., 2010). Quality and quantity are key concepts in any "diet." Just as parents encourage healthy, nutrient-rich foods (although still in moderation), it is important to steer our children toward educational, positive media choices.

Parents concerned about choosing quality media products and programs for children are wise to consult a variety of available resources.

There are excellent educational or entertaining DVDs, cable television, or broadcast television programs available; a parent must only take the time to seek out and research these products.

- Create a collection of videotapes and DVDs or borrow them from the local library; the public library is a rich resource for parents.
- Check websites for organizations with suggestions for educational DVDs or video games (www.cmch.tv; www.commonsense media.org; National Institute on Media and the Family, www.mediafamily.org).
- Several organizations create newsletters for parents that contain suggestions for educational or entertaining products for children.

Children Now, reviewing the state of E/I programming, list six criteria of highly educational children's TV shows. Parents can use these criteria in choosing programming for the family (and should notify the FCC if the standards are not met; Wilson et al., 2008)

- *Clarity*—what is the primary lesson?
- *Integration*—how well is the primary lesson woven into the program?
- *Involvement*—how engaging and interesting is the lesson?
- *Applicability*—is the lesson relevant to the real world?
- *Importance*—how valuable/useful is the primary lesson to the child?
- *Positive reinforcement*—is effort or successful learning rewarded?

With creativity and planning, television and other media programs can be positive learning experiences for children and adults (Christakis & Zimmerman, 2006). Parents can use a television image as a window of opportunity for reinforcing a family belief or dispelling a stereotype. Many shows transport children to new lands and allow a wide range of experience; parents can amplify these programs with simple observations and discussions. Some simple guidelines for choosing television programs, movies, or videos for children include the following:

- Seek programs without gender, racial, ethnic, or other negative, stereotypic portrayals.
- Choose programs that foster discussion.

- Choose programs that are consistent with your family beliefs and priorities.
- Select a program that will teach your child something new or exciting.

Selected video games and computer software programs can educate, stimulate, and reinforce family, prosocial values. Easily available online resources offer help to parents when selecting products for their children (www .mediafamily.org; www.pta.org; Public Broadcasting Service, www.pbs.org/parents/children andmedia).

- Games should require mental ability, not just a quick finger.
- Thought and problem-solving skills should be challenged.
- Ideally, skills should be applicable to real life.
- Games should enhance creativity and curiosity.
- Games with violent or sexual themes should be avoided.

As important as choosing appropriate programs and products, parents also may have to act as censors within the home, forbidding inappropriate programming for some children in some age groups. This could include: the evening newscast, often featuring lurid or violent current events ("if it bleeds, it leads"); prime-time television shows; daytime "tell-all" or the new genre of "reality" television shows; or some music television.

Anecdotally, many adolescents under age 17 attend (or rent) popular R-rated movies. Movie theaters and managers are ill equipped to check the ages of all theater patrons, and many young people slip into inappropriate movies without parental consent. Others purchase tickets to PG or PG-13 movies and attend the R-rated feature instead. Still more bothersome, many parents bring young children to R-rated movies rife with violence, graphic sexual themes, and lurid language, perhaps not realizing the potential impact on the immature viewer. Choosing appropriate media content and programming for children and teens extends to the movie theater. Firm, consistent parental rules and optimal surveillance by theater workers are important measures to ensure appropriate exposure.

Be a Positive Media Role Model

Parental roles of guiding children toward positive media choices and forbidding inappropriate media will help them to internalize the concept of choosing quality programs and products by themselves.

Children learn through imitation and reinforcement; media habits are no exception. If parents (the primary role models) hope to engender positive media habits in children, they must limit their own time in front of the screen and model planning and their own good choices in their lives (Jordan et al., 2006). Parents who value active pursuits, love to read, enjoy time with friends and family, and tackle new hobbies with enthusiasm teach children far more powerful lessons than words ever could. In a related memo to pediatricians: Those who use more media themselves are more reluctant to recommend limiting media exposure for their young patients (Gentile et al., 2004).

Arrange Your Home to Be a Positive Media Environment

If the television sits on the dining room table and is on during dinner, if the computer is squirreled away in your daughter's bedroom, if each of your children has a personal television set in his or her bedroom, all of these media habits reinforce negative behaviors. Some simple, effective guidelines ensure a positive media environment in every home (Jordan et al., 2006; Walsh, 2007).

- Avoid having computers or television sets in children's bedrooms; having a central, family media area encourages coviewing and discussion and limits aimless time in front of the screen.
- If at all possible, television should not be used as an "electronic babysitter." Although child-care issues are extremely challenging for busy parents, safe, creative alternatives are preferred.
- Experts rightly believe that regular family time is important glue for today's busy families. Having the television on during mealtimes precludes a routine time for togetherness in many households; the TV should be off during meals.

- TV should not be used as "background noise." If not being accessed in a planned manner, the television should be off.
- TV and other media (computers, video games) should not be used as a reward or punishment; then, the medium assumes much greater importance in a child's worldview.
- Homework and other obligatory activities, such as chores, must be completed satisfactorily before media can be accessed.

Experience Media With Your Children: Encourage Media Education

Research teaches us that parents "coviewing" television programs and using other media products with their children are critical components of media education (Nathanson & Cantor, 2000). Knowing what their children are watching allows parents to be involved in choices, to make priorities clear, and to encourage media literacy. A coviewing parent, through astute observations and questions about media messages, can make a poor program a learning experience, whereas a wonderful program watched by a child without a parent in attendance may be a wasted opportunity for learning and enjoyment.

Another oft-suggested strategy of media literacy is to actively watch with children. Research on giving them information before, during, or after they experience media produces some interesting results. Short media-literacy "moments" while experiencing media can influence active cognition rather than passive absorption, which can empower decision making (McCannon, 2009).

Coviewing can:

- Influence a child's judgment about the representation of TV characters
- Facilitate children's understanding of plots and story lines
- Mediate potentially harmful effects of aggressive and violent content (when adult disapproval is expressed and discussion of nonviolent values is advanced)

The "4 Cs" (DeGaetano & Bander, 1996), detailed below, help parents think about encouraging media-educated children: critical thinking and viewing, communication, creativity, and choices.

Critical Thinking and Viewing

These are cornerstones of media education. (See Chapter 34 on media literacy in this volume). A child who is able to analyze media messages, "talk back" to characters and images, and dissect programs is truly media literate. These skills are lifelong and will serve children well through youth and into adulthood. Examples of critical thinking and viewing include the following:

- *Discuss and dissect violent scenes in cartoons, movies, programs, and previews.* Parents coviewing such a scene can seize the opportunity to talk with a child about alternative conflict-resolution techniques, the technology used to "fake" scary or violent scenes, and voice disapproval of the violence.
- *Discuss stereotypic portrayals of female characters in situation comedies or primetime shows.* Parents can propose alternative character traits and strengths and dispel prevalent myths about gender.
- *Discuss the portrayal of persons of color, the elderly, or people with disabilities on television shows.* Coviewing adults have the opportunity to point out that media misrepresent the real world and can engage children in dialogue about more realistic views of society.
- *Discuss the overemphasis on police officers, lawyers, and doctors as professionals on television.* Where is everyone else?
- *Discuss techniques used in advertisements for beer, cars, candy, or toys.* How does the advertiser "grab" our attention? Do we get all the information we need, or is anything left out?
- *Analyze the presentation of news stories.* Why do violent news events lead the newscast? How are people involved in the news interviewed? Do we receive all the pertinent information? How do news producers grab our attention?

Helping children become critical thinkers and viewers is facilitated by thoughtful questions posed by parents. The behind-the-scenes and technical/creative aspects of media production offer great opportunities for discussion and insight (McCannon, 2009).

- Describe the people involved in creating the media message (writers, photographers, producers, special effects people, and advertisers).
- Talk about the visual effects, sound effects, and other special techniques used in creating the media message.
- Discuss the purpose of the message. Is the purpose to urge you to buy something? To entertain you? To inform you?
- What does the child or teen viewer think about the message?
- Encourage children to notice details of programs (e.g., clothing, scenery, characteristics of people involved, and time of year), sequence or plot, cause and effect, and symbolism.
- Challenge young viewers to predict the outcome of media messages, whether programs or advertisements, and to infer why characters behave the way they do.

Deconstruction, or dissection, of media is fun and instructive. This technique works for television programs, advertisements, movies, video games, and music lyrics—all forms of media. The only skills parents need to encourage critical thinking are communication and creativity.

Communication

Family discussions about media make critical thinking the valuable exercise that it is. Encouraging children and adolescents to share their ideas in an interested, supportive manner is part of media education. Media-educated children are likely to share their insights with a friend or sibling. Once children feel comfortable with the basics of media education and critical thinking, they will incorporate their skills into everyday life, applying a critical eye to media messages and images all around. Parents and children who openly and honestly discuss media messages and images can parlay these skills into a willingness to discuss all manner of hot topics.

Creativity

Parents become excited about media education as they see their efforts come to fruition through the enlightenment of children. Creativity is an essential aspect of media education, making the process even more rewarding for the family. Creativity involves weaving media education skills into everyday life, suggesting new and fun ways to interact with media using the family's collective imagination

to manage media in the home. The ideas for incorporating creativity into media education are limitless and include the following:

- Borrow a book from the library about a movie or program you plan to watch on television and read aloud in preparation for the event.
- Dress in costumes reflecting a movie the family plans to watch.
- Allow each family member (no matter how old) to lead a discussion after a family-watched television program or movie.
- Turn off the TV sound and make up your own family dialogue.
- Design your own commercials for a favorite product.
- Create counter-advertisements for unhealthy products such as beer or tobacco.
- Turn off a movie on videotape or DVD before the ending and have each family member predict the ending.
- Put on a family play and videotape the event.

Creativity also means pursuing nonmedia activities with gusto: taking family field trips to local zoos and museums, reading nightly from a chapter of a book, engaging in cooking adventures, and allowing time to daydream.

Choices

As emphasized above, making active, positive media choices is a key part of media education. Whether browsing the Internet, renting videos at the local store or online, or hunkering down for a night of television, media use should be a limited, planned, and conscious activity, and only a small slice of the life of an active, creative, curious child.

Understand and Use Current Ratings Systems

For many years, the age-based Motion Picture Association of America (MPAA) ratings system has been in place for movies produced in the United States, and parents, over the years, have become familiar with the meaning behind a G-, PG-, PG-13-, R-, or NC-17-rated film. (See Chapter 30 in this volume on ratings.) This familiarity with the ratings does not imply that parents always agree with the ratings; in fact, studies have shown that a significant percentage of parents disagree. Many professional organizations, as well as parents, would still prefer a content-based ratings system for all forms of media (Gentile, Humphrey, & Walsh, 2005; Strasburger et al., 2009).

In 1997, the television industry, under pressure from parents, advocacy groups, and some government leaders, instituted an age-based ratings system for many television programs. This system, reminiscent of the MPAA system for movies, allows producers to voluntarily rate their own shows (Cantor, 1998; Gentile et al., 2005).

With the advent of the highly touted V-chip, parents with this technology are able to block certain undesirable programs in their homes. However, the television rating system is far from ideal: News and sports programs are not rated; not all networks agreed to use the system; and the programs are still rated by a not-disinterested producer. Only the most intense level of content is displayed on the TV screen and determines the overall rating; content existing at lower levels is not displayed (Cantor, 1998). In addition, the rating flashes on the screen at the beginning of the program and may be missed by parents. For undesirable Internet content, various blocking software has been developed; this may be effective technology for some adult sites. No blocking software is completely effective or foolproof, and sometimes, informational sites are inappropriately blocked (Strasburger et al., 2009).

Some video games and software also carry voluntary ratings for parents to use in deciding about the suitability of a product for a child (Strasburger et al., 2009). The Entertainment Software Association (which established the Entertainment Software Rating Board or ESRB) developed a ratings system in response to a request made during congressional hearings held on the subject in 1994 (see Table 33.2). Research shows that 87% of parents with children who play video game are aware of the ESRB rating system, and 76% say they regularly check the rating before buying computer and video games for their children (Federal Trade Commission, 2007; www.ftc.gov). The ESRB ratings for video and computer games include age-based rating symbols that appear on the front of the box and content descriptors that appear on the back of the box and indicate elements in a game that may have triggered a particular

rating and/or may be of interest or concern. For example, an E10+ rating indicates that a game has "content that may be suitable for ages 10 and older" and "may contain more cartoon, fantasy or mild violence, mild language and/or minimal suggestive themes" (Entertainment Software Rating Board, 2010). Additionally, more than 30 content descriptors are applied to games that warrant them, ranging from Fantasy Violence and Intense Violence to Sexual Themes and Strong Language (Entertainment Software Rating Board, 2010). Similarly, music CDs may carry labels warning about explicit lyrics, once again as a cue for concerned parents. Some products also include the lyrics in narrative form. This is a mixed blessing; in the case of explicit or suggestive music lyrics, many young people are unaware of the meaning of these lyrics (or do not catch the lyrics at all)!

Studies have shown that, for some children (particularly young boys), a mature rating, whether for television or movies, increases the young viewer's incentive to watch the show or movie—the "forbidden fruit" quandary (Cantor, 1998). Ratings, including video game ratings, do not predict the appropriateness of a product or program for a particular child. These shortcomings underscore the important role parents play in mediating the media choices of children. Whether a television show or movie is rated G or higher, or a video game is rated E for everyone, a parent knows the unique fears and sensitivities of a child or adolescent and should exercise the option of forbidding viewing of that program or playing that video game. Similarly, in some cases, a show with a prohibitive rating may be appropriate or educational at a given time and place for a given child. For example, a historical TV program on the Holocaust, the civil rights movement, or other major events, violence not withstanding, may be a rich experience for a child coviewing with an interested parent.

Encourage Alternative Activities to Electronic Media

Hours in front of a screen mean time is not being spent with a good book, friends, coloring materials, or an active outdoor game.

Table 33.2	ESRB Ratings for Computer and Video Games
EC	**Early Childhood**: Titles rated EC have content that may be suitable for ages 3 and older. Contains no material a parent would find inappropriate.
E	**Everyone:** Titles rated E have content that may be suitable for ages 6 and older. Titles in this category may contain minimal cartoon, fantasy, or mild violence and/or frequent use of mild language.
E10+	**Everyone 10+:** Titles rated E10+ have content that may be suitable for ages 10 and older. Titles in this category may contain more cartoon, fantasy, or mild violence, mild language, and/or minimal suggestive themes.
T	**Teen:** Titles rated T have content that may be suitable for ages 13 and older. Titles in this category may contain violence, suggestive themes, crude humor, minimal blood, simulated gambling, and/or infrequent use of strong language.
M	**Mature**: Titles rated M have content that may be suitable for persons ages 17 and older. Titles in this category may contain intense violence, blood and gore, sexual content, and/or strong language.
AO	**Adults Only:** Titles rated AO have content that should only be played by persons 18 and older. Titles in this category may include prolonged scenes of intense violence and/or graphic sexual content, and nudity.
RP	**Rating Pending**: Titles listed as RP are awaiting final rating by the ESRB.

Source: Entertainment Software Rating Board (2010).

Parents interested in media literacy also encourage activities unrelated to media, building strong bodies, agile minds, and lasting relationships (Ginsburg & Jablow, 2006). Research tells us that children who are regular or heavy viewers of TV tend to engage in scripted, imitative play, suggested by characters or plots in favorite programs. Playing freely and creatively, making up scenarios, characters, and plot lines is conducive to developing a rich imagination. Whether building with clay or mud, writing a story, crafting a village out of blocks, or playing dress-up, creative pursuits allow children to unlock minds and imaginations, exploring the possibilities offered in their environment (Singer & Singer, 2008). Television and other media activities are generally passive: Viewers watch make-believe characters living their scripted lives.

Parents should read to children beginning in early infancy, sharing a love of books with an assortment of characters and plots. Reading aloud fosters listening skills, an active imagination, ease with language, an introduction to symbols, and a love of books for life. Parents should also encourage children to read alone.

Providing a library card or regularly adding editions to the home bookshelves enables children and adolescents to curl up with a book and be transported on endless journeys.

Engaging in exercise and sports is a healthy alternative for children, adolescents, and adults who are increasingly suffering from obesity, sedentary lifestyles, and the panoply of health problems accompanying these lifestyle risks. Running, biking, and participating in competitive sports are fun activities and essential for healthy bodies. Friendships and strong self-concepts are built and nurtured through physical pursuits.

Finally, social time with friends and family promotes emotional well-being and enhances the sense of self. Watching television often precludes conversation and interchange with others. Although video games may involve more than one player, the communication involved may be competitive and counterproductive for friendship and growth. Family rituals, including daily mealtimes together, bond the members and perpetuate identity and satisfaction. If, instead of sharing joys and experiences of everyone's day or plans for tomorrow or hashing out a family problem, everyone's eyes are glued to the TV at dinner, valuable relationship-building opportunities are lost.

Evaluate the Family's Media Use and Habits Regularly

Keeping a media diary or log helps families to record and analyze media use habits in the home. How many hours is our TV on each day? Are we making wise choices in our TV use? Our computer time? What kinds of programs have we enjoyed as a family? Since thinking about media time and media planning, have we changed our priorities as a family? Are we finding plenty of other pursuits to keep us engaged and challenged?

Parents and children can evaluate family discussions. Have certain TV programs or other media programs offered opportunities for critical thinking? Have any family members had a revelation about media images and messages? Are we better, smarter, more critical viewers now? It is important for families to continually self-examine the role media literacy plays in the family's everyday life.

Other Forms of Media: Specific Issues for Parents

Video Games

Although television is the most ubiquitous of the media, other forms of electronic media commonly reside in homes across the country. For young people 8 to 18 years old, 87% have a dedicated video game system at home; the average home has 2.3 consoles (Rideout et al., 2010). On an average day, 60% of these young people play video games and those who play spend almost 2 hours daily; about half play on a console, but 29% use handheld video game players and 23% use their cell phones (Rideout et al., 2010). More boys than girls play video games, but the market for games aimed at young girls is burgeoning. Concerns have been raised about the content of many of these home video games, especially violence, sexual content, and stereotypical characters. (See Chapters 3, 4, and 13 in this volume.) Many experts are concerned

about the rewarding of violent behavior and the frequency of violent and sexual portrayals commonly seen in video game products (Anderson et al., 2010), but new research finds that prosocial video games, across cultures and countries, can encourage prosocial behavior (Gentile et al., 2009).

Parents, although commonly much less facile than their young children in the operation of these games, should attempt to play the games with youngsters and use the opportunity for critical discussion about content and characters. Firm guidelines about time limits on video game play and restriction of play until homework is completed complement rules about television viewing and computer use. Careful selection of video games and use of existing ratings systems can optimize the use of these popular media in the home.

Music

Music videos, MTV, and rock music lyrics continue to engender much passion on both sides of the debate. (See Chapter 23 in this volume.) The scenes in music videos and on MTV commonly contain violence (often with guns), sexual themes, or juxtapose both violence and sex. Issues about explicit-lyric warning labels on CDs, raised earlier, include the lack of data about the effect of the warnings on youth and concern about the "forbidden fruit" response. Unfortunately, despite the fact that "rock'n'roll is middle aged" and MTV has been around for decades, little research links music lyrics or music videos to harmful behavior. "Clearly, for a small minority of teenagers, certain music may serve as a biological marker for psychological distress" (Strasburger et al., 2009, p. 365).

Statistics suggest that adolescents listen to many hours of music daily (an average of 2 hours and 19 minutes), often while doing homework (even over the protests of parents) or interacting with peers. Unlike other forms of media, music may provide comforting background music for teens and may act as an important definition of "who I am," allowing a teen to feel membership in a larger group. Music is accessed by radio, but more often on an iPod, MP3 player, CD player, cell phone, or computer (Rideout et al., 2010).

For youth having trouble in school or socially, examining the time spent alone in a room listening to music (and not doing homework) is an essential parental role. However, unlike the situation with television viewing or video game playing, adolescents typically use another medium while listening to music—or work on classroom assignments with headphones or ear buds in place. Many youth (43%) listen to music while engaged in another task most of the time, while 30% report multitasking with media some of the time. Trying to enforce rules about listening to music, a seemingly integral part of personal and social development during adolescence, is challenging (Rideout et al., 2010).

Computers

More and more families are online, and increasing numbers of children are spending hours they used to spend in front of the TV screen with a mouse and computer screen. Many young children navigate the World Wide Web with confidence, and teenagers gather useful data for elusive research projects and investigate health questions, but the perils cannot be ignored.

- Hours spent in front of the computer, again, are hours away from friends, physical activity, books, and happy daydreaming.
- Websites with explicit sexual images are a mere click away, sometimes encountered unwittingly.
- Websites sell products and advertise substances such as alcoholic beverages and cigarettes freely.
- Children's and, consequently, family privacy are not guaranteed on the Internet; children may unconsciously provide confidential information about family finances and priorities.

Blocking devices for computers are imperfect and often preclude legitimate use of the Internet. Rather than censorship, parents and media education provide the most effective, simplest means to deal with the control of the computer. Basic media education tenets should apply to computer use for children and adolescents of all ages, including limiting time spent with the computer, mandating

parental supervision, encouraging discussion, and, if reasonable, keeping the computer at a central site in the family home. Parents should become as computer sophisticated as possible; children today are getting a big head start in the computer race.

Depending on interest and developmental capability, children are ready to begin computer activities at different ages. The family computer need not play a role in the life of children under 2. By age 3 or 4, manipulating the mouse and using simple child-friendly software provide a wonderful introduction to the computer. Allow children to see the rest of the family using this technology for information gathering and enjoyment. Older children require adult supervision and encouragement while playing computer games and exploring the many facets of this technology. Proper computer ethics and safety should be demonstrated and reinforced. Limiting time online, discussing privacy and avoidance of mature material, and other house rules must be emphasized. As children get older, parents and teachers partner to maximize use of the computer for learning, projects, and communication. Although older children and adolescents need more independence, parental rules and co-use are still vital to healthy computer habits. These young people should be encouraged to discuss their impressions of information learned, pursue new interests, and explore the technology as a rich resource for learning and communication. Today, 93% of teens are online, using this power for a variety of means, including 63% who seek out political news and current events, 48% who purchase items, and 31% who gather health, dieting, or fitness information (another 17% search out answers to sensitive questions, such as drug use or sexual health; Lenhart et al., 2010).

Especially for tweens and teens, social networking sites offer compelling ways to stay connected with friends and create a self-identity, a vital task for these age groups. Growing numbers of American teens, now about 73%, actively visit the most popular social networking sites, Facebook and MySpace (Lenhart et al., 2010). Three computer activities claim most online time for young people: the social networking sites (25%), computer games (19%), and watching videos on sites like YouTube (16%; Rideout et al., 2010). Parents face a barrage of advice and warnings about the dangers of the Internet, not only the popular social networking sites but also chat rooms and discussion boards. Recent data suggest that parental fears (while certainly understandable) may be overblown and that sexual solicitation is, in fact, in decline, and most online solicitations come from persons known to the child or adolescent (Tynes, 2007). Tynes proposes that parents and other adults reframe concerns about young people online, especially females, and recognize the potential educational and supportive opportunities available. Youth learn to sift through and prioritize information, develop critical thinking and argumentation skills, and seek support and/or gain self-awareness from peers. Autonomy and intimacy are two of the major tasks of the adolescent years; "whether constructing their profiles in MySpace, creating a video and posting it on YouTube, or talking in chat rooms, teens are constantly creating, recreating, and honing their identities" (Tynes, 2007).

In an effort to protect young people from real or perceived online threats, blocking software, as noted before, is an option. Parents may also locate computers in family areas in the home and place limits on time and amount of Internet use. As with other forms of media, media education offers strategies to help parents, children, and youth explore cyberspace safely and effectively (Tynes, 2007).

- *Maintain an open and honest dialogue* about potential Internet risks, both at home and in the school setting. Share your concerns with your children.
- *Help youths protect their privacy online* by learning about the privacy controls available on Facebook and MySpace. Privacy settings can limit or block contacts. Adults should discuss safety measures with young Internet users, such as knowing what information is safe to share and what is not.
- *Develop an exit strategy.* Adults may help tweens and teens recognize the telltale behavior of predators or bullies online and

know how to respond. Young people need to be able to report uncomfortable behavior to a trusted adult and/or authorities.

Make Your Voice Heard: Advocacy and Activism

Parents, schools, and communities share a common goal to make media positive, educational, and prosocial for children and adolescents. These groups are natural collaborators. (See Chapter 35 in this volume.) Some of the most effective voices for change in media have risen from grassroots campaigns, including the now defunct Action for Children's Television and the ongoing National TV-Turnoff Week, sponsored by TV-Free America based in Washington.

There are many simple collaborative efforts parents can encourage, including the following:

- Support alternative, community-based activities for children, especially after school and on weekends.
- Publicize and promote TV-Turnoff Week in neighborhoods; make this fun and inviting for families.
- Publish a simple newsletter about alternatives to TV, perhaps including some ideas for educational videotapes, DVDs, and good upcoming TV shows.
- Commit with other parents to not using TV as a babysitter in homes or play groups.
- Ensure that all children and adolescents have access to appropriate technology in the classroom to optimize learning. In this new millennium, every child should have education about and access to computers and the Internet, not only to explore new material and ideas but also to create his or her own products.
- Parents should seek out the E/I symbol on the TV screen and complain to the FCC (Federal Communications Commission) if a program does not meet educational or informational standards (Wilson et al., 2008).

Networks and local affiliates listen when many parents call with complaints (or compliments) about television shows. Using the phone or writing a letter about a stereotypic portrayal, show, or other negative message and encouraging friends and family to write can influence a local television station manager. Advertisers and sponsors of shows should also be contacted about negative programming; refusal to buy products associated with sponsors of offensive programs can also influence programming choices. The media are big, profitable businesses, and networks and sponsors depend on the support and money of the listening and viewing audience.

Many organizations across the United States are committed to media education and healthy children and teens. These groups feel strongly that parents play a key role as mediators and role models of appropriate media use for young people. Not only can these organizations be effective lobbyists and advocates on a local and national level, but they can also be a source of educational materials for parents.

Correlation of Health and Behavior Problems With Media Use Habits

Pediatricians and parents increasingly worry about the impact of media exposure on children and adolescents. For most children, living in a loving home with consistent messages, fair discipline, and strong attachments between family members lessens the potentially harmful effects of media. However, some children may present disturbing behavior symptoms or signs of ill health; in some cases, the association between these problems and media habits is apparent. Pediatricians and their national organization, the American Academy of Pediatrics (AAP), have long been concerned about the impact of media, especially television, on children (American Academy of Pediatrics, 1998; Christakis & Zimmerman, 2006; Council on Communications and Media, 2010; Strasburger et al., 2010).

Specific examples of problem behaviors or health concerns include the following:

- Aggressive behavior on the playground displayed by a 6-year-old child who watches violent cartoons and videos at home
- Substance use such as early initiation of cigarette smoking in a young girl who has seen lead characters in her favorite movies smoking in a glamorous, "natural" way
- School problems in a 10-year-old boy who is typically online more than 6 hours per day
- Obesity in a young teen viewing many hours of TV daily while snacking on highly caloric and nonnutritional foods
- Difficulty making friends for a male teen who listens to hours of heavy metal music in his room every day while playing violent video games
- Fear of going to bed in a 4-year-old who saw scary previews for a popular movie on television
- A 12-year-old female found texting explicit self-photographs ("sexting") to classmates; parental concern about sexual activity

Using anticipatory guidance, pediatricians can suggest media education techniques to parents of young children to prevent media problems from ever arising. Together, the family and the pediatrician can explore a detailed, relevant "media history." If health or behavioral concerns are present, as in some of the scenarios above, the pediatrician–parent team develops a plan to alter media use habits, employ media education techniques in the home, and follow the concerns closely.

Conclusions and Recommendations

Families—parents, children, and adolescents—live in a media world. We are surrounded by media in various forms and inundated by messages and images, many of them potentially harmful to the health and well-being of young people. Positive and healthy media programs and products also exist but may be unrecognized and overwhelmed by the sheer weight of popular media. And, in this new millennium, new media devices and applications appear at breakneck pace. Children and adolescents are, on one hand, more interconnected and interdependent but, on the other, also isolated within their headphones or staring at the small screen.

In each individual home, parents and children should become media educated and set about creating a positive media environment. Time spent using media should be limited and alternative activities encouraged, including reading, physical activity, and creative and social pursuits. Television sets are ideally situated in a busy family space, not in a child's bedroom. Families, depending on their unique values, interests, and needs, should carefully choose the media consumed in the home, whether television programs, movies, DVDs, music, video games, or computer programs. Parents, in addition to being positive role models, should actively coview programs with children, using this golden opportunity for discussion and deconstruction. A media-educated child—a wise, selective, critical media consumer—has learned a valuable lifelong skill.

Parents and other adult caregivers invested in the health and well-being of children and adolescents best provide role modeling, monitoring, and encouragement of media education in the home. Keenly aware of the special needs and developmental path of each child and imbued with respect and authority, parents, in partnership with other parents, schools, advocacy groups, and pediatricians, can lessen the potentially harmful impact of media on children and allow the untapped prosocial benefits to be realized.

References

American Academy of Pediatrics. (1998). *Media education in the practice setting.* Elk Grove Village, IL: Media Matters.

Anderson, C. A., Shibuya, A., Ihori, N., Swing, E. L., Bushman, B. J., Sakamoto, A. et al., (2010). Violent video game effects on aggression, empathy, and prosocial behavior in Eastern and Western countries: A meta-analytic review. *Psychological Bulletin, 136,* 151–173.

Campaign for a Commercial-Free Childhood. (2009). *CCFC victory: Disney offers refunds on Baby Einstein videos.* Boston: Author. Online at www.commercialfreechildhood.org.

Cantor, J. (1998). *"Mommy, I'm scared!"* San Diego, CA: Harcourt Brace.

Center for Media and Child Health. Children's Hospital Boston, Harvard Medical School, Harvard School of Public Health. Boston, MA: CMCH. (www.cmch.tv).

Christakis, D. A. (2009). The effects of infant media usage: What do we know and what should we learn? *Acta Paediatrica, 98,* 8–16.

Christakis, D. A. & Garrison, M. M. (2009). Preschool-aged children's television viewing in child care settings. *Pediatrics, 124,*1627–1632.

Christakis, D. A., & Zimmerman, F. J. (2006). *The elephant in the living room: Make television work for your kids.* New York: Rodale Press.

Committee on Public Education, American Academy of Pediatrics. (1999). Media education. *Pediatrics, 104,* 341–343.

Common Sense Media. San Francisco, CA. Online at www.commonsensemedia.org.

Council on Communications and Media, American Academy of Pediatrics. (2010). Media education. *Pediatrics, 126,* 1012–1017.

DeGaetano, G., & Bander. K. (1996). *Screen smarts: A family guide to media literacy.* New York: Houghton Mifflin.

Entertainment Software Rating Board. (2010). *ESRB rating symbols.* New York: Author.

Federal Trade Commission. (2007). Online at www.ftc.gov/reports/violence/070421market ingviolentechildren.pdf.

Gentile, D. A., Anderson, C. A., Yawaka, S., Ihori, N., Saleem, M., Ming, L. K. et al., (2009). The effects of prosocial video games on prosocial behavior: International evidence from correlational, longitudinal, and experimental studies. *Personality and Social Psychological Bulletin, 35,* 752–763.

Gentile, D. A., Humphrey, J., & Walsh, D. A. (2005). Media ratings for movies, music, video games, and television: A review of the research and recommendations for improvements. *Adolescent Medicine Clinics, 16,* 427–446.

Gentile, D. A., Oberg, C., Sherwood, N. E., Story, M., Walsh, D. A., & Hogan, M. (2004). Well-child visits in the video age: Pediatricians and the American Academy of Pediatrics' guidelines for children's media use. *Pediatrics, 114,* 1235–1241.

Ginsburg, K. R., & Jablow, M. M. (2006). *A parent's guide to building resilience in children and teens: Giving your child roots and wings.* Elk Grove Village, IL: American Academy of Pediatrics.

Hogan, M. J. (2010). What pediatricians can and should be doing about media. *Pediatric Annals, 39,* 574–577.

Hogan, M. J., & Strasburger, V. C. (2008). Media and prosocial behavior in children and adolescents. In L. Nucci & D. Narvaez (Eds.), *Handbook of moral and character education* (pp. 537–553). Mahwah, NJ: Lawrence Erlbaum.

Huston, A. C., Donnerstein, E., Fairchild, H., Feshbach, N. D., Katz, P. A., Murray, J. P.

et al., (1992). *Big world, small screen.* Lincoln: University of Nebraska Press.

Jordan, A., Hersey, J., McDivitt, J., & Heitzler, C. (2006). Reducing children's television viewing time: A qualitative study of parents and their children. *Pediatrics, 18,* e1303–e1310.

Kunkel, D., Cope, K. M., Farinola, W. J. M., Biely, E., Rollin, E., & Donnerstein, E. (1999). *Sex on TV: A biennial report to the Kaiser Family Foundation.* Santa Barbara: University of California Press.

Lenhart, A. (2009). *Teens and sexting: Pew Internet and American life project.* Washington, DC: Pew Research Center.

Lenhart, A., Purcell, K., Smith, A., & Zickuhr, K. (2010). *Social media and young adults: Pew Internet and American life project.* Washington, DC: Pew Research Center.

McCannon, R. (2009). Media literacy/media education: Solution to big media? A review of the literature. In V. C. Strasburger, B. J. Wilson, & A. B. Jordan (Eds.), *Children, adolescents, and the media* (pp. 519–569). Thousand Oaks, CA: Sage.

McDonough, P. (2010). TV viewing among kids at an eight-year high. *Nielsen Wire* (blog). New York: Nielsen Company.

McGee, M. (Producer/writer). (1984, October 1). *On television: The violence factor.* New York: Channel WNYC.

Mohr, P. J. (1976). *Television, children, and parents—A report of the viewing habits, program preferences and parental guidance of school children in the fourth through ninth grades in Sedgwick County, Kansas* [on microfiche]. Wichita, KS: Wichita State University.

Mohr, P. J. (1979). Parental guidance of children's viewing of evening television programs. *Journal of Broadcasting, 23,* 213–228.

Moreno, M. A., VanderStoep A., Parks, M. R., Zimmerman, F. J., Kurth, A., & Christakis, D. A. (2009). Reducing at-risk adolescents' display of risk behavior on a social networking web site. *Archives of Pediatric and Adolescent Medicine, 163,* 35–41.

Nathanson, A. I., & Cantor, J. (2000). Reducing the aggression-promoting effect of violent cartoons by increasing children's fictional involvement with the victim. *Journal of Broadcasting and Electronic Media, 44,* 125–142.

National Institute on Media and the Family. Minneapolis, MN. Online at www.mediafamily.org.

National Parent Teacher Association. (2009). *Media Safety.* Chicago, IL: Author. Online at www.pta.org.

New York Times. (2010, March 24). Prosecutors gone wild (editorial). *New York Times.*

Public Broadcasting Service. *PBS parents.* Arlington, VA. Online at www.pbs.org/parents/childrenandmedia.

Rideout, V. J., Foehr, U. G., & Roberts, D. F. (2010). *Generation M²: Media in the lives of 8- to 18-year olds.* Menlo Park, CA: Henry J. Kaiser Family Foundation.

Singer, D. C., & Singer, J. L. (2008). Imaginative play, creativity, and fantasy: Links to children's media exposure. In S. L. Calvert & B. J. Lewis (Eds.), *Handbook of child development and the media* (pp. 290–308). Boston: Wiley-Blackwell.

Stanger, J. D., & Gridina, N. (1999). *Media in the home 1999: The fourth annual survey of parents and children.* Philadelphia: University of Pennsylvania, Annenberg Public Policy Center.

Strasburger, V. C., Jordan, A. B., & Donnerstein, E. (2010). Health effects of media on children and adolescents. *Pediatrics, 125,* 756–767.

Strasburger, V. C., Wilson, B. J., & Jordan, A. B. (2009). *Children, adolescents, and media* (2nd ed.). Thousand Oaks, CA: Sage.

Tynes, B. M. (2007). Internet safety gone wild? Sacrificing the educational and psychosocial benefits of online social environments. *Journal of Adolescent Research, 22,* 575–584.

Walsh, D. A. (2007). *No: Why kids of all ages need to hear it and ways parents can say it* (pp. 257–274). New York: Free Press.

Wilson, B. J., Kunkel, D., & Drogos, K. L. (2008). *Educationally insufficient: An analysis of the availability and educational quality of children's E/I programming.* Oakland, CA: Children Now.

Zimmerman, F. J., & Christakis, D. A. (2005). Children's television viewing and cognitive outcomes: A longitudinal analysis of national data. *Archives of Pediatric and Adolescent Medicine, 159,* 619–625.

Zimmerman, F. J., Christakis, D. A., & Meltzoff, A. N. (2007). Association between media viewing and language development in children under age two years. *Journal of Pediatrics, 151,* 364–368.

CHAPTER 34

Media Literacy and Media Education

MAMI KOMAYA
Showa Women's University

Children growing up today in homes where they are exposed almost constantly to the TV and other screen-based media come face to face with both the conveniences and dangers of our information society. Inevitably, young children absorb large amounts of information from the media: Some of this information is positive for children and enriches their lives, but some of it is erroneous or incomplete and has negative effects. These are the so-called dangerous three Cs of unprotected media exposure: inaccurate *content*, multiple *contacts* with anonymous or indefinite strangers, and intentional *commerce* aimed at children with a blurring of the differences between advertising and noncommercial content (Carrick-Davies, 2004).

There is a growing consensus that children need to gain media literacy through media education to survive unscathed in our advanced information society. The need for providing children with media education has gradually been recognized around the world, and considerable energy has been devoted to developing theoretical frameworks as well as effective teaching strategies and resources.

This chapter summarizes some of the trends that have been developed around the world for media literacy and media education for young children and focuses on screen-based media. The first half of the chapter outlines integral definitions and concepts of media literacy, and the latter half offers typical examples of the essentials for successful media education such as curriculum design, assessment, and support, including teacher training and other materials.

Media Literacy

What is media literacy? While this is a very a simple question, answering it proves to be unexpectedly difficult because definitions of media literacy have been developed in a diverse number of contexts from the grassroots level in community organizations to national and international levels. In addition, definitions vary depending on social, cultural, economic, historical, and technological context. However, common theoretical frameworks of media literacy can be classified into two main domains according to their primary foci: *definitions* and *foundational concepts*. Due to limited space, only those definitions and foundational concepts pertaining to media literacy in young children will be addressed here.

Major Definitions That Focus on Skills

There are a variety of definitions of media literacy that refer to skill acquisition such as technical, critical-viewing, and communication skills (Hargrave, 2010). We can identify two types of subcategories of media literacy definitions that emphasize skills: those that look at different skills and those that focus on skills specialized by media forms (Komaya, 2006). Initially, basic definitions stressed the multidimensional skills of media literacy with simple explanations, "the ability to access, analyze, evaluate and communicate messages in a variety of forms" (Aufderheide, 1992; Hobbs, 1997; Media Literacy Project, 2010) or "the ability to access, understand and create communications in a variety of contexts" (The Office of Communication [Ofcom], 2004).

Although there are many definitions of media literacy, because children begin life as receivers of media and therefore need critical thinking skills, this chapter will limit itself to definitions focusing on the skill of critical analysis in media literacy. For example, Silverblatt and Eliceiri (1997) link media literacy to individual empowerment: "critical thinking skills empower people to make independent judgments and informed decisions in response to information conveyed through the channels of mass communications" (Silverblatt & Eliceiri, 1997, p. 40). Hobbs (1997) defines media literacy in a similar way but includes a user perspective. Here, media literacy is the ability to critically analyze media messages as well as learning methods for transmitting messages (Hobbs, 1997). Some definitions link media literacy with the ability to be a critical or discerning consumer. According to both Desmond (1997) and Rafferty (1999), media literacy involves the acquisition of skills necessary for becoming a consumer able to approach entertainment and advertising information with evaluative judgment.

Secondly, there are definitions that focus on media forms, with a tendency to relate this to a single medium, often screen-image media, with TV the most common. This is because TV is the first screen-based medium to which children are exposed. What we are talking about here is visual literacy and defined variously as the power of "viewing" at the moment of deciphering and transmitting image media (Adams & Hamm, 2001) and "an understanding of representational conventions through which the users of media create and share meanings" (Messaris, 1998, p. 70). On the other hand, as children grow up, they are exposed more and more to new developments in information and communication technologies. Thus, media literacy can be defined as the ability to skillfully analyze and utilize the full range of media from print media (such as newspapers) to film, radio, television, computers, and interactive real-time media such as the Internet (Brown, 1998; Johnson, 2001; Tyner, 1998).

The European Commission (EC) has integrated these various definitions, which encompass all age levels from very small children to the elderly. For example, media literacy is defined as:

> the ability to access the media, to understand and to critically evaluate different aspects of the media and media contents to create communications in a variety of contexts. Media literacy relates to all media, including television and film, radio and recorded music, print media, the Internet and all other new digital communication technologies. It is a fundamental competence not only for the young generation but also for adults and elderly people, for parents, teachers and media professionals. (EC, 2010, Media Literacy site)

Here we see the emergence of media literacy as a skill that adults, children, professionals, and nonprofessionals all need to develop. It is now considered a "fundamental competence."

Recently, the pioneering concept of media and information literacy (MIL) was introduced by United Nations Educational, Scientific and Cultural Organization (UNESCO) at the World Summit on Media for Children and Youth 2010 in Karlstad, Sweden, to present a basic and common understanding of media literacy. MIL represents a creative fusion of media literacy and information literacy.

According to UNESCO, "MIL represents essential competencies and skills to equip citizens in the 21st century with the abilities to engage with media and information systems effectively and develop critical thinking and life-long learning skills to socialize and become citizens" (UNESCO, 2008, p. 4). UNESCO is trying to encourage the unity of media literacy policies by introducing MIL to the world. This definition indicates a movement toward the acquisition of media literacy by all children in the 21st century.

Representative Concepts Focused on Media Reality

Looking at the major media literacy conceptual models, it is clear that there is a common base in terms of one key constructive concept, a form of virtual reality, generated by media structure and content. To better understand media literacy, we need to focus on interpretations of media reality during different periods of a child's life. From a psychological angle, the preschool years are that stage where a child first starts to understand reality generally (Buckingham, 1993, 2003; Potter, 2005; Schmitt, Anderson & Collins, 1999), and in the elementary school years, he or she becomes involved with reality through engagement in social activities.

Children growing up in this multimedia age frequently confuse reality and fantasy. It is difficult for them to distinguish between things happening in the real world and those occurring in a media world. Children need to be able to draw a line between the real world and the world of media; they need a passport to allow them to escape the mixing up of fantasy and reality. This passport is media literacy, which acts as a strategy conducive to understanding media reality. Below are outlined the most representative concepts involved in the idea of media reality as it relates to children.

Masterman's Conceptual Model

In *Teaching the Media* (1985), Len Masterman, based in the United Kingdom, clearly specifies that media reality is a key constructive concept in media literacy. He defines it as the first principle of media education and argues that "the media are actively involved in the processes of constructing or representing 'reality' rather than simply transmitting or reflecting it" (Masterman, 1985, p.20). It should be noted that in the United Kingdom the term *media education* is preferred to *media literacy* or *media literacy education*.

Masterman (1995) initially identified 18 basic principles of media education that he used to construct a general model of media literacy. Subsequently, following an analysis of media literacy trends in Europe between 1970 and 1990, he reduced this list to eight key component ideas (Masterman, 1997). The following two components are particularly relevant to the concept of media reality and children's acquisition of media literacy: "1. The media do not reflect reality but represent it. 2. A central purpose of media education is to create an understanding that media messages are constructions and do not occur naturally" (Masterman, 1997, p. 40). Masterman does not view children's enjoyment of the media negatively but calls for a practical media literacy that understands the text from a contextualization of its meaning in order to encourage awareness, critically and subjectively, of the values and ideology embedded in the media text. Encouraging an understanding of media reality should not lead to a lessening of the enjoyment of various media forms; rather, it should create the conditions for heightening enjoyment through an understanding of any text on multiple levels.

The Ontario Ministry of Education Constructive Conceptual Model and Media Analysis Model

In 1987, the Ontario Ministry of Education was the first government ministry in the world to introduce media education into the curriculum. In 1989, in cooperation with the Association for Media Literacy (AML), it produced the *Media Literacy; Resource Guide* as a teaching resource. Although influenced by the ideas of Masterman mentioned above, the *Resource Guide* defined media education in a novel way (AML, 2010; Ontario Ministry of Education, 1989). The Ontario Ministry of Education model is constructed on the basis of eight key concepts (KC), with the foremost being media reality

(Ontario Ministry of Education, 1989). The following outlines the original key concepts and interpretations by Pungente, one of the writers of the *Resource Guide*. (Pungente, 2010a, Media Awareness Network, Media Literacy Key Concepts site):

> KC1. *All media are constructions.* The media do not present simple reflections of external reality. Rather, they present carefully crafted constructions that reflect many decisions and result from many determining factors.
>
> KC2. *The media construct versions of reality.* The media are responsible for the majority of the observations and experiences from which we build up our personal understandings of the world and how it works . . . The media, to a great extent, give us our sense of reality.
>
> KC3. *Audiences negotiate meaning in media.*
>
> KC4. *Media messages have commercial implications.*
>
> KC5. *Media messages contain ideological and value messages.*
>
> KC6. *Media messages contain social and political implications.*
>
> KC7. *Form and content are closely related in media messages.*
>
> KC8. *Each medium has a unique aesthetic form.*

The significance of the Ontario Ministry of Education model is to codify concisely that understanding media reality is a universal and essential element of media literacy. More than 20 years have passed since the model was created, and it has become a standard for the development of media literacy curricula throughout Canada. What is important in this model is the two most important key concepts relating to children's understanding of the media reality.

Moreover, in *Scanning Television* (Anderson, Tyner, & Pungente, 2003) the Ontario Ministry of Education's model and the media triangle model, developed by Eddie Dick of the Scottish Film Council (1989), have been combined to create the media analysis model and introduced into media literacy curriculum (Anderson et al., 2003). This model makes it easy to visualize the importance of media literacy for children.

As shown in Figure 34.1, the media analysis model is divided into three domains,

Text, Audience, and Production, within which 23 subcategories of conceptual elements connected to the media have been created and set alongside the Ontario Ministry of Education's eight key concepts (KC) in a triangular relationship. With media reality at the core of the triangle, the model represents media in the following ways. As modes of representation vary according to the genre—image and print, for example—within the domain of Text, attention is given to the particular language (code, rhetoric) of each. It seeks to elucidate the values and ideology embedded in products and to analyze the overt and covert meanings they contain. In the domain of Production, the focus of the content of study is largely on the process of creating a product. For example, there is an analysis of the kind of products that are produced by the media. The flow between media management, distribution, sales, and laws and regulations concerning media content and management is illustrated as well as the way that these components change. The focus of analysis is on the characteristics of domain audiences. There is an examination of the way in which factors such as the social background, psychological factors tied in with the media, previous experience, the form of media used, and skill at reading media text all impact audience understandings (Anderson et al., 2003; Dick, 1989).

The British Film Institute's Cineliteracy Model and Buckingham's Conceptual Model

The British Film Institute (BFI), which is a major platform for media education in the United Kingdom, drew on its long history and experience in the field to build on Masterman's ideas to create a model of cineliteracy (BFI, 1999). This model is based on three conceptual dimensions of what the BFI refer to as "moving-image" media, including film, video, and television (FVT); that of Film Language, Producers and Audiences, and Messages and Values. It is noteworthy that media reality is incorporated into the final dimension of Messages and Values. This dimension is concerned with the effects of the media on "ideas, values and beliefs" and especially focuses on the relationship between moving-image FVT texts and "reality."

Figure 34.1 Media Analysis Model

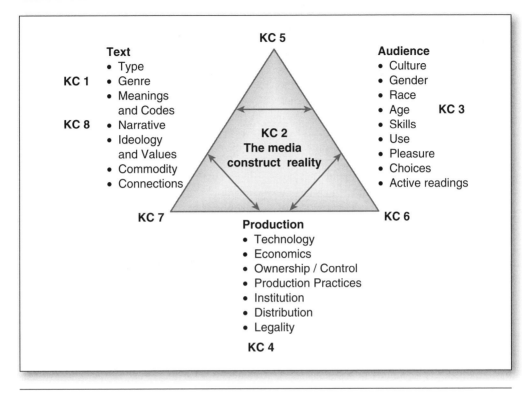

Source: Adapted from *Scanning Television* (Anderson, Tyner, & Pungente, 2003).

The following illustrates five stages of learning progression and examples of certain learning outcomes that are expected at various stages in the Messages and Values dimension of the Cineliteracy model (BFI, 1999; Buckingham, 2003).

Stage 1

- Identify and talk about different levels of "realism," for example, in naturalistic drama vs. cartoon animation.
- Use key words such as *shot, cut, zoom, close-up*, and *focus* in order to refer to film language when explaining personal responses and preferences.
- Identify devices such as flashback, dream sequences, and exaggeration—discuss why they are needed and what they convey.

Stage 2

- Use key words such as *violence* and *magic* to identify ways in which FVT can show things that have not really happened.

- Explore the reasons for and against censorship, age classifications, and the broadcasting watershed.

Stage 3

- Use key words such as *stereotype, authentic,* and *representation* to explain how social groups, events, and ideas are presented in FVT.
- Explain and justify aesthetic judgments and personal responses.
- Argue for alternative ways of representing a group, events, or idea.

Stage 4

- Use key words such as *propaganda* and *ideology* to discuss and evaluate FVT texts with strong social or ideological messages.

Stage 5

- Use key words such as *hegemony* and *diegesis* to discuss and evaluate ideological messages in mainstream FVT texts.

- Describe and account for different levels of realism in FVT texts.
- Explain relationships between aesthetic style and social/political meaning.

(BFI, 1999; Buckingham, 2003, pp. 40–41).

A key feature of this model is that it is stage based rather than age specific. It allows for the evaluation of "learning outcomes" at each stage based on the normative content of each level. As a result, when it comes to media reality, all learners should pass through the stages outlined above, but they will go at their own pace, and the model promotes a diversified pattern of learning. It is noteworthy that children's media literacy acquisition is divided into five distinct stages and that children ascend these stages as they better understand media reality.

Building on the BFI's cineliteracy model, Buckingham (2003) creates a theoretical framework that can be applied not only to new media but also to older media and indicates that within this, the single most important principle is that of media reality. Buckingham uses four key concepts: Production, Language, Representation, and Audience. The domain of Representation corresponds to Messages and Values in the cineliteracy model, which in turn corresponds to the idea of media reality. Media are regarded not a "window on the world," but they re-present the real world. The following seven study items are included in the domain Representation (Buckingham, 2003).

- *Realism.* Is this text intended to be realistic? Why do some texts seem more realistic than others?
- *Telling the truth.* How do media claim to tell the truth about the world? How do they try to seem authentic?
- *Presence and absence.* What is included and excluded from the media world? Who speaks, and who is silenced?
- *Bias and objectivity.* Do media texts support particular views about the world? Do they put across moral or political values?
- *Stereotyping.* How do media represent particular social groups? Are those representations accurate?
- *Interpretations.* Why do audiences accept some media representations as true or reject others as false?
- *Influences.* Do media representations affect our views of particular social groups or issues? (Buckingham, 2003, p. 58)

In addition to understanding media literacy as involving critical thinking skills and the creation of specific abilities, Buckingham makes clear that studying "media representation," as outlined, should help children understand from a critical viewpoint the relationship between television and reality.

Potter's Typological Conceptual Model[1]

Potter (2010) emphasizes what he regards as the two most important characteristics of media literacy: Media literacy is multidimensional and is on a continuum. Especially, the idea that media literacy is not something you either have or not but a set of skills that are developed on the basis of a continuum is recognized as foundational for cognitive, emotional, aesthetic, and moral developments of media literacy. Potter's typology of media literacy relating to children is summarized below and indicates how they become media literate and can understand media reality through eight stages, moving back and forth. It is meaningful that Potter has linked the typology of media literacy to the developmental stages of children.

Acquiring Fundamentals Stage (lower level, this process starts during the first year of life)

- Learning that there are human beings and other physical things apart from one's self; these things look different and serve different functions.
- Learn the meaning of facial expressions and natural sounds.
- Recognize shapes, form, size, color, movement, and spatial relations.
- Rudimentary concept of time—regular patterns.

Language Acquisition Stage (lower level, and starts during the 2nd and 3rd years of life)

- Recognize speech sounds and attach meaning to them.
- Be able to reproduce speech sounds.
- Orient to visual and audio media.
- Make emotional and behavior responses to music and sounds.
- Recognize certain characters in visual media and follow their movement.

Narrative Acquisition Stage (lower level, this starts during the 3rd to 5th years of life)

- Develop understanding of differences: Fiction vs. nonfiction, Ads vs. entertainment, and Real vs. make-believe.
- Understand how to connect plot elements: By time sequencing, by motive-action-consequence.

Developing Skepticism Stage (middle level, this starts during the 5th to 9th year of life)

- Discount claims made in ads.
- Sharpen differences between likes and dislikes for TV shows, characters, and actions.
- Make fun of certain characters even through those characters are not presented as foils in their shows.

Intensive Development Stage (middle level, ongoing an indefinite period)

- Strong motivation to seek out information on certain topics.
- Developing a detailed set of information on particular topics (sports, politics, etc.).
- High awareness of utility of information and quick facility in processing information judged to be useful. (Potter, 2010, pp. 22–23).

The remaining three stages (advanced level) do not apply to young children and therefore have been omitted (see Note). The significance of Potter's typological model is that it demonstrates the developmental process of media literacy acquisition. It is crucial for young children to understand media reality, which they do by moving back and forth as they learn between the lower level, Narrative Acquisition Stage, to middle levels, Developing Skepticism and Intensive Development stages.

Media Education

As the conceptual models above make clear, media literacy is an essential life-long skill, and children do not automatically gain critical perspectives on the media for understanding media reality. They need developmentally appropriate education to become media literate. When it comes to this education, however, there is a confusing array of terminology such as *media literacy*, *media literacy education*, *media studies*, and *media education*, and a variety of ideas about what these areas involve. Here, the term *media education* refers to programs aimed at developing media literacy in children, young people, or adults.

UNESCO understands media education in a very broad sense to mean education about the media targeting millions of people around the world. Summarizing the opinions of media educators and researchers from 33 countries, UNESCO highlighted seven key points relating to the understanding of media reality, two of which are particularly worth mentioning here. The first is that media education must "enable people to gain an understanding of the way media act and operate in society," and the second is that it "must ensure that people learn how to analyze and critically reflect upon media messages" (von Feilitzen & Bucht, 2001, p. 71).

The Essentials for Successful Media Education

Based on Thoman's four steps to success in media literacy (1995) and Pungente's nine criteria for a successful media education program (Pungente, 2010b, Center for Media Literacy, Criteria for a Successful Media Education Program site), we can highlight three main factors that contribute to the success of media education: appropriate curriculum development, assessment, and support, including teaching materials and teacher training. Given space limitations, only the representative programs or projects in media education are examined.

Representative National Curricula

The importance of developing culturally appropriate media education curricula that is also age appropriate cannot be overstated. Media education is still a new endeavor for many teachers around the world; therefore, the creation of learning outcomes by teachers for implementing media education is an essential task. Providing sample curricula can help teachers gain an image of how to teach media literacy in their classrooms, deliver media activities to children, and assess the children's work (Buckingham & Domaille, 2009). Countries with well-established traditions incorporate media education into a part of the compulsory educational curriculum. Canada, the United Kingdom, and Australia are especially noteworthy because they have included media literacy acquisition in their national curricula. Media education in these three countries is covered from the preschool years through to the senior high school years, indicating an understanding of the importance of child development in media literacy. Moreover, the shared first goal of these curricula is for children to understand the special characteristics of screen-based media and to differentiate between reality and fantasy. These child-centered curricula support the early development of children's understanding of media reality. Let us now look briefly at each of these three countries' media education programs.

Canada is described as a world leader in media education and therefore deserves a slightly more detailed overview. As previously mentioned, the Ontario Ministry of Education in 1987 became the first government body in the world to introduce media education, and this curriculum has been taken as a model elsewhere, too. Media education was initially introduced as a part of the national language arts curriculum for Grades 7 through 12. The conceptual "critical thinking skill" framework of the curriculum was developed by the Association for Media Literacy (AML). In 1995, media education was introduced into Ontario's Common Curriculum: Policies and Outcomes for Grades 1 through 8. In 2006 and 2007, the Ontario Ministry of Education revised the curriculum to mandate media literary for Grades 1 through 12. Media literacy is now a distinct strand in the language program at the elementary level (Grades 1–8) and in the English program at the secondary level (Grades 9–12; Buckingham & Domaille, 2009; Media Awareness Network, 2010; Silverblatt & Eliceiri, 1997; Wilson & Duncan, 2009;). In the language program of the revised curriculum, two of the four goals of the media literacy strand are for students to "demonstrate an understanding of a variety of media texts, and identify some media forms and explain how the conventions and techniques associated with them are used to create meaning" (Ontario Ministry of Education, 2006, p. 14). Even curricula at the kindergarten level have been updated, with the revised 2006 curriculum expecting children to "begin to respond critically to animated works, . . . communicate their ideas verbally and non-verbally about a variety of media materials, . . . and view and listen to a variety of media materials and respond critically to them" (Ontario Ministry of Education, 2010, p. 39). Following Ontario's lead, all 10 Canadian provinces now include media literacy in their curricula (Silverblatt & Eliceiri, 1997).

The United Kingdom is frequently heralded as the birthplace of media education. Since its establishment in 1933, the British Film Institute (BFI) has creatively worked in the art form of the moving image, such as film and television. BFI has developed a conceptual moving-image framework for media education (Buckingham & Domaille, 2009). The BFI's cineliteracy model fits in with the Key Stages of the National Curriculum. Since 1990, the National Curriculum in England has required students in Key Stages 3 and 4 (ages 11–16) to learn about media and moving-image texts as part of their English curriculum. Subsequently, Wales, Northern Ireland, and even Scotland, which does not have a national curriculum, have introduced some requirements for learning about the media as part of their respective language curricula. In 1999, the national curriculum in England was revised and broadened the types of media text from printed matter to Internet. Importantly, young children in the primary curriculum begin to reinforce critical approaches to listening, watching, and responding to the media and eventually discuss media texts appropriately for each grade level (EC, 2007a).

Australia has been referred to as having the most comprehensive approach for media education due to the fact that the Government of Western Australia Curriculum Council introduced the world's first integrated media education curriculum covering kindergarten to 12th grade in the mid-1990s (Quin & McMahon, 2001). The conceptual viewing framework that runs through this curriculum was influenced by the BFI (Brown, 1998; Buckingham & Domaille, 2009; Potter, 2010). One of the nine English Learning Area Outcomes for kindergarten through to Grade 12 is for "students to view a wide range of visual texts with purpose, understanding and critical awareness" (Government of Western Australia Curriculum

Council, 1998, p. 90). Kindergarten through Grade 3 builds on the children's previous exposure to visual texts and existing interpretive skills. Teachers provide time in the classroom for children to interpret, discuss, and reflect on various media texts. They consider symbolism and begin to discover that the "visual texts are constructed by people to represent real and imaginary experiences" (p. 95). In subsequent stages, children are exposed to ever more complex visual texts. They consider how medium and genre influence texts and how social factors play a role in the production and the audiences' interpretation of texts. Children engage in self-reflection vis-à-vis how their own social contexts influence their responses to texts. Children learn to approach media independently and critically and to weigh a text's "relevance and reliability, identifying evidence of such factors as selectivity, emphasis, distortion, bias and vested interest" (Government of Western Australia Curriculum Council, 1998, pp. 100–101).

It is clearly evident that the underlying core values of media education in these three pioneering countries are substantial curricula that cover early childhood through the teen years that place emphasis on the understanding of the special characteristics of moving images and the ability to differentiate between reality and fantasy. The success of these curricula has been demonstrated by the positive assessment of children's progress and is discussed later in the chapter.

Assessment of Children's Outcomes

Assessments by teachers are necessary to evaluate children's learning after implementing media education curricula. They not only indicate how effective the learning has been but can also serve as a tool for professional development for teachers and further stimulate children's development of media literacy as a result of reflection on learning. While assessment is necessary, in reality, there are two fundamental difficulties that have to be overcome. First, assessment in media education frequently has no connection to curricula. Second, it tends to be based on vague standards at best. Children's work is very often used to develop writing or speaking skills and not critical thinking skills (Buckingham & Domaille, 2009, p. 25). In other words, assessment is not always aligned with learning outcomes. Furthermore, because media literacy as a school subject does not naturally produce a traditional written product, as is typical in core subjects, teachers are not always clear how to frame any assessment (Worsnop, 2010). "The absence of structured assessment procedure has contributed to lack of status afforded to media education" (Buckingham & Domaille, 2009, p. 26). However, Canada, Australia, and the UK have been successful at solving the problem of assessment by making clear assessment standards that are connected to the curriculum.

In Canada, assessment is based on the Ontario Language Curriculum (Ontario Ministry of Education, 2006).

> Assessment is the process of gathering of information from a variety of sources (including assignments, day-to-day observations, conversations or conferences, demonstrations, projects, performances, and tests) that accurately reflects how well a student is achieving the curriculum expectations in a subject . . . Evaluation refers to the process of judging the quality of student work on the established criteria, and assigning a value to represent that quality. (Ontario Ministry of Education, 2006, p. 15)

The "provincial standard" for expected outcomes is presented in the Achievement Chart for Language, which "guides the development of assessment tasks and tools (including rubrics)." This chart provides criteria such as "Thinking: the use of critical and creative thinking skills and/or processes" from with limited effectiveness at Level 1 to a high degree of effectiveness at Level 4 (Ontario Ministry of Education, 2006, p. 20). The teachers can crosscheck this chart with the curriculum expectations, for example, "by the end of Grade 6, students will explain how a variety of media texts address their intended purpose and audience" in the strand of Media Literacy of each grade to assess children's outcomes in the classroom (Ontario Ministry of Education, 2006, p. 117).

In Australia, Quin and McMahon developed the Monitoring Standards Assessment Program in Media Analysis Skills for the

Western Australian Ministry of Education (Brown, 2001; Quin & McMahon, 1994; Silverblatt & Eliceiri, 1997). In the method of assessment used in kindergarten through to the seventh grade, there is a "*content strand*," which assesses the student's knowledge of language and narrative, and a "*context strand*," which assesses the students' understanding of production/circulation, audiences, and values (Silverblatt & Eliceiri, 1997, pp. 7–8).

In the UK, BFI's cineliteracy curricula provides teachers with assessment criteria based on the National Curriculum model's 5 Key-stage scale with key words, as previously mentioned (Buckingham, 2003). This assessment, in turn, reveals the key to effective teaching in media education; namely, if an assessment is carried out in line with expected curricula learning outcomes, the key, we can gain an accurate picture of children's understanding of media reality as critical thinking processes.

Support

Support in the form of teacher training and teaching materials is essential if we are to see more media education with appropriate assessment in schools around the world. In particular, a wide variety of support can create high motivation and ensure continuation of media education programs. This is already happening at the global/international level, the academic research level, and the media industry level. In addition, collaboration and partnerships between teachers, parents, communities, researchers, media professionals, and the abovementioned organizations can contribute to the stable establishment and continuation of media education. Sometimes teacher training courses and teaching materials are provided as part of support, collaborations, or partnerships (e.g., Media Smart in the UK and Advertising Elementary School in Japan). Educators who teach media education as specialists are still in the minority, and they are often isolated. Others involved in media education are nonspecialists who can only introduce a limited curriculum, often making room for it in their teaching of conventional subjects such as language, history, or social studies (Brown, 2003). Given these conditions, it makes sense for people who have an interest in media education to gather in one place, help each other, and share information across occupational and national boundaries. Below are some notable examples of support, collaboration, and partnerships that have been successful.

UNESCO, EC, and UN are key players in the development of media education as they manage networks and exchange on media literacy around the world. In 2008, UNESCO developed a Media and Information Literacy (MIL) Curriculum for Teachers (UNESCO, 2008). As a result, UNESCO was involved in providing "critical knowledge and analytical tools" to the international community, which, in turn, empowers "media consumers to function as autonomous and rational citizens, and enabling them to critically make use of the media" (UNESCO, 2010, Media and Information Literacy site). The EC collects and provides up-to-date information on the situation surrounding media education in Europe. For example, the EC has released individual EU member country profiles assessing the development of media education, media literacy-related policies and actions, and media education in school curricula (EC, 2007b). After identifying the strengths and weaknesses of media education in each country, the EC provided the document *A Study on Assessment Criteria for Media Literacy Levels*, which is a comprehensive overview of the concept of media literacy (EC, 2009). The UN Alliance of Civilizations has developed a website, the Media Literacy Education Clearinghouse, that offers worldwide resources relevant to media education from organizations, university departments, associations, groups, and individuals who are developing new pedagogical tools, strategies, and theories that take into consideration the challenges of the information society (UN Alliance of Civilizations, 2010, Media Literacy Education Clearinghouse site). The Ofcom is the world's first government-funded body established as an "independent regulator and competition authority for the UK communications industries" (Ofcom, 2010, home page). It seeks to protect children as consumers through regulation of the media, produce concrete regulatory measures, and help children think critically about the media.

Many local or nonprofit-level organizations have participated in the development of concrete and effective programs/tools of media education corresponding to the various needs of educators in different countries. For example, the BFI in the UK, the Association for Media Literacy (AML) in Canada, Australian Teachers of Media (ATOM), the Center for Media Literacy (CML), and the National Association for Media Literacy Education (NAMLE) in the United States have a variety of initiatives that include: (1) providing a network for media literacy teachers throughout the world; (2) publishing an online newsletter for their members; (3) organizing workshops and conferences; (4) publishing curriculum anthologies and other support material for media education teachers; (5) lobbying and communicating with government, school boards, and the media industry about mutual concerns (AML, 2010; ATOM Queensland, 2010; CML, 2010; EC, 2007a, p.12; NAMLE, 2010; Silverblatt & Eliceiri, 1997, pp. 12–13;). As some of these grassroots organizations have strong relationship to teachers, they can respond to teachers' exact needs to help them implement media education while creating their own classroom lessons.

Academic researchers often verify the results and the effectiveness of media education projects and use these data to modify and improve media education curricula (Strasburger & Wilson, 2002). Representative examples of media education curricula and projects that have been developed specifically for preschool level through to Grade 12 will be introduced here.

Targeting elementary school children, randomly assigned to control and experimental groups, in Grades 3 to 5, Singer and colleagues (1980, 1981) created a program to understand how television works, focusing on fantasy and reality in television, camera effects and special effects, commercials and the television industry, the tendency to identify with TV characters, stereotyping, and violence and aggressiveness. A posttest compared to a pretest checked the target groups' general understanding of television. Results proved the program's effectiveness for those children in the experimental group. The control group then received the media literacy training, and when tested, this group also made significant gains in the understanding of the media.

Dorr, Graves, and Phelps (1980) developed and implemented an industry curriculum and a process curriculum for preschool through to Grade 3 in elementary school. The industry curriculum was structured to help young children acquire knowledge of entertainment programs and the TV industry. It was structured around four themes: (1) structuring a plot; (2) characters are actors; (3) incidents are fabricated; and (4) the backdrop scenery is frequently constructed. The process curriculum seeks to develop in young children critical evaluation of TV content and methods on the following themes: (1) the construction of entertainment programs; (2) there is more diversity in real life than in programs; (3) viewers can judge the reality level of entertainment programs themselves; and (4) we should try to judge the content of television based on a comparison with other information sources (personal experience, what other people have told us, other media). It was found that, as a result of these curricula, the participating children were found to have acquired basic critical viewing skills.

Hobbs (2000) developed a ML education curriculum and the textbook *Assignment: Media Literacy (AML)* for elementary, junior high, and senior high school students. The AML curriculum has helped in fostering critical thinking and creative communication skills. In elementary school, for example, children could learn the fundamental concepts of media and narrative, the predictability of language in media messages, journalistic criteria, how social context influences an audience's interpretation of media messages, the role of ratings, and ultimately the important role that different media play in their lives.

Focusing on mother–child interactions at home in early childhood and teacher–child or peer interactions at elementary school, Komaya (2006) developed separate media literacy materials for use in these two learning environments in Japan. The results suggest that media literacy materials should be adapted to reflect the media literacy abilities of each targeted age group. Furthermore, the results also revealed that acquisition of media literacy does not destroy children's beliefs, as in the Santa fantasy.

While there is a limit to the scale and number of participants that can be involved with university-level research, it is still possible to develop productive methods for enhancing children's media literacy levels. The International Clearinghouse on Children, Youth and Media at Nordicom, University of Gothenburg, supports its academic researchers by collecting and documenting research and other information on children, youth, and media from across the world. By means such as yearbooks, newsletters, and survey articles, the Clearinghouse aims at broadening and contextualizing this knowledge, thereby increasing awareness and media literacy (EC, 2007b, p. 14).

Media-related industries have an inherent responsibility to contribute to developing children's media literacy (Hobbs, 2008). Broadcasting organizations like the BBC in the UK, Channel 1 in the United States, and NHK in Japan provide rich educational online resources for learning support of media education. Additionally, they provide teachers' resources, activities, lesson plans, worksheets, and teachers' packs and practical reports. The BBC's materials fit the Key Stages of the National Curriculum. Teachers can easily choose a level and a topic and play in the classroom one or more of many video clips available online. Children can develop their critical thinking skills by viewing programs and discussing them in the classroom (BBC, 2010, Learning Teachers site; Channel One News, 2010, teaching tools site; NHK, 2010, NHK Digital Curriculum site). Other broadcasting companies also play an active part in media education by providing stations tours. In Japan, TV Asahi provides "delivery lessons" where TV producers or announcers visit primary and secondary schools and universities to show what happens behind the scenes. This provides students with a good opportunity to understand in depth a media literacy key concept: The media are constructed by people (Komaya, 2010a).

Teaching materials focusing on advertising like Media Smart in the UK and Advertising Elementary School in Japan (Dentsu) are effective components of media education for elementary school children. They can use real commercials in their materials because they are funded by the advertising business as part of corporate social responsibility (CSR) endeavors. Children can foster critical viewing skills and critical perception skills toward advertising through watching and understanding authentic commercials (Dentsu, 2010; Media Smart, 2010).

Future Challenges of Media Education

This chapter has offered a general overview of front-line concepts, research, movements, and activities that guide media education in the world. In order for media education to keep progressing and for children to develop media literacy deeply and comprehensively, there are two points of view to consider: a microscopic perspective, the so-called ant's-eye view, and a macroscopic perspective, the so-called bird's-eye view.

From the ant's-eye view, media education from early childhood should be ensured. The younger the children, the more they leave themselves vulnerable to the dangerous three Cs of unprotected media exposure as mentioned in the beginning of this chapter. They need to develop media literacy, or resistance to the negative influence of media, for which media education acts as a vaccine. For children who display varying degrees of understanding of media reality, we can easily imagine effective media education during the preschool years being carried out at the microsystem level in either the home or the preschool setting, be it a day-care center or a kindergarten. Yet in order to avoid separating learning and practice in media education, and from the perspective of where young children spend most of their time, the home appears to be the more appropriate location. The important point is that cooperation between home and school should be required to reinforce early childhood media education, because good balance of teaching young children both at home and school could bring in the three E advantages of media education: enjoyment, "edutainment," and empowerment (Komaya, 2006). It is necessary to focus on transitional periods in young children's development (between the ages of 5 and 6) and take this time to reinforce media literacy skills. Komaya (2010b) presents detailed results of research showing how a unified and continuous spiral curriculum from the preschool through the elementary school years best accomplishes this. Therefore, from an ant's-eye view, we should focus on specific periods in children's development.

At the same time, all educators, regardless of location, should take a bird's-eye view of media education and fully understand their roles. This means, first of all, that worldwide networks of media education should be strengthened by all sectors that have investments in media education and opened to all educators around the world. The 2010 World Summit on Media for Children and Youth discussed recommendations such as "creation of a platform for different actors (governments, teachers, social workers, youth . . .)" and the "establishment of common global conditions for children to participate" (World Summit on Media for Children and Youth, 2010, Challenges and Recommendations site). Establishing nationwide and worldwide networks is vital to accomplishing these goals. These networks act as bridges to the world for beginning educators. Finally, by joining networks of media education, educators will have more opportunities for discussing and realizing the "importance of developing critical thinkers" (World Summit on Media for Children and Youth, 2010, Challenges and Recommendations site). In order for these goals to be realized and take hold, it is necessary to establish an umbrella organization of accreditation that will verify whether quality and continuity are maintained in media education programs.

Note

[1] Potter's typology of media literacy has a more advanced level: the Experiential Exploring Stage (seeking out different forms of content and narratives), the Critical Appreciation Stage (accepting messages on their own terms, then evaluating them within that sphere), the Social Responsibility Stage (taking a moral stand that certain messages are more constructive for society than others. This is a multidimensional perspective based on thorough analyses of the media landscape; Potter, 2010, p. 23).

References

Adams, D., & Hamm, M. (2001). *Literacy in a multimedia age*. Norwood, MA: Christopher-Gordon.

Anderson, N., Tyner, K., & Pungente, J. (2003). *Scanning television* (2nd Ed). Toronto, ONT: Harcourt Canada.

Association for Media Literacy (AML). (2010). Home page. Retrieved October 4, 2010, from http://www.aml.ca/home/.

Aufderheide, P. (1992). *A report of the national leadership conference on media literacy*. Eugene: University of Oregon, Center for Advanced Technology in Education.

Australian Teachers of Media Queensland (ATOM). (2010). ATOM home page. Retrieved October 4, 2010, from http://www.atomqld.org/.

BBC. (2010). Learning Teachers site. Retrieved October 4, 2010, from http://www.bbc.co.uk/schools/teachers/.

British Film Institute (BFI). (1999). *Making movies matter: Report of the Film Education Working Group*. Retrieved October 4, 2010, from http://www.bfi.org.uk/education/research/advocacy/mmm/pdf/fewg.pdf.

Brown, J. A. (1998). Media literacy perspectives. *Journal of Communication*, 48(1), 44–57.

Brown, J. A. (2001). Media literacy and critical television viewing in education. In D. G. Singer & J. L. Singer (Eds.), *Handbook of children and the media* (pp. 681–697). Thousand Oaks, CA: Sage.

Buckingham, D. (1993). *Children talking television: The making of television literacy*. London: Falmer Press.

Buckingham, D. (2003). *Media education: Literacy, learning and contemporary culture*. Cambridge, UK: Polity Press.

Buckingham, D., & Domaille, K. (2009). Making media education happen: A global view. In C. Cheung (Ed.), *Media education in Asia* (pp. 19–30). New York: Springer Science + Business Media.

Carrick-Davies, S. (2004, January). *The dangers to children about Internet by Childnet International, U.K. at Children and Internet Forum*. Retrieved October 4, 2010, from http://www.iajapan.org/seminar/2004forumpdf/Stephen.pdf.

Channel One News. (2010). Teaching tools site. Retrieved October 4, 2010, from http://www.channelone.com/teachers/.

Center for Media Literacy. (2010). CML site. Retrieved October 4, 2010, from http://www.medialit.org/.

Dentsu. (2010). *Advertising elementary school*. Retrieved October 4, 2010, from http://www.dentsu.co.jp/komainu/.

Desmond, R. (1997). TV viewing, reading, and media literacy. In J. Flood, S. B. Heath, & D. Lapp (Eds.), *Handbook of research on teaching literacy through the communication and visual arts* (pp. 23–30). New York: Macmillan.

Dick, E. (1989). The media triangle. Retrieved October 4, 2010, from http://www.frankwbaker.com/mediatriangle.htm.

Dorr, A., Graves, S. B., & Phelps, E. (1980). Television literacy for young children. *Journal of Communication, 30*(3), 71–83.

European Commission (EC). (2007a). Country profiles. United Kingdom. In *Study on the current trends and approaches to media literacy in Europe.* Retrieved October 4, 2010, from http://ec.europa.eu/culture/media/literacy/docs/studies/country/uk.pdf.

European Commission. (2007b). Media Literacy profile—EUROPE. In *Study on the current trends and approaches to media literacy in Europe.* Retrieved October 4, 2010, from http://ec.europa.eu/culture/media/literacy/docs/studies/country/europe.pdf.

European Commission. (2009). *Study on assessment criteria for media literacy levels—A comprehensive view of the concept of media literacy and an understanding of how media literacy level in Europe should be assessed.* Retrieved October 4, 2010, from http://ec.europa.eu/culture/media/literacy/docs/studies/eavi_study_assess_crit_media_lit_levels_europe_finrep.pdf.

EC. (2010). Media literacy site. Retrieved October 4, 2010, from http://ec.europa.eu/culture/media/literacy/index_en.htm.

Government of Western Australia Curriculum Council. (1998). *Curriculum framework for kindergarten to year 12 education in Western Australia.* Osborne Park, Western Australia: Curriculum Council.

Hargrave, A. M. (2010). Media literacy in the digital age. *NHK Broadcasting Studies, An International Annual of Broadcasting Science, 8,* 189–209.

Hobbs, R. (1997). Expanding the concept of literacy. In R. Kubey (Ed.), *Media literacy in the information age: Current perspectives, information, and behavior* (Vol. 6, pp. 163–183). New Brunswick, NJ: Transaction.

Hobbs, R. (2000). *Assignment: Media literacy.* Retrieved October 4, 2010, from http://mediaeducationlab.com/assignment-media-literacy.

Hobbs, R. (2008). Debates and challenges facing new literacies in the 21st century. In K. Drotner & S. Livingstone (Eds.), *The international handbook of children, media and culture* (pp. 431–447). Thousand Oaks, CA: Sage.

Johnson, L. L. (2001). *Media, education, and change.* New York: Peter Lang.

Komaya, M. (2006). *Youjiki karajidouki niokeru media riterashi kyouiku no kaihatsu kenkyu. [Development Research on ML Education from early childhood through later childhood].* (Doctoral Dissertation, Ochanomizu University, 2006).

Komaya, M. (2010a). Media riterashi oyako sannkagata purojekuto "Roppon Natsuyasumi" no jissenteki kenkyu. [A study of parent–child participation in the "Roppon Summer Holidays" media literacy project: A collaborative project with the University of Tokyo and TV Asahi]. *Gakuen, 833,* 49–67.

Komaya, M. (2010b). *New media literacy education project "Fun with Media!" for Japanese kindergarteners and elementary school children.* Poster session presented at the World Summit on Media for Children and Youth 2010, in Karlstad, Sweden. This project is funded by Grants-in-Aid for Scientific Research by Ministry of Education, Culture, Sports, Science and Technology-Japan, 2007–2009.

Masterman, L. (1985). *Teaching the media.* London: Comedia Publishing Group.

Masterman, L. (1995). 18 principles of media education. Retrieved October 4, 2010, from http://www.media-awareness.ca/english/resources/educational/teaching_backgrounders/media_literacy/18_principles.cfm. Reprinted with permission from *Mediacy, the newsletter of Ontario's Association for Media Literacy, 17*(3, Summer).

Masterman, L. (1997). A rationale for media education. In R. Kubey (Ed.), *Media literacy in the information age: Current perspectives, information, and behavior* (Vol. 6, pp. 15–68). New Brunswick, NJ: Transaction.

Media Awareness Network. (2010). Media education in Ontario site. Retrieved October 4, 2010, from http://www.media-awareness.ca/english/teachers/media_education/ont_curricular_overview.cfm.

Media Literacy Project. (2010). About us site. Retrieved October 4, 2010, from http://www.nmmlp.org/about_us/index.html.

Media Smart. (2010). About us site. Retrieved October 4, 2010, from http://www.mediasmart.org.uk/about.php.

Messaris, P. (1998). Visual aspects of media literacy. *Journal of Communication, 48*(1), 70–80.

National Association for Media Literacy Education (NAMLE). (2010). About NAMLE site Retrieved October 4, 2010, from http://www.nmmlp.org/about_us/index.html.

NHK. (2010). NHK digital curriculum site. Retrieved October 4, 2010, from http://www.nhk.or.jp/school/english/index.html.

Ofcom. (2004). *Ofcom's strategy and priorities for the promotion of media literacy: A statement.* Retrieved October 4, 2010, from http://stakeholders.ofcom.org.uk/binaries/consultations/strategymedialit/summary/strat_prior_statement.pdf.

Ofcom. (2010). Ofcom home page. Retrieved October 4, 2010, from http://www.ofcom.org.uk/.

Ontario Ministry of Education. (1989). *Media literacy: Resource guide, intermediate and senior divisions*. Ontario: Ontario Ministry of Education.

Ontario Ministry of Education. (2006). *The Ontario curriculum grades 1–8 language.* Retrieved October 4, 2010, from http://www .edu.gov.on.ca/eng/curriculum/elementary/ language18currb.pdf.

Ontario Ministry of Education. (2010). The full-day early learning–kindergarten program. Retrieved October 4, 2010, from http://www .edu.gov.on.ca/eng/curriculum/elementary/ kindergarten_english_june3.pdf.

Potter, W. J. (2005). *Media literacy* (3rd ed.). Thousand Oaks, CA: Sage.

Potter, W. J. (2010). *Media literacy* (5th ed.). Thousand Oaks, CA: Sage.

Pungente, J. (2010a). *Media literacy key concepts.* In the site of Media Awareness Network. Retrieved October 4, 2010, from http://www .media-awareness.ca/english/teachers/media_ literacy/key_concept.cfm.

Pungente, J. (2010b). *Criteria for a successful media education program.* In the site of Center for Media Literacy. Retrieved October 4, 2010, from http://www.medialit.org/reading_room/ article118.html.

Quin, R., & McMahon, B. (1994). Media assessment. Groundbreaking assessment from Australia. Source: Strategies for media literacy. Excerpts digested from *Media Analysis: Performance in Media in Western Australian Government Schools 1991,* by Robyn Quin & Barrie McMahon. Retrieved October 4, 2010, from http://www.huntel.net/rsweetland/litera ture/media/assessment.htm.

Quin, R., & McMahon, B. (2001). Living with the tiger: Media curriculum issues. In R. Kubey (Ed.), *Media literacy in the information age: Current perspectives. Information and behavior* (pp. 307–321), 6. New Brunswick, NJ: Transaction.

Rafferty, C. S. (1999). Literacy in the information age. *Education Leadership, 57*(2), 22–26.

Schmitt, K. L., Anderson, D. R., & Collins, P. A. (1999). Form and content: Looking at visual features of television. *Developmental Psychology, 35,* 1156–1167.

Silverblatt, A., & Eliceiri, E. M. E. (1997). *Dictionary of media literacy.* Westport, CT: Greenwood Press.

Singer, D. G., Zuckerman, D. M., & Singer, J. L. (1980). Helping elementary school children learn about TV. *Journal of Communication, 30*(3), Summer, 84–93.

Singer, D. G., Singer, J. L., & Zuckerman, D. M. (1981). *Getting the most out of TV.* Santa Monica, CA: Goodyear.

Strasburger, V. C., & Wilson, B. J. (2002). *Children, adolescents, & the media.* Thousand Oaks, CA: Sage.

Thoman, E. (1995). *Four steps to success in media literacy* in the site of Center for Media Literacy. Retrieved October 4, 2010, from http://www .medialit.org/reading_room/article125.html.

Tyner, K. (1998). *Literacy in a digital world: Teaching and learning in the age of information.* Mahwah, NJ: Lawrence Erlbaum.

UNESCO. (2008, June). *Teacher training curricula for media and information literacy.* Background strategy paper, International Expert Group Meeting, Paris, UNESCO Headquarters.

UNESCO. (2010). *Media and information literacy* in the site of UNESCO. Retrieved October 4, 2010, from http://portal.unesco.org/ci/en/ev.php -URL_ID=31267&URL_DO=DO_TOPIC &URL_SECTION=201.html.

UN Alliance of Civilizations. (2010). *Media literacy education clearinghouse.* Retrieved October 4, 2010, from http://www.aocmedi aliteracy.org/.

von Feilitzen, C., & Bucht, C. (2001). Media education, literacy, communication. In *Outlooks on children and media, children and media violence yearbook 2001* (pp. 69–71). The UNESCO International Clearinghouse on Children and Violence on the Screen at Nordicom, Gothenburg.

Wilson, C., & Duncan, B. (2009). Implementing mandates in media education: The Ontario experience. In D. Frau-Meigs & J. Torrent (Eds.), *Mapping media education policies in the world: Visions, programmes and challenges* (pp. 127–140). New York: United Nations-Alliance of Civilizations in co-operation with Grupo Comunicar.

Worsnop, C. (2010). *Using rubrics to assess media work in the classroom.* In the site of Teaching Backgrounder, Media Awareness Network. Retrieved October 4, 2010, from http://www .media-awareness.ca/english/resources/edu cational/teaching_backgrounders/media_ literacy/using_rubrics.cfm.

World Summit on Media for Children and Youth. (2010, June). *Challenges and recommendations.* Retrieved October 4, 2010, from http:// www.wskarlstad2010.se/filer/challenges_and_ recommendations.pdf.

CHAPTER 35

Children's Advocacy Groups

A History and Analysis

Laurie A. Trotta

The Television Phenomenon

Just a few short years after World War II, television eclipsed radio as America's favorite form of electronic entertainment. The radio broadcast networks were already well established as the leaders in delivering programming to millions of Americans, and many of the programs and genres established on radio—including soap operas, game shows, Westerns, news and public affairs, and children's shows—made the transformation to the small screen as well.

As the networks took primary control of television programming, the public was left to devise its own methods for responding meaningfully to their offerings and for changing images considered troublesome. And, from the earliest days of the television industry, parents, church, social, and education groups have voiced concern over the influence this new force would have on viewers.

During the nascent era, most concern was centered on the effects of viewing violence. A few individuals, some journalists, and at times established institutions began working

to influence the images on TV. Over time, key media advocacy groups emerged and grew to serve as articulate voices on issues such as violence, stereotyping, mediocre programming, and blatant consumerism. The effects of these on shaping the values and behaviors of children were always of greatest concern. Eventually, organizations arose that focused on all issues as they relate to children and the media in its many forms. These have included gender and sexual health, disabilities, racial and cultural stereotypes, ageism and sexism, childhood obesity, consumerism, fighting the digital divide on the Internet, and understanding effects of all forms of on-screen entertainment.

These advocacy groups adopted a variety of approaches, both radical and conservative, for working to change what we see on TV, to inform the public about its rights, and to educate both the entertainment industry as well as the public on the effects of media on viewers.

Have the efforts of media advocates made a difference in what we see in filmed entertainment? Is our media landscape somehow a better place because they toiled? Where does the future lie for media advocacy? This chapter will trace the roots of children's media advocacy since the beginning of the television era. It will utilize texts, interviews, Internet data, and journalistic and scholarly reports as well as personal accounts from professionals to trace the trajectory and nature of media advocacy and the challenges for the future of these organizations. Finally, we will look at the new breed of social issues workers raised on the Internet with goals designed to carry media advocacy well into the mid-21st century. It is hoped that the exploration of where we have been will help illuminate the road ahead for future generations.

Radio Roots: A Brief History of How TV Got to Where It Is Today

Debate over whether electronic communications have educational value or are simply vehicles of commercialization goes back to the post–World War I era, when radio became readily available (Trotta, 2007). Commercial enterprises (e.g., Westinghouse and AT&T) as well as educational, community, and religious groups were granted licenses to broadcast over the public airwaves, but public-service stations were soon outdone by the wealthier commercial stations, which could offer professional-quality, continuous programming. Mass commercialization of the medium soon resulted. In response to this turn of events, the government ruled that commercial stations must offer airtime to serve the public interest (Trotta, 2007).

In the early years of radio, direct advertising was considered unpalatable by key government and broadcasting officials. This opinion was voiced at the First Radio Conference, called by Secretary of Commerce Herbert Hoover in 1922 (Head & Sterling, 1982). National Broadcasting Company (NBC) president David Sarnoff compared the network he envisioned with the great public institutions of the day, such as libraries, and made no mention of advertising as a great profit

maker for his company (Head & Sterling, 1982). The idea of radio sponsorship evolved several years later, as advertising agencies seized the opportunity to fill programming voids by creating shows sponsored by their client companies. The 1928 to 1929 radio broadcast season is considered the first full-scale network advertising year, although the practice of direct advertising, wherein programming actually stopped and a commercial took its place, did not take hold until the mid-1930s (Head & Sterling, 1982).

Television Takes Center Stage

The years 1948 to 1952 represent television's critical growth period, as the number of sets in American households rose from 250,000 to 17 million (Head & Sterling, 1982); the medium soon pushed radio aside as America's favorite source of broadcast entertainment.

The first signs of heightened controversy over violent content on TV occurred in the early 1950s following a rise in crime and juvenile delinquency that had swept the country. *Time* and *Newsweek* magazines published research indicating children's fare was among the most violent on the air, while the early advocacy group National Association for Better Radio and Television (NAFBRAT) reported that "the amount of crime on television should dismay all parents" (Turow, 1981, p. 20). This drew attention to the need for more quality programming.

In 1952, Congress held the first of decades of hearings on broadcast violence, examining both radio and television as possible instigators of real-world violence. This was at a time when only 23.5% of families owned television sets and only the major urban areas of the country could receive any visual broadcasts at all (Turow, 1981). The networks argued there was no proven link between mayhem in society and onscreen violence. Meanwhile, the National Association of Broadcasters (NAB) included a section entitled Responsibility to Children in the first edition of its Television Code in 1952 but offered no specific guidelines or framework to help broadcasters make responsible choices for the nation's youth (Turow, 1981).

The Wasteland

In 1960, the Federal Communications Commission (FCC) broached the concept of children constituting a special audience in need of particular sensitivities, although it issued no specific rules regarding content (Head & Sterling, 1982). One year later, then-FCC Chairman Newton Minow admonished programmers at the national NAB conference for failing to create a range of informative and inspirational programs that served the public interest, coining the much-used descriptive of the television landscape as "a vast wasteland" (Minow, 1961).

That same year, a new spate of television violence hearings took place on Capitol Hill, this time led by Senator Thomas Dodd of Connecticut. These hearings were derailed when the networks again countered the reports that the action-adventure violence on TV was promoting juvenile delinquency, reasserting that no causal link actually existed between the two. Meanwhile, in the halls of academe, University of Pennsylvania Professor George Gerbner began work in 1967 on the Media Violence Index, a more than 30-year study of violence on TV, while in 1972, the Surgeon General issued a major report documenting a link between screen violence and aggressive behavior, a study that was updated a decade later.

Action for Children's Television (ACT)

In 1968, a new organization called Action for Children's Television (ACT) was formed by a group of women in the Boston area who wanted to increase the diversity of television choices available to children. ACT was to become a powerful voice for children and the media in a series of government battles that lasted through the next quarter-century.

ACT first persuaded the FCC to hold hearings of proposed rule making that would govern certain aspects of children's programming. "People say the FCC was impenetrable, but in reality, we went to Washington in 1970 and were able to meet with six of the seven commissioners," said Peggy Charren, ACT's long time president (P. Charren, personal interview,

August 17, 1999). Specifically, ACT members wanted rules requiring at least 7 hours of children's programming scheduled throughout the week, not just on weekend mornings. ACT also put forth the notion that children's programs should be developed for specific age groups, each with its own developmental sensibilities.

After holding extensive hearings, the FCC rejected ACT's rule-making request. Instead, it issued a policy statement in 1974 urging broadcasters to voluntarily improve children's programming along the lines of the ACT proposals. One result was the NAB Television Code Board's adoption of special advertising rules for children's programs shortly thereafter (Head & Sterling, 1982).

Several years later, the FCC, still under pressure from ACT and other groups such as the national PTA, appointed a Children's Television Task Force to explore the extent to which broadcasters had complied with the 1974 policy statement. The task force studies found some improvement in advertising practices but little in the programming area (Head & Sterling, 1982). The FCC re-examined the issue in 1979, inviting comments on a number of possible steps that might be taken. However, before any action was taken, incoming FCC chair Mark Fowler ceased all attempts at regulation, advocating instead total deregulation for television programming, including children's.

Advocates then took the cause to Congress, and a decade later, the Children's Television Act of 1990 (CTA) was passed to improve educational broadcast programming for children. Congress did so after concluding that television has a significant impact on children and that it can be used as a tool to complement traditional education, help young people learn specific skills, or help prepare for formal schooling (Trotta, 1998).

The FCC was left the task of creating the specific rules necessary to enforce the Act, thus adopting the Children's TV Rules of 1996, a new set of standards designed to strengthen and implement the CTA. The guidelines outlined the number of hours television stations must air children's educational programming; sharpened the definition of educational programming; and adopted measures to improve public access to the programming. Although stations that do not comply with the rules risk losing their operating licenses, it falls to citizens and media advocates to watch the broadcasters' progress, as no government agency is monitoring the educational programming.

Peggy Charren closed ACT in 1993, and the collection of ACT's papers, tapes, and books is now housed in the Monroe C. Guttman Library at the Harvard Graduate School of Education.

At about the same time ACT was conducting its campaign before the FCC, advocates, researchers, and other concerned individuals were gathering forces on other fronts. The National Association for Better Broadcasting (NABB), a group opposed to violence in children's programming, in 1969 announced a "spectacular milestone" in broadcast consumerism (Head & Sterling, 1982, p. 504). Here, KTTV-TV in Los Angeles agreed to ban from its programming all episodes of the syndicated series *Batman, Superman,* and *Aquaman,* as well as to provide a "caution to parents" notice before airing any of 81 other series if scheduled before 8:30 PM (Head & Sterling, 1982, p. 504). The FCC struck down this agreement, citing censorship issues; subsequently, the agency adopted a policy statement that set up guidelines for such agreements in the future.

In 1975, the National Parent Teacher Association adopted a resolution demanding that networks and local television stations reduce the amount of violence in programs and commercials. The following year, the American Medical Association House of Delegates characterized television violence as an environmental hazard, while other leading medical groups, including the American Psychiatric Association and the American Academy of Pediatrics (AAP), issued statements on the risks of media violence and took steps to educate members as well as parents. More recently, the AAP garnered front-page coverage in *The New York Times* when its members agreed to urge their patients to limit TV watching (Mifflin, 1999).

During the late 1970s and 1980s, a new phenomenon occurred wherein court cases were initiated to explore the liability of the media in cases of real-world violence. For example, in *Zamora v. CBS et al.* (1979), parents of a Florida 15-year-old convicted of murdering a neighbor unsuccessfully sued all three networks for negligence for failing to prevent him from imitating television violence (UCLA Center for Communication Policy, 1995). Several other cases followed, and in 1999, parents of three students killed at a Kentucky high school filed a $130 million lawsuit against the entertainment industry asserting that media violence had inspired the boy who shot their children.

The Reagan era's policy of deregulation in television galvanized media advocates and created a wellspring of new academic research on the subject. In 1980, the National Coalition on Television Violence was formed, and literally dozens of children's media advocacy groups soon followed.

The industry also sponsored research in these areas. The National Television Violence Study (NTVS, 1996), sponsored by the National Cable Television Association and conducted by a team assembled by the nonprofit organization Mediascope, examined depictions across thousands of hours of television and reported that the types of televised violence most often portrayed on TV lead to desensitization, increased fear of being victimized, and learning aggressive attitudes and behaviors. At the same time, the UCLA Center for Communications Policy released a network-sponsored study that found the networks were reducing violence on screen (UCLA Center for Communication Policy, 1995).

Congress soon responded, passing the Telecommunications Act of 1996 that mandated V-chip screening devices for all televisions manufactured after 1999 and the creation of a rating system to identify video programming that contains sexual, violent, or other indecent material (U.S. Senate TCA, 1996), Meanwhile, on Capitol Hill in 1998, the Senate Judiciary Committee led by Senator Orrin G. Hatch once again examined the issue in its report, Children, Violence and the Media, and the NTVS (NTVS, 1998) revealed that 68% of all children's programming contains violence in a humorous context, considered a key factor in desensitizing children to real world violence.

On September 9, 2004, the Federal Communications Commission (FCC) issued new rules to improve children's television as the nation's broadcasters prepared to make the transition to digital television (DTV). By a unanimous vote, the five FCC commissioners established rules to help ensure that children have access to educational television programming and parents are able to identify educational shows (Trotta, 2007).

Today, parents, educators, civic and religious groups, academics, and politicians can add the prospect of mobile devices that make 24-hour Internet access for children a reality. In 2009, the FCC again entered the arena, proposing a Letter of Inquiry, *Empowering Parents and Protecting Children in an Evolving Media Landscape*, calling for information to explore the scope and potential benefits and detriments to children.

On June 4, 2010, a government report that reviewed and evaluated the status of industry, government, law enforcement, education and nonprofit efforts to promote online safety for children was published. *Youth Safety on a Living Internet* was submitted on behalf of the Online Safety and Technology Working Group (OSTWG) of the National Telecommunications and Information Administration and listed more than 100 advocacy, government and industry programs to educate and assist the public around online safety for children. Issues included cyberbullying, identity theft and online predators as well as the efficacy of blocking technologies, labeling and other means of shielding children from inappropriate content. OSTWG recommendations include:

- Keep up with the youth-risk and social-media research, and create a web-based clearinghouse that makes this research accessible to all involved with online safety education at local, state, and federal levels.
- Coordinate Federal Government educational efforts.
- Provide targeted online-safety messaging and treatment.
- Avoid scare tactics and promote the social-norms approach to risk prevention.
- Promote digital citizenship in pre-K–12 education as a national priority.
- Promote instruction in digital media literacy and computer security in pre-K–12 nationwide.

Approaches by Media Advocates

Approaches used by children's media advocates generally fall into broad categories and target different audiences. For example, a group of organizations now exists that works directly with the creative community, using positive, industry-friendly reinforcement based on public health research to inspire change for children. Other groups use sophisticated techniques to lobby government officials, while others effectively serve teachers, parents, and community groups by providing media literacy materials.

Impassioned individuals and groups have led landmark campaigns that helped in many ways to change what we see in the media, and we will examine their continuing efforts more fully below. Their work hinges on tactics that involve taking on the existing power structure: the networks, studios, judicial system, and federal government. The court established print and electronic news media to report on their issues, form coalitions with like-minded organizations, and fight what is akin to hand-to-hand combat with those who wield the power to create, legislate, and change media. Although variances in type, audience served, focus, budget, and size are the norm, some commonalties of approach do exist. Most of the organizations tend to weave together several of these approaches to create a mosaic of activities and initiatives that span audiences as well as methodologies.

The following methods for initiating change on television and other forms of screened entertainment have been used by media advocates (Trotta, 2007):

1. Working through government channels to effect policy change, for example, lobbying Congress and the Federal Communication Commission (FCC), testifying before government hearings, and filing FCC petitions to deny broadcast licenses or petitions of proposed rule making

2. Mobilizing the public around its rights under public interest clauses of broadcasting regulations

3. Sponsoring informational opportunities (e.g., conferences, workshops, and seminars) for industry executives and creative professionals to raise awareness and offering positive reinforcement in the forms of awards and seals of approval for perceived excellence in programming

4. Conducting research of parents on media-related issues in which the results are used

to inform the public, parents, government, journalists, and the creative community and broadcasters

5. Offering technical and consultative services or referrals to the entertainment industry to provide information on sensitive depictions in early stages of a project's development

6. Educating parents, teachers, and children of the hazards of media overconsumption through media literacy efforts (e.g., publishing and training)

7. Organizing consumer-based initiatives (e.g., letter-writing campaigns, boycotts) to exert pressure on advertisers, sponsors, and broadcasters to prohibit screening of individual episodes or movies

8. Orchestrating news media campaigns against individual programs, networks, or issues to help build awareness among the general public as well as in pressuring advertisers and broadcasters to effect change

The effects of advocacy groups on influencing entertainment have been sporadic and have historically ebbed and flowed along with the tides of popular opinion, politics, and personal relationships with individuals in the entertainment industry. It is difficult to gauge progress made by advocacy efforts. Much of the social change in the broadcast industry has occurred slowly due to the results of a gathering of many forces and pressures over time. Government has displayed a history of voicing concern over programming issues but has taken a very precautionary approach toward regulation. The commitment an advocate brings to the issue is often fraught with challenges. The often underfunded nonprofit consumer groups are engaging politically with some of the largest media corporations in the world, which possess economic and political infrastructures that present formidable obstacles (Montgomery, 2007).

Yet progress has been made. For example, individual producers and writers in children's television have come forth with truly educational and entertaining programming for children, especially the younger set. Nickelodeon/Noggin now offers 24 hours a day of commercial-free programming for preschoolers. PBS continues its educational fare for children for a segment of each programming day, while Discovery Kids, Disney, and other niche cable providers have greatly

increased the selections for children. Meanwhile, the old networks offer a host of weekend shows for young children greatly devoid of the violent subject matter that during the 1980s was regular fare. Programs such as Nickelodeon's *Blue's Clues*, PBS's *Cyberchase*, which teaches math concepts to middle schoolers, and Discovery's *Magic School Bus* are just a few that have proven that television can be both educational and entertaining. "When I was working in Children's Programming in the '80s it was really more about selling to the kids, and there was a lot of violence," veteran children's producer Nancy Steingard said. "But there has been a pulling back from this way of thinking today and there is some truly fine programming out there now. It may have been the results of advocacy groups in part, but these changes really must come down from the top" (N. Steingard, personal interview, January 12, 2007). In summarizing the strides made by advocacy efforts, Steingard adds:

> Clearly, the advocacy movement has had an effect on building awareness of issues, motivating and inspiring industry professionals, and utilizing government processes to lobby for change. It must be noted that the underlying commerciality of the television business will—unless enormous structural changes to the system are made—most likely remain a primary consideration in the industry. However, advocates represent the public, which votes by its viewing selections, supporting quality programming for children when available. Advocates have successfully exerted government pressure in the past, and as their ranks grow, those changes will happen more quickly. (N. Steingard, personal interview, January 12, 2007)

Meeting the expenses of advocacy work has always been a struggle and remains so. In order to fund their efforts, most advocates turn to the world of philanthropy. Farsighted organizations such as the Carnegie Corporation, the Robert Wood Johnson Foundation, the Markle Foundation, the Henry J. Kaiser Family Foundation, and dozens of others fund media advocacy work, either on a project-by-project scale or through general program support. However, funding has always presented challenges to advocates, who are resigned to spending a percentage of their time writing grants, hiring development professionals, and cultivating relationships with philanthropic organizations. Kathryn C. Montgomery, a professor at American University, is the former director of the influential Center for Media Education, now defunct. She recalls:

> It was hard to raise money. We were successful at it, but it was a real challenge. Some funders may simply not be interested, others change their focus, leadership and missions, and so you constantly have to be very creative and develop projects that are attractive to them. And sometimes this means that your core projects are only held together by your own passion and dedication. (K. C. Montgomery, personal interview, January 19, 2007)

Further complicating the issue of fundraising for media advocates is the sense that the funding world constitutes a "small pond" wherein many of the advocates working toward similar goals are, in fact, competing for the same pot of money from key philanthropies.

Another challenge has been the lack of continuity. Organizations rise and fall as issues come to the fore and then recede, and follow-up efforts sometimes fall by the wayside. In 2000, a survey was conducted of 33 media advocacy organizations working in the United States (Trotta, 2007). Of these, nine were regarded as having a visible presence in Hollywood and were considered the major groups working to effect change. Today, only three are still working in entertainment industry advocacy and two no longer exist, while the others have changed focus away from Hollywood or work in media literacy only. Each of these organizations had expertise in advocating in a focused area. When they moved on, if no remaining group stepped in to fill the gap, a vacuum ensued.

"An organization has its time," says Kathy Montgomery (personal interview, January 19, 2007), who has gone on to teach what she sees as the next generation of advocates. She further states,

> But continuity is an ongoing concern. When we first formed CME we saw a void in the media reform leadership, which had been so strong in the 1970s. Why did this happen? Strong leaders had gone to work in the Carter Administration, deregulation cut

them down, funders left . . . There was major jockeying on the part of the powerful media corporations in the policy arena, but very little representation of the public interest. When we closed CME, several organizations picked up aspects of our work, but not all of it continued. It's a real problem. (Kathy Montgomery, personal interview, January 19, 2007)

Influencing Media Content

Public health experts have long established the value of communicating with the public through entertainment products. Studies have shown that learning occurs through storytelling, and the learning is heightened when lessons are voiced by characters about whom viewers care (Trotta, 1998). Thus, it remains vital for advocacy groups to bring their messages to established media.

During the 1980s and 1990s, many advocacy groups—and even the federal government—began to internalize the importance of these ideas. A number of nonprofit organizations exist today whose primary mission is to work with the entertainment industry on depictions of a variety of social and health issues. These range from gender and race to teen sexuality, violence, population, environment, and mental health. These organizations generally work directly with the creative community, providing accurate information on health issues in a positive, industry-friendly fashion. National organizations whose primary mission is directly health care related, such as the American Medical Association, the American Academy of Pediatrics, and the Centers for Disease Control and Prevention, strongly believe in the value of reaching out to the entertainment industry and have created media information programs (W. E. Duke & Company, 2001).

Many health and nonprofit groups hired people with various backgrounds—from academia, entertainment, marketing, public relations, and journalism—to begin to reach out to entertainment industry professionals who create content. The mission of these entertainment resource professionals, as they are known, is to encourage the creative community to incorporate story lines, information, and characters into their products that will, in an entertaining way, educate the viewing public about certain issues. In this way, public health information can reach the public, and television and film creators could serve not only as entertainers, but—albeit as a secondary byproduct—educators as well.

But the points of entry are sometimes difficult to determine. Filmed entertainment is collaborative. It is created through a unique amalgamation of associations, partnerships, and alliances between the major studios, mini majors, networks, distribution companies, the stars themselves, and a group of writers, directors, and producers who drive the creative process. Advocates attempting this work need, first and foremost, to understand the business to which they are attempting to gain entry as well as the nature of most of television and film: to entertain. Personal relationships are key. For example, a media advocate met the executive producer of a hit network police show at a cocktail party in Los Angeles. During the course of their conversation, the advocate mentioned her work in violence and public health, and the producer expressed interest. Information was sent to him the next day, and a link was forged between the issue of violence depiction and a prime-time program.

Sensitive issues can emerge when any outside force attempts to influence an artist or artistic endeavor. Issues of censorship can arise, especially when one of the nonprofit organizations has government affiliations. This was illustrated in the experiment by the Office of National Drug Control Policy in the 2000 programming year to offer incentives for programs that used antidrug messages. Most writers consider themselves artists, and any whiff of attempting to unduly influence their work, as opposed to offering helpful ideas, will be rebuffed immediately.

The people conducting this pioneering work of reaching out to the entertainment industry with information for many multicultural and health issues have begun to build the methodology for success in their field. In 2006, organizers in Los Angeles formed a collegial association, Entertainment Resources Professional Association (ERPA), in which colleagues share information, strategies, and ideas. Members of ERPA range from the Gay & Lesbian Alliance Against Defamation to the National Youth Anti-Drug Campaign, the American Association of Pediatrics, and Suicide Awareness Violence in Education.

"Nonprofits attempting to bring their issue to the entertainment industry must first understand the special audience they are attempting to reach," says Lisa Cho Allen (personal interview, January 3, 2007), who cofounded ERPA in 2006 with Deborah Glick, Sc.D., Director of the Health and Media Research Center, University of California, Los Angeles (UCLA), School of Public Health, and Rachel Flores, also of UCLA. Furthermore, Allen observes,

> Writers for entertainment products are interested in emotional truth. If an issue cannot be dramatized and integrated into a story, then it most likely will not make it into programming. Executives at advocacy organizations must realize that the types of communications in entertainment outreach are different from a more traditional outreach campaign. The entertainment industry has the ability to dramatize an issue, to create empathy, a sense of shared understanding, as no other outreach work can do. But advocates will not get the message across in the same manner as they would in a traditional print or outreach campaign. (Lisa Cho Allen, personal interview, January 3, 2007)

Allen also suggests that success in this field does not have to be entire story lines built around issues. Simply having a character in passing comment on the importance, for example, of a health issue, can "reach literally millions of viewers and has the potential to open a window for them."

Unlike a few decades ago when caution was exercised to gain access to the industry, the work of advocates today is more valued and out in the open, Allen observes (personal interview, January 6, 2007). Indeed, an April 7, 2010, *Wall Street Journal* article featured network executives casually and somewhat proudly referencing the concept of "behavior placement," wherein characters from NBC shows such as *30 Rock* and *The Office* act out eco-friendly behaviors that advertisers hope will sway viewers' behavior.

At the same time this professional field is developing to work as partners in entertainment and health, advocates are becoming more savvy about the varied ways to access media. The power of groups of individuals networking on social media sites such as Facebook and Twitter must certainly be considered for their potential impact as influencers of social change. Says Allen: "If you are smart and want to be involved in advocacy you can reach around Hollywood."

Allen continues,

> Youth are multi-consuming media at a much faster rate than ever before—Instant Messaging and Web-surfing and watching TV and talking on their cell all at the same time. Being aware that this is happening and taking advantage of these opportunities is important to keep in mind. You can work with filmmakers at all different levels, post your own series of animation on your own site, and create your own content. This is an exciting time to be working in this field. The possibilities are endless. (Lisa Cho Allen, personal interview, January 5, 2007)

Further, a shift in approaches to funding advocacy efforts is slowly taking shape, moving away from philanthropies that provide funding toward ventures that are run like corporations and that are designed to do good but also to be self-sustaining entities, paving the way for more projects and forming a snowball effect for social change. Indeed, the Internet—which has already opened up pathways to media access never before imagined—also is making new funding sources available for advocates. Literally billions of dollars wielded by post–Baby Boomer entrepreneurs who have built vast fortunes around innovative ideas for using this new technology have become available. A new breed of technologically savvy philanthropist is emerging who wants to apply the knowledge gleaned from online business success to address today's problems. As one of these new waves of advocates proudly states in its advertising campaign, "Social Change is Changing" (Hollywood Hill, 2006/2007, p. 12).

A New Breed of Activism

As the 21st century pulses forward, a new breed of activists may be just on the horizon. Celebrities such as Bono, Drew Barrymore, Geena Davis, and others are using the power of fame to push social activism to the fore. Others working behind the scenes in Hollywood are using the power of global media to promote their causes. These new organizations are self-sustaining, savvy, and sometimes run as for-profit businesses. Their ideas are bold, and even their language represents a new dramatic approach. Ariel Hauter is a 20-something Los Angelino who cofounded The Hollywood Hill, a group of entertainment industry heavy hitters prepared to use the power of entertainment, the Internet, and new technologies to help solve social ills. Their website states,

> A new generation of Hollywood activists is taking over. But their focus is not on the Democratic Party . . . they have set their sights much higher. The world is now small and flat. And with new technologies, sciences, and the Internet, these world-renowned creators and powerbrokers are exercising their muscle to truly change the world. Considering the current threats against humanity, it's not a minute too soon. (Hollywood Hill, 2007)

According to Hollywood Hill (n.d.), "Hollywood is in transition" and "[Leaders] are looking for the corporate version of marching down the streets. Hollywood has matured into a business savvy industrial complex complete with large financial resources, tremendous influence, and yet a strong sense of social responsibility" (Hollywood Hill, 2007). Hollywood Hill (n.d.) further states,

> Such an ambitious project is not for the faint of heart. It's for those who understand the days of "Save the Whales" are over. Affecting change in a global community controlled by many far-reaching power centers requires having a solid foundation, a self-sustaining model, and serious talent and resources. It also requires a new mode of thinking . . . a hybrid approach, based on proven techniques, but adapted to a new marketplace with new tools.

Another exciting model for social change that utilizes the power of media is that of Participant Media, founded by Internet millionaire Jeff Skoll, the first president of eBay. This film production company blasted onto the scene in 2004 with an agenda to create entertaining films with a social mission but also to create full-fledged social action campaigns around each of its products. Participant has racked up several Academy Award nominations—and wins—with its roster of socially aware entertainment. Recent highly acclaimed films include *FOOD Inc.* and *Darfur Now*; *Syriana* (in partnership with Warner Bros.); *An Inconvenient Truth*; *Good Night, And Good Luck* (with Warner Independent Pictures, Section 8 and 2929 Entertainment); and *Fast Food Nation*. Participant (n.d.) states,

> . . . a good story well told can truly make a difference in how one sees the world. Whether it is a feature film, documentary or other form of media, Participant exists to tell compelling, entertaining stories that also create awareness of the real issues that shape our lives. We seek to entertain our audiences first, then to invite them to participate in making a difference next. (Participant Media, n.d.)

Furthermore,

> The company seeks to entertain audiences first, then to invite them to participate in making a difference. To facilitate this, Participant creates specific social action campaigns for each film and documentary designed to give a voice to issues that resonate in the films. Participant teams with social sector organizations, non-profits and corporations who are committed to creating an open forum for discussion, education and who can, with Participant, offer specific ways for audience members to get involved. These include action kits, screening programs, educational curriculums and classes, house parties, seminars, panels and other activities and are ongoing "legacy" programs that are updated and revised to continue beyond the film's domestic and international theatrical, DVD and television windows. To date, Participant has developed active, working relationships with 156 non-profits who collectively have the potential of reaching over 75 million people. (Participant Media, n.d.)

Time will tell whether these groups and others like them will use the power of media to effect real social change. Whatever their successes, they represent a new breed of entrepreneurial-style activists ready to harness the power of corporate America and technology to circumvent the traditional paths of advocacy and spur change on a massive scale.

Conclusions

The struggle between advocates and the media will continue and now includes broader definitions of entertainment such as Internet, gaming,

and all digital media. As the forms of media become more engaging and the time spent interacting with media is ever increasing, the efforts of advocacy groups must keep pace. Advocates must find ways to keep the flame burning from one leader to the next, and they must continue to keep abreast of new ways of reaching audiences through nontraditional methods such as entertainment industry outreach and direct campaigns through new media. They must find new modes of funding, ideally self-sustaining, that allow them to focus on the important work at hand. At the same time, bold new forms of advocacy are bringing new tactics to activism, using entertainment products and the Internet and adopting corporate models to bring causes directly to millions of potential allies on a global scale. Time will see what accomplishments they will bring and where they will take us.

Major Advocacy Groups and Their Philosophies

Following is a compendium of 20 media advocacy organizations working today in the United States (one is focused internationally). The organizations are organized by approach, methodology, and the audiences they primarily serve, although great overlap exists. The material in each instance was taken directly from the organization's website and/or published materials. The list is by no means complete and is only as up to date as the date of this printing, as new organizations rise and fall along with issues, economic environments, and the lives of founders and leaders. Since the first issue of this list was first complied in 2000, 13 once-thriving organizations are no longer operating in the field of media advocacy. Please also note that major university programs, as well as regional and state literacy programs, are not covered herein.

I. The following six organizations have a visible presence in Hollywood and can be considered the major groups working on a myriad of levels and with diverse audiences to affect change in entertainment for children. Audiences range from producers, writers, and directors to academicians to the general public. Methods include work in policy, outreach, direct contact with the creative community, and independent research:

American Center for Children and Media

http://www.centerforchildrenandmedia.org/
The American Center for Children and Media—an "executive roundtable" for TV and digital industry leaders—anticipates, analyzes, and acts regarding research findings, evolving technologies, social shifts, and the volatile marketplace. The result is positive initiatives in the service of audience needs and a coordinated response when the industry has to speak out against attacks or inaccuracies. In other words, the Center leads its constituents to "do well by doing good." The Kaiser Family Foundation and the American Center for Children and Media sponsor a roundtable discussion to focus on what proposals, policies, or practices are likely to emerge during the Obama Administration concerning children's media content and delivery.
Strategies:

1. Convenes its Executive Roundtable for forthright discussion of industry issues and to consider solutions or strategies that are child friendly, responsible, and sustainable

2. Offers insight and guidance on emerging and ongoing issues that influence the entertainment craft and business, challenging current practices as necessary

3. Serves as a public voice for the children's media industries where feasible

4. Continually amasses up-to-date research, news, and writings about children and media, from which it digests, analyzes, and disseminates information on trends and themes

Children Now: Children and the Media Program

www.childrennow.org
Works to improve the quality of news and entertainment media both for children and about children's issues through media literacy outreach, independent research, and public policy. Children Now is a nonpartisan, independent voice for children, working to translate the nation's commitment to children and families into action.

Strategies:

1. Media industry conferences: Annual national conference and 1-day symposia bring media industry leaders, children's advocates, and academic experts together to help better understand the impact media have on children

2. Public opinion surveys of kids and parents

3. Independent research on television and print media

4. Newsletter: current research on media as they pertain to children

5. Press workshops on important children's issues

6. Entertainment industry briefings: Encourages constructive story lines by briefing writers and producers on issues concerning children

7. Public policy development: Monitors legislation and regulations affecting children's media

8. Uses communication strategies to bring children into the national conversation. Newspaper and magazine features, radio and television coverage, advertising campaigns, community partnerships, and reader-friendly publications focus attention on children's needs and propose ways to meet them

9. Website disseminates information and stimulates action on behalf of children

Entertainment Industries Council, Inc. (EIC)

EIC is a nonprofit organization founded in 1983 by leaders in the entertainment industry to provide information, awareness, and understanding of major health and social issues among the entertainment industries and to audiences at large. Board of trustees hail from entertainment industries and other fields. EIC educates, serves as a resource to, and recognizes the writers, directors, producers, performers, and others who are committed to making a difference through their art.
Strategies:

1. Encouraging the entertainment industry to more effectively address and accurately depict major health and social issues

2. Serving as a bridge for information between the entertainment industry and public policy members

3. Being instrumental in affecting social change through providing educational materials, research, and training for entertainment industries

4. Promoting and recognizing the accomplishments of the entertainment industry in addressing public health and social issues

5. Developing programs to foster volunteerism to support public and private partnerships designed to serve the entertainment industry workplace and further enhance the industry's outreach to the general public

Entertainment Resource Professional Association

http://entertainmentresource.org

The Entertainment Resource Professionals Association (ERPA) is a coalition of independent organizations and individuals who work to inspire cause-specific story ideas within entertainment media and to provide accurate and unbiased public health information to members of television, film, and video game industries. ERPA's primary purpose is to serve as a support system and resource for its participants working in the new and growing field of entertainment outreach. ERPA participants hail from academia, government, and both the commercial and nonprofit sectors. Members can be educators, researchers, public health officials, public relations professionals, writers, journalists, publicists, advertisers, and media professionals, among others.

Strategies:

1. Network of health and media professionals provides film and television writers with free expert, unbiased research and fact-based information on issues relevant to its members

2. Holds monthly networking and informational meetings with guest speakers

Henry J. Kaiser Family Foundation: Entertainment Media and Public Health Program

www.kff.org

A leader in health policy and communications, the Kaiser Family Foundation is a nonprofit, private foundation focusing on major health care issues. Kaiser develops and runs its own research and communications programs, sometimes in partnership with other nonprofit research organizations or major media companies. Current partners in the United States include MTV, BET, Univision, Viacom/CBS, and Fox. Together, Kaiser's campaigns reach tens of millions of people annually and have won multiple Emmy and Peabody Awards in recent years.

The partnerships take a comprehensive communications approach, combining targeted public service messages with longer-form special programming, the integration of information and messaging into popular shows, extensive use of new media, and places to go for more information such as toll-free hotlines, information brochures, and websites. Kaiser establishes a contractual relationship with each of its media partners and works collaboratively to provide both expert substantive guidance and management of production and operations. Kaiser has also helped launch broadcast media initiatives around the world in Russia and India, as well as coordinated first-of-their-kind regional initiatives in Africa and the Caribbean now involving more than 100 broadcasters working together in almost 50 countries. Kaiser also serves as a nonpartisan source of facts, information, and analysis for policy makers the media, the health care community, and the public.

Strategies:

1. Provides information to those in the entertainment media who are incorporating public health issues into their programs

2. Offers both group and one-on-one briefings to media writers and producers on health issues as a way of encouraging more story lines on these issues

3. Conducts surveys of the public

4. Works with media researchers to measure content and impact of media depictions

5. Helps produce and evaluate public service announcements

6. Engages in partnerships with media producers to create special media campaigns

Population Communications International (PCI)

www.population.org

Works creatively with international media, nongovernmental organizations (NGOs), foreign health agencies, and other organizations to motivate individuals and communities to make choices that will influence population trends encouraging sustainable development and environmental protection. PCI works to integrate social messages into the story lines of programming, primarily soap operas, in developing countries around the globe.

Strategies:

1. Provides technical assistance and training for radio and television soap operas that feature social themes, particularly in developing countries. The characters in their productions become role models for the elevation of the status of women, use of family planning, small family size, AIDS prevention, and other related values.

2. Programs encourage professionals in the entertainment industry—including soap operas, talk shows, and computer games—to recognize the positive contributions they can make to increasing public awareness of important social and public health issues.

II. The following three organizations work to inform parents and educators by providing evaluations, guidelines, reviews, and other resources for navigating the media landscape; several have devised their own film and television ratings to further assist parents in making media choices.

Coalition for Quality Children's Media (CQCM)—KidsFirst

www.kidsfirst.org

The Coalition for Quality Children's Media is a national, nonprofit organization founded in 1991 whose mission is to teach children critical viewing skills and to increase the visibility and availability of quality children's media. The Coalition is a voluntary collaboration comprising more than 100,000 media professionals, lobbyists, policy makers, child advocates, educators, parents, and families nationwide.

Strategies:

1. Operates KIDS FIRST, a program that evaluates and rates videos, CD-ROMs, and television for children aged infant to 18 years as well as conducting critical viewing workshops. Titles submitted are reviewed by volunteer jurors nationwide.

2. A collaboration of more than 100,000 concerned adults

3. KIDS FIRST! endorsements and recommendations

4. KIDS FIRST! film festival

5. KIDS FIRST! junior film critics club

6. KIDS FIRST! top 100 kids' films list—on Amazon.com

Common Sense Media

http://www.commonsensemedia.org/

Common Sense Media is dedicated to improving the lives of kids and families by providing the trustworthy information, education, and independent voice they need to thrive in a world of media and technology.

Strategies:

1. Website offers reviews of films, television, music, and video games

2. Promotes digital literacy and citizenship

3. Works to improve consumer tools and ratings to empower families to make smarter media choices

4. Federal and state policy work includes white papers

Dove Foundation

www.dove.org

A nonprofit encouraging the creation, production, distribution, and consumption of wholesome family movies and videos.

Strategies:

1. Awards a Dove Seal to any movie or video that is rated "family friendly" by its film review board

2. Selects certain high-quality PG, PG-13, and R-rated films and recommends their release in family-edited versions

3. Rallies consumer support to encourage filmmakers to produce more wholesome family-scripted movies

4. Holds Dove Family Film Festivals throughout the country

5. Provides young hospitalized children with educational programming through its Children's Hospital Dove Movie Channel

Focus on the Family—Plugged In

http://www.pluggedin.com/

The Christian organization Focus on the Family hosts a comprehensive media site, Plugged In, that reviews television, films, videos, music, and video games. Reviewers work through the prism of their religious views, but parents interested in learning about possibly objectionable materials in entertainment products may find this site helpful.

Strategies:

1. Movie, video, television, music, and game reviews for parents with a Christian perspective

2. Newsletter on media issues

3. Conducts polls

III. A specific network of groups operating across the country is striving to build media literacy among parents and teachers and to educate the public on the issues surrounding media and their health effects on our nation's children. The following 11 organizations were examined; those marked by an asterisk represent coalitions:

Action Alliance for Children (AAC)

www.4children.org

A nonprofit information agency committed to educating and empowering people who work with and for children. AAC serves as a resource for policy makers, children's service providers and advocates, and the media. AAC provides information on current trends and public policy issues affecting children and their families. In addition, the agency facilitates dialogue among diverse community groups (child-care workers, educators, parents, human service providers, advocates, media, and policy makers). AAC is committed to improving the lives of children and families and believes that sharing information is the first step towards that goal.

Strategies:

1. Conducts conferences, media dialogues, workshops, and training on current child-related issues. AAC's media forums enable children's advocates and the press to discuss effective ways to disseminate information about children's issues.

American Academy of Pediatrics (AAP): Media Matters

www.aap.org

For more than 30 years, the AAP has addressed the impact of the media on children and adolescents. In 1997, the AAP launched Media Matters, a national campaign to make pediatricians, parents, and children more aware of the influence that media can have on children, both mentally and behaviorally, positively and negatively. A key element is to teach basic media literacy and to be more discriminating about media use. Media Matters addresses all media and covers a range of issues including the use of tobacco, alcohol, and illicit drugs; aggression and violence; sex and sexual exploitation; nutritional issues; and self-image.

Strategies:

1. Provides materials, training, and events for parents, entertainment industry, and health professionals on topical media issues

2. Makes available a media history form to give pediatricians concrete information about a child's media exposure

3. Has developed policy statement on media education that focuses on the public health impact of the media and how the medical community can address such impact

4. Letter-writing campaign aims to prevent children from seeing potentially harmful violent or sexually explicit content by encouraging the public to send letters to theaters and retailers in their communities and asking them to provide quality family entertainment and to enforce the rating system

5. Sponsors Turnoff Week and Back to School

Center for Media Literacy

www.medialit.org

The Center for Media Literacy (CML) is an educational organization that provides leadership, public education, professional development, and educational resources nationally. Dedicated to promoting and supporting media literacy education as a framework for accessing, analyzing, evaluating, creating, and participating with media content, CML works to help citizens, especially the young, develop critical thinking and media production skills needed to live fully in the 21st-century media culture. The ultimate goal is to make wise choices possible.

Strategies:

1. Develops and distributes, via a printed and online catalog, media literacy materials to teachers, schools, parents, youth and community leaders, and others

2. Designs, develops, and conducts media literacy workshops, teacher training, seminars, and special events, as well as cosponsors national conferences

Center for Screen-time Awareness

http://www.tvturnoff.org/

Working to make screen-time reduction a vital and integral part of all plans that improve health, education, and wellness while building stronger families and communities.

Strategies:

1. *National TV-Turnoff Week:* An annual event initiated in 1995 that encourages Americans to voluntarily turn off their TV sets for 7 days and rediscover that life can be more constructive, rewarding, healthy,—even informed—with more time and less TV

2. Encourages game nights in the family, school, and community as an alternative to media viewing, along with other family-friendly, community-building events

3. Extensive website, forums, and information

Just Think Foundation

www.justthink.org

Founded in 1995 as a concerned response to the ever-increasing deluge of messages youth receive from television, radio, film, print media, electronic games, and the Internet, Just Think teaches young people media literacy skills for the 21st century. Just Think has been successfully creating and delivering in-school, after-school, and online media arts and technology education locally, nationally, and internationally for 13 years. Works to stimulate critical thinking about popular media and strives to equip young people with literacy tools that will be crucial in their future. These tools include the ability to comprehend the content of media and master

the technical skills to produce media messages in various forms, from broadcast public service announcements to websites.

Strategies:

1. Producing innovative media arts and technology curricula that ignite young minds and encourage critical thinking

2. Delivering exciting in-school and after-school programs that teach essential media literacy concepts and vital media arts and technology skills to youth and their caring adults

KIDSNET

www.kidsnet.org

National nonprofit computerized clearinghouse and information center devoted to children's television, radio, audio, video, and multimedia. Helps children, families, and educators intelligently access the educational opportunities available from television, radio, and multimedia sources by encouraging media literacy in children and a commitment to educational excellence in broadcasters.

Strategies:

Works with health and social service professionals, community organizations, and educators, as well as media professionals and parents, to create and disseminate educational materials for children ages preschool through high school. Some of KIDSNET's outreach activities include:

1. A monthly media guide describing programs for children, families, and educators referenced by air date, curriculum areas, grade levels, supplemental materials, related multimedia, off-air taping rights, and sources for more information

2. Media News, a quarterly resource of awards, events, legislation, regulation, technology, services, research, grants, and competitions related to children's media

3. The production and distribution of study guides to be used in conjunction with programming for children and families. Study guides are designed for various curriculum areas including science, literature, history, social studies, and health. These are distributed to a targeted list of teachers, librarians, health workers, and social service professionals free of charge.

4. Provides a unique forum for dialogue on areas of mutual interest with producers and networks representing commercial, cable, and public television

5. Offers consulting and technical assistance to children's programmers and broadcasters in education and public affairs

Media Education Foundation (MEF)

http://www.mediaed.org

The Media Education Foundation produces and distributes documentary films and other educational resources to inspire critical reflection on the social, political, and cultural impact of American mass media.

Strategies:

1. Produces and disseminates award-winning resources for students of media literacy, educators, parents, and community leaders

2. Conducts research on timely media issues

National Association of Media Literacy Education*

http://www.amlainfo.org/

The National Association for Media Literacy Education (formerly Alliance for a Media Literate America) is a national membership organization dedicated to advancing the field of media literacy education in the United States. Membership includes K–12 teachers, academics, health care professionals, community activists, and students.

Strategies:

1. Brings together a broad-based coalition of media literacy practitioners and advocates from diverse fields, professions, and perspectives in a national, nonprofit membership organization to act as a key force in bringing high-quality media literacy education to all students in the United States, their parents, teachers, health care providers, counselors, clergy, political representatives, and communities.

National PTA: Family and Community Critical Viewing Project

www.pta.org

The PTA is the nation's largest volunteer child-advocacy organization, with nearly seven million members, committed to uniting the home, school, and community in promoting the education, health, and welfare of children and families. PTA leaders have been involved with the issue of violence on television in both community programs and in the legislative arena since the 1970s.

Strategies:

1. National PTA leaders play a pivotal role in representing members at key meetings of educational groups, government organizations, the media, and other child advocacy groups.

2. Provides extensive publications and website information, tipsheets for parents on viewing habits, safety strategies, video gaming information, and more.

Parents Television Council (PTC)

www.parentstv.org

Established in 1995 by television legend Steve Allen to encourage positive, family-oriented television programming to the entertainment industry, PTC encourages grassroots mobilization to restore television to its roots as an independent and socially responsible entertainment medium.

Strategies:

1. Organizes a group of entertainment industry leaders to serve as members of the advisory board. These individuals address issues relating to television entertainment and its impact on American families and assist in representing the interests of the PTC in Hollywood.

2. Monitors prime-time television for areas of concern

3. Publishes special reports focusing on topics relating to the content of television

4. *Family Guide to Prime Time*: Profiles sitcoms and dramas on ABC, CBS, Fox, NBC, UPN, and WB; provides information on subject matter that is inappropriate for children; offers comprehensive study of prime-time content that clearly identifies shows that promote family-friendly themes. Uses an easy "traffic light" rating system (red, yellow, and green) to signal a show's suitability for children based on language, violence, and sexual situations, as well as overall content.

*Teachers Resisting Unhealthy
Entertainment (TRUCE)**

http://www.truceteachers.org/
Teachers Resisting Unhealthy Children's
Entertainment is a national group of educators deeply concerned about how children's
entertainment and toys are affecting the play
and behavior of children in our classrooms.
Strategies:

1. To raise public awareness about the nega-
    tive effects of violent and stereotyped toys
    and media on children, families, schools,
    and society

2. To work to limit the harmful influence of
    unhealthy children's entertainment

3. To provide children with toys and activities
    that promote healthy play and nonviolent
    behavior at home and school

4. To create a broad-based effort to eliminate
    marketing to children and to reduce the sale
    of toys of violence

5. To support parents' and teachers' efforts to
    deal with the issues regarding media

References and Additional Readings

Advocates for Youth. (2007). *Advocacy for adolescent reproductive and sexual health.* Retrieved
February 22, 2007, from www.advocatesfor
youth.org/advocacy.htm.

Barber, B. R. (1995). *Jihad vs. McWorld.* New York:
Ballantine Books.

Brown, L. (1971). *Television: The business behind
the box.* New York: Harcourt Brace Jovanovich,
Inc.

Brown, L. (1979). *Keeping your eye on television.*
New York: Pilgrim Press.

Chozick, A. (2010, April 7). What your TV is telling
you to do. *Wall Street Journal.*

DeGaetano, G., & Grossman, D. (1999). *Uncorrected
proof: Stop teaching our kids to kill: A call to
action against TV, movies & video game violence.* New York: Crown.

Federal Communications Commission. (2009).
*Empowering parents and protecting children
in an evolving media landscape.* MB Docket
No. 09-194 (2009). Retrieved April 15, 2010,
from http://hraunfoss.fcc.gov/edocs_public/
attachmatch/FCC-09-94A1_Rcd.pdf.

Gerbner, G. (1998). *Casting the American scene: A
look at the characters on prime time and daytime television from 1994–1998* (Screen Actors
Guild Report, December 1998). Retrieved April
5, 2007, from http://www.media-awareness
.ca/english/resources/research_documents/
reports/diversity/american_scene.cfm.

Head, S. W., & Sterling, C. H. (1982). *Broadcasting in
America: A survey of television, radio, and new
technologies* (4th ed.). Boston: Houghton Mifflin.

Hobbes, R. (2010). *A trip to the FCC: Advocating for net neutrality.* Media Education Lab,
retrieved April 20, 2010, from http://media
educationlab.com/blog/trip-fcc-advocating-
net-neutrality.

Hollywood Hill. (2006/2007, Dec./Jan.). *Moving
Pictures Magazine*, p. 12.

Hollywood Hill. (n.d.). *Our mission.* Retrieved
February 22, 2007, from www.hhill.org/hill/
about_mission.

Kotler, P., & Roberto, E. L. (1989). *Social marketing: Strategies for changing public behavior.*
New York: Free Press.

Mifflin, L. (1999, Aug. 4). Pediatrics group offers
tough rules for television. *New York Times.*

Minow, N. N. (1961). *Television and the public
interest.* Speech delivered May 9, 1961, to
the National Association of Broadcasters in
Washington, DC. Retrieved May 25, 2010, from
http://www.americanrhetoric.com/speeches/
newtonminow.htm.

Minow, N. N., & Lamay, C. L. (1995). *Abandoned
in the wasteland: Children, television and the
first amendment.* New York: Hill and Wang.

Montgomery, K. C. (1989). *Target: Prime time.*
New York: Oxford University Press.

Montgomery, K. C. (2007). Advocating children's
television. In J. A Bryant, *The children's television community* (pp. 229–257). Mahwah, NJ:
Lawrence Erlbaum.

Murray, J. P., & Salomon, G. (Eds.). (1984). *The
future of children's television.* Boys Town, NE:
Boys Town.

*National Television Violence Study (NTVS) Executive
Summary (1994–1995).* (1996). Studio City,
CA: Mediascope.

*National Television Violence Study (NTVS) Executive
Summary (Vol. 3).* (1998). Thousand Oaks,
CA: Sage.

Online Safety and Technology Working Group.
(2011). *Youth Safety on a Living Internet.*
Retrieved June 12, 2011, from http://www
.ntia.doc.gov/reports/2010/OSTWG_Final_
Report_070610.pdf

Participant Media. (n.d.). *About Participant.*
Retrieved April 28, 2010, from http://www
.participantmedia.com/company/about_us.php.

The social effects of electronic interactive games; an annotated bibliography. (1996). Studio City, CA: Mediascope.

Trotta, L. (1998). *Building blocks: A guide for creating children's educational television.* Studio City, CA: Mediascope.

Trotta, L. (2007). The changing landscape: Media advocacy for the new millennium. In J. K. Asamen, G. L. Berry, & M. L. Ellis (Eds.), *Handbook of child development, multiculturalism, and media* (pp. 419–432). Thousand Oaks, CA: Sage.

Turow, J. (1981). *Entertainment, education, and the hard sell: Three decades of network children's television.* New York: Praeger.

UCLA Center for Communication Policy. (1995). *The UCLA television violence monitoring report.* Los Angeles, CA: Author.

U.S. Senate. (1996). *Telecommunications Act (TCA) of 1996,* 104th Congress 2d Session. Washington, DC: U.S. Government Printing Office.

U.S. Senate (Judiciary Committee). (1999, September 14). *Children, violence and the media: A report for parents and policy makers.* [Online]. Available: http://www.senate.gov/~judiciary/mediavio.html [9 August 1999].

Valenti, F. M. (2000). *More than a movie: Ethics in entertainment.* Boulder, CO: Westview Press.

W. E. Duke & Company. (2001). *Script doctors? Developing a Hollywood health information service for the entertainment industry.* Retrieved April 29, 2010, from www.rwjf.org/reports/grr/038104.htm?gsa=1#int_grantinfo.

A Final Word From the Editors

The Future of Literacy and of Pictorial Consciousness

We introduced this handbook by calling attention to the fact that, even though written language and human reading have a 6,000-year history, really widespread popular literacy is largely a 19th- and 20th-century phenomenon. The emergence of the electronic media in the 20th century overlapped with an increase in reading and writing for great masses of children in Japan, the Soviet Union, and China, as well as many other Asian and Central European nations. Universal literacy on our planet has yet to be achieved, however. Sadly, there remain seemingly modern cultures in which male leaders continue to resist the education of women.

Learning to read fluently takes children several years of sustained motivation and effort. By contrast, listening to radio or recorded music and watching films or television provide an almost immediate impact. That direct influence may explain why the electronic media have leapfrogged over the slower-paced acquisition of literacy in attracting the attention of children and youth around the world. Once, the young Abe Lincoln, Charles Dickens, and Mary Ann Evans (George Eliot), to name but a few, found their imaginations soaring as they sat by the fire and pored over the densely written, small-print, sparsely illustrated books of the 1800s. Today, almost certainly reflecting our early exposure to film

and television, we and our children prefer more lavishly illustrated books. The staid *New York Times,* long resistant to the flashy, brief television news summaries or to the encapsulated journalism of *USA Today,* now presents many shorter reports and vivid, color photographs. Will we become a chiefly pictorial society, hardly reading at all, in the 21st century?

The amazing upsurge of computer usage not only by adults but also by children in just the last few years provides a challenge to such a view. Although the Internet is replete with graphics and even with the newest software such as CDs and video-moving images, reading written text and engaging in sequential information processing remains critical for effective use of computers by children. Campaign rhetoric in the United States and even President Clinton's State of the Union Address in 2000 referred to the "digital divide," a recognition that not only relative economic affluence but also literacy is necessary for providing *all* children with the benefits of computer usage at home or at school. As computers become cheaper and more routinely available in most homes and schools, they will represent a countervalent force against the drift toward a purely pictorial, nonlinear-thinking society that some have feared as television has taken over the world. The amazing surge in computer-based commercialism that has characterized the past few years has the potential for both economic and social exploitation of child users (see Chapter 31). At the same time, however, the very attractiveness of the cultural novelties, the games, the educational and social features of e-mail and benign chat rooms, blogs, Twitter, and iPads are influences that can motivate improving reading skills and other basic educational competencies. Letter writing, once so central a feature of the social experience of educated children and adults across the life span, had become almost a lost art in the last half of the 20th century. We suddenly see its modified return and attractiveness for the young with the proliferation of worldwide e-mail and texting communication.

Voice-comprehension technology is nearly perfected. Children can speak to a computer that will respond with still graphics and moving pictures so that we might envision a future where even the crude abbreviated written language of texting may no longer be necessary. Oral verbiage and the visual interchanges, now available through Skype, may suffice as a means of communication as they once did for the great majority of our species. A "bookless" prospect was already anticipated by novelists in the years just before the emergence of computers. As had been the case from ancient Egypt through the Middle Ages, in those stories, only a small cadre of an elite literate class will be needed to upgrade software and to design new technology. Even in these days when we already see university libraries being restructured to eliminate their huge book collections, we are not ready to accept this Aldous Huxley, George Orwell, or Ray Bradbury pessimistic view of the human future. Our contributors indicate that research has already begun to examine the impact of the "computer–television complex." We can expect more studies comparing (with appropriate demographic controls) children who spend several hours a day just with television, others who combine TV and computers, and others who use only computers (taking into account, of course, content variations in these media). We can see if, over a period from ages 4 or 5 to 8 or 9, we can observe differential literacy trends. Even with the great increase in home and school computer availability, there is enough variability in the timing of these developments across homes and schools that we may still be able to identify well-matched groups whom we can follow up on in the next decade.

Many of the research studies reviewed in the handbook were generated by concerns that the electronic media would severely affect the slow human gains in literacy and formal education or in logical, orderly thought. Even though the scientific data suggested that such a risk might be real in a world in which only passive viewing of entertainment television prevailed, the computer society that must still spread to children all over the planet seems likely to mitigate that danger. With increased use of home theaters, large screens, and large numbers of diversified cable channels but also computers integrated with the television medium through "boxes" and keypads, we may be forging a new kind of consciousness. Smell transmittal is already technologically feasible, so Aldous Huxley's 1930s *Brave New World* fantasy of "smellovision" may soon be a reality. Yes, we may be more pictorial and sensory, but we may also find that we cannot be effective in this emerging electronic society unless we are also literate. Parents will have to confront their responsibility to monitor media usage by children and also to support and extend the tremendous educational potential of the visual, written, and auditory messages that come into the home. Our educators will have to build *media literacy* into their curricula not only as "add-ons" to prevent harmful influences of violent television content but also as fundamental skills in computer usage, as crucial for children as reading, writing, and arithmetic. Such media literacy, however, will be ineffective without the three Rs. Teacher preparation will continue to require more training in computer mastery and media literacy. We can expect great changes in traditional pedagogical education and perhaps, eventually, even in classroom organization.

We completed a study sponsored by the U.S. Department of Education regarding computer availability and usage in public libraries. We found that every one of the 98 libraries surveyed in each state of the union now had computers and that librarians were willing to help in the use of computers and software. Every library in our survey also had a preschool program, and practically all permitted borrowing videos for home use. We can take the optimistic view that books may not disappear from libraries but that libraries may also begin to play a role in training children and their parents for media literacy as well as reading.

Even with the accelerating increases in accessibility of computer-based attractions for children, the most recent reports, such as that by the Kaiser Family Foundation (described in several chapters of this volume) and our own 16-nation study cited in our Introduction, make clear that broadcast television continues to be by far the most attractive medium for entertainment of children. The combination of federal government intervention through legislation and FCC rule making has yielded what might be called a growth spurt in children's television (Mifflin, 1999). The large networks and their affiliates have joined the Public Broadcasting Corporation in providing educationally slanted entertainment shows. The proliferation of cable channels has also opened new directions for child-oriented programming spearheaded by the congressional legislation; the Nickelodeon channel may have led the way, followed by the Disney Channel, the Discovery Kids' Channel, and others. The commercial success of Nickelodeon and, alas, the recognition of the vast sales generated by licensing toys, games, and dolls or action figures derived from televised children's shows on both public and commercial outlets have encouraged producers to present more child-directed shows that at least have some educational and socially constructive features. The result is that there has been an increase in children's viewing of child-oriented programming and somewhat less viewing of adult-oriented shows.

What conclusions about writing and producing children's programming can we draw from the chapters of this handbook? A series of suggestions about the programming of entertaining children's material that can be reasonably age specific, educational, reasonably constructive in its influence, and relatively free of those serious hazards of TV viewing for children so well brought out

in Chapters 11 to 23 of this handbook can be found in *Public Broadcasting: Ready to Teach*, which we prepared many years ago as a report to Congress for the Corporation for Public Broadcasting (CPB; Corporation for Public Broadcasting, 1993). We believe the same suggestions in this report apply to videos, CD-ROMs, and computer games and websites, although more research evidence for these media has yet to be accumulated. Practical suggestions along similar lines can also be found in Chapters 6 through 10 and in a number of advocacy chapters in Part III.

Growing Up in an Electronic Environment: Implications for Child Development and for Research

Recent studies suggest that computer involvement is reflected in less time spent with family and friends, less out-of-home store shopping, and, if anything, more time being spent on work at home after regular workplace hours (Markoff, 2000; Richtel, 2010). What impact will this trend, if it continues, have on children, not only through their experiencing computer-focused parents but also through their mimicking this adult behavior themselves and growing up either watching more television or spending more solitary time in front of the computer? The concept of home-theater rooms in which the TV is integrated with computer-driven boxes is spreading. Will we see a growing "real human" social isolation among children? The virtual social contacts of e-mail and chat rooms may not really compensate for direct communication and play with peers. Even if organized sports like Little League or "Moms' Soccer" continue to be fostered on weekends, will there be time for just spontaneous play and fooling around with family members and peers?

The challenge for research suggested a decade ago in our handbook generated new studies that tracked children's attention, comprehension, and social interaction patterns in settings where both television viewing and computer activity are part of their daily experience. We see some meaningful use of computers by children and how such experience predicts later school readiness as well as general computer skills. Can we assume that the relative ease of television watching will, to some degree, displace the time needed to master the more interactive computer skills? Will we be able to identify with more certainty groups of children whose involvement with television *and* computers, even with the video contacts of Skype, may be putting them at risk for social isolation? It may turn out that our human capacity for adjustment to new technologies may preclude such a possibility, but we will need careful research observation to reassure us on that point.

An intermediary stop between complete engrossment of children in the TV screen and the more interactive features of e-mail or computer games may emerge as educationally oriented websites proliferate on the Internet. According to some estimates, 93% of U.S. children between 12 and 17 years old are online; 87% of 8- to 18-year-olds in the United States live in a home with at least one video game console; and 79% of 13- to 19-year-olds have a mobile device (see Chapter 4). Websites for children that include some learning materials, follow-ups on televised programming, or specific games and education sites are expanding and ideally may serve as the bridge between home and school. Some of these websites are free to subscribers; others depend on subscriptions and advertising. We can recommend that parents and educators investigate PBS Online, the Children's Television Workshop Online, Nickelodeon Online, and primarily for pure entertainment, the Disney Online websites. On the positive side, in addition to educationally useful material presented in an enjoyable fashion, one can also note that most of these websites *do not* collect or distribute personal information from children. Such websites do, however, include *advertising* and promotion of products derived from their TV programming. Chapter 13 in this volume discusses the laws and safeguards for young children related to Internet advertising. Until our society respects children enough to subsidize such important educational outlets free of commercialism, we may have to accept advertising as a major source of revenue. Still

another burden of monitoring the sites and educating children about commercialism to prevent undue exploitation will fall on parents, child care workers, and educators.

The research studies reviewed in our handbook point to significant hazards for children who watch violent content and, to a lesser extent, sexually provocative content on television. Will such content be as prevalent in the new, more differentiated cable programming now emerging? What risks may follow, especially with the high level of sexual content one can easily stumble on when surfing the 'Net? What new dangers may emerge when frequent levels of "risky" TV viewing are combined with computer game playing or the use of the Web and chat rooms by early school-age or pubescent children?

The chapters in this handbook also have pointed to many potentially constructive uses of television. One can anticipate even more effective prosocial and constructive learning possibilities when judicious TV viewing is combined with the exploration of learning materials specially prepared for the computer. How can we maximize such engagement and opportunities for children? What role can parents, educators, and producers play in enhancing the socially adaptive employment of computers by children across the spectrum?

Special problems regarding the protection of children are raised by the largely unregulated nature of the Internet and World Wide Web. How can children be protected from child abuse or unwarranted exposure to sexual or commercial exploitation in the upcoming combinations of television and computer use? There have already been a few cases of child molestation set up through initial chat-room exposure. Here, the computer's impact is even more potentially negative than the research has shown for mere exposure from television viewing because of the Internet's interactive nature. Will we need new laws, blocking procedures, and, necessarily, increasing parental or other adult caregiver education to establish suitable controls? Linda Sanchez, a Congresswoman from California, recently introduced the Megan Meier Cyberbullying Prevention Act that would make it a federal crime to cause emotional distress to others through use of the Internet (Singer, 2009).

Beyond the risk of sexual molestation or product-purchase exploitation via chat rooms and websites, there is still a further hazard for children—*privacy*. Protection of children in the online environment has been the focus, since 1999, of a succession of Safer Internet programs implemented by the European Commission (the executive body of the European Union). It is the only pan-European initiative relating to child protection online and has several actions that have proved effective. As part of its actions, the program has initiated a number of European networks bringing together different stakeholders such as nongovernmental organizations (NGOs), industry, researchers, and law enforcement agencies in order to facilitate dialogue and exchange of best practice on specific issues (European Commission, 2010). The European Union has led the way in establishing guidelines for limiting what personal data can be collected from the computer nets. These data must involve unambiguous consent or completion of a contract. They must be specifically required by law or necessary for law enforcement. Data on ethnic origins, political opinions, religious or philosophical beliefs, union membership, health, or sex life are prohibited from collection without explicit consent. We need legal specifications of children's ages of consent and protections for them lest they be lured into providing such data.

There is a great challenge for research in the next decade to examine how such privacy issues are affecting children. This issue, at best, was less critical when the focus was only the more passive nature of television viewing. Now with but the click of a mouse, millions of children may be on the brink of significant losses of privacy or legal involvement that can put the whole family in jeopardy (see Chapter 31). Because children and adults put so much personal information on the Internet, "researchers at the University of Washington are developing a new technology called Vanish that makes electronic data—email messages as well as photos and text posted on the Web—'self-destruct' after a specified period of time" (Rosen, 2010, p. 36).

We believe that the research reviewed herein and the advocacy issues raised are critical in guiding us to confront the needed research and policy questions that will be emerging in the next decades. The questions raised about how children at various ages attend to and comprehend television content suggest that youngsters are active participants rather than passive absorbers of the content and structure of video materials. Will they be able to adapt to the even more active roles demanded by the combinations of TV and computers? How will the liveliness and arousal values of digital stimulation affect children's ability to learn from computerized material? Will the uses of computers lead to greater alienation (Markoff, 2000) or to more effective social networking (Weise, 2000)?

We have ample evidence of the potential hazards of unregulated television watching by children. Will the greater complexity and interaction required for computer use minimize these hazards? We think that is likely. Yet we cannot discount the possibility that websites and chat rooms may emerge that not only present children with graphic and explicit sexual content but may also teach them very specific and tempting ways to use guns, knives, or other destructive weapons. What will we need to demonstrate such possibilities by research, and what kinds of controls will be called for to avoid such risks? We believe many of the chapters in this handbook provide a full range of research approaches that can be applied to the new wave of electronic media combining television and computers. The task of compiling regular annual records of violent content on network TV programming that was possible for the Annenberg group, led by George Gerbner in the 1970s and 1980s, will have to be substantially modified to provide systematic indications of such content on the vast cyberspace universe. More ingenuity may be needed to obtain from children or parents what actual content they watch or become involved with, as well as sampling the array of content available. Students of child development will be challenged to determine how children across the age spans choose and react to the great variety of Internet possibilities.

In summary, we believe that, despite some hesitations, false starts, and missed opportunities for research and policy making demonstrated in our history, industry, and advocacy chapters, a great deal has been accomplished in the half-century since television use began to spread across the world. We believe that the research, the policy questions and government and industry actions, and the advocacy efforts reviewed in this handbook can open the way for more reasoned and carefully planned approaches to scientific studies and effective interventions in this new century. Such efforts can help children to grow up effectively in a digital, "wired" world of electronic media.

References

Corporation for Public Broadcasting. (1993). *Public broadcasting: Ready to teach: A report to the 103rd Congress and the American people. Pursuant to P.L. 102-356.* Washington, DC: Author.

European Commission. (2010). *Safer Internet programme: Empowering and protecting children online.* Retrieved September 25, 2010, from http://www.euractiv.com/en/infosociety/internet-security/article-162834.

Markoff, J. (2000, February 16). A newer, lonelier crowd emerges in Internet study. *New York Times,* pp. A1, A18.

Mifflin, L. (1999, April 19). A growth spurt is transforming TV for children. *New York Times,* pp. Al, A19.

Richtel, M. (2010, June 7). Hooked on gadgets, and paying a mental price. *The New York Times*, pp. A1, A12–A13.

Rosen, J. (2010, July 25). The end of forgetting. *New York Times Magazine*, pp. 30–37, 44–45.

Singer, D. G. (2009, Summer). Play and the search for identity in the cyberspace community. *Washington and Lee Law Review 66*(3), 1003–1031.

Weise, E. (2000, February 22). A circle unbroken by surveys. *USA Today,* p. 3D.

Author Index

Note: In page references, f indicates figures and t indicates tables.

Subject Index

Note: In page references, f indicates figures and t indicates tables.

SAGE Research Methods Online

The essential tool for researchers

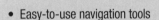